The series Lecture Notes in Computer Science (LNCS), including its subseries Lecture Notes in Artificial Intelligence (LNAI) and Lecture Notes in Bioinformatics (LNBI), has established itself as a medium for the publication of new developments in computer science and information technology research, teaching, and education.

LNCS enjoys close cooperation with the computer science R & D community, the series counts many renowned academics among its volume editors and paper authors, and collaborates with prestigious societies. Its mission is to serve this international community by providing an invaluable service, mainly focused on the publication of conference and workshop proceedings and postproceedings. LNCS commenced publication in 1973.

T0189688

Lecture Notes in Computer Science 14154

Founding Editors

Gerhard Goos
Juris Hartmanis

Thomas Johansson · Daniel Smith-Tone
Editors

Post-Quantum Cryptography

14th International Workshop, PQCrypto 2023
College Park, MD, USA, August 16–18, 2023
Proceedings

 Springer

Editors
Thomas Johansson
Lund University
Lund, Sweden

Daniel Smith-Tone
National Institute of Standards
and Technology
Gaithersburg, MD, USA

University of Louisville
Louisville, KY, USA

ISSN 0302-9743   ISSN 1611-3349 (electronic)
Lecture Notes in Computer Science
ISBN 978-3-031-40002-5   ISBN 978-3-031-40003-2 (eBook)
https://doi.org/10.1007/978-3-031-40003-2

This Springer imprint is published by the registered company Springer Nature Switzerland AG
The registered company address is: Gewerbestrasse 11, 6330 Cham, Switzerland

Preface

PQCrypto 2023, the 14th International Conference on Post-Quantum Cryptography, was held at the University of Maryland, College Park, Maryland, USA on the dates of August 16–18, 2023. The PQCrypto conference series provides a venue for the communication of research results on cryptography under the assumption that large-scale quantum computers are available to adversaries. Since its inception, the conference focus has grown to serve not only academic and theoretical work in post-quantum cryptography, but also applied and technical work, further developing the science and advancing the practical aspects of implementation and deployment of post-quantum cryptographic schemes.

Continuing in the same model as its previous iterations, PQCrypto 2023 utilized a two-stage submission process in which authors registered their papers one week before the final submission deadline. The conference received 55 submissions. Other than papers that were withdrawn by the authors, every paper was reviewed in a single-blind process by at least three Program Committee members. The Committee then engaged in an intensive discussion phase, conducted online. Through this process, the Program Committee selected a total of 25 papers for inclusion in the technical program and for publication in these proceedings. The diverse array of accepted articles found in these proceedings discuss multiple research areas within the scope of the conference, including code-based cryptography, group-action-based cryptography, isogeny-based cryptography, lattice-based cryptography, multivariate cryptography, quantum algorithms, quantum cryptanalysis, quantum random oracle model (QROM) proofs, post-quantum protocols, and side-channel cryptanalysis and countermeasures.

In addition to the 25 contributed presentations, the program was highlighted by four invited lectures on topics of significant contemporary relevance. These talks were delivered by Thibauld Feneuil, CryptoExperts and Sorbonne Université, France (on "MPC-in-the-head" digital signature schemes), Sophie Schmieg, Google, USA (on the transition and deployment issues of post-quantum cryptography), Jean-Pierre Tillich, INRIA, France (on code-based cryptography), and Benjamin Wesolowski, ENS-Lyon, France (on isogeny-based cryptography).

The success of this iteration of PQCrypto was due to the efforts of many individuals and organizations. We are indebted to everyone who contributed to make PQCrypto 2023 a success. We owe thanks to the many scientists, engineers, and authors who submitted their work (of notably high average quality) to our conference. We would like to thank all 49 members of the Program Committee and the 21 external reviewers whose commitment and labor-intensive efforts in evaluating and discussing the submissions allowed us to compile a technical program of such high quality.

We thank our organizers and hosts, the Joint Center for Quantum Information and Computer Science and the University of Maryland Institute for Advanced Computer Studies. The organizers wish to express a special thanks to the following industry sponsors:

- Silver Sponsor

  - Amazon Web Services, Inc.

- Bronze Sponsors

  - Cisco Systems, Inc.
  - Isara Corporation
  - PQSecure Technologies, LLC
  - PQShield, Ltd.
  - SandboxAQ

We would like to thank Rene Peralta for organizing student travel stipends, Kelly Hedgepeth for arranging travel itineraries for the invited speakers, and Andrea Svejda for her help in setting up our conference management. We would also like to express, on behalf of the entire community, how very indebted we are to Yi-Kai Liu, whose efforts in organizing the meeting--- coordinating with sponsors, managing the conference website, overseeing local preparations, arranging publicity, etc.— allowed PQCrypto to return to the superior format of an in-person event. We also wish to express our gratitude to the team at Springer for handling the publication of these conference proceedings.

August 2023

Thomas Johansson
Daniel Smith-Tone

Organization

General Chair

Yi-Kai Liu — Joint Center for Quantum Information and Computer Science, USA and University of Maryland Institute for Advanced Computer Studies, USA and National Institute of Standards and Technology, USA

Program Committee Chairs

Thomas Johansson — Lund University, Sweden
Daniel Smith-Tone — National Institute of Standards and Technology, USA and University of Louisville, USA

Program Committee

Magali Bardet — University of Rouen Normandy, France
Daniel J. Bernstein — University of Illinois at Chicago, USA and Ruhr University Bochum, Germany and Academia Sinica, Taiwan
Olivier Blazy — École Polytechnique, France
Daniel Cabarcas — Universidad Nacional de Colombia, Colombia
Ryann Cartor — Clemson University, USA
André Chailloux — Inria, France
Anupam Chattopadhyay — NTU Singapore, Singapore
Chen-Mou Cheng — BTQ, Taiwan
Jung Hee Cheon — Seoul National University, South Korea
Jan-Pieter D'Anvers — KU Leuven, Belgium
Jintai Ding — Tsinghua University, China
Scott Fluhrer — Cisco Systems, USA
Philippe Gaborit — University of Limoges, France
Tommaso Gagliardoni — Kudelski Security, Switzerland
Qian Guo — Lund University, Sweden
Tim Güneysu — Ruhr University Bochum, DFKI, Germany
Andreas Hülsing — Eindhoven University of Technology, The Netherlands

David Jao	University of Waterloo, Canada
John Kelsey	National Institute of Standards and Technology, USA and KU Leuven, Belgium
Howon Kim	Pusan National University, South Korea
Jon-Lark Kim	Sogang University, South Korea
Kwangjo Kim	Korea Advanced Institute of Science and Technology, South Korea
Elena Kirshanova	TII, UAE
Tanja Lange	Eindhoven University of Technology, The Netherlands and Academia Sinica, Taiwan
Changmin Lee	KIAS, South Korea
Christian Majenz	Technical University of Denmark, Denmark
Dustin Moody	National Institute of Standards and Technology, USA
Michele Mosca	University of Waterloo and Perimeter Inst., Canada
Ray Perlner	NIST, USA
Thomas Pöppelmann	Infineon, Germany
Thomas Prest	PQShield Ltd., UK
Angela Robinson	National Institute of Standards and Technology, USA
Palash Sarkar	ISI, India
Nicolas Sendrier	Inria, France
Jae Hong Seo	Hanyang University, South Korea
Benjamin Smith	Inria, France
Yongsoo Song	Seoul National University, South Korea
Damien Stehlé	CryptoLab, France
Rainer Steinwandt	University of Alabama in Huntsville, USA
Tsuyoshi Takagi	University of Tokyo, Japan
Atsushi Takayasu	University of Tokyo, Japan
Jean-Pierre Tillich	Inria, France
Keita Xagawa	NTT, Japan
Bo-Yin Yang	Academia Sinica, Taiwan
Yang Yu	Université de Rennes, CNRS, IRISA, France
Yu Yu	Shanghai Jiao Tong University, China
Aaram Yun	Ewha Womans University, South Korea

Additional Reviewers

Francois Arnault
Anubhab Baksi
Maxime Bros
Wonhee Cho
Heewon Chung
Reo Eriguchi
Anirban Ghatak
Jai Hyun Park
Minsik Kang
Jiseung Kim
Markus Krausz

Georg Land
Jeeun Lee
Hyunbum Lee
Charles Meyer-Hilfiger
Tomoki Moriya
Kirill Morozov
Kaushik Nath
Hiroshi Onuki
Jan Richter-Brockmann
Olivier Ruatta

Contents

Multivariate Cryptography

Quantum Algorithms, Cryptanalysis and Models

Post-Quantum Protocols

Side-Channel Cryptanalysis and Countermeasures

Code-Based Cryptography

An Extension of Overbeck's Attack with an Application to Cryptanalysis of Twisted Gabidulin-Based Schemes

Alain Couvreur[1,2]($\boxtimes$) and Ilaria Zappatore[3]

[1] Inria, Saclay, France
alain.couvreur@inria.fr
[2] LIX, CNRS UMR 7161, École Polytechnique, Institut Polytechnique de Paris,
1 rue Honoré d'Estienne d'Orves, 91120 Palaiseau Cedex, France
[3] XLIM, CNRS UMR 7252, Université de Limoges, 123, avenue Albert Thomas,
87060 Limoges Cedex, France
ilaria.zappatore@unilim.fr

Abstract. In this article, we discuss the decoding of Gabidulin and related codes from a cryptographic point of view, and we observe that these codes can be decoded solely from the knowledge of a generator matrix. We then extend and revisit Gibson and Overbeck attacks on the generalized GPT encryption scheme (instantiated with the Gabidulin code) for different ranks of the distortion matrix. We apply our attack to the case of an instantiation with twisted Gabidulin codes.

Keywords: Code-based cryptography · rank metric codes · Gabidulin codes · Overbeck's attack · twisted Gabidulin codes

Introduction

The most promising post-quantum alternatives to RSA and elliptic curve cryptography are based on error–correction based paradigms. The metric which quantifies the amount of noise, can be either Euclidean (lattice–based cryptography), Hamming (code–based cryptography) or the rank metric. The latter has been much less investigated than the first two. However, it offers an interesting range of primitives with rather short keys [1–3]. In addition, the Gabidulin code family benefits from a decoder that corrects any error up to a fixed threshold. This makes it possible to design schemes with a zero failure rate, such as RQC [1]. Although no rank–based submission was selected for standardization, NIST encouraged the community to continue the research efforts in the design and security of rank–metric based primitives.

The authors are funded by the French Agence Nationale de la Recherche through the France 2023 ANR project ANR-22-PETQ-0008 PQ-TLS and the ANR-21-CE39-0009-BARRACUDA.

T. Johansson and D. Smith-Tone (Eds.): PQCrypto 2023, LNCS 14154, pp. 3–37, 2023.
https://doi.org/10.1007/978-3-031-40003-2_1

Historically, the first primitive based on rank metric was proposed by Gabidulin, Paramonov and Tretjakov [22]. It was a McEliece–like scheme where the structure of a Gabidulin code is hidden. This scheme was first attacked in exponential time by Gibson [26,27]. Then, Gabidulin and Ourivski proposed an improvement of the system that was resistant to Gibson's attack [21,38]. Later, Overbeck [39,40] proposed a polynomial time attack which breaks both GPT and its improvements. Gabidulin *et al.* then introduced several variants of the GPT based on a different column scrambler $\boldsymbol{P}$, so that some entries of $\boldsymbol{P}^{-1}$ can be in $\mathbb{F}_{q^m}$ [17,20,46]. However, in [37] the authors proved that for all of the aforementioned versions, the shape of the public key is in fact unchanged and remains subject to Overbeck–type attacks.

The natural approach to circumvent Overbeck's attack is to replace the Gabidulin codes with another family equipped with an efficient decoding algorithm. However, only a few such families exist. On the one hand, there are the LRPC codes [23] which lead to the ROLLO scheme [2]. On the other hand, one can in a way deteriorate the structure of the Gabidulin codes, at the cost of a loss of efficiency of the decoder. Loidreau [34] proposed to encrypt with a Gabidulin code perturbed by some $\mathbb{F}_{q^m}$–linear operation. This proposal was subject to polynomial–time attacks for the smallest parameters [11,25,41], while, for larger parameters, it remains secure so far. In another direction, Puchinger *et al.* [43] proposed to replace Gabidulin codes with twisted Gabidulin codes. However their proposal was only partial, since they could not provide an efficient decoder correcting up to half the minimum distance.

Our Contributions. The contribution we make in this article is threefold.

First, we discuss the decoding of Gabidulin codes and twisted Gabidulin codes. Using the result of [8], we explain how to correct errors for such codes without always being able to correct up to half of the minimum distance. From a cryptographic point of view, we highlight an important observation: if in Hamming metric, decoding Reed–Solomon codes requires the knowledge of the evaluation sequence, in the rank metric, Gabidulin codes can be decoded solely from the knowledge of a generator matrix. This observation extends to twisted Gabidulin codes as soon as the decoding radius is below a certain threshold.

Second, we revisit the Overbeck's attack and propose an extension. Specifically, from a public code $\mathscr{C}_{\mathrm{pub}}$, the original Overbeck's attack is based on the computation of $\Lambda_i(\mathscr{C}_{\mathrm{pub}}) = \mathscr{C}_{\mathrm{pub}} + \mathscr{C}_{\mathrm{pub}}^q + \cdots + \mathscr{C}_{\mathrm{pub}}^{q^i}$. For the attack to succeed, a trade–off on the parameter i must be satisfied. On the one hand, i must be large enough to rule out the random part (called *distortion matrix*) in $\mathscr{C}_{\mathrm{pub}}$ used to mask the hidden code. On the other hand, i must be small enough so that $\Lambda_i(\mathscr{C}_{\mathrm{pub}})$ does not to fill in the ambient space. In the this article, we propose an extension of the Overbeck's attack that limits our goal to the smallest possible i, namely $i = 1$. This relaxation is based on calculations on a certain automorphism algebra of the code $\Lambda_1(\mathscr{C}_{\mathrm{pub}})$ and extends the range of the attack.

Third, we investigate in depth the behavior of twisted Gabidulin codes with respect to the Λ_i operator.

The aforementioned contributions lead to an attack on a variant of GPT proposed by Puchinger, Renner and Wachter–Zeh [43]. In this variant, the authors used two techniques to resist Overbeck's attack. First, they mask the code with a *distortion matrix* of very low rank. Second, they replace Gabidulin codes with twisted Gabidulin codes. The authors chose twisted Gabidulin codes $\mathscr{C}$ so that for any positive i, the code $\Lambda_i(\mathscr{C})$ may never have co-dimension 1 (see [43, Theorem 6]). In this article, we prove that the latter property is not a strong enough security assessment for twisted Gabidulin codes and that the aforementioned contributions lead directly to an attack on the Puchinger *et al.*'s variant of GPT.

Outline of the Article. The article is organized as follows. Section 1 introduces some basic notations used in this paper, as well as Gabidulin codes, their twisted version and the GPT cryptosystem. In Sect. 2 we first discuss the decoding of Gabidulin codes and propose an algorithm (Algorithm 1), which does not need to know the evaluation sequence. We then explain how to decode twisted Gabidulin codes, under a certain decoding radius. In Sect. 3, we revisit the Overbeck's attack on the GPT scheme instantiated with Gabidulin codes and we make some remarks on the structure of the generator matrix of the code obtained by applying the q-sum operator to the public key. In Sect. 4, we propose an extension of the Overbeck's attack to the GPT scheme instantiated with either Gabidulin or twisted Gabidulin codes. Finally, in Sect. 5 we examine the behavior of the q-sum operator applied to the public key of the GPT system instantiated with twisted Gabidulin codes. We then show that we can exploit the structure of its generator matrix to break the corresponding scheme using either the Overbeck's attack, or more generally, its previously proposed extension.

1   Prerequisites

In this section we introduce the basic notions we will use throughout the paper, starting with the notations used. Then, we briefly introduce the Gabidulin codes and their twisted version, and finally the GPT cryptosystem.

1.1   Notation

Let q be a prime power, $\mathbb{F}_q$ be a finite field of order q, and $\mathbb{F}_{q^m}$ be the extension field of $\mathbb{F}_q$ of degree m. In this article, vectors are represented by lowercase bold letters: $\boldsymbol{a}, \boldsymbol{b}, \boldsymbol{x}$, and matrices by uppercase bold letters $\boldsymbol{M}, \boldsymbol{G}, \boldsymbol{H}$. We also denote the space of $m \times n$ matrices with entries in a general field $\mathbb{K}$, by $\mathcal{M}_{m,n}(\mathbb{K})$. In the square case, *i.e.* $m = n$, we simplify the notation by writing $\mathcal{M}_n(\mathbb{K})$, and we denote by $\mathbf{GL}_n(\mathbb{K})$ the group of $n \times n$ invertible matrices.

1.2   Rank Metric Codes

Given $x = (x_1, \ldots, x_n)$ a vector in $\mathbb{F}_{q^m}^n$, we can define its *support* as,

$$\mathrm{Supp}(x) \stackrel{\text{def}}{=} \mathbf{Span}_{\mathbb{F}_q}\{x_1, \ldots, x_n\}$$

and

$$\mathbf{rank}_q(x) \stackrel{\text{def}}{=} \dim(\mathrm{Supp}(x)).$$

The *rank distance* (briefly *distance*) of two vectors $x, y \in \mathbb{F}_{q^m}^n$ is

$$\mathrm{d}(x, y) \stackrel{\text{def}}{=} \mathbf{rank}_q(x - y).$$

A *rank metric code* $\mathscr{C}$ of *length* n and *dimension* k is an $\mathbb{F}_{q^m}$-vector subspace of $\mathbb{F}_{q^m}^n$. Its *minimum distance* is defined as,

$$\mathrm{d}_{min}(\mathscr{C}) \stackrel{\text{def}}{=} \min_{x \in \mathscr{C} \setminus \{0\}} \{\mathbf{rank}_q(x)\}.$$

By choosing an $\mathbb{F}_q$-basis $\mathcal{B}$ of $\mathbb{F}_{q^m}$, any codeword $c \in \mathscr{C}$ can be written as a matrix $M_{\mathcal{B}}(c) \in \mathcal{M}_{m,n}(\mathbb{F}_q)$ by representing any element $c_i \in \mathbb{F}_{q^m}$ as a column vector whose entries are its coefficients in the basis $\mathcal{B}$. With this point of view, one can introduce a second notion of support which is less considered in the literature but will be useful in the sequel.

Definition 1. *The* row support *$RowSupp(c)$ of a vector $c \in \mathbb{F}_{q^m}^n$ is the row span of the $m \times n$ matrix $M_{\mathcal{B}}(c)$.*

Note that the row support of a vector is an intrinsic notion that does not depend on the choice of the basis $\mathcal{B}$. Moreover, as for the support, the rank of a vector equals its row support.

Remark 1. One could have defined rank metric codes as spaces of matrices endowed with the same rank metric. Such a framework is more general than ours since a matrix subspace of $\mathcal{M}_{m,n}(\mathbb{F}_q)$ is not $\mathbb{F}_{q^m}$–linear in general. But considering such rank metric codes would be useless in what follows.

Two codes $\mathscr{C}, \mathscr{D} \subseteq \mathbb{F}_{q^m}^n$ are said to be *right equivalent* if there exists $P \in \mathbf{GL}_n(\mathbb{F}_q)$ such that for any $c \in \mathscr{C}$, $cP \in \mathscr{D}$. We denote this as "$\mathscr{C}P = \mathscr{D}$". We emphasize that P should have its entries in $\mathbb{F}_q$ and **not** in $\mathbb{F}_{q^m}$. In this way, the map $x \mapsto xP$ is rank–preserving, *i.e.* is an isometry with respect to the rank metric.

Finally, the *dual* $\mathscr{C}^\perp$ of a code $\mathscr{C} \in \mathbb{F}_{q^m}^n$ is the *orthogonal* of $\mathscr{C}$ with respect to the canonical inner product in $\mathbb{F}_{q^m}$,

$$\begin{cases} \mathbb{F}_{q^m} \times \mathbb{F}_{q^m} \longrightarrow \mathbb{F}_{q^m} \\ (x, y) \longmapsto \sum_{i=1}^n x_i y_i. \end{cases}$$

We frequently apply the *component-wise Frobenius map* to vectors and codes:, given $\boldsymbol{c} = (c_1, \ldots, c_n) \in \mathbb{F}_{q^m}^n$ and $0 \leqslant i \leqslant m - 1$, we denote

$$\boldsymbol{c}^{[i]} \stackrel{\text{def}}{=} (c_1^{q^i}, \ldots, c_n^{q^i}).$$

Given an $[n, k]$ code $\mathscr{C} \subset \mathbb{F}_{q^m}^n$, we write

$$\mathscr{C}^{[i]} \stackrel{\text{def}}{=} \{\boldsymbol{c}^{[i]} \mid \boldsymbol{c} \in \mathscr{C}\}.$$

We also define the *(i-th) q-sum* of $\mathscr{C}$ as,

$$\Lambda_i(\mathscr{C}) \stackrel{\text{def}}{=} \mathscr{C} + \mathscr{C}^{[1]} + \cdots + \mathscr{C}^{[i]}.$$

We notice that if $\boldsymbol{G} \in \mathcal{M}_{k,n}(\mathbb{F}_{q^m})$ is a generator matrix of $\mathscr{C}$, the matrix

$$\begin{pmatrix} \boldsymbol{G} \\ \boldsymbol{G}^{[1]} \\ \vdots \\ \boldsymbol{G}^{[i]} \end{pmatrix} \in \mathcal{M}_{(i+1)k,n}(\mathbb{F}_{q^m}) \tag{1}$$

is a generator of the q-sum of $\mathscr{C}$, *i.e.* $\Lambda_i(\mathscr{C})$. By abuse of notation we sometimes denote the matrix of (1) as $\Lambda_i(\boldsymbol{G})$.

1.3   Gabidulin Codes

q-polynomials were first introduced in [36]. They are defined as $\mathbb{F}_{q^m}$-linear combinations of the monomials $X, X^q, X^{q^2}, \ldots, X^{q^i}, \ldots$ respectively denoted by $X, X^{[1]}, X^{[2]}, \ldots, X^{[i]}, \ldots$ Formally, a nonzero q-polynomial F is defined as,

$$F = \sum_{i=0}^{d} f_i X^{[i]}$$

assuming that $f_d \neq 0$. The integer d is called *q–degree* of F and we denote it $\deg_q f$. We equip the space of q–polynomial with a non-commutative algebra structure, where the multiplication law is the composition of polynomials. In particular, the product law is given by the following relations extended by $\mathbb{F}_{q^m}$–linearity:

$$\forall i, j \in \mathbb{N}, \ \forall a \in \mathbb{F}_{q^m}, \quad X^{[i]} X^{[j]} = X^{[i+j]} \quad \text{and} \quad X^{[i]} a = a^{q^i} X^{[i]}.$$

Any q–polynomial F induces an $\mathbb{F}_q$–endomorphism $\mathbb{F}_{q^m} \to \mathbb{F}_{q^m}$ and the *rank of* F will be defined as the rank of its induced endomorphism.

Denote by $\mathcal{L}$ the ring of all q–polynomial and by $\mathcal{L}^{<e}$ the $\mathbb{F}_{q^m}$–linear space of q–polynomials of q–degree less than e, namely:

$$\mathcal{L}^{<e} \stackrel{\text{def}}{=} \{f \in \mathcal{L} \mid \deg_q f < e\}.$$

Given two positive integers k, n, with $k < n \leqslant m$ and $\boldsymbol{g} \in \mathbb{F}_{q^m}^n$ of $\mathbf{rank}_q(\boldsymbol{g}) = n$, the *Gabidulin code* of length n and dimension k is defined as

$$\mathscr{G}_k(\boldsymbol{g}) \stackrel{\text{def}}{=} \{(F(g_1), \dots, F(g_n)) \mid F \in \mathcal{L}^{<k}\}.$$

A *generator matrix of this code* is a *Moore matrix* (see for instance [28, § 1.3]), *i.e.* a matrix of the form

$$\mathbf{M}_k(\boldsymbol{g}) \stackrel{\text{def}}{=} \begin{pmatrix} \boldsymbol{g} \\ \boldsymbol{g}^{[1]} \\ \vdots \\ \boldsymbol{g}^{[k-1]} \end{pmatrix} = \begin{pmatrix} g_1 & g_2 & \cdots & g_n \\ g_1^q & g_2^q & \cdots & g_n^q \\ \vdots & \vdots & \cdots & \vdots \\ g_1^{q^{k-1}} & g_2^{q^{k-1}} & \cdots & g_n^{q^{k-1}} \end{pmatrix}. \tag{2}$$

Gabidulin codes are *Maximum Rank Distance* (MRD) codes, *i.e.* their minimum distance is $d_{\min}(\mathscr{G}_k(\boldsymbol{g})) = n - k + 1$ and they benefit from a decoding algorithm correcting up to half the minimum distance (see [33]).

We now recall the following classical lemmas, that will be useful in the rest of the paper.

Lemma 1. *Let $\mathscr{G}_k(\boldsymbol{g})$ be a Gabidulin code and $\boldsymbol{T} \in \mathbf{GL}_n(\mathbb{F}_q)$. Then $\mathbf{M}_k(\boldsymbol{g})\boldsymbol{T}$ is a generator matrix of the Gabidulin code $\mathscr{G}_k(\boldsymbol{gT})$.*

In short, a right–equivalent code to a Gabidulin code is a Gabidulin code with another evaluation sequence.

Lemma 2 ([18, **Theorem 7**]). *The dual of the Gabidulin code $\mathscr{G}_k(\boldsymbol{g})$ is the Gabidulin code $\mathscr{G}_{n-k}(\boldsymbol{y}^{[-n+k+1]})$, where $\boldsymbol{y}$ is a nonzero vector in $\mathscr{G}_{n-1}(\boldsymbol{g})^{\perp}$.*

1.4   Twisted Gabidulin Codes

Twisted Gabidulin codes were first introduced in [48] and contain a broad family of MRD codes that are not equivalent to Gabidulin codes. The construction of these codes was then generalized in [42,43]. We consider the q–polynomials of the form

$$F = \sum_{i=0}^{k-1} f_i X^{[i]} + \sum_{j=1}^{\ell} \eta_j f_{h_j} X^{[k-1+t_j]}, \tag{3}$$

where the f_i'a are in $\mathbb{F}_{q^m}$, $\ell \leqslant n-k$, $\boldsymbol{h} \in \{0, \dots, k-1\}^\ell$, $\boldsymbol{t} \in \{1, \dots, n-k\}^\ell$ (with distinct t_i) and $\boldsymbol{\eta} \in (\mathbb{F}_{q^m}^*)^\ell$. We denote by $\mathcal{L}_{t,h,\eta}^{n,k}$ the space of all q–polynomials of the form (3) with parameters $\boldsymbol{h}, \boldsymbol{t}, \boldsymbol{\eta}$. Now, given a vector $\boldsymbol{g} \in \mathbb{F}_{q^m}^n$, with $\mathbf{rank}_q(\boldsymbol{g}) = n$, the $[\boldsymbol{g}, \boldsymbol{t}, \boldsymbol{h}, \boldsymbol{\eta}]$-*twisted Gabidulin code* of *length* n, dimension k, ℓ twists, *hook vector* $\boldsymbol{h}$, *twist vector* $\boldsymbol{t}$ and *evaluation sequence* $\boldsymbol{g}$ is defined as

$$\mathscr{C}_{\boldsymbol{g},\boldsymbol{t},\boldsymbol{h},\boldsymbol{\eta}}[n,k] \stackrel{\text{def}}{=} \{(F(g_1), \dots, F(g_n)) \mid F \in \mathcal{L}_{t,h,\eta}^{n,k}\}.$$

We observe that in [48], Sheekey introduced a simplified version of these codes with just one twist, *i.e.* $n = m, \ell = 1, \boldsymbol{h} = (0), \boldsymbol{t} = (1)$.

Assumption 1. *Throughout this paper, according to [43], we consider a* $[g, t, h, \eta]$*-twisted Gabidulin code with ℓ twists, and with the following parameters,*

- $t_i \overset{def}{=} (i+1)(\delta+1)$, *where* $\delta \overset{def}{=} \frac{n-k-\ell}{\ell+1}$,
- $0 < h_1 < h_2 < \ldots < h_\ell < k-1$ *and* $|h_i - h_{i-1}| > 1$.

for any i, $1 \leqslant i \leqslant \ell$.

This choice is particularly relevant because it allows us to quantify the dimension of the q-sum operator applied to these codes (see Proposition 2).

We now observe that in general, a generator matrix of a $\mathscr{C}_{g,t,h,\eta}[n,k]$ is

$$
\begin{pmatrix}
g \\
g^{[1]} \\
\vdots \\
g^{[h_1-1]} \\
g^{[h_1]} + \eta_1 g^{[k-1+t_1]} \\
g^{[h_1+1]} \\
\vdots \\
g^{[h_\ell-1]} \\
g^{[h_\ell]} + \eta_\ell g^{[k-1+t_\ell]} \\
g^{[h_\ell+1]} \\
\vdots \\
g^{[k-1]}
\end{pmatrix}.
\tag{4}
$$

The decoding of twisted Gabidulin codes such as their *additive variants* has recently been studied in [29–32, 44, 45]. However, in [45] there were proposed some algorithms which allow to decode twisted Gabidulin codes with only one twist and $t = (1)$, for some special choices of parameters. They manage to correct up to $\lfloor \frac{n-k-1}{2} \rfloor$ errors. But their decoding up to half of the minimum distance remains an open problem.

To the best of our knowledge, the decoding of twisted Gabidulin codes with multiple twists, or one twist with $t_1 > 1$ has not been studied in the literature. We address this point in Sect. 2 for decoding radii that remain below half the minimum distance.

1.5   GPT System and Variants

The GPT cryptosystem was introduced in 1991 by Gabidulin, Paramonov and Tretjakov [22]. This system is a *rank-metric* variant of the classical *McEliece* cryptosystem [35], in which the Goppa codes are replaced by Gabidulin codes. The first version of GPT was first broken by Gibson in [26]. Gabidulin proposed a new version in [19], which was later attacked again by Gibson in [27].

In this work we present the generalized version of GPT proposed by Gabidulin and Ourivski in [21, 38].

– *Key Generation.* Let,
- $\mathscr{G}_k(\boldsymbol{g})$ an $[n,k]$-Gabidulin code with generator matrix $\boldsymbol{G}_{\mathrm{sec}}$ (as in (2));
- $\boldsymbol{S}$ a random invertible matrix in $\mathcal{M}_k(\mathbb{F}_{q^m})$,
- $\boldsymbol{X}$ a random matrix in $\mathcal{M}_{k,\lambda}(\mathbb{F}_{q^m})$ of fixed rank $1 \leqslant s \leqslant \lambda$, called *distortion matrix*,
- $\boldsymbol{P}$ a random matrix in $\mathbf{GL}_{n+\lambda}(\mathbb{F}_q)$, called *column scrambler.*

The *secret key* is the triple,

$$(\boldsymbol{S}, \boldsymbol{G}_{\mathrm{sec}}, \boldsymbol{P})$$

and the *public key* is,

$$\boldsymbol{G}_{pub} \stackrel{\mathrm{def}}{=} \boldsymbol{S}(\boldsymbol{X} \mid \boldsymbol{G}_{\mathrm{sec}})\boldsymbol{P}, \tag{5}$$

where $(\boldsymbol{X} \mid \boldsymbol{G}_{\mathrm{sec}}) \in \mathcal{M}_{k,n+\lambda}(\mathbb{F}_{q^m})$ denotes the matrix whose columns are the concatenations of those of $\boldsymbol{X}$ and of $\boldsymbol{G}_{\mathrm{sec}}$. We denote $\mathscr{C}_{\mathrm{pub}}$ the linear code with $\boldsymbol{G}_{\mathrm{pub}}$ as generator matrix.

– *Encryption.* To encode a plaintext $\boldsymbol{m} \in \mathbb{F}_{q^m}^k$, choose a random vector $\boldsymbol{e} \in \mathbb{F}_{q^m}^{n+\lambda}$ of $\mathbf{rank}_q(\boldsymbol{e}) = t$, where $t = \lfloor \frac{n-k}{2} \rfloor$ and compute the ciphertext as,

$$\boldsymbol{c} \stackrel{\mathrm{def}}{=} \boldsymbol{m}\boldsymbol{G}_{\mathrm{pub}} + \boldsymbol{e}.$$

– *Decryption.* Apply the chosen decoding algorithm for Gabidulin codes to the last n components of the vector,

$$\boldsymbol{c}\boldsymbol{P}^{-1} = \boldsymbol{m}\boldsymbol{S}[\boldsymbol{X}|\boldsymbol{G}_{\mathrm{sec}}] + \boldsymbol{e}\boldsymbol{P}^{-1}.$$

Since $\boldsymbol{P} \in \mathbf{GL}_{n+\lambda}(\mathbb{F}_q)$, then $\mathbf{rank}_q(\boldsymbol{e}\boldsymbol{P}^{-1}) = t$ and in particular, the rank (over $\mathbb{F}_q$) of the last n rows of this matrix is at most t. So, the decoder computes $\boldsymbol{m}\boldsymbol{S}$, and by inverting $\boldsymbol{S}$, the initial message can be finally encrypted.

The description of the secret key as the triple $(\boldsymbol{S}, \boldsymbol{G}_{\mathrm{sec}}, \boldsymbol{P})$ is not the most relevant one when it comes to instantiating the scheme with Gabidulin or twisted Gabidulin codes. In particular, once we know the secret code $\mathscr{C}_{\mathrm{sec}}$ of the generator matrix $\boldsymbol{G}_{\mathrm{sec}}$ and the scrambling matrix, we are able to decode. So, the knowledge of $\boldsymbol{S}$ is not relevant. Thus, in the following, we assume that $\boldsymbol{G}_{\mathrm{pub}}$ as

$$\boldsymbol{G}_{\mathrm{pub}} = (\boldsymbol{X} \mid \boldsymbol{G}_{\mathrm{sec}})\boldsymbol{P}. \tag{6}$$

Remark 2. The previous scheme is instantiated with Gabidulin codes but can actually be instantiated with any code family equipped with a decoder that corrects up to t errors.

Remark 3. The original GPT scheme [22] did not involve the distortion matrix $\boldsymbol{X}$ as it is. The seminal proposal was to use either a random generator matrix $\boldsymbol{G}$ of a Gabidulin code or a matrix $\boldsymbol{G} + \boldsymbol{X}_0$, where $\boldsymbol{X}_0$ had low rank. The latter version required to reduce the weight of the error term in the encryption process. In the following, we no longer consider this masking technique. The use of a distortion matrix with a column scrambler appeared only ten years later with the works of Ourivski and Gabidulin [21,38].

2   On the Decoding of Gabidulin Codes and Their Twists

In this section, we discuss further the decoding of Gabidulin and twisted Gabidulin codes. We show that, although decoding twisted Gabidulin codes up to half the minimum distance remains an open problem, their decoding up to a smaller radius is possible, using the same decoder as for Gabidulin codes. This approach was developed in [8] and is related to that of Gaborit, Ruatta and Schrek in [24, § V–VI].

We begin by examining the decoding of Gabidulin codes.

2.1   An Important Remark on the Decoder of Gabidulin Codes

It is well–known that the Gabidulin codes have a decoder that corrects up to half the minimum distance (see for instance [33]). This algorithm is analogous to the Welch–Berlekamp algorithm for Reed–Solomon codes. An important fact from a cryptographic point of view is that, given a Reed–Solomon code

$$\mathbf{RS}(k) \stackrel{\text{def}}{=} \{(f(x_1), \ldots, f(x_n)) \mid f \in \mathbb{F}_q[X],\ \deg f < k\},$$

where $x = (x_1, \ldots, x_n) \in \mathbb{F}_q^n$ has distinct entries, the knowledge of the vector x is necessary to run the decoding algorithm. However, given a Gabidulin code $\mathscr{G}_k(g)$, it is possible to decode without knowing g. Indeed, given as input $y = c + e$ where $c \in \mathscr{G}_k(g)$ and $\mathbf{rank}_q(e) \leqslant t \stackrel{\text{def}}{=} \frac{n-k}{2}$, the decoding algorithm first consists in finding a q–polynomial $P(x)$ of degree at most t which vanishes at the entries of e. This can be done by solving the $\mathbb{F}_{q^m}$–linear system

$$P(y) \stackrel{\text{def}}{=} (P(y_1), \ldots, P(y_n)) \in \mathscr{G}_{k+t}(g) \tag{7}$$

whose unknowns are the coefficients of $P \in \mathcal{L}^{\leqslant t}$. Next, the code $\mathscr{G}_{k+t}(g)$ can be computed by simply knowing a generator matrix of $\mathscr{G}_k(g)$, thanks to the following well–known statement.

Proposition 1 ([40, **Lem. 5.1**]). *Let $g \in \mathbb{F}_{q^m}^n$, with $\mathbf{rank}_q(g) = n$ and $\mathscr{G}_k(g)$ an $[n, k]$ Gabidulin code. Then,*

$$\Lambda_i(\mathscr{G}_k(g)) = \mathscr{G}_{k+i}(g).$$

In particular,

$$\dim(\Lambda_i(\mathscr{G}_k(g))) = \min\{n, k+i\}.$$

Next, for any P satisfying (7), we have $P(y) = P(c) + P(e)$. By construction, $P(c) \in \Lambda_t(\mathscr{G}_k(g)) = \mathscr{G}_{k+t}(g)$ and hence, $P(e) \in \mathscr{G}_{k+t}(g)$. Moreover, we have $\mathbf{rank}_q(P(e)) \leqslant \mathbf{rank}_q(e) \leqslant t$, while $\Lambda_t(\mathscr{G}_k(g)) = \mathscr{G}_{k+t}(g)$ has minimum distance $n-k-t+1$. Therefore, for $t \leqslant \frac{n-k}{2}$, which entails $t < n-k-t+1$, we should have $P(e) = 0$ for any P satisfying (7). Thus, the kernel of P contains the support of e and the knowledge of the support of the error allows to solve the decoding problem by solving a linear system. See for instance [24, § IV.a], [4, § III.A].

Algorithm 1: Decoding algorithm of Gabidulin codes without knowing the evaluation sequence

---

Input: A Gabidulin code $\mathscr{C}$ represented by a generator matrix G, an integer t and a vector $\boldsymbol{y} \in \mathbb{F}_{q^m}^n$

Output: A vector $\boldsymbol{c} \in \mathscr{C}$ such that $\mathbf{rank}_q(\boldsymbol{y} - \boldsymbol{c}) \leqslant t$ if exists and '?' otherwise.

1 Compute $P \in \mathcal{L}^{\leqslant t} \setminus \{0\}$ such that $P(\boldsymbol{y}) \in \Lambda_t(\mathscr{C})$
2 Compute (if exists) $\boldsymbol{e} \in \mathbb{F}_{q^m}$ such that $\mathrm{Supp}(\boldsymbol{e}) \subseteq \ker(P)$ and $\boldsymbol{y} - \boldsymbol{e} \in \mathscr{C}$
3 **if** $\boldsymbol{e}$ *exists* **then**
4 $\quad \lfloor$ Return $\boldsymbol{y} - \boldsymbol{e}$

5 **else**
6 $\quad \lfloor$ Return '?'

Algorithm 1 summarizes the previous discussion. Note that, with the knowledge of the evaluation sequence $\boldsymbol{g}$, the algorithm could be terminated by performing an Euclidean division or using the Extended Euclidean Algorithm in the non-commutative ring $\mathcal{L}$ instead of using [24, § IV.a], [4, § III.A].

The key observation here is the following: **decoding a Gabidulin code $\mathscr{G}_k(\boldsymbol{g})$ is possible without knowing the vector $\boldsymbol{g}$.**

Remark 4. In GPT original public key encryption scheme [22] the public code is a Gabidulin code with no distortion matrix. In this situation, the previous discussion shows that this proposal is immediately broken without trying to compute a description (*i.e.* an evaluation sequence) of the public code.

2.2 Decoding Twisted Gabidulin Codes

If some twisted Gabidulin codes are proven to be MRD without being equivalent to Gabidulin codes, the question of decoding them up to half the minimum distance remains open. For *twisted Reed–Solomon codes*, the Hamming metric analogues introduced in [7], it is shown in [6] how they can be decoded up to half the minimum distance at the cost of an exhaustive search on the terms associated with the twists. Thus, the decoding complexity of a twisted Reed–Solomon code with ℓ twists is $O(q^\ell)$ times the complexity of the decoding of a Reed–Solomon code. This can be transposed to twisted Gabidulin codes but the cost overhead is $O(q^{m\ell})$ times the cost of decoding a Gabidulin code, which is exponential in m and so in the code length n (since $n \leqslant m$).

Although one does not know how to efficiently decode twisted Gabidulin codes up to half the minimum distance, one can apply the Algorithm 1 to them. Given $\boldsymbol{y} = \boldsymbol{c} + \boldsymbol{e}$, where $\boldsymbol{c}$ is a codeword of a twisted Gabidulin code $\mathscr{C}$ and $\mathbf{rank}_q(\boldsymbol{e}) \leqslant t$ for some t we will discuss later, compute $P \in \mathcal{L}^{\leqslant t}$ such that

$$P(\boldsymbol{y}) \overset{\text{def}}{=} (P(y_1), \ldots, P(y_n)) \in \Lambda_t(\mathscr{C}). \tag{8}$$

Such a solution P satisfies $P(e) \in \Lambda_t(\mathscr{C})$. The difference with the Gabidulin case is that we do not have an *a priori* lower bound on the minimum distance of $\Lambda_t(\mathscr{C})$. However we have the following result.

Proposition 2 ([43, **Theorem 4**]). *Given a twisted Gabidulin code $\mathscr{C}_{g,t,h,\eta}[n,k]$ (where parameters are chosen according to Assumption 1), then*

$$\forall i \geqslant 0, \quad \dim(\Lambda_i(\mathscr{C}_{g,t,h,\eta}[n,k])) = \min\{k + i + \ell(i+1), n\}.$$

Proposition 2 entails that for a twisted Gabidulin code $\mathscr{C}$ with ℓ twists, we have

$$\dim_{\mathbb{F}_{q^m}} \Lambda_t(\mathscr{C}) \leqslant k - 1 + (t+1)(\ell+1). \tag{9}$$

Now, denote by $\mathscr{E}$ the 1-dimensional code generated by e and let us consider the dimension of $\Lambda_t(\mathscr{E})$. Since $\Lambda_t(\mathscr{E})$ is the image of $\mathcal{L}^{\leqslant t}$ by the map $Q \mapsto Q(e)$, we have

$$\dim_{\mathbb{F}_{q^m}} (\Lambda_t(\mathscr{E})) = \dim_{\mathbb{F}_{q^m}} (\mathcal{L}^{\leqslant t}) - \dim_{\mathbb{F}_{q^m}} \{Q \in \mathcal{L}^{\leqslant t} \mid Q(e) = 0\}.$$

First, $\dim(\mathcal{L}^{\leqslant t}) = t + 1$. Second, recall that there exists a unique monic q–polynomial P of q–degree $\mathrm{rank}_q(e)$ such that $P(e) = 0$. Therefore,

$$\{Q \in \mathcal{L}^{\leqslant t} \mid Q(e) = 0\} = \{F \circ P \mid F \in \mathcal{L}^{\leqslant t - \mathrm{rank}_q(e)}\}$$

and the latter space has dimension $t - \mathrm{rank}_q(e) + 1 \geqslant 1$. Putting all together, we deduce that

$$\dim_{\mathbb{F}_{q^m}} (\Lambda_t(\mathscr{E})) \leqslant t.$$

We claim that if

$$\dim_{\mathbb{F}_{q^m}} \Lambda_t(\mathscr{C}) + t \leqslant n, \tag{10}$$

the spaces $\Lambda_t(\mathscr{C})$ and $\Lambda_t(\mathscr{E})$ are very likely to have a zero intersection. The validity of this claim are given in Sect. 2.3. This would entail that for any $P \in \mathcal{L}^{\leqslant t}$ satisfying (8), we have $P(e) = 0$. Therefore, from (9) and (10) we can conclude that if,

$$t \leqslant \frac{n - k - \ell}{\ell + 2}.$$

then we can decode twisted Gabidulin codes as classical Gabidulin codes: form the kernel of P, we get the error support and finally the error itself is deduced using [24, § IV.a], [4, § III.A]. This decoding radius is rather pessimistic since the dimension of $\Lambda_t(\mathscr{C})$ may be much smaller depending on the way the twists are chosen. Therefore, the above bound is what we can expect in the worst case.

2.3 Discussion About the Claim

Suppose that the error e is obtained as follows: draw a uniformly random subspace $V \subseteq \mathbb{F}_q^n$ of dimension t and then draw a uniformly random vector e among the vector with row support contained in V. One can easily prove that all the elements of $\Lambda_t(e)$ have their row support contained in V.

Therefore, the intersection $\Lambda_t(\mathscr{E}) \cap \Lambda_t(\mathscr{C})$ consists in elements of $\Lambda_t(\mathscr{C})$ whose row support is in V. So, consider the subcode $\mathrm{Sh}_V(\Lambda_t(\mathscr{C}))$ called *shortening of* $\Lambda_t(\mathscr{C})$ defined as the subcode of $\Lambda_t(\mathscr{C})$ of vectors whose row support is contained in V. This space can be obtained as follows. Consider a basis $(\boldsymbol{v}_1, \ldots, \boldsymbol{v}_{n-t})$ of the dual $V^\perp \subseteq \mathbb{F}_q^n$ of V for the canonical inner product. Then, $\mathrm{Sh}_V(\Lambda_t(\mathscr{C}))$ is the kernel of the map

$$\begin{cases} \Lambda_t(\mathscr{C}) \longrightarrow & \mathbb{F}_{q^m}^{n-t} \\ \boldsymbol{c} \longmapsto (\boldsymbol{c} \cdot \boldsymbol{v}_1^\top, \ldots, \boldsymbol{c} \cdot \boldsymbol{v}_{n-t}^\top). \end{cases}$$

Remark 5. Note that in the above equation, $\boldsymbol{c}$ and the $\boldsymbol{v}_i$'s have different nature, $\boldsymbol{c}$ has entries in $\mathbb{F}_{q^m}$ while the $\boldsymbol{v}_i$'s have their entries in $\mathbb{F}_q$.

Finally, since V is uniformly random, and $\dim \Lambda_t(\mathscr{C}) \leqslant n - t$, it is likely that the above map is injective and hence its kernel $\mathrm{Sh}_V(\Lambda_t(\mathscr{C}))$ is likely to be zero. Since the latter kernel contains $\Lambda_t(\mathscr{E}) \cap \Lambda_t(\mathscr{C})$, we conclude that this intersection is likely to be zero.

2.4   A Remark on the Code that is Actually Decoded

To conclude, let us notice an important fact for the sections to follow. The previously described decoder may decode a slightly larger code than $\mathscr{C}$ defined below.

Definition 2. *Let $\mathscr{C} \subseteq \mathbb{F}_{q^m}^n$ be a code and s be a positive integer. We denote by $\overline{\mathscr{C}}^s$ the largest code $\mathscr{C}'$ containing $\mathscr{C}$ such that $\Lambda_s(\mathscr{C}) = \Lambda_s(\mathscr{C}')$.*

It is easy to check that, the aforementioned decoder actually decodes $\overline{\mathscr{C}}^t$ and not only $\mathscr{C}$.

Remark 6. It can be proved that for a random code $\mathscr{C}$ with dimension $k < \frac{n}{s}$, then $\mathscr{C} = \overline{\mathscr{C}}^s$ with a high probability. It ca also be proved that a Gabidulin code $\mathscr{C}$ of dimension k satisfies $\overline{\mathscr{C}}^i = \mathscr{C}$ for any $i < n - k$.

Remark 7. An alternative definition of $\overline{\mathscr{C}}^s$ is given by.

$$\overline{\mathscr{C}}^s \overset{\mathrm{def}}{=} \bigcap_{j=0}^s (\Lambda_s(\mathscr{C}))^{[-j]}$$

3   Revisiting Overbeck's Attack

In this section we revisit the Overbeck's attack of GPT instantiated with Gabidulin codes to introduce the extension presented in Sect. 4, which will allow us to break [43].

3.1 A Distinguisher

The core of the Overbeck's attack consists in the application of the q-sum operator, which allows to *distinguish* Gabidulin codes from random ones. In particular, the following proposition observes the behavior of random codes *w.r.t.* the i-th q-sum operator.

Proposition 3 ([10, **Prop. 1**]). *If $\mathscr{C} \subset \mathbb{F}_{q^m}^n$ is a k-dimensional random code, then for any $0 < i < k$,*

$$\dim(\Lambda_i(\mathscr{C})) \leqslant \min\{n, (i+1)k\}.$$

Moreover, for any $a \geqslant 0$, we have

$$\mathbf{Prob}(\dim(\Lambda_i(\mathscr{C})) \leqslant \min\{n, (i+1)k\} - a) = O(q^{-ma}).$$

Gabidulin codes have a significantly different behavior with respect to the q-sum compared to random codes (see Proposition 1). In fact, we observe that if $i < n - k$,

$$\dim(\Lambda_i(\mathscr{G}_k(\boldsymbol{g}))) = k + i < (i+1)k = \dim(\Lambda_i(\mathscr{C})),$$

where $\mathscr{G}_k(\boldsymbol{g})$ is a n-Gabidulin code of dimension k, and $\mathscr{C}$ is a random code, and we know from the previous proposition that the last equality is true with high probability.

In the Overbeck's attack, the operator $\Lambda_i(\cdot)$ is used for two related reasons.

1. It provides a distinguisher on the public key based on the peculiar behavior of Gabidulin codes with respect to $\Lambda_i(\cdot)$. This permits to rule out the distortion matrix [40] and to recover a decomposition of the form (6), in order to decrypt any ciphertext computed with this public key.
2. Once we have discarded the distortion matrix, we have access to the secret Gabidulin code and we can recover its hidden structure, *i.e.* an evaluation sequence.

We observe that the second step is not necessary since, using Algorithm 1, one can directly decode any message, without knowing the evaluation sequence. Thus, in the sequel, we focus on the first step.

3.2 The Structure of $\Lambda_i(G_{\mathrm{pub}})$

Let i be a positive integer and $\boldsymbol{G}_{\mathrm{pub}} = (\boldsymbol{X} \mid \boldsymbol{G}_{\mathrm{sec}})\boldsymbol{P}$ a public key as in (6). Recall that, in the present section, we suppose that $\boldsymbol{G}_{\mathrm{sec}}$ is a generator matrix of a Gabidulin code. Observe that, since $\boldsymbol{P} \in \mathbf{GL}_{n+\lambda}(\mathbb{F}_q)$, we have $\boldsymbol{P}^{[i]} = \boldsymbol{P}$ and hence,

$$\Lambda_i(\boldsymbol{G}_{\mathrm{pub}}) = (\Lambda_i(\boldsymbol{X}) \mid \Lambda_i(\boldsymbol{G}_{\mathrm{sec}}))\boldsymbol{P}. \tag{11}$$

We now assume that $i < n-k$ and we focus on the matrix $(\Lambda_i(\boldsymbol{X}) \mid \Lambda_i(\boldsymbol{G}_{\mathrm{sec}}))$. If we denote the distortion matrix $\boldsymbol{X}$ according to its rows, *i.e.*

$$\boldsymbol{X} = \begin{pmatrix} \boldsymbol{x}_0 \\ \boldsymbol{x}_1 \\ \vdots \\ \boldsymbol{x}_{k-1} \end{pmatrix},$$

where $\boldsymbol{x}_j \in \mathbb{F}_{q^m}^{\lambda}$ for any $0 \leqslant j \leqslant k-1$, then

$$(\Lambda_i(\boldsymbol{X}) \mid \Lambda_i(\boldsymbol{G}_{\mathrm{sec}})) = \left(\begin{array}{c|c} \begin{matrix} \boldsymbol{x}_0 \\ \boldsymbol{x}_1 \\ \vdots \\ \boldsymbol{x}_{k-1} \\ \vdots \\ \boldsymbol{x}_0^{[i]} \\ \boldsymbol{x}_1^{[i]} \\ \vdots \\ \boldsymbol{x}_{k-1}^{[i]} \end{matrix} & \begin{matrix} \boldsymbol{g} \\ \boldsymbol{g}^{[1]} \\ \vdots \\ \boldsymbol{g}^{[k-1]} \\ \vdots \\ \boldsymbol{g}^{[i]} \\ \boldsymbol{g}^{[i+1]} \\ \vdots \\ \boldsymbol{g}^{[k-1+i]} \end{matrix} \end{array} \right).$$

Now, after performing some row elimination, we finally get

$$\left(\begin{array}{c|c} \begin{matrix} \boldsymbol{x}_0 \\ \boldsymbol{x}_1 \\ \vdots \\ \boldsymbol{x}_{k-1} \\ \vdots \\ \boldsymbol{x}_{k-1}^{[i]} \\ \vdots \\ \boldsymbol{x}_0^{[i]} - \boldsymbol{x}_1^{[i-1]} \\ \boldsymbol{x}_1^{[i]} - \boldsymbol{x}_2^{[i-1]} \\ \vdots \\ \boldsymbol{x}_{k-2}^{[i]} - \boldsymbol{x}_{k-1}^{[i-1]} \end{matrix} & \begin{matrix} \boldsymbol{g} \\ \boldsymbol{g}^{[1]} \\ \vdots \\ \boldsymbol{g}^{[k-1]} \\ \vdots \\ \boldsymbol{g}^{[k-1+i]} \\ \vdots \\ \boldsymbol{0} \\ \boldsymbol{0} \\ \vdots \\ \boldsymbol{0} \end{matrix} \end{array} \right).$$

Thus, we have the following.

Lemma 3. *Let $i < n-k$. Then, up to row elimination,*

$$(\Lambda_i(\boldsymbol{X}) \mid \Lambda_i(\boldsymbol{G}_{sec})) = \begin{pmatrix} \boldsymbol{X}' & \mathbf{M}_{k+i}(\boldsymbol{g}) \\ \Lambda_{i-1}(\boldsymbol{X}'') & \mathbf{0} \end{pmatrix}, \tag{12}$$

where,

$$X' = \begin{pmatrix} x_0 \\ \vdots \\ x_{k-1} \\ x_{k-1}^{[1]} \\ \vdots \\ x_{k-1}^{[i]} \end{pmatrix} \quad and \quad X'' = X_{\{0,\dots,k-2\}}^{[1]} - X_{\{1,\dots,k-1\}}.$$

In detail, $X_{\{0,\dots,k-2\}}^{[1]}$ *is the submatrix of* $X^{[1]}$ *composed by its first* $k-1$ *rows and* $X_{\{1,\dots,k-1\}}$ *is the submatrix of* X *composed by its rows starting from the second one.*

We now observe that the row space of X'', denoted $\mathbf{RowSp}_{\mathbb{F}_{q^m}}(X'')$, is contained in the sum of the row spaces of X and $X^{[1]}$, which is $\mathbf{RowSp}_{\mathbb{F}_{q^m}}(\Lambda_1(X))$ and so $\mathbf{rank}(X'') \leqslant \min\{2s, \lambda\}$, where we recall that $s = \mathbf{rank}(X)$.

More generally, $\mathbf{RowSp}_{\mathbb{F}_{q^m}}(\Lambda_{i-1}(X'')) \subseteq \mathbf{RowSp}_{\mathbb{F}_{q^m}}(\Lambda_i(X))$ for any $i \geqslant 1$. And $\mathbf{rank}(\Lambda_{i-1}(X'')) \leqslant \min\{(i+1)s, \lambda\}$.

3.3   Overbeck's Attack

The attack consists in finding an $i < n - k$, for which $\mathbf{rank}(\Lambda_{i-1}(X'')) = \lambda$. In this case,

$$\dim(\Lambda_i(\mathscr{G}_{pub})) = k + i + \lambda$$

and the dimension of the dual is

$$\dim(\Lambda_i(\mathscr{G}_{pub})^\perp) = n - k - i.$$

So, the code $\Lambda_i(\mathscr{G}_{pub})$ admits a parity check of this form

$$(\mathbf{0} \mid \boldsymbol{H}_i)(\boldsymbol{P}^{-1})^\top, \tag{13}$$

where $\boldsymbol{H}_i$ is a parity check matrix of $\Lambda_i(\mathscr{G}_k(\boldsymbol{g})) = \mathscr{G}_{k+i}(\boldsymbol{g})$.

After finding such an i, we can easily find a *valid* column scrambler $\boldsymbol{T} \in \mathbf{GL}_{n+\lambda}(\mathbb{F}_q)$, which will allow us to attack the system (see Theorem 2 ([40, Thm 5.3])).

Therefore, **the crucial part of the Overbeck's attack consists in finding (if there exists) a positive integer** i, **for which** $\dim(\Lambda_{i-1}(X'')) = \lambda$ **and** $\Lambda_i(\mathscr{C}_{sec}) \neq \mathbb{F}_{q^m}^n$ **or equivalently** $\dim(\Lambda_i(\mathscr{C}_{pub})) = \dim(\Lambda_i(\mathscr{C}_{sec})) + \lambda$.

Remark 8. If for $i = n - k - 1$, we have $\dim(\Lambda_{n-k-1}(\mathscr{C}_{pub}))^\perp = 1$, then we can perform the attack quite straightforwardly. Indeed, in this case there exists $\boldsymbol{v} \in \mathbb{F}_{q^m}^n$ which spans the entire dual. Many papers in the literature describe the attack just for this choice i, claiming that we can perform it only if $\dim(\Lambda_{n-k-1}(\mathscr{C}_{pub}))^\perp = 1$. We stress out that **this is not the only possible choice for** i: one only needs an $i < n - k$ for which $\Lambda_i(\mathscr{C}_{pub})^\perp$ has the structure (13).

Description of the Attack. We now briefly detail the procedure of the attack (partially presented in the proof of [40, Thm. 5.3]).

We know that $\Lambda_i(\mathscr{C}_{pub})$ admits a parity check matrix $\boldsymbol{H}_{\mathrm{pub}}$ (for simplicity, we omit the dependency on i) of the form (13). Thus, we look for some $\boldsymbol{T} \in \mathbf{GL}_{n+\lambda}(\mathbb{F}_q)$ for which

$$\boldsymbol{H}_{\mathrm{pub}}\boldsymbol{T}^{\top} = (\mathbf{0} \mid \boldsymbol{H}') \qquad (14)$$

The matrix $\boldsymbol{T}$ is not unique. Furthermore, the following statement taken from [40, Thm 5.3] asserts that every invertible $\boldsymbol{T}$ satisfying (14) is suitable to complete the attack. For the sake of completeness, we give the proof of this result.

Theorem 2 ([40, Thm 5.3]). *If there exists a positive integer $i < n - k$ for which the dimension of $\Lambda_i(\mathscr{G}_{pub})^{\perp}$ is $n - k - i$ and if we denote by $\boldsymbol{H}_{pub}$ a generator matrix of this dual, then any $\boldsymbol{T} \in \mathbf{GL}_{n+\lambda}(\mathbb{F}_q)$ such that*

$$\boldsymbol{H}_{pub}\boldsymbol{T}^{\top} = (\mathbf{0} \mid \boldsymbol{H}')$$

for some $\boldsymbol{H}' \in \mathcal{M}_{n-k-i,n}(\mathbb{F}_{q^m})$ is a valid column scrambler, i.e. there exists $\boldsymbol{Z} \in \mathcal{M}_{k,\lambda}(\mathbb{F}_{q^m})$ and $\boldsymbol{g}^{\star} \in \mathbb{F}_{q^m}^n$ of rank n, such that

$$\boldsymbol{G}_{pub} = \boldsymbol{S}(\boldsymbol{Z} \mid \mathbf{M}_k(\boldsymbol{g}^{\star}))\boldsymbol{T},$$

where $\mathbf{M}_k(\boldsymbol{g}^{\star})$ denotes the Moore matrix with generator vector $\boldsymbol{g}^{\star}$ (see (2)).

Proof. Since $\dim(\Lambda_i(\mathscr{G}_{pub})^{\perp}) = n - k - i$, then this dual admits a generator matrix of the form (13). Now, consider $\boldsymbol{T} \in \mathbf{GL}_{n+\lambda}(\mathbb{F}_q)$ such that

$$(\mathbf{0} \mid \boldsymbol{H}_i)(\boldsymbol{P}^{-1})^{\top}\boldsymbol{T}^{\top} = (\mathbf{0} \mid \boldsymbol{H}') \qquad (15)$$

for some $\boldsymbol{H}' \in \mathcal{M}_{n-k-i,n}(\mathbb{F}_{q^m})$. Denote,

$$\boldsymbol{T}\boldsymbol{P}^{-1} = \begin{pmatrix} \boldsymbol{A} \ \boldsymbol{B} \\ \boldsymbol{C} \ \boldsymbol{D} \end{pmatrix}$$

where $\boldsymbol{A} \in \mathcal{M}_{\lambda}(\mathbb{F}_q)$, $\boldsymbol{B} \in \mathcal{M}_{\lambda,n}(\mathbb{F}_q)$, $\boldsymbol{C} \in \mathcal{M}_{n,\lambda}(\mathbb{F}_q)$ and $\boldsymbol{D} \in \mathcal{M}_n(\mathbb{F}_q)$. From (15), we have that

$$\boldsymbol{H}_i\boldsymbol{B}^{\top} = 0 \implies \boldsymbol{B} = 0.$$

Since $\boldsymbol{P}\boldsymbol{T}^{-1}$ is invertible, this entails in particular that $\boldsymbol{A} \in \mathbf{GL}_{\lambda}(\mathbb{F}_q)$ and $\boldsymbol{D} \in \mathbf{GL}_n(\mathbb{F}_q)$. Then, we have that

$$(\boldsymbol{T}\boldsymbol{P}^{-1})^{-1} = \boldsymbol{P}\boldsymbol{T}^{-1} = \begin{pmatrix} \boldsymbol{A}^{-1} & \mathbf{0} \\ -\boldsymbol{D}^{-1}\boldsymbol{C}\boldsymbol{A}^{-1} \ \boldsymbol{D}^{-1} \end{pmatrix}$$

and so we get,

$$\boldsymbol{G}_{\mathrm{pub}}\boldsymbol{T}^{-1} = \boldsymbol{S}(\boldsymbol{X} \mid \mathbf{M}_k(\boldsymbol{g}))\boldsymbol{P}\boldsymbol{T}^{-1} = \boldsymbol{S}(\boldsymbol{Z} \mid \boldsymbol{G}')$$

for some matrix $\boldsymbol{Z}$, where $\boldsymbol{G}'$ is a generator matrix of $\mathscr{G}_k(\boldsymbol{g})\boldsymbol{D}^{-1}$, which also equals $\mathscr{G}_k(\boldsymbol{g}\boldsymbol{D}^{-1})$ since $\boldsymbol{D}$ is nonsingular with entries in $\mathbb{F}_q$ (see Lemma 1). $\square$

In order find such a T, we compute the space of the matrices $T \in \mathcal{M}_{n+\lambda}(\mathbb{F}_q)$ such that the λ leftmost columns of $H_{\mathrm{pub}} T^\top$ are zero. Then, we need to extract a nonsingular matrix from this solution space. This last step can be done by picking random elements in this space until we find a nonsingular matrix.

Once such a column scrambler T is computed, we can compute cT^{-1} and remove the leftmost λ entries. By Theorem 2, each of these T's is a valid column scrambler and it suffices to apply the Gabidulin codes decoder to the former vector to recover the plaintext. Recall that, from Sect. 2.1, the decoder works independently on the knowledge of g.

3.4   Analyzing the Dimension of $\Lambda_i(\mathscr{C}_{\mathrm{pub}})$ for Small i's

In this section we study what happens if we apply the q-sum operator to the public key for small i's, namely $i = 1$. In particular, we will see that in this case we can always attack the system by applying either strategies described in Sect. 4 or the classical Overbeck attack.

First, we recall that, by Lemma 3, the matrix $(\Lambda_1(X) \mid \Lambda_1(G))$ (see (12)) can be transformed into a matrix

$$\begin{pmatrix} X' & \mathbf{M}_{k+1}(g) \\ X'' & 0 \end{pmatrix} \tag{16}$$

In this case, $\mathbf{rank}(X'') \leqslant \min\{2s, \lambda\}$, where $s = \mathbf{rank}(X)$. We now introduce the following useful lemma.

Lemma 4. *If $k \geqslant 4s + 1$, then, up to row multiplications,*

$$[\Lambda_1(X) \mid \Lambda_1(G)] = \begin{pmatrix} \mathbf{0} & \mathbf{M}_{k+1}(g) \\ X'' & \mathbf{0} \end{pmatrix} \tag{17}$$

with a high probability.

Proof. We need to prove that $\mathbf{RowSp}_{\mathbb{F}_{q^m}}(X') \subseteq \mathbf{RowSp}_{\mathbb{F}_{q^m}}(X'')$. We first claim that $\mathbf{RowSp}_{\mathbb{F}_{q^m}}(X'') = \mathbf{RowSp}_{\mathbb{F}_{q^m}}(\Lambda_1(X))$ with a high probability. We consider the submatrix of X'' in $\mathcal{M}_{\lfloor \frac{k-1}{2} \rfloor, \lambda}(\mathbb{F}_{q^m})$ obtained by selecting alternate rows of X''. This is a uniformly random matrix in $\mathcal{M}_{\lfloor \frac{k-1}{2} \rfloor, \lambda}(\mathbb{F}_{q^m})$. By the assumption $\frac{k-1}{2} \geqslant 2s$, it has rank equal to $\min\{2s, \lambda\} = \mathbf{rank}(\Lambda_1(X))$ with a high probability (by Proposition 3). Thus, $\mathbf{rank}(X'') \geqslant \mathbf{rank}(\Lambda_1(X))$ with a high probability and so the claim follows. The result derives from remarking that $\mathbf{RowSp}_{\mathbb{F}_{q^m}}(X') \subseteq \mathbf{RowSp}_{\mathbb{F}_{q^m}}(\Lambda_1(X))$. ☐

We remark that if $\mathbf{rank}(X) = s \geqslant \lambda/2$, then $\mathbf{rank}(X'') = \lambda$ with high probability and so we can apply straightforwardly the Overbeck's attack (Sect. 3). One could then think that it suffices to take a sufficiently small s in order to repair the system. In the following section we show that thanks to the structure of the matrix (17), we can construct an attack, which is an extension of the Overbeck's one, which allows us to break the system independently from the rank of the distortion matrix, even for the twisted Gabidulin GPT scheme.

Remark 9. The condition $k \geqslant 4s + 1$ required in Lemma 4, yields a range of parameters for which we can assert the validity of the result. Nevertheless, it is probably highly conservative and one could expect result to hold for smaller k or equivalently larger s.

3.5   Puchinger, Renner and Wachter–Zeh Variant of GPT

In [43], the authors use simultaneously two distinct techniques in order to resist to Overbeck's attack:

1. they impose the distortion matrix to have a low rank (*e.g.* $s = 1$ or 2),
2. they replace Gabidulin codes by twisted ones (with parameters specified in Assumption 1).

The rationale behind the use of twisted Gabidulin codes is that, one step of Overbeck's attack consists in obtaining $\Lambda_{n-k-1}(\mathscr{C}_{\text{sec}})$ where $\mathscr{C}_{\text{sec}}$ is the hidden Gabidulin code. Then the dual $\Lambda_{n-k-1}(\mathscr{C})$ has dimension 1 and immediately provides the evaluation sequence. Based on this observation, the authors select parameters for twisted Gabidulin codes such that none of the $\Lambda_i(\mathscr{C}_{\text{sec}})$'s for $i > 0$ may have codimension 1 (see [43, Thm. 6]).

Table 1. Parameters from [43]

q	k	n	m	ℓ	λ	s
2	18	26	104	2	6	1
2	21	33	132	2	8	1
2	32	48	192	2	12	2

As mentioned in Remark 8, the choice of computing $\Lambda_{n-k-1}(\mathscr{C}_{\text{sec}})$ is only technical and can be circumvented in many different ways. In fact, once the distortion matrix $\boldsymbol{X}$ is discarded, we can access to $\mathscr{C}_{\text{sec}}$ and, using the discussion in Sect. 2.2, just knowing this code is generally enough to decode. However, their approach presents another difficulty for the attacker if one wants to apply Overbeck's attack. Indeed, the proposed parameters consider a distortion matrix of low rank, *e.g.* $s = 1$ or 2 (see Table 1). Then, to get for $\Lambda_i(\mathscr{C}_{\text{pub}})$ a generator matrix of the form (17) with $\Lambda_{i-1}(\boldsymbol{X}'')$ of full rank, one needs i to be large, while the dimensions of the $\Lambda_i(\mathscr{C}_{\text{sec}})$ increase faster than for a Gabidulin code. Thus, for some parameters it is possible that the computation of the successive $\Lambda_i(\mathscr{C}_{\text{pub}})$ provide successive codes with generator matrices of the form (17), so that $\Lambda_i(\mathscr{C}_{\text{sec}})$ becomes the full code $\mathbb{F}_{q^m}^n$ before $\Lambda_{i-1}(\boldsymbol{X}'')$ reaches the full rank λ. The core of our extension in Sect. 4 is the observation that there is no need for $\boldsymbol{X}''$ to have full rank to break the scheme.

Example 1. According to the Table 1, suppose that $n = 26$, $k = 18$, $\lambda = 6$ and $s = 1$. Then, for $\boldsymbol{X}''$ to have full rank $\lambda = 6$, while $\boldsymbol{X}$ has rank 1, we need to compute $\Lambda_6(\mathscr{C}_{\text{pub}})$. But since the secret code has dimension 18 and it is a twisted Gabidulin code, we deduce that $\dim \Lambda_6(\mathscr{C}_{\text{sec}}) \geqslant 26$ and, since $n = 26$, this code is nothing else than $\mathbb{F}_{q^m}^{26}$. Thus, for such parameters, we cannot apply the Overbeck's attack. In fact, even if instantiated with a Gabidulin code, the Overbeck's attack would fail for such parameters.

4   An Extension of Overbeck's Attack

As explained earlier, Overbeck's technique consists in applying the q–sum operator Λ_i to the public code, for an i such that the public code has a generator matrix of the form

$$\begin{pmatrix} \boldsymbol{I}_\lambda & \boldsymbol{0} \\ \boldsymbol{0} & \Lambda_i(\boldsymbol{G}_{\text{sec}}) \end{pmatrix} \boldsymbol{P}, \tag{18}$$

where $\Lambda_i(\mathscr{C}_{\text{sec}}) \neq \mathbb{F}_{q^m}^n$. This entails that the dual code has a generator matrix of the form

$$(\boldsymbol{0} \mid \boldsymbol{H})\,(\boldsymbol{P}^{-1})^\top, \tag{19}$$

where $\boldsymbol{H}^\top$ is a parity–check matrix of $\Lambda_i(\mathscr{C}_{\text{sec}})$. Then, a valid column scrambler can be computed by solving a linear system. The point of this section is to prove that one can relax the constraint on i and only expect $\Lambda_i(\boldsymbol{G}_{\text{pub}})$ to have a generator matrix "splitting in two blocks", *i.e.*

$$\begin{pmatrix} \boldsymbol{Y} & \boldsymbol{0} \\ \boldsymbol{0} & \Lambda_i(\boldsymbol{G}_{\text{sec}}) \end{pmatrix} \boldsymbol{P}, \tag{20}$$

without requiring $\boldsymbol{Y}$ to have full rank λ.

   Note that the above-described setting is precisely what happens to $\Lambda_1(\boldsymbol{G}_{\text{pub}})$ when $s = \mathbf{rank}(\boldsymbol{X}) < \lambda/2$, see Sect. 3.4, Example 1 or Sect. 5.3.

Example 2. Back to Example 1, for such parameters, even instantiated with a Gabidulin code, the Overbeck's attack fails because there is not any $i > 0$ which gives a matrix of the shape (18). However, under some assumptions on the parameters of the code, it is likely that $\Lambda_1(\boldsymbol{G}_{\text{pub}})$ has a generator matrix of the shape (20). See for instance Lemmas 4 and 6.

4.1   Sketch of the Attack

Now, let us explain how to find the hidden splitting structure (20) without any knowledge of the scrambling matrix $\boldsymbol{P}$. Assume that $\Lambda_i(\mathscr{C}_{\text{pub}})$ has a generator matrix of the form

$$\begin{pmatrix} \boldsymbol{Y} & \boldsymbol{0} \\ \boldsymbol{0} & \boldsymbol{G}_i \end{pmatrix} \boldsymbol{P}, \tag{21}$$

where $\boldsymbol{Y}$ is a matrix with λ columns, $\boldsymbol{G}_i$ is a generator matrix of $\Lambda_i(\mathscr{C}_{\text{sec}})$ and $\mathscr{C}_{\text{sec}}$ is the hidden code of dimension k. The code $\mathscr{C}_{\text{sec}}$ could be either a Gabidulin code in the case of classical GPT or a twisted Gabidulin code (see respectively Sect. 1.5 and the beginning of Sect. 5).

The idea consists in computing the *right stabilizer algebra* of $\Lambda_i(\mathscr{C}_{\mathrm{pub}})$:

$$\mathrm{Stab}_{\mathrm{right}}(\Lambda_i(\mathscr{C}_{\mathrm{pub}})) \overset{\mathrm{def}}{=} \{ M \in \mathcal{M}_{n+\lambda}(\mathbb{F}_q) \mid \Lambda_i(\mathscr{C}_{\mathrm{pub}}) M \subseteq \Lambda_i(\mathscr{C}_{\mathrm{pub}}) \}.$$

This algebra can be computed by solving a linear system (see Sect. 4.2). It turns out that it contains two peculiar matrices, namely:

$$E_1 = P^{-1} \begin{pmatrix} I_\lambda & 0 \\ 0 & 0 \end{pmatrix} P \quad \text{and} \quad E_2 = P^{-1} \begin{pmatrix} 0 & 0 \\ 0 & I_n \end{pmatrix} P. \tag{22}$$

The core of the attack consists in computing these two matrices, or more precisely conjugates of these matrices, and then consider the code $\mathscr{C}_{\mathrm{pub}} E_2$ which is somehow right equivalent to $\mathscr{C}_{\mathrm{sec}}$. In particular, the right multiplication by E_2 will annihilate the distortion matrix X. Let us now present the approach in more detail.

4.2   Some Algebraic Preliminaries

Split and Indecomposable Codes. The first crucial notion is that of *split* or *decomposable* codes.

Definition 3. *A code $\mathscr{C} \subseteq \mathbb{F}_{q^m}^n$ of dimension k is said to* split *if it has a generator matrix of the form*

$$\begin{pmatrix} G_1 & 0 \\ 0 & G_2 \end{pmatrix} Q,$$

for some matrices $G_1 \in \mathcal{M}_{a,b}(\mathbb{F}_{q^m}), G_2 \in \mathcal{M}_{k-a,n-b}(\mathbb{F}_{q^m})$ and $Q \in \mathbf{GL}_n(\mathbb{F}_q)$. If no such block–wise decomposition exists, then the code is said to be indecomposable.

Remark 10. Considering the code as a space of matrices, being split means that the code is the direct sum of two subcodes whose row supports (*i.e.* the sum of the row spaces of their elements) are in direct sum. This is the rank metric counterpart of Hamming codes which are the direct sum of two subcodes with disjoint Hamming supports. Note that this property is very rare and corresponds to somehow very *degenerated* codes.

Stabilizer Algebras and Conductors. We now define the notions that we will use throughout this section. Stabilizers are useful invariants of codes, also called *idealizers* in the literature. Conductors, are used for instance in [12] and have often been used in cryptanalysis of schemes based on algebraic Hamming metric codes, for instance [5,13,14].

Definition 4. *Let $\mathscr{C} \subseteq \mathbb{F}_{q^m}^{n_1}$ and $\mathscr{D} \subseteq \mathbb{F}_{q^m}^{n_2}$ be two $\mathbb{F}_{q^m}$–linear codes of respective length n_1, n_2. The conductor of $\mathscr{C}$ into $\mathscr{D}$ is defined as:*

$$\mathrm{Cond}(\mathscr{C}, \mathscr{D}) \overset{\mathrm{def}}{=} \{ A \in \mathcal{M}_{n_1,n_2}(\mathbb{F}_q) \mid \forall c \in \mathscr{C}, \ cA \in \mathscr{D}. \}$$

It is an $\mathbb{F}_q$-vector subspace of $\mathcal{M}_{n_1,n_2}(\mathbb{F}_q)$. Moreover, when $\mathscr{C} = \mathscr{D}$, then the conductor is an algebra which is usually called right stabilizer *or* right idealizer *of $\mathscr{C}$ and denoted*

$$Stab_{right}(\mathscr{C}) \stackrel{def}{=} Cond(\mathscr{C}, \mathscr{C}) = \{ A \in \mathcal{M}_{n_1}(\mathbb{F}_q) \mid \forall c \in \mathscr{C}, \ cA \in \mathscr{C} \}.$$

Relation to Our Problem. The first important point is that almost any code of length $n + \lambda$ has a *trivial right stabilizer*, *i.e.* a stabilizer of the form $\{ \alpha I_{n+\lambda} \mid \alpha \in \mathbb{F}_q \}$. However, the stabilizer of $\Lambda_i(\mathscr{C}_{pub})$ is non trivial, since it contains the matrices (22).

The second point is that $Stab_{right}(\Lambda_i(\mathscr{C}_{pub}))$ can be computed by solving a linear system. In general, given a parity–check matrix H for $\mathscr{C}$, the elements of $Stab_{right}(\mathscr{C})$ are nothing but the solutions $M \in \mathcal{M}_{n+\lambda}(\mathbb{F}_q)$ of the system

$$GMH^\top = 0. \tag{23}$$

Idempotents and Decomposition of the Identity. The matrices E_1 and E_2 of (22) are *idempotents* of the right stabilizer algebra of $\Lambda_i(\mathscr{C}_{pub})$, *i.e.* elements satisfying $E_1^2 = E_1$ and $E_2^2 = E_2$. In addition, they provide what is usually called *a decomposition of the identity with orthogonal idempotents*. The general definition is given below.

Definition 5. *In a matrix algebra $\mathcal{A} \subseteq \mathcal{M}_n(\mathbb{F}_q)$, a tuple $E_1, \ldots, E_r$ of nonzero idempotents are said to be a* decomposition of the identity into orthogonal idempotents *if they satisfy,*

$$\forall 1 \leqslant i, j \leqslant r, \ E_i E_j = 0 \quad and \quad E_1 + \cdots + E_r = I.$$

Such a decomposition is said to be minimal *if none of the E_i's can be written as a sum of two nonzero orthogonal idempotents.*

Proposition 4. *A code $\mathscr{C} \subseteq \mathbb{F}_{q^m}^n$ is split if and only if $Stab_{right}(\mathscr{C})$ has a non-trivial decomposition of the identity into orthogonal idempotents.*

Proof. Suppose that $Stab_{right}(\mathscr{C})$ contains such a decomposition of the identity into orthogonal idempotents $I = E_1 + \cdots + E_r$. Since the E_i's commute pairwise and are diagonalizable (indeed, being idempotent, they all cancelled by the split polynomial $X^2 - X$), they are simultaneously diagonalizable. Thus, there exists $Q \in \mathbf{GL}_n(\mathbb{F}_q)$ such that

$$E_1 = Q^{-1} \begin{pmatrix} I_{n_1} & & (0) \\ & \ddots & \\ (0) & & (0) \end{pmatrix} Q, \ldots, \ E_r = Q^{-1} \begin{pmatrix} (0) & & (0) \\ & \ddots & \\ (0) & & I_{n_r} \end{pmatrix} Q,$$

for some positive integers $n_1, \ldots, n_r$ such that $n_1 + \cdots + n_r = n$.

The code $\mathscr{C}' = \mathscr{C}Q$ has the matrices

$$E'_1 = \begin{pmatrix} I_{n_1} & & (0) \\ & \ddots & \\ (0) & & (0) \end{pmatrix}, \ldots, E'_r = \begin{pmatrix} (0) & & (0) \\ & \ddots & \\ (0) & & I_{n_r} \end{pmatrix} \tag{24}$$

in its right stabilizer algebra, and one can easily check that $\mathscr{C}' = \mathscr{C}'E'_1 \oplus \cdots \oplus \mathscr{C}'E'_r$, leading to a block–wise generator matrix of $\mathscr{C}'$. Thus, $\mathscr{C}$ has a generator matrix of the form

$$\begin{pmatrix} G_1 & & (0) \\ & \ddots & \\ (0) & & G_r \end{pmatrix} Q^{-1}. \tag{25}$$

Conversely, if $\mathscr{C}$ has a generator matrix as in (25), one can easily deduce a decomposition of the identity in $\mathrm{Stab}_{\mathrm{right}}(\mathscr{C})$ into the idempotents (24). □

In particular, a code is indecomposable if and only if its right stabilizer algebra has no nontrivial idempotent. Such an algebra is said to be *local*.

A crucial aspect of minimal decompositions of the identity is the following, sometimes referred to as the Krull–Schmidt Theorem.

Theorem 3 ([15, Thm. 3.4.1]). *Let $\mathcal{A} \subseteq \mathcal{M}_n(\mathbb{F}_q)$ be a matrix algebra and $E_1, \ldots, E_r$ and $F_1, \ldots, F_s$ be two minimal decompositions of the identity into orthogonal idempotents. Then, $r = s$ and there exists $A \in \mathcal{A}^\times$ such that, after possibly re-indexing the F_i's, we have $F_i = AE_iA^{-1}$, for any $i \in \{1, \ldots, s\}$.*

In short: a minimal decomposition of the identity into idempotents is unique up to conjugation.

Algorithmic Aspects. Given a matrix algebra, a decomposition of the identity into minimal idempotents can be efficiently computed using Friedl and Ronyái's algorithms [16, 47]. Such a calculation is presented in the case of stabilizer algebras of codes in [12]. Further, in Sect. 4.5, we present the calculation in a simple case which turns out to be the generic situation for our cryptanalysis.

4.3 Description of Our Extension of Overbeck's Attack

The attack summarizes as follows. Recall that the public code $\mathscr{C}_{\mathrm{pub}}$ has a generator matrix

$$G_{\mathrm{pub}} = (X \mid G_{\mathrm{sec}})P.$$

Step 1. Compute i so that the code $\Lambda_i(\mathscr{C}_{\mathrm{pub}})$ splits as in (21), *i.e.* has the shape

$$\begin{pmatrix} Y & 0 \\ 0 & G_i \end{pmatrix} P \tag{26}$$

where G_i is a generator matrix of $\Lambda_i(\mathscr{C}_{\text{sec}})$ and P the column scrambler. In the sequel, **we suppose that** $\Lambda_i(\mathscr{C}_{\text{sec}})$ **is indecomposable.** This assumption is discussed further in Sect. 4.5.

Step 2. Compute $\text{Stab}_{\text{right}}(\Lambda_i(\mathscr{C}_{\text{pub}}))$. We know that this algebra contains the matrices

$$E_1 = P^{-1} \begin{pmatrix} I_\lambda & 0 \\ 0 & 0 \end{pmatrix} P \quad \text{and} \quad E_2 = P^{-1} \begin{pmatrix} 0 & 0 \\ 0 & I_n \end{pmatrix} P. \tag{27}$$

Next, using the algorithms described in [12,16,47], compute a minimal decomposition of the identity of $\text{Stab}_{\text{right}}(\Lambda_i(\mathscr{C}_{\text{pub}}))$ into orthogonal idempotents. The following statement relates any such minimal decomposition to the matrices E_1 and E_2 in (27).

Lemma 5. *Assume that $\lambda < n$. Under the assumption that $\Lambda_i(\mathscr{C}_{\text{sec}})$ is an indecomposable code, any minimal decomposition of the identity into orthogonal idempotents in $\Lambda_i(\mathscr{C}_{\text{pub}})$ contains a unique element F of rank n. Moreover, there exists $A \in \text{Stab}_{right}(\Lambda_i(\mathscr{C}_{\text{pub}}))^\times$ such that $F = A^{-1}E_2 A$ where E_2 is the matrix introduced in (27).*

Proof. Consider the pair E_1, E_2 introduced in (27). The matrix E_2 has rank n and projects the code $\Lambda_i(\mathscr{C}_{\text{pub}})$ onto the code with generator matrix $(0 \ G_i)P$, where G_i is a generator matrix of $\Lambda_i(\mathscr{C}_{\text{sec}})$. Since $\Lambda_i(\mathscr{C}_{\text{pub}})$ is supposed to be indecomposable, E_2 cannot split into $E_2 = E_{21} + E_{22}$ such that $E_{21}E_{22} = E_{22}E_{21} = 0$, since this would contradict the indecomposability of $\Lambda_i(\mathscr{C}_{\text{sec}})$. Next, either E_1, E_2 is a minimal decomposition or, E_1 splits into a sum of orthogonal idempotents (if the code with generator matrix Y splits). In the latter situation, one deduces a minimal decomposition of the identity of the form $E_{11}, \ldots, E_{1r}, E_2$. Now, Theorem 3, permits to conclude that any other minimal decomposition is conjugate to the previous one and hence contains a unique element of rank n which is conjugate with E_2.   □

Step 3. Once we have computed a minimal decomposition of the identity into minimal idempotents, according to Lemma 5 and Theorem 3, we have computed $F \in \text{Stab}_{\text{right}}(\Lambda_i(\mathscr{C}_{\text{pub}}))$ of rank n satisfying $F = A^{-1}E_2 A$ for some unknown matrix $A \in \text{Stab}_{\text{right}}(\Lambda_i(\mathscr{C}_{\text{pub}}))^\times$.

Proposition 5. *The code, $\mathscr{C}_{\text{pub}}F$ is contained in the code with generator matrix*

$$\left(0 \mid \overline{G}_{sec}^i \right) PA,$$

where $\overline{G}_{sec}^i$ is a generator matrix of the code $\overline{\mathscr{C}}_{sec}^i$ introduced in Definition 2.

Before proving the previous statement, let us discuss it quickly. The result may seem disappointing since, even if we discarded the distortion matrix, we do not recover exactly the secret code. However,

1. the approach is relevant for small i's, and if $i \leqslant t$, where t is the rank of the error term in the encryption process, then, the algorithm described in Sect. 2.2 decodes $\overline{\mathscr{C}}_{\mathrm{sec}}^{t}$ (and hence $\overline{\mathscr{C}}_{\mathrm{sec}}^{i}$ since it is contained in $\overline{\mathscr{C}}_{\mathrm{sec}}^{t}$) as efficiently as $\mathscr{C}_{\mathrm{sec}}$ itself.
2. In Sect. 4.5, we provide some heuristic claiming that, most of the time, $\mathscr{C}_{\mathrm{pub}}\boldsymbol{F}$ is nothing but the code with generator matrix

$$(\mathbf{0} \mid \boldsymbol{G}_{\mathrm{sec}})\,\boldsymbol{P}\boldsymbol{A}.$$

Proof (of Proposition 5). Recall that $\boldsymbol{F} = \boldsymbol{A}^{-1}\boldsymbol{E}_2\boldsymbol{A}$ for some matrix $\boldsymbol{A} \in \mathrm{Stab}_{\mathrm{right}}(\Lambda_i(\mathscr{C}_{\mathrm{pub}}))$. Then, since $\boldsymbol{A}$ is invertible, we deduce that $\Lambda_i(\mathscr{C}_{\mathrm{pub}})\boldsymbol{A}^{-1} = \Lambda_i(\mathscr{C}_{\mathrm{pub}})$. Therefore,
$$\Lambda_i(\mathscr{C}_{\mathrm{pub}})\boldsymbol{F} = \Lambda_i(\mathscr{C}_{\mathrm{pub}})\boldsymbol{E}_2\boldsymbol{A}.$$

From (26) and (27), the code $\Lambda_i(\mathscr{C}_{\mathrm{pub}})\boldsymbol{E}_2$ has a generator matrix of the form $(\mathbf{0} \mid \boldsymbol{G}_i)\boldsymbol{P}$ and hence the code $\Lambda_i(\mathscr{C}_{\mathrm{pub}})\boldsymbol{F}$ has a generator matrix

$$(\mathbf{0} \mid \boldsymbol{G}_i)\boldsymbol{P}\boldsymbol{A}. \tag{28}$$

Next, the code $\mathscr{C}_{\mathrm{pub}}$ is contained in $\Lambda_i(\mathscr{C}_{\mathrm{pub}})$ but also in $\overline{\Lambda_i(\mathscr{C}_{\mathrm{pub}})}^{i}$. Moreover, according to Remark 7, we have

$$\mathscr{C}_{\mathrm{pub}} \subseteq \overline{\mathscr{C}}_{\mathrm{pub}}^{i} = \bigcap_{j=0}^{i} (\Lambda_i(\mathscr{C}_{\mathrm{pub}}))^{[-j]}.$$

Since both $\boldsymbol{P}$ and $\boldsymbol{A}$ have their entries in $\mathbb{F}_q$, they commute with the operations of raising to any q–th power and we deduce that

$$\mathscr{C}_{\mathrm{pub}}\boldsymbol{F} \subseteq \overline{\Lambda_i(\mathscr{C}_{\mathrm{pub}})}^{i}\boldsymbol{F}.$$

Then, from (28), we deduce that $\mathscr{C}_{\mathrm{pub}}\boldsymbol{F}$ is contained in the code with generator matrix
$$\left(\mathbf{0} \mid \overline{\boldsymbol{G}}_{\mathrm{sec}}^{i}\right)\boldsymbol{P}\boldsymbol{A}.$$

$\square$

Step 5. With the previous results at hand, given a ciphertext $\boldsymbol{y} = \boldsymbol{m}\boldsymbol{G}_{\mathrm{pub}} + \boldsymbol{e}$ with $\mathbf{rank}(\boldsymbol{e}) \leqslant t$, we can compute

$$\boldsymbol{y}\boldsymbol{F} = \boldsymbol{m}\boldsymbol{G}_{\mathrm{pub}}\boldsymbol{F} + \boldsymbol{e}\boldsymbol{F}.$$

Then, we remove its λ leftmost entries. Since $\boldsymbol{F}$ has its entries in $\mathbb{F}_q$, $\mathbf{rank}(\boldsymbol{e}\boldsymbol{F}) \leqslant \mathbf{rank}(\boldsymbol{e})$. Next, $\boldsymbol{m}\boldsymbol{G}_{\mathrm{pub}}\boldsymbol{F}$ with the λ leftmost entries removed is a codeword in $\overline{\Lambda_i(\mathscr{C}_{\mathrm{sec}})}^{i}$ which can be decoded using the algorithm introduced in 2.2. This yields the plaintext $\boldsymbol{m}$.

Algorithm 2: Summary of the attack

Input: G_{pub}, a ciphertext y and the rank of the error term t
Output: A pair $(m e) \in \mathbb{F}_{q^m}^k \times \mathbb{F}_{q^m}^n$ such that $\mathbf{rank}(e) = t$ and $y = m G_{\mathrm{pub}} + e$
or '?' if fails

1 Compute a generator matrix of $\Lambda_i(\mathscr{C}_{\mathrm{pub}})$ for the least i for which the code splits.
2 **if** *no such i exists* **then**
3   ⌊ Return '?'
4 Compute a minimal decomposition of the identity of $\mathrm{Stab}_{\mathrm{right}}(\Lambda_i(\mathscr{C}))$ and extract its unique term F of rank n.
5 **if** *no such F exists* **then**
6   ⌊ Return '?'
7 Compute $y F$ and apply to it the decoder described in 2.2.
8 return the output m of the decoder (possibly '?' if the decoder fails).

4.4 Summary of the Attack

According to the description in Sect. 4.3, the attack is now summarized in Algorithm 2 below.

4.5 Discussions and Simplifications

For the attack presented in Algorithm 2 to work, several assumptions are made. Here we discuss these assumptions and their rationale. We also point out that in our specific case, the algebra $\mathrm{Stab}_{\mathrm{right}}(\Lambda_i(\mathscr{C}_{\mathrm{pub}}))$ will be very specific. This may permit to avoid to consider the difficult cases of Friedl Ronyái's algorithms.

Indecomposability of $\Lambda_i(\mathscr{C}_{\mathrm{sec}})$. An important assumption for the attack to succeed is that $\Lambda_i(\mathscr{C}_{\mathrm{sec}})$ does not split. Note first that in the classical GPT case, $\mathscr{C}_{\mathrm{sec}}$ is a Gabidulin code. And so, this always holds as soon as $i < n - k$.

This is a consequence of the following statement and the fact that if $\mathscr{C}_{\mathrm{sec}}$ is a Gabidulin code, and so for any $i > 0$, also $\Lambda_i(\mathscr{C}_{\mathrm{sec}})$ is a Gabidulin code. Thus, according to the following statement it is indecomposable.

Proposition 6. *An MRD code $\mathscr{C} \subsetneq \mathbb{F}_{q^m}^n$ never splits.*

Proof. Let $\mathscr{C} \subseteq \mathbb{F}_{q^m}^n$ be an MRD code of dimension k. Suppose it splits into a direct sum of two codes $\mathscr{C}_1, \mathscr{C}_2$ of respective lengths n_1, n_2 and dimensions k_1, k_2. Then, $\mathscr{C}_1$ has codewords of rank weight $n_1 - k_1 + 1$ and $\mathscr{C}_2$ has words of weight $n_2 - k_2 + 1$. Such words are also words of $\mathscr{C}$ and, since $\mathscr{C}$ is MRD, we have

$$n_1 - k_1 + 1 \geqslant n - k + 1$$
$$n_2 - k_2 + 1 \geqslant n - k + 1$$

Summing up these two inequalities and using the fact that $n_1 + n_2 = n$ and $k_1 + k_2 = k$, we get a contradiction. $\qquad\square$

In the general case of twisted Gabidulin codes the situation is more complicated. However, twisted Gabidulin codes are contained in Gabidulin codes of larger dimensions, hence so are their images by the Λ_i operator. It seems very unlikely that a Gabidulin code could contain large subcodes that split.

On the Structure of $\mathrm{Stab}_{\mathrm{right}} \Lambda_i(\mathscr{C}_{\mathrm{pub}})$. A crucial step of the attack is the computation of a decomposition of the identity of $\mathrm{Stab}_{\mathrm{right}}(\Lambda_i(\mathscr{C}_{\mathrm{pub}}))$ into a sum of orthogonal idempotents. For this, we referred to Friedl Ronyái [16,47]. Actually, our setting is rather specific and the structure of this stabilizer algebra is pretty well understood. Let us start with a proposition.

Proposition 7. *Let $\mathscr{C}$ be an $\mathbb{F}_{q^m}$–linear code of length $n + \lambda$ and dimension K with a generator matrix of the shape (21), i.e.*

$$\begin{pmatrix} G_1 & 0 \\ 0 & G_2 \end{pmatrix},$$

with $G_1 \in M_{k_1, \lambda}(\mathbb{F}_{q^m})$ for some integer k_1 and $G_2 \in M_{k_2, n}(\mathbb{F}_{q^m})$ for some integer k_2 so that $k_1 + k_2 = K$. Denote by $\mathscr{C}_1$ and $\mathscr{C}_2$ the codes with respective generator matrices G_1 and G_2. Then any $M \in \mathrm{Stab}_{right}(\mathscr{C})$ has the shape

$$M = \begin{pmatrix} A & B \\ C & D \end{pmatrix},$$

where $A \in \mathrm{Stab}_{right}(\mathscr{C}_1)$, $B \in \mathrm{Cond}(\mathscr{C}_2, \mathscr{C}_1)$, $C \in \mathrm{Cond}(\mathscr{C}_1, \mathscr{C}_2)$ and $D \in \mathrm{Stab}_{right}(\mathscr{C}_2)$. □

Proof. Let $c_1 \in \mathscr{C}_1$, then $(c_1 \ 0) \in \mathscr{C}$ and by definition of M, $(c_1 \ 0)M = (c_1 A \ c_1 B) \in \mathscr{C}$. By definition of $\mathscr{C}$, we have $c_1 A \in \mathscr{C}_1$ and $c_1 B \in \mathscr{C}_2$. Since the previous assertions hold for any $c_1 \in \mathscr{C}_1$, then we deduce that $A \in \mathrm{Stab}_{right}(\mathscr{C}_1)$ and $B \in \mathrm{Cond}(\mathscr{C}_1, \mathscr{C}_2)$.

The result for C, D is obtained in the same way by considering $(0 \ c_2)M$ for $c_2 \in \mathscr{C}_2$. □

Consequently considering the generator matrix (26) of $\Lambda_i(\mathscr{C}_{\mathrm{pub}})$, elements of $\mathrm{Stab}_{\mathrm{right}}(\Lambda_i(\mathscr{C}_{\mathrm{pub}}))$ have the shape

$$\begin{pmatrix} A & B \\ C & D \end{pmatrix}, \tag{29}$$

where $A \in \mathrm{Stab}_{\mathrm{right}}(\mathscr{C}_Y)$ ($\mathscr{C}_Y$ being the code with generator matrix Y), $B \in \mathrm{Cond}(\Lambda_i(\mathscr{C}_{\mathrm{sec}}), \mathscr{C}_Y)$, $C \in \mathrm{Cond}(\mathscr{C}_Y, \Lambda_i(\mathscr{C}_{\mathrm{sec}}))$ and $D \in \mathrm{Stab}_{\mathrm{right}}(\Lambda_i(\mathscr{C}_{\mathrm{sec}}))$.

Here again, we claim that is very likely that the stabilizer algebras of $\mathscr{C}_Y$ and $\Lambda_i(\mathscr{C}_{\mathrm{pub}})$ are trivial, *i.e.* contain only scalar multiples of the identity matrix and that the conductors $\mathrm{Cond}(\mathscr{C}_Y, \Lambda_i(\mathscr{C}_{\mathrm{sec}}))$ and $\mathrm{Stab}_{\mathrm{right}}(\Lambda_i(\mathscr{C}_{\mathrm{sec}}))$ are zero. This claim is discussed further in Sect. 4.7.

In such a situation, we have:

$$\mathrm{Stab}_{\mathrm{right}}(\Lambda_i(\mathscr{C}_{\mathrm{pub}})) = \left\{ P^{-1} \begin{pmatrix} a I_\lambda & 0 \\ 0 & b I_n \end{pmatrix} P \ \middle| \ a, b \in \mathbb{F}_q \right\}. \tag{30}$$

Hence this algebra has dimension 2 and the calculation of the matrix

$$P^{-1} \begin{pmatrix} 0 & 0 \\ 0 & I_n \end{pmatrix} P \tag{31}$$

can be performed as follows.

1. First extract a singular matrix of $\mathrm{Stab}_{\mathrm{right}}(\Lambda_i(\mathscr{C}_{\mathrm{pub}}))$. For that, take U, V a basis of $\mathrm{Stab}_{\mathrm{right}}(\Lambda_i(\mathscr{C}_{\mathrm{pub}}))$. If V is singular we are done. Otherwise, compute a root of the univariate polynomial $\det(U + XV)$. This yields a singular element R of $\mathrm{Stab}_{\mathrm{right}}(\Lambda_i(\mathscr{C}_{\mathrm{pub}}))$ corresponding either to $a = 0$ or $b = 0$ in the description (30).
2. Next, rescale R as νR in order to get an idempotent element. If the obtained idempotent has rank n set $F = \nu R$, otherwise (it will have rank λ), set $F = I_{n+\lambda} - \nu R$.

The obtained matrix F is nothing but the target matrix in (31). Therefore, one can even skip the proof of Proposition 5 and observe that the code $\mathscr{C}_{\mathrm{pub}} F$ will be **exactly** the code with generator matrix

$$(0 \mid G_{\mathrm{sec}}) P.$$

4.6 Complexity

Considering the previous simple case which remains very likely, we analyze the cost of the various computation steps.

– The computation of $\Lambda_i(\mathscr{C}_{\mathrm{pub}})$ can be done by iterating i successive Gaussian eliminations (we assume that raising an element of $\mathbb{F}_{q^m}$ to the q–th power can be done for free, for instance by representing $\mathbb{F}_{q^m}$ with a normal basis). Thus, a cost $O(in^\omega)$ operations in $\mathbb{F}_{q^m}$ and hence $O(im^2 n^\omega)$ operations in $\mathbb{F}_q$. Here, ω denotes the usual exponent for the cost of the product of two $n \times n$ matrices.
– The computation of $\mathrm{Stab}_{\mathrm{right}}(\Lambda_i(\mathscr{C}_{\mathrm{pub}}))$ is done by solving the linear system (23). The system has n^2 unknowns in $\mathbb{F}_q$ and $k_i(n - k_i) = O(n^2)$ equations in $\mathbb{F}_{q^m}$ and hence $O(mn^2)$ equations in $\mathbb{F}_q$. This yields a cost of $O(mn^{2\omega})$ operations in $\mathbb{F}_q$ (see [9, Thm. 8.6] for the complexity of the resolution of a non square linear system).

In the aforementioned simple case, the remaining operations are negligible compared to the calculation of the stabilizer algebra, which turns out to be the bottleneck of the calculation. This overall cost is hence in

$$O(mn^{2\omega}) \text{ operations in } \mathbb{F}_q.$$

4.7 Discussion About the Claims on Conductors and Stabilizers

Back to the description (29) of the elements of $\mathrm{Stab}_{\mathrm{right}}(\Lambda_i(\mathscr{C}_{\mathrm{pub}}))$. Let us discuss the validity of the claim.

Conductors are Likely to be Zero. Let $C \in \mathrm{Cond}(\mathscr{C}_Y, \Lambda_i(\mathscr{C}_{\mathrm{sec}}))$, then the code $\mathscr{C}_Y C$ is a subcode of $\Lambda_i(\mathscr{C}_{\mathrm{sec}})$ and one proves easily that any element of $\mathscr{C}_Y C$ has a row support contained in the row space of C. Since $C \in \mathcal{M}_{\lambda,n}(\mathbb{F}_q)$, its rank is at most equal to λ and hence the code $\mathscr{C}_Y C$ has a row space contained in a space of dimension $\leqslant \lambda$. It seems unlikely that the code $\Lambda_t(\mathscr{C}_{\mathrm{sec}})$ contains such a space. In particular, this cannot happen if the minimum distance of $\Lambda_i(\mathscr{C}_{\mathrm{sec}})$ exceeds λ.

Now, consider $B \in \mathrm{Cond}(\Lambda_i(\mathscr{C}_{\mathrm{sec}}), \mathscr{C}_Y)$. Suppose first that B has full rank. Since $\dim(\Lambda_i(\mathscr{C}_{\mathrm{sec}})) \gg \lambda$, the code $\Lambda_i(\mathscr{C}_{\mathrm{sec}})B$ is likely to be equal to $\mathbb{F}_{q^m}^{\lambda}$ and hence cannot be contained in $\mathscr{C}_Y$, a contradiction. If B has not full rank, then, the code $\Lambda_i(\mathscr{C}_{\mathrm{sec}})B$ is likely to be equal to the subspace of $\mathbb{F}_{q^m}^{\lambda}$ of all the vectors whose row support is in the row space of B and we can assume that $\mathscr{C}_Y$ has no such subspace. Indeed, if it did, it would entail that $\mathscr{C}_Y^{\perp}$ (and hence $\Lambda_i(\mathscr{C}_{\mathrm{pub}})^{\perp}$ too) would have a parity-check matrix of the form $(\mathbf{0} \mid \boldsymbol{H}')(\boldsymbol{P}^{-1})^{\top}$ as in (19). Details are left to the reader.

Stabilizers are Likely Restrict to Scalar Matrices. For $\mathscr{C}_Y$, this code is close to be random and random codes have trivial stabilizer algebras with a high probability.

For $\Lambda_i(\mathscr{C}_{\mathrm{sec}})$ the right stabilizer algebra might be a larger one. Indeed, regarding the proof of Proposition 2 (see [43, Thm. 4]) we can see that $\Lambda_t(\mathscr{C})$ is a code generated by the evaluations of q-monomials and such a code, when $n = m$ has a right stabilizer algebra equal to a matrix representation of $\mathbb{F}_{q^m}$. This is a consequence of the fact that an $\mathbb{F}_{q^m}$–space spanned by q–monomials is $\mathbb{F}_{q^m}$–linear on the left but also on the right. Thus, $\mathrm{Stab}_{\mathrm{right}}(\Lambda_i(\mathscr{C}_{\mathrm{sec}}))$ might be such a larger algebra. In this situation, the calculation of a decomposition of the identity into orthogonal idempotents is slightly more complicated but remains definitely possible in polynomial time using Friedl Ronyái algorithms.

5   Don't Twist Again

In this section we first show that, even for twisted Gabidulin codes, the application of the q-sum operator allows to *distinguish* them from random codes. It is therefore possible to apply the attack described in Sect. 4 to the GPT cryptosystem instantiated with these codes. In the first part of this section we discuss the behaviour of raw twisted Gabidulin codes with respect to the operator Λ_i or equivalently, how the use of Λ_i allows to distinguish them from random codes. In the second part, we focus on q-operator applied to the corresponding public key and we will prove that even in this case, we have a generator matrix with a structure similar to (16) and that the corresponding codes split. This allows us to apply the results of Sect. 4.

5.1 A Distinguisher

First, recall Propositions 2 and 3 about the dimension of the q-sum operator applied respectively to twisted Gabidulin codes and to random codes. In particular, recall that if $\mathscr{C}$ is a random code, $\dim(\Lambda_i(\mathscr{C})) = (i+1)k$ with high probability. Then, we remark that, if $i < \frac{n-k-\ell}{\ell+1}$

$$\dim(\Lambda_i(\mathscr{C}_{g,t,h,\eta}[n,k])) = k+i+\ell(i+1) < (i+1)k = \dim(\Lambda_i(\mathscr{C})) \quad (32)$$
$$\Longleftrightarrow i > \ell/(k-\ell-1), \quad (33)$$

where $\mathscr{C}_{g,t,h,\eta}[n,k]$ is a twisted Gabidulin code (see Sect. 1.4).

Thus, the inequality $i > \ell/(k-\ell-1)$ is satisfied by any positive i, if $k > 2\ell+1$. We notice that this is often the case if we consider a small number of twists as in Table 1. This means that, even if the dimension of the q-sum applied to these codes is greater than that of the q-sum of a Gabidulin code, we can however still distinguish them for random codes.

Thus, this distinguisher can be exploited to construct an attack against the GPT cryptosystem instantiated with twisted Gabidulin codes, instead of classical ones.

5.2 The Structure of $\Lambda_i(\mathscr{G}_{Tpub})$

From now on, we consider the GPT cryptosystem instantiated with a twisted Gabidulin code $\mathscr{C}_{g,t,h,\eta}[n,k]$ with the parameters defined in Assumption 1. We denote by $\boldsymbol{G}_{\mathrm{Tpub}}$ the corresponding public key, obtained as (5) by just replacing $\boldsymbol{G}_{\mathrm{sec}}$ with a generator matrix $\boldsymbol{G_T}$ (of the form (4)) of the code $\mathscr{C}_{g,t,h,\eta}[n,k]$ and by $\mathscr{G}_{\mathrm{Tpub}}$ the linear code which has $\boldsymbol{G}_{\mathrm{Tpub}}$ as generator matrix. Again, as for the Gabidulin codes scheme, we can discard the matrix $\boldsymbol{S}$.

We now apply the q-sum operator to $\boldsymbol{G}_{\mathrm{Tpub}}$, and as (11), we get

$$\Lambda_i(\boldsymbol{G}_{\mathrm{Tpub}}) = [\Lambda_i(\boldsymbol{X})|\Lambda_i(\boldsymbol{G_T})]\boldsymbol{P},$$

where $\boldsymbol{P} \in \mathbf{GL}_{n+\lambda}(\mathbb{F}_q)$ is the column scrambler.

Let $i < \frac{n-\ell-k}{l+1}$ and write $\boldsymbol{X}$ (as in Sect. 3.2) according to its rows.

Now, for simplicity we consider that $\ell = 1$, $\eta_1 = 1$ and $i = 1$. Recall that the structure of G_T is given in (4). Then, we have

$$(\Lambda_1(X) \mid \Lambda_1(G_T)) = \begin{pmatrix} x_0 & g \\ x_1 & g^{[1]} \\ \vdots & \vdots \\ x_{h_1} & g^{[h_1]} + g^{[k-1+t_1]} \\ \vdots & \vdots \\ x_{k-1} & g^{[k-1]} \\ \hline x_0^{[1]} & g^{[1]} \\ x_1^{[1]} & g^{[2]} \\ \vdots & \vdots \\ x_{h_1-1}^{[1]} & g^{[h_1]} \\ x_{h_1}^{[1]} & g^{[h_1+1]} + g^{[k+t_1]} \\ \vdots & \vdots \\ x_{k-2}^{[1]} & g^{[k-1]} \\ x_{k-1}^{[1]} & g^{[k]} \end{pmatrix} \longrightarrow \begin{pmatrix} x_0 & g \\ x_1 & g^{[1]} \\ \vdots & \vdots \\ x_{h_1-1} & g^{[h_1-1]} \\ x_{h_1-1}^{[1]} & g^{[h_1]} \\ x_{h_1+1} & g^{[h_1+1]} \\ \vdots & \vdots \\ x_{k-1} & g^{[k-1]} \\ x_{k-1}^{[1]} & g^{[k]} \\ \hline x_0^{[1]} & g^{[1]} \\ x_1^{[1]} & g^{[2]} \\ \vdots & \vdots \\ x_{h_1-2}^{[1]} & g^{[h_1-1]} \\ x_{h_1} & g^{[h_1]} + g^{[k-1+t_1]} \\ x_{h_1}^{[1]} & g^{[h_1+1]} + g^{[k+t_1]} \\ x_{h_1+1}^{[1]} & g^{[h_1+2]} \\ \vdots & \vdots \\ x_{k-2}^{[1]} & g^{[k-1]} \end{pmatrix}$$

where the second matrix is obtained by permuting the rows of the first one. We now observe that the first block of the second matrix can be rewritten as $[\tilde{X}' \mid \mathbf{M}_{k+1}(g)]$ and so, after performing row elimination, we get

$$\begin{pmatrix} \tilde{X}' & \mathbf{M}_{k+1}(g) \\ \hline x_{h_1} - x_{h_1-1}^{[1]} & g^{[k-1+t_1]} \\ x_{h_1}^{[1]} - x_{h_1+1} & g^{[k+t_1]} \\ \hline x_0^{[1]} - x_1 & 0 \\ x_1^{[1]} - x_2 & 0 \\ \vdots & \vdots \\ x_{h_1-2}^{[1]} - x_{h_1-1} & 0 \\ x_{h_1+1}^{[1]} - x_{h_1+2} & 0 \\ \vdots & \vdots \\ x_{k-2}^{[1]} - x_{k-1} & 0 \end{pmatrix}$$

Therefore, we have the following result.

Lemma 6. Let $i < \frac{n-\ell-k}{\ell+1}$. Then, up to row elimination

$$(\Lambda_i(X) \mid \Lambda_i(G_T)) = \begin{pmatrix} Y & \Lambda_i(G_T) \\ \tilde{X} & 0 \end{pmatrix} \tag{34}$$

where,

$$\tilde{X} = \begin{cases} \left(X_T''\right) \in \mathcal{M}_{k-1-2\ell}(\mathbb{F}_{q^m}) & \text{if } i = 1 \\ \begin{pmatrix} \Lambda_{i-1}(X_T'') \\ X''' \end{pmatrix} \in \mathcal{M}_{i(k-1-2\ell)+(i-1)\ell}(\mathbb{F}_{q^m}) & \text{if } i > 1 \end{cases}$$

$Y \in \mathcal{M}_{k+i+\ell(i+1),\lambda}(\mathbb{F}_{q^m})$ *and the matrix* X_T'' *is defined as,*

$$X_T'' = X^{[1]}_{\{0,\ldots,k-2\}\backslash\{h_i-1,h_i|1\leqslant i\leqslant\ell\}} - X_{\{1,\ldots,k-1\}\backslash\{h_i,h_i+1|1\leqslant i\leqslant\ell\}}, \quad (35)$$

where $X^{[1]}_{\{0,\ldots,k-2\}\backslash\{h_i-1,h_i|1\leqslant i\leqslant\ell\}}$ *is a submatrix of* $X^{[1]}$ *composed by the first* $k-1$ *rows except all the* (h_i-1)*-th,* h_i*-th rows and* $X_{\{1,\ldots,k-1\}\backslash\{h_i,h_i+1|1\leqslant i\leqslant\ell\}}$ *is a submatrix of* X *determined by all the rows, starting from the second one, except the* h_i*-th,* h_i+1*-th ones. Finally,* $X''' \in \mathcal{M}_{i-1,\lambda}(\mathbb{F}_{q^m})$.

Proof. Using the same elimination techniques as before, we can extend the proof to the case $\ell > 1$, $\boldsymbol{\eta} \in (\mathbb{F}_{q^m} \backslash \{0\})^\ell$ and $i > 1$.   □

Even in this case, we show that it suffices to consider $i = 1$ to attack the corresponding GPT scheme.

5.3   Attacking the System for Small i's

We now consider $i = 1$. Then by Lemma 6, $(\Lambda_i(\boldsymbol{X}) \mid \Lambda_i(\boldsymbol{G}_T))$ can be transformed into

$$\begin{pmatrix} \boldsymbol{Y} & \Lambda_1(\boldsymbol{G_T}) \\ \boldsymbol{X}_T'' & 0 \end{pmatrix}$$

As in Sect. 3.4 (see Lemma 4), under some assumptions on the parameters, we can split the previous matrix into two blocks.

Lemma 7. *If* $k \geqslant 4s + 2\ell + 1$, *then, with a high probability,*

$$\begin{pmatrix} 0 & \Lambda_1(\boldsymbol{G_T}) \\ \boldsymbol{X}_T'' & 0 \end{pmatrix} \quad (36)$$

up to row eliminations.

Proof. The proof is analogous to the proof of Lemma 4. First we prove that $\mathbf{RowSp}_{\mathbb{F}_{q^m}}(\boldsymbol{X}_T'') = \mathbf{RowSp}_{\mathbb{F}_{q^m}}(\Lambda_1(\boldsymbol{X}))$ with a high probability. Again, we consider the submatrix of $\boldsymbol{X}_T''$ in $\mathcal{M}_{\lfloor\frac{k-1-2\ell}{2}\rfloor}(\mathbb{F}_{q^m})$ obtained by alternatively selecting rows of $\boldsymbol{X}_T''$. This matrix is uniformly random and by Proposition 3, if $\frac{k-1-2\ell}{2} \geqslant 2s$ (which is true by assumption), it has rank equal to the rank of $\Lambda_1(\boldsymbol{X})$ with a high probability. Thus the equality $\mathbf{RowSp}_{\mathbb{F}_{q^m}}(\boldsymbol{X}_T'') = \mathbf{RowSp}_{\mathbb{F}_{q^m}}(\Lambda_1(\boldsymbol{X}))$ holds.

The result follows by noting that $\mathbf{RowSp}_{\mathbb{F}_{q^m}}(\boldsymbol{Y}) \subseteq \mathbf{RowSp}_{\mathbb{F}_{q^m}}(\Lambda_1(\boldsymbol{X}))$.   □

Therefore we can apply the attack of Sect. 4 in order to break the corresponding GPT cryptosystem.

Remark 11. Notice that, if $\mathbf{rank}(\boldsymbol{X}) = s \geqslant \lambda/2$, then $\mathbf{rank}(\boldsymbol{X}_T) = \lambda$ with high probability and we can apply the Overbeck's attack to this scheme. In fact, in this case (as in Sect. 3.3), $\dim(\Lambda_1(\mathscr{G}_{Tpub})^{\perp}) = n - k - 1 - 2\ell$, and so the code $\Lambda_1(\mathscr{G}_{Tpub})$ admits a parity check matrix whose first λ columns are $\boldsymbol{0}$. We can then compute a valid column scrambler and attack the system.

More generally, we can apply this attack to any $i < \frac{n-\ell-k}{\ell+1}$ for which

$$\mathbf{rank}(\tilde{\boldsymbol{X}}) = \lambda,$$

where $\tilde{\boldsymbol{X}}$ is defined in Lemma 6.

Conclusion

In this paper, we present new observations on the decoding of Gabidulin codes. These allow us to introduce a decoder for twisted Gabidulin codes up to a certain threshold, which may be less than half of the minimum distance.

We then propose an extension of the Overbeck's attack on GPT-like systems instantiated on Gabidulin or related codes such as twisted Gabidulin codes. This attack is efficient as soon as the secret code $\Lambda_i(\mathscr{C}_{\mathrm{sec}})$ has a small dimension compared to the dimension of $\Lambda_i(\mathscr{C})$, where $\mathscr{C}$ is a random code. One of the interesting things about our approach is that it succeeds even when the distortion matrix has a low rank, which might cause the Overbeck's attack fails. Our attack extension allows to break the proposal of [43].

References

1. Aguilar Melchor, C., et al.: Rank quasi cyclic (RQC). Second Round submission to NIST Post-Quantum Cryptography call (2020). https://pqc-rqc.org
2. Aragon, N., et al.: ROLLO (merger of Rank-Ouroboros, LAKE and LOCKER). Second round submission to the NIST post-quantum cryptography call (2019). https://pqc-rollo.org
3. Aragon, N., Blazy, O., Gaborit, P., Hauteville, A., Zémor, G.: Durandal: a rank metric based signature scheme. In: Ishai, Y., Rijmen, V. (eds.) EUROCRYPT 2019. LNCS, vol. 11478, pp. 728–758. Springer, Cham (2019). https://doi.org/10.1007/978-3-030-17659-4_25
4. Aragon, N., Gaborit, P., Hauteville, A., Tillich, J.P.: A new algorithm for solving the rank syndrome decoding problem. In: 2018 IEEE International Symposium on Information Theory, ISIT 2018, Vail, CO, USA, 17–22 June 2018, pp. 2421–2425. IEEE (2018). https://doi.org/10.1109/ISIT.2018.8437464
5. Barelli, É., Couvreur, A.: An efficient structural attack on NIST submission DAGS. In: Peyrin, T., Galbraith, S. (eds.) ASIACRYPT 2018. LNCS, vol. 11272, pp. 93–118. Springer, Cham (2018). https://doi.org/10.1007/978-3-030-03326-2_4
6. Beelen, P., Bossert, M., Puchinger, S., Rosenkilde, J.: Structural properties of twisted Reed-Solomon codes with applications to cryptography. In: 2018 IEEE International Symposium on Information Theory (ISIT), pp. 946–950 (2018). https://doi.org/10.1109/ISIT.2018.8437923

7. Beelen, P., Puchinger, S., Rosenkilde né Nielsen, J.: Twisted Reed-Solomon codes. In: 2017 IEEE International Symposium on Information Theory (ISIT), pp. 336–340 (2017). https://doi.org/10.1109/ISIT.2017.8006545

8. Bombar, M., Couvreur, A.: Decoding supercodes of Gabidulin codes and applications to cryptanalysis. In: Cheon, J.H., Tillich, J.-P. (eds.) PQCrypto 2021 2021. LNCS, vol. 12841, pp. 3–22. Springer, Cham (2021). https://doi.org/10.1007/978-3-030-81293-5_1

9. Bostan, A., et al.: Algorithmes Efficaces en Calcul Formel. Frédéric Chyzak (auto-édit.), Palaiseau (2017). https://hal.archives-ouvertes.fr/AECF/

10. Coggia, D., Couvreur, A.: On the security of a Loidreau's rank metric code based encryption scheme. In: Workshop on Coding Theory and Cryptography, WCC 2019, Saint-Jacut-de-la-Mer, France (2019)

11. Coggia, D., Couvreur, A.: On the security of a Loidreau's rank metric code based encryption scheme. Des. Codes Cryptogr. **88**, 1941–1957 (2020)

12. Couvreur, A., Debris-Alazard, T., Gaborit, P.: On the hardness of code equivalence problems in rank metric (2020). https://hal.archives-ouvertes.fr/hal-02997801. Working paper or preprint

13. Couvreur, A., Márquez-Corbella, I., Pellikaan, R.: Cryptanalysis of McEliece cryptosystem based on algebraic geometry codes and their subcodes. IEEE Trans. Inform. Theory **63**(8), 5404–5418 (2017)

14. Couvreur, A., Otmani, A., Tillich, J.P.: Polynomial time attack on wild McEliece over quadratic extensions. IEEE Trans. Inform. Theory **63**(1), 404–427 (2017)

15. Drodz, Y.A., Kirichenko, V.V.: Finite Dimensional Algebras. Springer, Heidelberg (1994). Original Russian edition published by: Publisher of Kiev State University, Kiev 1980, Translated by V. Dlab

16. Friedl, K., Rónyai, L.: Polynomial time solutions of some problems of computational algebra. In: Proceedings of the Seventeenth Annual ACM Symposium on Theory of Computing, STOC 1985, pp. 153–162. Association for Computing Machinery, New York (1985). https://doi.org/10.1145/22145.22162

17. Gabidulin, E., Rashwan, H., Honary, B.: On improving security of GPT cryptosystems. In: Proceedings of the IEEE International Symposium Information Theory - ISIT, pp. 1110–1114. IEEE (2009)

18. Gabidulin, E.M.: Theory of codes with maximum rank distance. Problemy Peredachi Informatsii **21**(1), 3–16 (1985)

19. Gabidulin, E.M.: Public-key cryptosystems based on linear codes over large alphabets: efficiency and weakness. In: Farrell, P.G. (ed.) 4th IMA Conference on Cryptography and Coding, the Institute of Mathematics and its Applications, pp. 17–31 (1993)

20. Gabidulin, E.M.: Attacks and counter-attacks on the GPT public key cryptosystem. Des. Codes Cryptogr. **48**(2), 171–177 (2008)

21. Gabidulin, E.M., Ourivski, A.V.: Modified GPT PKC with right scrambler. Electron. Notes Discret. Math. **6**, 168–177 (2001). https://doi.org/10.1016/S1571-0653(04)00168-4

22. Gabidulin, E.M., Paramonov, A.V., Tretjakov, O.V.: Ideals over a non-commutative ring and their application in cryptology. In: Davies, D.W. (ed.) EUROCRYPT 1991. LNCS, vol. 547, pp. 482–489. Springer, Heidelberg (1991). https://doi.org/10.1007/3-540-46416-6_41

23. Gaborit, P., Murat, G., Ruatta, O., Zémor, G.: Low rank parity check codes and their application to cryptography. In: Proceedings of the Workshop on Coding and Cryptography WCC 2013, Bergen, Norway (2013). www.selmer.uib.no/WCC2013/pdfs/Gaborit.pdf

24. Gaborit, P., Ruatta, O., Schrek, J.: On the complexity of the rank syndrome decoding problem. IEEE Trans. Inform. Theory **62**(2), 1006–1019 (2016)
25. Ghatak, A.: Extending Coggia-Couvreur attack on Loidreau's rank-metric cryptosystem. Des. Codes Cryptogr. **90**, 215–238 (2022)
26. Gibson, K.: Severely denting the Gabidulin version of the McEliece public key cryptosystem. Des. Codes Cryptogr. **6**(1), 37–45 (1995)
27. Gibson, K.: The security of the Gabidulin public key cryptosystem. In: Maurer, U. (ed.) EUROCRYPT 1996. LNCS, vol. 1070, pp. 212–223. Springer, Heidelberg (1996). https://doi.org/10.1007/3-540-68339-9_19
28. Goss, D.: Basic Structures of Function Field Arithmetic, Ergebnisse der Mathematik und ihrer Grenzgebiete (3) [Results in Mathematics and Related Areas (3)], vol. 35. Springer, Berlin (1996)
29. Kadir, W.K., Li, C.: On decoding additive generalized twisted Gabidulin codes. Cryptogr. Commun. **12**(5), 987–1009 (2020). https://doi.org/10.1007/s12095-020-00449-9
30. Kadir, W.K., Li, C., Zullo, F.: On interpolation-based decoding of a class of maximum rank distance codes (2021). https://arxiv.org/abs/2105.03115
31. Li, C.: Interpolation-based decoding of nonlinear maximum rank distance codes. In: 2019 IEEE International Symposium on Information Theory (ISIT), pp. 2054–2058 (2019). https://doi.org/10.1109/ISIT.2019.8849472
32. Li, C., Kadir, W.K.: On decoding additive generalized twisted Gabidulin codes. In: Proceedings of the International Workshop on Coding and Cryptography, WCC 2019 (2019)
33. Loidreau, P.: A Welch–Berlekamp like algorithm for decoding Gabidulin codes. In: Ytrehus, Ø. (ed.) WCC 2005. LNCS, vol. 3969, pp. 36–45. Springer, Heidelberg (2006). https://doi.org/10.1007/11779360_4
34. Loidreau, P.: Designing a rank metric based McEliece cryptosystem. In: Sendrier, N. (ed.) PQCrypto 2010. LNCS, vol. 6061, pp. 142–152. Springer, Heidelberg (2010). https://doi.org/10.1007/978-3-642-12929-2_11
35. McEliece, R.J.: A Public-Key System Based on Algebraic Coding Theory, pp. 114–116. Jet Propulsion Lab (1978). dSN Progress Report 44
36. Ore, Ø.: On a special class of polynomials. Trans. Am. Math. Soc. **35**(3), 559–584 (1933)
37. Otmani, A., Talé-Kalachi, H., Ndjeya, S.: Improved cryptanalysis of rank metric schemes based on Gabidulin codes. CoRR abs/1602.08549 (2016). http://arxiv.org/abs/1602.08549
38. Ourivski, A.V., Gabidulin, E.M.: Column scrambler for the GPT cryptosystem. Discret. Appl. Math. **128**(1), 207–221 (2003). International Workshop on Coding and Cryptography (WCC 2001)
39. Overbeck, R.: A new structural attack for GPT and variants. In: Dawson, E., Vaudenay, S. (eds.) Mycrypt 2005. LNCS, vol. 3715, pp. 50–63. Springer, Heidelberg (2005). https://doi.org/10.1007/11554868_5
40. Overbeck, R.: Structural attacks for public key cryptosystems based on Gabidulin codes. J. Cryptol. **21**(2), 280–301 (2008)
41. Pham, B., Loidreau, P.: An analysis of Coggia-Couvreur attack on Loidreau's rank-metric public-key encryption scheme in the general case. In: Twelfth International Workshop on Coding and Cryptography, WCC 2022 (2022). https://www.wcc2022.uni-rostock.de/storages/uni-rostock/Tagungen/WCC2022/Papers/WCC_2022_paper_38.pdf

42. Puchinger, S., Rosenkilde né Nielsen, J., Sheekey, J.: Further generalisations of twisted Gabidulin codes. In: Workshop on Coding Theory and Cryptography, WCC 2017 (2017). https://arxiv.org/abs/1703.08093
43. Puchinger, S., Renner, J., Wachter-Zeh, A.: Twisted Gabidulin codes in the GPT cryptosystem (2018). http://arxiv.org/abs/1806.10055
44. Randrianarisoa, T.: A decoding algorithm for rank metric codes. Preprint (2017). https://arxiv.org/abs/1712.07060
45. Randrianarisoa, T., Rosenthal, J.: A decoding algorithm for twisted Gabidulin codes. In: 2017 IEEE International Symposium on Information Theory, pp. 2771–2774 (2017). https://doi.org/10.1109/ISIT.2017.8007034
46. Rashwan, H., Gabidulin, E., Honary, B.: Security of the GPT cryptosystem and its applications to cryptography. Secur. Commun. Netw. 4(8), 937–946 (2011)
47. Rónyai, L.: Computing the structure of finite algebras. J. Symb. Comput. 9(3), 355–373 (1990)
48. Sheekey, J.: A new family of linear maximum rank distance codes. Adv. Math. Commun. 10(3), 475–488 (2016)

Cryptanalysis of Rank-Metric Schemes Based on Distorted Gabidulin Codes

Pierre Briaud[1,2(✉)] and Pierre Loidreau[3]

[1] Sorbonne Universités, UPMC Univ Paris 06, Paris, France
[2] Inria, Team COSMIQ, Paris, France
pierre.briaud@inria.fr
[3] DGA and IRMAR, Univ. Rennes, Rennes, France
pierre.loidreau@univ-rennes.fr

Abstract. In this work, we introduce a new attack for the Loidreau scheme [PQCrypto 2017] and its more recent variant LowMS. This attack is based on a constrained linear system for which we provide two solving approaches:

- the first one is an enumeration algorithm inspired from combinatorial attacks on the Rank Decoding (RD) Problem. While the attack technique remains very simple, it allows us to obtain the best known structural attack on the parameters of these two schemes.
- the second one is to rewrite it as a bilinear system over $\mathbb{F}_q$. Even if Gröbner basis techniques on this second system seem infeasible, we provide a detailed analysis of the first degree fall polynomials which arise when applying such algorithms.

1 Introduction

The idea of building rank-metric cryptography relying on Gabidulin codes is over 30 years old. It dates back to the seminal GPT scheme [15]. The initial goal of Gabidulin was to use the properties of the rank metric in order to propose a scheme with a public-key size one order of magnitude smaller than that of the original McEliece cryptosystem [20]. However, this proposal and following variants have suffered structural attacks [22] tending to show that masking these codes is difficult.

The Loidreau cryptosystem introduced in [19] is based on a different type of masking. Along with the LowMS variant [1], it is arguably one of the few reparations which resists cryptanalysis for well-chosen parameters.

On the one hand, this scheme offers nice features compared to other modern PKEs and especially to those proposed at the NIST post-quantum standardization process. First, decryption is deterministic. Second, regarding performance, the key is between one and two orders of magnitude smaller than that of non-structured Hamming-based cryptosystems. It even favorably compares with that of PKEs based on unstructured lattices. Similarly, the ciphertext is small compared to that of unstructured lattice proposals and it compares favourably with that of structured lattices.

T. Johansson and D. Smith-Tone (Eds.): PQCrypto 2023, LNCS 14154, pp. 38–56, 2023.
https://doi.org/10.1007/978-3-031-40003-2_2

On the other hand, its security analysis is not yet sufficiently stabilized. This is mainly due to the new type of masking, which calls for assessing the difficulty of distinguishing the public code from a random one. This code is a Gabidulin code distorted with a non-singular matrix with coefficients in a small-dimensional secret subspace of $\mathbb{F}_{q^m}$. A conjecture was made in [19] concerning the complexity of solving the problem, for parameters not impacted by the Coggia-Couvreur attack.

Contributions. First, we improve upon the enumeration approach of Loidreau presented as an extended abstract at the WCC 2022 conference. We adapt techniques from combinatorial attacks on RD [2] showing that it is more efficient to enumerate over vector spaces of larger dimension than that of the original secret subspace. This allows us to obtain the best complexity for this type of technique.

Second, we propose an algebraic approach to find a distinguisher by modeling the original problem as a bilinear system over $\mathbb{F}_q$. Even if the solving by Gröbner bases does not seem promising from our experiments, we manage to analyze precisely the first steps of the computation. In particular, we show that there exist degree falls of the same nature as in [4,6] due to the specific structure of the system.

2   Preliminaries on the Rank Metric

Rank-metric cryptography relies on codes which are $\mathbb{F}_{q^m}$-linear, where $\mathbb{F}_{q^m}$ is an extension of degree m over $\mathbb{F}_q$. In this context, the *rank* (or *weight*) of a vector $\mathbf{a} = (a_1, \ldots, a_n) \in \mathbb{F}_{q^m}^n$ denoted by $\mathrm{Rk}(\mathbf{a})$ is the dimension of the $\mathbb{F}_q$-subspace of $\mathbb{F}_{q^m}$ generated by the components of $\mathbf{a}$, *i.e.*,

$$\mathrm{Rk}(\mathbf{a}) \overset{def}{=} \dim \langle a_1, \ldots, a_n \rangle_{\mathbb{F}_q}.$$

Gabidulin codes were first constructed by Delsarte as extremal object in Bose-Mesner algebra [10]. Some years later, Gabidulin presented an algebraic theory as well as a polynomial-time decoding algorithm [14]. These codes can be viewed as analogues of Reed-Solomon codes in the rank metric, where polynomials are replaced by linearized polynomials.

Notation 1 *In the whole paper, we will denote by $(a_{i,j})_{1 \leq i \leq n_r, 1 \leq j \leq n_c}$ the $n_r \times n_c$ matrix whose entry in row i and column j is equal to $a_{i,j}$ for $i \in \{1..n_r\}$ and $j \in \{1..n_c\}$ or simply $(a_{i,j})$ when the sizes are already clear from the context.*

Definition 1 *For integers $k \leq n \leq m$, let $\mathbf{g} = (g_1, \ldots, g_m) \in \mathbb{F}_{q^m}^n$ such that $Rk(\mathbf{g}) = n$. The k-dimensional Gabidulin code with support vector $\mathbf{g}$, denoted $\mathcal{G}_k(\mathbf{g})$, is the $\mathbb{F}_{q^m}$-linear code generated by the matrix $(g_j^{[i-1]})_{1 \leq i \leq k, 1 \leq j \leq n}$, where $[i] \overset{def}{=} q^i$.*

Finally, the following proposition shows that the dual of a Gabidulin code is a Gabidulin code.

Proposition 1 ([14]) *Let $\mathcal{G}_k(\mathbf{g}) \subset \mathbb{F}_{q^m}^n$, then there exists $\mathbf{h} \in \mathbb{F}_{q^m}^n$ of rank n such that $\mathcal{G}_{n-k}(\mathbf{h}) = \mathcal{G}_k(\mathbf{g})^{\perp}$ for the usual scalar product in $\mathbb{F}_{q^m}$*

3   Loidreau Cryptosystem

The Loidreau scheme was introduced in [19] with $q = 2$ but it can be declined for any prime power q. For positive integers m, n and an $\mathbb{F}_q$-vector space $\mathcal{A}$, let $\mathcal{M}_{m,n}(\mathcal{A})$ be the vector space of matrices of size $m \times n$ with entries in $\mathcal{A}$ and let $\mathrm{GL}_n(\mathbb{F}_{q^m})$ be the group of non-singular matrices of size n with entries in $\mathbb{F}_{q^m}$.

3.1   Description of the Scheme

The parameters are integers $k \leq n \leq m$ related to the underlying Gabidulin code as well as $\lambda \in \mathbb{N}$ related to the masking. The value of λ is chosen such that $\lambda < \lfloor (n-k)/2 \rfloor$ for correctness and $\lambda \geq 3$ to avoid the polynomial attack of [8]. The three standard building blocks of a public encryption scheme are the following:

KeyGen(1^{ν})

1. Construct $\mathcal{G} \subset \mathbb{F}_{q^m}^n$ a k-dimensional Gabidulin code.
2. Pick $\mathbf{G} \in \mathcal{M}_{k,n}(\mathbb{F}_{q^m})$ random in the set of full-rank generator matrices for $\mathcal{G}$. A usual way to do it is to choose a matrix under canonical form, say the one given by Definition 1 and then multiply on the left by a randomly chosen matrix in $\mathrm{GL}_k(\mathbb{F}_{q^m})$.
3. Pick $\mathcal{V} \subset \mathbb{F}_{q^m}$ a random λ-dimensional $\mathbb{F}_q$-subspace of $\mathbb{F}_{q^m}$.
4. Pick $\mathbf{P}$ a random element in $\mathrm{GL}_n(\mathbb{F}_{q^m}) \cap \mathcal{M}_{n,n}(\mathcal{V})$.
5. **return** $\mathbf{G}_{pub} = \mathbf{G}\mathbf{P}^{-1}$ and $\mathbf{sk} = (\mathbf{G}, \mathbf{P})$.

Let $\mathbf{p} \in \mathbb{F}_{q^m}^k$ be the plaintext to be encrypted.

Encrypt($\mathbf{p}, \mathbf{G}_{pub}$)

1. Pick $\mathbf{e} \in \mathbb{F}_{q^m}^n$ such that $\mathrm{Rk}(\mathbf{e}) \leq \lfloor (n-k)/2\lambda \rfloor$.
2. **return** $\mathbf{c} = \mathbf{p}\mathbf{G}_{pub} + \mathbf{e}$.

Decrypt($\mathbf{c}, \mathbf{sk}$)

– **return** Decode($\mathbf{c}\mathbf{P}, \mathbf{G}$), where Decode($*, \mathbf{G}$) stands for any decoding algorithm for a Gabidulin code with generator matrix $\mathbf{G}$ decoding up to the error-correcting capability $\lfloor (n-k)/2 \rfloor$.

3.2   Security

Let $\mathcal{C}_{pub} \subset \mathbb{F}_{q^m}^n$ be the $\mathbb{F}_{q^m}$-linear code of dimension k generated by the public matrix $\mathbf{G}_{pub}$. The IND-CPA security of the scheme is related to the difficulty of solving the two following problems:

– Distinguish the code $\mathcal{C}_{pub}$ from a random $\mathbb{F}_{q^m}$-linear code with the same parameters.
– Solve a generic instance of the Rank Decoding problem whose parameters are $(m, n, k, t \stackrel{def}{=} \lfloor (n-k)/(2\lambda) \rfloor)$.

In addition to these assumptions, note that LowMS also relies on the Rank Support Learning problem [16].

We address the hardness of the first problem which is used in both [1,19]. We even go further since we provide an attack enabling to decrypt. For these schemes, our work also shows that the Gabidulin code itself can be considered as a parameter (meaning that $\mathbf{G}$ generating $\mathcal{G}$ is public) without security loss. This leads to a simplification of the key-generation procedure that can be rewritten as

KeyGen()

1. Pick $\mathcal{V} \subset \mathbb{F}_{q^m}$ a random λ-dimensional $\mathbb{F}_q$-subspace of $\mathbb{F}_{q^m}$.
2. Pick $\mathbf{P}$ randomly in $\mathrm{GL}_n(\mathbb{F}_{q^m}) \cap \mathcal{M}_{n,n}(\mathcal{V})$.
3. **return** $\mathbf{G}_{pub} = \mathbf{pk} = \mathbf{GP}^{-1}$ and $\mathbf{sk} = \mathbf{P}$.

4   A Constrained Linear System for Decryption

In this section, we introduce a constrained linear system (Proposition 3) whose solution allows to devise a polynomial time decryption algorithm for the public code $\mathcal{C}_{pub}$. Note that this trivially implies that one has designe a distinguisher for the public code. The issue of solving this system will be addressed in the next sections in two different ways.

Let $r \stackrel{def}{=} n - k$. In the following, we overline with a hat data known to an attacker. For instance, let $\widehat{\mathbf{H}}_{pub} \in \mathcal{M}_{r,n}(\mathbb{F}_{q^m})$ an arbitrary parity-check matrix for $\mathcal{C}_{pub}$ and for $\alpha \in \mathbb{F}_{q^m}$ a normal element, let $\widehat{\mathbf{H}}_{norm}$ be the matrix $(\alpha^{[i+j-2]})_{1 \leq i \leq r, 1 \leq j \leq m}$. Note that

$$\widehat{\mathcal{A}} \stackrel{def}{=} \{\alpha^{[i]}, \ i = 0, \ldots, m-1\}$$

is a basis of $\mathbb{F}_{q^m}$ over $\mathbb{F}_q$. From Proposition 1, there exists a vector $\mathbf{h} \in \mathbb{F}_{q^m}^n$ such

that $\mathbf{H} \stackrel{def}{=} \begin{pmatrix} \mathbf{h}^{[0]} \\ \vdots \\ \mathbf{h}^{[r-1]} \end{pmatrix} \in \mathcal{M}_{r,n}(\mathbb{F}_{q^m})$ is a parity-check matrix for the Gabidulin code $\mathcal{G}$. Then, it is easy to see that there exists a unique $\mathbf{S} \in \mathrm{GL}_r(\mathbb{F}_{q^m})$ such that

$$\mathbf{S}\widehat{\mathbf{H}}_{pub} = \mathbf{HP}^t. \tag{1}$$

We indeed have $\mathbf{HP}^t\mathbf{G}_{pub}^t = \mathbf{HP}^t(\mathbf{P}^t)^{-1}\mathbf{G}^t = \mathbf{HG}^t = \mathbf{0}$, so that $\mathbf{HP}^t$ is a parity-check matrix for $\mathcal{C}_{pub}$. Finally, any parity-check matrix and, a fortiori, $\widehat{\mathbf{H}}_{pub}$, is obtained with a basis transformation induced by a non-singular matrix over $\mathbb{F}_{q^m}$. Another straightforward proposition is

Proposition 2 *Let $\mathbf{H}$ be a parity check matrix for $\mathcal{G}$ under canonical form. There exists a q-ary matrix $\mathbf{M} \in \mathcal{M}_{m,n}(\mathbb{F}_q)$ of rank n such that*

$$\mathbf{H} = \widehat{\mathbf{H}}_{norm}\mathbf{M}.$$

Proof. Let $\mathbf{h} = (h_1, \ldots, h_n)$ be the first row of $\mathbf{H}$. We consider the matrix $\mathbf{M}$ whose i-th column corresponds to the m-dimensional q-ary vector formed by the coordinates of h_i in the basis $\widehat{\mathcal{A}}$, for $1 \leq i \leq n$. By construction we have $\mathbf{H} = \widehat{\mathbf{H}}_{norm}\mathbf{M}$ and moreover $h_1, \ldots, h_n$ are linearly independent over $\mathbb{F}_q$ by construction of Gabidulin codes. This shows that $\mathbf{M}$ has full rank.

Now Eq. (1) can be rewritten as

$$\mathbf{S}\widehat{\mathbf{H}}_{pub} = \widehat{\mathbf{H}}_{norm}\mathbf{T}, \tag{2}$$

where the matrix $\mathbf{T} \stackrel{def}{=} \mathbf{MP}^t$ is full rank in $\mathcal{V}^{m \times n}$ since $\mathbf{M}$ is a q-ary matrix of full rank n and since $\mathbf{P} \in \mathrm{GL}_n(\mathcal{V})$. Finally, the following proposition shows that any solution to the constrained linear system described by (2) indeed yields a polynomial-time decryption algorithm.

Proposition 3 *Let $r = n-k$ and let $\widehat{\mathbf{H}}_{pub}$ be a parity-check matrix for $\mathcal{C}_{pub}$. Let $\alpha \in \mathbb{F}_{q^m}$ be a normal element and let $\widehat{\mathbf{H}}_{norm}$ be the matrix $(\alpha^{[i+j-2]})_{1 \leq i \leq r, 1 \leq j \leq m}$. From the knowledge of any non-singular matrix $\mathbf{V} \in \mathcal{M}_{r \times r}(\mathbb{F}_{q^m})$ and $\mathbf{W} \in \mathcal{M}_{m \times n}(\mathcal{W})$ of rank n such that*

$$\mathbf{V}\widehat{\mathbf{H}}_{pub} = \widehat{\mathbf{H}}_{norm}\mathbf{W} \tag{3}$$

and where $\mathcal{W}$ is $\mathbb{F}_q$-vector subspace of $\mathbb{F}_{q^m}$ of dimension $\leq \lambda$, it is possible to decrypt any ciphertext in polynomial time.

Proof. Recall that a ciphertext is $\mathbf{c} = \mathbf{p} \cdot \mathbf{G}_{pub} + \mathbf{e} \in \mathbb{F}_{q^m}^n$, where $\mathrm{Rk}(\mathbf{e}) = \lfloor (n-k)/(2\lambda) \rfloor$. Thus $\widehat{\mathbf{H}}_{pub}\mathbf{c}^t = \widehat{\mathbf{H}}_{pub}\mathbf{e}^t$ and

$$\mathbf{V}\widehat{\mathbf{H}}_{pub}\mathbf{e}^t = \widehat{\mathbf{H}}_{norm}\underbrace{\mathbf{We}^t}_{\mathbf{e}'^t}.$$

Since $\mathcal{W}$ has dimension $\leq \lambda$, this implies that and $\mathrm{Rk}(\mathbf{e}') \leq \lambda\mathrm{Rk}(\mathbf{e}) \leq \lfloor (n-k)/2 \rfloor$. Therefore by decoding in the public Gabidulin code with parity-check matrix $\widehat{\mathbf{H}}_{norm}$, one recovers $\mathbf{e}'^t = \mathbf{We}^t$. Since $\mathbf{W}$ has rank $n \leq m$, $\mathbf{e} \mapsto \mathbf{W}^t\mathbf{e}$ is one-to-one and $\mathbf{e}$ can be uniquely recovered. The vector $\mathbf{p}$ such that $\mathbf{p} \cdot \mathbf{G}_{pub} = \mathbf{c} - \mathbf{e}$ can also be uniquely recovered. $\qquad\square$

To conclude this section, note that a first naive solving approach would be to enumerate all solutions $(\mathbf{V}, \mathbf{W}) \in \mathcal{M}_{r \times r}(\mathbb{F}_{q^m}) \times \mathcal{M}_{m \times n}(\mathbb{F}_{q^m})$ to (3) and to test if they satisfy the constraint, *i.e.*, the $\mathbf{W}$ matrix has its entries in a small dimensional $\mathbb{F}_q$-vector subspace of $\mathbb{F}_{q^m}$. Even if one takes into account the fact that there may be multiple possibilities, this effort lies beyond the capacities of any computer even for moderate parameters. Indeed, a first difficulty is that the solution space to (3) is an $\mathbb{F}_{q^m}$-vector space of dimension at least $r^2 + (m - r)n$ without the imposed condition.

5   Combinatorial Approach

A first idea to take advantage of this extra information is to enumerate candidate bases $\boldsymbol{\mu} \in \mathbb{F}_{q^m}^{\lambda}$ for the secret vector space $\mathcal{V}$. Any such candidate is then completed into a basis of $\mathbb{F}_{q^m}$ in which we express the coefficients of $\boldsymbol{V}$ and $\boldsymbol{W}$ in order to write down the linear system (3) over $\mathbb{F}_q$. We assume that each entry in $\boldsymbol{W}$ belongs to the $\mathbb{F}_q$-vector space spanned by $\boldsymbol{\mu}$ and thus we introduce only λmn unknowns over $\mathbb{F}_q$ instead of m^2n for this matrix. Since we typically have $rmn \gg \lambda mn + mr^2$, this initial guess can be tested by solving the resulting linear equations over $\mathbb{F}_q$ to check if they have a non-zero solution. As is usual for this type of approach, the total cost contains two factors:

– an exponential one coming from enumerating the bases;
– a polynomial one which corresponds to the linear system solving over $\mathbb{F}_q$.

Proposed Algorithm. We can in fact obtain a better exponential factor by relying on the same techniques as used in combinatorial attacks on the Rank Decoding problem [2,17,21]. The rationale is that it is enough to know (a basis for) a γ-dimensional vector space $\mathcal{U}$ which contains $\mathcal{V}$ for $\gamma \geq \lambda$ to apply the same algorithm, provided that γ is not too large. The advantage is that it is always easier to find such a $\mathcal{U}$ than to guess a basis of $\mathcal{V}$ directly, the extreme case being $\gamma = m$ for which we succeed with probability 1. Here, we even note that a vector space $\mathcal{U}$ which contains an arbitrary multiple $x\mathcal{V}$ for $x \in \mathbb{F}_{q^m}^*$ instead of simply $\mathcal{V}$ is enough for our purposes. This is because any pair $(x\boldsymbol{V}, x\boldsymbol{W})$ is a solution to the constrained linear system. The following Proposition 4 gives the condition on γ for our attack to succeed.

Proposition 4 *Assume that $\gamma \geq \lambda \in \mathbb{N}$ is such that*

$$rn \geq \gamma n + r^2. \tag{4}$$

If $\boldsymbol{\nu} \in \mathbb{F}_{q^m}^{\gamma}$ is a basis for a vector space $\mathcal{U}$ which contains a multiple $x\mathcal{V}$ for $x \in \mathbb{F}_{q^m}^*$, the linear system over $\mathbb{F}_q$ derived from (3) by writing the coefficients of the secret matrix $\boldsymbol{W}$ in the basis $\boldsymbol{\nu}$ is expected to have a solution space of dimension 1. If $\boldsymbol{\nu}$ does not correspond to such a basis, this linear system will not have a non-zero solution with overwhelming probability.

From this proposition, we can then use the same algorithm as sketched at the beginning of Sect. 5 with γ instead of λ provided that $\gamma \leq r(1 - r/n)$.

Estimated Cost. The exponential factor of this approach is given by the inverse of the probability that a fixed subspace $\mathcal{U}$ of dimension γ contains a subspace of the form $x\mathcal{V}$ for some $x \in \mathbb{F}_{q^m}^*$. According to [2, B.], it can be estimated by $q^{m-\lambda(m-\gamma)} = q^{-(\lambda-1)m+\lambda\gamma}$. We assume that the optimal complexity corresponds to the optimal exponential factor and thus we consider the highest possible value for γ. By Eq. (4), this leads to choose $\gamma \overset{def}{=} \lfloor r(1 - r/n) \rfloor$.

The linear system solving step can be performed by applying Gaussian elimination on a matrix of size $rnm \times (\gamma n + r^2)m$ over $\mathbb{F}_q$. The corresponding cost in $\mathbb{F}_q$-operations can be estimated by $\mathcal{O}((\gamma n + r^2)m)^\omega)$, where ω is the linear algebra constant. However, checking that a linear system is consistent does not require to compute a row echelon form. We can actually apply the Wiedemann algorithm [9], which may offer an advantage since the input matrix is sparse. Indeed, equations have weight $m(r+\gamma)$ but they contain $m(r^2+\gamma n) \gg m(r+\gamma)$ unknowns. In particular, we lower bound the complexity of linear algebra by considering the cost of computing the kernel of a sparse square matrix of size $m(\gamma n + r^2)$ corresponding to the number of unknowns with a number of non-zero coefficients roughly equal to $m^2(r+\gamma)(\gamma n+r^2)$. An estimation of this lower bound is

$$m^3(r + \gamma)(\gamma n + r^2)^2 > m^3 r^5$$

q-ary operations. Recalling that $r = n - k$ and by introducing the code rate $R \overset{def}{=} k/n$, a lower bound of the overall complexity of this precise attack is then given by

$$W_{\text{Spec\_Inf}} = m^3(n - k)^5 q^{(\lambda-1)m-\lambda\lfloor n(1-R)R \rfloor}. \tag{5}$$

Application to Some Parameters. Finally, we instantiate our bound with the parameters of the WCC 2022 abstract and the ones of LowMS [1]. We believe that the comparison is fair since they have been obtained from the content the abstract. In Table 1, column *Lower bound* contains the value of the binary logarithm of the cost of Eq. (5). Our results always improve the cost of the best structural attack. If it becomes below the one of attacks on RD, this might lead to re-evaluate parameters in [1,19].

Table 1. Cost estimate on former parameters.

(m, n, k, λ)	Security	Source	Lower bound	Former
$(128, 128, 20, 3)$	128	WCC 2022	263	311
$(128, 128, 44, 3)$	128	WCC 2022	225	308
$(59, 50, 25, 3)$	128	LowMS	**123**	158
$(67, 66, 33, 4)$	128	LowMS	180	244
$(83, 74, 37, 3)$	192	LowMS	**157**	211
$(79, 78, 39, 4)$	192	LowMS	206	282

Note however that we do not claim that the lower bound is on all possible algorithms which would solve the same problem. The lower bound in our case only deals with the linear algebra part when using Wiedemann's algorithm. It is a lower bound relatively to the state of the art of research in this field.

6   A Bilinear System

Instead of guessing a basis for $\mathcal{V}$ or for a vector space which contains it as in Sect. 5, our second approach consists in solving a bilinear system over $\mathbb{F}_q$ (**System 1**). These former quantities attached to $\mathcal{V}$ still appear in the system as an unknown block of variables but we will not fix them in the first place.

Let $\widehat{\mathcal{B}}$ denote an arbitrary basis of $\mathbb{F}_{q^m}$ over $\mathbb{F}_q$. For an element $a \in \mathbb{F}_{q^m}$, we consider $\vec{a}$ the m-dimensional vector of its coordinates over $\widehat{\mathcal{B}}$, so that $\widehat{\mathcal{B}}\vec{a} = a$. For $\mu \in \mathbb{F}_{q^m}$, we also define $\mathbf{M}_\mu \in \mathcal{M}_{m \times m}(\mathbb{F}_q)$ the matrix of the multiplication by μ in the basis $\widehat{\mathcal{B}}$. This matrix is such that

$$\forall a, \ b \in \mathbb{F}_{q^m}, \ b = \mu a, \text{ then } \vec{b} = \mathbf{M}_\mu \vec{a}.$$

The claimed bilinear system is as follows:

System 1 *Let* $\widehat{\mathbf{H}}_{pub} = (\widehat{h}_{ij})$ *and let* $\widehat{\mathbf{H}}_{norm} = (\alpha^{[i+j-2]})$. *We consider the bilinear system over* $\mathbb{F}_q$ *in the non-zero unknowns* $\vec{v_{iu}}$, $b_{ij}^{(\ell)}$ *and linearly independent* $\vec{\mu_\ell} \in \mathbb{F}_q^m$, *whose equations are given by*

$$\forall \begin{cases} i \in \{1..r\} \\ j \in \{1..n\} \end{cases}, \quad \sum_{u=1}^r \mathbf{M}_{\widehat{h}_{uj}} \vec{v_{iu}} = \sum_{u=1,\ell=1}^{m,\lambda} b_{uj}^{(\ell)} \mathbf{M}_{\alpha^{[i+u-2]}} \vec{\mu_\ell}. \tag{6}$$

System 1 contains mrn affine equations over $\mathbb{F}_q$. The linear parts involve mr^2 variables $\vec{v_{iu}}$ while the bilinear parts involve $\lambda mn + \lambda m$ variables $b_{uj}^{(\ell)}$ and $\vec{\mu_\ell}$ respectively. Proposition 5 states that the solutions to this system are actually equivalent to the ones of the constrained linear equations (3).

Proposition 5 *Let* $\widetilde{\mathbf{V}} = (v_{ij}) \in \mathcal{M}_{r \times r}(\mathbb{F}_{q^m})$ *and* $\widetilde{\mathbf{W}} = (w_{ij}) \in \mathcal{M}_{m \times n}(\mathbb{F}_{q^m})$ *which satisfy the constrained linear equations (3) and let* $\mathcal{W}$ *a*[1] λ-*dimensional subspace of* $\mathbb{F}_{q^m}$ *which contains the entries of* $\widetilde{\mathbf{W}}$. *Let* $(\mu_1, \ldots, \mu_\lambda) \in \mathbb{F}_{q^m}^\lambda$ *be a basis for* $\mathcal{W}$ *and*

$$w_{ij} \stackrel{def}{=} \sum_{\ell=1}^\lambda b_{ij}^{(\ell)} \mu_\ell \tag{7}$$

be the unique decomposition of w_{ij} *in this basis. Then* $\vec{v_{iu}} \in \mathbb{F}_q^m$, $b_{ij}^{(\ell)}$ *and* $\vec{\mu_\ell}$ *are a solution to* **System 1**. *Conversely, any solution* $\vec{v_{iu}}$, $b_{ij}^{(\ell)}$, $\vec{\mu_\ell}$ *to* **System 1** *gives a pair of matrices* $\widetilde{\mathbf{V}} = (v_{ij})$, $\widetilde{\mathbf{W}} = (w_{ij})$ *solution to the constrained linear equations (3), where* w_{ij} *is defined by Eq. (7).*

---

[1] Concretely, "the".

If (V, W) stands for the genuine couple of matrices which is implicit from the description of the scheme, we have already mentioned that any $(\widetilde{V}, \widetilde{W}) \overset{def}{=}$ (xV, xW) for $x \in \mathbb{F}_{q^m}^*$ allows to decrypt. Concretely, to reduce the number of solutions to **System** 1, we will thus:

– fix μ_1 to 1 and choose a basis $\widehat{\mathcal{B}}$ such that $\hat{b}_1 = 1$;
– target a basis in systematic form, $i.e.$,

$$(1, \mu_2, \ldots, \mu_\lambda)^\mathsf{T} \overset{def}{=} \begin{pmatrix} & \mathbf{0}_{1 \times (m-\lambda)} \\ \mathbf{I}_\lambda & \\ & \mathbf{R}' \end{pmatrix} \widehat{\mathcal{B}}^\mathsf{T}, \tag{8}$$

where $\mathbf{R}' \in \mathcal{M}_{(\lambda-1) \times (m-\lambda)}(\mathbb{F}_q)$. We cannot always guarantee to have a solution in this way but the success probability is constant.

Note that similar strategies to fix variables had already been suggested in previous works, see for instance [7, §3.4] or [21, §3.1].

Solving by Gröbner Bases. To solve **System** 1, one may be tempted to use Gröbner basis techniques [11–13]. However, our practical experiments for this method were not conclusive. A reason is that there is a great imbalance between the two blocks of variables $\vec{\mu}_\ell$ and $b_{ij}^{(\ell)}$ since $(\lambda - 1)(m - \lambda) \ll mn\lambda$. This also explains why it was quite natural in Sect. 5 to proceed by enumeration on the smallest block $\vec{\mu}_\ell$ (corresponding to an unknown basis for $\mathcal{V}$) in order to obtain linear equations.

7   Tools to Analyze System 1

Even if the Gröbner basis approach seems infeasible, this section gives some background to partially explain the early steps of such an algorithm. More specifically, in Sect. 8, we will characterize the first degree fall polynomials (see Definition 2) which arise in the computation.

   Gröbner basis solvers [11–13] had already been analyzed by [13] in the context of generic bilinear systems. However, in our case, we need to use the fact that **System** 1 admits a much stronger structure than being merely bilinear. It turns out that its analysis is much closer to the one performed in [4,23] on bilinear modelings of MinRank and of the Rank Decoding problem. Indeed, a common feature in such systems is that the equations can be viewed as the entries of a matrix $M = AXY$, where A is a matrix of scalars and where X and Y are matrices of unknowns x and y respectively. It is easy to see that our equations exhibit a similar shape. Using the notation from **System** 1, we can indeed write each column $w_j = (w_{1,j}, \ldots, w_{m,j}) \in \mathbb{F}_{q^m}^m$ of the unknown W as

$w_j^\mathsf{T} = C_j(\mu_1, \ldots, \mu_\lambda)^\mathsf{T} = C_j R \widehat{\mathcal{B}}^\mathsf{T}$, where $C_j \overset{def}{=} (b_{i,j}^{(\ell)})_{1 \le i \le m, 1 \le \ell \le \lambda}$ and where the rows of $R \in \mathcal{M}_{\lambda \times m}(\mathbb{F}_q)$ are the $\vec{\mu}_\ell$'s for $1 \le \ell \le \lambda$. We then obtain

System 0 *For* $j \in \{1..n\}$*, let* $\widehat{\boldsymbol{h}_j} \in \mathbb{F}_{q^m}^r$ *denote the* j*-th column in* $\widehat{\mathbf{H}}_{pub}$*. There are* r *bilinear equations in the entries of* $\widetilde{\boldsymbol{V}}$*,* $\boldsymbol{R}$ *and* $\boldsymbol{C}_j$ *from the equality*

$$\widetilde{\boldsymbol{V}}\widehat{\boldsymbol{h}_j}^{\mathsf{T}} = \widehat{\mathbf{H}}_{norm}\boldsymbol{C}_j\boldsymbol{R}\widehat{\mathcal{B}}^{\mathsf{T}}. \tag{9}$$

By considering all columns, we obtain an affine bilinear system with

- rn *equations over* $\mathbb{F}_{q^m}$.
- r^2 *unknowns* v_{ij} *over* $\mathbb{F}_{q^m}$ *and* $\lambda mn + \lambda m$ *unknowns over* $\mathbb{F}_q$.

Note that **System 1** captures exactly the same information as the system over $\mathbb{F}_q$ obtained from **System 0** by taking as unknowns the $\vec{v_{iu}}$'s instead of the v_{ij}'s and then by projecting over the base field. We may adopt the latter for the theoretical analysis since it is more convenient.

7.1 Algebraic Background

Let us start with some necessary facts on Gröbner bases techniques applied to bilinear systems.

Syzygies and Degree Falls. For a polynomial sequence $\mathcal{F} = (f_1, \ldots, f_M)$, a *syzygy* is a polynomial combination $\sum_{i=1}^{M} g_i f_i = 0$. Its degree is defined by $\max_{i=1}^{M} (\deg(g_i f_i))$. In our systems, recall that any polynomial is of the form $f_i = b_i + l_i$ where b_i is bilinear and l_i is linear. In particular, a syzygy $\sum_{i=1}^{M} g_i b_i = 0$ of degree d for $(b_1, \ldots, b_M)$ typically yields an equation $\sum_{i=1}^{m} g_i f_i = \sum_{i=1}^{M} g_i l_i = 0$ of degree $d - 1$ in the ideal. This is a particular case of

Definition 2 (Degree fall polynomial) *A degree fall polynomial for a sequence* $\mathcal{F} = (f_1, \ldots, f_M)$ *is a non-zero polynomial combination* $\sum_{i=1}^{M} g_i f_i$ *whose degree* δ *is strictly less than* $d \stackrel{def}{=} \max_{i=1}^{M} (\deg(g_i f_i))$*. We may also refer to it as a degree fall from degree* d *to degree* δ*.*

Such an equation will be meaningful if and only if it is not a linear combination between previously considered equations of degree $\leq d-1$. Some actually prefer to include this extra constraint already in Definition 2. Degree fall polynomials for affine systems play a similar role to that of syzygies for homogeneous equations. Their study is thus instrumental to understand the complexity of solving such affine equations.

Bilinear Systems [13]. Let $\mathcal{B} = (b_1, \ldots, b_M) \subset \mathbb{F}[\boldsymbol{x}, \boldsymbol{y}]$ be the homogeneous bilinear sequence in two blocks of variables $\boldsymbol{x}$ and $\boldsymbol{y}$ over a field $\mathbb{F}$ which contains the degree 2 parts of an affine bilinear sequence $\mathcal{F}$. As we have just said, degree fall polynomials for $\mathcal{F}$ are directly related to syzygies for $\mathcal{B}$. Let us now consider the Jacobian matrices which are defined by

$$\text{Jac}_{\boldsymbol{x}}(\mathcal{S}) \stackrel{def}{=} \left(\frac{\partial b_i}{\partial x_j}\right)_{1 \leq i \leq M, \ 1 \leq j \leq n_x}$$

and

$$\mathrm{Jac}_{\boldsymbol{y}}(\mathcal{S}) \stackrel{def}{=} \left(\frac{\partial b_i}{\partial y_j}\right)_{1 \le i \le M,\ 1 \le j \le n_y}.$$

Their entries are linear forms in $\mathbb{F}[\boldsymbol{y}]$ and $\mathbb{F}[\boldsymbol{x}]$ respectively. The study of these Jacobians is motivated by the following Lemma 1, which states that generic syzygies for $\mathcal{S}$ are provided by vectors in the left kernel of these matrices.

Lemma 1 *Let* $\mathcal{S} \stackrel{def}{=} (b_1, \ldots, b_M) \subset \mathbb{F}[\boldsymbol{x}, \boldsymbol{y}]$ *be a homogeneous bilinear sequence and let* $\mathcal{G} \stackrel{def}{=} (g_1, \ldots, g_M) \subset \mathbb{F}[\boldsymbol{y}]^M$ *be a polynomial sequence. We have* $\sum_{i=1}^{M} g_i b_i = 0$ *if and only if* $\mathcal{G}$ *belongs to the left kernel of* $\mathrm{Jac}_{\boldsymbol{x}}(\mathcal{S})$.

Proof. Let $\mathcal{G} = (g_1, \ldots, g_M)$ be an arbitrary polynomial sequence. Since we have

$$\mathcal{G}\mathrm{Jac}_{\boldsymbol{x}}(\mathcal{S})\boldsymbol{x}^{\mathsf{T}} = \sum_{i=1}^{M} g_i b_i,$$

we obtain a syzygy from any kernel vector of $\mathrm{Jac}_{\boldsymbol{x}}(\mathcal{S})$. The converse statement is only valid for $\mathcal{G} \subset \mathbb{F}[\boldsymbol{y}]^M$. For such a vector of polynomials, the product by $\mathrm{Jac}_{\boldsymbol{x}}(\mathcal{S})$ is still a row vector of elements in $\mathbb{F}[\boldsymbol{y}]$. The only possibility for it to be 0 when multiplied by $\boldsymbol{x}^{\mathsf{T}}$ is that it is already 0, *i.e.*, $\mathcal{G} \in \ker(\mathrm{Jac}_{\boldsymbol{x}}(\mathcal{S}))$. $\square$

The following Lemma 2 gives kernel vectors for these Jacobian matrices regardless of their structure.

Lemma 2 (Lemma 3.1 in [13]) *Let* $\boldsymbol{M} \in \mathcal{M}_{M \times t}(\mathbb{F}[\boldsymbol{y}])$ *be a matrix whose entries are linear forms with* $t < M$. *Let*

$$\boldsymbol{V}_J \stackrel{def}{=} (\ldots, \underbrace{0}_{j \notin J}, \ldots, \underbrace{(-1)^{\ell+1}|\boldsymbol{M}|_{J \setminus j_\ell, *}}_{j = j_\ell}, \ldots),$$

where $J = \{j_1 < \cdots < j_{t+1}\} \subset \{1..M\}$. *These vectors are such that* $\boldsymbol{V}_J \boldsymbol{M} = 0$.

Generically, the vectors $\boldsymbol{V}_J$ generate the left kernel of such a matrix $\boldsymbol{M}$, see for instance [13, Conjecture 4.1]. Also, for a bilinear random $\mathcal{S}$, the entries of the matrix $\mathrm{Jac}_{\boldsymbol{x}}(\mathcal{S})$ are random linear forms in $\mathbb{F}[\boldsymbol{y}]$. Lemma 2 was thus used in [13] to have a complete description of its left kernel. Based on this result, they show that the degree of regularity of a generic bilinear system is such that $d_{\mathrm{reg}} \le \min(n_{\boldsymbol{x}} + 1, n_{\boldsymbol{y}} + 1)$.

However, the bilinear equations relevant to us are not generic and we will have to analyze the structure of the Jacobians.

A Useful Lemma. Consider a matrix equation $\boldsymbol{M} = \boldsymbol{A}\boldsymbol{X}\boldsymbol{Y} \in \mathcal{M}_{p \times n}(\mathbb{F}[\boldsymbol{x}, \boldsymbol{y}])$ as in the beginning of this section, where $\boldsymbol{A} \in \mathcal{M}_{p \times m}(\mathbb{F})$ is a matrix of scalars and where $\boldsymbol{X} \in \mathcal{M}_{m \times r}(\mathbb{F}[\boldsymbol{x}])$ and $\boldsymbol{Y} \in \mathcal{M}_{r \times n}(\mathbb{F}[\boldsymbol{y}])$ are matrices of unknowns $\boldsymbol{x}$ and $\boldsymbol{y}$ respectively. Let us define the row vector $\left(\boldsymbol{M}_{\{1\},*} \cdots \boldsymbol{M}_{\{m\},*}\right)$ formed by the concatenation of the rows of $\boldsymbol{M}$ and similarly $\mathrm{col}(\boldsymbol{M}) \stackrel{def}{=} \mathrm{row}(\boldsymbol{M}^{\mathsf{T}})$. Then we have the following lemma

Lemma 3 *The Jacobian matrix of a system $\boldsymbol{AXY} = \boldsymbol{0}_{p \times n}$ with respect to the $\boldsymbol{x}$ variables is given by*

$$\mathrm{Jac}_{row(\boldsymbol{X})}\left(row(\boldsymbol{AXY})\right) = \boldsymbol{A} \otimes \boldsymbol{Y}^\mathsf{T} \in \mathcal{M}_{np \times mr}(\mathbb{F}[\boldsymbol{y}]),$$
$$\mathrm{Jac}_{col(\boldsymbol{X})}\left(col(\boldsymbol{AXY})\right) = \boldsymbol{Y}^\mathsf{T} \otimes \boldsymbol{A} \in \mathcal{M}_{np \times mr}(\mathbb{F}[\boldsymbol{y}]).$$

Proof. See [4, Lemma 1]. $\square$

7.2   Understanding the Projection Over $\mathbb{F}_q$

In addition to the matrix product structure, another particularity comes from the extension field. Indeed, recall that **System 1** can be seen as the projection over $\mathbb{F}_q$ of **System 0** whose equations have coefficients in $\mathbb{F}_{q^m}$ but where the variables involved in the bilinear parts belong to $\mathbb{F}_q$. In that respect, this system is obtained in the exact same manner as in [3,4,6] which aim at solving the Rank Decoding Problem and the Rank Support Learning Problem.

In the case of [3,4,6], the analysis of the full system over $\mathbb{F}_q$ can be boiled down to the one of the initial system over $\mathbb{F}_{q^m}$. On our side, however, the situation is less simple. For instance, it is not sufficient to analyze **System 0** to understand the computation on **System 1** over $\mathbb{F}_q$. This might be due to the following simple fact: by choosing $\widehat{\mathcal{B}} = \mathcal{A} = \{1, \alpha^{[1]}, \ldots, \alpha^{[m-1]}\}$ to express **System 0**, we actually recover the first row of $\widehat{\mathbf{H}}_{norm}$. This gives another interesting property which was not present in [3,4,6].

As explained after the definition of **System 0**, projecting this system yields equations over $\mathbb{F}_q$ which generate the same system as **System 1**. Let us denote by $\{b_1, \ldots, b_m\}$ the set of m equations over $\mathbb{F}_q$ obtained by projecting the bilinear part b of an equation of **System 0**. Also, let us extend the Frobenius map to polynomials by reducing modulo the field equations of the small field since all variables belong to $\mathbb{F}_q$, namely $b^{[\ell]} \overset{def}{=} b^{q^\ell} \bmod \langle x_i^q - x_i \rangle_i$. For a matrix $\boldsymbol{M} = (m_{ij})$ over $\mathbb{F}_{q^m}$ (or over a polynomial ring with base field $\mathbb{F}_{q^m}$), we also denote by $\boldsymbol{M}^{[\ell]}$ the matrix $\left(m_{ij}^{[\ell]}\right)$. Finally, in our analysis, we will use the fact that the algebraic properties[2] of both sequences $(b_1, \ldots, b_m)$ and $(b, \ldots, b^{[m-1]})$ are the same. In particular, it will be relevant to consider the following **System 2** which is equivalent to **System 1**.

System 2 *For $j \in \{1..n\}$, let $\widehat{\boldsymbol{h}_j} \in \mathbb{F}_{q^m}^r$ denote the j-th column in $\widehat{\mathbf{H}}_{pub}$. For any $0 \le \ell \le m-1$, we consider the r equations obtained by applying the Frobenius ℓ times on Eq. (9). They are given by*

$$\boldsymbol{V}^{[\ell]}\left(\widehat{\boldsymbol{h}_j^{[\ell]}}\right)^\mathsf{T} = \widehat{\mathbf{H}}_{norm}^{[\ell]} \boldsymbol{C}_j \boldsymbol{R}\left(\widehat{\mathcal{B}^{[\ell]}}\right)^\mathsf{T}. \tag{10}$$

---

[2] Syzygies, etc.

We stress that **System** 2 has essentially a theoretical value. In particular, it would not be suitable to solve it by using naive Gröbner basis algorithms since the equations have very high degree in the $v_{i,j}$ variables.

8   Degree Fall Polynomials from Jacobians

This final section aims at studying the Jacobians associated to the bilinear parts of our equations. We will show in Lemma 4 and Lemma 5 that their kernels provide two types syzygies in degree $\lambda + 2$, hence degree fall polynomials of degree $\lambda + 1$ for the original affine equations. Moreover, our experiments suggest that these are the only ones at this degree and that these are the *first*, *i.e.*, no one appear at a lower degree.

Interestingly enough, we do not need to wait the degree $\lambda + 2$ step of a Gröbner basis algorithm on **System** 0 or **System** 1 for a graded order to obtain these polynomials. They can indeed be pre-computed as maximal minors of public matrices of linear forms. In that respect, the situation is quite similar to the one of algebraic attacks on the Rank Decoding problem [4–6, 21]. For instance, the so-called MaxMinors equations introduced in [4] were originally obtained as degree fall polynomials for the former bilinear modeling of Ourivski-Johansson [21] but they can also be computed directly.

For the sake of simplicity, we give the results for the non-specialized version of our systems. They can be easily adapted if we fix μ_1 to 1 and if we choose a matrix $\boldsymbol{R}$ in systematic form as presented above.

8.1   Jacobian with Respect to the $\boldsymbol{R}$ Variables

We start from the Jacobian matrices with respect to the block of $\boldsymbol{R}$ variables. We will see that their structure is similar to the one encountered in [4, §5.1]. As in their work, we also observed that all degree falls over $\mathbb{F}_q$ from these matrices were obtained by projecting over $\mathbb{F}_q$ degree fall polynomials whose coefficients are in $\mathbb{F}_{q^m}$. This means that we can focus on **System** 0 rather than on **System** 1 for this part of the analysis, the situation being different in Sect. 8.2.

If we restrict ourselves to the bilinear parts in **System** 0, a direct application of Lemma 3 for $1 \leq j \leq n$ with $\boldsymbol{X} \overset{def}{=} \boldsymbol{R}$, $\boldsymbol{A} \overset{def}{=} \widehat{\mathbf{H}}_{norm} \boldsymbol{C}_j$ and $\boldsymbol{Y} \overset{def}{=} \widehat{\mathcal{B}}^{\mathsf{T}}$ yields

$$\mathrm{Jac}_{\mathrm{row}(\boldsymbol{R})}(\mathrm{row}(\widehat{\mathbf{H}}_{norm} \boldsymbol{C}_j \boldsymbol{R} \widehat{\mathcal{B}}^{\mathsf{T}})) = \widehat{\mathbf{H}}_{norm} \boldsymbol{C}_j \otimes \widehat{\mathcal{B}}. \tag{11}$$

The full system can also be viewed as the following matrix product

$$\left(\boldsymbol{I}_n \otimes \widehat{\mathbf{H}}_{norm} \right) \begin{pmatrix} \boldsymbol{C}_1 \\ \vdots \\ \boldsymbol{C}_n \end{pmatrix} \boldsymbol{R} \widehat{\mathcal{B}}^{\mathsf{T}},$$

and thus we obtain in the same manner

$$\mathrm{Jac}_{\mathrm{row}(R)}\left(\left(I_n \otimes \widehat{\mathbf{H}}_{norm}\right)\begin{pmatrix}C_1\\ \vdots \\ C_n\end{pmatrix}R\widehat{\mathcal{B}}^{\mathsf{T}}\right)$$

$$= \begin{pmatrix}\widehat{\mathbf{H}}_{norm}C_1\\ \vdots \\ \widehat{\mathbf{H}}_{norm}C_n\end{pmatrix} \otimes \widehat{\mathcal{B}}. \tag{12}$$

Recall from Lemma 1 that the kernel of such Jacobians provides syzygies for the bilinear parts whose coefficients are polynomials in the C_j variables. In our case, we can obtain

Lemma 4 *In* **System** *0, there are at least* $\binom{nr}{\lambda+1}$ *degree falls from degree* $\lambda + 2$ *to* $\lambda + 1$. *Indeed, some of them are already given by the maximal minors of the matrix*

$$\mathcal{M} \overset{def}{=} \begin{pmatrix}\widetilde{\boldsymbol{V}\widehat{h_1}}^{\mathsf{T}} & \widehat{\mathbf{H}}_{norm}C_1\\ & \vdots & \\ \widetilde{\boldsymbol{V}\widehat{h_n}}^{\mathsf{T}} & \widehat{\mathbf{H}}_{norm}C_n\end{pmatrix}. \tag{13}$$

Among these equations, we may find in particular the maximal minors of the matrix

$$\mathcal{M}_j \overset{def}{=} \mathcal{M}_{\{1+r(j-1)..rj\},*} = \left(\widetilde{\boldsymbol{V}\widehat{h_j}}^{\mathsf{T}} \quad \widehat{\mathbf{H}}_{norm}C_j\right), \tag{14}$$

for $1 \leq j \leq n$.

Even before giving the proof of Lemma 4, it is easy to see from Eq. (9) that all $\mathcal{M}_j$ matrices are not full-rank (a fortiori, $\mathcal{M}$) if and only if $(\widetilde{\boldsymbol{V}}, C_1, \ldots, C_n)$ are components of a solution to **System** 0.

Proof. (Analogous to [4]). We do the proof for a single matrix $\mathcal{M}_j$. Using Eq. (11), it is sufficient to look at the left kernel of $\widehat{\mathbf{H}}_{norm}C_j$. We then compute the kernel vectors $\boldsymbol{V}_J$ of Lemma 2 for this matrix of linear forms, namely

$$\boldsymbol{V}_J \overset{def}{=} \left(\underbrace{0}_{j \notin J}, \ldots, \underbrace{(-1)^{\ell+1}\left|\widehat{\mathbf{H}}_{norm}C_j\right|_{J\setminus\{j\},*}}_{j=j_\ell \in J}, \ldots\right), \quad \#J = \lambda + 1, \ J \subset \{1..r\}.$$

The degree falls are then obtained by multiplying these vectors by the linear parts of the equations, *i.e.* $(\boldsymbol{V}_J) \cdot \widetilde{\boldsymbol{V}\widehat{h_j}}^{\mathsf{T}}$. Finally, the latter actually coincides with the maximal minor $|\mathcal{M}_j|_{J,*}$ using Laplace expansion along the first column. The reasoning is similar for $\mathcal{M}$ if we replace Eq. (11) by Eq. (12).   □

Bilinear Structure. The degree fall polynomials given by Lemma 4 have degree $\lambda+1$. Moreover, Laplace expansion along the first column of $\mathcal{M}$ in Eq. (13) shows that these equations are *bilinear* in the entries of $\widetilde{V}$ (which belong to $\mathbb{F}_{q^m}$) and in the maximal minors of the matrix

$$D \overset{def}{=} \begin{pmatrix} C_1 \\ \vdots \\ C_n \end{pmatrix},$$

whose coefficients are in $\mathbb{F}_q$. Similarly, the maximal minors of $\mathcal{M}_j$ are simply bilinear in the entries of $\widetilde{V}$ and in the $\binom{m}{\lambda}$ maximal minors of C_j. Such a structure had already been encountered in the bilinear systems of [5,6] to attack the Rank Decoding Problem and MinRank. In particular, note that the newly introduced bilinear modeling of [5] ([5, Modeling 4]) has exactly the same shape as it involves a block of *linear variables* over the extension field $\mathbb{F}_{q^m}$ and a block of *minor variables* over $\mathbb{F}_q$.

Projection Over $\mathbb{F}_q$. In **System** 1, we observed $m\binom{nr}{\lambda+1}$ (linearly independent) degree falls from degree $\lambda+2$ to degree $\lambda+1$ which involve these variables[3] in our experiments. Clearly, they should coincide with the projection over $\mathbb{F}_q$ of the degree fall polynomials described in Lemma 4 for **System** 0. To project the equations, note that we also have to express the entries of $\widetilde{V}$ over $\mathbb{F}_q$. This yields r^2m variables $v_{iu}^{\rightarrow}$ and thus $r^2m\binom{mn}{\lambda}$ degree 2 monomials among these degree fall polynomials (but only $r^2m\binom{m}{\lambda}$ if we restrict ourselves to one matrix C_j).

8.2   Jacobian with Respect to the C_j Variables

Contrary to the systems of [4–6] to solve the Rank Decoding Problem, a specificity of **System** 1 is that the Jacobian with respect to the other block of variables also yields degree fall polynomials of low degree, for instance $\lambda+1$. One cannot grasp them by studying **System** 0 only.

Absence of Degree Falls for System 0. First, let us explain why we do not expect degree fall polynomials of small degree coming from this Jacobian for **System** 0. Note that the set $\mathcal{S}$ of bilinear parts of the equations from this system can be written as $\mathcal{S} \overset{def}{=} \cup_{j=1}^{n}\mathcal{S}_j$, where the polynomials in $\mathcal{S}_j$ are defined as the entries of the matrix $\widehat{\mathbf{H}}_{norm}C_j R\widehat{\mathcal{B}}^{\mathsf{T}}$ at the right hand side of Eq. (9). The $R\widehat{\mathcal{B}}^{\mathsf{T}}$ part being independent of j, we already obtain $\mathrm{Jac}_{\mathrm{row}(C_j)}(\mathrm{row}(\mathcal{S}_j)) = \mathrm{Jac}_{\mathrm{row}(C_1)}(\mathrm{row}(\mathcal{S}_1))$ for any j and thus

$$\mathrm{Jac}_{\mathrm{row}(C)}(\mathrm{row}(\mathcal{S})) = I_n \otimes \mathrm{Jac}_{\mathrm{row}(C_1)}(\mathrm{row}(\mathcal{S}_1)).$$

Then, to compute $\mathrm{Jac}_{\mathrm{row}(C_1)}(\mathrm{row}(\mathcal{S}_1))$, we apply Lemma 3 once again this time with $X \overset{def}{=} \widehat{\mathbf{H}}_{norm}$, $A \overset{def}{=} C_1$ and $Y \overset{def}{=} R\widehat{\mathcal{B}}^{\mathsf{T}}$. This yields

$$\mathrm{Jac}_{\mathrm{row}(C_1)}(\mathrm{row}(\mathcal{S}_1)) = \widehat{\mathbf{H}}_{norm} \otimes \widehat{\mathcal{B}}R^{\mathsf{T}}. \tag{15}$$

---

[3] Section 8.2 will give another type of degree falls in the same degree.

This matrix is of size $r \times m\lambda$ and its entries are linear forms in the $\mathbf{R}$ variables. However, we cannot apply Lemma 2 since $r < m\lambda$. We expect a trivial left kernel for this matrix.

Additional Degree Falls for System 1. We analyze the situation over $\mathbb{F}_q$ by studying the **System** 2 introduced in Sect. 7.2, which contains the same information as **System** 1. From now on we fix $\widehat{\mathcal{B}} = \mathcal{A}$. As in the previous section, we can clearly reason in a similar way for all indexes $1 \le j \le n$. For $1 \le j \le n$ and $0 \le \ell \le m-1$, let us consider Eq. (10) and for $1 \le u \le r$, let us denote by $g_{u,\ell,j}$ the bilinear polynomial

$$g_{u,\ell,j} \overset{def}{=} \left(\widehat{\mathbf{H}}_{norm}^{[\ell]} \right)_{u,*} \mathbf{C}_j \mathbf{R} \left(\mathcal{A}^{[\ell]} \right)^{\mathsf{T}} = \left(\mathcal{A}^{[\ell+u-1]} \right) \mathbf{C}_j \mathbf{R} \left(\mathcal{A}^{[\ell]} \right)^{\mathsf{T}}.$$

We also keep track of the corresponding linear part $L_{u,\ell,j} \overset{def}{=} \mathbf{V}_{u,*}^{[\ell]} \left(\widehat{\mathbf{h}_j^{[\ell]}} \right)^{\mathsf{T}}$, so that the whole equation reads $g_{u,\ell,j} - L_{u,\ell,j} = 0$. We then group the equations according to the value of $v \overset{def}{=} u+\ell-1 \bmod m$. We obtain the following equality, where all ℓ indexes are modulo m,

$$\left(L_{1,v,j} \; L_{2,v-1,j} \; \ldots \; L_{r,v-r+1,j} \right) = \left(g_{1,v,j} \; \ldots \; g_{r,v-r+1,j} \right)$$

$$\widehat{\mathbf{h}_j^{[\ell]}} \left(\mathbf{V}^{[\ell]} \right)^{\mathsf{T}} = \mathcal{A}^{[v]} \mathbf{C}_j \mathbf{R} \left(\left(\mathcal{A}^{[v]} \right)^{\mathsf{T}} : \left(\mathcal{A}^{[v-r+1]} \right)^{\mathsf{T}} \right)$$

$$= \mathcal{A}^{[v]} \mathbf{C}_j \mathbf{R} \left(\widehat{\mathbf{H}}_{inv}^{[v]} \right)^{\mathsf{T}},$$

and where

$$\widehat{\mathbf{H}}_{inv} \overset{def}{=} \begin{pmatrix} \mathcal{A} \\ \ldots \\ \mathcal{A}^{-[r-1]} \end{pmatrix} \in \mathcal{M}_{m,r}(\mathbb{F}_{q^m}).$$

Using Lemma 3, we then compute the Jacobian matrix of these equations with respect to the $\mathbf{C}_j$ variables with $\mathbf{A} \overset{def}{=} \mathcal{A}^{[v]}$, $\mathbf{X} \overset{def}{=} \mathbf{C}_j$ and $\mathbf{Y} \overset{def}{=} \mathbf{R} \left(\widehat{\mathbf{H}}_{inv}^{[v]} \right)^{\mathsf{T}}$. This gives

$$\mathrm{Jac}_{\mathrm{row}(\mathbf{C}_j)} \left(g_{1,\ell_1,j} \; \ldots \; g_{r,\ell_r,j} \right) = \mathcal{A}^{[v]} \otimes \widehat{\mathbf{H}}_{inv}^{[v]} \mathbf{R}^{\mathsf{T}}.$$

We can continue as above to obtain Lemma 5, whose proof is analogous to the one of Lemma 4.

Lemma 5 *For any fixed column $\mathbf{h}_j$ in $\mathbf{H}_{pub}$, for $0 \le \ell \le m-1$ and for a modulus $0 \le v \le m-1$, there are $\binom{r}{\lambda+1}$ degree falls from degree $\lambda+2$ to $\lambda+1$ which are given by the maximal minors of the matrix*

$$\mathcal{N}_{j,\ell,v} \overset{def}{=} \begin{pmatrix} \widehat{\mathbf{h}_j^{[\ell]}} \left(\mathbf{V}^{[\ell]} \right)^{\mathsf{T}} \\ \mathbf{R} \left(\widehat{\mathbf{H}}_{inv}^{[v]} \right)^{\mathsf{T}} \end{pmatrix}, \tag{16}$$

where

$$\widehat{\mathbf{H}}_{inv} \stackrel{def}{=} \begin{pmatrix} \mathcal{A} \\ \dots \\ \mathcal{A}^{-[r-1]} \end{pmatrix}.$$

By gathering the equations for all columns $\boldsymbol{h}_j$ in $\boldsymbol{H}_{\mathrm{pub}}$, all indexes ℓ and all moduli v, we obtain a system of $nm^2 \binom{r}{\lambda+1}$ polynomials of degree $\lambda+1$. Similarly to the above, these polynomials have a bilinear structure: they are bilinear in the entries of the $\boldsymbol{V}^{[\ell]}$'s and in the maximal minors r_T of $\boldsymbol{R}$. Coming back to the **System** 1 over $\mathbb{F}_q$ that we want to solve, this will correspond to an extra set of $nm^2 \binom{r}{\lambda+1}$ polynomials of degree $\lambda+1$ which are produced in degree $\lambda+2$ by the computation. They can also be seen as an affine bilinear system involving $mr^2 \binom{m}{\lambda}$ quadratic monomials.

8.3 Approach Based on Degree Fall Polynomials

Instead of simply solving the original bilinear system, our results suggest another method by focusing on a system of degree fall polynomials of degree $\lambda+1$. It would consist of the one given by Lemma 4, Lemma 5 or a subset of such equations. As we have just seen, this approach would benefit from the compactness of these polynomials since they have a specific bilinear structure. Its analysis is left for future work, including the study of linear dependencies and the possibility of using hybrid techniques.

In the case of the Rank Decoding Problem, solving the system given by the MaxMinors equations [6] lead to a significant improvement compared to attacks based on Ourivski-Johansson [4,21]. In our case, however, the same will not necessarily hold. First, the ratio between equations and variables in Lemma 4 or Lemma 5 seems less favorable than in [6]. Second, our experiments suggest that the degree falls polynomials in degree $\lambda+2$ do not mark the end of the computation on the original system in general, whereas it was often the case for the Rank Decoding Problem [4,18].

9 Conclusion

In the paper we presented two different approaches to *distinguish* a public-key from random.

The combinatorial approach seems to have reached its limits as is the case for the problem of decoding in rank metric and we do not expect significant gain (say non-polynomial improvements on the complexity) from further improvements, except if there is a major theoretical breakthrough, but who would probably also extend to the problem of decoding in rank metric.

Concerning the algebraic approach, it is more difficult to ascertain that no significant improvements are to be expected. Namely, as is the case for solving non-linear system, a smarter approach to rewrite the system could lead to major improvements. Anyway it is certainly an interesting field of research to obtain a finer analysis of system solving.

References

1. Aragon, N., Dyseryn, V., Gaborit, P., Loidreau, P., Renner, J., Wachter-Zeh, A.: LowMS: a new rank metric code-based KEM without ideal structure. Cryptology ePrint Archive, Paper 2022/1596 (2022). https://eprint.iacr.org/2022/1596
2. Aragon, N., Gaborit, P., Hauteville, A., Tillich, J.P.: A new algorithm for solving the rank syndrome decoding problem. In: 2018 IEEE International Symposium on Information Theory (ISIT 2018), Vail, CO, USA, 17–22 June 2018, pp. 2421–2425. IEEE (2018). https://doi.org/10.1109/ISIT.2018.8437464
3. Bardet, Magali, Briaud, Pierre: An algebraic approach to the rank support learning problem. In: Cheon, Jung Hee, Tillich, Jean-Pierre. (eds.) PQCrypto 2021 2021. LNCS, vol. 12841, pp. 442–462. Springer, Cham (2021). https://doi.org/10.1007/978-3-030-81293-5_23
4. Bardet, M., et al.: An algebraic attack on rank metric code-based cryptosystems. In: Canteaut, Anne, Ishai, Yuval (eds.) EUROCRYPT 2020. LNCS, vol. 12107, pp. 64–93. Springer, Cham (2020). https://doi.org/10.1007/978-3-030-45727-3_3
5. Bardet, M., Briaud, P., Bros, M., Gaborit, P., Tillich, J.P.: Revisiting algebraic attacks on MinRank and on the rank decoding problem. Cryptology ePrint Archive, Paper 2022/1031 (2022). https://eprint.iacr.org/2022/1031
6. Bardet, M., et al.: Improvements of algebraic attacks for solving the rank decoding and MinRank problems. In: Moriai, Shiho, Wang, Huaxiong (eds.) ASIACRYPT 2020. LNCS, vol. 12491, pp. 507–536. Springer, Cham (2020). https://doi.org/10.1007/978-3-030-64837-4_17
7. Chabaud, F., Stern, J.: The cryptographic security of the syndrome decoding problem for rank distance codes. In: Kim, K., Matsumoto, T. (eds.) ASIACRYPT 1996. LNCS, vol. 1163, pp. 368–381. Springer, Heidelberg (1996). https://doi.org/10.1007/BFb0034862
8. Coggia, D., Couvreur, A.: On the security of a Loidreau rank metric code based encryption scheme. Des. Codes Crypt. **88**(9), 1941–1957 (2020). https://doi.org/10.1007/s10623-020-00781-4
9. Coppersmith, D.: Solving homogeneous linear equations over GF(2) via block Wiedemann algorithm. Math. Comput. **62**, 333–350 (1994)
10. Delsarte, P.: Bilinear forms over a finite field, with applications to coding theory. J. Comb. Theory Ser. A **25**(3), 226–241 (1978)
11. Faugère, J.C.: A new efficient algorithm for computing Gröbner bases (F4). J. Pure Appl. Algebra **139**(1–3), 61–88 (1999)
12. Faugère, J.C.: A new efficient algorithm for computing Gröbner bases without reduction to zero: F5. In: Proceedings ISSAC 2002, pp. 75–83. ACM Press (2002)
13. Faugère, J.C., Safey El Din, M., Spacodecrenlehauer, P.J.: Gröbner bases of bihomogeneous ideals generated by polynomials of bidegree (1,1): algorithms and complexity. J. Symbolic Comput. **46**(4), 406–437 (2011)
14. Gabidulin, E.M.: Theory of codes with maximum rank distance. Problemy Peredachi Informatsii **21**(1), 3–16 (1985)
15. Gabidulin, E.. M.., Paramonov, A.. V.., Tretjakov, O.. V..: Ideals over a noncommutative ring and their application in cryptology. In: Davies, Donald W.. (ed.) EUROCRYPT 1991. LNCS, vol. 547, pp. 482–489. Springer, Heidelberg (1991). https://doi.org/10.1007/3-540-46416-6_41
16. Gaborit, Philippe, Hauteville, Adrien, Phan, Duong Hieu, Tillich, Jean-Pierre.: Identity-based encryption from codes with rank metric. In: Katz, Jonathan, Shacham, Hovav (eds.) CRYPTO 2017. LNCS, vol. 10403, pp. 194–224. Springer, Cham (2017). https://doi.org/10.1007/978-3-319-63697-9_7

17. Gaborit, P., Ruatta, O., Schrek, J.: On the complexity of the rank syndrome decoding problem. IEEE Trans. Inf. Theory **62**(2), 1006–1019 (2016)
18. Levy-dit-Vehel, F., Perret, L.: Algebraic decoding of rank metric codes. Talk at the Special Semester on Gröbner Bases - Workshop D1, pp. 1–19 (2006). https://ricamwww.ricam.oeaw.ac.at/specsem/srs/groeb/download/Levy.pdf
19. Loidreau, Pierre: A new rank metric codes based encryption scheme. In: Lange, Tanja, Takagi, Tsuyoshi (eds.) PQCrypto 2017. LNCS, vol. 10346, pp. 3–17. Springer, Cham (2017). https://doi.org/10.1007/978-3-319-59879-6_1
20. McEliece, R.J.: A Public-Key System Based on Algebraic Coding Theory, pp. 114–116. Jet Propulsion Lab (1978). dSN Progress Report 44
21. Ourivski, A.V., Johansson, T.: New technique for decoding codes in the rank metric and its cryptography applications. Probl. Inf. Transm. **38**(3), 237–246 (2002). https://doi.org/10.1023/A:1020369320078
22. Overbeck, R.: A new structural attack for GPT and variants. In: Dawson, E., Vaudenay, S. (eds.) Mycrypt 2005. LNCS, vol. 3715, pp. 50–63. Springer, Heidelberg (2005). https://doi.org/10.1007/11554868_5
23. Verbel, Javier, Baena, John, Cabarcas, Daniel, Perlner, Ray, Smith-Tone, Daniel: On the complexity of "superdetermined" minrank instances. In: Ding, Jintai, Steinwandt, Rainer (eds.) PQCrypto 2019. LNCS, vol. 11505, pp. 167–186. Springer, Cham (2019). https://doi.org/10.1007/978-3-030-25510-7_10

A High-Performance Hardware Implementation of the LESS Digital Signature Scheme

Luke Beckwith[1,2](✉), Robert Wallace[1], Kamyar Mohajerani[1], and Kris Gaj[1]

[1] George Mason University, Fairfax, VA 22030, USA
{lbeckwit,rwalla,mmohajer,kgaj}@gmu.edu
[2] PQSecure Technologies, Boca Raton, FL 33431, USA
luke.beckwith@pqsecurity.com

Abstract. In 2022, NIST selected the first set of four post-quantum cryptography schemes for near-term standardization. Three of them - CRYSTALS-Kyber, CRYSTALS-Dilithium, and FALCON - belong to the lattice-based family and one - SPHINCS+ - to the hash-based family. NIST has also announced an "on-ramp" for new digital signature candidates to add greater diversity to the suite of new standards. One promising set of schemes - a subfamily of code-based cryptography - is based on the linear code equivalence problem. This well-studied problem can be used to design flexible and efficient digital signature schemes. One of these schemes, LESS, was submitted to the NIST standardization process in June 2023. In this work, we present a high-performance hardware implementation of LESS targeting Xilinx FPGAs. The obtained results are compared with those for the state-of-the-art hardware implementations of CRYSTALS-Dilithium, SPHINCS+, and FALCON.

Keywords: Code-Based Cryptography · Post-Quantum Cryptography · Hardware Acceleration · FPGA · Digital Signatures

1 Introduction

The first set of post-quantum cryptography schemes was selected for standardization by NIST in 2022 [3]. These algorithms are intended to replace current public key standards, such as RSA and Elliptic Curve Cryptosystems, which are vulnerable to quantum attacks through the use of Shor's algorithm [28]. These new standards are built upon computationally hard problems that are secure against classical and quantum computing attacks. Three of the new standards are lattice-based algorithms: CRYSTALS-Kyber, CRYSTALS-Dilithium, and FALCON. The fourth, SPHINCS+, is a hash-based algorithm. CRYSTALS-Dilithium, FALCON, and SPHINCS+ are all digital signature schemes, while CRYSTALS-Kyber is a Key Encapsulation Mechanism (KEM). The primary recommendations from NIST and the NSA for most applications are CRYSTALS-Kyber and CRYSTALS-Dilithium due to their relatively small key sizes and high

© The Author(s), under exclusive license to Springer Nature Switzerland AG 2023
T. Johansson and D. Smith-Tone (Eds.): PQCrypto 2023, LNCS 14154, pp. 57–90, 2023.
https://doi.org/10.1007/978-3-031-40003-2_3

performance [3,23]. FALCON is well suited for applications that require small signatures and fast verification but has complex and slow key generation and signing. Compared to the other selected algorithms, SPHINCS$^+$ has lower performance and larger signatures. However, it has a mature security basis making it a more conservative option [3].

NIST intends to standardize additional algorithms to diversify the suite of new standards. This intent includes algorithms optimized for specific types of applications and algorithms of different cryptographic families. There are currently three code-based KEMs that have advanced to the fourth round for further evaluation, and NIST announced an "on-ramp" for new digital signature candidates with the submission deadline on June 1, 2023.

One of these new digital signature algorithms is LESS [8], a code-based digital signature scheme. Unlike many previous code-based algorithms, which are based on the Syndrome Decoding Problem (SDP), LESS builds its security on the difficulty of determining the linear isometry between two codes [12]. This security basis allows the use of smaller parameters than those typically required for algorithms based on SDP, enabling more practical key and signature sizes.

In this work, we present a high-performance hardware implementation of the LESS digital signature scheme. Our hardware architecture implements all base parameter sets and provides substantial improvements over the software implementation. The hardware implementation is also protected against timing attacks as all operations are constant-time with respect to the secret values. The implementation is publicly available at github.com/GMUCERG/LESS.

2   Previous Work

Since LESS is built using a different framework than previous code-based digital signature schemes, there are no existing hardware implementations we can make a direct comparison to. However, there are at least partial implementations of all the algorithms selected for standardization.

The NIST-selected digital signature algorithms have received varying levels of implementation work. CRYSTALS-Dilithium has received the most effort with several high-performance and lightweight hardware implementations [10,11,17,21,32]. A unified hardware design for CRYSTALS-Dilithium and Saber was presented in [1]. A similar work on a unified implementation of CRYSTALS-Kyber and CRYSTALS-Dilithium was presented in [2]. Additionally, software/hardware co-designs of CRYSTALS-Dilithium were reported in [20,22,33,34]. Of particular relevance to this paper is the pure hardware implementation by Zhao et al. [32], which is the highest performance implementation reported thus far. SPHINCS$^+$ has one full implementation which targets high performance [4]. FALCON has received considerably less effort, with the only hardware implementation reported thus far being the implementation of the verification operation [11]. Additionally, a software/hardware co-design of the verification operation of FALCON was reported in [20].

Hardware implementations of Gaussian elimination over $GF(p)$, performing an operation similar to that of the Row Reduced Echelon Form unit described in this paper, were reported in [18, 19]. Additionally, hardware implementations of Gaussian elimination over a different class of fields, $GF(2^m)$, were reported in [6, 7, 13, 15, 25–27, 29–31].

None of the previously reported designs can be easily adapted for the implementation of the LESS signature scheme. The major differences stem from the use of a) much larger matrix dimensions, which prevent the use of systolic array architectures, b) different field, which affects the complexity of addition, subtraction, multiplication, and inversion, and c) different expected output - the row reduced echelon form, rather than the (unreduced) row echelon form, also known as the upper triangular matrix.

3 Background

3.1 Generator, Permutation, and Monomial Matrices

As this work discusses the code-based cryptosystem LESS, there are several important concepts from coding theory that must be defined.

A fundamental object in coding theory is the generator matrix. A generator matrix $G \in \mathbb{F}^{k \times n}$ defines an $[n, k]$-code by the operation $c = mG$, where $m \in \mathbb{F}^k$ is the message and $c \in \mathbb{F}^n$ is the corresponding codeword. The same code can also be defined using the parity check matrix $H \in \mathbb{F}^{(n-k) \times n}$. The parity check matrix can be used to check if a given vector c is a codeword by verifying that $Hc^T = 0$.

The generator matrix is said to be in standard form if the k leftmost columns are the identity matrix, that is if $G = (I_k | M)$ with $M \in \mathbb{F}^{(k-n) \times n}$. If G is in standard form, the corresponding parity matrix can be expressed as $H = [-M^T | I_{n-k}]$. If the generator is in standard form, the first k entries of any code word will simply be the message itself. Thus, the code is said to be systematic in its first k positions.

For applications that use the functionality of the code, it is beneficial to represent the generator matrix in its standard form because it enables easy derivation of the parity check matrix. For LESS, however, we are only concerned with determining if two matrices produce equivalent codes. That is, is there an invertible matrix $S \in GL_k(q)$ for $G, G' \in \mathbb{F}^{k \times n}$ such that $G = SG$. Thus, converting to any unique representation of a code is sufficient. The standard form representation is unique and thus would work for this purpose, but it is not required. The Reduced Row Echelon Form (RREF) is also a unique representation.

RREF is an extension of Row Echelon Form (REF), which is defined as follows: a matrix is in row echelon form if the following properties hold: (1) All rows consisting of only zeroes are at the bottom of the matrix, (2) the leading entry of every non-zero row is to the right of the leading entry of every row above it. That is, they form a staircase pattern. A matrix is then in RREF if it meets all the requirements of REF, all of the leading entries of non-zero rows are 1, and each column containing a leading 1 has zeros in all of its other entries. Pseudocode for converting a matrix to RREF is provided in Algorithm 1.

Other important concepts for LESS are permutation and monomial matrices. A permutation matrix is a square binary matrix that has exactly one entry of 1 in each row and each column and 0s elsewhere. A monomial matrix is a matrix with the same non-zero pattern as a permutation matrix. However, unlike a permutation matrix, where the non-zero entry must be 1, in a monomial matrix, the non-zero entry can be any non-zero value in F_q^*.

Algorithm 1: Converting a $k \times n$ matrix to Reduced Row Echelon Form (RREF)

Input: Matrix $G \in \mathbb{Z}_q^{k \times n}$
Output: Matrix $G \in \mathbb{Z}_q^{k \times n}$

1 **for** row_id_to_reduce $\in [0, k-1]$ **do**
2 $\quad$ valid_pivot $\leftarrow 0$
3 $\quad$ **for** col_id $\in$ [row_id_to_reduce, $n-1$] **do**
4 $\quad\quad$ **for** row_id $\in$ [row_id_to_reduce, $k-1$] **do**
5 $\quad\quad\quad$ **if** $(G[\text{row\_id}][\text{col\_id}] > 0)$ *and* (valid_pivot $== 0$) **then**
6 $\quad\quad\quad\quad$ pivot_row_id $\leftarrow$ row_id
7 $\quad\quad\quad\quad$ pivot_col_id $\leftarrow$ col_id
8 $\quad\quad\quad\quad$ valid_pivot $\leftarrow 1$
9 $\quad$ swap_row($G[\text{row\_id\_to\_reduce}], G[\text{pivot\_row\_id}]$)
10 $\quad$ $m \leftarrow G[\text{row\_id\_to\_reduce}][\text{pivot\_col\_id}]^{-1} \bmod q$
11 $\quad$ **for** col_id $\in [0, n-1]$ **do**
12 $\quad\quad$ $G[\text{row\_id\_to\_reduce}][\text{col\_id}] \leftarrow m \cdot G[\text{row\_id\_to\_reduce}][\text{col\_id}]$ $\bmod q$
13 $\quad$ **for** row_id $\in [0, k-1]$ **do**
14 $\quad\quad$ **if** row_id $\neq$ row_id_to_reduce **then**
15 $\quad\quad\quad$ $m \leftarrow G[\text{row\_id}][\text{pivot\_col\_id}]$
16 $\quad\quad\quad$ **for** col_id $\in$ [pivot_col_id, $n-1$] **do**
17 $\quad\quad\quad\quad$ tmp $\leftarrow m \cdot G[\text{row\_id\_to\_reduce}][\text{col\_id}] \bmod q$
18 $\quad\quad\quad\quad$ $G[\text{row\_id}][\text{col\_id}] \leftarrow G[\text{row\_id}][\text{col\_id}] - \text{tmp} \bmod q$

3.2 LESS

LESS is a code-based digital signature scheme based on the difficulty of the Linear Equivalence Problem (LEP). LESS was first introduced by Biasse et al. [12] and was later expanded upon by Barenghi et al. [9] and Persichetti [24]. This work focuses on the most recent version of the scheme that was submitted to the NIST standardization process [8]. The linear equivalence problem can be defined as follows: given two generator matrices $G, G' \in \mathbb{F}_q^{k \times n}$ which generate codes $\mathbb{C}, \mathbb{C}'$, determine if the two corresponding codes are linearly equivalent. That is, does there exist matrices $S \in GL_k(q)$ and $P \in M_n$ such that $G' = SGP$.

The digital signature scheme is created by first defining a sigma protocol using the linear equivalence problem and then converting it to a non-interactive signature using the Fiat-Shamir transformation [16]. In the sigma protocol, there are two users involved: the prover, who is attempting to prove they know the

Table 1. Parameter sets for LESS and resulting data sizes.

NIST Cat.	Parameter Set	Code Params			Prot. Params			pk (KiB)	sig (KiB)
		n	k	q	t	ω	s		
1	LESS-1b	252	126	127	247	30	2	13.7	8.4
	LESS-1i				244	20	4	41.1	6.1
	LESS-1s				198	17	8	95.9	5.2
3	LESS-3b	400	200	127	759	33	2	34.5	18.4
	LESS-3s				895	26	3	68.9	14.1
5	LESS-5b	548	274	127	1352	40	2	64.6	32.5
	LESS-5s				907	37	3	129.0	26.1

secret corresponding to a public key, and a verifier, who is trying to confirm the identity of the prover. The private key is a monomial matrix $Q \in M_n$, and the public key is $G_1 = RREF(G_0 Q)$, where G_0 is a publicly available generator matrix. The prover first generates a commitment by sampling a random monomial $\tilde{Q}$ and calculating $\tilde{G} = RREF(G_0 \tilde{Q})$. They then hash $\tilde{G}$ and send the hash to the verifier as the commitment. The verifier then responds with a single-bit challenge. If the challenge is 0, then the prover responds with $\tilde{Q}$, and the verifier checks the response by checking that the hash of G_0 multiplied by the response equals the commitment. If the challenge is 1, the prover responds with $Q^{-1}\tilde{Q}$, and the verifier checks the response by verifying that the product of G_1 and the response matches the commitment. Note that this holds true because $G_1 Q^{-1}\tilde{Q} = G_0 Q Q^{-1}\tilde{Q} = G_0 \tilde{Q}$, which matches the commitment.

With each round of the protocol, an imposter has a $\frac{1}{2}$ chance of deceiving the verifier by guessing what the challenge will be. The difficulty of deceiving the verifier can be increased by repeating the protocol multiple times or by creating additional pairs of public and private matrices. LESS takes advantage of both approaches. This protocol can be converted into a digital signature scheme by having the prover pre-compute numerous commitments and then using an agreed-upon function to self-generate an unpredictable challenge. In the case of LESS, this is accomplished by hashing the commitment matrices with the message appended and using a variant of the Fisher-Yates shuffle to generate a challenge with a fixed number of non-zero entries.

The parameters for the version of LESS this work implements are described in Table 1. Parameters are provided for three security levels corresponding to the NIST-defined security levels 1, 3, and 5. There are multiple parameter sets for each security level. They aim for different optimization metrics. The balanced parameter sets, denoted by "b", seek to minimize the combined size of the public key and signature. The small parameter sets, denoted by "s", aim to minimize the signature size. Level 1 also has an intermediate parameter set, denoted by "i". The first three parameters relate to the codes used in LESS: n and k define the dimensions of the generator matrices, and q is the modulus of the coefficients. The following three relate to the LESS protocol: t defines the number of challenges, i.e., how many rounds of the sigma protocol are simulated. The number of non-zero challenges is defined by ω, and the number of pairs in the key is defined by s.

The short parameter sets reduce the signature size by increasing the number of pairs in the key. This means fewer iterations of the protocol are required to reach the security threshold, and consequently, the number of responses in the signature is smaller. However, this comes at the cost of larger keys.

The descriptions of key generation, signing, and verification for LESS are provided in Algorithms 2, 3, and 4. In a key generation, the user generates s key pairs. The first pair is simply the public parameter G_0 and the identity matrix. All following pairs are generated by sampling a random Q_i and calculating $G_i = RREF(G_0 Q_i)$. Note that Q_i is assumed to be inverted when sampled, so for the calculation of the public key, we must invert the monomial before multiplication. This assumption removes the need for inverting the monomial in signature generation. The seeds used to sample the secret monomials are all derived from a single input seed $seed_{sk}$. The calculated matrices are serialized to minimize their size in the public key.

Algorithm 2: LESS-KEYGEN() [8]

Input: None

Output: $\mathsf{sk} = (\mathsf{seed}_1, \ldots, \mathsf{seed}_{s-1})$: private key, where $\mathsf{seed}_i \in \{0,1\}^\lambda$ is employed to derive $\mathbf{Q}_i^{-1}$. The first entry of the private key $\mathbf{Q}_0 = \mathbf{I}_n$ is not stored.
$\mathsf{pk} = (\mathsf{seed}_0, \mathbf{G}_1, \ldots, \mathbf{G}_{s-1})$: public key, where $\mathbf{G}_i \in \mathbb{F}_q^{k \times n}$ is stored as the non-pivot columns and their positions via the COMPRESSRREF subroutine.

Data: CSPRNG($seed, \mathbb{S}_{\mathsf{RREF}}$): Samples a generator matrix in RREF from the output of SHAKE using the provided seed.
CSPRNG($seed, \mathsf{M}_n$): Samples a monomial matrix from the output of SHAKE using the provided seed.
RREF($\mathbf{G}$): Converts input generator into RREF.
COMPRESSRREF($\mathbf{G}_i$): Encodes pivot locations and non-pivot columns of generator matrix in RREF.

1 $\mathbf{G}_0 \leftarrow$ CSPRNG($\mathsf{pk}[0], \mathbb{S}_{\mathsf{RREF}}$)
2 **for** $i \leftarrow 1$ **to** $s - 1$ **do**
3 $\quad$ $\mathsf{sk}[i] \xleftarrow{\$} \{0,1\}^\lambda$
4 $\quad$ $\mathbf{Q} \leftarrow$ CSPRNG($\mathsf{sk}[i], \mathsf{M}_n$)
5 $\quad$ $\mathbf{Q}_i \leftarrow \mathbf{Q}^{-1}$
6 $\quad$ $\mathbf{G}_i \leftarrow$ RREF($\mathbf{G}_0 \mathbf{Q}_i$)
7 $\quad$ $\mathsf{pk}[i] \leftarrow$ COMPRESSRREF($\mathbf{G}_i$)
8 **return** $(\mathsf{sk}, \mathsf{pk})$

In a slightly simplified approach to signing, first t commitments are generated by sampling random monomials $\tilde{Q}_i$ and calculating $\tilde{G}_i = RREF(G_0\tilde{Q}_i)$. All the commit matrices are then encoded and hashed with the message to generate the challenge seed d. The challenge seed is then used to seed the XOF function from which the challenge is parsed. For the zero challenges, the seed used to sample the corresponding monomial serves as the response. For the non-zero challenges, $Q_{x_i}^{-1}Q_i$ is the response. The signatures are composed of the challenge seed and all responses.

An optimization can be performed that significantly reduces the size of the signatures. Instead of transmitting the entire monomial for the non-zero challenges, we can instead transmit only the columns corresponding to the pivot columns of the result. This reduces the transmission overhead of these monomials by a factor of two. However, to recover from the missing information of the monomial, additional processing is required after the RREF operation. The non-pivot columns are lexicographically minimized and sorted to remove the impact of the scaling and permutation operations of the monomial multiplication. These operations are combined into a single function called `PrepareDigestInput`. For further details, we refer to the LESS specification [8].

Another optimization is used for the seeds of the challenge monomials. Rather than defining the seeds using simple expansion of a root seed by an XOF, the seeds are defined as the leaves of a binary tree derived from the root seed. So, the seeds are generated by recursively hashing an input seed until the required number of leaves is reached. Then the signature size can be reduced by sending the tree nodes needed to recreate the target leaves rather than sending the leaves themselves.

In verification, the challenge seed is first expanded into the challenge in the same manner as in signing, and the leaves of the seed tree are regenerated from the path. For all responses t, the monomial is decoded or resampled and multiplied by the corresponding generator matrix. When the monomial is sampled from a seed, we use the same `PrepareDigestInput` algorithm to regenerate the commitment. When the monomial is decoded from the response, we use the standard RREF operation and minimize and sort the non-pivot columns of the result. All the generator matrices are then hashed, and the result is compared with the challenge seed in the signature. If they match, the signature is accepted.

4 Hardware Architecture

In this section, we discuss the design of our implementation of LESS. We begin with a brief description of the top-level architecture before discussing the details of the submodules and operation schedule. The datapath of packed matrices and seeds is $W = 64$. For all parameter sets, $n > q$. So for portions of the design that transmit data of both width $\lceil \log_2(n) \rceil$ and $\lceil \log_2(q) \rceil$, we use a width of $\lceil \log_2(n) \rceil$.

Algorithm 3: LESS-SIGN(sk, msg, pk) [8]

Input: sk = $(\text{seed}_1, \ldots, \text{seed}_{s-1})$: private key, where $\text{seed}_i \in \{0, 1\}^\lambda$ is employed
to derive $\mathbf{Q}_i^{-1}$. The first entry of the private key which is the identity
matrix $\mathbf{Q}_0 = \mathbf{I}$ is not stored.
pk[0] = seed_0: first element of the public key employed to derive $\mathbf{G}_0$ in
RREF at runtime
msg: message to be signed, as a sequence of bits

Output: $\sigma = (\text{rsp}_1, \ldots, \text{rsp}_t, \mathbf{d})$: signature composed by a salt salt, ω ZKID
protocol responses $\text{rsp}_i, 0 \leq i < t$, the seed-tree path treepath and a
digest $\mathbf{d}$

Data: CSPRNG$(seed, \mathbb{S}_{t,\omega})$: Samples the fixed weight challenge from the
output of SHAKE.
PREPAREDIGESTINPUT$(\mathbf{G}, \widetilde{\mathbf{Q}})$: Calculates the RREF of $\mathbf{G}\widetilde{\mathbf{Q}}$ and returns
the lexicographically sorted and minimized values of the non-pivot
columns of the result as well as the corresponding entries of the
monomial.
SEEDTREELEAVES(seed, salt): Generates seed tree using SHAKE.
SEEDTREEPATHS$(seed, (x_0, \ldots, x_{t-1}))$: Calculates nodes of path for the
target leaves of the seed tree.
COMPRESSMONOMACTION$(\mathbf{Q}\overline{\mathbf{Q}})$: Encodes the relevant permutation and
coefficients of the monomial matrix.

1   $\mathbf{G}_0 \leftarrow$ CSPRNG(pk[0], $\mathbb{S}_{\text{RREF}}$)

2   rootSeed $\xleftarrow{\$} \{0, 1\}^\lambda$

3   salt $\xleftarrow{\$} \{0, 1\}^\lambda$

4   $(\text{seed}[0], \ldots, \text{seed}[t-1]) \leftarrow$ SEEDTREELEAVES(rootSeed, salt)

5   **for** $i \leftarrow 0$ **to** $t - 1$ **do**

6      $\widetilde{\mathbf{Q}}_i \leftarrow$ CSPRNG(seed[i], M_n)

7      $(\mathbf{V}_i, \overline{\mathbf{Q}_i}) \leftarrow$ PREPAREDIGESTINPUT$(\mathbf{G}_0, \widetilde{\mathbf{Q}}_i)$

8   $\mathbf{d} \leftarrow$ HASH$(\mathbf{V}_0 || \ldots || \mathbf{V}_{t-1} || \text{msg} || \text{salt})$

9   $(x_0, \ldots, x_{t-1}) \leftarrow$ CSPRNG$(\mathbf{d}, \mathbb{S}_{t,\omega})$

10   treepath $\leftarrow$ SEEDTREEPATHS$(\text{rootSeed}, (x_0, \ldots, x_{t-1}))$

11   $j \leftarrow 0$

12   **for** $i \leftarrow 0$ **to** $t - 1$ **do**

13   **if** $x_i \neq 0$ **then**

14          $\mathbf{Q} \leftarrow \text{sk}[x_i]$

15          $\text{rsp}_j \leftarrow$ COMPRESSMONOMACTION$(\mathbf{Q}\overline{\mathbf{Q}_i})$

16          $j \leftarrow j + 1$

17   **return** $(\text{salt}, \text{treepath}, \text{rsp}_0, \ldots, \text{rsp}_{\omega-1}, \mathbf{d})$

4.1   Top Level Architecture

The top-level datapath of the hardware architecture is shown in Fig. 1. The
hardware modules implementing all the operations of LESS are partitioned into
five major submodules: the seed generator, monomial arithmetic unit, generator

---

Algorithm 4: LESS-VERIFY($\mathsf{pk}, \sigma, \mathsf{msg}$) [8]

Input: $\mathsf{pk} = (\mathbf{G}_0, \ldots, \mathbf{G}_{s-1})$: public key, where $\mathbf{G}_i \in \mathbb{F}_q^{k \times n}$
$\sigma = (\mathsf{salt}, \mathsf{treepath}, \mathsf{rsp}_0, \ldots, \mathsf{rsp}_{\omega-1}, \mathbf{d})$: signature composed by a salt
salt, *omega* ZKID protocol responses $\mathsf{rsp}_i, 0 \le i < t$, the seed-tree path
treepath and a digest $\mathbf{d}$
msg: message to be signed, as a sequence of bits

Output: Boolean value indicating whether the signature is valid

Data: REBUILDSEEDTREELEAVES($\mathsf{treepath}, (x_0, \ldots, x_{t-1}), \mathsf{salt}$): Regenerates
the target leaves of the seed tree using the path nodes.
EXPANDTOMONOMACTION(rsp): Decodes the encoded coefficients and
permutation values from the monomial.
LEXMIN($\mathbf{v}$): lexicographically minimizes the input vector.
LEXSORTCOLUMNS($\mathbf{V}$): lexicographically sorts the set of the input
vectors.

1 $\mathbf{G}_0 \leftarrow$ CSPRNG($\mathsf{pk}[0], \mathbb{S}_{\mathsf{RREF}}$)
2 $(x_0, \ldots, x_{t-1}) \leftarrow$ CSPRNG($\mathbf{d}, \mathbb{S}_{t,\omega}$)
3 $(\mathsf{seed}[0], \ldots, \mathsf{seed}[t-1]) \leftarrow$
   REBUILDSEEDTREELEAVES($\mathsf{treepath}, (x_0, \ldots, x_{t-1}), \mathsf{salt}$)

4 **for** $i \leftarrow 0$ **to** $t-1$ **do**
5 $\quad$ **if** $x_i = 0$ **then**
6 $\quad\quad$ $\tilde{\mathbf{Q}}_i \leftarrow$ CSPRNG($\mathsf{seed}[i], \mathsf{M}_n$)
7 $\quad\quad$ $(\mathbf{V}_i, \overline{\mathbf{Q}_i}) \leftarrow$ PREPAREDIGESTINPUT($\mathbf{G}_0, \tilde{\mathbf{Q}}_i$)
8 $\quad$ **else**
9 $\quad\quad$ $\overline{\mathbf{Q}}_i \leftarrow$ EXPANDTOMONOMACTION(rsp_i)
10 $\quad\quad$ $\mathbf{G}_i \leftarrow \mathsf{pk}[x_i]$
11 $\quad\quad$ $\overline{\mathbf{G}}_i \leftarrow \mathbf{G}_i \overline{\mathbf{Q}}_i$
12 $\quad\quad$ $[\mathbf{I}\ \mathbf{V}_i] \leftarrow$ RREF($\overline{\mathbf{G}}_i$) // $\mathbf{V}_i = [\mathbf{v}_0\ \mathbf{v}_1\ \cdots\ \mathbf{v}_{n-k-1}]$
13 $\quad\quad$ **for** $j \leftarrow 0$ **to** $(n-k)-1$ **do**
14 $\quad\quad\quad$ $\mathbf{v}_j \leftarrow$ LEXMIN($\mathbf{v}_j$)
15 $\quad\quad$ $\mathbf{V}_i \leftarrow$ LEXSORTCOLUMNS($\mathbf{V}_i$)
16 $\mathbf{d}' \leftarrow$ HASH($\mathbf{V}_0 || \ldots || \mathbf{V}_{t-1} || \mathsf{msg} || \mathsf{salt}$)

17 **if** ($\mathbf{d} = \mathbf{d}'$) **then**
18 $\quad$ **return** true
19 **return** false

---

arithmetic unit, RREF unit, and challenge generator. The seed generator is responsible for expanding the input seeds into the seeds used for sampling of monomial and generator matrices. This includes the simple expansions of the secret key seed as well as all seed tree operations. The monomial arithmetic unit performs the sampling, inversion, multiplication, encoding, and decoding of monomial matrices. It receives input from the seed generator when sampling and transfers the monomial matrices to the generator module as needed. The generator module performs the generator-monomial multiplication, encoding, as

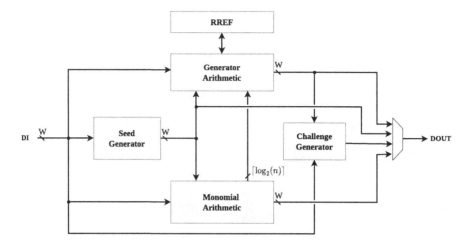

Fig. 1. Top-Level Block Diagram of LESS Hardware Architecture.

well as lexicographic sorting. The RREF unit converts the matrix multiplication result into RREF. The challenge parser hashes the commitment matrices and uses the result to generate the challenge.

During most operations, only a single generator matrix needs to be stored throughout the entire operation. For example, during key generation and signing, only G_0 needs to be used multiple times. All other generator matrices are immediately hashed or unloaded from the accelerator. The exception is verification, where all public keys may be required to check the authenticity of the signature. For the balanced parameter sets, which only uses two generator matrices, this does not cause any issues. However, for the short parameter sets, there are eight matrices in the public key. Due to the large size of these matrices, this requires a significant amount of memory resources. To address this limitation, we assume that the system that is connected to the accelerator holds the full public key. The accelerator requests the generator matrices as they are needed during verification.

4.2   Submodule Design

Seed Generator. All operations of LESS require the generation of various seeds for the sampling of monomial and generator matrices. The architecture of this module can be seen in Fig. 2. The SHA-3 module used is a publicly available implementation [14]. During key generation, the generation of seeds is done by expanding the λ-bit seed into $s-1$ λ-bit seeds using the XOF. The SHA-3 module is configured to run the appropriate variant of SHAKE. The core ingests the input seed and produces the appropriate number of output bits which are stored back in memory. These seeds can then be used to initialize the XOF for sampling as needed.

During signature generation and verification, the seed tree operations are also utilized. This includes the generation of the seed tree by recursively hashing the root seed, generation of the path nodes needed for the signature, and recreation of the relevant leaves using the path nodes. The seed tree operation is implemented in a straightforward manner using breadth-first traversal of the tree and hashing the current node into two child nodes until the required number of leaves is generated. The seed path generation is performed in two steps. During the first step, the tree is traversed from the leaves up, and a flag is set for each seed to indicate whether or not it is in the path of the target seeds. For the leaves themselves, they are considered target seeds if they are not part of the non-zero challenges. For the node seeds, they are included if both of their children are included. Once the flags of all seeds are set, the tree is traversed again, and seeds are included in the path if their flag is set but their parent node is not. The entire seed tree is kept in memory after the initial generation, so no hashing is required during this operation. During the regeneration of the leaves, the first step from path generation is repeated. For the second step, the tree is traversed in the same manner, but once a seed that is in the path is reached, it is hashed to generate its child nodes.

All of these operations can be performed using a very simple datapath shown in Fig. 2. The controller is responsible for tracking the current location during tree traversal and setting the $flgi$ signal, which is used to set the flag for each seed as needed during the seed tree operations.

All operations performed by the seed generator are constant time with respect to the sensitive data. Hashing requires a constant number of cycles. Thus seed expansion does not leak any information. The generation and usage of the seed tree path are non-constant time, but the variation of the latency depends on the public challenge, not the secret seeds.

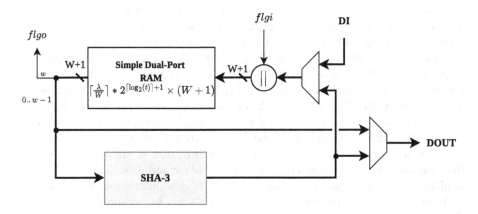

Fig. 2. Top-level Diagram of Seed Generator Submodule

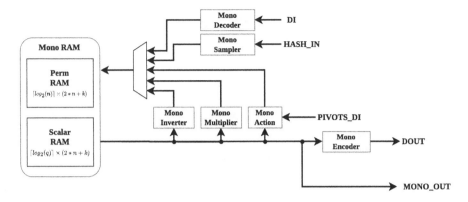

Fig. 3. Top-level Diagram of Monomial Submodule

Monomial Arithmetic. The top-level architecture of the monomial arithmetic unit is shown in Fig. 3. This section of the hardware consists of two memories and five submodules related to the monomial matrices.

Monomial sampling is required in key generation for the creation of the secret key and in signing for the generation of the ephemeral secrets used to create the commitments. The hardware architecture implementing monomial sampling is shown in Fig. 4. The monomial is represented as two lists, one representing the scalar values and one representing the permutation. The scalar values are generated using rejection sampling on $\lceil \log_q(q) \rceil$ bits of pseudorandom input at a time. Samples are accepted if they are in the range $[0, q - 2]$ and then are incremented by one to shift them into the range $[1, q - 1]$. Since the latency of monomial sampling is negligible in comparison to the latency of the RREF operation, only one sample is processed per cycle. The permutation coefficients are generated using a simple shuffling algorithm. The shuffler module contains a $N \times \lceil \log_2(n) \rceil$ RAM module, which is initialized to hold the array $[0, 1, ..., n-1]$. This array is then shuffled using n random samples in the range $[0, n - 1]$.

Monomial encoding is a straightforward serialization of the permutation and scalar values. This is accomplished using a variable-rate bus width converter, which can receive input at a rate of $\lceil \log_2(n) \rceil$ or $\lceil \log_2(q) \rceil$ and produces an output of length W. Figure 5 shows the architecture of this module. The decoding module follows a similar architecture with the modification that the input is W bits and the output can optionally be $N \times \lceil \log_2(n) \rceil$ or $N \times \lceil \log_2(q) \rceil$ bits.

Monomial inversion involves element-wise inversion of the scalar values of the monomial as well as calculation of the inverse permutation. The architecture implementing this operation is shown in Fig. 6. The inverse permutation b of permutation a can be calculated by $b_{a_i} = i$. This can be accomplished by using the input permutation as the address of a memory while writing values sequentially from $0, ..., n - 1$. In the hardware module shown, the input permutation is used as the address input when writing the sequential values coming from a counter. After the entire permutation is loaded in, the RAM will contain the

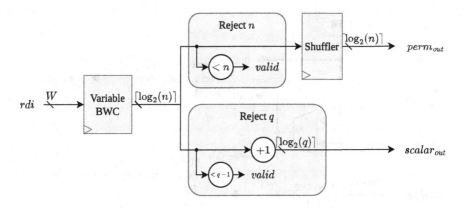

Fig. 4. Monomial Sampler Block Diagram

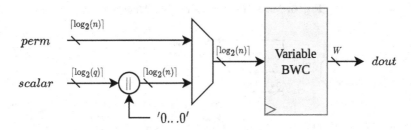

Fig. 5. Monomial Encoder Block Diagram

inverse permutation, which can be read out sequentially using the counter to drive the address input. Since the modulus is small, inversion of the coefficient values can be done inexpensively using a Look-Up-Table one coefficient at a time. The ordering of the coefficients must also be adjusted to match the new permutation so the coefficients are written into RAM in the same manner as the permutation.

Monomial multiplication involves combinations of both the permutations and the scalar values of the two input monomials. The resulting permutation is calculated by reading the permutation of the left operand with the permutation of the right operand. In the hardware architecture shown in Fig. 7, this is accomplished by first writing the left operand's permutation into a RAM and then unloading using the right operand's permutation as the address. The scalar values are calculated by first applying the right operand's permutation to the scalar values of the left-operand and then multiplying coefficient-wise with the left operand's coefficients. This is accomplished in the hardware by writing the left operand's scalar values into memory and then using the right operand's permutation to drive the address when performing the multiplication.

The monomial operations are also constant time with respect to the sensitive data. Monomial inversion, multiplication, encoding, and decoding are all constant time operations, as their latency depends only on the dimension of the

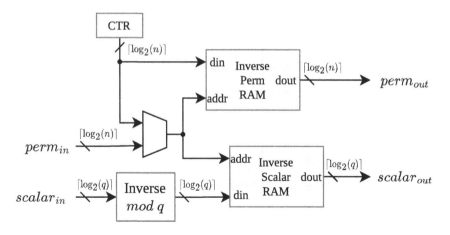

Fig. 6. Monomial Inverter Block Diagram

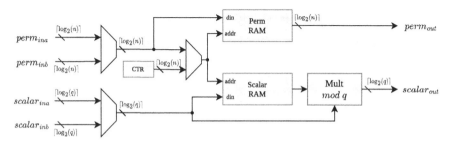

Fig. 7. Monomial Multiplier Block Diagram

matrices and not on the values within them. Monomial sampling is not strictly constant time as it uses rejection sampling. However, the difference in latency caused by rejection does not leak any information about the value of the accepted samples. Thus it is not vulnerable to timing attacks.

Generator Arithmetic. The generator arithmetic module, shown in Fig. 8, has three primary functions: 1) preparing the generator for processing by decoding a matrix from the public key or sampling it from a seed, 2) performing the monomial multiplication while loading the generator into the RREF module, and 3) performing the post-processing of sorting and encoding the non-pivot columns after RREF.

Generator encoding and decoding is similar to monomial encoding in that it is a straightforward serialization of elements, one being a set of n bits representing whether each column is a pivot or not and the other being the $\lceil \log_2(q) \rceil$ bit coefficients. The list of pivot locations is serialized first at the beginning of the encoded string. Then the coefficients of the non-pivot columns are serialized row-wise.

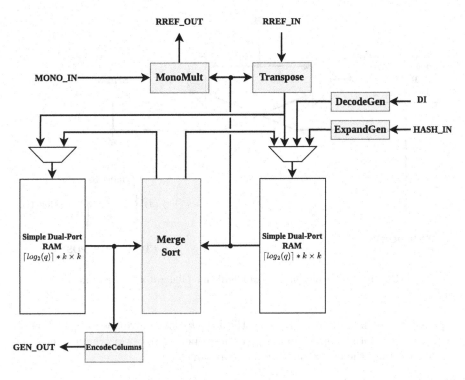

Fig. 8. Top-level Diagram of Generator Submodule

The monomial multiplication is performed when loading the matrix into the RREF module. An entire row can be accessed from memory at once. The permutation is applied using several $k \times 1$ multiplexers to read the row coefficients using the monomial permutation. The selected row coefficients are then scaled by the monomial coefficients before they are loaded into the RREF module.

During the lexicographic sorting operation, the matrix must be sorted column-wise. However, the operations of RREF and encoding are performed row-wise. Therefore we have a module which transposes the matrix when it is received from the RREF module. The columns are then sorted using an implementation of merge sort. During this operation, the entire column is accessible from the memories, so the comparison operation can be performed in a single cycle. Since merge sort requires additional memory overhead during processing, both memories are used during the sorting process. The sorted columns are then transposed back before encoding of the columns.

All operations performed by the generator arithmetic module are secure against timing attacks. The latencies of decoding, monomial multiplication, and transposition are determined by the dimension of the matrix and always take the exact same number of cycles. The expansion of the generator is a public operation. Merge sort was selected as the approach for sorting the columns because of its excellent performance in hardware and because it is very straightforward to

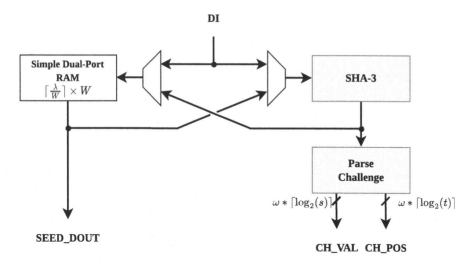

Fig. 9. Top-level Diagram of Challenge Generator Submodule

implement in constant time. Each of the $\log_2(k)$ layer involves exactly k read, write, and comparison operations. Since these operations always require the same amount of time, the entire operation is constant time.

Challenge Generator. The challenge generator module, shown in Fig. 9, is responsible for hashing the commitment matrices and parsing the signature element d into the fixed-weight challenge. The challenge is parsed by first sampling the values of the ω non-zero entries. When s is two, this stage can be skipped since 1 is the only possible value. These samples are written into the top ω entries of a t entry memory. They are then randomly permuted using a variant of the Fisher-Yates shuffle. A counter p is initialized to $t - \omega$, and then samples are repeatedly generated in the range $[0, p-1]$ using rejection sampling to determine where to shuffle the value at index p. This is repeated until all ω samples have been shuffled into the challenge. Since the parsing of the challenge is a public operation, it is not a target for timing attacks.

RREF. The RREF operation converts a matrix to row reduced echelon form. The typical complexity of this operation on a $k \times n$ matrix is $O(nk^2)$, where all k rows must be reduced, and each reduction requires all $k \times n$ elements to be operated on.

The reduction of a matrix to RREF is described in Algorithm 1. Four major steps of the algorithm can be identified. They are: (1) pivot search, (2) row swap, (3) rescaling a pivot row, and (4) reduce other rows. These steps are repeated k times, once for every row, so that all rows of the matrix are fully reduced. The first step is identifying a pivot element. The pivot of a row is the leftmost non-zero element such that after the reduction of the matrix, the pivot will be

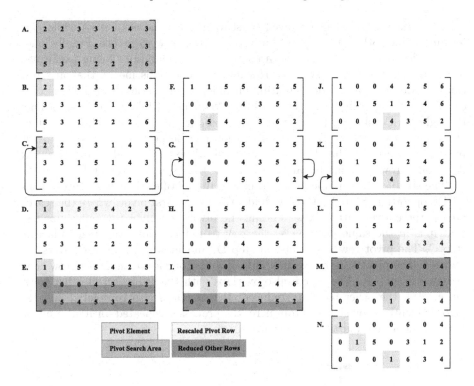

Fig. 10. RREF Example: $n = 7, k = 3, q = 7$

1, and all elements below it, in the same column, will be 0. The pivot search step is described in lines 2–8 of Algorithm 1. After finding the pivot (which is not guaranteed to be in the row to reduce), a row swap is performed so the row to reduce always contains the pivot. Next, the pivot row is rescaled so that the pivot element is 1. This is achieved by multiplying the entire row by a multiplier equal to the inverse of the pivot element modulo q. This operation is described in lines 11–12 of Algorithm 1. Finally, all other rows are reduced so that the elements in the same column as the pivot, above and below, are set to 0. This operation is described in lines 13–18 of the Algorithm 1.

There are several features of this algorithm that can be taken advantage of for optimization. When performing an arithmetic operation on a row, such as rescaling a pivot row or reducing a non-pivot row, there is no sequential dependence between elements. Arithmetic operations can be performed on all elements of a row at the same time. This parallelism reduces the time complexity of the algorithm to $O(k^2)$ and creates an $O(n)$ area cost in hardware. Additionally, the rows involved in the pivot search are always bounded by the row to reduce and k. This means that each time a pivot search is performed, the pivot row will always be between the row to reduce and k, and the search will require less time, each iteration, at a constant rate. Also, the current iteration's reduce other row's results are the elements that are searched during the pivot search in the next row to reduce. Cycles can be saved by searching for the next pivot while performing reduce other rows operation of the current row to reduce. Finally, once the rescale pivot row step has been completed, all operations being performed in the reduce other rows step are row-independent. This means that any row can be reduced in any order, creating an independent series of operations that can be pipelined to increase the hardware frequency, while maintaining a high throughput. Combining these observations about the pivot search and reduce other rows, the reduce other rows operation can be performed on rows in the pivot search area so that the next pivot will always be found before the next iteration of row reducing begins, masking the time spent searching for a pivot.

The small scale example provided in Fig. 10 identifies the key features of the RREF operation. Step A. starts with identifying the first pivot, where the search area is the entire matrix. After finding the pivot, the pivot row is swapped so that it is in the same position as the row to reduce, this swap takes place in step C. The pivot row is rescaled in step D, and in step E, all other rows are reduced. The pivot search area in step E includes one less column and row than the area in step A. The search also overlaps with the reduction of other rows. Once all of the other rows are reduced, the search is also completed and the pivot is identified by step F. From here, the process is repeated until all k pivots have be identified and their rows reduced.

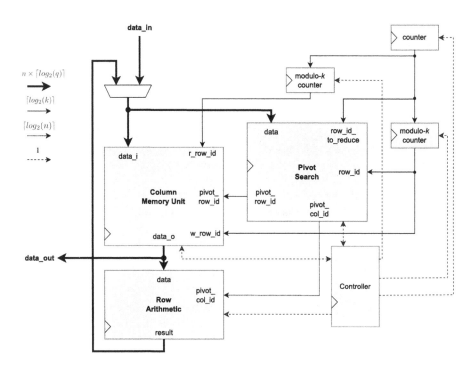

Fig. 11. RREF Top-Level Block Diagram

The hardware implementation of RREF aims to take advantage of each of the identified characteristics. The top-level module is split into three main parts: column memory unit, pivot search, and row arithmetic. The top level block diagram is presented in Fig. 11. Each part operates on an entire row of the input matrix at once. The pivot search unit is designed to search only rows that are within the search area for a specific row to reduce. This feature is in line with the row arithmetic unit's write back, so the search for the pivot of the next row to reduce occurs during the operations on the current row to reduce. The column memory unit provides separate read and write ports to enable pipelining of the rescale arithmetic which supports its highly parallel nature.

The column memory unit provides a wide interface to enable reading/writing to an entire row in a memory single access. The block diagram for the column memory unit is presented in Fig. 12. It is built up of n simple dual-port RAMs with synchronous read operating in parallel. Additionally, when addressing the memory, an address translation table is used. The table is built of a true dual-port RAM to enable the swapping of rows without needing to access the entire memory. A separate translation table is required for both the read and write ports of the column memory unit so the pipelined accesses do not need to target the same row. Any access to this memory unit will require two cycles, one for the address translation and another for the data access.

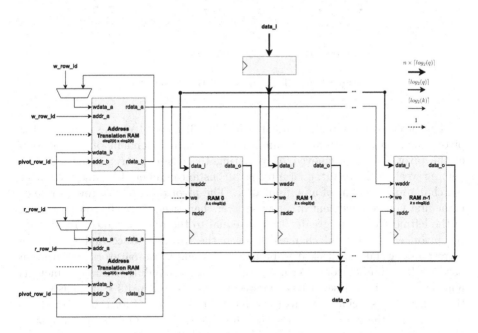

Fig. 12. RREF Column Memory Unit Block Diagram

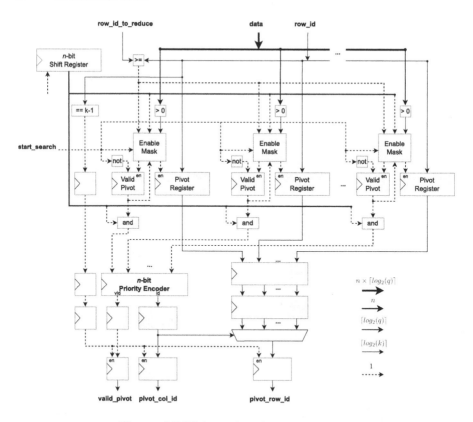

Fig. 13. RREF Pivot Search Block Diagram

The pivot search circuit, presented in Fig. 13, guarantees the results of the
pivot search in a deterministic number of cycles, independent of the location
of the pivot. This is achieved by requiring the entire matrix to be searched
before revealing the result, guaranteeing a constant number of clock cycles spent
searching, independent of any input data. The pivot of a specific row to reduce
is the first non-zero element in a row, greater than or equal to the row to reduce,
in the leftmost column, greater than or equal to the row to reduce. To identify
the pivot, as the row id changes between the row to reduce and $k - 1$, the
corresponding data is checked to be non-zero using n comparators operating in
parallel. If a comparator determines that its corresponding column element is
non-zero, then it will set a flag and record the row id in its own register. At
this point, that specific columns pivot has been determined for a row to reduce,
meaning that there are now n registers holding the row id of the first non-zero
element in a column and a flag to identify if the column contains a non-zero
element. An n-bit priority encoder is used on all n flag bits to determine the
leftmost column that contains a pivot. These flags are masked so that only a
column id greater than or equal to the row to reduce is identified. The encoded
column id is then used to read from the corresponding register to identify the

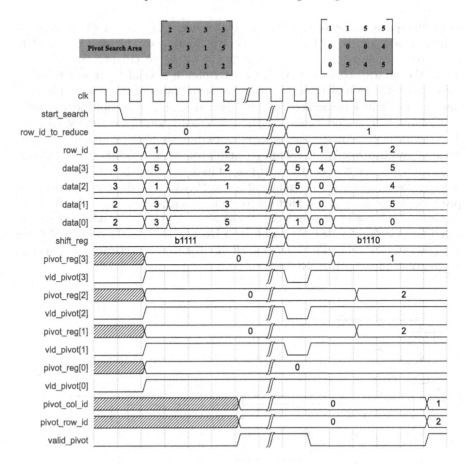

Fig. 14. RREF Pivot Search Example

row id of the pivot element in that column. By the time all k rows have been iterated over, the circuit will have determined the pivot row id and pivot column id for the corresponding row id to reduce. There is a three-cycle latency for the results of the pivot search to be accessible by the rest of the module to support a higher frequency. This latency will be masked away by the top-level pipeline.

An example of the pivot search circuit in operation, with $n = 4$, is provided in Fig. 14. After the start_search signal is set, the valid pivot flip-flops (vld_pivot[i]) are cleared. This action initializes the circuit to begin a search. If the data in a column within the search area is non-zero, then the corresponding pivot register will store the index of the first (lowest-index) row containing a non-zero element. Each valid pivot flip-flop will store a value indicating whether there exists at least one non-zero element in the search area of a given column. The priority encoder uses the flags of each column and a mask, driven by the shift register, to identify the lowest column id with a valid pivot. The mask, stored in shift_reg, makes it possible to shrink the search area when iterating over subsequent values of the row_id_to_reduce. Once the pivot_column_id is determined, the row id from the corresponding pivot register is routed to the output register, pivot_row_id, of the pivot search circuit. The valid signal of the priority encoder is used to determine if a valid pivot was found in the current iteration of the algorithm. The search area of the next iteration of row_id_to_reduce is smaller than the previous one. It does not include row 0 and column 0. The start_search signal is asserted again to clear the valid pivot flip-flops corresponding to the columns located inside of the search area. In the iteration when row_id is 1, columns 1 and 2 contain zeros, this causes the corresponding pivot registers and valid pivot flip-flops to not be updated. When a non-zero value occurs in a column and row within the search area, and the valid pivot flag is not already set, then the row index is captured, and the valid pivot flag is raised. If the pivot search circuit cannot find a pivot, the RREF controller will halt operation and signal that an error has occurred. In the context of LESS key generation, signing, and verifying, all input matrices to the RREF operation are guaranteed to have an RREF.

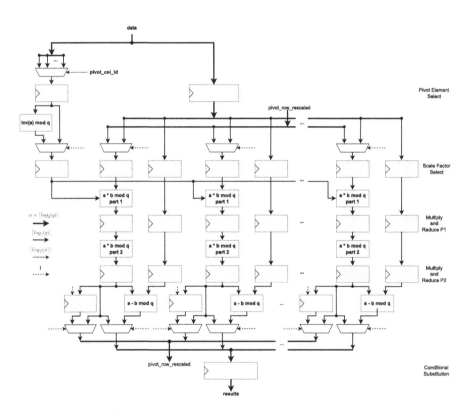

Fig. 15. RREF Row Arithmetic Block Diagram

The row arithmetic circuit, shown in Fig. 15, is used to perform multiplication, subtraction, and reduction modulo q of all elements in a row. It can be controlled to switch between rescaling a pivot row and reducing other rows. The circuit contains n arithmetic units to operate on an entire row in parallel. To support higher clock frequencies, the circuit takes advantage of the parallel nature of the rescaling operation by implementing several pipeline registers. The arithmetic pipeline has 5 stages: pivot element select, scale factor select, two stages of multiply and reduce, and conditional subtract. The pivot row must be rescaled before the reduction of other rows can begin. The bypass of the last row of registers and the feedback loop allow starting the reduction of other rows a couple of cycles earlier than the when the rescaled pivot row is written back to memory. The pipeline bypass consistently occurs independent of input data, so this circuit will always complete its operation in a constant number of clock cycles.

The RREF order of operations is demonstrated in Fig. 16. While data is being loaded into the RREF internal memory, the first pivot search occurs. Once all rows of the matrix are loaded in, then the RREF pipeline begins by performing a swap, if no swap is required, the clock cycle is spent swapping in place. The rescale pivot row and reduce other rows operations follow, while performing the next pivot search during the reduce other rows. These operations repeat until the matrix is fully reduced.

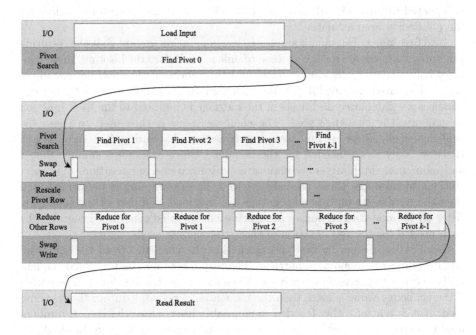

Fig. 16. RREF Operation Scheduling

All loops within the RREF algorithm described in Algorithm 1 are bounded by constants and do not exit early due to any results. This enables a fixed latency to perform all operations of RREF. Additionally, memory access also has a fixed latency, regardless of the data. Therefore the RREF operation is completed in constant time, regardless of the input matrix. The required cycles to perform the operation, for any parameter set, not including loading the input matrix and unloading the output matrix, can be represented by $k^2 + 3k + 58$.

4.3   Operation Scheduling

The schedule of operations used to perform the algorithms of LESS is described in Figs. 17, 18, and 19. The figures provide insight into the order of operations and which of them can be performed in parallel, but the duration of the operations is not to scale. In the key generation, the operation begins with the module receiving the secret key seed and the parameter generator matrix G_0. The seed is expanded into $s - 1$ seeds which are used to sample the secret key monomial matrices. The inversion of the first monomial matrix is performed in parallel with the sampling of the generator matrix. Then the generator matrix is multiplied by the monomial matrix before being written loading into the RREF module. The RREF operation is then started, and the next monomial is sampled and inverted in parallel with the operation. Once RREF completes, the resulting generator matrix is encoded and unloaded from the hardware. This loop of RREF is repeated in parallel with monomial sampling until all generator matrices for the public key are calculated.

The first stage of signing is similar to key generation, except that the resulting generator matrices are hashed instead of unloaded. Before the hashing, these non-pivot columns are transposed, sorted, and then encoded. The sorting, encoding, and hashing are performed in parallel with the RREF operation. Once t generator matrices are calculated and hashed, the message is ingested to the hash function to generate the challenge seed. The challenge seed is then used to parse the challenge itself. There are t monomial matrices sampled during the commitments. However, only ω are needed for the response. Since ω is much smaller than t and monomial sampling is a computationally inexpensive operation, it is more efficient to resample these needed matrices. The resampling is performed, and then the results are multiplied together and encoded as a part of the signature. After all the non-zero responses are calculated, the seed generator generates the path needed for the regeneration of the zero-response seeds.

Verification begins by first reconstructing the challenge from the signature and decoding the monomial matrices. The responses must be processed sequentially in order to successfully recreate the challenge seed. Thus, for each response, if the challenge value is zero, then the monomial is resampled from the response seed. If it is nonzero, the decoded monomial is used. Once the response monomial is prepared, the public key generator matrix corresponding to the challenge value is decoded and multiplied with the monomial before being loaded into the RREF module. The post-processing is performed in the same manner as in signing. The next monomial and generator matrix are prepared in parallel with

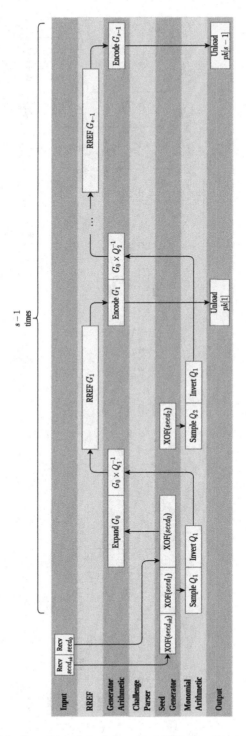

Fig. 17. Operation Scheduling for LESS Key Generation

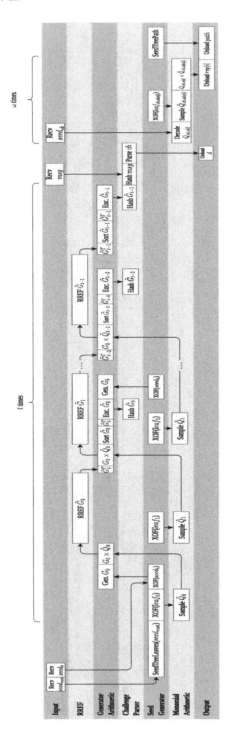

Fig. 18. Operation Scheduling for LESS Sign

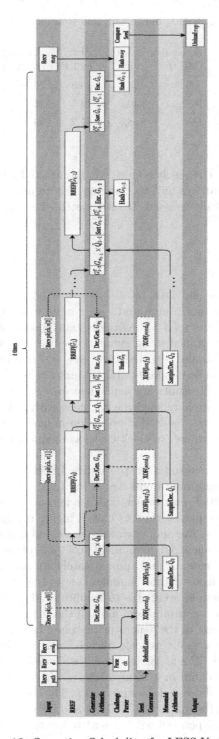

Fig. 19. Operation Scheduling for LESS Verify

Table 2. RREF Implementation Results on Artix-7

k	n	q	Frequency (MHz)	LUTs ($\times 10^3$)	FFs ($\times 10^3$)	BRAM (36 Kbit)	Cycles ($\times 10^3$)
126	252	127	200	27.1	26.8	26.5	16.3
200	400	127	167	40.3	43.5	41	40.7
274	548	127	143	58.8	61.2	56.5	75.9

the RREF operation. The result is encoded and ingested into the hash function. After all generator matrices and the message are hashed, the resulting hash is compared with the challenge seed. If they match, the signature is accepted. If not, it is rejected.

5 Results

Hardware performance and area results are reported for Artix-7 FPGA. The device used for generating timing and area results was XC7A200TFBG484-3. Xilinx Vivado 2022.2 was used for synthesis and implementation. Performance cycle counts were determined using simulation. All hardware implementations included for comparison also reported their area and timing for Artix-7 FPGA.

The implementation results for the RREF unit are listed in Table 2. The area and operating frequency results are dependent on n. A large n will result in a greater area, due to more parallel elements, along with a slower clock frequency, due to large multiplexers. The RREF operation in hardware is executed in constant time, where the number of clock cycles is uniquely dependent on the size of k.

The implementation results for the entire LESS scheme are provided in Tables 3 and 4. The maximum frequency of the LESS module is limited by the critical path of the RREF unit, which is dependent on the size of the generator matrix. Thus the lower parameter sets have a higher maximum frequency. The RREF module consumes the majority of resources and takes up the most significant portion of the latency. Approximately 50%–56% of the LUTs of the design are used in the RREF module, and approximately 80% of the cycles in sign and verification are spent in the RREF module. Due to the computational intensity of RREF, all other modules were able to be optimized for the low area.

With respect to area consumption, most of the change in resource consumption is related to the size of the generator matrices. In particular, the resources of RREF and generator modules scale linearly with the size of these matrices. This is because the RREF and sorting modules always perform their operations on an entire row or column in a single cycle, so the number of processing elements within these modules scales with n and k. The memory also scales directly with the dimension of the matrices. The LUT and FF resources of the remaining modules are mostly independent with respect to the size of the matrices, but the memories within these modules do increase for the larger matrices.

Table 3. Comparison of Hardware Area for Relevant PQC Implementations. *TW* refers to this work.

Algorithm	Implementer	Platform	Parameter Set	Frequency	LUTs ($\times 10^3$)	FFs ($\times 10^3$)	DSP	BRAM (36 Kbit)
LESS	TW	Artix-7	L1-{b,i,s}	200	54.8	39.9	0	59.5
			L3-{b,s}	167	76.7	57.9	0	102.5
			L5-{b,s}	143	104.3	76.7	0	167.5
FALCON	Beckwith et al.	Artix-7	L1	142	14.5	7.3	4	2
			L5		13.9	6.7	4	2
Dilithium	Zhao et al.	Artix-7	L2	96.9	30	10.4	10	11
			L3					
			L5					
SPHINCS+	Amiet et al.	Artix-7	128s-simple	250 & 500	48.2	72.5	0	11.5
			128s-robust		49.1	73.1	0	15.5
			128f-simple		48.0	72.5	1	11.5
			128f-robust		48.9	73.0	1	15.5
			192s-simple		48.7	72.5	0	17
			192s-robust		50.1	74.5	0	22.5
			192f-simple		48.4	73.5	1	17
			192f-robust		47.2	74.3	1	22.5
			256s-simple		51.1	74.6	1	22.5
			256s-robust		50.1	75.7	1	30
			256f-simple		51.0	74.5	1	22.5
			256f-robust		50.3	75.7	1	30

Table 4. Performance Results for Relevant PQC Implementations on Artix-7. *TW* refers to this work.

Design			Algorithm Details			Performance Results					
Algorithm	Implementer	Parameter Set	Public Key (KB)	Signature (KB)	Frequency	Keygen		Sign		Verify	
						Cycles ($\times 10^3$)	Latency (μs)	Cycles ($\times 10^3$)	Latency (μs)	Cycles ($\times 10^3$)	Latency (μs)
LESS	TW	L1-b	13.7	8.4	200	29.1	145.3	5,204.0	26,023.0	5,156.2	25,780.9
		L1-i	41.1	6.1		77.5	387.7	5,126.4	25,631.8	5,093.2	25,465.8
		L1-s	95.9	5.2		174.5	872.5	4,166.1	20,830.6	4,137.2	20,685.9
		L3-b	34.5	18.4	167	72.1	432.8	39,237.4	235,424.4	39,146.0	234,875.7
		L3-s	68.9	14.1		132.8	796.7	46,216.7	277,300.0	46,142.8	276,856.9
		L5-b	64.6	32.5	143	134.4	941.1	129,885.6	909,199.5	129,726.1	908,082.6
		L5-s	129	26.1		247.9	1,735.5	87,161.5	610,130.3	87,013.8	609,096.4
FALCON	Beckwith et al.	L1	0.897	0.666	142	N/A	N/A	N/A	N/A	2.4	16.8
		L5	1.79	1.28	142					4.7	32.8
Dilithium	Zhao et al.	L2	1.31	2.4	96.9	4.1	41	28.1	281	4.4	44
		L3	1.95	3.3		5.9	59	44.7	447	6.2	62
		L5	2.59	4.6		8.8	88	49.0	490	9.0	90
SPHINCS+	Amiet et al.	128s-simple	0.032	7.9	250 & 500	N/A	N/A	N/A	12,400	N/A	70
		128s-robust	0.032	7.9					21,100		110
		128f-simple	0.032	17.1					1,010		160
		128f-robust	0.032	17.1					1,640		230
		192s-simple	0.048	16.3					21,400		100
		192s-robust	0.048	16.3					38,300		150
		192f-simple	0.048	35.7					1,170		190
		192f-robust	0.048	35.7					2,120		310
		256s-simple	0.064	29.8					19,300		140
		256s-robust	0.064	29.8					36,100		200
		256f-simple	0.064	49.9					2,520		210
		256f-robust	0.064	49.9					4,680		340

Table 5. Performance Comparison with AVX2 Implementation

Parameter Set	Platform	Frequency	Keygen		Sign		Verify	
			Latency (μs)	HW Speedup	Latency (μs)	HW Speedup	Latency (μs)	HW Speedup
L1-b	Artix-7	200 MHz	145.3	×**1.5**	26,023.0	×**2.5**	25,780.9	×**2.5**
L1-i			387.7	×**1.4**	25,631.8	×**2.7**	25,465.8	×**2.7**
L1-s			872.5	×**1.4**	20,830.6	×**2.6**	20,685.9	×**2.6**
L3-b		167 MHz	432.8	×**1.4**	235,424.4	×**2.5**	234,875.7	×**2.5**
L3-s			796.7	×**1.4**	277,300.0	×**2.5**	276,856.9	×**2.5**
L5-b		143 MHz	941.1	×**1.4**	909,199.5	×**2.6**	908,082.6	×**2.6**
L5-s			1,735.5	×**1.3**	610,130.3	×**2.5**	609,096.4	×**2.5**
L1-b	Software (AVX2)	3.9 GHz	222.7		64,653.9		68,500.4	
L1-i			557.5		68,689.0		68,689.0	
L1-s			1,185.8		54,835.1		54,835.1	
L3-b			610.7		584,660.7		584,660.7	
L3-s			1,099.8		683,915.5		683,915.5	
L5-b			1,306.4		2,348,707.0		2,348,707.0	
L5-s			2,333.3		1,547,110.1		1,547,110.1	

5.1   Software Comparison

Table 5 provides a comparison between our hardware accelerator running on
Artix-7 and the optimized AVX2 implementation running on an AMD Ryzen
5 5600G desktop CPU. The software was compiled with GCC 12.2 with -O3
-march=native -mtune=native optimization flags and the measurements were
taken with hyperthreading and frequency-scaling (Turbo Core) disabled. The
CPU was running at 3.9 GHz, which is $19.5 - 27.3\times$ faster than the hardware.

Despite this significant difference in clock frequency, the hardware outperforms the software for all parameter sets. The key generation operation is 1.4×
faster in hardware. Signing and verification are both 2.5× faster. The performance could be increased further through the use of a higher-end FPGA, which
can enable high clock frequencies, or through implementation as an ASIC.

5.2   Comparison with Other Digital Signature Schemes

In Tables 3 and 4, we provide comparisons with the best high-performance hardware architectures for CRYSTALS-Dilithium, FALCON, and SPHINCS[+].

When comparing both performance and area, the two lattice-based algorithms CRYSTALS-Dilithium and FALCON both outperform the implementation of LESS. Both algorithms require significantly fewer resources, with the
exception of DSPs, and have significantly lower latency. The DSP usage is
required in these algorithms for modular multiplication because the moduli are
too large to effectively perform in LUTs without a significant increase in the
critical path of the design, whereas the small modulus of LESS allows for multiplication to be implemented using LUTs.

A more relevant comparison is with SPHINCS$^+$, which is the only non-lattice-based signature scheme selected by NIST for standardization to date. Both algorithms provide parameter sets optimizing for different metrics. For SPHINCS$^+$, the "s" and "f" notations correspond to "smaller signature but slower signing" and "faster signing but larger signature", respectively. The "simple" parameter set has higher performance but a less conservative security argument than the "robust" parameter set [5].

When comparing the parameter sets for LESS and SPHINCS$^+$, we can observe that the signature size of LESS varies from 30%–106%, 39%–112%, and 52%–109% of the size of SPHINCS$^+$'s signatures for security levels 1, 3, and 5, respectively. Both algorithms have multiple parameter sets with different trade-offs for the signature size. The small signature parameter set of LESS always has a smaller signature size then that of SPHINCS$^+$, but the public key is significantly larger. The latency for SPHINCS$^+$ is lower for all levels except when comparing SPHINC$^+$ 128s-robust to LESS L1-s, in which LESS is slightly shorter.

The area of the LESS design is comparable to SPHINCS$^+$ for most parameter sets. LESS uses similar LUTs at level 1 to all levels of SPHINCS$^+$, slightly more at level 2, and substantially more at level 3. The flip-flop utilization of LESS is less or very similar to all parameter sets of SPHINCS+. The BRAM utilization is much larger for LESS than SPHINCS$^+$ due to the optimization of RREF operating on an entire row of the matrix.

6 Conclusions

This work presents a high-performance hardware implementation of LESS, a recently-proposed code-based digital signature scheme, which was submitted to the NIST post-quantum cryptography standardization process. A key component is a constant-time, highly parallel unit implementing conversion of an arbitrary $k \times n$ matrix over $GF(p)$ to the reduced row echelon form. This conversion is by far the most computationally intensive operation of LESS. The hardware implementation running on Artix-7 FPGA outperforms optimized software running on a modern desktop CPU by factors ranging between 1.3 and 2.7 depending on a variant and security level. The entire hardware implementation of LESS is resistant to timing attacks.

Acknowledgments. This work has been partially supported by the National Science Foundation under Grant No.: CNS-1801512 and by the US Department of Commerce (NIST) under Grant No.: 70NANB18H218.

References

1. Aikata, et al.: A unified cryptoprocessor for lattice-based signature and key-exchange. IEEE Trans. Comput. 1–13 (2022). https://doi.org/10.1109/TC.2022.3215064

2. Aikata, A., Mert, A.C., Imran, M., Pagliarini, S., Roy, S.S.: KaLi: a crystal for post-quantum security using Kyber and Dilithium. IEEE Trans. Circuits Syst. I Regul. Pap. **70**(2), 747–758 (2023). https://doi.org/10.1109/TCSI.2022.3219555

3. Alagic, G., et al.: Status Report on the Third Round of the NIST Post-Quantum Cryptography Standardization Process. National Institute of Standards and Technology Interagency or Internal Report NIST IR 8413-upd1, National Institute of Standards and Technology (2022). https://doi.org/10.6028/NIST.IR.8413-upd1

4. Amiet, D., Leuenberger, L., Curiger, A., Zbinden, P.: FPGA-based SPHINCS+ implementations: mind the glitch. In: 2020 23rd Euromicro Conference on Digital System Design (DSD), Kranj, Slovenia, pp. 229–237. IEEE (2020). https://doi.org/10.1109/DSD51259.2020.00046

5. Aumasson, J.P., et al.: SPHINCS+ Specification v3.1 (2022). https://sphincs.org/data/sphincs+-r3.1-specification.pdf

6. Balasubramanian, S., Carter, H.W., Bogdanov, A., Rupp, A., Ding, J.: Fast multivariate signature generation in hardware: the case of Rainbow. In: 16th International Symposium on Field-Programmable Custom Computing Machines, FCCM 2008, pp. 25–30 (2008)

7. Balasubramanian, S.R.: A parallel hardware architecture for fast signature generation of Rainbow. Master's thesis, University of Cincinnati, Cincinnati, OH (2007)

8. Baldi, M., et al.: LESS: Linear Equivalence Signature Scheme. https://www.less-project.com/

9. Barenghi, A., Biasse, J.-F., Persichetti, E., Santini, P.: LESS-FM: fine-tuning signatures from the code equivalence problem. In: Cheon, J.H., Tillich, J.-P. (eds.) PQCrypto 2021 2021. LNCS, vol. 12841, pp. 23–43. Springer, Cham (2021). https://doi.org/10.1007/978-3-030-81293-5_2

10. Beckwith, L., Nguyen, D.T., Gaj, K.: High-performance hardware implementation of CRYSTALS-Dilithium. In: 2021 International Conference on Field-Programmable Technology (ICFPT), Auckland, New Zealand, pp. 1–10. IEEE (2021). https://doi.org/10.1109/ICFPT52863.2021.9609917

11. Beckwith, L., Nguyen, D.T., Gaj, K.: High-performance hardware implementation of lattice-based digital signatures (2022). https://eprint.iacr.org/2022/217

12. Biasse, J.-F., Micheli, G., Persichetti, E., Santini, P.: LESS is more: code-based signatures without syndromes. In: Nitaj, A., Youssef, A. (eds.) AFRICACRYPT 2020. LNCS, vol. 12174, pp. 45–65. Springer, Cham (2020). https://doi.org/10.1007/978-3-030-51938-4_3

13. Bogdanov, A., Eisenbarth, T., Rupp, A., Wolf, C.: Time-area optimized public-key engines: $\mathcal{MQ}$-cryptosystems as replacement for elliptic curves? In: Oswald, E., Rohatgi, P. (eds.) CHES 2008. LNCS, vol. 5154, pp. 45–61. Springer, Heidelberg (2008). https://doi.org/10.1007/978-3-540-85053-3_4

14. CERG: SHAKE. https://github.com/GMUCERG/SHAKE

15. Ferozpuri, A., Gaj, K.: High-speed FPGA implementation of the NIST round 1 Rainbow signature scheme. In: 2018 International Conference on ReConFigurable Computing and FPGAs (ReConFig), Cancun, Mexico, pp. 1–8. IEEE (2018). https://doi.org/10.1109/RECONFIG.2018.8641734

16. Fiat, A., Shamir, A.: How to prove yourself: practical solutions to identification and signature problems. In: Odlyzko, A.M. (ed.) CRYPTO 1986. LNCS, vol. 263, pp. 186–194. Springer, Heidelberg (1987). https://doi.org/10.1007/3-540-47721-7_12

17. Gupta, N., Jati, A., Chattopadhyay, A., Jha, G.: Lightweight hardware accelerator for post-quantum digital signature CRYSTALS-Dilithium. IEEE Trans. Circuits Syst. I: Regular Pap. 1–10 (2023). https://doi.org/10.1109/TCSI.2023.3274599

18. Hochet, B., Quinton, P., Robert, Y.: Systolic solution of linear systems over GF(p) with partial pivoting. In: 1987 IEEE 8th Symposium on Computer Arithmetic (ARITH), Como, Italy, pp. 161–168. IEEE (1987). https://doi.org/10.1109/ARITH.1987.6158700

19. Hochet, B., Quinton, P., Robert, Y.: Systolic Gaussian elimination over GF(p) with partial pivoting. IEEE Trans. Comput. **38**(9), 1321–1324 (1989). https://doi.org/10.1109/12.29471

20. Karl, P., Schupp, J., Fritzmann, T., Sigl, G.: Post-quantum signatures on RISC-V with hardware acceleration. ACM Trans. Embed. Comput. Syst. (2023). https://doi.org/10.1145/3579092

21. Land, G., Sasdrich, P., Güneysu, T.: A hard crystal - implementing Dilithium on reconfigurable hardware. In: Grosso, V., Püppelmann, T. (eds.) CARDIS 2021. LNCS, vol. 13173, pp. 210–230. Springer, Cham (2022). https://doi.org/10.1007/978-3-030-97348-3_12

22. Nannipieri, P., Di Matteo, S., Zulberti, L., Albicocchi, F., Saponara, S., Fanucci, L.: A RISC-V post quantum cryptography instruction set extension for number theoretic transform to speed-up CRYSTALS algorithms. IEEE Access **9**, 150798–150808 (2021). https://doi.org/10.1109/ACCESS.2021.3126208

23. NSA: Cybersecurity Advisory Announcing the Commercial National Security Algorithm Suite 2.0 (2022). https://media.defense.gov/2022/Sep/07/2003071834/-1/-1/0/CSA_CNSA_2.0_ALGORITHMS_.PDF

24. Persichetti, E.: LESS: Digital Signatures from Linear Code Equivalence (2023). https://csrc.nist.gov/Projects/post-quantum-cryptography/workshops-and-timeline/pqc-seminars

25. Preucil, T.: Implementation of the signature scheme Rainbow on SoC FPGA. Master's thesis, Uppsala University, Uppsala, Sweden (2022). http://urn.kb.se/resolve?urn=urn:nbn:se:uu:diva-484811

26. Preucil, T., Socha, P., Novotny, M.: Implementation of the Rainbow signature scheme on SoC FPGA. In: 2022 25th Euromicro Conference on Digital System Design (DSD), Maspalomas, Spain, pp. 513–519. IEEE (2022). https://doi.org/10.1109/DSD57027.2022.00074

27. Rupp, A., Eisenbarth, T., Bogdanov, A., Grieb, O.: Hardware SLE solvers: efficient building blocks for cryptographic and cryptanalytic applications. Integration **44**(4), 290–304 (2011). https://doi.org/10.1016/j.vlsi.2010.09.001

28. Shor, P.: Algorithms for quantum computation: discrete logarithms and factoring. In: Proceedings 35th Annual Symposium on Foundations of Computer Science, Santa Fe, NM, USA, pp. 124–134. IEEE Computer Society Press (1994). https://doi.org/10.1109/SFCS.1994.365700

29. Tang, S., Yi, H., Ding, J., Chen, H., Chen, G.: High-speed hardware implementation of Rainbow signature on FPGAs. In: Yang, B.-Y. (ed.) PQCrypto 2011. LNCS, vol. 7071, pp. 228–243. Springer, Heidelberg (2011). https://doi.org/10.1007/978-3-642-25405-5_15

30. Yi, H., Li, W.: Small FPGA implementations for solving systems of linear equations in finite fields. In: 2015 6th IEEE International Conference on Software Engineering and Service Science (ICSESS), Beijing, China, pp. 561–564. IEEE (2015). https://doi.org/10.1109/ICSESS.2015.7339120

31. Yi, H., Nie, Z.: High-speed hardware architecture for implementations of multivariate signature generations on FPGAs. EURASIP J. Wirel. Commun. Netw. **2018**(1), 1–9 (2018). https://doi.org/10.1186/s13638-018-1117-2

32. Zhao, C., et al.: A compact and high-performance hardware architecture for CRYSTALS-Dilithium. IACR Trans. Cryptogr. Hardw. Embed. Syst. **2022**(1), 270–295 (2021). https://doi.org/10.46586/tches.v2022.i1.270-295
33. Zhao, Y., Xie, R., Xin, G., Han, J.: A high-performance domain-specific processor with matrix extension of RISC-V for module-LWE applications. IEEE Trans. Circuits Syst. I Regul. Pap. **69**(7), 2871–2884 (2022). https://doi.org/10.1109/TCSI.2022.3162593
34. Zhou, Z., He, D., Liu, Z., Luo, M., Choo, K.K.R.: A software/hardware co-design of CRYSTALS-Dilithium signature scheme. ACM Trans. Reconfigurable Technol. Syst. **14**(2), 11:1–11:21 (2021). https://doi.org/10.1145/3447812

Wave Parameter Selection

Nicolas Sendrier[(✉)]

Inria, Paris, France
nicolas.sendrier@inria.fr

Abstract. Wave is a provably EUF-CMA (existential unforgeability under adaptive chosen message attacks) digital signature scheme based on codes [15]. It is a hash-and-sign primitive and its security is built according to a GPV-like framework [19] under two assumptions related to coding theory: (i) the hardness of finding a word of prescribed Hamming weight and prescribed syndrome, and (ii) the pseudo-randomness of ternary generalized $(U|U+V)$ codes. Forgery attacks (i)—or message attacks—consist in solving the ternary decoding problem for large weight [7], while, to the best of our knowledge, key attacks (ii) will try to exhibit words that are characteristic of $(U|U+V)$ codes, which are called type-U or type-V codewords in the present paper. In the current state-of-the-art, the best known attacks both reduce to various flavours of Information Set Decoding (ISD) algorithms for different regime of parameters. In this paper we give estimates for the complexities of the best known ISD variants for those regimes. Maximizing the computational effort, thus the security, for both attacks lead to conflicting constraints on the parameters. We provide here a methodology to derive optimal trade-offs for selecting parameters for the Wave signature scheme achieving a given security. We apply this methodology to the current state-of-the-art and propose some effective parameters for Wave. For $\lambda = 128$ bits of classical security, the signature is 737 bytes long, scaling linearly with the security, and the public key size is 3.6 Mbytes, scaling quadratically with the security.

1 Introduction

The signature scheme Wave is built from a family of trapdoor one-way preimage sampleable function [15]. It is a hash-and-sign digital signature scheme and, in contrast with [12], it easily scales with the security parameter. It is provably EUF-CMA under code-based hardness assumptions, namely the hardness of decoding and the indistinguishability of generalized ternary $(U|U+V)$ codes. The scheme enjoys some very attractive features: (1) very short signatures, less than 1 kbyte for 128 bits of security, and (2) fast verification, less than 1 millisecond [2]. The main drawback is a very large public key, of several megabytes.

This work has been partially supported by the French Agence Nationale de la Recherche through the France 2030 program under grant agreement No. ANR-22-PETQ-0008 PQ-TLS.

Project-Team COSMIQ, Inria de Paris, 2 rue Simone Iff, 75012 Paris.

T. Johansson and D. Smith-Tone (Eds.): PQCrypto 2023, LNCS 14154, pp. 91–110, 2023.
https://doi.org/10.1007/978-3-031-40003-2_4

In this paper we explore the best known attacks on the Wave signature scheme and provide some practical parameters based on the current state-of-the-art, as well as a methodology to adjust those parameters to any target security or if the state-of-the-art evolves. There are two ways to attack the Wave scheme:

1. Message attacks, or forgery attacks, which consist in solving a generic decoding problem. Those problems are for ternary codes and for large weights, and the best solver [7] uses information set decoding (ISD) [27] combined with Wagner's generalized birthday algorithm (GBA) [31].
2. Structural attacks, or key attacks, which consist in defeating the indistinguishability assumption. To the best of our knowledge, the most efficient way to achieve that is to exhibit codewords in the public code (*i.e.* the code deriving from the public key) that have an expectedly low, or high, weight. Such codewords are likely to be among the, so-called, type-U or type-V codewords, and are susceptible to reveal information about the hidden $(U|U + V)$ structure. In practice, those key attacks boil down to finding codewords of specified weight in a generic code, for which the best solvers again derive from ISD.

We will observe that the two classes of attacks above provide conflicting constraints on the system parameters, and the choice of secure parameters derives from a trade-off between those constraints.

Related Works. Code-based digital signatures first appeared in [30]: the Stern authentication protocol using the Fiat-Shamir transform [17]. The first hash-and-sign signature based on codes was proposed in [12] but does not scale very well, making it unpractical. There have been improvements to Stern's scheme, [1] using cyclic codes and a 5-pass protocol, and more recently [16] using the MPC-in-the-head paradigm [20]. The latter allows schemes with signatures shorter than the latter, around 10 kbytes or a bit less. Those techniques have relatively larger signature sizes compared to Wave, but much smaller public keys. Let us also mention the LESS scheme [4] with similar characteristic but a security based on the hardness of code equivalence rather than the hardness of decoding.

The paper is organized as follows. We first recall in Sect. 2 basic information about codes and hard problems, the definition of $(U|U+V)$ codes and their main properties, and a description of the Wave signature scheme. Then in Sect. 3 we give a framework to estimate the cost of ISD in the q-ary case, adapted from existing literature, presenting the variants that are relevant for the study of Wave's security. Finally, in Sect. 4, we provide estimates for the computational cost of the best known attacks and a methodology to derive practical parameters for the Wave digital signature scheme.

2   Preliminaries

Many statements in this section are often admitted as coding theory folklore. We point out [14] to the reader for a precise and rigorous presentation of some of those statements.

NOTATION

$\mathbf{F}_q$	The q-ary finite field
$\mathbf{x} \in \mathbf{F}_q^n$	$\mathbf{x} = (x_0, \ldots, x_n)_{0 \leq i < n} \in \mathbf{F}_q^n$, vectors generally use bold letters
$|\mathbf{x}|$	Hamming weight of $\mathbf{x} \in \mathbf{F}_q^n$, $|\mathbf{x}| = |\{i, 0 \leq i < n \mid x_i \neq 0\}|$
$\mathcal{E}_{q;n,t}$	$\mathcal{E}_{q;n,t} = \{\mathbf{e} \in \mathbf{F}_q^n, |\mathbf{e}| = t\}$
$\mathbf{x} \star \mathbf{y}$	Component-wise product $\mathbf{x} \star \mathbf{y} = (x_i y_i)_{0 \leq i < n}$, $\mathbf{x}, \mathbf{y} \in \mathbf{F}_q^n$

$\mathbf{M} \in \mathbf{F}_q^{r \times n}$	$(M_{i,j})_{0 \leq i < r, 0 \leq j < n}$, $r \times n$ matrix over $\mathbf{F}_q$
$\langle \mathbf{M} \rangle$	The vector space spanned by the rows of matrix $\mathbf{M}$
	A matrix $\mathbf{M} \in \mathbf{F}_q^{r \times n}$ is in systematic form if its writes as $\mathbf{M} = (\mathbf{Id} \mid \mathbf{R})$ where $\mathbf{Id}$ is the $r \times r$ identity matrix
Reduced row echelon form	
	A matrix in $\mathbf{F}_q^{r \times n}$ is in reduced row echelon form if its r leftmost independent columns form an identity matrix
$\mathbf{x} \star \mathbf{M}$	Row-wise star product $\mathbf{x} \star \mathbf{M} = (x_j M_{i,j})_{0 \leq i < r, 0 \leq j < n} \in \mathbf{F}_q^{r \times n}$, $\mathbf{x} \in \mathbf{F}_q^n$, $\mathbf{M} = \mathbf{F}_q^{r \times n}$

$\mathcal{S}_n$	Group of permutations of $\{0, \ldots, n-1\}$
$\mathbf{x}^\pi$	$\mathbf{x}^\pi = (x_{\pi(i)})_{i \leq 0 < n}$, $\mathbf{x} \in \mathbf{F}_q^n$, $\pi \in \mathcal{S}_n$
$\mathbf{M}^\pi$	$\mathbf{M}^\pi = (M_{i,\pi(j)})_{0 \leq i < r, 0 \leq j < n}$, $\mathbf{M} \in \mathbf{F}_q^{r \times n}$, $\pi \in \mathcal{S}_n$
$\mathcal{X}^\pi$	$\mathcal{X}^\pi = \{\mathbf{x}^\pi \mid \mathbf{x} \in \mathcal{X}\}$, $\mathcal{X} \subset \mathbf{F}_q^n$, $\pi \in \mathcal{S}_n$

2.1   Error Correcting Code

A q-ary linear $[n, k]$ code C is a k-dimensional subspace of $\mathbf{F}_q^n$. A *generator matrix* $\mathbf{G} \in \mathbf{F}_q^{k \times n}$ of C is such that $\langle \mathbf{G} \rangle = C$ and a *parity check matrix* $\mathbf{H} \in \mathbf{F}_q^{(n-k) \times n}$ of C is such that $\langle \mathbf{H} \rangle^\perp = C$, *i.e.*

$$C = \{\mathbf{xG} \mid \mathbf{x} \in \mathbf{F}_q^k\} \text{ and } C = \{\mathbf{y} \in \mathbf{F}_q^n \mid \mathbf{yH}^\mathsf{T} = 0\}.$$

For any $\mathbf{y} \in \mathbf{F}_q^n$ the quantity $\mathbf{yH}^\mathsf{T}$ is called the *syndrome* of $\mathbf{y}$ (relatively to $\mathbf{H}$). The *dual code* of C is $C^\perp = \langle \mathbf{H} \rangle$, the orthogonal of C.

Weight Distribution. When the code C is chosen uniformly at random, the expected number of its codewords of weight i is asymptotically [14]:

$$W_i(C) = \mathbb{E}\left[|\{\mathbf{c} \in C \mid |\mathbf{c}| = i\}|\right] = \frac{\binom{n}{i}(q-1)^i}{q^{n-k}}.$$

The actual number of codewords of a specific weight might differ for structured codes. If this difference is measurable, this could be used to distinguish a given code C from random.

2.2   Decoding Problem

The decoding problem over $\mathbf{F}_q$ is defined as follows:

Problem 1 (Decoding Problem – DP$(q; n, k, t)$). A finite field $\mathbf{F}_q$ and three integers n, k, t such that $n > k > 0$ and $0 \leq t \leq n$.
Instance: $(\mathbf{H}, \mathbf{s}) \in \mathbf{F}_q^{(n-k) \times n} \times \mathbf{F}_q^{n-k}$
Solution: $\mathbf{e} \in \mathbf{F}_q^n$ such that $|\mathbf{e}| = t$ and $\mathbf{e}\mathbf{H}^\mathsf{T} = \mathbf{s}$.

We denote $\mathrm{Dec}(q; \mathbf{H}, \mathbf{s}, t)$ an instance of the above problem and also, for convenience, the set of its solutions.

The problem DP$(q; n, k, t)$ is hard if solving $\mathrm{Dec}(q; \mathbf{H}, \mathbf{s}, t)$ is hard on average with $\mathbf{H}$ uniformly distributed in $\mathbf{F}_q^{(n-k) \times n}$ and $\mathbf{s} = \mathbf{x}\mathbf{H}^\mathsf{T}$ with $\mathbf{x}$ uniformly distributed in $\mathcal{E}_{q;n,t}$, the set of words of weight t. When the cardinality of $\mathcal{E}_{q;n,t}$ is (sufficiently) larger than q^{n-k}, this is the same as having $\mathbf{s}$ uniformly distributed $\mathbf{F}_q^{n-k}$, see for instance [14, Section 2.5].

In practice, when k/n and t/n are positive constants, the best known algorithms have an average complexity exponential in n when $t < \frac{q-1}{q}(n - k)$ or $t > k + \frac{q-1}{q}(n - k)$ and polynomial in n when $\frac{q-1}{q}(n - k) \leq t \leq k + \frac{q-1}{q}(n - k)$.

Codeword Finding. Finding codewords of given weight correspond to instances of DP with a zero syndrome $\mathbf{s}$. This problem is also hard and, in practice and in the general case, solvers are the same as for DP.

Decoding One Out of Many. The variant of the decoding problem with multiple instances is relevant for the security of code-based signature schemes. This problem was considered in the binary case in [21,28].

Problem 2 (DOOM Problem – DP$_N(q; n, k, t)$). A finite $\mathbf{F}_q$ field and three integers n, k, t such that $n > k > 0$ and $0 \leq t \leq n$. A number $N > 0$ of instances.
Instance: $(\mathbf{H}, \mathbf{s}_1, \ldots, \mathbf{s}_N) \in \mathbf{F}_q^{(n-k) \times n} \times \left(\mathbf{F}_q^{n-k}\right)^N$
Solution: $\mathbf{e} \in \mathbf{F}_q^n$ such that $|\mathbf{e}| = t$ and $\mathbf{e}\mathbf{H}^\mathsf{T} \subset \{\mathbf{s}_1, \ldots, \mathbf{s}_N\}$.

By extension, we denote $\mathrm{DP}_\infty(q; n, k, t)$ the *unlimited* DOOM problem in which the solver is free to decide the value of N. If we denote WF_N the average computational effort for solving $\mathrm{DP}_N(q; n, k, t)$, we have $\mathrm{WF}_N \geq \max(N, \mathrm{WF}_1/N)$ and it follows that $\mathrm{WF}_\infty \geq \sqrt{\mathrm{WF}_1}$. The unlimited DOOM problem cannot be easy if the corresponding Decoding Problem is hard.

2.3   Generalized Ternary $(U|U + V)$ Code

We consider integers n, k, k_U, k_V with n even such that $n > k > 0$, $k = k_U + k_V$, $0 < k_U < n/2$, and $0 < k_V < n/2$. Let $\mathbf{a}, \mathbf{b}, \mathbf{c}, \mathbf{d}$ denote vectors in $\mathbf{F}_3^{n/2}$ such that

$$\forall i, 0 \leq i < n/2, \begin{cases} a_i c_i \neq 0 \\ a_i d_i - b_i c_i \neq 0 \end{cases}. \tag{1}$$

Let $\mathbf{H}_U \in \mathbf{F}_3^{(\frac{n}{2}-k_U)\times\frac{n}{2}}$ and $\mathbf{H}_V \in \mathbf{F}_3^{(\frac{n}{2}-k_V)\times\frac{n}{2}}$ denote parity check matrices of the ternary linear codes U and V of length $n/2$ and dimension respectively k_U and k_V. The generalized ternary $(U|U+V)$ code $\mathcal{C}$ associated to $(\mathbf{H}_U, \mathbf{H}_V, \mathbf{a}, \mathbf{b}, \mathbf{c}, \mathbf{d})$ admits the following parity check matrix

$$\mathbf{H} = \begin{pmatrix} \mathbf{d}\star\mathbf{H}_U & -\mathbf{b}\star\mathbf{H}_U \\ -\mathbf{c}\star\mathbf{H}_V & \mathbf{a}\star\mathbf{H}_V \end{pmatrix} \in \mathbf{F}_3^{(n-k)\times n}. \tag{2}$$

Dual Code. If $\mathcal{C}$ is a generalized ternary $(U|U+V)$ code $\mathcal{C}$ associated to $(\mathbf{H}_U, \mathbf{H}_V, \mathbf{a}, \mathbf{b}, \mathbf{c}, \mathbf{d})$, then its dual is also a generalized $(U|U+V)$ code, associated to $(\mathbf{G}_V, \mathbf{G}_U, -\mathbf{c}, \mathbf{d}, \mathbf{a}, -\mathbf{b})$ where $\mathbf{G}_V$ and $\mathbf{G}_U$ are generator matrices of V and U, that is, equivalently, parity check matrices of the dual codes $V^\perp$ and $U^\perp$.

Decoder for Large Weights. A probabilistic decoding procedure for $\mathcal{C}$ is described in [15]:

$$\begin{aligned} \Phi_{\mathcal{C},w} : \mathbf{F}_3^{n-k} &\longrightarrow \mathbf{F}_3^n \\ \mathbf{s} &\longmapsto \mathbf{e} \quad \text{such that } \mathbf{e}\mathbf{H}^\mathsf{T} = \mathbf{s}, |\mathbf{e}| = w. \end{aligned} \tag{3}$$

It makes use of the $(U|U+V)$ structure and runs in polynomial time for some weight $w > k + \frac{2}{3}(n-k)$ such that the decoding problem $\mathrm{DP}(3; n, k, w)$ is hard.

2.4 The Wave Signature Scheme

1. Main parameters: code-length n, dimension k, error weight w,
2. Public Key: $\mathbf{H}_{\mathrm{pub}} \in \mathbf{F}_3^{(n-k)\times n}$,
3. Signature: $\mathbf{e} \in \mathbf{F}_3^n$ such that $|\mathbf{e}| = w$ and $\mathbf{e}\mathbf{H}_{\mathrm{pub}}^\mathsf{T} = \mathrm{Hash}(\mathrm{Message}) \in \mathbf{F}_3^{(n-k)}$.

The matrix $\mathbf{H}_{\mathrm{pub}}$ is the reduced row echelon form of the parity check matrix of a generalized ternary $(U|U+V)$ code $\mathcal{C}$ of length n and dimension k, randomly permuted by $\pi \in \mathcal{S}_n$. The secret key is a decoding procedure, $\Psi : \mathbf{F}_3^{n-k} \to \mathbf{F}_3^n$, to solve $\mathrm{Dec}(\mathbf{H}_{\mathrm{pub}}, \mathbf{s}, w)$ which easily derives from $\Phi_{\mathcal{C},w}$, see (3), and the permutation π. It involves the parameters k_U, k_V for the $(U|U+V)$ structure, see Sect. 2.3, and g, called the *gap*, which is used by the decoder. We will refer to the integers (k_U, k_V, g) as the secondary parameters, they are public but are only used for signing.

4. The secondary parameters (k_U, k_V, g) verify

$$k_U = g + \frac{3}{2}w - n, k_V = k - k_U \text{ and } 0 \le g \le \frac{\lambda}{\log_2 3} \tag{4}$$

where λ is the security parameter[1].

---

[1] *e.g.* $\lambda = 128$ corresponds to a scheme about as secure as AES-128.

An additional condition is required to build a secure signature scheme: essentially the distribution of $\Psi(\mathbf{s})$, or equivalently of $\Phi_{\mathcal{C},w}(\mathbf{s})$, must be uniform over $\mathcal{E}_{3;n,w}$ when the input $\mathbf{s}$ is uniformly distributed over $\mathbf{F}_3^{n-k}$. This involves a choice of internal distributions and possibly some rejection sampling. It is shown in [15] that with a gap $g = \lambda/\log_2 3$ it is possible to implement the decoder so that the statistical distance between the distribution of its output and the uniform distribution over $\mathcal{E}_{3;n,w}$ do not exceed $2^{-\lambda}$.

Depending on the adversarial model and on the security assumptions, the value of the gap g might be lower than $\lambda/\log_2 3$ without reducing the computational security. We will consider various scenarios for the value of g ranging from 0 to $\lambda/\log_2 3$ and examine how they impact the scheme parameters. This is discussed further in Sect. 4.3.

Wave Security Reduction. With the above notations, and assuming that the decoder's output is properly distributed, the Wave signature scheme is EUF-CMA secure under the following assumptions:

1. The unlimited DOOM problem $\mathrm{DP}_\infty(3; n, k, w)$ is hard.
2. Permuted generalized ternary $(U|U + V)$ codes of parameters (n, k_U, k_V) are computationally indistinguishable from random.

2.5   Weight Distribution and $(U|U + V)$-Specific Codewords

Let $\mathcal{C}$ denote a ternary generalized $(U|U + V)$ code, presumably used as an instance of Wave, associated to $(\mathbf{H}_U, \mathbf{H}_V, \mathbf{a}, \mathbf{b}, \mathbf{c}, \mathbf{d})$. We examine below how its weight distribution differs from that of a random code. We denote U and V the codes of respective parity check matrices $\mathbf{H}_U$ and $\mathbf{H}_V$. We call respectively type-U and type-V codewords, the elements of the following subcodes of $\mathcal{C}$

$$\mathcal{U}(\mathcal{C}) = \{(\mathbf{a} \star \mathbf{u}, \mathbf{c} \star \mathbf{u}) \mid \mathbf{u} \in U\},$$
$$\mathcal{V}(\mathcal{C}) = \{(\mathbf{b} \star \mathbf{v}, \mathbf{d} \star \mathbf{v}) \mid \mathbf{v} \in V\}.$$

We refer to $\mathbf{u}$ and $\mathbf{v}$ above as the component words. Except for the contribution of the type-U and type-V codewords, the weight distribution of $\mathcal{C}$ is as for a random ternary linear $[n, k]$ code, see [13] for precise statements. We partition type-U and type-V codewords according to the Hamming weight of their component words and define

$$\mathcal{U}(\mathcal{C}, j) = \{(\mathbf{a} \star \mathbf{u}, \mathbf{c} \star \mathbf{u}) \mid \mathbf{u} \in U, |\mathbf{u}| = j\},$$
$$\mathcal{V}(\mathcal{C}, j) = \{(\mathbf{b} \star \mathbf{v}, \mathbf{d} \star \mathbf{v}) \mid \mathbf{v} \in V, |\mathbf{v}| = j\},$$

whose respective expected cardinalities are

$$\mathbb{E}\left[|\mathcal{U}(\mathcal{C}, j)|\right] = W_j(U) = \frac{\binom{n/2}{j} 2^j}{3^{n/2 - k_U}} \text{ and } \mathbb{E}\left[|\mathcal{V}(\mathcal{C}, j)|\right] = W_j(V) = \frac{\binom{n/2}{j} 2^j}{3^{n/2 - k_V}}.$$

The words of $\mathcal{U}(\mathcal{C}, j)$ all have a Hamming weight $t = 2j$ while the words of $\mathcal{V}(\mathcal{C}, j)$ have a Hamming weight $j \leq t \leq 2j$ depending on the intersection of the component word support with the supports of $\mathbf{b}$ and $\mathbf{d}$. If $(\mathbf{a}, \mathbf{b}, \mathbf{c}, \mathbf{d})$ are uniformly distributed with the condition (1), then, on average, three quarters of the b_i and d_i are non zero. So the typical weight of a word of $\mathcal{V}(\mathcal{C}, j)$ is $t = 3j/2$.

Codewords of type-U or type-V are very few, less than $3^{k_U} + 3^{k_V}$ among $3^k = 3^{k_U + k_V}$ codewords. However, for a particular weight t, it may happen that most codewords of weight t of type-U or type-V. For typical Wave parameters it may happen, see Fig. 1, that, either for small or for large values of t, type-U codewords dominate. We also observe in Fig. 1 that the type-V codewords never dominate, regardless of the weight. This also holds for other possible choices of code parameters k_U, k_V for Wave.

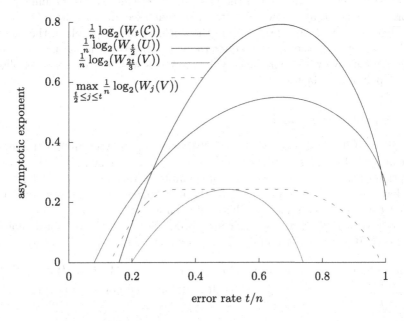

Fig. 1. (Expected) Number of codewords of weight t in $\mathcal{C}$ (black), of type-U (blue), or type-V (red), for Wave parameters $k_U = 0.693 \cdot \frac{n}{2}$, $k_V = 0.307 \cdot \frac{n}{2}$, $k = \frac{n}{2}$ and $w = 0.894 \cdot n$ (Color figure online)

Example: Lets consider words of weight $t = 0.209 \cdot n$ in a ternary $(U|U + V)$ code $\mathcal{C}$ of length n, dimension $k = 0.5 \cdot n$, and $k_U = 0.693 \cdot \frac{n}{2}$ (the vertical line in Fig. 1). We expect to find $2^{0.231 \cdot n}$ words of weight $t/2$ in a random ternary linear $[n/2, k_U]$ code (the blue curve) and "only" $2^{0.156 \cdot n}$ in a random ternary linear $[n, k]$ code (the black curve). From [13], the weight of codewords which are not of type-U or type-V is distributed as for a random code, so, if one can somehow sample a (random) word of weight $t = 0.209 \cdot n$ in $\mathcal{C}$ as above, it will almost certainly be a type-U codeword.

3 q-ary Information Set Decoding (ISD)

Information Set Decoding was first introduced by Prange in 1962 [27] and is one of the main algorithmic techniques to solve the decoding problem. It was later improved in many ways, in particular: birthday paradox [29], representation technique in [23], nearest neighbors in [24]. The current state-of-the-art in the binary case is [5,6,9]. Variants using the Generalized Birthday Algorithm [31] (GBA) are also of interest. GBA was first used for decoding in [11], and for some regime of parameters it can be efficiently used within ISD. This is the case in particular for the decoding of large weights in the non binary case [7].

Few contributions are available in the q-ary case, let us mention [7,8,26]. The interested reader may also refer to [14, Ch. 3] for a comprehensive survey of ISD for any alphabet size. In general the analysis is very similar to the binary case, we briefly revisit that below. Note that, as remarked in [26], there is a factor $\sqrt{q-1}$ to be gained that derives from the linearity of the problem: the identity $\mathbf{e}_0\mathbf{H}_0^\mathsf{T} = \mathbf{s}_0$ remains true up to a non-zero factor, and this can be used to speed-up the search. We will ignore this in the sequel as we only consider complexity up to a polynomial factor.

3.1   An ISD Framework

We will describe and analyze several ISD variants that fit in the framework described in [18]. This is the case of most known variants, with the notable exception of the latest and best known asymptotic variants [5,6,9]. Those variants have not been generalized yet to the non-binary case, and moreover they are not considered as practical. This could change in the future.

The ISD framework we consider here is described as follows. For a choice of parameters $0 \le \ell \le n - k$ and $0 \le p \le t$, solve $\mathrm{Dec}(\mathbf{H}_0, \mathbf{s}_0, t)$ by repeating:

1. Pick a permutation σ uniformly in $\mathcal{S}_n$ and compute $(\mathbf{H}, \mathbf{H}', \mathbf{s}, \mathbf{s}') \in \mathbf{F}_q^{\ell\times(k+\ell)} \times \mathbf{F}_q^{(n-k-\ell)\times(k+\ell)} \times \mathbf{F}_q^\ell \times \mathbf{F}_q^{n-k-\ell}$ such that for some non singular matrix $\mathbf{U} \in \mathbf{F}_q^{(n-k)\times(n-k)}$,

$$\mathbf{U}\mathbf{H}_0^\sigma = \left(\begin{array}{c|c}\mathrm{Id}_{n-k-\ell} & \mathbf{H}' \\ \hline 0 & \mathbf{H}\end{array}\right) = \mathbf{U}\mathbf{s}_0^\mathsf{T} = \left(\begin{array}{c}\mathbf{s}'^\mathsf{T} \\ \mathbf{s}^\mathsf{T}\end{array}\right). \tag{5}$$

2. Use a SubISD routine to compute $\mathcal{E}_\mathrm{isd} \subset \mathcal{E} = \{\mathbf{e} \in \mathcal{E}_{q;k+\ell,p}, |\mathbf{e}| = p, \mathbf{e}\mathbf{H}^\mathsf{T} = \mathbf{s}\}$.
3. For all $\mathbf{e} \in \mathcal{E}_\mathrm{isd}$, check $\mathbf{e}_0 = (\mathbf{e}, \mathbf{s}' - \mathbf{e}\mathbf{H}'^\mathsf{T})$.

Variants of ISD differ in the SubISD routine used at the second step. Every $\mathbf{e}_0$ of weight t at step 3 is a valid solution, the algorithm may either exit there, or continue until a prescribed number of iterations is executed. ISD algorithms are probabilistic and the successive iterations are independent. We will view the sets $\mathcal{E}$ and $\mathcal{E}_\mathrm{isd}$ of step 2 as random variables. For convenience, we denote

$$\mathcal{F} = \left\{(\mathbf{e}, \mathbf{s}' - \mathbf{e}\mathbf{H}'^\mathsf{T})^{\sigma^{-1}}, \mathbf{e} \in \mathcal{E}\right\} \text{ and } \mathcal{F}_\mathrm{isd} = \left\{(\mathbf{e}, \mathbf{s}' - \mathbf{e}\mathbf{H}'^\mathsf{T})^{\sigma^{-1}}, \mathbf{e} \in \mathcal{E}_\mathrm{isd}\right\} \subset \mathcal{F}.$$

The first set $\mathcal{F}$ above has, a priori, the same size as $\mathcal{E}$ and is the maximal search space for a particular iteration. If $\mathbf{x}$ belongs to $\mathrm{Dec}(\mathbf{H}_0, \mathbf{s}_0, t)$, then the permutation σ is "good for $\mathbf{x}$" if $\mathbf{x} \in \mathcal{F}$. The second set $\mathcal{F}_{\mathrm{isd}}$ is possibly smaller than $\mathcal{F}$ and is the effective search space for a particular iteration and a particular SubISD routine, generally $\mathcal{F}_{\mathrm{isd}}$ is close to $\mathcal{F}$.

Let $\mathcal{A}$ denote a variant of ISD, we define the following three quantities

1. For all $\mathbf{x} \in \mathbf{F}_q^n$ such that $\mathbf{x}\mathbf{H}_0^{\mathsf{T}} = \mathbf{s}_0$, we define the probability

$$\pi_{\ell,p}(\mathbf{x}) = \mathrm{Pr}\left(\mathbf{x} \in \mathcal{F}\right) = \frac{\binom{n-k-\ell}{|\mathbf{x}|-p}\binom{k+\ell}{p}}{\binom{n}{|\mathbf{x}|}}, \quad \pi_{\ell,p}(i) = \frac{\binom{n-k-\ell}{i-p}\binom{k+\ell}{p}}{\binom{n}{i}}.$$

As it only depends of the weight of $\mathbf{x}$ we overload the notation and define $\pi_{\ell,p}(|\mathbf{x}|) = \pi_{\ell,p}(\mathbf{x})$. This quantity is the same for all ISD variants. It is in fact the probability that the permutation σ drawn at step 1 properly splits the support of $\mathbf{x}$ with exactly p non-zero coordinates in the $k + \ell$ rightmost coordinates after permutation.

2. For a given SubISD routine at step 2, we define the *decimation factor* as

$$\mu_{\mathcal{A}} = \frac{\mathbb{E}[|\mathcal{E}_{\mathrm{isd}}|]}{\mathbb{E}[|\mathcal{E}|]} \leq 1.$$

This is the proportion of solutions of the decoding problem $\mathrm{Dec}(\mathbf{H}, \mathbf{s}, p)$ that are discovered on average by the SubISD routine at step 2. The decimation factor is also equal to $\mathbb{E}[|\mathcal{F}_{\mathrm{isd}}|]/\mathbb{E}[|\mathcal{F}|]$ and this quantity is independent of the target weight t.

3. The average cost of one iteration is denoted $C_{\mathcal{A}}$. It is also independent of the target weight t.

For every particular instance $\mathcal{A}$ of the ISD framework, that is for every choice of (ℓ, p) and of the SubISD routine, the computational cost can be estimated, depending on the task that $\mathcal{A}$ should solve (single or multiple targets, see below). The cost will next be minimized over all choices of (ℓ, p) and possibly other parameters of the SubISD routine.

Single Solution. For any $\mathbf{x} \in \mathrm{Dec}(\mathbf{H}_0, \mathbf{s}_0, t)$, the probability to discover that particular solution in a particular iteration is

$$P = \mathrm{Pr}(\mathbf{x} \in \mathcal{F}_{\mathrm{isd}}) = \mu_{\mathcal{A}} \cdot \mathrm{Pr}(\mathbf{x} \in \mathcal{F}) = \mu_{\mathcal{A}} \cdot \pi_{\ell,p}(t)$$

so we expect to make $1/P$ iterations to find $\mathbf{x}$ and the expected computational effort is

$$\mathrm{WF}_{\mathcal{A}}(n, k, t, 1) = \frac{C_{\mathcal{A}}}{\mu_{\mathcal{A}} \cdot \pi_{\ell,p}(t)} \tag{6}$$

up to a constant factor.

Multiple Solutions. Let $\mathcal{X}$ denote a subset of cardinality N of all solutions of $\mathrm{Dec}(\mathbf{H}_0, \mathbf{s}_0, t)$. The probability to discover an element of $\mathcal{X}$ in a particular iteration is

$$P_{\mathcal{A}}(t, N) = \mathrm{Pr}(\mathcal{X} \cap \mathcal{F}_{\mathrm{isd}} \neq \emptyset) \leq 1 - \prod_{\mathbf{x} \in \mathcal{X}} (1 - \mathrm{Pr}(\mathbf{x} \in \mathcal{F}_{\mathrm{isd}} \neq \emptyset)) \tag{7}$$

$$\leq 1 - (1 - \mu_{\mathcal{A}} \cdot \pi_{\ell,p}(t))^N$$

$$\leq \min(1, N \cdot \mu_{\mathcal{A}} \cdot \pi_{\ell,p}(t))$$

so the expected computational effort to find an element of $\mathcal{X}$ is

$$\mathrm{WF}_{\mathcal{A}}(n, k, t, N) = \frac{C_{\mathcal{A}}}{P_{\mathcal{A}}(t, N)} \geq \frac{C_{\mathcal{A}}}{\min(1, N \cdot \mu_{\mathcal{A}} \cdot \pi_{\ell,p}(t))}. \tag{8}$$

The inequality (7) derives from the union bound. The equality holds when the events "$\mathbf{x} \in \mathcal{F}$" are all independent. In some situation, for instance if $\mathcal{X}$ is a set of type-U codewords as in Sect. 2.5, the actual probability might be smaller and the actual computational effort larger.

Effective Workfactor. The workfactor formula (6) or (8) depends on the parameters p and ℓ, and possibly other parameters stemming from the subroutine used in the variant. The effective workfactor corresponds to the choice of parameters that will minimize the formula. The corresponding optimization problem can be difficult and has to be solved for each particular problem, that is for given values of n, k, t, and N.

3.2   ISD-MMT

The generalization of the MMT algorithm [23] to the q-ary case is relatively straightforward. We briefly sketch the algorithm and its analysis in the q-ary case, the interested reader may wish to check the relevant literature for a more comprehensive presentation.

We consider the framework of the previous section. After permuting the coordinates and computing a partial Gaussian elimination as in (5), we consider the routine of step 2, which attempts to recover all, or as many as possible, elements of the search space $\mathcal{E} = \left\{ \mathbf{e} \in \mathbf{F}_q^{k+\ell}, |\mathbf{e}| = p, \mathbf{e}\mathbf{H}^{\mathsf{T}} = \mathbf{s} \right\}$.

We denote $L = \binom{k+\ell}{p}(q-1)^p$ and $L_0 = \binom{(k+\ell)/2}{p/4}(q-1)^{p/4}$. We call syndrome of $\mathbf{y} \in \mathbf{F}_q^{k+\ell}$ the quantity $\mathbf{y}\mathbf{H}^{\mathsf{T}}$. An additional parameter ℓ_2, $0 \leq \ell_2 \leq \ell$ is introduced. The routine runs as follows:

1. Build 4 lists of size L_0 of words in $\mathbf{F}_q^{k+\ell}$ of weight $p/4$
2. Merge the above lists pairwise to obtain 2 lists of size L_0^2/q^{ℓ_2} of words in $\mathbf{F}_q^{k+\ell}$ of weight $p/2$ with a prescribed value on ℓ_2 coordinates of their syndromes
3. Merge the above 2 lists to obtain a list of size $L_0^4/q^{\ell+\ell_2}$ of words in $\mathbf{F}_q^{k+\ell}$ of weight p with a prescribed value on the other $\ell - \ell_2$ coordinates of their syndromes

The cost of this procedure is, up to a constant factor, the maximum of all the above list sizes. The optimal choice of ℓ_2 is such that $q^{\ell_2} = L/L_0^4$ and L_0 is usually negligible for parameters of interest.

Using the fact that $\binom{k+\ell}{p/2}(q-1)^{p/2} = \Omega(\sqrt{p}) \cdot L_0^2$, the iteration cost becomes

$$C_{\mathrm{MMT}} = \binom{k+\ell}{p}(q-1)^p \cdot \max\left(\frac{1}{\binom{k+\ell}{p/2}(q-1)^{p/2}}, \frac{1}{q^\ell}\right)$$

which is minimal when the two terms in the max are equal. Finally the characteristic quantities of ISD-MMT are

$$C_{\mathrm{MMT}} = \binom{k+\ell}{p}(q-1)^p q^{-\ell} \text{ and } \mu_{\mathrm{MMT}} = 1 \text{ with } q^\ell = \binom{k+\ell}{p/2}(q-1)^{p/2} \quad (9)$$

up to a polynomial factor.

3.3 ISD-GBA

Wagner's Generalized Birthday Algorithm (GBA) [31] can be used as SubISD routine. Again, we only briefly sketch the algorithm, the interested reader may refer to [7,25] for more details. The GBA of order a builds a binary tree, with 2^a leaves. Lists attached to siblings are merged and attached to the parent node. The list attached to the root is returned.

1. At level a: build 2^a lists of L words of weight $p/2^a$ in $\mathbf{F}_q^{k+\ell}$
2. At level i, $0 \leq i < a$: merge pairwise the 2^{i+1} lists of level $i+1$ to obtain 2^i lists of L words of weight $p/2^i$ in $\mathbf{F}_q^{k+\ell}$ with a prescribed value on ℓ/a coordinates of their syndromes
3. At level 0: output the final list of L words of weight p with a prescribed syndrome

With the constraint that $L = q^{\ell/a}$ and $L^{2^a} \leq \binom{k+\ell}{p}(q-1)^p$. In practice, a should be an integer ≥ 2, but the algorithm can be smoothed, see [7,18], and we may consider the real value a such that

$$q^{\ell/a} = \left(\binom{k+\ell}{p}(q-1)^p\right)^{\frac{1}{2^a}}. \quad (10)$$

Even though this value of a does not correspond to an actual GBA tree as above, it provides meaningful bounds. Putting everything together, the characteristic quantities of GBA are the following:

$$C_{\mathrm{GBA}} = (2^{a+1} - 1) \cdot q^{\ell/a} \text{ and } \mu_{\mathrm{GBA}} = \frac{q^{\frac{a+1}{a}\ell}}{\binom{k+\ell}{p}(q-1)^p} \quad (11)$$

up to a polynomial factor.

The DOOM Variant. The DOOM problem, Problem 2, is relevant in the case of the security against forgery of a signature scheme, as the adversary can build any number of messages and be happy to sign only one of them.

The best known way to exploit multiple instance with GBA is to fill one of the 2^a lists of level a with target syndromes. The characteristic quantities of GBA-DOOM verify (11), but instead of (10) the optimal order a will be such that

$$q^{\ell/a} = \left(\binom{k+\ell}{p} (q-1)^p \right)^{\frac{1}{2^a-1}}. \tag{12}$$

4   Best Known Attacks on Wave

We consider an instance of Wave of main parameters (n, w, k), public key $\mathbf{H}_{\mathrm{pub}} \in \mathbf{F}_3^{(n-k)\times n}$, and secondary parameters (k_U, k_V, g). The public code is $\mathcal{C}_{\mathrm{pub}} = \mathcal{C}^\pi = \langle \mathbf{H}_{\mathrm{pub}} \rangle^\perp$ where π is a secret permutation and $\mathcal{C}$ is a generalized $(U|U+V)$ code. The type-U and type-V codewords of $\mathcal{C}$, denoted $\mathcal{U}(\mathcal{C})$ and $\mathcal{V}(\mathcal{C})$, are defined in Sect. 2.5. To ease the statements we will also call type-U and type-V codewords the elements of $\mathcal{C}_{\mathrm{pub}}$ which belong to $\mathcal{U}(\mathcal{C})^\pi$ and $\mathcal{V}(\mathcal{C})^\pi$ respectively.

- **Forgery Attack.** Without knowledge about the secret, the adversary is reduced to solve $\mathrm{DP}_\infty(3; n, k, w)$ on average. The target weight w is large, close to the block length n. In this regime, the best known attack is Information Set Decoding using the Generalized Birthday Algorithm as subroutine, see [7].
- **Key Attack.** The best known method for recovering the secret key, or at least distinguishing the public key from a random matrix, will consist in exhibiting a type-U codeword in $\mathcal{C}_{\mathrm{pub}}$ or in $\mathcal{C}_{\mathrm{pub}}^\perp$.

4.1   Forgery Attack

This problem was addressed in [7]. We want to solve the unlimited DOOM problem $\mathrm{DP}_\infty(3; n, k, w)$ when w is close to n. The workfactor is (larger than)

$$\frac{C_{\mathrm{GBA}}}{\min(1, N \cdot \mu_{\mathrm{GBA}} \cdot \pi_{\ell,p}(w))}$$

with $N = \binom{n}{w} 2^w / 3^{n-k}$ the expected number of solutions, C_{GBA} and μ_{GBA} defined in (11), minimized over all choices of ℓ, p, a such that (12).

Optimization. It is optimal to choose $p = k + \ell$ in this regime, this was already remarked in [7]. We also notice that the workfactor is minimal when the success probability of an iteration is constant (*i.e.* one or a small number of iterations is enough). This happens, asymptotically, when $N \cdot \mu_{\mathrm{GBA}} \cdot \pi_{\ell,p}(t) = 1$. Finally, the minimal workfactor is $\mathrm{WF}_{\mathrm{GBA}} = q^{\ell/a}$ when ℓ and a verify

$$3^{\ell/a} = 2^{(k+\ell)/(2^a-1)} = \frac{3^{n-k-\ell}}{\binom{n-k-\ell}{w-k-\ell} 2^{w-k-\ell}}.$$

4.2   Key Attack

The key attack we consider here consists in searching a type-U or a type-V codeword in either the public $[n, k]$ code $\mathcal{C}_{\text{pub}}$ or its dual. This is done by applying a generic decoding technique (*e.g.* ISD and variants) for a target error weight t and the zero syndrome.

Limiting the Codeword Search:

– We will not consider type-V codewords. In fact, for all Wave parameters of interest, the situation is similar to what we observe in Fig. 1, the type-V codewords (red curve) are always dominated by the type-U codewords. So it will always be easier to find a type-U.
– We will not consider type-U codewords of high weight. We observe in Fig. 1 that, for large weights, the blue curve of type-U codewords is above the expected number of codewords of that weight, in black. This phenomenon even amplifies when the code rate k decrease. Even though, those words are always harder to find in practice.

Note that to be thorough, the designer must check the above cases a posteriori, which can easily be done when the parameters are known. The purpose of the above limitation is to reduce the parameters selection to a trade-off between the forgery attack of Sect. 4.1 and the search of type-U codewords of small weight.

Finding type-U Codewords of Small Weight. This search will consist in finding a word of weight t, to be determined, in the code $\mathcal{C}_{\text{pub}}$ or $\mathcal{C}_{\text{pub}}^{\perp}$. The adversary wins if it was able to obtain at least one type-U codeword of such weight. That is:

– either search a type-U codeword in $\mathcal{C}_{\text{pub}}$, one among $N_U(t) = \binom{n/2}{t/2} 2^{\frac{t}{2}} / 3^{\frac{n}{2} - k_U}$;
– or search a type-U codeword in $\mathcal{C}_{\text{pub}}^{\perp}$, one among $N_V(t) = \binom{n/2}{t/2} 2^{\frac{t}{2}} / 3^{k_V}$.

The workfactor is minimized over those two cases and over all possible even values of t. The corresponding computational effort when the generic decoding algorithm is ISD-MMT [23] is

$$\min \left(\min_{t,\ell} \left(\text{WF}_{\text{MMT}}(n, k, t, N_U(t)) \right), \min_{t,\ell} \left(\text{WF}_{\text{MMT}}(n, n - k, t, N_V(t)) \right) \right) \quad (13)$$

whose value derives from (8) and (9). The optimization parameters p and ℓ are related when the optimum is reached in ISD-MMT, see (9), here we write p as a function of ℓ, and ℓ is used to minimize the expression.

Remark: the optimal value of t, that is the weight for which it is easiest to find a type-U codeword, is a non trivial trade-off. For instance for $(k/n, w/n) = (0.5, 0.894)$ and $k_U = 0.693\, n/2$, the easiest target weight is not, as one could expect, the Gilbert-Varshamov distance ($t/n = 0.081$ where the blue curve meets the horizontal axis in Fig. 1) but is much larger ($t/n = 0.209$ shown by the small vertical black line in Fig. 1).

4.3   Wave Parameter Selection

We consider here asymptotic estimates. Relative parameters are considered, *e.g.* k/n, w/n..., and polynomial factors are not considered. Our purpose is to find the good proportion between the scheme parameters, main and secondary. As the security scales linearly with code-length n, the target security is obtained as a final step by scaling n.

1. Let λ be the target (classical) security or the "number of security bits", *e.g.* $\lambda = 128$.
   We want that all attacks against the scheme require a computational effort at least equal to 2^λ.
2. Select the main parameters (k, w).
   (guidelines: $0.35 \leq k/n \leq 0.7$ and $0.85 \leq w/n \leq 0.95$)
   The forgery attack requires a computational effort

$$\mathrm{WF_{GBA}}(n, k, w) \geq 2^{c \cdot n}$$

   where c only depends on k/n and w/n.
   We may now relate the code-length and the security as we want to reach $c \cdot n = \lambda$ where λ is the "number of (classical) security bits".
3. The secondary parameters (k_U, k_V) derive from the main ones:

$$k_U = g + \frac{3}{2}w - n \text{ and } k_V = k - k_U.$$

4. The gap g is used in [15] to unconditionally ensure a uniformity condition needed to formally reach the EUF-CMA security, its value is $g = \lambda / \log_2 3 = 0.631 c \cdot n$ for "λ bits of (classical) security". Using $g = 0$ is probably safe but, at the moment, would require an additional heuristic assumption. We will favor an intermediate value $g = 0.315\, c \cdot n$ and admit that it corresponds to an adversary limited to $2^{\lambda/2}$ queries to a signing oracle, *e.g.* a scheme with 128 bits of security with an adversary allowed to at most 2^{64} queries to a signing oracle, corresponding to a gap $g \approx 40$.
5. The corresponding computational effort for the key attack derives from (13) and Sect. 4.2. If we denote $\mathrm{WF_{key}}$ this quantity, the corresponding asymptotic exponent is $c' = \frac{1}{n}\log_2(\mathrm{WF_{key}})$ which only depends of the relative value k/n and k_U/n. Finally k_U is related to w and to the gap g.

Example: In Fig. 2, we consider $k/n = 0.5$. The asymptotic exponent is given for forgery attack, the increasing curve in black, and for the key attack, the decreasing curves in dotted red, solid blue, dashed green, corresponding to various choices for the gap. The optimal choice will correspond to the curves intersections whose numerical values are given in Table 1.

We observe that, even though the gap does not change the order of magnitude, it has a significant impact on the system parameters. In the sequel we will consider the "half gap" scenario, corresponding to $g = 40$ when the target security is $\lambda = 128$.

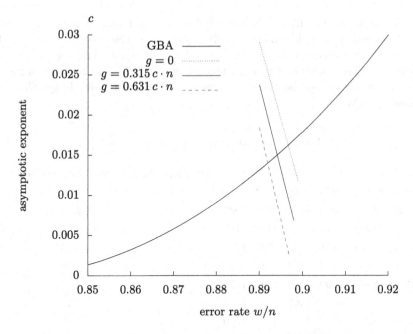

Fig. 2. Security Exponent for Best Known Forgery Attacks (black) and Key Attacks (blue) *vs.* Error Weight for a Code Rate $k = 0.5$ (Color figure online)

Table 1. Wave Parameters *vs.* Gap for $k = 0.5$

asymptotic parameters			Wave parameters, $\lambda{=}128$					
	w/n	c	n	k	w	k_U	k_V	g
no gap	0.89665	0.0162184	7904	3952	7077	2763	1183	0
half gap	0.89412	0.0150016	8532	4266	7629	2951	1315	40
full gap	0.89193	0.0139887	9150	4575	8161	3132	1443	81

4.4   Sizes

The public key can be provided in systematic form, so its size is equal to $k(n-k)\log_2 3$ bits. The signature is a ternary vector **e** of length n and weight w. As explained in [2, §2.5], when the public key is in systematic form, it is enough to provide the last k coordinates of **e**. Moreover those coordinates can be compressed to a size $k \cdot h_3(w/n)$ bits, where $h_3(x) = -x\log_2 x - (1-x)\log_2(1-x) + x$ is the ternary entropy function.

For a security level $\lambda = 128$ and the intermediate gap $g = 40$ we give in Table 2 Wave parameters for a code rate between 0.38 and 0.70. We also give in Fig. 3 the signature length and the public key size for the same range of code rates. We observe that if k/n decrease below 0.43 or increases above 0.66 then both the signature length and the key size increase. So the effective range for the code rate is rather narrow. In practice $k = 0.5$ seems to offer a rather good trade-off, the signature length is very close the minimum, 737 bytes for a minimum of 723 bytes, while the public key has a size of 3.6 MB, not much larger than the minimal 3.04 MB.

Table 2. Wave parameters for $(\lambda, g) = 128, 40$

k/n	n	k	w	k_U	k_V	signature length (bytes)	key size (MB)
0.38	10464	3976	8918	2953	1023	724	5.11
0.41	9792	4015	8454	2928	1087	723	4.60
0.44	9262	4075	8095	2920	1155	724	4.19
0.47	8846	4158	7822	2927	1231	729	3.86
0.50	8526	4263	7623	2949	1314	737	3.60
0.53	8318	4409	7516	2995	1414	751	3.41
0.56	8184	4583	7469	3059	1524	768	3.27
0.59	8124	4793	7485	3143	1650	791	3.16
0.62	8136	5044	7564	3249	1795	818	3.09
0.65	8226	5347	7713	3383	1964	852	3.05
0.68	8402	5713	7942	3550	2163	894	3.04
0.70	8574	6002	8146	3685	2317	928	3.06

4.5   Scaling Security

All parameters scale linearly with the security. The signature length also scales linearly, the key size however is quadratic. So Table 2 can be used to deduce parameters offering a higher security level, *e.g.* $\lambda \in \{192, 256\}$. This scaling will also increase the gap while in some situations, for instance in the NIST call for postquantum primitives, some capabilities of the adversary are limited regardless of the target security. Let us assume then that the adversary is limited to 2^{64} calls to a signing oracle and we want to reach security levels 192 or 256. It is possible to do slightly better than just scaling Table 2 (Table 3)

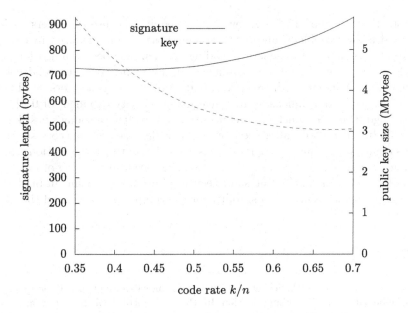

Fig. 3. Signature Length and Public Key Size *vs.* Code Rate for a Security $\lambda = 128$ and a Gap $g = 40$

Table 3. Scaling Wave Parameters with a Gap $g = 40$

λ	g	n	k	w	k_U	k_V	signature length	key size
128	40	8526	4263	7623	2949	1314	737 bytes	3.60 MB
192	40	12476	6238	11165	4311	1927	1076 bytes	7.71 MB
256	40	16424	8212	14705	5673	2539	1416 bytes	13.36 MB

4.6 Quantum Security

All attacks that are involved in the parameter selection process derive from ISD. So far quantum speedup of ISD variants [3,10,22] never managed to reduce the security exponent by more than a factor 2 and thus, from Sect. 4.5, scaling the scheme to resist to quantum cryptanalysis will be straightforward.

5 Conclusion

Wave is the first scalable hash-and-sign signature scheme based on codes. It enjoys short signature and fast verification, whereas signing time is average, hundreds of milliseconds, and the public key large, several megabytes.

We propose here some practical parameters for the scheme, based on the current knowledge of the underlying hard problems. Our proposed methodology would easily adapt to any evolution of the best known solvers for those problems.

Note that all known attacks eventually require the use of solvers for the generic decoding problem, and even though those solvers are used in unusual regime of parameters, the generic decoding problem has been studied for more than half a century without any significant improvement. For instance, decoding at the Gilbert-Varshamov distance at rate 0.5, *i.e.* $t = 0.11 \cdot n$ errors in a binary code of length n and dimension $n/2$, features a security exponent of 0.12 with Prange algorithm [27] which only reduces to about 0.09 with today's best known solver [5]. In other words, after sixty years, any code-based scheme corresponding to this regime of parameters, as for the instance the Stern authentication scheme [30] and related signatures, as [16] for instance, need an increase of only 25% of its block size to maintain the same security. Very few problems in public key cryptography can claim such a stability for the computational cost of their best known attacks.

References

1. Aguilar, C., Gaborit, P., Schrek, J.: A new zero-knowledge code based identification scheme with reduced communication. In: Proceedings of IEEE Information Theory Workshop- ITW 2011, pp. 648–652. IEEE (2011)
2. Banegas, G., Debris-Alazard, T., Nedeljković, M., Smith, B.: Wavelet: code-based postquantum signatures with fast verification on microcontrollers. Cryptology ePrint Archive, Report 2021/1432 (2021). https://ia.cr/2021/1432
3. Bernstein, D.J.: Grover vs. McEliece. In: Sendrier, N. (ed.) PQCrypto 2010. LNCS, vol. 6061, pp. 73–80. Springer, Heidelberg (2010). https://doi.org/10.1007/978-3-642-12929-2_6
4. Biasse, J.-F., Micheli, G., Persichetti, E., Santini, P.: LESS is more: code-based signatures without syndromes. In: Nitaj, A., Youssef, A. (eds.) AFRICACRYPT 2020. LNCS, vol. 12174, pp. 45–65. Springer, Cham (2020). https://doi.org/10.1007/978-3-030-51938-4_3
5. Both, L., May, A.: Optimizing BJMM with nearest neighbors: full decoding in $2^{2/21n}$ and McEliece security. In: WCC Workshop on Coding and Cryptography (2017). http://wcc2017.suai.ru/Proceedings_WCC2017.zip
6. Both, L., May, A.: Decoding linear codes with high error rate and its impact for LPN security. In: Lange, T., Steinwandt, R. (eds.) PQCrypto 2018. LNCS, vol. 10786, pp. 25–46. Springer, Cham (2018). https://doi.org/10.1007/978-3-319-79063-3_2
7. Bricout, R., Chailloux, A., Debris-Alazard, T., Lequesne, M.: Ternary syndrome decoding with large weight. In: Paterson, K.G., Stebila, D. (eds.) SAC 2019. LNCS, vol. 11959, pp. 437–466. Springer, Cham (2020). https://doi.org/10.1007/978-3-030-38471-5_18
8. Canto Torres, R.: Asymptotic analysis of ISD algorithms for the $q-$ary case. In: Proceedings of the Tenth International Workshop on Coding and Cryptography WCC 2017 (2017). http://wcc2017.suai.ru/Proceedings_WCC2017.zip
9. Carrier, K., Debris-Alazard, T., Meyer-Hilfiger, C., Tillich, J.: Statistical decoding 2.0: reducing decoding to LPN. In: Agrawal, S., Lin, D. (eds.) ASIACRYPT 2022. LNCS, vol. 13794, pp. 477–507. Springer, Cham (2022). https://doi.org/10.1007/978-3-031-22972-5_17

10. Chailloux, A., Debris-Alazard, T., Etinski, S.: Classical and quantum algorithms for generic syndrome decoding problems and applications to the lee metric. In: Cheon, J.H., Tillich, J.-P. (eds.) PQCrypto 2021 2021. LNCS, vol. 12841, pp. 44–62. Springer, Cham (2021). https://doi.org/10.1007/978-3-030-81293-5_3

11. Coron, J.S., Joux, A.: Cryptanalysis of a provably secure cryptographic hash function. IACR Cryptology ePrint Archive, Report 2004/013 (2004). http://eprint.iacr.org/

12. Courtois, N.T., Finiasz, M., Sendrier, N.: How to achieve a McEliece-based digital signature scheme. In: Boyd, C. (ed.) ASIACRYPT 2001. LNCS, vol. 2248, pp. 157–174. Springer, Heidelberg (2001). https://doi.org/10.1007/3-540-45682-1_10

13. Debris-Alazard, T.: Cryptographie fondée sur les codes : nouvelles approches pour constructions et preuves ; contribution en cryptanalyse. Theses, Sorbonne Université (2019). https://tel.archives-ouvertes.fr/tel-02424234

14. Debris-Alazard, T.: Code-based cryptography: Lecture notes. arXiv:2304.03541 (2023)

15. Debris-Alazard, T., Sendrier, N., Tillich, J.-P.: Wave: a new family of trapdoor one-way preimage sampleable functions based on codes. In: Galbraith, S.D., Moriai, S. (eds.) ASIACRYPT 2019. LNCS, vol. 11921, pp. 21–51. Springer, Cham (2019). https://doi.org/10.1007/978-3-030-34578-5_2

16. Feneuil, T., Joux, A., Rivain, M.: Syndrome decoding in the head: Shorter signatures from zero-knowledge proofs. In: Dodis, Y., Shrimpton, T. (eds.) CRYPTO 2022, vol. 13508, pp. 541–572. Springer, Cham (2022). https://doi.org/10.1007/978-3-031-15979-4_19

17. Fiat, A., Shamir, A.: How to prove yourself: practical solutions to identification and signature problems. In: Odlyzko, A.M. (ed.) CRYPTO 1986. LNCS, vol. 263, pp. 186–194. Springer, Heidelberg (1987). https://doi.org/10.1007/3-540-47721-7_12

18. Finiasz, M., Sendrier, N.: Security bounds for the design of code-based cryptosystems. In: Matsui, M. (ed.) ASIACRYPT 2009. LNCS, vol. 5912, pp. 88–105. Springer, Heidelberg (2009). https://doi.org/10.1007/978-3-642-10366-7_6

19. Gentry, C., Peikert, C., Vaikuntanathan, V.: Trapdoors for hard lattices and new cryptographic constructions. In: Proceedings of the Fortieth Annual ACM Symposium on Theory of Computing, pp. 197–206. ACM (2008)

20. Ishai, Y., Kushilevitz, E., Ostrovsky, R., Sahai, A.: Zero-knowledge from secure multiparty computation. In: Johnson, D.S., Feige, U. (eds.) STOC 2007, pp. 21–30. ACM (2007). https://doi.org/10.1145/1250790.1250794

21. Johansson, T., Jönsson, F.: On the complexity of some cryptographic problems based on the general decoding problem. IEEE Trans. Inform. Theory **48**(10), 2669–2678 (2002)

22. Kachigar, G., Tillich, J.-P.: Quantum information set decoding algorithms. In: Lange, T., Takagi, T. (eds.) PQCrypto 2017. LNCS, vol. 10346, pp. 69–89. Springer, Cham (2017). https://doi.org/10.1007/978-3-319-59879-6_5

23. May, A., Meurer, A., Thomae, E.: Decoding random linear codes in $\tilde{\mathcal{O}}(2^{0.054n})$. In: Lee, D.H., Wang, X. (eds.) ASIACRYPT 2011. LNCS, vol. 7073, pp. 107–124. Springer, Heidelberg (2011). https://doi.org/10.1007/978-3-642-25385-0_6

24. May, A., Ozerov, I.: On computing nearest neighbors with applications to decoding of binary linear codes. In: Oswald, E., Fischlin, M. (eds.) EUROCRYPT 2015. LNCS, vol. 9056, pp. 203–228. Springer, Heidelberg (2015). https://doi.org/10.1007/978-3-662-46800-5_9

25. Minder, L., Sinclair, A.: The extended k-tree algorithm. In: Mathieu, C. (ed.) Proceedings of SODA 2009, pp. 586–595. SIAM (2009)

26. Peters, C.: Information-set decoding for linear codes over Fq. In: Sendrier, N. (ed.) PQCrypto 2010. LNCS, vol. 6061, pp. 81–94. Springer, Heidelberg (2010). https:// doi.org/10.1007/978-3-642-12929-2_7
27. Prange, E.: The use of information sets in decoding cyclic codes. IRE Trans. Inf. Theory **8**(5), 5–9 (1962). https://doi.org/10.1109/TIT.1962.1057777
28. Sendrier, N.: Decoding one out of many. In: Yang, B.-Y. (ed.) PQCrypto 2011. LNCS, vol. 7071, pp. 51–67. Springer, Heidelberg (2011). https://doi.org/10.1007/ 978-3-642-25405-5_4
29. Stern, J.: A method for finding codewords of small weight. In: Cohen, G., Wolfmann, J. (eds.) Coding Theory 1988. LNCS, vol. 388, pp. 106–113. Springer, Heidelberg (1989). https://doi.org/10.1007/BFb0019850
30. Stern, J.: A new identification scheme based on syndrome decoding. In: Stinson, D.R. (ed.) CRYPTO 1993. LNCS, vol. 773, pp. 13–21. Springer, Heidelberg (1994). https://doi.org/10.1007/3-540-48329-2_2
31. Wagner, D.: A generalized birthday problem. In: Yung, M. (ed.) CRYPTO 2002. LNCS, vol. 2442, pp. 288–304. Springer, Heidelberg (2002). https://doi.org/10. 1007/3-540-45708-9_19

Group-Action-Based Cryptography

SPDH-Sign: Towards Efficient, Post-quantum Group-Based Signatures

Christopher Battarbee[1]([✉]), Delaram Kahrobaei[1,2,3,4], Ludovic Perret[5],
and Siamak F. Shahandashti[1]

[1] Department of Computer Science, University of York, York, UK
kit.battarbee@york.ac.uk
[2] Departments of Computer Science and Mathematics, Queens College, City
University of New York, New York, USA
[3] Initiative for the Theoretical Sciences, Graduate Center,
City University of New York, New York, USA
[4] Department of Computer Science and Engineering, Tandon School of Engineering,
New York University, New York, USA
[5] Sorbonne University, CNRS, LIP6, PolSys, Paris, France

Abstract. In this paper, we present a new diverse class of post-quantum group-based Digital Signature Schemes (DSS). The approach is significantly different from previous examples of group-based digital signatures and adopts the framework of group action-based cryptography: we show that each finite group defines a group action relative to the semidirect product of the group by its automorphism group, and give security bounds on the resulting signature scheme in terms of the group-theoretic computational problem known as the Semidirect Discrete Logarithm Problem (SDLP). Crucially, we make progress towards being able to efficiently compute the novel group action, and give an example of a parameterised family of groups for which the group action can be computed for any parameters, thereby negating the need for expensive offline computation or inclusion of redundancy required in other schemes of this type.

Keywords: Group-based Signature · Post-quantum Signature · Group Action Based Cryptography · Post-quantum Group-based Cryptography

Introduction

Since the advent of Shor's algorithm and related quantum cryptanalysis, it has been a major concern to search for quantum-resistant alternatives to traditional public-key cryptosystems. The resultant field of study is known today as Post-Quantum Cryptography (PQC), and has received significant attention since the announcement of the NIST standardisation.

One of the goals of PQC is to develop a quantum-resistant Digital Signature Scheme (DSS), a widely applicable class of cryptographic scheme providing certain authenticity guarantees. Following multiple rounds of analysis, NIST have

T. Johansson and D. Smith-Tone (Eds.): PQCrypto 2023, LNCS 14154, pp. 113–138, 2023.
https://doi.org/10.1007/978-3-031-40003-2_5

selected three such schemes for standardisation, two of which are based on the popular algebraic notion of a lattice. Nevertheless, stressing the importance of diversity amongst the post-quantum roster, a call for efficient DSS proposals not based on lattices was issued in 2022 [30]. A potential source of post-quantum hard computational problems come from group-based cryptography; for a comprehensive survey of the field including examples of DSSs, see the work of Kahrobaei et al. in [18,19].

Recall that a finite commutative group action consists of a finite abelian group G, a finite set X, and a function mapping pairs in $G \times X$ into G. Another promising framework for PQC has its origins in the so-called *Hard Homogenous Spaces* of Couveignes[1] [10]: one considers a family of group actions for which all the 'reasonable' operations - for example, evaluating the group action function, and sampling uniformly from the group - can be done efficiently, but a natural analogue of the discrete logarithm problem called the Vectorisation Problem is computationally difficult. Given such a group action, one can exploit the commutativity of the group operation to construct a generalisation of the Diffie-Hellman Key Exchange protocol based on the difficulty of the Vectorisation Problem, which is believed to be post-quantum hard.

As well as this analogue of Diffie-Hellman, the group action framework is used to construct an interactive proof of identity, which is effectively a standard three-pass identification scheme. In his doctoral thesis [36], Stolbunov uses this identification scheme to obtain a signature scheme by applying the standard Fiat-Shamir heuristic; we will here follow the convention of referring to this scheme as the CRS[2] Digital Signature Scheme (CRS-DSS). In order to specify a practical signature scheme it remains to specify a group action: very roughly, CRS-DSS uses the celebrated example, coming from the theory of isogenous elliptic curves, of a finite abelian group called the 'class group' acting on a set of elliptic curves.

CRS-DSS did not recieve much attention for a number of years, for two key reasons: first, it was demonstrated that the scheme admits an attack of quantum subexponential complexity [7] (in fact, this attack applies to all group-action based cryptography). This might in itself be tolerable; much more troubling is that the original version of CRS-DSS is unacceptably slow. There has, however, been a resurgence of interest in schemes similar to CRS-DSS following the discovery in [6] of a much faster isogeny-based group action; on the other hand, the computation of the class group is in general thought to be computationally difficult. In fact this is quite a significant problem: without random sampling the security proofs, which rely on group elements hiding secrets to have the appropriate distribution, break down. Two approaches to solving this problem have been suggested: in [12], one uses the 'Fiat-Shamir with aborts' technique developed by Lyubashevsky [22], at the cost of rendering the scheme considerably less space efficient; in [3], a state-of-the-art computation of a class group is performed and the resulting group action is used as the platform for CRS-DSS. However, it is important to note that here the computation of *a* class group is performed, and

---

[1] Similar notions were arrived at independently by Rostovstev and Stolbunov [34,35].
[2] Couveignes, Rostovstev and Stolbunov.

so one is restricted in terms of tweaking parameters. In particular, the introduction of new parameters would require another extremely expensive offline class group computation.

A potential third solution is to dispense with the isogeny-based group action altogether, and search for different examples of group actions for which computing the appropriate group - and therefore uniform sampling - is efficient. Historically speaking, there has not been much research in this direction since non-trivial examples of cryptographically interesting group actions have not been available - though this work is predated by a general framework for actions by semigroups in [27], and an example semigroup action arising from semirings in [24]. In this paper we make an important step in the search for efficient group actions; in particular we show that every finite group gives rise to a group action on which CRS-DSS-type signatures can be constructed, and that the respective group is cyclic and has order dividing a known quantity. These group actions arise from the group-theoretic notion of the semidirect product, and were first studied in the context of a generalisation of Diffie-Hellman [15] - note, however, that it was not known at the time that the proposed framework was an example of a group action. Indeed, the link was only discovered rather recently [2], and prompted the isogeny-style renaming of the key exchange in [15] as **S**emidirect **P**roduct **D**iffie-**H**ellman, or SPDH (to be pronounced 'spud'). With this in mind, in this paper we propose a hypothetical family of digital signature schemes which we christen SPDH-Sign.

It is important to note that we do not provide concrete security parameters, nor do we claim a security improvement over similar schemes: instead, the paper has two key contributions. First, we notify the community of a promising step towards efficient, scalable sampling in cryptographic group actions: our Theorem 4 shows that for each group action we construct there is quite a severe restriction on the possible sizes of the cyclic group acting. Since sampling from a cyclic group is trivial if we know its order, we have provided a large class of candidate group actions for which sampling is efficient. As such we also carry out the standard methodology of defining a resulting signature scheme, and give a security proof in the random oracle model that bounds the security of the signature scheme in terms of our central algorithmic problem in more explicit terms than comparable proofs.

The second key contribution is the proposal of a specific group as an example of a group in which one can efficiently sample in the resulting group action whilst maintaining resistance to related (but not known equivalent) cryptanalysis. Here we see an example of our Theorem 4 in action - the size of the crucial parameter needed for efficient sampling can be one of only 12 values, and we can check the validity of each of these values in logarithmic time.

Related Work

The following is a short note to emphasise the novelty of our contribution with respect to related areas of the literature.

The idea of defining cryptography based on the action of a semigroup on a set, and the resulting "semigroup action problem" (SAP), is proposed in Chris Monico's thesis [27], and is referenced by Han and Zhuang in their recent paper [16]. Certainly this idea of a semigroup action predates our establishment of a cryptographically relevant group action arising from topics in group theory. We therefore clarify that our contribution is not the novel proposal of a group action of this type, but the explicit connection between cryptographic group actions and the problems arising from semidirect product key exchange, which originally appears in [15].

In [16], SAP and the semidirect product key exchange are mentioned in the same breath in the introduction. This, however, does not constitute the explicit connection of the problem originally appearing in the discussion of semidirect product key exchange and cryptographic group actions - where this connection is one of the claimed novel aspects of our paper - but a list of problems related to the semigroup DLP. Moreover, none of the semidirect product key exchange-adjacent literature we are aware of mentions SAP, including proposals of semidirect product key exchange [15,20,31,32] and cryptanalysis of the semidirect product key exchange authored by Monico himself [25,26]. Accordingly, we believe that establishing the connection between semidirect product key exchange and group-action based cryptography is a novel contribution to the area.

1   Preliminaries

1.1   The Semidirect Product

The term 'semidirect' product refers, generally speaking, to a rather deep family of notions describing the structure of one group with respect to two other groups. For our purposes we are interested in a rather specific case of the semidirect product, defined as follows:

Definition 1. *Let G be a finite group and $Aut(G)$ its automorphism group. Suppose that the set $G \times Aut(G)$ is endowed with the following operation:*

$$(g, \phi)(g', \phi') = (\phi'(g)g', \phi'\phi)$$

where the multiplication is that of the underlying group G, and the automorphism $\phi'\phi$ is the automorphism obtained by first applying ϕ, and then ϕ'. We denote this group $G \ltimes Aut(G)$.

A few facts about this construction are standard.

Proposition 1. *Let G be a finite group and $\Phi \leq Aut(G)$ (where Φ can be any subgroup, including $Aut(G)$ itself). One has the following:*

1. *$G \ltimes \Phi$ is a finite group of size $|G||\Phi|$*
2. *Let $(g, \phi) \in G \ltimes \Phi$. One has*

$$(g, \phi)^{-1} = (\phi^{-1}(g^{-1}), \phi^{-1})$$

1.2   Proofs of Knowledge and Identification Schemes

Roughly speaking, the idea of the Fiat-Shamir class of signatures is as follows: we interactively convince an 'honest' party that we possess a certain secret. We can then transform this interactive paradigm to a non-interactive digital signature scheme by applying the Fiat-Shamir transform. A primary motivation for this approach is that the resulting signature scheme inherits its security at rather low cost from security properties of the underlying interactive scheme - as such, it is necessary for us now to review some of these security notions.

First, let us define exactly what we mean by these interactive proof of knowledge protocols. The idea of communicating a 'secret' is neatly captured by the notion of a binary relation; that is, for two sets W and S, consider a set $\mathcal{R} \subset W \times S$. Given a pair $(w, s) \in \mathcal{R}$, we say s is the *statement* and w is the *witness*. In general, for a given statement a party called the 'prover' wishes to demonstrate their knowledge of a valid witness (that is, given s we wish to prove that we possess a w such that $(w, s) \in \mathcal{R}$) to a party called the *verifier*. Of course, one can do this trivially by simply revealing the witness, so we add the crucial requirement that *no information about the witness is revealed.*

We refer more or less to this idea when discussing identification schemes, with the caveat that the prover should be able to compute an arbitrary pair of the binary relation. If the prover cannot generate an arbitrary pair of the binary relation, and instead is to demonstrate his knowledge of some given element of the binary relation, we have instead a 'zero-knowledge proof'. A notable class of zero-knowledge proofs are the so-called 'sigma protocols'. One can always turn a zero-knowledge proof into an identification scheme by providing the prover with an algorithm capable of generating an arbitrary pair of the binary relation; our definition of identification schemes in fact refers only to those arrived at by transforming a sigma protocol into an identification scheme.

Notice that the idea of a binary relation serves as a neat generalisation of the usual notion of a public and private key pair. The algorithm used by the identification scheme to generate binary relation instances is therefore denoted by KeyGen, and produces a pair (sk, pk). We also require, in some sense to be made precise later, that recovering an appropriate witness from a statement is computationally difficult.

Definition 2 (Identification Scheme). *Let $\mathcal{R} \subset S \times P$ be a binary relation. An identification scheme is a triple of algorithms (KeyGen, P, V), where*

- KeyGen *takes as input a security parameter n and generates a pair $(sk, pk) \in \mathcal{R}$, publishes pk, and passes sk to* P
- P *is an interactive algorithm initialised with a pair $(sk, pk) \in \mathcal{R}$*
- V *is an interactive algorithm initialised with a statement $pk \in P$. After the interaction,* V *outputs a decision 'Accept' or 'Reject'.*

The interaction of P *and* V *runs as follows:*

1. P *generates a random 'commitment' I from the space of all possible commitments $\mathcal{I}$ and sends it to* V

2. *Upon receipt of I,* V *chooses a 'challenge' c from the space of all possible challenges C at random and sends it to* P
3. P *responds with a 'response' p*
4. V *calculates an 'Accept' or 'Reject' response as a function of* (I, c, p) *and the statement pk.*

The interaction of P *and* V *is depicted in Fig. 1.*

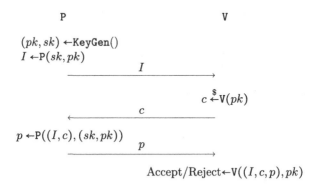

Fig. 1. An identification scheme.

Definition 3. *Let (*KeyGen, P, V*) be an identification scheme. The triple* (I, c, p) *of exchanged values between* P *and* V *is called a 'transcript'; if a prover (resp. verifier) generates* I, p *(resp c) with the algorithm* P *(resp.* V*), they are called 'honest'. An identification scheme is 'complete' if a transcript generated by two honest parties is always accepted by the verifier.*

Turning our attention to the security of identification protocols, let us define the framework we wish to work with. As we will see later, it suffices for signature security to only consider identification schemes for which we have an honest verifier - in other words, it suffices to consider only a cheating prover. Let us do so in the form of the following attack games, which are [4, Attack Game 18.1] and [4, Attack Game 18.2] respectively.

Definition 4 (Direct Attack Game). *Let* ID = *(*KeyGen, P, V*) be an identification scheme and* $\mathcal{A}$ *be an adversary. Consider the following game:*

1. *The challenger obtains* (sk, pk)←KeyGen *and passes pk to* $\mathcal{A}$*.*
2. *The adversary interacts with the challenger who generates responses with* V*. At the end, the challenger outputs 'Accept/Reject' as a function of the generated transcript and pk; the adversary wins the game if* V *outputs 'Accept'.*

The Direct Attack game is depicted in Fig. 2. We denote the advantage of the adversary in this game with ID *as the challenger by* dir-adv$(\mathcal{A}, ID)$*.*

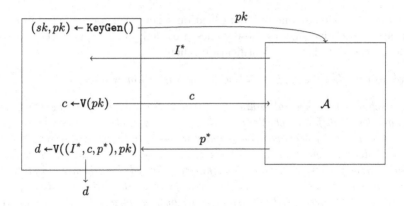

Fig. 2. The direct attack game.

Definition 5 (Eavesdropping Attack). *Let* ID = *(*KeyGen, P, V*) be an identification scheme and* $\mathcal{A}$ *be an adversary. Consider the following game:*

1. *The challenger obtains* (sk, pk)←KeyGen *and passes* pk *to* $\mathcal{A}$.
2. *The adversary enters into an 'eavesdropping' phase, whereby they can request honestly-generated transcripts from a transcript oracle* $\mathcal{T}$ *possessing the same* (sk, pk) *pair generated in the previous step.*
3. *The adversary interacts with the challenger who generates responses with* V. *At the end, the challenger outputs 'Accept/Reject' as a function of the generated transcript and* pk; *the adversary wins the game if* V *outputs 'Accept'.*

The Eavesdropping Attack game is depicted in Fig. 3. We denote the advantage of the adversary in this game with ID *as the challenger by* eav-adv*(*$\mathcal{A}$,ID*).*

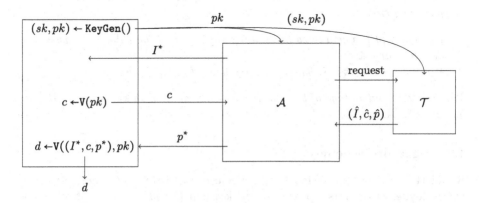

Fig. 3. The eavesdropping attack game.

In practice, given a concrete identification scheme it is possible to bound the advantage of an adversary in these games provided one can prove the following two properties hold for the identification scheme:

Definition 6. *Let (*KeyGen*, P, V) be an identification scheme.*

- *The scheme has 'special soundness' if two transcripts with the same commitment and different challenges allow recovery of the witness sk; that is, if $(I, c, p), (I, c^*, p^*)$ are two transcripts generated with $(sk, pk) \leftarrow$ KeyGen, there is an efficient algorithm taking these transcripts as input that returns sk.*
- *The scheme has 'special honest verifier zero knowledge' if, given a statement pk and a challenge c, there is an efficient algorithm to generate a passing transcript (I^*, c, p^*) with the same distribution as a legitimately generated transcript.*

Before moving on there is one final security notion to explore. Notice that if the underlying binary relation of an identification scheme is such that one can easily recover a valid witness from the public statement, an adversary can easily succeed in either of the above games simply by honestly generating the proof p with the appropriate value of sk. We have loosely discussed the notion that recovering a witness should therefore be difficult; it is nevertheless so far not clear how precisely this difficulty is accounted for. In fact, there are a number of ways to get round this. For our purposes, and in our application of the Fiat-Shamir transform, we will invoke the system outlined in [4, Section 19.6]. The idea is basically thus: provided the properties in Definition 6 hold, it is possible to set up the security proof such that all the difficulty of recovering a witness is 'priced in' to the key generation algorithm. Again, we will need a precise definition to make this rigorous later on: the following is [4, Attack Game 19.2]

Definition 7 (Inversion Attack Game). *Let* KeyGen *be a key generation algorithm for a binary relation $\mathcal{R} \subset \mathcal{S} \times \mathcal{P}$ and $\mathcal{A}$ be an adversary. Consider the following game:*

1. *A pair (sk, pk) is generated by running* KeyGen*, and the value pk is passed to the adversary $\mathcal{A}$.*
2. *$\mathcal{A}$ outputs some $\hat{sk} \in \mathcal{S}$. The adversary wins if $(\hat{sk}, pk) \in \mathcal{R}$.*

We denote the advantage of the adversary in this game with kg *as the challenger by* inv-adv*($\mathcal{A}$,kg).*

1.3   Signature Schemes

Recall that a 'signature scheme' is a triple of algorithms (KeyGen, Sg, Vf), where KeyGen() outputs a private-public key pair (sk, pk) upon input of a security parameter. For some space of messages $\mathcal{M}$, Sg takes as input sk and some $m \in \mathcal{M}$, producing a 'signature' σ. Vf takes as input pk and a pair (m, σ), and outputs either 'Accept' or 'Reject'. We have the obvious correctness requirement that for a key pair (sk, pk) generated by KeyGen we can expect, for any $m \in \mathcal{M}$, that one has

$$\text{Vf}(pk, (m, \text{Sg}(sk, m))) = \text{Accept}$$

The security of a signature scheme is defined with respect to the following attack game, which is [4, Attack Game 13.1] (but is widely available).

Definition 8 (Chosen Message Attack). *Let* S = *(KeyGen, Sg, Vf) be a signature scheme and* $\mathcal{A}$ *be an adversary. Consider the following game:*

1. *The challenger obtains* $(sk, pk) \leftarrow$ KeyGen *and passes pk to* $\mathcal{A}$.
2. *The adversary enters into an 'querying' phase, whereby they can obtain signatures* $\sigma_i = \text{Sg}(sk, m_i)$ *from the challenger, for the adversary's choice of message* m_i. *The total number of messages queried is denoted* Q.
3. *The adversary submits their attempted forgery - a message-signature pair* (m^*, σ^*) *- to the challenger. The challenger outputs* $\text{Vf}(pk, (m^*, \sigma^*))$; *the adversary wins if this output is 'Accept'.*

The Chosen Message Attack game is depicted in Fig. 4. We denote the advantage of the adversary in this game with S *as the challenger by* cma-adv*($\mathcal{A}$,S).*

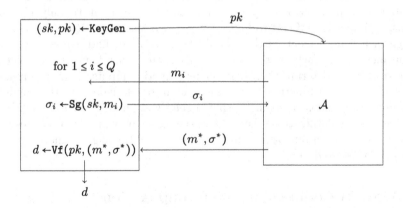

Fig. 4. The chosen message attack game.

A signature scheme S for which **cma-adv**($\mathcal{A}$,S) is bounded favourably[3] from above for any efficient adversary $\mathcal{A}$ is sometimes called **euf-cma** secure, or 'existentially unforgeable under chosen message attacks'.

It remains to briefly define the well-known notion of the Fiat-Shamir transform, initially presented in [14]:

Definition 9 (Fiat-Shamir). *Let* ID = *(KeyGen, P, V) be an identity scheme with commitment space* $\mathcal{I}$ *and* $\mathcal{C}$. *We define a signature scheme* FS*(ID)* = *(KeyGen, Sg, Vf) on the message space* $\mathcal{M}$ *given access to a public function* $H : \mathcal{M} \times \mathcal{I} \rightarrow \mathcal{C}$:

---

[3] 'Favourably' here usually means as a negligible function of a security parameter.

1. KeyGen *is exactly the key generation algorithm of* ID *and outputs a pair* (sk, pk), *where pk is made public*
2. Sg *takes as input* $m \in \mathcal{M}$ *and the key pair* (pk, sk) *and outputs a signature* (σ_1, σ_2):

$$I \leftarrow P((sk, pk))$$
$$c \leftarrow H(m, I)$$
$$p \leftarrow P((I, c), (sk, pk))$$
$$(\sigma_1, \sigma_2) \leftarrow (I, p)$$
$$\textbf{return } (\sigma_1, \sigma_2)$$

3. Vf *takes as input a message-signature pair* $(m, (\sigma_1, \sigma_2))$ *and outputs a decision* d, *which is 'Accept' or 'Reject'*:

$$c \leftarrow H(I, \sigma_1)$$
$$d \leftarrow V((\sigma_1, c, \sigma_2), pk)$$
$$\textbf{return } d$$

Intuitively, we can see that Sg is simulating an interactive protocol non-interactively with a call to the function H; in order to inherit the security properties of the identification scheme, this function H should have randomly distributed outputs on fresh queries and should be computationally binding - that is, it should be difficult to find a value $I' \neq I$ such that $H(m, I) = H(m, I')$; and given a commitment $c \in \mathcal{C}$ it should be difficult to find a message m and commitment $I \in \mathcal{I}$ such that $H(m, I) = c$. On the other hand, for correctness we need H to be deterministic on previously queried inputs. Such a function is modelled by a hash function under the random oracle model: in this model, it was famously demonstrated in [1] that a relatively modest security notion for the underlying identification scheme gives strong security proofs for the resulting signature scheme. In our own security proof we use the slightly more textbook exposition presented in [4].

2   A Novel Connection to a Group Action

Our first task is to demonstrate the existence of the claimed group action, for any finite group. A very similar structure was outlined in [2] - with the important distinction that *semi*groups are insisted upon. Indeed, it turns out that allowing invertibility changes the structure in a way that we shall outline below.

Definition 10. *Let* G *be a finite group, and* $\Phi \leq Aut(G)$. *Fix some* $(g, \phi) \in G \rtimes \Phi$. *For any* $x \in \mathbb{Z}$, *the function* $s_{g,\phi} : \mathbb{Z} \to G$ *is defined as the group element such that*

$$(g, \phi)^x = (s_{g,\phi}(x), \phi^x)$$

The group action of interest arises from the study of the set $\{s_{g,\phi}(i) : i \in \mathbb{Z}\}$. Certainly $1 \in \{s_{g,\phi}(i) : i \in \mathbb{Z}\}$, since there is some $n \in \mathbb{N}$ such that $(s_{g,\phi}(n), \phi^n) = (g, \phi)^n = (1, id)$, but one cannot immediately deduce that this is the smallest integer for which $s_{g,\phi}$ is 1. Indeed, even if the order n of (g,ϕ) is the smallest integer such that $s_{g,\phi}(n)=1$, we are not necessarily guaranteed that every integer up to n is mapped to a distinct elements of G by $s_{g,\phi}$. Before resolving these questions let us introduce some terminology.

Definition 11. *Let G be a finite group, and $\Phi \leq Aut(G)$. Fix some $(g,\phi) \in G \ltimes \Phi$. The set*

$$\mathcal{X}_{g,\phi} := \{s_{g,\phi}(i) : i \in \mathbb{Z}\}$$

is called the cycle of (g,ϕ), and its size is called the period of (g,ϕ).

In the interest of brevity we will also assume henceforth that by (g,ϕ) we mean some pair occurring in a semidirect product group as described above. For any such pair (g,ϕ), note that $\mathcal{X}_{g,\phi}$ is not necessarily closed under the group operation - we can, nevertheless, implement addition in the argument of $s_{g,\phi}$ as follows:

Theorem 1. *Let $i,j \in \mathbb{Z}$ and suppose $(g,\phi) \in G \ltimes \Phi$ in the usual way. One has that*

$$\phi^j(s_{g,\phi}(i))s_{g,\phi}(j) = s_{g,\phi}(i+j)$$

Proof. Following the definitions one has

$$\begin{aligned}
(s_{g,\phi}(i+j), \phi^{i+j}) &= (g,\phi)^{i+j} \\
&= (g,\phi)^i (g,\phi)^j \\
&= (s_{g,\phi}(i), \phi^i)(s_{g,\phi}(j), \phi^j) \\
&= (\phi^j(s_{g,\phi}(i))s_{g,\phi}(j), \phi^{i+j})
\end{aligned}$$
$\square$

Put another way, we can use integers to map $\mathcal{X}_{g,\phi}$ to itself. This idea is sufficiently important to earn its own notation:

Definition 12. *Let $i \in \mathbb{Z}$. The function $* : \mathbb{Z} \times \mathcal{X}_{g,\phi} \to \mathcal{X}_{g,\phi}$ is given by*

$$i * s_{g,\phi}(j) := \phi^j(s_{g,\phi}(i))s_{g,\phi}(j)$$

We have seen that $i * s_{g,\phi}(j) = s_{g,\phi}(i+j)$; accordingly, we pronounce the $*$ symbol as 'step'. An immediate consequence is the presence of some degree of 'looping' behaviour; that is, supposing $s_{g,\phi}(n) = 1$ for some $n \in \mathbb{Z}$, one has

$$\begin{aligned}
s_{g,\phi}(n+1) = 1 * s_{g,\phi}(n) &= 1 * 1 \\
&= \phi(1)s_{g,\phi}(1) \\
&= s_{g,\phi}(1)
\end{aligned}$$

Generalising this idea we get a more complete picture of the structure of the cycle.

Theorem 2. *Let G be a finite group and $\Phi \leq Aut(G)$ an automorphism subgroup. Fix $(g,\phi) \in G \ltimes Aut(G)$, and let n be the smallest positive integer for which $s_{g,\phi}(n) = 1$. One has that $|\mathcal{X}_{g,\phi}| = n$, and*

$$\mathcal{X}_{g,\phi} = \{1, g, ..., s_{g,\phi}(n-1)\}$$

Proof. First, let us demonstrate that the values $1 = s_{g,\phi}(0), s_{g,\phi}(1), ..., s_{g,\phi}(n-1)$ are all distinct. Suppose to the contrary that there exists $0 \leq i < j \leq n-1$ such that $s_{g,\phi}(i) = s_{g,\phi}(j)$; then some positive $k < n$ must be such that $i + k = j$. In other words:

$$i * s_{g,\phi}(k) = s_{g,\phi}(j) \Rightarrow \phi^i(s_{g,\phi}(k))s_{g,\phi}(i) = s_{g,\phi}(j)$$
$$\Rightarrow \phi^i(s_{g,\phi}(k)) = 1$$
$$\Rightarrow s_{g,\phi}(k) = 1$$

which is a contradiction, since $k < n$. It remains to show that every integer is mapped by $s_{g,\phi}$ to one of these n distinct values - but this is trivial, since we can write any integer i as $kn + j$ for some integer k and $0 \leq j < n$. It follows that

$$s_{g,\phi}(i) = s_{g,\phi}(j)$$

where $s_{g,\phi}(j)$ is one of the n distinct values.   □

It follows that we can write $i * s_{g,\phi}(j) = s_{g,\phi}(i + j \mod n)$. In fact, the latter part of the above argument demonstrates something slightly stronger: not only is every integer mapped to one of n distinct values by $s_{g,\phi}$, but every member of a distinct residue class modulo n is mapped to the *same* distinct value. It is this basic idea that gives us our group action.

Theorem 3. *Let G be a finite group and $\Phi \leq Aut(G)$. Fix a pair $(g, \phi) \in G \times Aut(G)$, and let n be the smallest positive integer such that $s_{g,\phi}(n) = 1$. Define the function as*

$$\circledast: \quad \mathbb{Z}_n \times \mathcal{X}_{g,\phi} \to \mathcal{X}_{g,\phi}$$
$$[i]_n \circledast s_{g,\phi}(j) = i * s_{g,\phi}(j)$$

The tuple $(\mathbb{Z}_n, \mathcal{X}_{g,\phi}, \circledast)$ is a free, transitive group action.

Proof. First, let us see that $\circledast$ is well-defined. Suppose $i \cong j \mod n$, then $i = j + kn$ for some $k \in \mathbb{Z}$. For some arbitrary $\mathcal{X}_{g,\phi}$, say $s_{g,\phi}(l)$ for $0 \leq l < n$, one has

$$i * s_{g,\phi}(l) = (j + kn) * s_{g,\phi}(l)$$
$$= j * s_{g,\phi}(l + kn)$$
$$= j * s_{g,\phi}(l)$$

We also need to verify that the claimed tuple is indeed a group action. In order to check that the identity in $\mathbb{Z}_n$ fixes each $\mathcal{X}_{g,\phi}$, by the well-definedness just demonstrated, it suffices to check that $0 * s_{g,\phi}(l) = s_{g,\phi}(l)$ for each $0 \leq l < n$ - which indeed is the case. For the compatibility of the action with modular addition, note that for $0 \leq i, j, k < n-1$ one has

$$[k]_n \circledast ([j]_n \circledast s_{g,\phi}(i)) = [k]_n \circledast s_{g,\phi}(i + j \mod n)$$
$$= s_{g,\phi}(i + j + k \mod n)$$
$$= [j + k]_n \circledast s_{g,\phi}(i)$$

as required. It remains to check that the action is free and transitive. First, suppose $[i]_n \in \mathbb{Z}_n$ fixes each $s_{g,\phi}(j) \in \mathcal{X}_{g,\phi}$. By the above we can assume without loss of generality that $0 \leq i < n-1$, and we have $\phi^j(s_{g,\phi}(i))s_{g,\phi}(j) = s_{g,\phi}(j)$. It follows that $s_{g,\phi}(i) = 1$, so we must have $i = 0$ as required. For transitivity, for any pair $s_{g,\phi}(i), s_{g,\phi}(j)$ we have $[j-i]_n \circledast s_{g,\phi}(i) = s_{g,\phi}(j)$, and we are done. $\square$

Recalling that the set $\mathcal{X}_{g,\phi}$ and the period n are a function of the pair (g, ϕ), we have actually shown the existence of a large family of group actions. Nevertheless, we have only really shown the existence of the crucial parameter n - it is not necessarily clear how this value should be calculated. With this in mind let us conclude the section with a step in this direction:

Theorem 4. *Fix a pair $(g, \phi) \in G \ltimes Aut(G)$. Let n be the smallest integer such that $s_{g,\phi}(n) = 1$, then n divides the order of the pair (g, ϕ) as a group element in $G \ltimes Aut(G)$.*

Proof. Suppose $m = ord((g, \phi))$. Certainly $s_{g,\phi}(m) = 1$, and by definition one has $m \geq n$. We can therefore write $m = kn + l$, for $k \in \mathbb{N}$ and $0 \leq l < n$. It is not too difficult to verify that $s_{g,\phi}(x) = \phi^{x-1}(g)...\phi(g)g$ for any $x \in \mathbb{N}$. It follows that

$$s_{g,\phi}(m) = \phi^{kn}(s_{g,\phi}(l))\phi^{(k-1)n}(s_{g,\phi}(n))...\phi^n(s_{g,\phi}(n))s_{g,\phi}(n)$$

Since $s_{g,\phi}(m) = s_{g,\phi}(n) = 1$, we must have $s_{g,\phi}(l) = 1$. But $l < n$ and so $l = 0$ by the minimality of n, which in turn implies that $n|m$ as required. $\square$

2.1 Semidirect Discrete Logarithm Problem

Given a group G and a pair $(g, \phi) \in G \ltimes Aut(G)$, observe that as a consequence of Theorem 1 and Definition 12, for any two integers $i, j \in \mathbb{N}$ we have that $s_{g,\phi}(i + j) = j * s_{g,\phi}(i) = i * s_{g,\phi}(j)$. A Diffie-Hellman style key exchange immediately follows[4]; indeed, a key exchange based on this idea first appears in [15], and is known as Semidirect Product Key Exchange. In the same way that the security of Diffie-Hellman key exchange is related to the security of the Discrete Logarithm Problem, to understand the security of Semidirect Product Key Exchange we should like to study the difficulty of the following task:

Definition 13 (Semidirect Discrete Logarithm Problem). *Let G be a finite group, and let $(g, \phi) \in G \times Aut(G)$. Suppose, for some $x \in \mathbb{N}$, that one is given $(g, \phi), s_{g,\phi}(x)$; the Semidirect Discrete Logarithm Problem (SDLP) with respect to (g, ϕ) is to recover the integer x.*

The complexity of SDLP is relatively well understood, in large part due to the connection with group actions highlighted above. We will see later on that the security game advantages for our identification and signature schemes can

---

[4] Historically speaking, the key exchange predates the more abstract treatment in this paper.

be bounded in terms of the advantage of an adversary in solving SDLP; indeed, for the SDLP attack game defined in the obvious way, we write the advantage of an adversary $\texttt{sdlp-adv}(\mathcal{A},(g,\phi))$.

Before we move on to study the signature schemes resulting from each group action we note that the convention in the area is to restrict a finite group G to be a finite, *non-abelian* group G. This was in part to preclude a trivial attack on the related key exchange for a specific choice of ϕ - nevertheless, throughout the rest of the paper we adopt this convention.

3   SPDH-Sign

3.1   An Identification Scheme

Recall that our strategy is to set up an honest-verifier identification scheme, to which we can apply the well-known Fiat-Shamir heuristic and obtain strong security guarantees in the ROM. The central idea of this identification scheme is as follows: suppose we wish to prove knowledge of some secret $\mathbb{Z}_n$ element, say $[s]_n$. We can select an arbitrary element of $\mathcal{X}_{g,\phi}$, say X_0, and publish the pair $X_0, X_1 := [s]_n \otimes X_0$. An honest party wishing to verify our knowledge of the secret $[s]_n$ might invite us to commit to some group element $[t]_n$, for $[t]_n$ sampled uniformly at random from $\mathbb{Z}_n$. We can do this by sending the element $I = [t]_n \otimes X_0$ - note that as a consequence of the free and transitive properties, $[t]_n$ is the unique group element such that $I = [t]_n \otimes X_0$. However, with our knowledge of the secret $[s]_n$ and the commitment $[t]_n$, we can calculate the element $[p]_n = [t-s]_n$ such that $[p]_n \otimes X_1 = I$, where this equation holds by the group action axioms: one has $[t-s]_n \otimes ([s]_n \otimes X_0) = [t]_n \otimes X_0 = I$.

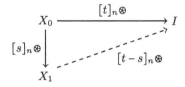

Fig. 5. Paths to the commitment.

Interpreted graph-theoretically (as depicted in Fig. 5), an honest verifier can ask to see one of two paths to the commitment value. Consider a dishonest party attempting to convince the verifier that they possess the secret $[s]_n$. In attempting to impersonate the honest prover, our dishonest party can generate their own value of $[t]_n$, and so can certainly provide the correct path in one of the two scenarios. Assuming, however, that recovering the appropriate group element is difficult, without knowledge of the secret $[s]_n$ this party succeeds in their deception with low probability.

This intuition gives us the following non-rigorous argument of security in the framework described in Sect. 1.2. First, recall that we are in the honest verifier scenario, and so a challenge bit c will be 0 with probability $1/2$, in which case a cheating prover succeeds with probability 1. Supposing that ε is the probability of successfully recovering the value $[t-s]_n$, it follows that a cheating prover succeeds with probability $(1+\varepsilon)/2$ - that is, with probability larger than $1/2$. We can quite easily counter this by requiring that N instances are run at the same time. In this case, if N zeroes are selected the prover wins with probability 1 by revealing their dishonestly generated values of $[t]_n$ - otherwise, they are required to recover at least 1 value of $[t-s]_n$. Assuming for simplicity that the probability of doing so remains consistent regardless of the number of times such a value is to be recovered, since the honest verifier selects their challenges uniformly at random the cheating prover succeeds with probability

$$\frac{1}{2^N} + \sum_{i=1}^{2^N-1} \frac{\varepsilon}{2^N} = \frac{1}{2^N} + \varepsilon \frac{2^N-1}{2^N}$$

which tends to ε as $N \to \infty$.

The actual proof of security operates within the security games defined in the preliminaries. As a step towards this formalisation, we need to specify the binary relation our identification scheme is based on. Choose some finite non-abelian group G: given a fixed pair $(g, \phi) \in G \times Aut(G)$ we are interested, by Theorem 3, in a subset $\mathcal{R}$ of $\mathbb{Z}_n, \mathcal{X}_{g,\phi}$, where n is the smallest integer such that $s_{g,\phi}(n) = 1$. In fact, legislating for N parallel executions of the proof of knowledge, to each tuple $(X_1, ..., X_N)$ is associated a binary relation

$$\mathcal{R} \subset \mathbb{Z}_n^N \times \mathcal{X}_{g,\phi}^N$$

where $(([s_1]_n, ..., [s_N]_n), (Y_1, ..., Y_N)) \in \mathcal{R}$ exactly when $(Y_1, ..., Y_N) = ([s_1]_n * X_1, ..., [s_N]_n * X_N)$.

With all this in mind let us define our identification scheme. The more rigorous presentation should not distract from the intuition that we describe N parallel executions of the game in Fig. 5.

Protocol 1. Let G be a finite non-abelian group and $(g, \phi) \in G \ltimes Aut(G)$. Suppose also that $n \in \mathbb{N}$ is the smallest integer such that $s_{g,\phi}(n) = 1$. The identification scheme SPDH-ID$_{g,\phi}(N)$ is a triple of algorithms

$$(\text{KeyGen}_{g,\phi}, \text{P}_{g,\phi}, \text{V}_{g,\phi})$$

such that

1. KeyGen$_{g,\phi}$ takes as input some $N \in \mathbb{N}$.

   $(X_1, ..., X_N) \leftarrow \mathcal{X}_{g,\phi}^N$
   $([s_1]_n, ..., [s_N]_n) \leftarrow \mathbb{Z}_n^N$
   $(Y_1, ..., Y_N) \leftarrow ([s_1]_n \circledast X_1, ..., [s_N]_n \circledast X_N)$

   KeyGen$_{g,\phi}$ outputs the public key $((X_1, ..., X_N), (Y_1, ..., Y_N))$ and passes the secret key $([s_1]_n, ..., [s_N]_n)$ to the prover $\text{P}_{g,\phi}$. The public key and the value of N used is published.

2. $\text{P}_{g,\phi}$ and $\text{V}_{g,\phi}$ are interactive algorithms that work as depicted in Fig. 6:

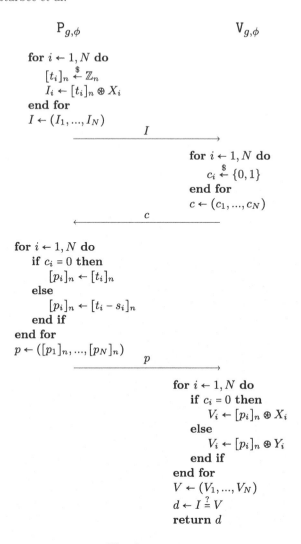

Fig. 6. SPDH-ID

Security. In this section we demonstrate that SPDH-ID is secure against eavesdropping attacks in the following sense: the advantage of an adversary in the eavesdropping attack game can be bounded by that of the adversary in the SDLP game. First, let us check that the desirable properties of an identification scheme hold:

Theorem 5. SPDH-ID *has the following properties:*

1. *Completeness*
2. *Special soundness*
3. *Special honest-verifier zero knowledge.*

Proof. Note that in order to prove each of these properties on the N-tuples comprising the transcripts generated by SPDH-ID, we need to prove that the properties hold for each component of the tuple; but since each component is independent of all the others, it suffices to demonstrate the stated properties for a single arbitrary component. In other words, we show that the stated properties hold when $N = 1$, and the general case immediately follows.

1. If $b = 0$ then $[p]_n = [t]_n$, and trivially we are done. If $b = 1$ then $[p]_n = [t-s]_n$; doing the bookkeeping we get that

$$\begin{aligned}
[p]_n \otimes S_1 &= [p]_n \otimes ([s]_n \otimes S_0) \\
&= ([t-s]_n [s]_n) \otimes S_0 \\
&= ([s]_n \otimes S_0) = I
\end{aligned}$$

2. Two passing transcripts with the same commitment are $(I, 0, [t]_n)$ and $(I, 1, [t-s]_n)$. Labelling the two responses x^{p_1}, x^{p_2}, we recover the secret as $(x^{p_2})^{-1}(x^{p_1})$.

3. It suffices to show that one can produce passing transcripts with the same distribution as legitimate transcripts, but without knowledge of $[s]_n$. We have already discussed how to produce these transcripts; if a simulator samples $[t]_n$ uniformly at random, then the transcript $([t]_n \otimes S_b, b, [t]_n)$ is valid regardless of the value of b. Moreover, if $b = 0$, trivially the transcripts have the same distribution; if $b=1$, since $[s]_n$ is fixed and $[t]_n$ is sampled uniformly at random, the distribution of a legitimate passing transcript is also uniformly random. □

We are now ready to bound on the security of our identification scheme.

Theorem 6. *Let G be a finite abelian group and let $(g, \phi) \in G \ltimes Aut(G)$. For some $N \in \mathbb{N}$, consider the identification scheme $\text{SPDH-ID}_{g,\phi}(N)$ and an efficient adversary $\mathcal{A}$. There exists an efficient adversary $\mathcal{B}$ with $\mathcal{A}$ as a subroutine, such that with $\varepsilon = \text{sdlp-adv}(\mathcal{B}, (g, \phi))$, we have*

$$\text{eav-adv}(\mathcal{A}, \text{SPDH-ID}_{g,\phi}(N)) \leq \sqrt{\varepsilon} + \frac{1}{2^N}$$

Proof. This is just a straightforward application of two results in [4]. By [4, Theorem 19.14], since $\text{SPDH-ID}_{g,\phi}(N)$ has honest verifier zero knowledge, there exists an efficient adversary $\mathcal{B}'$ with $\mathcal{A}$ as a subroutine such that

$$\text{eav-adv}(\mathcal{A}, \text{SPDH-ID}_{g,\phi}(N)) = \text{dir-adv}(\mathcal{B}', \text{SPDH-ID}_{g,\phi}(N))$$

Moreover, let

$$\delta = \text{inv-adv}(\mathcal{B}', \text{KeyGen}_{g,\phi})$$

Since SPDH-ID$_{g,\phi}(N)$ has special soundness, [4, Theorem 19.13] gives

$$\texttt{dir-adv}(\mathcal{B}, \texttt{SPDH-ID}_{g,\phi}(N)) \leq \sqrt{\delta} + \frac{1}{M}$$

where M is the size of the challenge space. It is easy to see that $M = 2^N$; it remains to relate the quantities ε and δ. We do so eschewing some of the detail since the argument is straightforward; note that by definition of the binary relation underpinning KeyGen$_{g,\phi}$, we can think of the inversion attack game as a security game in which one solves N independent SDLP instances in parallel. Call the advantage in this game N-sdlp-adv$(\mathcal{B}', (g, \phi))$, and suppose an adversary $\mathcal{B}$ in the standard SDLP attack game runs $\mathcal{B}'$ as an adversary. $\mathcal{B}$ can simply provide $\mathcal{B}'$ with N copies of its challenge SDLP instance, and succeeds whenever $\mathcal{B}'$ does. It follows that $\delta \leq \varepsilon$, and we are done.   □

3.2   A Digital Signature Scheme

It remains now to apply the Fiat-Shamir transform to our identification scheme. Doing so yields the signature scheme claimed in the title of this paper.

Protocol 2 (SPDH-Sign). Let G be a finite non-abelian group and let $(g, \phi) \in G \times Aut(G)$ be such that n is the smallest integer for which $s_{g,\phi}(n) = 1$. For any $N \in \mathbb{N}$ and message space $\mathcal{M}$, suppose we are provided a hash function $H : \mathcal{X}_{g,\phi}^N \times \mathcal{M} \to \{0,1\}^N$. We define the signature scheme

$$\texttt{SPDH-Sign}_{g,\phi}(N) = (\texttt{KeyGen}, \texttt{Sg}, \texttt{Vf})$$

as in Fig. 7.

It is easy to see that given the identification scheme SPDH-ID$_{g,\phi}(N)$, the signature scheme SPDH-Sign$_{g,\phi}(N)$ is exactly FS(SPDH-ID$_{g,\phi}(N)$). Before we can use this fact to prove the security of the signature, we require that the hash function gives outputs distributed at 'random', in some sense. This is accounted for by the 'Random Oracle Model': every time we wish to compute the hash function H, we suppose that an oracle function of the appropriate dimension selected at random is queried. Any party can query the random oracle at any time, and the number of these queries is kept track of. We also note that we do not in this paper account for the quantum-accessible random oracle model required for post-quantum security - equivalent security proofs in the quantum-accessible random oracle model are provided, for example, in [3].

With this heuristic in place we can prove the security of our signature scheme relative to SDLP with a simple application of [4, Theorem 19.15] and its corollaries:

Theorem 7. *Let G be a finite non-abelian group; $(g, \phi) \in G \ltimes Aut(G)$; and $n \in \mathbb{N}$ be the smallest integer such that $s_{g,\phi}(n) = 1$. Consider the chosen message attack game in the random oracle model, where Q_s is the number of signing queries made and Q_{ro} is the number of random oracle queries. For any efficient*

KeyGen(N):
  for $i \leftarrow 1, N$ do
    $X_i \overset{\$}{\leftarrow} \mathcal{X}_{g,\phi}$
    $[s_i]_n \overset{\$}{\leftarrow} \mathbb{Z}_n$
    $Y_i \leftarrow [s_i]_n \circledast X_i$
  end for
  $sk \leftarrow ([s_1]_n, ..., [s_N]_n)$
  $pk \leftarrow ((X_1, ..., X_N), (Y_1, ..., Y_N))$
  return (sk, pk)

Sg(m, (sk, pk)):
  for $i \leftarrow 1, N$ do
    $[t_i]_n \overset{\$}{\leftarrow} \mathbb{Z}_n$
    $I_i \leftarrow [t_i]_n \circledast X_i$
  end for
  $I \leftarrow (I_1, ..., I_N)$
  $c \leftarrow H(I, m)$
  for $i \leftarrow 1, N$ do
    if $c_i = 0$ then
      $p_i \leftarrow [t_i]_n$
    else
      $p_i \leftarrow [t_i - s_i]_n$
    end if
  end for
  $p \leftarrow (p_1, ..., p_N)$
  $(\sigma_1, \sigma_2) \leftarrow (I, p)$
  return (σ_1, σ_2)

Vf(m, (σ_1, σ_2), pk):
  $c \leftarrow H(\sigma_1, m)$
  for $i \leftarrow 1, N$ do
    if $c_i = 0$ then
      $V_i \leftarrow p_i \circledast X_i$
    else
      $V_i \leftarrow p_i \circledast Y_i$
    end if
  end for
  $V \leftarrow (V_1, ..., V_N)$
  $d \leftarrow V \overset{?}{=} I$
  return d

Fig. 7. SPDH-Sign

adversary $\mathcal{A}$ and $N \in \mathbb{N}$, there exists an efficient adversary $\mathcal{B}$ running $\mathcal{A}$ as a subroutine such that the signature scheme SPDH-Sign$_{g,\phi}(N)$ has

$$\delta \le \frac{Q_s}{n}(Q_s + Q_{ro} + 1) + \frac{Q_{ro}}{2^N} + \sqrt{(Q_{ro} + 1)\text{sdlp-adv}(\mathcal{B}, (g, \phi))}$$

where $\delta = \text{cma-adv}^{\text{ro}}(\text{SPDH-Sign}_{g,\phi}(N), \mathcal{A})$ is the advantage of the signature scheme in the random oracle model version of the chosen message attack game.

Proof. Applying [4, Theorem 19.15] and [4, Equation 19.21], since the underlying identification scheme has honest verifier zero knowledge there is an efficient adversary $\mathcal{B}'$ running $\mathcal{A}$ as a subroutine such that

$$\delta \le \gamma Q_s(Q_s + Q_{ro} + 1) + \frac{Q_{ro}}{|\mathcal{C}|} + \sqrt{(Q_{ro} + 1)\text{inv-adv}(\mathcal{B}, \text{KeyGen}_{g,\phi})}$$

where γ is the probability that a given commitment value appears in a transcript, and KeyGen$_{g,\phi}$ is the key generation algorithm of the underlying identification scheme. Since choosing a random group element corresponds to choosing a random element of $\mathcal{X}_{g,\phi}$, each commitment value in $\mathcal{X}_{g,\phi}$ has probability $1/|\mathcal{X}_{g,\phi}| = 1/n$ of being selected. We have already seen in the proof of Theorem 6 that the advantage of an adversary in the inversion attack game against this key generation algorithm is bounded by the advantage in an SDLP attack game, and the result follows. □

The above theorem provides a concrete estimate on the advantage of an adversary in the chosen message attack game; nevertheless, a plain English rephrasing is a useful reflection on these results. Essentially, we now know that the `euf-cma` security of our signature scheme is reliant on the integer n corresponding to the pair (g, ϕ), the size of N, and the difficulty of SDLP relative to the pair (g, ϕ). We can discount the reliance on N, which can be 'artificially' inflated as we please; note also that we can intuitively expect the size of n and the difficulty of SDLP for (g, ϕ) to be at least somewhat correlated, since a small value of n trivially renders the associated SDLP instance easy by brute force. In essence, then, we have shown that we can expect the signature scheme corresponding to (g, ϕ) to be secure provided the associated SDLP instance is difficult.

4   On the Difficulty of SDLP

For any finite non-abelian group G, we have shown the existence of signature scheme for any pair $(g, \phi) \in G \times Aut(G)$. It is now clear from Theorem 7 that if the signature is defined with respect to a pair (g, ϕ), SDLP with respect to (g, ϕ) should be difficult. In this section we discuss sensible choices of G with respect to this criterion.

As alluded to in the title of this paper we are interested in post-quantum hard instances of SDLP; that is, if an instance of SDLP has a known reduction to a quantum-vulnerable problem we should consider it to be easy.

There are three key strategies in the literature for addressing SDLP. Two of them, at face value, appear to solve a problem instead related to SDLP: let us explore the gap between the problems below.

4.1   Dihedral Hidden Subgroup Problem

It should first be noted that, as with all group action-based cryptography, the Dihredral Hidden Subgroup Problem will be highly relevant. Indeed, we can bound the complexity of SDLP above by appealing to Kuperberg's celebrated quantum algorithm for the Abelian Hidden Shift Problem [21], defined as follows:

Definition 14. *Let A be an abelian group and S be a set. Consider two injective functions $f, g : A \to S$ such that for some $h \in A$, we have $f(a) = g(a+h)$ for all $a \in A$. We say that the functions f, g 'hide' h, and the Abelian Hidden Shift Problem is to recover h via queries to f, g.*

Adapting an argument seen throughout the literature, but first codified in its modern sense in [7], gives us the following result.

Theorem 8. *Let G be a finite non-abelian group and let $(g, \phi) \in G \ltimes Aut(G)$; and $n \in \mathbb{N}$ be the smallest integer such that $s_{g,\phi}(n) = 1$. Given (g, ϕ) and a group element $s_{g,\phi}(x)$, there is a quantum algorithm that recovers x in time $2^{\mathcal{O}(\sqrt{\log n})}$.*

Proof. If the relevant abelian group has size n we have the claimed complexity for an abelian hidden shift problem by [21, Proposition 6.1]. It suffices to show that one can solve SDLP provided one can solve the abelian hidden shift problem - the argument goes as follows. Define $f, g : \mathbb{Z}_n \to \mathcal{X}_{g,\phi}$ by

$$f([z]_n) = [z]_n \otimes s_{g,\phi}(x) \quad g([z]_n) = [z]_n \otimes s_{g,\phi}(1)$$

We have for all $[z]_n \in \mathbb{Z}_n$ that

$$\begin{aligned} f([z]_n) &= [z]_n \otimes s_{g,\phi}(x) \\ &= [z]_n \otimes ([x-1]_n \otimes s_{g,\phi}(1)) \\ &= ([z]_n + [x-1]_n) \otimes s_{g,\phi}(1) \\ &= g([z]_n + [x-1]_n) \otimes s_{g,\phi}(1) \end{aligned}$$

so f and g hide $[x-1]_n$, from which $x \in \mathbb{N}$ can be recovered trivially. □

A small amount of detail is suppressed in the above proof: namely, that we have tacitly assumed knowledge of the quantity n. Since the best algorithm for the abelian hidden shift problem is quantum anyway, we need not be reticent to compute n with a quantum algorithm - and since the function $s_{g,\phi}$ is periodic in n, certainly such Shor-like techniques are available, such as [8, Algorithm 5]. On the other hand, the ability to compute n efficiently and classically is both desirable and addressed later in this paper.

4.2   Semidirect Computational Diffie-Hellman

The other major body of work related to the analysis of SDLP addresses the following related problem:

Definition 15 (Semidirect Computational Diffie-Hellman). *Let G be a finite abelian group, and let $(g, \phi) \in G \ltimes Aut(G)$. Let $x, y \in \mathbb{N}$ and suppose we are given the data $(g, \phi), s_{g,\phi}(x)$ and $s_{g,\phi}(y)$. The Semidirect Computational Diffie-Hellman problem (SCDH) is to compute the value $s_{g,\phi}(x + y)$.*

Recall our discussion of Semidirect Product Key Exchange in Sect. 2.1. Notice that SCDH is, similarly to the role of the classic CDH, precisely the problem of key recovery in Semidirect Product Key Exchange, and moreover that the relationship between SCDH and SDLP is not immediately obvious. Of course, one can solve SCDH if one can solve SDLP, but the converse does not follow *a priori*.

There are two general approaches for solving SCDH:

The Dimension Attack. The general form of this argument appears in [29]; we prefer the slightly more purpose-built exposition of [33]. The idea is basically that if our group G can be embedded as a multiplicative subgroup of a finite-dimensional algebra over a field, and if the automorphism ϕ can be extended to preserve addition on this algebra, we can solve SCDH for some pair (g, ϕ) using Gaussian elimination.

The Telescoping Attack. In [5], it is noticed that $1 * s_{g,\phi}(x) = \phi^x(g)s_{g,\phi}(x)$. Since we know $s_{g,\phi}(x)$ we can calculate $1 * s_{g,\phi}(x)$ and solve for $\phi^x(g)$. In some cases - notably, in the additive structure given in [31] - this suffices for recovery of $s_{g,\phi}(x + y)$.

We comment that a method of efficiently converting an SCDH solver to an SDLP solver is not currently known. On the other hand, a recent result of Montgomery and Zhandry [28] shows that a computational problem underpinning SDLP and a computational problem underpinning SCDH[5] are (surprisingly) quantum equivalent. We therefore cautiously conjecture that there exists some efficient quantum method of converting an SCDH solver to an SDLP solver.

5   A Candidate Group

We propose the following group of order p^3, where p is an odd prime, for use with SPDH-Sign.

Definition 16. *Let p be an odd prime. The group G_p is defined by*

$$G_p = \left\{ \begin{pmatrix} a & b \\ 0 & 1 \end{pmatrix} : a, b \in \mathbb{Z}_{p^2}, a \equiv 1 \mod p \right\}$$

As discussed in [9], this group is one of two non-abelian groups of order p^3 for an odd prime up to isomorphism. It has presentation

$$G_p = \langle x, y : y^p = 1, [x, y] = x^p = :z \in Z(G_p), z^p = 1 \rangle$$

as described in [23]; moreover, its automorphism group is known and has size $(p-1)p^3$ by [11, Theorem 3.1].

With respect to the various matters discussed in this paper, we briefly present the advantages of employing such a group.

Sampling. Recall that our security proof for SPDH-Sign relied heavily on the underlying identification scheme being honest-verifier zero knowledge, which in turn relied on the 'fake' transcripts to have the same distribution as honestly generated transcripts. For a pair (g, ϕ), it is therefore important to be able to sample uniformly at random from the group $\mathbb{Z}_n$, where n is the smallest integer for which $s_{g,\phi}(n) = 1$ - in our case, to do so it clearly suffices to compute n.

Here we recall Theorem 4, which tells us basically that, thinking of (g, ϕ) as a member of the semidirect product group $G \ltimes Aut(G)$, n must divide the order of (g, ϕ). We therefore have the following

Theorem 9. *Let $(g, \phi) \in G_p \times Aut(G_p)$, where p is an odd prime. Suppose n is the smallest integer for which $s_{g,\phi}(n) = 1$. Then*

$$n \in \{p, p^2, p^3, p^4, p^5, p^6, (p-1), p(p-1), p^2(p-1), p^3(p-1), p^4(p-1), p^5(p-1)\}$$

---

[5] More precisely, the Vectorisation and Parallelisation problems of Couveignes [10], respectively.

Proof. By Theorem 4 we know that $n|ord((g,\phi))$, and it is standard that

$$ord((g,\phi)) \quad | \quad |G_p \ltimes Aut(G)|.$$

We know from the discussion at the outset of this section that $|G_p| = p^3$ and $|Aut(G_p)| = p^3(p-1)$. It follows that $n|p^3p^3(p-1)$. Since p is prime, and assuming that (g,ϕ) is not the identity, the claimed set is a complete list of divisors of $p^6(p-1)$ - excluding $p^6(p-1)$ itself, since this would imply $G_p \ltimes Aut(G_p)$ is cyclic.

It follows that for an arbitrary pair (g, ϕ) in $G_p \ltimes Aut(G_p)$, in order to compute the smallest n for which $s_{g,\phi}(n) = 1$, and therefore the group $\mathbb{Z}_n$, one has to compute $s_{g,\phi}(i)$ for at most 12 values of i. Moreover, by square-and-multiply each computation requires $\mathcal{O}(\log p)$ applications of the group operation in the semidirect product group. In other words, we can compute a complete description of $\mathbb{Z}_n$ efficiently.

SDLP. By Theorem 8 and Theorem 9 we know SDLP in $G_p \ltimes Aut(G_p)$ has time complexity at most $2^{\mathcal{O}(\sqrt{\log poly(p)})} = 2^{\mathcal{O}(\sqrt{\log p})}$. Taking the security parameter to be the length of an input, we can represent a pair $(g, \phi) \in G_p \ltimes Aut(G_p)$ with a bitstring of length $\mathcal{O}(\log p^2) = \mathcal{O}(\log p)$. Asymptotically, then, with k as the security parameter we estimate the time complexity of the main quantum attack on SDLP as $2^{\mathcal{O}(\sqrt{k})}$. On the other hand, in order to derive a concrete estimate for specific security parameters - say, those required by NIST - one would have to check the associated constants much more carefully. Although this is outside the scope of this paper, we refer the reader to [6, Section 7.2 'Subexponential vs Practical'] for an idea of type of spirited research carried out in pursuit of a satisfactory resolution to deriving concrete security estimates - one should note, however, that this exposition deals with specific artefacts of the isogeny framework.

The Dimension Attack. Supposing an efficient method of converting an SCDH solver to an SDLP solver can be found, one solves SDLP efficiently provided one can efficiently embed G_p in an algebra over a field. However, as argued in [20], the following result of Janusz [17] limits the effectiveness of such an approach: the smallest dimension of an algebra over a field in which a p-group with an element of order p^n can be embedded is $1 + p^{n-1}$. In our case, certainly G_p has an element of order p^2, and so since the attack relies on Gaussian elimination we expect the dimension attack for G_p to have complexity polynomial in $(p+1)^3 = \mathcal{O}(p^3)$. Since the G_p elements can be represented by a bitstring of order $4\log p^2 = 8\log p$, with k the security parameter the dimension attack runs in time $\mathcal{O}(2^{3k/8})$.

The Telescoping Attack. In general, the explicit method of deducing $s_{g,\phi}(x+y)$ from $s_{g,\phi}(y)$ and $\phi^x(g)$ relies on the group G being the abelian group of a matrix alegbra over a field under addition. In particular, an extension outside of this linear context is not known - we would expect, however, that such an extension would rely on equation solving techniques available only in an algebra over a field, rather than over a ring, and therefore that arguments on the efficiency of a representation discussed above would also apply.

Efficiency. Multiplication in G_p consists of 8 multiplication operations and 4 addition operations in $\mathbb{Z}_{p^2}$, for a total of $\mathcal{O}(8 \log p^2) = \mathcal{O}(\log p)$ operations. Assuming that applying an automorphism ϕ has about the same complexity as multiplication[6]. It follows by standard square-and-multiply techniques that calculating $s_{g,\phi}$ and evaluating the group action is very roughly of complexity $\mathcal{O}((\log p)^2)$.

The signatures are also rather short, consisting of N elements of $\mathcal{X}_{g,\phi}$ and N elements of $\mathbb{Z}_n$. Since $\mathcal{X}_{g,\phi} \subset G_p$ we can represent $\mathcal{X}_{g,\phi}$ elements as bitstrings of length $4 \log(p^2) = 8 \log p$; and since $n = p^i(p-1)^j$ for some $1 \le i \le 5$ and $0 \le j \le 1$, $\mathbb{Z}_n$ elements can be represented by bitstrings of length $\log p^i(p-1)^j$. It follows that we get signatures of length

$$N((8 + i) \log p + j \log(p-1))$$

6   Conclusion

We have given a constructive proof that a few elementary definitions give rise to a free, transitive group action; such a group action naturally gives rise to an identification scheme and a signature scheme. Moreover, well-known tools allow us to phrase the security of this signature scheme in terms of the semidirect discrete logarithm problem, which is itself a special case of Couveignes' Vectorisation Problem.

Our main contributions are as follows: firstly, the generality of the construction gives an unusually diverse family of signature schemes - indeed, a signature scheme of the SPDH-Sign type is defined for each finite group. Much further study on the relative merits of different choices of finite non-abelian group in different use cases is required to fully realise the potential of this diversity.

Second, our Theorem 4 essentially gives us information about how to compute the group in our group action. In Theorem 9, we saw one particular case where the result was enough to completely describe how to efficiently compute the group, thereby yielding an example of a group-action based key exchange in which efficient sampling is possible from the whole group, without appealing to techniques inducing additional overhead, most notably the 'Fiat-Shamir with aborts' technique of Lyubashevsky.

The paper notably does not address concrete security estimates or recommend parameter sizes for a signature scheme. In order to do so we would need to carefully check the constants in the asymptotic security estimates - we consider the scale of this task, along with that of providing an implementation of the scheme, as sufficient to merit a separate paper.

At a late stage of the preparation of this manuscript the authors were made aware of work in [13] discussing the security of group action-induced computational problems, particularly in a quantum sense. The arguments therein should be addressed when discussing the difficulty of SDLP in subsequent work.

Acknowledgements. We would like to thank the anonymous reviewers who provided useful feedback on this manuscript.

---

[6] This is indeed the case if the automorphism is inner.

References

1. Abdalla, M., An, J.H., Bellare, M., Namprempre, C.: From identification to signatures via the Fiat-Shamir transform: minimizing assumptions for security and forward-security. In: Knudsen, L.R. (ed.) EUROCRYPT 2002. LNCS, vol. 2332, pp. 418–433. Springer, Heidelberg (2002). https://doi.org/10.1007/3-540-46035-7_28

2. Battarbee, C., Kahrobaei, D., Perret, L., Shahandashti, S.F.: A subexponential quantum algorithm for the semdirect discrete logarithm problem. In: 4th PQC NIST Conference 2022, pp. 1–27 (2022). https://csrc.nist.gov/csrc/media/Events/2022/fourth-pqc-standardizationconference/documents/papers/a-subexpoenential-quantum-algorithm-pqc2022.pdf

3. Beullens, W., Kleinjung, T., Vercauteren, F.: CSI-FiSh: efficient isogeny based signatures through class group computations. In: Galbraith, S.D., Moriai, S. (eds.) ASIACRYPT 2019. LNCS, vol. 11921, pp. 227–247. Springer, Cham (2019). https://doi.org/10.1007/978-3-030-34578-5_9

4. Boneh, D., Shoup, V.: A graduate course in applied cryptography. Draft 0.5 (2020)

5. Brown, D., Koblitz, N., Legrow, J.: Cryptanalysis of 'MAKE'. J. Math. Cryptol. **16**(1), 98–102 (2022)

6. Castryck, W., Lange, T., Martindale, C., Panny, L., Renes, J.: CSIDH: an efficient post-quantum commutative group action. In: Peyrin, T., Galbraith, S. (eds.) ASIACRYPT 2018. LNCS, vol. 11274, pp. 395–427. Springer, Cham (2018). https://doi.org/10.1007/978-3-030-03332-3_15

7. Childs, A., Jao, D., Soukharev, V.: Constructing elliptic curve isogenies in quantum subexponential time. J. Math. Cryptol. **8**(1), 1–29 (2014)

8. Childs, A.M., Van Dam, W.: Quantum algorithms for algebraic problems. Rev. Mod. Phys. **82**(1), 1 (2010)

9. Conrad, K.: Groups of Order p^3. https://kconrad.math.uconn.edu/blurbs/grouptheory/groupsp3.pdf

10. Couveignes, J.-M.: Hard homogeneous spaces. Cryptology ePrint Archive (2006). https://eprint.iacr.org/2006/291.pdf

11. Curran, M.J.: The automorphism group of a nonsplit metacyclic p-group. Arch. Math. **90**, 483–489 (2008)

12. De Feo, L., Galbraith, S.D.: SeaSign: compact isogeny signatures from class group actions. In: Ishai, Y., Rijmen, V. (eds.) EUROCRYPT 2019. LNCS, vol. 11478, pp. 759–789. Springer, Cham (2019). https://doi.org/10.1007/978-3-030-17659-4_26

13. Duman, J., Hartmann, D., Kiltz, E., Kunzweiler, S., Lehmann, J., Riepel, D.: Generic models for group actions. Cryptology ePrint Archive (2023). https://eprint.iacr.org/2022/1230

14. Fiat, A., Shamir, A.: How to prove yourself: practical solutions to identification and signature problems. In: Odlyzko, A.M. (ed.) CRYPTO 1986. LNCS, vol. 263, pp. 186–194. Springer, Heidelberg (1987). https://doi.org/10.1007/3-540-47721-7_12

15. Habeeb, M., Kahrobaei, D., Koupparis, C., Shpilrain, V.: Public key exchange using semidirect product of (semi)groups. In: Jacobson, M., Locasto, M., Mohassel, P., Safavi-Naini, R. (eds.) ACNS 2013. LNCS, vol. 7954, pp. 475–486. Springer, Heidelberg (2013). https://doi.org/10.1007/978-3-642-38980-1_30

16. Han, J., Zhuang, J.: DLP in semigroups: algorithms and lower bounds. J. Math. Cryptol. **16**(1), 278–288 (2022)

17. Janusz, G.J.: Faithful representations of p-Groups at characteristic p. Represent. Theory Finite Groups Relat. Top. **21**, 89 (1971)

18. Kahrobaei, D., Flores, R., Noce, M.: Group-based cryptography in the quantum era. Not. Am. Math. Soc. **70**(5), 752–763 (2023)
19. Kahrobaei, D., Flores, R., Noce, M., Habeeb, M., Battarbee, C.: Applications of Group Theory in Cryptography: Post-quantum Group-based Cryptography. The Mathematical Surveys and Monographs Series of the American Mathematical Society (2023, forthcoming)
20. Kahrobaei, D., Shpilrain, V.: Using semidirect product of (semi)groups in public key cryptography. In: Beckmann, A., Bienvenu, L., Jonoska, N. (eds.) CiE 2016. LNCS, vol. 9709, pp. 132–141. Springer, Cham (2016). https://doi.org/10.1007/978-3-319-40189-8_14
21. Kuperberg, G.: A subexponential-time quantum algorithm for the dihedral hidden subgroup problem. SIAM J. Comput. **35**(1), 170–188 (2005)
22. Lyubashevsky, V.: Fiat-Shamir with aborts: applications to lattice and factoring-based signatures. In: Matsui, M. (ed.) ASIACRYPT 2009. LNCS, vol. 5912, pp. 598–616. Springer, Heidelberg (2009). https://doi.org/10.1007/978-3-642-10366-7_35
23. Mahalanobis, A.: The MOR cryptosystem and extra-special p-groups. J. Discret. Math. Sci. Cryptogr. **18**, 201–208 (2015)
24. Maze, G., Monico, C., Rosenthal, J.: Public key cryptography based on semigroup actions. arXiv preprint cs/0501017 (2005). SPDHSign 27
25. Monico, C.: Remarks on MOBS and cryptosystems using semidirect products. arXiv preprint arXiv:2109.11426 (2021)
26. Monico, C., Mahalanobis, A.: A remark on MAKE–a matrix action key exchange. arXiv preprint arXiv:2012.00283 (2020)
27. Monico, C.J.: Semirings and semigroup actions in public-key cryptography. University of Notre Dame (2002)
28. Montgomery, H., Zhandry, M.: Full quantum equivalence of group action DLog and CDH, and more. In: Agrawal, S., Lin, D. (eds.) ASIACRYPT 2022. LNCS, vol. 13791, pp. 3–32. Springer, Cham (2022). https://doi.org/10.1007/978-3-031-22963-3_1 ISBN 978-3-031-22962-6
29. Myasnikov, A., Roman'kov, V.: A linear decomposition attack. Groups Complex. Cryptol. **7**(1), 81–94 (2015)
30. PQC Standardization Process: Announcing Four Candidates to be Standardized, Plus Fourth Round Candidates. https://csrc.nist.gov/News/2022/pqc-candidates-to-be-standardized-and-round-4#newcall
31. Rahman, N., Shpilrain, V.: MAKE: a matrix action key exchange. J. Math. Cryptol. **16**(1), 64–72 (2022)
32. Rahman, N., Shpilrain, V.: MOBS: matrices over bit strings public key exchange (2021). https://eprint.iacr.org/2021/560
33. Roman'kov, V.: Linear decomposition attack on public key exchange protocols using semidirect products of (semi) groups arXiv preprint arXiv:1501.01152 (2015)
34. Rostovtsev, A., Stolbunov, A.: Public-key cryptosystem based on isogenies. Cryptology ePrint Archive (2006). https://eprint.iacr.org/2006/145
35. Stolbunov, A.: Constructing public-key cryptographic schemes based on class group action on a set of isogenous elliptic curves. Adv. Math. Commun. **4**(2), 215–235 (2010)
36. Stolbunov, A.: Cryptographic schemes based on isogenies. Ph.D. thesis (2012). https://doi.org/10.13140/RG.2.2.20826.44488

Isogeny-Based Cryptography

A Tightly Secure Identity-Based Signature Scheme from Isogenies

Jiawei Chen[1]([✉]), Hyungrok Jo[2], Shingo Sato[2], and Junji Shikata[1,2]

[1] Graduate School of Environment and Information Sciences, Yokohama National University, Yokohama, Japan
`chen-jiawei-hm@ynu.jp, shikata-junji-rb@ynu.ac.jp`
[2] Institute of Advanced Sciences, Yokohama National University, Yokohama, Japan
`{jo-hyungrok-xz,sato-shingo-zk}@ynu.ac.jp`

Abstract. We present a tightly secure identity-based signature (IBS) scheme based on the supersingular isogeny problems. Although Shaw and Dutta proposed an isogeny-based IBS scheme with provable security, the security reduction is non-tight. For an IBS scheme with concrete security, the tightness of its security reduction affects the key size and signature size. Hence, it is reasonable to focus on a tight security proof for an isogeny-based IBS scheme.

In this paper, we propose an isogeny-based IBS scheme based on the lossy CSI-FiSh signature scheme and give a tight security reduction for this scheme. While the existing isogeny-based IBS has the square-root advantage loss in the security proof, the security proof for our IBS scheme avoids such advantage loss, due to the properties of lossy CSI-FiSh. Moreover, we show that the user key size and signature size of our scheme are better than those sizes of existing isogeny-based IBS schemes, under suitable parameter settings.

Keywords: Identity-based signature · Isogeny-based cryptography · Post-quantum cryptography

1 Introduction

Post-Quantum Cryptography (PQC, for short) is a next-generation cryptographic system that differs from widely used cryptographic systems based on the hardness of integer factorization problems, and is globally popularized and used. It is based on various mathematically hard problems that are resistant to attacks by Shor's quantum algorithm [37] and has been actively researched by many researchers. Isogeny-based cryptography is one of the promising candidates for PQC, along with lattice-based cryptography, code-based cryptography, multivariate-based cryptography, and hash-based cryptography. The National Institute of Standards and Technology (NIST) is currently working to standardize practical post-quantum cryptography systems that offer sufficient security and practicality, with the aim of promoting and using these next-generation

T. Johansson and D. Smith-Tone (Eds.): PQCrypto 2023, LNCS 14154, pp. 141–163, 2023.
https://doi.org/10.1007/978-3-031-40003-2_6

cryptographic systems in the near future. In July 2022, NIST released the results of its third round of selection [29], with CRYSTALS-Kyber being chosen for the KEM category and CRYSTALS-Dilithium, Falcon, and SPHINCS+ selected for the signature category. In the KEM category, SIKE based on the hardness of the supersingular isogeny problem, along with BIKE, Classic McEliece, and HQC, made it to the fourth round. However, in September 2022, SIKE was unfortunately excluded from the candidates due to several known attacks [9,28,33]. As the fundamental computational hardness problem in isogeny-based cryptographic systems remains unsolved, cryptographic systems like CSIDH [10] and SQI-Sign [15] that do not rely on auxiliary point information in their basic structure or have a different cryptographic construction than SIDH, continue to be considered secure.

Recently, there have been several new isogeny-based cryptographic systems that are considered resistant to attacks on SIDH, such as primeSIDH [27] and M(D)-SIDH [20]. Additionally, Dartois et al. [14] have proposed an improved signature scheme called SQI-SignHD, which utilizes the algorithmic breakthrough underlying the attack [33] on SIDH. By representing isogenies of arbitrary degrees as components of a higher dimensional isogeny, SQI-SignHD provides more efficiency compared to its predecessor. Thus, the field of isogeny-based cryptography is continuously evolving with the development of new and improved systems.

Meanwhile, isogeny-based cryptographic system have often been considered less practical compared to other cryptographic systems, resulting in a limited number of proposals for advanced functional isogeny-based encryption schemes [6,31,36]. However, when it comes to the essential perspective of identity-based cryptography, isogeny-based cryptographic systems can have advantages in constructing identity-based schemes due to their compact key size compared to other post-quantum cryptography candidates. In particular, for identity-based cryptosystems, it can be advantageous when a user joins a network. The Key Generation Center (KGC) issues the master key and user key based on the user's identity (e.g., e-mail, social security number, credit card number, smart card, MAC address, IO/EO, etc.) and is not involved in the subsequent process.

Identity-Based Signatures from the CSIDH Setting. Shamir [35] suggested the first identity-based signature schemes, which are signature schemes with the public key of a user as his/her identity. Instead of conducting the role of Public Key Infrastructures (PKI), a trusted KGC issues the corresponding secret key. CSIibs, proposed by Peng et al. [31], is the first identity-based signature scheme based on the supersingular isogeny assumption. However, Shaw and Dutta [36] pointed out a flaw in the main structure of CSIibs and proposed a new identity-based signature scheme based on supersingular isogeny assumption that includes the forward secrecy feature to address the issue. Both Peng et al. and Shaw and Dutta's identity-based signature schemes are based on CSIDH and use SeaSign [19] and CSI-FiSh [7] as their ID protocols. In addition, there is a generic construction starting from two signature schemes (e.g., see [3,24,26]). Thus, it is possible to obtain an isogeny-based IBS scheme by applying an isogeny-based signature scheme to this generic construction.

CSI-FiSh and Lossy CSI-FiSh. Isogeny-based cryptography was initially proposed by Couveignes [12] and by Rostovtsev and Stolbunov [34]. These proposals are known to be weakened by the quantum attack of Childs, Jao and Soukarev [11] against their based hardness assumptions on isogeny between ordinary elliptic curves. Instead of ordinary elliptic curves, Jao and De Feo [23] and Castryck et al. [10] proposed the Diffie-Hellman key exchanges using supersingular elliptic curves. As mentioned above, SIDH was broken by mainly Castryck and Decru [9] and subsequently Robert [28], Maino and Martindale [33]. These attacks do not apply to CSIDH-based schemes as SeaSign [19], CSI-FiSh [7], CSI-RAShi [5], Sashimi [13] and CSI-SharK [2]. Kaafarani et al. [17] proposed the lossy version of CSI-FiSh to achieve a tight reduction. The efficiency of the CSIDH-based schemes mainly depends on the precomputation of the related class-group structure which is restrained by a specific set of CSIDH parameters by the time being, named CSIDH-512. However, there are some controversies over the real post-quantum security level of CSIDH-512 [8]. Hence for expected post-quantum security, we may need a larger class group. Recently, De Feo et al. [18] proposed SCALLOP based on group action of isogenies of oriented supersingular curves where a larger class group structure can be easily computed. Since this is a recent result, and more analysis for SCALLOP is needed, we utilize the lossy CSI-FiSh as the underlying signature scheme in this paper instead.

Our Contributions. We suggest the identity-based signature (IBS) scheme from isogenies with tight security.

The existing isogeny-based IBS scheme with provable security is the CSI-FiSh-based scheme proposed by Shaw and Dutta [36]. However, their scheme does not achieve tight security. This one is constructed by applying their proposed identity-based identification scheme to the Fiat-Shamir transformation. In order to prove the security of this IBS, it is necessary to employ the *forking lemma* and adaptive re-programming of random oracles [4,32]. Because of this, the security reduction for the existing one is not tight. For the similar IBS schemes based on other hardness assumptions [3], one can remedy the security loss by using the larger parameters. However, CSI-FiSh is based on a GAIP (Group Action Inverse Problem) defined for only 128-bit security with CSIDH-512 parameters. As of now, no other parameter sets have been computed to yield suitable algebraic structure for CSI-FiSh. Hence, we cannot claim any level of security for the IBS proposed by Shaw and Dutta [36] when a 128-bit security level is desired.

In order to construct an isogeny-based IBS scheme with tight security, our proposed scheme is based on lossy CSI-FiSh [17] which is a lossy identification scheme based on CSI-FiSh. Due to the result of [1], it is known that we can construct a signature scheme with tight security by applying a lossy identification scheme to the Fiat-Shamir transformation. Hence, it is reasonable to utilize lossy CSI-FiSh in order to construct a tightly secure IBS scheme.

Table 1. Comparison of Isogeny-based IBS schemes

Scheme	MPK-size (bit)	USK-size (bit)	Signature-size (bit)	Security bound
SD [36]	$S_0\lceil\log p\rceil$	$T_1S_1S_1\delta\lceil\log N\rceil$ $+S_1\delta$	$T_1S_1\lceil\log p\rceil$ $+T_1T_2\lceil\log N\rceil$ $+T_2\delta'$	$\sqrt{q\cdot\epsilon}+\mathsf{negl}$
PW [26]+ [30]	$S_0\lceil\log p\rceil$	$4S_0\lceil\log p\rceil$ $+(T_1+$ $S_0)\lceil\log N\rceil$ $+\delta$	$4S_0\lceil\log p\rceil$ $+3T_1\lceil\log N\rceil$ $+3\delta$	$2S_0\cdot\epsilon+\mathsf{negl}$
Our Scheme	$(2S_0+2)\lceil\log p\rceil$	$T_1S_1\lceil\log N\rceil$ $+S_1\delta$	$T_1S_1\lceil\log p\rceil$ $+T_1T_2\lceil\log N\rceil$ $+T_2\delta'$	$S_0\cdot\epsilon+\mathsf{negl}$

MPK and USK denote the master public key and user's secret key respectively. SD is the isogeny-based IBS scheme proposed in [36], and PW is the IBS scheme constructed by applying the isogeny-based signature scheme [30] to the generic construction of [26]. We assume that the above IBS schemes use supersingular curves over $\mathbb{F}_p$. N is an odd order of an ideal cyclic group. ϵ is the maximum probability of breaking the underlying computational problem (i.e., the GAIP or D-CSIDH assumtpion). q is the maximum number of queries issued to (random) oracles. negl is a negligible function in a security parameter. S_0, S_1 are parameters of the corresponding computational assumptions. T_1, T_2 are the numbers of parallel executions of the underlying (lossy) identification scheme. For 128-bit security, $\delta = T_1\lceil\log(S_0+1)\rceil$ and $\delta' = T_1\lceil\log(S_1+1)\rceil$.

Technical Overview. Although the construction of our proposed IBS is similar to that of the existing IBS [36], the security proof for ours is not obvious. To prove the security for a signature scheme constructed from a lossy identification scheme, we employ the following properties required to that identification scheme: *Indistinguishability of keys* and *lossy soundness*. A lossy identification scheme has two key generation algorithms: The ordinary (public-secret) key generation and *lossy key generation* which produces a (public) lossy key which is impossible to distinguish from a real public key. When a generated public key is lossy (called *lossy mode*), *lossy soundness* ensures that generating a valid response to a random challenge is statistically impossible after producing a commitment. When proving the security for a signature scheme from a lossy identification scheme, we replace a real public key with a lossy key by utilizing the standard hybrid argument (i.e., the sequence-of-games approach). However, we cannot employ lossy soundness in the straightforward way, when proving the security for our IBS scheme. This is because regarding IBSs, there is no notion corresponding to the lossy mode. Since an IBS scheme does not generate any public-secret key pair, we cannot employ the proof approach of [1].

In order to resolve this, we utilize the proof technique similar to the technique used for a tight security reduction of a DDH-based IBS scheme [21]. Regarding our proposed scheme, the key derivation algorithm produces a signature on an identity as a user secret key, and the signing algorithm generates a signature on an identity-message pair. These signatures are generated by using (a variant of) a lossy CSI-FiSh-based signature scheme. Informally, to prove the security, we simulate those signatures (i.e., those user secret key and signature on an identity and a message) without using a secret key of lossy CSI-FiSh. This is possible by utilizing a property of lossy CSI-FiSh and the sequence-of-games proof approach. Namely, we can replace real signatures with signatures generated in a lossy mode-like way, via tight security reductions. Hence, it is possible to give a tight security proof for our IBS scheme, by employing properties of lossy CSI-FiSh.

Comparison. We present a comparison of different isogeny-based IBS schemes based on key-size, signature-size, and security bound in Table 1. For our comparison, we consider a direct construction of [36] and a scheme obtained by applying a tightly secure isogeny-based signature scheme [30] to the generic construction [26] of IBS. Our proposed scheme has a significantly tighter security proof than the direct construction of SD [36], with equivalent USK-size and Signature-size. Therefore, our scheme has improved concrete security compared to SD. When compared to the scheme of PW [26]+ [30], our security bound is asymptotically equivalent, and we need to compare the concrete USK-size and Signature-size of PW and ours.

Table 2 presents the USK-size and Signature-size of our isogeny-based IBS scheme, obtained from the optimized parameter setting in Peng et al.'s [31], and from the parameter values derived using the correlation analysis method in Shaw and Dutta's [36], both providing 128-bit security level. Our results show that, for the large parameter $S_1 = 2^{16} - 1$, the USK-size and Signature-size of PW are smaller than those of our scheme, as our scheme's USK-size and Signature-size grow linearly with S_1 (see Table 1). On the other hand, under smaller parameter settings with $S_1 \leq 2^8 - 1$, our scheme outperforms PW and provides a more compact user key and signature.

Remark 1. For the security parameter λ, (T_0, T_1, S_0, S_1) needs to satisfy the following two inequalities, due to the parameter setting of [31]:

$$T_1 \lceil \log S_0 + 1 \rceil \geq \lambda,$$
$$T_1 T_2 \lceil \log S_1 + 1 \rceil \geq \lambda.$$

Hence, for the sake of efficiency, when given fixed S_0 and S_1, we first choose T_1 as small as possible such that T_1 satisfies the first inequality above and then choose T_2 as small as possible such that T_2 satisfies the second inequality above.

Remark 2. Since the direct construction of SD is based on the CSIDH-512 parameters and its security reduction is loose, there are no known parameters for SD to achieve 128-bit security. Hence we only give a comparison between PW and our scheme in Table 2.

Remark 3. In Table 2, our scheme achieves EUF-ID-CMA-MK security while the scheme of PW satisfies stronger security, owing to the result of [26].

In summary, our proposed scheme achieves a better key-size and signature-size than the existing one under suitable parameter settings, while providing a similar level of security as PW. Therefore, we can claim that our scheme achieves an optimal balance between security and efficiency. However, it is important to note that decreasing S_1 in our scheme leads to an increase the execution time of the user key and signature generation algorithms. Thus, our proposed scheme can be seen as an isogeny-based IBS scheme with a compact user key and signature, provided that suitable parameters are chosen.

Table 2. A comparison of USK-size and signature-size for 128-bit security parameters

(T_1, T_2, S_0, S_1)	PW [26]+ [30]		Our Scheme	
	USK	Signature	USK	Signature
(16, 3, 255, 7)	74.0 KB	66.9 KB	3.7 KB	8.7 KB
(16, 2, 255, 15)	74.0 KB	66.9 KB	8.0 KB	16.4 KB
(8, 2, 65535, 255)	18.9 MB	16.8 MB	69.9 KB	131.1 KB
(8, 1, 65535, 65535)	18.9 MB	16.8 MB	18.0 MB	33.6 MB

This paper is organized as follows. In Sect. 2, we give the preliminaries for the CSIDH setting, lossy identification schemes, identity-based signatures and hardness assumptions. In Sect. 3, we describe the construction of the lossy CSI-FiSh by [17]. In Sect. 4, we suggest the tightly secure identity-based signature from the lossy CSI-FiSh.

2 Preliminaries

2.1 Elliptic Curve and Ideal Class Group

We give some notations and preliminaries for using the CSIDH setting, which is based on [10,17,38]. Let E be an elliptic curve over a finite field $\mathbb{F}_p$ with a prime $p \geq 5$, and O_E denote the point at infinity on E. Let E and E' be the two elliptic curves over $\mathbb{F}_p$. It is called an *isogeny* φ between E and E' if $\varphi : E \to E'$ is a non-constant morphism satisfying $\varphi(0_E) = 0_{E'}$. A *separable* isogeny (it induces a separable extension of function fields) having $\{0_E\}$ as kernel is an isomorphism; an isogeny having the same domain and range is an endomorphism.

Ideal Class Group. The set of all endomorphisms of an elliptic curve E, together with the zero map, form a ring under pointwise addition and composition. Such a ring is called the *endomorphism ring* of E and it is denoted by $\text{End}(E)$. If $\text{End}(E)$ is an order in a quaternion algebra, the curve is said to be *supersingular*, if otherwise it is said to be *ordinary*. The restriction $\text{End}_p(E)$ to the endomorphisms defined over $\mathbb{F}_p$ forms a subring, which is isomorphic to an order in the quadratic field $\mathbb{K} = \mathbb{Q}(\sqrt{-p})$. An order is a subring of $\mathbb{Q}(\sqrt{-p})$ which is also a finitely-generated $\mathbb{Z}$-module containing a basis of $\mathbb{K}$ as a $\mathbb{Q}$-vector space. The set $\mathbb{Z}[\sqrt{-p}] = \{m + n\sqrt{-p} \mid m, n \in \mathbb{Z}\}$ satisfies the above three conditions, and we will denote it by $\mathcal{O}$. We then consider the set $\mathcal{E}\ell\ell_p(\mathcal{O}, \pi)$ containing all supersingular curves E defined over $\mathbb{F}_p$ - modulo isomorphisms defined over $\mathbb{F}_p$ - such that there exists an isomorphism between $\mathcal{O}$ and $\text{End}_p(E)$

mapping $\sqrt{-p} \in \mathcal{O}$ into the Frobenius endomorphism $(x, y) \mapsto (x^p, y^p)$. Each isomorphism class in $\mathcal{E}\ell\ell_p(\mathcal{O}, \pi)$ can be uniquely represented by a single element of $\mathbb{F}_p$ if $p \geq 5$ is a prime such that $p \equiv 3 \pmod 8$.

A *fractional ideal* $\mathfrak{a}$ of $\mathcal{O}$ is a finitely generated $\mathcal{O}$-submodule of $\mathbb{K}$. When $\mathfrak{a}$ is contained in $\mathcal{O}$, it is said to be *integral*; when $\mathfrak{a} = \alpha\mathcal{O}$ for some $\alpha \in \mathbb{K}$, it is said to be *principal*; when there exists a fractional ideal $\mathfrak{b}$ such that $\mathfrak{a}\mathfrak{b} = \mathcal{O}$, it is called *invertible*. The set of invertible fractional ideals of $\mathcal{O}$ forms an abelian group under ideal multiplication. Its quotient by the subgroup composed by principal fractional ideals is a finite group called *ideal class group* of $\mathcal{O}$, usually denoted by $\mathcal{C}\ell(\mathcal{O})$, which cardinality is the class number of $\mathcal{O}$.

The ideal class group $\mathcal{C}\ell(\mathcal{O})$ acts freely and transitively on the set $\mathcal{E}\ell\ell_p(\mathcal{O}, \pi)$ via a group action, which denote by $\star$.

$$\star : \mathcal{C}\ell(\mathcal{O}) \times \mathcal{E}\ell\ell_p(\mathcal{O}, \pi) \to \mathcal{E}\ell\ell_p(\mathcal{O}, \pi)$$
$$(\mathfrak{a}, E) \mapsto \mathfrak{a} \star E.$$

For convenience, we use representatives instead of equivalence classes to denote elements of $\mathcal{C}\ell(\mathcal{O})$ and $\mathcal{E}\ell\ell_p(\mathcal{O}, \pi)$. When p is of the form $4\ell_1\ell_2 \cdots \ell_s - 1$, where $\ell_1, \ldots, \ell_s$ are small odd primes, a special integral ideal $\mathfrak{J}_{\ell_i} \subset \mathcal{O}$ corresponds to each prime ℓ_i. These ideals allow an efficient computation of the group action. In particular, the action of $\mathfrak{J}_{\ell_i}$ on a curve $E \in \mathcal{E}\ell\ell_p(\mathcal{O}, \pi)$ is determined by an isogeny having as kernel the unique rational ℓ_i-torsion subgroup of E.

The CSIDH Setting [10]. The general variant of the CSIDH key-exchange scheme relies on the heuristic assumption that the equivalence classes of certain ideals generate the entire ideal class group $\mathcal{C}\ell(\mathcal{O})$. Castryck et al. proposed a *non-interactive* key exchange with using of supersingular elliptic curves over $\mathbb{F}_p$ with $p \equiv 3 \pmod 8$. The scheme starts with the curve $E_0 : y^2 = x^3 + x$ and its $\mathcal{C}\ell(\mathcal{O})$-orbit, which contains all supersingular Montgomery curves $E_A : y^2 = x^3 + Ax^2 + x$ over $\mathbb{F}_p$, where the $\mathbb{F}_p$-isomorphism class is uniquely determined by A. The small public key size is achieved using a single $\mathbb{F}_p$-element A to check for supersingularity.

Throughout this paper, we use the following notation: For a positive integer n, let $[n] = \{1, 2, \ldots, n\}$. For n values $x_1, \ldots, x_n$, let $(x_i)_{i \in [n]} = (x_1, \ldots, x_n)$. For a function $f : \mathbb{N} \to \mathbb{R}$, f is negligible in λ if $f(\lambda) = o(\lambda^{-c})$ for any constant $c > 0$ and sufficiently large $\lambda \in \mathbb{N}$. Then, we write $f(\lambda) = \mathsf{negl}(\lambda)$. A probability is an overwhelming probability if it is $1 - \mathsf{negl}(\lambda)$. "Probabilistic polynomial-time" is abbreviated as PPT. For a positive integer λ, let $\mathsf{poly}(\lambda)$ be a universal polynomial of λ.

2.2 Lossy Identification Schemes

Following [1,17], we describe the definition of lossy identification schemes.

Definition 1 (Lossy Identification Scheme). *A lossy identification scheme for a relation* $\mathcal{R} \subseteq \mathcal{X} \times \mathcal{Y}$ *consists of five polynomial-time algorithms* (IGen,

LossyIGen, P = (P$_1$, P$_2$), V): *Let* ComSet, ChSet, *and* ResSet *be the commitment space, the challenge space, and the response space, respectively.*

Key Generation. *The randomized algorithm* IGen *takes as input a security parameter* 1^λ *and outputs a statement-witness pair* $(X, W) \in \mathcal{R}$.
Lossy Key Generation. *The randomized algorithm* LossyIGen *takes as input a security parameter* 1^λ *and outputs a statement* $X_{los} \in \mathcal{X}$.
Prover. *The prover protocol* P *is split into two randomized algorithms* (P$_1$, P$_2$):
- *The randomized algorithm* P$_1$ *takes as input a statement-witness pair* (X, W) *and outputs a commitment* $com \in$ ComSet.
- *The randomized or deterministic algorithm* P$_2$ *takes as input a statement-witness pair* $(X, W) \in \mathcal{R}$, *a commitment* $com \in$ ComSet, *and a challenge* $ch \in$ ChSet, *and it outputs a response* $resp \in$ ResSet.
Verifier. *The deterministic algorithm* V *takes as input a statement* X, *a commitment* $com \in$ ComSet, *a challenge* $ch \in$ ChSet, *and a response* $resp \in$ ResSet, *and it outputs* 1 *(accept) or* 0 *(reject).*

In addition, following [1], we describe the transcript generation protocol $\mathsf{Trans}_{X,W}^{\mathsf{LossyID}}$ for a lossy identification scheme (IGen, LossyIGen, P = (P$_1$, P$_2$), V). For every $(X, W) \leftarrow$ IGen(λ), $\mathsf{Trans}_{X,W}^{\mathsf{LossyID}}()$ generates a transcript $(com, ch, resp) \in$ ComSet $\times$ ChSet $\times$ ResSet $\cup \{(\bot, \bot, \bot)\}$, in the following way:

1. Compute $com \leftarrow$ P$_1(X, W)$.
2. Choose $ch \xleftarrow{\$}$ ChSet.
3. Compute $resp \leftarrow$ P$_2((X, W), com, ch)$.
4. If $resp = \bot$, set $(com, ch) \leftarrow (\bot, \bot)$.
5. Output $(com, ch, resp)$.

The required properties for a lossy identification scheme are as follows:

Definition 2. *A lossy identification scheme* LossyID = (IGen, LossyIGen, P = (P$_1$, P$_2$), V) *is required to satisfy the following properties:*

Completeness. *For every* $(X, W) \leftarrow$ IGen(1^λ), *it holds that*

$$\Pr\left[V(X, com, ch, resp) = 1 \,\middle|\, \begin{array}{c} com \leftarrow \text{P}_1(X, W); ch \xleftarrow{\$} \text{ChSet}; \\ resp \leftarrow \text{P}_2(X, W, com, ch) \end{array} \right] = 1.$$

Honest-Verifier Zero-Knowledge. *For every* $(X, W) \leftarrow$ IGen(1^λ), *there exists a PPT simulator* Sim *which, on input a statement* X, *outputs transcripts* $\{(com, ch, resp)\}$ *whose distributions are statistically indistinguishable from those of the transcripts generated by* $\mathsf{Trans}_{X,W,\lambda}^{\mathsf{LossyID}}$.
Indistinguishability of Lossy Statements. *For any PPT adversary* $\mathcal{A}$ *against* IDS, *its advantage*

$$\mathsf{Adv}_{\mathsf{IDS},\mathcal{A}}^{\mathsf{ind\text{-}stmt}}(\lambda) := |\Pr[\mathcal{A}(X) = 1 \mid (X, W) \leftarrow \mathsf{IGen}(1^\lambda)]$$
$$- \Pr[\mathcal{A}(X_{los}) = 1 \mid X_{los} \leftarrow \mathsf{LossyIGen}(1^\lambda)]|$$

is negligible in λ.

Lossy Soundness. LossyID *satisfies* ϵ_{los}-lossy soundness *if for any unbounded adversary $\mathcal{A}$ against* LossyID, *its advantage*

$$\mathsf{Adv}^{\text{los-imp-pa}}_{\mathsf{LossyID},\mathcal{A}}(\lambda) = \Pr[\mathsf{Expt}^{\text{los-imp-pa}}_{\mathsf{LossyID},\mathcal{A}}(\lambda) = 1]$$

is less than ϵ_{los}, where $\mathsf{Expt}^{\text{los-imp-pa}}_{\mathsf{LossyID},\mathcal{A}}(\lambda)$ *is the following experiment:*

1. *A challenger generates $X_{los} \leftarrow \mathsf{LossyIGen}(1^\lambda)$ and gives X_{los} to the adversary $\mathcal{A}$.*
2. *$\mathcal{A}$ submits a commitment com $\in$ ComSet to the challenger. The challenger returns a challenge ch $\overset{\$}{\leftarrow}$ ChSet.*
3. *$\mathcal{A}$ outputs a response resp $\in$ ResSet. The challenger returns $b \leftarrow \mathsf{V}(X_{los}, com, ch, resp)$.*

2.3 Identity-Based Signatures

Following [22,39], we describe the syntax and a security definition for identity-based signatures (IBSs), as follows:

Definition 3 (IBS). *An IBS scheme consists of polynomial-time algorithms* (Setup, KeyDer, Sign, Vrfy): *For a security parameter λ, let $\mathcal{ID} = \mathcal{ID}(\lambda)$ be the identity space, let $\mathcal{M} = \mathcal{M}(\lambda)$ be the message space, and let $\mathcal{USK} = \mathcal{USK}(\lambda)$ be the user secret key space.*

Setup. *The randomized algorithm* Setup *takes as input a security parameter 1^λ and outputs a master public key* mpk *and a master secret key* msk.

Key Derivation. *The randomized algorithm* KeyDer *takes as input a master public key* mpk, *a master secret key* msk, *and an identity* id, *and it outputs a user secret key* $\mathsf{usk}_{id} \in \mathcal{USK}$.

Signing. *The randomized or deterministic algorithm* Sign *takes as input a master public key* mpk, *a user secret key* $\mathsf{usk}_{id} \in \mathcal{USK}$, *and a message* m $\in \mathcal{M}$, *and it outputs a signature σ.*

Verification. *The deterministic algorithm* Vrfy *takes as input a master public key* mpk, *an identity* id $\in \mathcal{ID}$, *a message* m $\in \mathcal{M}$, *and a signature σ, and it outputs 1 (accept) or 0 (reject).*

We require an IBS scheme to be *correct*, as follows:

Definition 4. *An IBS scheme* (Setup, KeyDer, Sign, Vrfy) *is* correct, *if for every* (mpk, msk) $\leftarrow$ Setup(1^λ), *every* id $\in \mathcal{ID}$, *and every* m $\in \mathcal{M}$, *it holds that* Vrfy(mpk, id, m, σ) = 1, *where* $\mathsf{usk}_{id} \leftarrow$ KeyDer(mpk, msk, id) *and* $\sigma \leftarrow$ Sign(mpk, usk_{id}, m).

As a security notion of IBSs, we describe the definition of *existential unforgeability against chosen identity and chosen message attacks under the multi-key setting* (called EUF-ID-CMA-MK security) [39].

Definition 5 (EUF-ID-CMA-MK security). *An IBS scheme* IBS = (Setup, KeyDer, Sign, Vrfy) *is* EUF-ID-CMA-MK *secure, if for any PPT adversary $\mathcal{A}$ against* IBS, *its advantage* $\mathsf{Adv}^{\text{euf-id-cma}}_{\mathsf{IBS},\mathcal{A}}(\lambda) := \Pr[\mathsf{Expt}^{\text{euf-id-cma}}_{\mathsf{IBS},\mathcal{A}}(\lambda) = 1]$ *is negligible in λ, where the experiment* $\mathsf{Expt}^{\text{euf-id-cma}}_{\mathsf{IBS},\mathcal{A}}(\lambda)$ *is defined as follows:*

Setup. *The challenger generates* $(\mathsf{mpk}, \mathsf{msk}) \leftarrow \mathsf{Setup}(1^\lambda)$ *and sets the four lists* $\mathcal{L}_{\mathsf{id}} \leftarrow \emptyset$, $\hat{\mathcal{L}}_{\mathsf{id}} \leftarrow \emptyset$, $\mathcal{L}_{\mathsf{usk_{id}}} \leftarrow \emptyset$, *and* $\mathcal{L}_{\mathsf{m}} \leftarrow \emptyset$. *It gives* mpk *to the adversary* $\mathcal{A}$.

Queries. $\mathcal{A}$ *is given access to the following oracles:*

- *Key derivation oracle* $\mathsf{O}_{\mathsf{KeyDer}}$: *On input a key derivation query* $\mathsf{id} \in \mathcal{ID}$, $\mathsf{O}_{\mathsf{KeyDer}}$ *outputs* $\perp$ *if* $\mathsf{id} \in \hat{\mathcal{L}}_{\mathsf{id}}$. *Then, it checks whether* $(\mathsf{id}, \cdot) \in \mathcal{L}_{\mathsf{usk_{id}}}$. *If* $(\mathsf{id}, \mathsf{usk_{id}}) \in \mathcal{L}_{\mathsf{usk_{id}}}$ *for some* $\mathsf{usk_{id}} \in \mathcal{USK}$, *it returns* $\mathsf{usk_{id}}$. *Otherwise, it returns* $\mathsf{usk_{id}} \leftarrow \mathsf{KeyDer}(\mathsf{mpk}, \mathsf{msk}, \mathsf{id})$ *and sets the two lists* $\mathcal{L}_{\mathsf{usk_{id}}} \leftarrow \mathcal{L}_{\mathsf{usk_{id}}} \cup \{(\mathsf{id}, \mathsf{usk_{id}})\}$, $\mathcal{L}_{\mathsf{id}} \leftarrow \mathcal{L}_{\mathsf{id}} \cup \{\mathsf{id}\}$.
- *Signing oracle* $\mathsf{O}_{\mathsf{Sign}}$: *On input a signing-query* $(\mathsf{id}, \mathsf{m}) \in \mathcal{ID} \times \mathcal{M}$, $\mathsf{O}_{\mathsf{Sign}}$ *sets* $\mathcal{L}_{\mathsf{m}} \leftarrow \mathcal{L}_{\mathsf{m}} \cup \{(\mathsf{id}, \mathsf{m})\}$ *and checks whether* $(\mathsf{id}, \mathsf{usk_{id}}) \in \mathcal{L}_{\mathsf{usk_{id}}}$:
  - *If* $(\mathsf{id}, \mathsf{usk_{id}}) \in \mathcal{L}_{\mathsf{usk_{id}}}$ *for some* $\mathsf{usk_{id}} \in \mathcal{USK}$, *it returns* $\sigma \leftarrow \mathsf{Sign}(\mathsf{mpk}, \mathsf{usk_{id}}, \mathsf{m})$.
  - *If there does not exist* $(\mathsf{id}, \mathsf{usk_{id}}) \in \mathcal{L}_{\mathsf{usk_{id}}}$ *such that* $\mathsf{usk_{id}} \in \mathcal{USK}$, *it computes* $\mathsf{usk_{id}} \leftarrow \mathsf{KeyDer}(\mathsf{mpk}, \mathsf{msk}, \mathsf{id})$, *sets* $\mathcal{L}_{\mathsf{usk_{id}}} \leftarrow \mathcal{L}_{\mathsf{usk_{id}}} \cup \{(\mathsf{id}, \mathsf{usk_{id}})\}$, $\hat{\mathcal{L}}_{\mathsf{id}} \leftarrow \hat{\mathcal{L}}_{\mathsf{id}} \cup \{\mathsf{id}\}$, *and returns* $\sigma \leftarrow \mathsf{Sign}(\mathsf{mpk}, \mathsf{usk_{id}}, \mathsf{m})$.

Output. $\mathcal{A}$ *outputs a forgery* $(\mathsf{id}^*, \mathsf{m}^*, \sigma^*)$. *The challenger outputs* 1 *if* $\mathsf{id}^* \notin \mathcal{L}_{\mathsf{id}} \wedge (\mathsf{id}^*, \mathsf{m}^*) \notin \mathcal{L}_{\mathsf{m}} \wedge \mathsf{Vrfy}(\mathsf{mpk}, \mathsf{id}^*, \mathsf{m}^*, \sigma^*) = 1$, *and* 0 *otherwise.*

2.4 Hardness Assumptions

We describe the definitions of the computational assumptions related to our IBS scheme's security: The *decisional CSIDH* and *fixed-curve multi-decisional CSIDH* assumptions.

Following [17], we describe the decisional CSIDH (D-CSIDH) and fixed-curve multi-decisional CSIDH (FCMD-CSIDH) assumptions, as follows:

Definition 6 (Decisional CSIDH Assumption). *Given the set* $\mathcal{Ell}_p(\mathcal{O}, \pi)$ *and the ideal class group* $\mathcal{Cl}(\mathcal{O})$, *the decisional CSIDH (*D-CSIDH*) problem is to distinguish between the following distributions:*

- $(E, H, \mathfrak{a} \star E, \mathfrak{a} \star H)$, *where the supersingular elliptic curves* E *and* H *are sampled uniformly from* $\mathcal{Ell}_p(\mathcal{O}, \pi)$, *and* $\mathfrak{a}$ *is sampled uniformly from* $\mathcal{Cl}(\mathcal{O})$,
- (E, H, E', H'), *where* E, H, E', H' *are supersingular elliptic curves sampled uniformly from* $\mathcal{Ell}_p(\mathcal{O}, \pi)$.

We say that the D-CSIDH *assumption holds if for any PPT algorithm* $\mathcal{A}$, *its advantage* $\mathsf{Adv}_{\mathcal{A}}^{\mathsf{D\text{-}CSIDH}}(\lambda)$ *is negligible in* λ, *where* $\mathsf{Adv}_{\mathcal{A}}^{\mathsf{D\text{-}CSIDH}}(\lambda)$ *is the advantage of* $\mathcal{A}$ *distinguishing the above two distributions.*

Definition 7 (Fixed-Curve Multi-Decisional CSIDH Assumption). *Let* S *be a positive integer. Given the ideal class group* $\mathcal{Cl}(\mathcal{O})$ *and the set* $\mathcal{Ell}_p(\mathcal{O}, \pi)$, *the fixed-curve multi-decisional CSIDH (*FCMD-CSIDH*) problem with* S *is to distinguish the following distributions:*

- $(E, H, (\mathfrak{a}_i \star E, \mathfrak{a}_i \star H)_{i \in [S]})$, *where the supersingular elliptic curves* E *and* H *are sampled uniformly from* $\mathcal{Ell}_p(\mathcal{O}, \pi)$, *and for* $i \in [S]$, $\mathfrak{a}_i$ *are sampled uniformly from* $\mathcal{Cl}(\mathcal{O})$,

- $(E, H, (E_i', H_i')_{i \in [S]})$, where E, H, E_i', H_i' for $i \in [S]$ are supersingular elliptic curves sampled from $\mathcal{E}\ell\ell_p(\mathcal{O}, \pi)$ uniformly at random.

We say that the FCMD-CSIDH assumption with parameter S holds if for any PPT algorithm $\mathcal{A}$, its advantage $\mathsf{Adv}_{\mathcal{A},S}^{\mathsf{FCMD\text{-}CSIDH}}(\lambda)$ is negligible in λ, where $\mathsf{Adv}_{\mathcal{A},S}^{\mathsf{FCMD\text{-}CSIDH}}(\lambda)$ is the advantage of $\mathcal{A}$ distinguishing the above two distributions.

From a result of [17], the following relationship between the above two assumptions was shown:

Lemma 1 D-CSIDH to FCMD-CSIDH ([17]). *Let S be a positive integer. If there exists any PPT algorithm $\mathcal{A}$ solving the FCMD-CSIDH problem with parameter S, then there exists a PPT algorithm $\mathcal{B}$ solving the D-CSIDH problem such that*

$$\mathsf{Adv}_{\mathcal{A},S}^{\mathsf{FCMD\text{-}CSIDH}}(\lambda) \leq S \cdot \mathsf{Adv}_{\mathcal{B}}^{\mathsf{D\text{-}CSIDH}}(\lambda).$$

3 The Lossy CFI-FiSh Scheme

In this section, we first recall the construction of the lossy CFI-FiSh identification scheme [17].

3.1 The Lossy CFI-FiSh

The lossy CFI-FiSh identification scheme $(\mathsf{IGen}, \mathsf{LossyIGen}, \mathsf{P}_1, \mathsf{P}_2, \mathsf{V})$ is constructed as follows:

The following system parameter of the lossy CSI-FiSh is set: Assume the ideal class group $\mathcal{C}\ell(\mathcal{O})$ is cyclic with a known order N and generator $\mathfrak{g}$. Let E_0 be the base curve defined by $y^2 = x^3 + x$. Let $\mathcal{X}$ be a finite set of pairs $((E_1^{(0)}, E_2^{(0)}), (E_1^{(1)}, E_2^{(1)}))$ where $E_1^{(0)}, E_2^{(0)}, E_1^{(1)}, E_2^{(1)}$ are being run over $\mathcal{E}\ell\ell_p(\mathcal{O}, \pi)$. Here, $\mathcal{Y} = \mathbb{Z}_N$ is the set of witnesses. Consider the relation

$$\mathcal{R} := \{(((E_1^{(0)}, E_2^{(0)}), (E_1^{(1)}, E_2^{(1)})), a) \in \mathcal{X} \times \mathcal{Y} \mid E_1^{(1)} = \mathfrak{g}^a \star E_1^{(0)}, E_2^{(1)} = \mathfrak{g}^a \star E_2^{(0)}\},$$

where $((E_1^{(0)}, E_2^{(0)}), (E_1^{(1)}, E_2^{(1)})) \in \mathcal{X}$ is a statement, and $a \in \mathcal{Y}$ is a witness.

- The IGen algorithm samples $a, b, c \in \mathbb{Z}_N$ uniformly at random and outputs a pair $(X, W) \in \mathcal{R}$ where $X = ((E_1^{(0)} = \mathfrak{g}^b \star E_0, E_2^{(0)} = \mathfrak{g}^c \star E_0), (E_1^{(1)} = \mathfrak{g}^a \star E_1^{(0)}, E_2^{(1)} = \mathfrak{g}^a \star E_2^{(0)}))$ and $W = a$

- The $\mathsf{LossyIGen}$ algorithm chooses $a, a', b, c \in \mathbb{Z}_N$ uniformly at random and outputs a lossy statement $X_{ls} = ((E_1^{(0)} = \mathfrak{g}^b \star E_0, E_2^{(0)} = \mathfrak{g}^c \star E_0), (E_1^{(1)} = \mathfrak{g}^a \star E_1^{(0)}, E_2^{(1)} = \mathfrak{g}^{a'} \star E_2^{(0)}))$

- The P_1 algorithm takes (X, W) as input and generates a uniformly random $r \in \mathbb{Z}_N$. This algorithm outputs the commitment $com = (F_1 = \mathfrak{g}^r \star E_1^{(0)}, F_2 = \mathfrak{g}^r \star E_2^{(0)})$.
- The P_2 algorithm, on input $((X, W), com, ch)$ where $ch \in \{0, 1\}$, outputs the response $resp = r$ if $ch = 0$, else $resp = r - a$.
- The V algorithm given $(X, com, ch, resp)$ accepts if the following equations hold (Fig. 1):

$$\begin{cases} \mathfrak{g}^{resp} \star E_1^{(0)} = F_1, \mathfrak{g}^{resp} \star E_2^{(0)} = F_2, & \text{if } ch = 0 \\ \mathfrak{g}^{resp} \star E_1^{(1)} = F_1, \mathfrak{g}^{resp} \star E_2^{(1)} = F_2, & \text{if } ch = 1 \end{cases}$$

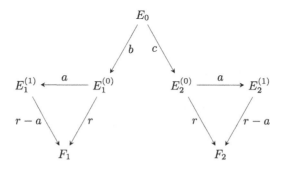

Fig. 1. The base lossy CFI-FiSh identification scheme in [17]

From results of [17], the following proposition was proved:

Proposition 1 ([17]). *The above lossy identification scheme* LossyID^{base} *satisfies* completeness *and* honest-verifier zero-knowledge *property.*

- LossyID^{base} satisfies indistinguishability of lossy statements *if the* D-CSIDH *assumption holds. In particular, we have* $\text{Adv}_{\mathcal{A}, \text{LossyID}^{\text{base}}}^{\text{ind-stmt}}(\lambda) = \text{Adv}_{\mathcal{B}}^{\text{D-CSIDH}}(\lambda)$, *where* $\mathcal{A}$ *is a PPT algorithm against* LossyID^{base}, *and* $\mathcal{B}$ *is a PPT algorithm against the* D-CSIDH *problem.*
- LossyID^{base} satisfies ϵ_{los}-lossy soundness *for* $\epsilon_{\text{los}} = 1/(2N)$, *where* $N = |\mathcal{C}\ell(\mathcal{O})|$.

The above lossy identification scheme has only one-bit challenge. To improve the security, we need to execute the base lossy identification scheme in parallel rounds. To decrease the signature size of the resulting Fiat-Shamir signature scheme, a method in [19] is applied which need to satisfy the size of public key. The concrete construction is as follows: As the security parameter, let $\mathbf{X} = \{(E_1^{(0)}, E_2^{(0)}), (E_1^{(1)}, E_2^{(1)}), \cdots, (E_1^{(S)}, E_2^{(S)}) \mid E_i^{(j)} \in \mathcal{E}\ell\ell_p(\mathcal{O})\}, Y = \{a_1, a_2, \cdots, a_S \mid a_i \in \mathbb{Z}_N\}$. E_0 is defined the same as the base lossy CFI-FiSh.

- The algorithm IGen takes $\{a_i\}_{i \in [S]}, b, c \in \mathbb{Z}_N$ and outputs a pair $(X, W) \in \mathcal{R}$ where $X = ((E_1^{(0)} = \mathfrak{g}^b \star E_0, E_2^{(0)} = \mathfrak{g}^c \star E_0), (E_1^{(1)} = \mathfrak{g}^{a_1} \star E_1^{(0)}, E_2^{(i)} = \mathfrak{g}^{a_1} \star E_2^{(0)}), \cdots, (E_1^{(S)} = \mathfrak{g}^{a_S} \star E_1^{(0)}, E_2^{(S)} = \mathfrak{g}^{a_S} * E_2^{(0)}))$ and $W = \{a\}_i$

- The algorithm LossyIGen takes $a_1, a_2, \cdots, a_S, a_1', a_2', \cdots, a_S', b, c \in \mathbb{Z}_N$ and outputs a lossy statement $X_{ls} = ((E_1^{(0)} = \mathfrak{g}^b \star E_0, E_2^{(0)} = \mathfrak{g}^c \star E_0), (E_1^{(1)} = \mathfrak{g}^{a_1} \star E_1^{(0)}, E_2^{(1)} = \mathfrak{g}^{a_1'} \star E_2^{(0)}), \cdots, (E_1^{(S)} = \mathfrak{g}^{a_S} \star E_1^{(0)}, E_2^{(S)} = \mathfrak{g}^{a_S'} \star E_2^{(0)}))$

- P_1 takes the output (X, W) of the algorithm IGen and then generates t random $r_i \in \mathbb{Z}_N$. The output of P_1 is the commitment $com = (F_1^{(i)} = \mathfrak{g}^r \star E_1^{(0)}, F_2^{(i)} = \mathfrak{g}^r \star E_2^{(0)})$

- P_2 takes $((X, W), com, ch)$ where $ch = b_1 \| b_2 \| \cdots \| b_t$, each $b_i \in \{0, 1, \cdots, S\}$ and outputs the response $resp = resp_1 \| resp_2 \| \cdots \| resp_t$, $resp_i = r_i$ if $b_i = 0$, else $resp_i = r_i - a_i$.

- The algorithm V takes $(X, com, ch, resp)$ and accepts if the following equations hold

$$\begin{cases} \mathfrak{g}^{resp_i} \star E_1^{(0)} = F_1, \mathfrak{g}^{resp_i} \star E_2^{(0)} = F_2, & \text{if } b_i = 0 \\ \mathfrak{g}^{resp} \star E_1^{(1)} = F_1, \mathfrak{g}^{resp} \star E_2^{(1)} = F_2, & \text{if } b_i \neq 0 \end{cases}$$

4   Tightly Secure IBS from Lossy CSI-FiSh

4.1   Construction

In this section, we describe our proposed IBS scheme with tight security. This scheme is based on the lossy CSI-FiSh scheme and IBS scheme in [36]. Informally, our IBS is described as follows:

- The master public key mpk and the master secret key msk are a public key $(E_1^{(i)}, E_2^{(i)})_{i \in \{0, \ldots, S_0\}}$ and a secret key $(a_i)_{i \in [S_0]}$ of the lossy CSI-FiSh scheme, respectively.
- When generating a user's secret key $\mathsf{usk_{id}}$, a lossy CSI-FiSh's signature $(F_1^{(i,j)}, F_2^{(i,j)}, resp_{i,j})_{i \in [T_1], j \in [S_1]}$ on id is generated by using msk. Then, this signature corresponds to $\mathsf{usk_{id}}$ in our scheme.
- The Sign algorithm on input $\mathsf{usk_{id}}$ and a message m generates a signature on (id, m), which consists of the commitment $(F_1^{(i,j)}, F_2^{(i,j)})_{i \in [T_1], j \in [S_1]}$ and a new lossy CSI-FiSh's signature $(\widehat{ch}_{i,j}, \widehat{resp}_{i,j})_{i \in [T_1], j \in [T_2]}$ computed by using $\mathsf{usk_{id}}$.
- The Vrfy algorithm checks the validity-check of the given signature on (id, m), by following the verification algorithm of the lossy CSI-FiSh scheme.

Concretely, our proposed IBS scheme $\mathsf{IBS_{LCSI\text{-}FiSh}}$ = (Setup, KeyDer, Sign, Vrfy) is constructed as follows: As the system parameter of $\mathsf{IBS_{LCSI\text{-}FiSh}}$, let E_0 be the base curve, let $T_1, T_2, S_0 = 2^{\eta_0} - 1, S_1 = 2^{\eta_1} - 1$

be positive integers, where η_0, η_1 are positive integers, and $T_1 < S_0, T_2 < S_1$. Let $H : \{0,1\}^* \to \{0,\ldots,S_0\}^{T_1 S_1}$ and $\hat{H} : \{0,1\}^* \to \{0,\ldots,S_1\}^{T_1 T_2}$ be random oracles. $\mathcal{ID} = \{0,1\}^*$ and $\mathcal{M} = \{0,1\}^*$ are the identity space and the message space, respectively.

- (mpk, msk) $\leftarrow$ Setup(1^λ):
  1. Choose $b \xleftarrow{\$} \mathbb{Z}_N$ and $c \xleftarrow{\$} \mathbb{Z}_N$.
  2. Compute $E_1^{(0)} = \mathfrak{g}^b \star E_0$ and $E_2^{(0)} = \mathfrak{g}^c \star E_0$.
  3. For $i \in \{1,\ldots,S_0\}$, choose $a_i \xleftarrow{\$} \mathbb{Z}_N$ and compute $E_1^{(i)} = \mathfrak{g}^{a_i} \star E_1^{(0)}$, $E_2^{(i)} = \mathfrak{g}^{a_i} \star E_2^{(0)}$.
  4. Output mpk $= ((E_1^{(0)}, E_2^{(0)}), (E_1^{(i)}, E_2^{(i)})_{i \in [S_0]})$ and msk $= \{b, c, (a_1, \ldots, a_{S_0})\}$.
- usk$_{id}$ $\leftarrow$ KeyDer(mpk, msk, id):
  1. Parse $((E_1^{(0)}, E_2^{(0)}), (E_1^{(i)}, E_2^{(i)})_{i \in [S_0]})$ and msk $= (a_1, \ldots, a_{S_0})$.
  2. Let $a_0 \leftarrow 0$.
  3. For $i \in [T_1]$ and $j \in [S_1]$, choose $r_{i,j} \xleftarrow{\$} \mathbb{Z}_N$ and compute $F_1^{(i,j)} = \mathfrak{g}^{r_{i,j}} \star E_1^{(0)}$, $F_2^{(i,j)} = \mathfrak{g}^{r_{i,j}} \star E_2^{(0)}$.
  4. Compute $(ch_i)_{i \in [T_1 S_1]} = H((F_1^{(i,j)}, F_2^{(i,j)})_{i \in [T_1], j \in [S_1]} \parallel id)$.
  5. For $i \in [T_1]$ and $j \in [S_1]$, compute $resp_{i,j} = r_{i,j} - a_{ch_i}$.
  6. Output usk$_{id}$ $= (id, (F_1^{(i,j)}, F_2^{(i,j)})_{i \in [T_1], j \in [S_1]}, (resp_{i,j})_{i \in [T_1], j \in [S_1]})$.
- $\sigma \leftarrow$ Sign(mpk, usk$_{id}$, m):
  1. Parse mpk $= ((E_1^{(0)}, E_2^{(0)}), (E_1^{(i)}, E_2^{(i)})_{i \in [S_0]})$ and usk$_{id}$ $= (id, (F_1^{(i,j)}, F_2^{(i,j)})_{i \in [T_1], j \in [S_1]}, (resp_{i,j})_{i \in [T_1], j \in [S_1]})$.
  2. For $i \in [T_1]$, set $resp_{i,0} = 0$.
  3. Compute $(ch_i)_{i \in [T_1 S_1]} = H((F_1^{(i,j)}, F_2^{(i,j)})_{i \in [T_1], j \in [S_1]} \parallel id)$.
  4. For $i \in [T_1]$ and $j \in [T_2]$, choose $\hat{r}_{i,j} \xleftarrow{\$} \mathbb{Z}_N$ and compute $\hat{F}_1^{(i,j)} = \mathfrak{g}^{\hat{r}_{i,j}} \star E_1^{(ch_i)}$, $\hat{F}_2^{(i,j)} = \mathfrak{g}^{\hat{r}_{i,j}} \star E_2^{(ch_i)}$.
  5. Compute $(\widehat{ch}_{i,j})_{i \in [T_1], j \in [T_2]} = \hat{H}((\hat{F}_1^{(i,j)}, \hat{F}_2^{(i,j)})_{i \in [T_1], j \in [T_2]} \parallel id \parallel m)$.
  6. For $i \in [T_1]$ and $j \in [T_2]$, compute $\widehat{resp}_{i,j} = \hat{r}_{i,j} - resp_{i, \widehat{ch}_{i,j}}$.
  7. Output $\sigma = ((F_1^{(i,j)}, F_2^{(i,j)})_{i \in [T_1], j \in [S_1]}, (\widehat{ch}_{i,j})_{i \in [T_1], j \in [T_2]}, (\widehat{resp}_{i,j})_{i \in [T_1], j \in [T_2]})$.
- $1/0 \leftarrow$ Vrfy(mpk, id, m, σ):
  1. Parse mpk $= ((E_1^{(0)}, E_2^{(0)}), (E_1^{(i)}, E_2^{(i)})_{i \in [S_0]})$ and $\sigma = ((F_1^{(i,j)}, F_2^{(i,j)})_{i \in [T_1], j \in [S_1]}, (\widehat{ch}_{i,j})_{i \in [T_1], j \in [T_2]}, (\widehat{resp}_{i,j})_{i \in [T_1], j \in [T_2]})$.
  2. Compute $(ch_i)_{i \in [T_1 S_1]} = H((F_1^{(i,j)}, F_2^{(i,j)})_{i \in [T_1], j \in [S_1]} \parallel id)$.
  3. For $i \in [T_1]$ and $j \in [T_2]$, compute
     - $\hat{F}_1^{(i,j)\prime} = \mathfrak{g}^{\widehat{resp}_{i,j}} \star E_1^{(ch_i)}$ and $\hat{F}_2^{(i,j)\prime} = \mathfrak{g}^{\widehat{resp}_{i,j}} \star E_2^{(ch_i)}$ if $\widehat{ch}_{i,j} = 0$, and
     - $\hat{F}_1^{(i,j)\prime} = \mathfrak{g}^{\widehat{resp}_{i,j}} \star F_1^{(i, \widehat{ch}_{i,j})}$ and $\hat{F}_2^{(i,j)\prime} = \mathfrak{g}^{\widehat{resp}_{i,j}} \star F_2^{(i, \widehat{ch}_{i,j})}$ if $\widehat{ch}_{i,j} > 0$.
  4. Output 1 if $(\widehat{ch}_{i,j})_{i \in [T_1], j \in [T_2]} = \hat{H}((\hat{F}_1^{(i,j)\prime}, \hat{F}_2^{(i,j)\prime})_{i \in [T_1], j \in [T_2]} \parallel id \parallel m)$, and 0 otherwise.

We show the correctness of our scheme IBS$_{\mathsf{LCSI\text{-}FiSh}}$, as follows:

Proposition 2. *The IBS scheme* $\mathsf{IBS}_{\mathsf{LCSI\text{-}FiSh}}$ *is* correct.

Proof. Let $\mathsf{mpk} = ((E_1^{(0)}, E_2^{(0)}), (E_1^{(i)}, E_2^{(i)})_{i \in [S_0]})$ and $\mathsf{msk} = (a_1, \ldots, a_{S_0})$, where $(\mathsf{mpk}, \mathsf{msk}) \leftarrow \mathsf{Setup}(1^\lambda)$. For an identity $\mathsf{id} \in \mathcal{ID}$ and a message $\mathsf{m} \in \mathcal{M}$, let $\mathsf{usk}_{\mathsf{id}} = (\mathsf{id}, (F_1^{(i,j)}, F_2^{(i,j)})_{i \in [T_1], j \in [S_1]}, (resp_{i,j})_{i \in [T_1], j \in [S_1]}) \leftarrow$ $\mathsf{KeyDer}(\mathsf{mpk}, \mathsf{msk}, \mathsf{id})$ and let $\sigma = ((F_1^{(i,j)}, F_2^{(i,j)})_{i \in [T_1], j \in [S_1]}, (\widehat{ch}_{i,j})_{i \in [T_1], j \in [T_2]},$ $(\widehat{resp}_{i,j})_{i \in [T_1], j \in [T_2]}) \leftarrow \mathsf{Sign}(\mathsf{mpk}, \mathsf{usk}_{\mathsf{id}}, \mathsf{m})$.

Then, we show that the verification algorithm Vrfy accepts the valid message-signature pair (m, σ) on id.

In the case $\widehat{ch}_{i,j} = 0$, for $(i, j) \in [T_1] \times [T_2]$ and $k \in \{1, 2\}$, we have

$$
\begin{aligned}
\hat{F}_k^{(i,j)\prime} &= \mathfrak{g}^{\widehat{resp}_{i,j}} \star E_k^{(ch_i)} \\
&= \mathfrak{g}^{\hat{r}_{i,j} - resp_{i,\widehat{ch}_{i,j}}} \star E_k^{(ch_i)} \\
&= \mathfrak{g}^{\hat{r}_{i,j} - resp_{i,0}} \star E_k^{(ch_i)} \\
&= \mathfrak{g}^{\hat{r}_{i,j}} \star E_k^{(ch_i)} = \hat{F}_k^{(i,j)}.
\end{aligned}
$$

In the case $\widehat{ch}_{i,j} > 0$, we have the following for $(i, j) \in [T_1] \times [T_2]$ and $k \in \{1, 2\}$:

$$
\begin{aligned}
\hat{F}_k^{(i,j)\prime} &= \mathfrak{g}^{\widehat{resp}_{i,j}} \star F_k^{(i,\widehat{ch}_{i,j})} \\
&= \mathfrak{g}^{\hat{r}_{i,j} - resp_{i,\widehat{ch}_{i,j}}} \star (\mathfrak{g}^{r_{i,\widehat{ch}_{i,j}}} \star E_k^{(0)}) \\
&= \mathfrak{g}^{\hat{r}_{i,j} - (r_{i,\widehat{ch}_{i,j}} - a_{ch_i})} \star (\mathfrak{g}^{r_{i,\widehat{ch}_{i,j}}} \star E_k^{(0)}) \\
&= \mathfrak{g}^{\hat{r}_{i,j}} \star (\mathfrak{g}^{a_{ch_i}} \star E_k^{(0)}) \\
&= \mathfrak{g}^{\hat{r}_{i,j}} \star E_k^{(ch_i)} = \hat{F}_k^{(i,j)}.
\end{aligned}
$$

From the above, we obtain the following equation:

$$
\begin{aligned}
(\widehat{ch}_{i,j})_{i \in [T_1], j \in [T_2]} &= \hat{H}((\hat{F}_1^{(i,j)}, \hat{F}_2^{(i,j)})_{i \in [T_1], j \in [T_2]} \parallel \mathsf{id} \parallel \mathsf{m}) \\
&= \hat{H}((\hat{F}_1^{(i,j)\prime}, \hat{F}_2^{(i,j)\prime})_{i \in [T_1], j \in [T_2]} \parallel \mathsf{id} \parallel \mathsf{m}).
\end{aligned}
$$

Therefore, if a signature σ on an identity-message pair $(\mathsf{id}, \mathsf{m})$ is generated correctly, the Vrfy algorithm accepts this signature. The proof is completed. □

4.2 Security Analysis

The following theorem shows the security of our proposed IBS scheme $\mathsf{IBS}_{\mathsf{LCSI\text{-}FiSh}}$:

Theorem 1. *If the* FCMD-CSIDH *assumption with parameter* S_0 *holds, then the IBS scheme* $\mathsf{IBS}_{\mathsf{LCSI\text{-}FiSh}}$ *is* EUF-ID-CMA-MK *secure in the random oracle model.*

Proof. Let $\mathcal{A}$ be a PPT adversary against the EUF-ID-CMA-MK security of $\mathsf{IBS_{LCSI\text{-}FiSh}}$. Let q_s, q_k, q_h, and $q_{\hat{h}}$ be the maximum numbers of queries issued to $\mathsf{O_{Sign}}$, $\mathsf{O_{KeyDer}}$, H, and $\hat{H}$, respectively. Let $\sigma^* = ((F_1^{(i,j)*}, F_2^{(i,j)*})_{i\in[T_1],j\in[S_1]}$, $(\widehat{ch}_{i,j}^*)_{i\in[T_1],j\in[T_2]}, (\widehat{resp}_{i,j}^*)_{i\in[T_1],j\in[T_2]})$ be the signature generated by $\mathcal{A}$ in the **Output** phase.

In order to prove Theorem 1, we consider a sequence of the security games $\mathsf{Game_0}, \mathsf{Game_1}, \mathsf{Game_2}, \mathsf{Game_3}$. For $i \in \{0,1,2,3\}$, let W_i be the event that the experiment outputs 1 in Game_i.

$\underline{\mathsf{Game_0}}$: This game is the same as the ordinary EUF-ID-CMA-MK security game. Then, we have $\mathsf{Adv}_{\mathsf{IBS_{LCSI\text{-}FiSh}},\mathcal{A}}^{\text{euf-id-cma}}(\lambda) = \Pr[W_0]$.

$\underline{\mathsf{Game_1}}$: This game is the same as $\mathsf{Game_0}$ except that the key-derivation oracle $\mathsf{O_{KeyDer}}$ generates a user secret key $\mathsf{usk_{id}}$ for $\mathsf{id} \in \mathcal{ID}$, as follows:

1. For $i \in [T_1 S_1]$, choose $ch_i \xleftarrow{\$} \{0,\ldots,S_0\}$.
2. For $i \in [T_1]$, set $resp_{i,0} = 0$.
3. For $i \in [T_1]$ and $j \in [S_1]$, choose $resp_{i,j} \xleftarrow{\$} \mathbb{Z}_N$.
4. For $i \in [T_1]$ and $j \in [S_1]$, compute $F_1^{(i,j)} = \mathfrak{g}^{resp_{i,j}} \star E_1^{(ch_i)}$ and $F_2^{(i,j)} = \mathfrak{g}^{resp_{i,j}} \star E_2^{(ch_i)}$.
5. Program $(ch_i)_{i\in[T_1 S_1]} = H((F_1^{(i,j)}, F_2^{(i,j)})_{i\in[T_1],j\in[S_1]} \| \mathsf{id})$ if the hash value of $((F_1^{(i,j)}, F_2^{(i,j)})_{i\in[T_1],j\in[S_1]} \| \mathsf{id})$ is not defined. Otherwise abort.
6. Let $\mathsf{usk_{id}} = (\mathsf{id}, (F_1^{(i,j)}, F_2^{(i,j)})_{i\in[T_1],j\in[S_1]}, (resp_{i,j})_{i\in[T_1],j\in[S_1]})$.

First, we show that the $\mathsf{O_{KeyDer}}$ oracle is correctly simulated in $\mathsf{Game_1}$ unless the aborting event occurs. Let $\sigma = ((F_1^{(i,j)}, F_2^{(i,j)})_{i\in[T_1],j\in[S_1]}, (\widehat{ch}_{i,j})_{i\in[T_1],j\in[T_2]}, (\widehat{resp}_{i,j})_{i\in[T_1],j\in[T_2]}) \leftarrow \mathsf{Sign}(\mathsf{mpk}, \mathsf{usk_{id}}, \mathsf{m})$ be a signature generated in $\mathsf{Game_1}$. We analyze the output of the Vrfy algorithm. In the case $\widehat{ch}_{i,j} = 0$, Vrfy computes the following for $(i,j) \in [T_1] \times [T_2]$ and $k \in \{1,2\}$:

$$\hat{F}_k^{(i,j)\prime} = \mathfrak{g}^{\widehat{resp}_{i,j}} \star E_k^{(ch_i)} = \mathfrak{g}^{\hat{r}_{i,j} - resp_{i,\widehat{ch}_{i,j}}} \star E_k^{(ch_i)}$$
$$= \mathfrak{g}^{\hat{r}_{i,j} - resp_{i,0}} \star E_k^{(ch_i)} = \mathfrak{g}^{\hat{r}_{i,j}} \star E_k^{(ch_i)} = \hat{F}_k^{(i,j)}.$$

In the case $\widehat{ch}_{i,j} > 0$, for $(i,j) \in [T_1] \times [T_2]$ and $k \in \{1,2\}$, Vrfy computes the following for a valid signature:

$$\hat{F}_k^{(i,j)\prime} = \mathfrak{g}^{\widehat{resp}_{i,j}} \star F_k^{(i,\widehat{ch}_{i,j})}$$
$$= \mathfrak{g}^{\hat{r}_{i,j} - resp_{i,\widehat{ch}_{i,j}}} \star (\mathfrak{g}^{resp_{i,\widehat{ch}_{i,j}}} \star E_k^{(ch_i)})$$
$$= \mathfrak{g}^{\hat{r}_{i,j}} \star E_k^{(ch_i)} = \hat{F}_k^{(i,j)}.$$

The second equation holds because for any $\widehat{ch}_{i,j} = \hat{j} > 0$, the $\mathsf{O_{KeyDer}}$ oracle sets $F_k^{(i,\hat{j})} = \mathfrak{g}^{resp_{i,\hat{j}}} \star E_k^{(ch_i)}$.

We next estimate the upper bound of the probability that the O_{KeyDer} oracle aborts, that is, the probability that $((F_1^{(i,j)}, F_2^{(i,j)})_{i \in [T_1], j \in [S_1]} \| \text{id})$ has been queried to H when defining $H((F_1^{(i,j)}, F_2^{(i,j)})_{i \in [T_1], j \in [S_1]} \| \text{id})$.

As the worst-case scenario, $q_h + 1$ queries are issued to H at the beginning of the experiment. Then, the probability that O_{KeyDer} aborts for the i-th query is at most $(i + q_h)/N$. In addition, the total number of queries issued to H is at most $q_s + q_k$, since O_{Sign} and O_{KeyDer} call H at most q_s and q_k times, respectively. The probability of guessing a collision of H each time is at most $(q_s + q_k + q_h + 1)/N$. Hence, the probability of aborting Game_1 is at most $(q_s + q_k)(q_s + q_k + q_h + 1)/N$ over all $(q_s + q_k)$ extraction queries, and we have $|\Pr[W_0] - \Pr[W_1]| \leq (q_s + q_k)(q_s + q_k + q_h + 1)/N$.

$\underline{\text{Game}_2}$: This game is the same as Game_1 except that the signing oracle O_{Sign} generates a signature σ on (id, m), as follows:

1. Parse $\text{usk}_{\text{id}} = (\text{id}, (F_1^{(i,j)}, F_2^{(i,j)})_{i \in [T_1], j \in [S_1]}, (resp_{i,j})_{i \in [T_1], j \in [S_1]})$.
2. Compute

   $(ch_i)_{i \in [T_1 S_1]} = H((F_1^{(i,j)}, F_2^{(i,j)})_{i \in [T_1], j \in [S_1]} \| \text{id})$.
3. For $i \in [T_1]$ and $j \in [T_2]$, choose $\widehat{ch}_{i,j} \xleftarrow{\$} \{0, \ldots, S_1\}$ and $\widetilde{resp}_{i,j} \xleftarrow{\$} \mathbb{Z}_N$.
4. For $i \in [T_1]$ and $j \in [T_2]$, compute
   - $\hat{F}_1^{(i,j)} = \mathfrak{g}^{\widetilde{resp}_{i,j}} \star E_1^{(ch_i)}$ and $\hat{F}_2^{(i,j)} = \mathfrak{g}^{\widetilde{resp}_{i,j}} \star E_2^{(ch_i)}$ if $\widehat{ch}_{i,j} = 0$, and
   - $\hat{F}_1^{(i,j)} = \mathfrak{g}^{\widetilde{resp}_{i,j}} \star F_1^{(i, \widehat{ch}_{i,j})}$ and $\hat{F}_2^{(i,j)} = \mathfrak{g}^{\widetilde{resp}_{i,j}} \star F_2^{(i, \widehat{ch}_{i,j})}$ if $\widehat{ch}_{i,j} > 0$.
5. Program $(\widehat{ch}_{i,j})_{i \in [T_1], j \in [T_2]} = \hat{H}((\hat{F}_1^{(i,j)}, \hat{F}_2^{(i,j)})_{i \in [T_1], j \in [T_2]} \| \text{id} \| \text{m})$ if the hash value of $((\hat{F}_1^{(i,j)}, \hat{F}_2^{(i,j)})_{i \in [T_1], j \in [T_2]} \| \text{id} \| \text{m})$ has not been defined. Otherwise abort.
6. Let $\sigma = ((F_1^{(i,j)}, F_2^{(i,j)})_{i \in [T_1], j \in [S_1]}, (\widehat{ch}_{i,j})_{i \in [T_1], j \in [T_2]}, (\widetilde{resp}_{i,j})_{i \in [T_1], j \in [T_2]})$.

We show that Game_1 and Game_2 are identical unless the aborting event occurs. All signatures generated by O_{Sign} in Game_2 are valid, because O_{Sign} computes

- $\hat{F}_1^{(i,j)} = \mathfrak{g}^{\widetilde{resp}_{i,j}} \star E_1^{(ch_i)}$ and $\hat{F}_2^{(i,j)} = \mathfrak{g}^{\widetilde{resp}_{i,j}} \star E_2^{(ch_i)}$ if $\widehat{ch}_{i,j} = 0$, and
- $\hat{F}_1^{(i,j)} = \mathfrak{g}^{\widetilde{resp}_{i,j}} \star F_1^{(i, \widehat{ch}_{i,j})}$ and $\hat{F}_2^{(i,j)} = \mathfrak{g}^{\widetilde{resp}_{i,j}} \star F_2^{(i, \widehat{ch}_{i,j})}$ if $\widehat{ch}_{i,j} > 0$.

That is, the Vrfy algorithm always accepts a signature generated by O_{Sign} since Vrfy computes the values above in the same way as O_{Sign}. Then, the distributions of $\hat{F}_1^{(i,j)}$ and $\hat{F}_2^{(i,j)}$ are uniform, since $\widetilde{resp}_{i,j}$ and $\widehat{ch}_i$ are uniformly random (where $i \in [T_1]$ and $j \in [T_2]$). Hence, as long as the aborting event does not occur, Game_2 is identical to Game_1.

In the same way as the proof of the indistinguishability between Game_0 and Game_1, the probability of aborting is at most $(q_s + q_k)(q_s + q_k + q_{\hat{h}} + 1)/N$. Therefore, we obtain $|\Pr[W_1] - \Pr[W_2]| \leq (q_s + q_k)(q_s + q_k + q_{\hat{h}} + 1)/N$.

$\underline{\text{Game}_3}$: This game is the same as Game_2 except that the challenger generates $E_1^{(i)} = \mathfrak{g}^{a_i} \star E_1^{(0)}$ and $E_2^{(i)} = \mathfrak{g}^{a_i'} \star E_2^{(0)}$ for $i \in [S_0]$ instead of $E_1^{(i)} = \mathfrak{g}^{a_i} \star E_1^{(0)}$ and $E_2^{(i)} = \mathfrak{g}^{a_i} \star E_2^{(0)}$, when generating a master public key and a master secret key.

It is possible to show the indistinguishability between Game_2 and Game_3, by constructing a PPT reduction algorithm solving the FCMD-CSIDH problem. In both Game_2 and Game_3, the $\mathsf{O}_{\mathsf{KeyDer}}$ and $\mathsf{O}_{\mathsf{Sign}}$ oracles can be simulated without msk. Thus, it is possible to set the given FCMD-CSIDH instance as mpk. Then, if the given values are valid FCMD-CSIDH instances, Game_2 can be simulated. If those values are random FCMD-CSIDH instances, Game_3 is also simulated. Hence, by using $\mathcal{A}$, we can construct a PPT algorithm $\mathcal{B}$ solving the FCMD-CSIDH problem such that $|\Pr[W_2] - \Pr[W_3]| \leq \mathsf{Adv}_{\mathcal{B},S_0}^{\mathsf{FCMD\text{-}CSIDH}}(\lambda)$, in the straightforward way.

We show that the winning probability in Game_3 is negligible. In order to do this, we consider the following two events:

- [Reuse]: $\mathcal{A}$ outputs a valid forgery $(\mathsf{id}^*, \mathsf{m}^*, \sigma^*)$ by reusing some value of $(F_1^{(i,j)}, F_2^{(i,j)})_{i \in [T_1], j \in [S_1]}$ generated by $\mathsf{O}_{\mathsf{Sign}}$. Namely, it holds that

$$(F_1^{(i,j)*}, F_2^{(i,j)*})_{i \in [T_1], j \in [S_1]} = (F_1^{(i,j)}, F_2^{(i,j)})_{i \in [T_1], j \in [S_1]}$$

for $\sigma^* = ((F_1^{(i,j)*}, F_2^{(i,j)*})_{i \in [T_1], j \in [S_1]}, (\widehat{ch}_{i,j}^*)_{i \in [T_1], j \in [T_2]}, (\widehat{resp}_{i,j}^*)_{i \in [T_1], j \in [T_2]})$.
- [¬Reuse]: $\mathcal{A}$ outputs a valid forgery $(\mathsf{id}^*, \mathsf{m}^*, \sigma^*)$ without reusing any value of $(F_1^{(i,j)}, F_2^{(i,j)})_{i \in [T_1], j \in [S_1]}$ generated by $\mathsf{O}_{\mathsf{Sign}}$ given $(\mathsf{id}^*, \mathsf{m}^*)$. Namely, it holds that $(F_1^{(i,j)*}, F_2^{(i,j)*})_{i \in [T_1], j \in [S_1]} \neq (F_1^{(i,j)}, F_2^{(i,j)})_{i \in [T_1], j \in [S_1]}$ for any value of $(F_1^{(i,j)}, F_2^{(i,j)})_{i \in [T_1], j \in [S_1]}$ generated by $\mathsf{O}_{\mathsf{Sign}}$.

We first estimate the upper bound of the probability $\Pr[W_3 \wedge \neg\mathsf{Reuse}]$. In order to do this, for the generated public key $\mathsf{mpk} = ((E_1^{(0)}, E_2^{(0)}), (E_1^{(i)} = \mathfrak{g}^{a_i} \star E_1^{(0)}, E_2^{(i)} = \mathfrak{g}^{a_i'} \star E_2^{(0)})_{i \in [S_0]})$, we define $\mathcal{X}_{\mathsf{bad}}$ as the subset of $\mathcal{X}$ (the statement set of lossy CSI-FiSh) which satisfies the following condition for all distinct $i, j \in [S_0]$: $a_i \neq a_i' \wedge a_j - a_i \neq a_j' - a_i'$. Then, for each $(a_i, a_i') \in (\mathbb{Z}_N)^2$ $(i \in [S_0])$, there are at most $N(N-i)$ pairs satisfying this condition. Hence, $|\mathcal{X}_{\mathsf{bad}}| = N^{S_0+2}(N-1) \cdots (N-S_0)$ holds, and we have $\Pr[\mathsf{mpk} \in \mathcal{X}_{\mathsf{bad}}] = (N-1) \cdots (N-S_0)/N^{S_0}$.

We estimate the upper bound of the winning probability in the case where the event $[\neg\mathsf{Reuse} \wedge \mathsf{mpk} \in \mathcal{X}_{\mathsf{bad}}]$ occurs. Let $\sigma^* = ((F_1^{(i,j)*}, F_2^{(i,j)*})_{i \in [T_1], j \in [S_1]}, (\widehat{ch}_{i,j}^*)_{i \in [T_1], j \in [T_2]}, (\widehat{resp}_{i,j}^*)_{i \in [T_1], j \in [T_2]})$ be the signature generated by $\mathcal{A}$. Note that

$$H((F_1^{(i,j)*}, F_2^{(i,j)*})_{i \in [T_1], j \in [S_1]} \| \mathsf{id}^*) = (ch_i^*)_{i \in [T_1 S_1]}$$

and

$$\hat{H}((\hat{F}_1^{(i,j)*}, \hat{F}_2^{(i,j)*})_{i \in [T_1], j \in [T_2]} \| \mathsf{id}^* \| \mathsf{m}^*) = (\widehat{ch}_{i,j}^*)_{i \in [T_1], j \in [T_2]}$$

are defined, due to the definition of Game_3. We consider the case $\widehat{ch}_{i,j} = 0$ and assume that there exist two hash values $(ch_i^*)_{i \in [T_1 S_1]}$ and $(ch_i)_{i \in [T_1 S_1]}$ such that the corresponding values $(\widehat{resp}_{i,j}^*)_{i \in [T_1], j \in [T_2]}$ and $(\widehat{resp}_{i,j})_{i \in [T_1], j \in [T_2]}$ satisfy the condition of Vrfy. Then, we have

$$
\begin{cases}
\hat{F}_1^{(i,j)*} = \mathfrak{g}^{\widetilde{resp}^*_{i,j}} \star E_1^{(ch_i^*)}, \;\; \hat{F}_2^{(i,j)*} = \mathfrak{g}^{\widetilde{resp}^*_{i,j}} \star E_2^{(ch_i^*)}, \\
\hat{F}_1^{(i,j)*} = \mathfrak{g}^{\widetilde{resp}_{i,j}} \star E_1^{(ch_i)}, \;\; \hat{F}_2^{(i,j)*} = \mathfrak{g}^{\widetilde{resp}_{i,j}} \star E_2^{(ch_i)},
\end{cases}
$$
$$
\Leftrightarrow E_1^{(ch_i^*)} = \mathfrak{g}^{\widetilde{resp}_{i,j}-\widetilde{resp}^*_{i,j}} \star E_1^{(ch_i)}, \;\;\; E_2^{(ch_i^*)} = \mathfrak{g}^{\widetilde{resp}_{i,j}-\widetilde{resp}^*_{i,j}} \star E_2^{(ch_i)}.
$$

This contradicts the condition of $\mathcal{X}_{\mathsf{bad}}$. We consider the case $\widehat{ch}^*_{i,j} > 0$ and assume that there exist the two hash values $(ch_i^*)_{i\in[T_1 S_1]}$ and $(ch_i)_{i\in[T_1 S_1]}$ such that the corresponding values

$$
((resp^*_{i,j})_{i\in[T_1],j\in[S_1]}, (\widetilde{resp}^*_{i,j})_{i\in[T_1],j\in[T_2]})
$$

and

$$
((resp_{i,j})_{i\in[T_1],j\in[S_1]}, (\widetilde{resp}_{i,j})_{i\in[T_1],j\in[T_2]})
$$

satisfy the acceptance condition of Vrfy. Due to the change of Game_1, we have

$$
\begin{cases}
\hat{F}_1^{(i,j)*} = \mathfrak{g}^{\widetilde{resp}^*_{i,j}} \star F_1^{(i,\widehat{ch}^*_{i,j})*}, \;\; \hat{F}_2^{(i,j)*} = \mathfrak{g}^{\widetilde{resp}^*_{i,j}} \star F_2^{(i,\widehat{ch}^*_{i,j})*}, \\
\hat{F}_1^{(i,j)*} = \mathfrak{g}^{\widetilde{resp}_{i,j}} \star F_1^{(i,\widehat{ch}_{i,j})}, \;\; \hat{F}_2^{(i,j)*} = \mathfrak{g}^{\widetilde{resp}_{i,j}} \star F_2^{(i,\widehat{ch}_{i,j})}.
\end{cases}
$$
$$
\Leftrightarrow
\begin{cases}
\hat{F}_1^{(i,j)*} = \mathfrak{g}^{\widetilde{resp}^*_{i,j}+resp^*_{i,j}} \star E_1^{(ch_i^*)}, \;\; \hat{F}_2^{(i,j)*} = \mathfrak{g}^{\widetilde{resp}^*_{i,j}+resp^*_{i,j}} \star E_2^{(ch_i^*)}, \\
\hat{F}_1^{(i,j)*} = \mathfrak{g}^{\widetilde{resp}_{i,j}+resp_{i,j}} \star E_1^{(ch_i)}, \;\; \hat{F}_2^{(i,j)*} = \mathfrak{g}^{\widetilde{resp}_{i,j}+resp_{i,j}} \star E_2^{(ch_i)}.
\end{cases}
$$
$$
\Leftrightarrow
\begin{cases}
E_1^{(ch_i^*)} = \mathfrak{g}^{(\widetilde{resp}_{i,j}+resp_{i,j})-(\widetilde{resp}^*_{i,j}+resp^*_{i,j})} \star E_1^{(ch_i)}, \\
E_2^{(ch_i^*)} = \mathfrak{g}^{(\widetilde{resp}_{i,j}+resp_{i,j})-(\widetilde{resp}^*_{i,j}+resp^*_{i,j})} \star E_2^{(ch_i)}.
\end{cases}
$$

This also contradicts the condition of $\mathcal{X}_{\mathsf{bad}}$. Hence, there exists at most one $(ch_i^*)_{i\in[T_1 S_1]}$ that satisfies the condition of Vrfy, and we have $\Pr[W_3 \mid \neg\mathsf{Reuse} \wedge \mathsf{mpk} \in \mathcal{X}_{\mathsf{bad}}] \leq 1/(S_0 + 1)^{T_1 S_1}$. Therefore, we obtain

$$
\begin{aligned}
\Pr[W_3 \wedge \neg\mathsf{Reuse}] &= \Pr[W_3 \wedge \neg\mathsf{Reuse} \wedge \mathsf{mpk} \in \mathcal{X}_{\mathsf{bad}}] + \Pr[W_3 \wedge \neg\mathsf{Reuse} \wedge \mathsf{mpk} \notin \mathcal{X}_{\mathsf{bad}}] \\
&\leq \Pr[W_3 \mid \neg\mathsf{Reuse} \wedge \mathsf{mpk} \in \mathcal{X}_{\mathsf{bad}}] \cdot \Pr[\mathsf{mpk} \in \mathcal{X}_{\mathsf{bad}}] + \Pr[\mathsf{mpk} \notin \mathcal{X}_{\mathsf{bad}}] \\
&\leq \frac{1}{(S_0 + 1)^{T_1 S_1}} \cdot \frac{(N - 1)\cdots(N - S_0)}{N^{S_0}} \\
&\quad + \left(1 - \frac{(N - 1)\cdots(N - S_0)}{N^{S_0}}\right).
\end{aligned}
$$

Next, we estimate the upper bound of the probability $\Pr[W_3 \wedge \mathsf{Reuse}]$. Let $\sigma^* = ((F_1^{(i,j)*}, F_2^{(i,j)*})_{i\in[T_1],j\in[S_1]}, (\widehat{ch}^*_{i,j})_{i\in[T_1],j\in[T_2]}, (\widetilde{resp}^*_{i,j})_{i\in[T_1],j\in[T_2]})$ be the signature on $(\mathsf{id}^*, \mathsf{m}^*)$, which is generated by $\mathcal{A}$. If $\widehat{ch}^*_{i,j} = 0$, we have

$$
\hat{F}_1^{(i,j)*} = \mathfrak{g}^{\widetilde{resp}^*_{i,j}} \star E_1^{(ch_i^*)}, \;\; \hat{F}_2^{(i,j)*} = \mathfrak{g}^{\widetilde{resp}^*_{i,j}} \star E_2^{(ch_i^*)}.
$$

Thus, $\mathsf{mpk} \in \mathcal{X}_{\mathsf{bad}}$ always holds since $a_{ch_i^*} \neq a'_{ch_i^*}$ in Game_3.

If $\widehat{ch}^*_{i,j} > 0$, it is shown that there exists at most one $(ch_i^*)_{i\in[T_1 S_1]}$ which satisfies the winning condition, in the same way as the case $[W_3 \wedge \neg\mathsf{Reuse}]$.

Hence, it holds that

$$\Pr[W_3 \wedge \mathsf{Reuse}] = \Pr[W_3 \wedge \mathsf{Reuse} \wedge \mathsf{mpk} \in \mathcal{X}_{\mathsf{bad}}] + \Pr[W_3 \wedge \mathsf{Reuse} \wedge \mathsf{mpk} \notin \mathcal{X}_{\mathsf{bad}}]$$
$$\leq \Pr[W_3 \mid \mathsf{Reuse} \wedge \mathsf{mpk} \in \mathcal{X}_{\mathsf{bad}}] \cdot \Pr[\mathsf{mpk} \in \mathcal{X}_{\mathsf{bad}}]$$
$$\leq \frac{1}{(S_0 + 1)^{T_1 S_1}} \cdot \frac{(N - 1) \cdots (N - S_0)}{N^{S_0}}.$$

Therefore, we have

$$\Pr[W_3] = \Pr[W_3 \wedge \mathsf{Reuse}] + \Pr[W_3 \wedge \neg\mathsf{Reuse}]$$
$$\leq \frac{2}{(S_0 + 1)^{T_1 S_1}} \cdot \frac{(N - 1) \cdots (N - S_0)}{N^{S_0}} + \left(1 - \frac{(N - 1) \cdots (N - S_0)}{N^{S_0}}\right).$$

From the discussion above, the inequality

$$\mathsf{Adv}_{\mathsf{IBS}_{\mathsf{LCSI\text{-}FiSh}}, \mathcal{A}}^{\mathsf{euf\text{-}id\text{-}cma}}(\lambda) \leq \sum_{i=0}^{2} |\Pr[W_i] - \Pr[W_{i+1}]| + \Pr[W_3]$$
$$\leq \mathsf{Adv}_{\mathcal{B}, S_0}^{\mathsf{FCMD\text{-}CSIDH}}(\lambda) + \frac{(q_s + q_k)(2q_s + 2q_k + q_h + q_{\hat{h}} + 2)}{N}$$
$$+ \frac{2}{(S_0 + 1)^{T_1 S_1}} \cdot \frac{(N - 1) \cdots (N - S_0)}{N^{S_0}}$$
$$+ \left(1 - \frac{(N - 1) \cdots (N - S_0)}{N^{S_0}}\right)$$

is obtained.   □

Finally, we have the following result due to Lemma 1 and Theorem 1:

Corollary 1. *If the* D-CSIDH *assumption holds, then the IBS scheme* IBS$_{\mathsf{LCSI\text{-}FiSh}}$ *is* EUF-ID-CMA-MK *secure in the random oracle model. Concretely, for a PPT adversary* $\mathcal{A}$ *against the* EUF-ID-CMA-MK *security of* IBS$_{\mathsf{LCSI\text{-}FiSh}}$, *then there exists a PPT algorithm* $\mathcal{B}$ *against the* D-CSIDH *problem such that*

$$\mathsf{Adv}_{\mathsf{IBS}_{\mathsf{LCSI\text{-}FiSh}}, \mathcal{A}}^{\mathsf{euf\text{-}id\text{-}cma}}(\lambda) \leq S_0 \cdot \mathsf{Adv}_{\mathcal{B}}^{\mathsf{D\text{-}CSIDH}}(\lambda) + \frac{(q_s + q_k)(2q_s + 2q_k + q_h + q_{\hat{h}} + 2)}{N}$$
$$+ \frac{2}{(S_0 + 1)^{T_1 S_1}} \cdot \frac{(N - 1) \cdots (N - S_0)}{N^{S_0}}$$
$$+ \left(1 - \frac{(N - 1) \cdots (N - S_0)}{N^{S_0}}\right),$$

where q_s, q_k, q_h, *and* $q_{\hat{h}}$ *are the maximum numbers of queries to* $\mathsf{O}_{\mathsf{Sign}}$, $\mathsf{O}_{\mathsf{KeyDer}}$, H, *and* $\hat{H}$, *respectively.*

Therefore, we have given a tight security proof for the proposed IBS scheme.

5   Conclusion

In this paper, we have proposed an identity-based signature scheme based on the lossy CSI-FiSh and proved a tight security reduction for this scheme. Furthermore, we have showed that our scheme has more compact user keys and signatures than existing suitable schemes by choosing appropriate parameters. We leave the construction of IBS based on other isogeny-based hard problems, e.g. Endomorphism Ring Problem [15,16,25] for future works.

Acknowledgements. This research was in part conducted under a contract of "Research and development on new generation cryptography for secure wireless communication services" among "Research and Development for Expansion of Radio Wave Resources (JPJ000254)", which was supported by the Ministry of Internal Affairs and Communications, Japan. This work was in part supported by JSPS KAKENHI Grant Number JP22H03590. The authors would like to thank the anonymous reviewers for their helpful comments.

References

1. Abdalla, M., Fouque, P., Lyubashevsky, V., Tibouchi, M.: Tightly secure signatures from lossy identification schemes. J. Cryptol. **29**(3), 597–631 (2016)
2. Atapoor, S., Baghery, K., Cozzo, D., Pedersen, R.: CSI-SharK: CSI-FiSh with sharing-friendly keys. Cryptology ePrint Archive (2022)
3. Bellare, M., Namprempre, C., Neven, G.: Security proofs for identity-based identification and signature schemes. J. Cryptol. **22**(1), 1–61 (2009)
4. Bellare, M., Neven, G.: Multi-signatures in the plain public-key model and a general forking lemma. In: CCS, pp. 390–399. ACM (2006)
5. Beullens, W., Disson, L., Pedersen, R., Vercauteren, F.: CSI-RAShi: distributed key generation for CSIDH. In: Cheon, J.H., Tillich, J.-P. (eds.) PQCrypto 2021 2021. LNCS, vol. 12841, pp. 257–276. Springer, Cham (2021). https://doi.org/10.1007/978-3-030-81293-5_14
6. Beullens, W., Katsumata, S., Pintore, F.: Calamari and Falafl: logarithmic (linkable) ring signatures from isogenies and lattices. In: Moriai, S., Wang, H. (eds.) ASIACRYPT 2020. LNCS, vol. 12492, pp. 464–492. Springer, Cham (2020). https://doi.org/10.1007/978-3-030-64834-3_16
7. Beullens, W., Kleinjung, T., Vercauteren, F.: CSI-FiSh: efficient isogeny based signatures through class group computations. In: Galbraith, S.D., Moriai, S. (eds.) ASIACRYPT 2019. LNCS, vol. 11921, pp. 227–247. Springer, Cham (2019). https://doi.org/10.1007/978-3-030-34578-5_9
8. Bonnetain, X., Schrottenloher, A.: Quantum security analysis of CSIDH. In: Canteaut, A., Ishai, Y. (eds.) EUROCRYPT 2020. LNCS, vol. 12106, pp. 493–522. Springer, Cham (2020). https://doi.org/10.1007/978-3-030-45724-2_17
9. Castryck, W., Decru, T.: An efficient key recovery attack on SIDH (preliminary version). Cryptology ePrint Archive (2022)
10. Castryck, W., Lange, T., Martindale, C., Panny, L., Renes, J.: CSIDH: an efficient post-quantum commutative group action. In: Peyrin, T., Galbraith, S. (eds.) ASIACRYPT 2018. LNCS, vol. 11274, pp. 395–427. Springer, Cham (2018). https://doi.org/10.1007/978-3-030-03332-3_15

11. Childs, A., Jao, D., Soukharev, V.: Constructing elliptic curve isogenies in quantum subexponential time. J. Math. Cryptol. **8**(1), 1–29 (2014)
12. Couveignes, J.M.: Hard homogeneous spaces. Cryptology ePrint Archive (2006)
13. Cozzo, D., Smart, N.P.: Sashimi: cutting up CSI-FiSh secret keys to produce an actively secure distributed signing protocol. In: Ding, J., Tillich, J.-P. (eds.) PQCrypto 2020. LNCS, vol. 12100, pp. 169–186. Springer, Cham (2020). https://doi.org/10.1007/978-3-030-44223-1_10
14. Dartois, P., Leroux, A., Robert, D., Wesolowski, B.: SQISignHD: new dimensions in cryptography. Cryptology ePrint Archive (2023)
15. De Feo, L., Kohel, D., Leroux, A., Petit, C., Wesolowski, B.: SQISign: compact post-quantum signatures from quaternions and isogenies. In: Moriai, S., Wang, H. (eds.) ASIACRYPT 2020. LNCS, vol. 12491, pp. 64–93. Springer, Cham (2020). https://doi.org/10.1007/978-3-030-64837-4_3
16. Eisenträger, K., Hallgren, S., Lauter, K., Morrison, T., Petit, C.: Supersingular isogeny graphs and endomorphism rings: reductions and solutions. In: Nielsen, J.B., Rijmen, V. (eds.) EUROCRYPT 2018. LNCS, vol. 10822, pp. 329–368. Springer, Cham (2018). https://doi.org/10.1007/978-3-319-78372-7_11
17. El Kaafarani, A., Katsumata, S., Pintore, F.: Lossy CSI-FiSh: efficient signature scheme with tight reduction to decisional CSIDH-512. In: Kiayias, A., Kohlweiss, M., Wallden, P., Zikas, V. (eds.) PKC 2020. LNCS, vol. 12111, pp. 157–186. Springer, Cham (2020). https://doi.org/10.1007/978-3-030-45388-6_6
18. Feo, L.D., et al.: SCALLOP: scaling the CSI-FiSh. In: Boldyreva, A., Kolesnikov, V. (eds.) PKC 2023. LNCS, vol. 13940, pp. 345–375. Springer, Cham (2023). https://doi.org/10.1007/978-3-031-31368-4_13
19. De Feo, L., Galbraith, S.D.: SeaSign: compact isogeny signatures from class group actions. In: Ishai, Y., Rijmen, V. (eds.) EUROCRYPT 2019. LNCS, vol. 11478, pp. 759–789. Springer, Cham (2019). https://doi.org/10.1007/978-3-030-17659-4_26
20. Fouotsa, T.B., Moriya, T., Petit, C.: M-SIDH and MD-SIDH: countering SIDH attacks by masking information. Cryptology ePrint Archive (2023)
21. Fukumitsu, M., Hasegawa, S.: A Galindo-Garcia-like identity-based signature with tight security reduction, revisited. In: CANDAR, pp. 92–98. IEEE Computer Society (2018)
22. Galindo, D., Garcia, F.D.: A Schnorr-like lightweight identity-based signature scheme. In: Preneel, B. (ed.) AFRICACRYPT 2009. LNCS, vol. 5580, pp. 135–148. Springer, Heidelberg (2009). https://doi.org/10.1007/978-3-642-02384-2_9
23. Jao, D., De Feo, L.: Towards quantum-resistant cryptosystems from supersingular elliptic curve isogenies. In: Yang, B.-Y. (ed.) PQCrypto 2011. LNCS, vol. 7071, pp. 19–34. Springer, Heidelberg (2011). https://doi.org/10.1007/978-3-642-25405-5_2
24. Kiltz, E., Neven, G.: Identity-based signatures. In: Identity-Based Cryptography, Cryptology and Information Security Series, vol. 2, pp. 31–44. IOS Press (2009)
25. Kohel, D.R.: Endomorphism Rings of Elliptic Curves over Finite Fields. University of California, Berkeley (1996)
26. Lee, Y., Park, J.H., Lee, K., Lee, D.H.: Tight security for the generic construction of identity-based signature (in the multi-instance setting). Theoret. Comput. Sci. **847**, 122–133 (2020)
27. Leroux, A.: A new isogeny representation and applications to cryptography. In: Agrawal, S., Lin, D. (eds.) ASIACRYPT 2022. LNCS, vol. 13792, pp. 3–35. Springer, Cham (2022). https://doi.org/10.1007/978-3-031-22966-4_1
28. Maino, L., Martindale, C.: An attack on SIDH with arbitrary starting curve. Cryptology ePrint Archive (2022)

29. NIST: National Institute of Standards and Technology Interagency (2022). https://doi.org/10.6028/NIST.IR.8413

30. Pan, J., Wagner, B.: Lattice-based signatures with tight adaptive corruptions and more. In: Hanaoka, G., Shikata, J., Watanabe, Y. (eds.) PKC 2022. LNCS, vol. 13178, pp. 347–378. Springer, Cham (2022). https://doi.org/10.1007/978-3-030-97131-1_12

31. Peng, C., Chen, J., Zhou, L., Choo, K.R., He, D.: CsiIBS: a post-quantum identity-based signature scheme based on isogenies. J. Inf. Secur. Appl. **54**, 102504 (2020)

32. Pointcheval, D., Stern, J.: Security arguments for digital signatures and blind signatures. J. Cryptol. **13**(3), 361–396 (2000)

33. Robert, D.: Breaking SIDH in polynomial time. Cryptology ePrint Archive (2022)

34. Rostovtsev, A., Stolbunov, A.: Public-key cryptosystem based on isogenies. Cryptology ePrint Archive (2006)

35. Shamir, A.: Identity-based cryptosystems and signature schemes. In: Blakley, G.R., Chaum, D. (eds.) CRYPTO 1984. LNCS, vol. 196, pp. 47–53. Springer, Heidelberg (1985). https://doi.org/10.1007/3-540-39568-7_5

36. Shaw, S., Dutta, R.: Identification scheme and forward-secure signature in identity-based setting from isogenies. In: Huang, Q., Yu, Yu. (eds.) ProvSec 2021. LNCS, vol. 13059, pp. 309–326. Springer, Cham (2021). https://doi.org/10.1007/978-3-030-90402-9_17

37. Shor, P.W.: Polynomial-time algorithms for prime factorization and discrete logarithms on a quantum computer. SIAM Rev. **41**(2), 303–332 (1999)

38. Silverman, J.H.: The Arithmetic of Elliptic Curves, vol. 106. Springer, Cham (2009). https://doi.org/10.1007/978-0-387-09494-6

39. Zhang, X., Liu, S., Gu, D., Liu, J.K.: A generic construction of tightly secure signatures in the multi-user setting. Theor. Comput. Sci. **775**, 32–52 (2019)

Lattice-Based Cryptography

New NTRU Records with Improved Lattice Bases

Elena Kirshanova[1,3]($\boxtimes$) (iD), Alexander May[2]($\boxtimes$) (iD), and Julian Nowakowski[2]($\boxtimes$) (iD)

[1] Technology Innovation Institute, Abu Dhabi, UAE
`elenakirshanova@gmail.com`
[2] Ruhr-University Bochum, Bochum, Germany
`{alex.may,julian.nowakowski}@rub.de`
[3] I.Kant Baltic Federal University, Kaliningrad, Russia

Abstract. The original NTRU cryptosystem from 1998 can be considered the starting point of the great success story of lattice-based cryptography. Modern NTRU versions like NTRU-HPS and NTRU-HRSS are round-3 finalists in NIST's selection process, and also CRYSTALS-KYBER and especially FALCON are heavily influenced by NTRU.

Coppersmith and Shamir proposed to attack NTRU via lattice basis reduction, and variations of the Coppersmith-Shamir lattice have been successfully applied to solve official NTRU challenges by Security Innovations, Inc. up to dimension $n = 173$.

In our work, we provide the tools to attack modern NTRU versions, both by the design of a proper lattice basis, as well as by tuning the modern *BKZ with lattice sieving* algorithm from the G6K library to NTRU needs.

Let n be prime, $\Phi_n := (X^n - 1)/(X - 1)$, and let $\mathbb{Z}_q[X]/(\Phi_n)$ be the cyclotomic ring. As opposed to the common belief, we show that switching from the Coppersmith-Shamir lattice to a basis for the cyclotomic ring provides benefits. To this end, we slightly enhance the *LWE with Hints* framework by Dachman-Soled, Ducas, Gong, Rossi with the concept of projections against *almost-parallel hints*.

Using our new lattice bases, we set the first cryptanalysis landmarks for NTRU-HPS with $n \in [101, 171]$ and for NTRU-HRSS with $n \in [101, 211]$. As a numerical example, we break our largest HPS-171 instance using the cyclotomic ring basis within 83 core days, whereas the Coppersmith-Shamir basis requires 172 core days.

We also break one more official NTRU challenges by Security Innovation, Inc., originally worth 1000\$, in dimension $n = 181$ in 20 core years. Our experiments run up to BKZ blocksizes beyond 100, a regime that has not been reached in analyzing cryptosystems so far.

Keywords: NTRU · Cryptanalysis · BKZ · Sieving

1 Introduction

Lattice-based cryptography has evolved as the most favourable candidate for building *efficient* post-quantum cryptosystems, because lattices seem to

© The Author(s), under exclusive license to Springer Nature Switzerland AG 2023
T. Johansson and D. Smith-Tone (Eds.): PQCrypto 2023, LNCS 14154, pp. 167–195, 2023.
https://doi.org/10.1007/978-3-031-40003-2_7

provide sufficiently hard problems in reasonable dimensions. This is in contrast to coding-based cryptography [ABB+20, MAB+21, ABC+20] that usually requires significantly larger dimensions. However, when compared to code-based schemes, precisely estimating the security of lattice-based schemes is much more difficult, since the behavior of lattice reduction algorithms is not yet fully understood. Their analysis remains a tricky business that heavily relies on experimental data that sharpens the accuracy of lattice estimators.

The NTRU cryptosystem [HPS98] from 1998 can be considered a blueprint for most efficient lattice-based constructions [BDK+18, FHK+18]. Therefore, it may not come as a surprise that NTRU received a significant amount of cryptanalytic attention, both from the theoretical side as well as from experimental evaluations.

Lattice Attacks in Theory. NTRU is defined over the convolution polynomial ring $\mathbb{Z}_q[X]/(X^n - 1)$. An NTRU secret key consists of two small norm polynomials $f, g \in \mathbb{Z}_q[X]/(X^n - 1)$, f being invertible, with corresponding NTRU public key $h = f^{-1}g$. In 1997, Coppersmith and Shamir [CS97] already showed how to use h for defining a basis for a $2n$-dimensional lattice $\mathcal{L}_{CS}$. Let $\mathbf{f}, \mathbf{g}$ denote the coefficient vectors of f, g. Then $(\mathbf{f}, \mathbf{g}) \in \mathcal{L}_{CS}$, and $(\mathbf{f}, \mathbf{g})$ is presumably a shortest (non-zero) vector in $\mathcal{L}_{CS}$.

The lattice $\mathcal{L}_{CS}$ does not only contain $(\mathbf{f}, \mathbf{g})$, but also n rotations of $(\mathbf{f}, \mathbf{g})$. Observe that $X^i f \cdot h = X^i g$ for all $0 \le i < n$. By construction, the coefficient vectors of $X^i f, X^i g$ are also contained in $\mathcal{L}_{CS}$. Since we work modulo $X^n - 1$, a multiplication by X^i simply defines a cyclic rotation of the coefficient vector by i positions, and therefore all coefficient vectors have identical norm. These rotations were first used in May, Silverman [MS01] to speed up lattice basis reduction by dimension reduction. However, recently [DDGR20] showed that lattice reduction already benefits internally from the presence of many short rotations (i.e., it benefits even without dimension reduction).

Moreover, the n rotations of $(\mathbf{f}, \mathbf{g})$ define an n-dimensional sublattice $\mathcal{L}_{f,g} \subset \mathcal{L}_{CS}$. Kirchner and Fouque [KF17] observed that for sufficiently large q, called the *overstretched* NTRU regime, lattice basis reduction finds a basis for $\mathcal{L}_{f,g}$ significantly earlier than predicted by the analysis for *secret key recovery* (SKR) of $(\mathbf{f}, \mathbf{g})$ in $\mathcal{L}_{CS}$. Since $\mathcal{L}_{f,g}$ contains n exceptionally small vectors, we call $\mathcal{L}_{f,g}$ a *dense* sublattice of $\mathcal{L}_{CS}$, and the detection of a basis of $\mathcal{L}_{f,g}$ when reducing $\mathcal{L}_{CS}$ a *dense sublattice discovery* (DSD). Ducas and van Woerden [DvW21] showed that the overstretched regime, for which DSD happens early, requires $q = \Omega(n^{2.484})$.

NTRU with Hints. By design, NTRU parameters may fulfill further relations. E.g., for correctness of decryption most NTRU variants require $g(1) = 0$, or equivalently $\langle \mathbf{g}, \mathbf{1}^n \rangle = 0$. In the framework of [DDGR20] such a secret key relation is called a *perfect hint*. [DDGR20] provide a method for reducing the lattice dimension by 1 for every perfect hint.

For some parameter settings, we have $h(1) = 0$ implying the relation $\langle \mathbf{h}, \mathbf{1}^n \rangle = 0$. This implies that the short vector $\mathbf{v} = (\mathbf{1}^n, \mathbf{0}^n)$ is contained in the Coppersmith-Shamir lattice $\mathcal{L}_{CS}$. Although $\mathbf{v}$ is very short, it is useless for a cryptanalyst. [DDGR20] provide a method to *project a lattice basis against* such useless vectors, thereby removing them from the lattice. [DDGR20] call this a *short vector hint*.

This projection also reduces the lattice dimension by 1, but may come at the cost of decreasing the lattice determinant, since a projection usually decreases vector lengths. Thus, it is not clear whether a *projection against* a useless lattice vector decreases the run time for finding a secret key in a lattice.

Lattice Attacks in Practice. There has been reasonable cryptanalytic effort for breaking instantiations of the original NTRU cryptosystem. This was further encouraged by *Security Innovation, Inc.* by publishing 11 challenges in dimensions $107 \leq n \leq 211$ with a prize money of 1000\$ each [Incb]. These challenges stimulated the development of new attack techniques and their efficient implementations, such as Howgrave-Graham's lattice-hybrid technique [How07] that lead to the break of two challenges in dimension $n \in \{107, 113\}$. With Bounded Distance Decoding of Liu, Nguyen [LN13] five more challenges with $n \in \{131, 139, 149, 163, 173\}$ were solved by Ducas, Nguyen [Inca].

In their experiments, Ducas and Nguyen used *BKZ 2.0 lattice reduction with extreme pruning* [GNR10, CN11]. In the meantime, there has been significant progress in computing shortest vectors in theory via sieving [NV08, MV10, Duc18] and also in its practical G6K implementation [ADH+19, DSvW21] as a subroutine in BKZ reduction. This algorithmic improvement has however not led to improved NTRU cryptanalysis, though.

Moreover, modern NTRU versions such as the NIST round-3 finalists NTRU-HRS and NTRU-HPSS [HRSS17, CDH+19] have not yet experienced extensive practical cryptanalysis.

1.1 Our Results

Cyclotomic Ring. The polynomial $X^n - 1$ factors into $X^n - 1 = \prod_{d|n} \Phi_d$, where Φ_d denotes the *d-th cyclotomic polynomial*. Gentry [Gen01] showed that in the case of composite n, where $X^n - 1$ has many divisors, attacks on NTRU can improve significantly, when switching from the Coppersmith-Shamir lattice to a lattice defined over some ring $\mathbb{Z}_q[X]/(p)$, where $p \mid (X^n - 1)$ and $1 \ll \deg p \ll n$.

As a countermeasure against Gentry's attack, modern NTRU variants use prime n. In that case $X^n - 1$ has only the two divisors $\Phi_1 = X - 1$ and

$$\Phi_n = \frac{X^n - 1}{X - 1} = X^{n-1} + X^{n-2} + \ldots + X + 1.$$

Both Φ_1 and Φ_n have either too small or too large degree to successfully mount Gentry's attack.

Nevertheless, as an attacker, one still might be temped to work over the so-called *cyclotomic* ring $\mathbb{Z}_q[X]/(\Phi_n)$. Since Φ_n has degree $n - 1$, a canonical lattice for the cyclotomic ring analogous to the Coppersmith-Shamir lattice $\mathcal{L}_{CS}$

has dimension only $2(n-1)$, thereby saving two dimensions over $\mathcal{L}_{\mathsf{CS}}$. However, the rotations of $(\mathbf{f}, \mathbf{g})$ modulo Φ_n have in general norm larger than $(\mathbf{f}, \mathbf{g})$ itself. Therefore, [DDGR20] conclude that the effect of saving two dimensions is likely outweighed by the increase in norm.

To avoid this issue, we define a new $2(n-2)$-dimensional lattice that retains the norm of all cyclic rotations. To this end, we take a closer look at the arithmetic of the cyclotomic ring $\mathbb{Z}_q[X]/(\Phi_n)$ and additionally introduce the following new concept of lattice hints, enriching the hint methodology of [DDGR20].

Almost-Parallel Hint. Assume that we are looking for a short secret lattice vector $(\mathbf{f}, \mathbf{g})$ in a lattice $\mathcal{L}$, and we know another vector $\mathbf{v}$ (not necessarily in $\mathcal{L}$) *almost parallel to* $(\mathbf{f}, \mathbf{g})$. Then we may project $(\mathbf{f}, \mathbf{g})$ against $\mathbf{v}$, thereby eliminating the (long) component of $(\mathbf{f}, \mathbf{g})$ parallel to $\mathbf{v}$, and leaving the (short) component of $(\mathbf{f}, \mathbf{g})$ orthogonal to $\mathbf{v}$. As a result, our short lattice vector $(\mathbf{f}, \mathbf{g})$ is projected into an even shorter lattice vector, making the projection potentially easier to find by lattice reduction algorithms.

HPS, HRSS Results. Using our techniques, we define different lattice bases for NTRU-HPS and NTRU-HRSS, for $\mathbb{Z}_q[X]/(X^n-1)$ and the cyclotomic ring $\mathbb{Z}_q[X]/(\Phi_n)$. Additionally, we include lattice hints by the design criteria of HPS and HRSS. We experimentally show that our lattice basis for the cyclotomic ring that retains rotation norms via an almost-parallel hint performs significantly better than the standard basis for $\mathcal{L}_{\mathsf{CS}}$. That is, we require smaller BKZ blocksizes to achieve secret key recovery (SKR), or if we are in the overstretched regime, for dense sublattice discovery (DSD).

Our smaller blocksizes result in a significant runtime decrease, e.g., we break HPS-161 with our cyclotomic lattice in 15 core days instead of 39 core days for $\mathcal{L}_{\mathsf{CS}}$, and HPS-171 in 83 core days instead of 172 core days. For HRSS the savings over $\mathcal{L}_{\mathsf{CS}}$ are even larger. As an example, we solved HRSS-161 with our cyclotomic lattice in 4 core hours versus 20 core hours for $\mathcal{L}_{\mathsf{CS}}$.

181-Challenge. Using our techniques, we are also able to solve an unbroken NTRU Challenge proposed by Security Innovation, Inc [Incb] with $n = 181$, thereby improving upon the previous $n = 173$ record of Ducas, Nguyen.

G6K Implementation. For the first time we apply the *BKZ with sieving* implementation G6K for NTRU cryptanalysis. We measure complexity by the minimal BKZ blocksize β that is required to achieve SKR or DSD. The current turnover point, where BKZ with sieving is superior to enumeration lies around $\beta = 65$ – for our implementations and our parallel hardware. In our experiments, we go beyond $\beta = 100$, a regime where sieving is clearly favourable, and that has not been reached so far for attacks on real-world lattice schemes. For NTRU-HPS we provide the first cryptanalysis landmarks in the range $101 \leq n \leq 171$ using ring modulus $q = 512$. For NTRU-HRSS we use the recommended larger moduli $q = 2048$ and $q = 4096$, which in turn allow us to break instances even in the range $101 \leq n \leq 211$.

1.2   Future Work

Existent estimators for NTRU [DDGR20, DvW21] consider the Coppersmith-Shamir lattice $\mathcal{L}_{CS}$. It appears to be difficult to translate these estimators to our new lattices. In particular, the Fatigue estimator from [DvW21] crucially relies on the circulant structure of $\mathcal{L}_{f,g}$, which is not preserved in our new lattices. We leave the estimates for our lattices and comparison with the existent ones for future work.

1.3   Organization of Our Paper

In Sect. 2 we provide some basic lattice facts and recall lattice estimates. Section 3 defines NTRU-HPS and NTRU-HRSS, as submitted to the NIST PQC competition [CDH+19]. In Sect. 4, we generalize the *LWE with a hint* framework of [DDGR20] and introduce our new concept of *almost-parallel hints*. Using the results of Sect. 4, we describe in Sect. 5 how to properly design a lattice basis over the cyclotomic ring for attacking NTRU-HPS and NTRU-HRSS, and we discuss its benefits over the Coppersmith-Shamir lattice in detail. Finally, in Sect. 6 we provide an extensive overview of our experimental results and discuss potential implications for the security of NTRU-HPS and NTRU-HRSS. We end in Sect. 7 with the details of our new record computation for $n = 181$.

The implementation accompanying our work, including a detailed documentation, can be found at https://github.com/ElenaKirshanova/ntru_with_sieving.

2   Preliminaries

2.1   Notations

We denote by $\mathbb{Z}_n$ the ring of integers modulo n and by $\mathbb{Z}_n^*$ its group of units. Lower case bold letters represent (row-)vectors. Upper case bold letters represent matrices. We denote by $\mathbf{I}_n$ the $n \times n$ identity matrix. The n-dimensional all-zero and all-one vectors are denoted by $\mathbf{0}^n$ and $\mathbf{1}^n$, respectively. For a polynomial $p \in \mathbb{Z}[X]$, we denote by $\mathbf{p}$ its coefficients vector. Conversely, for a vector $\mathbf{v} = (v_0, v_1, \ldots, v_n) \in \mathbb{Z}^{n+1}$, we denote by v the corresponding polynomial $v = \sum_{i=0}^n v_i X^i$. If a polynomial has coefficients in $\{0, 1, -1\}$, we call the polynomial and its coefficient vector *ternary*.

The Euclidean norm and the Euclidean inner product are denoted by $\|\cdot\|$ and $\langle \cdot, \cdot \rangle$, respectively. For a vector $\mathbf{w} \in \mathbb{R}^n$, we denote by $\mathbf{w}^\perp \subseteq \mathbb{R}^n$ the subspace orthogonal to $\mathbf{w}$. We call $\mathbf{w}^\perp$ the orthogonal complement of $\mathbf{w}$.

For $\mathbf{v} \in \mathbb{R}^n$ we denote by $\pi_{\mathbf{w}}(\mathbf{v}) \in \mathbf{w}^\perp$ the orthogonal projection of $\mathbf{v}$ onto $\mathbf{w}^\perp$,

$$\pi_{\mathbf{w}}(\mathbf{v}) := \mathbf{v} - \frac{\langle \mathbf{v}, \mathbf{w} \rangle}{\|\mathbf{w}\|^2} \mathbf{w}. \tag{1}$$

We call the projection $\pi_{\mathbf{w}}$ onto $\mathbf{w}^\perp$ a projection *against* $\mathbf{w}$.

2.2 Lattices

For $\mathbf{B} \in \mathbb{Q}^{n \times m}$, we define $\mathcal{L}(\mathbf{B})$ as the lattice generated by the *rows* of $\mathbf{B}$:

$$\mathcal{L}(\mathbf{B}) := \{\mathbf{xB} \mid \mathbf{x} \in \mathbb{Z}^n\},$$

keeping our notation consistent with commonly used implementations of lattice-reduction algorithms. If the rows of $\mathbf{B}$ are linearly independent, we call $\mathbf{B}$ a *basis matrix* of $\mathcal{L}(\mathbf{B})$. The number of rows in a basis matrix is called the *dimension* of a lattice, denoted $\dim \mathcal{L}(\mathbf{B})$. The *determinant* of a lattice $\mathcal{L}$ with basis matrix $\mathbf{B}$ is defined as

$$\det \mathcal{L} := \det \sqrt{\mathbf{BB}^T}.$$

Both the dimension and the determinant do not depend on the basis choice.

Let $\mathbf{b}_1, \ldots, \mathbf{b}_n$ denote the rows of a basis matrix $\mathbf{B}$. *Hadamard's inequality* states

$$\det \mathcal{L}(\mathbf{B}) \leq \prod_{i=1}^n \|\mathbf{b}_i\|.$$

The *dual* of a lattice $\mathcal{L} = \mathcal{L}(\mathbf{B})$ is defined as

$$\mathcal{L}^* := \{\mathbf{v} \in \mathrm{span}(\mathbf{B}) \mid \forall \mathbf{w} \in \mathcal{L} : \langle v, w \rangle \in \mathbb{Z}\}.$$

A vector $\mathbf{v} \in \mathcal{L}$ is called *primitive* with respect to some lattice $\mathcal{L}$, if it is not a multiple of a lattice vector, i.e., for every integer $k \geq 2$ it holds that $\frac{1}{k}\mathbf{v} \notin \mathcal{L}$.

A lattice $\mathcal{L} \subset \mathbb{Z}^n$ is called *q-ary*, if it contains $q\mathbb{Z}^n$.

2.3 Lattice Reduction

Every lattice of dimension at least two has infinitely many bases. In many applications (such as cryptanalysis), one wants to compute a *good* basis of a lattice, i.e., a basis consisting of short and almost orthogonal vectors.

The LLL lattice reduction algorithm [LLL82] computes in polynomial time a relatively good basis, whose shortest vector is exponentially (in the lattice dimension) longer than a shortest lattice vector. Its generalization, the BKZ algorithm [Sch87, CN11, AWHT16] provides a trade-off between runtime and basis quality.

The most important parameter of BKZ is the so-called *blocksize* β. The BKZ algorithm computes shortest vectors in projected sub-lattices of dimension β. This dominates the runtime of BKZ. The security of lattice-based cryptosystems is therefore usually measured in the required blocksize β to find a shortest vector. There are two main approaches to find a shortest vector: enumeration algorithms [Kan83, ABF+20] implemented in [dt21a], and sieving algorithms [AKS01, NV08] implemented in [dt21b]. Sieving algorithms find a shortest vector in time and memory $2^{\mathcal{O}(n)}$, while enumeration requires $2^{\mathcal{O}(n \log n)}$ time and only $\mathrm{poly}(n)$ memory. Experiments with publicly available implementations of sieving and enumeration suggest [ADH+19] that sieving algorithms are superior to enumeration starting from dimension ≈ 65.

Estimating the required β for a given lattice is an active area of research. The *NTRU Fatigue estimator* [DvW21] provides the most accurate estimates for NTRU lattices. It is based on the *probabilistic simulation method* introduced in [DDGR20], which in turn is a refinement of the so-called *2016 estimate* or *GSA intersect method* introduced in [ADPS16].

As the name suggests, this method is based on the *geometric series assumption (GSA)* [Sch03], which states that in a random lattice the Gram-Schmidt norms of the vectors of a BKZ-reduced basis decay geometrically. Intuitively, the 2016 estimate states, if a lattice $\mathcal{L}$ contains a sufficiently short vector $\mathbf{s}$, then for sufficiently large β, the GSA cannot hold. Hence, in that case the BKZ behaves differently than on a random lattice and therefore likely recovers $\mathbf{s}$.

More precisely, the 2016 estimate states that BKZ with blocksize β recovers a short vector $\mathbf{s}$ in a d-dimensional lattice $\mathcal{L}$, provided that

$$\sqrt{\beta/d}\|\mathbf{s}\| < \delta_\beta^{2\beta-d-1} \cdot \det(\mathcal{L})^{1/d},$$

where

$$\delta_\beta \approx \left(\frac{\beta}{2\pi e}(\pi\beta)^{1/\beta}\right)^{1/(2(\beta-1))}.$$

We refer the reader to the survey by Albrecht and Ducas [AD21] for further details.

A straight-forward calculation shows that for $\|\mathbf{s}\| := \gamma\sqrt{d}\det(L)^{1/d}$ with $0 < \gamma < 1$, the 2016 estimate predicts

$$\beta = \frac{d\log(d)}{\log(d) - 2\log(\gamma)} + o(d). \tag{2}$$

Hence, if $\|\mathbf{s}\|$ is very close to the so-called *Minkowski bound* of $\sqrt{d}\det(L)^{1/d}$, then the 2016 estimate predicts $\beta \approx d$. Conversely, if $\|\mathbf{s}\|$ is significantly smaller than $\sqrt{d}\det(L)^{1/d}$, then the estimate predicts $\beta \ll d$. As a consequence, it gets the easier for BKZ to find a shortest vector $\mathbf{s}$ in $\mathcal{L}$, the smaller the dimension d, the larger the determinant $\det\mathcal{L}$, and the shorter $\mathbf{s}$.

3   NTRU

In this section, we recall the definition of the NTRU cryptosystem, as defined in the submission to the NIST PQC competition [CDH+19], as well as the NTRU challenges published by Security Innovation, Inc [Incb].

3.1   NIST Submission

Let n be a prime number, where the order of both 2 and 3 in $\mathbb{Z}_n^*$ is $n-1$. We denote the set of all such primes by $\mathcal{N}$. The primes $n \in \mathcal{N}$ with $n \leq 1000$ are exactly the elements of the following set

$$\mathcal{N}_{\leq 1000} := \{5, 19, 29, 53, 101, 139, 149, 163, 173, 197,$$
$$211, 269, 293, 317, 379, 389, 461, 509, 557,$$
$$653, 677, 701, 773, 797, 821, 859, 907, 941\}.$$

The NTRU specification [CDH+19] defines

$$\Phi_n := \frac{X^n - 1}{X - 1} = X^{n-1} + X^{n-2} + \ldots + X + 1,$$

$$\mathcal{T} := \left\{ \sum_{i=0}^{n-2} v_i X^i \mid v_i \in \{-1, 0, 1\} \right\},$$

$$\mathcal{T}_+ := \left\{ \sum_{i=0}^{n-2} v_i X^i \in \mathcal{T} \mid \sum_i v_i v_{i+1} \geq 0 \right\},$$

$$\mathcal{T}(\omega) := \left\{ \sum_{i=0}^{n-2} v_i X^i \in \mathcal{T} \mid \begin{array}{l} v_i = +1 \text{ for } \frac{\omega}{2} \text{ coefficients } v_i, \\ v_i = -1 \text{ for } \frac{\omega}{2} \text{ coefficients } v_i \end{array} \right\}, \quad (3)$$

where ω is an even positive integer. Notice, since n is prime, Φ_n is the n-th cyclotomic polynomial.

An NTRU private key is a tuple (n, q, f, g), where $n \in \mathcal{N}$, $q \in \mathbb{N}$ is a power of two and $f, g \in \mathbb{Z}[X]$ are polynomials with *small* coefficients. The corresponding public key is a tuple (n, q, h), where

$$h := 3g f_q \quad \mod (q, X^n - 1) \quad (4)$$

and

$$f_q := f^{-1} \quad \mod (q, \Phi_n). \quad (5)$$

If f is sampled from (a subset of) $\mathcal{T} \setminus \{0\}$, then the following lemma shows that f_q is well-defined.

Lemma 3.1. *Let $n \in \mathcal{N}$, $f \in \mathcal{T} \setminus \{0\}$ and let $q \in \mathbb{N}$ be a power of two. Then f is invertible in $\mathbb{Z}_q[X]/(\Phi_n)$.*

Proof. By definition of $\mathcal{N}$, the order of 2 in $\mathbb{Z}_n^*$ is $n - 1$. This implies that the n-th cyclotomic polynomial Φ_n is irreducible over $\mathbb{Z}_2$. (This easily follows from the fact that the subgroup $\{2^i \mod n \mid i \in \mathbb{Z}\} \subseteq \mathbb{Z}_n^*$ is isomorphic to the Galois group of the field extension $\mathbb{Z}_2 \subset \mathbb{Z}_2(\zeta_n)$, where ζ_n denotes a formal primitive n-th root of unity.) Hence, $\mathbb{Z}_2[X]/(\Phi_n)$ is a finite field. Since $f \in \mathcal{T}$ and $f \neq 0$, it follows that $f \not\equiv 0 \mod (2, \Phi_n)$. Therefore, f is invertible in $\mathbb{Z}_2[X]/(\Phi_n)$ and consequently also in $\mathbb{Z}_q[X]/(\Phi_n)$.   □

The NTRU submission defines two different variants of the scheme, called *NTRU-HPS* and *NTRU-HRSS*. The variants use slightly different sample spaces for f and g, and have different constraints on q.

NTRU-HPS. In the HPS variant, the modulus q may be set to any power of 2. The polynomials f and g are sampled from the following two sets

$$\mathcal{L}_{f,\mathsf{HPS}} := \mathcal{T},$$

$$\mathcal{L}_{g,\mathsf{HPS}} := \mathcal{T}(\omega), \quad (6)$$

where $\omega := \min\{q/8 - 2, 2\lfloor n/3 \rfloor\}$. The specification recommends to either use $q = 2048$ and $n \in \{509, 677\}$ or $q = 4096$ and $n = 821$. (The former imposes $\omega = 254$, the latter $\omega = 510$).

NTRU-HRSS. In the HRSS variant, the modulus q is

$$q := 2^{\lceil 7/2 + \log_2(n) \rceil}. \tag{7}$$

The polynomials f, g are sampled from the following two sets

$$\begin{aligned}\mathcal{L}_{f,\mathsf{HRSS}} &:= \mathcal{T}_+, \\ \mathcal{L}_{g,\mathsf{HRSS}} &:= (X - 1) \cdot \mathcal{T}_+.\end{aligned} \tag{8}$$

The specification recommends to set $n = 701$. (This imposes $q = 8192$).

The NTRU Key Equation. From the definitions of $\mathcal{L}_{g,\mathsf{HPS}}$ and $\mathcal{L}_{g,\mathsf{HRSS}}$ it follows that in both NTRU-HPS and NTRU-HRSS $g(1) = 0$ and by Eq. (4) consequently also $h(1) \equiv 0 \mod q$. Hence, from the Chinese remainder theorem

$$\mathbb{Z}_q[X]/(X^n - 1) \simeq \mathbb{Z}_q[X]/(\Phi_n) \times \mathbb{Z}_q[X]/(X - 1)$$

it follows that in both variants the keys satisfy the *NTRU key equation*

$$fh \equiv 3g \mod (q, X^n - 1). \tag{9}$$

3.2 NTRU Challenges

When compared to the NTRU variants submitted to NIST PQC competition, the NTRU challenges by Security Innovation, Inc. use a quite different key format. Let $n \in \mathbb{N}$ and define

$$\mathcal{T}_{\mathsf{Ch.}}(d_i) := \left\{ \sum_{i=0}^{n-1} v_i X^i \;\middle|\; \begin{array}{l} v_i = +1 \text{ for } d_i\text{-many } v_i, \\ v_i = -1 \text{ for } d_i\text{-many } v_i \end{array} \right\} \tag{10}$$

for some parameter $d_i \in \mathbb{N}$.[1]

The sample spaces for the secret polynomials f and g are defined as follows

$$\mathcal{L}_{f,\mathsf{Ch.}}(d_1, d_2, d_3) := \{f_1 f_2 + f_3 \mod X^n - 1 \,|\, f_i \in \mathcal{T}_{\mathsf{Ch.}}(d_i)\}, \tag{11}$$

$$\mathcal{L}_{g,\mathsf{Ch.}}(d_g) := \left\{ \sum_{i=0}^{n-1} g_i X^i \;\middle|\; \begin{array}{l} g_i = +1 \text{ for } (d_g + 1)\text{-many } g_i, \\ g_i = -1 \text{ for } d_g\text{-many } g_i \end{array} \right\}, \tag{12}$$

where $d_1, d_2, d_3, d_g \in \mathbb{N}$ are some positive integers.

The public polynomial h is defined via the equation

$$(1 + 3f)h \equiv g \mod (q, X^n - 1),$$

where q is a power of two.

Security Innovation, Inc. published 27 different challenges. 11 of the challenges used to be worth 1000\$ each, the other 16 challenges used to be worth 5000\$ each. The concrete parameters for all 1000\$ challenges are given in Table 1.

---

[1] As opposed to the set $\mathcal{T}(\omega)$, defined in Eq. (3), the elements of $\mathcal{T}_{\mathsf{Ch.}}(d_i)$ are of degree at most $n - 1$, instead of $n - 2$. In addition, they have $2d_i$ non-zero coefficients, instead of ω.

Table 1. Parameters of the 1000\$ NTRU challenges.

n	q	d_1	d_2	d_3	d_g	Solved by
107	512	4	4	4	36	Howgrave-Graham
113	1024	5	4	3	38	Howgrave-Graham
131	1024	5	4	4	44	Ducas, Nguyen
139	1024	5	5	3	46	Ducas, Nguyen
149	1024	5	5	3	50	Ducas, Nguyen
163	1024	5	5	4	54	Ducas, Nguyen
173	1024	6	5	4	58	Ducas, Nguyen
181	1024	6	5	4	60	**This work**
191	1024	6	5	4	64	–
199	1024	6	5	6	66	–
211	1024	6	6	4	70	–

4   Lattice Reduction with a Hint

When attacking a cryptographic lattice $\mathcal{L}$, one often knows some side information about the secret short vector $\mathbf{s} \in \mathcal{L}$. Dachman-Soled, Ducas, Gong and Rossi (DDGR) introduced in [DDGR20] a framework for integrating such *hints* into $\mathcal{L}$ to improve the performance of lattice reduction algorithms. In this section, we recall two types of hints and additionally introduce a new type of hint.

Perfect Hints. Suppose we know a vector $\mathbf{v}$, which is orthogonal to the secret vector $\mathbf{s}$, i.e.,

$$\langle \mathbf{s}, \mathbf{v} \rangle = 0.$$

This type of hint is called a *perfect hint*.

Instead of searching for $\mathbf{s}$ in $\mathcal{L}$, we can then search in the sub-lattice $\mathcal{L} \cap \mathbf{v}^{\perp}$. As shown by DDGR, this may make reducing the lattice a bit easier, since it decreases the dimension by one and additionally may increase the determinant (assuming that $\mathbf{v}$ is not too far from being primitive with respect to the dual):

Lemma 4.1 (Generalization of Lemma 12 in [DDGR20]). *Let $\mathcal{L}$ be a lattice and let $\mathbf{v} \in \mathcal{L}^*$. Let $k \in \mathbb{N}$ such that $\frac{1}{k}\mathbf{v}$ is primitive with respect to $\mathcal{L}^*$. Then $\mathcal{L} \cap \mathbf{v}^{\perp}$ is a lattice of dimension $\dim \mathcal{L} - 1$. Its determinant is given by*

$$\det(\mathcal{L} \cap \mathbf{v}^{\perp}) = \frac{\|\mathbf{v}\|}{k} \cdot \det \mathcal{L}.$$

Worth noting, if k is significantly larger than $\|\mathbf{v}\|$, incorporating a perfect hint may actually be counterproductive for lattice reduction algorithms, as the disadvantage of having a smaller determinant then may outweigh the benefit of losing one dimension. DDGR heuristically assume that k always equals 1. However, in Sect. 5.3 we show that this is not the case for typical NTRU lattices.

Given a basis $\mathbf{B}$ for $\mathcal{L}$, DDGR suggest the following polynomial time algorithm to compute a basis for the sub-lattice $\mathcal{L} \cap \mathbf{v}^\perp$.

1. Compute the dual basis $\mathbf{D}$ of $\mathbf{B}$. (Recall that $\mathbf{D}$ is given by $\mathbf{D} = (\mathbf{B}^+)^T$, where $\cdot^+$ and $\cdot^T$ denote the Moore-Penrose pseudoinverse and transpose, respectively.)
2. Compute $\mathbf{D}_\perp := \pi_{\mathbf{v}}(\mathbf{D})$, where $\pi_{\mathbf{v}}$ is applied row-wise to $\mathbf{D}$.
3. Apply the LLL algorithm to $\mathbf{D}_\perp$ to eliminate linear dependencies. Then delete the first (all-zero) row.
4. Output the dual of the resulting matrix.

Short Vector Hints. Many cryptographic lattices contain short-ish vectors that neither reveal the secret key, nor help the decryption. For instance, in some NTRU variants, the lattices contain the all-one vector. Even though this vector is very short, it cannot be used for decryption. Futhermore, almost all cryptographic lattices are q-ary for some small $q \in \mathbb{N}$ and thus contain the rather short q-vectors $(0, \ldots, 0, q, 0, \ldots, 0)$.

It can be sometimes beneficial for lattice reduction algorithms to *remove* these vectors from the lattice, i.e., to project the lattice onto their orthogonal complement. DDGR call this a *short vector hint*.

The benefit of projecting a lattice $\mathcal{L}$ against $\mathbf{v} \in \mathcal{L}$ is that the dimension decreases by one. However, as the following lemma shows, at the same time the determinant shrinks by a factor of $\|\mathbf{v}\|$. A short vector hint is therefore always a trade-off between decreased dimension and decreased determinant.

Lemma 4.2 (Fact 14 in [DDGR20]). *Let $\mathcal{L}$ be a lattice and let $\mathbf{v} \in \mathcal{L}$ be primitive with respect to $\mathcal{L}$. Then*

$$\det(\pi_{\mathbf{v}}(\mathcal{L})) = \det(\mathcal{L})/\|\mathbf{v}\|.$$

In contrast to a perfect hint, where the constraint on $\mathbf{v}$ being primitive is a potential disadvantage, this is not the case for a short vector hint: if $\mathbf{v}$ is not primitive, i.e., if there exists $k \geq 2$, such that $\frac{1}{k}\mathbf{v}$ is a primitive vector of $\mathcal{L}$, then projecting actually shrinks the determinant by less than a $\|\mathbf{v}\|$-factor, since in that case we have

$$\det(\pi_{\mathbf{v}}(\mathcal{L})) = \det(\pi_{\frac{1}{k}\mathbf{v}}(\mathcal{L})) = k \cdot \frac{\det(\mathcal{L})}{\|\mathbf{v}\|} > \frac{\det(\mathcal{L})}{\|\mathbf{v}\|}.$$

A potential drawback from projecting against $\mathbf{v}$ is a loss of information. While $\mathbf{s}$ is contained in $\mathcal{L}$, the projection $\pi_{\mathbf{v}}(\mathcal{L})$ only contains $\pi_{\mathbf{v}}(\mathbf{s})$, from which one has to recover $\mathbf{s}$.

Almost-Parallel Hints (New). In our attacks, the secret vector $\mathbf{s}$ is sometimes *almost parallel* to some known vector $\mathbf{v}$ (not necessarily included in our lattice), i.e., it has a decomposition into

$$\mathbf{s} = c\mathbf{v} + \mathbf{s}',$$

for some vector $\mathbf{s}'$ significantly shorter than $\mathbf{s}$, and some scalar c. We call this an *almost-parallel hint*.

Projecting the lattice against $\mathbf{v}$ makes the secret target vector $\mathbf{s}$ significantly shorter:

$$\|\pi_{\mathbf{v}}(\mathbf{s})\| = \|\pi_{\mathbf{v}}(\mathbf{s}')\| \leq \|\mathbf{s}'\|.$$

In addition, by integrating an almost-parallel hint, we also decrease the dimension of $\mathcal{L}$ by one.[2]

As with a short vector hint, using an almost-parallel hint also comes with a disadvantage: both types of hints decrease the determinant. In fact, the following straight-forward generalization of Lemma 4.2 shows, in contrast to a short vector hint, where the determinant only shrinks by a $\|\mathbf{v}\|$-factor, an almost-parallel may shrink way more significantly (assuming that only large multiples of $\mathbf{v}$ are contained in $\mathcal{L}$):

Lemma 4.3. *Let $\mathcal{L}$ be lattice and let $\mathbf{v}$ be a vector. If there exists $\lambda \in \mathbb{R}$ such that $\lambda\mathbf{v}$ is a primitive lattice vector of $\mathcal{L}$, then*

$$\det(\pi_{\mathbf{v}}(\mathcal{L})) = \det(\mathcal{L})/(\lambda\|\mathbf{v}\|).$$

Notice that for an integral vector $\mathbf{v} \in \mathbb{Z}^n \backslash \mathbf{0}^n$ and a q-ary lattice $\mathcal{L}$ we shrink, however, at most by a $q\|\mathbf{v}\|$-factor, because in that case there exists $\lambda \in \{1, 2, \ldots, q\}$, such that $\lambda\mathbf{v}$ is primitive.

As in the case of short vector hints we potentially lose information with projecting against $\mathbf{v}$, since $\mathcal{L}$ contains $\mathbf{s}$, whereas $\pi_{\mathbf{v}}(\mathcal{L})$ only contains $\pi_{\mathbf{v}}(\mathbf{s})$. However, in our applications of almost-parallel hints we are always able to efficiently recover $\mathbf{s}$ from its projection $\pi_{\mathbf{v}}(\mathbf{s})$.

5   Choosing Lattices for NTRU-HPS and NTRU-HRSS

5.1   The Coppersmith-Shamir Lattice

Let (n, q, h) be an NTRU-HPS or NTRU-HRSS public key with corresponding secret key (n, q, f, g). The most straight-forward approach for attacking NTRU is to consider the following lattice

$$\mathcal{L}_{\mathsf{CS}} := \{(\mathbf{v}, \mathbf{w}) \in \mathbb{Z}^{2n} \mid vh \equiv 3w \mod (q, X^n - 1)\},$$

which was first introduced by Coppersmith and Shamir (CS) in [CS97]. A basis matrix for $\mathcal{L}_{\mathsf{CS}}$ is given by

$$\mathbf{B}_{\mathsf{CS}} := \begin{pmatrix} \mathbf{I}_n & \mathbf{H} \\ \mathbf{0} & q\mathbf{I}_n \end{pmatrix}, \tag{13}$$

---

[2] We assume that a multiple of $\mathbf{v}$ is included in $\mathcal{L}$. For an integral vector $\mathbf{v}$ and a q-ary lattice $\mathcal{L}$, this certainly is the case, since $q\mathbf{v} \in \mathcal{L}$. If $\mathcal{L}$ contains no multiple of $\mathbf{v}$, then $\pi_{\mathbf{v}}(\mathcal{L})$ might not be a lattice.

where for $i = 0, \ldots, n - 1$, the $(i + 1)$-st row of $\mathbf{H} \in \mathbb{Z}^{n \times n}$ is defined as the coefficient vector of

$$3^{-1} X^i h \mod (q, X^n - 1).$$

By Eq. (9), $\mathcal{L}_{\mathsf{CS}}$ contains the vector $(\mathbf{f}, \mathbf{g}) \in \mathbb{Z}^{2n}$ corresponding to the secret polynomials f and g. Since f and g have very small coefficients, $(\mathbf{f}, \mathbf{g})$ likely is a shortest vector in $\mathcal{L}_{\mathsf{CS}}$. Hence, we can compute the secret key by running lattice reduction on $\mathbf{B}_{\mathsf{CS}}$.

Presence of Many Short Vectors. A remarkable property of $\mathcal{L}_{\mathsf{CS}}$ is that the lattice not only contains the short vector $(\mathbf{f}, \mathbf{g})$, but also all *rotations* of the secret key, i.e., the coefficient vectors corresponding to $X^i f$ and $X^i g$ for every $i \in \{0, 1, \ldots, n - 1\}$. It is well known that the rotations also serve as valid secret keys.

Notice that the rotations have the same norm as $(\mathbf{f}, \mathbf{g})$, since multiplication by X in $\mathbb{Z}_q[X]/(X^n - 1)$ simply corresponds to a rotation of the coefficients. As discussed in [DDGR20, Section 6.3], the presence of these many short vectors makes finding the secret key a bit easier than it would be in a lattice containing (up to sign) only one short vector. Intuitively this is caused by the fact that the probability of BKZ finding *at least one* of the short vectors is higher than the probability of finding *one fixed* short vector.

Dense Sublattice. The rotations of the secret key generate an n-dimensional sub-lattice $\mathcal{L}_{f,g} \subset \mathcal{L}_{\mathsf{CS}}$. This sub-lattice is unusually *dense* for a sublattice of $\mathcal{L}_{\mathsf{CS}}$, i.e., its determinant is much smaller than what we would expect from a random lattice: using Hadamard's inequality, we find that the determinant is upper bounded by

$$\det \mathcal{L}_{f,g} \leq \|(\mathbf{f}, \mathbf{g})\|^n.$$

As shown in [KF17] and refined in [DvW21], if q is sufficiently large, the presence of such a dense sub-lattice violates a prediction on the behavior of sublattices based on the GSA and thus forces BKZ to behave differently on $\mathcal{L}_{\mathsf{CS}}$, than it would on a random lattice. Indeed, it turns out that we can recover the secret key in that case using significantly smaller blocksizes.

According to the 2016 estimate, *secret key recovery (SKR)* normally would happen at blocksize $\beta = \tilde{\Theta}(n / \ln q)$. However, as shown in [KF17, Theorem 9], if q is large, BKZ recovers at significantly smaller blocksize $\beta = \tilde{\Theta}(n / \ln^2 q)$ a basis $\mathcal{B}_{f,g}$ for $\mathcal{L}_{f,g}$ – from which one easily obtains the secret key. (This event is called *dense sub-lattice discovery (DSD)*.) For instance, instead of running BKZ on the $2n$-dimensional lattice $\mathcal{L}_{\mathsf{CS}}$, one then may run it on the n-dimensional sub-lattice $\mathcal{L}_{f,g}$, which is significantly easier.

NTRU parameters, that have this property, are called *overstretched*. Ducas and van Woerden [DvW21, Claim 3.5] showed that NTRU variants with $\|(\mathbf{f}, \mathbf{g})\| = \mathcal{O}(n^{1/2})$ (such as HPS and HRSS) become overstretched when $q = \Omega(n^{2.484})$. As shown in [DvW21, Section 5.3], the asymptotic bound already holds for reasonably small values of n.

5.2   The Cyclotomic Lattice and the Projected Cyclotomic Lattice

The NTRU key equation holds not only over the convolution polynomial ring $\mathbb{Z}_q[X]/(X^n - 1)$, but also over the cyclotomic polynomial ring $\mathbb{Z}_q[X]/(\Phi_n)$. Instead of working with the CS lattice, one might therefore be tempted to work with the following lattice

$$\mathcal{L}_\Phi := \{(\mathbf{v}, \mathbf{w}) \in \mathbb{Z}^{2(n-1)} \mid vh \equiv 3w \mod (q, \Phi_n)\},$$

which we call the *cyclotomic lattice*. Analogously to the CS lattice, one can easily compute a basis matrix for $\mathcal{L}_\Phi$ as

$$\mathbf{B}_\Phi := \begin{pmatrix} \mathbf{I}_{n-1} & \mathbf{H}_\Phi \\ \mathbf{0} & q\mathbf{I}_{n-1} \end{pmatrix}, \tag{14}$$

where for $i = 0, \ldots, n - 2$, the $(i + 1)$-st row of $\mathbf{H}_\Phi$ is defined as the coefficient vector of

$$3^{-1}X^i h \mod (q, \Phi_n).$$

Since the cyclotomic lattice has dimension only $2(n-1)$ instead of $2n$, one might hope that reducing it may be a bit easier than reducing the CS lattice.

Dachman-Soled, Ducas, Gong and Rossi [DDGR20, Section 6.3], however, doubt whether using $\mathcal{L}_\Phi$ really is beneficial. They argue, since multiplication by X in $\mathbb{Z}[X]/(\Phi_n)$ does not correspond to a simple rotation of the coefficients (as it does in $\mathbb{Z}[X]/(X^n - 1)$), the length of the vectors corresponding to $X^i f$, $X^i g$ may be increased "significantly" in $\mathcal{L}_\Phi$. Accordingly, $\mathcal{L}_\Phi$ will contain fewer short secret key vectors than $\mathcal{L}_{\mathsf{CS}}$ and recovering them should therefore probably be harder.

This issue, however, can easily be fixed. To this end, let us take a closer look at the arithmetic in $\mathbb{Z}[X]/(\Phi_n)$.

Lemma 5.1. *Let $p = \sum_i p_i X^i$ be a polynomial of degree at most $n - 2$. For every $k \in \{0, 1, \ldots, n - 1\}$ it holds that*

$$X^k p \equiv \sum_{i=0}^{k-2} p_{i+n-k} X^i + \sum_{i=k}^{n-2} p_{i-k} X^i - \sum_{i=0}^{n-2} p_{n-k-1} X^i \mod \Phi_n. \tag{15}$$

Furthermore, for every $k \in \mathbb{N}$ it holds that

$$X^k p \equiv X^{(k \mod n)} p \mod \Phi_n. \tag{16}$$

Proof. From $X^n - 1 = \Phi_n(X - 1) \equiv 0 \mod \Phi_n$ it follows that

$$X^n \equiv 1 \mod \Phi_n. \tag{17}$$

Notice that this already proves Eq. (16).

Writing $\Phi_n = X^{n-1} + X^{n-2} + \ldots X + 1$, we obtain

$$X^{n-1} \equiv -(X^{n-2} + X^{n-3} + \ldots X + 1) \mod \Phi_n. \tag{18}$$

To prove Eq. (15), we now simply apply Eqs. (17) and (18) to the following identity:

$$X^k p = \sum_{i=k}^{n-2} p_{i-k} X^i + p_{n-k-1} X^{n-1} + \sum_{i=0}^{k-2} p_{i+n-k} X^{n+i}.$$

□

From Lemma 5.1 it follows that the arithmetic in $\mathbb{Z}[X]/(\Phi_n)$ is actually quite similar to that in $\mathbb{Z}[X]/(X^n - 1)$. First, in both rings multiplication by X is n-periodic. Second, while in $\mathbb{Z}[X]/(\Phi_n)$ a multiplication by X does not perfectly correspond to a rotation of the coefficients, one might still view it as a *rotation with an extra step*: in $\mathbb{Z}[X]/(X^n - 1)$, we have the following identity[3]

$$X^k p = \sum_{i=0}^{k-2} p_{i+n-k} X^i + \sum_{i=k}^{n-1} p_{i-k} X^i \quad \mod X^n - 1. \tag{19}$$

Comparing Eq. (19) with Eq. (15), we find that in $\mathbb{Z}[X]/(\Phi_n)$ the coefficients first get rotated exactly as they would in $\mathbb{Z}[X]/(X^n - 1)$, but then the leading coefficient p_{n-k-1} gets removed and is instead subtracted from all other coefficients.

Let us illustrate with an example. Consider the polynomial

$$p := 1 + X^2 - X^3.$$

The coefficient vectors of $X^0 p, \ldots, X^4 p$ modulo $X^5 - 1$ are

$$(1, 0, 1, -1, 0),$$
$$(0, 1, 0, 1, -1),$$
$$(-1, 0, 1, 0, 1),$$
$$(1, -1, 0, 1, 0).$$

The coefficient vectors modulo Φ_5 on the other hand are

$$(1, 0, 1, -1) - 0 \cdot (1, 1, 1, 1) = (1, 0, 1, -1),$$
$$(0, 1, 0, 1) - (-1) \cdot (1, 1, 1, 1) = (1, 2, 1, 2),$$
$$(-1, 0, 1, 0) - 1 \cdot (1, 1, 1, 1) = (-2, -1, 0, -1),$$
$$(1, -1, 0, 1) - 0 \cdot (1, 1, 1, 1) = (1, -1, 0, 1),$$
$$(0, 1, -1, 0) - 1 \cdot (1, 1, 1, 1) = (-1, 0, -2, -1).$$

Hence, the rotations of p modulo Φ_n are the sum of a short vector and a multiple of 1^{n-1}, i.e., the rotations are *almost parallel* to 1^{n-1}.

This suggests to incorporate two almost-parallel hints to $\mathcal{L}_\Phi$, i.e., to work with the following lattice, which we call the *projected cyclotomic lattice*

$$\mathcal{L}_{\Phi,\perp} := \{(\pi_{1^{n-1}}(\mathbf{v}), \pi_{1^{n-1}}(\mathbf{w})) \in \mathbb{Z}^{2(n-1)} \mid vh \equiv 3w \mod (q, \Phi_n)\}$$
$$= \pi_{(0^{n-1}, 1^{n-1})} \left(\pi_{(1^{n-1}, 0^{n-1})} (\mathcal{L}_\Phi) \right).$$

---

[3] Notice that there is no monomial of degree $k-1$ in Eq. (19), since p has no monomial of degree $n - 1$.

Remark 5.2. Since $\pi_{\mathbf{1}^{n-1}}(\cdot)$ maps into $\frac{1}{n-1} \cdot \mathbb{Z}^{n-1}$, one may want to work in practice with the scaled lattice $(n-1) \cdot \mathcal{L}_{\Phi,\perp}$ to avoid a non-integral basis.

Remark 5.3. We can easily recover the secret $\mathbf{f}$ from its projection $\pi_{\mathbf{1}^{n-1}}(\mathbf{f})$, by simply brute-forcing the inner product $\langle \mathbf{f}, \mathbf{1}^{n-1} \rangle$ (which is a small integer between $-(n-1)$ and $n-1$) and then obtain $\mathbf{f}$ via Eq. (1).

Remark 5.4. Interestingly, Coppersmith and Shamir similarly suggest to project the vectors in their lattice $\mathcal{L}_{CS}$ orthogonally against $\mathbf{1}^n$ – although for a completely different reason: they showed that any vector $\mathbf{v}$, which is almost parallel to $\mathbf{1}^n$ (i.e., for which $\pi_{\mathbf{1}^n}(\mathbf{v})$ is short), already serves as a valid NTRU private key. If $\mathcal{L}_{CS}$ contains (besides the rotations of the secret key) additional such vectors, then BKZ has an increased success probability for finding a secret key on the projected variant of the CS lattice. However, in practice, we never encountered such vectors.

As opposed to the (non-projected) cyclotomic lattice, the projected cyclotomic lattice still contains *many* short vectors. In addition, it has a smaller dimension than both $\mathcal{L}_{CS}$ and $\mathcal{L}_\Phi$. Indeed, it has dimension only $2n-4$: we lose two dimensions by working modulo Φ_n, and two more dimensions by projecting. (The latter follows from the fact that the q-ary lattice $\mathcal{L}_\Phi$ contains the vectors $q(\mathbf{1}^{n-1}, \mathbf{0}^{n-1})$ and $q(\mathbf{0}^{n-1}, \mathbf{1}^{n-1})$, see also the discussion on almost-parallel hints in Sect. 4).

We may therefore hope that attacks using the projected cyclotomic lattice outperform the other two lattices.

It should be noted, however, that $\mathcal{L}_{\Phi,\perp}$ has the smallest determinant out of our three lattices.

Theorem 5.5. *The determinant of $\mathcal{L}_{\Phi,\perp}$ equals*

$$\det \mathcal{L}_{\Phi,\perp} = \frac{q^{n-3}}{n-1}.$$

Proof. Let $d := n - 1$. We define a polynomial

$$v := \left((3^{-1} \mod q) \cdot h \cdot \sum_{i=0}^{n-2} X^i \right) \mod \Phi_n. \tag{20}$$

Notice that the coefficient vector $\mathbf{v} \in \mathbb{Z}^d$ of v is the sum over the rows of the matrix $\mathbf{H}_\Phi$ in Eq. (14). Hence, by Eq. (14) we have the following equivalence for any $s \in \mathbb{Z}$:

$$s(\mathbf{1}^d, \mathbf{0}^d) \in \mathcal{L}_\Phi \iff s\mathbf{v} \in q\mathbb{Z}^d \iff \frac{s}{q}\mathbf{v} \in \mathbb{Z}^d. \tag{21}$$

Using this equivalence we now compute the smallest integer $s > 0$, that satisfies $s(\mathbf{1}^d, \mathbf{0}^d) \in \mathcal{L}_\Phi$.

From Eqs. (20), (4) and (5), it follows that

$$v \equiv 3^{-1} \cdot h \cdot \sum_{i=0}^{n-2} X^i \equiv g \cdot f^{-1} \cdot \sum_{i=0}^{n-2} X^i \mod (q, \Phi_n).$$

By Lemma 3.1, both g and $\sum_{i=0}^{n-2} X^i$ are invertible in the ring $\mathbb{Z}_q[X]/(\Phi_n)$.[4] As f^{-1} is obviously also invertible, v is invertible as well. In particular, it follows that at least one coefficient of v is odd. (Since q is a power of 2, polynomials with only even coefficients are not invertible in $\mathbb{Z}_q[X]/(\Phi_n)$.) Combing this observation with Eq. (21), it follows that the smallest $s > 0$, satisfying $s(\mathbf{1}^d, \mathbf{0}^d) \in \mathcal{L}_\Phi$, is $s = q$.

This shows that $q(\mathbf{1}^d, \mathbf{0}^d)$ is primitive with respect to $\mathcal{L}_\Phi$. Together with Lemma 4.3 this yields

$$\det\left(\pi_{(\mathbf{1}^d, \mathbf{0}^d)}(\mathcal{L}_\Phi)\right) = \frac{\det \mathcal{L}_\Phi}{\|q(\mathbf{1}^d, \mathbf{0}^d)\|} = \frac{q^{n-2}}{\sqrt{d}}. \tag{22}$$

Let us now compute the smallest integer $t > 0$, satisfying $t(\mathbf{0}^d, \mathbf{1}^d) \in \pi_{(\mathbf{1}^d, \mathbf{0}^d)}(\mathcal{L}_\Phi)$.

From Eq. (14) it follows that $\pi_{(\mathbf{1}^d, \mathbf{0}^d)}(\mathcal{L}_\Phi)$ is generated by the following matrix

$$\mathbf{B}_\pi := \begin{pmatrix} \pi_{\mathbf{1}^d}(\mathbf{I}_d) & \mathbf{H}_\Phi \\ \mathbf{0} & q\mathbf{I}_d \end{pmatrix}, \tag{23}$$

where $\pi_{\mathbf{1}^d}$ is applied row-wise to $\mathbf{I}_d$. Let $(\mathbf{w}_1, \mathbf{w}_2) \in \mathbb{Z}^{2d}$, such that

$$(\mathbf{w}_1, \mathbf{w}_2) \cdot \mathbf{B}_\pi = t(\mathbf{0}^d, \mathbf{1}^d) \tag{24}$$

for the smallest possible integer $t > 0$. Using Eq. (23), we conclude that

$$\mathbf{w}_1 \in \ker \pi_{\mathbf{1}^d} \cap \mathbb{Z}^d = \mathbb{Z} \cdot \mathbf{1}^d.$$

Hence, there exists $m \in \mathbb{Z}$, such that $\mathbf{w}_1 = m \cdot \mathbf{1}^d$. This implies that $\mathbf{w}_1$ is the coefficient vector of $m \cdot \sum_{i=0}^{n-2} X^i$. Using Eq. (24) it follows that

$$\left(m \cdot \sum_{i=0}^{n-2} X^i \right) \cdot \left(3^{-1} \cdot h \right) \equiv t \cdot \sum_{i=0}^{n-2} X^i \mod (q, \Phi_n).$$

By Lemma 3.1, the ternary polynomial $\sum_{i=0}^{n-2} X^i$ is invertible, so we may divide it from the above congruence and obtain

$$m \cdot 3^{-1} \cdot h \equiv t \mod (q, \Phi_n). \tag{25}$$

Multiplying the polynomial $3^{-1} \cdot h$ by an integer m can result in another integer t, if and only if t is congruent to 0 modulo q. Hence, the smallest $t > 0$, for which Eq. (25) can hold is $t = q$.

By definition of m, this implies that the smallest $t > 0$, satisfying $t(\mathbf{0}^d, \mathbf{1}^d) \in \pi_{(\mathbf{1}^d, \mathbf{0}^d)}(\mathcal{L}_\Phi)$, is $t = q$. Hence, $q(\mathbf{0}^d, \mathbf{1}^d)$ is primitive with respect to $\pi_{(\mathbf{1}^d, \mathbf{0}^d)}(\mathcal{L}_\Phi)$.

---

[4] Even though g is not a ternary polynomial in NTRU-HRSS, Lemma 3.1 still implies that g is invertible, since g is the product of two ternary (and therefore invertible) polynomials, see Eq. (8).

Now applying Lemma 4.3 and using Eq. (22), we finish the proof:

$$\det \mathcal{L}_{\Phi,\perp} = \det \left(\pi_{(0^d,1^d)} \left(\pi_{(1^d,0^d)} \left(\mathcal{L}_\Phi \right) \right) \right)$$
$$= \frac{\det \left(\pi_{(1^d,0^d)}(\mathcal{L}_\Phi) \right)}{\| q(0^d, 1^d) \|} = \frac{q^{n-3}}{n-1}.$$

$\square$

Recall that by Eq. (2), the required BKZ blocksize does not directly depend on the determinant of the lattice, but on its *root-determinant*. Since we have

$$(\det \mathcal{L}_{\mathsf{CS}})^{1/(2n)} = \sqrt{q},$$

and by Theorem 5.5

$$(\det \mathcal{L}_{\Phi,\perp})^{1/(2(n-2))} = \frac{1}{((n-1)q)^{1/(2n-4)}} \sqrt{q},$$

the root-determinants only differ by a factor $\frac{1}{((n-1)q)^{1/(2n-4)}}$, which rapidly converges to 1. Thus, the decrease in determinant should not significantly effect the required blocksize, and instead should be outweighed by the decrease in secret's norm and lattice dimension. Our experimental results in Sect. 6 confirm that this is the case.

5.3   Further Improvement by Exploiting Design Choices

For correctness of decryption, it is necessary in both NTRU-HPS and NTRU-HRSS that 1 is a root of g. HPS ensures this property by simply distributing 1's and -1's evenly among the coefficients of g, see Eq. (6). HRSS, on the other hand, defines g as a product of $X - 1$ and a ternary polynomial, see Eq. (8). We can exploit these properties by incorporating them into our lattices.

NTRU-HRSS. Since the secret polynomial g is the product of $X - 1$ and a ternary polynomial, the coefficient vector $\frac{g}{X-1}$ is significantly shorter than the coefficient vector of g. Instead of searching for a short vector $(\mathbf{v}, \mathbf{w})$ with

$$vh \equiv 3w \quad \mathrm{mod}\ (q, \Phi_n),$$

we should therefore rather search for $(\mathbf{v}, \mathbf{w}')$ with

$$vh \equiv 3(X - 1)w' \quad \mathrm{mod}\ (q, \Phi_n),$$

To do so, we simply replace the matrix $\mathbf{H}_\Phi$ in Eq. (14) by a matrix $\mathbf{H}'_\Phi$, where for $i = 0, \ldots, n - 2$, the $(i + 1)$-st row of $\mathbf{H}'_\Phi$ is defined as the coefficient vector of

$$3^{-1}(X - 1)^{-1}X^i h \quad \mathrm{mod}\ (q, \Phi_n).$$

Notice that by Lemma 3.1, $X - 1$ is indeed invertible in $\mathbb{Z}_q[X]/(\Phi_n)$.

Interestingly, we cannot as easily apply this trick when working modulo $X^n - 1$, since $X - 1$ is not invertible modulo $X^n - 1$. In fact, we fail to see how to explicitly compute a basis for the lattice

$$\mathcal{L}_{\mathsf{HRSS}} := \{(\mathbf{v}, \mathbf{w}) \in \mathbb{Z}^{2n} \mid vh \equiv 3(X - 1)w \ \mathrm{mod}\ (q, X^n - 1)\}. \tag{26}$$

NTRU-HPS. Even though g is also divisible by $X-1$ in NTRU-HPS, we should not divide that factor out here, because the resulting polynomial would not have as small coefficients. We can nevertheless still incorporate the fact $g(1) = 0$ to our lattice, by instead interpreting it as a perfect hint.

Geometrically, the equation $g(1) = 0$ is equivalent to the fact that the coefficient vector of g is orthogonal to the all-one vector. Hence, instead of working directly with the CS lattice or the projected cyclotomic lattice, we may first intersect them with $(\mathbf{0}^n, \mathbf{1}^n)^\perp$ or $(\mathbf{0}^{n-1}, \mathbf{1}^{n-1})^\perp$, respectively, i.e., we may work with the following lattices

$$\mathcal{L}_{\mathsf{CS},\cap} := \mathcal{L}_{\mathsf{CS}} \cap (\mathbf{0}^n, \mathbf{1}^n)^\perp,$$

$$\mathcal{L}_{\Phi,\perp,\cap} := \pi_{(\mathbf{1}^{n-1},\mathbf{0}^{n-1})} \left(\pi_{(\mathbf{0}^{n-1},\mathbf{1}^{n-1})} \left(\mathcal{L}_\Phi \cap (\mathbf{0}^{n-1}, \mathbf{1}^{n-1})^\perp \right) \right).$$

We would like to point out that Dachman-Soled, Ducas, Gong and Rossi [DDGR20, Section 6.3] also suggest to incorporate the fact $g(1) = 0$ as a perfect hint for NTRU-HPS. Worth noting, they claim that, according to Lemma 4.1 (respectively Lemma 12 in their work), this increases the determinant of the CS lattice by a factor of $\sqrt{n}$. This claim, however, is not correct. It would be correct if the vector $(\mathbf{0}^n, \mathbf{1}^n)$ was primitive with respect to the dual of $\mathcal{L}_{\mathsf{CS}}$. This is, however, not the case:

Theorem 5.6. *The vector $(\mathbf{0}^n, \mathbf{1}^n)$ is not primitive with respect to the dual of $\mathcal{L}_{\mathsf{CS}}$, but $\frac{1}{q}(\mathbf{0}^n, \mathbf{1}^n)$ is.*

Proof. Since $g(1) = 0$, it follows from Eq. (4) that $h(1) \equiv 0 \mod q$. This implies that the sum over all coefficients of h is a multiple of q. Hence, for every row $\mathbf{H}_i$ of $\mathbf{H}$, as defined in Eq. (13), the inner product between $\frac{1}{q}\mathbf{1}^n$ and $\mathbf{H}_i$ is an integer. Clearly, the inner product between $\frac{1}{q}\mathbf{1}^n$ and a row of $q\mathbf{I}_n$ is also an integer (namely 1).

Combing these two observations with Eq. (13), it follows that for every vector $\mathbf{v} \in \mathcal{L}_{\mathsf{CS}}$ the inner product $\langle \frac{1}{q}(\mathbf{0}^n, \mathbf{1}^n), \mathbf{v} \rangle$ is an integer. Hence, $\frac{1}{q}(\mathbf{0}^n, \mathbf{1}^n)$ lies in the dual of $\mathcal{L}_{\mathsf{CS}}$.

To finish the proof, it remains to show that for any $k \geq 2$, the vector $\frac{1}{kq}(\mathbf{0}^n, \mathbf{1}^n)$ is not included in $\mathcal{L}_{\mathsf{CS}}^*$. This easily follows from the fact that for any such k, the inner product between $\frac{1}{kq}(\mathbf{0}^n, \mathbf{1}^n)$ and the q-vector $(\mathbf{0}^n, q, \mathbf{0}^{n-1}) \in \mathcal{L}_{\mathsf{CS}}$ equals $\frac{1}{k}$ and thus is non-integral. $\qquad\square$

According to Lemma 4.1 and Theorem 5.6, the hint $g(1) = 0$ does not increase the determinant by a factor of $\sqrt{n}$, but decreases it by a factor of $\sqrt{n}/q$.

6   Experimental Results for HRSS and HPS

We implemented all the lattices described in Sect. 5. The source code is available at https://github.com/ElenaKirshanova/ntru_with_sieving.

We provide an interface to generate NTRU-HPS and NTRU-HRSS keys as specified in the documentation [CDH+19]. Our interface also allows to input explicit public parameters n, q, h, instead of generating random instances, e.g. in order to solve the challenges from [Incb].

Our implementation supports the following types of lattices: the Coppersmith-Shamir lattice $\mathcal{L}_{CS}$, the cyclotomic lattice $\mathcal{L}_{\Phi}$, the projected cyclotomic lattice $\mathcal{L}_{\Phi,\perp}$ as well as the lattices $\mathcal{L}_{CS,\cap}$ and $\mathcal{L}_{\Phi,\perp,\cap}$. Upon receiving the type of the NTRU lattice together with the parameters n, q (and optionally h), our implementation constructs the corresponding basis and starts lattice reduction.

We use progressive BKZ [AWHT16] that internally calls either enumeration from the FPyLLL library [dt21a] (with the default pruning strategies [GNR10] for enumeration), or sieving from the G6K library [ADH+19]. Choosing which SVP oracle to use is left to the user. In our experiments, for BKZ blocksizes higher than 65, we use sieving. For smaller blocksizes we run enumeration.[5]

For each BKZ tour, we check either of the two events: *dense sublattice discovery* (DSD) or *secret key recovery* (SKR). In case of DSD, we extract the dense sublattice, which is half of the dimension of the original lattice, and continue with progressive BKZ on this smaller lattice until we find the NTRU secret key.

In all our experiments we use an AMD EPYC 7763 with 1 TB of RAM, as well as an AMD EPYC 7742 processor with 2 TB of RAM. Each EPYC is equipped with 128 physical cores that with parallelization give 256 threads. This number of cores was mostly used to run multiple parallel experiments.

6.1   NTRU-HRSS

Unlike in most other NTRU variants, the parameter q cannot be chosen freely in NTRU-HRSS. Instead, it is fixed to $q = 2^{\lceil 7/2 + \log_2(n) \rceil}$, as specified in Eq. (7). For medium sized values of n, this formula sets q to a value significantly larger than n. For instance, for $91 \leq n \leq 181$, it sets $q = 2048$. (In contrast, for NTRU-HPS such a large q is recommended for $n \in \{509, 677\}$.) As a consequence, NTRU-HRSS parameters with medium sized n lie in the overstretched regime. Indeed, according to the NTRU Fatigue estimator, all NTRU-HRSS parameters with $n < 261$ are overstretched.

We would like to stress that all HRSS parameters, that we can currently attack in a reasonable amount of time, are therefore overstretched. The recommended parameters $n = 701$ and $q = 8192$, on the other hand, are not overstretched.

We ran experiments from $n = 101$ up to $n = 211$ for NTRU-HRSS. Note that only $n = 101, 211$ are elements of $\mathcal{N}$, as defined in Sect. 3, but we are not exploiting any structure for speeding up lattice reduction for $n \notin \mathcal{N}$.

---

[5] In [ADH+19], the crossover point between enumeration and sieving was observed at dimension 70. However, we gain additional speed-up from parallelized sieving.

As expected, in 100% of our experiments the DSD event occurred, confirming that NTRU-HRSS with medium sized n indeed is overstretched. Once the DSD event was detected at blocksize β, the SKR event followed within the next 5 blocksizes, i.e., at blocksize at most $\beta + 5$. In larger dimensions $n \geq 151$, the SKR event usually happened even in the next progressive BKZ call. In some experiments, DSD and SKR events happened at the exact same block size.[6]

Observed Speedup from $\mathcal{L}_{\Phi,\perp}$. In our experiments, we tried all different types of lattices that our implementation supports. Out of all lattices, the Coppersmith-Shamir lattice $\mathcal{L}_{\mathsf{CS}}$ performs worst, whereas the projected cyclotomic lattice $\mathcal{L}_{\Phi,\perp}$ performs best. In the left half of Fig. 1, we plot the required average blocksize β for DSD on $\mathcal{L}_{\mathsf{CS}}$ and on $\mathcal{L}_{\Phi,\perp}$ for $101 \leq n \leq 171$. The exact numbers are given in Table 2. As the figure and table show, $\mathcal{L}_{\Phi,\perp}$ performs significantly better than $\mathcal{L}_{\mathsf{CS}}$.

Changing to the cyclotomic ring and using almost-parallel hints therefore is indeed beneficial for lattice reduction algorithms. As expected, the benefits are not outweighed by decreasing the determinant from q^n to $q^{n-3}/(n-1)$, see Theorem 5.5.

Average blocksize β

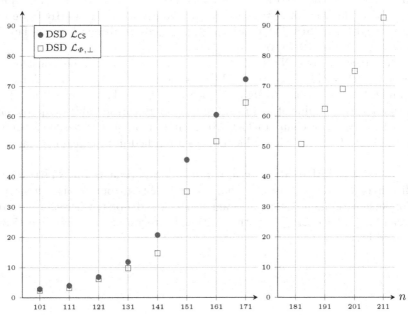

Fig. 1. Comparison between $\mathcal{L}_{\mathsf{CS}}$ and $\mathcal{L}_{\Phi,\perp}$ in the overstretched regime of NTRU-HRSS with $q = 2048$ (left) and $q = 4096$ (right). Averaged over 32 keys each for every $n \leq 171$. For $n = 191, 201$, the average is taken over 20 experiments. For $n = 211$, the blocksize is averaged over 5 experiments.

[6] When DSD and SKR happen at the same blocksize, we are still in the overstretched regime. We are in the non-overstretched regime only if SKR happens *before* DSD.

For $n \geq 183$, we ran experiments only on the superior lattice $\mathcal{L}_{\Phi,\perp}$. The results are shown in the right half of Fig. 1. Comparing both halves of Fig. 1, the reader may notice that for $n = 161$ and $n = 183$ we require roughly the same blocksize $\beta \approx 51$. This is due to the increase in q, caused by Eq. (7): for $n \geq 182$, we switch from $q = 2048$ to $q = 4096$.

Table 2. Average required blocksizes for NTRU-HRSS, as per Fig. 1

n	101	111	121	131	141	151	161	171
$\beta_{\Phi,\perp}$	2.4	3.3	6.3	9.8	14.7	35.1	51.7	64.5
β_{CS}	2.9	4.0	6.9	11.8	20.7	45.6	60.5	72.3

6.2 NTRU-HPS

In contrast to our NTRU-HRSS experiments, we used for NTRU-HPS a significantly smaller modulus $q = 512$ to ensure that we are far off from the overstretched regime. As one might expect, this decrease in q results in significantly larger required BKZ blocksizes. For instance, with NTRU-HPS we require for $n = 131$ a blocksize of $\beta \approx 57$ for SKR, whereas with NTRU-HRSS we require only $\beta \approx 10$ for DSD. Therefore, we cannot provide results for n as large as in NTRU-HRSS ($n = 211$), but only up to $n = 171$.

Nevertheless, our NTRU-HPS computations can still be considered new records in the field of practical NTRU cryptanalysis: The former NTRU record computation by Ducas and Nguyen [Inca] were in similar dimension $n = 173$, but with a larger modulus of $q = 1024$, and therefore (presumably) required smaller blocksizes than our computations. We go up to blocksizes $\beta > 100$, a regime that to the best of our knowledge has not been reached in practical cryptanalysis so far.

As with NTRU-HRSS, we also ran our experiments on NTRU-HPS with all different types of lattices, that are available in our implementation. The Coppersmith-Shamir lattice $\mathcal{L}_{\mathsf{CS}}$ again performed worst, whereas the projected cyclotomic lattice $\mathcal{L}_{\Phi,\perp,\cap}$ (with additional integrated hints, see Sect. 5.3) performed best.

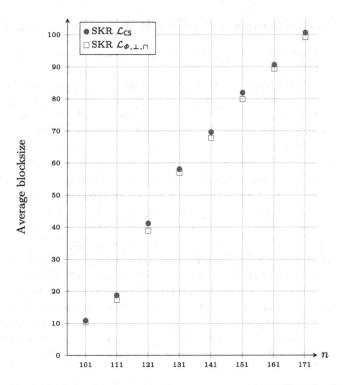

Fig. 2. Required blocksize for the secret key recovery on NTRU-HPS with $q = 512$. Averaged over 32 keys each for every n.

Observed Speedup from $\mathcal{L}_{\Phi,\perp,\cap}$. In Fig. 2, we plot the average required β for $\mathcal{L}_{CS}$ and $\mathcal{L}_{\Phi,\perp,\cap}$. In contrast to NTRU-HRSS, the gap between the two lattices here is not as large. (See Sect. 6.3 for an explanation.)

Table 3. Average required blocksizes for NTRU-HPS, as per Fig. 2

n	101	111	121	131	141	151	161	171
β_{CS}	10.9	18.7	41.1	58.0	69.6	81.9	90.7	100.6
$\beta_{\Phi,\perp,\cap}$	10.4	17.3	38.9	56.8	67.8	79.9	89.4	99.2

In Table 3, we provide all averaged blocksizes β_{CS} and $\beta_{\Phi,\perp,\cap}$ required for SKR in $\mathcal{L}_{CS}$ and $\mathcal{L}_{\Phi,\perp,\cap}$, respectively. While the differences in blocksizes may seem rather small, we note that the difference in runtimes is still significant in practice. For instance, in our $n = 171$ experiment, $\mathcal{L}_{CS}$ required on average 172 core days, whereas $\mathcal{L}_{\Phi,\perp,\cap}$ took on average only 83 core days.

As expected, and similarly as in NTRU-HRSS, the benefits of reducing the dimension thus outweigh the disadvantage of a decreased determinant also in NTRU-HPS.

6.3   Comparison Between HRSS and HPS, and Implications

Let us now explain why the gap between β's is significantly larger for HRSS than it is for HPS.

Recall that we decrease the dimension in HRSS by 4 (by switching to the projected cyclotomic lattice) and in HPS by 5 (by additionally integrating one perfect hint). In both variants, we decrease the root determinant only by a negligible amount. With respect to dimension and determinant, both lattices are thus very similar.

The main difference between our lattices for HRSS and HPS is that $\mathcal{L}_{\mathsf{CS}}$ contains for HRSS the polynomial g that is a multiple of $(X - 1)$ and ternary polynomial, see Eq. (8). As proposed in Sect. 5.3, in the construction of $\mathcal{L}_{\Phi,\perp}$ we divide out $(X - 1)$. This reduces g's norm by roughly a $\sqrt{2}$-factor. Hence, for HRSS we not only decrease the dimension of the lattice, but also decrease the norm of the shortest vectors – which results in a larger gap between β's.

We note that in the HRSS specification [CDH+19] the authors analyzed the lattice $\mathcal{L}_{\mathsf{HRSS}}$ as defined in Eq. (26). Although [CDH+19] does not explicitly provide a basis for $\mathcal{L}_{\mathsf{HRSS}}$ – and constructing one might actually be hard – $\mathcal{L}_{\mathsf{HRSS}}$ was nevertheless used in [CDH+19] to conservatively estimate HRSS security. (In other words, the authors of [CDH+19] already anticipated our improvement in lattice basis construction.) Since the $(X - 1)$ factor is already divided out in $\mathcal{L}_{\mathsf{HRSS}}$, the gap in β's thus do not imply a security loss for HRSS.

7   New NTRU Record: $n = 181$

7.1   Choosing a Lattice for the NTRU Challenges

Due to the different key format in the NTRU challenges, the lattices introduced in Sect. 5 are not the best choice for attacking the challenges. While in NTRU-HPS and NTRU-HRSS the keys satisfy the equation

$$fh \equiv 3g,$$

in the NTRU challenges they satisfy

$$(1 + 3f)h \equiv g. \tag{27}$$

Hence, for the challenges, it is likely not the optimal strategy to search for a short vector $(\mathbf{v}, \mathbf{w})$ satisfying

$$vh \equiv w,$$

since such a vector would be significantly longer than the coefficient vector $(\mathbf{f}, \mathbf{g})$.

As a better strategy, Ducas and Nguyen interpreted Eq. (27) in their record computations as an instance of the *bounded distance decoding problem (BDD)*. They constructed a variant of the CS lattice, namely

$$\mathcal{L}_{\mathsf{DN}} := \{(\mathbf{v}, \mathbf{w}) \in \mathbb{Z}^{2n} \mid 3vh \equiv w \mod (q, X^n - 1)\}, \tag{28}$$

and then searched for a lattice vector $(\mathbf{v}, \mathbf{w}) \in \mathcal{L}_{\mathsf{DN}}$, close to the (non-lattice) vector $(\mathbf{0}^n, \mathbf{h})$. With this strategy one likely finds the vector $(\mathbf{f}, \mathbf{g} - \mathbf{h}) \in \mathcal{L}_{\mathsf{DN}}$, since it is close to $(\mathbf{0}^n, \mathbf{h})$.

We choose to follow a different strategy based on the framework of lattice reduction with hints. Instead of interpreting Eq. (27) as a BDD instance, we choose to interpret it as an almost-parallel hint. The equation implies that $\mathcal{L}_{\mathsf{DN}}$ contains with $(\mathbf{f}, \mathbf{g} - \mathbf{h})$ a vector almost parallel to $(\mathbf{0}^n, \mathbf{h})$. This suggests to project $\mathcal{L}_{\mathsf{DN}}$ orthogonally against $(\mathbf{0}^n, \mathbf{h})$ and then search for

$$\pi_{(\mathbf{0}^n, \mathbf{h})}\big((\mathbf{f}, \mathbf{g} - \mathbf{h})\big) = (\mathbf{f}, \pi_{\mathbf{h}}(\mathbf{g})). \tag{29}$$

as a shortest vector.

We can further improve this lattice, by additionally incorporating a perfect hint. From Eq. (11) we know that f satisfies $f(1) = 0$, since f is composed out of three polynomials f_1, f_2, f_3, which all satisfy $f_i(1) = 0$ (see Eq. (10)). Hence, we have $\langle \mathbf{f}, \mathbf{1}^n \rangle = 0$. Thus, to improve the attack we may intersect $\mathcal{L}_{\mathsf{DN}}$ with $(\mathbf{1}^n, \mathbf{0}^n)^{\perp}$.

Remark 7.1. Similarly as with the projected cyclotomic lattice, one may want to work with the scaled lattice $\|\mathbf{h}\|^2 \cdot \pi_{(\mathbf{0}, \mathbf{h})}\big((\mathcal{L}_{\mathsf{DN}} \cap (\mathbf{1}^n, \mathbf{0}^n)^{\perp})\big)$ in practice to avoid a non-integral basis (see also Remark 5.2).

Remark 7.2. Here we do not have to worry, whether we can efficiently invert the projection against $(\mathbf{0}, \mathbf{h})$, since the left half of the secret still contains the (non-projected) vector $\mathbf{f}$, see Eq. (29).

On Further Possible Improvements. As in Sect. 3.1, we could theoretically further improve our lattice, by working over the cyclotomic ring $\mathbb{Z}_q[X]/(\varPhi_n)$ and incorporating the two almost parallel hints of $(\mathbf{1}^{n-1}, \mathbf{0}^{n-1})$ and $(\mathbf{0}^{n-1}, \mathbf{1}^{n-1})$. However, in that case we would already project our lattice against three vectors in total. This would make the denominators of the coefficients of our lattice vectors very large (or equivalently it would require scaling the lattice by a large factor). To avoid issues of numerical stability in practice, we therefore choose to not include these improvements.

One might ask, whether we can use special properties of g to further improve our lattice (since we have only used the structure of f and the almost-parallel hint of $(\mathbf{0}, \mathbf{h})$ so far).

From Eq. (12) it follows that $g(1) = 1$ or, equivalently,

$$\langle \mathbf{g}, \mathbf{1}^n \rangle = 1.$$

Theoretically, we could also incorporate such a non-homogeneous type of perfect hint into our lattice by using the framework of [DDGR20]. However, for that we would first have to embed our NTRU problem into a non-homogeneous LWE problem, see [DDGR20, Sect. 4.1]. This would increase the lattice dimension by one and therefore negate the effect of introducing the perfect hint $\langle \mathbf{f}, \mathbf{1}^n \rangle = 0$.

As an alternative, one may try to obtain a short vector hint from the structure of g: Applying $f(1) = 0$ and $g(1) = 1$ to Eq. (27), it follows that

$$h(1) = 1 \mod q. \tag{30}$$

Combining this with the fact that for every polynomial $p \in \mathbb{Z}_q[X]/(X^n - 1)$ it holds that[7]

$$(X^{n-1} + \ldots + X + 1) \cdot p \equiv (X^{n-1} + \ldots + X + 1) \, p(1), \tag{31}$$

we obtain

$$(X^{n-1} + X^{n-2} \ldots + X + 1) \cdot h \equiv X^{n-1} + X^{n-2} \ldots + X + 1.$$

Hence, by Eq. (28), the lattice $\mathcal{L}_{\mathsf{DN}}$ contains the short vector $(\mathbf{1}^n, \mathbf{3}^n)$.

One might be tempted to incorporate this fact as a short vector hint. Unfortunately, we have, however, already removed the vector $(\mathbf{1}^n, \mathbf{3}^n)$ from our lattice, because we intersected it with $(\mathbf{1}^n, \mathbf{0}^n)^\perp$.

Interestingly, both the perfect hint $\langle \mathbf{f}, \mathbf{1}^n \rangle = 0$ and the short vector hint $(\mathbf{1}^n, \mathbf{3}^n)$ therefore decrease the dimension by one by *removing* $(\mathbf{1}^n, \mathbf{3}^n)$ from the lattice. The following theorem shows, however, that the perfect hint is superior:

Theorem 7.3. *The determinants of the lattices* $\pi_{(\mathbf{1}^n, \mathbf{3}^n)}(\mathcal{L}_{\mathsf{DN}})$ *and* $\mathcal{L}_{\mathsf{DN}} \cap (\mathbf{1}^n, \mathbf{0}^n)^\perp$ *are given by*

$$\det \left(\mathcal{L}_{\mathsf{DN}} \cap (\mathbf{1}^n, \mathbf{0}^n)^\perp \right) = \sqrt{n} q^n, \tag{32}$$

and

$$\det \left(\pi_{(\mathbf{1}^n, \mathbf{3}^n)}(\mathcal{L}_{\mathsf{DN}}) \right) = \frac{q^n}{\sqrt{10n}}. \tag{33}$$

Proof. Since $\mathcal{L}_{\mathsf{DN}} \subset \mathbb{Z}^{2n}$ is an integer lattice, the vector $(\mathbf{1}^n, \mathbf{3}^n) \in \mathcal{L}_{\mathsf{DN}}$ clearly is primitive with respect to $\mathcal{L}_{\mathsf{DN}}$. Hence, Eq. (33) immediately follows from Lemma 4.2.

To prove Eq. (32), it suffices to show that $(\mathbf{1}^n, \mathbf{0}^n)$ is primitive with respect to the dual $\mathcal{L}_{\mathsf{DN}}^*$, see Lemma 4.1. This, in turn, easily follows from the fact that for every integer $k \geq 2$ the inner product between $\frac{1}{k}(\mathbf{1}^n, \mathbf{0}^n)$ and the lattice vector $(1, \mathbf{0}^{n-1}, 3\mathbf{h}) \in \mathcal{L}_{\mathsf{DN}}$ (see Eq. (28)) equals $\frac{1}{k}$ and thus is not integral.   □

7.2   Record Computation Details

The idea of incorporating almost-parallel hints enables us to establish a new record for the NTRU challenges from [Incb]. The former record holders are Ducas and Nguyen [Inca] who managed to solve NTRU with $n = 173$. We went up one challenge further and solved NTRU for $n = 181$ with $q = 1024$. These parameters do not lie in the overstretched regime. To solve the challenge, we implemented

---

[7] Equation (31) easily follows from the Chinese Remainder Theorem.

the approach described above. That is, we run BKZ on the lattice $\mathcal{L}_{DN}$ from Eq. (28) intersected with $(\mathbf{1}^n, \mathbf{0}^n)^\perp$ and projected orthogonally against $(\mathbf{0}^n, \mathbf{h})$. The shortest vector of the form (f, g) was found at blocksize $\beta = 109$ after 20 core years of computations. The solution is posted at https://github.com/ElenaKirshanova/ntru_with_sieving.

Acknowledgments. Elena Kirshanova is supported by the Russian Science Foundation grant N 22-41-04411, https://rscf.ru/project/22-41-04411/. Alexander May and Julian Nowakowski are funded by the Deutsche Forschungsgemeinschaft (DFG, German Research Foundation) – grant 465120249. Alexander May is additionally supported by grant 390781972.

References

[ABB+20] Aragon, N., et al.: BIKE: bit flipping key encapsulation (2020). https://bikesuite.org/files/v5.0/BIKE_Spec.2022.10.10.1.pdf

[ABC+20] Albrecht, M.R., et al.: Classic McEliece: conservative code-based cryptography (2020). https://classic.mceliece.org/nist/mceliece-20201010.pdf

[ABF+20] Albrecht, M.R., Bai, S., Fouque, P.-A., Kirchner, P., Stehlé, D., Wen, W.: Faster enumeration-based lattice reduction: root Hermite factor $k^{1/(2k)}$ Time $k^{k/8+o(k)}$. In: Micciancio, D., Ristenpart, T. (eds.) CRYPTO 2020. LNCS, vol. 12171, pp. 186–212. Springer, Cham (2020). https://doi.org/10.1007/978-3-030-56880-1_7

[AD21] Albrecht, M.R., Ducas, L.: Lattice attacks on NTRU and LWE: a history of refinements, pp. 15–40 (2021)

[ADH+19] Albrecht, M.R., Ducas, L., Herold, G., Kirshanova, E., Postlethwaite, E.W., Stevens, M.: The general sieve kernel and new records in lattice reduction. In: Ishai, Y., Rijmen, V. (eds.) EUROCRYPT 2019. LNCS, vol. 11477, pp. 717–746. Springer, Cham (2019). https://doi.org/10.1007/978-3-030-17656-3_25

[ADPS16] Alkim, E., Ducas, L., Pöppelmann, T., Schwabe, P.: Post-quantum key exchange - a new hope. In: 25th USENIX Security Symposium, pp. 327–343 (2016)

[AKS01] Ajtai, M., Kumar, R., Sivakumar, D.: A sieve algorithm for the shortest lattice vector problem. In: STOC 2001, pp. 601–610 (2001)

[AWHT16] Aono, Y., Wang, Y., Hayashi, T., Takagi, T.: Improved progressive BKZ algorithms and their precise cost estimation by sharp simulator. In: Fischlin, M., Coron, J.-S. (eds.) EUROCRYPT 2016. LNCS, vol. 9665, pp. 789–819. Springer, Heidelberg (2016). https://doi.org/10.1007/978-3-662-49890-3_30

[BDK+18] Bos, J.W., et al.: CRYSTALS - Kyber: a CCA-secure module-lattice-based KEM. In: 2018 IEEE EuroS&P, pp. 353–367 (2018)

[CDH+19] Chen, C., et al.: PQC round-3 candidate: NTRU. technical report (2019). https://ntru.org/f/ntru-20190330.pdf

[CN11] Chen, Y., Nguyen, P.Q.: BKZ 2.0: better lattice security estimates. In: Lee, D.H., Wang, X. (eds.) ASIACRYPT 2011. LNCS, vol. 7073, pp. 1–20. Springer, Heidelberg (2011). https://doi.org/10.1007/978-3-642-25385-0_1

[CS97] Coppersmith, D., Shamir, A.: Lattice attacks on NTRU. In: Fumy, W. (ed.) EUROCRYPT 1997. LNCS, vol. 1233, pp. 52–61. Springer, Heidelberg (1997). https://doi.org/10.1007/3-540-69053-0_5

[DDGR20] Dachman-Soled, D., Ducas, L., Gong, H., Rossi, M.: LWE with side information: attacks and concrete security estimation. In: Micciancio, D., Ristenpart, T. (eds.) CRYPTO 2020. LNCS, vol. 12171, pp. 329–358. Springer, Cham (2020). https://doi.org/10.1007/978-3-030-56880-1_12

[DSvW21] Ducas, L., Stevens, M., van Woerden, W.: Advanced lattice sieving on GPUs, with tensor cores. In: Canteaut, A., Standaert, F.-X. (eds.) EUROCRYPT 2021. LNCS, vol. 12697, pp. 249–279. Springer, Cham (2021). https://doi.org/10.1007/978-3-030-77886-6_9

[dt21a] The FPLLL development team. FPYLLL, a Python wraper for the FPLLL lattice reduction library, Version: 0.5.7 (2021). https://github.com/fplll/fpylll

[dt21b] The G6K development team. The general sieve kernel (G6K) (2021). https://github.com/fplll/g6k

[Duc18] Ducas, L.: Shortest vector from lattice sieving: a few dimensions for free. In: Nielsen, J.B., Rijmen, V. (eds.) EUROCRYPT 2018. LNCS, vol. 10820, pp. 125–145. Springer, Cham (2018). https://doi.org/10.1007/978-3-319-78381-9_5

[DvW21] Ducas, L., van Woerden, W.: NTRU fatigue: how stretched is overstretched? In: Tibouchi, M., Wang, H. (eds.) ASIACRYPT 2021. LNCS, vol. 13093, pp. 3–32. Springer, Cham (2021). https://doi.org/10.1007/978-3-030-92068-5_1

[FHK+18] Fouque, P.-A., et al.: FALCON: fast-Fourier lattice-based compact signatures over NTRU (2018). https://www.di.ens.fr/~prest/Publications/falcon.pdf

[Gen01] Gentry, C.: Key recovery and message attacks on NTRU-composite. In: Pfitzmann, B. (ed.) EUROCRYPT 2001. LNCS, vol. 2045, pp. 182–194. Springer, Heidelberg (2001). https://doi.org/10.1007/3-540-44987-6_12

[GNR10] Gama, N., Nguyen, P.Q., Regev, O.: Lattice enumeration using extreme pruning. In: Gilbert, H. (ed.) EUROCRYPT 2010. LNCS, vol. 6110, pp. 257–278. Springer, Heidelberg (2010). https://doi.org/10.1007/978-3-642-13190-5_13

[How07] Howgrave-Graham, N.: A hybrid lattice-reduction and meet-in-the-middle attack against NTRU. In: Menezes, A. (ed.) CRYPTO 2007. LNCS, vol. 4622, pp. 150–169. Springer, Heidelberg (2007). https://doi.org/10.1007/978-3-540-74143-5_9

[HPS98] Hoffstein, J., Pipher, J., Silverman, J.H.: NTRU: a ring-based public key cryptosystem. In: Buhler, J.P. (ed.) ANTS 1998. LNCS, vol. 1423, pp. 267–288. Springer, Heidelberg (1998). https://doi.org/10.1007/BFb0054868

[HRSS17] Hülsing, A., Rijneveld, J., Schanck, J., Schwabe, P.: High-speed key encapsulation from NTRU. In: Fischer, W., Homma, N. (eds.) CHES 2017. LNCS, vol. 10529, pp. 232–252. Springer, Cham (2017). https://doi.org/10.1007/978-3-319-66787-4_12

[Inca] NTRU Securty Innovation Inc. NTRU challenge - answers. https://web.archive.org/web/20151229220714/https://www.securityinnovation.com/uploads/ntru-challenge-parameter-sets-and-public-keys-answers.pdf

[Incb] NTRU Securty Innovation Inc. NTRU challenge parameter sets and public keys. https://web.archive.org/web/20160310141551/https://www.securityinnovation.com/uploads/ntru-challenge-parameter-sets-and-public-keys-new.pdf

[Kan83] Kannan, R.: Improved algorithms for integer programming and related lattice problems. In: STOC 1983 (1983)

[KF17]   Kirchner, P., Fouque, P.-A.: Revisiting lattice attacks on overstretched
          NTRU parameters. In: Coron, J.-S., Nielsen, J.B. (eds.) EUROCRYPT
          2017. LNCS, vol. 10210, pp. 3–26. Springer, Cham (2017). https://doi.
          org/10.1007/978-3-319-56620-7_1

[LLL82]   Lenstra, A.K., Lenstra, H.W., Lovász, L.: Factoring polynomials with ratio-
          nal coefficients. Math. Ann. **261**, 515–534 (1982)

[LN13]   Liu, M., Nguyen, P.Q.: Solving BDD by enumeration: an update. In: Daw-
          son, E. (ed.) CT-RSA 2013. LNCS, vol. 7779, pp. 293–309. Springer, Hei-
          delberg (2013). https://doi.org/10.1007/978-3-642-36095-4_19

[MAB+21] Melchor, C.A., et al.: Hamming quasi-cyclic (HQC) (2021). https://pqc-
          hqc.org/doc/hqc-specification_2021-06-06.pdf

[MS01]   May, A., Silverman, J.H.: Dimension reduction methods for convolution
          modular lattices. In: Silverman, J.H. (ed.) CaLC 2001. LNCS, vol. 2146,
          pp. 110–125. Springer, Heidelberg (2001). https://doi.org/10.1007/3-540-
          44670-2_10

[MV10]   Micciancio, D., Voulgaris, P.: Faster exponential time algorithms for the
          shortest vector problem. In: SODA 2010, pp. 1468–1480 (2010)

[NV08]   Nguyen, P.Q., Vidick, T.: Sieve algorithms for the shortest vector problem
          are practical. J. Math. Cryptol. **2**(2), 181–207 (2008)

[Sch87]   Schnorr, C.-P.: A hierarchy of polynomial time lattice basis reduction algo-
          rithms. Theor. Comput. Sci. **53**, 201–224 (1987)

[Sch03]   Schnorr, C.P.: Lattice reduction by random sampling and birthday meth-
          ods. In: Alt, H., Habib, M. (eds.) STACS 2003. LNCS, vol. 2607, pp. 145–
          156. Springer, Heidelberg (2003). https://doi.org/10.1007/3-540-36494-
          3_14

On the Hardness of Scheme-Switching Between SIMD FHE Schemes

Karim Eldefrawy[1], Nicholas Genise[2(✉)], and Nathan Manohar[3]

[1] SRI International, Menlo Park, USA
karim.eldefrawy@sri.com
[2] Duality Technologies, Maplewood, USA
ngenise@dualitytech.com
[3] IBM T.J. Watson Research Center, Yorktown Heights, USA
nmanohar@ibm.com

Abstract. Fully homomorphic encryption (FHE) schemes are either lightweight and can evaluate boolean circuits or are relatively heavy and can evaluate arithmetic circuits on encrypted vectors, i.e., they perform single instruction multiple data operations (SIMD). SIMD FHE schemes can either perform exact modular arithmetic in the case of the Brakerski-Gentry-Vaikuntanathan (BGV) and Brakerski-Fan-Vercauteren (BFV) schemes or approximate arithmetic in the case of the Cheon-Kim-Kim-Song (CKKS) scheme. While one can homomorphically switch between BGV/BFV and CKKS using the computationally expensive bootstrapping procedure, it is unknown how to switch between these schemes without bootstrapping. Finding more efficient methods than bootstrapping of converting between these schemes was stated as an open problem by Halevi and Shoup, Eurocrypt 2015 [33,34].

In this work, we provide strong evidence that homomorphic switching between BGV/BFV and CKKS is *as hard as* bootstrapping. In more detail, if one could efficiently switch between these SIMD schemes, then one could bootstrap these SIMD FHE schemes using a single call to a homomorphic scheme-switching algorithm *without applying homomorphic linear transformations*. Thus, one cannot hope to obtain significant improvements to homomorphic scheme-switching without also significantly improving the state-of-the-art for bootstrapping.

We also explore the relative hardness of computing homomorphic comparison in these same SIMD FHE schemes as a secondary contribution. We show that given a comparison algorithm, one can bootstrap these schemes using a few calls to the comparison algorithm for typical parameter settings. While we focus on the comparison function in this work, the overall approach to demonstrate relative hardness of computing specific functions homomorphically extends beyond comparison to other useful functions such as min/max or ReLU.

Keywords: Fully Homomorphic Encryption · Lattice-Based Cryptography · Post-Quantum Cryptography

N. Manohar—This work was done while the second and third authors were at SRI International.

T. Johansson and D. Smith-Tone (Eds.): PQCrypto 2023, LNCS 14154, pp. 196–224, 2023.
https://doi.org/10.1007/978-3-031-40003-2_8

1 Introduction

Fully homomorphic encryption (FHE) enables a client to encrypt their data, send it to a cloud server, and have the server compute any function on the client's encrypted data without knowledge of the decryption key. This client-server setting for outsourcing computation is especially useful when the client has limited computational capabilities, and the server has significantly more resources. FHE was first proposed in 1978 by Rivest et al. [57], but it was not until Gentry's breakthrough in 2009 [26,27] that the cryptographic community saw a plausible, (truly) fully homomorphic[1] encryption scheme. Gentry's breakthrough in 2009 focused on schemes with limited homomorphic capabilities that also possessed a simple decryption circuit. Such schemes can homomorphically evaluate their decryption circuits to re-encrypt, or "bootstrap", their ciphertexts. Gentry showed that a fully homomorphic encryption scheme can be obtained from any scheme that can homomorphically evaluate a NAND gate together with its decryption circuit [27]. Further, Gentry based his scheme on ideal lattices since decryption in lattice-based cryptosystems boils down to decoding noisy lattice points back to the public lattice (linear operations followed by a rounding step).

FHE has gone through many iterations towards practicality since Gentry's breakthrough in 2009. Today, there are three main FHE cryptoschemes using (ring) lattices: FHEW/TFHE [17,20] which encrypt one bit, or a scalar, at a time and the BGV/BFV or CKKS schemes which pack (up to) thousands of plaintext values into each ciphertext. The former, FHEW/TFHE, schemes are relatively lightweight but can only perform one nonlinear boolean or small-number operations for each lightweight bootstrapping. On the other hand, the packed schemes, BGV/BFV and CKKS, can perform thousands of arithmetic operations in parallel using ciphertext packing and also support computations between ciphertext slots using the underlying field's Galois automorphisms. After a fixed number of multiplications (referred to as the "depth"), these schemes need to perform a more expensive bootstrapping operation to increase the size of the ciphertext modulus (and lower the relative noise level in the ciphertext in the case of BGV/BFV).

In this work, we focus on the SIMD FHE schemes. BGV and BFV are schemes which perform exact modular arithmetic modulo some prime power whereas CKKS performs approximate arithmetic on fixed-point numbers. It is well-known that homomorphic scheme-switching between BGV and BFV can be computed efficiently by scalar multiplications [2]. However, it is not known how to efficiently switch between CKKS and BGV/BFV without bootstrapping.

Given the differing plaintext spaces, switching between schemes can be useful in a variety of applications. For example, say the majority of a computation is done in CKKS until the underlying plaintext has lost a set number of precision bits. Then, one could homomorphically convert the CKKS ciphertexts into

---

[1] Many schemes beforehand had limited homomorphic capabilities. They either had ciphertexts grow exponentially with operations [3,23,54] or they had limited homomorphism [6,40]. See Chap. 3 of Gentry's dissertation [26] for a survey of previous schemes.

BGV/BFV ciphertexts to continue the rest of the computation and avoid any further loss in precision. Alternatively, a computation may consist of several stages where some stages are required to be computed exactly and others can be computed approximately. One could compute homomorphically using CKKS for the approximate stages of the computation and use BGV/BFV for the exact stages of the computation. This is a natural setting since CKKS is much more efficient than BGV/BFV for performing real and complex arithmetic computations. Another setting is to develop a general cross-scheme bootstrapping technique where efficient homomorphic scheme-switching is the first step [34]. Then, for example, an ASIC on a server for one scheme could be used for multiple FHE schemes.

Recently, there has been a flurry of work in scheme-specific hardware acceleration for SIMD schemes [1,22,24,58,59]. This gives a clear motivation for efficient homomorphic scheme-switching since a server might have a specialized ASIC for one scheme (CKKS) but has many ciphertext stored encrypted in another scheme (BFV). Ideally, the server could homomorphically switch the ciphertexts into the main scheme used in the ASIC without bootstrapping.

It is folklore that one can switch between schemes using bootstrapping. This is done, essentially, by homomorphically evaluating the decryption circuit of one scheme inside the other. Unfortunately, bootstrapping is computationally expensive, and, thus, it is desirable to obtain more efficient methods of scheme-switching. Finding scheme-switching between BGV/BFV and CKKS methods without bootstrapping was explicitly stated as an open problem by Halevi and Shoup Eurocrypt 2015 [33,34]. The recent library OpenFHE [4] and the recent work [19] also both explicitly mention that scheme-switching between BGV/BFV and CKKS as an open problem.

1.1 Our Results

We provide strong evidence that homomorphic scheme-switching between the aforementioned SIMD FHE schemes is *as hard as* bootstrapping. In fact, we show that a weak variant of homomorphic scheme-switching between these schemes which ignores the differences in the plaintext encoding can bootstrap these SIMD schemes in one call to such an algorithm *without applying homomorphic linear transformations*. We model this homomorphic scheme-switcher as an oracle.

In more detail, both BGV/BFV and CKKS have ciphertexts of the form $\mathsf{ct} = (c_0, c_1) \in R_Q^2$, where $R := \mathbb{Z}[X]/(X^N + 1)$ is a cyclotomic ring of integers, $Q \in \mathbb{Z}^+$ is a ciphertext modulus, and $R_Q := R/(QR)$. Since converting between BGV and BFV can be done by simply multiplying by a constant [2], we will focus on BGV in this work, but the results hold for BFV as well. In both BGV and CKKS, (homomorphic) decryption begins by computing $(c_0 + c_1 \cdot s(X)) \bmod Q$ for a secret $s(X) \in R$. In BGV, this results in $p \cdot e(X) + m(X) \in R$, where p is the plaintext modulus. In CKKS, this gives $\Delta m(X) + e(X) \in R$ for some scaling factor Δ. A weak scheme-switcher from BGV to CKKS takes as input a BGV ciphertext $(c_0, c_1) \in R_Q^2$ where $(c_0 + c_1 \cdot s(X)) \bmod Q = pe(X) + m(X)$ and outputs a

CKKS ciphertext $(c_0', c_1') \in R_{Q'}^2$ where $(c_0' + c_1' \cdot s(X)) \bmod Q' = \Delta m(X) + e'(X)$. (A weak homomorphic scheme-switcher from CKKS to BGV is defined analogously.) We refer to such a scheme-switcher as *weak* because it homomorphically switches schemes with respect to the same ring polynomial $m(X)$ without dealing with the fact that BGV and CKKS have different plaintext encodings. Recall, in BGV, the plaintext polynomial $m(X) \in R_p$ is related to $(\mathbb{Z}_p)^k$ or $(\mathbb{F}_{p^r})^k$ via a ring isomorphism [29], whereas in CKKS, the plaintext polynomial $\Delta m(X) + e(X)$ is embedded into $\mathbb{C}^{N/2}$ via the canonical embedding [14]. Thus, in order to homomorphically switch between these schemes in practice, one would also need to deal with the differences in plaintext encodings. This is done by applying homomorphic linear transformations where the matrix is represented by plaintext polynomials [13,32]. However, we show this weaker variant of homomorphic scheme-switching already implies an immediate bootstrapping algorithm *without applying homomorphic linear transformations*. We model the weak scheme-switchers as oracles $\mathcal{O}_{C \hookrightarrow B}$ and $\mathcal{O}_{B \hookrightarrow C}$. Informally, we show the following main results.

Theorem 1.1 (Informal). *If there exists a weak homomorphic scheme-switching algorithm from BGV to CKKS, $\mathcal{O}_{B \hookrightarrow C}$, then there exists a CKKS bootstrapping algorithm with the same time complexity plus the time to perform one CKKS rescaling operation.*

Theorem 1.2 (Informal). *If there exists a weak homomorphic scheme-switching algorithm from CKKS to BGV, $\mathcal{O}_{C \hookrightarrow B}$, then there exists a BGV bootstrapping algorithm with the same time complexity plus the time to perform one BGV plaintext multiplication, one plaintext addition, and one modulus switching operation.*

As a secondary contribution, we also explore the relative hardness of computing homomorphic comparison in these SIMD FHE schemes. Prior works [15, 16, 39, 46] focused on computing homomorphic comparison (and other related functions such as max/min and ReLU) in these SIMD FHE schemes since these functions are useful to compute for many machine-learning applications. Computing comparisons in these SIMD schemes is difficult since comparison is not easily expressible as a shallow arithmetic circuit. We model the homomorphic comparison functionality as an oracle $\mathcal{O}_{\geq}$ and show how to use several calls to this oracle to bootstrap these SIMD FHE schemes. We focus on comparison in this work, but our approach extends to other related functions such as max/min and ReLU. Unlike our primary contribution on the hardness of homomorphic scheme-switching, this secondary result is somewhat expected because bootstrapping requires some form of digit extraction.

1.2   Technical Overview

Fig. 1. Visualization of a weak scheme-switching oracle from BGV to CKKS. This process is called *weak* because homomorphic scheme-switching using this oracle requires us to call BGV's slots-to-coefficient algorithm, a homomorphic linear transformation, before we call the oracle and CKKS's coefficient-to-slots algorithm, another homomorphic linear transformation, after we call the oracle. We show this "weak" process is surprisingly powerful: it allows for bootstrapping CKKS ciphertexts *without* homomorphic linear transformations.

A simplified view of a weak scheme-switching oracle, $\mathcal{O}_{B \hookrightarrow C}$, is shown in Fig. 1. The main intuition is that any non-trivial bit-wise manipulations on an RLWE encryption's message/error polynomial's coefficients are the most expensive operations performed in bootstrapping. This is seen in BGV's decryption circuit: there is a linear operation on the ciphertext over R_Q, $d := c_0 + c_1 \cdot s \mod Q$, followed by some nonlinear rounding, $d \mod p$. In essence, we show the homomorphic nonlinear rounding in either BGV or CKKS can be achieved by (homomorphically) moving around contiguous bits of the message/error polynomial's coefficients, weakly switching the plaintext encoding of the encrypted plaintext. Hence, a weak converter is quite powerful in the FHE setting. We sketch the case from BGV to CKKS using $\mathcal{O}_{B \hookrightarrow C}$ since it is simpler. Recall the main idea of bootstrapping a CKKS ciphertext [13]: we have a CKKS ciphertext $\mathsf{ct} = (c_0, c_1) \in R_q^2$ which we implicitly treat as a ciphertext with respect to a larger ciphertext modulus $Q > q$ with $q \mid Q$. That is, we view ct as a pair of elements in R_Q^2. We need to compute the $y(X) \mapsto y(X) \mod q$ function (where the mod is taken on all the coefficients of $y(X)$) homomorphically on ct to obtain a $\mathsf{ct}' \in R_Q^2$ that decrypts to approximately the same value as ct under the same secret key for some ciphertext modulus $Q' > q$. Observe that $c_0 + c_1 \cdot s(X) = \Delta m(X) + e(X) + I(X)q$ where each coefficient of $\Delta m(X) + e(X)$ is $\ll q$. Notice that bootstrapping in CKKS reduces to clearing the high order bits of the plaintext polynomial's coefficients (the $I(X)q$ term). Standard CKKS bootstrapping moves these coefficients to the plaintext slots via discrete Fourier transform (DFT), computes the mod q function via a polynomial approximation, and then moves the result back to the coefficients.

However, there is a much more efficient algorithm for performing the $y \mapsto y \mod q$ function on a CKKS ciphertext's coefficients given the oracle in Fig. 1. If we simply treat the input CKKS ciphertext $\mathsf{ct} \in R_Q^2$ as a BGV ciphertext with plaintext modulus q, we observe that ct is a valid BGV encryption of

$\Delta m(X) + e(X)$ with error $I(X)q$ for some small integer polynomial $I(X)$. The oracle $\mathcal{O}_{B \to C}$ applied to this BGV encryption outputs a CKKS encryption of $\Delta'(\Delta m(X) + e(X)) + e'(X)$ with ciphertext modulus $Q' \gg q$ and some other error $e'(X)$, noting that $q > \Delta m(X)$. Therefore, we perform one CKKS rescaling operation and return the result as the new bootstrapped ciphertext of CKKS encrypting $m(X)$. The CKKS to BGV case is similar.

1.3 Related Works

Switching between BGV/BFV and CKKS without bootstrapping was first mentioned as an open problem in the updated version of [33,34] as it pertains to a potential cross-scheme bootstrapping technique.

The problem of switching between FHEW/TFHE and BGV/BFV and CKKS is an orthogonal problem since once you apply homomorphic linear transformations on the latter, the rest is up to extracting the coefficients as separate lightweight FHEW/TFHE ciphertexts. This was done explicitly in [8,52], respectively called Chimera and Pegasus, and was partially done in the original FHEW/TFHE works [17,20] while interfacing the homomorphic accumulator and LWE Regev encryptions [55,56]. Chimera [8] and Pegasus [52] consider methods of scheme-switching between CKKS and TFHE via bootstrapping. Moreover, Chimera [8] also considers scheme-switching from BFV to TFHE by bootstrapping. Chimera handles the differing plaintext spaces by using the underlying ring's coefficient packing, similar to our approach. Kim et al. [43] take this idea further and apply FHEW/TFHE techniques to packed schemes, BGV/BFV and CKKS. Liu, Micciancio, and Polyakov [51] developed a high precision FHEW functional bootstrapping with the CKKS-to-FHEW/TFHE application in mind, building on Chillotti et al. [18].

Additionally, several works [15,16,39,46] have focused on methods of computing comparison (and other related functions such as max/min and ReLU) in these SIMD FHE schemes since these functions are useful to compute for applications, but are not easily expressible as arithmetic circuits.

We note the security model likely changes when going from BGV/BFV to CKKS, since the latter is an approximate FHE scheme [49], if the user publishes decryption results. One must apply noise flooding when switching to CKKS in applications where the noisy CKKS decryption value is publicly available or published [50].

1.4 Organization

In Sect. 2, we cover the necessary background and preliminaries. Scheme-switching oracles are defined in Sect. 3. We also show how to transform a weak scheme-switching oracle, which works on coefficients, into a strong scheme-switching oracle, which inputs a packed BGV (resp. CKKS) ciphertext and outputs a packed CKKS (resp. BGV) ciphertext, in this section. In Sect. 4, we give the main results of our paper in Theorems 4.1 and 4.2. In Sect. 5, we show how one can bootstrap BGV and CKKS with a few calls to comparison oracles. We conclude in Sect. 6.

2 Preliminaries

We denote the integers as $\mathbb{Z}$, the rationals as $\mathbb{Q}$, the reals as $\mathbb{R}$, and the complex numbers as $\mathbb{C}$. For polynomials or vectors of real numbers, we use the notation $\lceil v \rfloor$ to denote coefficient-wise rounding to the integers. For an integer z, we denote its balanced remainder modulo q as $[z]_q \in [-q/2, q/2)$ and its p-digit decomposition as $z = \sum_i z\langle i \rangle p^i$ where $z\langle i \rangle \in [-p/2, p/2)$. We denote an integer z's k-through-j middle digits as $z\langle j, \ldots, k \rangle = \sum_{i=k}^{j} z\langle i \rangle p^i$ for $k < j$. Throughout the paper, we use power of two cyclotomic rings[2] (fields), $R := \mathbb{Z}[X]/(X^N + 1)$ $(F := \mathbb{Q}[X]/(X^N + 1))$ is the cyclotomic ring (field) of order $2N$, where N is a power of two. We often view these rings in their coefficient embedding. That is, $a(X) = \sum_{i=0}^{N-1} a_i X^i \in R$ embeds as $a(X) \leftrightarrow (a_0, \ldots, a_{N-1}) \in \mathbb{Z}^N$ and the analogous embedding for the cyclotomic field. We denote the ℓ_∞ norm of a polynomial in $a(X) = \sum_{i=0}^{N-1} a_i X^i \in R$ as $\|a\|_\infty = \max_i |a_i|$. Any two polynomials $f, g \in R$ satisfy $\|fg\|_\infty \leq N\|f\|_\infty\|g\|_\infty$. This worst-case bound is rarely met when the polynomials are distributed as in FHE ciphertexts and $\|fg\|_\infty \leq 2\sqrt{N}\|f\|_\infty\|g\|_\infty$ is often seen in practice with high probability [31].

2.1 RLWE SIMD Schemes

Here we discuss the main SIMD schemes used in practice: CKKS [14], BGV [10], and BFV [9,21]. These schemes are RLWE-based crypto-systems [53] and use ciphertext packing [29,60], which allows a ciphertext to hold up to thousands of plaintext scalars for common parameters. Even though BGV and BFV can encrypt elements from an extension field of $\mathbb{Z}_p$, we focus on the case where they encrypt scalar elements for simplicity. BGV/BFV and CKKS differ greatly in their plaintext spaces even with this simplification. The former have each plaintext scalar in $\mathbb{Z}_p$, and the latter has each in $\mathbb{R}$ (or even $\mathbb{C}$) via fixed-point approximations. Since we can always switch between BFV and BGV with the same plaintext spaces cheaply with scalar multiplications [2,44], we will often focus on BGV in this work, but our results also apply for BFV.

Let $R := \mathbb{Z}[X]/(X^N + 1)$ be the $2N$-th cyclotomic ring for N a power of two and let $R_Q := R/QR$ be the ciphertext space where Q is a positive integer. When sampling ring elements, we refer to them by their coefficient representations in the appropriate space (i.e. $\mathbb{Z}^N, \mathbb{Z}_Q^N, \mathbb{Z}_p^N$). We will work with residue classes in the balanced representation (so elements of $\mathbb{Z}_Q$ are represented by $[-Q/2, Q/2) \cap \mathbb{Z}$).

BGV. A BGV encryption is defined as follows.

---

[2] All of our results apply to arbitrary cyclotomic fields. See [36] for the full details of BGV in general cyclotomics.

Definition 2.1. *Fix a ciphertext modulus Q, a plaintext modulus p (typically a prime power), and a ring dimension N. Further, p and Q must be coprime integers. A BGV encryption of $m \in R_p$ for a secret $s \in R$ with small norm, and a noise distribution χ, is a pair of ring elements $ct = (c_0, c_1) \in R_Q^2$ where $c_0 = as + pe + m$, $c_1 = -a$, and $e \leftarrow \chi$. To decrypt, one computes $(c_0 + c_1 s \bmod Q) \bmod p$. For correctness of decryption, we require that $\|pe + m\|_\infty < Q/2$. We denote the set of BGV ciphertexts that decrypt to m, under some fixed s and χ, as $\mathsf{BGV}^s(m)_{p,Q} \subset R_Q^2$.*

Note that we leave χ unspecified since the error distribution is affected by homomorphic operations. The appropriate χ for a particular ciphertext will be clear from context.

BFV. A BFV encryption is defined as follows.

Definition 2.2. *Fix a ciphertext modulus Q, a plaintext modulus p (typically a prime power), and a ring dimension N. A BFV encryption of $m \in R_p$ for a secret $s \in R$ with small norm, and a noise distribution χ, is a pair of ring elements $ct = (c_0, c_1) \in R_Q^2$ where $c_0 = as + \lceil \Delta m \rfloor + e$, for $\Delta = \frac{Q}{p} \in \mathbb{Q}$, $c_1 = -a$, and $e \leftarrow \chi$. To decrypt, one computes*

$$m' = \left\lceil \lceil (c_0 + c_1 s \bmod Q)/\Delta \rfloor \right\rceil.$$

For correctness of decryption, we require that $\|e\|_\infty < Q/(2p) - 1/2 = (\Delta - 1)/2$.

See [44] for more details on BFV, its optimized version, and its relation to BGV.

A key noise management operation in BGV is modulus-switching, defined as follows. Note, we focus on the case where the moduli, Q and Q', satisfy $Q = DQ'$, as all feasible BGV implementations include a chain of ciphertext moduli satisfying this divisibility requirement, e.g., HELib [36].

Definition 2.3 ([10,29]). *Let $ct \in \mathsf{BGV}^s(m)_{p,Q}$ be a BGV ciphertext and $Q = Q'D$ be a positive integer coprime with p, and $Q \bmod p = Q' \bmod p = 1$. Then, the BGV modulus-switching operation is*

$$ct' \leftarrow \lceil (Q'/Q) \cdot (ct + \delta) \rfloor_p \in R_{Q'}^2,$$

where $\delta = p \cdot ([-c_0/p]_D, [-c_1/p]_D) \in R^2$ and $\lceil \frac{Q'}{Q} z \rfloor_p$ maps an integer $z \in [-Q/2, Q/2)$ to the nearest integer, z', in $[-Q'/2, Q'/2)$ such that $z' \equiv z \mod p$. We write $ct' \leftarrow \mathsf{BGV.ModSwitch}(ct)_{Q \to Q'} \in \mathsf{BGV}^s(m)_{p,Q'}$ as shorthand for BGV modulus-switching.

Modulus-switching is the main noise-management technique used in BGV besides bootstrapping. The following lemma states its effect on ciphertext noise precisely.

Lemma 2.1 ([10,29]). *If $ct \in \mathsf{BGV}^s(m)_{p,Q}$ is a BGV ciphertext satisfying*

$$\|c_0 + c_1 s \bmod Q\|_\infty \leq \frac{Q}{2} - \frac{pD(1 + N\|s\|_\infty)}{2},$$

then $\mathsf{ct}' \leftarrow \mathsf{BGV.ModSwitch}(\mathsf{ct})_{Q \to Q'} \in \mathsf{BGV}^s(m)_{p,Q'}$ is a BGV ciphertext with error norm $\|e'\|_\infty$ at most $\|e\|_\infty/D + (1 + N\|s\|_\infty)/2$, where $Q'D = Q$ and $e \in R$ is the error for the input ciphertext ct.

CKKS Scheme. A CKKS encryption with respect to a scaling parameter $\Delta \in \mathbb{Z}$ is defined as follows.

Definition 2.4. *Fix a ciphertext modulus Q, $\Delta \in \mathbb{Z}^+$, and a ring dimension N. A CKKS encryption of $m \in R$ with scaling factor $\Delta \in \mathbb{Z}^+$ is a pair of ring elements $\mathsf{ct} = (c_0, c_1) \in R_Q^2$ where $c_0 = as + e + \Delta m$, $c_1 = -a$. To decrypt, one computes $\lceil (c_0 + c_1 s \bmod Q)/\Delta \rfloor$. For correctness of decryption, we require that $\|\Delta m + e\|_\infty < Q/2$. We denote the set of CKKS ciphertexts, under some fixed s and χ, as $\mathsf{CKKS}^s(m)_{\Delta,Q} \subset R_Q^2$.*

The flexibility in choosing Δ, together with ciphertext packing, allows CKKS encryption to encrypt fixed-point approximations of numbers. Next, we describe the analogous noise-management technique in CKKS to BGV's modulus switching.

Definition 2.5 ([14]). *Given a CKKS ciphertext $\mathsf{ct} \in \mathsf{CKKS}^s(m)_{\Delta,Q}$ with a ciphertext modulus $Q = Q'D$, CKKS rescaling is the following operation:*

$$\mathsf{ct}' \leftarrow \lceil (Q'/Q) \cdot \mathsf{ct} \rfloor \in R_{Q'}^2,$$

where multiplication is done over $\mathbb{Q}$. We use $\mathsf{CKKS.Rescale}(\mathsf{ct})_{Q \to Q'}$ as shorthand for the above operation.

Rescaling and modulus switching are the nearly same operation, but the rounding factor in BGV has entries as large as $\pm p/2$ wheres the rounding factor in CKKS has smaller entries in $[\pm 1/2]$. Next, we give the change in ciphertext noise under the infinity metric of the coefficients.

Lemma 2.2 ([14]). *Let $\mathsf{ct} \in \mathsf{CKKS}^s(m)_{\Delta,Q}$ be a CKKS ciphertext satisfying*

$$\|c_0 + c_1 s \bmod Q\|_\infty \leq Q/2 - D(N\|s\|_\infty + 1)/2$$

and let $Q = Q'D$. Then, the operation, $\mathsf{ct}' \leftarrow \mathsf{CKKS.Rescale}(\mathsf{ct})_{Q \to Q'} \in R_{Q'}^2$, is a CKKS encryption, $\mathsf{ct}' \in \mathsf{CKKS}^s(m)_{\Delta/D,Q'}$. Furthermore, if the error term e in $\mathsf{ct} = (as + \Delta m + e, -a)$ has norm $\|e\|_\infty$, then ct' has an error norm $\|e'\|_\infty$ with norm at most $\|e\|_\infty/D + (N\|s\|_\infty + 1)/2$.

It is easy to see that if ct satisfies

$$\|c_0 + c_1 s \bmod Q\|_\infty \leq Q/2 - D(N\|s\|_\infty + 1)/2,$$

then you can always decrypt after rescaling. The same holds true for BGV modulus-switching if the input ciphertext satisfies

$$\|c_0 + c_1 s \bmod Q\|_\infty \leq Q/2 - pD(N\|s\|_\infty + 1)/2.$$

Homomorphic Operations. Adding and multiplying ciphertexts in BGV and CKKS are given by the following simple operations: if $\mathsf{ct} = (c_0, c_1) \in \mathsf{BGV}^s(m)_{p,Q}$ and $\mathsf{ct}' = (c_0', c_1') \in \mathsf{BGV}^s(m')_{p,Q}$, then addition over R_Q^2 ($\mathsf{ct} + \mathsf{ct}'$) gives a ciphertext in $\mathsf{BGV}^s(m + m')_{p,Q}$. We can multiply a BGV (CKKS) ciphertext by a plaintext polynomial $\alpha \in R_p$ ($\alpha \in R$) by simply returning $\mathsf{ct} \leftarrow \alpha \cdot \mathsf{ct} \in R_Q^2$. It is easy to see how this increases the noise from $\|e\|_\infty$ to $\|\alpha\|_\infty \|e\|_\infty$. Multiplying BGV or CKKS ciphertexts is given by $(d_0, d_1, d_2) = (c_0 c_0', c_0 c_1' + c_0' c_1, c_1 c_1') \in R_Q^3$. In BGV, we get the following:

$$(c_0 + c_1 s)(c_0' + c_1' s) = c_0 c_0' + s(c_0 c_1' + c_0' c_1) + s^2 c_1 c_1'$$
$$= p(pee' + em' + e'm) + mm'$$
$$= mm' \bmod p.$$

We have the following analogous equations for multiplying two CKKS ciphertexts:

$$(c_0 + c_1 s)(c_0' + c_1' s) = c_0 c_0' + s(c_0 c_1' + c_0' c_1) + s^2 c_1 c_1'$$
$$= \Delta^2 mm' + (\Delta me' + \Delta m'e + ee').$$

Therefore, we "re-linearize" the ciphertext after multiplication with a key-switching operation to get a ciphertext represented with two polynomials again in R_Q encrypting mm'. For simplicity, we use the Gentry-Halevi-Smart method [30] for relinearization: The *relinearization key* is an RLWE encryption of s^2 under the original key s under a larger modulus, $Q' = PQ$ where Q is the largest modulus allowed for ciphertexts. That is, the evaluation key is $evk := (-as + Ps^2 + pe, a) \in R_{P \cdot Q}^2$. Then, we relinearize (d_0, d_1, d_2) by returning

$$(d_0, d_1) + \mathsf{BGV}.\mathsf{ModSwitch}(d_2 \cdot evk)_{PQ \to Q}.$$

For CKKS, we have the same operations but the evaluation key does not have its RLWE error scaled by p: $evk := (-as + Ps^2 + e, a) \in R_{PQ}^2$.

See [10, 14, 29] for the full details of the BGV and CKKS schemes.

2.2 Useful Lemmas

Here we list some useful lemmas used throughout the paper. First, we list a core lemma to the state of the art in BGV bootstrapping's digit extraction procedure. We list the case simplified to the plaintext space being a prime $p \neq 2$.

Lemma 2.3 ([34]). *Let $p > 1$, $r \geq 1$, and $\tilde{q} = p^r + 1$ be integers with p being an odd prime. Let z be an integer such that $|z/q| + |[z]_q| < (q-1)/2$. Then,*

$$[z]_q = z\langle 0 \rangle - z\langle r \rangle \bmod p.$$

Next, we list a lemma which summarizes the complexity to perform homomorphic digit extraction in BFV and BGV. Digit extraction is a crucial step in these schemes' state-of-the-art bootstrapping algorithms.

Lemma 2.4 ([12]). *Let p be prime, $v < e$ be positive integers, u be an integer input modulo p^e with digits*

$$u = u\langle e-1, \ldots, 0\rangle = \sum_{i=0}^{e-1} u_i p^i.$$

Then, there is an algorithm with $\sqrt{2pev}$ multiplications and arithmetic depth $v \log p + \log e$ which returns

$$u\langle e-1, \ldots, v\rangle = \sum_{i=v}^{e-1} u\langle i\rangle p^i.$$

2.3   Bootstrapping Circuits for BGV and CKKS

Here we describe the state of the art in BGV (BFV) and CKKS bootstrapping. The linear portion of the RLWE decryption function is $c_0 + c_1 s \bmod q$ for both BGV and CKKS. However, BGV further performs a modulo p operation, for plaintext p coprime to q, so

$$m = (c_0 + c_1 s \bmod q) \bmod p = (m + pe) \bmod p.$$

CKKS takes a ciphertext at the lowest level, $(c_0, c_1) \in R_q^2$ just like BGV, but implicitly treats the ciphertext as a high level ciphertext in R_Q^2. Then,

$$c_0 + c_1 s \bmod q = \Delta m + e + Iq$$

for some small polynomial $I = I(X) \in R$. Therefore, the majority of CKKS bootstrapping is spent computing the $y \mapsto y \bmod q$ homomorphically.

Both CKKS and BGV use plaintext packing which enables SIMD arithmetic. CKKS packing is given by the canonical embedding modulo complex conjugation: $a(X) \in R$ can be represented by $(a(\delta), a(\delta^{i_1}), \ldots, a(\delta^{i_{N/2-1}})) \in \mathbb{C}^{N/2}$ where δ is a complex root of $X^N + 1$ and $i_1, \ldots, i_{N/2-1}$ are representatives of $\mathbb{Z}_{2N}^* / \{\pm 1\}$. BGV ciphertext packing is given by the analogous representation modulo p: $(a(\zeta^{k_1}), a(\zeta^{k_2}), \ldots, a(\zeta^{k_j})) \in \mathbb{F}_{p^d}^j$ where $\zeta \in \mathbb{Z}_p$ is a root of $X^N + 1 \bmod p$, d is the order of p in $\mathbb{Z}_{2N}^*$, and $\{\zeta^{k_j}\}$ are coset representatives of $\mathbb{Z}_{2N}^* / \langle p \rangle$ [36]. Switching between coefficient reprensetation and these evaluation representations is done by linear transformations over $\mathbb{C}$ and $\mathbb{Z}_p$, respectively. Both can be performed homomorphically on a ciphertext, where the former is approximate. These linear transformations are a key step in bootstrapping and can be evaluated with constant multiplicative depth [13,32].

BGV. In more detail, BGV bootstrapping is given by:

1. Modulus-switch to a special ciphertext modulus of the form $\tilde{q} = p^r + 1$ [34].
2. Perform a homomorphic inner-product with an encrypted version of the secret key at the highest level (also called the bootstrapping hint). Here, the input ciphertext is treated as a plaintext to the bootstrapping hint.

3. Unpack the ciphertext with a homomorphic linear transformation (constant depth, but time-intensive). This moves the ciphertext coefficients to the ciphertext slots. Depending on parameters, these values may require multiple ciphertexts.
4. Homomorphically compute the function $x \mapsto (x \bmod \tilde{q}) \bmod p$ via the state-of-the-art digit extraction polynomials [12].
5. Repack the ciphertext with the inverse of the homomorphic linear transformation from the second step above with respect to the smaller, original plaintext modulus p.

See [25] for more details and the state of the art in BGV and BFV bootstrapping.

CKKS. For CKKS, we perform the following:

1. Treat the ciphertext as a larger modulus ciphertext $(Q \gg q)$.
2. Unpack the ciphertext with a homomorphic linear transformation. This moves the coefficients into the plaintext slots. If the ciphertext is fully packed, this will need to output 2 ciphertexts to store the N coefficients. If $\leq N/4$ slots are used, then we can fit all the coefficients in the slots of a single ciphertext. See [13] for more details. This step is referred to as CoeffsToSlots.
3. Compute an approximation of the $y \mapsto y \bmod q$ homomorphically [11, 13, 38, 41, 42, 47, 48].
4. Re-pack the ciphertext with a homomorphic linear transformation. This step is referred to as SlotsToCoeffs.

Another optimization in CKKS bootstrapping was recently given in [5] where they treat bootstrapping as a black box and bootstrap twice in order to reduce the error induced strictly from bootstrapping. Recently, [45] showed how to save a few ciphertext levels in the overall CKKS bootstrapping procedure by computing the EvalRound function homomorphically instead of EvalMod.

3   Homomorphic Scheme-Switching

In this section, we define variants of scheme-switching oracles. First, we define weak scheme-switching oracles. A weak scheme-switching oracle takes a CKKS (resp. BGV) ciphertext encrypting a ring polynomial $m(X)$ and outputs a BGV (resp. CKKS) ciphertext encrypting the same ring polynomial $m(X)$. We call the scheme-switching oracles *weak* because they fix the encrypted message in its coefficient form, instead of the evaluation representation (slots), and do not handle the fact that BGV and CKKS have different message encodings. In other words, we would still have to call the CKKS (resp. BGV) slots-to-coefficients function before calling the oracle and re-pack the BGV ciphertext homomorphically after calling the oracle. Next, we define strong scheme-switching oracles which switch packed ciphertexts. We conclude with showing how to transform a weak oracle into a strong oracle with homomorphic linear transformations.

3.1   Weak Scheme-Switching Oracles

Here we define two weak scheme-switching oracles needed for our main result: one that takes a BGV ciphertext encrypting some message polynomial $m(X)$ and outputs a CKKS ciphertext for $m(X)$ (with respect to some scaling factor Δ) and another which takes a CKKS ciphertext encrypting some message polynomial $m(X)$ (with respect to some scaling factor Δ) and outputs a BGV ciphertext encrypting $m(X)$. Ideally, these oracles are black boxes parameterized by BGV and CKKS parameters which have the same functionality as decrypting a BGV (resp. CKKS) ciphertext and re-encrypting the message polynomial in CKKS (resp. BGV) without direct access to the secret key.

Regarding noise and ciphertext moduli, these oracles potentially lower the quality (i.e., the noise magnitude to modulus ratio) of the ciphertexts they convert, just as a real FHE computation would. We have the oracles take as input a ciphertext with noise from an error distribution χ_{in} and return a ciphertext with noise from an error distribution χ. Note that an oracle returning a ciphertext with a smaller modulus and the same noise magnitude as the input is analogous to an oracle returning a ciphertext with the same ciphertext modulus but with a larger noise magnitude since we can always modulus-switch or rescale the oracle's output without the secret key.

First, we define the weak scheme-switching oracle from BGV to CKKS:

Definition 3.1. *Let $\mathcal{O}_{B \to C}(\mathsf{ct}_{in}; p, \Delta, Q, Q', \chi_{in}, \chi)$ denote the BGV-to-CKKS oracle that takes as input a BGV ciphertext $\mathsf{ct}_{in} = (c_0, c_1)$ encrypting some m, i.e., $c_0 + c_1 s \bmod Q = m + pe$ for error distributed as $e \sim \chi_{in}$, and is parameterized by a BGV plaintext modulus $p \in \mathbb{Z}^+$, a CKKS scaling factor Δ, an input ciphertext modulus Q, an output ciphertext modulus Q', an input noise distribution χ_{in}, and an output noise distribution χ, potentially a randomized function of χ_{in}, $\chi = f(\chi_{in})$. The oracle returns a CKKS encryption of m, $\mathsf{ct}_{out} = (c_0', c_1') \in R_{Q'}^2$, i.e., $c_0' + c_1' s \bmod Q' = \Delta m + e_\chi$, for a potentially smaller modulus $Q' \leq Q$ and an error e_χ, where $e_\chi = f(e)$, under the same secret key as the input ciphertext.*

Observe that since we allow f to be a randomized function in the above definition, Definition 3.1 captures instantiations of the oracle where χ is independent of χ_{in}, and f simply ignores the input noise distribution χ_{in}. However, by defining the oracle in this manner, we also capture situations where χ is dependent on χ_{in}, which is also possible depending on the oracle instantiation. The other scheme-switching oracles in this paper are defined analogously for the same reason.

Next, we define the analogous oracle for switching from CKKS to BGV.

Definition 3.2. *Let $\mathcal{O}_{C \to B}(\mathsf{ct}_{in}; \Delta, p, Q, Q', \chi_{in}, \chi)$ denote the CKKS-to-BGV oracle that takes as input a CKKS ciphertext $\mathsf{ct}_{in} = (c_0, c_1) \in R_Q^2$ encrypting some m, i.e., $c_0 + c_1 s \bmod Q = \Delta m + e$ for error distributed as $e \sim \chi_{in}$, a CKKS scaling factor Δ, and is parameterized by a BGV plaintext modulus $p \in \mathbb{Z}^+$, an input ciphertext modulus Q, an output ciphertext modulus Q', an input noise* *distribution* χ_{in}, *and an output noise distribution* χ, *potentially a randomized function of* χ_{in}, $\chi = f(\chi_{in})$. *The oracle returns a BGV encryption of* m, $\mathsf{ct}_{out} = (c'_0, c'_1) \in R^2_{Q'}$, *where* $c'_0 + c'_1 s \bmod Q' = m + p e_\chi$, *for a potentially smaller modulus* $Q' \le Q$ *and an error* e_χ, *where* $e_\chi = f(e)$, *under the same secret key as the input ciphertext.*

Observe that in order to preserve $m(X)$, the oracles must be called with appropriate parameters. For example, when calling $\mathcal{O}_{B\hookrightarrow C}$, if $\|e_\chi\|_\infty > \Delta$, then the least significant bits of $m(X)$ will be destroyed by the error (we would only have an approximation of $m(X)$). This is commonplace in CKKS encryption and why CKKS is often referred to as an "approximate" FHE scheme. When calling $\mathcal{O}_{C\hookrightarrow B}$, the returned ciphertext is a BGV encryption of $m(X) \bmod p$. Thus, the higher-order bits of the coefficients of $m(X)$ will be lost if their magnitude is larger than $p/2$.

3.2   Strong Scheme-Switching Oracles

Here we discuss strong scheme-switching oracles, which take packed ciphertexts as input and return a packed ciphertext in another SIMD scheme. First, we define strong scheme-switching oracles. Then, we show how to transform a weak scheme-switching oracle into a strong one via homomorphic linear transformations.

Recall the BGV plaintext encoding in its simplest form, where p is a prime with $p = 1 \bmod 2N$. Here, the RLWE plaintext space is $\mathbb{Z}_p[X]/(X^N + 1)$, and $X^N + 1$ splits modulo p. This means that $\mathbb{Z}_p[X]/(X^N + 1) \cong \mathbb{Z}_p^N$ by evaluating a polynomial at the primitive roots of unity modulo p via the discrete Fourier transform (DFT) over the field. Let $\mathbf{D}$ denote this matrix. Then, given an input vector $\mathbf{v} \in \mathbb{Z}_p^N$, one packs it into a polynomial by treating it as the evaluation of some polynomial over the roots of unity and recovers the polynomial by taking the inverse modulo p: $m(X) := \mathbf{D}^{-1}\mathbf{v}$. In general, the cyclotomic polynomial might not split modulo p, but it will factor into degree k polynomials. Then, the plaintext space is $\mathbb{F}_{p^k}^\ell$ where $N = k \cdot \ell$, and the packing is similar. See Appendix C of [29] or [36] for the full details. Given a vector $\mathbf{v} \in \mathbb{Z}_p^N$, we denote the BGV encoding algorithm as $m(X) = \mathsf{encode}_{\mathsf{BGV}}(\mathbf{v})$ with $m(X) \in R_p$. The inverse is denoted by $\mathbf{v} = \mathsf{decode}_{\mathsf{BGV}}(m(X))$.

CKKS packing is done analogously but with the primitive complex roots of unity. Here, the roots of $X^N + 1$ over $\mathbb{C}$ are all N primitive roots of unity of order $2N$. Evaluating a polynomial at all of these roots leads to an element in the conjugate space $\mathbb{H} = \{\mathbf{z} = (z_j)_{j \in \mathbb{Z}_{2N}^*} : z_j = \overline{z_{-j}}\} \subset \mathbb{C}^N$ where one half of the vector $\mathbf{z}$ is the conjugate of the other half and $\mathbb{Z}_{2N}^*$ denotes the unit group of $\mathbb{Z}_{2N}$. Call this map τ. CKKS encoding only uses one half of these vectors by projecting down to $\mathbb{C}^{N/2}$. Call this projection π. CKKS encoding is the inverse of this process: given a vector $\mathbf{v} \in \mathbb{C}^{N/2}$, take the inverse DFT corresponding to the projected portion of the symmetric space $\mathbb{H}$. Since this only gives us an element in $\mathbb{R}[X]/(X^N + 1)$, CKKS encoding scales and rounds this element to $R = \mathbb{Z}[X]/(X^N + 1)$. This is done in the canonical embedding space $\mathbb{H}$ by scaling up by some scaling factor Δ and rounding to the ring R: $m(X) = \lfloor \tau^{-1}(\Delta\pi^{-1}(\mathbf{v})) \rceil$ where the projection π is invertible on the image of $\mathbb{H}$. Further, we often write the scaled CKKS message as $\Delta m(X)$ by linearity and since we can add the rounding error into the RLWE error. Representing the message as $\Delta m(X)$ helps gauge the number of bits left for homomorphic operations, roughly $\log(Q) - \log(\Delta)$ for small m. Given a vector $\mathbf{v} \in \mathbb{C}^{N/2}$, we denote the CKKS encoding algorithm as $m(X) = \mathsf{encode}_{\mathsf{CKKS}}(\mathbf{v}, \Delta)$, $m(X) \in R$. The (lossy) inverse is denoted by $\mathbf{v}' = \mathsf{decode}_{\mathsf{CKKS}}(m(X), \Delta)$.

Given a BGV or CKKS ciphertext encrypting a packed polynomial, one can homomorphically rotate the slots by performing a field automorphism σ to the ciphertext. For example, if $\mathsf{ct} = (c_0, c_1) \in R_Q^2$ is a BGV ciphertext encrypting $m(X) = \mathsf{encode}_{\mathsf{BGV}}(\mathbf{v})$, then $(\sigma_i(c_0), \sigma_i(c_1))$ encrypts

$$m'(X) = \sigma_i(m) = \mathsf{encode}_{\mathsf{BGV}}((v_i, v_{i+1}, \ldots, v_{N-1-i \bmod N}))$$

under the secret key $\sigma_i(s)$. That is, σ_i is the Galois automorphism that cyclically shifts the vector by i positions. We then key-switch back to a ciphertext encrypted under s using an operation similar to relinearization.(Relinearization is a special case of key-switching).

Now consider a strong homomorphic scheme-switching algorithm. Given a BGV ciphertext $(as + pe + m, -a)$ where $m = m(X) = \mathsf{encode}_{\mathsf{BGV}}(\mathbf{v})$ encodes N elements in $\mathbb{Z}_p$, the goal is to switch to either one or two packed CKKS ciphertexts encrypting the elements of v. We say potentially two ciphertexts since we expect applications to use BGV for exact multiplication before overflow modulo p and the spaces $\mathbb{C}$ and $\mathbb{F}_p^2$ are incompatible in terms of arithmetic operations. For simplicity, assume we want to pack them into one CKKS ciphertext. Then, given $(as + pe + m, -a)$, the output is a ciphertext $(a's + e' + \Delta m', -a')$ where $m' = m'(X) = \mathsf{encode}_{\mathsf{CKKS}}(\mathbf{v}, \Delta)$. This yields the following definitions.

We denote $\Re(y)$ and $\Im(y)$ as the respective real and imaginary part of a complex number, $y \in \mathbb{C}$, and $\Re(\mathbf{y})$, $\Im(\mathbf{y})$ as the function applied component-wise to a vector $\mathbf{y} \in \mathbb{C}^m$. We define the strong scheme-switching oracles below:

Definition 3.3. *Let $\mathcal{O}_{B \to C}^{\mathsf{strong}}(\mathsf{ct}_{\mathsf{in}}; p, \Delta, Q, Q', \chi_{\mathsf{in}}, \chi)$ denote the strong BGV-to-CKKS oracle that takes as input a BGV ciphertext $\mathsf{ct}_{\mathsf{in}} = (c_0, c_1)$ encrypting some m, i.e., $c_0 + c_1 s \bmod Q = m + pe$ for $m = m(X) = \mathsf{encode}_{\mathsf{BGV}}(\mathbf{v})$, $\mathbf{v} \in \mathbb{Z}_p^N$ with error distributed as $e \sim \chi_{\mathsf{in}}$, and is parameterized by a BGV plaintext modulus $p \in \mathbb{Z}^+$, a CKKS scaling factor Δ, an input ciphertext modulus Q, an output ciphertext modulus Q', an input noise distribution χ_{in}, and an output noise distribution χ, potentially a randomized function of χ_{in}, $\chi = f(\chi_{\mathsf{in}})$. The oracle returns a CKKS encryption of m, $\mathsf{ct}_{\mathsf{out}} = (c'_0, c'_1) \in R_{Q'}^2$, i.e., $c'_0 + c'_1 s \bmod Q' = \Delta m' + e_\chi$ where $m' = \mathsf{encode}_{\mathsf{CKKS}}(\mathbf{v}, \Delta)/\Delta$, for a potentially smaller modulus $Q' \leq Q$ and an error e_χ, where $e_\chi = f(e)$, under the same secret key as the input ciphertext.*

Definition 3.4. *Let $\mathcal{O}_{C \to B}^{\mathsf{strong}}(\mathsf{ct}_{\mathsf{in}}; \Delta, p, Q, Q', \chi_{\mathsf{in}}, \chi)$ denote the CKKS-to-BGV oracle that takes as input a CKKS ciphertext $\mathsf{ct}_{\mathsf{in}} = (c_0, c_1) \in R_Q^2$ encrypting some m, i.e., $c_0 + c_1 s \bmod Q = \Delta m + e$ for $m = m(X) =$*

$\mathsf{encode_{CKKS}}(\mathbf{v}, \Delta)/\Delta$, $\mathbf{v} \in \mathbb{C}^{N/2}$ *with error distributed as* $e \sim \chi_{in}$, *a CKKS scaling factor* Δ, *and is parameterized by a a BGV plaintext modulus* $p \in \mathbb{Z}^+$, *an input ciphertext modulus* Q, *an output ciphertext modulus* Q', *an input noise distribution* χ_{in}, *and an output noise distribution* χ, *potentially a randomized function of* χ_{in}, $\chi = f(\chi_{in})$. *The oracle returns a BGV encryption of* m, *i.e.,* $\mathsf{ct_{out}} = (c'_0, c'_1) \in R_{Q'}^2$ *where* $c'_0 + c'_1 s \bmod Q' = m' + pe_\chi$ *with* $m' = \mathsf{encode_{BGV}}(\mathbf{v}')$ *where* $\mathbf{v}' = (\Re(\mathbf{v}), \Im(\mathbf{v}))$, *for a potentially smaller modulus* $Q' \leq Q$ *and an error* e_χ, *where* $e_\chi = f(e)$, *under the same secret key as the input ciphertext.*

Next, we show how to take a weak scheme-switcher and transform it into a strong scheme-switcher using homomorphic linear transformations. We will use the following two lemmas on homomorphically encoding and decoding in CKKS and BGV. The following algorithms/lemmas are given in terms of minimal plaintext-ciphertext depth for simplicity. Note, homomorphically applying the BGV and CKKS encoding/decoding algorithms can be done with homomorphic linear transformations where the matrix is stored as plaintexts polynomials. In the case of CKKS, this is an approximate linear transformation due to the CKKS encoding function. We summarize this in Lemmas 3.1 and 3.2 below.

Lemma 3.1 ([32]). *Given a BGV ciphertext* $\mathsf{ct} = (c_0, c_1) \in R_Q^2$, $c_0 + c_1 s = m + pe$ *for* $m(X) = \mathsf{encode_{BGV}}(\mathbf{v})$, $\mathbf{v} \in \mathbb{Z}_p^N$, *together with its public evaluation key evk, one can homomorphically transform* ct *into a BGV ciphertext* ct', *under the same secret key, encrypting* $\mathbf{v}$ *in the coefficients of* $m'(X)$, *in a plaintext-ciphertext multiplicative depth one circuit and* $N/2$ *ciphertext rotations.*

Lemma 3.2 (Algorithm 1 in [13]). *Given a CKKS ciphertext* $\mathsf{ct} = (c_0, c_1) \in R_Q^2$, $c_0 + c_1 s = \Delta m + e$ *for* $m(X) = \mathsf{encode_{CKKS}}(\mathbf{v}, \Delta)/\Delta$, $\mathbf{v} \in \mathbb{C}^{N/2}$, *together with its public evaluation key evk, one can homomorphically transform* ct *into a CKKS ciphertext* $\mathsf{ct}' \in R_{Q'}^2$, *under the same secret key, encrypting* $\mathbf{v}$ *in the coefficients of* $m'(X)$, *in a plaintext-ciphertext multiplicative depth one circuit and* $N/2$ *ciphertext rotations. The resulting ciphertext modulus* $Q' \leq Q$ *depends on the precision to which this approximate computation is performed, which a more precise computation resulting in* ct' *having a smaller* Q'.

See Chen et al. [11] or Han et al. [37] for a faster algorithm for homomorphic encoding and decoding using an FFT-like algorithm with a deeper circuit. Further efficiency optimizations can be found in [7]. The algorithms in Lemmas 3.1 and 3.2 encode each linear transformation's matrix by N (resp., $N/2$) diagonals as plaintext polynomials and apply the matrix-vector multiplication homomorphically. See [13,32] for more details.

If the input ciphertext in Lemma 3.1 (resp., Lemma 3.2) has distribution χ_{in}, then denote the output distribution as $T_B(\chi_{in})$ (resp., $T_C(\chi_{in})$). In practice, the noise growth from applying the homomorphic linear transformations is relatively small, but the homomorphic computation involved is time-intensive.

We now show how to take a weak scheme-switching oracle and turn it into a strong scheme-switching oracle at the cost of two levels of plaintext-ciphertext multiplicative depth.

Theorem 3.1. *Given a weak scheme-switching oracle from BGV to CKKS, $\mathcal{O}_{B \to C}(\mathsf{ct_{in}}; p, \Delta, Q, Q', T_B(\chi_{in}), \chi)$, there exists a strong scheme-switching oracle from BGV to CKKS, $\mathcal{O}_{B \to C}^{\mathsf{strong}}(\mathsf{ct_{in}}; p, \Delta, Q, Q'', \chi_{in}, T_C(\chi))$, where Q'' is related to Q' by the instantiation of Lemma 3.2.*

Proof. Let $\mathsf{ct''} = (c_0'', c_1'') \in R_Q^2$ be a BGV ciphertext where $c_0'' + c_1'' s = m'' + p e''$ and $m'' = m''(X) = \mathsf{encode_{BGV}}(\mathbf{v})$ for some vector $\mathbf{v} \in \mathbb{Z}_p^N$. Let χ'' denote the input error's distribution, $e'' \sim \chi''$. Compute the following:

1. Run the algorithm in Lemma 3.1 to get a ciphertext $\mathsf{ct'} = (c_0', c_1')$ where $c_0' + c_1' s = m' + p e'$ encrypts $\mathbf{v}$ as the coefficients in m': $m'(X) = v_0 + v_1 X + \cdots + v_{N-1} X^{N-1}$. Denote the error distribution of $\mathsf{ct'}$ by $T_B(\chi'')$.
2. Call the weak scheme-switching oracle on $\mathsf{ct'}$,

$$\hat{\mathsf{ct}} \leftarrow \mathcal{O}_{B \to C}(\mathsf{ct'}; p, \Delta, Q, Q', T_B(\chi''), \chi),$$

   to get $\hat{\mathsf{ct}} = (\hat{c}_0, \hat{c}_1) \in R_{Q'}^2$ where $\hat{c}_0 + \hat{c}_1 s = \Delta m' + \hat{e}$.
3. Let $\mathbf{v}' \in \mathbb{C}^{N/2}$ denote $\mathbf{v}$'s entries stored as a complex vector. Run the algorithm in Lemma 3.2 to get $\mathsf{ct} = (c_0, c_1) \in R_{Q''}^2$ where $c_0 + c_1 s = \Delta m + e$ and $m = m(X) = \mathsf{encode_{CKKS}}(\mathbf{v}', \Delta)/\Delta$. The error distribution of e is $T_C(\chi)$.

$\square$

Theorem 3.2. *Given a weak scheme-switching oracle from CKKS to BGV, $\mathcal{O}_{C \to B}(\mathsf{ct_{in}}; \Delta, p, Q', Q'', T_C(\chi_{in}), \chi)$, there exists a strong scheme-switching oracle from CKKS to BGV, $\mathcal{O}_{C \to B}^{\mathsf{strong}}(\mathsf{ct_{in}}; \Delta, p, Q, Q'', \chi_{in}, T_B(\chi))$, where Q' is related to Q by the instantiation of Lemma 3.2.*

Proof. The proof is analogous to that of Theorem 3.1. $\square$

4   Bootstrapping via a Weak Scheme-Switching Oracle

In this section, we show our main results that one can bootstrap a BGV (resp., CKKS) ciphertext using a single call to a weak scheme-switching oracle *without* computing homomorphic linear transformations. Recall that since BFV ciphertexts can be simply converted to BGV ciphertexts via scalar multiplication [2], our result for BGV also applies to BFV.

We show two directions:

1. Using a BGV to CKKS weak scheme-switching oracle, one can bootstrap a CKKS ciphertext using one oracle query and
2. Using a CKKS to BGV weak scheme-switching oracle, one can bootstrap a BGV ciphertext using one oracle query.

To bootstrap a CKKS ciphertext, we only need to perform one CKKS rescaling in addition to the oracle call. To bootstrap a BGV ciphertext, we only need to perform a homomorphic inner product and one BGV modulus-switching in addition to the oracle call. Thus, we provide powerful evidence that scheme-switching is at least as hard as bootstrapping and improvements to scheme-switching should lead to improvements to bootstrapping.

4.1 Bootstrapping in CKKSfrom a BGV-to-CKKS Oracle

We begin by showing that a weak BGV-to-CKKS scheme-switching oracle allows one to bootstrap a CKKS ciphertext immediately. As mentioned above, this allows the user to bootstrap a CKKS ciphertext *without* the costly coefficients-to-slots homomorphic linear transformation or its inverse. In the reduction, we are calling $\mathcal{O}_{B \to C}$ with a BGV plaintext modulus equal to the input ciphertext modulus q. We emphasize that treating the lowest level ciphertext modulus as a plaintext modulus is common in BGV bootstrapping. See [28,34] for more details.

Theorem 4.1. *Fix some CKKS parameters: $R = \mathbb{Z}[X]/(X^N + 1)$, $\Delta, \Delta_{\text{in}}$ positive integers, and $q \ll Q'' \leq Q' \leq Q$ as ciphertext moduli with $q \mid \Delta Q'' = Q' \mid Q$. Let the ciphertext $\text{ct} \in \text{CKKS}^s(m)_{\Delta_{\text{in}},q}$ be the input. Then, the existence of a BGV to CKKS weak scheme-switching oracle, $\mathcal{O}_{B \to C}(\ \cdot\ ; q, \Delta, Q, Q', \chi', \chi)$, implies the existence of a CKKS bootstrapping algorithm where the time to bootstrap is the time complexity of the oracle plus the time complexity to rescale from Q' to Q'/Δ, and the output ciphertext has noise at most $\|e\|_\infty + \frac{\|e_\chi\|_\infty}{\Delta} + (N\|s\|_\infty + 1)/2$, where e is the error term of ct and e_χ is the error term in the output of $\mathcal{O}_{B \to C}$.*

Proof. Let $\text{ct} = (c_0, c_1) \in R_q^2$ be the input ciphertext in $\text{CKKS}^s(m)_{\Delta_{\text{in}},q}$. That is, the ciphertext satisfies $c_0 + c_1 s \bmod q = \Delta_{\text{in}} m + e$. By embedding c_0, c_1 into R_Q, it follows that this new ciphertext with modulus Q satisfies $c_0 + c_1 s \bmod Q = \Delta_{\text{in}} m + e + I(X)q$ where $I(X)$ is an integer polynomial that depends on the Hamming weight and norm of the secret key, $s \in R$. Note that $I(X) \cdot q \ll Q$ for common parameter settings. Then, the reduction simply calls the weak scheme-switching oracle with BGV plaintext $p = q$, where χ' is the implicit error distribution of viewing ct as a BGV ciphertext in the above manner. Let

$$\text{ct}^{(1)} = \mathcal{O}_{B \to C}(\text{ct}; q, \Delta, Q, Q', \chi', \chi).$$

Notice that $\text{ct}^{(1)} \in R_{Q'}^2$ satisfies

$$c_0^{(1)} + c_1^{(1)} s \bmod Q' = \Delta(\Delta_{\text{in}} m + e) + e_\chi$$

where $e_\chi \sim \chi$. Therefore, we simply call the CKKS rescale function and return the result $\text{ct}^{(2)} \leftarrow \text{CKKS.Rescale}(\text{ct}^{(1)}, \Delta)$. The output $\text{ct}^{(2)} \in R_{Q''}^2$, $Q'' = Q'/\Delta$, now satisfies $c_0^{(2)} + c_1^{(2)} s \bmod Q'' = \Delta_{\text{in}} m + e''$ with $\|e''\|_\infty \leq \|e\|_\infty + \frac{\|e_\chi\|_\infty}{\Delta} + (N\|s\|_\infty + 1)/2$ by the rescaling lemma, Lemma 2.2. An illustration of the proof is given in Fig. 2. $\qquad\square$

4.2 Bootstrapping in BGVfrom a CKKS-to-BGV Oracle

In this subsection, we show how to use a weak CKKS-to-BGV scheme-switching oracle to bootstrap a BGV ciphertext. At a high level, bootstrapping a BGV ciphertext consists of linear operations and then digit extraction. The digit extraction step involves taking a BGV encryption of a message z with plaintext modulus p^{r+1} and computing a BGV encryption of the message $z\langle r \rangle$ with plaintext modulus p, where $z\langle r \rangle$ is the rth digit in the base-p decomposition of z. By viewing the BGV encryption of z as a CKKS encryption with $\Delta = p^r$, the CKKS-to-BGV oracle will output a BGV encryption of $z\langle r \rangle$ with plaintext modulus p.

Theorem 4.2 below uses the same bootstrapping hint as the state-of-the-art BGV bootstrapping algorithm. That is, if we wish to refresh a ciphertext $\mathsf{ct} = (c_0, c_1) \in \mathsf{BGV}^s(m)_{p,q}$ to a larger modulus Q, we first modulus-switch to a smaller modulus of a special form, $\tilde{q} = p^r + 1$, yielding a ciphertext in $\mathsf{BGV}^s(m)_{p,\tilde{q}}$. Then, we use a bootstrapping hint, an encryption of the secret key under the target ciphertext modulus and a larger plaintext modulus $\mathsf{BGV}^s(s)_{p^{r+1},Q}$, to get the encrypted inner product in the larger ciphertext space $\mathsf{BGV}^s(c_0 + c_1 s)_{p^{r+1},Q}$. This is done by treating the ciphertext in $\mathsf{BGV}^s(m)_{p,\tilde{q}}$ as *plaintext* to the bootstrapping hint in $\mathsf{BGV}^s(s)_{p^{r+1},Q}$. See Halevi and Shoup's 2015 paper, [34], for the full details.

Theorem 4.2. *Fix some BGV parameters: $R = \mathbb{Z}[X]/(X^N + 1)$, p a prime, and $\tilde{q} = p^r + 1 \ll Q' \le Q$ are ciphertext moduli. Let $\mathsf{ct} \in \mathsf{BGV}^s(m)_{p,\tilde{q}}$ be the input ciphertext and let $\mathsf{hint} = (h_0, h_1) \in \mathsf{BGV}^s(s)_{p^{r+1},Q}$ be a bootstrapping hint where $s \in R$ is ct's secret key. Then, the existence of a CKKS to BGV weak scheme-switching oracle, $\mathcal{O}_{C \hookrightarrow B}(\,\cdot\,; \Delta, p, Q, Q', \chi', \chi)$, implies the existence of a BGV bootstrapping algorithm with time complexity that of the oracle plus the time complexity to modulus-switch from Q to Q' and the time complexity to perform a homomorphic inner product between ct and hint, where ct's polynomials are treated as plaintext to the hint. The output ciphertext has noise as most $\frac{Q'}{Q}\tilde{q}^2 \|e_{\mathsf{hint}}\|_\infty + (1 + N\|s\|_\infty)/2 + e_\chi$, where e_{hint} is the noise of hint and e_χ is the noise of the output of $\mathcal{O}_{C \hookrightarrow B}$.*

Proof. Let $\mathsf{ct} = (c_0, c_1) \in \mathsf{BGV}^s(m)_{p,\tilde{q}}$ be the input ciphertext and $\mathsf{hint} = (h_0, h_1) \in \mathsf{BGV}^s(s)_{p^{r+1},Q}$ be the bootstrapping hint for ct's secret key, $s \in R$. The reduction is as follows.

1. First, perform the homomorphic inner product to get an encryption of $z = \langle \mathsf{ct}, (1, s) \rangle$:
$$\mathsf{ct}^{(1)} = c_1 \cdot \mathsf{hint} + (c_0, 0) \in \mathsf{BGV}^s(z)_{p^{r+1},Q}.$$

2. Next, call the oracle on the resulting ciphertext with $\Delta = p^r$, where χ' is the implicit error distribution of $\mathsf{ct}^{(1)}$ when viewed as a CKKS ciphertext:
$$\mathsf{ct}^{(2)} \leftarrow \mathcal{O}_{C \hookrightarrow B}(\mathsf{ct}^{(1)}; p^r, p, Q, Q', \chi', \chi).$$

3. View $\mathsf{ct}^{(1)}$ as a ciphertext with plaintext modulus p and mod switch to Q', $\mathsf{ct}^{(3)} \leftarrow \mathsf{BGV.ModReduce}(\mathsf{ct}^{(1)}, Q, Q')$, and return the difference

$$\mathsf{ct}_{\mathsf{out}} = \mathsf{ct}^{(2)} - \mathsf{ct}^{(3)} \quad \mathrm{mod}\ Q' \in \mathsf{BGV}^s(m)_{p,Q'}.$$

Correctness is as follows. Recall, the operation $(z \mod \tilde{q}) \mod p$ is $z\langle 0\rangle - z\langle r\rangle$ mod p by Lemma 2.3. The oracle treats the input ct as a CKKS ciphertext where the least significant digit is in the r-th position (the lower digits are considered as part of the error). Then, we treat $\mathsf{ct}^{(1)}$ as implicitly encrypting $z\langle 0\rangle$ modulo p, and the result follows.

To analyze the error associated with $\mathsf{ct}_{\mathsf{out}}$, let e_{hint} denote the error associated with the ciphertext hint. It follows that $\|e^{(1)}\|_\infty \leq \tilde{q}\|e_{\mathsf{hint}}\|_\infty$. $\mathsf{ct}^{(2)}$ has associated error e_χ given by the oracle and plaintext modulus p. By Lemma 2.1, $\|e^{(3)}\|_\infty \leq \frac{Q'}{Q}\tilde{q}^2\|e_{\mathsf{hint}}\|_\infty + (1+N\|s\|_\infty)/2$. Note that the correctness condition for Lemma 2.1 holds since $\tilde{q}^2\|e_{\mathsf{hint}}\|_\infty \ll Q/2$ for reasonable parameters. Thus,

$$\|e_{\mathsf{out}}\|_\infty \leq \frac{Q'}{Q}\tilde{q}^2\|e_{\mathsf{hint}}\|_\infty + (1+N\|s\|_\infty)/2 + e_\chi.$$

$\square$

We note that the above proofs adapt easily to the case where the BGV plaintext modulus is a power of p. See Fig. 2 and Fig. 3 for pictorial illustrations representing the reductions in Theorem 4.1 and Theorem 4.2.

4.3   Switching Between Schemes Using Bootstrapping

Here, for completeness, we briefly sketch how to switch between schemes using bootstrapping. The main idea is that a coefficient-packed BFV ciphertext can be seen as an "exhausted" coefficient-packed CKKS ciphertext and vice versa. If we have an algorithm that bootstraps a coefficient-packed CKKS ciphertext, which is easily obtained from a SIMD-packed CKKS bootstrapping algorithm via homomorphic linear transformations [35], then we can treat a coefficient-packed BFV ciphertext as a CKKS ciphertext and bootstrap using the aforementioned algorithm. The output will be a CKKS ciphertext with the inputted BFV ciphertext's message as its plaintext polynomial. The other direction is analogous. We can treat a coefficient-packed CKKS ciphertext as a coefficient-packed BFV ciphertext and use a BFV bootstrapping algorithm to convert the inputted ciphertext to a BFV ciphertext. Lastly, we can convert between BGV and BFV cheaply with a scalar multiplication [2]. This shows how to convert between BGV/BFV and CKKS with bootstrapping.

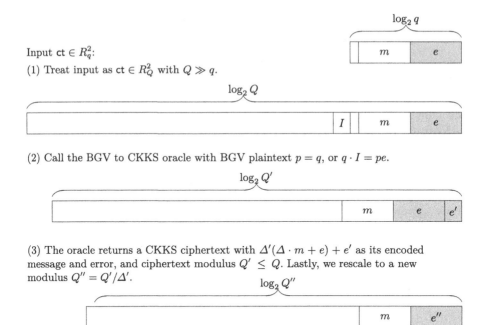

Fig. 2. CKKS bootstrapping using a BGV to CKKS weak scheme-switching oracle. Our input is a CKKS ciphertext with small modulus q. We call the weak scheme-switching oracle on the input ciphertext with BGV plaintext modulus equal to the input CKKS ciphertext modulus.

5   Bootstrapping via a Comparison Oracle

The SIMD FHE schemes discussed in this work are capable of natively evaluating arithmetic circuits homomorphically in a SIMD fashion over an encrypted vector of plaintext values. However, there are various functions, such as comparison, that are useful to compute for applications, but are not easily expressible as an arithmetic circuit. Several prior works [15,16,39,46] have focused on methods of computing comparison (and other related functions such as max/min and ReLU) in these SIMD FHE schemes.

In this section, we explore the relative hardness of homomorphically evaluating the comparison function in these SIMD FHE schemes by showing how to bootstrap in these schemes using several calls to a comparison oracle. In particular, we show how to bootstrap packed CKKS ciphertexts and thinly packed BGV ciphertexts. At a high level, our comparison oracles (one for CKKS and one for BGV) will take as input a ciphertext ct encrypting a vector of plaintext values $(m_1, \ldots, m_t)$ and a value α and output a new ciphertext ct' that encrypts the value 1 in its i-th slot if $m_i \geq \alpha$ and 0 otherwise. We observe that a comparison oracle only outputs the encryption of a single bit in each slot and, thus, it is much weaker than the scheme-switching oracles in Sect. 3. In particular, we will have to make several calls to the comparison oracle in order to bootstrap (as

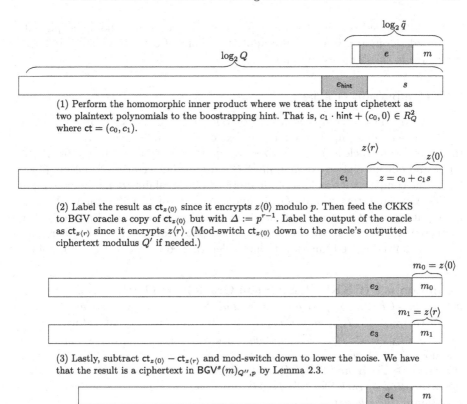

Fig. 3. BGV bootstrapping using a CKKS to BGV weak scheme-switching oracle.

opposed to only a single call to the weak scheme-switching oracles in Sect. 4). Moreover, we will also have to apply the homomorphic linear transformations CoeffsToSlots and SlotsToCoeffs in order to bootstrap, which was not required previously when using the weak scheme-switching oracles. While we focus on comparison in this section, our approach also extends to related functions such as max/min and ReLU.

To see how a comparison oracle could be used to bootstrap, we will sketch the intuition for the CKKS case as it is slightly simpler than the BGV case. Recall that CKKS bootstrapping begins by taking a ciphertext $\mathsf{ct} \in R_q^2$ and viewing it as a ciphertext with respect to the largest modulus Q. Viewed this way, ct now decrypts to $\Delta m + e + I(X)q$, and thus, we now need to homomorphically compute the mod q function on the coefficients of the encrypted polynomial. If we call the CoeffsToSlots homomorphic linear transform, we can put the coefficients of this polynomial in the ciphertext slots. Let K denote an upper bound on $\|I\|_\infty$. Then, using $\log K$ calls to a comparison oracle, we can homomorphically compute the mod q function to remove the Iq term. This is done by clearing one bit of I at a time starting from the most significant bit by comparing to an appropriate power of 2 and subtracting the two ciphertexts. Once we have homomorphically computed the mod q function, we apply the SlotsToCoeffs homomorphic linear transform to finish bootstrapping.

5.1 Comparison Oracles

Here, we define the comparison oracles rigorously in the same manner as in Sect. 3. The oracles' inputs are a ciphertext ct $\in R_Q^2$ and a scalar α. For CKKS, the comparison oracle is parameterized by input and output scaling factors Δ, Δ', input and output ciphertext moduli Q, Q', and output error distribution χ. For BGV, the comparison oracle is parameterized by the plaintext modulus p, input and output ciphertext moduli Q, Q', and output error distribution χ. We omit the input error distribution χ_{in} from the parameters of these oracles as it is clear from context. Recall from Sect. 3 that the output error distribution χ is related to χ_{in} via a randomized function f that is determined by the instantiation of the oracle.

Definition 5.1 (CKKS Comparison Oracle). *Let $\mathcal{O}_\geq(\mathsf{ct}, \alpha; \Delta, \Delta', Q, Q', \chi)$ denote the CKKS comparison oracle that takes as input a ciphertext $\mathsf{ct} \in \mathsf{CKKS}^s(m)_{\Delta,Q} \subset R_Q^2$ that decrypts to $\Delta m + e = v$ and returns $\mathsf{ct}' \in \mathsf{CKKS}^s(m')_{\Delta',Q'} \subset R_{Q'}^2$. The output ciphertext $\mathsf{ct}' = (c_0', c_1')$ satisfies $c_0' + c_1' s \bmod Q' = \Delta' m' + e_\chi = v'$ where v' is a polynomial with $\mathsf{Slot}_i(v') \approx \Delta'$ if $\mathsf{Slot}_i(v) \geq \Delta \cdot \alpha$ and $\mathsf{Slot}_i(v') \approx 0$ otherwise and $e_\chi \sim \chi$. The error in the approximation of each $\mathsf{Slot}_i(v')$ is determined by the error polynomial e_χ's contribution to the ith slot.*

Definition 5.2 (BGV Comparison Oracle). *Let $\mathcal{O}_\geq(\mathsf{ct}, \alpha; p, Q, Q', \chi)$ denote the BGV comparison oracle that takes as input a ciphertext $\mathsf{ct} \in \mathsf{BGV}^s(m)_{p,Q} \subset R_Q^2$ and returns $\mathsf{ct}' \in \mathsf{BGV}^s(m')_{p,Q'} \subset R_{Q'}^2$. The output ciphertext $\mathsf{ct}' = (c_0', c_1')$ satisfies $c_0' + c_1' s \bmod Q' = m' + p e_\chi$ where m' is a polynomial with $\mathsf{Slot}_i(m') = 1$ if $\mathsf{Slot}_i(m) \geq \alpha$ and $\mathsf{Slot}_i(m') = 0$ otherwise and $e_\chi \sim \chi$.*

5.2 Bootstrapping in CKKS from Comparisons

We first show how to bootstrap a CKKS ciphertext using a CKKS comparison oracle. For ease of exposition, we will focus on the case where the ciphertext moduli and scaling factors are powers of two. We show the following theorem.

Theorem 5.1. *Let R, Q, Δ be CKKS parameters. Let $\mathsf{ct} = (c_0, c_1) \in R_q^2$ be a CKKS ciphertext such that $c_0 + c_1 s = \Delta m + e + I(X)q$ over the ring R with $\|I(X)\|_\infty \leq K$. Then assuming the existence of a list of CKKS comparison oracles $\mathcal{O}_\geq$ from Definition 5.1, with parameters*

$$\mathcal{O}_\geq(\mathsf{ct}'_{i-1}, K/2^i; q, K/2^{i-1} \cdot q, Q_{i-1}, Q_i, \chi)$$

satisfying $Q_i \mid Q_{i-1}$ for $i = 1$ to $\log K$, there is a CKKS bootstrapping algorithm that makes $\log_2 K$ calls to the oracles together with the CoeffsToSlots and SlotsToCoeffs homomorphic linear transformations for CKKS bootstrapping.

Proof. Let $\mathsf{ct} = (c_0, c_1) \in R_q^2$ be the input ciphertext in $\mathsf{CKKS}^s(m)_{\Delta,q}$. That is, the ciphertext satisfies $c_0 + c_1 s \bmod q = \Delta m + e$. By embedding c_0, c_1 into R_Q, it follows that this new ciphertext with modulus Q satisfies $c_0 + c_1 s \bmod Q = \Delta m + e + I(X)q$ where $I(X)$ is an integer polynomial that depends on the Hamming weight and norm of the secret key, $s \in R$. Note that $I(X) \cdot q \ll Q$ for commonly used parameter settings. Let K be an upper bound on the magnitude of a coefficient of $I(X)$. WLOG, assume that K is a power of 2. First, we run the $\mathsf{CoeffsToSlots}$ step of the CKKS bootstrapping procedure (see Sect. 2.3) to obtain a ciphertext $\mathsf{ct}' \in R_{Q'}^2$ that encrypts the coefficients of $\Delta m + e + I(X)q$ in its slots. Note that if ct was a fully packed ciphertext, this would require two ciphertexts to store all the coefficients. For simplicity, we will assume that ct is not fully packed so that the coefficients can all be encrypted in a single ciphertext ct'.

Each coefficient of $I(X)$ can be expressed as $\sum_{i=0}^{\log K - 1} 2^i \cdot I_i$ with $I_i \in \{0, 1\}$. Let $\mathsf{ct}' = \mathsf{ct}'_0$. For $i = 1$ to $\log K$, call

$$\mathcal{O}_{\geq}(\mathsf{ct}'_{i-1}, K/2^i; q, K/2^{i-1} \cdot q, Q_{i-1}, Q_i, \chi)$$

to obtain ct_i with ciphertext modulus Q_i. Then, mod down ct'_{i-1} to modulus Q_i to obtain ct''_{i-1}. Set $\mathsf{ct}'_i = \mathsf{ct}''_{i-1} - \mathsf{ct}_i$.

Observe that $\mathsf{ct}'_{\log K}$ is a ciphertext with modulus $Q_{\log K}$ that has the coefficients of $\Delta m + e_{\log K}$ in its slots. Call $\mathsf{SlotsToCoeffs}$ to obtain a bootstrapped ciphertext. $\qquad\square$

5.3   Bootstrapping in BGV from Comparisons

We now show how to bootstrap a BGV ciphertext using a BGV comparison oracle. We show the following theorem.

Theorem 5.2. *Let R, q, p be BGV parameters and let $\mathsf{ct} \in \mathsf{BGV}^s(m)_{p,q}$ be an input ciphertext. Then, the existence of oracles $\mathcal{O}_{\geq}(\mathsf{ct}, \alpha; p^{r+1}, Q_{i-1}, Q_i, \chi)$, for $Q_i \gg q$, $p^{r+1} < q$, implies the existence of a BGV bootstrapping algorithm that makes $\lceil \log p \rceil - 1$ calls to the oracles and also computes a homomorphic inner product and the homomorphic linear transformations $\mathsf{CoeffsToSlots}$ and $\mathsf{SlotsToCoeffs}$ for BGV bootstrapping.*

Proof. First, we calculate the homomorphic inner product with standard techniques: The input is a BGV ciphertext $\mathsf{ct} \in \mathsf{BGV}^s(m)_{p,q}$, and we switch to the modulus $\tilde{q} = p^r + 1$,

$$\mathsf{ct}' \leftarrow \mathsf{ModSwitch}(\mathsf{ct}, \tilde{q}).$$

Using the bootstrapping hint, $\mathsf{hint} \in \mathsf{BGV}^s(s)_{Q,p^{r+1}}$, calculate the homomorphic inner product

$$\mathsf{ct}'' = c_1' \cdot \mathsf{hint} + (c_0', 0) \in \mathsf{BGV}^s(z)_{p^{r+1},Q}.$$

Now we have a BGV ciphertext in $\mathsf{BGV}^s(z)_{Q,p^{r+1}}$, and we can call the homomorphic linear transformation $\mathsf{CoeffsToSlots}$ to move these coefficients to the slots modulo p^{r+1}. Call this ciphertext ct_0. Notice that in each slot, we want to next extract the largest p-digit in $z = p^r z\langle r \rangle + p^{r-1}(\text{lowerdigits})$. Let $k = \lceil \log_2 p \rceil$. Now we use the oracle to extract

$$z\langle r \rangle = \sum_{i=0}^{K-1} 2^i z_i^r,$$

for $z_i^r \in \{0,1\}$, bit-by-bit.

Initialize $\mathsf{ct_{sum}} \leftarrow (0,0)$. For $i = 1, \ldots, k-1$, let

$$\mathsf{ct}_i' \leftarrow \mathcal{O}_{\geq}(\mathsf{ct}_{i-1}, p^r \cdot 2^{k-i}; p^{r+1}, Q_{i-1}, Q_i, \chi)$$

and let $\mathsf{ct}_i = \mathsf{ModSwitch}(\mathsf{ct}_{i-1}, Q_i) - (p^r 2^{k-i}) \cdot \mathsf{ct}_i'$ and $\mathsf{ct_{sum}} \leftarrow 2^{k-i} \cdot \mathsf{ct}_i' + \mathsf{ModSwitch}(\mathsf{ct}_i', Q_i)$. Finally, $\mathsf{ct_{sum}}$ is an encryption of $z\langle r \rangle$ modulo p so we compute the ciphertext

$$\mathsf{ModSwitch}(\mathsf{ct}_{k-1}, Q_{k-1}) - \mathsf{ct_{sum}}$$

and then call the homomorphic linear transformation SlotsToCoeffs to move the slots modulo p to the coefficients and return the resulting ciphertext.

Correctness follows from Lemma 2.3.

6   Conclusion

In this work, we provide strong evidence that homomorphic scheme-switching between the BGV/BFV and CKKS SIMD FHE schemes is as hard as bootstrapping. We achieve this by showing how to bootstrap both BGV/BFV and CKKS ciphertexts with a single call to such an algorithm (in fact, only a weak scheme-switching algorithm that does not convert the differences in packings between the schemes) without having to perform homomorphic linear transformations. In addition, we show how homomorphic comparisons are analogously powerful by bootstrapping with a few calls to a SIMD comparison algorithm. The fact that we can bootstrap with one call to a weak scheme-switching oracle is surprising since weak scheme-switching appears much simpler than bootstrapping.

References

1. Agrawal, R., et al.: FAB: an FPGA-based accelerator for bootstrappable fully homomorphic encryption. In: HPCA, pp. 882–895. IEEE (2023)
2. Alperin-Sheriff, J., Peikert, C.: Practical bootstrapping in quasilinear time. In: Canetti, R., Garay, J.A. (eds.) CRYPTO 2013. LNCS, vol. 8042, pp. 1–20. Springer, Heidelberg (2013). https://doi.org/10.1007/978-3-642-40041-4_1
3. Armknecht, F., Sadeghi, A.: A new approach for algebraically homomorphic encryption. IACR Cryptol. ePrint Arch., p. 422 (2008)
4. Badawi, A.A., et al.: OpenFHE: open-source fully homomorphic encryption library. Cryptology ePrint Archive, Paper 2022/915 (2022). https://eprint.iacr.org/2022/915

5. Bae, Y., Cheon, J.H., Cho, W., Kim, J., Kim, T.: Meta-BTS: bootstrapping precision beyond the limit. Cryptology ePrint Archive, Paper 2022/1167 (2022). https://eprint.iacr.org/2022/1167. To Appear in CCS 2022
6. Boneh, D., Goh, E.-J., Nissim, K.: Evaluating 2-DNF formulas on ciphertexts. In: Kilian, J. (ed.) TCC 2005. LNCS, vol. 3378, pp. 325–341. Springer, Heidelberg (2005). https://doi.org/10.1007/978-3-540-30576-7_18
7. Bossuat, J.-P., Mouchet, C., Troncoso-Pastoriza, J., Hubaux, J.-P.: Efficient bootstrapping for approximate homomorphic encryption with non-sparse keys. In: Canteaut, A., Standaert, F.-X. (eds.) EUROCRYPT 2021. LNCS, vol. 12696, pp. 587–617. Springer, Cham (2021). https://doi.org/10.1007/978-3-030-77870-5_21
8. Boura, C., Gama, N., Georgieva, M., Jetchev, D.: CHIMERA: combining ring-LWE-based fully homomorphic encryption schemes. J. Math. Cryptol. 14(1), 316–338 (2020)
9. Brakerski, Z.: Fully homomorphic encryption without modulus switching from classical GapSVP. In: Safavi-Naini, R., Canetti, R. (eds.) CRYPTO 2012. LNCS, vol. 7417, pp. 868–886. Springer, Heidelberg (2012). https://doi.org/10.1007/978-3-642-32009-5_50
10. Brakerski, Z., Gentry, C., Vaikuntanathan, V.: (Leveled) fully homomorphic encryption without bootstrapping. In: ITCS, pp. 309–325. ACM (2012)
11. Chen, H., Chillotti, I., Song, Y.: Improved bootstrapping for approximate homomorphic encryption. In: Ishai, Y., Rijmen, V. (eds.) EUROCRYPT 2019. LNCS, vol. 11477, pp. 34–54. Springer, Cham (2019). https://doi.org/10.1007/978-3-030-17656-3_2
12. Chen, H., Han, K.: Homomorphic lower digits removal and improved FHE bootstrapping. In: Nielsen, J.B., Rijmen, V. (eds.) EUROCRYPT 2018. LNCS, vol. 10820, pp. 315–337. Springer, Cham (2018). https://doi.org/10.1007/978-3-319-78381-9_12
13. Cheon, J.H., Han, K., Kim, A., Kim, M., Song, Y.: Bootstrapping for approximate homomorphic encryption. In: Nielsen, J.B., Rijmen, V. (eds.) EUROCRYPT 2018. LNCS, vol. 10820, pp. 360–384. Springer, Cham (2018). https://doi.org/10.1007/978-3-319-78381-9_14
14. Cheon, J.H., Kim, A., Kim, M., Song, Y.: Homomorphic encryption for arithmetic of approximate numbers. In: Takagi, T., Peyrin, T. (eds.) ASIACRYPT 2017. LNCS, vol. 10624, pp. 409–437. Springer, Cham (2017). https://doi.org/10.1007/978-3-319-70694-8_15
15. Cheon, J.H., Kim, D., Kim, D.: Efficient homomorphic comparison methods with optimal complexity. In: Moriai, S., Wang, H. (eds.) ASIACRYPT 2020, Part II. LNCS, vol. 12492, pp. 221–256. Springer, Cham (2020). https://doi.org/10.1007/978-3-030-64834-3_8
16. Cheon, J.H., Kim, D., Kim, D., Lee, H.H., Lee, K.: Numerical method for comparison on homomorphically encrypted numbers. In: Galbraith, S.D., Moriai, S. (eds.) ASIACRYPT 2019, Part II. LNCS, vol. 11922, pp. 415–445. Springer, Cham (2019). https://doi.org/10.1007/978-3-030-34621-8_15
17. Chillotti, I., Gama, N., Georgieva, M., Izabachène, M.: Faster fully homomorphic encryption: bootstrapping in less than 0.1 seconds. In: Cheon, J.H., Takagi, T. (eds.) ASIACRYPT 2016. LNCS, vol. 10031, pp. 3–33. Springer, Heidelberg (2016). https://doi.org/10.1007/978-3-662-53887-6_1
18. Chillotti, I., Ligier, D., Orfila, J.-B., Tap, S.: Improved programmable bootstrapping with larger precision and efficient arithmetic circuits for TFHE. In: Tibouchi, M., Wang, H. (eds.) ASIACRYPT 2021. LNCS, vol. 13092, pp. 670–699. Springer, Cham (2021). https://doi.org/10.1007/978-3-030-92078-4_23

19. Drucker, N., Moshkowich, G., Pelleg, T., Shaul, H.: BLEACH: cleaning errors in discrete computations over CKKS. Cryptology ePrint Archive, Paper 2022/1298 (2022). https://eprint.iacr.org/2022/1298

20. Ducas, L., Micciancio, D.: FHEW: bootstrapping homomorphic encryption in less than a second. In: Oswald, E., Fischlin, M. (eds.) EUROCRYPT 2015. LNCS, vol. 9056, pp. 617–640. Springer, Heidelberg (2015). https://doi.org/10.1007/978-3-662-46800-5_24

21. Fan, J., Vercauteren, F.: Somewhat practical fully homomorphic encryption. IACR Cryptol. ePrint Arch., p. 144 (2012)

22. Feldmann, A., et al.: F1: a fast and programmable accelerator for fully homomorphic encryption (extended version). CoRR abs/2109.05371 (2021)

23. Fellows, M., Koblitz, N.: Combinatorial cryptosystems galore! (1994)

24. Geelen, R., et al.: BASALISC: flexible asynchronous hardware accelerator for fully homomorphic encryption. IACR Cryptol. ePrint Arch., p. 657 (2022)

25. Geelen, R., Vercauteren, F.: Bootstrapping for BGV and BFV revisited. IACR Cryptol. ePrint Arch., p. 1363 (2022)

26. Gentry, C.: A fully homomorphic encryption scheme. Diss. Stanford University (2009)

27. Gentry, C.: Fully homomorphic encryption using ideal lattices. In: STOC, pp. 169–178. ACM (2009)

28. Gentry, C., Halevi, S., Smart, N.P.: Better bootstrapping in fully homomorphic encryption. In: Fischlin, M., Buchmann, J., Manulis, M. (eds.) PKC 2012. LNCS, vol. 7293, pp. 1–16. Springer, Heidelberg (2012). https://doi.org/10.1007/978-3-642-30057-8_1

29. Gentry, C., Halevi, S., Smart, N.P.: Fully homomorphic encryption with polylog overhead. In: Pointcheval, D., Johansson, T. (eds.) EUROCRYPT 2012. LNCS, vol. 7237, pp. 465–482. Springer, Heidelberg (2012). https://doi.org/10.1007/978-3-642-29011-4_28

30. Gentry, C., Halevi, S., Smart, N.P.: Homomorphic evaluation of the AES circuit. In: Safavi-Naini, R., Canetti, R. (eds.) CRYPTO 2012. LNCS, vol. 7417, pp. 850–867. Springer, Heidelberg (2012). https://doi.org/10.1007/978-3-642-32009-5_49

31. Halevi, S., Polyakov, Y., Shoup, V.: An improved RNS variant of the BFV homomorphic encryption scheme. In: Matsui, M. (ed.) CT-RSA 2019. LNCS, vol. 11405, pp. 83–105. Springer, Cham (2019). https://doi.org/10.1007/978-3-030-12612-4_5

32. Halevi, S., Shoup, V.: Algorithms in HElib. In: Garay, J.A., Gennaro, R. (eds.) CRYPTO 2014. LNCS, vol. 8616, pp. 554–571. Springer, Heidelberg (2014). https://doi.org/10.1007/978-3-662-44371-2_31

33. Halevi, S., Shoup, V.: Bootstrapping for HElib. IACR Cryptol. ePrint Arch., p. 873 (2014)

34. Halevi, S., Shoup, V.: Bootstrapping for HElib. In: Oswald, E., Fischlin, M. (eds.) EUROCRYPT 2015. LNCS, vol. 9056, pp. 641–670. Springer, Heidelberg (2015). https://doi.org/10.1007/978-3-662-46800-5_25

35. Halevi, S., Shoup, V.: Faster homomorphic linear transformations in HElib. In: Shacham, H., Boldyreva, A. (eds.) CRYPTO 2018. LNCS, vol. 10991, pp. 93–120. Springer, Cham (2018). https://doi.org/10.1007/978-3-319-96884-1_4

36. Halevi, S., Shoup, V.: Design and implementation of HElib: a homomorphic encryption library. IACR Cryptol. ePrint Arch., p. 1481 (2020)

37. Han, K., Hhan, M., Cheon, J.H.: Improved homomorphic discrete Fourier transforms and FHE bootstrapping. IEEE Access **7**, 57361–57370 (2019)

38. Han, K., Ki, D.: Better bootstrapping for approximate homomorphic encryption. In: Jarecki, S. (ed.) CT-RSA 2020. LNCS, vol. 12006, pp. 364–390. Springer, Cham (2020). https://doi.org/10.1007/978-3-030-40186-3_16

39. Iliashenko, I., Zucca, V.: Faster homomorphic comparison operations for BGV and BFV. Proc. Priv. Enhancing Technol. **2021**(3), 246–264 (2021). https://doi.org/10.2478/popets-2021-0046

40. Ishai, Y., Paskin, A.: Evaluating branching programs on encrypted data. In: Vadhan, S.P. (ed.) TCC 2007. LNCS, vol. 4392, pp. 575–594. Springer, Heidelberg (2007). https://doi.org/10.1007/978-3-540-70936-7_31

41. Jutla, C.S., Manohar, N.: Modular lagrange interpolation of the mod function for bootstrapping of approximate HE. Cryptology ePrint Archive, Report 2020/1355 (2020). https://eprint.iacr.org/2020/1355

42. Jutla, C.S., Manohar, N.: Sine series approximation of the mod function for bootstrapping of approximate HE. In: Dunkelman, O., Dziembowski, S. (eds.) EUROCRYPT 2022. LNCS, vol. 13275, pp. 491–520. Springer, Cham (2022). https://doi.org/10.1007/978-3-031-06944-4_17

43. Kim, A., et al.: General bootstrapping approach for rlwe-based homomorphic encryption. IACR Cryptol. ePrint Arch., p. 691 (2021)

44. Kim, A., Polyakov, Y., Zucca, V.: Revisiting homomorphic encryption schemes for finite fields. In: Tibouchi, M., Wang, H. (eds.) ASIACRYPT 2021. LNCS, vol. 13092, pp. 608–639. Springer, Cham (2021). https://doi.org/10.1007/978-3-030-92078-4_21

45. Kim, S., Park, M., Kim, J., Kim, T., Min, C.: EvalRound algorithm in CKKS bootstrapping. In: Agrawal, S., Lin, D. (eds.) ASIACRYPT 2022. LNCS, vol. 13792, pp. 161–187. Springer, Cham (2022). https://doi.org/10.1007/978-3-031-22966-4_6, https://eprint.iacr.org/2022/1256

46. Lee, E., Lee, J.W., Kim, Y.S., No, J.S.: Optimization of homomorphic comparison algorithm on RNS-CKKS scheme. Cryptology ePrint Archive, Paper 2021/1215 (2021). https://eprint.iacr.org/2021/1215

47. Lee, J.-W., Lee, E., Lee, Y., Kim, Y.-S., No, J.-S.: High-precision bootstrapping of RNS-CKKS homomorphic encryption using optimal minimax polynomial approximation and inverse sine function. In: Canteaut, A., Standaert, F.-X. (eds.) EUROCRYPT 2021. LNCS, vol. 12696, pp. 618–647. Springer, Cham (2021). https://doi.org/10.1007/978-3-030-77870-5_22

48. Lee, Y., Lee, J.W., Kim, Y.S., Kim, Y., No, J.S., Kang, H.: High-precision bootstrapping for approximate homomorphic encryption by error variance minimization. In: Dunkelman, O., Dziembowski, S. (eds.) EUROCRYPT 2022. LNCS, vol. 13275, pp. 551–580. Springer, Cham (2022). https://doi.org/10.1007/978-3-031-06944-4_19

49. Li, B., Micciancio, D.: On the security of homomorphic encryption on approximate numbers. In: Canteaut, A., Standaert, F.-X. (eds.) EUROCRYPT 2021. LNCS, vol. 12696, pp. 648–677. Springer, Cham (2021). https://doi.org/10.1007/978-3-030-77870-5_23

50. Li, B., Micciancio, D., Schultz, M., Sorrell, J.: Securing approximate homomorphic encryption using differential privacy. In: Dodis, Y., Shrimpton, T. (eds.) CRYPTO 2022. LNCS, vol. 13507, pp. 560–589. Springer, Cham (2022). https://doi.org/10.1007/978-3-031-15802-5_20

51. Liu, Z., Micciancio, D., Polyakov, Y.: Large-precision homomorphic sign evaluation using FHEW/TFHE bootstrapping. In: Agrawal, S., Lin, D. (eds.) ASIACRYPT 2022. LNCS, vol. 13792, pp. 130–160. Springer, Cham (2022). https://doi.org/10.1007/978-3-031-22966-4_5

52. Lu, W., Huang, Z., Hong, C., Ma, Y., Qu, H.: PEGASUS: bridging polynomial and non-polynomial evaluations in homomorphic encryption. In: IEEE Symposium on Security and Privacy, pp. 1057–1073. IEEE (2021)

53. Lyubashevsky, V., Peikert, C., Regev, O.: On ideal lattices and learning with errors over rings. In: Gilbert, H. (ed.) EUROCRYPT 2010. LNCS, vol. 6110, pp. 1–23. Springer, Heidelberg (2010). https://doi.org/10.1007/978-3-642-13190-5_1

54. Melchor, C.A., Gaborit, P., Herranz, J.: Additively homomorphic encryption with d-operand multiplications. In: Rabin, T. (ed.) CRYPTO 2010. LNCS, vol. 6223, pp. 138–154. Springer, Heidelberg (2010). https://doi.org/10.1007/978-3-642-14623-7_8

55. Regev, O.: On lattices, learning with errors, random linear codes, and cryptography. In: STOC, pp. 84–93. ACM (2005)

56. Regev, O.: On lattices, learning with errors, random linear codes, and cryptography. J. ACM **56**(6), 34:1–34:40 (2009)

57. Rivest, R.L., Adleman, L., Dertouzos, M.L., et al.: On data banks and privacy homomorphisms. Found. Secure Comput. **4**(11), 169–180 (1978)

58. Samardzic, N., et al.: F1: a fast and programmable accelerator for fully homomorphic encryption. In: MICRO, pp. 238–252. ACM (2021)

59. Samardzic, N., et al.: CraterLake: a hardware accelerator for efficient unbounded computation on encrypted data. In: ISCA, pp. 173–187. ACM (2022)

60. Smart, N.P., Vercauteren, F.: Fully homomorphic SIMD operations. Des. Codes Cryptogr. **71**(1), 57–81 (2014)

Classical and Quantum 3 and 4-Sieves to Solve SVP with Low Memory

André Chailloux[(⊠)] and Johanna Loyer[(⊠)]

Inria Paris, EPI COSMIQ, Paris, France
andre.chailloux@inria.fr, johanna.loyer@gmail.com

Abstract. The Shortest Vector Problem (SVP) is at the foundation of lattice-based cryptography. The fastest known method to solve SVP in dimension d is by lattice sieving, which runs in time $2^{td+o(d)}$ with $2^{md+o(d)}$ memory for constants $t, m \in \Theta(1)$. Searching reduced vectors in the sieve is a problem reduced to the configuration problem, *i.e.* searching k vectors satisfying given constraints on their pairwise scalar products.

In this work, we present a framework for k-sieve algorithms: we filter the input list of lattice vectors using a code structure modified from [Bec+16] to get lists centred around k codewords summing to the null-vector. Then, we solve a simpler instance of the configuration problem in the k filtered lists. Based on this framework, we describe classical sieves for $k = 3$ and 4 that introduce new time-memory trade-offs. We also use the k-Lists algorithm [Kir+19] inside our framework, and this improves the time for $k = 3$ and gives new trade-offs for $k = 4$.

Keywords: Shortest Vector Problem (SVP) · Lattice sieving · Locality-sensitive filtering (LSF) · Configuration problem

1 Introduction

The Shortest Vector Problem (SVP) is a central problem in lattice-based cryptography. For a given d-dimensional lattice, SVP asks to find a shortest non-zero vector in the lattice. This problem admits a variety of derived problems such as SIS, LWE and their modular or ring versions, on which several of the (believed to be) quantum-resistant cryptographic protocols rely, such as Dilithium [Duc+19] and Kyber [Bos+18] both winners of the NIST standardization process. It is therefore crucial to estimate the hardness of these constructions both in classical and quantum models.

There are two main families of algorithms for SVP: those based on enumeration [FP85, Kan83, Poh81] and those based on sieving [NV08, MV10]. The former does not have good asymptotic running but requires a small amount of memory and has good performances in practice. The latter has much better asymptotic running time - especially with heuristics that improve the analysis of these algorithms - but requires a very large amount of memory, sometimes as much as

T. Johansson and D. Smith-Tone (Eds.): PQCrypto 2023, LNCS 14154, pp. 225–255, 2023.
https://doi.org/10.1007/978-3-031-40003-2_9

the running time. Despite these strong memory requirements, the current best algorithms for SVP in practice are based on sieving methods[1]

The rough idea of sieving algorithms is the following: we start from a list of lattice points of large norm and sum them in order to find shorter lattice points, and repeat until we find a short vector. However, the number of points we have to start with is very large, which explains the large memory requirements. For example, in 2-sieve algorithms, where we start from a list of N points and build shorter points by summing pairs, we need to take $N = 2^{0.2075d+o(d)}$ in order to be able to build enough shorter lattice points.

Reducing this memory requirement makes the attack more materially practical, and a way to do it is by the k-sieve introduced in [BLS16] and then improved by [HK17,HKL18,Kir+19]. The idea is to sum k lattice points instead of pairs at each sieving step in order to find shorter ones. This decreases the number N of lattice points that we need at each step to find the same number N of shorter lattice points. However, this will drastically increase the time to perform the sieving step. For instance, a naive exhaustive search of each k-tuple takes time $O(N^k)$, and the fact that N is smaller does not outweigh this increased exponent, see Table 1.

Table 1. N is the number of points needed for k-sieving. N^k is the running time of a naive exhaustive search for k-sieving.

k	2	3	4	5	6
$\frac{\log_2(N)}{d}$	0.2075	0.1887	0.1724	0.1587	0.1473
$\frac{\log_2(N^k)}{d}$	0.4150	0.5661	0.6896	0.7935	0.8838

There are two main ideas that significantly improve the complexity of k-sieving algorithms:

- For 2-sieving, perform locality-sensitive filtering (LSF). The idea is to regroup lattice points into filters for which pairs are more likely to be reducible than random pairs. The most efficient known way to perform LSF for 2-sieve is to construct a code that behaves as a random code but which is efficiently decodable. In [Bec+16], the authors use a random product code to achieve this. Then, filters will correspond to all lattice points which will be close to a given code point.
- For $k > 2$, one can replace the reducibility constraint $\|\vec{x}_1 + \cdots + \vec{x}_k\| \leq R$ (starting from vectors of norm R) with constraints of the form $\langle \vec{x}_i | \vec{x}_j \rangle \leq C_{i,j}$ for some well-chosen $C_{i,j}$. This is known as the configuration problem. The main advantage is that we now only have constraints on pairs of points instead of k-tuples and we can use much more efficient algorithms, including the LSF idea presented above.

---

[1] See https://www.latticechallenge.org/svp-challenge/.

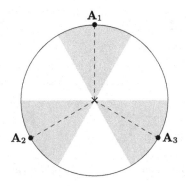

Fig. 1. $\mathbf{A}_1 + \mathbf{A}_2 + \mathbf{A}_3 = \vec{0}$ with $\langle \mathbf{A}_i | \mathbf{A}_j \rangle = -\frac{1}{2}$ for $i \neq j$.

In this work, we add an extra idea that gives better time-memory trade-offs for 3-sieve and 4-sieve algorithms, both in the classical and quantum regimes, and introduce the notion of LSF tailored for k-sieving. In previous algorithms, we first start from a configuration problem and then use LSF only on pairs of points. Here, we first use LSF in a way to construct many lists of lattice points $L_1, \ldots, L_k$ such that k-tuples $(\vec{x}_1, \ldots, \vec{x}_k) \in L_1 \times \cdots \times L_k$ are more likely to reduce than random k-tuples.

We illustrate briefly this with an example: in 3-sieve algorithms, we look for triplets of lattice points $(\vec{x}_1, \vec{x}_2, \vec{x}_3)$ each of norm R such that $\|\vec{x}_1 + \vec{x}_2 + \vec{x}_3\| \leq R$. Instead of directly translating this condition into a configuration problem, we first perform a filtering step as follows: consider a list-decodable code that contains many triples of words $\mathbf{A}_1, \mathbf{A}_2, \mathbf{A}_3$ such that $\mathbf{A}_1 + \mathbf{A}_2 + \mathbf{A}_3 = \vec{0}$ (see Fig. 1). If we consider lists of lattice points L_1, L_2, L_3 such that each L_i contains lattice points close to $\mathbf{A}_i$, then triplets of points $(\vec{x}_1, \vec{x}_2, \vec{x}_3) \in L_1 \times L_2 \times L_3$ of norm R are more likely to satisfy $\|\vec{x}_1 + \vec{x}_2 + \vec{x}_3\| \leq R$ than random triplets. We then use known algorithms on configuration search on these triplets of lists to find reducible triplets.

We summarize our contributions below.

- We show how to extend the construction of random product codes of [Bec+16] as a means of performing LSF tailored for k-sieving. Our code will also be efficiently decodable and the set of codewords can be partitioned into sets $\{\mathbf{A}_1, \ldots, \mathbf{A}_k\}$ each of size k such that $\mathbf{A}_1 + \cdots + \mathbf{A}_k = \vec{0}$.
- We analyze classical and quantum algorithms for 3 and 4-sieving using this k-sieve tailored filtering, and get improved time-memory trade-offs for these algorithms.

We first analyze our results for classical algorithms (see Fig. 2). For the 3-sieve, our algorithm performs better in the minimal memory regime. In the main text, we also present other time-memory trade-offs. However, when we do not restrict memory, we obtain the same running time $2^{0.3041d+o(d)}$ as in [HKL18] and our method does not give improvements here. For 4-sieve algorithms, the

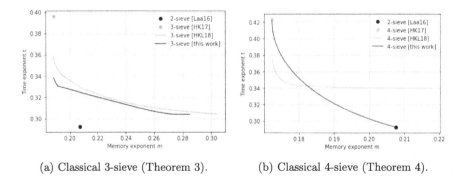

(a) Classical 3-sieve (Theorem 3).   (b) Classical 4-sieve (Theorem 4).

Fig. 2. Time $T = 2^{td+o(d)}$ for classical algorithms as a function of available memory $2^{md+o(d)} = 2^M$.

situation is a little different. We use a different algorithm than the ones studied in previous work. We essentially combine sequentially two 2-sieve algorithms. However, we first perform our tailored LSF on 4-tuples of points to speed up this process. As Fig. 2 shows, this algorithm does not perform well in the minimal memory regime ($M = 2^{0.1723d+o(d)}$) but then works much better for slightly larger memories, outperforming our 3-sieve algorithm and also the best previously known running time for 4-sieve, which used more memory.

We must notice however that it is hard to make direct comparisons with previous work in the classical setting as those are mainly done for Gauss-sieve and we present results for NV-sieve which has better time-memory trade-offs asymptotically. However, our results do show that tailored LSF significantly improves the algorithms we study, and we leave it as future work to extend this idea to the Gauss sieve.

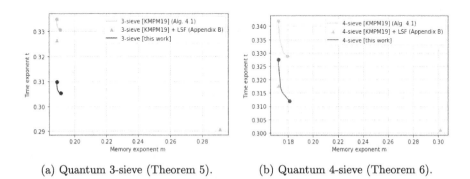

(a) Quantum 3-sieve (Theorem 5).   (b) Quantum 4-sieve (Theorem 6).

Fig. 3. Time $T = 2^{td+o(d)}$ for quantum 3 and 4-sieves algorithms as a function of available memory $2^{md+o(d)} = 2^M$.

In the quantum setting (see Fig. 3), we use the same algorithms as in [Kir+19] so the comparison can be made more directly. Our algorithm uses our tailored filtering and then applies Algorithm 4.1 of [Kir+19], which is not the best algorithm for the configuration problem for low values of k. What we show is that this algorithm benefits from this prefiltering. The results should be compared with the state-of-the-art Algorithm B.2 of [Kir+19]. However, only the extremities of the trade-offs of their algorithm were given, represented by triangles on the graphs of Fig. 3. For $k = 3$ in the minimal memory regime $M = 2^{0.1887d+o(d)}$, we achieve time $T = 2^{0.3098d+o(d)}$ improving the time $T = 2^{0.3266d+o(d)}$ of Algorithm B.2 in [Kir+19]. For $k = 4$, our algorithm does not work well for the lowest memory regime but gives a new interesting time-memory trade-off.

Notice that as in previous algorithms cited here, our quantum algorithms require quantumly accessible classical memory (QRACM) and poly(d) qubits.

Outline of the Article. Sect. 2 introduces the helpful preliminaries on quantum computing and lattice sieving. Section 3 presents the new code structure for the filtering step tailored for k-sieving. Then, we present a framework to solve SVP by sieving in Sect. 4, and describe some instances within this framework in the classical model in Sect. 5 and in the quantum model in Sect. 6.

2   Preliminaries

Notations. We designate the elements of $\mathbb{R}^d$ as vectors as well as points. The norm considered in this work is Euclidean and is denoted by $\| \cdot \|$. We denote by $\mathcal{S}^{d-1} = \{\vec{x} \in \mathbb{R}^d : \|\vec{x}\| = 1\}$ the d-dimensional unit sphere. For two vectors $\vec{x}_1, \vec{x}_2 \in \mathbb{R}^d$, $\langle \vec{x}_1 | \vec{x}_2 \rangle$ denotes their scalar product and $\theta(\vec{x}_1, \vec{x}_2) = \arccos(\frac{\langle \vec{x}_1 | \vec{x}_2 \rangle}{\|\vec{x}_1\| \|\vec{x}_2\|})$ denotes their angle. We use the notation $\widetilde{\mathcal{O}}$ to denote running times $T = \widetilde{\mathcal{O}}(2^{cd})$, which ignores sub-exponential factors in d.

2.1   Quantum Computing

QRAM Model. The Quantum Random Access Memory (QRAM) is an operation added to the quantum circuit model. We consider here only quantum-accessible classical memory (sometimes denoted as QRACM in the literature). Consider N classical registers $x_1, ..., x_N \in \{0, 1\}^d$ stored in memory. A QRAM operation consists of applying the following unitary

$$U_{\text{QRAM}} : |i\rangle |y\rangle \rightarrow |i\rangle |x_i \oplus y\rangle.$$

This work relies on the QRAM model, meaning that the above unitary can be constructed efficiently. In particular, we assume that given list L there exists an efficient quantum circuit for $\frac{1}{\sqrt{|L|}} \sum_i |i\rangle |0\rangle \rightarrow \frac{1}{\sqrt{|L|}} \sum_i |i\rangle |L[i]\rangle$. With a QRAM access to L, this can be done by applying Hadamard gates to state $|0\rangle$ to create a superposition over all indices, and then by querying $L[i]$ for each i in the superposition.

Proposition 1 (Grover's algorithm [Gro96]**).** *We are given QRAM access to a list* $L = \{x_1, ...x_\ell\}$. *We consider a function* $f : L \to \{0,1\}$, *associated to its unitary* $O_f : |x\rangle |y\rangle \to |x\rangle |y \oplus f(x)\rangle$, *such that there are* t *elements* $x_i \in L$ *said "marked" verifying* $f(x_i) = 1$. *The value* t *is not necessarily known. There exists a quantum algorithm, called Grover's algorithm, that returns a marked element with probability greater than* $1/2$ *using* $\mathcal{O}(\sqrt{|L|/t})$ *calls to* O_f. *Classically, this problem cannot be solved with a better average complexity than* $\Theta(|L|/t)$ *queries in the black box model.*

Proposition 2 (Quantum Amplitude amplification [Bra+02]**).** *Let* $\mathcal{A}$ *be an algorithm without measurements that finds a solution* $x \in L$ *such that* $f(x) = 1$ *with a success probability* p. *Quantum amplitude amplification returns a solution with probability* $1/2$ *using* $\mathcal{O}(1/\sqrt{p})$ *calls to* O_f.

Moreover, one can make the success probability of these algorithms go exponentially close to 1 by repeating them k times:

Proposition 3. *Grover's algorithm (resp. Quantum Amplitude Amplification) described above can have a success of* $1 - 2^{-\eta}$ *with* $\mathcal{O}(\eta\sqrt{|L|/t})$ *(resp.* $\mathcal{O}(\eta/\sqrt{p})$*) calls to* O_f.

2.2 Lattice Sieving

Definition 1 (Lattice). *Given a basis* $B = (\vec{b}_1, ...\vec{b}_m) \in \mathbb{R}^d$ *of linearly independent vectors, the lattice generated by* B *is defined as* $\mathcal{L}(B) = \left\{\sum_{i=1}^m z_i \vec{b}_i, z_i \in \mathbb{Z}\right\}$. *For simplicity, we work with lattices of full rank, i.e.* $d = m$.

Definition 2 (Shortest Vector Problem). *Given a basis* B, *the Shortest Vector Problem (SVP) asks to find a shortest non-zero vector of* $\mathcal{L}(B)$. *By Minkowski's theorem, the Euclidean norm of a shortest vector of* $\mathcal{L}(B)$ *is upper-bounded by* $\sqrt{d} \cdot \det(B)^{1/d}$.

Sieving Algorithms. The sieving algorithms, introduced by [NV08], are a class of heuristic algorithms that solves SVP. Given a list of lattice vectors of norm at most R and a reducing factor $\gamma < 1$, a sieving step will return a list of lattice vectors of norm at most γ. To obtain these reduced vectors, it computes all the differences between pairs of vectors of the input list and fills the output list with those which are of norm at most γ. Then, it iteratively builds lists of shorter lattice vectors by applying this sieve step. The first list of lattice vectors can be sampled with Klein's algorithm [Kle00] for example. Because the norms of the list vectors reduce with a factor by $\gamma < 1$ at each sieve step, the output list will hopefully contain a non-zero shortest lattice vector after a polynomial number of iterations.

We present here two simplifications of notation. First, we will only consider the case $R = 1$. Indeed, all the algorithms we consider will be independent of R. Also, in practice, we have $\gamma \approx 1$ (typically $\gamma = 1 - \frac{1}{\text{poly}(d)}$). For simplicity of

---

Algorithm 1. NV-sieve step

Require: List L of N lattice vectors of norm at most 1, a reducing factor $\gamma < 1$.
Ensure: List L_{out} of N lattice vectors of norm at most γ.
   for $(\vec{x}_1, \vec{x}_2) \in L$ **do**
      if $\|\vec{x}_1 - \vec{x}_2\| \leq \gamma$ **then** add $\vec{x}_1 - \vec{x}_2$ to L_{out}
   return L_{out}

Algorithm 2. Solve SVP by the sieving method

Require: basis B of a lattice $\mathcal{L}$, a reducing factor $\gamma < 1$.
Ensure: a shortest vector of $\mathcal{L}$ (probably)
   $L \leftarrow$ generate N lattice vectors of norm at most 1 using Klein's algorithm on B
   while L does not contain a short vector **do**
      $L \leftarrow$ **Sieve-step**(L, γ) ▷ Any sieve step algorithm.
   return $\min(L)$

---

notations, we will fix $\gamma = 1$ which doesn't change the overall analysis of these algorithms.

There is also another family of sieving algorithms called Gauss-sieve. These have worse asymptotic time-memory trade-offs so we don't analyze them in this work since we are interested in the best asymptotic time-memory trade-offs. However, they are usually faster in practice and it is an interesting follow-up to look at how our new ideas for sieving apply in this setting.

The sieving algorithms stand under the following heuristic.

Heuristic 1. *Lattice points behave like uniform points.*

Notice that uniform vectors of norm at most 1 are with a high probability of norm close to 1. So we will consider that the lattice vectors are lying on the sphere $\mathcal{S}^{d-1}$. The relevance of this heuristic has been studied in [NV08]. It becomes invalid when the vectors become short, but in this case, we can assume we have solved SVP. In practice, the faster algorithms to solve SVP rely on this heuristic.

Tuple-Sieve and k-List Algorithms. The NV-sieve described above can be generalized to the k-sieve.

Definition 3 (Approximate k-Lists problem). *Given k lists $L_1..., L_k$ of equal exponential (in d) size N and whose elements are i.i.d. uniformly chosen vectors from $\mathcal{S}^{d-1}$, the approximate k-List problem is to find N k-tuples $(\vec{x}_1, \ldots, \vec{x}_k) \in L_1 \times \cdots \times L_k$ satisfying $\|\vec{x}_1 + \cdots + \vec{x}_k\| \leq 1$.*

Volume of Spherical Cap / Hypercone Filter. We define the spherical cap of center $\vec{s}$ and angle α as follows:

$$\mathcal{H}_{\vec{s}, \alpha} := \{\vec{x} \in \mathcal{S}^{d-1} \mid \theta(\vec{x}, \vec{s}) \leq \alpha\}.$$

In order to compute the complexity of sieving algorithms, we will need the following value.

Proposition 4 *([Bec+16], Lemma 2.1) For an angle $\alpha \in [0, \pi/2]$ and a vector $\vec{v} \in \mathcal{S}^{d-1}$, the ratio of the volume of a spherical cap $\mathcal{H}_{\vec{v},\alpha}$ to the volume of the sphere $\mathcal{S}^{d-1}$ is*

$$\mathcal{V}(\alpha) := \text{poly}(d) \cdot \sin^d(\alpha).$$

2.3 Configurations

In the approximate k-list problem, we have the condition $\|\vec{x}_1 + \cdots + \vec{x}_k\| \leq 1$. Notice that we can rewrite

$$\|\vec{x}_1 + \cdots + \vec{x}_k\|^2 = \sum_{i=1}^{k} \|\vec{x}_i\|^2 + 2 \sum_{i,j \neq i}^{k} \langle \vec{x}_i | \vec{x}_j \rangle.$$

This means that the condition on $\|\vec{x}_1 + \cdots + \vec{x}_k\|$ can be verified if some constraints on the $\langle \vec{x}_i | \vec{x}_j \rangle$ are verified. This motivates the following definition:

Definition 4 (Configuration) *The configuration C of k points $\vec{x}_1, \ldots, \vec{x}_k \in \mathcal{S}^{d-1}$ is the Gram matrix of the $\vec{x}_i$'s, i.e. $C_{i,j} = \langle \vec{x}_i | \vec{x}_j \rangle$.*

A configuration is said balanced when for $i \neq j$, $C_{i,j} = -1/k$ and $C_{i,i} = 1$. In this case, the tuple points will form together the summits of a regular polyhedron inscribed in the sphere.

For $I \subset [k]$, we denote by $C[I]$ the $|I| \times |I|$ submatrix of C obtained by restricting C to the rows and columned whose indexes are in I.

Definition 5 (Configuration problem) *Let $k \in \mathbb{N}$ and $\epsilon > 0$. Suppose we are given a target configuration $C \in \mathbb{R}^{k \times k}$. Given lists $L_1, \ldots, L_k$ all of exponential (in d) size $|L|$ whose elements are i.i.d. uniform from $\mathcal{S}^{d-1}$, the configuration problem consists of finding a $1 - o(1)$ fraction of all solutions, where a solution is a k-tuple $(\vec{x}_1, \ldots, \vec{x}_k)$ with $\vec{x}_i \in L_i$ such that $\langle \vec{x}_i | \vec{x}_j \rangle \leq C_{i,j}$ for all i, j.*

[HK17] showed that the approximate k-Lists problem (Definition 3) can be reduced to the configuration problem.

Proposition 5 ([HK17]). *The probability that a k-tuple of i.i.d. uniformly random points on $\mathcal{S}^{d-1}$ satisfies a given configuration $C \in \mathbb{R}^{k \times k}$ is $\det(C)^{d/2}$.*

After a sieving step on a list L, we want to get $|L|^k \cdot \det(C)^{d/2}$ k-tuples satisfying the chosen configuration C, so that they are reducing k-tuples. We need this number of solutions to be equal to $|L|$. So we can deduce the required size of L, in function of the target configuration:

$$|L| = \widetilde{\mathcal{O}}\left(\left(\frac{1}{\det(C)} \right)^{\frac{d}{2(k-1)}} \right). \tag{1}$$

For a fixed k, the minimum value of $|L|$ is reached when the configuration C is balanced. In particular, for a balanced configuration with $k = 2$ we require $(4/3)^{d/2} = 2^{0.2075d+o(d)}$ points ; for $k = 3$, $(27/16)^{d/4} = 2^{0.1887d+o(d)}$ points and for $k = 4$, $(256/125)^{d/6} = 2^{0.1724d+o(d)}$ points. See Table 1 for the other values of k. We see that this value decreases with k, and that is the main interest of the k-sieve: to reduce the minimum memory we require to solve SVP. Considering non-balanced configurations leads to not reaching the lower bound for memory, but it can allow decreasing time by adding a little memory. This is useful to get better time-memory trade-offs.

Proposition 6 (Size of the filtered lists $L_i(x_j)$ given $C_{i,j}$ [Kir+19]). *We are given a configuration $C \in \mathbb{R}^{k \times k}$ and lists $L_1, \ldots L_k \subset \mathcal{S}^{d-1}$ each of size $|L_j|$. For $\vec{x}_1, \ldots, \vec{x}_i \in \mathcal{S}^{d-1}$, we denote*

$$L_j(\vec{x}_1, \ldots, \vec{x}_i) := \{\vec{x}_j \in L_j \ : \ \langle \vec{x}_1 | \vec{x}_j \rangle \leq C_{1,j}, \ \ldots, \langle \vec{x}_i | \vec{x}_j \rangle \leq C_{i,j}\}.$$

Then, for a i-tuple $\vec{x}_1, \ldots, \vec{x}_i$ satisfying the configuration $C[1 \ldots i]$, the expected size of $L_j(\vec{x}_1, \ldots, \vec{x}_j)$ is

$$\mathbb{E}(|L_j(\vec{x}_1, \ldots, \vec{x}_i)|) = |L_j| \cdot \left(\frac{\det(C[1, \ldots, i, j])}{\det(C[1, \ldots, i])} \right)^{d/2}.$$

And in particular,

$$\mathbb{E}(|L_j(\vec{x}_i)|) = |L_j| \cdot \left(1 - C_{i,j}^2 \right)^{d/2}.$$

3   Code Structure and Filtering

3.1   Locality Sensitive Filtering

Random Product Code (RPC). We assume $d = m \cdot b$, for $m = O(\text{polylog}(d))$ and a block size b. The vectors in $\mathbb{R}^d$ will be identified with tuples of m vectors in $\mathbb{R}^b$. A random product code $\mathfrak{C}$ of parameters $[d, m, B]$ on subsets of $\mathbb{R}^d$ and of size B^m is defined as a code of the form

$$\mathfrak{C} = Q \cdot (\mathfrak{C}_1 \times \mathfrak{C}_2 \times \cdots \times \mathfrak{C}_m)$$

where Q is a uniformly random rotation over $\mathbb{R}^d$ and the subcodes $\mathfrak{C}_1, \ldots, \mathfrak{C}_m$ are sets of B vectors, sampled uniformly and independently random over the sphere $\sqrt{1/m} \cdot \mathcal{S}^{b-1}$, so that codewords are points of the sphere $\mathcal{S}^{d-1}$. We can have a full description of $\mathfrak{C}$ by storing mB points corresponding to the codewords of $\mathfrak{C}_1, \ldots, \mathfrak{C}_m$ and by storing the rotation Q. When the context is clear, $\mathfrak{C}$ will correspond to the description of the code or to the set of codewords.

The code points of $\mathfrak{C}$ behave like random points of the sphere $\mathcal{S}^{d-1}$. This was argued in [Bec+16], see for instance Lemma 5.1 and Appendix C therein. Random product codes can be easily decoded in some parameter range, as the following proposition shows.

Proposition 7 ([Bec+16]). *Let $\mathfrak{C}$ be a random product code of parameters (d, m, B) with $m = log(d)$ and $B^m = N^{O(1)}$. For any $\vec{x} \in \mathcal{S}^{d-1}$ and angle α, one can compute $\mathcal{H}_{\vec{x},\alpha} \cap \mathfrak{C}$ in time $N^{o(1)} \cdot |\mathcal{H}_{\vec{x},\alpha} \cap \mathfrak{C}|$, where $\mathcal{H}_{\vec{x},\alpha}$ is defined in Proposition 4.*

Definition 6 (Hypercone filter). *Given a center $\mathbf{A}_i^j \in \mathcal{S}^{d-1}$ and an angle α, the filter $f_{\mathbf{A}_i^j,\alpha}$ is the set of all points in $\mathcal{S}^{d-1}$ of angle at most α with $\mathbf{A}_i^j$.*

Random Product Codes are useful tools to search reducing pairs of lattice vectors in a sieving step (Algorithm 1). Indeed, given a list of lattice vectors on $\mathcal{S}^{d-1}$ and a Random Product Code $\mathfrak{C}$, we can efficiently compute for a given vector all its nearest codewords. In this way, we construct lists that contain vectors from the input list close to the codewords. Each codeword is considered the center of a filter. Then, we can search in the same filter two vectors $\vec{x}_1, \vec{x}_2$ such that $\vec{x}_1 - \vec{x}_2$ is reduced. By adding Locality Sensitive Filtering using Random Product Codes [Bec+16, Laa16] in a sieving step, this provides the actual best algorithms to solve SVP. The sieve with LSF reaches time $2^{0.292d+o(d)}$ in the classical model [Bec+16], in time $2^{0.257d+o(d)}$ in the quantum model [CL21, Hei21, Bon+22].

However, a k-sieve structure for $k > 2$ searches k-tuples such that $\vec{x}_1 + \cdots + \vec{x}_k$ is reduced. Then, searching within one unique filter does not permit to quickly find a solution without having to check a lot of non-reducing elements. So we will slightly modify the construction of the random product code in order to take into account a configuration.

k-Random Product Code. In order to describe our k-Random Product Code construction, we start with the case $k = 3$. Instead of constructing fully random codes $\mathfrak{C}_1, \ldots, \mathfrak{C}_m$, we will construct random codes $\mathfrak{C}_i$ which have the following property:

$$\forall \mathbf{A}_1 \in \mathfrak{C}_i, \exists \mathbf{A}_2, \mathbf{A}_3 \in \mathfrak{C}_i \ st. \ \mathbf{A}_1 + \mathbf{A}_2 + \mathbf{A}_3 = \vec{0}.$$

More formally, we assume $d = m \cdot b$, for $m = O(\text{polylog}(d))$ and a block size b. The vectors in $\mathbb{R}^d$ will be identified with tuples of m vectors in $\mathbb{R}^b$. A random product code with triangles $\mathfrak{C}$ of parameters $[d, m, B]$ on subsets of $\mathbb{R}^d$ and of size B^m is defined as a code of the form

$$\mathfrak{C} = Q \cdot (\mathfrak{C}_1 \times \mathfrak{C}_2 \times \cdots \times \mathfrak{C}_m)$$

where Q is a uniformly random rotation over $\mathbb{R}^d$ and the subcodes $\mathfrak{C}_1, \ldots, \mathfrak{C}_m$ are each constructed as follows:

1. Sample $B/3$ random vectors $\mathbf{A}_1^1, \ldots, \mathbf{A}_1^{B/3}$ sampled uniformly at random over the sphere $\sqrt{1/m} \cdot \mathcal{S}^{b-1}$.
2. For each $i \in [B/3]$, pick a random vector $\mathbf{A}_2^j$ sampled uniformly at random over the sphere $\sqrt{1/m} \cdot \mathcal{S}^{b-1}$ with the condition that $\langle \mathbf{A}_1^j | \mathbf{A}_2^j \rangle = -\frac{1}{2m}$.

3. For each $i \in [B/3]$, let $\mathbf{A}_3^j$ be the unique point on the sphere $\sqrt{1/m} \cdot \mathcal{S}^{b-1}$ st. $\mathbf{A}_1^j + \mathbf{A}_2^j + \mathbf{A}_3^j = \vec{0}$.

The code $\mathbf{C}$ is then the set of points $\{\mathbf{A}_1^1, \mathbf{A}_2^1, \mathbf{A}_3^1, \ldots, \mathbf{A}_1^{B/3}, \mathbf{A}_2^{B/3}, \mathbf{A}_3^{B/3}\}$.

Notice that $\mathbf{A}_3^j = -(\mathbf{A}_1^j + \mathbf{A}_2^j)$ is of the correct norm $\frac{1}{\sqrt{m}}$. Indeed,

$$\|\mathbf{A}_3^j\|^2 = \| - (\mathbf{A}_1^j + \mathbf{A}_2^j)\|^2 = \|\mathbf{A}_1^j\|^2 + \|\mathbf{A}_2^j\|^2 + 2\langle\mathbf{A}_2^j|\mathbf{A}_1^j\rangle = \frac{2}{m} - \frac{2}{2m} = \frac{1}{m}.$$

We can generalize this construction for any constant k to get a k-RPC of codewords $\{\mathbf{A}_i^j\}_{i\in[k],j\in[B/3]}$ such that

$$\forall \mathbf{A}_1 \in \mathbf{C}_i, \exists \mathbf{A}_2, \ldots \mathbf{A}_k \in \mathbf{C}_i \ st. \ \sum_{i=1}^{k} \mathbf{A}_i = \vec{0}.$$

1. Sample B/k random vectors $\mathbf{A}_1^1, \ldots, \mathbf{A}_1^{B/k}$ sampled uniformly at random over the sphere $\sqrt{1/m} \cdot \mathcal{S}^{b-1}$.
2. For each $j \in [B/k]$, pick a random vector $\mathbf{A}_2^j$ sampled uniformly at random over the sphere $\sqrt{1/m} \cdot \mathcal{S}^{b-1}$ with the condition that $\langle\mathbf{A}_1^j|\mathbf{A}_2^j\rangle = -\frac{1}{(k-1)m}$.
   Then, for $i \in [|2, k-1|]$, pick random vectors $\mathbf{A}_i^j$ such that for each previous $i' \in [i]$, $\langle\mathbf{A}_i^j|\mathbf{A}_{i'}^j\rangle = -\frac{1}{(k-1)m}$.
3. For each $j \in [B/k]$, let $\mathbf{A}_k^j$ be the unique point on the sphere $\sqrt{1/m} \cdot \mathcal{S}^{b-1}$ such that $\sum_{i=1}^{k} \mathbf{A}_i^j = \vec{0}$. The code $\mathbf{C}$ is then the set of points $\{\mathbf{A}_i^j\}_{i\in[k],j\in[B/3]}$.

As before, we can check that $\mathbf{A}_k^j = -\sum_{j=1}^{k-1} \mathbf{A}_i^j$ is of the correct norm $\frac{1}{\sqrt{m}}$:

$$\|\mathbf{A}_k^j\|^2 = \sum_{j=1}^{k-1} \|\mathbf{A}_i^j\|^2 + \sum_{i=1}^{k-1}\sum_{\substack{i'=1 \\ i' \neq i}}^{k-1} \langle\mathbf{A}_i^j|\mathbf{A}_{i'}^j\rangle$$

$$= \frac{k-1}{m} + (k-1)(k-2) \cdot \frac{-1}{(k-1)m} = \frac{k-1}{m} - \frac{k-2}{m} = \frac{1}{m}.$$

For each $j \in [B/k]$, we actually take $\langle\mathbf{A}_i^j|\mathbf{A}_{i'}^j\rangle = -1/(k-1)$ for $i \neq i'$, because this balanced configuration optimizes the number of k-tuples whose vectors are respectively close to the centers $\mathbf{A}_i^j$ (See Proposition 5).

Proposition 8. *Let $\mathbf{C}$ be a random product code with triangles of parameters $[d, m, B]$ with $m = log(d)$ and $B^m = N^{O(1)}$. For any $\vec{x} \in \mathcal{S}^{d-1}$ and angle α, one can compute $\mathcal{H}_{\vec{x},\alpha} \cap \mathbf{C}$ in time $N^{o(1)} \cdot |\mathcal{H}_{\vec{x},\alpha} \cap \mathbf{C}|$.*

Proof. The decoding algorithm of Proposition 7 presented in [Bec+16] uses only the product structure of the code and not how the codes $\mathbf{C}_1, \ldots, \mathbf{C}_m$ are constructed. The same algorithm will therefore also efficiently decode random product codes with triangles. □

Definition 7 (Tuple-filter). *Let $\mathbf{C}$ be a k-RPC with codewords $(\mathbf{A}_i^j)$ for $i \in [k]$ and $j \in [|\mathbf{C}|/k]$ such that $\forall j \in [|\mathbf{C}|/k], \sum_{i=1}^{k} \mathbf{A}_i^j = \vec{0}$. Given angle α, we call a tuple-filter $(f_{\alpha,\mathbf{A}_1^j}, \ldots, f_{\alpha,\mathbf{A}_k^j})$, with $f_{\alpha,\mathbf{A}_i^j}$ filters (see Definition 6).*

3.2   Residual Vectors in Filter

Proposition 9 ([HKL18], **Lemma 3**). *We are given vectors i.i.d. uniformly random over $\mathcal{S}^{d-1}$ and a filter of center $\boldsymbol{A}$ and angle α. Then the vectors of angle at most α with $\boldsymbol{A}$ are i.i.d. uniformly random over the border of the filter. Their residual vectors are i.i.d. uniformly random over the (d-1)-dimensional sphere $\{\vec{\boldsymbol{y}} \in \mathbb{R}^d : \|\vec{\boldsymbol{y}}\| = 1, \theta(\vec{\boldsymbol{y}}, \boldsymbol{A}_i) = \alpha\}$.*

Then for a random $\vec{\boldsymbol{x}} \in \mathcal{S}^{d-1}$ of angle α with a center of filter $\boldsymbol{A}$, we can write for some $\vec{\boldsymbol{y}} \perp \boldsymbol{A}$,

$$\vec{\boldsymbol{x}} = \cos(\alpha)\boldsymbol{A} + \sin(\alpha)\vec{\boldsymbol{y}}.$$

We call $\vec{\boldsymbol{y}}$ the residual vector of $\vec{\boldsymbol{x}}$ on the filter of center $\boldsymbol{A}$ and angle α.

We are given a list L of lattice vectors assumed to be i.i.d. uniformly random over $\mathcal{S}^{d-1}$. We choose an angle α and sample a k-RPC $\mathfrak{C}$ having $1/\mathcal{V}(\alpha)$ codewords. Going through the $\vec{\boldsymbol{x}}$'s in the list L, we decode $\vec{\boldsymbol{x}}$ to its nearest unique codeword $\boldsymbol{A} \in \mathfrak{C}$. This step, called prefiltering, separates L into disjoint sublists, each one of size $N \cdot \mathcal{V}(\alpha)$. We focus on only one chosen tuple of filters of centers $\boldsymbol{A}_1, \ldots, \boldsymbol{A}_k$ respectively associated to the lists $L_1, \ldots, L_k$. By Proposition 9, with high probability the angle between any $\vec{\boldsymbol{x}} \in L_i$ and $\boldsymbol{A}_i$ is α.

While filling the list L_i with the $\vec{\boldsymbol{x}}$, we fill in parallel a list R_i with their residual vectors $\vec{\boldsymbol{y}}$ in the filter of center $\boldsymbol{A}_i$. Note that the points in L_i are i.i.d. uniformly random over the (d-1)-dimensional sphere $\{\vec{\boldsymbol{y}} \in \mathbb{R}^d : \|\vec{\boldsymbol{y}}\| = 1, \theta(\vec{\boldsymbol{y}}, \boldsymbol{A}_i) = \alpha\}$. See Fig. 4 for illustration.

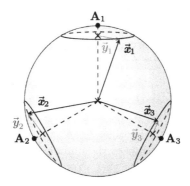

Fig. 4. List vectors $\vec{\boldsymbol{x}}_i \in L_i$ in their filters of centers $\boldsymbol{A}_i$ and their respective residual vectors $\vec{\boldsymbol{y}}_i \in R_i$, where for $i \neq j$, $\langle \boldsymbol{A}_i | \boldsymbol{A}_j \rangle = -\frac{1}{2}$.

Proposition 10. *Using the above notations for the lists L_i's and R_i's, a k-tuple $\vec{\boldsymbol{x}}_1, \ldots, \vec{\boldsymbol{x}}_k \in L_1 \times \cdots \times L_k$ is reducing iff. their residual vectors $\vec{\boldsymbol{y}}_1, \ldots, \vec{\boldsymbol{y}}_k \in R_1 \times \cdots \times R_k$ satisfy*

$$\sum_{1 \leqslant i < j \leqslant k} \langle \vec{\boldsymbol{y}}_i | \vec{\boldsymbol{y}}_j \rangle \leqslant \frac{1 - k\cos^2(\alpha)}{2\sin^2(\alpha)} := I_k(\alpha). \tag{2}$$

Proof. By Proposition 9, we can consider that for $i \neq j$, $\langle \mathbf{A}_i | \vec{\boldsymbol{y}}_j \rangle = 0$. And for $i \neq j$, $\vec{\boldsymbol{x}}_i \in L_i$ and $\vec{\boldsymbol{x}}_j \in L_j$, we obtain:

$$\langle \vec{\boldsymbol{x}}_i | \vec{\boldsymbol{x}}_j \rangle = \cos^2(\alpha) \langle \mathbf{A}_i | \mathbf{A}_j \rangle + \sin^2(\alpha) \langle \vec{\boldsymbol{y}}_i | \vec{\boldsymbol{y}}_j \rangle.$$

Then we have

$$\left\| \sum_{i=1}^{k} \vec{\boldsymbol{x}}_i \right\|^2 = \left\| \sum_{i=1}^{k} \sin(\alpha) \vec{\boldsymbol{y}}_i \right\|^2 = k \sin^2(\alpha) + 2 \sin^2(\alpha) \left(\sum_{1 \leqslant i < j \leqslant k} \langle \vec{\boldsymbol{y}}_i | \vec{\boldsymbol{y}}_j \rangle \right). \tag{3}$$

In the case the tuple $(\vec{\boldsymbol{x}}_1, \ldots, \vec{\boldsymbol{x}}_k)$ is reducing, we have $\left\| \sum_{i=1}^{k} \vec{\boldsymbol{x}}_i \right\|^2 \leqslant 1$, hence the wanted result. Notice also that we can translate the norm condition $\left\| \sum_{i=1}^{k} \vec{\boldsymbol{x}}_i \right\|^2 \leqslant 1$ directly into a norm condition of the residual vectors $\left\| \sum_{i=1}^{k} \vec{\boldsymbol{y}}_i \right\|^2 \leqslant \frac{1}{\sin^2(\alpha)}$. □

Lemma 1. *Let be a configuration $C \in \mathbb{R}^{k \times k}$ and an angle α. If a k-tuple $\vec{\boldsymbol{x}}_1, \ldots, \vec{\boldsymbol{x}}_k$ satisfies C then their residual vectors $\vec{\boldsymbol{y}}_1, \ldots, \vec{\boldsymbol{y}}_k$ on a filter of angle α satisfies the configuration $C'(\alpha)$ with for $i \neq j$,*

$$C'_{i,j}(\alpha) = -\frac{1}{\sin^2(\alpha)} \left(C_{i,j} + \frac{\cos^2(\alpha)}{k-1} \right).$$

Proof. As written in the previous proof, for $i \neq j$ we have $\langle \vec{\boldsymbol{x}}_i | \vec{\boldsymbol{x}}_j \rangle = \cos^2(\alpha) \langle \mathbf{A}_i | \mathbf{A}_j \rangle + \sin^2(\alpha) \langle \vec{\boldsymbol{y}}_i | \vec{\boldsymbol{y}}_j \rangle$. The configuration C gives constraints over the $\vec{\boldsymbol{x}}_i$'s, and $C'(\alpha)$ over the $\vec{\boldsymbol{y}}_i$'s ; and $\langle \mathbf{A}_i | \mathbf{A}_j \rangle$ is fixed at $-1/(k-1)$. □

If we consider a balanced configuration C for the $\vec{\boldsymbol{x}}_i$'s, then we have for $i \neq j$, $C_{i,j} = -1/k$ all equal. For residual vectors on a filter of angle α, this also implies $C'_{i,j}(\alpha)$ all equal for $i \neq j$. There are $C'_{i,j}$ at number $\sum_{i=1}^{k-1} i = k \cdot (k-1)/2$. Thus for $i \neq j$ we will have $C'_{i,j}(\alpha) = \frac{2}{k \cdot (k-1)} \cdot I_k(\alpha)$, with $I_k(\alpha)$ as defined in Proposition 10.

4 Framework

The idea behind the framework of our sieving algorithms is the following:

1. Prefilter the list vectors,
2. Search all reduced tuples within each filter,
3. Repeat steps 1. and 2. until all the reduced points are found.

Parameters. The algorithm takes into its input an angle α, and a configuration $C \in \mathbb{R}^{k \times k}$ that defines constraints over the lattice vectors. We will discuss later how to choose them optimally. From α and C, we can compute the configuration $C'(\alpha)$ over the residual vectors on filters of angle α using Lemma 1. From C, we also know the number of vectors we require to achieve the sieve step, which gives by Proposition 5 the minimum memory requirement $|L| = \widetilde{\mathcal{O}}(\det(C)^{-\frac{d}{2(k-1)}})$.

Algorithm 3. Framework for our new k-sieves

Require: List L of lattice vectors of norm at most R ; reducing factor $\gamma < 1$.
    Parameters: $k \in \mathbb{N}$; angle $\alpha \in (0, \pi/2]$; target configuration C.
Ensure: List L_{out} of lattice vectors of norm at most γR.
    $L_{out} = \emptyset$
    while $|L_{out}| < |L|$ **do** $\triangleright$ NbRep$_{\alpha,C}$ repeats
      Sample a k-RPC code $\mathfrak{C}$ having $k \cdot 1/\mathcal{V}(\alpha)$ codewords
      $L_i^j = \emptyset$ for $i \in [k], j \in [|\mathfrak{C}|/k]$
      for each $\vec{x} \in L$ **do**
        $\mathbf{A}_i^j \leftarrow \textbf{Decode}(\vec{x}, \mathfrak{C})$ $\triangleright$ Algorithm from Proposition 7.
        $\vec{y} \leftarrow 1/\sin(\alpha) \cdot (\vec{x} - \cos(\alpha)\mathbf{A}_i^j)$ $\triangleright$ Residual vector of $\vec{x}$ in the filter of center $\mathbf{A}_i^j$
        $L_i^j \leftarrow L_i^j \cup \{\vec{x}\}$; $R_i^j \leftarrow R_i^j \cup \{\vec{y}\}$
      for each tuple-filter numbered $j \in [|\mathfrak{C}|/k]$ **do**
        $Sol_{\vec{y}} \leftarrow \textbf{FindAllSolutionsWithinFilter}\left((R_i^j)_i, C'(\alpha)\right)$ $\triangleright$ Find all $(\vec{y}_i)_i \in R_1^j \times$
      $\cdots \times R_k^j$ satisfying $C'(\alpha)$
        $Sol_{\Sigma\vec{x}} \leftarrow \left\{\sum_{i=1}^k \vec{x}_i : (\vec{y}_i)_i \in Sol_{\vec{y}}\right\}$ $\triangleright$ $\vec{x}_i \in L_i^j$ and $\vec{y}_i \in R_i^j$ share the same
      index in their respective lists
        $L_{out} \leftarrow L_{out} \cup Sol_{\Sigma\vec{x}}$
    return L_{out}

---

1. Prefiltering. We start by sampling a k-RPC $\mathfrak{C}$ (Defined in Part 3.1) of size $k \cdot 1/\mathcal{V}(\alpha)$. Its codewords are denoted $(\mathbf{A}_i^j)_{i,j}$ for $i \in [k]$ and $j \in [|\mathfrak{C}|/k]$ (we suppose these values are integers by simplicity). For a fixed $j \in [|\mathfrak{C}|/k]$ and for $i_1 \neq i_2 \in [k]$ we have $\langle \mathbf{A}_{i_1}^j | \mathbf{A}_{i_2}^j \rangle = -\frac{1}{k-1}$, that implies $\sum_{i=1}^k \mathbf{A}_i^j = \vec{0}$.

Once the code is sampled, we can start the so-called prefiltering step. For each vector $\vec{x} \in L$, we efficiently compute its nearest codeword in $\mathfrak{C}$ using the algorithm from Proposition 8. If it returns center $\mathbf{A}_i^j$, then we add $\vec{x}$ to its associated list L_i^j. We also compute $\vec{x}$'s residual vector $\vec{y} = 1/\sin(\alpha) \cdot (\vec{x} - \cos(\alpha)\mathbf{A}_i^j)$ (by Proposition 9) and we add it to list R_i^j. Given a residual vector in R_i^j, we will be able to recover its corresponding vector in L_i^j by just looking at the same index.

There are tuple-filters $(\mathbf{A}_i^j)_{i\in[k]}$ at number

$$\text{NbFilters} := |\mathfrak{C}|/k = \mathcal{O}\left(\frac{1}{\mathcal{V}(\alpha)}\right). \tag{4}$$

As we compute the nearest filter in amortized time $\mathcal{O}(1)$ for each vector in L, the prefiltering step takes times $|L|$.

2. Find All Solutions Within a Tuple-Filter. We started with a list L and we wanted to solve a configuration problem, and after the prefiltering step, we can consider easier instances of the configuration problem on the sublists of L. The subroutine **FindAllSolutionsWithinFilter** solves one of these instances at a time, and we run it over each of the $1/\mathcal{V}(\alpha)$ tuple-filters.

Let's fix some $j \in [|\mathfrak{C}|/k]$ and consider the instance of configuration problem on the k lists $(R_i^j)_i$ with configuration $C'(\alpha)$. The subroutine then has to find all the k-tuples within $R_1^j \times \cdots \times R_k^j$ that satisfies the configuration $C'(\alpha)$. As we focus on only one filter at a time, in the following we will no longer write the j in exponent to lighten the notations.

The number of solutions the subroutine has to return is given by the following lemma.

Lemma 2. *With the same notations as before and for fixed $j \in [|\mathfrak{C}|/k]$, the expected number of tuples in the tuple-filter associated with the lists $R_1 \times \cdots \times R_k$ satisfying configuration $C'(\alpha)$ is on average*

$$|Sol_f| = \mathcal{O}\left(|R_1|^k \cdot \det(C'(\alpha))^{d/2}\right) = \mathcal{O}\left(|L|^k \mathcal{V}(\alpha)^k \cdot \det\left(C'(\alpha)\right)^{d/2}\right).$$

Proof. There are $|R_1|^k$ tuples in $R_1 \times \ldots \times R_k$ as the lists are all of same size $|R_1| = |L| \cdot \mathcal{V}(\alpha)$. Any tuple $(\vec{y}_1, ..., \vec{y}_k)$ from this set has probability $\det(C'(\alpha))^{d/2}$ to satisfy configuration $C'(\alpha)$. Hence the expected number of tuples satisfying $C'(\alpha)$. □

Any subroutine with these inputs and outputs may suit the framework. For example, in the case $k = 2$, [CL21] describes a 2-sieve under this framework, where the subroutine uses quantum random walks to find the reducing pairs of vectors. We denote the time complexity of the subroutine **FindAllSolutionsWithinFilter** with parameters α and C by $T(\mathbf{FAS}_{C'(\alpha)})$.

3. Number of repeats. After searching all the solutions within every tuple-filters, we expect to find the following number of solutions:

$$|Sol_{all}| = |L|^k \cdot det(C)^{d/2}. \tag{5}$$

To complete the sieve step, we require to find $|L|$ reduced lattice vectors. Thus steps 1. and 2. have to be repeated until enough solutions have been found. The missed solutions are the ones such that a part of the solution is in one tuple-filter and the rest is in another. By doing a new prefiltering, it changes the partitions of the sphere, and this allows to find some of these missing solutions.

Lemma 3. *The number of repetitions in the while loop is*

$$NbRep_{\alpha,C} = \mathcal{O}\left(\max\left\{1, \frac{|Sol_{all}|}{|Sol_f| \cdot NbFilters}\right\}\right)$$

$$= \mathcal{O}\left(\max\left\{1, \frac{|L_1|^k \det(C)^{d/2}}{|L_1|^k \mathcal{V}^k(\alpha) \det\left(C'(\alpha)\right)^{d/2} \cdot \frac{1}{\mathcal{V}(\alpha)}}\right\}\right)$$

$$= \mathcal{O}\left(\max\left\{1, \frac{\det(C)^{d/2}}{\mathcal{V}^{k-1}(\alpha) \det\left(C'(\alpha)\right)^{d/2}}\right\}\right).$$

The overall time complexity of an algorithm based on this framework is given in the following theorem.

Theorem 2. *Let $\alpha \in (0, \pi/2]$ be an angle and a configuration $C \in \mathbb{R}^{k \times k}$, and $C'(\alpha)$ the configuration on the residual vectors (See Lemma 1). Given an algorithm that solves the configuration problem $C'(\alpha)$ for k lists in time $T(\mathbf{FAS}_{C'(\alpha)})$, Algorithm 3 solves SVP in time*

$$T(k\text{-}sieve) := NbRep_{\alpha,C} \cdot \left(|L| + NbFilters_\alpha \cdot T(\mathbf{FAS}_{C'(\alpha)}) \right)$$

where $NbRep_{\alpha,C}$ is given by Lemma 3 and $NbFilters_\alpha = \mathcal{O}(\frac{1}{\mathcal{V}(\alpha)})$ by Eq. 4.

The above theorem is the main technical contribution of our work. The main novelty is the angle α which can be freely chosen. Taking an angle $\alpha = \pi/2$ means that we do not perform any tailored LSF.

Optimization of the Parameters. So the $C_{i,j}$'s are parameters to optimize to get the minimal overall time of the k-sieve, and they obey to the constraints on memory and reduceness of the tuples. We also require that the inner algorithm for solving the configuration problem with $C'(\alpha)$ uses at most memory M. There is as well the prefiltering angle $\alpha \in (0, \pi/2]$ that has to be optimized. In the next sections, we will present algorithms that fit in the framework 3 and for each one we will specify the optimal values for C and α we have obtained by numerical optimization. The code is available on https://github.com/johanna-loyer/3-4-sieve.

5   Classical Sieving

We present here our 3-sieve and 4-sieve classical algorithms. In both cases, we use Theorem 2 so the only thing to explicit is the inner algorithm running in time $T(\mathbf{FAS}_{C'(\alpha)})$ as well as the parameters C and α. Actually, in both cases, the inner algorithm will use a classical 2-sieve algorithm so we first give formulas for the configuration problem with $k = 2$.

5.1   Classical 2-Sieve

We present here the best-known algorithm for classical 2-sieve. While these are known results, we will need this analysis for our 3-sieve and 4-sieve algorithms. We can actually derive the best-known algorithms (in terms of asymptotic time and memory) from our framework.

Proposition 11. *Take $k = 2$, lists L_1, L_2 of random points of norm 1 with $|L_1| = |L_2|$, a target configuration $C = \begin{pmatrix} 1 & C_{12} \\ C_{12} & 1 \end{pmatrix}$. Let α st. $\mathcal{V}(\alpha) = \frac{1}{|L_1|}$.*

Algorithm 3 with parameter α constructs a list L_{out} of pairs of points $(\vec{x}_1, \vec{x}_2)$ with $(\vec{x}_1, \vec{x}_2) \in L_1 \times L_2$ st. $\langle \vec{x}_1 | \vec{x}_2 \rangle \leq C_{12}$, in time T using memory M st.

$$|L_{out}| = \mathcal{O}\left(|L_1|^2 \det(C)^{d/2}\right) = \mathcal{O}\left(|L_1|^2 \left(1 - C_{12}^2\right)^{d/2}\right)$$

$$T = \mathcal{O}\left(|L_1|^2 \frac{\det(C)^{d/2}}{\det\left(C'(\alpha)\right)^{d/2}}\right) = \mathcal{O}\left(|L_1|^2 \frac{(1 - C_{12}^2)^{d/2}}{(1 - C_{12}'(\alpha)^2)^{d/2}}\right).$$

$$M = \mathcal{O}\left(\max\{|L_1|, |L_{out}|\}\right)$$

where recall that $C_{12}'(\alpha) = \frac{1}{\sin^2(\alpha)} \cdot \left(C_{12} + \cos^2(\alpha)\right)$. Notice that $|L_{out}|$ corresponds asymptotically to all the pairs $(\vec{x}_1, \vec{x}_2) \in L_1 \times L_2$ st. $\langle \vec{x}_1 | \vec{x}_2 \rangle \leq C_{12}$ so we find here asymptotically all solutions.

Proof. We use Theorem 2 with $k = 2$ and some parameter α to get

$$T = \mathcal{O}\left(NbRep_{\alpha, C_{12}} \cdot \left(|L_1| + \frac{1}{\mathcal{V}(\alpha)} T(\mathbf{FAS}_{C_{12}'(\alpha)})\right)\right). \tag{6}$$

Recall that here, $\mathbf{FAS}_{C_{12}'(\alpha)}$ computes the running time of finding all solution pairs with inner product smaller than $C_{12}'(\alpha)$ when starting with lists of size $|R_1| = |L_1|\mathcal{V}(\alpha)$. We perform an exhaustive search on the pairs of points to find all solutions so

$$T(\mathbf{FAS}_{C_{12}'(\alpha)}) = \mathcal{O}\left(\max\{1, |L_1|^2 \mathcal{V}^2(\alpha)\}\right).$$

We take α st. $\mathcal{V}(\alpha) = \frac{1}{|L_1|}$ so Eq. 6 becomes $T = \mathcal{O}\left(NbRep_{\alpha, C_{12}} \cdot |L_1|\right)$. Finally, from Lemma 3, we have

$$NbRep_{\alpha, C_{12}} = \mathcal{O}\left(\max\left\{1, \frac{\det(C)^{d/2}}{V^{k-1}(\alpha) \det\left(C'(\alpha)\right)^{d/2}}\right\}\right) = |L_1| \frac{\det(C)^{d/2}}{\det\left(C'(\alpha)\right)^{d/2}},$$

which allows us to conclude that

$$T = \mathcal{O}\left(|L_1|^2 \frac{\det(C)^{d/2}}{\det\left(C'(\alpha)\right)^{d/2}}\right).$$

$\square$

As a special case, we can take $|L_1| = |L_2| = 2^{0.2075d}$, $C_{12} = -1/3$ which gives $L_{out} = |L_1|$, $T = 2^{0.292d}$ and $M = |L_1|$ which is the best-known algorithm asymptotically.

5.2   Classical 3-Sieve

So we now consider the case of $k = 3$. Our inner algorithms will construct the following intermediate lists:

1. Construct $L_{12} = \{(\vec{x}_1, \vec{x}_2) \in L_1 \times L_2 : \langle \vec{x}_1 | \vec{x}_2 \rangle \leq C_{12}\}$ and $L_{13} = \{(\vec{x}_1, \vec{x}_3) \in L_1 \times L_3 : \langle \vec{x}_1 | \vec{x}_3 \rangle \leq C_{23}\}$.
2. For each $\vec{x}_1 \in L_1$, let $L_{12}(\vec{x}_1) = \{\vec{x}_2 \in L_2 : (\vec{x}_1, \vec{x}_2) \in L_{12}\}$ and $L_{13}(\vec{x}_1) = \{\vec{x}_3 \in L_3 : (\vec{x}_1, \vec{x}_3) \in L_{13}\}$.
3. For each $\vec{x}_1 \in L_1$, compute $L_{123}(\vec{x}_1) = \{(\vec{x}_2, \vec{x}_3) \in L_{12}(\vec{x}_1) \times L_{13}(\vec{x}_1) : \langle \vec{x}_2 | \vec{x}_3 \rangle \leq C_{23}\}$. For each $\vec{x}_1 \in L_1$, triples $(\vec{x}_1, \vec{x}_2, \vec{x}_3)$ are solution when $(\vec{x}_2, \vec{x}_3) \in L_{123}(\vec{x}_1)$.

Now that we defined all intermediate lists, we can write the algorithm we use for solving the inner configuration problem with $k = 3$.

Algorithm 4. FindAllSolutionsWithinFilter classical 3-sieve

Require: lists L_1, L_2, L_3 of vectors i.i.d. in $\mathcal{S}^{d-1}$ with $|L_1| = |L_2| = |L_3|$; target configuration $C \in \mathbb{R}^{3 \times 3}$.
Ensure: list L_{out} of all 3-tuples in $L_1 \times L_2 \times L_3$ satisfying configuration C.
$\quad L_{out} := \emptyset$.
$\quad$ construct L_{12} and L_{13} using a 2-sieve algorithm with angle parameter α', from which you can recover lists $L_{12}(\vec{x}_1)$ and $L_{13}(\vec{x}_1)$
$\quad$ **for each** $\vec{x}_1 \in L_1$:
$\quad\quad$ compute $L_{123}(\vec{x}_1)$ using a 2-sieve algorithm with angle parameter α''
$\quad\quad$ for each $(\vec{x}_2, \vec{x}_3) \in L_{123}(\vec{x}_1)$, do $L_{out} := L_{out} \cup \{(\vec{x}_1, \vec{x}_2, \vec{x}_3)\}$.
$\quad$ **return** L_{out}

Complexity of Algorithm 4. *Construction of the Lists L_{12} and L_{13}.* As a direct consequence of Proposition 11, we have:

Lemma 4. *Let T_{12} (resp. T_{13}) be the time to compute L_{12} (resp. L_{13}). Let α such that $|L_1| = 1/\mathcal{V}(\alpha)$. We have*

$$T_{12} = \mathcal{O}\left(|L_1|^2 \frac{\left(1 - C_{12}^2\right)^{d/2}}{\left(1 - C_{12}'(\alpha)^2\right)^{d/2}}\right)$$

$$T_{13} = \mathcal{O}\left(|L_1|^2 \frac{\left(1 - C_{13}^2\right)^{d/2}}{\left(1 - C_{13}'(\alpha)^2\right)^{d/2}}\right)$$

Construction of the Lists $L_{23}(\vec{x}_1)$. For a fixed $\vec{x}_1$, notice that the lists $L_2(\vec{x}_1)$ and $L_3(\vec{x}_1)$ do not contain points uniformly distributed on the sphere since they have an inner-product constraint with $\vec{x}_1$ so we cannot apply Proposition 11 directly. Fix $\vec{x}_1 \in L_1$ and let $\vec{x}_2 \in L_2$ and $\vec{x}_3 \in L_3$. For simplicity of calculations, we consider the case where $\langle \vec{x}_1 | \vec{x}_2 \rangle = C_{12}, \langle \vec{x}_1 | \vec{x}_3 \rangle = C_{13}$ and $\langle \vec{x}_2 | \vec{x}_3 \rangle = C_{23}$. This approximation is justified from Heuristic 1. So we write

$$\vec{x}_2 = C_{12}\vec{x}_1 + \sqrt{1 - C_{12}^2}\vec{y}_2 \quad ; \quad \vec{x}_3 = C_{13}\vec{x}_1 + \sqrt{1 - C_{13}^2}\vec{y}_3 \tag{7}$$

where $\vec{y}_2, \vec{y}_3$ are orthogonal to $\vec{x}_1$. Also, if $\vec{x}_2$ (resp. $\vec{x}_3$) is a random vector satisfying $\langle \vec{x}_1 | \vec{x}_2 \rangle = C_{12}$ (resp. $\langle \vec{x}_1 | \vec{x}_3 \rangle = C_{13}$) then $\vec{y}_2$ (resp. $\vec{y}_3$) is a random unit vectors. Let $Y_{23} := \langle \vec{y}_2 | \vec{y}_3 \rangle$. We have

$$\langle \vec{x}_2 | \vec{x}_3 \rangle = C_{12} C_{13} + \sqrt{1 - C_{12}^2} \sqrt{1 - C_{13}^2} Y_{23}$$

which implies

$$Y_{23} = \frac{C_{23} - C_{12} C_{13}}{\sqrt{1 - C_{12}^2} \sqrt{1 - C_{13}^2}}.$$

We can now use Proposition 11 to give the running time of computing $R_{23}(\vec{x}_1)$, which gives the running time $T_{23}(\vec{x}_1)$ of computing $L_{23}(\vec{x}_3)$. Let $Y = \begin{pmatrix} 1 & Y_{23} \\ Y_{23} & 1 \end{pmatrix}$ and let α'' st. $\mathcal{V}(\alpha') = \frac{1}{|L_2(\vec{x}_1)|}$. We have

$$T_{23}(\vec{x}_1) = \mathcal{O}\left(NbRep_{\alpha',Y} \cdot |L_2(\vec{x}_1)| \right).$$

Now, let T_{23} be the running of computing all the lists $L_{23}(\vec{x}_1)$ since the number of $\vec{x}_1$ is $|L_1|$, we have

$$T_{23} = |L_1| T_{23}(\vec{x}_1) = \mathcal{O}\left(|L_1| NbRep_{\alpha',Y} \cdot |L_2(\vec{x}_1)| \right) \tag{8}$$

$$= |L_1| |L_2(\vec{x}_1)|^2 \frac{\left(1 - Y_{23}^2\right)^{d/2}}{\left(1 - Y_{23}'(\alpha')^2\right)^{d/2}} \tag{9}$$

with $Y_{23}'(\alpha) = \frac{1}{\sin^2(\alpha)} \left(Y_{23} + \cos^2(\alpha') \right)$. Putting everything together, we have the following

Proposition 12. *Let $|L_1|$ a list size and C a 3×3 configuration matrix with negative non-diagonal entries. Let $|L_2(\vec{x}_1)| = |L_1|(1 - C_{12}^2)^{d/2}$. Let α' st. $\mathcal{V}(\alpha') = \frac{1}{|L_2(\vec{x}_1)|}$. Algorithm 4 solves $\mathbf{FAS}_3^c(|L_1|, C)$ in time $T_{12} + T_{13} + T_{23}$ with*

$$T_{12} = T_{23} = \mathcal{O}\left(|L_1|^2 (1 - C_{12}^2)^{d/2} \right)$$

$$T_{123} = |L_1| |L_2(\vec{x}_1)|^2 \frac{\left(1 - Y_{23}^2\right)^{d/2}}{\left(1 - Y_{23}'(\alpha')^2\right)^{d/2}}$$

where

$$Y_{23} = \frac{1}{\sqrt{1 - C_{12}^2} \sqrt{1 - C_{13}^2}} \cdot (C_{23} + C_{12} C_{13})$$

$$Y_{23}'(\alpha) = \frac{1}{\sin^2(\alpha)} \left(Y_{23} + \cos^2(\alpha') \right).$$

Let $|L_{12}| = |L_1|^2 \left(1 - C_{12}^2\right)^{d/2}$. This algorithm uses memory $M = \max\{|L_1|, |L_{12}|\}$.

Complexity of the Classical 3-Sieve. The above was the analysis of the classical 3-sieve after the first filtering. We now apply Theorem 2 with $k = 3$ in order to obtain the running of our classical 3-sieve algorithm within our framework.

Theorem 3. *There is a classical algorithm with parameter α that solves the 3-sieve problem for a configuration C and lists of size $|L|$ that runs in time T and that uses memory M with*

$$T = \mathcal{O}\left(NbRep_{\alpha,C} \cdot \left(|L| + \frac{1}{\mathcal{V}(\alpha)} \cdot T\left(\mathbf{FAS}_3^c\left(|L_1|, C'(\alpha)\right)\right) \right) \right),$$

and

$$M = \max\{|L|, |L_1|, |L_{12}|, |L_{123}|\}.$$

where $|L_1| = |L| \cdot \mathcal{V}(\alpha)$, $|L_{12}|, |L_{123}|$ can be taken from Proposition 6 and $\mathbf{FAS}_3^c(|L_1|, C) = T_{12} + T_{13} + T_{123}$ where each T_{12}, T_{13}, T_{123} can be taken from Proposition 12.

Proposition 13. *There exists a classical algorithm for SVP using 3-sieve that runs in time $2^{0.338d+o(d)}$ and uses memory $2^{0.1887d+o(d)}$.*

Proof. Take the above proposition with a configuration matrix C st. $C_{12} = C_{13} = C_{23} = -\frac{1}{3}$, $\alpha = 1.2954 rad$ and $|L| = 2^{0.1887d}$. We apply Proposition 3; We write $C'_{12}(\alpha) = C'_{13}(\alpha) = C'_{23}(\alpha) \approx -0.32$ and $|L_1| = |L| \cdot \mathcal{V}(\alpha) = 2^{0.133d}$. We have, (omitting $o(d)$ factors in the exponent)

$$NbRep_{\alpha,C} = 2^{0.070d} \quad ; \quad \frac{1}{\mathcal{V}(\alpha)} = 2^{0.055d} \quad ; \quad T\left(\mathbf{FAS}_3^c(|L_1|, C')\right) = 2^{0.213d}$$

Putting everything together, we indeed have a running time of $2^{0.070d} \cdot 2^{0.055d} \cdot 2^{0.213d} = 2^{0.338d}$. The memory $M = \max\{|L|, |L_{out}|, |L_{int}|\}$ where L_{int} is the intermediate list used in $\mathbf{FAS}_3^c(|L_1|, C'(\alpha))$. We have

$$|L_{int}| = |L_1|^2 \left(1 - C'_{12}(\alpha)^2\right)^{d/2} = 2^{0.1887d}.$$

This implies that the memory used is $M = 2^{0.1887d}$.   □

Space-Time Trade-Off. We also extend this algorithm where we fix the available memory to something more than the minimal memory $2^{0.1887d}$. We present here a list of points that we obtain, showing the general behaviour of our algorithm (Table 2):

Table 2. Time complexity of our classical 3-sieving algorithm for a fixed memory constraint. α is the optimal angle used in the first prefiltering. Also see Fig. 2a for a plot corresponding to this algorithm.

$\frac{1}{d}\log_2$(Memory)	0.1887	0.19	0.2	0.2075	0.22	0.24	0.26	0.272	0.286
$\frac{1}{d}\log_2$(Time)	0.338	0.334	0.328	0.325	0.320	0.313	0.307	0.304	0.304
α (rad)	1.2954	1.305	1.329	1.346	1.366	1.408	1.470	$\pi/2$	$\pi/2$

5.3   Classical 4-Sieve

We now consider the case $k = 4$. For our inner algorithms, we start with 4 lists L_1, L_2, L_3, L_4. There are actually several strategies of merging the lists. Here we choose to perform the following merges:

1. Construct $L_{12} = \{(\vec{x}_1, \vec{x}_2) \in L_1 \times L_2 : \langle \vec{x}_1 | \vec{x}_2 \rangle \leq C_{12}\}$ and $L_{34} = \{(\vec{x}_3, \vec{x}_4) \in L_3 \times L_4 : \langle \vec{x}_3 | \vec{x}_4 \rangle \leq C_{34}\}$.
2. Construct $L_{1234} = \{((\vec{x}_1, \vec{x}_2), (\vec{x}_3, \vec{x}_4)) \in L_{12} \times L_{34} : (\vec{x}_1, \vec{x}_2, \vec{x}_3, \vec{x}_4)$ satisfies configuration $C\}$.

Using these lists, we consider the following algorithm:

Algorithm 5. FindAllSolutionsWithinFilter classical 4-sieve

Require: lists L_1, L_2, L_3, L_4 of vectors i.i.d. in $\mathcal{S}^{d-1}$ with $|L_1| = |L_2| = |L_3| = |L_4|$; target configuration $C \in \mathbb{R}^{4 \times 4}$ with $C_{12} = C_{34}$ and $C_{13} = C_{14} = C_{23} = C_{24}$.
Ensure: list L_{out} of all 4-tuples $(\vec{x}_1, \vec{x}_2, \vec{x}_3, \vec{x}_4) \in L_1 \times L_2 \times L_3 \times L_4$ satisfying configuration C.
   Construct L_{12} and L_{34} using our classical 2-sieve algorithm.
   Start from L_{12} and L_{34} and use our classical 2-sieve algorithm to compute L_{1234}.
   return L_{1234}.

We then use the above algorithm as the **FindAllSolutionsWithinFilter** subroutine in Algorithm 3 to describe our entire algorithm for 4-sieve. The algorithm presented here is usually inefficient in memory because the lists L_{12} and L_{13} are large. However, thanks to our initial α-filtering, we start from smaller lists L_1, L_2, L_3, L_4 so the intermediate lists will be small as well.

Complexity of Algorithm 5.

Lemma 5.   *Let T_{12} be the time to compute L_{12} (which is also the time to compute L_{34} by symmetry). Let α st. $\mathcal{V}(\alpha) = \frac{1}{|L_1|}$. Then*

$$T_{12} = \mathcal{O}\left(|L_1|^2 \frac{\left(1 - C_{12}^2\right)^{d/2}}{\left(1 - C_{12}'(\alpha)^2\right)^{d/2}}\right)$$

This comes directly from the analysis of our simplified 2-sieve algorithm. The size of the intermediate lists L_{12} and L_{34} is then

$$|L_{12}| = |L_1|^2 \cdot \left(1 - C_{12}^2\right)^{d/2} \tag{10}$$

We now look at the time to compute L_{1234}. Elements of L_{12} are of squared norm $R^2 = 2 + 2C_{12}$, using $\|\vec{x}_1 + \vec{x}_2\|^2 = \|\vec{x}_1\|^2 + \|\vec{x}_2\|^2 + 2\langle \vec{x}_1 | \vec{x}_2 \rangle$. We write

Lemma 6. *Let $\vec{z}_{12} \in L_{12}$ and $\vec{z}_{34} \leq L_{34}$. If $Angle(\vec{z}_{12}, \vec{z}_{34}) = \arccos\left(\frac{\sin^2(\alpha)}{2R'^2} - 1\right)$ then $\|\vec{z}_{12} + \vec{z}_{34}\|^2 \leq \sin^2(\alpha)$.*

Proof. We write

$$\|\vec{z}_{12} + \vec{z}_{34}\|^2 = \|\vec{z}_{12}\|^2 + \|\vec{z}_{34}\|^2 + 2\langle\vec{z}_{12}|\vec{z}_{34}\rangle$$

By taking $\langle\vec{z}_{12}|\vec{z}_{34}\rangle = R^2(\frac{r_0^2}{2R^2} - 1)$, we obtain indeed $\|\vec{z}_{12} + \vec{z}_{34}\|^2 \le r_0^2$.   □

Lemma 7. *Let T_{1234} be the time to compute L_{1234}. Let $Y = \frac{r_0}{4+4C_{12}} - 1$. Let α' st. $\mathcal{V}(\alpha') = \frac{1}{|L_{12}|}$. We have*

$$T_{1234} = \mathcal{O}\left(|L_{12}|^2 \frac{\left(1 - Y^2\right)^{d/2}}{\left(1 - Y'(\alpha')^2\right)^{d/2}}\right),$$

with $Y'(\alpha') = \frac{1}{\sin^2(\alpha)}\left(T + \cos^2(\alpha')\right)$.

By combining the above 2 propositions, we have

Theorem 4. *Algorithm 5 runs in time $T = 2T_{12} + T_{1234}$ where T_{12} and T_{1234} can be taken respectively from Lemma 5 and Lemma 7.*

To conclude, we can plug this theorem again in Theorem 2 to get our results. Recall that we work with 4-tuples of residual vectors after an initial α-filtering so we look for 4-tuples of residual points $(\vec{y}_1, \vec{y}_2, \vec{y}_3, \vec{y}_4)$ st. $\|\vec{y}_1 + \vec{y}_2 + \vec{y}_3 + \vec{y}_4\| \le \frac{1}{\sin(\alpha)}$ (see Eq. 3). This means we take $r_0 = \frac{1}{\sin(\alpha)}$. Regarding memory requirements, we have that the memory M of our algorithm satisfies $M = \max\{|L_1|, |L_{12}|, |L_{1234}|\}$.

This algorithm gives smooth time-memory trade-off to the points where the memory is $2^{0.0275d}$ and the time is $2^{0.292d}$, corresponding precisely to the complexity of the 2-sieve algorithm (and indeed corresponds to the case where our 4-sieve algorithm performs independently two 2-sieve algorithms). When looking at the minimal memory setting, so $M = 2^{0.1724d}$, this algorithm performs poorly, as the time is $2^{0.418d}$. However, when looking at intermediate memory requirements, there are some ranges when the algorithm performs quite well. For example, when taking $M = 2^{0.1887d}$, this algorithm performs better than the 3-sieve classical algorithm we presented before. We put below a list of values of interest. As in the previous case, the less memory we are allowed, the more it is interesting to perform a tailored prefiltering step. We put below a list of values and the corresponding angle α used in the prefiltering step (Table 3).

Table 3. Time complexity of our classical 4-sieving algorithm for a fixed memory constraint. α is the optimal angle used in the prefiltering. Also see Fig. 2b for a plot corresponding to this algorithm.

$\log_2(\text{Memory})/d$	0.1724	0.175	0.18	0.1887	0.193	0.198	0.203	0.2075
$\log_2(\text{Time})/d$	0.418	0.380	0.352	0.324	0.315	0.306	0.298	0.2925
α (rad)	1.278	1.315	1.350	1.401	1.425	1.457	1.494	$\pi/2$

6   Quantum Sieving

We now study how our framework impacts quantum algorithms. In the quantum setting, Theorem 2 also applied and once again, we only need to describe the running time and amount of memory used for the inner configuration problem.

The input lists L_i are stored classically and are assumed to be quantumly accessible, *i.e.* for any given list L, we can efficiently construct the uniform superposition over all its elements $|\psi_L\rangle := \frac{1}{\sqrt{|L|}} \sum_\ell |\ell\rangle |L[\ell]\rangle$. In the following, we will not necessarily write the first register for simplicity[2].

6.1   Quantum 3-Sieve

For the **FindAllSolutionsWithinFilter** quantum subroutine in case $k = 3$, we start with classical lists L_1, L_2, L_3 that are quantumly accessible. The algorithm outputs a list containing all triples in $L_1 \times L_2 \times L_3$ satisfying a given target configuration C.

To find one solution, our algorithm constructs a uniform quantum superposition over all triples, and then applies two Grover's algorithms in order to get a "filtered" quantum superposition. This whole process is then repeated inside an amplitude amplification to get a superposition over the solutions, that we measure, and we repeat this whole process until we have found all the solutions.

As a reminder (See Proposition 6), given a configuration C, we use the following notation: for $i, j \in [k]$, $i \neq j$ and $\vec{y}_j \in L_j$,

$$L_i(\vec{y}_j) := \{\vec{y}_i \in L_i : \langle \vec{y}_i | \vec{y}_j \rangle \leq C_{i,j}\}.$$

Algorithm 6. FindAllSolutionsWithinFilter quantum 3-sieve

Require: lists L_1, L_2, L_3 of vectors i.i.d. in $\mathcal{S}^{d-1}$ with $|L_1| = |L_2| = |L_3|$; a target configuration $C \in \mathbb{R}^{3 \times 3}$.
Ensure: list L_{out} containing all 3-triples in $L_1 \times L_2 \times L_3$ satisfying configuration C.
 $\quad L_{out} := \emptyset$
 $\quad$**while** $|L_{out}| < |Sol|$ **do**
 $\quad\quad$Construct state $|\psi_{L_1}\rangle |\psi_{L_2}\rangle |\psi_{L_3}\rangle$
 $\quad\quad$Apply **Grover** on the second register to get state $|\psi_{L_1}\rangle |\psi_{L_2(\vec{y}_1)}\rangle |\psi_{L_3}\rangle$
 $\quad\quad$Apply **Grover** on the third register to get state $|\psi_{L_1}\rangle |\psi_{L_2(\vec{y}_1)}\rangle |\psi_{L_3(\vec{y}_1)}\rangle$
 $\quad\quad$Apply Amplitude Amplification to get state $|\psi_{Sol}\rangle$, the uniform superposition of all solutions
 $\quad\quad$Take a measurement and get some $(\vec{y}_1, \vec{y}_2, \vec{y}_3)$
 $\quad\quad$**if** $(\vec{y}_1, \vec{y}_2, \vec{y}_3)$ satisfies configuration C **then** add it to L_{out}
 $\quad$**return** L_{out}

---

[2] This simplification was already done in [Kir+19]. At no point do we use the fact that we do not have the first register, this is just for simplicity of notations.

Complexity of Algorithm 6. We first analyse the complexity to find one solution during one single iteration from the while-loop.

Initialization. We assume that lists L_1, L_2 and L_3 of i.i.d. random points are classically stored and quantumly accessible. So the state $|\psi_{L_1}\rangle |\psi_{L_2}\rangle |\psi_{L_3}\rangle$ can be constructed efficiently.

Grover on the Second Register. The algorithm then applies Grover's algorithm on the second register such that the two first registers become

$$|\psi_{L_1}\rangle |\psi_{L_2(\vec{y}_1)}\rangle = \frac{1}{\sqrt{|L_1|}} \frac{1}{\sqrt{|L_2(\vec{y}_1)|}} \sum_{\vec{y}_1 \in L_1} \sum_{\vec{y}_2 \in L_2(\vec{y}_1)} |\vec{y}_1\rangle |\vec{y}_2\rangle.$$

It only keeps in the quantum superposition the elements $\vec{y}_2 \in L_2$ such that $\langle \vec{y}_1 | \vec{y}_2 \rangle \leq C_{12}$ for each superposed $\vec{y}_1$ from the first register. So the state ends up with a quantum superposition of all pairs in $L_1 \times L_2$ eligible to form the beginning of a triple-solution. This application of Grover's algorithm takes time $T_2 = \sqrt{\frac{|L_2|}{|L_2(\vec{y}_1)|}} = (1 - C_{12})^{-d/4}$ by Proposition 6.

Grover on the Third Register. Similarly, we also apply Grover's algorithm on the third register to get the state $|\psi_{L_1}\rangle |\psi_{L_2(\vec{y}_1)}\rangle |\psi_{L_3(\vec{y}_1)}\rangle$ equal to

$$\frac{1}{\sqrt{|L_1|}} \frac{1}{\sqrt{|L_2(\vec{y}_1)|}} \frac{1}{\sqrt{|L_3(\vec{y}_1)|}} \sum_{\vec{y}_1 \in L_1} \sum_{\vec{y}_2 \in L_2(\vec{y}_1)} \sum_{\vec{y}_3 \in L_3(\vec{y}_1)} |\vec{y}_1\rangle |\vec{y}_2\rangle |\vec{y}_3\rangle$$

in time $T_3 = \sqrt{\frac{|L_3|}{|L_3(\vec{y}_1)|}} = (1 - C_{13})^{-d/4}$. The sizes $|L_2(\vec{y}_1)|$ and $|L_3(\vec{y}_1)|$ do not depend on the choice of $\vec{y}_1$, that is why we can write their corresponding normalizing factors before the sum over the $\vec{y}_1$'s.

Amplitude Amplification. The goal is now to construct a uniform quantum superposition over all elements of the set of solutions $Sol := \{(\vec{y}_1, \vec{y}_2, \vec{y}_3) \in L_1 \times L_2 \times L_3$ satisfying $C\}$, by applying a quantum amplitude amplification. Let $\mathcal{A}$ be unitary that maps $|0\rangle |0\rangle |0\rangle$ to the state $|\psi_{L_1}\rangle |\psi_{L_2(\vec{y}_1)}\rangle |\psi_{L_3(\vec{y}_1)}\rangle$ constructed so far.

Lemma 8. *The operation $\mathcal{A} : |0\rangle |0\rangle |0\rangle \rightarrow |\psi_{L_1}\rangle |\psi_{L_2(\vec{y}_1)}\rangle |\psi_{L_3(\vec{y}_1)}\rangle$ is repeated T_{AA} times inside the amplitude amplification to construct state $|\psi_{Sol}\rangle$ (with probability $1 - o(1)$), where*

$$T_{AA} = \mathcal{O}\left(\sqrt{|L_1|/|Sol|} \cdot \sqrt{|L_2(\vec{y}_1)|}\sqrt{|L_3(\vec{y}_1)|}\right)$$
$$= \mathcal{O}\left(\sqrt{|L_i^3|/|Sol|} \cdot (1 - C_{12})^{d/4}(1 - C_{13})^{d/4}\right).$$

Proof. Performing a measurement of state $|\psi_{L_1}\rangle\,|\psi_{L_2(\vec{y}_1)}\rangle\,|\psi_{L_3(\vec{y}_1)}\rangle$ gives a triplet solution $(\vec{y}_1, \vec{y}_2, \vec{y}_3)$ with some probability p, we are going to specify. There are $|L_1|$ possible $\vec{y}_1$ and $|Sol|$ "good" ones belonging to a solution, so the probability of measuring a good $\vec{y}_1$ is $|Sol|/|L_1|$. Then given a $\vec{y}_1$, a pair $(\vec{y}_2, \vec{y}_3) \in L_2(\vec{y}_1) \times L_3(\vec{y}_1)$ forms the solution together with $\vec{y}_1$ with probability $\frac{1}{|L_2(\vec{y}_1)|} \frac{1}{|L_3(\vec{y}_1)|}$.

Finally, the probability to measure a solution is thus $p = |Sol|/|L_1| \cdot \frac{1}{L_2(\vec{y}_1)} \frac{1}{L_3(\vec{y}_1)}$. By Theorem 3, the number of iterations of amplitude amplification is $\mathcal{O}\left(1/\sqrt{p}\right)$, hence the top line. The bottom line is obtained by expressing the sizes of $L_2(\vec{y}_1)$ and $L_3(\vec{y}_1)$ using Proposition 6.   □

Subroutine Complexity.

Proposition 14 (*FindAllSolutionsWithinFilter* quantum 3-sieve). *Let $|L_1|$ a list size and C a 3×3 configuration matrix with negative non-diagonal entries. Algorithm 6 solves* $\mathbf{FAS}_3^q(|L_1|, C)$ *in time* $|Sol| \cdot (T_2 + T_3) \cdot T_{AA}$ *where*

$$|Sol| = |L_1|^3 \cdot \det(C)^{d/2}$$

$$T_2 = (1 - C_{12})^{-d/4} \quad ; \quad T_3 = (1 - C_{13})^{-d/4}$$

$$T_{AA} = \mathcal{O}\left(\sqrt{|L_i^3|/|Sol|} \cdot (1 - C_{12})^{d/4}(1 - C_{13})^{d/4}\right)$$

After simplification, the time complexity of Algorithm 6 can be written

$$T(\mathbf{FAS}_3^q(|L_1|, C)) = \sqrt{|L_i|^3 \cdot |Sol|} \cdot \left((1 - C_{12}^2)^{d/2} + (1 - C_{13}^2)^{d/2}\right).$$

This algorithm uses classical memory $|L_1|$ *and quantum memory* poly(d) *qubits.*

Complexity of the Quantum 3-Sieve. The above was the analysis of the algorithm we use as the subroutine **FindAllSolutionsWithinFilter** in Algorithm 3 for quantum 3-sieve. The lists given in input of Algorithm 6 are then the lists of residual vectors R_1, R_2, R_3, which are of size $|R_1| = |L_1| = |L| \cdot \mathcal{V}(\alpha)$; and it return residual vectors that satisfy the target configuration $C'(\alpha)$. Using Theorem 2 in the case $k = 3$, we recover the overall time complexity of our quantum 3-sieve algorithm.

Theorem 5. *There is a quantum algorithm with parameter α that solves the 3-sieve problem for a configuration $C \in \mathbb{R}^{3\times 3}$ and lists of size $|L|$, that runs in time*

$$T = \mathcal{O}\left(NbRep_{\alpha,C}\left(|L| + \frac{1}{\mathcal{V}(\alpha)} \cdot T(\mathbf{FAS}_3^q(|L_1|, C'(\alpha)))\right)\right)$$

where $|L_1| = |L| \cdot \mathcal{V}(\alpha)$ and $T(\mathbf{FAS}_3^q(|L_1|, C'(\alpha)))$ given by Proposition 14. This algorithm uses quantum-accessible classical memory $M = |L|$ and quantum memory poly(d).

Minimal Memory Parameters.

Proposition 15. *There is a quantum algorithm that solves SVP in dimension d using 3-sieve that runs in time $T = 2^{0.3098d+o(d)}$, quantum-accessible classical memory $M = 2^{0.1887d+o(d)}$ and poly(d) quantum memory.*

Proof. We take a balanced configuration C with $C_{12} = C_{13} = C_{23} = -1/3$, $\alpha = 1.2343$rad and $|L| = 2^{0.1887d} = M$. We apply Proposition 5: We write $C'_{12}(\alpha) = C'_{13}(\alpha) = C'_{23}(\alpha) \approx -0.31$ and $|L_1| = |L| \cdot \mathcal{V}(\alpha) = 2^{0.1055d}$. We have

$$\text{NbRep}_{\alpha,C} = 2^{0.1055d} \quad ; \quad \frac{1}{\mathcal{V}(\alpha)} = 2^{0.0832d} \quad ; \quad T(\mathbf{FAS}_3^q(|L_1|, C')) = 2^{0.1210d}.$$

Putting everything together, we indeed have a running time of $2^{0.1055d} \cdot 2^{0.0832d} \cdot 2^{0.1210d} = 2^{0.3098d}$. □

Space-Time Trade-Offs. We also extend this algorithm where we fix the available memory to something more than the minimal memory $2^{0.1887d}$ (Table 4).

Table 4. Time complexity of our quantum 3-sieving algorithm for a fixed memory constraint. α is the optimal angle used in the prefiltering. Also see Fig. 3a for a plot corresponding to this algorithm.

$\log_2(\text{Memory})/d$	0.1887	0.189	0.190	0.1907
$\log_2(\text{Time})/d$	0.3098	0.3073	0.3056	0.3053
α (rad)	1.2346	1.2341	1.2336	1.2331

6.2   Quantum 4-Sieve

This algorithm and its analysis are very similar to Algorithm 6. As previously, we first analyse the complexity to find one solution during one single iteration from the while-loop.

Complexity of Algorithm 7.

Initialization. Lists L_i for $i = 1, 2, 3, 4$ are assumed stored classically and quantumly accessible, so we can construct the state $|\psi_{L_1}\rangle |\psi_{L_2}\rangle |\psi_{L_3}\rangle |\psi_{L_4}\rangle$.

Grover Over the Second Register. The algorithm applies Grover's algorithm over the second register such that the two first registers become

$$|\psi_{L_1}\rangle |\psi_{L_2(\vec{y}_1)}\rangle = \frac{1}{\sqrt{|L_1|}} \frac{1}{\sqrt{|L_2(\vec{y}_1)|}} \sum_{\vec{y}_1 \in L_1} \sum_{\vec{y}_2 \in L_2(\vec{y}_1)} |\vec{y}_1\rangle |\vec{y}_2\rangle,$$

which takes time $\sqrt{\frac{|L_2|}{|L_2(\vec{y}_1)|}} = (1 - C_{12}^2)^{-d/4}$.

Algorithm 7. FindAllSolutionsWithinFilter quantum 4-sieve

Require: lists L_1, L_2, L_3, L_4 of vectors i.i.d. in $\mathcal{S}^{d-1}$ with $|L_1| = |L_2| = |L_3| = |L_4|$;
a target configuration $C \in \mathbb{R}^{4 \times 4}$.
Ensure: list L_{out} containing all 4-triples in $L_1 \times L_2 \times L_3 \times L_4$ satisfying configuration
C.

$L_{out} := \emptyset$
while $|L_{out}| < |Sol|$ **do**
$\quad$ Construct $|\psi_{L_1}\rangle |\psi_{L_2}\rangle |\psi_{L_3}\rangle |\psi_{L_4}\rangle$
$\quad$ Apply **Grover** on the second register to get state $|\psi_{L_1}\rangle |\psi_{L_2(\vec{y}_1)}\rangle |\psi_{L_3}\rangle |\psi_{L_4}\rangle$
$\quad$ Apply **Grover** on the third register to get state $|\psi_{L_1}\rangle |\psi_{L_2(\vec{y}_1)}\rangle |\psi_{L_3(\vec{y}_1,\vec{y}_2)}\rangle |\psi_{L_4}\rangle$
$\quad$ Apply **Grover** on the fourth register to get state:

$$|\psi_{L_1}\rangle |\psi_{L_2(\vec{y}_1)}\rangle |\psi_{L_3(\vec{y}_1,\vec{y}_2)}\rangle |\psi_{L_4(\vec{y}_1,\vec{y}_2)}\rangle$$

$\quad$ Apply Amplitude Amplification to get state $|\psi_{Sol}\rangle$, the uniform superposition of
all solutions
$\quad$ Take a measurement and get some $(\vec{y}_1, \vec{y}_2, \vec{y}_3, \vec{y}_4)$
$\quad$ **if** $(\vec{y}_1, \vec{y}_2, \vec{y}_3, \vec{y}_4)$ satisfies configuration C **then** add it to L_{out}
return L_{out}

Grover Over the Third Register. Another Grover's algorithm is then performed
over the third register $|\psi_{L_3}\rangle$ such that it becomes the quantum superposition
over all elements of $L_3(\vec{y}_1, \vec{y}_2)$, for $\vec{y}_1 \in L_1$ and $\vec{y}_2 \in L_2(\vec{y}_1)$ being elements
in quantum superposition in the two first registers. Let $Z = |L_1| \cdot |L_2(\vec{y}_1)| \cdot |L_3(\vec{y}_1, \vec{y}_2)|$. The three first registers then become the state

$$|\psi_{L_1}\rangle |\psi_{L_2(\vec{y}_1)}\rangle |\psi_{L_3(\vec{y}_1,\vec{y}_2)}\rangle = \frac{1}{\sqrt{Z}} \sum_{\vec{y}_1 \in L_1} \sum_{\vec{y}_2 \in L_2(\vec{y}_1)} \sum_{\vec{y}_3 \in L_3(\vec{y}_1,\vec{y}_2)} |\vec{y}_1\rangle |\vec{y}_2\rangle |\vec{y}_3\rangle \cdot$$

Performing this Grover's algorithm takes time $T_3 = \sqrt{\frac{|L_3|}{|L_3(\vec{y}_1,\vec{y}_2)|}}$. Propo-
sition 6 gives $|L_3(\vec{y}_1, \vec{y}_2)| = |L_3| \cdot \left(\frac{\det(C[1,2,3])}{\det(C[1,2])}\right)^{d/2}$. Note that these nota-
tions for partial configurations are given in Definition 4. So we can rewrite
$T_3 = \left(\frac{\det(C[1,2,3])}{\det(C[1,2])}\right)^{-d/4}$.

Grover Over the Fourth Register. Analogously to what was done over the third
register, we perform Grover's algorithm over the fourth one $|\psi_{L_4}\rangle$. For $Z' = |L_1| \cdot |L_2(\vec{y}_1)| \cdot |L_3(\vec{y}_1, \vec{y}_2)| \cdot |L_4(\vec{y}_1, \vec{y}_2)|$, this operation allows to construct the
state $|\psi_{L_1}\rangle |\psi_{L_2(\vec{y}_1)}\rangle |\psi_{L_3(\vec{y}_1,\vec{y}_2)}\rangle |\psi_{L_4(\vec{y}_1,\vec{y}_2)}\rangle$ equal to

$$\frac{1}{\sqrt{Z'}} \sum_{\vec{y}_1 \in L_1} \sum_{\vec{y}_2 \in L_2(\vec{y}_1)} \sum_{\vec{y}_3 \in L_3(\vec{y}_1,\vec{y}_2)} \sum_{\vec{y}_4 \in L_4(\vec{y}_1,\vec{y}_2)} |\vec{y}_1\rangle |\vec{y}_2\rangle |\vec{y}_3\rangle |\vec{y}_4\rangle,$$

in time $T_4 = \left(\frac{\det(C[1,2,4])}{\det(C[1,2])}\right)^{-d/4}$.

Amplitude Amplification. We then want to construct a uniform quantum superposition over all elements of the set of solutions $Sol := \{(\vec{y}_1, \vec{y}_2, \vec{y}_3, \vec{y}_4) \in L_1 \times L_2 \times L_3 \times L_4 \text{ satisfying } C\}$, by applying a quantum amplitude amplification.

Lemma 9. *The operation* $|0\rangle |0\rangle |0\rangle |0\rangle \rightarrow |\psi_{L_1}\rangle |\psi_{L_2(\vec{y}_1)}\rangle |\psi_{L_3(\vec{y}_1, \vec{y}_2)}\rangle |\psi_{L_4(\vec{y}_1, \vec{y}_2)}\rangle$ *is repeated* T_{AA} *times inside the amplitude amplification to construct state* $|\psi_{Sol}\rangle$ *(with probability* $1 - o(1))$*, where*

$$T_{AA} = \sqrt{\frac{|L_1|}{|Sol|}} \sqrt{|L_2(\vec{y}_1)|} \sqrt{|L_3(\vec{y}_1, \vec{y}_2)|} \sqrt{|L_4(\vec{y}_1, \vec{y}_2)|}$$

$$= \frac{|L_i|^2}{\sqrt{|Sol|}} \cdot (1 - C_{12}^2)^{d/4} \cdot \left(\frac{\det(C[1,2,3])}{\det(C[1,2])} \right)^{d/4} \cdot \left(\frac{\det(C[1,2,4])}{\det(C[1,2])} \right)^{d/4}$$

where notation $C[I]$ *with a set of indexes* I *was introduced in Definition 4.*

Proof. The reasoning is the same as for the proof of Lemma 8. Performing a measurement of state $|\psi_{L_1}\rangle |\psi_{L_2(\vec{y}_1)}\rangle |\psi_{L_3(\vec{y}_1, \vec{y}_2)}\rangle |\psi_{L_4(\vec{y}_1, \vec{y}_2)}\rangle$ gives a 4-tuple solution $(\vec{y}_1, \vec{y}_2, \vec{y}_3, \vec{y}_4)$ with some probability p, we are going to specify. The probability of measuring a good $\vec{y}_1$ is $|Sol|/|L_1|$. Then given a $\vec{y}_1$, a triple $(\vec{y}_2, \vec{y}_3, \vec{y}_4)$ forms the solution together with $\vec{y}_1$ with probability $1/(|L_2(\vec{y}_1)| \cdot |L_3(\vec{y}_1, \vec{y}_2)| \cdot |L_4(\vec{y}_1, \vec{y}_2)|)$.

Finally, the probability of success to measure a solution is thus $p = \frac{|Sol|}{|L_1|} \cdot 1/ (|L_2(\vec{y}_1)| \cdot |L_3(\vec{y}_1, \vec{y}_2)| \cdot |L_4(\vec{y}_1, \vec{y}_2)|)$. By Theorem 3, the number of iterations of amplitude amplification is $\mathcal{O}\left(1/\sqrt{p}\right)$, hence the top line. The bottom line is obtained by expressing the sizes of $L_2(\vec{y}_1)$, $L_3(\vec{y}_1, \vec{y}_2)$ and $L_4(\vec{y}_1, \vec{y}_2)$ using Proposition 6.   □

Measurement gives a 4-tuple $(\vec{y}_1, \vec{y}_2, \vec{y}_3, \vec{y}_4)$ solution to the configuration problem. We need to repeat this whole process until we find all the solutions at number $|Sol|$.

Notice that the same operations are performed over L_3 and over L_4, which implies that an optimal configuration will necessarily respect the symmetry $C_{13} = C_{14}$ and $C_{23} = C_{24}$.

In the end, this subroutine **FindAllSolutionsWithinFilter** runs in time

$$T(\mathbf{FAS}_4^q) = |Sol| \cdot (T_2 + T_3 + T_4) \cdot T_{AA},$$

and this leads to the following theorem.

Proposition 16. *Given lists* $L_1, L_2, L_3, L_4 \subset \mathcal{S}^{d-1}$ *of same size* $|L_i|$ *with i.i.d. uniformly random vectors, and a configuration* $C \in \mathbb{R}^{4 \times 4}$ *with* $C_{13} = C_{14}$ *and* $C_{23} = C_{24}$*, there exists an algorithm that finds all the* $|Sol|$ *4-tuples in* $L_1 \times L_2 \times L_3 \times L_4$ *satisfying configuration* C *in time*

$$T(\mathbf{FAS}_4^q) = |L_i|^2 \sqrt{|Sol|} \left(\left(\frac{1}{1 - C_{12}^2} \right)^{d/2} + \left(\frac{\det(C[1,2,3])}{1 - C_{12}^2} \right)^{d/4} \right).$$

Complexity of the Quantum 4-Sieve. The above was the analysis of the quantum 4-sieve after the prefiltering. We use this algorithm as the subroutine in our framework for $k = 4$. Using Theorem 2 in this case, we recover the overall time complexity of our quantum 4-sieve algorithm.

Theorem 6. *There is a quantum algorithm with parameter α that solves the 3-sieve problem for a configuration C and lists of size $|L|$ that runs in time T with*

$$T = \mathcal{O}\left(NbRep_{\alpha,C} \left(|L| + \frac{1}{\mathcal{V}(\alpha)} T(\boldsymbol{FAS}_4^q(|L_1|, C'(\alpha))) \right) \right)$$

and uses quantum-accessible classical memory $M = |L|$ and quantum memory poly(d), and where $|L_1| = |L| \cdot \mathcal{V}(\alpha)$ and $T(\boldsymbol{FAS}_4^q(|L_1|, C'(\alpha)))$ given by Proposition 16.

Minimal Memory Parameters.

Proposition 17. *There is a quantum algorithm that solves SVP in dimension d using 4-sieve that runs in time $T = 2^{0.3276d+o(d)}$ using quantum-accessible classical memory $M = 2^{0.1724d+o(d)}$ and quantum memory poly(d).*

Proof. We take a balanced configuration C with $C_{i,j} = -1/4$ for $i \neq j$, $\alpha \approx 1.3131$rad and $|L| = 2^{0.1724d} = M$. We apply Theorem 6: We write $C'_{i,j} \approx -0.244$ for $i \neq j$ and $|L_1| = |L| \cdot \mathcal{V}(\alpha) = 2^{0.124d}$. We have

$$NbRep_{\alpha,C} = 2^{0.1069d} \quad ; \quad \frac{1}{\mathcal{V}(\alpha)} = 2^{0.0484d} \quad ; \quad T(\boldsymbol{FAS}_4^q(|L_1|, C')) = 2^{0.1722d}.$$

Putting everything together, we indeed have a running time of $2^{0.1069d} \cdot 2^{0.0484d} \cdot 2^{0.1722d} = 2^{0.3276d}$. □

Time-Optimizing Parameters.

Proposition 18. *There exists an algorithm that solves SVP in dimension d in time $T = 2^{0.3120d+o(d)}$ using quantum-accessible classical memory $M = 2^{0.1813d+o(d)}$ and quantum memory poly(d).*

Proof. We take a configuration C with $C_{12} \approx -0.3859$, $C_{13} = C_{14} \approx -0.2294$, $C_{23} = C_{24} \approx -0.2297$ and $C_{34} \approx -0.1998$. We take $\alpha \approx 1.313$rad and $|L| = 2^{0.1813d} = M$. We apply Proposition 6: We write $C'_{12} \approx -0.3859$, $C'_{13} = C'_{14} \approx -0.2210$, $C'_{23} = C'_{24} \approx -0.2215$ and $C'_{34} \approx -0.1892$. We set $|L_1| = |L| \cdot \mathcal{V}(\alpha) = 2^{0.1259d}$. We have

$$NbRep_{\alpha,C} = 2^{0.1254d} \quad ; \quad \frac{1}{\mathcal{V}(\alpha)} = 2^{0.0554d} \quad ; \quad \boldsymbol{FAS}_4^q(|L_1|, C') = 2^{0.1312d}.$$

Putting everything together, we indeed have a running time of $2^{0.1254d} \cdot 2^{0.0554d} \cdot 2^{0.1312d} = 2^{0.3120d}$ (Table 5). □

Table 5. Time complexity of our quantum 4-sieving algorithm for a fixed memory constraint. For the prefiltering, we have an optimal $\alpha \approx 1.3131$rad. Also see Fig. 3b for a plot corresponding to this algorithm.

$\log_2(\text{Memory})/d$	0.1724	0.175	0.180	0.1813
$\log_2(\text{Time})/d$	0.3276	0.3153	0.3127	0.3120

Code Used for Our Results. All our results have been obtained using Sage-Math and the code is available on https://github.com/johanna-loyer/3-4-sieve.

References

[Bec+16] Becker, A., Ducas, L., Gama, N., Laarhoven, T.: New directions in nearest neighbor searching with applications to lattice sieving. In: Proceedings of the 2016 Annual ACM-SIAM Symposium on Discrete Algorithms (2016)

[BLS16] Bai, S., Laarhoven, T., Stehlé, D.: Tuple lattice sieving. LMS J. Comput. Math. **19**, 146–162 (2016)

[Bon+22] Bonnetain, X., Chailloux, A., Schrottenloher, A., Shen, Y.: Finding many collisions via reusable quantum walks (2022)

[Bos+18] Bos, J., et al.:. CRYSTALS-Kyber: a CCA-secure module-lattice-based KEM. IEEE (2018)

[Bra+02] Brassard, G., Hoeyer, P., Mosca, M., Tapp, A.: Quantum amplitude amplification and estimation. In: Quantum Computation and Quantum Information: A Millennium, vol. 305, pp. 53–74 (2002)

[CL21] Chailloux, A., Loyer, J.: Lattice sieving via quantum random walks. In: Tibouchi, M., Wang, H. (eds.) ASIACRYPT 2021. LNCS, vol. 13093, pp. 63–91. Springer, Cham (2021). https://doi.org/10.1007/978-3-030-92068-5_3

[Duc+19] Ducas, L.: Crystals-dilithium, algorithm specifications and supporting documentation. NIST (2019)

[FP85] Fincke, U., Pohst, M.: Improved methods for calculating vectors of short length in a lattice. Math. Comput. **44**(170), 463–471 (1985)

[Gro96] Grover, L.: A fast quantum mechanical algorithm for database search. In: Proceedings of the 28th Annual ACM Symposium on the Theory of Computing STOC, pp. 212–219 (1996)

[Hei21] Heiser, M.: Improved quantum hypercone locality sensitive filtering in lattice sieving. preprint (2021)

[HK17] Herold, G., Kirshanova, E.: Improved algorithms for the approximate k-list problem in Euclidean norm. In: Fehr, S. (ed.) PKC 2017. LNCS, vol. 10174, pp. 16–40. Springer, Heidelberg (2017). https://doi.org/10.1007/978-3-662-54365-8_2

[HKL18] Herold, G., Kirshanova, E., Laarhoven, T.: Speed-ups and time–memory trade-offs for tuple lattice sieving. In: Abdalla, M., Dahab, R. (eds.) PKC 2018. LNCS, vol. 10769, pp. 407–436. Springer, Cham (2018). https://doi.org/10.1007/978-3-319-76578-5_14

[Kan83] Kannan, R.: Improved algorithms for integer programming and related lattice problems. In: Proceedings of the 15th Symposium on the Theory of Computing (STOC), ACM Press, pp. 99–108 (1983)

[Kir+19] Kirshanova, E., Mårtensson, E., Postlethwaite, E.W., Moulik, S.R.: Quantum algorithms for the approximate k-list problem and their application to lattice sieving. In: Galbraith, S.D., Moriai, S. (eds.) ASIACRYPT 2019. LNCS, vol. 11921, pp. 521–551. Springer, Cham (2019). https://doi.org/10.1007/978-3-030-34578-5_19

[Kle00] Klein, P.: Finding the closest lattice vector when it's unusually close. SODA, pp. 937–941 (2000)

[Laa16] Laarhoven, T.: Search problems in cryptography, from fingerprinting to lattice sieving (2016)

[MV10] Micciancio, D., Voulgaris, P.: Faster exponential time algorithms for the shortest vector problem. SODA, pp. 1468–1480 (2010)

[NV08] Nguyen, P.Q., Vidick, T.: Sieve algorithms for the shortest vector problem are practical. J. Math. Crypt. **2**, 181–207 (2008)

[Poh81] Pohst, M.E.: On the computation of lattice vectors of minimal length, successive minima and reduced bases with applications. ACM SIGSAM Bull. **15**(1), 37–44 (1981)

NTRU in Quaternion Algebras of Bounded Discriminant

Cong Ling and Andrew Mendelsohn[✉]

Department of EEE, Imperial College London, London SW7 2AZ, UK
{c.ling,andrew.mendelsohn18}@imperial.ac.uk

Abstract. The NTRU assumption provides one of the most prominent problems on which to base post-quantum cryptography. Because of the efficiency and security of NTRU-style schemes, structured variants have been proposed, using modules. In this work, we create a structured form of NTRU using lattices obtained from orders in cyclic division algebras of index 2, that is, from quaternion algebras. We present a public-key encryption scheme, and show that its public keys are statistically close to uniform. We then prove IND-CPA security of a variant of our scheme when the discriminant of the quaternion algebra is not too large, assuming the hardness of Learning with Errors in cyclic division algebras.

Keywords: post-quantum cryptography · NTRU · quaternion algebras

1 Introduction

NTRU schemes provide one of the most efficient post-quantum cryptographic frameworks. While attacks such as lattice reduction can be used, known attacks are ineffective against NTRU with well-chosen parameters. This absence of decisive attacks against well-chosen parameters over a long period of time has led NTRU to have a prominent place in the geography of post-quantum cryptography. This is illustrated by two NTRU-based schemes reaching the third round of NIST's post-quantum standardization effort [13,19]. Moreover, partial security reductions for NTRU have been given in [18,46], lending further weight to NTRU as a platform for cryptography.

The NTRU problem can be formulated as follows: if f and g are 'short' ring elements, and $h := g \cdot f^{-1}$, find (f, g) from $h \bmod q$, for some modulus $q \in \mathbb{Z}$. Typical choices of rings are polynomial rings of the form $\mathbb{Z}[x]/(x^p - 1)$, $\mathbb{Z}[x]/(x^{2^k} + 1)$, and $\mathbb{Z}[x]/(x^p - x - 1)$ [9,19,24]. These enjoy fast algorithms for multiplication and low storage requirements. Moreover, a simple public-key encryption scheme can be based on the hardness of the NTRU problem.

The cryptanalytic history of NTRU is lengthy, beginning with lattice reduction attacks [17] and including meet-in-the-middle attacks [27], hybrid attacks [25], attacks based on decryption failures [26], and subfield attacks [2]. These often exploit particular design choices of specific NTRU schemes (such as a choice of ternary secrets, or an 'overstretched' choice of modulus, or the use of rings with many subrings), and hence these weak(er) instances or parameters can be avoided by careful design. As a result, after 25 years of cryptanalysis, the NTRU assumption remains a trusted basis for cryptography.

The reliability and speed of NTRU has also prompted work exploring alternatively structured variants of NTRU [15,16]. Whereas NTRU uses multiplication of elements in polynomial rings, these constructions use operations in modules over polynomial rings, and aim to instantiate efficient and compact NTRU schemes while enabling greater flexibility with parameter choices. However, neither of [15,16] give a full proof of security: in [16], it is shown that module NTRU public keys are (asymptotically) close to uniform, if the modulus factors into only two prime ideals in the ring - yet the scheme uses primes which completely split in the ring; and the authors of [15] give no such proof.

Our Contributions. In this work we study the NTRU problem in the context of quaternion algebras over number fields. In particular, we define NTRU in cyclic division algebras (CDAs) when the ring of scalars (the 'center') of the algebra is a cyclotomic field with power of two conductor. We call this NTRU variant 'CNTRU'. The dimension of these algebras over their center is a square, d^2, and the positive square-root of this dimension, d, is called the index of the algebra. When the index is 1, the CDA is equal to its center, and so in our case is a cyclotomic field; when the index is 2, the CDA is called a quaternion algebra. These quaternion algebras enjoy particularly nice properties (see e.g. [56]) and the proof of our main result on the uniformity of our NTRU public keys appears to fail when $d > 2$. This is because when $d = 2$ and the center is a cyclotomic field of power-of-two conductor, the number of roots of unity in the CDAs used equals the dimension of certain lattices $\mathcal{L}$ concerned, so letting λ_i denote the ith successive minimum of a lattice $\mathcal{L}$, we have $\lambda_1(\mathcal{L}) = \lambda_{[\mathcal{L}:\mathbb{Z}]}(\mathcal{L})$ and can make use of results such as Lemma 3; when $d > 2$, we can no longer apply such lemmas.

The specific algebras in which we consider our NTRU variant are constructed as follows: let m be a prime power, $K = \mathbb{Q}(\zeta_m)$ be a cyclotomic field of conductor m, and $M = \mathbb{Q}(\zeta_{\ell m})$, for some prime ℓ such that $\ell \equiv 1 \bmod m$ and $\ell \not\equiv 1 \bmod pm$ for any prime divisor p of m. Then M/K is cyclic Galois, with Galois group generated by (say) σ. Let L be the intermediate field fixed by σ^2; this can be written explicitly as $L = \mathbb{Q}(\zeta_m, \sqrt{\ell})$ when m is a power of two. Set u to be an element such that $u^2 = \zeta_m$ and $ux = \theta(x)u$ for all $x \in L$, where $\mathrm{Gal}(L/K) = \langle \theta \rangle$. Then $\mathcal{A} = (L/K, \theta, \zeta_m) = L + uL$ is a quaternion algebra. We define $\Lambda := \mathcal{O}_L + u\mathcal{O}_L$ and $\Lambda_q := \Lambda/q\Lambda$ for some prime q. We denote the units of Λ_q by $\Lambda_q^\times$, and the center of Λ by $\mathcal{Z}(\Lambda)$. We then prove, for these quaternion algebras,

Theroem 4. Let $\epsilon > 0$, q be a completely split prime, $p \in \mathcal{Z}(\Lambda_q^\times)$, and $\sigma \geq 4n^{3/2}\sqrt[4]{\ell}\sqrt{2\ln(32nq)}q^{\frac{1}{2}+2\epsilon}$. Let $y_i \in \Lambda_q$ and $z_i = -y_i p^{-1} \bmod q$ for $i = 1, 2$, and $D_{\sigma,z_i}^\times$ denote $D_{\Lambda,\sigma}$ restricted by rejection to $\Lambda_q^\times + z_i$. Then when $d = 2$,

$$\Delta\left(\frac{y_1 + pD_{\sigma,z_1}^\times}{y_2 + pD_{\sigma,z_2}^\times} \bmod q, U\left(\Lambda_q^\times\right)\right) \leq 2^{22n}q^{-8n\epsilon}.$$

To achieve this, we prove a number of new results on q-ary lattices obtained from orders in CDAs (of a particular form). These results can be stated for any $d \geq 1$, but we restrict them to the case of interest, $d = 2$.

We then proceed to study algorithms to encrypt and decrypt messages based on the NTRU problem in these quaternion algebras. We prove that if there is an efficient indistinguishability-under-chosen-plaintext attack (IND-CPA) algorithm for CNTRU, there is an algorithm with non-negligible advantage for decision CLWE [21], a structured form of learning with errors (LWE) in CDAs. The uniformity of CNTRU public keys (over invertible elements) forms a crucial part of the proof of this result. Moreover, this connection is in part a motivation for the particular CDAs we define NTRU over: the existence of a security proof for CLWE in these particular algebras linking SIVP on lattices obtained from ideals of Λ to CLWE allows us to link SIVP and NTRU, too (it should be noted that the reduction from SIVP to CLWE holds for a (slightly) restricted space of secrets). We obtain

Lemma 1. *Let $n \geq 8$ be a power of 2, $d = 2$, $\ell \leq Cn$, and $q \geq 8n$ a prime such that $x^n + 1$ splits completely modulo q. Let $\delta > 0$, $p \in \mathcal{Z}\left(\Lambda_q^\times\right)$ and $\sigma \geq 2n^{3/2}\sqrt[4]{\ell}\sqrt{\ln(32nq)}q^{\frac{1}{2}+2\epsilon}$ satisfy the conditions of Lemma 18 and Theorem 4. If there exists an IND-CPA attack algorithm $\mathcal{A}$ against CNTRU, running in time T with advantage δ, then there exists an algorithm to solve decision-CLWE$_{\mathrm{HNF}}^\times$ that runs in time $T' = T + O(\mathrm{poly}(n))$ with success probability $\delta' = \delta - q^{-\Omega(n)}$.*

Note the condition $\ell \leq Cn$ for a constant C: we impose a bound on ℓ in order to allow for a precise statement on the correctness of the decryption algorithm (see Lemma 18). This is necessary because of the form of L. Consider the square of field element $1 + \sqrt{\ell}$; this is an element of small ℓ_2-norm when using $1, \sqrt{\ell}$ as a basis of L/K, but its square, $1 + \ell + 2\sqrt{\ell}$, may potentially be large indeed, if ℓ is large. This constraint amounts to a bound on the discriminant of the quaternion algebra, which has discriminant which we bound by $(n\sqrt{\ell})^{4n}$ (Lemma 2); when $\ell \leq Cn$, this becomes a function solely in $n = [K : \mathbb{Q}]$.

In practice, we have not found this imposition difficult to satisfy for small values of C. The interested reader is directed to [21, §3.4] and Appendix B of this paper for further discussion on parameter selection.

We also sketch a KEM and a signature scheme based on NTRU in CDAs in the appendix, to give examples of greater functionality from CNTRU (Table 1).

Table 1. Comparison of Cyclotomic NTRU Variants

	Cyclotomic NTRU [57]	ModFalcon [16]	This work
Ambient space	$\mathbb{Q}(\zeta_n)$, any n	$\mathbb{Q}(\zeta_{2^r})^2$	$\mathcal{A} = L \oplus uL, L = \mathbb{Q}(\zeta_{2^r}, \sqrt{\ell})$
$\mathbb{Z}$-Dimension	$\varphi(n)$	2^r	2^{r+1}
Recommended q	$q \equiv 1 \bmod n$	$q \equiv 1 \bmod 2^r$	q completely split in L
Provably secure q	$q \equiv 1 \bmod n$	$q \equiv 3 \bmod 8$	q completely split in L

Previous Work. There have been many algebraic variants of NTRU proposed over the years: in CTRU [20], the usual polynomials were replaced with elements from the ring $\mathbb{F}_2[T][X]/(X^n - 1)$; this was later subjected to a polynomial-time attack in [33], which also introduced NTRU over the Gaussian Integers. This idea was expanded by [41] and [51], which introduced NTRU over the Eisenstein integers (ETRU) and the ring of integers of $\mathbb{Q}(\sqrt{-7})$ (KTRU) respectively. More details on ETRU can be found in [40] and [29]. A version of NTRU using ideal lattices can be found in [30], an attempt to secure CTRU can be found in [4], and an attempt to further secure ETRU can be found in [5].

There have also been more exotic attempts to improve NTRU: some of these include non-commutative variants such as [6,35,53,54]; NTRU over group rings in [58]; non-associative schemes in [34] and [52]; and a variant with different invertibility conditions in [7]. A useful comparison of some of these schemes can be found in [47]. An overview of NTRU can be found in [50].

Despite this flood of NTRU variants, we note that few of them generalise NTRU, in the sense that they do not offer a broader framework from which the traditional form of NTRU can emerge; rather, they simply replace the underlying ring, or make other subtle amendments. Two papers [15,16] do develop general (module) versions of NTRU; these are compared to the construction featured in this paper below. Finally, we note recent works [10,18,46] which provide reductions between various (module) NTRU problems, and also module LWE.

Paper Organization. In the next section we state the mathematical background necessary for the rest of the paper. In Sect. 3 we introduce NTRU, in Sect. 4 CDAs, and combine these in Sect. 5. We then begin the mathematical work of the paper: Sect. 6 is dedicated to q-ary lattices obtained from CDAs, Sect. 7 to the CNTRU key generation algorithm, Sect. 8 to proving IND-CPA security of CNTRU (subject to the CLWE assumption). In the appendix we give possible parameters and sketch a KEM and signature scheme.

2   Preliminaries

Lattices. An n-dimensional lattice is a discrete additive subgroup of $\mathbb{R}^n$. One can consider a lattice $\mathcal{L}$ to be the set of integer linear combinations of a set of vectors $B = \{\mathbf{b}_1, \ldots, \mathbf{b}_k\}$ that are linearly independent, for some $k \leq n$, written $\mathcal{L}(B) = \left\{ \sum_{i=1}^{k} z_i \mathbf{b}_i : z_i \in \mathbb{Z} \right\}$. All lattices in this work will have $k = n$.

Definition 1. Let $\mathcal{L}$ be a lattice, and $\mathbb{R}^n$ be endowed with inner product $\langle \cdot, \cdot \rangle$. Then the set $\mathcal{L}^* = \{v \in \mathbb{R}^n : \langle \mathcal{L}, v \rangle \subset \mathbb{Z}\}$ is called the *dual lattice* of $\mathcal{L}$.

Recall $\lambda_i(\mathcal{L})$, the 'ith successive minimum of $\mathcal{L}$', is the minimum length of a set of i linearly independent vectors in $\mathcal{L}$, where the length of a set of vectors $\{\mathbf{x}_1, \ldots, \mathbf{x}_n\}$ is $\max_i (\|\mathbf{x}_i\|)$, for some norm $\|\cdot\|$.

Discrete Gaussians. For vector space $V \subset \mathbb{R}^n$ equipped with (Euclidean) norm $\|\cdot\|$, $\mathbf{c} \in V$, and $r > 0$, we define the *Gaussian function* $\rho_{r,c} : V \to (0, 1]$ by $\rho_{r,c}(\boldsymbol{x}) = \exp\left(-\pi\|\boldsymbol{x} - \mathbf{c}\|/r^2\right)$. If $\mathbf{c} = \mathbf{0}$, we write ρ_r.

The spherical Gaussian distribution D_r over $\mathbb{R}^n$ outputs a vector $\mathbf{v}$ with probability proportional to $\rho_r(\mathbf{v})$, and an elliptical Gaussian $D_{\mathbf{r}}$ can be sampled as follows: fix a basis $\mathbf{b}_1, \ldots, \mathbf{b}_n$ of $\mathbb{R}^n$, and a vector $\mathbf{r} = (r_1, \ldots, r_n)$. Sample $x_i \leftarrow D_{r_i}$ (independently for $i \neq j$) and output $\sum_{i=1}^n x_i \mathbf{b}_i$.

The discrete Gaussian distribution $D_{\mathcal{L}, r, \mathbf{c}}$, defined over a lattice $\mathcal{L}$, outputs $\mathbf{x}$ with probability $\frac{\rho_{r,c}(\mathbf{x})}{\rho_{r,c}(\mathcal{L})}$ for each $\mathbf{x} \in \mathcal{L}$.

The *smoothing parameter*, defined below, will be used throughout this work:

Definition 2. Let $\mathcal{L}$ be a lattice and $\varepsilon > 0$. Then the *smoothing parameter* $\eta_\varepsilon(\mathcal{L})$ of $\mathcal{L}$ is the smallest $r > 0$ such that $\rho_{1/r}(\mathcal{L}^* \setminus \{\mathbf{0}\}) \leq \varepsilon$.

We will use the following bounds on the smoothing parameter:

Lemma 2 *[44, Lemma 3.5]. For any full-rank lattice $\mathcal{L} \subseteq \mathbb{R}^n$ and $\epsilon \in (0, 1)$, we have $\eta_\epsilon(\mathcal{L}) \leq \sqrt{\ln(2n(1 + 1/\epsilon))/\pi} \cdot \frac{1}{\lambda_1^\infty(\mathcal{L}^*)}$.*

Lemma 3 *[37, Lemma 3.3]. For any full-rank lattice $\mathcal{L} \subseteq \mathbb{R}^n$ and $\epsilon \in (0, 1)$, we have $\eta_\epsilon(\mathcal{L}) \leq \sqrt{\ln(2n(1 + 1/\epsilon))/\pi} \cdot \lambda_n(\mathcal{L})$.*

The *statistical distance* between distributions D, D' over a discrete set S is denoted $\Delta(D, D') = \frac{1}{2} \sum_{x \in S} |D(x) - D'(x)|$. We also need the following lemmas:

Lemma 4 *[37, Lemma 4.1]. For a lattice $\mathcal{L}$ over $\mathbb{R}^n$, $\varepsilon > 0$, $r \geq \eta_\varepsilon(\mathcal{L})$, and $\boldsymbol{x} \in \mathbb{R}^n$, the statistical distance between $(D_r + \boldsymbol{x}) \bmod \mathcal{L}$ and the uniform distribution modulo $\mathcal{L}$ is bounded above by $\varepsilon/2$. Equivalently, $\rho_r(\mathcal{L} + \boldsymbol{x}) \in \left[\frac{1-\varepsilon}{1+\varepsilon}, 1\right] \cdot \rho_r(\mathcal{L})$*

Lemma 5 *[14, Theorem 1]. For any positive definite Σ, vector $\mathbf{c}$, lattice coset $A := \Lambda + \mathbf{a} \subset \mathbf{c} + \mathrm{span}(\Sigma)$, and injective linear transformation $\mathbf{T}$, we have*

$$\mathbf{T}\left(D_{A, \sqrt{\Sigma}, \mathbf{c}}\right) = D_{\mathbf{T}A, \mathbf{T}\sqrt{\Sigma}, \mathbf{T}\mathbf{c}}.$$

Lemma 6 *[37, Lemma 4.4]. For any full-rank lattice $\mathcal{L} \subseteq \mathbb{R}^n$, $\mathbf{c} \in \mathbb{R}^n$, $\delta \in (0, 1)$ and $\sigma \geq \eta_\delta(\mathcal{L})$, we have $\mathrm{Pr}_{\boldsymbol{b} \leftarrow D_{\mathcal{L}, \sigma, \mathbf{c}}}[\|\boldsymbol{b}\| \geq \sigma\sqrt{n}] \leq \frac{1+\delta}{1-\delta}2^{-n}$.*

Number Fields. A number field is a finite field-extension of $\mathbb{Q}$. We will be especially interested in cyclotomic fields, $\mathbb{Q}(\zeta_n)$, where ζ_n is such that the smallest integer m such that $\zeta_n^m = 1$ is $m = n$. In this setting the degree $[\mathbb{Q}(\zeta_n) : \mathbb{Q}] = \varphi(n)$, where φ is the totient function. We recall that $\varphi(p^r) = p^{r-1}(p-1)$.

A degree-n number field K is Galois over $\mathbb{Q}$ if the set of K-automorphisms fixing $\mathbb{Q}$ pointwise, $\mathrm{Gal}(K/\mathbb{Q})$, forms a group. The automorphisms $\sigma_i \in \mathrm{Gal}(K/\mathbb{Q})$ extend to embeddings $\sigma_i : K \hookrightarrow \mathbb{C}$. Using these embeddings, we embed $K \hookrightarrow \mathbb{C}^n$ via $\sigma_K : x \mapsto (\sigma_1(x), ..., \sigma_n(x))$. Defining a space $H = \{x \in \mathbb{C}^n : x_i = \overline{x_{n-i}} \text{ for } i \in [n]\}$, we have $\sigma_K(K) \subset H$, and $\mathbb{R}^n \cong H$ as an inner product space. Thus the image of any discrete additive subgroup of K under σ_K can be considered a lattice. The map σ_K is called the *canonical embedding*. These definitions extend straightforwardly to a finite extension of number fields L/K.

An alternative way to embed a Galois number field into $\mathbb{R}^n$ is to write $K = \mathbb{Q}(\alpha)$ for some element α and writing $x = x_1\alpha + ... + x_n\alpha^n$ for $x \in K, x_i \in \mathbb{Q}$. The element x can then be mapped to $(x_1, ..., x_n) \in \mathbb{R}^n$. This is called the *coefficient embedding* of x, denoted $\mathrm{coeff}(x)$.

Any Galois number field K contains a subring called the ring of integers of the field, which consists of the field elements which are the root of a monic polynomial with integral coefficients. We denote this subring $\mathcal{O}_K$. For any ideal $\mathcal{I}$ of $\mathcal{O}_K$, we define the dual ideal $\mathcal{I}^\vee = \{x \in K : T_{K/\mathbb{Q}}(x\mathcal{I}) \subset \mathbb{Z}\}$. Here $T_{K/\mathbb{Q}}(\cdot) = \sum_{\sigma \in \mathrm{Gal}(K/\mathbb{Q})} \sigma(\cdot)$.

Bases of Real Quadratic Extensions of Cyclotomics. We consider an extension L/K, where $K = \mathbb{Q}(\zeta_{2^r})$, $L = K(\sqrt{\ell}) = \mathbb{Q}(\zeta_{2^r}, \sqrt{\ell})$ and $\gcd(2, \ell) = 1$. With $n = [K : \mathbb{Q}]$ and $m = 2^r$, $\varphi(m) = n$. Define the *powerful basis* of $L/\mathbb{Q}$ as

$$\overrightarrow{p} = (1, \zeta_m, ..., \zeta_m^{n-1}, \sqrt{\ell}, \zeta_m\sqrt{\ell}, ..., \zeta_m^{n-1}\sqrt{\ell}).$$

We obtain a matrix from this by applying the canonical embedding to each entry:

$$\sigma_L(\overrightarrow{p}) = (\sigma_L(1), \sigma_L(\zeta_m), ..., \sigma_L(\zeta_m^{n-1}), \sigma_L(\sqrt{\ell}), \sigma_L(\zeta_m\sqrt{\ell}), ..., \sigma_L(\zeta_m^{n-1}\sqrt{\ell})).$$

This is a $2n \times 2n$ matrix. To find the singular values of this matrix, we compute $\sigma_L(\overrightarrow{p})^*\sigma_L(\overrightarrow{p})$. This is diagonal with two blocks: the top left $n \times n$ diagonal entries are all equal to m, and the bottom right $n \times n$ to $m\ell$. The eigenvalues of a diagonal matrix are its non-zero entries, so the singular values of $\sigma_L(\overrightarrow{p})$ are $\sqrt{[L : \mathbb{Q}]}$, $\sqrt{[L : \mathbb{Q}]\ell}$. Denoting the largest singular value by $s_1(\overrightarrow{p})$ and the smallest by $s_{2n}(\overrightarrow{p})$, we have $s_1(\overrightarrow{p}) = \sqrt{[L : \mathbb{Q}]\ell}$, $s_{2n}(\overrightarrow{p}) = \sqrt{[L : \mathbb{Q}]}$. Since

$$\sigma_L(x) = \sigma_L(\overrightarrow{p}) \cdot \mathrm{coeff}(x),$$

for $x \in L$, we find $\|\sigma_L(x)\| \leq s_1(\overrightarrow{p})\|x\|_{\overrightarrow{p}}$, where $\|\cdot\|_{\overrightarrow{p}}$ is the norm obtained by writing x in the $\overrightarrow{p}$ basis and taking the coefficient embedding. Conversely,

$$\|x\|_{\overrightarrow{p}} \leq \frac{1}{s_{2n}(\overrightarrow{p})}\|\sigma_L(x)\| = \frac{1}{\sqrt{[L : \mathbb{Q}]}}\|\sigma_L(x)\|.$$

The $s_i(\overrightarrow{p})$ can in practice be taken to be polynomial in n, if desired. We will be interested in the above for integral elements $x \in \mathcal{O}_L$, which has powerful basis

$$(1, \zeta_m, ..., \zeta_m^{n-1}, \frac{1+\sqrt{\ell}}{2}, \zeta_m \frac{1+\sqrt{\ell}}{2}, ..., \zeta_m^{n-1} \frac{1+\sqrt{\ell}}{2}),$$

when $\ell \equiv 1 \bmod 4$. Upon computing the singular values of $\sigma(\overrightarrow{p})$, we find that

Proposition 1. *Let* $n = 2^{r-1}$, $\ell \equiv 1 \bmod 2^r$ *a prime, and* $L = \mathbb{Q}(\zeta_{2^r}, \sqrt{\ell})$. *Then, using the powerful basis of* $\mathcal{O}_L$, *we have*

$$s_1(\overrightarrow{p}) = \frac{\sqrt{n}}{2}\sqrt{\ell + 5 + \sqrt{\ell^2 - 6\ell + 25}} \ \& \ s_{2n}(\overrightarrow{p}) = \frac{\sqrt{n}}{2}\sqrt{\ell + 5 - \sqrt{\ell^2 - 6\ell + 25}}$$

Proof. The symmetric matrix $\sigma(\overrightarrow{p})^*\sigma(\overrightarrow{p})$ has a block form: the top left block is $[L : \mathbb{Q}] \cdot I_{2^{r-1}}$, where $I_{2^{r-1}}$ is the $2^{r-1} \times 2^{r-1}$ identity matrix, the lower right block is $2^{r-2} \cdot (\ell + 1)$, and the top right and lower left blocks are $2^{r-1} \cdot I_{2^{r-1}}$. The eigenvalues of this matrix are $\lambda_i = 2^{r-2} \cdot \frac{\ell + 5 \pm \sqrt{\ell^2 - 6\ell + 25}}{2}$. So the singular values are $s_i(\overrightarrow{p}) = \sqrt{2^{r-2} \cdot \frac{\ell + 5 \pm \sqrt{\ell^2 - 6\ell + 25}}{2}} = \frac{\sqrt{n}}{2}\sqrt{\ell + 5 \pm \sqrt{\ell^2 - 6\ell + 25}}$. □

If $\overrightarrow{d}$ is the dual of $\overrightarrow{p}$, we obtain $s_1(\overrightarrow{d}) = \frac{1}{s_{2n}(\overrightarrow{p})}$, $s_{2n}(\overrightarrow{d}) = \frac{1}{s_1(\overrightarrow{p})}$. We will use bounds in terms of this 'decoding basis'; in particular, for $x \in \mathcal{O}_L^\vee$,

$$\|x\|_{\overrightarrow{d}} \leq \frac{1}{s_{2n}(\overrightarrow{d})}\|\sigma_L(x)\| = \frac{\sqrt{n}}{2}\sqrt{\ell + 5 + \sqrt{\ell^2 - 6\ell + 25}}\|\sigma_L(x)\|.$$

When ℓ is bounded by some integer multiple of n, say $\ell \leq Cn$ for $C \geq 2$, we can use the bound $s_1(\overrightarrow{p}) < 2Cn$, when $n \geq 4$.

Discretisation. We will need the following distribution:

Definition 3. [39] Denote by Bern the Bernoulli distribution and let $a \in \mathbb{R}$. The univariate *Reduction distribution* $\mathrm{Red}(a) = \mathrm{Bern}(\lceil a \rceil - a) - (\lceil a \rceil - a)$ is defined

$$\mathrm{Red}(a) := \begin{cases} 1 + a - \lceil a \rceil, & \text{with probability } \lceil a \rceil - a, \\ a - \lceil a \rceil, & \text{with probability } 1 + a - \lceil a \rceil. \end{cases}$$

A random variable $\boldsymbol{R} = (R_1, \cdots, R_n)^T \in \mathbb{R}^n$ has a multivariate Reduction distribution $R \sim \mathrm{Red}(\boldsymbol{a})$ on $\mathbb{R}^n$ for parameter $\boldsymbol{a} = (a_1, \cdots, a_n)^T$ if $R_j \sim \mathrm{Red}(a_j)$ for $j = 1, \cdots, n$ are independent univariate Reduction random variables.

Definition 4. Let $\mathcal{L} = \mathcal{L}(B)$ be an n-dimensional lattice under the canonical embedding. For $c \in H$, the coordinatewise randomized rounding (CRR) discretisation $\lfloor X \rceil_{\mathcal{L}+c}^B$ of random variable X to $\mathcal{L} + c$ is defined by

$$\lfloor X \rceil_{\mathcal{L}+c}^B = X + B\,\mathrm{Red}\left(B^{-1}(c - X)\right).$$

Extend this to H^d by applying the discretisation in each coordinate. The discretisation variable on H is 0-subgaussian:

Definition 5. For any $\delta \geq 0$, a multivariate random variable X on $\mathbb{R}^n$ (resp. H) is δ-subgaussian with standard parameter $b \geq 0$ if

$$E\left(e^{\langle t, X \rangle}\right) \leq e^\delta e^{\frac{1}{2} b^2 \|t\|^2}, \quad \text{for all } t \in \mathbb{R}^n \text{ (resp. } t \in H).$$

Extend this to H^d by saying a multivariate random variable Z on H^d is δ-subgaussian with standard parameter $b \geq 0$ if Z is δ-subgaussian with standard parameter $b \geq 0$ in each H-coordinate ($H^d \cong \mathbb{R}^{nd^2}$ as $\mathbb{R}$-vector spaces). Formally,

Definition 6. A multivariate random variable Z on H^d is δ-subgaussian with standard parameter $b \geq 0$ if

$$E\left(e^{\langle t, Z \rangle}\right) \leq e^\delta e^{\frac{1}{2} b^2 \|t\|^2}, \quad \text{for all } t \in H^d$$

Definition 7. A random variable Z on $\mathbb{R}^n$ (or H) is noncentral subgaussian with noncentrality $\|E(Z)\| \geq 0$ and deviation $d \geq 0$ if the centered random variable $Z_0 = Z - E(Z)$ is 0-subgaussian with standard parameter d.

We will need the following lemmas:

Lemma 7. [38] *Suppose that B is a column basis matrix for a lattice in H with largest singular value $s_1(B)$ and Z is an independent noncentral subgaussian random variable with deviation d_Z. The CRR discretisation of Z, $\lfloor Z \rceil_{\Lambda+c}^B$ is noncentral subgaussian with noncentrality $\|E(Z)\|$ and deviation $\left(d_Z^2 + \left(\frac{1}{2}\right)^2 s_1(B)^2\right)^{\frac{1}{2}}$.*

When $L = \mathbb{Q}(\zeta_n, \sqrt{\ell})$ for n a power of two, $\gcd(n, \ell) = 1$, this becomes

Lemma 8. *Suppose that B is a column basis matrix for a lattice in H^d with largest singular value $s_1(B)$ and Z is an independent noncentral subgaussian random variable with deviation d_Z. The CRR discretisation of Z to $\lfloor Z \rceil_{\Lambda+c}^B$ is noncentral subgaussian with noncentrality $\|E(Z)\|$ and deviation $\left(d_Z^2 + \frac{1}{2} s_1(B)^2\right)^{\frac{1}{2}}$.*

Proof. As in [38, Theorem 2], but with an extra factor of $\sqrt{2}$ from taking the matrix norm of the basis. □

3   NTRU

We begin by defining the problem underlying schemes based on NTRU.

The NTRU Assumption

Definition 8 (NTRU instances). Let $\mathcal{R}$ be a ring and $q \in \mathbb{Z}_{\geq 2}$ a modulus. An instance of NTRU is an element $h \in \mathcal{R}_q$ such that $h \cdot f = g \bmod q\mathcal{R}$ for some pair of non-zero elements $(f, g) \in \mathcal{R}$.

We are interested in the following problem, based off NTRU instances:

Definition 9 (The NTRU problem). Let $\mathcal{R}$ and q be as above, and $\epsilon > 0$. Let $\mathcal{D}$ be a distribution over instances of NTRU. The NTRU problem is, given $h \leftarrow \mathcal{D}$, to find non-zero (f, g) such that $h \cdot f = g \bmod q\mathcal{R}$ and $\|f\|, \|g\| \leq \frac{\sqrt{q}}{\epsilon}$.

The hardness of the NTRU problem varies significantly, depending on ϵ.

Connection to Lattices. The solutions over $\mathcal{R}$ to the defining equation $hf \equiv g \bmod q$ form a lattice, denoted

$$\mathcal{L}_{h,q} = \{(x, y) \in \mathcal{R}^2 : hx - y \equiv 0 \bmod q\}.$$

The sum of two solutions to the defining equation is again a solution, and one can also observe that for any $z \in \mathcal{R}$ and $(f, g) \in \mathcal{L}_{h,q}$, $z(f, g)$ satisfies $zhf - zg \equiv z(hf - g) \equiv 0 \bmod q$. Thus $\mathcal{L}_{h,q}$ is a $\mathcal{R}$-module of rank 2, and the NTRU problem can be rephrased as a shortest vector problem in the NTRU lattice $\mathcal{L}_{h,q}$.

Encryption Scheme. The NTRU encryption scheme, as in [24], runs as follows:

KeyGen: Let $\mathcal{S}_f$, $\mathcal{S}_g$, $\mathcal{S}_\phi$, and $\mathcal{S}_M$ be sets of polynomials in $\mathcal{R} = \mathbb{Z}[x]/(t(x))$ for some degree-N polynomial $t(x)$. Let $q \gg p \in \mathbb{Z}$ be coprime. Select f from $\mathcal{S}_f$ and g from $\mathcal{S}_g$, such that f is invertible modulo both q and p. Compute $h = g \cdot f^{-1} \bmod q$; this polynomial h is the public key, and (f, g) the private key.
Encryption: Suppose the message is M, taken from $\mathcal{S}_M$. Then to encrypt M, select ϕ from $\mathcal{S}_\phi$ and compute $c = p\phi \cdot h + M \bmod q$. This is the ciphertext.
Decryption: To decrypt c, first compute $a = f \cdot c \bmod q$. Then compute $f^{-1} \cdot a \bmod p$, to recover $M \bmod p$. This decryption holds provided the coefficients of a lie in the correct interval. Otherwise, there is a small chance of *decryption failure*. Parameters can be chosen to eliminate the chance of decryption failure.
Correctness: Observe that

$$a = f \cdot c \bmod q = f \cdot (p\phi \cdot h + M) \bmod q = p\phi \cdot g + f \cdot M \bmod q,$$

so that finally $f^{-1} \cdot a \bmod p = f^{-1} \cdot (p\phi g + f \cdot M) \bmod p = f^{-1} \cdot (fM) \bmod p = M \bmod p$, provided that when we reduce a modulo q (taking the coefficients between $\frac{-q}{2}$ and $\frac{q}{2}$), we obtain simply the polynomial a.

Further Discussion of NTRU. There are a variety of parameter choices currently used to instantiate NTRU. In the paper initially proposing the NTRU problem [24], the ring $\mathcal{R} = \mathbb{Z}[x]/(x^N - 1)$ was used, with N prime (and the authors recommended using Sophie Germain primes). Of the two final round NTRU-based schemes in NIST's post-quantum standardization process, NTRU [13] samples f and g from $\mathbb{Z}[x]/(t(x))$ with $t(x) = \Phi_n(x)$, where n is prime and $\Phi_n(x)$ is the nth cyclotomic polynomial. This is contrasted by NTRU Prime [9], which uses $t(x) = x^p - x - 1$ for some prime p (not to be confused with the modulus of the previous section), such that $\mathbb{Z}_q[x]/(x^p - x - 1)$ is a field.

We also note here that f and g are often chosen to be binary or ternary polynomials (i.e. coefficients are in $\{0,1\}$, $\{-1,0,1\}$ respectively), which increases efficiency, but which has been subjected to meet-in-the-middle attacks [25].

Structured Forms of NTRU. Two papers have proposed structured forms of NTRU using modules [15,16]. The authors construct NTRU modules of the following form, where $\mathcal{R} = \mathcal{O}_K$ for a number field K:

$$\mathcal{L}_{\mathbf{h},q} = \{(\mathbf{f},g)^T \in \mathcal{R}^{d+1} : \langle \mathbf{f},\mathbf{h}\rangle - g \equiv 0 \bmod q\}.$$

Here g is a ring element and $\mathbf{f}$ is an d-dimensional vector over $\mathcal{R}$, and embedding the lattice (via either coefficients or ring embeddings) yields lattices in $\mathbb{R}^{(d+1)n}$, where $\dim_{\mathbb{Z}}(\mathcal{R}) = n$. Multiple samples can be taken and written in the following form, where we have chosen d samples to obtain square matrices for convenience of expression (note squareness of the matrices involved is not required):

$$\mathcal{L}_{\mathbf{h},q} = \{(\mathbf{F},\mathbf{g})^T \in \mathcal{R}^{d\times(d+1)} : \mathbf{F}\mathbf{h} - \mathbf{g} \equiv \mathbf{0} \bmod q\}.$$

These are more general objects than those considered in this work. However, the authors of [16] are able to prove uniformity of their NTRU public keys only for certain prime moduli, those splitting into two prime ideals in $\mathcal{R}$ (those congruent to 3 modulo 8), which are usually not the primes used in practice - and their recommended parameters are completely split primes and a module rank of 2, over a power-of-two cyclotomic field. They prove:

Theorem 1 (Theorem A.1, [16]). *Let K be a cyclotomic number field of degree d and maximal order R. Let $n \geq m \geq 1$. Let q be a prime integer which factors as $qR = \mathfrak{p}_1\mathfrak{p}_2$, where the $\mathfrak{p}_i$'s have algebraic norm $q^{d/2}$. For $s \geq 2dq^{m/(n+m)+2/(d(n+m))}$, we have:*

$$\Delta\left(\mathcal{E}_s, U\left(R_q^{n\times m}\right)\right) \leq 2^{-\Omega(d)},$$

where $\mathcal{E}_s$ is the distribution of $\mathbf{F}^{-1}\mathbf{G} \bmod q$, for $\mathbf{F}, \mathbf{G}$ with entries chosen according to discrete Gaussians.

In contrast, restricting ourselves to more structured modules, we obtain a full proof of uniformity of our public keys, for completely split primes in rank 2. Our modules are obtained from *cyclic division algebras*.

4   Cyclic Division Algebras

In this section we define the cyclic algebras we will use to generalise NTRU.

Definition 10. Let $K/\mathbb{Q}$ be a number field of degree n, and L/K be a Galois extension of degree d with cyclic Galois group, i.e. $\mathrm{Gal}(L/K) = \langle \theta \rangle$ for some automorphism θ. Consider the direct sum

$$\bigoplus_{i=0}^{d-1} u^i L = L \oplus uL \oplus u^2 L \oplus \dots \oplus u^{d-1} L,$$

subject to the relations $u^d = \gamma \in \mathcal{O}_K$, and $x \cdot u = u \cdot \theta(x)$, for all $x \in L$.

We denote this direct sum $\mathcal{A} = (L/K, \theta, \gamma)$, which is a *cyclic algebra*.

Definition 11. A cyclic algebra $\mathcal{A} = (L/K, \theta, \gamma)$ is a *division algebra* if for every element $a \in \mathcal{A}$, there exists an inverse element $a^{-1} \in \mathcal{A}$ such that $a \cdot a^{-1} = 1$.

In order to ensure that our algebras are division, we will need to ensure they meet the following condition, known as the *non-norm* condition:

Lemma 9. [1] *Let $\mathcal{A} = (L/K, \theta, \gamma)$ be a CDA. Then $\mathcal{A}$ is a division algebra if and only if γ is a non-norm element, i.e. $\nexists x \in L : N_{L/K}(x) = \gamma$.*

The construction of non-norm elements is therefore crucial in finding division algebras. In [21], much discussion was given to finding such elements - we recap this below, after the following definitions.

In NTRU, polynomials are often sampled from subrings of fields. We now define the corresponding mathematical object within cyclic algebras from which it is suitable to sample elements.

Definition 12. A $\mathbb{Z}$-*order*, $\mathcal{O}$, in $\mathcal{A} = (L/K, \theta, \gamma)$ is a finitely generated $\mathbb{Z}$-module such that $\mathcal{O} \cdot \mathbb{Q} = \mathcal{A}$ and $\mathcal{O}$ is a subring of $\mathcal{A}$ with the same identity element as $\mathcal{A}$. Note $\mathcal{O} \cdot \mathbb{Q} = \{\sum_{i=1}^{m} a_i q_i : a_i \in \mathcal{O}, q_i \in \mathbb{Q}, m \in \mathbb{Z}_{\geq 1}\}$.

Definition 13. Define the *natural order* to be the order of the form

$$\Lambda = \bigoplus_{i=0}^{d-1} u^i \mathcal{O}_L = \mathcal{O}_L \oplus u\mathcal{O}_L \oplus u^2 \mathcal{O}_L \oplus \dots \oplus u^{d-1} \mathcal{O}_L,$$

where $\mathcal{O}_L$ denotes the ring of integers of L.

Given a prime $q \in \mathbb{Z}$, we can take the quotient of Λ to obtain

$$\Lambda_q = \Lambda/q\Lambda = \bigoplus_{i=0}^{d-1} u^i (\mathcal{O}_L/q\mathcal{O}_L)$$

$$= \mathcal{O}_L/q\mathcal{O}_L \oplus u(\mathcal{O}_L/q\mathcal{O}_L) \oplus u^2(\mathcal{O}_L/q\mathcal{O}_L) \oplus \dots \oplus u^{d-1}(\mathcal{O}_L/q\mathcal{O}_L).$$

When $R = \mathbb{Z}[x]/\Phi_n(x)$, R is the ring of integers of the nth cyclotomic field, say L; then $R_q = \mathcal{O}_L/q\mathcal{O}_L$. So Λ_q can be seen as a tuple of elements of R_q, equipped with a noncommutative multiplication induced by multiplication by u.

Fixing the L-basis of $\mathcal{A}$, $\{u^i\}_{i\geq 0}$, we can express an element as the linear map $\phi(x)$ given by left multiplication on the u^i. For example, if $x = \oplus_{i=0}^{d-1} u^i x_i \in \mathcal{A}$,

$$\phi(x) = \begin{pmatrix} x_0 & \gamma\theta(x_{d-1}) & \dots & \gamma\theta^{d-1}(x_1) \\ x_1 & \theta(x_0) & \dots & \gamma\theta^{d-1}(x_2) \\ \dots & \dots & \dots & \dots \\ x_{d-1} & \theta(x_{d-2}) & \dots & \theta^{d-1}(x_0) \end{pmatrix}.$$

This is called the left regular representation.

If we denote the n embeddings $K \hookrightarrow \mathbb{C}$ by α, we can extend these to embeddings of L (which, in an abuse of notation, we also denote by α). It can be seen that all the nd embeddings of L are obtained from the set $\{\alpha \circ \theta^i\}_{\alpha,i}$. So we may form a vector in $\mathbb{R}^{nd^2}$ from x by concatenating the vectorized images of the $\alpha(\phi(x))$ for all $\alpha \in \text{Emb}(K)$. Then the image of any discrete additive subgroup of $\mathcal{A}$ is mapped to a lattice in $\mathbb{R}^{nd^2}$. Finally, we define two norms on $\mathcal{A}$: we set $\|x\|_p^p = \sum_{\alpha \in \text{Emb}(K)} \sum_{i,j} |\alpha(\phi(x)_{i,j})|^p$, and $\|x\|_\infty = \max_{\alpha,i,j} |\alpha(\phi(x)_{i,j})|$, where $\phi(x)_{i,j}$ denotes the i,jth entry of $\phi(x)$. We may use $\|\cdot\|$ to denote $\|\cdot\|_2$.

Let $\text{Tr}(\cdot)$ be the map $\text{Tr}(x) = T_{K/\mathbb{Q}} \circ \text{trace}(\phi(x))$, for $x \in \mathcal{A}$. This map is symmetric and additive. The dual of an ideal $\mathcal{I}$ is the set

$$\mathcal{I}^\vee = \{x \in \mathcal{A} : \text{Tr}(x\mathcal{I}) \subset \mathbb{Z}\}.$$

We also define a multiplicative norm on ideals. Let $\mathcal{I}$ be an integral ideal of a maximal order $\mathcal{O}$; then $N_{\mathcal{A}/\mathbb{Q}}(\mathcal{I}) := |\mathcal{O}/\mathcal{I}|$.

We now outline the construction of CDAs using cyclotomic fields as in [21]. Let $m = p^r$ be a prime power, $K = \mathbb{Q}(\zeta_m)$ and $M = \mathbb{Q}(\zeta_{\ell m})$, for a prime ℓ such that $\ell \equiv 1 \bmod m$ and $\ell \not\equiv 1 \bmod pm$. Then M/K is cyclic Galois, with Galois group generated by (say) θ. Let L be the intermediate field fixed by θ^d. It can be verified that ζ_m is not the norm of any element of L, so $(L/K, \theta, \zeta_m)$ is a division algebra. Moreover, Λ is maximal with respect to inclusion in $\mathcal{A}$. Security reductions for LWE in these algebras were given; here we investigate the properties of NTRU implemented in such an algebra.

In the case $d = 2$, L is the compositum of K and the unique quadratic subfield of $\mathbb{Q}(\zeta_\ell)$, which is $\mathbb{Q}(\sqrt{\ell})$. Thus $L = \mathbb{Q}(\zeta_m, \sqrt{\ell})$ and $\Lambda = \mathcal{O}_L + u\mathcal{O}_L$. We now prove an upper bound on the discriminant of Λ:

Definition 14. $\text{disc}(\Lambda/\mathbb{Z}) := \left\{ \det \left(\text{Tr}(x_i x_j) \right)_{i,j=1}^{nd^2} \mid (x_1, \dots, x_{nd^2}) \in \Lambda^{nd^2} \right\}.$

It was proved in [55, Lemma 2.9] that $\text{disc}(\Lambda/\mathcal{O}_K) = \text{disc}(L/K)^d \gamma^{d(d-1)}$. Since in our case γ is a root of unity, this simplifies to $\text{disc}(\Lambda/\mathcal{O}_K) = \text{disc}(L/K)^d$.

Proposition 2. Let $L = \mathbb{Q}(\zeta_{2^r}, \sqrt{\ell})$, $r \geq 2$, $\ell \equiv 1 \bmod 2^r$, and $K = \mathbb{Q}(\zeta_{2^r})$. Then

$$\text{disc}(\Lambda/\mathbb{Z}) \leq (n\sqrt{l})^{4n}.$$

Proof. Since $u^i \mathcal{O}_L$ and $u^j \mathcal{O}_L$ are orthogonal with respect to the trace form, except when $i + j \equiv 0 \bmod 2$, we have

$$\det\left(\operatorname{Tr}\left(u x_k u x_\ell\right)\right)_{k,\ell=1}^{2n} = \det\left(u^2 \operatorname{Tr}\left(x_k x_\ell\right)\right)_{k,\ell=1}^{2n} = \gamma^{nd} \det\left(\operatorname{Tr}\left(x_k x_\ell\right)\right)_{k,\ell=1}^{2n}$$

$$= \det\left(\operatorname{Tr}\left(x_k x_\ell\right)\right)_{k,\ell=1}^{2n} = \operatorname{disc}(L/\mathbb{Q}),$$

for some $x_i \in \mathcal{O}_L$, since $\gamma = \zeta_n$.

It now suffices to prove that $\operatorname{disc}(L/\mathbb{Q}) \leq (n\sqrt{\ell})^{2n}$. Since L is the compositum of $K = \mathbb{Q}(\zeta_{2^r})$ and $\mathbb{Q}(\sqrt{\ell})$, we can apply a general formula on the discriminants of composita (e.g. [36, ex. 23(c)]) to obtain

$$\operatorname{disc}(L/\mathbb{Q}) = \operatorname{disc}(K/\mathbb{Q})^2 \operatorname{disc}(\mathbb{Q}(\sqrt{\ell})/\mathbb{Q})^n.$$

We combine $\operatorname{disc}(K/\mathbb{Q}) \leq n^n$ with $\operatorname{disc}(\mathbb{Q}(\sqrt{\ell})/\mathbb{Q}) = \ell$ for the result. $\square$

Proposition 3 *[8, Proposition 2.5]. Let Λ be as above and $\mathcal{I} \subset \Lambda$ be an integral ideal. Then*

$$\operatorname{Vol}(\mathcal{I}) = N_{\mathcal{A}/\mathbb{Q}}(\mathcal{I})\sqrt{\operatorname{disc}(\Lambda/\mathbb{Z})}.$$

We will use the following bound on the shortest vector of a Λ-ideal lattice under the canonical embedding, with repect to a p-norm, $\lambda_1^p(\mathcal{L})$:

Proposition 4 *(cf. [45, Lemma 6.1]). Let $\mathcal{I}$ be an ideal of Λ. Then*

$$\lambda_1^p(\mathcal{I}) \leq (nd^2)^{1/p} N_{\mathcal{A}/\mathbb{Q}}(\mathcal{I})^{1/nd^2} \operatorname{disc}(\Lambda/\mathbb{Z})^{1/2nd^2}.$$

Proof. Since $\|x\|_p \leq \left(nd^2\right)^{\frac{1}{p}} \|x\|_\infty$, we bound $\|x\|_\infty$. Recall $\mathcal{A} \hookrightarrow H^d \subset (\mathbb{R}^{r_1} \times \mathbb{C}^{2r_2})^d$, with $r_1 + 2r_2 = nd$. Set $C = \{x \in H^d : \|x\|_\infty \leq 1\}$ and note $\operatorname{Vol}(C) = 2^{nd^2}\left(\frac{\pi}{2}\right)^{r_2 d}$. Then if $\beta^{nd^2} > \left(\frac{2}{\pi}\right)^{r_2 d} N_{\mathcal{A}/\mathbb{Q}}(\mathcal{I})\sqrt{\operatorname{disc}(\Lambda/\mathbb{Z})}$, we have

$$\operatorname{Vol}(\beta C) = \beta^{nd^2} \operatorname{Vol}(C) > \left(\frac{2}{\pi}\right)^{r_2 d} N_{\mathcal{A}/\mathbb{Q}}(\mathcal{I})\sqrt{\operatorname{disc}(\Lambda/\mathbb{Z})} 2^{nd^2}\left(\frac{\pi}{2}\right)^{r_2 d}$$

$$= N_{\mathcal{A}/\mathbb{Q}}(\mathcal{I})\sqrt{\operatorname{disc}(\Lambda/\mathbb{Z})} 2^{nd^2} = \operatorname{Vol}(\mathcal{I}) 2^{nd^2}.$$

By Minkowski's theorem, βC contains a lattice point from $\mathcal{I}$, so $\lambda_1^\infty(\mathcal{I}) \leq \beta$. $\square$

This implies that in the ℓ_2-norm, $\lambda_1(\Lambda) \leq (nd^2)^{1/2}(n\sqrt{\ell})^{1/2} = dn\sqrt[4]{\ell}$.

Proposition 5. *Let $\Lambda \subset \mathcal{A} = (L/K, \theta, \gamma)$ where $|\gamma| = 1$, $[L : K] = d$ and $[K : \mathbb{Q}] = n$. Then, for $x = \oplus_{i=0}^{d-1} u^i x_i \in \Lambda$, $\mathcal{I}$ an ideal of Λ,*

$$\|x\|_p \geq [\mathcal{A} : \mathbb{Q}]^{1/p} \cdot \left(\prod_{0 \leq i < d} |N_{L/\mathbb{Q}}(x_i)|\right)^{1/[\mathcal{A}:\mathbb{Q}]}.$$

When $\mathcal{I} = \mathfrak{J}\Lambda$ for some $\mathcal{O}_K$-ideal $\mathfrak{J}$ and $\bar{\mathcal{I}} := \mathcal{I} \cap \mathcal{O}_L$, then

$$\lambda_1^p(\mathcal{I}) \geq [\mathcal{A} : \mathbb{Q}]^{1/p} \cdot \left|N_{L/\mathbb{Q}}\left(\bar{\mathcal{I}}\right)\right|^{d/[\mathcal{A}:\mathbb{Q}]}, \quad \text{and } \lambda_1^\infty(\mathcal{I}) \geq \left(N_{L/\mathbb{Q}}(\bar{\mathcal{I}})\right)^{1/nd}.$$

Proof. See Appendix A.   □

Mapping Between Bases of $\mathcal{A}$. Let $d = 2$, so $\mathcal{A}$ embeds into H^2. Similarly as above, consider the block-diagonal matrix with each block equal to $\sigma(\overrightarrow{p})$, for $\overrightarrow{p}$ the powerful basis of L. Now, since $\Lambda = \mathcal{O}_L + u\mathcal{O}_L$, and $\mathcal{O}_L = \mathbb{Z}[\zeta_{2^r}, \frac{1+\sqrt{\ell}}{2}]$, $\Sigma(\Lambda) = (\sigma_L(\Lambda_0), \sigma_L(\Lambda_1))$, a matrix acting on a vector to map it to a coefficient embedding representation, should act on the first and second coordinates $\sigma_L(\Lambda_i)$ in the desired way. Thus the required transformation is $V_\Lambda = \begin{pmatrix} \sigma(\overrightarrow{p}) & 0 \\ 0 & \sigma(\overrightarrow{p}) \end{pmatrix}$.

Note if $\sigma(\overrightarrow{p})$ is invertible, so is V_Λ. We similarly extend $\overrightarrow{d}$ to Λ. We can then obtain bounds for norms defined over these bases: for $x \in \Lambda$ with $d = 2$ we obtain

$$\|x\|_{\sigma(\overrightarrow{d})} \le \sqrt{2} s_1(\overrightarrow{p})\|x\|.$$

Note that when $d = 1$, $K = L$ and $\mathcal{A} = K$. This is the fact that will enable us to generalise NTRU schemes which sample elements from $\mathbb{Z}[x]/(\Phi_{2^r}(x))$, using algebras of the form $\mathcal{A} = (L/\mathbb{Q}(\zeta_{2^r}), \theta, \zeta_n)$; when $d = 1$, we will recover the familiar families of polynomials in certain spaces, generalising NTRU, ETRU and others. If one uses CDAs over fields K where K is some other popular choice of field for NTRU, one obtains generalisations of those schemes too.

CLWE and Its Security. Below, we link the hardness of NTRU in CDAs to that of LWE in CDAs. Here we introduce CLWE, and begin by defining a distribution on the error distributions used to establish the hardness of CLWE:

Definition 15. Define the distributions Σ_α as the set of Gaussian distributions Σ over $\bigoplus_{i=0}^{d-1} u^i L_\mathbb{R}$ with Gaussian marginal distribution in the $(i,j)^{\text{th}}$ coordinate with parameter $r_{i,j} \le \alpha$. The error distribution Υ_α on the family of error distributions is sampled from by choosing $\Sigma \in \Sigma_\alpha$ and adding it to D_r, where each $r_i := \alpha \left((n \cdot d^2)^{1/4} \cdot \sqrt{y_i} \right)$ for $y_1, \dots, y_{n \cdot d^2}$ sampled from $\Gamma(2, 1)$.

Then the CLWE distribution, and decision CLWE problem, are as follows:

Definition 16. Let L/K be a Galois extension of number fields with $[L : K] = d$ and $[K : \mathbb{Q}] = n$, with $\text{Gal}(L/K)$ cyclic, generated by θ. Let $\mathcal{A} := (L/K, \theta, \gamma)$ be the resulting cyclic K-algebra with element u such that $u^d = \gamma \in \mathcal{O}_K$ and γ satisfying the non-norm condition. Let Λ be the natural order of $\mathcal{A}$. For an error distribution ψ over $\bigoplus_{i=0}^{d-1} u^i L_\mathbb{R}$, $q \ge 2$, and secret $s \in \Lambda_q^\vee$, a sample from the CLWE distribution $\Pi_{q,s,\psi}$ is obtained by sampling $a \leftarrow \Lambda_q$ uniformly at random, $e \leftarrow \psi$, and outputting $(a, b) = (a, (a \cdot s)/q + e \bmod \Lambda^\vee) \in \left(\Lambda_q, \bigoplus_{i=0}^{d-1} u^i L_\mathbb{R} \right)/\Lambda^\vee$.

Let Υ be as above and U_Λ the uniform distribution on $\left(\Lambda_q, \left(\bigoplus_{i=0}^{d-1} u^i L_\mathbb{R} \right)/\Lambda^\vee \right)$. Then the decision CLWE problem, DCLWE$_{q,\Upsilon}$, is on input a collection of independent samples from $\Pi_{q,s,\psi}$ for a random choice of $(s, \psi) \leftarrow U(\Lambda_q^\vee) \times \Upsilon$ or from U_Λ, to decide which is the case (with non-negligible advantage).

Recall the following security reductions for CLWE, from [21]:

Theorem 2. *Let $\mathcal{A}$ be a cyclic division algebra over a number field L with center K and natural, maximal order Λ with $|\gamma| = 1$. Let $\alpha = \alpha(n) \in (0,1)$ and $q = q(n) \geq 2$, unramified in L, be parameters such that $\alpha \cdot q \geq \omega(\sqrt{\log(nd^2)})$. Then, there is a polynomial-time quantum reduction from $\mathcal{A}$-$SIVP_\xi$ to search $CLWE_{q,\Sigma_\alpha}$ for any $\sqrt{8Nd} \cdot \xi = (\omega(\sqrt{dn})/\alpha)$.*

Theorem 3. *Let Λ be the natural order of a cyclic algebra $\mathcal{A} = (L/K, \theta, \gamma), q \in$ poly(n), and assume that $\alpha \cdot q \geq \eta_\varepsilon(\Lambda^\vee)$ for a negligible $\varepsilon = \varepsilon(n)$. Then, there is a probabilistic reduction from search $CLWE_{q,\Sigma_\alpha,G}$ for any pairwise different $G \subset \Lambda_q^\vee$ to decision $CLWE_q, \Upsilon_\alpha$ which runs in time polynomial in n.*

These reductions combine to ground the security of decision CLWE on SIVP over ideal lattices in CDAs. Thus if we connect the security of NTRU to that of CLWE, we will have connected the security of NTRU to SIVP. However, we require a particular variant of CLWE to which to reduce NTRU. Here we recall the variant of RLWE used in [48]. Let $s \in R_q$ and ψ be a distribution over R_q. Define $A_s^\times$ as the distribution obtained by sampling $(a, as + e)$ with $(a, e) \leftarrow U(R_q^\times) \times \psi$, where $R_q^\times$ is the set of invertible elements of R_q. When $q = \Omega(n)$, the probability of a uniform element of R_q being invertible is non-negligible, so RLWE is hard even when $A_{s,\psi}$ and $U(R_q \times R_q)$ are replaced by $A_{s,\psi}^\times$ and $U(R_q^\times \times R_q)$ respectively. Denote this variant by RLWE$^\times$.

It is known that s can be chosen from the same distribution as e without losing security (see [3]). The authors of [48] call the variant of RLWE when the secret and error are both chosen from the error distribution RLWE$_{\mathrm{HNF}}^\times$. To see this, let algorithm $\mathcal{A}$ be able to solve RLWE$_{\mathrm{HNF}}^\times$. One can transform samples $((a_i, b_i))_i$ into samples $\left((a_1^{-1}a_i, b_i - a_1^{-1}b_1a_i)\right)_i$, where inversion is performed in $R_q^\times$. This transformation maps $A_{s,\psi}^\times$ to $A_{-e_1,\psi}^\times$, and $U\left(R_q^\times \times R_q\right)$ to itself. Note that $b_i - a_1^{-1}b_1a_i = a_is + e_i - a_1^{-1}(a_1s + e_1)a_i = a_is + e_i - a_is - a_1^{-1}e_1a_i = -a_1^{-1}a_ie_1 + e_i$.

We can define CLWE$^\times$ analogously: let $s \in \Lambda_q$, $e \leftarrow \chi$, and $a \leftarrow U(\Lambda_q^\times)$. Output $(a, as + e) \in \Lambda_q^\times \times \oplus_{i=0}^{d-1} u^i L_{\mathbb{R}}$, and call the distribution obtained $A_{q,s,\chi}^\times$. We can take s from the same distribution as the error to obtain CLWE$_{HNF}^\times$; to see the transformation as in the RLWE case, transform CLWE$^\times$ samples into CLWE$_{HNF}^\times$ samples via the transformation $(a_i, b_i) \mapsto (a_ia_1^{-1}, b_i - a_ia_1^{-1}b_1)$.

5   NTRU in CDAs

In the following, we follow the method outlined in [24] to implement NTRU in CDAs. After demonstrating that the basic form of NTRU adapts easily to our context, we will go on to discuss the tweaks, improvements, and modifications that have arisen in the literature, and how they can be brought into CDAs. For convenience, we refer to NTRU in a cyclic division algebra as *CNTRU*.

NTRU Instances in CDAs.

Definition 17 (CNTRU instances). Let $\mathcal{A} = (L/K, \theta, \gamma)$ be an algebra as constructed above, and Λ the natural order. Let $q \in \mathbb{Z}_{\geq 2}$. An instance of CNTRU is an element $h \in \Lambda_q$ such that $f \cdot h = g \mod q\Lambda$ for non-zero pair $(f, g) \in \Lambda$.

We define the NTRU problem for CDAs, based off CNTRU instances:

Definition 18 (The CNTRU problem). Let Λ and q be as above, and $\epsilon > 0$. Let $\mathcal{D}$ be a distribution over instances of CNTRU. The CNTRU problem is, given $h \leftarrow \mathcal{D}$, to find non-zero (f, g) such that $f \cdot h = g \mod q\Lambda$ and $\|f\|, \|g\| \leq \frac{\sqrt{q}}{\epsilon}$.

NTRU Lattices from CDAs. We now consider the lattices generated by CNTRU instances. These lattices are a generalization of [16] and [15]'s lattices: take a private key $(f, g) \in \Lambda^2$ and public key $h = f^{-1}g \mod q\Lambda$. Observe that the pair (f, g) satisfies

$$fh - g = 0 \mod q\Lambda, \tag{1}$$

so in the same way as NTRU, the set $S = \{(f, g) \in \Lambda^2 : fh - g = 0 \mod q\Lambda\} \subset \Lambda^2$ is a left Λ-module (i.e. S is additively closed and closed under multiplication from Λ on the left). We can write a generator matrix for this Λ-module as $\begin{pmatrix} -h & 1 \\ q & 0 \end{pmatrix}$ where the columns generate the module over Λ^2. By fixing a basis $\{u^i\}_i$, we can then rewrite this matrix to obtain one with entries in $\mathcal{O}_L$, $\begin{pmatrix} -H & I_d \\ \hline qI_d & 0 \end{pmatrix}$ where

$$H = \begin{pmatrix} h_0 & \gamma\theta(h_{d-1}) & \gamma\theta^2(h_{d-2}) & \ldots & \gamma\theta^{d-1}(h_1) \\ h_1 & \theta(h_0) & \gamma\theta^2(h_{d-1}) & \ldots & \gamma\theta^{d-1}(h_2) \\ \ldots & \ldots & \ldots & \ldots & \ldots \\ h_{d-1} & \theta(h_{d-2}) & \theta^2(h_{d-3}) & \ldots & \theta^{d-1}(h_0) \end{pmatrix}.$$

Note that in the module NTRU examples referenced above, the element h defines a vector over a field, so appears in just one column of the corresponding matrix, whereas one sample of CNTRU for $[L : K] = d$ results in $h \mod q$ defining an NTRU-style matrix with d columns determined by h, as can be seen. This is (loosely) equivalent to d samples of module NTRU.

To make the comparison explicit, recall that module forms of NTRU rely on lattices of the form

$$\mathcal{L}_{\mathbf{h},q} = \{(\mathbf{F}, \mathbf{g}) \in \mathcal{R}^{d \times (d+1)} : \mathbf{Fh} - \mathbf{g} \equiv \mathbf{0} \mod q\}.$$

In this case, one can see that these $\mathcal{R}$-modules have a similar form to the CNTRU modules defined above as

$$\mathcal{L}_{h,q} = \{(f, g)^T \in \Lambda^2 : fh - g \equiv 0 \mod q\},$$

when ring multiplication is expanded in matrix-vector form using the regular representation of Λ:

$$\mathcal{L}_{h,q} = \{(\mathbf{f}, \mathbf{g})^T \in \mathcal{O}_L^{2d \times 1} : \phi(f)\mathbf{h} - \mathbf{g} \equiv 0 \mod q\}.$$

Thus we expect the hardness of NTRU problems in CDAs to lie between that of NTRU over rings and NTRU over modules. Moreover, because of the ring structure of Λ, one could use algorithms such as [11] to follow the analysis of [21] and gain (asymptotic) efficiency over standard forms of module NTRU. Finally, we note that the storage required for a CNTRU private key is much less than the module case (for multiple samples), because of the structure of $\phi(f)$ as compared with that of F, using the above notation. In particular, one only has to store the first column of $\phi(f)$, as opposed to the entire matrix.

NTRU-Based PKE. To develop encryption based on the CNTRU problem, we proceed as in [24]. Take the following setup: let $\mathcal{A} = (L/K, \theta, \gamma)$ be a CDA, and $\Lambda \subset \mathcal{A}$ the natural order, assumed to be maximal. Let $K = \mathbb{Q}(\zeta_{2^r})$, $[K : \mathbb{Q}] = n$, and $[L : K] = d$. Then $\Lambda = \mathcal{O}_L \oplus u\mathcal{O}_L \oplus ... \oplus u^{d-1}\mathcal{O}_L$. Denote by $\mathcal{S}_f$, $\mathcal{S}_g$, $\mathcal{S}_\phi$, and $\mathcal{S}_M$ sets of elements of Λ. Select $p, q \in \mathbb{Z}$ such that $\gcd(p, q) = 1$ and $p \ll q$.

Key creation: Select f from $\mathcal{S}_f$, and g from $\mathcal{S}_g$. Furthermore, ensure that f has inverses in Λ_q and in Λ_p. Set $(pk, sk) := (h, (f, g))$ where

$$h := f^{-1} \cdot g \bmod q\Lambda.$$

Encryption: Select a message M from $\mathcal{S}_M$ and ϕ from $\mathcal{S}_\phi$. Then use the public key, h, to form the element

$$c := ph \cdot \phi + M \bmod q\Lambda.$$

Decryption: To decrypt c, compute $a := f \cdot c \bmod q\Lambda$, then $f^{-1} \cdot a \bmod p\Lambda$.

Correctness. Note that

$$a = f \cdot c \bmod q = f \cdot (ph \cdot \phi + M) \bmod q = fph \cdot \phi + f \cdot M \bmod q$$
$$= pf \cdot (f^{-1} \cdot g) \cdot \phi + f \cdot M \bmod q = pg\phi + f \cdot M \bmod q,$$

since $f \cdot f^{-1} \equiv 1 \bmod q$. Then

$$f^{-1} \cdot a \bmod p = f^{-1}(pg \cdot \phi) + f^{-1}(f \cdot M) = p(f^{-1}g\phi) + (f^{-1} \cdot f) \cdot M \bmod p$$
$$= (f^{-1} \cdot f) \cdot M \bmod p = M \bmod p.$$

Remark: This is basically the same as NTRU, but we have to be careful about the order we multiply elements, because of noncommutativity.

Observe that when $d = 1$, we are in the usual set up for NTRU. We could choose the sets $\mathcal{S}_f$, $\mathcal{S}_g$ etc. to be analogous to the ring case, if for example we wanted f and g to be ternary.

Note that the original NTRU scheme doesn't meet the IND-CPA security condition (though [46] gives partial reductions for search and decision NTRU problems). Below we will state an adaptation to the above scheme, and mirror the security guarantee of [48].

6   Results on q-Ary Lattices

In this section we prove a regularity lemma on q-ary lattices obtained from the natural order of our family of CDAs.

Uniformity of the NTRU Public Key Distribution. We ultimately aim to demonstrate near-uniformity of the CNTRU public key distribution, focusing on the case $d = 2$. Almost all of the argument below holds for arbitrary d, but one step restricts us to $d = 2$; we leave the removal of this restriction as a topic of future research. We prove our result for completely split primes, but note that the proof can be adapted for any prime which is unramified in L.

Let Λ be the natural order of a CDA as above, where $[K : \mathbb{Q}] = n$ and $[L : K] = d$. Let $q \in \mathbb{Z}$ be prime, such that q is unramified in $\mathcal{O}_L$. Then:

Lemma 10 *[43, Proposition 4]. Suppose that $\mathcal{I} = \mathfrak{q}$ is a prime in $\mathcal{O}_K$, such that $\mathfrak{q}\mathcal{O}_L = \mathfrak{Q}_1\mathfrak{Q}_2 \cdots \mathfrak{Q}_g$ in L, with $\gamma \neq 0$ mod $\mathfrak{q}$. Then the only proper two-sided ideal of Λ containing $\mathcal{I}$ is $\mathcal{I}\Lambda = \oplus_{j=0}^{d-1} u^j \mathfrak{q}\mathcal{O}_L$.*

Since in our case Λ is a maximal order, ideals uniquely factorize into products of prime ideals and prime ideals are maximal. By the above lemma all unramified two-sided ideals of Λ factor into a product of ideals of the form $\mathfrak{q}\Lambda$, where $\mathfrak{q}$ lies in K. Thus any two-sided unramified ideal can be expressed as $\mathcal{I} = \prod_{i \in S} \mathfrak{q}_i \Lambda$, for some indexing set S. In the following, we will consider the ideals lying above $q\Lambda$, where q splits completely L: these have the form $\mathcal{I} = \prod_{i \in S} \mathfrak{q}_i \Lambda$ where $q\mathcal{O}_K = \prod_i^n \mathfrak{q}_i$ and $S \subset \{1, ..., n\}$. We now define the following module lattices:

Definition 19. Let $q \geq 2$ be a prime completely split in $\mathcal{O}_L$. Let $\mathcal{I}$ be an ideal of Λ of the form $\mathcal{I} = \prod_{i \in S} \mathfrak{q}_i \Lambda$ containing $q\Lambda$, and $\mathcal{I}_S$ be an ideal of Λ_q of the form $\mathcal{I}_S = \prod_{i \in S} \mathfrak{q}_i \Lambda / q\Lambda$ for some $S \subset \{1, ..., n\}$. Let $m \geq 2$ and $\boldsymbol{a} = (a_1, ..., a_m) \in \Lambda_q^m$.

$$\boldsymbol{a}^\perp(\mathcal{I}_S) := \{(t_1, ..., t_m) \in \mathcal{I}^m : \sum_i t_i a_i \equiv 0 \bmod q\}, \text{ and}$$

$$L(\boldsymbol{a}, \mathcal{I}_S) := \{(t_1, ..., t_m) \in (\Lambda^\vee)^m : t_i \equiv a_i s \bmod q\mathcal{I}^\vee \text{ for some } s \in \Lambda^\vee, \forall i\}.$$

Lemma 11. $\boldsymbol{a}^\perp(\mathcal{I}_S) = q(L(\boldsymbol{a}, \mathcal{I}_S))^\vee$, and $L(\boldsymbol{a}, \mathcal{I}_S) = q\left(\boldsymbol{a}^\perp(\mathcal{I}_S)\right)^\vee$.

Proof. To show $\boldsymbol{a}^\perp(\mathcal{I}_S) \subset q(L(\boldsymbol{a}, \mathcal{I}_S))^\vee$, we show that any $\boldsymbol{t} = (t_1, ..., t_m) \in \boldsymbol{a}^\perp(\mathcal{I}_S)$ has $Tr(\boldsymbol{t} \cdot \boldsymbol{z}) \equiv 0 \bmod q$ for any $\boldsymbol{z} \in L(\boldsymbol{a}, \mathcal{I}_S))^\vee$. Write $z_i = a_i s + qz_i'$, for $s \in \Lambda^\vee$ and $z_i' \in \mathcal{I}^\vee$. Then $Tr(\boldsymbol{t} \cdot \boldsymbol{z}) = Tr(\sum_i t_i z_i) = \sum_i Tr(t_i z_i) = \sum_i Tr(t_i a_i s) + Tr(q \cdot t_i z_i') = Tr(\sum_i (t_i a_i) s) + qTr(t_i z_i') \in q\mathbb{Z}$.

To show the reverse containment, let $x \in L(\boldsymbol{a}, \mathcal{I}_S))^\vee$. We show $\sum_i q x_i a_i \equiv 0 \bmod q$ and $q x_i \in \mathcal{I}$. Note $q \cdot (\mathcal{I}^\vee)^m \in L(\boldsymbol{a}, \mathcal{I}_S))^\vee$. Set v_i to be an element of $L(\boldsymbol{a}, \mathcal{I}_S)^\vee$ with zeroes everywhere except for the ith entry, which is qs' for $s' \in \mathcal{I}^\vee$. Then $Tr(x \cdot v_i) = Tr(q \cdot x_i s') \in \mathbb{Z}$, so $q x_i \in \mathcal{I}$. Moreover, for all $\boldsymbol{t} \in L(\boldsymbol{a}, \mathcal{I}_S))$, we have $Tr(\boldsymbol{x} \cdot \boldsymbol{t}) \in \mathbb{Z}$. Writing $t_i = a_i s + q t_i'$ where $t_i' \in \mathcal{I}^\vee$, we obtain $Tr(\boldsymbol{x} \cdot \boldsymbol{t}) = \sum_i Tr(x_i a_i s + q x_i t_i') = Tr((\sum_i x_i a_i) s) + \sum_i Tr(q x_i t_i') \in \mathbb{Z}$, and hence we have $Tr((\sum_i x_i a_i) s) \in \mathbb{Z}$. So $\sum_i x_i a_i \in \Lambda$, as required.   □

We now lower bound the shortest vector in $L(\boldsymbol{a}, \mathcal{I}_S))$, probabilistically. Recall the construction of our algebras: $K = \mathbb{Q}(\zeta_{2^r})$ with $[K : \mathbb{Q}] = n$, $M = \mathbb{Q}(\zeta_{2^r \cdot \ell})$ for a prime ℓ congruent to 1 mod 2^r, and L is intermediate of degree 2 over K.

Lemma 12. *Let* $S \subset \{1, ..., n\}$, $m \geq 2$, $d = 2$, *and* $\epsilon > 0$. *Then* $\lambda_1^\infty(L(\boldsymbol{a}, \mathcal{I}_S))) \geq B := q^\beta/(n\sqrt{\ell})$, *where* $\beta = (1 - \frac{|S|}{n})(\frac{3}{4} - \frac{1}{m}) - \epsilon$, *except with probability at most* $2^{(1+10m)n}q^{-4mn\epsilon}$, *where* $\boldsymbol{a} \leftarrow U(\Lambda_q^\times)^m$.

Proof. Set $P = Pr_{\boldsymbol{a} \leftarrow U((\Lambda_q^\times))^m} [L(\boldsymbol{a}, \mathcal{I}_S) \text{ contains } \boldsymbol{t} \neq \boldsymbol{0} : \|\boldsymbol{t}\|_\infty < q^\beta/nd]$. To bound this, consider $P(\boldsymbol{t}, s) := Pr_{\boldsymbol{a} \leftarrow U((\Lambda_q^\times)^m)} [t_i \equiv a_i s \bmod q\mathcal{I}^\vee, \forall i]$. This, because $\boldsymbol{t} \in (\Lambda^\vee)^m$ lies in $L(\boldsymbol{a}, \mathcal{I}_S)$ iff $t_i \equiv a_i s \bmod q\mathcal{I}^\vee$ for some $s \in \Lambda^\vee$. Since the a_i are sampled independently, we can rewrite this as $P(\boldsymbol{t}, s) = \prod_i^m P_i(t_i, s)$, where $P_i(t_i, s) := Pr_{a_i \leftarrow U(\Lambda_q^\times)} [t_i \equiv a_i s \bmod q\mathcal{I}^\vee]$. So we obtain

$$P \leq \sum_{\substack{\boldsymbol{t} \in (\mathcal{I}^\vee)^m : \\ 0 < \|t_i\|_\infty < B \ \forall i}} \sum_{s \in \Lambda^\vee/q\mathcal{I}^\vee} \prod_i^m P_i(t_i, s).$$

Now, since $\mathcal{I} = \prod_{i \in S} \mathfrak{q}_i \Lambda$, we have $\mathcal{I}^{-1} = \prod_{i \in S} \mathfrak{q}_i^{-1}\Lambda$, and $q\mathcal{I}^\vee = q\mathcal{I}^{-1}\Lambda^\vee = (\prod_{i=1}^n \mathfrak{q}_i \Lambda)(\prod_{i \in S} \mathfrak{q}_i^{-1}\Lambda)\Lambda^\vee = \prod_{i \in S'} \mathfrak{q}_i\Lambda^\vee$, where $S' = \{1, ..., n\} \setminus S$. By the CRT $\mathcal{I}^\vee/q\mathcal{I}^\vee \cong \mathcal{I}^\vee/\mathfrak{q}_{i_1}\Lambda^\vee \times ... \times \mathcal{I}^\vee/\mathfrak{q}_{i_{|S'|}}\Lambda^\vee$, for a subsequence $i_j \in S'$, $j = 1, ..., |S'|$.

We claim that if $P_i(t_i, s) \neq 0$ there exists a subset $S'' \subset S'$ such that t_i and $s \in \prod_{i \in S''} \mathfrak{q}_i\Lambda^\vee$ and $t_i, s \notin \mathfrak{q}_j\Lambda^\vee$ for any $j \in S' \setminus S''$. If this weren't the case, there would exist $j \in S'$ such that $s \equiv 0 \bmod \mathfrak{q}_j\Lambda^\vee$ and $t \not\equiv 0 \bmod \mathfrak{q}_j\Lambda^\vee$, or vice versa. But in either scenario $P_i(t_i, s) = 0$, because $a_i \in \Lambda_q^\times$. So such a S'' exists.

If $j \in S''$, $t_i \equiv a_i s \equiv 0 \bmod \mathfrak{q}_j\Lambda^\vee$ for all $a_i \in \Lambda_q^\times$. Alternatively, if $j \in S' \setminus S''$, $t_i \equiv a_i s \not\equiv 0 \bmod \mathfrak{q}_j\Lambda^\vee$, so there is a unique such $a_i \in \Lambda_q^\times$ satisfying the equation. Finally, for $j \in S$, there is no constraint on the a_i. So for a fixed set size $|S''| = d'$, the number of possible $a_i \in \Lambda_q^\times$ satisfying $t_i \equiv a_i s \bmod q\mathcal{I}^\vee$ is

$$\left(\prod_{i=0}^{d-1}(q^d - q^i)\right)^{n - (|S'| - |S''|)} = \left(\prod_{i=0}^{d-1}(q^d - q^i)\right)^{n + d' - |S'|},$$

and so

$$P_i(t_i, s) = \left(\prod_{i=0}^{d-1}(q^d - q^i)\right)^{n + d' - |S'|} / \left(\prod_{i=0}^{d-1}(q^d - q^i)\right)^n = \left(\prod_{i=0}^{d-1}(q^d - q^i)\right)^{d' - |S'|},$$

since $\Lambda/\mathfrak{q}_i\Lambda \cong M_d(\mathbb{F}_q)$, so $\Lambda_q \cong \prod_{i=1}^n M_d(\mathbb{F}_q)$ and $|\Lambda_q^\times| = \prod_{i=1}^n |Gl_d(\mathbb{F}_q)|$.

We can now rewrite P as follows, where $\mathfrak{h} = \prod_{i \in S''} \mathfrak{q}_i\Lambda^\vee$:

$$P \leq \sum_{\substack{0 \leq d' \leq |S'|}} \sum_{\substack{S'' \subset S' \\ |S''| = d'}} \sum_{\substack{\boldsymbol{t} \in (\mathcal{I}^\vee)^m : t_i \in \mathfrak{h} \\ 0 < \|t_i\|_\infty < B \ \forall i}} \sum_{s \in \Lambda^\vee/q\mathcal{I}^\vee \cap \mathfrak{h}} \prod_i^m \left(\prod_{i=0}^{d-1}(q^d - q^i)\right)^{d' - |S'|}.$$

The rest of the analysis divides into two cases, depending on the size of d'. In the first case, we consider $d' \geq \beta n$. Define $N(B, d') := \#\{t \in \mathcal{I}^\vee : \|t\|_\infty < B \text{ and } t \in \mathfrak{h}\}$. Observe that $\|t\|_\infty = \max_{\alpha,i,j} |\alpha((\phi(t))_{i,j})| \geq \lambda_1^\infty(\bar{\mathfrak{h}}) \geq N_{L/\mathbb{Q}}(\bar{\mathfrak{h}})^{1/nd}$, because $t \in \mathfrak{h}$, where $\bar{\mathfrak{h}} = \mathfrak{h} \cap L$. Observe that $\bar{\mathfrak{h}} = \prod_{i \in S''} \mathfrak{q}_i \Lambda^\vee \cap L = \prod_{i \in S''} \mathfrak{q}_i \mathcal{O}_L^\vee$, so

$$N_{L/\mathbb{Q}}(\bar{\mathfrak{h}})^{1/nd} = N_{L/\mathbb{Q}}(\prod_{i \in S''} \mathfrak{q}_i \mathcal{O}_L^\vee)^{1/nd} = N_{L/\mathbb{Q}}(\prod_{i \in S''} \mathfrak{q}_i \mathcal{O}_L)^{1/nd} N_{L/\mathbb{Q}}(\mathcal{O}_L^\vee)^{1/nd}$$

$$\geq \frac{q^{\frac{dd'}{nd}}}{n\sqrt{\ell}} = \frac{q^{\frac{d'}{n}}}{n\sqrt{\ell}} \geq \frac{q^\beta}{n\sqrt{\ell}} = B,$$

where we used $N_{L/\mathbb{Q}}(\mathcal{O}_L^\vee) = \mathrm{disc}(L)^{-1}$, and the bound $\mathrm{disc}(L) \leq (n^2\ell)^n$ (this bound holds for $d = 2$). Thus $N(B, d') = 0$ if $d' \geq \beta n$.

The second case is $d' < \beta n$. Set $\mathfrak{B}(l, c) = \{x \in H^d : \|x - c\|_\infty < l\}$. One can interpret $N(B, d')$ as the number of points of $\sigma_A(\mathfrak{h})$ in $\mathfrak{B}(B, 0)$. Set $\lambda := \lambda_1^\infty(\mathfrak{h})/2$. So $\mathfrak{B}(\lambda, v_2) \cap \mathfrak{B}(\lambda, v_2) = \emptyset$ for any distinct $v_1, v_2 \in \mathfrak{h}$. Moreover, if $v \in \mathfrak{B}(B, 0)$, it holds that $\mathfrak{B}(\lambda, v) \subseteq \mathfrak{B}(B + \lambda, 0)$. We can then say that

$$N(B, d') \leq \frac{Vol(\mathfrak{B}(B + \lambda, 0))}{Vol(\mathfrak{B}(B, \lambda, 0))} = \frac{(2(\lambda + B))^{nd^2}}{2\lambda^{nd^2}} = (\frac{B}{\lambda} + 1)^{nd^2}$$

$$\leq \left(\left(\frac{q^\beta}{n\sqrt{s}}\right) / \left(\frac{\lambda_1^\infty(\mathfrak{h})}{2}\right) + 1\right)^{nd^2} \leq (2q^{\beta - \frac{d'}{n}} + 1)^{nd^2} \leq 2^{2nd^2} q^{nd^2\beta - d'd^2}.$$

As we have $\mathfrak{h}/q\mathcal{I}^\vee = \prod_{i \in S''} \mathfrak{q}_i \Lambda^\vee / \prod_{i \in S'} \mathfrak{q}_i \Lambda^\vee \cong \prod_{i \in S''} \mathfrak{q}_i \Lambda / \prod_{i \in S'} \mathfrak{q}_i \Lambda$ $\cong \Lambda / \prod_{i \in S' \backslash S''} \mathfrak{q}_i \Lambda$, then $|\mathfrak{h}/q\mathcal{I}^\vee| = |\Lambda / \prod_{i \in S' \backslash S''} \mathfrak{q}_i \Lambda| = \prod_{i=1}^{|S' \backslash S''|} |M_d(\mathbb{F}_q)| = q^{d^2(|S'| - d')}$. Then

$$P \leq \sum_{\substack{0 \leq d' \leq \beta n}} \sum_{\substack{S'' \subset S' \\ |S''| = d'}} \sum_{\substack{t \in (\mathcal{I}^\vee)^m : t_i \in \mathfrak{h} \\ 0 < \|t_i\|_\infty < B \; \forall i}} \sum_{s \in \Lambda^\vee / q\mathcal{I}^\vee \cap \mathfrak{h}} \prod_i^m \left(\prod_{i=0}^{d-1}(q^d - q^i)\right)^{d' - |S'|}$$

$$\leq \max_{d' < \beta n} \frac{q^{d^2(|S'| - d')} N(B, d')^m 2^{|S'|}}{(\prod_{i=0}^{d-1}(q^d - q^i))^{m(|S| - d')}} \leq 2^{n(1 + dm + 2d^2m)} q^{-d^2 nm\epsilon},$$

for $\epsilon = (1 - \frac{|S|}{n})(\frac{d+1}{2d} - \frac{1}{m}) - \beta$, using $|Gl_d(\mathbb{F}_q)| > q^{\frac{d(d+1)}{2}}/2^d$. $\qquad \square$

In the above proof we used $\mathrm{disc}(L) \leq (n\sqrt{\ell})^{2n}$, where ℓ is the prime used to construct L. This only holds for our construction of L when $d = 2$. The above result can be proven for more values of d, but because of the restriction in place on a theorem below, we specialise to $d = 2$. We now prove a regularity result.

Lemma 13. *Let q be completely split in L, $d = 2$, $m \geq 2$, $\delta \in (0, 1/2)$, $\epsilon > 0$, $S \subset \{1, ..., n\}$, $c \in \Lambda^m$, and $t \leftarrow D_{\Lambda^m, \sigma, c}$ for $\sigma \geq \frac{n\sqrt{\ell}}{\sqrt{\pi}}\sqrt{\ln(8mn(1 + 1/\delta))}q^{-\beta}$, where $\epsilon = (1 - \frac{|S|}{n})(\frac{3}{4} - \frac{1}{m}) - \beta$. For all but a fraction less than $2^{n(1 + 10m)}q^{-4nm\epsilon}$ of $a \in (\Lambda_q^\times)^m$,*

$$\Delta\left(\boldsymbol{t} \bmod \boldsymbol{a}^{\perp}(\mathcal{I}_S), U\left(\Lambda^m/\boldsymbol{a}^{\perp}(\mathcal{I}_S)\right)\right) \leq 2\delta.$$

Proof. A direct combination of Lemmas 2, 4, 11, and 12. □

7 An NTRU Key Generation Algorithm

In [48] and [49], the authors published work improving the hardness guarantees of NTRU. They tweak the original version of NTRU, adding an error term that allows them to demonstrate IND-CPA security, assuming the hardness of a variant of RLWE. Here we adapt their work to our setting, following [57].

The Revised CNTRU Scheme. Recall $D_{\Lambda,\sigma}$ samples over $L_{\mathbb{R}}^2$ to enable us to sample elements of Λ_q, and $p \in \Lambda_q^{\times}$. We will sample the elements s, e from the same distribution, $\chi = \lfloor D_{\xi q} \rceil_{\Lambda^{\vee}}$, where $\lfloor \cdot \rceil_{\Lambda^{\vee}}$ is the CRR discretisation, $\xi = \alpha \left(\frac{2nk}{\log(4nk)}\right)^{\frac{1}{4}}$, $\alpha q \geq \omega(\sqrt{\log 4n})$, and $k = O(1)$.

KeyGen: Sample $f' \leftarrow D_{\Lambda,\sigma}$ and let $f = p \cdot f' + 1$; if $f \bmod q \notin \Lambda_q^{\times}$, resample. Sample $g \leftarrow D_{\Lambda,\sigma}$; if $g \bmod q \notin \Lambda_q^{\times}$, resample.
Return secret key $sk = (f, g)$ and public key $pk = h = f^{-1}pg \in \Lambda_q^{\times}$.
Encryption: Given $m \in \Lambda_p^{\vee}$, sample $s, e \hookleftarrow \chi$ and return $c = hs + pe + m \in \Lambda_q^{\vee}$.
Decryption: Given ciphertext c and secret key f, compute $c' = f \cdot c \in \Lambda_q$ and return $c' \bmod p$.
Correctness: $c' = fc = f(hs + pe + m) = fhs + fpe + fm = pgs + fpe + fm$. If the coefficients of $pgs + fpe + fm$ are small enough, reduction modulo q leaves the coefficients unchanged, and $c' \bmod p = m \bmod p$.

Recall that in an order of a CDA, if p is a central element, reduction by p works as usual; if $p \notin \mathcal{Z}(\Lambda)$, then we understand $(p) = \Lambda p \Lambda$.

We want to prove that if there is an IND-CPA attack on CNTRU, then a variant of CLWE can be broken. The following holds for the algebras used in CLWE, namely when $K = \mathbb{Q}(\zeta_{2r})$, $n = [K : \mathbb{Q}]$ and L is a finite cyclic extension of K of degree 2. We now show there is a high probability of selecting an appropriate value f for the public key.

Lemma 14 *[21, Lemma 17].* For a fixed d, the proportion of invertible elements of $M_d(\mathbb{F}_q)$ is at least $(1 - \frac{1}{q})^d$.

Lemma 15. Let $d = 2$, $0 < \epsilon < \frac{1}{2}$, $r \geq 2n\sqrt[4]{l}\sqrt{\frac{\ln 8n(1+1/\epsilon)}{\pi}} \cdot q^{\frac{1}{n}}$, $p \in \Lambda_q^{\times}$, $D_{\Lambda,r}$ a discrete Gaussian sampling Λ and $q \in \mathbb{Z}$ a prime that splits completely in K, i.e. $q\mathcal{O}_K = \prod_{i=1}^{[K:\mathbb{Q}]} \mathfrak{p}_i$. Then $\Pr_{f' \leftarrow D_r}[(pf' + 1 \bmod q\Lambda) \notin \Lambda_q^{\times}] \leq n\left(\frac{2}{q} - \frac{1}{q^2} + 2\epsilon\right)$.

Proof. We bound $\Pr_{f' \leftarrow D_r}[(pf' + 1 \bmod \mathfrak{p}_i\Lambda) \notin \Lambda/\mathfrak{p}_i\Lambda^{\times}]$. Since r is sufficiently large, $pf' + 1 \bmod \mathfrak{p}_i\Lambda$ is statistically close to the uniform distribution. Thus the probability that $pf' + 1$ is not invertible in $\Lambda/\mathfrak{p}_i\Lambda$ is 1 minus the proportion of invertible elements in $\Lambda/\mathfrak{p}_i\Lambda \cong M_d(\mathbb{F}_q)$ plus 2ϵ. Note $M_d(\mathbb{F}_q)$ has size $|M_d(\mathbb{F}_q)| = q^{d^2}$ and the set of invertible elements in R_i has size $|GL_d(q)| = \prod_{i=0}^{d-1}(q^d - q^i)$. By Lemma 14, this proportion is at least $(1 - \frac{1}{q})^d$, so with $d = 2$ we lower bound the probability with $1 - (1 - \frac{1}{q})^2$. The CRT and a union bound implies the result.

Regarding r, since when $d = 2$ and K is a cyclotomic field with power of 2 conductor, the number of roots of unity in Λ is equal to $[\mathcal{A} : \mathbb{Q}]$ and hence since $\mathfrak{p}_i\Lambda$ is a Λ-ideal, $\lambda_{nd^2}(\mathfrak{p}_i\Lambda) = \lambda_1(\mathfrak{p}_i\Lambda)$. We then apply Lemma 3 and compute $\eta_\epsilon(\mathfrak{p}_i\Lambda) \leq \sqrt{\ln(2nd^2(1 + 1/\epsilon))/\pi} \cdot \lambda_{nd^2}(\mathfrak{p}_i\Lambda) = \sqrt{\ln(2nd^2(1 + 1/\epsilon))/\pi} \cdot \lambda_1(\mathfrak{p}_i\Lambda) \leq \sqrt{\ln(2nd^2(1 + 1/\epsilon))/\pi} \cdot 2n\sqrt[4]{l}q^{1/n} = \sqrt{\ln(8n(1 + 1/\epsilon))/\pi} \cdot 2n\sqrt[4]{l}q^{1/n}$. □

If $q \geq n + 1$, then $(1 - \frac{1}{q})^{nd} \geq \left((1 - \frac{1}{n+1})^n\right)^d \geq e^{-d}$ and the proportion of invertible elements in Λ_q is non-negligible. We now show that with high likelihood the elements f and g used to construct the public key will not be too large.

Lemma 16. *Let $n \geq 8$ be a power of 2 such that $x^n + 1$ splits completely modulo $q \geq 8n$. Let $\mathcal{A} = (L/K, \theta, \gamma)$ with $K = \mathbb{Q}(\zeta_n)$, $[L : K] = 2$, $\delta > 0$, and $\sigma \geq 2n\sqrt[4]{l}\sqrt{\frac{2\ln(24n)}{\pi}} \cdot q^{1/n}$. The secret key polynomials f, g returned by the cyclic-NTRU algorithm satisfy, with probability $\geq 1 - 2^{4-4n}$,*

$$\|f\| \leq \sqrt{2}(1 + \sigma\|p\|_\infty\sqrt{2n}) \text{ and } \|g\| \leq 2\sigma\sqrt{n}.$$

Proof. When $d = 2$, $\lambda_{nd^2}(\Lambda) = \lambda_1(\Lambda) \leq d\sqrt{n} \cdot (\text{disc}(\Lambda))^{\frac{1}{2nd^2}} \leq 2n\sqrt[4]{l}$. If we set $\delta = \frac{1}{3n-1}$, then Lemma 3 implies $\eta_\delta(\Lambda) \leq \sqrt{\frac{2\ln(24n)}{\pi}} \cdot 2n\sqrt[4]{l}$. We can then use Lemma 6 to obtain $\text{Pr}_{x \leftarrow D_{\Lambda,\sigma}}(\|x\| \geq d\sqrt{n}\sigma) \leq \frac{3n}{3n-2}2^{-nd^2}$. Then

$$\text{Pr}_{g \leftarrow D_{\Lambda,\sigma}}\left(\|g\| \geq d\sqrt{n}\sigma \mid g \in \Lambda_q^\times\right) = \frac{\text{Pr}_{g \leftarrow D_{\Lambda,\sigma}}\left(\|g\| \geq d\sqrt{n}\sigma \text{ and } g \in \Lambda_q^\times\right)}{\text{Pr}_{g \leftarrow D_{\Lambda,\sigma}}\left(g \in \Lambda_q^\times\right)}$$

$$\leq \frac{\text{Pr}_{g \leftarrow D_{\Lambda,\sigma}}(\|g\| \geq d\sqrt{n}\sigma)}{\text{Pr}_{g \leftarrow D_{\Lambda,\sigma}}\left(g \in \Lambda_q^\times\right)}$$

$$\leq \frac{3n}{3n-2} \cdot 2^{-4n} \cdot \left(1/1 - n\left(\frac{2}{q} - \frac{1}{q^2} + 2\epsilon\right)\right)$$

$$\leq 2^{-4n} \cdot 16 \leq 2^{4-4n}.$$

This applies to both f' and g, so we have $\|f'\|, \|g\| \leq 2\sqrt{n}\sigma$ with probability at least $1 - 2^{4-4n}$. Finally, observe $\|f\| = \|pf' + 1\| \leq \|pf'\| + \|1\| \leq \|p\|_\infty\|f'\| + \sqrt{2} \leq \|p\|_\infty\sigma 2\sqrt{n} + \sqrt{2} = \sqrt{2}(1 + \sigma\|p\|_\infty\sqrt{2n})$ with probability $\geq 1 - 2^{4-4n}$. □

We now show near-uniformity of the required distribution, to ensure our NTRU public keys are statistically close to the uniform distribution over $\Lambda_q^\times$.

Theorem 4. *Let $\epsilon > 0$, q be a completely split prime, $p \in \mathcal{Z}(\Lambda_q^\times)$, and $\sigma \geq 4n^{3/2}\sqrt[4]{\ell}\sqrt{2\ln(32nq)}q^{\frac{1}{2}+2\epsilon}$. Let $y_i \in \Lambda_q$ and $z_i = -y_i p^{-1} \bmod q$ for $i = 1, 2$, and $D_{\sigma,z_i}^\times$ denote $D_{\Lambda,\sigma}$ restricted by rejection to $\Lambda_q^\times + z_i$. Then when $d = 2$,*

$$\Delta\left(\frac{y_1 + pD_{\sigma,z_1}^\times}{y_2 + pD_{\sigma,z_2}^\times} \bmod q, U\left(\Lambda_q^\times\right)\right) \leq 2^{22n}q^{-8n\epsilon}.$$

Proof. Let $P_a := Pr_{f_i \leftarrow D_{\sigma,z_i}^\times, i=1,2}\left[(y_1 + pf_1) \cdot (y_2 + pf_2)^{-1} = a\right]$, where $a \in \Lambda_q^\times$. We aim to show that $|P_a - \frac{1}{|\Lambda_q^\times|}| < \epsilon'$, for some small $\epsilon' > 0$, except for an exponentially small fraction of the $a \in \Lambda_q^\times$.

Let $\boldsymbol{a} = (a_1, a_2) \leftarrow U((\Lambda_q^\times)^2)$. When $z_i = -p^{-1}y_i \bmod q$, $(y_1 + pf_1) \cdot (y_2 + pf_2)^{-1} = -a_1^{-1}a_2 \bmod q$ is equivalent to $a_1f_1 + a_2f_2 = p^{-1}(-a_1y_1 - a_2y_2) \bmod q$, and so to $a_1f_1 + a_2f_2 = a_1z_1 + a_2z_2 \bmod q$. Since $-a_1^{-1}a_2 \in \Lambda_q^\times$ is uniform,

$$P_{-a_1^{-1}a_2} = P_a := Pr_{f_i \leftarrow D_{\sigma,z_i}^\times, i=1,2}[a_1f_1 + a_2f_2 = a_1z_1 + a_2z_2 \bmod q],$$

if $\boldsymbol{a} \in (\Lambda_q^\times)^2$. One can see that the set of solutions to $a_1f_1 + a_2f_2 = a_1z_1 + a_2z_2 \bmod q$ in Λ, taken from $D_{\sigma,z_i}^\times$, $i = 1, 2$, is $\boldsymbol{z} + \boldsymbol{a}^{\perp\times}$, where $\boldsymbol{a}^{\perp\times} = \boldsymbol{a}^\perp \cap (\Lambda_q^\times \cap q\Lambda)^2$, and $\boldsymbol{a}^\perp = \boldsymbol{a}^\perp(\Lambda_q)$. We can then write

$$P_a = \frac{D_{\Lambda^2,\sigma}(\boldsymbol{z} + \boldsymbol{a}^{\perp\times})}{D_{\Lambda,\sigma}(z_1 + \Lambda_q^\times + q\Lambda) \cdot D_{\Lambda,\sigma}(z_2 + \Lambda_q^\times + q\Lambda)}.$$

Now, let $\boldsymbol{t} \in \boldsymbol{a}^\perp$. Then $t_1a_1 + t_2 + a_2 \equiv 0 \bmod q$ implies that $t_2 = -t_1\frac{a_1}{a_2}$ and the t_i lie in a shared ideal of Λ_q. Denote this ideal by $\mathcal{I}_S$. Then

$$\boldsymbol{a}^{\perp\times} = \boldsymbol{a}^\perp \setminus \cup_{S \subset \{1,\ldots,n\}} \boldsymbol{a}^\perp(\mathcal{I}_S) \text{ and } \Lambda_q^\times + q\Lambda = \Lambda \setminus \cup_{S \subset \{1,\ldots,n\}\setminus\emptyset}(\mathcal{I}_S + q\Lambda).$$

Applying an inclusion-exclusion argument, we get two expressions to analyse:

$$D_{\Lambda^2,\sigma}(\boldsymbol{z} + \boldsymbol{a}^{\perp\times}) = \sum_{S \subset \{1,\ldots,n\}} (-1)^{|S|} D_{\Lambda^2,\sigma}(\boldsymbol{z} + \boldsymbol{a}^\perp(\mathcal{I}_S)), \text{ and} \qquad (2)$$

$$D_{\Lambda,\sigma}(z_i + \Lambda_q^\times + q\Lambda) = \sum_{S \subset \{1,\ldots,n\}} (-1)^{|S|} D_{\Lambda,\sigma}(z_i + \mathcal{I}_S + q\Lambda). \qquad (3)$$

We deal with (2) first, with two cases. If $|S| \leq \epsilon n$, use Lemma 13 with $m = 2$ and $\delta = q^{-nd^2 - \lfloor \epsilon n \rfloor d^2}$. Note that $q\Lambda^2 \subset \boldsymbol{a}^\perp(\mathcal{I}_S) \subset \Lambda^2$, so $|\Lambda^2/\boldsymbol{a}^\perp(\mathcal{I}_S)| = q^{d^2(n-|S|)}$. Then for all except a fraction less than $2^{n(1+4d^2+2d)}q^{-2d^2n\epsilon}$ of $\boldsymbol{a} \in (\Lambda_q^\times)^2$,

$$\left|D_{\Lambda^2,\sigma}(\boldsymbol{z} + \boldsymbol{a}^\perp(\mathcal{I}_S)) - \frac{q^{d^2(n-|S|)}}{q^{2nd^2}}\right| = \left|D_{\Lambda^2,\sigma}(\boldsymbol{z} + \boldsymbol{a}^\perp(\mathcal{I}_S)) - q^{-nd^2 - d^2 S}\right| \leq 2\delta.$$

In the second case, when $|S| > \epsilon n$, one can choose a subset $S'' \subset S'$ such that $|S''| = \lfloor \epsilon n \rfloor$. Then $\boldsymbol{a}^\perp(\mathcal{I}_S) \subset \boldsymbol{a}^\perp(\mathcal{I}_{S'})$, so $D_{\Lambda^2,\sigma}(\boldsymbol{z} + \boldsymbol{a}^\perp(\mathcal{I}_S)) \leq D_{\Lambda^2,\sigma}(\boldsymbol{z} + \boldsymbol{a}^\perp(\mathcal{I}_{S'}))$, so $D_{\Lambda^2,\sigma}(\boldsymbol{z} + \boldsymbol{a}^\perp(\mathcal{I}_S)) \leq 2\delta + q^{-nd^2 - d^2\lfloor \epsilon n \rfloor}$. We can now say that

$$\left| D_{\Lambda^2,\sigma}(\boldsymbol{z} + \boldsymbol{a}^{\perp\times}) - 2^{n(d-1)} \frac{|\Lambda_q^\times|}{|\Lambda_q|^2} \right|$$

$$\leq \left| \sum_{S \subset \{1,\dots,n\}} (-1)^{|S|} D_{\Lambda^2,\sigma}(\boldsymbol{z} + \boldsymbol{a}^\perp(\mathcal{I}_S)) - 2^{n(d-1)} \left(\frac{(q^{d^2}-1)^n}{2^{n(d-1)}q^{2nd^2}} \right) \right|$$

$$\leq \left| \sum_{S \subset \{1,\dots,n\}} (-1)^{|S|} D_{\Lambda^2,\sigma}(\boldsymbol{z} + \boldsymbol{a}^\perp(\mathcal{I}_S)) - \frac{(q^{d^2}-1)^n}{q^{2nd^2}} \right|$$

$$\leq \left| \sum_{S \subset \{1,\dots,n\}} (-1)^{|S|} D_{\Lambda^2,\sigma}(\boldsymbol{z} + \boldsymbol{a}^\perp(\mathcal{I}_S)) - \sum_{k=0}^{n} (-1)^k \binom{n}{k} q^{d^2(-n-k)} \right|$$

$$\leq \left| \sum_{S \subset \{1,\dots,n\}} (-1)^{|S|} D_{\Lambda^2,\sigma}(\boldsymbol{z} + \boldsymbol{a}^\perp(\mathcal{I}_S)) - \sum_{S \subset \{1,\dots,n\}} (-1)^{|S|} q^{-d^2(n+|S|)} \right|$$

$$\leq \left| \sum_{S \subset \{1,\dots,n\}} (-1)^{|S|} \left(D_{\Lambda^2,\sigma}(\boldsymbol{z} + \boldsymbol{a}^\perp(\mathcal{I}_S)) - q^{-d^2(n+|S|)} \right) \right|$$

$$\leq 2^n (2\delta + 2q^{-d^2(n+\lfloor \epsilon n \rfloor)}) \leq 2^{n+1}(\delta + q^{-d^2(n+\lfloor \epsilon n \rfloor)}),$$

except for a fraction of $\boldsymbol{a} \in (\Lambda_q^\times)^2$ less than $2^{n(2+2d+4d^2)}q^{-2d^2 n\epsilon}$. Writing

$$D_{\Lambda^2,\sigma}(\boldsymbol{z} + \boldsymbol{a}^{\perp\times}) = (1 + \delta_0) 2^{n(d-1)} \frac{|\Lambda_q^\times|}{|\Lambda_q|^2},$$

we find that $|\delta_0| \leq \frac{|\Lambda_q|^2}{|\Lambda_q^\times|} 2^{-n(d-1)} 2^{n+1}(\delta + q^{-d^2(n+\lfloor \epsilon n \rfloor)})$
$\leq 2^{nd} q^{nd^2} 2^{-n(d-1)} 2^{n+1}(\delta + q^{-d^2(n+\lfloor \epsilon n \rfloor)}) = 2^{2n+2} q^{-d^2 \lfloor \epsilon n \rfloor}$.

Moving on to (3), begin by observing that

$$\det(\mathcal{I}_S + q\Lambda) = N_{\mathcal{A}/\mathbb{Q}}(\mathcal{I})\sqrt{\operatorname{disc}(\Lambda)} = q^{|S|}\sqrt{\operatorname{disc}(\Lambda)}.$$

Moreover, $\lambda_{nd}(\mathcal{I}_S + q\Lambda) = \lambda_1(\mathcal{I}_S + q\Lambda) \leq d\sqrt{n} \cdot \det(\mathcal{I}_S + q\Lambda)^{1/nd^2} = d\sqrt{n} \cdot q^{|S|/nd^2} \operatorname{disc}(\Lambda)^{1/2nd^2}$. When $d = 2$ and n is a power of two, we in fact have $\lambda_{nd^2}(\mathcal{I}_S + q\Lambda) \leq d\sqrt{n} \cdot q^{|S|/nd^2} \operatorname{disc}(\Lambda)^{1/2nd^2}$. Since $\operatorname{disc}(\Lambda/\mathbb{Z}) \leq (n\sqrt{\ell})^{4n}$, we obtain $\lambda_{nd^2}(\mathcal{I}_S + q\Lambda) \leq d\sqrt{n}q^{|S|/nd^2}\sqrt{n}\sqrt[4]{\ell} = nd\sqrt[4]{\ell}q^{|S|/nd^2}$. Then Lemma 3 implies that $\eta_\delta(\mathcal{I}_S + q\Lambda) \leq \sqrt{\ln(2nd^2(1+1/\delta))/\pi}\lambda_{nd^2}(\mathcal{I}_S + q\Lambda)$, so we find $\eta_\delta(\mathcal{I}_S + q\Lambda) \leq \sqrt{\ln(2nd^2(1+1/\delta))/\pi}nd\sqrt[4]{\ell}q^{|S|/nd^2}$. Since σ is larger than this quantity for $|S| \leq n/2$ and $\delta = q^{-nd^2/2}$, we can apply Lemma 4 to obtain $|D_{\Lambda,\sigma}(z_i + \mathcal{I}_S + q\Lambda) - \frac{1}{|\Lambda/\mathcal{I}|}| = |D_{\Lambda,\sigma}(z_i + \mathcal{I}_S + q\Lambda) - \frac{1}{q^{d^2|S|}}| \leq 2\delta$. If $|S| > n/2$, we can pick a subset $S' \subset S$ such that $|S'| \leq n/2$, and then $D_{\Lambda,\sigma}(z_i + \mathcal{I}_S + q\Lambda) \leq D_{\Lambda,\sigma}(z_i + \mathcal{I}_{S'} + q\Lambda) \leq 2\delta + q^{-nd^2/2}$. We now justify a claim, before proceeding with the rest of the proof:

Claim. For $d \geq 2$ and $q \geq 5$, we have $\prod_{i=1}^{d}(q^i - 1) \geq (q^{\frac{d(d+1)}{2}} - 1)/2^{\frac{d-1}{2}}$.

To see this, induct on d. When $d = 2$, the claim simplifies to the statement $(q-1)(q^2-1) > (q^3-1)/\sqrt{2}$, which is true iff the polynomial $(\sqrt{2}-1)q^3 - \sqrt{2}q^2 - \sqrt{2}q + (1+\sqrt{2}) > 0$, which is true when $q \geq 5$. Suppose the claim is true for $d = k-1 \geq 2$, and consider $\prod_{i=1}^{k}(q^i - 1)$. By induction, $\prod_{i=1}^{k-1}(q^i - 1) \geq (q^{\frac{k(k-1)}{2}} - 1)/2^{\frac{k-2}{2}}$, and we can write

$$\prod_{i=1}^{k}(q^i - 1) \geq (q^{\frac{k(k-1)}{2}} - 1)(q^k - 1)/2^{\frac{k-2}{2}} = (q^{\frac{k(k+1)}{2}} - q^{\frac{k(k-1)}{2}} - q^k + 1)/2^{\frac{k-2}{2}}.$$

Then the claim is true if

$$(q^{\frac{k(k+1)}{2}} - q^{\frac{k(k-1)}{2}} - q^k + 1)/2^{\frac{k-2}{2}} > (q^{\frac{k(k+1)}{2}} - 1)/2^{\frac{k-1}{2}},$$

i.e. $(\sqrt{2}-1)q^{\frac{k(k+1)}{2}} - \sqrt{2}q^{\frac{k(k-1)}{2}} - \sqrt{2}q^k + \sqrt{2} + 1 > 0$, which holds if $q \geq 5$, $k \geq 2$.

The claim implies that $2^{\frac{n(d-1)}{2}}|\Lambda_q^{\times}|/(q^{d^2} - 1)^n > 1$, for appropriate d and q, which we will use below. Resuming the proof, we have

$$\left| D_{\Lambda,\sigma}(z_i + \Lambda_q^{\times} + q\Lambda) - 2^{\frac{n(d-1)}{2}} \frac{|\Lambda_q^{\times}|}{|\Lambda_q|} \right|$$

$$\leq \left| \sum_{S\subset\{1,\ldots,n\}} (-1)^{|S|} D_{\Lambda,\sigma}(z_i + \mathcal{I}_S + q\Lambda) - \frac{(q^{d^2} - 1)^n}{q^{nd^2}} \right|$$

$$= \left| \sum_{S\subset\{1,\ldots,n\}} (-1)^{|S|} D_{\Lambda,\sigma}(z_i + \mathcal{I}_S + q\Lambda) - \sum_{k=0}^{n}(-1)^k \binom{n}{k} q^{-d^2 k} \right|$$

$$= \left| \sum_{S\subset\{1,\ldots,n\}} (-1)^{|S|} D_{\Lambda,\sigma}(z_i + \mathcal{I}_S + q\Lambda) - \sum_{S\subset\{1,\ldots,n\}} (-1)^{|S|} q^{-d^2|S|} \right|$$

$$= \left| \sum_{S\subset\{1,\ldots,n\}} (-1)^{|S|} \left(D_{\Lambda,\sigma}(z_i + \mathcal{I}_S + q\Lambda) - q^{-d^2|S|} \right) \right|$$

$$\leq 2^n(2\delta + 2q^{-nd^2/2}) = 2^{n+1}(\delta + q^{-nd^2/2});$$

writing $D_{\Lambda,\sigma}(z_i + \Lambda_q^{\times} + q\Lambda) = (1+\delta_i)2^{\frac{n(d-1)}{2}} \frac{|\Lambda_q^{\times}|}{|\Lambda_q|}$, for $\epsilon < \frac{1}{2}$ we get the required bounds on the δ_i since $|\delta_i| \leq 2^{\frac{-n(d-1)}{2}} \frac{|\Lambda_q|}{|\Lambda_q^{\times}|} 2^{n+1}(\delta + q^{-nd^2/2}) \leq 2^{\frac{n(d+3)}{2}+2}q^{-nd^2/2}$.

Finally, we obtain that since $P_a = \dfrac{D_{\Lambda^2,\sigma}(z+a^{\perp\times})}{D_{\Lambda,\sigma}(z_1+\Lambda_q^\times+q\Lambda)\cdot D_{\Lambda,\sigma}(z_2+\Lambda_q^\times+q\Lambda)}$,

$$\left| P_a - \frac{1}{|\Lambda_q^\times|} \right| = \left| \frac{D_{\Lambda^2,\sigma}(z+a^{\perp\times})}{D_{\Lambda,\sigma}(z_1+\Lambda_q^\times+q\Lambda)\cdot D_{\Lambda,\sigma}(z_2+\Lambda_q^\times+q\Lambda)} - \frac{1}{|\Lambda_q^\times|} \right|$$

$$= \left| \frac{(1+\delta_0)2^{n(d-1)}\frac{|\Lambda_q^\times|}{|\Lambda_q|^2}}{(1+\delta_1)2^{\frac{n(d-1)}{2}}\frac{|\Lambda_q^\times|}{|\Lambda_q|}(1+\delta_2)2^{\frac{n(d-1)}{2}}\frac{|\Lambda_q^\times|}{|\Lambda_q|}} - \frac{1}{|\Lambda_q^\times|} \right|$$

$$= \left| \frac{(1+\delta_0)}{(1+\delta_1)(1+\delta_2)|\Lambda_q^\times|} - \frac{1}{|\Lambda_q^\times|} \right|,$$

and since the δ_i tend to 0, we obtain the result. $\qquad\square$

8 A Provably Secure NTRU-Based Scheme

In this section we provide a proof of IND-CPA security, subject to the hardness of LWE in CDAs, for the revised CNTRU scheme. Recall the definition of IND-CPA security:

Definition 20. [31] Let $\Pi = $ (Gen, Enc, Dec) be a PKE scheme, and $\mathcal{A}$ be an adversary. Say Π is *indistinguishable under chosen-plaintext attack* if a ppt. adversary in the following experiment $\mathrm{PubK}_{\mathcal{A},\Pi}(n)$ has negligible advantage:

1. Gen is run to obtain keys (pk, sk).
2. Adversary $\mathcal{A}$ is given pk, and outputs a pair of equal-length messages m_0, m_1 in the message space.
3. A uniform bit $b \in \{0,1\}$ is chosen, and then a ciphertext $c \leftarrow \mathrm{Enc}_{pk}(m_b)$ is computed and given to $\mathcal{A}$. We call c the challenge ciphertext.
4. $\mathcal{A}$ outputs a bit b'. The output of the experiment is 1 if $b' = b$, and 0 otherwise. If $b' = b$ we say that $\mathcal{A}$ succeeds.

That is, $\Pr\left[\mathrm{PubK}_{\mathcal{A},\Pi}(n) = 1\right] \le \frac{1}{2} + \mathrm{neg}(n)$.

Security Analysis. We first obtain a bound on the infinity norm of a discretised Gaussian sample under the canonical embedding with the following lemma:

Lemma 17. *Assume that* $\xi = \alpha\left(\frac{ndk}{\log(nd^2k)}\right)^{\frac{1}{4}}$, $\chi = \lfloor D_{\xi q}\rceil_{\Lambda^\vee}$, $\alpha q \ge \omega(\sqrt{\log nd^2})$ *and* $k = O(1)$. *Set* $\delta = \omega\left(\sqrt{nd\log nd^2}\cdot\alpha^2 q^2\right)$ *and* B *the decoding basis of* $\Lambda^\vee$. *Then for any* $t \in H^d$, $\Pr_{x\leftarrow\chi}\left(|\langle t, x\rangle| > \delta\|t\|^2\right) \le (nd^2)^{-\omega(\sqrt{nd\log nd^2})\|t\|^2}$.

Proof. A Gaussian random variable $x \hookleftarrow D_{q\xi}$ of mean $\mathbf{0}$ and standard deviation $\frac{q\xi}{\sqrt{2\pi}}$ has a noncentral subgaussian discretisation $\lfloor x\rceil$ with noncentrality 0 and deviation $\left(\frac{q^2\xi^2}{2\pi} + \frac{1}{2}s_1(B)^2\right)^{\frac{1}{2}}$ by Lemma 8. The definition of subgaussian gives

$$E\left(e^{\langle t, \lfloor x\rceil\rangle}\right) \le e^{\frac{1}{2}\left(\frac{q^2\xi^2}{2\pi} + \frac{1}{2}s_1(B)^2\right)\|t\|^2},$$

for any $t \in H^d$. A Chernoff bound then implies

$$\Pr\left(|\langle t, \lfloor x \rceil \rangle| > \delta\|t\|^2\right) = \Pr\left(e^{|\langle t, \lfloor x \rceil \rangle|} > e^{\delta\|t\|^2}\right)$$

$$\leq 2e^{\frac{1}{2}\left(\frac{q^2\xi^2}{2\pi} + \frac{1}{2}s_1(B)^2\right)\|t\|^2 - \delta\|t\|^2}.$$

$s_1(B) \leq 1$, so $\frac{1}{2}\left(\frac{q^2\xi^2}{2\pi} + \frac{1}{2}s_1(B)^2\right)\|t\|^2 = \Omega\left(\alpha^2 q^2 \sqrt{nd}\log(nd^2)^{-\frac{1}{2}} \cdot \|t\|^2\right)$. Thus

$$\Pr\left(|\langle t, \lfloor x \rceil \rangle| > \delta\|t\|^2\right) \leq (nd^2)^{-\omega(\sqrt{nd\log nd^2})\|t\|^2}.$$ $\square$

The above lemma gives an estimate for $\|x\|_\infty$ with $x \hookleftarrow \chi = \lfloor D_{q\cdot\xi} \rceil$:

$$Pr_{e \leftarrow \lceil \chi \rfloor}\left(\|e\|_\infty > \delta\right) \leq (nd^2)^{-\delta}, \tag{4}$$

where $\delta = \omega(\sqrt{nd\log nd^2}\alpha^2 q^2)$ and $\alpha q \geq \omega(\sqrt{\log nd^2})$. In the following, we make our assumption that $\ell \leq Cn$ for some constant $C \geq 2$; in this case, when C_1 and C_2 are bounds such that $\|\cdot\|^c \leq C_1\|\cdot\|$ and $\|\cdot\| \leq C_2\|\cdot\|^c$, we have $C_1 = \sqrt{2}s_1(\overrightarrow{p}) < 2\sqrt{2}Cn$, so $C_1 = O(n)$, and $C_2 = \sqrt{2}s_1(\overrightarrow{d}) < 1$.

Lemma 18. *Let $n \geq 8$ be a power of 2, $q \geq 8n$ split completely in L, $\ell \leq Cn$, $\sigma \geq 2n\sqrt[4]{l}\sqrt{\frac{2\ln(24n)}{\pi}}q^{1/n}$. The decryption algorithm outputs m with probability $1 - (4n)^{-\omega(\sqrt{2n\log 4n})}$ over s, e, f, g if $\omega\left(2\sqrt{2}n^2\sqrt{\log 4n}\alpha^2 q^2\right)\sigma\|p\|_\infty^2 \leq q/2$.*

Proof. Notice that $f \cdot h \cdot s = p \cdot g \cdot s \mod q\Lambda^\vee$, we have $fc = pgs + pfe + fm \mod q\Lambda^\vee \in \Lambda^\vee$. If $\|pgs + pfe + fm\|_\infty^c < \frac{q}{2}$, then we have fc has the representation of the form $pgs + pfe + fm$ in $\Lambda_q^\vee$. Hence, we have $m = (fc \mod q\Lambda^\vee) \mod p\Lambda^\vee$. It thus suffices to upper bound the probability that $\|pgs + pfe + fm\|_\infty^c \geq \frac{q}{2}$.

Note that $\|fc\|_\infty^c \leq \|fc\|^c \leq C_1\|fc\| = C_1\|pgs + pfe + fm\| \leq C_1(\|pgs\| + \|pfe\| + \|fm\|)$. By the choice of σ and Lemma 16, with probability larger than $1 - 2^{4-nd^2}$, $\|f\| \leq \sqrt{d}(1 + \sigma\|p\|_\infty\sqrt{nd})$ and $\|g\| \leq \sqrt{nd}\sigma$. Combining with (4),

$$\|pfe\| + \|pgs\| \leq \sqrt{d}(1 + \sigma\|p\|_\infty\sqrt{nd})\|p\|_\infty\|e\|_\infty + \sqrt{nd}\sigma\|p\|_\infty\|s\|_\infty$$

$$\leq 2\sigma\sqrt{nd}\|p\|_\infty^2\|e\|_\infty + \sqrt{nd}\sigma\|p\|_\infty\|s\|_\infty \leq \omega(nd^{3/2}\sqrt{\log nd^2}\alpha^2 q^2)\sigma\|p\|_\infty^2$$

with probability $1 - (nd^2)^{-\omega(\sqrt{nd\log nd^2})}$. Since $m \in \Lambda^\vee/p\Lambda^\vee$, by reducing modulo the $p\sigma(d)_i$, write $m = \sum_{i=1}^{nd^2}\varepsilon_i p\sigma(d)_i$ with $\varepsilon_i \in \left(-\frac{1}{2}, \frac{1}{2}\right]$. We have

$$\|m\| = \left\|\sum_{i=1}^{nd^2}\varepsilon_i p\sigma(d)_i\right\| \leq \|p\|_\infty\left\|\sum_{i=1}^{nd^2}\varepsilon_i\sigma(d)_i\right\| \leq \|p\|_\infty\frac{\sqrt{nd}}{2}C_2,$$

so $\|fm\| \leq \|f\|\|m\| \leq \sqrt{d}(1 + \sigma\|p\|_\infty\sqrt{nd}) \cdot \|p\|_\infty\frac{\sqrt{nd}}{2}C_2 \leq 2\sigma\sqrt{nd}\|p\|_\infty \cdot \|p\|_\infty\frac{\sqrt{nd}}{2}C_2 \leq nd^2\sigma\|p\|_\infty^2 C_2$ with probability $\geq 1 - 2^{4-n}$. All together, we have

$$\|fc\|_\infty^c \leq C_1\left(\omega(nd^{3/2}\sqrt{\log nd^2}\alpha^2 q^2)\sigma\|p\|_\infty^2 + nd^2\sigma\|p\|_\infty^2 C_2\right)$$

$$\leq \omega\left(n^2 d^{3/2}\sqrt{\log nd^2} \cdot \alpha^2 q^2\right)\sigma\|p\|_\infty^2$$

with probability $1 - (nd^2)^{-\omega(\sqrt{nd\log nd^2})}$, since $C_2 \leq 1$ and $C_1 = O(n)$. $\square$

We now attempt a proof of IND-CPA security. Recall the CLWE variant we will use: let $s, e \leftarrow \chi$, and $a \leftarrow U(\Lambda_q^\times)$. Here χ is the CRR discretisation of the usual CLWE distribution to $\Lambda_q^\vee$; [21] gave a reduction from CLWE to this variant. Output $(a, as + e) \in \Lambda_q^\times \times \Lambda_q^\vee$, and call this distribution $A_{q,s,\chi}^\times$. Define the usual search and decision problems over this distribution to obtain $\text{CLWE}_{HNF}^\times$.

Lemma 19. *Let $n \geq 8$ be a power of 2, $d = 2$, $\ell \leq Cn$, and $q \geq 8n$ a prime such that $x^n + 1$ splits completely modulo q. Let $\delta > 0$, $p \in \mathcal{Z}\left(\Lambda_q^\times\right)$ and $\sigma \geq 2n^{3/2} \sqrt[4]{\ell} \sqrt{\ln(32nq)} q^{\frac{1}{2}+2\epsilon}$ satisfy the conditions of Lemma 18 and Theorem 4. If there exists an IND-CPA attack algorithm $\mathcal{A}$ against CNTRU, running in time T with advantage δ, then there exists an algorithm to solve decision-$\text{CLWE}_{HNF}^\times$ that runs in time $T' = T + O(\text{poly}(n))$ with success probability $\delta' = \delta - q^{-\Omega(n)}$.*

Note that if $p \in \mathbb{Z}_q^\times$, the algorithm runs in time $T' = T + O(n)$.

Proof. The proof runs similarly to [48, Lemma 13], [57, Lemma 16]. We construct an algorithm $\mathcal{B}$ against $\text{CLWE}_{HNF}^\times$ as follows: let $\mathcal{O}$ be an oracle that samples from one of $U(\Lambda_q^\times \times \Lambda_q^\vee)$ and $A_{s,\chi}^\times$ for some previously chosen $s \leftarrow \chi$. $\mathcal{B}$ begins by obtaining a sample (h', c') from $\Lambda_q^\times \times \Lambda_q^\vee$ using $\mathcal{O}$. Then $\mathcal{B}$ runs $\mathcal{A}$ with public key $h = p \cdot h' \in \Lambda_q$. When $\mathcal{A}$ outputs messages $m_0, m_1 \in \Lambda_p^\vee$, then $\mathcal{B}$ samples $b \leftarrow U(\{0,1\})$, computes ciphertext $c = p \cdot c' + m_b$, and sends c to $\mathcal{A}$. Finally, $\mathcal{A}$ submits a guess b' for b, and if $b' = b$, $\mathcal{B}$ outputs 1. Else, $\mathcal{B}$ outputs 0.

Since h' is uniformly random in $\Lambda_q^\times$ and p is invertible mod q, so is h. Thus the public key given to $\mathcal{A}$ is within statistical distance $q^{-\Omega(n)}$ of the public key distribution in the genuine attack, by Theorem 4. Moreover, since $c' = h \cdot s + e$ with $s, e \leftarrow \chi$, the c given to $\mathcal{A}$ has the right distribution as in the IND-CPA attack. Overall, if $\mathcal{O}$ outputs samples from $A_{s,\chi}^\times$, then $\mathcal{A}$ succeeds and $\mathcal{B}$ returns 1 with probability $\geq 1/2 + \delta - q^{-\Omega(n)}$. If $\mathcal{O}$ outputs samples from $U(\Lambda_q^\times \times \Lambda_q^\vee)$, then since $p \in \Lambda_q^\times$, $p \cdot c'$ and hence c is uniformly random in $\Lambda_q^\vee$ and independent of b. Thus $\mathcal{B}$ outputs 1 with probability $1/2$, and has the claimed advantage. $\square$

If $K = \mathbb{Q}(\zeta_{2^r})$, $2^{r-1} = n \geq 8$, $L = \mathbb{Q}(\zeta_{2^r}, \sqrt{\ell})$ for prime $\ell : \ell \equiv 1 \bmod 2^r$, $\ell \leq Cn$ for some $C \geq 2$, $q \geq 8n$ a prime q split completely in L, $\alpha \in (0,1)$: $\alpha q \geq \omega(\sqrt{\log 4n})$, $\xi = \alpha \left(\frac{2nk}{\log(4nk)}\right)^{\frac{1}{4}}$ with $k = O(1)$, $\epsilon \in \left(0, \frac{1}{2}\right)$, $p \in \Lambda_q^\times$, $\sigma \geq 2n^{3/2} \sqrt[4]{\ell} \sqrt{\ln(32nq)} q^{\frac{1}{2}+2\epsilon}$ and $\omega \left(2\sqrt{2}n^2 \sqrt{\log 4n}\alpha^2 q^2\right) \sigma \|p\|_\infty^2 \leq q/2$, the security reduction to CLWE from ideal lattice problems holds, and CNTRU connects with SIVP (note that the CLWE reduction is valid for a restricted secret space).

9   Conclusion

In this work we have defined a general form of NTRU, and shown that for certain parameters the NTRU instances obtained are indistinguishable from samples chosen uniformly at random. We have given the cryptographic application of a public-key encryption scheme, and shown that an IND-CPA attack on the PKE scheme implies an efficient attack on decision CLWE. Along the way we have proved new results on q-ary lattices obtained from natural orders of CDAs.

Future work includes selecting parameters for the signature scheme and the KEM and implementing these schemes. Further cryptanalysis is required to better understand the security of CNTRU. It would also be desirable to see if one could lift the constraint '$d = 2$', and obtain results for higher degrees. As explained in the introduction, the methods of this work are constrained to degree-two extensions of power-of-two cyclotomic fields, and we do not currently know how to remove this restriction.

A   Proofs

Proof. (of Proposition 5). We have

$$\|x\|_p^p = \sum_{\alpha \in \mathrm{Emb}(K)} \sum_{1 \le i,j < d} |\alpha((\phi(x))_{i,j})|^p \ge d^2 \sum_{\alpha \in \mathrm{Emb}(K)} \left(\prod_{i,j} |\alpha((\phi(x))_{i,j})|^p \right)^{1/d^2}$$

$$\ge d^2 [K : \mathbb{Q}] \left(\prod_{\alpha \in \mathrm{Emb}(K)} \left(\prod_{0 \le i < d} |\alpha(N_{L/K}(x_i))|^p \right)^{1/d^2} \right)^{1/[K:\mathbb{Q}]}$$

$$= [\mathcal{A} : \mathbb{Q}] \left(\prod_{0 \le i < d} |N_{L/\mathbb{Q}}(x_i)| \right)^{p/[\mathcal{A}:\mathbb{Q}]}, \quad \text{and if } x \in \mathcal{I},$$

$$\|x\|_p^p \ge [\mathcal{A} : \mathbb{Q}] \left(\prod_{0 \le i < d} |N_{L/\mathbb{Q}}(x_i)| \right)^{p/[\mathcal{A}:\mathbb{Q}]} = [\mathcal{A} : \mathbb{Q}] \left| N_{L/\mathbb{Q}} \left(\prod_{0 \le i < d} x_i \right) \right|^{p/[\mathcal{A}:\mathbb{Q}]}$$

By assumption, the coefficients x_i lie in the ideal $\mathfrak{J}\mathcal{O}_L$. Thus $x_i \in \bar{\mathcal{I}} := \mathcal{I} \cap \mathcal{O}_L$ for $i = 0, ..., d-1$, and so $\prod_{0 \le i < d} x_i \in \bar{\mathcal{I}}^d$, and hence $\|x\|_p^p \ge [\mathcal{A} : \mathbb{Q}] \cdot |N_{L/\mathbb{Q}}(\bar{\mathcal{I}})|^{dp/[\mathcal{A}:\mathbb{Q}]}$. Finally, to see $\lambda_1^\infty(\mathcal{I}) \ge \left(N_{L/\mathbb{Q}}(\bar{\mathcal{I}}) \right)^{1/nd}$,
$\|x\|_\infty = \sup_{i,j,\alpha} |\alpha(\phi(x)_{i,j})| \ge \prod_{i,j,\alpha} |\alpha((\phi(x))_{i,j})|^{1/nd^2} = N_{L/\mathbb{Q}}(\prod_{0 \le i < d} x_i)^{1/nd^2}$. $\qquad \square$

B   Choosing Parameters and Number Fields

In this section, we give a brief overview of some parameters choices for NTRU, focusing on n and q, before giving possible parameters for CDAs. We note that many suggested parameters (including ours) are not chosen according to security proofs, but rather take into account considerations such as speed and efficiency. We note the analysis of [12], and [32] for LWE, and welcome similar analysis for provably secure NTRU variants and CNTRU.

Parameters for NTRU in Previous Works. NTRU [24] uses convolution rings $\mathbb{Z}[x]/(x^N - 1)$ with N prime, which are not ring of integers of algebraic number fields. This is the same as in [23, 28]; since CDAs are constructed from fields, the parameters used here do not adapt straightforwardly to our setting. This situation is mirrored in the NTRU finalist in NIST's post-quantum standardisation process, [13]. The authors use the rings $\mathbb{Q}(x)/(x-1)\Phi_n(x)$ with prime n, which are not fields. In this case, the polynomials '$\Phi_n(x)$' are cyclotomic, hence $x^n - 1 = (x-1)\Phi_n(x)$; and $(x-1)\Phi_n(x)$ is plainly not irreducible.

However, the authors of [48, 49] replace $x^n - 1$ by $x^n + 1$, for power-of-two n. These are the $2n$th cyclotomic polynomials, which are amenable to generalisation by CDAs. Since n is a power of two, natural choices are $n = 512$ or $n = 1024$. They also recommend $p = 3$ or $p = 2$. As for q, if $\alpha q > n^{0.75}$, the decryption algorithm recovers m with probability $1 - n^{\omega(1)}$. For the security proof to hold, one needs $q \equiv 1 \bmod 2n$. So in the context of CDAs, one could choose $n = 256$, $q = 7681$, or $n = 512$, $q = 12289$, if working with the same framework as [49].

Falcon [19] uses $n = 512$ for NIST Level I, and $n = 1024$ for NIST Level V, where n is the degree of the cyclotomic ring. They use $q = 12289$. ModFalcon [16] uses a rank two module over a power of two cyclotomic of degree 512, and also sets $q = 12289$. In contrast, ModNTRU [15] uses a rank three module over a power of two cyclotomic of degree 512, but uses $q = 2^{19}$, instead of prime q.

Parameters for NTRU in CDAs. We follow the module NTRU instances in using power of two cyclotomics. Although there has been some concern raised over the large number of subfields and automorphisms attached to these objects [42], there has not yet been an efficient attack against the NTRU problem exploiting these features (for non-'overstretched' parameters). We recommend using algebras of dimension approximately 1000 over $\mathbb{Q}$. Following the construction detailed above: $\mathcal{A} = (L/\mathbb{Q}(\zeta_n), \theta, \zeta_n)$ with $K \subset L \subset M = \mathbb{Q}(\zeta_{\ell n})$ for $\ell \equiv 1 \bmod n$, $\ell \not\equiv 1 \bmod pn$ for any prime $p \mid n$. Take q to be a prime completely split in L, not too large to avoid attacks exploiting 'overstretched' parameters. Example parameters might be $n = 1024$, $d = 2$, $\ell = 12289$, and $q = 13313$.

As for choosing the sets $\mathcal{S}_f$ and so on, one can take these to be binary or ternary with set weights for efficiency, as some other NTRU schemes do, if desired. We leave the precise analysis of choices of such sets as future work.

C   Sketched Cryptographic Functionality

KEM. Here we outline an CNTRU-based KEM. We follow the structure of the KEM in [13] closely. Denote the CNTRU key generation, encryption, and decryption algorithms by KeyGen, Encrypt, and Decrypt respectively.

KeyGen$_{KEM}$
1. $(pk', sk') = (h, (f, g, h)) \leftarrow$ KeyGen(seed)
2. $s \leftarrow_\$ \{0, 1\}^{nd^2}$
3. return $(pk, sk) = (pk', (sk', s)) = (h, (f, g, h, s))$

Below, $H_1(\cdot)$ and $H_2(\cdot)$ are hash functions. Correctness is straightforward.

Encapsulate(h)	Decapsulate$((f, g, h, s), c)$
1. $(r, m) \leftarrow \mathcal{L}_r \times \mathcal{L}_m$	1. $(r, m) \leftarrow$ Decrypt (sk, c)
2. $c \leftarrow$ Encrypt$(h, (r, m))$	2. $k_1 \leftarrow H_1(r, m)$, $k_2 \leftarrow H_2(s, c)$
3. $k_1 \leftarrow H_1(r, m)$	3. if $(r, m) \neq \perp$ return k_1
4. return (c, k_1)	4. else return k_2

Signatures. We now give a signature scheme for CNTRU, based on pqN-TRUSign [22]. Below are the key generation, signing, and verification algorithms. As usual, we fix coprime integers p and q with $q \gg p$. In [22], ternary polynomials are used, though we note this is not essential for the correctness of the scheme. Let $\mathcal{T}$ denote elements of Λ with ternary coefficients, i.e. $\mathcal{T} = \{f = \oplus_{i=0}^{d-1} u^i f_i \in \Lambda : f_i$ is ternary$\}$. Moreover, let $\mathcal{R} = \{h = \oplus_{i=0}^{d-1} u^i h_i : \|h_i\|_\infty \leq q/2, i = 0, ..., d-1\}$ and $\mathcal{S} = \{g = \oplus_{i=0}^{d-1} g_i \in \Lambda : \|g_i\|_\infty \leq p/2, i = 0, ..., d-1\}$.

KeyGen$_{Sign}$
1. $F \leftarrow \mathcal{T}$ and set $f = pF$.
2. If $f \notin \Lambda_q^\times$, resample F.
3. $g \leftarrow \mathcal{S}$.
4. If $g \notin \Lambda_q^\times$, resample g.
5. $h := f^{-1} g \bmod q$.
6. $(pk, sk) = (h, (f, g))$.

Like pqNTRUSign, we require a function H which takes a public key h and a message μ to be signed, and outputs a pair of elements with bounded norm, that is $H : \mathcal{R} \times \{0, 1\}^* \to \mathcal{S} \times \mathcal{S}$. The values B_s and B_t are bounds that can be changed to vary the security level and efficiency of the protocol.

Sign(μ): input $(pk, sk, \mu) = (h, (f, g), \mu)$
1. $(s_p, t_p) = H(h, \mu)$.
2. $r \leftarrow \Lambda : \|r\|_\infty \leq \left\lfloor \frac{q}{2p} + \frac{1}{2} \right\rfloor$, $i = 0, ..., d-1$.
3. $(s_0, t_0) := (s_p + pr, s_0 h \bmod q)$.
4. $a := (t_p - t_0) g^{-1} \bmod p$.
5. If $\|af\|_\infty > B_s$ or $\|ag\|_\infty > B_t$ or $\|s\|_\infty > \frac{q}{2} - B_s$ or $\|t\|_\infty > \frac{q}{2} - B_t$, restart.
6. $(s, t) := (s_0, t_0) + (af, ag)$.
7. Output $\sigma = (s, t, \mu)$.

The signing algorithm is nearly identical to that of pqNTRUSign. We do, however, have to be careful about how we multiply a and f, g. For correctness to hold, we use the pair (af, ag) in our algorithm, whereas in [22] one can use (fa, ga) or (af, ag). This is because the NTRU lattice is an $\mathcal{O}_L$-bimodule in the commutative case, whereas CNTRU lattices are only left Λ-modules.

> Verify(σ): input $(h, \sigma) = (h, (s, t, \mu))$
> 1. $(s_p, t_p) \leftarrow H(h, \mu)$.
> 2. Check $(s_p, t_p) \equiv (s, t) \bmod p$.
> 3. Check $t \equiv sh \bmod q$.
> 4. Check $\|s\|_\infty \leq \frac{q}{2} - B_s$ and $\|t\|_\infty \leq \frac{q}{2} - B_t$.
> 5. If all checks succeed, output *Valid*.

It is straightforward to show correctness for this scheme, for well chosen B_s, B_t.

We do not analyse the above schemes in detail; we include them to demonstrate that such functionality is obtainable from NTRU in noncommutative rings.

References

1. Albert, A.: Structure of Algebras, AMS colloquium publications, vol. 24. American Mathematical Society, Providence (1939)
2. Albrecht, M., Bai, S., Ducas, L.: A subfield lattice attack on overstretched NTRU assumptions. In: Robshaw, M., Katz, J. (eds.) CRYPTO 2016. LNCS, vol. 9814, pp. 153–178. Springer, Heidelberg (2016). https://doi.org/10.1007/978-3-662-53018-4_6
3. Applebaum, B., Cash, D., Peikert, C., Sahai, A.: Fast cryptographic primitives and circular-secure encryption based on hard learning problems. In: Halevi, S. (ed.) CRYPTO 2009. LNCS, vol. 5677, pp. 595–618. Springer, Heidelberg (2009). https://doi.org/10.1007/978-3-642-03356-8_35
4. Atani, R., Atani, S., Karbasi, A.: NETRU: a noncommutative and secure variant of CTRU cryptosystem. ISC Int. J. Inf. Sec. **10**, 45–53 (2018)
5. Atani, R., Atani, S., Karbasi, A.: A provably secure variant of ETRU based on extended ideal lattices over direct product of Dedekind domains. JCS **5**, 13–34 (2018). https://doi.org/10.22108/jcs.2018.106856.0
6. Bagheri, K., Sadeghi, M.-R., Panario, D.: A non-commutative cryptosystem based on quaternion algebras. Des. Codes Crypt. **86**(10), 2345–2377 (2017). https://doi.org/10.1007/s10623-017-0451-4
7. Banks, W.D., Shparlinski, I.E.: A variant of NTRU with non-invertible polynomials. In: Menezes, A., Sarkar, P. (eds.) INDOCRYPT 2002. LNCS, vol. 2551, pp. 62–70. Springer, Heidelberg (2002). https://doi.org/10.1007/3-540-36231-2_6
8. Bayer-Fluckiger, E., Cerri, J.P., Chaubert, J.: Euclidean minima and central division algebras. Int. J. Number Theory **5**(07), 1155–1168 (2009). https://doi.org/10.1142/S1793042109002614
9. Bernstein, D.J., Chuengsatiansup, C., Lange, T., van Vredendaal, C.: NTRU prime: reducing attack surface at low cost. In: Adams, C., Camenisch, J. (eds.) SAC 2017. LNCS, vol. 10719, pp. 235–260. Springer, Cham (2018). https://doi.org/10.1007/978-3-319-72565-9_12
10. Boudgoust, K., Jeudy, C., Roux-Langlois, A., Wen, A.: Entropic hardness of module-LWE from module-NTRU. In: Isobe, T., Sarkar, S. (eds.) INDOCRYPT 2022. LNCS, vol. 13774, pp. 78–99. Springer, Cham (2022). https://doi.org/10.1007/978-3-031-22912-1_4
11. Caruso, X., Borgne, J.L.: Fast multiplication for skew polynomials. In: ISSAC 2017, pp. 77–84. Association for Computing Machinery (2017). https://doi.org/10.1145/3087604.3087617

12. Chatterjee, S., Koblitz, N., Menezes, A., Sarkar, P.: Another look at tightness II: practical issues in cryptography. In: Phan, R.C.-W., Yung, M. (eds.) Mycrypt 2016. LNCS, vol. 10311, pp. 21–55. Springer, Cham (2017). https://doi.org/10.1007/978-3-319-61273-7_3

13. Chen, C., et al.: NTRU: algorithm specifications and supporting documentation (2019). https://ntru.org/f/ntru-20190330.pdf

14. Chen, Y., Genise, N., Mukherjee, P.: Approximate trapdoors for lattices and smaller hash-and-sign signatures. In: Galbraith, S.D., Moriai, S. (eds.) ASIACRYPT 2019. LNCS, vol. 11923, pp. 3–32. Springer, Cham (2019). https://doi.org/10.1007/978-3-030-34618-8_1

15. Cheon, J.H., Kim, D., Kim, T., Son, Y.: A new trapdoor over module-NTRU lattice and its application to id-based encryption. Cryptol. ePrint Archive, Rpt. 2019/1468 (2019). https://eprint.iacr.org/2019/1468

16. Chuengsatiansup, C., Prest, T., Stehlé, D., Wallet, A., Xagawa, K.: ModFalcon: compact signatures based on module-NTRU lattices, pp. 853–866. ASIA CCS 2020, Assoc. for Computing Machinery (2020). https://doi.org/10.1145/3320269.3384758

17. Coppersmith, D., Shamir, A.: Lattice attacks on NTRU. In: Fumy, W. (ed.) EUROCRYPT 1997. LNCS, vol. 1233, pp. 52–61. Springer, Heidelberg (1997). https://doi.org/10.1007/3-540-69053-0_5

18. Felderhoff, J., Pellet-Mary, A., Stehlé, D.: On module unique-SVP and NTRU. In: Agrawal, S., Lin, D. (eds.) ASIACRYPT 2022. LNCS, vol. 13793, pp. 709–740. Springer, Cham (2022). https://doi.org/10.1007/978-3-031-22969-5_24

19. Fouque, P.A., et al.: Falcon: Fast-Fourier lattice-based compact signatures over NTRU. https://falcon-sign.info/falcon.pdf

20. Gaborit, P., Ohler, J., Solé, P.: CTRU, a polynomial analogue of NTRU. Technical report RR-4621, INRIA (2002). https://inria.hal.science/inria-00071964

21. Grover, C., Mendelsohn, A., Ling, C., Vehkalahti, R.: Non-commutative ring learning with errors from cyclic algebras. J. of Cryptology **35**(3), 22 (2022). https://doi.org/10.1007/s00145-022-09430-6

22. Hoffstein, J., Pipher, J., Schanck, J.M., Silverman, J.H., Whyte, W.: Transcript secure signatures based on modular lattices. In: Mosca, M. (ed.) PQCrypto 2014. LNCS, vol. 8772, pp. 142–159. Springer, Cham (2014). https://doi.org/10.1007/978-3-319-11659-4_9

23. Hoffstein, J., Pipher, J., Schanck, J.M., Silverman, J.H., Whyte, W., Zhang, Z.: Choosing parameters for NTRUEncrypt. In: Handschuh, H. (ed.) CT-RSA 2017. LNCS, vol. 10159, pp. 3–18. Springer, Cham (2017). https://doi.org/10.1007/978-3-319-52153-4_1

24. Hoffstein, J., Pipher, J., Silverman, J.H.: NTRU: a ring-based public key cryptosystem. In: Buhler, J.P. (ed.) ANTS 1998. LNCS, vol. 1423, pp. 267–288. Springer, Heidelberg (1998). https://doi.org/10.1007/BFb0054868

25. Howgrave-Graham, N.: A hybrid lattice-reduction and meet-in-the-middle attack against NTRU. In: Menezes, A. (ed.) CRYPTO 2007. LNCS, vol. 4622, pp. 150–169. Springer, Heidelberg (2007). https://doi.org/10.1007/978-3-540-74143-5_9

26. Howgrave-Graham, N., et al.: The impact of decryption failures on the security of NTRU encryption. In: Boneh, D. (ed.) CRYPTO 2003. LNCS, vol. 2729, pp. 226–246. Springer, Heidelberg (2003). https://doi.org/10.1007/978-3-540-45146-4_14

27. Howgrave-Graham, N., Silverman, J., Whyte, W.: A meet-in-the-middle attack on an NTRU private key. Technical report, NTRU Cryptosystems (2003)

28. Howgrave-Graham, N., Silverman, J.H., Whyte, W.: Choosing parameter sets for NTRUEncrypt with NAEP and SVES-3. In: Menezes, A. (ed.) CT-RSA 2005. LNCS, vol. 3376, pp. 118–135. Springer, Heidelberg (2005). https://doi.org/10.1007/978-3-540-30574-3_10

29. Jarvis, K.: NTRU over the Eisenstein Integers. Master's thesis (2011). https://ruor.uottawa.ca/handle/10393/19862

30. Karbasi, A.H., Atani, R.: ILTRU: an NTRU-like public key cryptosystem over ideal lattices. Cryptology ePrint Archive, p. 549 (2015)

31. Katz, J., Lindell, Y.: Introduction to Modern Cryptography, 2nd edn. Chapman & Hall/CRC, Boca Raton (2014)

32. Koblitz, N., Samajder, S., Sarkar, P., Singha, S.: Concrete analysis of approximate ideal-SIVP to decision ring-LWE reduction. Adv. Math. Commun. (2022). https://doi.org/10.3934/amc.2022082

33. Kouzmenko, R.: Generalizations of the NTRU cryptosystem. Ph.D. thesis (2005)

34. Malekian, E., Zakerolhosseini, A.: OTRU: a non-associative and high speed public key cryptosystem. In: CADS 15, pp. 83–90 (2010). https://doi.org/10.1109/CADS.2010.5623536

35. Malekian, E., Zakerolhosseini, A., Mashatan, A.: QTRU: quaternionic version of the NTRU public-key cryptosystem. ISC Int. J. Inf. Secur. **3**, 29–42 (2011). https://doi.org/10.22042/isecure.2015.3.1.3

36. Marcus, D.A.: Number Fields. U, Springer, Cham (2018). https://doi.org/10.1007/978-3-319-90233-3

37. Micciancio, D., Regev, O.: Worst-case to average-case reductions based on Gaussian measures. In: FOCS 2004. SIAM Journal on Computing, vol. 37, pp. 372–381 (2004). https://doi.org/10.1109/FOCS.2004.72

38. Murphy, S., Player, R.: δ-subgaussian random variables in cryptography. In: Jang-Jaccard, J., Guo, F. (eds.) ACISP 2019. LNCS, vol. 11547, pp. 251–268. Springer, Cham (2019). https://doi.org/10.1007/978-3-030-21548-4_14

39. Murphy, S., Player, R.: Discretisation and product distributions in ring-LWE. J. Math. Cryptol. **15**(1), 45–59 (2021). https://doi.org/10.1515/jmc-2020-0073

40. Jarvis, K., Nevins, M.: ETRU: NTRU over the Eisenstein integers. Des. Codes Crypt. **74**(1), 219–242 (2013). https://doi.org/10.1007/s10623-013-9850-3

41. Nevins, M., KarimianPour, C., Miri, A.: NTRU in rings beyond $\mathbb{Z}$. Des. Codes Crypt. **56**, 65–78 (2009). https://doi.org/10.1007/s10623-009-9342-7

42. NTRU prime risk-management team: Risks of lattice KEMs (2021). https://ntruprime.cr.yp.to/warnings.html

43. Oggier, F., Sethuraman, B.A.: Quotients of orders in cyclic algebras and space-time codes. AMC **7**(4), 441–461 (2013). https://doi.org/10.3934/amc.2013.7.441

44. Peikert, C.: Limits on the hardness of lattice problems in ℓ_p norms. In: CCC 2007, pp. 333–346 (2007). https://doi.org/10.1109/CCC.2007.12

45. Peikert, C., Rosen, A.: Lattices that admit logarithmic worst-case to average-case connection factors. STOC 2007, pp. 478–487. Association for Computing Machinery (2007). https://doi.org/10.1145/1250790.1250860

46. Pellet-Mary, A., Stehlé, D.: On the hardness of the NTRU problem. In: Tibouchi, M., Wang, H. (eds.) ASIACRYPT 2021. LNCS, vol. 13090, pp. 3–35. Springer, Cham (2021). https://doi.org/10.1007/978-3-030-92062-3_1

47. Singh, S., Padhye, S.: Generalisations of NTRU cryptosystem. SCN **9**(18), 6315–6334 (2016). https://doi.org/10.1002/sec.1693

48. Stehlé, D., Steinfeld, R.: Making NTRU as secure as worst-case problems over ideal lattices. In: Paterson, K.G. (ed.) EUROCRYPT 2011. LNCS, vol. 6632, pp. 27–47. Springer, Heidelberg (2011). https://doi.org/10.1007/978-3-642-20465-4_4

49. Stehlé, D., Steinfeld, R.: Making NTRUEncrypt and NTRUSign as secure as standard worst-case problems over ideal lattices. Cryptology ePrint Archive (2013). https://eprint.iacr.org/2013/004

50. Steinfeld, R.: NTRU cryptosystem: Recent developments and emerging mathematical problems in finite polynomial rings. In: Niederreiter, H., Ostafe, A., Panario, D., Winterhof, A. (eds.) Algebraic Curves and Finite Fields, pp. 179–212. De Gruyter (2014). https://doi.org/10.1515/9783110317916.179

51. Thakur, K., Tripathi, B.: KTRU: NTRU over the Kleinian integers. J. Int. Acad. Phys. Sci. **20**(03), 177–183 (2016)

52. Thakur, K., Tripathi, B.P.: STRU: a non alternative and multidimensional public key cryptosystem. GJPAM **13**, 1447–1464 (2017). http://www.ripublication.com/Volume/gjpamv13n5.htm

53. Truman, K.: Analysis and extension of non-commutative NTRU. Ph.D. thesis (2007). https://drum.lib.umd.edu/handle/1903/7344

54. Vats, N.: NNRU, a noncommutative analogue of NTRU. CoRR abs/0902.1891 (2009). http://arxiv.org/abs/0902.1891

55. Vehkalahti, R., Hollanti, C., Lahtonen, J., Ranto, K.: On the densest MIMO lattices from cyclic division algebras. IEEE Trans. Inf. Theory **55**(8), 3751–3780 (2009). https://doi.org/10.1109/TIT.2009.2023713

56. Voight, J.: Quaternion Algebras. Graduate Texts in Mathematics, Springer, Cham (2021)

57. Wang, Y., Wang, M.: Provably secure NTRUEncrypt over any cyclotomic field. In: Cid, C., Jacobson, M., Jr. (eds.) SAC 2018. LNCS, vol. 11349, pp. 391–417. Springer, Cham (2018). https://doi.org/10.1007/978-3-030-10970-7_18

58. Yasuda, T., Anada, H., Sakurai, K.: Application of NTRU using group rings to partial decryption technique. In: Yung, M., Zhang, J., Yang, Z. (eds.) INTRUST 2015. LNCS, vol. 9565, pp. 203–213. Springer, Cham (2016). https://doi.org/10.1007/978-3-319-31550-8_13

Do Not Bound to a Single Position: Near-Optimal Multi-positional Mismatch Attacks Against Kyber and Saber

Qian Guo[1] and Erik Mårtensson[1,2(✉)]

[1] Department of Electrical and Information Technology, Lund University, Lund, Sweden
{qian.guo,erik.martensson}@eit.lth.se
[2] Selmer Center, Department of Informatics, University of Bergen, Bergen, Norway
erik.martensson@uib.no

Abstract. The ephemeral-key setting of a lattice-based Key Encapsulation Mechanism (KEM) scheme assumes critical importance when considering certain advanced functionalities, such as forward secrecy. Accidental reuse of the ephemeral key may compromise the scheme's security and thus underscores the need for examining its keypair-reuse resilience. Keypair-reuse attacks include key mismatch attacks as a special case.

In this paper, we propose new key mismatch attacks against Kyber and Saber, NIST's selected scheme to be standardized for encryption and one of the finalists in the third round of the NIST process, respectively. Our novel idea is to recover partial information of multiple secret entries in each mismatch oracle call. These multi-positional attacks greatly reduce the expected number of oracle calls needed to fully recover the secret key. They also have significance in side-channel analysis.

Regarding lower bounds, our new attacks falsify the Huffman bounds proposed in [Qin et al. ASIACRYPT 2021], where a one-positional mismatch adversary is assumed. Our new attacks can be bounded by the Shannon bounds, i.e., the entropy of the distribution generating each secret coefficient times the number of secret coefficients. The proposed attacks are »near-optimal« since their query complexities are close to the Shannon bounds.

Keywords: Lattice-based cryptography · Mismatch attacks · LWE · LWR · Kyber · Saber

1 Introduction

Post-quantum cryptography (PQC) has become essential due to the rapid advances in building quantum computers. Researchers in post-quantum cryptography investigate new cryptographic primitives that resist attacks (e.g. Shor's algorithm [44]) from large-scale quantum computers. There are five main branches in post-quantum cryptography, lattice-based, code-based, multi-variate-based, isogeny-based, and symmetric-based cryptography. Lattice-based cryptography [3,42] is arguably the most promising of them all.

T. Johansson and D. Smith-Tone (Eds.): PQCrypto 2023, LNCS 14154, pp. 291–320, 2023.
https://doi.org/10.1007/978-3-031-40003-2_11

In 2016, NIST (National Institute of Standards and Technology, U.S. Department of Commerce) started a standardization process [1], referred to as the NIST PQC project, to solicit new quantum-resistant public-key cryptographic standards. Recently the fourth round began and for the Public Key Encryption (PKE)/Key Encapsulation Mechanism (KEM) category the Learning With Errors (LWE)-based KEM Kyber [43] has been chosen as the primitive to be standardized. Other than Kyber the third round included two more lattice-based PKE/KEM finalists, the Learning With Rounding (LWR)-based KEM Saber [16], as well as NTRU [12]. The last finalist in the third round was the code-based KEM Classic McEliece [4].

NIST has established five security levels, ranging from NIST-I to NIST-V, based on the computational effort required to search for a key on a block cipher or to search for a collision on a hash function. For instance, the NIST-I parameter set is expected to withstand any attack that requires less computational resources than a key search on AES128. A similar design philosophy guides most PKE/KEM candidates in the NIST PQC project, i.e., using a Chosen Plaintext Attack (CPA) secure encryption primitive as their core and achieving Chosen Ciphertext Attack (CCA) security with a transform like Fujisaki-Okamoto (FO) [22]. The CCA-secure version of the scheme offers keypair reuse resilience, allowing a pair of keys to be used repeatedly. Conversely, the core CPA secure construction can stand alone in the ephemeral-key setting, which is attractive because the CCA transform is costly. The ephemeral-key setting is critical for transport layer network protocols that require advanced security functionalities such as forward secrecy.

In the call-for-proposal [2], NIST listed keypair-reuse resilience for ephemeral-only encryption/key establishment as one of the additional desirable security properties. In a keypair-reuse attack, a keypair of ephemeral-only (a.k.a. CPA-secure) encryption/KEM is reused multiple times. Such reuses may come from implementation errors made by software developers. It is important to understand the capability of the adversary who exploits such keypair reuses.

The focal point of this paper is a specific type of keypair-reuse attacks called mismatch attacks [19]. In a mismatch attack, one communicating party's public key is reused. The adversary impersonates the other party and recovers the secret key by repeatedly checking whether the two shared keys match. There is a long list of known mismatch attacks on lattice-based KEMs, e.g. [6,7,24,36–38]. We mainly target the LWE/LWR-based KEMs Kyber and Saber, since Kyber is the selected proposal for standardization and Saber is another important third round finalist which is similar to Kyber.

The main problem related to mismatch attacks in the NIST PQC project is evaluating the candidate's key reuse resilience, i.e., how many key reuses can be tolerated before the full secret key is recovered. Mismatch attacks are not only significant when evaluating key reuse resilience, but also in side-channel and fault analysis, because the mismatch attack oracle can be used to implement certain types of chosen-ciphertext side-channel attacks [18,26,38,41,46] and a fault-injection attack [47]. The authors in [38] proposed a generic method of transforming the problem of finding optimal mismatch attacks to finding an optimal binary recovery tree (BRT), and obtained the optimal BRT and the corresponding lower bounds by Huffman coding.

However, the lower bounds in [38] are derived under the assumption that the adversary only can recover partial information of one secret entry in each mismatch oracle call. Their bounds could be invalid for general adversaries who can recover partial secret information related to multiple positions in each call, since the one-dimensional Huffman coding bound cannot bound multi-dimensional/multi-positional attacks. However, it is challenging *to design a better attacking strategy to constructively beat the lower bound proposed in* [38].

1.1 Related Work

Chosen Ciphertext attacks (CCA) on CPA secure schemes can be traced back to Bleichenbacher's attacks on the RSA PKCS#1 [11]. In 1999, Hall, Goldberg, and Schneier [29] proposed the reaction attack model that checks if the decryption is successful or not. This model is a weaker model than the CCA model, and the reaction attacks of [29] can be used to recover messages for code-based schemes like McEliece [33] and private keys for early lattice-based schemes such as the Ajtai-Dwork [3] and the GGH [23] cryptosystems. Hoffstein and Silverman [31] extended these attacks to NTRU [30].

These attacks are thwarted by using CCA transforms, such as the famous Fujisaki-Okamoto (FO) transform [22]. Numerous works [10,15,17,20,25,27,28] in lattice-based and code-based cryptography demonstrate that the CCA protection can fail if the decryption error rate is not sufficiently small.

In 2016, Fluhrer [21] initiated key-reuse attacks against lattice-based encryption. Later, Ding, Fluhrer, and Saraswathy [19] extended the attacks to lattice-based key exchange and proposed a key mismatch attack. Similar attacks can be applied to many lattice-based KEMs and the query complexities are further improved in [7,8,24,32,36,37].

Regarding the lower bounds on the average number of queries needed to recover the full secret key in a mismatch attack, in EUROCRYPT 2019, Băetu et al. [6] proved that this number should be larger than the Shannon entropy of the secret distribution. This lower bound is referred to as the Shannon bound in this paper. In ASIACRYPT 2021, Qin et al. [38] proposed sharper lower bounds from Huffman coding theory for CPA-secure lattice-based KEMs and also presented improved constructive results with query complexities close to the proposed Huffman coding lower bounds.

1.2 Contributions

In this paper, we propose novel mismatch attacks against Kyber and Saber that beat the Huffman coding lower bounds proposed in [38], i.e., we falsify their lower bounds by providing better constructive results. Our techniques include novel

Table 1. Sample complexity of the new attack **v.s.** lower bounds.

	Shannon Bound(b_1)	Lower Bound (b_2) from [38]	Previous Best (n_{pb})			New Attack(n_{na})		
			n_{pb} from [38]	n_{pb}/b_1	n_{pb}/b_2	n_{na}	n_{na}/b_1	n_{na}/b_2
Kyber512	1195	1216	1312	1.098	1.079	1205	1.008	**0.991**
Kyber768	1560	1632	1776	1.138	1.088	1588	1.018	**0.973**
Kyber1024	2079	2176	2368	1.139	1.088	2118	1.019	**0.973**
LightSaber	1386	1412	1460	1.053	1.033	1410	1.017	**0.998**
Saber	1954	1986	2091	1.071	1.053	1985	1.015	**0.999**
FireSaber	2389	2432	2624	1.098	1.079	2411	1.009	**0.991**

attacking strategies that can recover partial information about multiple coefficients of the secret key in each query. We name the new attacks *multi-positional mismatch attacks*. The main contributions of the paper are the following.

1. We first study two-positional attacks on Kyber and Saber. We propose new methods to split the two-dimensional plane for two secret coefficients and decide from the mismatch oracle call which part the two coefficients belong to. We propose various splitting approaches and transform the problem of finding the most efficient splits into an optimization problem. For Kyber512, Kyber768, Kyber1024, and FireSaber we search for the best two-positional attacks manually. When the possible pairs of secret coefficients are too large, e.g. in the cases of LightSaber and Saber, we design a greedy algorithm to automatically solve the optimization problem. This greedy approach is extended to attacking more than two positions at a time.
   In Table 1 we present the new query complexities, which are compared with the Shannon bounds and the one-dimensional Huffman bounds proposed in [38]. Regarding the constructive side, the new attacks significantly improve the query complexities, e.g., reducing 107 queries for Kyber512 and 250 for Kyber1024, compared to the attacks in [38]. Regarding the theoretical bounds, our new methods beat the lower bounds in [38] for all the parameter sets of Kyber and Saber. The new attacks are "near-optimal" since their query complexities are close to the Shannon bound. For instance, for Kyber512, the constructive result is only larger than the Shannon bound by 10 queries (or by a factor of 0.8%). Thus, the room for further improvement is small.
2. We further employ the lattice estimator, a new version of the widely-used LWE estimator [5] to roughly estimate the query complexity when a certain amount (e.g., 2^{60}) of post-processing with lattice reduction is allowed. Our new multi-positional mismatch attacks also improve the query complexity in this scenario. Though it has been remarked in [38] that the derived lower bounds are invalid when post-processing is allowed, we present the first quantitative analysis of mismatch attacks with post-processing.

3. Last, our new multi-positional mismatch attacks can improve the efficiency of some side-channel attacks on CCA-secure implementations of Kyber and Saber. The reason is that these attacks require building an oracle from side-channel leakages, similar to some extent to a mismatch oracle. The new attack may also be applied to improve the fault-injection attack in [47]. We present discussions on the potential extensions, though side-channel attacks and fault-injection attacks are not the focus of our paper.

1.3   Organization

The rest of the paper is organized as follows. In Sect. 2, we present the necessary background including the CPA-secure versions of Kyber and Saber, the model of mismatch attacks and Huffman coding. In Sect. 3, we present the state-of-the-art mismatch attacks on Kyber and Saber proposed in [38]. We present our multi-positional attacks, that constructively beat the lower bounds from [38], in Sect. 4. This is followed by more discussions about using post-processing to further reduce the query complexity and the connection to side-channel and fault-injection analysis in Sect. 5. We conclude this paper and present possible future works in Sect. 6.

2   Background

In this section, we introduce CPA-secure instantiations of the KEMs Kyber and Saber. Note that in the official documents of Kyber and Saber, the CPA-secure versions are limited to ephemeral keys, but this constraint may be ignored in practice. We thus create these CPA-secure instantiations to assess their key reuse resilience. Our notations and terminology are similar to the ones in [38].

- Let $\mathbf{H}(\cdot)$ be a hash function and $\mathbf{x}||\mathbf{y}$ be the concatenation of two strings $\mathbf{x}$ and $\mathbf{y}$.
- The symbol $\leftarrow_\$$ denotes sampling from a distribution.
- Let $\mathbf{A}^{\mathrm{tr}}$ denote the transpose of the matrix $\mathbf{A}$.
- The distribution $\mathbf{B}_\eta$ is the central binomial distribution whose output is computed as $\sum_{i=1}^{\eta}(a_i - b_i)$, where a_i and b_i are independently and uniformly randomly sampled from $\{0, 1\}$.

2.1   CPA-Secure Version of Kyber

Kyber [43] is the KEM proposal of CRYSTALS (Cryptographic Suite for Algebraic Lattices), based on the Module Learning with Errors (MLWE) problem. In the fourth round NIST has selected Kyber as their scheme for PKE/KEM. Following the work of [38], we describe a potential instantiation of the CPA-secure Kyber KEM in Fig. 1 by invoking the functions of Kyber.CPAPKE from [43].

Let $\mathcal{R}_q$ be the polynomial ring $\mathbb{Z}_q[x]/(x^n + 1)$, where $q = 3329$ and $n = 256$, and let $\circ$ ($+$ or $-$) be the corresponding multiplication (addition or subtraction)

Alice	Bob
1. Generate matrix $\mathbf{a} \in \mathcal{R}_q^{l \times l}$	
$\mathbf{s}_A, \mathbf{e}_A \leftarrow_\$ \mathbf{B}_\eta^l$	2. $\mathbf{m} \leftarrow_\$ \{0,1\}^{256}$
$\mathbf{P}_A \leftarrow \mathbf{a} \circ \mathbf{s}_A + \mathbf{e}_A$	Generate matrix $\mathbf{a} \in \mathcal{R}_q^{l \times l}$
Output: $(\mathbf{s}_A, \mathbf{P}_A)$ $\xrightarrow{\quad \mathbf{P}_A \quad}$	$\mathbf{s}_B \leftarrow_\$ \mathbf{B}_\eta^l, \mathbf{e}_B \leftarrow_\$ \mathbf{B}_{\eta'}^l, \mathbf{e}_B' \leftarrow_\$ \mathbf{B}_{\eta'}$
	$\mathbf{P}_B \leftarrow \mathbf{a} \circ \mathbf{s}_B + \mathbf{e}_B$
	$v_B \leftarrow \mathbf{P}_A^{tr} \circ \mathbf{s}_B + \mathbf{e}_B'$
	$\quad + \mathbf{Decompress}_q(\mathbf{m}, 2)$
3. $\mathbf{u}_A \leftarrow \mathbf{Decompress}_q(\mathbf{c}_1, 2^{d_{\mathbf{P}_B}})$	$\mathbf{c}_1 \leftarrow \mathbf{Compress}_q(\mathbf{P}_B, 2^{d_{\mathbf{P}_B}})$
$v_A \leftarrow \mathbf{Decompress}_q(\mathbf{c}_c, 2^{d_{v_B}})$ $\xleftarrow{\mathbf{P}_B, \mathbf{c}_1, \mathbf{c}_2}$	$\mathbf{c}_2 \leftarrow \mathbf{Compress}_q(v_B, 2^{d_{v_B}})$
$\mathbf{m}' \leftarrow \mathbf{Compress}_q(v_A - \mathbf{s}_A^{tr} \circ \mathbf{u}_A, 2)$	$K_B \leftarrow \mathbf{H}(\mathbf{m} \| (\mathbf{P}_B, (\mathbf{c}_1, \mathbf{c}_2)))$
$K_A \leftarrow \mathbf{H}(\mathbf{m}' \| (\mathbf{P}_B, (\mathbf{c}_1, \mathbf{c}_2)))$	

Fig. 1. The CPA-secure version of Kyber.

in the ring. Let l denote the rank of the module, which is set to be $2, 3$, and 4, for the three different versions, Kyber512, Kyber768, and Kyber 1024. Alice and Bob generate a matrix $\mathbf{a}$ from a public seed by calling a pseudorandom function. As shown in Fig. 1, round-3 Kyber employs two central binomial distributions $\mathbf{B}_\eta$ and $\mathbf{B}_{\eta'}$. The designers pick $(\eta, \eta') = (3, 2)$ for Kyber512, and $(\eta, \eta') = (2, 2)$ for Kyber768 and Kyber1024. The $\mathbf{Compress}_q(x, p)$ function transforms x from module q to module p by

$$\mathbf{Compress}_q(x, p) = \lceil x \cdot p/q \rfloor \mod {}^+ p,$$

where $r' = r \mod {}^+ p$ represents the unique element r' in the range $-\frac{p}{2} < r' \le \frac{p}{2}$ such that $r' \equiv r \pmod{p}$. We also define the inverse function

$$\mathbf{Decompress}_q(x, p) = \lceil x \cdot q/p \rfloor.$$

If the first input to the function $\mathbf{Compress}_q(x, p)$ (or $\mathbf{Decompress}_q(x, p)$) is a vector/polynomial, then we call the function coefficient-wise.

2.2 CPA-Secure Version of Saber

Saber [16], whose security is based on the hardness of the Module Learning with Rounding Problem (MLWR), was a finalist candidate in the third round of the NIST PQC project. Similar to the CPA-secure version of the Kyber KEM, in Fig. 2 we present a possible instantiation of a CPA-secure Saber KEM by invoking the functions of Saber.PKE from [16].

We use the same notations as in Sect. 2.1, e.g. $\mathcal{R}_q$ denotes the polynomial ring $\mathbb{Z}_q[x]/(x^n + 1)$, where $n = 256$ and the rank of the module l is set to be 2

Alice	Bob
1. Generate matrix $\mathbf{a} \in \mathcal{R}_q^{l \times l}$	
$\mathbf{s}_A \leftarrow_\$ \mathbf{B}_\eta^l$	2. $\mathbf{m} \leftarrow_\$ \{0,1\}^{256}$
$\mathbf{P}_A \leftarrow ((\mathbf{a} \circ \mathbf{s}_A + \mathbf{h}) \mod q)$	Generate matrix $\mathbf{a} \in \mathcal{R}_q^{l \times l}$
$\qquad \gg (\epsilon_p - \epsilon_q) \in \mathcal{R}_p^{l \times 1}$	$\mathbf{s}_B \leftarrow_\$ \mathbf{B}_\eta^l$
Output: $(\mathbf{s}_A, \mathbf{P}_A))$ $\quad \xrightarrow{\;\;\mathbf{P}_A\;\;}$	$\mathbf{P}_B \leftarrow ((\mathbf{a} \circ \mathbf{s}_B + \mathbf{h}) \mod q)$
	$\qquad \gg (\epsilon_p - \epsilon_q) \in \mathcal{R}_p^{l \times 1}$
	$\mathbf{v}_B \leftarrow \mathbf{P}_A^{tr} \circ (\mathbf{s}_B \mod p) \in \mathcal{R}_p$
3. $\mathbf{v}_A \leftarrow \mathbf{P}_B^{tr} \circ (\mathbf{s}_A \mod p) \in \mathcal{R}_p$	$\mathbf{c} \leftarrow ((\mathbf{v}_B + \mathbf{h}_1 - 2^{\epsilon_p-1}\mathbf{m}) \mod p)$
$\mathbf{m}' \leftarrow ((\mathbf{v}_A + \mathbf{h}_2 - 2^{\epsilon_p-\epsilon_T}\mathbf{c}) \mod p)$ $\quad \xleftarrow{\;\mathbf{P}_B, \mathbf{c}\;}$	$\qquad \gg (\epsilon_p - \epsilon_T) \in \mathcal{R}_T$
$\qquad \gg (\epsilon_p - 1) \in \mathcal{R}_2$	$K_B \leftarrow \mathbf{H}(\mathbf{m} \| (\mathbf{P}_B, \mathbf{c}))$
$K_A \leftarrow \mathbf{H}(\mathbf{m}' \| (\mathbf{P}_B, \mathbf{c}))$	

Fig. 2. The CPA-secure version of Saber.

for LightSaber, 3 for Saber, and 4 for FireSaber. The matrix $\mathbf{a}$ is also generated from a public seed. The secret coefficients are generated from the central binomial distribution $\mathbf{B}_\eta$, where η is 5 for LightSaber, 4 for Saber, and 3 for FireSaber, respectively. Saber chooses three positive integers q, p, and T as powers of 2, i.e., $q = 2^{\epsilon_q}$, $p = 2^{\epsilon_p}$, and $T = 2^{\epsilon_T}$, respectively. In round-3 Saber, $\epsilon_q = 13$ and $\epsilon_p = 10$. The exponent ϵ_T is set to be 3 for LightSaber, 4 for Saber, and 6 for FireSaber, respectively.

We denote the bitwise right shift operation by $\gg$ and apply it to polynomials and matrices by calling it coefficient-wise. Saber also introduces two constant polynomials $\mathbf{h}_1 \in \mathcal{R}_q$ and $\mathbf{h}_2 \in \mathcal{R}_q$ with all coefficients set to $2^{\epsilon_q-\epsilon_p-1}$ and $2^{\epsilon_p-2} - 2^{\epsilon_p-\epsilon_T-1} + 2^{\epsilon_q-\epsilon_p-1}$, respectively, and one constant vector $\mathbf{h} \in \mathcal{R}_q^{l \times 1}$ with each polynomial set to $\mathbf{h}_1$.

2.3 The Threat Model – Mismatch Attack Model

In this work, we focus on the key mismatch threat model against an ephemeral-only KEM which reuses the keypair. We assume that Alice reuses her keypair $(\mathbf{s}_A, \mathbf{P}_A)$ and the adversary Eve impersonates Bob to recover Alice's secret key $\mathbf{s}_A$ by communicating with Alice. We can build an oracle to simulate the decapsulation of Alice with input including the pair $(\mathbf{P}_B, \mathbf{c})$ chosen by Eve and the corresponding shared key K_B. Here we denote $\mathbf{c}_1, \mathbf{c}_2$ by $\mathbf{c}$ for Kyber. The oracle denoted $\mathcal{O}$ calls Alice's decapsulation function and obtains the shared key K_A. It outputs 1 if the shared keys $K_A = K_B$ and 0 otherwise. The aim of a mismatch attack is to recover Alice's key by selecting the chosen pairs of the form $(\mathbf{P}_B, \mathbf{c})$ and iteratively querying the oracle $\mathcal{O}$.

2.4 Huffman Coding

Huffman coding refers to an algorithm that finds an efficient binary code used for lossless data compression. Given a symbol-by-symbol encoding of strings with independent and identically distributed symbols from a known distribution, Huffman coding creates an optimal code. Huffman coding works by iteratively building a binary tree from the bottom up by merging the two least probable symbols into a new symbol. Basic (one-dimensional) Huffman coding can be generalized to n dimensions and improved by considering each possible n-tuple of symbols from an alphabet as a new symbol and applying Huffman coding to these n-tuples. We refer the reader to a book on information theory (e.g., [13]) for more details.

3   One-Positional Mismatch Attacks

In a mismatch attack, Eve impersonates Bob and wants to recover Alice's secret key $\mathbf{s}_A$. As we can see in Fig. 1 and 2, given the pair $(\mathbf{P}_B, \mathbf{c})$, the keys K_A and K_B match if and only if Alice's computed $\mathbf{m}'$ matches Eve's chosen $\mathbf{m}$. Thus, for each query of the oracle Eve sets her parameters $\mathbf{m}$ and $(\mathbf{P}_B, \mathbf{c})$ such that the output of the oracle teaches her something about $\mathbf{s}_A$.

Previous works on mismatch attacks recover one position at a time. Let us explain in some detail how Eve retrieves one position at a time in these works and let us first focus on position 0. Let s_i denote the value of $\mathbf{s}_A$ on index i, when the subscript A is implied. Eve creates the message $\mathbf{m} = [1, 0, \ldots, 0]$. She sets her parameters $(\mathbf{P}_B, \mathbf{c})$ such that Alice's received message $\mathbf{m}'$ is 0 by design on all positions except for the position 0, whose value depends on the secret value s_0. By observing the output of the oracle, Eve learns some information about s_0. Repeating the process, Eve learns the exact value of s_0 and then continues the process to learn the other s_i values.

3.1   Kyber

Let us now describe the attack in some more detail, for Kyber1024[1]. Eve lets $\mathbf{P}_B = [\lceil \frac{q}{32} \rfloor, 0, \ldots, 0]$. She calculates $\mathbf{c}_1 = \mathbf{Compress}_q(\mathbf{P}_B, 2^{d_{\mathbf{P}_B}})$ and sets $\mathbf{c}_2 = [h, 0, \ldots, 0]$, where h is a parameter designed to extract different information about the secret, depending on the context. Alice calculates $\mathbf{u}_A = \mathbf{Decompress}_q(\mathbf{c}_1, 2^{d_{\mathbf{P}_B}}) = \mathbf{P}_B$ and $\mathbf{v}_A = \mathbf{Decompress}_q(\mathbf{c}_2, 2^{d_{\mathbf{v}_B}}) = [\lceil \frac{q}{32} h \rfloor, 0, \ldots, 0]$. Next, Alice calculates

$$\mathbf{m}'[0] = \mathbf{Compress}_q((\mathbf{v}_A - \mathbf{s}_A^{\mathrm{tr}} \mathbf{u}_A)[0], 2) \tag{1}$$

$$= \mathbf{Compress}_q(\mathbf{v}_A[0] - (\mathbf{s}_A^{\mathrm{tr}} \mathbf{u}_A)[0], 2) \tag{2}$$

$$= \left\lceil \frac{2}{q} \left(\left\lceil \frac{q}{32} h \right\rfloor - \mathbf{s}_A[0] \left\lceil \frac{q}{32} \right\rfloor \right) \right\rfloor \mod 2. \tag{3}$$

---

[1] To attack other versions of Kyber you just alter the attack parameters slightly.

Table 2. $\mathbf{m}'[0]$ as a function of s_0 for different values of h for Kyber1024.

h	s_0				
	-2	-1	0	1	2
7	1	0	0	0	0
8	1	1	0	0	0
9	1	1	1	0	0
10	1	1	1	1	0
22	0	1	1	1	1
23	0	0	1	1	1
24	0	0	0	1	1
25	0	0	0	0	1

The value of $\mathbf{m}'[0]$ depends on h and s_0 according to Table 2. Each query gives us partial information about s_0. Notice that we are not able to split the values of s_0 into all possible two subsets of values. All the possible combinations split the values into two adjacent intervals. Attempts at making any other type of split fail. Modifying the mismatch attack to allow for other splits with respect to s_0 leads to a situation where $\mathbf{m}'[i]$ is not always equal to 0 for $i \neq 0$.

Let us show why Alice's received message is equal to 0 by construction on all positions with non-zero index. Since $\mathbf{v}_A[i] = 0$, for index $i \neq 0$, Alice computes

$$\mathbf{m}'[i] = \mathbf{Compress}_q((\mathbf{v}_A - \mathbf{s}_A^{\mathrm{tr}}\mathbf{u}_A)[i], 2) \tag{4}$$

$$= \mathbf{Compress}_q(\mathbf{v}_A[i] - (\mathbf{s}_A^{\mathrm{tr}}\mathbf{u}_A)[i], 2) \tag{5}$$

$$= \left\lceil \frac{2}{q}\left(-\mathbf{s}_A[i]\left\lceil\frac{q}{32}\right\rfloor\right)\right\rfloor \quad \bmod 2. \tag{6}$$

The expression within the outer rounding function is bounded in absolute value by $2/3329 \cdot 2 \cdot 105 = 0.126\ldots < 1/2$. Hence the value is always equal to 0 when rounded to the nearest integer and thus $\mathbf{m}'[i] = 0$, for $i \neq 0$.

To modify the mismatch attack to recover s_i, where $1 \leq i \leq n$, we instead let $\mathbf{P}_B$ be equal to 0 on all positions, except for $\mathbf{P}_B[n-i] = -\lceil\frac{q}{32}\rfloor$.

As Kyber is based on module-LWE, $\mathbf{P}_b$ and $\mathbf{s}$ consist of l blocks, where each block has size n. The multiplication of them consists of a scalar product of two vectors with l polynomials each. Thus, to retrieve positions n to $2n-1$, we just shift the index of $\mathbf{P}_B$ by n positions. That is, we let all positions in $\mathbf{P}_B$ be equal to 0, except that $\mathbf{P}_B[n] = \lceil\frac{q}{32}\rfloor$, to retrieve s_n. To retrieve the value s_{n+i}, for $0 < i < n$, we let all positions of $\mathbf{P}_B$ be equal to 0, except that $\mathbf{P}_B[2n-i] = -\lceil\frac{q}{32}\rfloor$. To retrieve another block we just continue shifting another n positions and so on.

In Fig. 3 we illustrate the mismatch attacks from [38] on the different versions of Kyber.

Table 3. $\mathbf{m}'[0]$ as a function of s_0 for different values of h and k for FireSaber.

h	k	s_0						
		-3	-2	-1	0	1	2	3
15	5	1	0	0	0	0	0	0
15	7	1	1	0	0	0	0	0
15	13	1	1	1	0	0	0	0
16	4	1	1	1	1	0	0	0
16	2	1	1	1	1	1	0	0
17	7	1	1	1	1	1	1	0
47	5	0	1	1	1	1	1	1
47	7	0	0	1	1	1	1	1
47	13	0	0	0	1	1	1	1
48	4	0	0	0	0	1	1	1
48	2	0	0	0	0	0	1	1
49	7	0	0	0	0	0	0	1

3.2 Saber

A mismatch attack on Saber works similarly to a mismatch attack on Kyber. Let $\mathbf{c}$ be equal to 0 on all positions, except that $\mathbf{c}[0] = h$. Let H denote $2^{\epsilon_p-2} - 2^{\epsilon_p-\epsilon_T-1} + 2^{\epsilon_q-\epsilon_p-1}$. Finally, let $\mathbf{P}_B$ be equal to 0 on all positions except $\mathbf{P}_B[0] = k$. For the first index $i = 0$ we get

$$\mathbf{m}'[0] = ((k(s_i \mod p) + H - 2^{\epsilon_p-\epsilon_T}h) \mod p) \gg (\epsilon_p - 1). \tag{7}$$

For the indices $i \neq 0$ we get

$$\mathbf{m}'[i] = ((k(s_i \mod p) + H) \mod p) \gg (\epsilon_p - 1). \tag{8}$$

If we make k small enough, then we make sure that $\mathbf{m}'[i] = 0$ for all possible values of s_i. Table 3 shows parameters achieving different splits of $\mathbf{m}'[0]$, while making sure that $\mathbf{m}'[i] = 0$, for all $i \neq 0$, for FireSaber[2].

Note that the parameters differ a bit from the ones in [38]. We pick the minimal values of k that achieve each possible split. This allows our multi-positional attacks in Sect. 4 to use as many positions at the same time as possible.

To retrieve positions s_i, for $1 \leq i \leq n-1$, we make the adjustment that $\mathbf{c}$ is equal to 0 on all positions, except that $\mathbf{c}[n-i] = -k$, where k refers to a value used to achieve a specific split to retrieve the value s_0 for an implied value of h.

Just like Kyber, Saber is based on module-LWE and the mismatch attack retrieves the secret values in blocks of size n. Just like for Kyber, we shift the non-zero indices of $\mathbf{P}_B$ by n positions to retrieve each new block of secret values.

In Fig. 3 we illustrate the mismatch attacks from [38] on the different versions of Saber.

---

[2] To attack other versions of Saber you just alter the attack parameters slightly.

Table 4. Lower limits for key mismatch attacks on Kyber and Saber.

Scheme	s Range	Unknowns	Entropy Per Position	Shannon Bound	Huffman Bound
Kyber512	$[-3,3]$	512	2.3334	1195	1216
Kyber768	$[-2,2]$	768	2.0306	1560	1632
Kyber1024	$[-2,2]$	1024	2.0306	2079	2176
LightSaber	$[-5,5]$	512	2.7064	1386	1412
Saber	$[-4,4]$	768	2.5442	1954	1986
FireSaber	$[-3,3]$	1024	2.3334	2389	2432

3.3 The Lower Bounds from [38]

An obvious lower bound on the attack is the Shannon bound. In a pure mismatch attack, the number of queries cannot be lower than the entropy of the secret. As each position in the secret vector is independent of the other positions, the entropy is equal to the number of positions times the entropy of each position, leading to the Shannon bounds of Table 4.

Regarding their mismatch attacks the authors of [38] write "For simplicity, we assume the adversary recovers Alice's secret key s_A one coefficient block by one coefficient block." For Kyber and Saber, this means recovering one coefficient at a time. Under this restriction, the authors show that Huffman coding is optimal and leads to another lower bound for a pure mismatch attack. In our concrete setting, since not every possible splitting of the secret values into two subsets is possible using our available types of queries, there is no guarantee that we can reach the performance of the Huffman code in practice.

3.4 The Practical Mismatch Attacks from [38]

Figure 3 illustrates and summarizes the practical mismatch attacks on Kyber and Saber from [38]. The blue/red/green/yellow/brown/orange lines correspond to the 1st/2nd/3rd/4th/5th/6th splits respectively.

All the attacks on both Kyber and Saber follow the same strategy. Start with a query that splits the possibilities for the secret value s_i into two halves as equally probable as possible. Then no matter on which half of the secret values we end up, each of the remaining queries decides whether the s_i is equal to the remaining most probable value or any of the other values[3].

There are two interesting ways of viewing these mismatch attacks, which we generalize to higher dimensions in Sect. 4.4.

Partly, the attacks correspond to first making as even of a split as possible, and then for the remaining part of the attack making splits that correspond to

---

[3] The fact that all the mismatch attacks on Kyber and Saber follow this approach is due to the distribution of the s_i values. For another distribution, such as the uniform distribution, this would of course not be a sensible strategy.

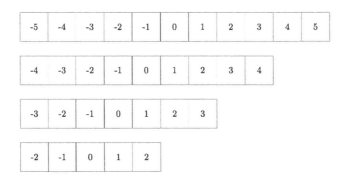

Fig. 3. Illustrations of the mismatch attacks on all versions of Kyber and Saber from [38]. Starting from the bottom of the figure and moving upwards the illustrations cover Kyber768/Kyber1024, Kyber512/FireSaber, Saber, and LightSaber, respectively.

Huffman coding[4]. In Sect. 4.4 we apply a similar strategy where we start with a couple of roughly even splits of the secret values and then apply steps that are identical to/close to Huffman coding. This approach is applied manually for attacks on all versions of Kyber and on FireSaber.

Another perspective on these mismatch attacks is that they are all greedy attacks. Each split for each attack is the split that divides up the remaining secret values into two as equally probable halves as possible. This approach is generalized in Sect. 4.4 for our attacks on Saber and LightSaber, systems where creating attacks by hand is tedious due to the s_i values taking a wider range of values.

3.5   On the Performance of the Mismatch Attacks from [38]

In Table 5 we list the expected number of queries used for the practical mismatch attacks from [38]. Notice that there are small deviations between our table and Table 6 of [38]. This is due to us avoiding premature rounding. Notice that for all deviations, our corrected values are closer to the experimental results of [38].

For Kyber and Saber we can argue that their approach is optimal given their restrictions.

1. By testing all parameter settings we find for both Kyber and Saber that the only possible splits divide the secret values into two adjacent intervals.
2. For the initial split it should be optimal to split the secret values as evenly as possible, that is, split into one interval of positive values, one interval of negative values, and put the value 0 in whichever of the two intervals.
3. For all versions of both Kyber and Saber, their approach after the initial split is identical to Huffman coding, which is optimal, given the restrictions.

---

[4] For all the attacks, after the initial split, the remaining splits correspond to Huffman coding for their respective half of the secret values. The possibility of this depends on the distribution of the s_i values. This is not possible for all secret distributions.

Table 5. Practical mismatch attacks compared to the Huffman bounds.

Scheme	s Range	Unknowns	Queries Per Position	Total Queries	Huffman Bound
Kyber512	$[-3,3]$	512	2.5625	1312	1216
Kyber768	$[-2,2]$	768	2.3125	1776	1632
Kyber1024	$[-2,2]$	1024	2.3125	2368	2176
LightSaber	$[-5,5]$	512	2.8515	1460	1412
Saber	$[-4,4]$	768	2.7226	2091	1986
FireSaber	$[-3,3]$	1024	2.5625	2624	2432

4 Multi-positional Mismatch Attacks

The main idea of this paper is to remove the constraint of recovering only one coefficient at a time. Let us begin by explaining how our idea works with two positions at a time and first explain it for Kyber.

4.1 Two-Positional Mismatch Attacks on Kyber

To start with we will show how to obtain s_0 and s_{128} (for the setting where $\mathbf{s}_A$ consists of blocks of size 256, which covers all versions of Kyber and Saber) and then later explain how to generalize this approach to obtain the other values of $\mathbf{s}_A$. Let us focus on Kyber1024[5]. Eve lets $\mathbf{m}$ have the value 0 on all positions, except that $\mathbf{m}[0] = 1$ and/or $\mathbf{m}[128] = 1$. Let $\mathbf{P}_B$ be 0 on all positions except that $\mathbf{P}_B[0] = b_1 \cdot \lceil \frac{q}{32} \rfloor$ and $\mathbf{P}_B[128] = b_2 \lceil \frac{q}{32} \rfloor$, where $b_1, b_2 \in \{-1, 0, 1\}$. Also, let $\mathbf{c}_2$ be 0 on all positions, except that $\mathbf{c}_2[0] = h_1 \lceil \frac{q}{32} \rfloor$ and $\mathbf{c}_2[128] = h_2 \lceil \frac{q}{32} \rceil$. Next, we calculate $\mathbf{m}'[0]$ and $\mathbf{m}'[128]$. We get

$$\mathbf{m}'[0] = \mathbf{Compress}_q(\mathbf{v}_A[0] - (\mathbf{s}_A^{\mathrm{tr}}\mathbf{u}_A)[0], 2) \tag{9}$$

$$= \left\lceil \frac{2}{q} \left(\left\lceil \frac{q}{32} h_1 \right\rfloor - \left(\mathbf{s}_A[0]b_1 \left\lceil \frac{q}{32} \right\rfloor - \mathbf{s}_A[128]b_2 \left\lceil \frac{q}{32} \right\rfloor \right) \right) \right\rfloor \mod 2 \tag{10}$$

and

$$\mathbf{m}'[128] = \mathbf{Compress}_q(\mathbf{v}_A[128] - (\mathbf{s}_A^{\mathrm{tr}}\mathbf{u}_A)[128], 2) \tag{11}$$

$$= \left\lceil \frac{2}{q} \left(\left\lceil \frac{q}{32} h_2 \right\rfloor - \left(\mathbf{s}_A[0]b_2 \left\lceil \frac{q}{32} \right\rfloor + \mathbf{s}_A[128]b_1 \left\lceil \frac{q}{32} \right\rfloor \right) \right) \right\rfloor \mod 2. \tag{12}$$

For an integer i, with $1 \leq i \leq 127$ we get

$$\mathbf{m}'[i] = \mathbf{Compress}_q(-(\mathbf{s}_A^{\mathrm{tr}}\mathbf{u}_A)[i], 2) \tag{13}$$

$$= \left\lceil \frac{2}{q} \left(- \left(\mathbf{s}_A[i]b_1 \left\lceil \frac{q}{32} \right\rfloor - \mathbf{s}_A[128 + i]b_2 \left\lceil \frac{q}{32} \right\rfloor \right) \right) \right\rfloor \mod 2 \tag{14}$$

---

[5] To attack other versions of Kyber you just alter the parameters of the attack slightly.

and

$$\mathbf{m}'[128+i] = \mathbf{Compress}_q(-(\mathbf{s}_A^{\mathrm{tr}}\mathbf{u}_A)[128+i], 2) \tag{15}$$

$$= \left\lceil \frac{2}{q}\left(-\left(\mathbf{s}_A[i]b_2\left\lceil \frac{q}{32}\right\rfloor + \mathbf{s}_A[128+i]b_1\left\lceil \frac{q}{32}\right\rceil\right)\right)\right\rfloor \mod 2. \tag{16}$$

For both of the latter two positions the expression within the outer rounding function is bounded in absolute value by $2/3329 \cdot 2 \cdot 2 \cdot 105 = 0.252\ldots < 1/2$. Hence these values are always equal to 0 when rounded to the nearest integer and thus $\mathbf{m}'[i] = 0$, for $i \neq 0, 128$.

To retrieve the positions s_i and s_{128+i}, where $1 \leq i \leq 127$, we can for example make the following adjustments. Let $\mathbf{m}$ be equal to 0 on all positions except that $\mathbf{m}[i] = 1$ and/or $\mathbf{m}[128+i] = 1$. Also, let $\mathbf{c}_2$ be 0 on all positions, except that $\mathbf{c}_2[i] = h_1\left\lceil \frac{q}{32}\right\rceil$ and $\mathbf{c}_2[128+i] = h_2\left\lfloor \frac{q}{32}\right\rfloor$.

Next, we will interpret our two-positional approach. We organize the possible pairs of values s_0, s_{128} in a two-dimensional grid. Let m_i' denote $\mathbf{m}'[i]$. For each cell we write the value of m_0', m_{128}' or $m' = m_0'\&m_{128}'$, depending on whether only $\mathbf{m}[0] = 1$, only $\mathbf{m}[128] = 1$ or if $\mathbf{m}[0] = \mathbf{m}[128] = 1$. Here of course the value of the bits depends in general on s_0, s_{128} and the chosen parameters b_1, b_2, h_1, h_2.

Planar Cuts. The most obvious split that can be achieved is the one where we cut with respect to only one of the variables. These planar cuts are achieved by letting $\mathbf{m}[0] = 1$, $\mathbf{m}[128] = 0$ and $h_2 = 0$. Two examples of such splits are shown in Fig. 4. To achieve a vertical split we let $b_2 = 0$ and $b_1 = 1$. In Fig. 4a, specifically we let $h_1 = 9$. To achieve a horizontal split we let $b_1 = 0$, $b_2 = -1$. In Fig. 4b specifically we let $h_1 = 24$. Horizontal and vertical splits are already the ones achieved in the mismatch attacks from [38], explained in detail in Sect. 3. In and of themselves, these two types of splits do not add anything to the mismatch attacks compared to previous work, but they are useful in combination with the other methods from this section.

Rectangular Cuts. We can also simultaneously cut horizontally and vertically. This allows us to cut out any rectangle of values, where at least one corner of the rectangle is at one of the corners of the grid. To do this we let $\mathbf{m}[0] = \mathbf{m}[128] = 1$. We let $b_1 = 1$ and $b_2 = 0$. In Fig. 5 we let $h_1 = 24$ and $h_2 = 9$. The figure shows m_0', m_{128}' and $m' = m_0'\&m_{128}'$ respectively. In other words, the vertical cut, the horizontal cut, and the resulting rectangular cut respectively.

Triangular Cuts. Our next type of split is a triangular cut, originating from any of the 4 corners of the grid. Here we let $\mathbf{m}[0] = 1$, $\mathbf{m}[128] = 1$ and $h_2 = 0$. See Fig. 6 for two examples of this type of cut. In Fig. 6a we let $h_1 = 10$, $b_1 = 1$ and $b_2 = -1$. In Fig. 6b we let $b_1 = b_2 = 1$ and $h_1 = 24$.

m'_0	s_0 -2	-1	0	1	2
-2	1	1	1	0	0
-1	1	1	1	0	0
s_{128} 0	1	1	1	0	0
1	1	1	1	0	0
2	1	1	1	0	0

(a) A vertical split.

m'_0	s_0 -2	-1	0	1	2
-2	0	0	0	0	0
-1	0	0	0	0	0
s_{128} 0	0	0	0	0	0
1	1	1	1	1	1
2	1	1	1	1	1

(b) A horizontal split.

Fig. 4. Two examples of planar splits of the secret values.

m'_0	s_0 -2	-1	0	1	2
-2	0	0	0	1	1
-1	0	0	0	1	1
s_{128} 0	0	0	0	1	1
1	0	0	0	1	1
2	0	0	0	1	1

(a) The vertical cut

m'_{128}	s_0 -2	-1	0	1	2
-2	1	1	1	1	1
-1	1	1	1	1	1
0	1	1	1	1	1
1	0	0	0	0	0
2	0	0	0	0	0

(b) The horizontal cut

m'	s_0 -2	-1	0	1	2
-2	0	0	0	1	1
-1	0	0	0	1	1
0	0	0	0	1	1
1	0	0	0	0	0
2	0	0	0	0	0

(c) The rectangular result

Fig. 5. The cuts with respect to m'_0, m'_{128} and the rectangular cut as their intersection.

Intersections of Two Triangular Cuts. Finally, by letting $\mathbf{m}[0] = \mathbf{m}[128] = 1$ and $b_1, b_2 \neq 0$, we create the intersection of two perpendicular triangular cuts. Notice that we are not able to create the intersection of all possible pairs of triangular cuts. The sign change and flip of b_1 and b_2 in (9) compared to (11) means that the two triangular cuts cannot originate from the same corner or from opposite corners. See Fig. 7 for an example of this type of cut. Here we let $b_1 = b_2 = 1$, $h_1 = 24$ and $h_2 = 10$.

			s_0		
m'_0	-2	-1	0	1	2
-2	0	1	1	1	1
-1	0	0	1	1	1
s_{128} 0	0	0	0	1	1
1	0	0	0	0	1
2	0	0	0	0	0

(a) A triangular cut of the secret values, originating from the upper right corner.

			s_0		
m'_0	-2	-1	0	1	2
-2	1	1	1	1	1
-1	1	1	1	1	1
s_{128} 0	1	1	1	1	0
1	1	1	1	0	0
2	1	1	0	0	0

(b) A triangular cut of the secret values, originating from the upper left corner.

Fig. 6. Two examples of triangular cuts.

			s_0		
m'_0	-2	-1	0	1	2
-2	1	1	1	1	1
-1	1	1	1	1	1
s_{128} 0	1	1	1	1	0
1	1	1	1	0	0
2	1	1	0	0	0

			s_0		
m'_{128}	-2	-1	0	1	2
-2	0	1	1	1	1
-1	0	0	1	1	1
0	0	0	0	1	1
1	1	0	0	0	1
2	0	0	0	0	0

			s_0		
m'	-2	-1	0	1	2
-2	0	1	1	1	1
-1	0	0	1	1	1
0	0	0	0	1	0
1	1	0	0	0	0
2	0	0	0	0	0

(a) First triangular cut   (b) Second triangular cut   (c) The intersection

Fig. 7. The cuts with respect to m'_0, m'_{128} and their intersection.

4.2   Two-Positional Mismatch Attacks on Saber

Two-positional mismatch attacks on Saber work similarly to the corresponding attacks on Kyber. We will briefly cover how to modify the parameters to make the attacks work to retrieve the values s_0 and s_{128}. The modifications used to recover the rest of the positions are analogous to the modifications covered in Sect. 4.1. Let $\mathbf{P}_B$ be equal to 0 on all positions, except that $\mathbf{P}_B[0] = k_1$ and $\mathbf{P}_B[128] = k_2$. Let $\mathbf{c}$ be equal to 0 on all positions, except that $\mathbf{c}[0] = h_1$ and $\mathbf{c}[128] = h_2$. For the index 0, we get

$$\mathbf{m}'[0] = ((k_1(s_0 \quad \bmod p) - k_2(s_{128} \quad \bmod p) + H - 2^{\epsilon_p - \epsilon_T} h_1) \quad \bmod p) \gg (\epsilon_p - 1). \tag{17}$$

For the index 128 we get

$$\mathbf{m}'[128] = ((k_1(s_{128} \quad \bmod p) + k_2(s_0 \quad \bmod p) + H - 2^{\epsilon_p - \epsilon_T} h_1) \quad \bmod p) \gg (\epsilon_p - 1). \tag{18}$$

Now, for an integer i, where $1 \leq i \leq 127$ we get

$$\mathbf{m}'[i] = ((k_1(s_i \mod p) - k_2(s_{128+i} \mod p) + H) \mod p) \gg (\epsilon_p - 1), \quad (19)$$

and

$$\mathbf{m}'[128 + i] = ((k_2(s_i \mod p) + k_1(s_{128+i} \mod p) + H) \mod p) \gg (\epsilon_p - 1). \quad (20)$$

For small values of k_1 and k_2 the expressions in (19) and (20) are equal to 0 for all secrets $\mathbf{s}_A$. Combining k_1 and k_2 with suitable values of h_1, h_2 we split the values in (17) and (18) correctly as a function of the values of s_0 and s_{128}.

Just like in the one-dimensional setting, all the splits that we have introduced for Kyber can also be done for Saber. Thus, when designing our mismatch attacks in Sect. 4.4 we only need to consider the distribution of $\mathbf{s}_A$.

4.3 Hyperrectangular Cuts

It is possible to generalize the idea of [38] in other ways. Instead of making planar cuts in one dimension at a time, we can make planar cuts with respect to an arbitrary number of positions at a time. Let us explain the idea for Kyber. Let $I \subset \{0, 1, \ldots, n-1\}$ be the set of indices that we want to make planar splits with respect to. Let $\mathbf{m}[i] = 1$, for $i \in I$, and $\mathbf{m}[i] = 0$, for $i \notin I$. Let $\mathbf{P}_B$ be equal to 0 on all positions except that $\mathbf{P}_B[0] = \lceil \frac{q}{32} \rfloor$. Let $\mathbf{c}_2[i] = 0$, for $i \notin I$ and $\mathbf{c}_2[i] = h_i$, for $i \in I$. Here h_i are the parameters deciding the precise planar cut with respect to each dimension. For $i \in I$ we now get

$$\mathbf{m}'[i] = \mathbf{Compress}_q(\mathbf{v}_A[i] - (\mathbf{s}_A^{tr}\mathbf{u}_A)[i], 2) \quad (21)$$

$$= \left\lceil \frac{2}{q} \left(\left\lceil \frac{q}{32}h_i \right\rfloor - \mathbf{s}_A[i] \left\lceil \frac{q}{32} \right\rfloor \right) \right\rfloor \mod 2. \quad (22)$$

For other indices we get

$$\mathbf{m}'[i] = \mathbf{Compress}_q(\mathbf{v}_A[i] - (\mathbf{s}_A^{tr}\mathbf{u}_A)[i], 2) \quad (23)$$

$$= \left\lceil \frac{2}{q} \left(-\mathbf{s}_A[i] \left\lceil \frac{q}{32} \right\rfloor \right) \right\rfloor \mod 2, \quad (24)$$

which simplifies to 0 as explained above. The idea works similarly for the Saber schemes, except the values of $\mathbf{m}'[i]$ are evaluated according to (7) for $i \in I$ (with the index 0 replaced by i) and (8) for $i \notin I$.

It is of course possible to create a lot of other cuts in higher dimensions. We briefly discuss the potential of these cuts in Sect. 5.1.

4.4 The Optimization Problem

Now we have introduced a set of cuts in the multi-positional setting and are ready to apply them to some schemes. In two dimensions, the optimization problem we now want to solve is, given our available planar, rectangular, triangular, and intersecting triangular splits, how do we come up with a splitting strategy, given the distribution of s_A, that minimizes the expected number of splits?

First, we will cover our attacks on all versions of Kyber and on FireSaber in detail. Then we will show how we devised a greedy algorithm to develop an attack on Saber and LightSaber.

Kyber1024 and Kyber768. In Kyber768 and Kyber1024 the s_i values are centered binomially distributed with $\eta = 2$. The probabilities of the possible value pairs (s_0, s_{128}) are according to Fig. 8.

The figure also shows the first four queries of the mismatch attack. For example, on the first query, represented by the blue lines, we learn whether the secret pair is among the nine positions in the lower left part or whether it is among the other sixteen positions. Depending on which is the case, the second query we make corresponds to either of the red splits and so on. The figure shows the first four queries.

Figure 9 then shows the next three queries. The positions that are filled in black are the positions that are found in less than or equal to four queries. Within seven queries the secret pair is guaranteed to be found. Notice for both figures that we do not always specify exactly which split we use. Given that the values of the secret pair are limited to a certain area, we only specify how the split works within that area. Given the lack of restrictions on the split's behavior outside of this area, most splits are not uniquely determined.

The overall strategy for choosing which splits to make is the following. Start by making a few splits that roughly divide up the possible secret pairs into equally probable blocks. Then make queries that perform identically/close to Huffman coding. This roughly generalizes the strategy of the mismatch attack on Kyber768/Kyber1024 in one dimension, as discussed in Sect. 3.4.

The number of queries needed to find all the different secret value pairs is found in Fig. 10. Using these figures together, we calculate the expected number of queries to recover two positions as $1059/256 \approx 4.1367$. This corresponds to roughly 2.0684 queries per position. We compare this query complexity against other algorithms and some boundaries in Sect. 4.5.

s_0

$256 \cdot P(s_0, s_{128})$	-2	-1	0	1	2
-2	1	4	6	4	1
-1	4	16	24	16	4
0	6	24	36	24	6
1	4	16	24	16	4
2	1	4	6	4	1

s_{128} labels the row index (leftmost column).

Fig. 8. The first part of the two-positional mismatch attack against Kyber768/Kyber1024. All the probabilities are multiplied by 256 for readability. The blue, red, green and yellow splits correspond to the first, second, third and fourth queries respectively. (Color figure online)

Kyber512 and FireSaber. In Kyber512 and FireSaber the values s_i are centered binomially distributed with $\eta = 3$. Thus, the probabilities of the possible value pairs (s_0, s_{128}) are according to Fig. 11. This figure also illustrates the first four queries of the mismatch attack. The remaining six queries are covered in Fig. 12. Just like for Kyber1024/Kyber768, the strategy is to start by making a couple of roughly even splits followed by using (close to) Huffman coding in latter queries. Also for these schemes, the strategy roughly mimics and generalizes the strategy of the mismatch attack on Kyber512/FireSaber in one dimension, as discussed in Sect. 3.4.

The number of queries needed to find all the different secret value pairs is found in Fig. 13. Using these figures together, we calculate the expected number of queries to recover two positions as $19285/4096 \approx 4.70825$. This corresponds to roughly 2.3541 queries per position. We compare this performance against other algorithms and some boundaries in Sect. 4.5.

The Automatic Greedy Approach. For Saber and LightSaber the number of possible pairs of secret values is too large to make manual optimization practical. To get a decent attack against these two schemes we make an automatic search for a solution instead. In two dimensions we apply a greedy attack, where the algorithm in each step chooses the query that splits the remaining positions as evenly as possible. It turns out that the algorithm performs better when only using planar and rectangular splits, compared to when adding triangular/triangular intersection splits. Using the latter types of splits makes the algorithm choose a worse local optimum.

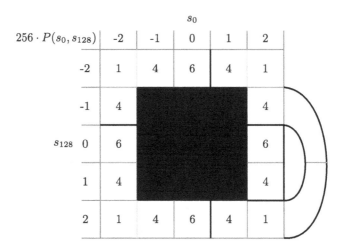

Fig. 9. The second part of the two-positional mismatch attack against Kyber768/Kyber1024. All the probabilities are multiplied by 256 for readability. The brown, orange and pink splits correspond to the fifth, sixth and seventh queries respectively. The positions that are filled in black correspond to the value pairs that are found after less than or equal to four queries. The curved path between the lower right and the upper right areas signals that these positions correspond to the same block after four queries. (Color figure online)

s_0

	-2	-1	0	1	2
-2	7	7	5	7	7
-1	6	4	4	4	6
s_{128} 0	6	3	3	4	5
1	6	4	3	4	5
2	7	7	6	6	6

Fig. 10. The number of queries needed to find the secret pair (s_0, s_{128}) for the different values of this pair for the two-positional mismatch attack on Kyber768/Kyber1024.

$4096 \cdot P(s_0, s_{128})$	s_0: -3	-2	-1	0	1	2	3
s_{128}: 3	1	6	15	20	15	6	1
2	6	36	90	120	90	36	6
1	15	90	225	300	225	90	15
0	20	120	300	400	300	120	20
-1	15	90	225	300	225	90	15
-2	6	36	90	120	90	36	6
-3	1	6	15	20	15	6	1

Fig. 11. The first part of the two-positional mismatch attack against Kyber512/FireSaber. All the probabilities are multiplied by 4096 for readability. The blue, red, green and yellow splits correspond to the first, second, third and fourth queries respectively. The green diagonal split decides whether the secret is $(0, 0)$ or any of the values in the upper left block. The yellow diagonal split decides whether the secret is $(0, -1)$ or $(-1, 0)$. (Color figure online)

We generalize this attack to three dimensions, where we allow for any types of cuboid splits (the hyperrectangular splits in three dimensions). This corresponds to letting $|I| \leq 3$ in Sect. 4.3. The performance of the attack in two and three dimensions is shown in Table 6.

Table 6. The performance of the greedy mismatch attacks in two and three dimensions on all versions of Kyber and Saber, measured in expected number of queries per secret position.

	Kyber512	Kyber768	Kyber1024	LightSaber	Saber	FireSaber
Two Dimensions	2.4561	2.0820	2.0820	2.7643	2.6256	2.4561
Three Dimensions	2.3771	2.0837	2.0837	2.7540	2.5839	2.3771

All the mismatch attacks in [38] on Kyber and Saber are hyperrectangular, greedy attacks in one dimension, making this type of greedy approach a pretty natural generalization. Perhaps not surprisingly, the greedy hyperrectangular attack mostly performs better in three dimensions than in two, and always

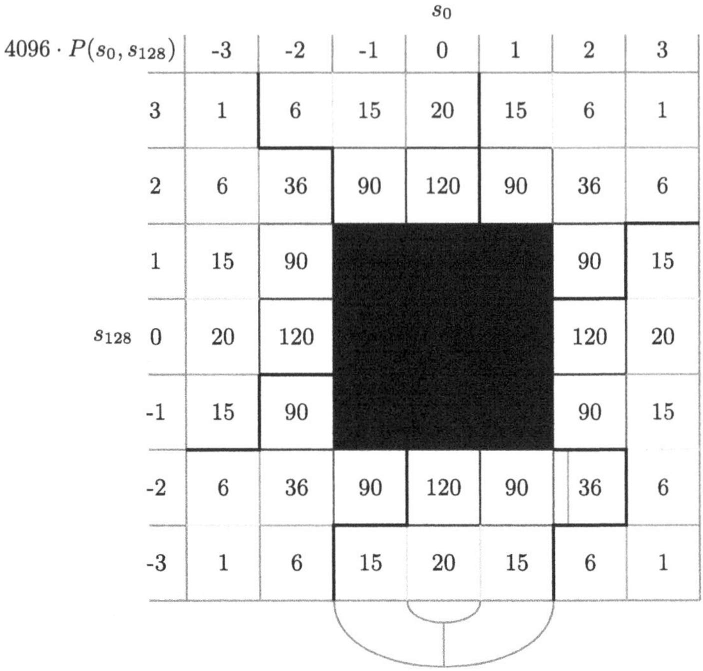

Fig. 12. The two-positional mismatch attack against Kyber512/FireSaber. The queries after the first four queries. The blue, red, green, yellow, brown and orange splits correspond to the fifth, sixth, seventh, eighth, ninth and tenth queries respectively. All the probabilities are multiplied by 4096 for readability. The green split inside the box to the lower right decides whether the secret pair is $(2, -2)$ or any of the other remaining values of the area. The brown split that crosses the curved lines decides whether the secret is $(-1, -3)$ or $(1, -3)$. (Color figure online)

better in two than in one. In three dimensions the attack performs slightly better than/slightly worse than the Huffman bound in one dimension, see Table 7 and Sect. 4.5 for a comparison of this approach to other algorithms and limits.

Notice that this is essentially the most obvious type of automatic attack. There is room for all sorts of improvements here, which we discuss in Sect. 5.1.

s_0

s_{128}	-3	-2	-1	0	1	2	3
3	10	8	8	7	8	10	10
2	10	7	6	5	6	7	9
1	9	6	4	4	4	5	8
0	9	5	4	3	4	5	8
-1	9	5	4	4	4	6	8
-2	8	7	6	5	6	7	9
-3	9	9	9	8	9	10	10

Fig. 13. The number of queries needed to find the secret pair (s_0, s_{128}) for the different values of this pair for the two-positional mismatch attack on Kyber512/FireSaber.

4.5 Comparisons

In Table 7 we compare our mismatch attacks against the previous state-of-the-art, previous lower bounds and new lower bounds. Our Result 1 refers to manual optimization in two dimensions. Our Result 2 refers to the best greedy attack from Sect. 4.4 for the different schemes[6]. The values in bold are the new state-of-the-art values. When performing two-positional attacks, the lower limit is Huffman coding in two dimensions. When performing three-positional attacks, the lower limit is Huffman coding in three dimensions. The performance of Huffman coding in one, two and three dimensions respectively is called Huffman Bound 1, 2 and 3 respectively. Finally, the Shannon Bound refers to the entropy of the secret, which is the theoretically best performance that you can achieve with a pure mismatch attack.

---

[6] Notice that for the greedy attacks in three dimensions the performance is marginally worse than the number of positions times the performance from Table 6. The secret is retrieved in blocks of 256 positions at a time. After finding $3 \cdot 84 = 252$ positions using the three-positional attack, the remaining 4 positions of the block have to be retrieved using two-positional steps, which are slightly worse for most schemes.

Table 7. Our results in expected number of queries to fully recover the secret compared to various bounds and previous practical attacks.

	Kyber512	Kyber768	Kyber1024	LightSaber	Saber	FireSaber
Previous Best [38]	1312	1776	2368	1460	2091	2624
Huffman Bound 1	1216	1632	2176	1412	1986	2432
Our Result 1	**1205.3**	**1588.5**	**2118**	–	–	**2410.6**
Our Result 2	1217.7	1599	2132	**1410.2**	**1984.9**	2435.4
Huffman Bound 2	1202.1	1575	2100	1395.9	1970.0	2404.3
Huffman Bound 3	1199.9	1569.8	2093.0	1391.7	1962.3	2399.7
Shannon Bound	1195	1560	2079	1386	1954	2389

Unlike the one-dimensional situation analyzed in Sect. 3.5, we do not claim that our strategy is optimal given our restrictions. Both developing an optimal strategy, and showing that a strategy is optimal, are much harder in our setting.

However, we can say that our results are fairly close to optimal. For all the schemes our attacks are much closer in performance to the Shannon bound than to [38]. We have thus made most of the possible improvements that can be made.

For all versions of Kyber and for FireSaber, we are very close to the Huffman bound in two dimensions, showing that there is very little room for improvement. Our greedy attacks against Saber and LightSaber are not optimal in our given context, but can still only be improved a little bit, as they both perform fairly close to the Huffman bound in three dimensions.

It should also be noted that due to not all imaginable splits being accessible in practice, even the optimal strategy performs worse than the Huffman bounds for the respective dimension, making our results even closer to optimal.

In Sect. 5.1 we discuss how improving our attacks probably makes it possible to reach the Shannon bound. In Sect. 5.2 we discuss how we can beat the Shannon bound by using post-processing.

5   Discussions

5.1   Room for Further Improvements

For the two-positional splits of Kyber, by letting $b_1 = 2$, $b_2 = 1$, vice versa or changing signs of one of the variables, we can create yet other cuts[7]. Similar extensions apply for Saber. These extensions create even more possible splits in two dimensions.

The hyperrectangular cuts from Sect. 4.3 only generalize the planar and rectangular splits. Of course, a lot of other splits are also possible in higher dimensions. Even limited to only hyperrectangular splits in higher dimensions our

---

[7] Notice that we cannot increase the values of b_1 and b_2 too much, because then the other indices of (13) are not guaranteed to be equal to 0.

fairly simple greedy attack can of course be improved with smarter approaches and/or by increasing the number of dimensions.

Thus, we conjecture that getting (arbitrarily close) to the Shannon bound is possible, because of the numerous potential improvements. Meanwhile, we emphasize that our current results are already close to the bound.

5.2   Post-processing with Lattice Reduction

Previous literature on mismatch attacks focuses on the number of queries needed to fully recover the secret s. However, the adversary also has access to LWE samples. Not taking advantage of this information in an attack is clearly sub-optimal. While [38] states "Secondly, what we talk about is recovering the full key, but obviously the recovery of the partial key also leaks information about the key, significantly decreasing the bit-security.", they did not study this hybrid approach in detail[8].

In principle, the optimal hybrid mismatch attack with post-processing chooses, given a limited number of queries, among all possible mismatch strategies, the strategy that minimizes the complexity of the post-processing. A paper that studied solving the LWE and NTRU problem with hints about the secret more generally is [14]. In our setting it is most likely optimal to find the exact value of as many positions as possible and, if the final few queries are not enough to completely know the final positions being queried, use the partial information we have on these positions.

We plot the relationship between the allowed number of queries using the best mismatch attack from Table 7 and the post-processing complexity in Fig. 14, for all versions of Kyber and Saber. We use the primal_bdd($\cdot$) function in the new Lattice-Estimator[9] [5] to estimate the cost of solving the corresponding LWE instance. Without post-processing, the right-most vertical line shows the query complexity of the current best two-positional attack and the second (dotted) vertical line to the right shows the Shannon lower bound. We can see that the two lines are fairly close, so our new attack is near-optimal in the information-theoretical sense. We also see that the query complexity can be highly reduced by using post-processing. For instance, the query complexity is reduced by a factor 2 for Kyber512, when the allowed post-processing cost is 2^{80}.

---

[8] Notice however that recently and independently of us, recovering the secret key using partial information from a mismatch attack was studied in [34]. Post-processing in a very similar setting was also concurrently studied in [40].

[9] https://github.com/malb/lattice-estimator.

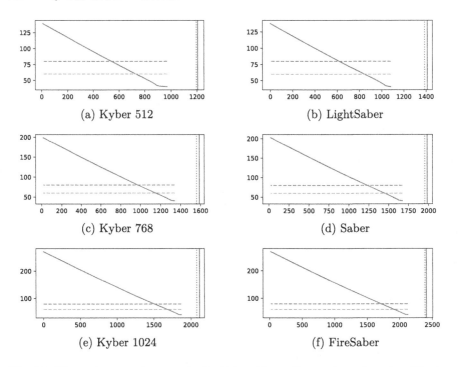

Fig. 14. The post-processing complexity in $\log_2(\cdot)$ **vs.** the number of queries. The two horizontal lines represent the post-processing complexity of 2^{80} (upper) and 2^{60} (lower), respectively. The right-most vertical line shows the current best multi-positional attack without post-processing and the second (dotted) vertical line shows the Shannon bound for the attacks without post-processing.

5.3 Relation to Side-Channel and Fault-Injection Attacks

Similar to the one-positional mismatch attacks proposed in [38], our multi-positional version can improve the query (or trace) complexity of PC-oracle-based chosen-ciphertext side-channel attacks on CCA-secure implementations of Kyber and Saber. The method of generating the chosen ciphertexts is the same as the approach of selecting ciphertexts described in Sect. 4. The improvement factor over the side-channel attack in [38] is close to that of our new mismatch attack (see Table 1) over its one-positional counterpart in [38]. Two recent papers [39,45] proposed improved side-channel attacks recovering multiple bits of information from the FO transform of one trace. We leave the problem of improving these two new attacks with our new idea to future research since side-channel attacks are not the focal point of the paper. The new attacks may also be applied to improve the fault-injection attack proposed in [47].

6   Conclusions and Future Work

In this paper, we have proposed novel multi-positional key mismatch attacks on Kyber and Saber, significantly improving the state-of-the-art mismatch attacks of [38]. Our new attacks even beat the lower bounds proposed in [38], and they are near-optimal since the query complexities are close to the Shannon bound. The new attacks can be applied to improve the efficiency of certain chosen-ciphertext side-channel attacks against Kyber and Saber and may also have significance in fault-injection attacks.

The new idea of targeting multiple secret coefficients simultaneously can be generalized to other lattice-based KEMs. This translation is probably straightforward for other LWE/LWR-based KEMs such as FrodoKEM [35], but might also be applicable to KEMs based on NTRU. e.g., NTRU [12] and NTRU prime [9].

We have also estimated how much the mismatch attacks can be improved by using post-processing, showing that we can clearly beat the Shannon bounds with this approach when having access to moderate computational resources.

As we conjecture in our paper, by improving the greedy algorithm and increasing the dimensions, it is likely possible to come arbitrarily close to the Shannon bound for all versions of Kyber and Saber. One interesting topic is to apply more advanced automatic tools, such as mixed integer linear programming (MILP) or constraint programming, to search for better mismatch attacks. On the other hand, our results are near-optimal, so the room for improvement is small in practice.

Acknowledgment. We would like to thank the anonymous reviewers of this paper. We would also like to thank Jonathan Sönnerup, whose excessive solution of an information theory course's project inspired some of the techniques of this paper. QG was funded by the Swedish Research Council (grant numbers 2019-04166 and 2021-04602), the Swedish Civil Contingencies Agency (grant number 2020-11632), the Swedish Foundation for Strategic Research (Grant No. RIT17-0005) and the Wallenberg AI, Autonomous Systems and Software Program (WASP) funded by the Knut and Alice Wallenberg Foundation. EM was funded by the project "Kvantesikker Kryptografi" from the National Security Authority of Norway.

References

1. NIST Post-Quantum Cryptography Standardization. https://csrc.nist.gov/Projects/Post-Quantum-Cryptography/Post-Quantum-Cryptography-Standardization. Accessed 24 Sept 2018
2. Submission Requirements and Evaluation Criteria for the Post-Quantum Cryptography Standardization Process. https://csrc.nist.gov/CSRC/media/Projects/Post-Quantum-Cryptography/documents/call-for-proposals-final-dec-2016.pdf. Accessed 18 Feb 2021
3. Ajtai, M., Dwork, C.: A public-key cryptosystem with worst-case/average-case equivalence. In: Proceedings of the Twenty-Ninth Annual ACM Symposium on Theory of Computing, STOC 1997, pp. 284–293. Association for Computing Machinery, New York (1997). https://doi.org/10.1145/258533.258604

4. Albrecht, M.R., et al.: Classic McEliece. Technical report, National Institute of Standards and Technology (2020). https://csrc.nist.gov/projects/post-quantum-cryptography/round-3-submissions

5. Albrecht, M.R., Player, R., Scott, S.: On the concrete hardness of learning with errors. J. Math. Cryptol. **9**(3), 169–203 (2015)

6. Băetu, C., Durak, F.B., Huguenin-Dumittan, L., Talayhan, A., Vaudenay, S.: Misuse attacks on post-quantum cryptosystems. In: Ishai, Y., Rijmen, V. (eds.) EURO-CRYPT 2019. LNCS, vol. 11477, pp. 747–776. Springer, Cham (2019). https://doi.org/10.1007/978-3-030-17656-3_26

7. Bauer, A., Gilbert, H., Renault, G., Rossi, M.: Assessment of the key-reuse resilience of NewHope. In: Matsui, M. (ed.) CT-RSA 2019. LNCS, vol. 11405, pp. 272–292. Springer, Cham (2019). https://doi.org/10.1007/978-3-030-12612-4_14

8. Bernstein, D.J., Groot Bruinderink, L., Lange, T., Panny, L.: HILA5 pindakaas: on the CCA security of lattice-based encryption with error correction. In: Joux, A., Nitaj, A., Rachidi, T. (eds.) AFRICACRYPT 2018. LNCS, vol. 10831, pp. 203–216. Springer, Cham (2018). https://doi.org/10.1007/978-3-319-89339-6_12

9. Bernstein, D.J., et al.: NTRU prime. Technical report, National Institute of Standards and Technology (2020). https://csrc.nist.gov/projects/post-quantum-cryptography/round-3-submissions

10. Bindel, N., Schanck, J.M.: Decryption failure is more likely after success. In: Ding, J., Tillich, J.-P. (eds.) PQCrypto 2020. LNCS, vol. 12100, pp. 206–225. Springer, Cham (2020). https://doi.org/10.1007/978-3-030-44223-1_12

11. Bleichenbacher, D.: Chosen ciphertext attacks against protocols based on the RSA encryption standard PKCS #1. In: Krawczyk, H. (ed.) CRYPTO 1998. LNCS, vol. 1462, pp. 1–12. Springer, Heidelberg (1998). https://doi.org/10.1007/BFb0055716

12. Chen, C., et al.: NTRU. Technical report, National Institute of Standards and Technology (2020). https://csrc.nist.gov/projects/post-quantum-cryptography/round-3-submissions

13. Cover, T.M., Thomas, J.A.: Elements of Information Theory. Wiley Series in Telecommunications and Signal Processing. Wiley-Interscience (2006)

14. Dachman-Soled, D., Ducas, L., Gong, H., Rossi, M.: LWE with side information: attacks and concrete security estimation. In: Micciancio, D., Ristenpart, T. (eds.) CRYPTO 2020. LNCS, vol. 12171, pp. 329–358. Springer, Cham (2020). https://doi.org/10.1007/978-3-030-56880-1_12

15. D'Anvers, J.-P., Guo, Q., Johansson, T., Nilsson, A., Vercauteren, F., Verbauwhede, I.: Decryption failure attacks on IND-CCA secure lattice-based schemes. In: Lin, D., Sako, K. (eds.) PKC 2019. LNCS, vol. 11443, pp. 565–598. Springer, Cham (2019). https://doi.org/10.1007/978-3-030-17259-6_19

16. D'Anvers, J.P., et al.: SABER. Technical report, National Institute of Standards and Technology (2020). https://csrc.nist.gov/projects/post-quantum-cryptography/round-3-submissions

17. D'Anvers, J.-P., Rossi, M., Virdia, F.: *(One) failure is not an option*: bootstrapping the search for failures in lattice-based encryption schemes. In: Canteaut, A., Ishai, Y. (eds.) EUROCRYPT 2020. LNCS, vol. 12107, pp. 3–33. Springer, Cham (2020). https://doi.org/10.1007/978-3-030-45727-3_1

18. D'Anvers, J.P., Tiepelt, M., Vercauteren, F., Verbauwhede, I.: Timing attacks on error correcting codes in post-quantum schemes. Cryptology ePrint Archive, Report 2019/292 (2019). https://eprint.iacr.org/2019/292

19. Ding, J., Fluhrer, S., Rv, S.: Complete attack on RLWE key exchange with reused keys, without signal leakage. In: Susilo, W., Yang, G. (eds.) ACISP 2018. LNCS,

vol. 10946, pp. 467–486. Springer, Cham (2018). https://doi.org/10.1007/978-3-319-93638-3_27

20. Fabšič, T., Hromada, V., Stankovski, P., Zajac, P., Guo, Q., Johansson, T.: A reaction attack on the QC-LDPC McEliece cryptosystem. In: Lange, T., Takagi, T. (eds.) PQCrypto 2017. LNCS, vol. 10346, pp. 51–68. Springer, Cham (2017). https://doi.org/10.1007/978-3-319-59879-6_4

21. Fluhrer, S.: Cryptanalysis of ring-LWE based key exchange with key share reuse. Cryptology ePrint Archive, Report 2016/085 (2016). https://eprint.iacr.org/2016/085

22. Fujisaki, E., Okamoto, T.: Secure integration of asymmetric and symmetric encryption schemes. In: Wiener, M. (ed.) CRYPTO 1999. LNCS, vol. 1666, pp. 537–554. Springer, Heidelberg (1999). https://doi.org/10.1007/3-540-48405-1_34

23. Goldreich, O., Goldwasser, S., Halevi, S.: Public-key cryptosystems from lattice reduction problems. In: Kaliski, B.S. (ed.) CRYPTO 1997. LNCS, vol. 1294, pp. 112–131. Springer, Heidelberg (1997). https://doi.org/10.1007/BFb0052231

24. Greuet, A., Montoya, S., Renault, G.: Attack on LAC key exchange in misuse situation. In: Krenn, S., Shulman, H., Vaudenay, S. (eds.) CANS 2020. LNCS, vol. 12579, pp. 549–569. Springer, Cham (2020). https://doi.org/10.1007/978-3-030-65411-5_27

25. Guo, Q., Johansson, T.: A new decryption failure attack against HQC. In: Moriai, S., Wang, H. (eds.) ASIACRYPT 2020. LNCS, vol. 12491, pp. 353–382. Springer, Cham (2020). https://doi.org/10.1007/978-3-030-64837-4_12

26. Guo, Q., Johansson, T., Nilsson, A.: A key-recovery timing attack on post-quantum primitives using the Fujisaki-Okamoto transformation and its application on FrodoKEM. In: Micciancio, D., Ristenpart, T. (eds.) CRYPTO 2020. LNCS, vol. 12171, pp. 359–386. Springer, Cham (2020). https://doi.org/10.1007/978-3-030-56880-1_13

27. Guo, Q., Johansson, T., Stankovski, P.: A key recovery attack on MDPC with CCA security using decoding errors. In: Cheon, J.H., Takagi, T. (eds.) ASIACRYPT 2016. LNCS, vol. 10031, pp. 789–815. Springer, Heidelberg (2016). https://doi.org/10.1007/978-3-662-53887-6_29

28. Guo, Q., Johansson, T., Yang, J.: A novel CCA attack using decryption errors against LAC. In: Galbraith, S.D., Moriai, S. (eds.) ASIACRYPT 2019. LNCS, vol. 11921, pp. 82–111. Springer, Cham (2019). https://doi.org/10.1007/978-3-030-34578-5_4

29. Hall, C., Goldberg, I., Schneier, B.: Reaction attacks against several public-key cryptosystem. In: Varadharajan, V., Mu, Y. (eds.) ICICS 1999. LNCS, vol. 1726, pp. 2–12. Springer, Heidelberg (1999). https://doi.org/10.1007/978-3-540-47942-0_2

30. Hoffstein, J., Pipher, J., Silverman, J.H.: NTRU: a ring-based public key cryptosystem. In: Buhler, J.P. (ed.) ANTS 1998. LNCS, vol. 1423, pp. 267–288. Springer, Heidelberg (1998). https://doi.org/10.1007/BFb0054868

31. Hoffstein, J., Silverman, J.H.: Protecting NTRU against chosen ciphertext and reaction attacks. NTRU Cryptosystems Technical Report 16 (2000)

32. Huguenin-Dumittan, L., Vaudenay, S.: Classical misuse attacks on NIST round 2 PQC. In: Conti, M., Zhou, J., Casalicchio, E., Spognardi, A. (eds.) ACNS 2020. LNCS, vol. 12146, pp. 208–227. Springer, Cham (2020). https://doi.org/10.1007/978-3-030-57808-4_11

33. McEliece, R.J.: A public-key cryptosystem based on algebraic coding theory. The deep space network progress report 42-44, Jet Propulsion Laboratory, California

Institute of Technology (1978). https://ipnpr.jpl.nasa.gov/progress_report2/42-44/44N.PDF

34. Mi, R., Jiang, H., Zhang, Z.: Lattice reduction meets key-mismatch: new misuse attack on lattice-based NIST candidate KEMs. Cryptology ePrint Archive, Paper 2022/1064 (2022). https://eprint.iacr.org/2022/1064

35. Naehrig, M., et al.: FrodoKEM. Technical report, National Institute of Standards and Technology (2020). https://csrc.nist.gov/projects/post-quantum-cryptography/round-3-submissions

36. Okada, S., Wang, Y., Takagi, T.: Improving key mismatch attack on NewHope with fewer queries. In: Liu, J.K., Cui, H. (eds.) ACISP 2020. LNCS, vol. 12248, pp. 505–524. Springer, Cham (2020). https://doi.org/10.1007/978-3-030-55304-3_26

37. Qin, Y., Cheng, C., Ding, J.: A complete and optimized key mismatch attack on NIST candidate NewHope. In: Sako, K., Schneider, S., Ryan, P.Y.A. (eds.) ESORICS 2019. LNCS, vol. 11736, pp. 504–520. Springer, Cham (2019). https://doi.org/10.1007/978-3-030-29962-0_24

38. Qin, Y., Cheng, C., Zhang, X., Pan, Y., Hu, L., Ding, J.: A systematic approach and analysis of key mismatch attacks on lattice-based NIST candidate KEMs. In: Tibouchi, M., Wang, H. (eds.) ASIACRYPT 2021. LNCS, vol. 13093, pp. 92–121. Springer, Cham (2021). https://doi.org/10.1007/978-3-030-92068-5_4

39. Rajendran, G., Ravi, P., D'Anvers, J.P., Bhasin, S., Chattopadhyay, A.: Pushing the limits of generic side-channel attacks on LWE-based KEMs-parallel PC oracle attacks on Kyber KEM and beyond. Cryptology ePrint Archive (2022)

40. Rajendran, G., Ravi, P., D'Anvers, J.P., Bhasin, S., Chattopadhyay, A.: Pushing the limits of generic side-channel attacks on LWE-based KEMs - parallel PC oracle attacks on Kyber KEM and beyond. IACR Trans. Cryptogr. Hardw. Embed. Syst. **2023**, 418–446 (2023)

41. Ravi, P., Roy, S.S., Chattopadhyay, A., Bhasin, S.: Generic side-channel attacks on CCA-secure lattice-based PKE and KEMs. IACR TCHES **2020**(3), 307–335 (2020). https://tches.iacr.org/index.php/TCHES/article/view/8592

42. Regev, O.: On lattices, learning with errors, random linear codes, and cryptography. In: Gabow, H.N., Fagin, R. (eds.) 37th ACM STOC, pp. 84–93. ACM Press (2005)

43. Schwabe, P., et al.: CRYSTALS-KYBER. Technical report, National Institute of Standards and Technology (2020). https://csrc.nist.gov/projects/post-quantum-cryptography/round-3-submissions

44. Shor, P.W.: Algorithms for quantum computation: discrete logarithms and factoring. In: 35th FOCS, pp. 124–134. IEEE Computer Society Press (1994)

45. Tanaka, Y., Ueno, R., Xagawa, K., Ito, A., Takahashi, J., Homma, N.: Multiple-valued plaintext-checking side-channel attacks on post-quantum KEMs. Cryptology ePrint Archive (2022)

46. Ueno, R., Xagawa, K., Tanaka, Y., Ito, A., Takahashi, J., Homma, N.: Curse of re-encryption: a generic power/EM analysis on post-quantum KEMs. IACR Trans. Cryptogr. Hardw. Embed. Syst. **2022**(1), 296–322 (2022). https://doi.org/10.46586/tches.v2022.i1.296-322

47. Xagawa, K., Ito, A., Ueno, R., Takahashi, J., Homma, N.: Fault-injection attacks against NIST's post-quantum cryptography round 3 KEM candidates. In: Tibouchi, M., Wang, H. (eds.) ASIACRYPT 2021. LNCS, vol. 13091, pp. 33–61. Springer, Cham (2021). https://doi.org/10.1007/978-3-030-92075-3_2

NTWE: A Natural Combination of NTRU and LWE

Joel Gärtner[✉]

KTH Royal Institute of Technology, Stockholm, Sweden
jgartner@kth.se

Abstract. Lattice-based cryptosystems are some of the primary post-quantum secure alternatives to the asymmetric cryptography that is used today. These lattice-based cryptosystems typically rely on the hardness of some version of either the NTRU or the LWE problem. In this paper, we present the NTWE problem, a natural combination of the NTRU and LWE problems, and construct a new lattice-based cryptosystem based on the hardness of the NTWE problem.

As with the NTRU and LWE problems, the NTWE problem naturally corresponds to a problem in a q-ary lattice. This allows the hardness of the NTWE problem to be estimated in the same way as it is estimated for the LWE and NTRU problems. We parametrize our cryptosystem from such a hardness estimate and the resulting scheme has performance that is competitive with that of typical lattice-based schemes.

In some sense, our NTWE-based cryptosystem can be seen as a less structured and more compact version of a cryptosystem based on the module-NTRU problem. Thus, parameters for our cryptosystem can be selected with the flexibility of a module-LWE-based scheme, while other properties of our system are more similar to those in an NTRU-based system.

Keywords: Lattice-based cryptography · Post-quantum cryptography · Public Key Encryption · NTRU · Learning With Errors

1 Introduction

The NIST standardization process for post-quantum cryptography has already resulted in four algorithms being selected for standardization. Three of these selected algorithms are lattice-based and the security of these schemes rely on the hardness of versions of either the LWE or the NTRU problem. The origins of the NTRU and LWE problems are quite different, but the concrete hardness of these problems is currently estimated in very similar ways.

NTRU was introduced more than 25 years ago as a ring-based public key cryptosystem [14]. The security of this system is based on the hardness of the NTRU problem which, with somewhat different parameters than those first proposed, has remained hard to solve in practice. While not originally stated as a lattice-based cryptosystem, an NTRU instance can easily be interpreted as

T. Johansson and D. Smith-Tone (Eds.): PQCrypto 2023, LNCS 14154, pp. 321–353, 2023.
https://doi.org/10.1007/978-3-031-40003-2_12

an instance a special type of structured lattice problem and the concrete security of current NTRU-based cryptosystems is typically estimated based on how efficiently this structured lattice problem can be solved.

The LWE problem is even more closely related to lattice problems. It was introduced in 2005 by Regev together with a quantum reduction from a worst-case lattice problem [22]. As such, the asymptotic security of LWE-based cryptosystems can be guaranteed as long as there exists instances of this lattice problem that are hard to solve with a quantum computer. This reduction does, however, say very little about the concrete security of typically considered parametrizations of LWE-based cryptosystems [5, 13]. Instead, LWE-based cryptosystems are usually parametrized in the same way as NTRU-based systems, based on a concrete hardness estimate for the natural lattice problem that corresponds to an LWE instance.

There are several different structured versions of the LWE problem, with the most prominent being the ring- and module-LWE problems. Especially the ring-LWE problem is very similar to the NTRU problem, as it essentially corresponds to an inhomogeneous version of the NTRU problem. The module-LWE problem can be seen as a somewhat less structured version of the ring-LWE problem and is thus also quite similar to the NTRU problem.

While there are results that relate the hardness of versions of the LWE problem to the hardness of versions of the NTRU problem [20, 26, 27], these results do not directly relate the security of concrete parametrizations of currently proposed cryptosystems. As such, given similar parametrization of an NTRU-based and an LWE-based cryptosystem, we can not directly determine if one of these schemes is more secure than the other. Although the security of both types of systems are based on similar assumptions, there is a possibility that an attack lowers the concrete security of schemes based on one of the assumptions, without directly impacting schemes based on the other assumption.

Thus, lattice-based cryptography is primarily based on the hardness of two similar, yet different problems. The worst-case to average-case reduction which were the reason for the introduction of the LWE problem does not support the concrete security of typical LWE-based cryptosystems. Furthermore, the understanding of lattice algorithms have improved significantly since the introduction of the NTRU system. Therefore, it is interesting to investigate what alternative problems we can base the security of similar cryptosystems on, and if this would allow any improvements compared to the schemes that are considered today.

1.1 Our Contribution

In this paper, we introduce and investigate the NTWE problem and create an NTWE-based cryptosystem. The NTWE problem can be seen as a natural combination of the NTRU and module-LWE problems. It is easily seen that as long as either the NTRU problem or the module-LWE problem is hard, then so is the NTWE problem.

We can thus parametrize our NTWE-based cryptosystem so that it is secure as long as either the corresponding NTRU- or LWE-based cryptosystem is secure.

As the NTRU and LWE problem are quite similar, one would typically not consider using a system that relies on an module-LWE-based and an NTRU-based cryptosystem in parallel. However, this type of parametrization of our NTWE-based cryptosystem is both more efficient and compact than simply combining an NTRU-based and a module-LWE-based cryptosystem and is therefore more interesting.

While we can guarantee that the NTWE problem is no easier than versions of the NTRU and the LWE problems, it actually seems to be significantly harder than the problems that we provably can relate it to. Similarly to the module-LWE problem, we consider a module version of the NTWE problem. A simple reduction shows that the rank k NTWE problem is no easier than the rank k module-LWE problem. However, we believe that the rank k NTWE problem is essentially as hard as a rank $k + 1$ module-LWE problem.

Similarly to the LWE and NTRU problems, the NTWE problem naturally corresponds to a lattice problem in a q-ary lattice. The lattice problem for the rank k NTWE problem is very similar to the lattice problem for the rank $k + 1$ module-LWE problem. This motivates our concrete hardness estimate for the rank k NTWE problem. Furthermore, we are able to show that a more structured version of the NTWE problem is at least as hard as the rank $k + 1$ module-NTRU problem, providing further motivation for our hardness estimate.

New hardness assumptions must be thoroughly analyzed before significant confidence can be placed in the security of cryptosystems that rely on them. However, any assumptions similar to the ones used today can be more easily trusted. As the NTWE problem naturally corresponds to a lattice problem, it directly benefits from analysis of similar lattice problems. Furthermore, due to the similarities between the rank k NTWE problem and the NTRU and LWE problems in rank $k + 1$ modules, we believe that any improved algorithms for the NTWE problem would also result in increased understanding of these other problems.

We furthermore provide concrete parametrizations of our NTWE-based cryptosystem. This includes parametrizations similar to the different parametrizations of CRYSTALS-Kyber [25], henceforth referred to only as Kyber. These parametrizations have essentially the same sized public-key and ciphertext as in the parametrizations of Kyber that target the same security level.

A large reason for the relatively small ciphertexts in Kyber is a method for ciphertext compression. This consists of discarding many of the bits of the ciphertext, allowing significantly smaller ciphertexts at the cost of somewhat larger decryption failure probability. In our scheme, we do not perform any such ciphertext compression but we still have a ciphertext size that is comparable to that of Kyber. Thus, compared to an LWE-based scheme without ciphertext compression, our scheme actually has significantly smaller ciphertexts.

There are multiple reasons to want to avoid ciphertext compression, one of which may be patent reasons. Although the method for ciphertext compression that is used in Kyber has not been patented, other versions of ciphertext compression seem to be protected by a patent. However, to which extent this patent actually covers the different methods for ciphertext compression that is performed in LWE-based schemes has not been entirely clear. This may be a reason to prefer our scheme where no such ciphertext compression is performed.

Another benefit of not having to use ciphertext compression is that it may allow more compact schemes that include a zero-knowledge proof that the ciphertext is correctly formed. Such a zero-knowledge proof seems to be incompatible with ciphertext compression, and such a scheme would therefore have to use uncompressed ciphertexts. Therefore, for these types of applications, the ciphertexts from our cryptosystem would be significantly smaller than the ciphertexts in a comparable LWE-based system. This advantage was one of the primary advantages of NTRU-based systems compared to LWE-based systems mentioned by Lyubashevsky and Seiler in a paper [18] developing a more efficient version of NTRU.

An advantage of our scheme compared to NTRU is its increased flexibility in allowing module versions of the problem. While module versions of the NTRU problem have been considered [8], this module-NTRU problem does not seem to be suitable for public key encryption. The size of the public key in such a module-NTRU-based encryption scheme would grow with the square of the module rank. This would result in a significantly larger public key than in a module-LWE based scheme, where the size of the public key depends linearly on the module rank. We can thus consider our NTWE-based cryptosystem as a more compact version of a cryptosystem based on the module-NTRU problem. Furthermore, whereas the NTRU problem is significantly easier in an overstretched parameter regime, it does not seem like there is such an overstretched parameter regime for the NTWE problem.

Another potential benefit of our NTWE-based cryptosystem compared to a system based on module-LWE is its resistance against dual lattice attacks. The two main attacks against LWE-based schemes are the primal and dual lattice attacks. Recent results have indicated that the dual attack may be more efficient against concrete cryptosystem parameters [12,19]. Although these results have been questioned [9], increased resistance against these dual attacks is still preferable.

While it is possible to perform a dual attack against the NTWE problem, a primal lattice attack against the NTWE problem seems to be significantly more efficient for the parameters that we consider in this paper. However, the dual attack against NTWE does seem to be more efficient than the primal attack against some parametrizations of this problem. Thus, the dual attack should still be considered when investigating the concrete hardness of specific NTWE instances.

For efficiency, we parametrize our cryptosystem using a ring R and modulos q that enable using the Number Theoretic Transform (NTT) to efficiently multiply ring elements. Similar to an NTRU-based system, we require computing inverses of a ring element f in both R_q and R_p, for an integer q and a small integer p, which we fix to be 2. While the inverse in R_q is efficiently computable by using the NTT, the inverse in R_2 is less efficient to compute. However, this primarily impacts the performance of key generation, and if the same public-key is used multiple times, this cost may be considered insignificant.

To improve the efficiency of key generation, we may select f from a distribution such that the inverse in R_2 is trivial, but such that the elements of f are a factor 2 larger. This trick results in schemes that are more efficient than the corresponding module-LWE-based schemes but with a larger decryption failure probability. If not using this trick to ensure that the inverse of f in R_2 is trivial, the resulting scheme actually has a lower decryption failure probability than a corresponding module-LWE-based scheme. Thus, compared to a corresponding module-LWE-based system, our NTWE-based cryptosystem is either more efficient with a larger decryption failure probability or less efficient with a smaller decryption failure probability.

1.2 Paper Outline

We begin the paper with some background in Sect. 2. Next, in Sect. 3, we introduce the NTWE problem and describe its relation to the LWE and NTRU problems.

In Sect. 4, we consider the concrete hardness of the natural lattice problems that correspond to the NTWE problem. For reference, we also briefly explain how lattice algorithms are used to solve the NTRU and LWE problems.

Next, in Sect. 5 we present our NTWE-based cryptosystem and compare it to NTRU-based and module-LWE-based cryptosystems and in Sect. 6 present some concrete parametrizations of this cryptosystem.

Finally, in Sect. 7, we have some final remarks, including a note regarding how investigating the concrete hardness of the NTWE problem could be interesting also due to implications for the LWE and NTRU problems.

2 Background

2.1 Notation

We denote real matrices by bold upper case letters $\boldsymbol{A}, \boldsymbol{B}$ and real vectors by bold lower case letters $\boldsymbol{s}, \boldsymbol{e}$. Vectors and matrices over a number field are denoted similarly, but with the letters overlined $\overline{\boldsymbol{A}}, \overline{\boldsymbol{s}}$.

We denote probability distributions by calligraphic letters $\mathcal{U}$ or by Greek letters ψ. In particular, we denote the uniform probability distribution over a set S by $\mathcal{U}(S)$.

For an arbitrary distribution ψ over a ring R, we let ψ^* be the same distribution restricted to the invertible elements of R. Rejection sampling from ψ, rejecting all non-invertible elements, allows sampling from this distribution. For the rings relevant in this work, only a small portion of the elements are not invertible.

2.2 Lattices

A lattice L is a discrete subgroup of $\mathbb{R}^d$. A lattice can always be described by a basis $\boldsymbol{B} \in \mathbb{R}^{d \times k}$ for $k \leq d$ with $L = L(\boldsymbol{B}) = \{\boldsymbol{B}\boldsymbol{x} : \boldsymbol{x} \in \mathbb{Z}^k\}$. The determinant of a lattice L is given by $\sqrt{\det(\boldsymbol{B}^T \boldsymbol{B})}$ for an arbitrary basis $\boldsymbol{B}$ of L.

We denote the length of the shortest non-zero vector in a lattice L by $\lambda_1(L)$. For a random d dimensional lattice, we expect the so called Gaussian Heuristic to hold. This heuristic predicts that the number of lattice points in a ball of volume V is $V/\det(L)$, which corresponds to estimating that

$$\lambda_1 \approx \mathrm{gh}(L) = \sqrt{\frac{d}{2\pi e}} \det(L)^{1/d}. \tag{1}$$

The Gaussian Heuristic is often assumed to approximately hold even in some lattices that are not sampled uniformly at random, such as in q-ary lattices.

2.3 Algebraic Number Theory

A number field K is a finite-degree field extension of the rational numbers $\mathbb{Q}$. This corresponds to $K = \mathbb{Q}(\zeta)$, the rational numbers adjoined with some element ζ that satisfies $f(\zeta) = 0$ for some irreducible polynomial $f \in \mathbb{Q}[x]$. This polynomial is called the minimal polynomial of ζ and the degree of the number field K is the degree of this polynomial. In this work, n denotes the degree of number fields where applicable.

The ring of integers $\mathcal{O}_K$ for a number field K is the set of algebraic integers in K, meaning that it is the elements in K that are a root of some monic polynomial in $\mathbb{Z}[x]$. For the concrete number fields we are considering in this paper, the ring of integers for the number field $K = \mathbb{Q}(\zeta)$ is always equal to $\mathbb{Z}(\zeta)$, but this is not the case in general. In particular, we only consider rings isomorphic to $\mathbb{Z}[X]/(X^n + 1)$ for $n = 2^\ell$ where ℓ is some integer. These are the rings of integers of power of two cyclotomic fields.

As we only consider rings of integers of power of two cyclotomic fields, a coefficient representation of elements in $\mathcal{O}_K$ is suitable. As such, we represent an element $\overline{v} \in \mathcal{O}_K$ by the vector $v \in \mathbb{Z}^n$ containing the coefficients of its natural representative in $\mathbb{Z}[X]/(X^n + 1)$. We let the norm $\|\overline{v}\|$ be given by the ℓ_2 norm of the coefficient vector, which we extend to modules $\mathcal{O}_K^k$ in the natural way. For an element $\overline{v}$ in R^k, we also consider a corresponding matrix in $\mathbb{Z}^{kn \times n}$, given by the coefficient vectors of $\overline{v}X^i$ for every integer i with $0 \le i < n$.

2.4 LWE and NTRU

The version of the Learning With Errors (LWE) problem considered in this work is defined in terms of a module-LWE distribution, as defined below.

Definition 1 (Module-LWE distribution). *Let q be a prime and R the ring of integers for a number field K. For $\overline{s} \in R_q^k$ and ψ some distribution on R_q, a sample from the module-LWE distribution $A_{\overline{s},\psi}$ is given by $(\overline{a}, b = \overline{a} \cdot \overline{s} + e)$, where $\overline{a} \leftarrow \mathcal{U}(R_q^k)$ and $e \leftarrow \psi$.*

In the original definition of module- and ring-LWE distributions and problems, the secrets have elements in the dual ideal $R_q^\vee$ and the error distribution has a continuous support. However, using secret elements in R_q is equivalent when R is the ring of integers of a power of two cyclotomic number field [17]. Furthermore, it is easily seen that the problem with a discretized error distribution is no easier than the original problem with a continuous distribution.

The version of the LWE problem that is relevant in this work is the normal-form decision module-LWE problem, as defined next.

Definition 2 (Normal form decision module-LWE problem). *Let q be a prime, R the ring of integers for a number field K and ψ be some distribution on R_q. Then, the normal form decision module-LWE problem is to distinguish samples from $A_{\overline{s},\psi}$ from uniformly random in $R_q^k \times R_q$ when $\overline{s}$ is a vector with elements sampled from ψ.*

We also use the following definition of a decision version of the NTRU problem, where multiple samples are provided from a distribution. The NTRU problem is not typically considered in terms of such a distribution from which it is possible to get multiple samples. However, this multi-sample problem has been considered previously [20,21] and does not seem to be significantly easier than the traditional, single sample, NTRU problem.

Our definition is for a module-version of the NTRU problem and a more traditional NTRU problem is recovered with module rank $k = 1$. The same module-NTRU problem, limited to at most k samples, is also considered in [8] as the basis for their scheme for public key encryption.

Definition 3 (Decision module-NTRU problem). *Let k be some integer, q be some prime, R be the ring of integers for some number field K and ψ be some distribution on R_q. Let $\overline{\overline{F}} \in R_q^{k \times k}$ have elements sampled from ψ and assume that $\overline{\overline{F}}$ is invertible. Then, the rank k decision module-NTRU problem is to distinguish samples of the form $\overline{h} = \overline{g} \cdot \overline{\overline{F}}^{-1} \in R_q^k$ from uniformly random in R_q^k where $\overline{g} \leftarrow \psi^k$.*

2.5 Lattice Reduction

In practice, the most efficient algorithm for finding relatively short vectors in a lattice is the lattice reduction algorithm BKZ [23,24]. BKZ works by iteratively improving the lattice basis by solving SVP instances in projected sublattices of dimension β.

The effectiveness of BKZ is often estimated through its Hermite factor δ_β, with BKZ finding a vector of length $\delta_\beta^d \det(L)^{1/d}$ in a d-dimensional lattice L. The specific value of this factor depends on the blocksize β BKZ is used with. A typical estimate is that

$$\delta_\beta = \left(\frac{\beta}{2\pi e}(\pi\beta)^{1/\beta} \right)^{\frac{1}{2(\beta-1)}} \tag{2}$$

which is heuristically proven to be the asymptotic performance of BKZ on random lattices [7].

In NTRU and LWE lattices, the secret vectors are significantly shorter than the shortest vector is expected to be in a random lattice. This enables BKZ to recover secret vectors faster than a simple estimate based on δ_β predicts. Instead, when estimating the hardness of these problems, one often considers the so called 2016 estimate [1,2] that predicts that BKZ with block size β finds an unusually short vector $\boldsymbol{v}$ in a d-dimensional lattice L if

$$\frac{\sqrt{\beta} \cdot \|\boldsymbol{v}\|}{\sqrt{d}} \leq \delta_\beta^{2\beta - d - 1} \det(L)^{1/d}. \tag{3}$$

A conservative estimate for the cost of using BKZ with block size β is the core SVP hardness, as introduced in [2]. This estimates that running BKZ with block-size β is no more expensive than solving a single SVP instance in dimension β. We further estimate the hardness of SVP in dimension β based on the performance of known algorithms.

For our parametrizations, we consider the performance of the best known classical algorithm for solving SVP, ignoring its memory requirements and subexponential factors in its running time. This performance is given by a heuristic algorithm [3] with complexity $\sqrt{3/2}^\beta \approx 2^{0.292\beta}$ for lattice dimension β. We represent the core SVP hardness by the logarithm of this, and thus given by 0.292β.

There are quantum algorithms that solve SVP more efficiently than this classical algorithm. However, these algorithms improve attacks against lattice-based cryptosystems less than Grover's quantum search algorithm improves attacks against symmetric primitives with comparable classical security. As such, when comparing the security of a lattice-based cryptosystem with the security of a symmetric primitive, the performance of current quantum attacks does not have to be considered. In this work, we therefore do not consider these quantum lattice algorithms, but we still claim that our system is post-quantum secure.

3   The NTWE Problem

The NTWE problem combines the NTRU and LWE problems in a natural way. Similarly to the NTRU problem, an instance of the NTWE problem is of the form $h = gf^{-1}$ where $g \leftarrow \psi_1$ and $f \leftarrow \psi_2$. However, unlike standard NTRU instances, we do not use similar distributions for ψ_1 and ψ_2, nor do we expect g to be a small element. Instead, we let the distribution ψ_1 be a module-LWE distribution and samples from this distribution are thus expected to be hard to distinguish from uniformly random.

A more formal definition of this problem follows, where we, similarly to the definition of the LWE problem, consider it in terms of an NTWE distribution. As with the module-LWE problem, we primarily consider the problem with the rank k some small integer, while the degree n of the underlying ring is fixed to some power of two, such as 256.

Definition 4 (NTWE distribution $\mathcal{W}(\overline{\boldsymbol{s}}, f, \psi)$). *Let q be a prime, k be an integer, n be some power of 2, $R = \mathbb{Z}[X]/(X^n + 1)$ and ψ be some distribution* *on R_q. Furthermore, let $\overline{s}$ be a vector in R_q^k and f be an invertible element in R_q. A sample from the NTWE distribution $\mathcal{W}(\overline{s}, f, \psi)$ is given by*

$$(\overline{a}, b = (\overline{a} \cdot \overline{s} + e)f^{-1}) \in R_q^k \times R_q$$

where $\overline{a} \leftarrow \mathcal{U}(R_q^k)$ and $e \leftarrow \psi$.

We consider an average case distribution of problem instances where the secret vector $\overline{s}$ and secret element f are sampled from the error distribution ψ. This is similar to the normal-form module-LWE problem. The definition of the search and decision versions of this average-case problem follows.

Definition 5 (Decision NTWE problem (DNTWE(ψ, h))). *Let ψ be some distribution on R_q and let h be some integer. An instance of the DNTWE(ψ, h) problem is given by an unknown distribution $\mathcal{D}$ that is either uniformly random or the $\mathcal{W}(\overline{s}, f, \psi)$ distribution for some $\overline{s} \leftarrow \psi^k$ and $f \leftarrow \psi^*$. The DNTWE(ψ, h) problem is to determine which is the case when given at most h samples from the unknown distribution.*

For the search version of the NTWE problem, the actual secrets $\overline{s}$ and f used to generate the NTWE distribution need not be recovered. Instead it suffices to recover $\overline{s}X^i$ and fX^i for some i as these alternative solutions would generate the same NTWE distribution as the actual secrets. Furthermore, for the rings R and error distributions ψ we consider, all of these solutions are equally likely to be sampled as secrets for the problem instance.

Definition 6 (Search NTWE problem SNTWE(ψ, h)). *Let ψ be some distribution on R_q and h be some integer. An instance of the SNTWE(ψ, h) problem is to recover $\overline{s}X^i$ and fX^i, for some i, when given at most h samples from the $\mathcal{W}(\overline{s}, f, \psi)$ distribution, where $\overline{s} \leftarrow \psi^k$ and $f \leftarrow \psi^*$.*

3.1   Relation to Other Problems

It is easily seen that an instance of the search/decision NTWE problem is at least as hard as an instance of the search/decision rank k module-LWE problem. This relation is formalized in the following lemma:

Lemma 1. *Assume that there is an algorithm W that is able to solve the (search/decision) NTWE problem with advantage ε. Then, using W once, with a negligible amount of additional computations, provides a solution to the corresponding (search/decision) normal form rank k module-LWE problem with advantage ε.*

Proof. Given an algorithm that solves the NTWE problem, we can easily solve the corresponding module-LWE problem. This is accomplished by sampling $f \leftarrow \psi^*$ and transforming samples from the input distribution in the module-LWE problem instance into $(\overline{a}, bf^{-1})$.

If the input samples are from a module-LWE distribution, the transformed samples are from an NTWE distribution. With these samples as input, an algorithm that solves the search NTWE problem recovers $\overline{s}X^i$ and fX^i for some i. As f is known, this allows recovering $\overline{s}$ and solving the search module-LWE problem.

If instead the input samples are from an uniformly random distribution, the transformed samples are also from a uniformly random distribution. As such, using an algorithm that solves the decision NTWE problem a single time provides a solution to the decision module-LWE problem with the same advantage.   □

It is also easily seen that the NTWE problem is no easier than a similarly parametrized version of the rank 1 module-NTRU problem.

Lemma 2. *Assume that there is an algorithm W that, when given h samples from the input distribution, is able to solve the (search/decision) NTWE problem with advantage ε. Then, using W once, with a negligible amount of additional computations, provides a solution to a rank 1 (search/decision) NTRU problem with advantage ε. This is accomplished by using $h + k$ samples from the input distribution in the given instance of the NTRU problem.*

Proof. Let $\overline{h} = \overline{g}f^{-1}$ be $h + k$ samples from the input distribution for the NTRU problem. By splitting $\overline{h}$ as $(\overline{s}f^{-1}, \overline{e}f^{-1}) \in R_q^k \times R_q^h$ and letting $\overline{A} \leftarrow \mathcal{U}(R_q^{h \times k})$, we can calculate $(\overline{A}\overline{s} + \overline{e})f^{-1}$. If the input is an NTRU distribution, this directly corresponds to h samples from an NTWE distribution. If instead the input is uniformly random, then so are the resulting h samples.

As such, any algorithm that solves the DNTWE(ψ, h) problem can be used to solve the decision NTRU problem by using $h + k$ NTRU samples. Similarly, any algorithm that solves the SNTWE(ψ, h) problem can be used to solve the search NTRU problem by using $h + k$ NTRU samples.   □

Lemma 2 ensures that the NTWE problem in rank k modules is at least as hard as the rank 1 NTRU problem with multiple samples. We do, however, expect something significantly stronger to hold, namely that the rank k NTWE problem is at least as hard as the rank $k + 1$ module-NTRU problem. Lemma 3 below provides motivation for such a statement, as it shows that if we can solve a special version of the rank k NTWE problem, then we can also solve the rank $k + 1$ module-NTRU problem.

This special version of the NTWE problem differs from an ordinary NTWE problem by using an $\overline{a}$ that is not sampled uniformly at random and instead from some other distribution. The specific distribution for which $\overline{a}$ is sampled from in these special NTWE instances is directly given by a rank $k + 1$ module-NTRU instance. As we do not have a good definition for this distribution besides for how it appears in the proof, we only define it as a part of the proof.

Although it is possible that the NTWE problem where $\overline{a}$ is non-uniform is a harder problem than NTWE with uniformly random $\overline{a}$, we have no reason to expect this to be the case. Instead, it seems more natural to assume the opposite, that samples with uniformly random $\overline{a}$ are harder to distinguish from uniformly random than those with $\overline{a}$ from some other distribution. As such, we consider this lemma to be a strong argument for why the concrete hardness of the rank k NTWE problem should be comparable to that of rank $k + 1$ module-NTRU. However, it should be noted that this lemma does not actually prove that the rank k NTWE problem, as we defined it, is at least as hard as a rank $k + 1$ NTRU problem.

Lemma 3. *Assume that there is an algorithm W that solves a decision version of the NTWE problem where $\overline{a}$ is not uniformly random and instead sampled from a special distribution, defined in the proof. If W achieves an advantage ε, then, using W once, with a negligible amount of additional computation, provides a solution to the decision rank $k + 1$ module-NTRU problem with advantage ε. This is accomplished by using h module-NTRU samples.*

Proof. We claim that a sample from a rank $k + 1$ module-NTRU instance $\overline{h} = \overline{g}\overline{F}^{-1}$ corresponds to a sample from a rank k NTWE instance with a special structure on $\overline{a}$. The $\overline{a}$ for this sample is the negation of the first k elements of $\overline{h}$, while the b part of the NTWE sample is the final element of $\overline{h}$.

To see this, we write $\overline{e} - \overline{h}\overline{F} = 0$ with $\overline{e} = \overline{g}$ and split $\overline{h}$ into $(-\overline{a}, b)$. Next, we rename the $k \times (k+1)$ dimensional submatrix of $\overline{F}$ that we multiply with $\overline{a}$ to $\overline{S}$, while the remaining $k+1$ dimensional row we call $\overline{f}$. Thus, $\overline{a}\overline{S} - b\overline{f} + \overline{e} = \overline{0}$, which corresponds to a sample from $k + 1$ different NTWE instance. These samples share the same $\overline{a}$ and have the same resulting b, but each NTWE instance uses different secrets $\overline{s}, f$ and errors e. This is seen by considering a single element, which is given by $\overline{a}\overline{s} - bf + e = 0$, or equivalently $(\overline{a}\overline{s} + e)f^{-1} = b$, if f is invertible.

Additional samples from the NTRU distribution also result in NTWE samples with the same $\overline{s}$ and f, but with different $\overline{a}$ and e. Furthermore, note that f, e and the elements in $\overline{s}$ are sampled from ψ, as expected for the NTWE instance.

The distribution of $\overline{a}$ in this constructed NTWE distribution is not uniformly random and instead given by the first k elements from a sample of the NTRU distribution. As such, each NTRU sample corresponds to a sample from an NTWE instance where the $\overline{A}$ matrix is generated with rows given by samples from an NTRU distribution. Furthermore, in this NTWE instance, the secrets $\overline{s}$ and f are part of the matrix $\overline{F}$ used to define the NTRU distribution used to generate the $\overline{A}$ matrix.

If instead given a sample from a uniformly random distribution, splitting the sample into $-\overline{a}$ and b obviously results in $\overline{a}$ and b that are uniformly random. Thus, if we are able to distinguish this special NTWE instance from uniformly random, then we are also able to distinguish a rank $k + 1$ module-NTRU instance from uniformly random. □

4   The NTWE Lattice Problems

Both the NTRU problem and the module-LWE problem can be solved by considering the naturally corresponding lattice problems. Currently, this approach leads to the best performing algorithms for solving these problems, and we recall the techniques used below. We expect that the NTWE problem similarly is best solved by considering lattice problems that naturally correspond to the NTWE problem. For context, we begin by briefly introducing the lattice problems for the NTRU and LWE lattice problems. We then present these NTWE lattice problems in Subsect. 4.3 below and compare them to the corresponding NTRU and LWE lattice problems.

We can not guarantee that there are no other, more efficient, attacks against the NTWE problem than the ones we consider here. However, its similarity to the LWE and NTRU problems motivates us to focus on attacks similar to the best performing attacks against these problems. In particular, we base the parametrizations of our cryptosystem on our assumption that these proposed lattice attacks against the NTWE problem actually are optimal. This is similar to how systems based on the hardness of the LWE or NTRU problems are typically parametrized.

In some sense, the NTWE lattice is a mix between an NTRU lattice and a module-LWE lattice. We therefore believe that it is likely that any improved attacks against the NTWE problem would improve our understanding of the NTRU and LWE problems. In particular, we believe that a specialized attack against the NTWE problem would likely have interesting implications for both the NTRU and LWE problem. Such an attack would serve as an indication that the LWE and NTRU problems are hard, but mixing them results in an easier problem.

4.1 NTRU Problem

In the module-NTRU problem, the input is a matrix $\overline{H} \in R_q^{h \times k}$. In the search version of the problem, the task is to recover $\overline{G} \in R_q^{h \times k}$, $\overline{F} \in R_q^{k \times k}$ such that $\overline{GF}^{-1} = \overline{H}$ and such that all elements in $\overline{G}$ and $\overline{F}$ are small. To state this as a lattice problem, we consider the integer matrices $F \in \mathbb{Z}^{kn \times kn}$ and $G, H \in \mathbb{Z}^{hn \times kn}$ corresponding to $\overline{F}, \overline{G}, \overline{H}$. Then, it can be seen that the $(h + k)n$-dimensional lattice spanned by the columns of

$$\begin{bmatrix} qI & H \\ 0 & I \end{bmatrix}$$

contains a dense kn-dimensional sublattice given by

$$\begin{bmatrix} qI & H \\ 0 & I \end{bmatrix} \begin{bmatrix} \star \\ F \end{bmatrix} = \begin{bmatrix} G \\ F \end{bmatrix}$$

where $\star$ represents the matrix corresponding to modular reduction. Using lattice reduction methods, this dense sublattice can be found, which solves both the search and decision NTRU problems.

Depending on the specific parametrization, the lattice reduction algorithms may directly find vectors that directly corresponds to elements of $\overline{F}$ and $\overline{G}$.

If the parameters are chosen in an overstretched regime, the lattice reduction may first find other vectors in the dense sublattice [10]. In either case, finding unusually short vectors in the lattice solves the decision NTRU problem and quickly leads to an attack against NTRU-based cryptosystems.

4.2 Module-LWE Problem

The Module-LWE problem is typically solved by using lattice reduction algorithms on one of two different types of lattices, corresponding to the dual and primal lattice attacks.

A Module-LWE instance with h samples is given by a uniformly random $\overline{A} \in R_q^{h \times k}$ and a vector $\overline{b} = \overline{A}\overline{s} + \overline{e} \in R_q^h$, where the elements of $\overline{e}$ are sampled from the error distribution ψ. In the normal form version of the problem, the elements of the secret vector $\overline{s}$ are also sampled from ψ. The lattices corresponding to this module-LWE instance are given by the integer matrices $A \in \mathbb{Z}^{hn \times kn}$ and $B \in \mathbb{Z}^{hn \times n}$ corresponding to $\overline{A}$ and $\overline{b}$.

In the primal attack, the relevant lattice is spanned by the columns of

$$\begin{bmatrix} qI & A & B \\ 0 & I & 0 \\ 0 & 0 & tI \end{bmatrix}$$

where t is a constant typically chosen to be 1. Furthermore, one typically do not consider this full $(h + k + 1)n$ dimensional lattice, instead only considering a single column b of the full matrix B, giving a $(h + k)n + 1$ dimensional lattice. Using lattice reduction, we can find the short lattice vector

$$\begin{bmatrix} e \\ -s \\ t \end{bmatrix} = \begin{bmatrix} qI & A & b \\ 0 & I & 0 \\ 0 & 0 & t \end{bmatrix} \begin{bmatrix} \star \\ -s \\ 1 \end{bmatrix}$$

where $\star$ gives the modular reductions and s and e are integer vectors representing $\overline{s}$ and $\overline{e}$ respectively. This short vector directly solves both the decision and search Module-LWE problems.

In the dual attack, the lattice given by

$$L^{\perp} = \{(x, y) \in \mathbb{Z}^{(h+k)n} : xA = y \mod q\}$$

is considered. The dual attack is based on using lattice reduction in order to find short vectors in $L^{\perp}$. Short vectors in $L^{\perp}$ can be used to distinguish between samples from a module-LWE instance and samples from a uniformly random distribution, solving the decision module-LWE problem.

Given a short vector w in $L^{\perp}$, the attack works by multiplying samples $b = As + e$ with w, resulting in $wb = y \cdot s + x \cdot e$ which is small if x, y, s and e all are short. By using these short lattice vectors, samples from a module-LWE distribution are thus transformed into small integers. Meanwhile, multiplying a uniformly random b with such a short vector results in a uniformly random integer in $\mathbb{Z}_q$. As such, short vectors in $L^\perp$ multiplied with samples from a distribution behave noticeably differently depending on if the distribution is uniformly random or a module-LWE distribution. Therefore, finding short vectors in $L^\perp$ provides a solution to the decision module-LWE problem.

4.3   NTWE Problem

We now present the natural lattices corresponding to the NTWE problem. These lattices correspond to the lattices used during primal and dual lattice attacks against the LWE problem. We therefore similarly denote our algorithms as the primal and dual attacks against the NTWE problem. Finding short vectors in these NTWE latices allows solving the NTWE problem.

Primal Attack. A primal attack against the NTWE problem uses the same lattice construction as for the primal attack against the LWE problem. In a rank k NTWE instance with h samples, we are given

$$(\overline{A}, \overline{b} = (\overline{A} \cdot \overline{s} + \overline{e}) \cdot f^{-1}) \in R_q^{h \times k} \times R_q^k$$

and are either supposed to distinguish these samples from uniformly random or use the samples to recover $\overline{s}$ and f. As with the primal attack against the LWE problem, this can be stated as finding a short vector in the lattice generated by the columns of

$$\begin{bmatrix} q\boldsymbol{I} & \boldsymbol{A} & \boldsymbol{B} \\ \boldsymbol{0} & \boldsymbol{I} & \boldsymbol{0} \\ \boldsymbol{0} & \boldsymbol{0} & t\boldsymbol{I} \end{bmatrix}$$

where $\boldsymbol{A} \in \mathbb{Z}^{hn \times kn}, \boldsymbol{B} \in \mathbb{Z}^{hn \times n}$ are the matrices corresponding to $\overline{A}$ and $\overline{b}$ respectively, while t is some small constant. In the primal attack against the module-LWE problem, it is sufficient to consider only a single column of the matrix $\boldsymbol{B}$. However, when solving the NTWE problem, the full matrix $\boldsymbol{B}$ must be accounted for.

This NTWE lattice contains the $(h + k + 1)n$ dimensional secret vector

$$\begin{bmatrix} \boldsymbol{e} \\ -\boldsymbol{s} \\ t\boldsymbol{f} \end{bmatrix} = \begin{bmatrix} q\boldsymbol{I} & \boldsymbol{A} & \boldsymbol{B} \\ \boldsymbol{0} & \boldsymbol{I} & \boldsymbol{0} \\ \boldsymbol{0} & \boldsymbol{0} & t\boldsymbol{I} \end{bmatrix} \begin{bmatrix} \star \\ -\boldsymbol{s} \\ \boldsymbol{f} \end{bmatrix}$$

where $\star$ gives the modular reduction while $\boldsymbol{s}$ and $\boldsymbol{f}$ are the integer vectors representing $\overline{s}$ and f.

Using $t = 1$, with an error distribution that has standard deviation σ, the secret vector is expected to have length approximately $\sigma \cdot \sqrt{(h + k + 1)n}$. By the 2016 estimate, detailed in (3), we deem such a short lattice vector to be recoverable by BKZ with block size β if

$$\sigma\sqrt{\beta} \le \delta_\beta^{2\beta - (h' + k + 1)n - 1} q^{h'/(h' + k + 1)} \tag{4}$$

for some $h' \leq h$ such that $h'n$ is an integer. Choosing $h' < h$ corresponds to ignoring rows of A and B, which decreases both the lattice dimension and its determinant and sometimes leads to a more efficient attack.

Although the NTWE lattice at first glance may seem similar to the lattice given by a rank k module-LWE instance with the full B matrix, there are some significant differences. The known basis for these lattices are of exactly the same form and, when constructed using the same number of samples, the lattices have the same determinant. However, in the rank k module-LWE lattice, the target vectors are shorter than in the NTWE lattice. Furthermore, in the rank k module-LWE lattice, each of the secret vectors is known to lie in a specific $(h+k)n+1$ dimensional sublattice, which is not the case in the NTWE problem. Due to these factors, we believe that the rank k NTWE problem is significantly harder than the rank k module-LWE problem.

The lattice constructed in the primal attack against the rank k NTWE problem is also very similar to the lattice used in the primal attack against the rank $k + 1$ module-LWE problem. Letting $t = 1$, and combining all but one column of B with A into $\tilde{A} \in \mathbb{Z}^{hn \times ((k+1)n-1)}$, the lattice is given by

$$\begin{bmatrix} qI & \tilde{A} & b \\ 0 & I & 0 \\ 0 & 0 & 1 \end{bmatrix}$$

where b is the remaining column of B. This lattice is one dimension smaller than the corresponding lattice for a rank $k + 1$ module-LWE problem and the $\tilde{A}$ matrix is not generated in the same way. However, with the same number of samples, the lattice determinant is the same as for the module-LWE lattice and the target vectors are of essentially the same length.

In some sense, due to the similarities of the corresponding lattices, the NTWE problem can be seen as a more structured version of the rank $k + 1$ module-LWE problem, with part of the $\tilde{A}$ matrix not sampled uniformly at random. Furthermore, by standard estimates for hardness of lattice problems, the primal attack against the rank k NTWE problem and against rank $k + 1$ module-LWE should require approximately as much work. We therefore believe that the concrete hardness of the rank k NTWE problem is comparable to that of the rank $k + 1$ module-LWE problem.

In particular, we can compare the primal attack against NTWE to the primal attack against Kyber [25]. Using the same notation as in our analysis of NTWE, the primal attack against Kyber with module rank $k + 1$ is estimated to be successful if

$$\sigma\sqrt{\beta} \leq \delta^{2\beta-(h'+k+1)n-2}q^{h'/(h'+k+1+1/n)}.$$

Besides the term $1/n$ in the denominator of the exponent of q and a difference of 1 in the exponent of δ_β, this is the same as the condition given by (4) for the primal attack against rank k NTWE.

Note also that, unlike in the lattice given by a module-LWE instance, in the NTWE lattice there is not only a single short vector to be found. Instead the NTWE lattice contains several short vectors that span a dense n dimensional sublattice. The existence of such a dense sublattice seems to be the reason for improved attacks against overstretched NTRU parameters [15].

In an NTRU lattice, there is a n-dimensional dense sublattice in a $2n$-dimensional lattice. Meanwhile, in the NTWE lattice there is an n-dimensional dense sublattice in a $(hn + kn + n)$-dimensional lattice. Due to the differences between the NTWE and NTRU lattices, we do not believe that the same type of overstretched parameters is a risk with the NTWE problem. As such, we do not believe that there are parameter choices for the NTWE problem such that it is significantly easier to find the dense sublattice in this NTWE lattice than it is to find the secret vector.

To motivate this belief, we note that an ordinary module-LWE lattice with the full $\boldsymbol{B}$ matrix included also contains a dense sublattice in the same way as the NTWE lattice. As such, if there is some parameter regime for the NTWE problem where there is a behavior similar to overstretched NTRU, the same behavior also applies to LWE instances. This limits the potential impact of an overstretched parameter regime on the NTWE problem, unless there also exists overstretched parameters for the LWE problem.

Finally, we note that the lattice for the primal attack against the NTWE problem is very similar to the lattice used when attacking the NTRU problem. With $h = k + 1$ and combining $\overline{\boldsymbol{A}}$ and $\overline{\boldsymbol{B}}$ into a $(k + 1) \times (k + 1)$ dimensional matrix $\overline{\boldsymbol{H}}$, the basis matrix for this primal attack is given by

$$\begin{bmatrix} q\boldsymbol{I} & \boldsymbol{H} \\ \boldsymbol{0} & \boldsymbol{I} \end{bmatrix}$$

with $\boldsymbol{H}$ the integer matrix representing $\overline{\boldsymbol{H}}$. This lattice is of exactly the same form as the lattice in a rank $k + 1$ module-NTRU instance, but with part of $\boldsymbol{H}$ uniformly random instead of given by $\boldsymbol{GF}^{-1}$. As such, the natural primal lattice for the rank k NTWE problem is essentially a less structured version of the rank $k + 1$ module-NTRU lattice, as suggested by Lemma 3.

Dual Attack. A dual attack against the NTWE problem is performed in a similar way to how the dual attack is performed against the LWE problem. By using a short vector in the lattice

$$L^{\perp} = \{(\boldsymbol{x}, \boldsymbol{y}) : \boldsymbol{x}\boldsymbol{A} = \boldsymbol{y} \mod q\}$$

we are able to transform $\overline{\boldsymbol{b}}$ from an NTWE distribution into what essentially corresponds to an NTRU sample. This is the case as if $\boldsymbol{w}$ is a short vector in $L^{\perp}$ and $\overline{\boldsymbol{w}}$ is the corresponding vector in R^k then

$$\overline{\boldsymbol{w}} \cdot \overline{\boldsymbol{b}} = \overline{\boldsymbol{w}} \cdot (\overline{\boldsymbol{A}} \cdot \overline{\boldsymbol{s}} + \overline{\boldsymbol{e}}) \cdot f^{-1} = (\overline{\boldsymbol{y}} \cdot \overline{\boldsymbol{s}} + \overline{\boldsymbol{x}} \cdot \overline{\boldsymbol{e}}) \cdot f^{-1} = gf^{-1}$$

where $g = \overline{\boldsymbol{y}} \cdot \overline{\boldsymbol{s}} + \overline{\boldsymbol{x}} \cdot \overline{\boldsymbol{e}}$ is a short element in R_q if $\overline{\boldsymbol{w}}$ is short. As such, $\overline{\boldsymbol{w}} \cdot \overline{\boldsymbol{b}} = gf^{-1}$ can be interpreted as an NTRU sample, although with different distributions for g and f.

Note that, as we consider the norm of the coefficient vector, the norm of g is dependent on the ring R. However, as we only consider the case where R is the ring of integers of a power of two cyclotomic field, we are guaranteed that the product $\overline{s} \cdot \overline{y}$ is a small element in R_q if both $\overline{y}$ and $\overline{s}$ are short.

In order for it to be reasonable to solve the constructed NTRU instance, we require that the vector given by (g, f) is significantly shorter than the shortest vector in a random q-ary $2n$-dimensional lattice without the NTRU structure. Such a lattice has determinant q^n and, by the Gaussian Heuristic, is expected to contain a vector of length $\sqrt{(qn)/(\pi e)}$.

On the other hand, the lattice corresponding to the constructed NTRU instance contains a short vector (g, f) where $g = \overline{y} \cdot \overline{s} + \overline{x} \cdot \overline{e}$ is expected to have length $\|(x, y)\| \cdot \sigma \sqrt{(h + k)n}$. Furthermore, we have that f is of expected length $\sigma \sqrt{n}$, and we can thus argue that in order for the constructed NTRU instance to actually contain an unusually short vector, we have the requirement that

$$\sigma^2 n \left((h + k) \|(x, y)\|^2 + 1 \right) \leq \frac{nq}{\pi e}$$

or equivalently

$$\|(x, y)\| \leq \sqrt{\frac{q}{(h + k)\pi e\sigma^2} - \frac{1}{h + k}}.$$

We can improve this attack by rebalancing the NTRU lattice so that we have to find a vector of length $L = \|(x, y)\| \cdot \sigma \sqrt{2(h + k)n}$, corresponding to $(g, f \cdot \sqrt{h + k} \|(x, y)\|)$. Although this vector is longer, the corresponding NTRU lattice also has a determinant that is $(\sqrt{h + k} \|(x, y)\|)^n$ times larger, meaning that it is not expected to contain as short vectors. This leads to the requirement that

$$2(h + k)n\sigma^2 \|(x, y)\|^2 \leq \frac{nq\sqrt{h + k} \|(x, y)\|}{\pi e} \tag{5}$$

in order for the dual attack to succeed, which corresponds to a requirement that

$$\sigma^2 \geq \frac{q}{2\pi e \|(\overline{x}, \overline{y})\| \sqrt{h + k}}$$

for the problem to not be solvable by a given $(\overline{x}, \overline{y})$ in $L^\perp$.

The lattice $L^\perp$ is $h + k$ dimensional and has determinant q^k. As such, BKZ with block-size β should be able to find a vector $(\overline{x}, \overline{y})$ of length $\delta_\beta^{(h+k)n} q^{k/(h+k)}$ in $L^\perp$. This means that, for the problem to be hard to solve, we require that

$$\sigma^2 \geq \frac{q^{h/(h+k)}}{2\pi e \cdot \delta_\beta^{(h+k)n} \cdot \sqrt{h + k}} \tag{6}$$

for every β that an adversary can afford to use as block-size.

While (5) is a necessary requirement for the constructed NTRU instance to be solvable via lattice reduction, a bounded adversary may still not be able to solve this NTRU instance. Therefore, we also estimate how short vectors can be found in the resulting $2n$-dimensional NTRU lattice.

In the resulting NTRU instance, there is an unusually short vector, with expected length $\ell = \sigma\sqrt{2(h+k)n} \cdot \delta_\beta^{(h+k)n} q^{k/(h+k)}$. By the 2016 estimate, detailed in (3), this vector is expected to be found by BKZ with block-size β in the $2n$-dimensional NTRU lattice with determinant $(q\ell)^n$ if

$$\ell \cdot \sqrt{\beta/(2n)} \le \delta_\beta^{2\beta-2n-1}\sqrt{q\ell}.$$

This gives that an adversary succeeds if

$$\ell\beta = \sigma\sqrt{2(h+k)n} \cdot \delta_\beta^{(h+k)n} \cdot q^{k/(h+k)} \cdot \beta \le 2nq\delta_\beta^{4\beta-4n-1}$$

which corresponds to the requirement that

$$\sigma \ge \delta_\beta^{4\beta-(4+h+k)n-1} \frac{q^{k/(h+k)}\sqrt{2n}}{\beta \cdot \sqrt{h+k}} \tag{7}$$

in order for the problem to not be solvable by an adversary that is able to run BKZ with block size β. However, this analysis is only applicable if the secret vector actually is unusually short in the NTRU lattice, and thus, for hardness of the NTWE problem, it is sufficient that either (6) or (7) is fulfilled.

It is not directly clear how this dual attack compares to the primal attack against the NTWE problem or to attacks against the NTRU and LWE problems. For the concrete parametrizations we present in Sect. 6, this approach for a dual-lattice attack against the NTWE problem seems to be significantly less efficient than the primal attack. However, for some other choices of parameters, this dual attack seems to be more efficient than the primal attack. In particular, by our estimates, the NTWE problem parametrized with $h = k = 1$ is often more efficiently solved with this dual attack than with the primal attack.

5   Our Cryptosystem

The procedures for key generation, encryption and decryption in our crypto-system are detailed in Algorithm 1. The system follows essentially the same idea as the LWE-based Lindner-Peikert scheme [16] but with decryption requiring using f in a similar way to how it is used in an NTRU based cryptosystem.

For encoding the message, we make use of a randomized rounding function $\lfloor \cdot \rceil_R$. For integers x, we let $\lfloor x \rceil_R = x$ while $\lfloor x + 1/2 \rceil_R$ is sampled from $\mathcal{U}(\{x, x+1\})$. For an element $e \in R$, we extend the definition to $\lfloor e/2 \rceil_R$ by considering each coefficient of e separately.

For our cryptosystem, we only consider the case where R is the ring of integers of a power of two cyclotomic field, but the system parametrized with other rings R could potentially also be interesting to investigate.

To improve the efficiency of our scheme, we prefer rings R and modulos q such that operations can be performed efficiently using the Number Theoretic Transform (NTT). With such a parametrization, it is very efficient to compute the inverse f^{-1} in R_q. However, computing the inverse in R_2 is a less efficient operation. If the public key is reused multiple times, this additional time for key generation can be acceptable.

During decryption, a product with f_2^{-1} must be computed, which can not be done efficiently by using the NTT. As such, this multiplication has a significant impact on the decryption efficiency in our PKE. For our PKE scheme, a large majority of the decryption time is spent on this multiplication. However, if some version of the Fujisaki-Okamoto transform is used to construct an IND-CCA secure KEM from this IND-CPA secure PKE, decryption in the resulting scheme also performs encryption of a message. Therefore, in this KEM, although the multiplication by f_2^{-1} still has a significant performance impact, it no longer constitutes a large majority of the decryption time.

In our parametrizations, we consider two different versions of the error distribution ψ_f from which f is sampled. For both versions of ψ_f, samples from this distribution, are always invertible in both R_2 and R_q. A sample from the first version of ψ_f is sampled from ψ_{gen} with rejection sampling ensuring that the result is invertible in both R_2 and R_q. In the second version, we let a sample be given by $f = 2f' + 1$, with $f' \leftarrow \psi_{\text{gen}}$ ensuring that f is the identity in R_2. By using rejection sampling, it is also ensured that samples from this version of ψ_f are invertible in R_q.

Selecting $f = 2f' + 1$ ensures that $f_2^{-1} = 1$ and therefore no expensive inverse has to be computed during key generation. Furthermore, this choice of f ensures that multiplication with f_2^{-1} is trivial, resulting in more efficient decryption. However, this comes at the cost of using a larger f, which results in a larger failure probability for the scheme. As the structure of how f is sampled is known, we can not argue that this larger f results in harder instances of the corresponding lattice problem.

For implementations, the matrix $\overline{A}$ may be sampled from a pseudorandom number generator. This allows a much more compact public key, as it only has to include the seed used to derive $\overline{A}$ instead of the full $\overline{A}$ matrix. Using a short seed to represent the public matrix $\overline{A}$ in this way is standard for LWE-based cryptosystems and is for example used in Kyber [25].

5.1 Security

The security of our cryptosystem relies on the hardness of both the NTWE problem and the module-LWE problem. Based on the assumed hardness of the decision NTWE problem, the public key in our cryptosystem is indistinguishable from uniformly random. Meanwhile, assuming the hardness of the decision module-LWE problem, the ciphertext completely masks the encrypted message. This is similar to a typical NTRU-based cryptosystem, where the public key is pseudorandomly generated as an NTRU instance, while the security of the ciphertexts relies on the hardness of a problem that can be seen as a variant of the ring-LWE problem.

In the following lemmas, we formalize how, assuming the computational hardness of the NTWE and module-LWE problems, the security of our cryptosystem is guaranteed. First we note that, assuming the hardness of the decision NTWE problem, the public key of our cryptosystem is indistinguishable from uniformly random.

Lemma 4. *Let W be an algorithm that, with advantage ε, can distinguish the public keys from our cryptosystem from uniformly random. Then, using W once with a negligible amount of additional computations provides a solution to the $DNTWE(\psi_{gen}, h)$ problem with advantage ε.*

Algorithm 1. Procedures for key generation, encryption and decryption for our cryptosystem

---

procedure KEY GENERATION
   $\overline{A} \leftarrow \mathcal{U}(R_q)^{h \times k}$
   $\overline{s} \leftarrow \psi_{\text{gen}}^k$
   $\overline{e} \leftarrow \psi_{\text{gen}}^h$
   $f \leftarrow \psi_{\text{f}}$
   $b = \left(\overline{A} \cdot \overline{s} + \overline{e}\right) \cdot f^{-1} \in R_q^h$
   Let f_2^{-1} be the inverse of f in R_2
   return $(pk = (\overline{A}, \overline{b}), sk = (\overline{s}, f, f_2^{-1}))$
end procedure
procedure ENCRYPTION$((\overline{A}, \overline{b}) = pk, m \in R_2)$
   $\overline{s}' \leftarrow \psi_{\text{enc}}^h$
   $e' \leftarrow \psi_{\text{enc}}$
   $\overline{e}'' \leftarrow \psi_{\text{enc}}^k$
   $c_1 = \overline{s}' \cdot \overline{b} + e' + \lfloor mq/2 \rceil_R$ ▷ With m interpreted as element in R
   $\overline{c}_2 = \overline{s}' \cdot \overline{A} + \overline{e}''$
   return $ct = (c_1, \overline{c}_2) \in R_q \times R_q^k$
end procedure
procedure DECRYPTION$((\overline{s}, f, f_2^{-1}) = sk, (c_1, \overline{c}_2) = ct)$
   Let $v = c_1 \cdot f - \overline{c}_2 \cdot \overline{s} \mod q$
   Interpret v as element in R with coefficients in $[0, q)$
   Let $u = \lfloor v \cdot 2/q \rceil$ interpreted as element in R_2
   return $v f_2^{-1} \in R_2$
end procedure

Proof. The public key in our cryptosystem consists of h NTWE samples. Thus, given h samples from an instance of the DNTWE(ψ_{gen}, h) problem, we can consider these as a public key for our system. If the samples are from an NTWE distribution, the public key is exactly distributed as for our actual cryptosystem. Thus, using W with these samples as the public key gives an algorithm that, with advantage ε, solves the DNTWE(ψ_{gen}, h) problem. □

The next lemma shows that, assuming the hardness of the rank h module-LWE problem, a version of our cryptosystem where a uniformly random public key is used is IND-CPA secure.

Lemma 5. *Assume that there is an adversary $\mathcal{A}$ that is able to achieve an advantage ε against the IND-CPA security of a version of our cryptosystem* *that uses uniformly random public keys. Then, using $\mathcal{A}$ once, with a negligible amount of additional computations, provides a solution to the rank h decision module-LWE problem with advantage ε.*

Proof. In a version of our system where the public key is uniformly random, the ciphertext is directly given by $k + 1$ samples from a rank h module-LWE distribution. The public key in this case is given by the $\overline{a}$ part of these module-LWE samples, while the ciphertext is constructed from the b part of the samples.

To encrypt the message encoded as $m \in R_2$, the ciphertext is constructed with $\overline{c}_2$ being the b part of k module-LWE samples. The corresponding $\overline{a}$ part of the module-LWE samples are used as the $\overline{A}$ matrix for the public key. The $\overline{a}$ part of the final module-LWE sample gives the $\overline{b}$ part of the public key for our cryptosystem with uniformly random public key. Meanwhile, the c_1 part of the ciphertext is given by the b part of this final module-LWE sample plus $\lfloor mq/2 \rceil_R$. This exactly corresponds to the ciphertext that encrypts m in a version of our cryptosystem that uses a uniformly random public key.

If instead given $k + 1$ samples from a uniformly random distribution, the ciphertext constructed in this way is uniformly random. As such, using $\mathcal{A}$ against these ciphertexts gives an advantage ε in distinguishing between the uniform distribution and a module-LWE distribution. $\qquad \square$

Finally, combining these lemmas shows that, assuming the hardness of both the NTWE problem and the rank h module-LWE problem, our cryptosystem is IND-CPA secure.

Lemma 6. *Assume that there is an adversary $\mathcal{A}$ that achieves an advantage 2ε against the IND-CPA security of our cryptosystem. Then, using $\mathcal{A}$ once, with a negligible amount of additional computations, provides a solution, with advantage ε, to either a rank h module-LWE problem or the rank k $DNTWE(\psi_{gen}, h)$ problem.*

Proof. An adversary $\mathcal{A}$ achieving advantage 2ε against the IND-CPA security of our cryptosystem could be used in order to solve either the relevant decision NTWE problem or the relevant decision ring-LWE problem with advantage ε. This follows from a simple hybrid argument and using Lemmas 4 and 5.

If $\mathcal{A}$ has advantage at least ε against a version of our cryptosystem with uniformly random public key, Lemma 5 provides an efficient algorithm for the decision module-LWE problem.

Otherwise, $\mathcal{A}$ has advantage 2ε against our cryptosystem but advantage less than ε against a version of our cryptosystem where the public key is uniformly random. This provides an ε distinguisher between our cryptosystem and a version of the system with uniformly random public key. Thus, by Lemma 4, we can use $\mathcal{A}$ to solve the DNTWE(ψ_{gen}, h) problem with advantage ε. $\qquad \square$

Our scheme only claims to be IND-CPA secure and, as with LWE- and NTRU-based schemes, it is vulnerable to a trivial chosen-ciphertext attack where the decryption oracle is used with the target ciphertext plus some small noise. Our PKE can, however, be used to construct an IND-CCA secure KEM by using some variant of the Fujisaki-Okamoto transform [11]. This approach to achieving IND-CCA security is also used in many of the submissions to the NIST post-quantum standardization process.

5.2   Correctness of Decryption

In the decryption algorithm, the value of v is given by

$$
\begin{aligned}
v &= c_1 \cdot f - \overline{c}_2 \cdot \overline{s} \\
&= ((\overline{s}' \cdot (\overline{A} \cdot \overline{s} + \overline{e}) f^{-1} + e') + \lfloor mq/2 \rceil_R) \cdot f - (\overline{s}' \cdot \overline{A} + \overline{e}'') \cdot \overline{s} \\
&= \overline{s}' \cdot \overline{e} - \overline{e}'' \cdot \overline{s} + (\lfloor mq/2 \rceil_R + e') \cdot f
\end{aligned}
$$

and we want $\lfloor v \cdot 2/q \rceil$ to equal mf, when both are interpreted as elements in R_2. This is the case if every coefficient of v is less than a distance $q/4$ from the corresponding coefficient in $(mq/2) \cdot f$ and we therefore want to bound this distance.

For adversarially chosen m, there can be quite a large difference between $\lfloor mq/2 \rfloor \cdot f$ and $(mq/2) \cdot f$, while the difference between $\lfloor mq/2 \rceil_R \cdot f$ and $(mq/2) \cdot f$ is unlikely to be very large. As the decryption failure probability relevant for the Fujisaki-Okamoto transform is for a worst-case message, this difference in decryption failure probability for an adversarially chosen message is important.

The worst-case message for the difference between $\lfloor mq/2 \rceil_R \cdot f$ and $(mq/2) \cdot f$ is if rounding occurs for all coefficients. In this case, the difference is rf, where each coefficient of r is sampled from $\mathcal{U}(\{-1/2, 1/2\})$. The decryption is correct if each coefficient of

$$
(r + e')f - \overline{e}'' \cdot \overline{s} + \overline{s}' \cdot \overline{e}
$$

is smaller than $q/4$.

As we consider power of two cyclotomic fields, the distribution of every coefficient of the resulting product is the same. We can therefore consider the corresponding integer vectors and bound the probability that

$$
\frac{q}{4} < |s' \cdot e + (r + e') \cdot f - e'' \cdot s| .
$$

To get a rough idea of the decryption failure probability of our system, we consider the case where ψ_{gen} and ψ_{enc} are discrete Gaussian distributions with standard deviations σ_{gen} and σ_{enc} respectively and where $\psi_{\text{f}} = \psi_{\text{gen}}$. Furthermore, we consider the case where we encrypt the all 0 message, meaning that $mq/2 = \lfloor mq/2 \rceil_R$ and we therefore do not have to consider contribution of r. This allows the following minor alteration of Lemma 3.1 from [16] to be used to bound the decryption failure probability.

Lemma 7. *The error probability per symbol (over the choice of secret key) when decrypting the all 0 message, is bounded from above by any desired δ as long as*

$$
\sigma_{gen} \cdot \sigma_{enc} \leq \frac{q}{8\sqrt{2(h + k + 1) \cdot n \cdot \ln(2/\delta)}}
$$

except for with a probability less than 2^{-n} over the randomness in the ciphertext.

For a more precise bound on the failure probability applicable for the different types of error distributions used in our concrete parametrizations, we numerically calculate the failure probability in the same way as done for the Kyber submission [25], by estimating the actual probability distribution for the error terms.

5.3   Comparison to Other Cryptosystems

In this section we compare the security, efficiency and compactness of our NTWE based cryptosystem to that of corresponding NTRU and LWE-based systems. For simplicity, these comparisons are between problems with the same ring R, modulos q and error distributions. Because of this, the schemes we compare do not necessarily have the same decryption error probability. For a comparison which also accounts for the difference in decryption error probability, we instead provide concrete parametrizations that are comparable to the different parametrizations of Kyber in Sect. 6.2.

Security. We believe that the NTWE problem in rank k is essentially as hard as the rank $k + 1$ module-LWE problem. This is motivated by the analysis in Sect. 4 of algorithms that solve the NTWE and module-LWE lattice problems. As such, based on our conjectured concrete hardness of the NTWE problem, our cryptosystem parametrized with $h = k + 1$ should have security comparable to that of a rank $k+1$ module-LWE-based system with the same error distributions. For general h, we believe that our system should have security comparable to a module-LWE-based system with a public key given by h samples from a rank $k+1$ module-LWE distribution with a ciphertext corresponding to $k+2$ samples from a rank h module-LWE distribution.

Compared to a rank $k + 1$ module-LWE-based system, our system exposes fewer module-LWE samples as part of the ciphertext. Whereas the ciphertext in our system consists of $k+1$ module-LWE samples, the ciphertext in the module-LWE-based system consists of $k + 2$ such samples. This could potentially be a reason for our system to be more secure than the corresponding module-LWE-based system. However, based on current understanding, this difference in the number of available module-LWE samples should not significantly impact the security of the system.

The public key in our system is a sample from an NTWE distribution while the public key in an NTRU-based system is given by an instance of the NTRU problem. As such, the security against key-recovery attacks in these systems is based on the hardness of the search-NTWE problem and the search-NTRU problems respectively. Furthermore, we believe that the NTWE problem is essentially as hard as the rank $k+1$ module-NTRU problem, as indicated by Lemma 3 and analyzed in Sect. 4.

The ciphertext for our system with $h = k + 1$ is also very similar to the ciphertext in a rank $k + 1$ module-NTRU-based cryptosystem. In the module-NTRU-based cryptosystem, the ciphertext consists of $k+1$ noisy inner products of public data with a secret vector. Similarly our system exposes $k+1$ such noisy inner products. As such, we also believe the security of our cryptosystem to be comparable to that of a rank $k+1$ module-NTRU-based cryptosystem.

Module-NTRU-based cryptosystems are typically not considered due to their large public keys. Therefore, a more fair comparison in the efficiency and compactness of our system is to that of an NTRU-based system that uses a ring of degree $(k+1)n$. The natural lattice problem for this NTRU problem is essentially the same as the rank $k+1$ module-NTRU problem and based on current understanding, the security of these systems should be essentially the same.

Efficiency. Besides calculation of inverses and an additional multiplication by f^{-1}, our cryptosystem performs the same operations as in a typical LWE-based cryptosystem and should thus have similar efficiency. When using $f = 2f' + 1$, all multiplications are efficiently computable in the NTT domain. Furthermore, calculating the inverse f^{-1} in R_q is also efficient in the NTT domain, meaning that these additional steps barely affect the performance of the scheme.

As we deem the rank k NTWE problem to be essentially as hard as a rank $k+1$ module-LWE problem, for the same security level our system should actually be more efficient than a comparable module-LWE-based system. Compared to a rank $k+1$ module-LWE-based system, our cryptosystem does not need as much uniformly random data for $\overline{A}$. Furthermore, in our system, we perform fewer additions and multiplications in key generation and encryption, and essentially the same number of these operations during decryption.

With $\overline{s}$ and f combined, the key generation samples as much data from error distributions as in the key generation of a rank $k+1$ module-LWE-based system with h samples in the public key. With $f = 2f' + 1$, we are guaranteed that f_2^{-1} is trivial. However, we are not guaranteed that f is invertible in R_q and may therefore have to sample multiple f' from ψ_{gen}. However, for the rings we consider, the probability that f is not invertible is small enough that this resampling has a negligible impact on the average running time of key generation.

Another reason our scheme can be more efficiently implemented than a module-LWE-based scheme is that we do not perform any ciphertext compression. This allows the ciphertexts in our system to be transmitted in NTT-form, decreasing the number of times we have to perform the transform and its inverse. This results in a speed-up both during the encryption of messages and the decryption of ciphertexts.

Compared to an NTRU-based scheme, it is easier to parametrize our scheme with rings that support efficient operations by using the NTT. This is the case as we may select a fixed base ring which supports efficient NTT operations and target different security levels by altering h and k. As module-NTRU-based systems are typically not considered due to their large public keys, having an NTRU-based system support efficient NTT operations imposes a restrictive condition on the possible rings that can be used. It is possible to construct NTRU-based systems that support NTT operations, as done in a paper by Lyubashevsky and Seiler [18]. However, the NTRU-based submissions for public key-encryption and key establishment in the third round of the NIST post-quantum standardization process did not support efficient NTT operations [4,6].

Compared to an NTRU-based scheme that does not use NTT, our key generation should be significantly more efficient, at least if using an f that given by $2f' + 1$. In this case, we have no expensive operations during key generation, as f_2^{-1} is trivial while the inverse in R_q is efficiently computed by using the NTT. Meanwhile, in an NTRU-based scheme that does not support the NTT, at least one expensive inverse must be computed. However, when our system samples f directly from ψ_{gen}, the inverse in f_2^{-1} must be computed. Therefore, this version of our system has performance for key generation that is more similar to that of an NTRU-based system.

It is harder to compare the performance of encryption and decryption for our system to that of an NTRU-based system. By using the NTT, general multiplications in our system are computed more efficiently than possible without using the NTT. However, NTRU-based systems typically only consider multiplications with certain classes of polynomials, which allows multiplications that have similar efficiency to that of our scheme. Furthermore, if our scheme is used with a seed for $\overline{A}$ instead of the full matrix in the public key, the full matrix must be generated both during key generation and encryption. This can be a somewhat costly operation that is not necessary in an NTRU-based system, where the public key is a single ring element.

Compactness. In a typical rank $k + 1$ module-LWE-based system, the ciphertext consists of a heavily compressed ring element and a somewhat compressed module element. In total, these are represented by using essentially as much space as it takes to represent a single rank $k + 1$ module element. The public-key in such a system is $k + 1$ ring elements and a uniformly random matrix that is typically represented by a small seed.

In our cryptosystem, the ciphertext consists of an uncompressed rank k module element and an uncompressed ring element. This is represented in the same amount of space as a single rank $k + 1$ module element, and our ciphertext size is therefore essentially the same as for a comparable module-LWE-based system. In our system, the public key consists of h ring elements and a uniformly random matrix. Thus, by using $h = k + 1$ and representing the uniformly random matrix by a small seed, our public key is of the same size as in the rank $k + 1$ module-LWE-based system.

In an NTRU-based system, both the public-key and the ciphertext consists of a single ring element. Representing an element of a degree $(k + 1)n$ ring takes as much space as representing $k + 1$ elements from a degree n ring. Thus, our cryptosystem has the same sized ciphertext as an NTRU-based system in a ring of degree $(k + 1)n$. Furthermore, our system with $h = k + 1$ and with $\overline{A}$ represented by a small seed has essentially the same sized public-key as this NTRU-based system, with the only difference being this small seed that is used to derive the $\overline{A}$ matrix.

6   Example Parametrizations

For our cryptosystem, described in Algorithm 1, we are able to choose ring R, integer q and error distributions $\psi_{gen}, \psi_{enc}, \psi_f$ relatively freely. To use Lemma 6 to argue for the security of our system, we require both that the relevant NTWE instance is hard and that a rank h module-LWE problem is hard.

One way to parametrize our system is to use $h = k$ and selecting ψ_{gen} and ψ_{enc} differently. By balancing the standard deviation on ψ_{gen} and ψ_{enc}, we can ensure that both problems seem to be equally hard to solve, and that the scheme achieves an acceptable decryption failure probability. This results in parametrizations that are similar to a rank $k + 1$ module-LWE-based scheme but where only k module-LWE samples are included in the public key.

By instead using $h = k + 1$ and $\psi_{gen} = \psi_{enc}$, the resulting parametrizations are more comparable to typical module-LWE-based schemes. We propose such parametrizations that support NTT calculations, using the same ring R and modulos q as in Kyber. This results in parametrizations with performance quite similar to Kyber, but which should allow for more efficient implementations and which do not have to use any ciphertext compression.

Another approach is to instantiate the system to only rely on the concrete hardness of the NTRU and ring-LWE problems, as these problems have already been thoroughly investigated. While there are relations between the NTRU and ring-LWE problems [20,26,27], these do not directly show that specific instantiations of a cryptosystem based on the NTRU problem or on some version of the LWE problem is more secure than another. However, our cryptosystem parametrized like this is essentially guaranteed to remain secure as long as either the corresponding NTRU- or module-LWE-based cryptosystem is secure.

For the concrete parametrization we propose, we let the $\overline{A}$ part of the public key be derived from a 256 bit seed using some cryptographically secure pseudorandom number generator. This significantly decreases the size of the public key as this 32 byte seed is sufficient to represent the full $\overline{A}$ matrix in the public key.

We consider two different versions for the distribution ψ_f, corresponding either directly to a sample from ψ_{gen} or from $2\psi_{gen} + 1$, as described in Sect. 5. The first version results in a less efficient key generation, as inverses in R_2 must be calculated, but with a smaller decryption failure probability δ. The second version ensures that key generation is efficient, but results in a larger decryption failure probability δ_2. In the parametrizations in Tables 1 and 2, we present both the decryption failure probabilities δ and δ_2 for these different choices of ψ_f.

The decryption failure probabilities δ, δ_2 and the core SVP security of the presented parametrizations have been calculated using a modified version of the script used to calculate the corresponding parameters for the Kyber specification.

6.1   Skewed Parameters

Here we consider parametrizations of the cryptosystem that use $h = k$, resulting in a public key that is significantly smaller than the ciphertext. This results in a system where the security of the public-key is based on the NTWE problem in rank k while the message security is based on the hardness of the rank k module-LWE problem. With the same error distribution, the rank k NTWE problem seems to be significantly harder than the rank k module-LWE problem. For these parametrizations, we therefore use error distributions with the standard deviation for ψ_{gen} significantly smaller than the standard deviation for ψ_{enc}.

We use the same NTT friendly ring $R = \mathbb{Z}[X]/(X^{256}+1)$ with $q = 3329$ as in Kyber. The error distributions are discrete Gaussian distributions with standard deviations σ_{gen} and σ_{enc} for key generation and encryption respectively. As we use a ring with degree 256, each ciphertext encrypts a 256-bit message. These parametrizations are detailed in Table 1.

A module-LWE based cryptosystem can also be parametrized with comparable parameters. This is achieved by letting the public key consist of k samples from a rank $k + 1$ module-LWE instance, while the ciphertext is given by samples from a rank k module-LWE instance. These skewed parametrizations of a module-LWE-based cryptosystem are, however, not typically considered. We also believe that other parametrizations of our NTWE-based cryptosystem are more interesting than these that use $h = k$.

6.2   Parameters Similar to Kyber

In Table 2 we present parametrizations of our scheme that have been selected to be similar to parametrizations of Kyber [25]. For comparison we also include relevant information about the different Kyber parametrizations in Table 3.

As the NTWE problem is used for key generation in our scheme, our parametrizations use a k that is one rank smaller than the module rank used in corresponding Kyber parametrizations, while still claiming that the problem is

Table 1. Some different parametrizations of our scheme with $h = k$. The table details the size of the public-key (PK) and ciphertext (CT). It also details the estimated Core SVP hardness, as described in Sect. 2.5, of the lattice problems underlying the public-key and ciphertext respectively.

Version	512	1024
Core SVP PK	144	280
Core SVP CT	140	276
$h = k$	2	4
q	3329	3329
σ_{gen}	0.49	0.42
σ_{enc}	9.62	8.04
PK size (bytes)	800	1568
CT size (bytes)	1152	1920
δ	$< 2^{-300}$	$< 2^{-300}$
δ_2	2^{-201}	2^{-272}

essentially as hard. This allows our parametrizations to have essentially the same public key and ciphertext size as the corresponding Kyber implementations, even though our scheme does not include any ciphertext compression.

In comparison to Kyber, encryption for these parametrizations is more efficient, as we use a smaller module-rank for an equivalent security level. Furthermore, if ψ_f is given by $2\psi_{gen} + 1$, key generation in our scheme is also more efficient than in Kyber, as we use a smaller module-rank and the inverse f^{-1} in R_q is efficiently computable via the NTT.

We do not have an optimized implementation of our scheme and we have not performed any extensive profiling in order to compare the performance of Kyber and our scheme. However, we have implemented our scheme by modifying an implementation of Kyber. With ψ_f given by $2\psi_{gen} + 1$, the combination of key generation, encryption and decryption runs in around 10% less time than for the original Kyber implementation.

The decryption failure probability of our schemes with ψ_f directly given by ψ_{gen} is somewhat smaller than for the corresponding Kyber parametrizations. For our schemes, we recover a noisy version of the encoded message, with noise corresponding to the sum of $h + k + 1 = 2(k + 1)$ products of two small polynomials. In the corresponding parametrization of Kyber, the noise is the sum of $2(k + 1)$ products of two small polynomials plus another small polynomial.

The contribution to the decryption failure probability of a single small polynomial is typically small. However, the ciphertext compression performed in Kyber increases the size of this small error polynomial, causing it to have a significant impact on the decryption failure probability. This means that, for a comparable decryption error probability, our scheme can be parametrized with a larger standard deviation for the error distributions than in Kyber. This allows us to parametrize our scheme to target somewhat higher security levels than in Kyber, at least when using ψ_f directly given by ψ_{gen}.

The error distribution used in these parametrizations is a centered binomial distribution $\mathcal{B}_k$, as in Kyber. A sample from this distribution is given by $\sum_{i=1}^{k}(x_i - y_i)$, where x_i and y_i are sampled from a Bernoulli distributed with equal probability for 0 and 1. As we are able to achieve a smaller decryption failure probability than in Kyber, we also include additional parametrizations that use larger error distributions than the ones used in Kyber.

All of these parametrizations use the same ring as in Kyber, namely $R = \mathbb{Z}[X]/(X^{256} + 1)$ and with the same modulos $q = 3329$. This allows efficient NTT operations in R_q. Furthermore, as the ring has degree 256, each ciphertext encrypts a 256-bit message.

Table 2. Parametrizations of our scheme comparable to Kyber. The table details the size of the public-key (PK) and ciphertext (CT). It also details the estimated Core SVP hardness, as described in Sect. 2.5, of the lattice problems underlying the public-key and ciphertext respectively.

Version	512-3	512-4	768-2	768-3	1024
Core SVP PK	118	123	182	193	256
Core SVP CT	118	124	183	191	253
k	1	1	2	2	3
m	2	2	3	3	4
$\psi = \psi_{\text{enc}} = \psi_{\text{gen}}$	$\mathcal{B}_3$	$\mathcal{B}_4$	$\mathcal{B}_2$	$\mathcal{B}_3$	$\mathcal{B}_2$
PK size (bytes)	800	800	1184	1184	1568
CT size (bytes)	768	768	1152	1152	1536
δ		2^{-190}	2^{-108}	2^{-291}	2^{-131}	2^{-224}
δ_2		2^{-102}	2^{-58}	2^{-182}	2^{-82}	2^{-153}

Table 3. Core SVP security estimate, sizes and decryption failure probability for the different Kyber parametrizations for comparison. All parametrizations of Kyber use modules over $\mathbb{Z}[X]/(X^{256} + 1)$ with $q = 3329$.

Version	Kyber512	Kyber768	Kyber1024
Core SVP	118	183	256
Module Rank	2	3	4
PK size (bytes)	800	1184	1568
CT size (bytes)	768	1088	1568
δ	2^{-139}	2^{-164}	2^{-174}

6.3   Parameters Combining NTRU and LWE

A conservative approach for parametrizing our cryptosystem is to use $k = h = 1$ and only rely on the hardness given by Lemmas 1 and 2. Although we believe this to be overly conservative, the resulting cryptosystem serves as an efficient hybrid between cryptosystems based on the NTRU and ring-LWE problems. This scheme should be secure if either the corresponding NTRU-based or ring-LWE-based cryptosystem is secure.

Our resulting system has the same public key size as the corresponding ring-LWE-based system. As we use a small seed to represent the $\overline{A}$ matrix, the public key is also only 32-bytes larger than for the corresponding NTRU-based systems. Meanwhile, the ciphertexts in this system are as large as in the corresponding ring-LWE-based system without ciphertext compression.

As an example, we can choose a parametrization similar to one of the parametrizations of the New Hope [2] system. Thus, we use the ring $\mathbb{Z}[X]/(X^{1024}+1)$ and $q = 12289$ which allow efficient computations via the NTT. Using the same error distribution, we can argue that our system should be at least as secure as New Hope, while it also should be at least as secure as a corresponding NTRU-based cryptosystem.

As we do not perform any ciphertext compression, this scheme has significantly larger ciphertexts than New Hope. Furthermore, if we sample f so that f_2^{-1} is trivial, the resulting scheme has significantly larger failure probability than the New Hope scheme. If we instead sample f directly from ψ_{gen}, the resulting scheme has significantly less efficient key generation than the New Hope scheme. As such, this scheme does not really compare favorably to New Hope by itself.

Compared to a system where NTRU and a ring-LWE-based system are used in parallel, our scheme does however have several advantages. Our scheme is more efficient than a combination of a ring-LWE-based and an NTRU-based cryptosystem. Furthermore, our scheme also has significantly smaller public key than that of a combined NTRU-based and ring-LWE-based scheme. The ciphertext is the same size as in a ring-LWE-based system without ciphertext compression, which is smaller than the size of the combined ciphertexts of an NTRU-based system and the New Hope cryptosystem.

For this parametrization of our NTWE-based cryptosystem, the ciphertext is computed in essentially the same way as in the New Hope cryptosystem. Neither the addition of multiplying the public key with f^{-1} nor the differences regarding ciphertext compression are expected to have any negative effect on the security of our NTWE-based cryptosystem. We can therefore more or less guarantee the IND-CPA security of our system if the New Hope system is secure.

Compared to the corresponding NTRU-based system, there are some differences which could impact the security. In particular, Lemma 2 only guarantees the hardness of the NTWE problem if the NTRU problem with multiple samples is hard. However, for the security of a typical NTRU-based cryptosystem, it is sufficient that the single sample NTRU problem is hard. However, we do not believe this difference to have any significant effect on the security of the system.

Furthermore, the ciphertext in an NTRU-based cryptosystem is a single noisy inner product while our ciphertext consists of two such products. Based on current understanding, the number of such noisy products, corresponding to ring-LWE samples, should not significantly impact how hard the products are to distinguish from uniformly random. As such, based on our current understanding, our system parametrized in this way is IND-CPA secure if New Hope is IND-CPA secure or if the corresponding NTRU-based system is IND-CPA secure.

7   Final Remarks

Based on our concrete hardness estimates for the NTWE problem, we parametrize our NTWE-based cryptosystem to have performance that is competitive to that of highly efficient module-LWE-based schemes. While the concrete hardness of the NTWE problem has not been analyzed before, we argue that its similarity to the NTRU and LWE problems provides some confidence in the security of these parametrizations.

As with the NTRU and LWE problems, the NTWE problem also naturally corresponds to a problem in a q-ary lattice. This NTWE lattice can be seen as a mix between an LWE lattice and a NTRU lattice, which motivates our belief in the hardness of the NTWE problem. We furthermore believe that any improved algorithms against the NTWE problem are likely to have interesting consequences for the NTRU and LWE problems as well. One possibility is that any such algorithm is directly applicable to the NTRU and LWE problems, which is of obvious interest. However, a specialized algorithm that is only applicable to the NTWE problem would also be interesting, in some sense indicating that the NTRU and LWE problems are hard, but a mix between them is easier than we expect.

Although not as suitable for a public-key cryptosystem, a generalization of the NTWE problem seems to even better capture this mix between the NTRU and LWE problems. An instance from this generalized problem is given by $(\overline{A}, \overline{B} = (\overline{A}\overline{S} + \overline{E})\overline{F}^{-1})$ for $\overline{F} \leftarrow (\psi^{t \times t})^*$, $\overline{A} \leftarrow \mathcal{U}(R_q^{h \times k})$, $\overline{S} \leftarrow \psi^{k \times t}$ and $\overline{E} \leftarrow \psi^{k \times t}$. With $k = 0$, this is exactly a rank t module-NTRU instance while the problem with $t = 1$ is a rank k NTWE instance. By instead considering the problem with $n = 1$ and $t = 1$, this problem is essentially the same as an unstructured LWE problem with secret dimension k.

The natural lattice for all of these instances is spanned by the columns of

$$\begin{bmatrix} qI & A & B \\ 0 & I & 0 \\ 0 & 0 & I \end{bmatrix}$$

where A, B are the integer matrix corresponding to $\overline{A}$ and $\overline{B}$. In this full class of problems, the solution is given by a short vector in this lattice, with the length of the target vector only dependent on the lattice dimension. As such, by current understanding, there should be no significant difference in how hard these lattice problems are to solve if hn and $(k + t)n$ are constant.

We believe that any algorithm against some version of this problem may provide interesting insights for other versions of this problem. In particular, an algorithm that is relevant against either the NTRU or the LWE problem, but not the other, will be applicable to some versions of this generalized NTWE problem. Investigating which versions such an algorithm is applicable to could potentially give a better understanding of the limitations and possibilities of such an algorithm. For example, it may be interesting to investigate how attacks against overstretched NTRU parameters fare against this larger class of problems and if such an attack can be used against versions of this problem that are more similar to the LWE problem.

Acknowledgment. This research has been supported in part by the Swedish Armed Forces and was conducted at KTH Center for Cyber Defense and Information Security (CDIS). The author would like to thank Johan Håstad and Martin Ekerå for their helpful feedback and comments.

References

1. Albrecht, M., Ducas, L.: Lattice attacks on NTRU and LWE: a history of refinements. Cryptology ePrint Archive, Report 2021/799 (2021). https://eprint.iacr.org/2021/799
2. Alkim, E., Ducas, L., Pöppelmann, T., Schwabe, P.: Post-quantum key exchange - a new hope. In: Holz, T., Savage, S. (eds.) USENIX Security 2016: 25th USENIX Security Symposium, Austin, TX, USA, 10–12 August 2016, pp. 327–343. USENIX Association (2016)
3. Becker, A., Ducas, L., Gama, N., Laarhoven, T.: New directions in nearest neighbor searching with applications to lattice sieving. In: Krauthgamer, R. (ed.) 27th Annual ACM-SIAM Symposium on Discrete Algorithms, Arlington, VA, USA, 10–12 January 2016, pp. 10–24. ACM-SIAM (2016)
4. Bernstein, D.J., et al.: NTRU prime. Technical report, National Institute of Standards and Technology (2020). https://csrc.nist.gov/projects/post-quantum-cryptography/post-quantum-cryptography-standardization/round-3-submissions
5. Chatterjee, S., Koblitz, N., Menezes, A., Sarkar, P.: Another look at tightness II: practical issues in cryptography. Cryptology ePrint Archive, Report 2016/360 (2016). https://eprint.iacr.org/2016/360
6. Chen, C., et al.: NTRU. Technical report, National Institute of Standards and Technology (2020). https://csrc.nist.gov/projects/post-quantum-cryptography/post-quantum-cryptography-standardization/round-3-submissions
7. Chen, Y.: Réduction de réseau et sécurité concrète du chiffrement complètement homomorphe. Ph.D. thesis, Université Paris Diderot (2013). 2013PA077242
8. Chuengsatiansup, C., Prest, T., Stehlé, D., Wallet, A., Xagawa, K.: ModFalcon: compact signatures based on module-NTRU lattices. In: Sun, H.-M., Shieh, S.-P., Gu, G., Ateniese, G. (eds.) ASIACCS 2020: 15th ACM Symposium on Information, Computer and Communications Security, Taipei, Taiwan, 5–9 October 2020, pp. 853–866. ACM Press (2020)
9. Ducas, L., Pulles, L.: Does the dual-sieve attack on learning with errors even work? Cryptology ePrint Archive, Report 2023/302 (2023). https://eprint.iacr.org/2023/302
10. Ducas, L., van Woerden, W.: NTRU fatigue: how stretched is overstretched? In: Tibouchi, M., Wang, H. (eds.) ASIACRYPT 2021. LNCS, vol. 13093, pp. 3–32. Springer, Cham (2021). https://doi.org/10.1007/978-3-030-92068-5_1
11. Fujisaki, E., Okamoto, T.: Secure integration of asymmetric and symmetric encryption schemes. In: Wiener, M. (ed.) CRYPTO 1999. LNCS, vol. 1666, pp. 537–554. Springer, Heidelberg (1999). https://doi.org/10.1007/3-540-48405-1_34
12. Guo, Q., Johansson, T.: Faster dual lattice attacks for solving LWE with applications to CRYSTALS. In: Tibouchi, M., Wang, H. (eds.) ASIACRYPT 2021. LNCS, vol. 13093, pp. 33–62. Springer, Cham (2021). https://doi.org/10.1007/978-3-030-92068-5_2
13. Gärtner, J.: Concrete security from worst-case to average-case lattice reductions. Cryptology ePrint Archive, Paper 2023/947 (2023). https://eprint.iacr.org/2023/947
14. Hoffstein, J., Pipher, J., Silverman, J.H.: NTRU: a ring-based public key cryptosystem. In: Buhler, J.P. (ed.) ANTS 1998. LNCS, vol. 1423, pp. 267–288. Springer, Heidelberg (1998). https://doi.org/10.1007/BFb0054868

15. Kirchner, P., Fouque, P.-A.: Revisiting lattice attacks on overstretched NTRU parameters. In: Coron, J.-S., Nielsen, J.B. (eds.) EUROCRYPT 2017. LNCS, vol. 10210, pp. 3–26. Springer, Cham (2017). https://doi.org/10.1007/978-3-319-56620-7_1

16. Lindner, R., Peikert, C.: Better key sizes (and attacks) for LWE-based encryption. In: Kiayias, A. (ed.) CT-RSA 2011. LNCS, vol. 6558, pp. 319–339. Springer, Heidelberg (2011). https://doi.org/10.1007/978-3-642-19074-2_21

17. Lyubashevsky, V., Peikert, C., Regev, O.: On ideal lattices and learning with errors over rings. Cryptology ePrint Archive, Report 2012/230 (2012). https://eprint.iacr.org/2012/230

18. Lyubashevsky, V., Seiler, G.: NTTRU: truly fast NTRU using NTT. IACR Trans. Cryptogr. Hardw. Embed. Syst. **2019**(3), 180–201 (2019). https://tches.iacr.org/index.php/TCHES/article/view/8293

19. MATZOV: Report on the security of LWE: improved dual lattice attack. Technical report, MATZOV (2022)

20. Peikert, C.: A decade of lattice cryptography. Cryptology ePrint Archive, Report 2015/939 (2015). https://eprint.iacr.org/2015/939

21. Pellet-Mary, A., Stehlé, D.: On the hardness of the NTRU problem. In: Tibouchi, M., Wang, H. (eds.) ASIACRYPT 2021. LNCS, vol. 13090, pp. 3–35. Springer, Cham (2021). https://doi.org/10.1007/978-3-030-92062-3_1

22. Regev, O.: On lattices, learning with errors, random linear codes, and cryptography. In: Gabow, H.N., Fagin, R. (eds.) 37th Annual ACM Symposium on Theory of Computing, Baltimore, MA, USA, 22–24 May 2005, pp. 84–93. ACM Press (2005)

23. Schnorr, C.P., Euchner, M.: Lattice basis reduction: improved practical algorithms and solving subset sum problems. Math. Program. **66**(1), 181–199 (1994). https://doi.org/10.1007/BF01581144

24. Schnorr, C.P.: A hierarchy of polynomial time lattice basis reduction algorithms. Theor. Comput. Sci. **53**(2), 201–224 (1987)

25. Schwabe, P., et al.: CRYSTALS-KYBER. Technical report, National Institute of Standards and Technology (2022). https://csrc.nist.gov/Projects/post-quantum-cryptography/selected-algorithms-2022

26. Stehlé, D., Steinfeld, R.: Making NTRU as secure as worst-case problems over ideal lattices. In: Paterson, K.G. (ed.) EUROCRYPT 2011. LNCS, vol. 6632, pp. 27–47. Springer, Heidelberg (2011). https://doi.org/10.1007/978-3-642-20465-4_4

27. Wang, Y., Wang, M.: Provably secure NTRUEncrypt over any cyclotomic field. In: Cid, C., Jacobson, M.J., Jr. (eds.) SAC 2018. LNSC, vol. 11349, pp. 391–417. Springer, Heidelberg (2019). https://doi.org/10.1007/978-3-030-10970-7_18

Multivariate Cryptography

Fast Enumeration Algorithm for Multivariate Polynomials over General Finite Fields

Hiroki Furue$^{(\boxtimes)}$ and Tsuyoshi Takagi

Department of Mathematical Informatics, The University of Tokyo, Tokyo, Japan
{furue-hiroki261,takagi}@g.ecc.u-tokyo.ac.jp

Abstract. The enumeration of all outputs of a given multivariate polynomial is a fundamental mathematical problem and is incorporated in some algebraic attacks on multivariate public key cryptosystems. For a degree-d polynomial in n variables over the finite field with q elements, solving the enumeration problem classically requires $O\left(\binom{n+d}{d} \cdot q^n\right)$ operations. At CHES 2010, Bouillaguet et al. proposed a fast enumeration algorithm over the binary field $\mathbb{F}_2$. Their proposed algorithm covers all the inputs of a given polynomial following the order of Gray codes and is completed by $O(d \cdot 2^n)$ bit operations. However, to the best of our knowledge, a result achieving the equivalent efficiency in general finite fields is yet to be proposed.

In this study, we propose a novel algorithm that enumerates all the outputs of a degree-d polynomial in n variables over $\mathbb{F}_q$ with a prime number q by $O(d \cdot q^n)$ operations. The proposed algorithm is constructed by using a lexicographic order instead of Gray codes to cover all the inputs. This result can be seen as an extension of the result of Bouillaguet et al. to general finite fields and is almost optimal in terms of time complexity. We can naturally apply the proposed algorithm to the case where q is a prime power. Notably, our enumeration algorithm differs from the algorithm by Bouillaguet et al. even in the case of $q = 2$.

Keywords: multivariate polynomial · finite fields · enumeration algorithm · exhaustive search · MQ problem · MPKC

1 Introduction

Currently used public key cryptosystems such as RSA and ECC can be broken in polynomial time by Shor's algorithm [19] using a quantum computer. Thus, the amount of research conducted on post-quantum cryptography (PQC), which is secure against quantum computing attacks, has been accelerating. Indeed, the U.S. National Institute for Standards and Technology (NIST) has initiated a PQC standardization project [18]. Among various PQC candidates, multivariate public key cryptosystem (MPKC) is one of the main categories. MPKCs are cryptosystems constructed based on the difficulty of solving a system of

© The Author(s), under exclusive license to Springer Nature Switzerland AG 2023
T. Johansson and D. Smith-Tone (Eds.): PQCrypto 2023, LNCS 14154, pp. 357–378, 2023.
https://doi.org/10.1007/978-3-031-40003-2_13

multivariate quadratic polynomial equations over a finite field (the multivariate quadratic (MQ) problem). The MQ problem is proven to be NP-complete [14] and is thus likely to be secure against quantum computers.

The security of MPKCs is strongly dependent on the difficulty of solving some algebraic problems in addition to the MQ problem. Especially, there have been proposed many key recovery attacks on MPKCs solving the MinRank problem [2,5,15,20,21], which finds one low-rank matrix from linear combinations of given matrices. An *enumeration problem* is also one of the algebraic problems relevant to the security of MPKCs. The enumeration problem is defined over the finite field $\mathbb{F}_q$ with a prime power q as follows: Given a single-degree-d polynomial f in $\mathbb{F}_q[x_1, \ldots, x_n]$, evaluate f over all the points in $\mathbb{F}_q^n$ (to find all the zeros of f). Indeed, there exist many algebraic attacks partly using enumeration algorithms, such as the hybrid approach [1,11], Crossbred algorithm [16], claw finding attack [4], and polynomial XL [13]. Therefore, improving the complexity of solving the enumeration problem directly improves the complexity of some algebraic attacks on MPKCs and strongly affects the security of MPKCs. In the rest of this paper, we focus on the theoretical asymptotic complexity of algorithms for solving the enumeration problems.

Fast Exhaustive Search over $\mathbb{F}_2$. At CHES 2010, Bouillaguet et al. [9] proposed a fast enumeration algorithm in $\mathbb{F}_2$ and a way of solving non-linear systems using this enumeration algorithm. Given a single-degree-d polynomial in n variables over $\mathbb{F}_2$, their enumeration algorithm requires $O(d \cdot 2^n)$ bit operations. This complexity is smaller than that of the classical exhaustive search $O\left(\binom{n}{d} \cdot 2^n\right)$. In their algorithms, all the inputs are covered in the order of Gray codes. Here, Gray codes are orderings of the elements of $\mathbb{F}_2^n$ such that two consecutive elements differ in only one bit. For consecutive two elements $\mathbf{x}_0$ and $\mathbf{x}_1$ in the order of Gray codes, which only differs in the k-th bit, their enumeration algorithm computes the output $f(\mathbf{x}_1)$ as follows using the derivative $\partial_k f$ with respect to the k-th variable

$$f(\mathbf{x}_1) = f(\mathbf{x}_0) + \partial_k f(\mathbf{x}_0),$$

where $+$ denotes addition in the binary field. By using this method recursively, outputs can be updated by $O(d)$ bit operations. Efficient implementations of their proposed algorithms are given in [8,10].

Our study aims to extend the results of Bouillaguet et al. to general finite fields. In [9], their enumeration algorithm uses one property of polynomials over $\mathbb{F}_2$ such that derivatives $\partial_k f$ do not include the variable x_k because polynomials over $\mathbb{F}_2$ are represented as a sum of monomials where the exponent of each variable is at most one (due to $x_i^2 = x_i$). Such a property does not hold over general finite fields, and this renders naturally extending the results of Bouillaguet et al. to general finite fields difficult. In [22], the authors proposed a practical enumeration algorithm in $\mathbb{F}_3$ with the Gray code order, but their algorithm requires more than $O(d)$ operations for each input.

Our Contributions. We propose a novel efficient enumeration algorithm over general finite fields $\mathbb{F}_q$ with a prime number q. Given a single-degree-d polynomial in n variables over $\mathbb{F}_q$, the proposed algorithm enumerates all the outputs of the given polynomial by $O(d \cdot q^n)$ operations after an initialization phase with $O\left(\binom{n+d}{d}^2\right)$ operations. This result achieves efficiency comparable to the enumeration algorithm proposed by Bouillaguet et al. Furthermore, we also show a method of applying the proposed algorithm to the case of $\mathbb{F}_{p^r}$ with a prime number p and a positive integer r in Remark 3.

From a theoretical point of view, the main difference between the proposed enumeration algorithm and one of Bouillaguet et al. is the order to cover all the inputs $\mathbb{F}_q^n$. The proposed algorithm uses a lexicographic order instead of Gray codes. For example, in the case of $q = 3$ and $n = 2$, all the inputs are ordered as follows: $(0,0) \to (0,1) \to (0,2) \to (1,0) \to (1,1) \to (1,2) \to (2,0) \to (2,1) \to (2,2)$. However, unlike the algorithm proposed by Bouillaguet et al., we de not compute all the outputs by adding some derivatives into the output to the last input. In the proposed algorithm, if an input has the form $(x_1, \ldots, x_k, 0, \ldots, 0)$ with $x_k \neq 0$, then the output to $(x_1, \ldots, x_k, 0, \ldots, 0)$ is computed as follows:

$$f(x_1, \ldots, x_k, 0, \ldots, 0) =$$
$$f(x_1, \ldots, x_k - 1, 0, \ldots, 0) + \partial_k f(x_1, \ldots, x_k - 1, 0, \ldots, 0).$$

The proposed algorithm following this rule covers all the inputs by a branching structure, unlike the algorithm proposed by Bouillaguet et al. (See Fig. 1 in Subsect. 4.2.) We then can achieve the time complexity limited to a small value as that proposed by Bouillaguet et al. Note that our enumeration algorithm differs from the algorithm proposed by Bouillaguet et al. even in the case of $q = 2$.

From a practical point of view, as we mentioned above, our enumeration algorithm can revise the complexity of attacks including the enumeration part, such as the claw finding attack, Crossbred, and polynomial XL, in finite fields with odd characteristics. This has an impact on MPKCs since some multivariate-based signature schemes in finite fields with odd characteristics have been proposed recently [3,12]. Furthermore, by using the method proposed in [9], our enumeration algorithm can be applied to solve systems of polynomial equations, and its complexity is estimated as $O(d^2 \cdot \log n \cdot q^n)$. (See Remark 4.)

We finally discuss the optimality of the proposed enumeration algorithm in terms of time complexity. A lower bound of the complexity of the exhaustive search is conjectured to be $O(q^n)$ because outputs have to be computed q^n times for all the inputs in $\mathbb{F}_q^n$. Therefore, in the case of $d \ll n$, the proposed enumeration algorithm with $O(d \cdot q^n)$ operations can be considered to be almost optimal in terms of time complexity.

Organizations. Section 2 reviews a classical enumeration algorithm and its complexity. After describing the enumeration algorithm proposed by Bouillaguet et al. in Sect. 3, the proposed algorithm is detailed in Sect. 4. Finally, Sect. 5 presents the conclusion, which summarizes the key points and suggests possible future directions.

2   Classical Approach

Let q be a prime power, and n and d be positive integers. This section deals with the enumeration problem on a polynomial $f \in \mathbb{F}_q[x_1, \ldots, x_n]$ with degree d. The conventional method to solve the enumeration problem is to evaluate the given polynomial f at all the points of $\mathbb{F}_q^n$. This section explains the conventional approach and its complexity.

Given a polynomial f in n variables with degree d, f can be decomposed as follows:

$$f(x_1, \ldots, x_n) = x_1 \cdot f_1(x_1, \ldots, x_n) + f_2(x_2, \ldots, x_n), \qquad (2.1)$$

where the degrees of $f_1(x_1, \ldots, x_n)$ and $f_2(x_2, \ldots, x_n)$ are at most $d - 1$ and d, respectively. Then, the output $f(x_1, \ldots, x_n)$ can be obtained by evaluating $f_1(x_1, \ldots, x_n)$ and $f_2(x_2, \ldots, x_n)$. Therefore, the enumeration problem in n variables with degree d can be reduced to the problem in n variables with degree $d - 1$ and the problem in $n - 1$ variables with degree d. From the discussion, the following theorem can be explained for evaluating complexity.

Lemma 1. *Let f be a polynomial in n variables with degree d over $\mathbb{F}_q$. Denoting by $T(n, d)$ an upper bound of the number of additions and multiplications over $\mathbb{F}_q$ for the evaluation of f for any input with the aforementioned approach, we have*

$$T(n, d) = 2 \cdot \left(\binom{n+d}{d} - 1 \right). \qquad (2.2)$$

Proof. The aforementioned statement can be proved by induction. We have $T(n, 0) = 0$ and $T(0, d) = 0$, which satisfy the aforementioned statement. We assume that, for $n, d \geq 1$, $T(n, d - 1)$ and $T(n - 1, d)$ satisfy Eq. (2.2). Since we have $T(n, d) = T(n, d - 1) + T(n - 1, d) + 2$ from Eq. (2.1), the following equation can be obtained:

$$
\begin{aligned}
T(n, d) &= 2 \cdot \left(\binom{n+d-1}{d-1} - 1 \right) + 2 \cdot \left(\binom{n-1+d}{d} - 1 \right) + 2 \\
&= 2 \cdot \left(\binom{n+d-1}{d-1} + \binom{n+d-1}{d} - 1 \right) \\
&= 2 \cdot \left(\binom{n+d}{d} - 1 \right).
\end{aligned}
$$

Thus, we confirmed $T(n, d)$ satisfies Eq. (2.2), and the aforementioned statement holds for any n and d. $\qquad \square$

From this lemma, the time complexity of the evaluation of f at each point of $\mathbb{F}_q^n$ is given as $O\left(\binom{n+d}{d} \right)$. Therefore, the complexity of the classical approach to the enumeration problem is given as follows:

$$O\left(\binom{n+d}{d} \cdot q^n \right).$$

3   Enumeration Algorithm of Bouillaguet et al.

This section describes an enumeration algorithm over the binary field proposed by Bouillaguet et al. [9]. After presenting some notations, we describe their enumeration algorithm in Subsect. 3.2. We change some notations from [9] for readability and consistency with the description of the proposed algorithm in Sect. 4.

3.1   Notations

We here give some notations about the vector space over the binary field, *Gray codes*, and *Derivatives*. These Gray codes and derivatives play crucial roles in their enumeration algorithm given in Subsect. 3.2.

Binary Vector. For the n-dimensional vector space $\mathbb{F}_2^n$ over the binary field, the indices are allocated from 1 to n from the most left bit to the most right bit such as $(x_1, \ldots, x_n)$. For a vector $\mathbf{a} \in \mathbb{F}_2^n$ and two integers $0 \leq i \leq 2^n - 1$ and $1 \leq k \leq n$, we use the following notations:

- $i_{(2)}$: an n-dimensional vector over $\mathbb{F}_2$ representing i in base-2
- $\mathbf{e}_k$: the k-th canonical basis vector in $\mathbb{F}_2^n$
- $\mathbf{a} \ll k$ (resp. $\mathbf{a} \gg k$): the binary left (resp. right) shift of a vector $\mathbf{a}$ by k bits.
- $\rho(\mathbf{a})$ (resp. $\sigma(\mathbf{a})$): the index of the most left (resp. right) nonzero bit of $\mathbf{a}$ (If $\mathbf{a} = \mathbf{0}$, then $\rho(\mathbf{a}) = \sigma(\mathbf{a}) = 0$.)

Gray Codes. The Gray code is an ordering of the binary vector space such that two successive values differ in only one bit. For the vector space $\mathbb{F}_2^n$, several orderings satisfy the aforementioned condition. However, in this study, we defined the Gray code $\mathrm{GC}(i)$ for $0 \leq i \leq 2^n - 1$ uniquely as follows:

$$\mathrm{GC}(i) = i_{(2)} + (i_{(2)} \gg 1). \tag{3.1}$$

Then, it can be easily confirmed that $\mathrm{GC}(i)$ and $\mathrm{GC}(i+1)$ differ in only one bit.

Derivatives. Finally, for an integer $1 \leq k \leq n$, $\mathbb{F}_2$ derivative $\partial_k f$ is defined as follows:

$$\partial_k f(\mathbf{x}) = f(\mathbf{x} + \mathbf{e}_k) + f(\mathbf{x}).$$

We can easily confirm that if the degree of f is d, then that of $\partial_k f$ is at most $d - 1$. For $a \in \mathbb{Z}_{\geq 0}$, $\partial_k^a f$ denotes the a-th derivative of f with respect to x_k, and for $\mathbf{a} = (a_1, \ldots, a_n) \in \mathbb{Z}_{\geq 0}^n$, $\partial^{\mathbf{a}} f = \partial_1^{a_1} \circ \cdots \circ \partial_n^{a_n} f$.

3.2   Enumeration Algorithm

This subsection recalls an enumeration algorithm proposed in [9]. The input f is a polynomial in $\mathbb{F}_2[x_1, \ldots, x_n]$ with degree d.

First, a method of storing some information through the enumeration is given. For any $\mathbf{a} = (a_1, \ldots, a_n) \in \mathbb{Z}_{\geq 0}^n$ with $|\mathbf{a}| = \sum_{i=1}^n a_i \leq d$, $D[\mathbf{a}]$ contains the information of the derivative $\partial^{\mathbf{a}} f$. Here, $\mathbf{a}$ is restricted by $|\mathbf{a}| \leq d$ because $\partial^{\mathbf{a}} f = 0$ for any $\mathbf{a}$ with $|\mathbf{a}| > d$. In their enumeration algorithm, three values can be read from $D[\mathbf{a}]$: $D[\mathbf{a}].\mathbf{x} \in \mathbb{F}_2^n$, $D[\mathbf{a}].y \in \mathbb{F}_2$, and $D[\mathbf{a}].i \in \mathbb{Z}_{>0}$. These invariants satisfy relationships that $D[\mathbf{a}].y = \partial^{\mathbf{a}} f(D[\mathbf{a}].\mathbf{x})$ and $D[\mathbf{a}].i$ is used to update $D[\mathbf{a}].\mathbf{x}$.

The enumeration algorithm is composed of three functions: INIT, MAIN, and NEXT. The main function MAIN first performs INIT and sets the initial values of each derivative. After the initialization phase, MAIN derives the outputs of f from D and uses NEXT to update D at each point. See Algorithm 1, 2, and 3 for details.

The main idea of this algorithm is to update the input $\mathbf{x}$ of f following Gray codes and obtain $f(\mathbf{x} + \mathbf{e}_i)$ by adding a derivative $\partial_i f(\mathbf{x})$ into $f(\mathbf{x})$. Such a construction is feasible because two successive values differ in only one bit in the Gray code order. In the following, we show a way of evaluating $\partial_i f$ for some inputs to update f. From the definition of the Gray code in Eq. (3.1), we have the following equation:

$$GC(i + 1) = GC(i) + \mathbf{e}_{\sigma((i+1)_{(2)})}.$$

From this equation, $GC(i + 1)$ is equal to $GC(i) + \mathbf{e}_k$ in the case where $i = j \cdot 2^{n-k+1} + 2^{n-k} - 1$ with $0 \leq j \leq 2^{k-1} - 1$. Namely, the enumeration algorithm requires the output of $\partial_k f$ at each point $\left(j \cdot 2^{n-k+1} + 2^{n-k} - 1\right)_{(2)}$ for $0 \leq j \leq 2^{k-1} - 1$. The following lemma can be easily derived from Lemma 3 in [9]

Lemma 2. *For* $0 \leq j \leq 2^{k-1} - 1$,

$$GC\left(j \cdot 2^{n-k+1} + 2^{n-k} - 1\right) = \begin{cases} GC(2^{n-k} - 1) + (GC(j) \ll (n - k + 1)) & (j \text{ is even}) \\ GC(2^{n-k} - 1) + (GC(j) \ll (n - k + 1)) + \mathbf{e}_k & (j \text{ is odd}) \end{cases}.$$

From this lemma, the first $(k - 1)$ bits of $GC\left(j \cdot 2^{n-k+1} + 2^{n-k} - 1\right)$ for $0 \leq j \leq 2^{k-1} - 1$ behaves like Gray codes in $(k - 1)$ variables, and the last $(n - k)$ bits of them are constants. The k-th bit of $GC\left(j \cdot 2^{n-k+1} + 2^{n-k} - 1\right)$ is determined by the parity of j. However, the k-th bit does not affect the value of $\partial_k f\left(GC\left(j \cdot 2^{n-k+1} + 2^{n-k} - 1\right)\right)$ because we have $\partial_k f(\mathbf{x} + \mathbf{e}_k) = \partial_k f(\mathbf{x})$ for any $\mathbf{x}$. Therefore, $\partial_k f\left(GC\left(j \cdot 2^{n-k+1} + 2^{n-k} - 1\right)\right)$ for $0 \leq j \leq 2^{k-1} - 1$ can be enumerated in the order of Gray codes in the first $(k - 1)$ variables. By applying this reduction recursively, the enumeration in the Gray code order can be realized for any $\partial^{\mathbf{a}} f$ with $|\mathbf{a}| \leq d$.

Following Theorem 1 in [9], the time and space complexities of the enumeration algorithm of Bouillaguet et al. are estimated as follows:

Algorithm 1. MAIN(f)

1: $D \leftarrow \text{INIT}(D, f, \mathbf{0}, \mathbf{0})$
2: **for** $i = 0, \ldots, 2^n - 1$ **do**
3:     "$f(D[0].\mathbf{x}) = D[0].y$"
4:     $D \leftarrow \text{NEXT}(D, \mathbf{0})$
5: **end for**

Algorithm 2. INIT($D, f, \mathbf{a}, \mathbf{x}_0$)

1: $D[\mathbf{a}].i \leftarrow 0$
2: $D[\mathbf{a}].\mathbf{x} \leftarrow \mathbf{x}_0$
3: $D[\mathbf{a}].y \leftarrow f(\mathbf{x}_0)$
4: **if** $|\mathbf{a}| < d$ **then**
5:     $k_0 \leftarrow \rho(\mathbf{a})$ ($k_0 \leftarrow n + 1$ if $\mathbf{a} = \mathbf{0}$.)
6:     **for** $k = 1, \ldots, k_0 - 1$ **do**
7:         $D \leftarrow \text{INIT}(D, \partial_k f, \mathbf{a} + \mathbf{e}_k, \mathbf{x}_0 + \mathbf{e}_{k+1})$ $(\mathbf{e}_{n+1} = \mathbf{0})$
8:     **end for**
9: **end if**
10: **return** D

Algorithm 3. NEXT($D, \mathbf{a}$)

1: $D[\mathbf{a}].i \leftarrow D[\mathbf{a}].i + 1$
2: $k \leftarrow \rho(\mathbf{a}) + \sigma((D[\mathbf{a}].i)_{(2)}) - n - 1$
3: $D[\mathbf{a}].\mathbf{x} \leftarrow D[\mathbf{a}].\mathbf{x} + \mathbf{e}_k$
4: $D[\mathbf{a}].y \leftarrow D[\mathbf{a}].y + D[\mathbf{a} + \mathbf{e}_k].y$
5: **if** $|\mathbf{a}| < d - 1$ **then**
6:     $D \leftarrow \text{NEXT}(D, \mathbf{a} + \mathbf{e}_k)$
7: **end if**
8: **return** D

Theorem 1. *All the zeros of a single polynomial f in n variables with degree d over the binary field can be found in essentially $O(d \cdot 2^n)$ bit operations, using $O(n^d)$ bits memory, after an initialization phase of negligible complexity $O(n^{2d})$.*

Remark 1 (Case of $\mathbb{F}_q$ with a prime number $q \neq 2$). It is critical to consider the extension of the enumeration algorithm in Subsect. 3.2 to general finite fields $\mathbb{F}_q$ with a prime number $q \neq 2$. Indeed, there exist Gray codes over $\mathbb{F}_q$ called q-array Gray codes, and derivatives are feasible over $\mathbb{F}_q$. However, the enumeration algorithm of Bouillaguet et al. cannot be simply extended to $\mathbb{F}_q$.

Subsection 3.2 reveals that some outputs of $\partial_k f$ required to enumerate f can be enumerated in the order of Gray codes. A similar result as Lemma 2 holds in $\mathbb{F}_q$ with $q \neq 2$. However, it does not hold that $\partial_k f(\mathbf{x} + \mathbf{e}_k) = \partial_k f(\mathbf{x})$ in $\mathbb{F}_q$, and thus, some required outputs of $\partial_k f$ cannot be enumerated using Gray codes in the first $(k-1)$ variables. Therefore, applying the proposed enumeration recursively for a polynomial in $\mathbb{F}_q$ is difficult.

4   Our Proposed Algorithms

This section proposes a novel efficient enumeration algorithm on a degree-d polynomial $f \in \mathbb{F}_q[x_1, \ldots, x_n]$ with a prime number q. This section is organized as follows: Subsect. 4.1 prepares some notations. Subsection 4.2 explains the order used in the proposed algorithm instead of Gray codes. Subsection 4.3 introduces the data structure used in the proposed algorithm. Subsection 4.4 prepares a function to classify the inputs used in the main algorithm. Subsection 4.5 describes the details of the proposed algorithm. Subsection 4.6 discusses the time and space complexities.

4.1   Notations

This subsection gives some notations for the proposed enumeration algorithm over $\mathbb{F}_q$ as in Subsect. 3.1 for the enumeration algorithm of Bouillaguet et al.

For the n-dimensional vector space over the finite field $\mathbb{F}_q$, the indices are allocated from 1 to n from the most left bit to the most right bit as described in Sect. 3. For a vector $\mathbf{a} \in \mathbb{F}_q^n$ and two integers $0 \leq i \leq q^n - 1$ and $1 \leq k \leq n$, we use the following notations

- $\mathbf{e}_k$: the k-th canonical basis vector in $\mathbb{F}_q^n$
- $\rho(\mathbf{a})$: the index of the most left nonzero bit of $\mathbf{a}$ (If $\mathbf{a} = \mathbf{0}$, then $\rho(\mathbf{a}) = n$.)

Furthermore, derivatives over $\mathbb{F}_q$ are defined as follows: For an integer $1 \leq k \leq n$, the $\mathbb{F}_q$ derivative $\partial_k f(\mathbf{x})$ for $\mathbf{x} \in \mathbb{F}_q^n$ is

$$\partial_k f(\mathbf{x}) = f(\mathbf{x} + \mathbf{e}_k) - f(\mathbf{x}).$$

For example, given $f(x_1, x_2) = 2x_1^2 + x_1 x_2 + x_1 + 2 \in \mathbb{F}_3[x_1, x_2]$, it holds $\partial_1 f(x_1, x_2) = x_1 + x_2$. As in the case of $\mathbb{F}_2$, if the degree of f is d, then that of $\partial_k f$ is at most $d - 1$. For $a \in \mathbb{Z}_{\geq 0}$, $\partial_k^a f$ denotes the a-th derivative of f with respect to x_k, and for $\mathbf{a} = (a_1, \ldots, a_n) \in \mathbb{Z}_{\geq 0}^n$, $\partial^{\mathbf{a}} f = \partial_1^{a_1} \circ \cdots \circ \partial_n^{a_n} f$.

4.2   Enumeration Order

We here introduce the order in all inputs $\mathbb{F}_q^n$ used to enumerate a given polynomial in the proposed algorithm. The enumeration of Bouillaguet et al. computes all the outputs of a polynomial consecutively in the order of Gray codes. On the other hand, the proposed algorithm follows a different order from Gray codes, a lexicographic order.

The proposed algorithm enumerates all the inputs in $\mathbb{F}_q^n$ following the a lexicographic order starting from $(0, \ldots, 0)$ to $(q - 1, \ldots, q - 1)$ as follows:

$$(0, \ldots, 0) \rightarrow (0, \ldots, 0, 1) \rightarrow \cdots \rightarrow (0, \ldots, 0, q - 1) \rightarrow$$
$$(0, \ldots, 0, 1, 0) \rightarrow \cdots \rightarrow (0, \ldots, 0, 1, q - 1) \rightarrow$$

$$\vdots$$

$$(q - 1, \ldots, q - 1, 0) \rightarrow \cdots \rightarrow (q - 1, \ldots, q - 1).$$

We then compute all the outputs in this order as follows: We first prepare $f(\mathbf{0})$ as an initial point. For any input with the form of $(x_1, \ldots, x_k, 0, \ldots, 0)$ with $x_k \neq 0$, the output is computed by

$$
\begin{aligned}
f(x_1, \ldots, x_k, 0, \ldots, 0) = \\
f(x_1, \ldots, x_k - 1, 0, \ldots, 0) + \partial_k f(x_1, \ldots, x_k - 1, 0, \ldots, 0),
\end{aligned}
\tag{4.1}
$$

using derivatives $\partial_k f$. If we have the value of $\partial_k f(x_1, \ldots, x_k - 1, 0, \ldots, 0)$, then this computation is clearly feasible since the value of $f(x_1, \ldots, x_k - 1, 0, \ldots, 0)$ is computed before the computation of $f(x_1, \ldots, x_k, 0, \ldots, 0)$ in the lexicographic order. In the rest of this paper, we call by a lexicographic order the order given above including the way of computation with derivatives like Eq. (4.1).

We also use the lexicographic order to enumerate each derivative $\partial^{\mathbf{a}} f$ with $\mathbf{a} \in \mathbb{Z}_{\geq 0}^n$. More specifically, we update $\partial^{\mathbf{a}} f$ as follows:

$$
\begin{aligned}
\partial^{\mathbf{a}} f(x_1, \ldots, x_k, 0, \ldots, 0) = \\
\partial^{\mathbf{a}} f(x_1, \ldots, x_k - 1, 0, \ldots, 0) + \partial^{\mathbf{a} + \mathbf{e}_k} f(x_1, \ldots, x_k - 1, 0, \ldots, 0),
\end{aligned}
\tag{4.2}
$$

as in Eq. (4.1) for any input $(x_1, \ldots, x_k, 0, \ldots, 0) \in A_{\mathbf{a}}$ with $x_k \neq 0$. To realize the enumeration of f, it is not necessary to evaluate $\partial^{\mathbf{a}} f$ at all the inputs in $\mathbb{F}_q^n$. Indeed, in the example on $f \in \mathbb{F}_3[x_1, x_2]$, $\partial_1 f$ and $\partial_2 f$ are only evaluated at $(0, 0), (1, 0)$ and $(0, 0), (0, 1), (1, 0), (1, 1), (2, 0), (2, 1)$, respectively. (See Fig. 1.) For any $\mathbf{a} = (a_1, \ldots, a_n) \in \mathbb{Z}_{\geq 0}^n$ with $|\mathbf{a}| \leq d$ satisfying $a_1, \ldots, a_{\alpha - 1} = 0$ and $a_\alpha \neq 0$, we then can define the subset $A_{\mathbf{a}} \subseteq \mathbb{F}_q^n$ composed by elements at which the proposed algorithm evaluates $\partial^{\mathbf{a}} f$ as follows:

$$
A_{\mathbf{a}} = \{(x_1, \ldots, x_\alpha, 0, \ldots, 0) \mid x_1, \ldots, x_{\alpha - 1} \in \mathbb{F}_q, x_\alpha \in \{0, \ldots, q - a_\alpha - 1\}\}. \tag{4.3}
$$

Lemma 3. *For a given function f in n variables with degree d over $\mathbb{F}_q$, our enumeration described in Eq. (4.2) requires outputs of $\partial^{\mathbf{a}} f$ at $A_{\mathbf{a}}$ for any $\mathbf{a} \in \mathbb{Z}_{\geq 0}^n$ with $|\mathbf{a}| \leq d$.*

Proof. First, we can clearly confirm the following two points:

- For any $\mathbf{a} \in \mathbb{Z}_{\geq 0}^n$, $A_{\mathbf{a}}$ can be covered by the lexicographic order.
- $A_{\mathbf{0}} = \mathbb{F}_q^n$.

The first point means that for any $(x_1, \ldots, x_k, 0, \ldots, 0) \in A_{\mathbf{a}}$ with $x_k \neq 0$, we have $(x_1, \ldots, x_k - 1, 0, \ldots, 0) \in A_{\mathbf{a}}$ from the definition of $A_{\mathbf{a}}$ in Eq. (4.3). The second point satisfies our purpose of evaluating f at all the inputs in $\mathbb{F}_q^n$. We then can confirm that to obtain the outputs of $\partial^{\mathbf{a}} f$ on $A_{\mathbf{a}}$ where $\mathbf{a} = (a_1, \ldots, a_n) \in \mathbb{Z}_{\geq 0}^n$ with $|\mathbf{a}| < d$ satisfying $a_1, \ldots, a_{\alpha - 1} = 0$ and $a_\alpha \neq 0$, our enumeration in the lexicographic order requires the outputs of $\partial^{\mathbf{a} + \mathbf{e}_k} f$ on $A_{\mathbf{a} + \mathbf{e}_k}$ for any $1 \leq k \leq \alpha$ from Eq. (4.2). Note that outputs of $\partial^{\mathbf{a} + \mathbf{e}_k} f$ with $1 \leq k \leq \alpha$ are used only to update $\partial^{\mathbf{a}} f$. From these discussions, we can confirm the correctness of the above statement. $\square$

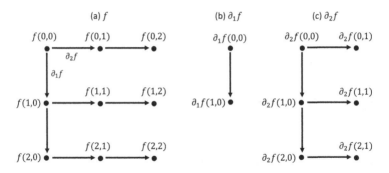

Fig. 1. The order of our proposed enumeration on a polynomial $f \in \mathbb{F}_3[x_1, x_2]$ with degree 2.

We finally prepare some subsets of $A_\mathbf{a}$ to realize our enumeration in the lexicographic order. For any $\mathbf{a} = (a_1, \ldots, a_n) \in \mathbb{Z}_{\geq 0}^n$ with $|\mathbf{a}| \leq d$ satisfying $a_1, \ldots, a_{\alpha-1} = 0$ and $a_\alpha \neq 0$, we define subsets $B_1^\mathbf{a}, \ldots, B_\alpha^\mathbf{a}$ of $A_\mathbf{a}$ as follows:

$$B_1^\mathbf{a} = \{(x_1, 0, \ldots, 0) \mid x_1 \in \mathbb{F}_q\},$$
$$B_i^\mathbf{a} = \{(x_1, \ldots, x_i, 0, \ldots, 0) \mid x_1, \ldots, x_{i-1} \in \mathbb{F}_q, x_i \neq 0\}. \quad (2 \leq i \leq \alpha - 1), \quad (4.4)$$
$$B_\alpha^\mathbf{a} = \{(x_1, \ldots, x_\alpha, 0, \ldots, 0) \mid x_1, \ldots, x_{\alpha-1} \in \mathbb{F}_q, x_\alpha \in \{1, \ldots, q - a_\alpha - 1\}\}.$$

We then have $B_i^\mathbf{a} \cap B_j^\mathbf{a} = \phi$ if $i \neq j$ and $B_1^\mathbf{a} \cup \cdots \cup B_\alpha^\mathbf{a} = A_\mathbf{a}$. In the proposed algorithm given in Subsect. 4.5 below, outputs for inputs in each $B_i^\mathbf{a}$ are stored separately to realize the branching structure due to the lexicographic order. (See Fig. 1.)

Remark 2. This remark shows the difference of our lexicographic order and Gray codes used in the enumeration algorithm of Bouillaguet et al. for a polynomial over the binary field $\mathbb{F}_2$. Figure 2 shows the difference of enumerating all the outputs $f \in \mathbb{F}_2$ in two variables. As displayed in Fig. 2, our enumeration order computes $f(0,1)$ and $f(1,0)$ by adding derivatives into $f(0,0)$ and computes $f(1,1)$ from $f(1,0)$. By contrast, the enumeration of Bouillaguet et al. computes all the outputs in the order $f(0,1)$, $f(0,1)$, $f(0,1)$, $f(0,1)$ successively. These examples indicate that the enumeration order and Gray codes are definitely different even in the case of the binary field.

4.3   Data Structure

Our proposed algorithm uses a different way of holding some data from the enumeration algorithm of Bouillaguet et al. For any $\mathbf{a} = (a_1, \ldots, a_n) \in \mathbb{Z}_{\geq 0}^n$ with $|\mathbf{a}| \leq d$, $D[\mathbf{a}]$ corresponding to the derivative $\partial^\mathbf{a} f$ stores the following values

- $\alpha \ (= \rho(\mathbf{a}))$: the index of the most left nonzero elements of $\mathbf{a}$ (If $\mathbf{a} = \mathbf{0}$, then $\alpha = n$.),

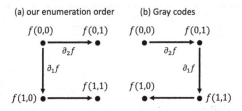

Fig. 2. Comparison of the order to cover all the outputs of $f \in \mathbb{F}_2[x_1, x_2]$ in our enumeration order and Gray codes

- $y_1, \ldots, y_\alpha \in \mathbb{F}_q$: an output of $\partial^{\mathbf{a}} f$ for an input as an element of each $B_1^{\mathbf{a}}, \ldots, B_\alpha^{\mathbf{a}}$,
- $i \in \{1, \ldots, \alpha\}$: the index that indicates that the input is an element of $B_i^{\mathbf{a}}$,
- $\mathbf{t} = (t_1, \ldots, t_n) \in \{0, \ldots, n-1\}^n$, $\mathbf{u} = (u_1, \ldots, u_n) \in \{0, \ldots, q-1\}^n$: two vectors used in the classification of elements of $A_{\mathbf{a}}$ into the subsets $B_1^{\mathbf{a}}, \ldots, B_\alpha^{\mathbf{a}}$.

Compared with the data structure used in the enumeration by Bouillaguet et al., we add some data to realize the enumeration in the lexicographic order given in Subsect. 4.2. Note that these additional data only provide a small cost of memory complexity as discussed in Subsect. 4.6 below.

4.4 Successive Classification of Inputs

We here prepare a subroutine CLASS used in the main algorithm described in Subsect. 4.5 below. This CLASS classifies given elements of $A_{\mathbf{a}}$ into the subsets $B_1^{\mathbf{a}}, \ldots, B_\alpha^{\mathbf{a}}$ defined in Eq. (4.4) successively in the lexicographic order in constant time. This computation is mainly equivalent to the successive computation of the index of the most right nonzero bit for vectors in $\mathbb{F}_q^{n-1}$ in the lexicographic order due to the definition of $B_1^{\mathbf{a}}, \ldots, B_\alpha^{\mathbf{a}}$. The following algorithm is constructed by revising an algorithm for Gray codes proposed in [6].

We first describe a way of successively computing the index of the lowest nonzero bit for vectors in $\mathbb{F}_q^{n-1}$ using a stack as the data structure. A stack is an abstract data type with two main operations as follows: *push* which adds an element to the collection and *pop* which removes the most recently added element. For a stack and $u_1, \ldots, u_{n-1} \in \{0, \ldots, q-1\}$, the computation is realized as follows: The stack initially contains $1, \ldots, n-1$ with the $n-1$ on top and we set $u_1 = \cdots = u_{n-1} = 0$. Next, the top element i is popped off and added into the sequence of the index to be found. If $a_i < q-2$, then the elements $i, \ldots, n-1$ are pushed onto the stack and we increase u_i by one. If $a_i = q - 2$, then the elements $i+1, \ldots, n-1$ are pushed onto the stack and we set $u_i = 0$. Comparing this algorithm with the algorithm proposed in [6], we introduce $u_1, \ldots, u_{n-1}$ to represent the structure of the base-q positional system.

In the above algorithm, the stack can be replaced by an array $t_1, \ldots, t_n \in \{0, \ldots, n-1\}$. For this array, t_j denotes the element below j on the stack if j is on the stack, t_j is set as $j - 1$ if j is not on the stack, and t_n points to the top

Algorithm 4. CLASS $(\mathbf{a} = (a_1, \ldots, a_n), \alpha, (t_1, \ldots, t_n), (u_1, \ldots, u_n))$

1: **if** $u_n < q - a_\alpha - 1$ **then**
2:    $i \leftarrow n$
3:    $u_n \leftarrow u_n + 1$
4: **else**
5:    $i \leftarrow t_n$
6:    **if** $\alpha + i - n = 0$ **then**
7:       **return** $0, (t_1, \ldots, t_n), (u_1, \ldots, u_n)$
8:    **end if**
9:    $u_n \leftarrow 0$
10:    $t_n \leftarrow n - 1$
11:    **if** $u_i < q - 2$ **then**
12:       $u_i \leftarrow u_i + 1$
13:    **else**
14:       $t_{i+1} \leftarrow t_i$
15:       $t_i \leftarrow i - 1$
16:       $u_i \leftarrow 0$
17:    **end if**
18: **end if**
19: **return** $\alpha + i - n, (t_1, \ldots, t_n), (u_1, \ldots, u_n)$

element of the stack. By following these rules, the way of updating the stack is changed as follows: If $u_i < q - 2$, then we set $t_n = n - 1$. On the other hand, in the case of $u_i = q - 2$, we set $t_n = n - 1$, $t_{i+1} = t_i$, and $t_i = i - 1$ since i is removed from the top and $i + 1, \ldots, n - 1$ are pushed onto the top.

Then, our classification algorithm is constructed by combining the above algorithm with $t_1, \ldots, t_n$ and $u_1, \ldots, u_{n-1}$ and one counter $u_n \in \{0, \ldots, q - 1\}$ to represent the structure of $A_{\mathbf{a}}$. In $A_{\mathbf{a}}$, only the $D[\mathbf{a}].\alpha$-th bit is carried up by $q - a_{D[\mathbf{a}].\alpha}$ from the definition, and u_n represents the value of this $D[\mathbf{a}].\alpha$-th bit. In the case where $u_n = q - a_{D[\mathbf{a}].\alpha} - 1$, we carry up the $D[\mathbf{a}].\alpha$-th bit, that is, we update $t_1, \ldots, t_n$ and $u_1, \ldots, u_{n-1}$ and set $u_n = 0$. By contrast, in the case where $u_n < q - a_{D[\mathbf{a}].\alpha} - 1$, we increase u_n by one and output $D[\mathbf{a}].\alpha$ as the index of $B_1^{\mathbf{a}}, \ldots, B_{D[\mathbf{a}].\alpha}^{\mathbf{a}}$.

Finally, we describe our classification algorithm CLASS. After two arrays $t_1, \ldots, t_n$ and $u_1, \ldots, u_n$ are initially set as $(0, 1, \ldots, n-1)$ and $(0, \ldots, 0)$, respectively, following the above discussion, these arrays are updated each time through CLASS. Other than these arrays, $\mathbf{a} = (a_1, \ldots, a_n)$ and α following the notation in Subsect. 4.3 are included in the inputs. The outputs are given as the classification index of $B_i^{\mathbf{a}}$ and the updated two arrays. (See Algorithm 4 for more details.)

4.5 Our Enumeration Algorithm

This subsection describes the proposed efficient enumeration algorithm over finite fields $\mathbb{F}_q$. As in the enumeration of Bouillaguet et al. in Subsect. 3.2, the proposed enumeration algorithm is composed of three functions, namely MAIN,

INIT, and NEXT. In the following, we will describe these three algorithms. See
Algorithm 5, 6, and 7 for more details.

Algorithm 5. MAIN(f)

1: $D \leftarrow \text{INIT}(D, f, \mathbf{0})$
2: **for** $\mathbf{x} \in \mathbb{F}_q^n$ (in the lexicographic order) **do**
3:     "$f(\mathbf{x}) = D[\mathbf{0}].y_{D[\mathbf{0}].i}$"
4:     $D \leftarrow \text{NEXT}(D, \mathbf{0})$
5: **end for**

Algorithm 6. INIT($D, f, \mathbf{a}$)

1: $D[\mathbf{a}].\alpha \leftarrow \rho(\mathbf{a})$
2: $D[\mathbf{a}].\mathbf{t} \leftarrow (0, 1, \ldots, n-1)$
3: $D[\mathbf{a}].\mathbf{u} \leftarrow (0, \ldots, 0)$
4: $D[\mathbf{a}].i \leftarrow 1$
5: **if** $|\mathbf{a}| < d$ **then**
6:     $D[\mathbf{a}].y_1 \leftarrow f(\mathbf{0})$
7:     **for** $k = 1, \ldots, \alpha$ **do**
8:         $D \leftarrow \text{INIT}(D, \partial_k f, \mathbf{a} + \mathbf{e}_k)$
9:     **end for**
10: **else**
11:     $D[\mathbf{a}].y_1, \ldots, y_\alpha \leftarrow f(\mathbf{0})$
12: **end if**
13: **return** D

Algorithm 7. NEXT($D, \mathbf{a} = (a_1, \ldots, a_n)$)

1: $D[\mathbf{a}].i, D[\mathbf{a}].\mathbf{t}, D[\mathbf{a}].\mathbf{u} \leftarrow \text{CLASS}(\mathbf{a}, D[\mathbf{a}].\alpha, D[\mathbf{a}].\mathbf{t}, D[\mathbf{a}].\mathbf{u})$
2: **if** $|\mathbf{a}| < d$ and $D[\mathbf{a}].i \neq 0$ **then**
3:     $i' \leftarrow D[\mathbf{a} + \mathbf{e}_{(D[\mathbf{a}].i)}].i$
4:     $D[\mathbf{a}].y_{(D[\mathbf{a}].i)} \leftarrow D[\mathbf{a}].y_{i'} + D[\mathbf{a} + \mathbf{e}_{(D[\mathbf{a}].i)}].y_{i'}$
5:     $D \leftarrow \text{NEXT}(D, \mathbf{a} + \mathbf{e}_{(D[\mathbf{a}].i)})$
6: **end if**
7: **return** D

MAIN. From Algorithm 1, our main algorithm differs in the following two points:
First, we cover all the inputs in $\mathbb{F}_q^n$ in the lexicographic order. Second, from the
definition, $D[\mathbf{0}]$ holds n outputs $y_1, \ldots, y_n$ and we select one output from them as
an output of f. The value $D[\mathbf{0}].i$ indicates that $y_{D[\mathbf{0}].i}$ is updated in the preceding
NEXT as an output for an input $\mathbf{x}$. Thus, we take $y_{D[\mathbf{0}].i}$ as an output in line 3.

INIT. As in Algorithm 2, the function INIT sets initial values for $D[\mathbf{a}]$. Line 1
sets α following the aforementioned definition. Line 2–3 set initial values for two
arrays $\mathbf{t}$ and $\mathbf{u}$ according to the description in Subsect. 4.4. Because $\mathbf{0} \in B_1^\mathbf{a}$, we
set $i = 1$ and store $f(\mathbf{0})$ in y_1. If $|\mathbf{a}| = d$, then we store $f(\mathbf{0})$ in $y_1, \ldots, y_\alpha$ for
convenience. In the case where $|\mathbf{a}| < d$, the function proceeds to $\partial_1 f, \ldots, \partial_\alpha f$
in line 8, because, for any element of $A_\mathbf{a}$, the last $n - \alpha$ values are always zeros
from the definition in (4.3).

NEXT. First, we show the basic strategy of the function NEXT. For any $\mathbf{a}$, we shift over an input $\mathbf{x}$ in $A_{\mathbf{a}}$ following the lexicographic order and store an output for the input in one of $y_1, \ldots, y_\alpha$ following the definition of $B_1^{\mathbf{a}}, \ldots, B_\alpha^{\mathbf{a}}$. In NEXT, every time updating outputs of $\partial^{\mathbf{a}} f$ using $\partial^{\mathbf{a}+\mathbf{e}_k} f$ as in Eq. (4.2) by NEXT$(D, \mathbf{a})$, we call NEXT$(D, \mathbf{a}+\mathbf{e}_k)$ and update outputs of $\partial^{\mathbf{a}+\mathbf{e}_k} f$. By doing so, we always have the following: When we try to add $\partial^{\mathbf{a}+\mathbf{e}_k} f(\mathbf{x})$ into $\partial^{\mathbf{a}} f(\mathbf{x})$ for the update of $\partial^{\mathbf{a}} f$, the output $\partial^{\mathbf{a}+\mathbf{e}_k} f(\mathbf{x})$ for $\mathbf{x}$ is the value updated in the last NEXT$(D, \mathbf{a}+\mathbf{e}_k)$. This is because every $A_{\mathbf{a}}$ is covered following the same order.

We then show a practical way of realizing the update like Eq. (4.2). The update requires two indices i and i' that denote

$$(x_1, \ldots, x_i, 0, \ldots, 0) \in B_i^{\mathbf{a}}, \ (x_1, \ldots, x_i - 1, 0, \ldots, 0) \in B_{i'}^{\mathbf{a}}.$$

If we have these two values, then the update is realized as follows:

$$D[\mathbf{a}].y_i \leftarrow D[\mathbf{a}].y_{i'} + D[\mathbf{a}+\mathbf{e}_k].y_{i'}.$$

From the definition, this i is represented as $D[\mathbf{a}].i$. Furthermore, from the above discussion, this i' is equal to the index i of $D[\mathbf{a}+\mathbf{e}_k]$ in the last time updating.

We finally explain the construction of Algorithm 7. We first determine the index $D[\mathbf{a}].i$ by using the classification algorithm CLASS described in Subsect. 4.4. In line 2–5, we update $D[\mathbf{a}].y_{(D[\mathbf{a}].i)}$, and the correctness of this part directly follows the aforementioned discussion. If $|\mathbf{a}| = d$, we do not update $D[\mathbf{a}].y_{(D[\mathbf{a}].i)}$ in line 2–5, because $\partial^{\mathbf{a}} f$ is constant. However, even in this case, we compute $D[\mathbf{a}].i$ for the correctness of NEXT$(D, \mathbf{a}')$ with $|\mathbf{a}'| = d - 1$.

4.6   Complexity

This subsection considers the time and space complexities of the initial part and the enumeration part of the proposed algorithm in Subsect. 4.5.

Theorem 2. *For a single polynomial f in n variables of degree d over $\mathbb{F}_q$ with a prime number q, the enumeration algorithm proposed in Subsect. 4.5 can be performed in $O(d \cdot q^n)$ operations after an initialization phase of negligible complexity $O\left(\binom{n+d}{d}^2\right)$ using $O\left(\log(q \cdot n) \cdot n \cdot \binom{n+d}{d}\right)$ bits memory.*

Proof. We first consider the time complexity of INIT. The computation of derivatives $\partial_k f$ in line 8 is clearly dominant in terms of the time complexity. This means that the time complexity of INIT is estimated as that of computing $\partial^{\mathbf{a}} f$ for any $\mathbf{a} \in \mathbb{Z}_{\geq 0}^n$ with $|\mathbf{a}| \leq d$. We here estimate that the number of $\mathbf{a}$ satisfying the condition of $|\mathbf{a}| \leq d$ is $\binom{n+d}{d}$ and the number of operations required to compute derivatives is at most $O\left(\binom{n+d}{d}\right)$. Therefore, the time complexity of the initial phase is given as $O\left(\binom{n+d}{d}^2\right)$ over $\mathbb{F}_q$.

We then estimate the time complexity of the enumeration part. The function NEXT can be performed in constant time excluding the recursive part in line 5, since the function CLASS is clearly completed by constant operations from Algorithm 4. Therefore, the time complexity of $\mathrm{NEXT}(D, \mathbf{0})$ is given as $O(d)$, and that of the enumeration part is estimated by $O(d \cdot q^n)$.

Finally, the space complexity of the proposed algorithm is discussed. Through the whole algorithm, for each $\mathbf{a}$, $D[\mathbf{a}]$ consumes $O\left(\log\left(q \cdot n\right) \cdot n\right)$ bit memory from the description in Subsect. 4.3. Therefore, the space complexity consumed by D is given as $O\left(\log\left(q \cdot n\right) \cdot n \cdot \binom{n+d}{d}\right)$. Other than memory consumption by D, we consider the space of derivatives $\partial^{\mathbf{a}} f$ consumed in INIT. From the description of Algorithm 6, we prepare the memory that can store polynomials of degree d to degree 0 simultaneously. The size of this memory is estimated as follows:

$$\log_2 q \cdot \left(\binom{n+d}{d} + \cdots + \binom{n+1}{1} + 1\right) = O\left(\log q \cdot \binom{n+d}{d}\right),$$

when $n \to \infty$. In conclusion, the space complexity of the proposed enumeration algorithm is given as $O\left(\log\left(q \cdot n\right) \cdot n \cdot \binom{n+d}{d}\right)$.   □

The comparison between these complexities and those of the enumeration algorithm of Bouillaguet et al. reveals that the proposed enumeration algorithm is as efficient as that of Bouillaguet et al. at the expense of a small amount $(O(n \log n))$ of memory consumption.

Remark 3 (Case of $q = p^r$). In this paper, we only discuss the case in which the number q of elements of the finite field is a prime number. This remark explains a method to apply the enumeration algorithm to the case of $q = p^r$ with a prime number p and a positive integer r.

One polynomial in n variables over $\mathbb{F}_{p^r}$ can be clearly regarded as r polynomials in $n \cdot r$ variables over $\mathbb{F}_p$ (i.e., if $\theta_1, \ldots, \theta_r$ are basis of $\mathbb{F}_{p^r}$ over $\mathbb{F}_p$, for each variable x_i over $\mathbb{F}_{p^r}$, we set r variables $x_1^{(i)}, \ldots, x_r^{(i)}$ over $\mathbb{F}_p$ satisfying $x_i = \sum_{j=1}^{r} x_j^{(i)} \theta_j$). After performing this transformation, our enumeration algorithm can be applied to each one of the resulting r polynomials over $\mathbb{F}_p$. Then, the time complexity is given as $O\left(r \cdot d \cdot p^{r \cdot n}\right) = O\left(r \cdot d \cdot q^n\right)$, whereas the space complexity is given as $O\left(r \cdot \log\left(p \cdot n \cdot r\right) \cdot n \cdot r \cdot \binom{n \cdot r + d}{d}\right)$.

Remark 4 (Application to solving polynomial equations). By using the method proposed in [9], our enumeration algorithm can be applied to solve systems of polynomial equations, and its complexity is estimated as $O\left(d^2 \cdot \log n \cdot q^n\right)$. (See Appendix A.) Unfortunately, this is not the theoretically best algorithm for solving multivariate non-linear systems, since Lokshtanov et al. [17] proposed an algorithm over general finite fields with the time complexity $O\left(q^{n \cdot (1-\epsilon)}\right)$, where $\epsilon > 0$. However, our method of solving non-linear systems would be more practical than the algorithm proposed by Lokshtanov et al. due to our simple structure as in the FES algorithm proposed by Bouillaguet et al. [9]. We leave optimizing our implementation as our future work.

5 Conclusion

This paper proposes a novel enumeration algorithm over finite fields $\mathbb{F}_q$ with a prime number q. Given a single-degree-d polynomial in n variables over $\mathbb{F}_q$, the proposed algorithm evaluates the given function at all the inputs with the time complexity $O(d \cdot q^n)$. The proposed enumeration algorithm is constructed by using a lexicographic order instead of Gray codes used in the enumeration algorithm by Bouillaguet et al. over $\mathbb{F}_2$. Compared with the enumeration algorithm by Bouillaguet et al., the proposed method achieves the equivalent efficiency with a small cost of memory consumption. Note that this small cost of the memory complexity is caused by our brunching structure of enumeration due to our lexicographic order. Furthermore, the proposed algorithm can be easily applied to the case where q is a prime power.

This paper discusses only the theoretical side, and thus one of our future works is to realize an efficient implementation of the proposed algorithm.

Acknowledgement. This work was supported by JST CREST Grant Number JPMJCR2113, Japan, and JSPS KAKENHI Grant Number JP22KJ0554, Japan.

A Application to Solving Polynomial Equations

In this section, we consider finding common zeros of m polynomials $f_1, \ldots, f_m$ in n variables with degree d. This section first recalls a way of applying the enumeration algorithm of Bouillaguet et al. described in Subsect. 3.2, and shows that our enumeration algorithm in Subsect. 4.5 is also applicable. We here only consider the case of $n = m$ case, because if $n > m$, then $n - m$ variables can be specified, and if $n < m$, then we can focus on n equations as they should have a constant number of solutions.

We here roughly describe the way of applying an enumeration algorithm to find common zeros of $f_1, \ldots, f_n$ proposed in [9]. Let Z_i be the set of common zeros of $f_1, \ldots, f_i$, and then it is clear that Z_n is the set of the solutions of the system. For an integer $1 \leq k \leq n$, the proposed algorithm is described as follows:

(1) Find Z_k using the enumeration algorithm on each $f_1, \ldots, f_k$.
(2) Compute $Z_{k+1}, \ldots, Z_n$ one by one by substituting each value of Z_i for f_{i+1}.

The enumeration algorithm in Sect. 4 can be clearly applied to find common zeros of $f_1, \ldots, f_n$ over $\mathbb{F}_q$ in a similar manner. In the following, we estimate the time complexity of solving a system. As estimated in [9], the time complexity of the first step is estimated by $O(k \cdot d \cdot q^n)$ from the statement of Theorem 2. Furthermore, because the expected cardinality of Z_i is q^{n-i}, the time complexity of the second step is given as $\sum_{i=k}^{n-1} \binom{n+d}{d} \cdot q^{n-i} \approx O\left(\binom{n+d}{d} \cdot q^{n-k}\right)$ due to the complexity of the classical evaluation described in Sect. 2. Therefore, the optimal k minimizing the complexity is given by solving $k \cdot d \cdot q^n = \binom{n+d}{d} \cdot q^{n-k}$, and k is estimated by $d \log n$ when $n \to \infty$. By substituting $k = d \log n$ in $k \cdot d \cdot q^n$, the whole complexity of solving a polynomial system is given as $O\left(d^2 \cdot \log n \cdot q^n\right)$ over $\mathbb{F}_q$.

B   Toy Example of Our Enumeration

We give an example of the behavior of the proposed enumeration algorithm on a concrete function. We take $f = x_1^2 + x_1 x_2 + x_2 + 2 \in \mathbb{F}_3[x_1, x_2]$ with degree $d = 2$ as an input. Then, derivatives of f are computed as follows:

$$\partial_1 f = 2x_1 + x_2 + 1,$$
$$\partial_2 f = x_1 + 1,$$
$$\partial_1^2 f = 2,$$
$$\partial_1 \partial_2 f = 1,$$
$$\partial_2^2 f = 0.$$

From these derivatives, for any $\mathbf{a} \in \mathbb{Z}_{\geq 0}$ with $|\mathbf{a}| \leq d = 2$, D is obtained as follows after $\text{INIT}(D, f, \mathbf{0}, \mathbf{0})$ in line 1 of Algorithm 5:

$$D[(0,0)].\,(\alpha, \mathbf{t}, \mathbf{u}, (y_1, y_2), i) = (2, (0,1), (0,0), (2, \cdot), 1),$$
$$D[(1,0)].\,(\alpha, \mathbf{t}, \mathbf{u}, y_1, i) = (1, (0,1), (0,0), 1, 1),$$
$$D[(0,1)].\,(\alpha, \mathbf{t}, \mathbf{u}, (y_1, y_2), i) = (2, (0,1), (0,0), (1, \cdot), 1),$$
$$D[(2,0)].\,(\alpha, \mathbf{t}, \mathbf{u}, y_1, i) = (1, (0,1), (0,0), 2, 1),$$
$$D[(1,1)].\,(\alpha, \mathbf{t}, \mathbf{u}, y_1, i) = (1, (0,1), (0,0), 1, 1),$$
$$D[(0,2)].\,(\alpha, \mathbf{t}, \mathbf{u}, (y_1, y_2), i) = (2, (0,1), (0,0), (0,0), 1).$$

Note that, for the case of $\mathbf{a} = (0,0)$ and $(0,1)$, $D[\mathbf{a}].y_2$ is not determined in $\text{INIT}(D, f, \mathbf{0}, \mathbf{0})$. In the following, we show how D is updated for each $\mathbf{x}$ in line 2–5 of Algorithm 5 after the aforementioned initialization phase. We here omit $D[\mathbf{a}].\alpha$ because this value is not changed through the algorithm. We also omit values stored in $D[(2,0)]$, $D[(1,1)]$, and $D[(0,2)]$ because $D[\mathbf{a}].i$ with $|\mathbf{a}| = 2$ does not change from 1 in this case due to the relationship of q and d. Here, D is updated as follows:

$\mathbf{x} = (0,1),$
$$D[(0,0)].\,(\mathbf{t}, \mathbf{u}, (y_1, y_2), i) = ((0,1), (0,1), (2,0), 2),$$
$$D[(1,0)].\,(\mathbf{t}, \mathbf{u}, y_1, i) = ((0,1), (0,0), 1, 1),$$
$$D[(0,1)].\,(\mathbf{t}, \mathbf{u}, (y_1, y_2), i) = ((0,1), (0,1), (1,1), 2),$$

$\mathbf{x} = (0,2),$
$$D[(0,0)].\,(\mathbf{t}, \mathbf{u}, (y_1, y_2), i) = ((0,1), (0,2), (2,1), 2),$$
$$D[(1,0)].\,(\mathbf{t}, \mathbf{u}, y_1, i) = ((0,1), (0,0), 1, 1),$$
$$D[(0,1)].\,(\mathbf{t}, \mathbf{u}, (y_1, y_2), i) = ((0,1), (1,0), (2,1), 1),$$

$\mathbf{x} = (1,0),$
$$D[(0,0)].\,(\mathbf{t}, \mathbf{u}, (y_1, y_2), i) = ((0,1), (1,0), (0,1), 1),$$
$$D[(1,0)].\,(\mathbf{t}, \mathbf{u}, y_1, i) = ((0,1), (0,1), 0, 1),$$
$$D[(0,1)].\,(\mathbf{t}, \mathbf{u}, (y_1, y_2), i) = ((0,1), (1,0), (2,1), 1),$$

$\mathbf{x} = (1, 1),$

$$D[(0,0)].\, (\mathbf{t}, \mathbf{u}, (y_1, y_2), i) = ((0, 1), (1, 1), (0, 2), 2),$$
$$D[(1,0)].\, (\mathbf{t}, \mathbf{u}, y_1, i) = ((0, 1), (0, 1), 0, 1),$$
$$D[(0,1)].\, (\mathbf{t}, \mathbf{u}, (y_1, y_2), i) = ((0, 1), (1, 1), (2, 2), 2),$$

$\mathbf{x} = (1, 2),$

$$D[(0,0)].\, (\mathbf{t}, \mathbf{u}, (y_1, y_2), i) = ((0, 1), (1, 2), (0, 1), 2),$$
$$D[(1,0)].\, (\mathbf{t}, \mathbf{u}, y_1, i) = ((0, 1), (0, 1), 0, 1),$$
$$D[(0,1)].\, (\mathbf{t}, \mathbf{u}, (y_1, y_2), i) = ((0, 0), (0, 0), (0, 2), 1),$$

$\mathbf{x} = (2, 0),$

$$D[(0,0)].\, (\mathbf{t}, \mathbf{u}, (y_1, y_2), i) = ((0, 0), (0, 0), (0, 1), 1),$$
$$D[(1,0)].\, (\mathbf{t}, \mathbf{u}, y_1, i) = ((0, 1), (0, 1), 0, 0),$$
$$D[(0,1)].\, (\mathbf{t}, \mathbf{u}, (y_1, y_2), i) = ((0, 0), (0, 0), (0, 2), 1),$$

$\mathbf{x} = (2, 1),$

$$D[(0,0)].\, (\mathbf{t}, \mathbf{u}, (y_1, y_2), i) = ((0, 0), (0, 1), (0, 0), 2),$$
$$D[(1,0)].\, (\mathbf{t}, \mathbf{u}, y_1, i) = ((0, 1), (0, 1), 0, 0),$$
$$D[(0,1)].\, (\mathbf{t}, \mathbf{u}, (y_1, y_2), i) = ((0, 0), (0, 1), (0, 0), 2),$$

$\mathbf{x} = (2, 2),$

$$D[(0,0)].\, (\mathbf{t}, \mathbf{u}, (y_1, y_2), i) = ((0, 0), (0, 2), (0, 0), 2),$$
$$D[(1,0)].\, (\mathbf{t}, \mathbf{u}, y_1, i) = ((0, 1), (0, 1), 0, 0),$$
$$D[(0,1)].\, (\mathbf{t}, \mathbf{u}, (y_1, y_2), i) = ((0, 0), (0, 1), (0, 0), 0).$$

Then, by seeing $D[(0,0)].\, \left(y_{D[(0,0)].i}\right)$ for each $\mathbf{x} \in \mathbb{F}_3^2$, one can confirm that the proposed algorithm enumerates the outputs of f correctly as follows:

$\mathbf{x}$	$(0,0)$	$(0,1)$	$(0,2)$	$(1,0)$	$(1,1)$	$(1,2)$	$(2,0)$	$(2,1)$	$(2,2)$
$f(\mathbf{x})$	2	0	1	0	2	1	0	0	0

C   Magma Code

We here provides a code of the proposed enumeration algorithm in Magma [7]. Note that this implementation is not an optimized one.

Listing 1.1. Magma code for the proposed algorithm

```
1 //q: the number of elements of the finite field
2 //n: the number of variables
3 //f: a given polynomial
4 //d: the degree of f
5
```

```
6  // Given a polynomial f and an index k,
7  // compute the k-th derivative of f.
8  function deriv(f,k)
9      P<[x]>:=Parent(f);
10     n:=#x;
11     Hom := hom<P->P|[x[i]: i in [1..k-1]] cat [x[k]+1] cat [x[i]:
           i in [k+1..n]]>;
12     ff:=Hom(f)-f;
13     return ff;
14 end function;
15
16 // Given a vector a representing the derivative \partial^a f and the
       degree d,
17 // compute the index of data structures corresponding to the
       derivatives of a.
18 function accD(a,d)
19     n:=#a;
20     b:=0;
21     c:=0;
22     for i in [1..n] do
23         b:=b+ &+([Binomial((n-i)+(d-c-j),(d-c-j)):j in [0..a[i
               ]-1]] cat [0]);
24         c:=c+a[i];
25     end for;
26     if c gt d then
27         return 0;
28     end if;
29     return b+1;
30 end function;
31
32 // Given a vector a,
33 // output the index of the most left nonzero bit of a.
34 function bit_a(a)
35     n:=#a;
36     for i in [1..n] do
37         if a[i] ne 0 then
38             return i;
39         end if;
40     end for;
41     return n;
42 end function;
43
44 //a: a vector representing the derivative \partial^a f
45 //D: outputs y_1,...y_\alpha for any a
46 //aa: \alpha=\rho(a) for any a
47 //ii: indices D[a].i for any a
48 //tt: vectors D[a].t for any a
49 //uu: vectors D[a].u for any a
50
51 function CLASS(q,n,d,a,aa,tt,uu)
52     k:=accD(a,d);
53     if uu[k][n] lt q-a[aa[k]]-1 then
54         i:=n;
55         uu[k][n]:=uu[k][n]+1;
56     else
```

```
57          i:=tt[k][n];
58          if aa[k]+i-n eq 0 then
59              return 0, tt, uu;
60          end if;
61          uu[k][n]:=0;
62          tt[k][n]:=n-1;
63          if uu[k][i] lt q-2 then
64              uu[k][i]:=uu[k][i]+1;
65          else
66              tt[k][i+1]:=tt[k][i];
67              tt[k][i]:=i-1;
68              uu[k][i]:=0;
69          end if;
70      end if;
71      return aa[k]+i-n, tt, uu;
72  end function;
73
74  function INIT(f,a,D,d,aa)
75      P<[x]>:=Parent(f);
76      n:=#x;
77      aa[accD(a,d)]:=bit_a(a);
78      if &+[a[i]:i in [1..n]] lt d then
79          D[accD(a,d)][1]:=Evaluate(f,[0: i in [1..n]]);
80          for k in [1..aa[accD(a,d)]] do
81              ab:=a;
82              ab[k]:=ab[k]+1;
83              D,aa:=INIT(deriv(f,k),ab,D,d,aa);
84          end for;
85      else
86          DD:=Evaluate(f,[0: i in [1..n]]);
87          for i in [1..aa[accD(a,d)]] do
88              D[accD(a,d)][i]:=DD;
89          end for;
90      end if;
91      return D,aa;
92  end function;
93
94  function NEXT(q,n,d,D,a,aa,ii,tt,uu)
95      ii[accD(a,d)],tt,uu:=CLASS(q,n,d,a,aa,tt,uu);
96      if &+[a[i]:i in [1..n]] lt d and ii[accD(a,d)] ne 0 then
97          a1:=a;
98          a1[ii[accD(a,d)]]:=a1[ii[accD(a,d)]]+1;
99          i1:=ii[accD(a1,d)];
100         D[accD(a,d)][ii[accD(a,d)]]:=D[accD(a,d)][i1]+D[accD(a1,d)
                ][i1];
101         D,ii,tt,uu:=NEXT(q,n,d,D,a1,aa,ii,tt,uu);
102     end if;
103     return D,ii,tt,uu;
104 end function;
105
106 function MAIN(q,n,d,f)
107     P:=Parent(f);
108     K:=BaseRing(P);
109     D:=ZeroMatrix(K,Binomial(n+d,d),n);
110     aa:=[0:i in [1..Binomial(n+d,d)]];
```

```
111    ii:=[1:i in [1..Binomial(n+d,d)]];
112    tt:=[[0..n-1]:i in [1..Binomial(n+d,d)]];
113    uu:=[[0: i in [1..n]]:i in [1..Binomial(n+d,d)]];
114    D,aa:=INIT(f,[0:i in [1..n]],D,d,aa);
115    solution:=[];
116    for i in [0..q^n-1] do
117        Append(~solution,D[accD([0:i in [1..n]],d)][ii[accD([0:i in
               [1..n]],d)]]);
118        D,ii,tt,uu:=NEXT(q,n,d,D,[0:i in [1..n]],aa,ii,tt,uu);
119    end for;
120    return solution;
121 end function;
```

References

1. Bettale, L., Faugère, J.-C., Perret, L.: Hybrid approach for solving multivariate systems over finite fields. J. Math. Cryptol. **3**, 177–197 (2009)

2. Beullens, W.: Improved cryptanalysis of UOV and rainbow. In: Canteaut, A., Standaert, F.-X. (eds.) EUROCRYPT 2021. LNCS, vol. 12696, pp. 348–373. Springer, Cham (2021). https://doi.org/10.1007/978-3-030-77870-5_13

3. Beullens, W.: MAYO: practical post-quantum signatures from oil-and-vinegar maps. In: AlTawy, R., Hülsing, A. (eds.) SAC 2021. LNCS, vol. 13203, pp. 355–376. Springer, Cham (2022). https://doi.org/10.1007/978-3-030-99277-4_17

4. Beullens, W., Campos, F., Celi, S., Hess, B., Kannwischer, M.: MAYO specification (2023). https://pqmayo.org/assets/specs/mayo.pdf

5. Billet, O., Gilbert, H.: Cryptanalysis of rainbow. In: De Prisco, R., Yung, M. (eds.) SCN 2006. LNCS, vol. 4116, pp. 336–347. Springer, Heidelberg (2006). https://doi.org/10.1007/11832072_23

6. Bitner, J.R., Ehrlich, G., Reingold, E.M.: Efficient generation of the binary reflected Gray code and its applications. Commun. ACM **19**(9), 517–521 (1976)

7. Bosma, W., Cannon, J., Playoust, C.: The Magma algebra system. I. The user language. J. Symb. Comput. **24**(3–4), 235–265 (1997)

8. Bouillaguet, C.: Boolean polynomial evaluation for the masses. Cryptology ePrint Archive, Paper 2022/1412 (2022). https://eprint.iacr.org/2022/1412

9. Bouillaguet, C., et al.: Fast exhaustive search for polynomial systems in $\mathbb{F}_2$. In: Mangard, S., Standaert, F.-X. (eds.) CHES 2010. LNCS, vol. 6225, pp. 203–218. Springer, Heidelberg (2010). https://doi.org/10.1007/978-3-642-15031-9_14

10. Bouillaguet, C., Cheng, C.-M., Chou, T., Niederhagen, R., Yang, B.-Y.: Fast exhaustive search for quadratic systems in $\mathbb{F}_2$ on FPGAs. In: Lange, T., Lauter, K., Lisoněk, P. (eds.) SAC 2013. LNCS, vol. 8282, pp. 205–222. Springer, Heidelberg (2014). https://doi.org/10.1007/978-3-662-43414-7_11

11. Courtois, N., Klimov, A., Patarin, J., Shamir, A.: Efficient algorithms for solving overdefined systems of multivariate polynomial equations. In: Preneel, B. (ed.) EUROCRYPT 2000. LNCS, vol. 1807, pp. 392–407. Springer, Heidelberg (2000). https://doi.org/10.1007/3-540-45539-6_27

12. Furue, H., Ikematsu, Y., Kiyomura, Y., Takagi, T.: A new variant of unbalanced oil and vinegar using quotient ring: QR-UOV. In: Tibouchi, M., Wang, H. (eds.) ASIACRYPT 2021. LNCS, vol. 13093, pp. 187–217. Springer, Cham (2021). https://doi.org/10.1007/978-3-030-92068-5_7

13. Furue, H., Kudo, M.: Polynomial XL: a variant of the XL algorithm using Macaulay matrices over polynomial rings. Cryptology ePrint Archive, Paper 2021/1609 (2021). https://eprint.iacr.org/2021/1609

14. Garey, M.-R., Johnson, D.-S.: Computers and Intractability: A Guide to the Theory of NP-Completeness. W. H. Freeman (1979)

15. Goubin, L., Courtois, N.T.: Cryptanalysis of the TTM cryptosystem. In: Okamoto, T. (ed.) ASIACRYPT 2000. LNCS, vol. 1976, pp. 44–57. Springer, Heidelberg (2000). https://doi.org/10.1007/3-540-44448-3_4

16. Joux, A., Vitse, V.: A crossbred algorithm for solving Boolean polynomial systems. In: Kaczorowski, J., Pieprzyk, J., Pomykała, J. (eds.) NuTMiC 2017. LNCS, vol. 10737, pp. 3–21. Springer, Cham (2018). https://doi.org/10.1007/978-3-319-76620-1_1

17. Lokshtanov, D., Paturi, R., Tamaki, S., Williams, R.R., Yu, H.: Beating brute force for systems of polynomial equations over finite fields. In: SODA 2017, pp. 2190–2202. SIAM (2017)

18. NIST: Post-quantum cryptography CSRC. https://csrc.nist.gov/Projects/post-quantum-cryptography/post-quantum-cryptography-standardization

19. Shor, P.W.: Polynomial-time algorithms for prime factorization and discrete logarithms on a quantum computer. SIAM J. Comput. **26**(5), 1484–1509 (1997)

20. Tao, C., Petzoldt, A., Ding, J.: Efficient key recovery for all HFE signature variants. In: Malkin, T., Peikert, C. (eds.) CRYPTO 2021. LNCS, vol. 12825, pp. 70–93. Springer, Cham (2021). https://doi.org/10.1007/978-3-030-84242-0_4

21. Verbel, J., Baena, J., Cabarcas, D., Perlner, R., Smith-Tone, D.: On the complexity of "superdetermined" Minrank instances. In: Ding, J., Steinwandt, R. (eds.) PQCrypto 2019. LNCS, vol. 11505, pp. 167–186. Springer, Cham (2019). https://doi.org/10.1007/978-3-030-25510-7_10

22. Yang, B.-Y., Wang, W.-J., Yang, S.-Y., Miou, C.-S., Cheng, C.-M.: Fast exhaustive search for polynomial systems over $\mathbb{F}_3$. Cryptology ePrint Archive, Paper 2023/731 (2023). https://eprint.iacr.org/2023/731

DME: A Full Encryption, Signature and KEM Multivariate Public Key Cryptosystem

Ignacio Luengo[(✉)], Martín Avendaño, and Pilar Coscojuela

Department of Algebra, Geometry and Topology, Faculty of Mathematics,
Universidad Complutense de Madrid, Madrid, Spain
{iluengo,mavend01,picoscoj}@ucm.es

Abstract. Multivariate public key cryptography is one of the most studied techniques used in post-quantum cryptography [21,24,28]. In [22] we introduced a new multivariate scheme DME that is based in the composition of linear and non linear maps as many other multivariate schemes, the main difference with other schemes is that the nonlinear components have very high degree and it can be used for KEM and signature. In this paper we present a new version of DME [23] that is simpler than the original in the sense that it uses only two fields $\mathbb{F}_q$ and $\mathbb{F}_{q^2}$ instead of three. The new design allows us to increase the number of exponentials to 3, 4 or more and it gives more resistance to decomposition attacks [18,35] while keeping a moderate number of monomials in the public key. With this setup the composition of exponentials and linear maps gives a deterministic trapdoor one way permutation which can be used for KEM and signature when combined with the standard padding OAEP and PSS [2,3] whose security is well understood.

In the paper we describe the setup of the scheme, the most important part of it is the Configuration Matrices ($\mathcal{CM}$) and the algorithm for the reduction of monomials. We give a preliminary security analysis of the resistance against Gröbner basis, Weil descent and structural attacks but more research on the security of DME is needed. We describe also the $\mathcal{CM}$ that we have implemented with three and four rounds, 8 variables and $q = 2^{64}$. We provide the SUPERCOP timings of DME-OAEP and DME-PSS00 for them and a comparison with NIST finalists. For NIST security level 5 the size of our ciphertext and signature is only 64 bytes.

1 Introduction

Multivariate Public Key Cryptography (MPKC) is one of the most studied techniques used post-quantum cryptography, they are based on the problem of solving systems of nonlinear equations. Since the paper of Imai-Matsumoto [24], many MPKC schemes have been proposed [14,28,29] and they has been extensively studied and attacked for more than 30 years [5,6,10,21,27,33]. In most of the schemes the public key consist in quadratic polynomials obtained as a

© The Author(s), under exclusive license to Springer Nature Switzerland AG 2023
T. Johansson and D. Smith-Tone (Eds.): PQCrypto 2023, LNCS 14154, pp. 379–402, 2023.
https://doi.org/10.1007/978-3-031-40003-2_14

composition of linear and non linear maps but cubic and other low degree polynomials has also been used. Different extension of fields has been used as well of the use of several round that combine linear and non linear maps.

There has been many direct attacks on MPKC using Gröbner basis and other methods to solve the polynomials system as well as structural attacks. As a consequence of such attacks many variants has been proposed for signatures (UOV, HFEv-, Rainbow, GeMSS, etc.) and 9 of them MPKC where present in the first round of the NIST competition. For the structural attacks the most powerful used the MinRank [4] and it has been useful against some of the NIST candidates [6].

For encryption and KEM there has been also interesting proposals such as ZHFE [30], the quadratic and cubic Simple Matrix Scheme [15] and l-Invertible Cycles [12], but only 3 where presented to NIST competition

The main new idea in [22] is to use birational exponential maps as non linear component which produces polynomials of very high degree. Birational maps where also used in [12,31] in a setup that gives low degree polynomials. In [22], we used two exponential maps, one over $\mathbb{F}_{q^2}$ and one over $\mathbb{F}_{q^3}$. DME with those parameters was broken in [1], but this attack do not work as it is if we change $\mathbb{F}_{q^3}$ by $\mathbb{F}_{q^4}$. W. Beullens suggested in the NIST PQC-Forum mail list to apply the decomposition algorithm of [18] and [35] to the polynomials over $\mathbb{F}_2$ obtained from the public key of DME by Weil descent. As we explain in the PQC-Forum mail list [26], the algorithm work if certain linear subspace in the vector space of cubic polynomials are equal (see [35] Thm. 5), but this equality does not hold for the polynomials obtained from the DME. Nevertheless we decided to increase the degree of the polynomials obtained by Weil descent and this is the main reason to increase the number of rounds in this new version of DME.

We also simplify the structure of DME by using only two fields $\mathbb{F}_q$ by $\mathbb{F}_{q^2}$ which allows us control the number of monomials more efficiently. In fact the number of monomials can be up to double exponential on the number of rounds r namely if all the rows of the E_i have two non zero entries then each component has 2^{2^r} monomials. We can reduce the number of monomials by imposing some linear conditions on the exponents e_i of the entries of the exponents matrices $\alpha_i = 2^{e_i}$ in such a way that some of the monomials become equal and the coefficient of the repeated monomial is a sum of several terms, giving us some defense against the structural cryptanalysis. The algorithm for the reduction of monomials is explained in Sect. 5.2 and also an efficient algorithm to compute the final polynomials of the public key using Kronecker product of matrices.

The final polynomials over $\mathbb{F}_q$ of the public key F are obtained as a composition of linear and exponential maps that gives a trapdoor permutation in a subset of $(\mathbb{F}_{q^2} \setminus \{0\})^{n/2}$. In the version we present here we use also affine translations in the linear part that can produce failure of decryption with a probability around $1/q^2$, see Proposition 43 for details. On the other hand, it is always possible to avoid the failure of verification of public signature (see Remark 44).

In Sect. 5, we explain the set up of DME, starting with the configuration matrices $\mathcal{CM}$ that is a list of r "skeleton" matrices E_i^* obtained from the exponential E_i by changing the non zero entries by 1. The configuration matrices $\mathcal{CM} = [E_1^*, \ldots E_r^*]$ determine the number of monomials of the public key F and the degree of the the polynomials over $\mathbb{F}_2$ obtained from the public key of DME by Weil descent. The configuration matrices $\mathcal{CM}$ determine also the linear conditions on the monomial reduction algorithm but the final number of monomials can only be determine when one computes F.

Section 6 is devoted to the security analysis of DME, starting with the well known upper bound of the complexity of computing a Gröbner basis of the ideal

$$I = \langle f_1(\underline{x}) - y_1, \ldots, f_n(\underline{x}) - y_n, x_1^{2^e} - x_1, \ldots, x_n^{2^e} - x_n \rangle$$

where $F(\underline{x}) = \underline{y}$. Let $sd(I)$ be the **solving degree of** I [8,13], we can safely assume that $2^e \leq sd(I)$, and the bound in the (2) give good security margin, for instance if $q = 2^{64}$ it would take $O(2^{1024})$ operations to solve the equations. The problem is that we do not know if the security estimate is accurate or not for this kind of ideals and further research is needed. The same is true for the determination of the complexity of a Weil descent attack. For instance for $q = 2^{64}$ and $\mathcal{CM}_2$ we have $d = 8$ and a precise estimation of the solving degree is needed. For instance if $sd((\tilde{I})) = 16$ then (2) gives a complexity of $O(2^{237})$.

For the structural cryptanalysis we try to invert F directly by starting with the inverse of the last linear map L_r. In order to do so we describe in the paragraph after Algorithm 3.1 how to obtain homogeneous equations on the unknown entries of L_{rk}^{-1} that will give us a solution up to a multiplicative constant λ_k. For instance, if we have $n = 8$ and $q = 2^{64}$, we have a choice of $O(2^{256})$ vectors $(\lambda_1, \lambda_2, \lambda_3, \lambda_4)$. Of course those are the first step on the structural cryptanalysis of the DME and more analysis is needed. For instance, how one can get the coefficients the polynomials on the previous round or which matrices give equivalent keys [34]. Given the high degrees of the polynomials in the public key it is not clear how MinRank or differential methods that are very successful versus quadratic schemes (see [4,20,30,32]) can be used against DME, but given the good performance and the small size signature/ciphertext of DME it is worth to continue the research on the security of DME.

As we said above, one of the main strengths of the DME is the very small size of the signatures. In addition to that, the implementation is very competitive with respect to running times with the other schemes that have been proposed for the first NIST call. We included a section with accurate timings, as measured by SUPERCOP, and a comparison with the cryptosystems selected initially for signature and KEM. At the level of security 5, DME takes almost the same time to sign than dilithium2, but one third of the time to verify.

2 Mathematical Description of DME

We present in this paper a new version of the multivariate public key cryptosystem DME based on the composition of linear and exponential maps that allow the polynomials of the public key to be of a very high degree. The main components of the DME cryptosystem are exponential maps $F_A : K^n \rightarrow K^n$

associated to matrices $A = (a_{ij}) \in \mathcal{M}_{n \times n}(\mathbb{Z})$, where K is a finite field, whose precise definition is given by the following formula:

$$F_A(x_1, \ldots, x_n) = (x_1^{a_{11}} \cdot \ldots \cdot x_n^{a_{1n}}, \ldots, x_1^{a_{n1}} \cdot \ldots \cdot x_n^{a_{nn}}). \qquad (1)$$

The following two facts are extremely useful and easy to verify:

a) If $A, B \in \mathcal{M}_{n \times n}(\mathbb{Z})$ and $C = B \cdot A$, then $F_C = F_B \circ F_A$.
b) If $\det(A) = \pm 1$, then the inverse matrix A^{-1} has integer entries, F_A is invertible on $(\mathbb{F}_q \setminus \{0\})^n$, and its inverse is given by $F_{A^{-1}}$.

The monomial maps are extensively used in Algebraic Geometry and produce birational maps. In Projective Geometry they are also called Cremona transformations. In [12] these transformations are used to produce a multivariate public key cryptosystem.

If $\det(A) \neq \pm 1$, the monomial map is not birational, for instance it is not difficult to prove using the Smith normal form the following fact that we will not use:

Proposition 21. *Let $F_A : K^n \to K^n$ be a monomial map as (1), where K is an algebraically closed field of characteristic zero. Then the monomial map F_A has geometric degree $d := |\det(A)|$ on $(K \setminus \{0\})^n$, that is, for a generic $x \in (K \setminus \{0\})^n$, the fiber $F_A^{-1}(x)$ has d preimages.*

Let $q = p^e$ be a prime power and $\mathbb{F}_q$ denote a finite field of q elements. It is not necessary to consider exponents greater than $q - 2$ since $x^{q-1} = 1$ for all $x \in \mathbb{F}_q \setminus \{0\}$. We take $A \in \mathcal{M}_{n \times n}(\mathbb{Z}_{q-1})$ and then we have:

Theorem 22. *Let $A \in \mathcal{M}_{n \times n}(\mathbb{Z}_{q-1})$ and $F_A : \mathbb{F}_q^n \to \mathbb{F}_q^n$ be the corresponding monomial map. If $\gcd(\det(A), q - 1) = 1$, and we set $b := \det(A)^{-1} \in \mathbb{Z}_{q-1}$ and $B := b\mathrm{Adj}(A)$, then $A^{-1} = B \in \mathcal{M}_{n \times n}(\mathbb{Z}_{q-1})$ and $F_A : (\mathbb{F}_q \setminus \{0\})^n \to (\mathbb{F}_q \setminus \{0\})^n$ is bijective with inverse $F_{A^{-1}}$.*

Proof. The proof is immediate since, as we mentioned above, we can reduce the exponents modulo $q - 1$. By construction, we have $b\det(A) = 1 + \lambda(q - 1)$, so $AB = b\det(A)I_n \equiv I_n \pmod{q - 1}$ and $\underline{x}^{AB} = \underline{x}^{I_n} = \underline{x}$.

The exponential maps F_A can be used to build a multivariate PKC in the standard way by putting powers of q in the non-zero entries of the matrix A. For instance, if each row has 2 non zero entries $q^{a_{ij}}$, then after composition with two linear maps at both ends, one gets a quadratic public key, if we allow 3 non zero entries, we get cubic polynomials, and so on. We made extensive computer tests leading to the conclusion that those systems are not safe against Gröbner basis attack for reasonable key size.

In order to make an scheme stronger against algebraic cryptanalysis we take $q = 2^e$ and allow the non-zero entries of A to be powers of 2 that are not powers of q. This choice produces final polynomials with degree up to $q - 1$ in each variable. The kernel of our scheme is a composition of r exponentials with n variables and $r + 1$ linear maps, that we denote by DME-$(r, n, 2^e)$. We have successfully built DME-$(r, n, 2^e)$ schemes with $n = 6, 8$ and $3 \leq r \leq 6$. For simplicity, we take $r = 4$ and $n = 8$ in the following description of the DME.

The DME-$(4, 8, 2^e)$ cryptosystem works with plain texts and cypher texts in $\mathbb{F}_q^8$ with $q = 2^e$. Let $u^2 + au + b \in \mathbb{F}_q[u]$ be an irreducible polynomial, consider the field extension $\mathbb{F}_{q^2} = \mathbb{F}_q[u]/\langle u^2 + au + b \rangle$ of degree two over $\mathbb{F}_q$. Let $\phi : \mathbb{F}_q^2 \to \mathbb{F}_{q^2}$ be the bijection defined by $(x, y) \mapsto x + y\bar{u}$ and let $\bar{\phi} : \mathbb{F}_q^8 \to (\mathbb{F}_{q^2})^4$ be the map $(x_1, \ldots, x_8) \mapsto (\phi(x_1, x_2), \phi(x_3, x_4), \phi(x_5, x_6), \phi(x_7, x_8))$. The values of e, a, b are fixed during the set up of the system.

The DME-$(4, 8, 2^e)$ cryptosystem combines 5 linear+affine maps $L_0, \ldots, L_4 :$ $\mathbb{F}_q^8 \to \mathbb{F}_q^8$ with 4 exponential maps $F_{E_1}, \ldots, F_{E_4} : (\mathbb{F}_{q^2})^4 \to (\mathbb{F}_{q^2})^4$. More precisely, the encryption map

$$F = \Psi(L_0, \ldots, L_4, E_1, \ldots, E_4) : \mathbb{F}_q^8 \to \mathbb{F}_q^8$$

is given by the composition

$$
\mathbb{F}_q^8 \xrightarrow{L_0} \mathbb{F}_q^8 \xrightarrow{\bar{\phi}} (\mathbb{F}_{q^2})^4 \xrightarrow{F_{E_1}} (\mathbb{F}_{q^2})^4 \longrightarrow
$$

$$
\xrightarrow{\bar{\phi}^{-1}} \mathbb{F}_q^8 \xrightarrow{L_1} \mathbb{F}_q^8 \xrightarrow{\bar{\phi}} (\mathbb{F}_{q^2})^4 \xrightarrow{F_{E_2}} (\mathbb{F}_{q^2})^4 \longrightarrow
$$

$$
\xrightarrow{\bar{\phi}^{-1}} \mathbb{F}_q^8 \xrightarrow{L_2} \mathbb{F}_q^8 \xrightarrow{\bar{\phi}} (\mathbb{F}_{q^2})^4 \xrightarrow{F_{E_3}} (\mathbb{F}_{q^2})^4 \longrightarrow
$$

$$
\xrightarrow{\bar{\phi}^{-1}} \mathbb{F}_q^8 \xrightarrow{L_3} \mathbb{F}_q^8 \xrightarrow{\bar{\phi}} (\mathbb{F}_{q^2})^4 \xrightarrow{F_{E_4}} (\mathbb{F}_{q^2})^4 \longrightarrow
$$

$$
\xrightarrow{\bar{\phi}^{-1}} \mathbb{F}_q^8 \xrightarrow{L_4} \mathbb{F}_q^8
$$

of the linear+affine and exponential maps interleaved with the bijections $\bar{\phi}$ and $\bar{\phi}^{-1}$.

Each linear+affine map L_i is made up of four linear maps $L_{i1}, \ldots, L_{i4} : \mathbb{F}_q^2 \to \mathbb{F}_q^2$ and four translation vectors $a_{i1}, \ldots, a_{i4} \in \mathbb{F}_q^2$, so that

$$L_i(x_1, \ldots, x_8) = (L_{i1}(x_1, x_2) + a_{i1}, L_{i2}(x_3, x_4) + a_{i2}, L_{i3}(x_5, x_6) + a_{i3}, L_{i4}(x_7, x_8) + a_{i4}).$$

The matrices of the blocks $L_{i1}, \ldots, L_{i4}$ are $A_{i1}, \ldots, A_{i4} \in \mathbb{F}_q^{2 \times 2}$, respectively.

If we like to avoid failures of decryption we should use translations in only one intermediate step $1 \leq i_0 < 4$ and set $a_{ij} = 0$ for all $i \neq i_0$, more technical details about this will be given in Sect. 4.

The exponential maps $F_{E_i} : (\mathbb{F}_{q^2})^4 \to (\mathbb{F}_{q^2})^4$ are defined by

$$(y_1, y_2, y_3, y_4) \mapsto F_{E_i}(y_1, y_2, y_3, y_4)$$

where $E_i = (\alpha_{i,k})_{1 \leq k \leq 16}$ is a 4×4 matrix with coefficients in $[0, q^2 - 1]$. It is not necessary to consider exponents greater than $q^2 - 1$ since $x^{q^2} = x$ for all $x \in \mathbb{F}_{q^2}$.

The linear+affine maps $L_i : \mathbb{F}_q^8 \to \mathbb{F}_q^8$ are invertible if and only if each of the four 2×2 blocks $L_{i1}, L_{i2}, L_{i3}, L_{i4}$ have non-zero determinant. In this case, the inverse of L_i is

$$L_i^{-1}(x_1, \ldots, x_8) = (L_{i1}^{-1}(x_1, x_2) - L_{i1}^{-1}a_{i1}, \ldots, L_{i4}^{-1}(x_7, x_8) - L_{i4}^{-1}a_{i4}),$$

i.e. L_i^{-1} is also a linear+affine map.

The exponential maps $F_{E_i} : (\mathbb{F}_{q^2})^4 \to (\mathbb{F}_{q^2})^4$ are not invertible in general. However, their restrictions to the torus $\widehat{F}_{E_i} : (\mathbb{F}_{q^2}^*)^4 \to (\mathbb{F}_{q^2}^*)^4$ are invertible if and only if

$$\gcd(\det(E_i), q^2 - 1) = 1.$$

The inverse of $\widehat{F}_{E_i}$ is also an exponential map $\widehat{F}_{E_i^{-1}} : (\mathbb{F}_{q^2}^*)^4 \to (\mathbb{F}_{q^2}^*)^4$, given by the inverse of the matrix E_i modulo $q^2 - 1$. This matrix has coefficients in $[0, q^2 - 2]$. Using the same matrix, we extend $\widehat{F}_{E_i^{-1}}$ to an exponential map $F_{E_i^{-1}} : (\mathbb{F}_{q^2})^4 \to (\mathbb{F}_{q^2})^4$.

The private key consists of the coefficients of the linear+affine maps $L_0, \ldots, L_4$ and exponential maps $F_{E_1}, \ldots, F_{E_4}$. That information is enough to apply all those maps in reverse, that is, to being able to decrypt. The public key is the polynomial representation of the composition of the maps,

$$F(x_1, \ldots, x_8) = (F_{4,1}, F_{4,2}, F_{4,3}, F_{4,4}, F_{4,5}, F_{4,6}, F_{4,7}, F_{4,8}).$$

3   Computing the Public Key F

3.1   Computing the Monomials of F

If $\underline{x} = (x_1, \ldots, x_8) \in \mathbb{F}_q^8$ are the initial coordinates, then the composition of all the maps allow us to compute the components of $F(\underline{x})$ as polynomials $F_{4,j} \in \mathbb{F}_q[x_1, \ldots, x_8]$. In order to keep the number of monomials small, we choose the matrices E_i with the following properties:

1. The entries of E_i are powers of 2.
2. Each row of E_i has one or two non zero entries.
3. If we define $d_i = \frac{1}{\det(E_i)} \mod q^2 - 1$, then we have that d_i has a big binary weight for some $1 < i \leq 4$.

The inverse map F^{-1} is also composition of 4 exponentials so if the number of monomials of F^{-1} is not very big, one can get the polynomial components of F^{-1} by interpolation, provided enough number of pairs $(\underline{x}, F(\underline{x}))$. To avoid this attack we take some i such that d_i has a big binary weight to ensure that the inverse E_i^{-1} has entries with big binary weight that will produce a big number of monomial of the inverse F^{-1} above a given security level.

It is possible to get the monomials of the F_i without computing the composition of all the maps. It is easy to verify that after exponential E_i plus $\bar{\phi}^{-1}$ the 8 resulting polynomials

$$F_{i,1}, F_{i,2}, F_{i,3}, F_{i,4}, F_{i,5}, F_{i,6}, F_{i,7}, F_{i,8}$$

verify that $F_{i,2k-1}$, $F_{i,2k}$ and $F_{i,2k-1} + \bar{u}.F_{i,2k}$ share the same monomials M_{ik} unless some coefficient vanish and also the same happens after we apply L_i.

Let $M = [m_1, \dots m_s]$ a list of monomials and α a power of 2, we define $M^\alpha = [m_1^\alpha, \dots, m_s^\alpha]$. If $M = [m_1, \dots, m_s]$ and $N = [n_1, \dots, n_t]$ are lists of monomials, we define

$$M^\alpha \otimes N^\beta = [m_i^\alpha \cdot n_j^\beta, 1 \le i \le s, 1 \le j \le t],$$

that is, $M^\alpha \otimes N^\beta$ is the Kronecker tensor product of M^α and N^β as row matrices.

It is easy to verify that $M_{ij}^\alpha \otimes M_{ik}^\beta$ is the list of monomials of the polynomial

$$(F_{i,2j-1} + \bar{u}.F_{i,2j})^\alpha \cdot (F_{i,2k-1} + \bar{u}.F_{i,2k})^\beta$$

since the exponents α and β are powers of 2.

Let $M_{01} = [x_1, x_2]$, $M_{02} = [x_3, x_4]$, $M_{03} = [x_5, x_6]$, $M_{04} = [x_7, x_8]$. We use the following notation for the entries of each matrix E_i: we call $\alpha_{i,2k-1}$ the first non zero entry of the row k and $\alpha_{i,2k}$ the second non zero entry. If there is only one non zero entry, we just set $\alpha_{i,2k} = 0$.

We reduce the list of monomials when some of them are repeated. Let us define an operation $Rm(M)$ on a list of monomials M that removes all duplicates, keeping only the first appearance of each monomial in the list and erasing the rest. The following algorithm, called MON, shows how to compute the lists of monomials of the F_{rj}.

The size of the lists M_{ri} can be up to double exponential on the number of rounds r for instance if all the rows of the E_i have two non zero entries then $card(M_{ri}) = 2^{2^r}$. We can reduce the size of the list of monomials by imposing some linear condition on the exponents $e_{i,j}$ of $\alpha_{i,j}$ ($\alpha_{i,j} = 2^{e_{i,j}}$), in such a way that some of the monomials become equal and the coefficient of the repeated monomial is a sum of several terms, which will give us a defense against the structural cryptanalysis. In fact, we need to take care of the following:

After the last exponential the final polynomials are obtained by computing $F_{(r-1)k_1}^{\alpha_{i,2k-1}} \cdot F_{(r-1)k_2}^{\alpha_{i,2k}}$. Let $F_{(r-1)k_1}^{\alpha_{i,2k-1}} = \sum B_i m_i$ and $F_{(r-1)k_2}^{\alpha_{i,2k}} = \sum C_j n_j$. Then,

$$F_{(r-1)k_1}^{\alpha_{i,2k-1}} \cdot F_{(r-1)k_2}^{\alpha_{i,2k}} = \left(\sum B_i m_i\right) \cdot \left(\sum C_j n_j\right) = \sum B_i C_j m_i n_j = \sum H_{ij} m_i n_j.$$

Algorithm 3.1. MON, compute the monomials in the public-key polynomials.

Input: $(E_1, \ldots, E_r)$
Output: $(M_{r1}, M_{r2}, M_{r3}, M_{r4})$
1: **for** $i = 0$ **to** $r - 1$ **do**
2:    **for** $k = 1$ **to** 4 **do**
3:       $M_{(i+1)k} = M_{ik_1}^{\alpha_{i,2k-1}} \otimes M_{ik_2}^{\alpha_{i,2k}}$, where $M_{ik_2} = [1]$ if $\alpha_{i,2k} = 0$
4:       $M_{(i+1)k} = Rm(M_{(i+1)k})$
5:       **if** $a_{(i+1)k} \neq 0$ **then**
6:          append 1 to the list $M_{(i+1)k}$
7:       **end if**
8:    **end for**
9: **end for**

Thus, we have $H_{ij} = B_i C_j$, it is clear now that the coefficients $H_{ij} \in \mathbb{F}_{q^2}$ satisfy $H_{ij} H_{kl} = H_{il} H_{kj}$, which will be called quadratic relations (QR) from now on. Since the coefficients of final polynomials $F_1, \ldots F_8$ are obtained applying $\bar{\phi}^{-1}$ and L_r, we can use the QR to compute equations for the coefficients of the components of inverse of L_r^{-1}. Given that the QR are homogeneous (of degree two), one can solve those equations to find L_r^{-1} and L_r up to a constant.

In order to eliminate the QR among the H_{ij}, the strategy is to force many coincidences among the final monomials, that is, if H_{ij} is a sum $= \sum B_k C_l$ it will by more difficult to get the quadratic relations or any polynomial relations among the H_{ij}. The implicit equations on the H_{ij} are obtained by computing the equations of the image of the map $Q = (Q_{ij})$, defined by $H_{ij} = Q_{ij}(B, C) = \sum B_k C_l$, that is by eliminating the B_1 and C_j from the system $\langle H_{ij} - \sum B_k C_l \rangle$

$$Q : \mathbb{F}_{q^2}[B_k, C_l] \longrightarrow \mathbb{F}_{q^2}[H_{ij}]$$

For instance, for the second component of Example 1 there are no QR, the source has 24 variables and the target 48.

Assume that we are at the step i of the algorithm MON and we are computing the list $M_{(i+1)k}$. We can force a reduction of the monomials only if there are two non zero entries $2^{e_{i,2k-1}}$ and $2^{e_{i,2k}}$ in the corresponding row of the matrix E_i, so we'll have to compute $M_{(i+1)k} = M_{ik_1}^{\alpha_{i,2k-1}} \otimes M_{ik_2}^{\alpha_{i,2k}}$. Now, we take a variable that is in both lists with exponent a power of 2, which for simplicity we'll assume it is x_1. More precisely, the monomial $x_1^{2^{l_1}} \cdot m_1$, where $l_1 = l_1(e_{j,l} : 1 \leq j \leq i - 1)$ is a linear form and m_1 is a monomial in the other variables would appear in M_{ik_1}, and $x_1^{2^{l_2}} \cdot m_2$ in the list M_{ik_2}. By the method that the lists are constructed (x_1 and x_2 play exactly the same role), we would also have the monomials $x_2^{2^{l_1}} \cdot m_1$ and $x_2^{2^{l_2}} \cdot m_2$ in the lists M_{ik_1} and M_{ik_2}, respectively.

Now, when we compute $M_{ik_1}^{\alpha_{i,2k-1}}$, the exponent of x_1 in the first monomial is $2^{l_1 + e_{i,2k-1}}$ and in the other list is $2^{l_2 + e_{i,2k}}$. We can force that $2^{l_1 + e_{i,2k-1}} = 2^{l_2 + e_{i,2k}}$ if we substitute $e_{i,2k}$ by $e_{i,2k-1} + l_1 - l_2$ and then the monomials in both lists became

$$x_1^{2^{l_1 + e_{i,2k-1}}} \cdot m_1^{2^{e_{i,2k-1}}}, \quad x_2^{2^{l_1 + e_{i,2k-1}}} \cdot m_1^{2^{e_{i,2k-1}}}$$

in the first list, and

$$x_1^{2l_1+e_{i,2k-1}} \cdot m_2^{2e_{i,2k-1}+l_1-l_2}, \quad x_2^{2l_1+e_{i,2k-1}} \cdot m_2^{2e_{i,2k-1}+l_1-l_2}$$

in the second.

When the tensor product of both lists is computed, we get that two of the four monomials are equal:

$$x_1^{2l_1+e_{i,j2k-1}} \cdot m_1^{2e_{i,j2k-1}} \cdot x_2^{2e_{i,j2k-1}+l_1-l_2} \cdot m_2^{2e_{i,j2k-1}+l_1-l_2}$$
$$= x_2^{2l_1+e_{i,j2k-1}} \cdot m_1^{2e_{i,2k-1j}} \cdot x_1^{2l_1+e_{i,j2k-1}} \cdot m_2^{2e_{i,j2k-1}+l_1-l_2}.$$

If there are other variables repeated in both lists that have different exponents after the change $e_{i,2k} = e_{i,2k-1} + l_1 - l_2$, we can repeat the same procedure of imposing a linear condition, but in this case the linear equations involves terms e_{jk} with $j \le i - 1$. In general, each linear condition will produce the reduction of many monomials, but the actual number depends of the structure of the matrices E_i and it is not possible to give a general formula for the final number of monomials of F. We call this algorithm RED, the input is the set $\{E_i\}$. Next, we present an example of the procedure.

Example 1: For this example, we take $q = 2^e$, $n = 6$ and following matrices over $\mathbb{Z}_{q^2-1}$:

$$E_1 = \begin{pmatrix} \alpha_{1,1} & 0 & \alpha_{1,2} \\ \alpha_{1,3} & \alpha_{1,4} & 0 \\ 0 & 0 & \alpha_{1,5} \end{pmatrix}, \quad E_2 = \begin{pmatrix} \alpha_{2,1} & \alpha_{2,2} & 0 \\ 0 & \alpha_{2,3} & \alpha_{2,4} \\ \alpha_{2,5} & 0 & \alpha_{2,6} \end{pmatrix}, \quad E_3 = \begin{pmatrix} \alpha_{3,1} & 0 & \alpha_{3,2} \\ \alpha_{3,3} & \alpha_{3,4} & 0 \\ 0 & \alpha_{3,5} & \alpha_{3,6} \end{pmatrix}.$$

As usual, $\alpha_{i,j} = 2^{e_{i,j}}$ and $e_{i,j} \le e - 1$. If the $e_{i,j}$ are generic, the lists of monomials after the first exponential (M_{11}, M_{12}, M_{13}) have size $(2^2, 2^2, 2)$, after the second exponential the lists (M_{21}, M_{22}, M_{23}) have size $(2^4, 2^3, 2^3)$, and after the third one the final lists (M_{31}, M_{32}, M_{33}) have size $(2^7, 2^7, 2^6)$. We can apply the method in this section and find 7 independent linear conditions on the $e_{i,j}$ as follows: after E_1, the lists (M_{11}, M_{12}, M_{13}) have size $(2^2, 2^2, 2)$, after E_2, we observe that the list M_{21} comes from tensoring M_{11} and M_{13}, which have x_1 and x_6 in common, so the linear condition $e_{2,2} = e_{1,1} + e_{2,1} - e_{1,3}$ reduces the number of monomials to 12. For M_{21} there are no common variables and for M_{23} we get the condition $e_{2,4} = -e_{2,5} + e_{2,6} - e_{1,1} + e_{1,3} + e_{2,3}$, that gives $(12, 2^3, 6)$ monomials. Finally, after E_3, the lists have size $(72, 96, 48)$. For the list M_{31} we get the condition $e_{3,2} = e_{3,1} + e_{2,1} - e_{2,5}$ that reduces the size of M_{31} to 32. For the list M_{32} we get the condition $e_{3,4} = e_{3,3} + e_{1,1} + e_{2,1} - e_{1,3} + e_{2,3}$ that reduces the size of M_{32} to 36. There is another independent linear equation $-e_{1,2} + e_{1,5} - e_{1,3} - e_{2,3} + e_{2,4}$ that reduce the size of M_{32} to 36. For the list M_{33} we get the condition $e_{3,6} = e_{3,5} - e_{1,1} + e_{1,3} - e_{2,5} + e_{2,3}$ that reduce the size of M_{33} to 24.

By making the above linear changes in the exponents of the E_i, new matrices E_i' and lists that have $(32, 36, 24)$ monomials appear, where one can verify that there are no quadratic relations among the coefficients H_{ij}. using a Computer Algebra System system one can compute binomial relations of the type $\prod(H_{ij}) - \prod(H_{kl})$ up to some degree. In this example we check with Maple that there are no binomial relations up to degree 10.

With this scheme three determinants $det(E_i')$ are a power of 2 and then the inverse F^{-1} can have a small number of monomials. If we do not use the last linear relation we get M_{33} with 48 monomials, and there are many QR which eventually will allow us to compute the last component the matrix L_3. A priori, this is not a problem for the security of the schema because the other two components of L_3 can not be obtained.

By checking the final lists of monomials, we can observe and interesting structure, if we make the changes of variables in S_1, S_2 and S_3:

$$S_1 = \begin{bmatrix} x_1^{2^{e_{1,1}+e_{1,1}+e_{2,1}}} = y_{11}, x_2^{2^{e_{1,1}+e_{1,1}+e_{2,1}}} = y_{12}, x_3^{2^{e_{1,4}+e_{1,1}+e_{2,1}-e_{1,3}+e_{3,1}}} = y_{13}, \\ x_4^{2^{e_{1,4}+e_{1,1}+e_{2,1}-e_{1,3}+e_{3,1}}} = y_{14}, x_5^{2^{e_{1,2}+e_{2,1}+e_{3,1}}} = y_{15}, x_6^{2^{e_{1,2}+e_{2,1}+e_{3,1}}} = y_{16} \end{bmatrix}$$

$$S_2 = \begin{bmatrix} x_1^{2^{e_{1,1}+e_{2,1}+e_{3,3}}} = y_{21}, x_2^{2^{e_{1,1}+e_{2,1}+e_{3,3}}} = y_{22}, x_3^{2^{e_{1,4}+e_{1,1}+e_{2,1}-e_{1,3}+e_{3,3}}} = y_{23}, \\ x_4^{2^{e_{1,4}+e_{1,1}+e_{2,1}-e_{1,3}+e_{3,3}}} = y_{24}, x_5^{2^{e_{1,2}+e_{2,1}+e_{3,3}}} = y_{24}, x_6^{2^{e_{1,2}+e_{2,1}+e_{3,3}}} = y_{26} \end{bmatrix}$$

$$S_3 = \begin{bmatrix} x_1^{2^{e_{1,3}+e_{2,3}+e_{3,5}}} = y_{31}, x_2^{2^{e_{1,3}+e_{2,3}+e_{3,5}}} = y_{32}, x_3^{2^{e_{1,4}+e_{2,3}+e_{3,5}}} = y_{33}, \\ x_4^{2^{e_{1,4}+e_{2,3}+e_{3,5}}} = y_{34}, x_5^{2^{e_{1,2}-e_{1,1}+e_{1,3}+e_{2,3}+e_{3,5}}} = y_{35}, x_6^{2^{e_{1,2}-e_{1,1}+e_{1,3}+e_{2,3}+e_{3,5}}} = y_{36} \end{bmatrix}$$

we get polynomials $\overline{F_i} = F_i(y) \in \mathbb{F}_q[y_{11}, \ldots y_{36}]$ of low degree 6 or 7. Therefore, using S_1, S_2, S_3 and $\overline{F_i}(y)$ instead of $F_i(x)$ as public key will make faster encryption for DME-KEM and faster signature verification for DME-SIGN.

3.2 Computing the Coefficients of the Public Key F

Once the list of monomials of the $F_{r,j}$ is obtained, one gets the coefficient of each group of polynomials by evaluating the polynomials $F_{r,1}, \ldots, F_{r,8}$. The set of pairs $(\underline{c}, F_{r,j}(\underline{c}))$ should be big enough to guarantee that the corresponding linear equations are independent. That is, if $Q_k = [q_1 \ldots q_d]$ and $F_{r,j} = \sum_{i=1}^{d} f_{rji} q_i(x)$, we take vectors $\underline{c}_1, \ldots, \underline{c}_R$ such that the linear equations on the coefficients f_{rij} in $F_k(c_e) = \sum f_{rji} q_i(c_e)$ are independent and can be solved to get the coefficients of the polynomials $F_{r,1}, \ldots, F_{r,8}$.

To compute the polynomials $F_{r,k}$ faster we can use the same idea used to compute the lists of monomials of the polynomial $(F_{i,2j-1} + \bar{u}F_{i,2j})^\alpha (F_{i,2k-1} + \bar{u}F_{i,2k})^\beta$, i.e. $M_{ij}^\alpha \otimes M_{ik}^\beta$. Let s_{ij} be the size of the list M_{ij}. Now, regard M_{ij} as a $1 \times s_{ij}$ matrix, which by abuse of notation, we will still write it as M_{ij}. We denote by C_{ij} the $s_{ij} \times 2$ matrix of the coefficients of the polynomials $F_{i,2j-1}$ and $F_{i,2j}$ on the monomials of M_{ij}, as shown in the following formula:

$$C_{ij} = \begin{bmatrix} c_{11}^{ij} & c_{12}^{ij} \\ c_{21}^{ij} & c_{22}^{ij} \\ \vdots & \vdots \\ c_{s_{ij}1}^{ij} & c_{s_{ij}2}^{ij} \end{bmatrix}$$

Now we have that $F_{i,2j-1} + \bar{u}F_{i,2j} = M_{ij} \cdot C_{ij} \cdot (1, \bar{u})^t$.

If $\alpha = 2^b$, then $(F_{i,2j-1} + \bar{u}F_{i,2j})^\alpha = M_{ij}^\alpha \cdot C_{ij}^\alpha \cdot (1, \bar{u}^\alpha)^t$.

Applying the mixed-product property of the Kronecker product we get:

$$
\begin{aligned}
(F_{i,2j-1} &+ \bar{u}F_{i,2j})^\alpha \cdot (F_{i,2k-1} + \bar{u}F_{i,2k})^\beta \\
&= (M_{ij}^\alpha \cdot C_{ij}^\alpha \cdot (1, \bar{u}^\alpha)^t) \otimes (M_{ik}^\beta \cdot C_{ik}^\beta \cdot (1, \bar{u}^\beta)^t) \\
&= (M_{ij}^\alpha \otimes M_{ik}^\beta) \cdot (C_{ij}^\alpha \otimes C_{ik}^\beta) \cdot (1, \bar{u}^\beta, \bar{u}^\alpha, \bar{u}^{\alpha+\beta})^t
\end{aligned}
$$

Let's call $U_{\alpha\beta}$ the 4×2 matrix defined by

$$(1, \bar{u}^\beta, \bar{u}^\alpha, \bar{u}^{\alpha+\beta})^t = U_{\alpha\beta} \cdot (1, \bar{u})^t.$$

Then, we have the following result:

Lemma 31. *The matrix of coefficients of* $(F_{i,2j-1}+\bar{u}F_{i,2j})^\alpha \cdot (F_{i,2k-1}+\bar{u}F_{i,2k})^\beta$ *with respect of the monomials* $M_{ij}^\alpha \otimes M_{ik}^\beta$ *is* $(C_{ij}^\alpha \otimes C_{ik}^\beta) \cdot U_{\alpha\beta}$.

Now, we can compute the coefficients of the $F_{r,j}$ with algorithms similar to Rm and MON. Given the matrices of coefficients (M, C) of a component we define $Rc(C)$ the matrix coefficient obtained by adding of the coefficient of a the same monomial in the case that is repeated in the monomial list M.

4 DME as a Trapdoor One Way Permutation

Let's assume that the public key is

$$F = \Psi(L_0, \dots, L_4, E_1, \dots, E_4) : \mathbb{F}_q^8 \to \mathbb{F}_q^8.$$

By construction, F is a composition of bijections of $(\mathbb{F}_{q^2} \setminus \{0\})^4$ and if there is no affine translations $a_{i,j} = 0$ for all i we have:

Remark 41. *Let* $\mathbb{U} = \bar{\phi}^{-1}((\mathbb{F}_{q^2} \setminus \{0\})^4) \subset \mathbb{F}_q^8$ *then* $F : \mathbb{U} \to \mathbb{U}$ *is a bijection.*

If we add an affine translation only in the step i_0, then given $\underline{x}_0 \in \mathbb{U}$ the translation $a_{i_0,j}$ can produce a 0 in the step i_0, which in turn will give $F(\underline{x}) \notin \mathbb{U}$, so F can not be inverted at $F(\underline{x})$. On the other hand, if $F(\underline{x}) \in \mathbb{U}$, then F is invertible at $F(\underline{x})$, that is, we have:

Algorithm 3.2. COE, compute the coefficients of the public-key polynomials.

Input: $(E_1, \ldots, E_r, L_0 \ldots L_r)$
Output: $(C_{r1}, C_{r2}, C_{r3}, C_{r4})$
1: $M_{01} \leftarrow [x_1, x_2], M_{02} \leftarrow [x_3, x_4], M_{03} \leftarrow [x_5, x_6], M_{04} \leftarrow [x_7, x_8]$
2: $C_{01} \leftarrow A_{01}, \ldots, C_{04} \leftarrow A_{04}$
3: **for** $i = 0$ **to** $r - 1$ **do**
4:     **for** $k = 1$ **to** 4 **do**
5:         **if** $\alpha_{i,2k} \neq 0$ **then**
6:             $C_{(i+1)k} = \left(C_{ik_1}^{\alpha_{i,2k-1}} \otimes C_{ik_2}^{\alpha_{i,2k}} \right) \cdot U_{\alpha_{i,2k-1}, \alpha_{i,2k}}$
7:         **else**
8:             $C_{(i+1)k} = C_{ik_1}^{\alpha_{i,2k-1}} \cdot (1, \bar{u}^\alpha)$
9:         **end if**
10:        $C_{(i+1)k} = Rc(C_{(i+1)k})$
11:        $C_{(i+1)k} = L_{(i+1)k} \cdot C_{(i+1)k} + a_{(i+1),k}$
12:    **end for**
13: **end for**

Theorem 42. *Let F be a public key map such that there is only one step $1 \leq i_0 < r$ with non-zero affine components then F is invertible at $F(\underline{x})$ if $F(\underline{x}) \in \mathbb{U}$. In other words,*

$$F : \mathbb{U} \cap F^{-1}(\mathbb{U}) \to \mathbb{U} \cap F(\mathbb{U})$$

is a bijection.

Proof. Let $\underline{x}$ and $\underline{y}^0 = (y_1^0, y_2^0, y_3^0, y_4^0) = \bar{\phi}(L_0(\underline{x})) \in (\mathbb{F}_{q^2} \setminus \{0\})^4$.

By construction, all the successive maps of which F is made up are bijections in $(\mathbb{F}_{q^2} \setminus \{0\})^4$ or $\mathbb{U}$ until we get the linear map L_{i_0}. If we have that $L_{i_0}(\underline{x}^{i_0}) \in \mathbb{U}$, this property is preserved by the rest of the maps, so $F(\underline{x}) \in \mathbb{U}$.

On the contrary, if $L_{i_0}(\underline{x}^{i_0}) \notin \mathbb{U}$, then there exist a k such that $L_{i_0 k}(x_{i_0,2k-1}, x_{i_0,2k}) + a_{i_0,k} = (0,0)$. As $det(E_i) \neq 0$, there is a non-zero entry $\alpha_{i_0 k}$ in the k-th column, $\underline{y}^{\alpha_{ik}} = 0$ and $F_{i_0+1}(x) \notin \mathbb{U}$ this property is preserved by the rest of the maps because there are no more translations, hence $F(\underline{x}) \notin \mathbb{U}$.

In this case, it is clear that there are some $\underline{x}$ such that $F(\underline{x}) \notin \mathbb{U}$ and therefore $F(\mathbb{U}) \not\subset \mathbb{U}$. This means that there will be messages that, after padding, $\underline{x} \in \mathbb{U}$ but can not be signed. By the same argument above, those messages can be detected because $F^{-1}(\underline{x}) \notin \mathbb{U}$ and the message can be signed by changing the padding. $\qquad\square$

In the case that there are affine translations in more than one step then it can be failure of decryption even if $F(\underline{x}) \in \mathbb{U}$. In Example 1, if we take $a_{11} \neq 0, a_{21} \neq 0, a_{22} \neq 0$ and the rest of the a_{ij} are zero, after L_1 we may have $(x_1^1, x_2^1) = (0,0)$ and $E_1(y^0)$ can not be inverted but as $a_{21} \neq 0$ and $a_{22} \neq 0$ then we may have $\underline{x}^2 \in \mathbb{U}$ and $F(\underline{x}) \in \mathbb{U}$, but clearly F is not invertible at $F(\underline{x})$. One can check that if we take $a_{13} \neq 0$ and $a_{21} \neq 0$ then F has the property that if $F(\underline{x}) \in \mathbb{U}$ then $F^{-1}(F(\underline{x})) = \underline{x}$, but the converse of this statement is not true because the matrices E_i^{-1} have all the entries different from zero.

Proposition 43. *There is a Zariski open set* $\mathbb{V} \subset (\mathbb{F}_{q^2} \setminus \{0\})^4$ *such that* $F : \mathbb{V} \to F(\mathbb{V})$ *is a bijection and the probability of* $\underline{x} \notin \mathbb{V}$ *is less than* b/q^2 *for small* b.

Proof. As we has seen in Thm 42 $F(\underline{x})$ fails to have an unique inverse if at some step his image is not in $(\mathbb{F}_{q^2} \setminus \{0\})^4$. It is clear that condition can be expressed in a finite number of equations $G_i(\underline{x})$ and if $\mathbb{W} = V(G_i)$ is its set of zeros then $\mathbb{V} = (\mathbb{F}_{q^2})^4 \setminus \mathbb{W}$. $\qquad\square$

If we have non zero affine translations only at one level $1 < i_0 \leq r - 1$, then $F : \mathbb{U} \cap F^{-1}(\mathbb{U}) \to \mathbb{U} \cap F(\mathbb{U})$ is a bijection and we can take $\mathbb{V} = \mathbb{U} \cap F^{-1}(\mathbb{U})$. In this case given a message m, we add some padding to get $\underline{x} \in \mathbb{U}$. If $F(\underline{x}) = pad(m) \notin \mathbb{U}$ there is a failure of decryption then we change the padding and try again. If there are non zero affine translations at more that one level then the failure of decryption can not be detected.

Remark 44. *For the signature it is always possible to avoid the failure of the signature verification. As the owner of the private key has the linear and non linear components of* F *it is possible to check at each step if the image is in* $(\mathbb{F}_{q^2} \setminus \{0\})^4$. *If is not the case one start again with a new padding until get one signature* $F^{-1}(pad(m))$ *that can be verified.*

In this paper, we are mainly interested into find out the performance and security of the DME and we will not elaborate more about padding. For padding, we use the standards OAEP [2] for PKE and KEM and PSS00 [3] for signature, and we will denote by DME-OAEP and DME-PSS the corresponding cryptosystem.

5   Set up of the DME

5.1   The Configuration Matrices

We define a **Configuration Matrices** $(\mathcal{CM})$ as a list of r matrices for the exponentials where the non zero entries are substituted by 1. We denote such matrices by E_i^*. Let $\mathcal{CM} = [E_r^*, \ldots E_1^*]$ be a configuration. Then, it is easy to get the number of monomials of the each component of F from $\mathcal{CM}$ if there are no repeated monomials, just compute $E^* = E_r^* \cdots E_1^*$ and let t_k be the sum of the entries in the $k - th$ row of E^*, in which case the number of monomials of the components F_{2k-1}, F_{2k} is 2^{t_k}. In the Example 1 we have

$$E^* = E_3^* \cdot E_2^* \cdot E_1^* = \begin{pmatrix} 3 & 1 & 3 \\ 3 & 2 & 2 \\ 2 & 1 & 3 \end{pmatrix}$$

and the corresponding number of monomials is $(2^7, 2^7, 2^6)$. The algorithm RED reduce number of monomials to $(32, 36, 24)$. Please notice that the output of algorithm RED depend only in the configuration $\mathcal{CM}$, we will denote it by $RED(\mathcal{CM})$.

Another example is the configuration $\mathcal{CM}_2$ that we study in the next section and we implemented with $q = 2^{64}$. The matrices of $\mathcal{CM}_2$ are:

$$E_1^* = \begin{pmatrix} 1 & 1 & 0 & 0 \\ 1 & 0 & 0 & 0 \\ 0 & 0 & 1 & 1 \\ 0 & 0 & 0 & 1 \end{pmatrix}, E_2^* = \begin{pmatrix} 1 & 1 & 0 & 0 \\ 0 & 1 & 0 & 0 \\ 1 & 0 & 0 & 1 \\ 0 & 0 & 1 & 0 \end{pmatrix}, E_3^* = \begin{pmatrix} 1 & 0 & 0 & 1 \\ 1 & 1 & 0 & 0 \\ 0 & 0 & 1 & 1 \\ 0 & 1 & 1 & 0 \end{pmatrix}, E_4^* = \begin{pmatrix} 1 & 1 & 0 & 0 \\ 0 & 1 & 1 & 0 \\ 0 & 1 & 0 & 1 \\ 0 & 0 & 1 & 1 \end{pmatrix}$$

$$E^* = E_4^* \cdot E_3^* \cdot E_2^* \cdot E_1^* = \begin{pmatrix} 5 & 2 & 1 & 1 \\ 4 & 2 & 1 & 2 \\ 5 & 2 & 0 & 1 \\ 3 & 2 & 1 & 3 \end{pmatrix}$$

and the number of monomials is $(2^9, 2^9, 2^8, 2^9)$. After imposing 8 linear conditions we reduce the number of monomials to $(72, 90, 36, 96)$ and there are no QR.

When we consider in 6.3 a possible attack of the DME by Weil descent, the t_k give also the degree of the components F_{2k-1}, F_{2k} when we express them as polynomials over $\mathbb{F}_2$. In fact one of the main reason to use 4 or more exponentials is to increase the values in the list (t_1, t_2, t_3, t_4).

5.2   Reduction of the Number of Monomials

Given a $\mathcal{CM}$, it is straightforward to use the algorithm $\mathrm{RED}(\mathcal{CM})$ in Sect. 3 to reduce drastically the number of monomials of the F_i, in fact the linear relations depends only on $\mathcal{CM}$ and they are easy to compute. It is more complicate to get the maximal reduction and simultaneously to produce a determinant $det(E_i)$ with a big binary weight so that E_i^{-1} yields a large number of monomials. Nevertheless, it is possible to get a few $\mathcal{CM}$ that verify that condition. Remember that the algorithm produce some linear condition on the exponents of the matrices that allow us to eliminate some parameters and find new matrices with exponents in the remainder parameters.

An important point for the security of the DME is that the final monomials depend on fewer parameters than the final matrices, this fact implies that given the monomials the public key F, we can deduce the parameters involved in the public key and the rest of free parameters will produce a big list of matrices with the same exponents as F. In Example 1, there are initially 17 parameters that reduce to 12 after the reduction of monomials and examining the lists of exponents that appear in $(F, S1, S2, S3)$ we can verify that the exponents of F depend only on 6 parameters as follows:

We make a list EX with the second exponent of the monomials in x_i in the lists $\{S_1, S_2, S_3\}$,

$$[e_{1,1} + e_{2,1} + e_{3,1}, e_{1,4} + e_{1,1} + e_{2,1} - e_{1,3} + e_{3,1}, e_{1,2} + e_{2,1} + e_{3,1}, e_{1,1} + e_{2,1} + e_{3,3},$$

$$e_{1,4} + e_{1,1} + e_{2,1} - e_{1,3} + e_{3,3}, e_{1,2} + e_{2,1} + e_{3,3}, e_{3,3} + e_{2,3} + e_{3,5},$$

$$e_{1,4} + e_{2,3} + e_{3,5}, e_{1,2} - e_{1,1} + e_{1,3} + e_{2,3} + e_{3,5}]$$

The 9 linear forms of EX define a linear map $H : \mathbb{Z}_{q^2-1}^{12} \to \mathbb{Z}_{q^2-1}^{9}$ that has rank 6. That is given the Public Key there are $12 - 6 = 6$ free parameter in the matrices of $\mathcal{CM}$ that produce the given PK because fixing $(F, S1, S2, S3)$ we fix a vector h_0 of the image of H and its anti image $H^{-1}(h_0)$ is an affine space of dimension 6. As the 6 remaining parameters verify that $1 < e_{ij} \le q^2-1$, given the exponents of the public key and the base field $\mathbb{F}_{2^e}$, there are $2^{6(\log_2(e)+1)}$ matrices that can produce those exponents. Let denote by l the number of remaining parameters that produces the above algorithm.

The above computation depends only on the configuration $\mathcal{CM}$ we can produce and algorithm that will gives the matrices with the free parameters with input $\mathcal{CM}$ and the monomials of $(F, S1, S2, S3)$, but we are mainly interested in the number of the remaining free parameters, Let denote by l this number, we get after the reduction of monomials $2^{l(\log_2(e)+1)}$ matrices that get the same monomials for F, and different sets of matrices will give different coefficients of the public key.

For the configuration $\mathcal{CM}_1$ in Sect. 7, we have initially 23 parameters and the reduction of exponent left 16 free parameters. Now the final exponents depend only on 8 parameters, that means that given the monomials of the public key there are $2^{8(\log_2(e)+1)}$ sets of matrices that produce the same monomials. This means that for $q = 2^{64}$, there are 2^{56} sets of matrices for a given public key.

For the configuration $\mathcal{CM}_2$ in Sect. 7 we start with 28 parameters $e_{i,j}$ corresponding to the non zero entries in $\mathcal{CM}_2$ and we impose 8 linear conditions to get $(72, 90, 36, 96)$ monomials. We fix F, in order to determine the monomials in F we need to give values to 8 of the remaining parameters that is after we fix F there are 12 free parameters. For instance if $q = 2^{64}$ the given F there are $2^{12(\log_2(e)+1)} = 2^{84}$ set of matrices from $\mathcal{CM}$ that give the same exponents as F.

6 Security of the DME

6.1 Gröbner Basis

To determine the resistance of a $\mathcal{CM}$ to the Gröbner basis attack, we have to estimate the complexity of computing the Gröbner basis of the ideal

$$I = \langle f_1(\underline{x}) - y_1, \ldots, f_n(\underline{x}) - y_n, x_1^{2^e} - x_1, \ldots, x_n^{2^e} - x_n \rangle$$

where $F(\underline{x}) = \underline{y}$. Let $sd(I)$ be the **solving degree of** I, i.e. the the highest degree of polynomials involved in the computation of the Gröbner basis. The complexity of computing the Gröbner basis using a algorithm like F4/F5 is bounded from above by

$$O\left(\binom{n + sd(I)}{n}^{\omega} \right) \tag{2}$$

(see [8,13,17]) where ω is the exponent in the complexity of matrix multiplication. It is easy to see that this upper bound is well above $O(2^{256})$, since $sd(I)$ is bounded below be degree of the initial basis I , $x_n^{2^e} - x_n \in I$ and a typical monomial of F has from 4 to 8 variables we can force the degree of I to be bounded below by 2^e. Now if we take a $\mathcal{CM}$ with 8 variables (2) is bounded below by 2^{16e}. If we use $q = 2^{64}$ then the complexity is bounded by $O(2^{1024})$.

We can safely assume that $2^e \leq sd(I)$, the problem is that we do not know if the bound (2) is accurate or not for the Gröbner basis computation of this kind of ideals. In order to make an experimental testing of the above bound, we used Magma [7] in a cluster with several fat nodes with 512 Gb of RAM each. After an extensive series of computations, Magma can find the Gröbner basis only for $q = 2^3$ and or $q = 2^4$. For $q = 2^5$ Magma exhausted the 512GB of RAM of our server before the end of the computation. Here are the conclusions that we get from our experiments.

- Given a $\mathcal{CM}$, the time of computing the Gröbner basis depends mainly on the exponents of F, but not of the actual matrices that give F.
- The initial basis I can be considered sparse because it has a low number of monomials by rapport to the degree but the intermediate computations of Magma show that the number of monomials can be very big.
- The upper bound (2) seems to be accurate, but further research is needed to confirm this fact.

Of course those conclusions can not be extrapolated for higher q. If any one can try to verify those conclusion for $e \geq 5$ we can provide them the basis for different $\mathcal{CM}$.

We can use the special form of the monomials that allow to substitute $F(\underline{x})$ by $F(y_{11}, \dots)$ as described in Example 1, but this will give a greater complexity because we will have much more variables but the degree will not decrease much. Let's explain this in the Example 1. We have now that $\bar{F}$ has 18 variables $\{y_{11}, \dots, y_{36}\}$. If we examine the relations among the x_i and the y_{jk} given by the lists S_1, S_2, S_3 we find, for instance, $x_1^{2^{e_{3,1}+e_{1,1}+e_{2,1}}} = y_{21}, x_1^{2^{e_{1,3}+e_{2,3}+e_{3,3}}} = y_{31}$, so we would get a relation $y_{31} = y_{21}^{2^a}$ for some $a \leq q$ and we would end with a basis $\bar{I}$ such that $sd(\bar{I}) \geq 2^e$ as before.

6.2   Weil Descent

Taking a base of $\mathbb{F}_q$ over $\mathbb{F}_2$, namely $B = \{v_1, \dots, v_e\}$, we can express the polynomial of F as polynomials $\tilde{F}$ in ne variables over $\mathbb{F}_2$. It is easy to verify that before the reduction of monomials, the degrees of the components of $\tilde{F}$ are $(t_1 \dots t_4)$. In fact the raise of the binary degree of the public key was one of the reasons to use more than two exponentials on the DME in order to avoid a decomposition attack as in [18]. As we explain in [26] the algorithm in [18] do not work (see also Thm. 5 in [35]). For binary polynomial of degree higher that four there is also an descomposition algorithms whose complexity can be controlled taking the degree high enough. For instance for $q = 2^{64}$ and the degree $t_i = 8$ theorem 4.2 of [19] gives a complexity $O(2^D)$ with $D > 243$.

The reduction of monomials can produce also a reduction of the degrees of $\tilde{F}$ and it is not possible to determine a priory the degrees of the $\tilde{F}$. One has to examine the list of monomials after the reduction and compute the degrees. For instance, in Example 1 the degrees are reduced from $(7, 7, 6)$ to $(5, 6, 6)$. For $\mathcal{CM}_2$ in Sect. 7 the degrees of $\tilde{F}$ are reduced from $(9, 9, 8, 9)$ to $(7, 8, 6, 7)$.

If $q = 2^{64}$ and the degree after Weil descent is $d = 8$ we will have $O(2^{56})$ monomial of degree up to 8. Our experiments suggest that the solving degree will be greater than 8 but more precise estimation of the solving degree are needed. For instance if $sd((I)) = 16$ then (2) gives a complexity of $O(2^{237})$. It is also interesting to use the Weil descend over different intermediate fields and to compute the complexity of solving the corresponding equations.

6.3   Estimation of the Number of Monomials of the Inverse

As we mentioned earlier we set that $1/det(A_i)$ has a big binary weight to get a number of monomials of the inverse big enough. Next we will do a more precise estimation of this number of monomial. Lets denote by C_i the matrix obtained from A_i^{-1} changing the non zero entries by 1. If the entries of A_i^{-1} were powers of two, then the number of monomials of F^{-1} is (s_1, s_2, s_3, s_4) where s_i is the sum of entries of de row i of $C^* = C_1^* \cdots C_r^*$ but now each entry in A_i^{-1} is multiplied by $1/det(A_i)$ or $-1/det(A_i)$. Let b_i the binary weight of $1/det(A_i)$ mod $q^2 - 1$ then $128 - b_i$ is the binary weight of $-1/det(A_i)$ mod $q^2 - 1$. We can impose that $b_i \leq 128 - b_i$ and then b_i is a lower bound for the binary weight of each entry of A_i^{-1}. It is easy to verify that the number of monomial is bounded below be $(s_1 b_i, s_2 b_i, s_3 b_i, s_4 b_i)$. If the $\mathcal{CM}$ has two matrices A_i, A_j with determinant not a power of 2 then one get the bound $(s_1 b_i b_j, s_2 b_i b_j, s_3 b_i b_j, s_4 b_i b_j)$.

For the configuration $\mathcal{CM}_1$ with 3 exponentials only A_3 has determinant not a power of 2. The computation of C^* gives

$$C^* = C_1^* \cdot C_2^* \cdot C_3^* = \begin{pmatrix} 3\,3\,3\,3 \\ 6\,6\,6\,6 \\ 7\,7\,7\,7 \\ 6\,6\,6\,6 \end{pmatrix}$$

This means that each polynomial has at least 2^{12b_3} monomials. If we take $b_3 = 10$ they have at least 2^{120} monomials that gives a complexity of $120w \geq 256$ bits.

For the configuration $\mathcal{CM}_2$ with 4 exponentials A_3 has determinant not a power of 2. The computation of C^* gives

$$C^* = C_1^* \cdot C_2^* \cdot C_3^* \cdot C_4^* = \begin{pmatrix} 1\ 4\ 4\ 4 \\ 3\ 9\ 9\ 9 \\ 4\ 12\ 12\ 12 \\ 9\ 9\ 9\ 9 \end{pmatrix}$$

This means that each polynomial has at least 2^{13b_3} monomials. If we take $b_3 = 9$ they have at least 2^{117} monomials that gives a complexity of $117w \geq 256$ bits .

6.4 Structural Cryptanalysis

We can try to invert F directly by starting with the inverse of the last linear map L_r. As we explained in Sect. 3, for each linear map L_{rk} we can use the the the relations $H_{ij} = Q_{ij}(B,C) = \sum B_k C_l$, to get homogeneous implicit equations for the H_{ij} that will give us homogeneous equations for the unknown entries of the matrices L_{rk}^{-1} and the translations a_{rk} by using that

$$B_i = B_{i1} + \bar{u}B_{i2} = L_{rk}^{-1}(D_i) - (a_{rk1} + \bar{u}a_{rk2})$$

where $D_i = D_{i1} + \bar{u}D_{i2}$ are the known coefficients of the corresponding monomial of the public key. It is not clear what is the complexity of the Gröbner basis computation for eliminate the B_k, C_l from the equations $H_{ij} = Q_{ij}(B,C)$ but the number of variables is high, for instance for the last component of $\mathcal{CM}_2$ we have $96 + 36 = 132$ variables.

We can give an upper bound of the cost using linear algebra as follows. Let n_1 the the number of variables H_{ij}, that is, the size of the corresponding list M_{rk} and let n_2 be the number of variables B_k, C_l. Let $P_d(H_{ij})$ a homogeneous polynomial of degree d, by making the substitution $Q_{2d}(B,C) = P_d(Q_{ij})$ we get a polynomial of degree $2d$, $Q_{2d}(B,C)$ in the variables B_k and C_l Taking the coefficients of $P_2(H_{ij}) = \sum c_{ij}H_{ij}$ as variables , the coefficients of $Q_{2d}(B,C)$ are linear forms on the c_{ij} and we can impose the condition $Q_{2d}(B,C) = 0$ by solving the corresponding linear equations. Let $HM(n,d) = \binom{n+d-1}{d}$ be the number of monomials of degree d in n variables. In our situation $HM(n_1,d) < HM(n_2,2d)$ for small d, but we can get $HM(n_1,d) > HM(n_2,2d)$ taking d big enough and the implicit equations on H_{ij} can be obtained by solving those linear equations. As the implicit equations that we get are homogeneous, for each $k \leq 4$ we would have a solution for the matrix L_{rk}^{-1} and the a_{rk} that is defined up to a multiplicative constant $\lambda_k \in \mathbb{F}_q$, and given $(\lambda_1, \ldots, \lambda_4) \in \mathbb{F}_q \setminus \{0\}$ we can find the inverse of the L_{3k} and a_{3k}.

7 Implementation and Timings

For test the timing we implemented two configuration matrices $\mathcal{CM}_1$ for DME-$(3,8,2^{64})$ and $\mathcal{CM}_2$ for DME-$(4,8,2^{64})$ for KEM (with OAEP as padding) and for SIGN (with PSS00 as padding) For the implementation, we used the special instructions that modern Intel processors have to perform arithmetic in finite fields, which gives th algorithm an impressive boost in performance. In all the cases, when a hash function was needed, we used the NIST approved standard SHA-2 function.

The matrices for $\mathcal{CM}_1$ with DME-$(3,8,2^{64})$ are the following:

$$E_1^* = \begin{pmatrix} 1&1&0&0 \\ 1&0&1&0 \\ 1&0&0&1 \\ 1&0&0&0 \end{pmatrix}, E_2^* = \begin{pmatrix} 1&1&0&0 \\ 1&0&1&0 \\ 1&0&0&1 \\ 0&0&1&1 \end{pmatrix}, E_3^* = \begin{pmatrix} 1&0&0&1 \\ 1&0&1&0 \\ 0&1&1&0 \\ 0&1&0&1 \end{pmatrix}$$

$$E^* = E_3^* \cdot E_2^* \cdot E_1^* = \begin{pmatrix} 4 & 1 & 1 & 1 \\ 4 & 2 & 1 & 0 \\ 4 & 2 & 0 & 1 \\ 4 & 1 & 0 & 2 \end{pmatrix}$$

The number of monomials of F before reduction is $(2^7, 2^7, 2^7, 2^7)$ and the binary degree $(7, 7, 7, 7)$. As we explain in Sect. 5.2 and in Example 1 in more detail, given the $\mathcal{CM}$, the linear equations that reduce the monomials are determined by matrices of the $\mathcal{CM}$. The only alternative is if we use all the linear equations for the reduction or we use all but one in order to ensure that $det(E_i)$ is not 0 or a power of 2. For this $\mathcal{CM}$ in particular, we get 9 linear equations, one for each row from the E_2 and E_3. By substituting the 9 equations one get $(40, 30, 30, 30)$, but then $det(E_3) = 0$ which is not valid. For this reason we drop the linear equation coming from the first row of E_3 and we get $(72, 30, 30, 30)$. The equations that we obtain with the algorithm RED are

$$e_{1,3} = e_{1,1},$$
$$e_{2,2} = e_{2,1},$$
$$e_{2,4} = e_{1,1} + e_{2,3} - e_{1,5},$$
$$e_{2,6} = e_{1,1} + e_{2,5} - e_{1,7},$$
$$e_{2,8} = e_{1,5} + e_{2,7} - e_{1,7},$$
$$e_{3,4} = e_{2,1} + e_{3,3} - e_{2,5},$$
$$e_{3,6} = e_{2,3} + e_{3,5} - e_{2,5},$$
$$e_{3,8} = e_{1,1} - e_{1,5} + e_{2,3} + e_{3,7} - e_{2,7}$$

The equation that we do not use is $e_{3,2} = e_{1,1} - e_{1,5} + e_{2,1} + e_{3,1} - e_{2,7}$. As in Example 1, we can make a change to the variables y_{ij}, which in this case are given by:

$$S_1 = \begin{bmatrix} x_1^{2^{e_{3,1}+e_{1,1}+e_{2,1}}} = y_{11}, & x_1^{2^{e_{3,2}+e_{1,5}+e_{2,7}}} = y_{12}, & x_2^{2^{e_{3,1}+e_{1,1}+e_{2,1}}} = y_{13}, & x_2^{2^{e_{3,2}+e_{1,5}+e_{2,7}}} = y_{14}, \\ x_3^{2^{e_{1,2}+e_{2,1}+e_{3,1}}} = y_{15}, & x_4^{2^{e_{1,2}+e_{2,11}+e_{3,1}}} = y_{16}, & x_5^{2^{e_{1,4}+e_{2,1}+e_{3,1}}} = y_{17}, & x_6^{2^{e_{1,4}+e_{2,1}+e_{3,1}}} = y_{18}, \\ x_7^{2^{e_{1,6}+e_{2,7}+e_{3,2}}} = y_{19}, & x_8^{2^{e_{1,6}+e_{2,7}+e_{3,2}}} = y_{1,10} \end{bmatrix}$$

$$S_2 = \begin{bmatrix} x_1^{2^{e_{1,1}+e_{2,1}+e_{3,3}}} = y_{21}, & x_2^{2^{e_{1,1}+e_{2,1}+e_{3,3}}} = y_{22}, & x_3^{2^{e_{1,2}+e_{2,1}+e_{3,3}}} = y_{23}, \\ x_3^{2^{e_{1,2}+e_{2,1}+e_{3,3}}} = y_{24}, & x_5^{2^{e_{1,4}+e_{2,11}+e_{3,3}}} = y_{25}, & x_6^{2^{e_{1,4}+e_{2,11}+e_{3,3}}} = y_{26} \end{bmatrix}$$

$$S_3 = \begin{bmatrix} x_1^{2^{e_{1,1}+e_{2,1}+e_{3,3}}} = y_{31}, & x_2^{2^{e_{1,1}+e_{2,1}+e_{3,3}}} = y_{32}, & x_3^{2^{e_{1,2}+e_{2,1}+e_{3,3}}} = y_{33}, \\ x_4^{2^{e_{1,2}+e_{2,1}+e_{3,3}}} = y_{34}, & x_5^{2^{e_{1,4}+e_{2,1}+e_{3,3}}} = y_{35}, & x_6^{2^{e_{1,4}+e_{2,1}+e_{3,3}}} = y_{36} \end{bmatrix}$$

$$S_4 = \begin{bmatrix} x_1^{2^{e_{1,1}+e_{2,3}+e_{3,7}}} = y_{41}, & x_2^{2^{e_{1,1}+e_{2,3}+e_{3,7}}} = y_{42}, & x_3^{2^{e_{1,2}+e_{2,3}+e_{3,7}}} = y_{43}, \\ x_4^{2^{e_{1,2}+e_{2,3}+e_{3,7}}} = y_{44}, & x_7^{2^{e_{1,6}+e_{1,1}+e_{2,3}-e_{1,5}+e_{3,7}}} = y_{45}, & x_8^{2^{e_{1,6}+e_{,11}+e_{2,3}-e_{1,5}+e_{3,7}}} = y_{46} \end{bmatrix}$$

With this changes the degrees of $\bar{F}$ aree $(5, 8, 7, 7)$ and the binary degrees of $\tilde{F}$ after Weil descent are $(7, 6, 6, 6)$. The translations are in the first component of the third linear map, yielding $(78, 36, 30, 30)$ monomials. The length of the secret key is 542 bytes, the length of the public key is 2739 bytes, and a ciphertext takes 64 bytes.

We take $n = 8$ and $q = 2^{64}$, we have a choice of $O(2^{256})$ vectors $(\lambda_1, \lambda_2, \lambda_3, \lambda_4)$ that are enough for the NIST level 5.

The matrices for $\mathcal{CM}_2$ with DME-$(4, 8, 2^{64})$ are the following:

$$
E_1^* = \begin{pmatrix} 1 1 0 0 \\ 1 0 0 0 \\ 0 0 1 1 \\ 0 0 0 1 \end{pmatrix}, E_2^* = \begin{pmatrix} 1 1 0 0 \\ 0 1 0 0 \\ 1 0 0 1 \\ 0 0 1 0 \end{pmatrix}, E_3^* = \begin{pmatrix} 1 0 0 1 \\ 1 1 0 0 \\ 0 0 1 1 \\ 0 1 1 0 \end{pmatrix}, E_4^* = \begin{pmatrix} 1 1 0 0 \\ 0 1 1 0 \\ 0 1 0 1 \\ 0 0 1 1 \end{pmatrix}
$$

,

$$
E^* = E_4^* \cdot E_3^* \cdot E_2^* \cdot E_1^* = \begin{pmatrix} 5 2 1 1 \\ 4 2 1 2 \\ 5 2 0 1 \\ 3 2 1 3 \end{pmatrix}
$$

The number of monomial of F before reductions is $(2^9, 2^9, 2^8, 2^9)$. After imposing 8 linear conditions we reduce the number of monomials to $(72, 90, 36, 96)$ and there are no QR. The equations that we obtain by method in Sect. 3 are:

$$
e_{2,2} = e_{1,1} + e_{2,1} - e_{1,3},
$$
$$
e_{3,4} = e_{1,1} - e_{1,3} + e_{2,1} - e_{2,3} + e_{3,3},
$$
$$
e_{3,6} = e_{1,7} - e_{1,6} + e_{2,6} - e_{2,7} + e_{3,5},
$$
$$
e_{3,8} = e_{1,3} - e_{1,1} + e_{2,3} - e_{2,5} + e_{3,7},
$$
$$
e_{4,2} = e_{3,1} - e_{3,4} + e_{4,1},
$$
$$
e_{4,4} = e_{2,1} - e_{2,5} + e_{3,3} - e_{3,5} + e_{4,3},
$$
$$
e_{4,6} = e_{1,1} - e_{1,3} + e_{2,1} - e_{2,3} + e_{3,3} - e_{3,7} + e_{4,5},
$$
$$
e_{4,8} = e_{1,1} - e_{1,3} + e_{2,5} - e_{2,5} + e_{3,5} - e_{3,7} + e_{4,7}
$$

As in the previous 3 round case one can make changes the to get the polynomials $\bar{F}(y_{ij})$ and after those changes the degrees of $\bar{F}$ are $(9, 9, 8, 9)$ and the binary degrees of $\tilde{F}$ after Weil descent are $(7, 8, 6, 7)$. Now we have a choice of $O(2^{256})$ vectors $(\lambda_1, \lambda_2, \lambda_3, \lambda_4)$ that are enough for the NIST level 5.

The translations are in the first component of the fourth linear map, yielding $(80, 90, 36, 96)$ monomials. The length of the secret key is 675 bytes, the length of the public key is 4843 bytes, and a ciphertext takes 64 bytes.

The timings of DME-KEM have also been measured with SuperCop, to allow a fair comparison with other schemes. The DME implementation has been optimized for processors with the special `clmul` operation (carry-less multiplication)

DME-$(3, 8, 2^{64})$-SIGN-PSS	
KeyGen	$380\mu s$
Sign	$37\mu s$
Verify	$7\mu s$
Public Key	2793 bytes
Secret Key	542 bytes
Signature	64 bytes

DME-$(3, 8, 2^{64})$-KEM-OAEP	
KeyGen	$384\mu s$
Decrypt	$36\mu s$
Encrypt	$7\mu s$
Public Key	2793 bytes
Secret Key	542 bytes
Shared Secret	32 bytes
Ciphertext	64 bytes

Fig. 1. Timings for DME-SIGN (100 byte messages) and DME-KEM

DME-$(4, 8, 2^{64})$-SIGN-PSS	
KeyGen	$931\mu s$
Sign	$44\mu s$
Verify	$9\mu s$
Public Key	4843 bytes
Secret Key	675 bytes
Signature	64 bytes

DME-$(4, 8, 2^{64})$-KEM-OAEP	
KeyGen	$929\mu s$
Decrypt	$43\mu s$
Encrypt	$9\mu s$
Public Key	4843 bytes
Secret Key	675 bytes
Shared Secret	32 bytes
Ciphertext	64 bytes

Fig. 2. Timings for DME-SIGN (100 byte messages) and DME-KEM

that gives a considerable speed-up in the arithmetic over finite fields of characteristic two. Currently, we are using a naive algorithm for computing inverses in $\mathbb{F}_q$ based on the binary exponentiation algorithm and the relation $a^{-1} = a^{q-2}$. Any optimization here would translate in further improvements in the timings (Figs. 1, 2, 3 and 4).

	NSL	KeyGen	Enc	Dec	PKey	SKey	SS	CText
dme-4r-8v-64b-oaep	5	3468004	80097	216374	4843	675	32	64
dme-3r-8v-64b-oaep	5	1510324	46929	224497	2793	542	32	64
kyber1024	5	137520	147921	112820	1568	3168	32	1568
ntrukem743	5	2002204	426806	610610	1023	1173	48	1023
mcelice348864	1	120686580	75741	278278	261120	6492	32	96
sikep751	5	23110975	37404352	40155660	564	644	32	596
bikel3	3	2729828	385831	8923861	3083	10105	32	3115

Fig. 3. Average CPU cycles for KEM as measured by SuperCop on an Intel(R) Core(TM) i7-1165G7 @ 2.80 GHz

	NSL	KeyGen	Sign	Verify	PKey	Skey	Signature
dme-4r-8v-64b-pss	5	4609827	222307	55484	4843	675	64
dme-3r-8v-64b-pss	5	1953078	182009	40197	2793	542	64
dilithium2	2	169935	238597	147235	1312	2544	2420
dilithium5	5	319828	617804	337222	2492	4880	4595
falcon1024dyn	5	78644060	2080846	310257	1793	2305	1330
sphincsf256shake256robust	5	23130618	530274683	25373313	64	128	49216

Fig. 4. Average CPU cycles for SIGN as measured by SuperCop on an Intel(R) Core(TM) i7-1165G7 @ 2.80 GHz (message length = 93 bytes)

References

1. Avendaño, M., Marco, M.: A structural attack to the DME-(3,2, q) cryptosystem. Finite Fields Their Appl. **71**, 101810 (2021)
2. Bellare, M., Rogaway, P.: Optimal asymmetric encryption. In: De Santis, A. (ed.) EUROCRYPT 1994. LNCS, vol. 950, pp. 92–111. Springer, Heidelberg (1995). https://doi.org/10.1007/BFb0053428
3. Bellare, M., Rogaway, P.: The exact security of digital signatures-how to sign with RSA and Rabin. In: Maurer, U. (ed.) EUROCRYPT 1996. LNCS, vol. 1070, pp. 399–416. Springer, Heidelberg (1996). https://doi.org/10.1007/3-540-68339-9_34
4. Bardet, M., et al.: Improvements of algebraic attacks for solving the rank decoding and MinRank problems. In: Moriai, S., Wang, H. (eds.) ASIACRYPT 2020. LNCS, vol. 12491, pp. 507–536. Springer, Cham (2020). https://doi.org/10.1007/978-3-030-64837-4_17
5. Bettale, L., Faugere, J.C., Perret, L.: Cryptanalysis of HFE, multi-HFE and variants for odd and even characteristic. Des. Codes Crypt. **69**(1), 1–52 (2013)
6. Beullens, W.: Improved cryptanalysis of UOV and rainbow. In: Canteaut, A., Standaert, F.-X. (eds.) EUROCRYPT 2021. LNCS, vol. 12696, pp. 348–373. Springer, Cham (2021). https://doi.org/10.1007/978-3-030-77870-5_13
7. Bosma, W., Cannon, J., Playoust, C.: The Magma algebra system. I. The user language. J. Symb. Comput. **24**(3–4), 235–265 (1997)
8. Gorla, E., Caminata, A.: Solving degree, last fall degree, and related invariants (with A. Caminata). J. Symb. Comput. **114**, 322–335 (2023)
9. Casanova, A., Faugere, J.C., Macario-Rat, G., Patarin, J., Perret, L., Ryckeghem, J.: GeMSS: a great multivariate short signature. NIST CSRC (2020). https://www-polsys.lip6.fr/Links/NIST/GeMSS-specification-round2.pdf
10. Courtois, N., Klimov, A., Patarin, J., Shamir, A.: Efficient algorithms for solving overdefined systems of multivariate polynomial equations. In: Preneel, B. (ed.) EUROCRYPT 2000. LNCS, vol. 1807, pp. 392–407. Springer, Heidelberg (2000). https://doi.org/10.1007/3-540-45539-6_27
11. Ding, J.: A new variant of the Matsumoto-Imai cryptosystem through perturbation. In: Bao, F., Deng, R., Zhou, J. (eds.) PKC 2004. LNCS, vol. 2947, pp. 305–318. Springer, Heidelberg (2004). https://doi.org/10.1007/978-3-540-24632-9_22
12. Ding, J., Wolf, C., Yang, B.-Y.: ℓ-invertible cycles for $\mathcal{M}$ultivariate $\mathcal{Q}$uadratic ($\mathcal{MQ}$) public key cryptography. In: Okamoto, T., Wang, X. (eds.) PKC 2007. LNCS, vol. 4450, pp. 266–281. Springer, Heidelberg (2007). https://doi.org/10.1007/978-3-540-71677-8_18

13. Ding, J., Schmidt, D.: Solving degree and degree of regularity for polynomial systems over a finite fields. In: Fischlin, M., Katzenbeisser, S. (eds.) Number Theory and Cryptography. LNCS, vol. 8260, pp. 34–49. Springer, Heidelberg (2013). https://doi.org/10.1007/978-3-642-42001-6_4

14. Ding, J., Chen, M.S., Petzoldt, A., Schmidt, D., Yang, B.Y.: Rainbow. NIST CSRC (2020). https://csrc.nist.gov/Projects/post-quantum-cryptography/round-3-submissions

15. Ding, J., Petzoldt, A., Wang, L.: The cubic simple matrix encryption scheme. In: Mosca, M. (ed.) PQCrypto 2014. LNCS, vol. 8772, pp. 76–87. Springer, Cham (2014). https://doi.org/10.1007/978-3-319-11659-4_5

16. Dubois, V., Fouque, P.-A., Shamir, A., Stern, J.: Practical cryptanalysis of SFLASH. In: Menezes, A. (ed.) CRYPTO 2007. LNCS, vol. 4622, pp. 1–12. Springer, Heidelberg (2007). https://doi.org/10.1007/978-3-540-74143-5_1

17. Faugere, J.C.: A new efficient algorithm for computing Gröbner bases (F4). J. Pure Appl. Algebra **139**, 61–88 (1999)

18. Faugere, J.C., Perret, L.: An efficient algorithm for decomposing multivariate polynomials and its applications to cryptography. J. Symb. Comput. **44**, 1676–1689 (2009)

19. Faugère, J.-C., Perret, L.: High order derivatives and decomposition of multivariate polynomials. In: Proceedings of ISSAC, pp. 207–214. ACM press (2009)

20. Fouque, P.-A., Granboulan, L., Stern, J.: Differential cryptanalysis for multivariate schemes. In: Cramer, R. (ed.) EUROCRYPT 2005. LNCS, vol. 3494, pp. 341–353. Springer, Heidelberg (2005). https://doi.org/10.1007/11426639_20

21. Kipnis, A., Shamir, A.: Cryptanalysis of the HFE public key cryptosystem by relinearization. In: Wiener, M. (ed.) CRYPTO 1999. LNCS, vol. 1666, pp. 19–30. Springer, Heidelberg (1999). https://doi.org/10.1007/3-540-48405-1_2

22. Luengo, I.: DME a public key, signature and KEM system based on double exponentiation with matrix exponents. https://csrc.nist.gov/CSRC/media/Presentations/DME/images-media/dme-April2018.pdf

23. I. Luengo, M. Avendaño : DME: a full encryption, signature and KEM multivariate public key cryptosystem. IACR preprint 2022/1538 (2022)

24. Matsumoto, T., Imai, H.: Public quadratic polynomial-tuples for efficient signature-verification and message-encryption. In: Barstow, D., et al. (eds.) EUROCRYPT 1988. LNCS, vol. 330, pp. 419–453. Springer, Heidelberg (1988). https://doi.org/10.1007/3-540-45961-8_39

25. Mohamed, M.S.E., Ding, J., Buchmann, J.: Towards algebraic cryptanalysis of HFE challenge 2. In: Kim, T., Adeli, H., Robles, R.J., Balitanas, M. (eds.) ISA 2011. CCIS, vol. 200, pp. 123–131. Springer, Heidelberg (2011). https://doi.org/10.1007/978-3-642-23141-4_12

26. NIST PQC Forum official comment. https://csrc.nist.gov/CSRC/media/Projects/Post-Quantum-Cryptography/documents/round-1/official-comments/DME-official-comment.pdf

27. Patarin, J.: Cryptanalysis of the Matsumoto and Imai public key scheme of Eurocrypt'88. In: Coppersmith, D. (ed.) CRYPTO 1995. LNCS, vol. 963, pp. 248–261. Springer, Heidelberg (1995). https://doi.org/10.1007/3-540-44750-4_20

28. Patarin, J.: Hidden fields equations (HFE) and isomorphisms of polynomials (IP): two new families of asymmetric algorithms. In: Maurer, U. (ed.) EUROCRYPT 1996. LNCS, vol. 1070, pp. 33–48. Springer, Heidelberg (1996). https://doi.org/10.1007/3-540-68339-9_4

29. Petzoldt, A., Chen, M.-S., Yang, B.-Y., Tao, C., Ding, J.: Design principles for HFEv- based multivariate signature schemes. In: Iwata, T., Cheon, J.H. (eds.) ASIACRYPT 2015. LNCS, vol. 9452, pp. 311–334. Springer, Heidelberg (2015). https://doi.org/10.1007/978-3-662-48797-6_14

30. Porras, J., Baena, J., Ding, J.: ZHFE, a new multivariate public key encryption scheme. In: Mosca, M. (ed.) PQCrypto 2014. LNCS, vol. 8772, pp. 229–245. Springer, Cham (2014). https://doi.org/10.1007/978-3-319-11659-4_14

31. Shamir, A.: Efficient signature schemes based on birational permutations. In: Stinson, D.R. (ed.) CRYPTO 1993. LNCS, vol. 773, pp. 1–12. Springer, Heidelberg (1994). https://doi.org/10.1007/3-540-48329-2_1

32. Smith-Tone, D.: On the differential security of multivariate public key cryptosystems. In: Yang, B.-Y. (ed.) PQCrypto 2011. LNCS, vol. 7071, pp. 130–142. Springer, Heidelberg (2011). https://doi.org/10.1007/978-3-642-25405-5_9

33. Tao, C., Petzoldt, A., Ding, J.: Efficient key recovery for All HFE signature variants. In: Malkin, T., Peikert, C. (eds.) CRYPTO 2021. LNCS, vol. 12825, pp. 70–93. Springer, Cham (2021). https://doi.org/10.1007/978-3-030-84242-0_4

34. Wolf, C., Preneel, B.: Equivalent keys in multivariate quadratic public key systems. J. Math. Cryptol. **4**(4), 375–415 (2011)

35. Zhao, S., Feng, R., Gao, X.: On functional decomposition of multivariate polynomials with differentiation and homogenization. J. Syst. Sci. Complexity **25**(2), 329–347 (2012)

Quantum Algorithms, Cryptanalysis and Models

On the Quantum Security of HAWK

Serge Fehr[1,2]($\boxtimes$) and Yu-Hsuan Huang[1]($\boxtimes$)

[1] Centrum Wiskunde & Informatica (CWI), Amsterdam, The Netherlands
serge.fehr@cwi.nl, yhh@cwi.nl
[2] Mathematical Institute, Leiden University, Leiden, The Netherlands

Abstract. In this paper, we prove the quantum security of the signature scheme HAWK, proposed by Ducas, Postlethwaite, Pulles and van Woerden (ASIACRYPT 2022). More precisely, we reduce its strong unforgeability in the quantum random oracle model (QROM) to the hardness of the one-more SVP problem, which is the computational problem on which also the classical security analysis of HAWK relies. Our security proof deals with the quantum aspects in a rather black-box way, making it accessible also to non-quantum-experts.

Keywords: quantum security · HAWK · digital signature · random oracle model

1 Introduction

Background. The discovery of Shor's algorithm has rendered most of the currently deployed public-key cryptosystems vulnerable to quantum attacks. As of 2016, the US National Institute of Standards and Technology (NIST) initiated the standardization process for post-quantum cryptography in the scope of key-encapsulation mechanism (KEM) and signature schemes. In 2022, the 3rd round winners were announced, but the process is still ongoing with the alternative KEM candidates and with a new call for signature schemes (see below). The selected signature schemes consist of Falcon [7] and Dilithium [4], which are lattice-based, and of SPHINCS+ [1], which is hash-based. For the sake of diversity, NIST has launched a new standardization process with a call for additional post-quantum signatures.

In 2022, [6] introduced a new cryptographic framework based on the *lattice-isomorphism problem (LIP)*. The framework can be used to build various post-quantum cryptographic schemes, including KEMs and signatures. One particularly interesting scheme is the signature scheme HAWK, proposed in [5]. It uses the simple lattice $\mathbb{Z}^{2n}$, endowed with the (module) structure of cyclotomic ring $\mathbb{Z}[x]/(x^n+1)$ for competitiveness. Due to this choice, the discrete Gaussian sampling (DGS), which is often the efficiency bottleneck, becomes much simpler and efficient. Indeed, by [5, Table 1], HAWK generally outperforms Falcon, which is considered to be one of the most efficient post-quantum signature schemes. It is

T. Johansson and D. Smith-Tone (Eds.): PQCrypto 2023, LNCS 14154, pp. 405–416, 2023.
https://doi.org/10.1007/978-3-031-40003-2_15

an "open secret" that HAWK will be submitted to the new NIST standardization process mentioned above.

The classical security of HAWK has been analyzed and rigorously proven (in the random oracle model), via a security reduction to the considered — and believed-to-be (quantum) hard — one-more SVP problem [5]. Especially in the light of being a candidate in the new NIST post-quantum competition, the *quantum* security of HAWK is of particular interest.

As is common for security proofs in the random oracle model, the classical security proof for HAWK from [5] does not carry over to the quantum setting, where the attacker can make quantum superposition queries to the random oracle. Also, HAWK does not follow a standard construction design, for which one could apply an off-the-shelf quantum-security result (like [3,9]). As a matter of fact, HAWK follows some non-standard randomized variant of the hash-and-sign paradigm, where first the hash $h := H(m, r)$ of the to-be-signed message m and some randomness r is computed, where r is then part of the signature $sig = (r, s)$, and the other part s is then sampled according to some distribution, which depends on the public key and on h, and that can be efficiently sampled if and (as far as we know) only if the secret key is given. The verification works by checking if some specific deterministic function of s and $H(m, r)$ satisfies some property (namely, is a non-zero short vector). Previous quantum analyses of generic hash-and-sign signature schemes, including the randomized variants considered in [2,10], which rely on preimage samplable functions, do not apply to HAWK (independent of whether one considers classical or quantum attacks). Thus, an explicit quantum security proof for HAWK is necessary to establish provable quantum security.

Contribution. In this work, we analyze the quantum security of HAWK in the random oracle model. In particular, we prove strong unforgeability against chosen-message attacks in the quantum random oracle model (QROM), where the quantum attacker is given superposition access to the random oracle. Our proof is in the form of a security reduction to the (same) one-more SVP problem, with an explicit security loss. Our result positively confirms that the claimed quantum security of HAWK lies on a firm theoretical foundation.

Our quantum security proof for HAWK recycles some elements of the classical proof from [5], but requires some new elements to deal with the quantum aspect. For example, we invoke the adaptive reprogramming technique from [8] as well as the optimality of Grover for preimage search. Our proof is rather modular, and from our quantum security proof one can easily extract a variant of the classical security proof as well (with a slightly improved bound compared to the original classical proof in [5]), simply by replacing the adaptive reprogramming and the preimage search parts by their classical counterparts. In particular, our quantum security proof is meant to be accessible to a large extent also to non-quantum-experts.

2 Preliminary

2.1 Setting up the Stage

Let $\mathcal{R}$ be the cyclotomic ring $\mathcal{R} = \mathbb{Z}[x]/(x^n + 1)$, which is isomorphic to $\mathbb{Z}^n$ as a $\mathbb{Z}$-module; later on, n will be restricted to be an integer power of 2. Furthermore, we fix the obvious inclusion map $\mathcal{R}/2\mathcal{R} \hookrightarrow \mathcal{R}$, and thus consider the reduction mod 2 as a map $\mathcal{R} \to \mathcal{R}/2\mathcal{R} \subset \mathcal{R}$.

In order to abstract away the technical details of the property sym-break from [5], we consider the function $\langle \cdot \rangle : \mathcal{R}^2 \to \mathcal{R}^2$ defined by

$$v = \begin{pmatrix} v_1 \\ v_2 \end{pmatrix} \mapsto \langle v \rangle := \begin{cases} -v \text{ if sym} - \mathsf{break}(v_1) = 1, \\ v \text{ otherwise,} \end{cases}$$

where, as defined in [5], sym-break$(v_1) = 1$ if and only if $v_1 \neq 0$ with the first nonzero coefficient being positive. It is convenient to think of $\langle v \rangle$ as a representation of the equivalence class $\{v, -v\}$, with the representation being unique if $v_1 \neq 0$. Indeed, what will be relevant is that

$$\langle v \rangle = \langle -v \rangle \in \{v, -v\} \quad \forall v \notin \{0\} \times \mathcal{R} , \tag{1}$$

while $\langle v \rangle = v$ for $v \in \{0\} \times \mathcal{R}$.

Let $\mathbf{B} \in \mathsf{GL}_2(\mathcal{R})$ be an invertible 2×2 matrix over $\mathcal{R}$, and let $\mathbf{Q} = \mathbf{B}^*\mathbf{B}$. Looking ahead, $\mathbf{B}$ will form the secret key and $\mathbf{Q}$ the public key in HAWK. Such a Hermitian matrix $\mathbf{Q}$ induces the norm $\|v\|_{\mathbf{Q}} := \mathsf{tr}\,(v^*\mathbf{Q}v)\,/n$. As the name suggests, this is a norm in the $\mathbb{Z}$-module $\mathcal{R}^2$, meaning $\|u + v\|_{\mathbf{Q}} \leq \|u\|_{\mathbf{Q}} + \|v\|_{\mathbf{Q}}$, $\|av\|_{\mathbf{Q}} = |a|\,\|v\|_{\mathbf{Q}}$ and $\|v\|_{\mathbf{Q}} = 0 \Rightarrow v = 0$ for all $u, v \in \mathcal{R}$ and $a \in \mathbb{Z}$.

For every $\sigma > 0$ and $h \in \mathcal{R}^2/2\mathcal{R}^2 \subset \mathcal{R}^2$, consider the following $\mathbf{Q}$-dependent distributions $D_\sigma^{\mathbf{B}}$, $\widetilde{D}_\sigma^{\mathbf{B}}[h]$ and $\widetilde{D}_\sigma^{\mathbf{B}}$. They can be efficiently sampled if the matrix $\mathbf{B}$ is known, which motivates the superscript-$\mathbf{B}$ notation.

Definition 1. *For every $\sigma > 0$ and $\mathbf{Q} = \mathbf{B}^*\mathbf{B}$ as specified above, define*

- $D_\sigma^{\mathbf{B}}$: *the discrete (σ-deviated) Gaussian distribution under $\mathbf{Q}$-norm centered at 0 and supported at $\mathcal{R}^2$.*
- $\widetilde{D}_\sigma^{\mathbf{B}}[h]$: *the discrete ($\sigma$-deviated) Gaussian distribution under $\mathbf{Q}$-norm centered at 0 and supported at $h + 2\mathcal{R}^2 \subset \mathcal{R}^2$.*
- $\widetilde{D}_\sigma^{\mathbf{B}}$: *with a random choice of $h \leftarrow \mathcal{R}^2/2\mathcal{R}^2$, sampling $D_\sigma'[h]$.*

Note that for every $h \in \mathcal{R}^2/2\mathcal{R}^2 \subset \mathcal{R}^2$ we have

$$v \bmod 2 = h \quad \forall v \in \mathsf{supp}\left(\widetilde{D}_\sigma^{\mathbf{B}}[h]\right) = h + 2\mathcal{R}^2 . \tag{2}$$

Furthermore, by Lemma 9 in the full version of [5], for every $\epsilon > 0$ and $\sigma \geq \eta_\epsilon(\mathbb{Z}^n)$, the statistical distance

$$\delta\left(D_{2\sigma}^{\mathbf{B}}, \widetilde{D}_{2\sigma}^{\mathbf{B}}\right) \leq \epsilon/(1 - \epsilon) , \tag{3}$$

where $\eta_\epsilon(\,\cdot\,)$ is as defined in [5, Definition 3]. This also implies that the distribution of $h := v \bmod 2$ for $v \leftarrow D_{2\sigma}^{\mathrm{B}}$ is close to uniformly random in $\mathcal{R}^2/2\mathcal{R}^2$, with statistical distance at most $\epsilon/(1-\epsilon)$. Furthermore, as a direct consequence of [5, Lemma 3], the guessing probability of $v \bmod 2$ for $v \leftarrow D_{2\sigma}^{\mathrm{B}}$ is bounded by

$$\mathrm{guess}(v \bmod 2) := \max_{h^\circ \in \mathcal{R}^2/2\mathcal{R}^2} \Pr[v \bmod 2 = h^\circ] \le 2^{-2n} \cdot \frac{1+\epsilon}{1-\epsilon}. \tag{4}$$

2.2 Geometric Units

Define the set of geometric units as $\mu_{\mathbb{K}} := \{x^1, \ldots, x^{2n}\} \subseteq \mathcal{R}$. The following Lemma 1 is recycled from the proof of Lemma 10 in the full version of [5], and will be useful in later analysis.

Lemma 1. *Let n be a power of 2, $\epsilon > 0$, $\sigma \ge \eta_\epsilon(\mathbb{Z}^n)$, and $h^\circ \in \mathcal{R}^2/2\mathcal{R}^2$. Consider $v \leftarrow D_{2\sigma}$ and set $h := v \bmod 2$. Then*

$$\Pr\left[\exists\, \alpha \in \mu_{\mathbb{K}} \setminus \{\pm 1\} : \tfrac{1}{2}(h + \alpha v) \in \mathcal{R}^2\right] \le 2^{-n} \cdot \frac{1+\epsilon}{1-\epsilon}, \quad and \tag{5}$$

$$\Pr\left[\exists\, \alpha \in \mu_{\mathbb{K}} : \tfrac{1}{2}(h^\circ + \alpha v) \in \mathcal{R}^2\right] \le n \cdot 2^{-2n} \cdot \frac{1+\epsilon}{1-\epsilon}. \tag{6}$$

Proof. For (5), note that $\tfrac{1}{2}(h + \alpha v) \in \mathcal{R}^2$ implies that $h + \alpha v \in 2\mathcal{R}^2$, and thus $\alpha v \equiv h \equiv v \pmod 2$. Furthermore, any $\alpha \in \mu_{\mathbb{K}} \setminus \{\pm 1\}$ satisfies $\alpha \equiv x^i \pmod 2$ for some $1 \le i < n$, and so we have $x^i v \equiv v \pmod 2$ and thus by repeated application

$$x^{ki}v = x^{(k-1)i}x^i v \equiv x^{(k-1)i}v = \cdots \equiv v \pmod 2 \tag{7}$$

for any positive integer k. Furthermore, exploiting that, by the choice of n as a power of 2, $n/2$ must be a multiple of $\gcd(i,n)$ and thus can be written as $n/2 = ki + \ell n$ (where one may choose k to be positive), and using that $x^n \equiv 1 \pmod 2$, we obtain that

$$x^{n/2}v \equiv v \pmod 2.$$

Thus, we conclude (5) by

$$\Pr\left[\exists\, \alpha \in \mu_{\mathbb{K}} \setminus \{\pm 1\} : \tfrac{1}{2}(h + \alpha v) \in \mathcal{R}^2\right]$$
$$\le \Pr\left[x^{n/2}v \equiv v \pmod 2\right]$$
$$\le \mathrm{guess}(v \bmod 2) \cdot \#\left\{v^\circ \in \mathcal{R}^2/2\mathcal{R}^2 \mid x^{n/2}v^\circ \equiv v^\circ \pmod 2\right\}$$
$$\le 2^{-2n} \cdot \frac{1+\epsilon}{1-\epsilon} \cdot 2^n$$
$$\le 2^{-n} \cdot \frac{1+\epsilon}{1-\epsilon},$$

where we exploited (4).

Similarly, for (6), note that $\tfrac{1}{2}(h^\circ + \alpha v) \in \mathcal{R}^2$ implies that $v \equiv \alpha^{-1}h^\circ \pmod 2$, and furthermore $\#\{\alpha^{-1}h^\circ \bmod 2 \mid \alpha \in \mu_{\mathbb{K}}\} \le n$. Together with (4), we conclude the claimed bound (6). $\qquad\square$

2.3   Adaptive Reprogramming Lemma

The following reprogramming lemma adapts from [8, Theorem 1], with a simpler proof. Intuitively, it states that, if the location x of a reprogramming is hard to guess prior to when it is taking place, then such a reprogramming is hard to notice.

Lemma 2 (Slight modification of [8, Theorem 1]). *Let $H : \mathcal{X} \to \mathcal{Y}$ be a random oracle, $\epsilon > 0$ and Ω be a family of distributions on $\mathcal{X}$ where every $\mathcal{D} \in \Omega$ is with guessing probability $guess(\mathcal{D}) := \max_{x^\circ} \Pr_{x \leftarrow \mathcal{D}} [x = x^\circ] \leq \epsilon$. Define the reprogramming oracle Repro_b for $b \in \{0,1\}$ that, on input (a suitable representation of) $\mathcal{D} \in \Omega$, works as below:*

$\mathsf{Repro}_0(\mathcal{D})$ $\mathsf{Repro}_1(\mathcal{D})$

1: $x \leftarrow \mathcal{D}$ *1:* $x \leftarrow \mathcal{D}$

2: $y := H(x)$ *2:* $H(x) := y \leftarrow \mathcal{Y}$

3: **return** (x, y) *3:* **return** (x, y)

Suppose $\mathcal{A}^{\mathsf{Repro}_b, H}$ for $b \in \{0,1\}$ makes at most q_R queries to the reprogramming oracle Repro_b, and at most q_H quantum queries to H before the last reprogramming query. Then,

$$\left| \Pr\left[1 \leftarrow \mathcal{A}^{\mathsf{Repro}_0, H} \right] - \Pr\left[1 \leftarrow \mathcal{A}^{\mathsf{Repro}_1, H} \right] \right| \leq 2 q_R \sqrt{(q_H + q_R) \cdot \epsilon} .$$

The intuition is quite simple: $\mathcal{A}$ can notice whether $H(x)$ gets reprogrammed or not only if it has queried x beforehand, which is unlikely the case since it is chosen with high entropy. The compressed oracle technique allows to make this line of reasoning rigorous, even when the queries to H are quantum: Before every Repro query we measure the compressed oracle to check whether x has been queried, we argue that the measurement outcome is "no" with overwhelming probability due to the high entropy in x, we conclude that the measurement caused little disturbance due to the gentle measurement lemma, and we observe that in case of a "no" outcome there is no difference between Repro_0 and Repro_1.

The full proof is based on the compressed oracle technique, but is rather standard. We refer readers to Appendix A for a detailed proof.

3   Brief Recap on HAWK and the One-More SVP

In the scope of HAWK, we take it as understood that the degree n of the cyclotomic ring $\mathcal{R}$ is a power of 2. Let $H : \mathcal{X} \to \mathcal{R}^2 / 2\mathcal{R}^2 \subseteq \mathcal{R}^2$ be a hash function, modelled as a random oracle, and let the parameters $\sigma_{\mathsf{pk}}, \sigma_{\mathsf{sign}}, \sigma_{\mathsf{ver}}, \mathsf{saltlen}$ be as specified in Lemma 10 in the full version of [5]. In particular, it holds that $\sigma_{\mathsf{sign}} \geq \eta_\epsilon(\mathbb{Z}^n)$ for some negligible $\epsilon > 0$. We write Gen for the (σ_{pk}-dependent) key generation procedure specified in [5], producing a public-secret key pair $(\mathbf{Q}, \mathbf{B})$ with $\mathbf{B} \in \mathsf{GL}_2(\mathcal{R})$ and $\mathbf{Q} = \mathbf{B}^* \mathbf{B}$

The signing $Sign_{\mathbf{B}}$ and verification $Vrfy_{\mathbf{Q}}$ of HAWK works as follows.

Remark 1. We take it as understood that $Vrfy_{\mathbf{Q}}$ implicitly checks that the signature $sig = (r, s)$ is well-formed, i.e. $r \in \{0,1\}^{\mathsf{saltlen}}$ and $s \in \mathcal{R}^2$.

$Sign_{\mathbf{B}}(m)$:
1: $r \leftarrow \{0,1\}^{\mathsf{saltlen}}$
2: $h := H(m,r)$
3: $v \leftarrow \widetilde{D}^{\mathbf{B}}_{2\sigma_{\mathsf{sign}}}[h]$
4: $s := \frac{1}{2}(h + \langle v \rangle) \in \mathcal{R}^2$
5: $\mathbf{return}\ sig := (r,s)$

$Vrfy_{\mathbf{Q}}(m, sig \in \{0,1\}^{\mathsf{saltlen}} \times \mathcal{R}^2)$:
1: $(r,s) := sig$
2: $h := H(m,r)$
3: $v := 2s - h$
4: $\mathbf{check}\ v = \langle v \rangle$ and $v \notin \{0\} \times \mathcal{R}$
5: $\mathbf{check}\ \|v\|_{\mathbf{Q}} \leq 2\sigma_{\mathsf{ver}} \cdot \sqrt{2n}$
6: $\mathbf{return}\ 1$ if all check pass

Fig. 1. $Sign_{\mathbf{B}}$ and $Vrfy_{\mathbf{Q}}$ of HAWK

Remark 2. The description in Fig. 1 matches the specification of HAWK (see [5, Algorithm 2 and Algorithm 3]) up to some small changes in the presentation (only). In particular, v as specified above coincides with $\frac{1}{2}\mathbf{B}^{-1}\mathbf{x}$ in the original specification of HAWK, and our definition of $s := \frac{1}{2}(h + \langle v \rangle)$ captures that $s := \frac{1}{2}h \mp \mathbf{B}^{-1}\mathbf{x}$, where the choice of the sign depends on $\mathsf{sym\text{-}break}(h_1 - 2s_2)$. Finally, the check $v = \langle v \rangle$ and $v \notin \{0\} \times \mathcal{R}$ is equivalent to checking $\mathsf{sym\text{-}break}(h_1 - 2s_1)$ as in the specification of HAWK.

Remark 3. Here we only concerns the uncompressed version of HAWK, while in practice an additional layer of compression is deployed for optimization. Nevertheless, it suffices to analyze the security of uncompressed HAWK because, according to [5, Section 3.2], the security of compressed HAWK follows immediately after.

Below, we describe the one-more SVP problem, as considered in [5], which considers an oracle algorithm $\mathcal{A}$ that makes at most q_S queries to the distribution $D^{\mathbf{B}}_{2\sigma_{\mathsf{sign}}}$. We stress that when considering $\mathcal{A}$ to be a quantum algorithm, the queries to the oracle/distribution $D^{\mathbf{B}}_{2\sigma_{\mathsf{sign}}}$ are restricted to be classical.

Definition 2. *Consider the one-more SVP game $G^{omSVP}_{\mathcal{A}}$, defined as follows:*

1: $(\mathbf{Q},\mathbf{B}) \leftarrow Gen$

2: $v^* \leftarrow \mathcal{A}^{D^{\mathbf{B}}_{2\sigma_{\mathsf{sign}}}}(\mathbf{Q})$ *// Write $v_1, \ldots, v_{q'_S}$ for the responses given by $D^{\mathbf{B}}_{2\sigma_{\mathsf{sign}}}$.*

3: $\mathbf{return}\ 1$ *if and only if* $0 < \|v^*\|_{\mathbf{Q}} \leq 2\sigma_{\mathsf{ver}}\sqrt{2n}$ *and*

$$v^* \notin \{\alpha \cdot v_i \mid (i,\alpha) \in [q'_S] \times \mu_{\mathbb{K}}\} . \tag{8}$$

The advantage $adv^{omSVP}_{\mathcal{A}}$ of winning the one-more SVP game is then defined as $adv^{omSVP}_{\mathcal{A}} := \Pr\left[1 \leftarrow G^{omSVP}_{\mathcal{A}}\right]$.

4   Quantum Security of HAWK

4.1   Warming Up: NMA Security

As a warm up, let $\mathcal{A}$ be an NMA attacker against HAWK, which on input the public key $\mathbf{Q}$ outputs a message-forgery pair (m^*, sig^*) with $sig^* = (r^*, s^*) \in$

$\{0,1\}^{\mathsf{saltlen}} \times \mathcal{R}^2$. Furthermore, consider the algorithm $\mathcal{E}$ that on input such a message-forgery pair (m^*, sig^*) computes

$$h^* := H(m^*, r^*) \qquad \text{and} \qquad v^* := 2s^* - h^* \tag{9}$$

and outputs v^*. Then $Vrfy_{\mathbf{Q}}(m^*, sig^*) = 1$ only if $0 < \|v^*\|_{\mathbf{Q}} \leq 2\sigma_{\mathsf{ver}} \cdot \sqrt{2n}$ by the definition of $Vrfy_{\mathbf{Q}}$. Thus, if $\mathcal{A}$ succeeds in forging a signature then $\mathcal{B} := \mathcal{E} \circ \mathcal{A}$ succeeds in finding a non-zero short vector. Formally,

$$adv_{\mathcal{A}}^{\mathsf{NMA}} := \Pr\left[Vrfy_{\mathbf{Q}}(m^*, sig^*) = 1 \,\middle|\, \begin{matrix} (\mathbf{Q}, \mathbf{B}) \leftarrow Gen \\ (m^*, sig^*) \leftarrow \mathcal{A}(\mathbf{Q}) \end{matrix} \right] \leq adv_{\mathcal{B}}^{\mathsf{omSVP}}.$$

We note that the above reasoning holds in the plain model with H being an arbitrary hash function, as well as in the random oracle model.

Remark 4. The reduction algorithm $\mathcal{B}$ here from NMA to one-more SVP does not make any query to $D_{2\sigma_{\mathsf{sign}}}^{\mathbf{B}}$.

4.2 Full CMA Quantum Security

Consider a CMA attacker $\mathcal{A}^{Sign_{\mathbf{B}}, H}(\mathbf{Q})$ against HAWK in the random oracle model, which on input the public key $\mathbf{Q}$ makes at most q_H queries to the random oracle H and at most q_S queries to the signing oracle $Sign_{\mathbf{B}}$, and eventually outputs a message-forgery pair (m^*, sig^*) with $sig^* = (r^*, s^*) \in \{0,1\}^{\mathsf{saltlen}} \times \mathcal{R}^2$. Without loss of generality, we assume $\mathcal{A}$ makes exactly q_H, q_S queries to $H, Sign_{\mathbf{B}}$ respectively.[1] The goal is to turn $\mathcal{A}$ into an algorithm $\mathcal{B}$ that solves the one-more-SVP problem.

Theorem 1 (Quantum Security of HAWK). *Let* HAWK *be as specified in Sect. 3, and let* $\mathcal{A}^{Sign_{\mathbf{B}}, H}(\mathbf{Q})$ *be a chosen-message attack making at most* q_S *queries to* $Sign_{\mathbf{B}}$ *and at most* q_H *quantum queries to* H *respectively. Then there exists an algorithm* $\mathcal{B}^{D_{2\sigma_{\mathsf{sign}}}^{\mathbf{B}}}$ *making* q_S *queries to solve one-more SVP, with running time* $\mathsf{TIME}(\mathcal{B}) \approx \mathsf{TIME}(\mathcal{A}) + \mathsf{Overhead}(q_S, q_H)$ *consisting of an additional overhead* $\mathsf{Overhead}(q_S, q_H)$ *of simulating* q_H, q_S *queries to* H *and* $Sim^{D_{2\sigma_{\mathsf{sign}}}^{\mathbf{B}}}$ *(specified in Fig. 2), such that*

$$adv_{\mathcal{A}}^{s\mathsf{UF}\text{-}\mathsf{CMA}} \leq adv_{\mathcal{B}}^{\mathsf{omSVP}} + \frac{q_S \epsilon}{1 - \epsilon} + 2q_S\sqrt{q_H + q_S} \cdot 2^{-\mathsf{saltlen}/2}$$

$$+ q_S\left(2^{-n} + (q_S - 1) \cdot n \cdot 2^{-2n}\right) \cdot \frac{1 + \epsilon}{1 - \epsilon} + O\left(q_H^2 \cdot n \cdot q_S/2^{2n}\right),$$

where the CMA advantage is defined as below:

$$adv_{\mathcal{A}}^{s\mathsf{UF}\text{-}\mathsf{CMA}} := \Pr\left[\begin{matrix} Vrfy_{\mathbf{Q}}(m^*, sig^*) = 1 \\ \forall i \in [q_S] : (m^*, r^*) \neq (m_i, sig_i) \end{matrix} \,\middle|\, \begin{matrix} (\mathbf{Q}, \mathbf{B}) \leftarrow Gen \\ (m^*, sig^*) \leftarrow \mathcal{A}^{Sign_{\mathbf{B}}, H}(\mathbf{Q}) \end{matrix} \right],$$

with (m_i, sig_i) *in the probability being the transcript produced at the ith signing query.*

---

[1] Otherwise, we let $\mathcal{A}$ make dummy queries to H and $Sign_{\mathbf{B}}$ respectively, with the dummy queries to $Sign_{\mathbf{B}}$ being on messages different from m^*, so that they do not affect the freshness of a forgery.

Simulating the Signing Queries. First, we show that we can replace the signing oracle $Sign$ by a particular simulator Sim that does not (explicitly) hold the secret key $\mathbf{B}$, but instead has access to the $\mathbf{Q}$-dependent distribution $D^{\mathbf{B}}_{2\sigma_{sign}}$, and that can reprogram the random oracle H; see Fig. 2 (right) below. Towards this goal, we also consider the oracle $Trans_{\mathbf{B}}$ as specified in Fig. 2 (left), and we show that

$$\mathcal{A}^{Sign_{\mathbf{B}},H}(\mathbf{Q}) \approx \mathcal{A}^{Trans_{\mathbf{Q}},H}(\mathbf{Q}) \approx \mathcal{A}^{Sim^{D^{\mathbf{B}}_{2\sigma_{sign}}},H}(\mathbf{Q}).$$

We have used subscript $\mathbf{Q}, \mathbf{B}$ to indicate that the oracle's execution depends on the keys, but for later convenience, we may also omit those subscripts based on the relevance of the context.

$Trans_{\mathbf{B}}(m)$:
1: $r \leftarrow \{0,1\}^{\mathsf{saltlen}}$
2: $H(m,r) := h \leftarrow (\mathcal{R}/2)^2$
3: $v \leftarrow \widetilde{D}^{\mathbf{B}}_{2\sigma_{sign}}[h]$
4: $s := \frac{1}{2}(h + \langle v \rangle) \in \mathcal{R}^2$
5: **return** $sig := (r,s)$

$Sim^{D^{\mathbf{B}}_{2\sigma_{sign}}}(m)$:
1: $r \leftarrow \{0,1\}^{\mathsf{saltlen}}$
2: $v \leftarrow D^{\mathbf{B}}_{2\sigma_{sign}}$
3: $H(m,r) := h := v \mod 2$
4: $s := \frac{1}{2}(h + \langle v \rangle) \in \mathcal{R}^2$
5: **return** $sig := (r,s)$

Fig. 2. Oracles $Trans_{\mathbf{B}}$ and $Sim^{D^{\mathbf{B}}_{2\sigma_{sign}}}$

Note that, the only difference between $Sign$ and $Trans$, is that the former computes $h := H(m,r)$ while the latter replaces it with reprogramming $H(m,r) := h \leftarrow \mathcal{R}^2/2\mathcal{R}^2$ for a freshly chosen h. It follows therefore directly from Lemma 2, with $\epsilon = 2^{-\mathsf{saltlen}}$ and $q_R = q_S$, that

$$\Pr\left[1 \leftarrow Vrfy^H \circ \mathcal{A}^{Sign,H}\right] - \Pr\left[1 \leftarrow Vrfy^H \circ \mathcal{A}^{Trans,H}\right] \leq 2q_S\sqrt{q_H + q_S}/2^{\mathsf{saltlen}/2}, \tag{10}$$

where it is understood that the verification $Vrfy^H$ is performed using the possibly reprogrammed H. Furthermore, by the closeness of the distributions $D^{\mathbf{B}}_{2\sigma_{sign}}$ and $\widetilde{D}^{\mathbf{B}}_{2\sigma_{sign}}$ (see Lemma 3 for the detailed reasoning), replacing the calls to $Trans$ one-by-one by calls to Sim, one obtains

$$\Pr\left[1 \leftarrow Vrfy^H \circ \mathcal{A}^{Trans,H}\right] - \Pr\left[1 \leftarrow Vrfy^H \circ \mathcal{A}^{Sim,H}\right] \leq \frac{q_S \cdot \epsilon}{1 - \epsilon}.$$

We thus conclude that the *validity* of a forgery is preserved when replacing the signing oracle $Sign$ by Sim, up to the sum of the two above probabilities.

Furthermore, the *freshness* of a forgery is also preserved, in that we can assume without loss of generality that $\mathcal{A}$ never outputs a forgery (m^*, sig^*) that matches the response of a signing query.

Lemma 3. *Let $\epsilon > 0$ and $\sigma_{sign} \geq \eta_\epsilon(\mathbb{Z}^n)$. Then the respective distributions of (r, h, s, v) in an execution of Sim and of Trans have statistical distance at most $\epsilon/(1 - \epsilon)$.*

Proof. First, we note that in *Trans*, right after the choice of $v \leftarrow \widetilde{D}_{2\sigma_{\text{sign}}}^{\mathbf{B}}[h]$ in line 3, we can redefine $H(m,r) := h := v \bmod 2$ with no effect, since $v \bmod 2 = h$ for $v \leftarrow \widetilde{D}_{2\sigma_{\text{sign}}}^{\mathbf{B}}[h]$ by (2). But now, the only difference between *Trans* and *Sim* is that in the former v is sampled by $\widetilde{D}_{2\sigma_{\text{sign}}}^{\mathbf{B}}$ and in the latter by $D_{2\sigma_{\text{sign}}}^{\mathbf{B}}$. The claim thus follows from (3). □

Extracting a Fresh Short Vector. Slightly abusing notation, we now consider the algorithm $\mathcal{B}^{D_{2\sigma_{\text{sign}}}^{\mathbf{B}}} := \mathcal{E}^{H} \circ \mathcal{A}^{Sim^{D_{2\sigma_{\text{sign}}}^{\mathbf{B}}},H}$ where, as before, $\mathcal{E}$ computes h^* and v^* as in (9) and outputs v^*, and where we take it as understood that the random oracle H is simulated by $\mathcal{B}$. As in the NMA case, it follows that if $\mathcal{A}^{Sim,H}$ succeeds in producing a valid forgery then $\mathcal{B}$'s output v^* is a short non-zero vector, i.e., $0 < \|v^*\|_{\mathbf{Q}} \leq 2\sigma_{\text{ver}} \cdot \sqrt{2n}$. It remains to show that v^* is fresh as well.

To show that this holds (almost with certainty), we assume that (m^*, sig^*) is a valid and fresh forgery (where the latter is without loss of generality), yet $v^* = \alpha v_j$ for some $(j, \alpha) \in [q_S] \times \mu_{\mathbb{K}}$, and we show that this implies an event that has negligible probability. For this purpose, let m_i, r_i, h_i, s_i, v_i be the transcripts m, r, h, s, v produced at the ith query to *Sim*, and let $sig^* = (r^*, s^*)$ be the signature output by $\mathcal{B}$. We distinguish between the following two cases.

Case $(m^*, r^*) = (m_i, r_i)$ for some $i \in [q_S]$, where we consider i to be maximal such that the equality holds.[2] Then $h^* = h_i$, and so

$$\mathcal{R}^2 \ni s^* = \frac{1}{2}(h^* + v^*) = \frac{1}{2}(h_i + \alpha v_j).$$

However, if $i \neq j$ then for any fixed choice of h_i, the probability over the choice of v_j of there being an $\alpha \in \mu_{\mathbb{K}}$ as above, is at most $n \cdot 2^{-2n} \cdot \frac{1+\epsilon}{1-\epsilon}$ by (6). On the other hand, if $i = j$ then we get that

$$\mathcal{R}^2 \ni s^* = \frac{1}{2}(h^* + v^*) = \frac{1}{2}(h_i + \alpha v_i).$$

Furthermore, $\alpha \neq \pm 1$ then; indeed, otherwise, $\langle v_i \rangle = \langle v^* \rangle = v^*$, where the second equality holds by the validity of sig^* and the first follows from $\{0\} \times \mathcal{R} \not\ni v^* = \pm v_i$ and (1), and so $s^* = \frac{1}{2}(h_i + \langle v_i \rangle) = s_i$ which contradicts the freshness of sig^*. However, the probability over the choice of v_i of there being an $\alpha \in \mu_{\mathbb{K}} \setminus \{\pm 1\}$ as above, is at most $2^{-n} \cdot \frac{1+\epsilon}{1-\epsilon}$ by (5).

In case $(m^*, r^*) \neq (m_i, r_i)$ for every $i \in [q_S]$, we must have that

$$\mathcal{R}^2 \ni s^* = \frac{1}{2}(h^* + v^*) = \frac{1}{2}(h^* + \alpha v_j),$$

and so $H(m^*, r^*) = h^* = \alpha v_j \bmod 2$; furthermore, H has not been reprogrammed throughout the execution at the location (m^*, r^*). Hence

$$H_{\text{init}}(m^*, r^*) = H(m^*, r^*) \in \{\alpha v_j \bmod 2 \mid (j, \alpha) \in [q_S] \times \mu_{\mathbb{K}}\} =: S, \qquad (11)$$

---

[2] If i is not the largest, it can be $(m^*, r^*) = (m_i, r_i)$ yet $h^* \neq h_i$ because h^* is computed via the possibly reprogramed H.

where H_{init} is the initial H before being reprogrammed. Thus, parsing $\mathcal{A}^{Sim,H}$ as $\mathcal{C}^{H_{\text{init}}}$, which runs the calls to Sim (for arbitrary but fixed samples $v_1, \ldots, v_{q_S}$ of $D_{2\sigma_{\text{sign}}}^{\mathrm{B}}$) and the reprogramming of H internally, we obtain a preimage-finding algorithm that finds a preimage under H_{init} of an element in S, making q_H queries to H_{init}. Given that $\#S \leq n \cdot q_S$, such an algorithm can succeed with probability at most $O(q_H^2 \cdot n \cdot q_S / 2^{2n})$ via the standard preimage finding bound.

Collecting all the different error terms, we obtain that

$$adv_{\mathcal{A}}^{\text{sUF-CMA}} \leq adv_{\mathcal{B}}^{\text{omSVP}} + \frac{q_S \epsilon}{1 - \epsilon} + 2q_S\sqrt{q_H + q_S} \cdot 2^{-\text{saltlen}/2}$$

$$+ q_S \left(2^{-n} + (q_S - 1) \cdot n \cdot 2^{-2n}\right) \cdot \frac{1 + \epsilon}{1 - \epsilon} + O(q_H^2 \cdot n \cdot q_S / 2^{2n}),$$

which concludes Theorem 1.

4.3   Classical Security

As our proof is modular, one may substitute certain part of the proof of Theorem 1 to obtain better bounds when considering the attacker $\mathcal{A}$ that only makes classical queries to H.

In (10) where the closeness between $Sign$ and $Trans$, one with and one without reprogramming, is argued, we may substitute the advantage by

$$\Pr\left[1 \leftarrow Vrfy^H \circ \mathcal{A}^{Sign,H}\right] - \Pr\left[1 \leftarrow Vrfy^H \circ \mathcal{A}^{Trans,H}\right] \leq 2q_S(q_H + q_S)/2^{\text{saltlen}}.$$

Moreover, to control the event (11) of finding a preimage of at most $n \cdot q_S$ elements, there is a better classical bound as well:

$$\Pr\left[H_{\text{init}}(m^*, r^*) \in S\right] \leq (q_H + 1) \cdot n \cdot q_S / 2^{2n}.$$

Putting things together, we obtain the classical security of HAWK as follows.

Theorem 2 (Classical Security of HAWK). *Let HAWK be as specified in Sect. 3, and let $\mathcal{A}^{Sign_{\mathrm{B}},H}(\mathbf{Q})$ be a chosen-message attack making at most q_S queries to $Sign_{\mathrm{B}}$ and at most q_H classical queries to H respectively. Then there exists an algorithm $\mathcal{B}^{D_{2\sigma_{\text{sign}}}^{\mathrm{B}}}$ making q_S queries to solve one-more SVP, with running time $\text{TIME}(\mathcal{B}) \approx \text{TIME}(\mathcal{A}) + \text{Overhead}(q_S, q_H)$ consisting of an additional overhead $\text{Overhead}(q_S, q_H)$ of respectively simulating q_H, q_S queries to H and $Sim^{D_{2\sigma_{\text{sign}}}^{\mathrm{B}}}$ (specified in Fig. 2), such that*

$$adv_{\mathcal{A}}^{sUF\text{-}CMA} \leq adv_{\mathcal{B}}^{omSVP} + \frac{q_S \epsilon}{1 - \epsilon} + 2q_S(q_H + q_S)/2^{\text{saltlen}}$$

$$+ q_S \left(2^{-n} + (q_S - 1) \cdot n \cdot 2^{-2n}\right) \cdot \frac{1 + \epsilon}{1 - \epsilon} + (q_H + 1) \cdot n \cdot q_S / 2^{2n}.$$

Acknowledgement. The authors thank Jelle Don and Eamonn W. Postlethwaite, Ludo N. Pulles for their useful discussions. Yu-Hsuan Huang is supported by the Dutch Research Agenda (NWA) project HAPKIDO (Project No. NWA.1215.18.002), which is financed by the Dutch Research Council (NWO).

A   More Proofs

Proof of Lemma 2. Without loss of generality, assume $\mathcal{A}$ makes exactly q_R queries to the reprogramming oracle Repro_b by doing additional dummy queries if otherwise. Define a sequence of hybrid games $\mathcal{G}_i$ that replaces the first i reprogramming queries of $\mathcal{A}^{\mathsf{Repro}_1,H}$ to querying Repro_0, where by definition $\mathcal{G}_0$ and $\mathcal{G}_{q_R}$ run as $\mathcal{A}^{\mathsf{Repro}_1,H}$ and $\mathcal{A}^{\mathsf{Repro}_0,H}$ respectively.

It suffices to show the closeness $\mathcal{G}_i \approx \mathcal{G}_{i+1}$ for every $0 \leq i < q_R$, where we refer to the only query that differs as the crucial query. For the sake of analysis, we consider the random oracle H to be (perfectly) simulated via compressed oracle in a designated database register D, which, within the crucial query before $y := H(x)$ or $H(x) := y \leftarrow \mathcal{Y}$, is decompressed and measured in the computational basis to obtain the oracle H to be used later.

Define $\mathcal{G}', \mathcal{G}''$ to respectively run as $\mathcal{G}_i, \mathcal{G}_{i+1}$ except additionally doing a binary measurement $\{M_0, M_1\}$ where $M_1 := \sum_{D(x)=\perp} |D\rangle \langle D|_{\mathsf{D}}$ right after $x \leftarrow \mathcal{D}$ being sampled but before $y := H(x)$ or $H(x) := y \leftarrow \mathcal{Y}$, and abort if the outcome does not match M_1. $\mathcal{G}'$ and $\mathcal{G}''$ behaves identically because on non-abort, the database register D collapses into $|\perp\rangle_{\mathsf{D}(x)}$, for which the reprogramming $H(x) := y \leftarrow \mathcal{Y}$ do not affect the decompressed-and-measured distribution of $\mathsf{D}(x)$. The closeness of $\mathcal{G}' \approx \mathcal{G}_i$ and $\mathcal{G}'' \approx \mathcal{G}_{i+1}$ follows from the gentle-measurement lemma, together with the fact that there has been at most $q_H + q_R$ queries of interaction with H prior to the crucial query, so $\Pr[\mathcal{G}' \text{ aborts}] = \Pr[\mathcal{G}'' \text{ aborts}] \leq (q_H + q_R)\epsilon$. This concludes the proof, which can be summarized by the following chain of closeness

$$\mathcal{G}_i \overset{\sqrt{(q_H+q_R)\epsilon}}{\approx} \mathcal{G}' \overset{0}{\approx} \mathcal{G}'' \overset{\sqrt{(q_H+q_R)\epsilon}}{\approx} \mathcal{G}_{i+1} \ .$$

$\square$

References

1. Bernstein, D.J., et al.: SPHINCS: practical stateless hash-based signatures. In: Oswald, E., Fischlin, M. (eds.) EUROCRYPT 2015. LNCS, vol. 9056, pp. 368–397. Springer, Heidelberg (2015). https://doi.org/10.1007/978-3-662-46800-5_15
2. Boneh, D., Dagdelen, Ö., Fischlin, M., Lehmann, A., Schaffner, C., Zhandry, M.: Random oracles in a quantum world. In: Lee, D.H., Wang, X. (eds.) ASIACRYPT 2011. LNCS, vol. 7073, pp. 41–69. Springer, Heidelberg (2011). https://doi.org/10.1007/978-3-642-25385-0_3
3. Don, J., Fehr, S., Majenz, C., Schaffner, C.: Security of the Fiat-Shamir transformation in the quantum random-oracle model. In: Boldyreva, A., Micciancio, D. (eds.) CRYPTO 2019. LNCS, vol. 11693, pp. 356–383. Springer, Cham (2019). https://doi.org/10.1007/978-3-030-26951-7_13
4. Ducas, L., et al.: CRYSTALS-dilithium: a lattice-based digital signature scheme. IACR Trans. Cryptographic Hardw. Embed. Syst. **2018**, 238–268 (2018)
5. Ducas, L., Postlethwaite, E.W., Pulles, L.N., van Woerden, W.: Hawk: Module LIP makes lattice signatures fast, compact and simple. In: Agrawal, S., Lin, D. (eds.) ASIACRYPT 2022. LNCS, vol. 13794, pp. 65–94. Springer, Cham (2022). https://doi.org/10.1007/978-3-031-22972-5_3

6. Ducas, L., van Woerden, W.: On the lattice isomorphism problem, quadratic forms, remarkable lattices, and cryptography. In: Dunkelman, O., Dziembowski, S. (eds.) EUROCRYPT 2022. LNCS, vol. 13277, pp. 643–673. Springer, Cham (2022). https://doi.org/10.1007/978-3-031-07082-2_23

7. Fouque, P.A., et al.: Falcon: fast-Fourier lattice-based compact signatures over NTRU. Submission NIST's Post-quantum Cryptography Stand. Process **36**(5), 1–75 (2018)

8. Grilo, A.B., Hövelmanns, K., Hülsing, A., Majenz, C.: Tight adaptive reprogramming in the QROM. In: Tibouchi, M., Wang, H. (eds.) ASIACRYPT 2021. LNCS, vol. 13090, pp. 637–667. Springer, Cham (2021). https://doi.org/10.1007/978-3-030-92062-3_22

9. Liu, Q., Zhandry, M.: Revisiting post-quantum Fiat-Shamir. In: Boldyreva, A., Micciancio, D. (eds.) CRYPTO 2019. LNCS, vol. 11693, pp. 326–355. Springer, Cham (2019). https://doi.org/10.1007/978-3-030-26951-7_12

10. Zhandry, M.: Secure identity-based encryption in the quantum random oracle model. Int. J. Quantum Inf. **13**(04), 1550014 (2015)

Non-Observable Quantum Random Oracle Model

Navid Alamati[1], Varun Maram[2(✉)], and Daniel Masny[3]

[1] VISA Research, Palo Alto, USA
[2] Department of Computer Science, ETH Zürich, Zürich, Switzerland
vmaram@inf.ethz.ch
[3] Meta Research, Menlo Park, USA

Abstract. The random oracle model (ROM), introduced by Bellare and Rogaway (CCS 1993), enables a formal security proof for many (efficient) cryptographic primitives and protocols, and has been quite impactful in practice. However, the security model also relies on some very strong and non-standard assumptions on how an adversary interacts with a cryptographic hash function, which might be unrealistic in a real world setting and thus could lead one to question the validity of the security analysis. For example, the ROM allows adaptively programming the hash function or observing the hash evaluations that an adversary makes.

We introduce a substantially weaker variant of the random oracle model in the post-quantum setting, which we call the *non-observable quantum random oracle model* (NO QROM). Our model uses weaker heuristics than the quantum random oracle model by Boneh *et. al.* (Asiacrypt 2011) or the non-observable random oracle model proposed by Ananth and Bhaskar (ProvSec 2013). At the same time, we show that our model is a viable option for establishing the post-quantum security of many cryptographic schemes by proving the security of important primitives such as extractable non-malleable commitments, digital signatures and chosen-ciphertext secure public-key encryption in the NO QROM.

Keywords: quantum random oracle model · non-observability · extractable non-malleable commitments · digital signatures · CCA security

1 Introduction

The random oracle model (ROM), introduced by Bellare and Rogaway [5], is an influential tool to argue the *heuristic* security of advanced cryptographic primitives such as existentially-unforgeable (EUF-CMA secure) digital signature schemes and chosen-ciphertext secure (CCA-secure) public-key encryption (PKE). In the ROM, a hash function is modeled as a random function, i.e. with

---

V. Maram—Parts of work done while the author was an intern at VISA Research.
D. Masny—Parts of work done while the author was at VISA Research.

T. Johansson and D. Smith-Tone (Eds.): PQCrypto 2023, LNCS 14154, pp. 417–444, 2023.
https://doi.org/10.1007/978-3-031-40003-2_16

a random truth table. This paradigm has turned out to be very useful in constructing very efficient and practically relevant cryptographic schemes [18,21,34]. Constructions that establish similar results without using ROs are typically very inefficient and thus seem to have less practical relevance [11,33].

Nevertheless, the model has a negative side in that there are signature and PKE schemes that are secure in the ROM but become insecure when the random oracle is replaced with any concrete hash function [12]. Therefore, we need to treat security arguments in the ROM with caution. Despite this weakness of the ROM, many results also require strong properties of the ROM: for example, the model allows security arguments to *"program"* the random oracle or to *observe* the queries made to the oracle by an adversary. These seem to be rather strong assumptions, or in other words, seem to significantly limit the class of adversaries against which security holds. Therefore, there have been proposals to weaken the ROM to *non-programmability* [20] or *non-observability* [3]. In this paper, we will be focusing on the latter aspect.

Specifically, the non-observable ROM (NO ROM) [3] has received less attention (at least compared to its non-programmable counterpart [20]) and there are almost no non-trivial positive results known in the model. For example, Ananth and Bhaskar [3] have proposed a secure *extractable* commitment scheme in the NO ROM but unfortunately it is much less efficient when compared to standard commitment schemes in the plain ROM. Hence, this raises the following question:

Does security of cryptographic primitives, such as extractable commitment schemes, in the NO ROM necessarily come with a significant loss in efficiency?

A different line of research arose with the rising threat of quantum computers, which extended the ROM to the quantum ROM (QROM) [8]. In the QROM, an adversary is allowed to make superposition queries to a quantum random oracle (QRO). This models the ability of a quantum algorithm to evaluate a hash function over an input in superposition. It was also shown that the QROM is a strictly weaker model than the ROM [37], in the sense that we make strictly weaker assumptions with respect to an adversary in the former. At the same time, many security proofs in the ROM have been adapted to hold in the QROM with respect to important cryptographic primitives such as digital signatures [15,16,29] and CCA-secure PKE schemes [23,25,35,41]. However, similar to our discussion of the ROM above, most of these security proofs in the QROM crucially rely on a strong property of the model: namely, that one can observe – or more precisely, *measure* – the quantum queries made by an adversary to the random oracle. This raises another pressing question.

Can we prove security of cryptographic primitives, such as digital signatures and CCA-secure PKE schemes, in the QROM without relying on measuring/observing queries?

1.1   Our Contributions

In this paper, we make significant progress towards answering the above questions by obtaining the following results.

New Model: "NO QROM". We first introduce a new post-quantum security model which we call the *non-observable quantum random oracle model (NO QROM)*. Essentially, the model is a weakened version of the NO ROM of [3], in terms of the heuristics used, which also accounts for quantum adversaries. In the original NO ROM, the random oracle is modeled with a Turing machine that can have a state which could be, for example, a list of random elements and the first query would be answered with the first element in the list. However, such a state is inherently incompatible with queries over superpositions. We therefore adapt the NO ROM to the quantum setting via NO QROM which allows superposition queries as in the QROM, while at the same time, forbids observing/measuring adversarial queries in the security proofs as in the NO ROM. The NO QROM therefore relies on weaker assumptions than the NO ROM and the QROM. In other words, security proofs in the NO QROM also hold in both the NO ROM and the QROM.

Efficient Extractable Commitments. Regarding the first question above on whether security of basic cryptographic primitives such as extractable commitments in the NO ROM is inherently tied with a loss in efficiency, we answer it in the negative. In fact, we go one step further and answer the same question in the weaker NO QROM; as mentioned previously, our results hold in the classical NO ROM as well.

Specifically, the previous extractable commitment scheme in the NO ROM [3] has some significant drawbacks. Namely, to commit to a message of size $|m|$ it requires a commitment of size $2\omega(\log \kappa) \cdot |m|$ using $|m|$ hash evaluations for security parameter κ. Furthermore, their security proof does not seem to translate to the quantum setting. That is, in their corresponding reduction, the outcome of a random oracle query solely depends on how many queries have been made before. But it is unclear how this strategy could translate to queries in quantum superposition, where multiple queries could be made in parallel.

In our work, by leveraging well-known techniques from the QROM setting [6,38,39], we show that the standard "textbook" commitment scheme $H(r, m)$ is in fact extractable in the NO QROM and significantly more efficient. It is computationally binding for a length $|m| + 2\omega(\log \kappa)$ with perfect extraction. We achieve a length of $|m| + \omega(\log \kappa)$ for a *computationally* binding, extractable commitment scheme[1] under the drawback that the extractor has either at most an inverse polynomial (in κ) success probability or runs in superpolynomial time.

---

[1] $|m| + \omega(\log \kappa)$ is optimal for a statistically binding commitment since for every message, there need to be at least $2^{\omega(\log \kappa)}$ many commitments to not violate hiding and each of these commitments is a commitment to a unique message.

Additionally, as mentioned in [10], $H(r, \mathsf{m})$ is also a *non-malleable* commitment [14] in the ROM. We show that $H(r, \mathsf{m})$ is also non-malleable in the NO QROM whenever $H(r, \mathsf{m})$ is statistically binding as required by the notion of non-malleability with respect to commitments [14,32]. However, intuitively $H(r, \mathsf{m})$ also seems non-malleable in the computationally binding setting. Hence, we make this intuition concrete by first weakening the definition of [14,32] by a slight adaptation and then showing that $H(r, \mathsf{m})$ is non-malleable with respect to our slightly weaker definition whenever the commitment is computationally binding. Furthermore, we give bounds on the commitment length for the commitment being statistically binding and show how this could be significantly improved using a NO QRO that is a permutation.

EUF-CMA Secure Signatures. We now consider our second question above on the NO QROM security of advanced cryptographic primitives such as digital signatures and CCA-secure PKE schemes. Focusing on the former primitive, in the classical setting, a well-known class of ROM digital signatures called *full-domain hash (FDH)* signature schemes [5] is known to be secure in the NO ROM [3]. However, in the quantum setting, their security proof breaks down if the adversary is also allowed to query the random oracle in a quantum superposition. One of the reasons is the inherent incompatibility of maintaining a state with respect to a random oracle in a quantum setting, as mentioned previously. Another reason is that, at a high level, the previous proof strategy [3] crucially relies on working with a polynomial number of inputs/outputs of the random oracle. But in the quantum setting, an adversary's random oracle query can be a superposition over *exponentially* many inputs.

Fortunately, Zhandry [39] overcame the above barrier using a novel technique related to indistinguishability of quantum random oracles, and subsequently proved the security of FDH signatures in the QROM. In this work, we adapt Zhandry's proof in the context of "non-observability" to show that the FDH signatures are also secure in the weaker NO QROM. In other words, our result shows that we don't need the full "machinery" of QROM – i.e., observability – to prove the post-quantum security of FDH signatures, and that relying on *weaker* heuristics is sufficient.

However one caveat is that there are no known instantiations of FDH signatures from *concrete* post-quantum assumptions. Fortunately, Boneh *et. al.* [8] identified a broader class of ROM signature schemes whose security can be shown in the QROM setting. To be specific, such a class of signatures have their classical ROM security proofs following a general structure known as *history-free reductions* [8]; roughly speaking, such reductions answer adversarial random oracle queries independently of the history of previous queries. And it was shown in [8] that history-free reductions lift ROM security of the corresponding signatures to QROM security. More importantly, the above class of "history-free signatures" include schemes with concrete post-quantum instantiations (in contrast to FDH signatures) – e.g., the lattice-based GPV signatures [22]. In our work, we extend the lifting theorem of [8] to show that such history-free signatures are in-fact secure in the NO QROM. Put differently, we *explicitly* establish that weaker heuristics are sufficient to prove post-quantum security of the above broad class of signatures with history-free reductions.

Hinting PRGs and CCA-Secure Encryption. We show that any CPA secure PKE can be transformed into a CCA secure PKE in the NO QROM. More specifically, we first provide a simple and efficient construction of a special cryptographic primitive in the NO QROM called a *hinting pseudorandom generator (PRG)*. This primitive was introduced by Koppula and Waters [27], and was mainly used to boost not only the "CPA-to-CCA" security of PKE, but also more advanced encryption systems such as *attribute-based encryption* and *one-sided predicate encryption* schemes. Therefore, we obtain the above CCA-secure encryption systems also in the NO QROM.

By proving the security of widely used cryptographic primitives in NO QROM, we establish the NO QROM paradigm as a viable option for analyzing the post-quantum security of cryptographic schemes with the advantage that it uses a weaker heuristic than the ROM, QROM and NO ROM. Nevertheless, we emphasize that the NO QROM does not resolve the uninstantiability of the ROM [12] since in their result, they do not rely on observing oracle queries.

1.2 Related Work

Regarding post-quantum security of extractable commitment schemes, Don et. al. recently made significant progress with respect to online-extractability in the QROM [17]; however, their techniques rely on measuring the adversarial random oracle queries. In another recent work, Bitansky, Lin, and Shmueli [7] proposed a $\log^*(\kappa)$ round non-malleable commitment based on the quantum hardness of LWE and quantum fully homomorphic encryption. Furthermore, they construct non-malleable commitments with polynomial rounds from post-quantum oblivious transfer or post-quantum one-way functions. Their constructions are the first non-malleable commitments secure against quantum attacks in the standard model. Since our construction is unconditionally secure in the NO QROM, our non malleable commitments are also secure against quantum attacks. At the same time our commitment is non-interactive.

Lombardi *et. al.* [30] observe that in many natural applications of extractable commitments in the context of post-quantum secure zero knowledge protocols, we require an additional property of the extractable commitments wherein the extractor E (cf. Definition 10) must also simulate the adversary $\mathcal{A}$'s view, in addition to extracting the message m from $\mathcal{A}$'s commitment c; the authors use the term *"state-preserving" extractable commitments* for such enhanced commitments, and proceed to give constructions in the standard model. We note that our analysis of the standard hash-based commitment $H(r, m)$ in the NO QROM (Theorems 1 and 2) also imply this stronger "state-preserving" extractability notion because of the simple fact that there is no rewinding of the adversary $\mathcal{A}$ in the online setting we consider.

In this work, we consider both statistical and computational binding proper-ties for commitments. However when it comes to the latter property, Unruh [36] argues that the "classical" definition of computational binding of commitments (cf. Definition 3) in the post-quantum setting is inadequate – at-least in the context of constructing post-quantum zero knowledge protocols. He proceeds to give a more satisfactory definition for computationally binding commitments in the quantum setting called *"collapse-binding"*, and then provides simple con-structions in the plain QROM. Specifically, he shows a black-box construction of collapse-binding commitments from so-called "collapsing" hash-functions, and later shows that quantum random oracles are indeed collapsing. Unruh essen-tially bases his latter result on a related result of Zhandry [40] which shows that quantum random oracles are collision-resistant. Given than Zhandry's analysis does not use the *observability* nor the *adaptive-programmability* features of the QROM, we expect one can extend Unruh's results to construct collapse-binding commitments in the weaker NO QROM heuristic – especially given their impor-tance in post-quantum zero knowledge applications.

Recently, Zhandry [42] argued that there is little theoretical justification for preferring the NO ROM of Ananth and Bhaskar [3] over the standard ROM. The reason is that certain "ROM failures" also apply to the NO ROM. Specifically, for any concrete hash function H, there exists a cryptographic scheme with a (NO) ROM security proof such that instantiating the random oracle with H will make the scheme insecure (Zhandry termed them "Type 2 failures" [42]). And it's not hard to see that the example scheme used by Zhandry to exhibit the above failure – namely, the *Encrypt-with-Hash* transform of [4] – can also be used to exhibit a similar failure in our NO QROM.

However, when it comes to the specific cryptographic schemes that we con-sider in this paper: namely, *hash-based extractable commitments*, *full domain hash signatures*, *hinting pseudorandom generators* and *CCA-secure encryption systems*, it is not so clear if these schemes fall under the above failure with respect to the NO QROM. Yet our security analysis of these schemes is still going to be heuristic at the end of the day. But the main goal of this paper, as already out-lined previously, is to *weaken* such heuristics – while not completely eliminating them. Unfortunately at the current state of art, we still need heuristics in order to not lose the efficiency nor a formal (even though heuristic) security analysis of widely adopted cryptographic schemes.

2   Preliminaries

κ denotes the security parameter. For a positive integer k, we write $[k] = \{1, \ldots, k\}$. For $n \in \mathbb{N}$, we use 0^n to denote the zero string of length n. For finite set X, we write $x \leftarrow \mathsf{X}$ to denote that x is uniformly at random sampled from X; also $|\mathsf{X}|$ denotes the cardinality of X. For a set element $x \in \mathsf{X}$ and an operation $+$ that might not be defined over X, we define $x + 0^*$ as x. For an algorithm $\mathcal{A}$ and oracle $\mathcal{O}$, we use $\mathcal{A}^{\mathcal{O}}$ to denote $\mathcal{A}$ with oracle access to $\mathcal{O}$. "ppt" stands for probabilistic polynomial time.

2.1   Quantum Random Oracle Model (QROM)

(We refer the reader to [31] for the basics of quantum computation and information.) In the QROM, we model hash functions as ideal functionalities called random oracles, which can be quantumly accessible. Namely, an adversary is allowed to query a random oracle $H : \{0,1\}^n \to \{0,1\}^\ell$ on an arbitrary quantum superposition of inputs, where we use the mapping $|x\rangle |y\rangle \mapsto |x\rangle |y \oplus H(x)\rangle$ with input register $x \in \{0,1\}^n$ and output register $y \in \{0,1\}^\ell$. Refer to [8] for a more detailed description of the model.

Now the following lemma describes the collision-resistance of such quantum random oracles.

Lemma 1 ([40, **Theorem 3.1**]). *There is a universal constant C such that the following holds. Let $H : \{0,1\}^n \to \{0,1\}^\ell$ be a random oracle. If an unbounded algorithm $\mathcal{A}$ makes a query to H at most q times, then*

$$\Pr[H(x) = H(x')] \leq C(q+1)^3/2^\ell,$$

where $(x, x') \leftarrow \mathcal{A}^H$ and $x, x' \in \{0,1\}^n$ with $x \neq x'$. Here the oracle accesses of $\mathcal{A}$ to H can be quantum.

The next three lemmas describe techniques to simulate quantum random oracles, which come in handy in security proofs. The first lemma uses $2q$-wise independent functions, the second uses so-called small-range distributions as defined in [38], and the third uses so-called semi-constant distributions [39].

Lemma 2 ([39, **Theorem 6.1**]). *Interpreting the set $\{0,1\}^\ell$ as the finite field $\mathbb{F}_{2^\ell}$, let $f : \{0,1\}^\ell \to \{0,1\}^\ell$ be an oracle drawn uniformly at random from the set of $(2q - 1)$-degree polynomials over $\mathbb{F}_{2^\ell}$. Then the advantage any quantum algorithm making at most q quantum queries to f has in distinguishing f from a truly random oracle $H : \{0,1\}^\ell \to \{0,1\}^\ell$ is identically zero.*

In general, if $\hat{f} : \{0,1\}^n \to \{0,1\}^\ell$ is an oracle implementing a $2q$-wise independent function, then it is perfectly indistinguishable from a uniformly random oracle $H : \{0,1\}^n \to \{0,1\}^\ell$ w.r.t. a quantum algorithm making at most q quantum oracle queries.

Definition 1 (Small-Range Distributions). *An oracle with an η-range distribution $(\eta \ll 2^\ell)$ $\mathsf{SR}_\eta : \{0,1\}^n \to \{0,1\}^\ell$ is defined with the following output distribution on image $\{0,1\}^\ell$:*

- *For each $i \in [\eta]$, choose a uniformly random value $y_i \in \{0,1\}^\ell$.*
- *For each $x \in \{0,1\}^n$, pick a uniformly random $i \in [\eta]$ and set $\mathsf{SR}_\eta(x) := y_i$.*

We also define the range $\mathbb{I}_\eta$ associated to SR_η as follows: $\mathbb{I}_\eta = \{y_i \mid i \in [\eta]\}$.

Lemma 3 ([38, **Corollary 7.5**]). *The statistical distance of output distributions of a quantum algorithm making q quantum queries either to $\mathsf{SR}_\eta : \{0,1\}^n \to \{0,1\}^\ell$ or a random oracle $H : \{0,1\}^n \to \{0,1\}^\ell$ is bounded by $f(q)/\eta$, where $f(q) = \pi^2(2q)^3/6 < 14q^3$.*

Definition 2 (Semi-Constant Distributions). *An oracle with a λ-constant distribution $\mathsf{SC}_\lambda : \{0,1\}^n \to \{0,1\}^\ell$ is defined with the following output distribution:*

- *First, fix a uniformly random value $y \in \{0,1\}^\ell$.*
- *For each $x \in \{0,1\}^n$, do:*
  - *Set $\mathsf{SC}_\lambda(x) := y$ with probability λ.*
  - *Otherwise (with probability $1 - \lambda$), set $\mathsf{SC}_\lambda(x)$ to be a uniformly random element in $\{0,1\}^\ell$.*

Note that $\mathsf{SC}_0 : \{0,1\}^n \to \{0,1\}^\ell$ is just a uniformly random oracle.

Lemma 4 ([39, **Corollary 4.3**]). *The statistical distance of output distributions of a quantum algorithm making q quantum queries either to $\mathsf{SC}_\lambda : \{0,1\}^n \to \{0,1\}^\ell$ or a random oracle $(\mathsf{SC}_0 =)H : \{0,1\}^n \to \{0,1\}^\ell$ is bounded by $\frac{8}{3}q^4\lambda^2$.*

The following lemma provides a generic reduction from a hiding-style property (indistinguishability) to a one-wayness-style property (unpredictability) in the (NO) QROM.

Lemma 5 ([2, **Theorem 1, adapted**]). *Let $H : \{0,1\}^n \to \{0,1\}^\ell$ be a random oracle, $\hat{x} \leftarrow \{0,1\}^n$ be a uniformly random value and y be a random bitstring which is independent of $\hat{x}$. Then, for any function $G : \{0,1\}^n \to \{0,1\}^\ell$ satisfying $\forall x \in \{0,1\}^n \setminus \{\hat{x}\}$, $G(x) = H(x)$ that might depend on $(\hat{x}, y)$, and any algorithm $\mathcal{A}$ making at most q queries,*

$$|\Pr[\mathcal{A}^H(y) = 1] - \Pr[\mathcal{A}^G(y) = 1]| \le 4\sqrt{\frac{q(q+1)}{2^n}}.$$

2.2 Commitments

We recap the syntax and basic properties of commitments such as hiding, binding and non-malleability.

Definition 3. *A commitment scheme is a tuple of ppt algoritms $(\mathsf{Com}, \mathsf{Open})$ and a message space M with the following syntax.*

Com: *Takes as input 1^κ, $\mathsf{m} \in \mathsf{M}$ and outputs a commitment c and an opening o.*
Open: *Takes as input a commitment c and an opening o and outputs a message $\mathsf{m} \in \mathsf{M}$ or $\perp$, such that $\mathsf{Open}(\mathsf{Com}(1^\kappa, \mathsf{m})) = \mathsf{m}$.*

Additionally, it suffices two properties, hiding and binding.

Hiding: *For any ppt adversary $\mathcal{A}$ and any $\mathsf{m}_0, \mathsf{m}_1 \in \mathsf{M}$,*

$$|\Pr[\mathcal{A}(1^\kappa, \mathsf{c}_0) = 1] - \Pr[\mathcal{A}(1^\kappa, \mathsf{c}_1) = 1]| \le \mathsf{negl}.$$

where $(\mathsf{c}_0, \mathsf{o}_0) \leftarrow \mathsf{Com}(1^\kappa, \mathsf{m}_0)$ and $(\mathsf{c}_1, \mathsf{o}_1) \leftarrow \mathsf{Com}(1^\kappa, \mathsf{m}_1)$.

Binding: *For any ppt adversary* $\mathcal{A}$,

$$\Pr[\mathsf{Open}(\mathsf{c}, \mathsf{o}_0) = \mathsf{m}_0 \wedge \mathsf{Open}(\mathsf{c}, \mathsf{o}_1) = \mathsf{m}_1] \leq \mathsf{negl},$$

where $(\mathsf{c}, \mathsf{o}_0, \mathsf{o}_1) \leftarrow \mathcal{A}(1^\kappa)$ *and* $\mathsf{m}_0, \mathsf{m}_1 \in \mathsf{M}$ *with* $\mathsf{m}_0 \neq \mathsf{m}_1$.

We call it statistically hiding (binding) if hiding (binding) holds even for any unbounded algorithm $\mathcal{A}$ *and unbounded oracle algorithm* $\mathcal{A}^{\mathcal{O}}$ *that is allowed to make an unbounded amount of queries to the oracle* $\mathcal{O}$.

Concurrent Non-Malleability. We follow the definition of non-malleable commitments of Pass and Rosen [32] with the slight change that we include the view of the man-in-the-middle adversary as input for the distinguisher similar to the definition of [28]. Notice that an adversary can include its view in the input through committed messages. Further, for the sake of simplicity, we use the weaker definition in which an adversary only receives a single commitment. As shown by [32], this implies the stronger version in which he receives many commitments. We recap the formal definition now.

Definition 4 (Concurrent Non-Malleability). *Let the random variables* mim *and* sim *be defined as follows.*

$\mathsf{mim}_{\mathsf{com}}^{\mathcal{A}}(z, \mathsf{m})$: *The man-in-the-middle adversary* $\mathcal{A}$ *receives a commitment* c *to a message* m *and auxiliary input* z. $\mathcal{A}$ *then generates* m *commitments* $\mathsf{c}_1, \ldots, \mathsf{c}_m$. *For every* $i \in [m]$, m_i *is defined as the unique committed message in* c_i *or* $\bot$ *if no such message exists. Since we consider statistically binding commitments, there will be only one message except with negligible probability. When there are more than one message or when* $\mathsf{c}_i = \mathsf{c}$, *we define* $\mathsf{m}_i := \bot$. *The random variable entails the view of* $\mathcal{A}$ *and messages* $\mathsf{m}_1, \ldots, \mathsf{m}_m$.

$\mathsf{sim}_{\mathsf{com}}^{\mathsf{S}}(z)$: *The simulator* S *receives an auxiliary input* z *and generates* m *commitments* $\mathsf{c}_1, \ldots, \mathsf{c}_m$. *As previously, for all* $i \in [m]$, *we define* m_i *as the unique committed message in* c_i *except if it is not unique or no such message exists. In that case, it is defined as* $\mathsf{m}_i := \bot$. *Further,* S *can set any* $\mathsf{m}_i := \bot$.

We call a commitment scheme ε-*concurrent non-malleable with respect to commitments if for any ppt adversary* $\mathcal{A}$ *there exists a ppt simulator* S *such that for any ppt distinguisher* D, *message* $\mathsf{m} \in \mathsf{M}$, *polynomial* $m \in \mathbb{N}$ *and any polynomial size auxiliary input* z,

$$|\Pr[\mathsf{D}(\mathsf{mim}_{\mathsf{com}}^{\mathcal{A}}(z, \mathsf{m})) = 1] - \Pr[\mathsf{D}(\mathsf{sim}_{\mathsf{com}}^{\mathsf{S}}(z) = 1)]| \leq \varepsilon.$$

A commitment scheme that is non-malleable is also computationally hiding, since otherwise an adversary could extract some information about m and a simulator which is independent of m could not simulate the view of such an adversary. This would break non-malleability. Therefore, showing non-malleability is sufficient for showing computationally hiding.

We extend Definition 4 to commitments that are not statistically binding. This allows to formalize that $H(r, \mathsf{m})$ is still non-malleable in an intuitive sense and it should be hard to change a commitment $H(r, \mathsf{m})$ to a commitment $H(r, \mathsf{m}')$ for a related message m'.

Definition 5 (weak Concurrent Non-Malleability). *We define the random variables* $\mathsf{wmim}^{\mathcal{A}}_{\mathsf{com}}(z, \mathsf{m})$ *and* $\mathsf{wsim}^{\mathsf{S}}_{\mathsf{com}}(z)$ *as* $\mathsf{mim}^{\mathcal{A}}_{\mathsf{com}}(z, \mathsf{m})$ *and* $\mathsf{sim}^{\mathsf{S}}_{\mathsf{com}}(z)$ *with the difference that they include all messages* $\mathsf{m}_{i,j}$ *for which there exists an opening* $\mathsf{o}_{i,j}$ *such that* c_i *opens to* $\mathsf{m}_{i,j}$.

We call a commitment scheme ε-*weak-concurrent non-malleable with respect to commitments if for any ppt adversary* $\mathcal{A}$ *there exists a ppt simulator* S *such that for any ppt distinguisher* D, *message* $\mathsf{m} \in \mathsf{M}$, *polynomial* $m \in \mathbb{N}$ *and any polynomial size auxiliary input* z,

$$|\Pr[\mathsf{D}(\mathsf{wmim}^{\mathcal{A}}_{\mathsf{com}}(z, \mathsf{m})) = 1] - \Pr[\mathsf{D}(\mathsf{wsim}^{\mathsf{S}}_{\mathsf{com}}(z) = 1)]| \leq \varepsilon.$$

Definition 5 is weaker than Definition 4 because it does not cover that an adversary can generate a commitment to a related message by simply copying the commitment. More specifically, a commitment c could be a commitment for message m and m'. Clearly, these two messages are related messages in the sense that given $\mathsf{c} = \mathsf{c}(\mathsf{m}') = \mathsf{c}(\mathsf{m})$, m cannot take every value in M unless the commitment is statistically hiding. Thus, unless it is hiding, a simulator that has no access to m could not simulate such a commitment. Definition 5 ignores this issue since the distinguisher receives $\perp$ instead of the committed messages in c and therefore does not offer security for this case.

Nevertheless, just copying the commitment does not seem a significant attack against the intuitive notion of malleability and by the computationally binding property of the commitment, an adversary would not be able to open the commitment to any other message m'. Due to this fact, we can use the same reasoning that non-malleability with respect to commitments implies non-malleability with respect to openings [13, 19] to argue that weak non-malleability with respect to commitments together with computational binding implies non-malleability with respect to openings.

Random-Oracle Based Commitments. For commitment schemes whose security properties rely on modeling their underlying hash functions as random oracles, the corresponding security definitions of hiding, binding and non-malleability above need to be modified accordingly in the QROM. Namely, we additionally need to give the involved parties (i.e., adversaries, simulators and distinguishers) quantum access to the random oracle(s) associated to the commitment scheme.

2.3 Other Basic Cryptographic Primitives

Definition 6 (Pseudorandom Functions). *A pseudorandom function (PRF) is a function* $\mathsf{PRF} : \mathcal{K} \times \mathcal{X} \to \mathcal{Y}$ *with* $\mathcal{K}$ *being the key-space, and* $\mathcal{X}$ *and* $\mathcal{Y}$ *being the domain and range respectively. Additionally,* PRF *is said to be post-quantum (resp., quantum) secure if no polynomial-time quantum adversary* $\mathcal{A}$ *making classical (resp., quantum) queries can distinguish between a truly random function and the function* $\mathsf{PRF}(k, \cdot)$ *for a random key* k.

More formally, for every such adversary $\mathcal{A}$, we have

$$\left| \Pr_{k \leftarrow \mathcal{K}}[\mathcal{A}^{\mathsf{PRF}(k,\cdot)}() = 1] - \Pr_{H \leftarrow \mathcal{Y}^{\mathcal{X}}}[\mathcal{A}^H() = 1] \right| \leq \mathsf{negl}.$$

Definition 7 (Signatures). *A signature scheme is a tuple of ppt algorithms* (Gen, Sign, Ver) *with the following syntax.*

Gen: *Takes as input 1^κ and generates a public/secret key pair* (pk, sk).
Sign: *Takes as input the secret key* sk *and a message* m *and outputs a signature σ on it.*
Ver: *Takes as input the public key* pk, *a message* m *and a signature σ, and outputs* acc *or* rej, *such that* Ver(pk, m, Sign(sk, m)) = acc.

To define security, we will use the standard chosen message attack (CMA) game:

- *The challenger generates* (pk, sk) $\leftarrow$ Gen(1^κ) *and sends* pk *to adversary $\mathcal{A}$.*
- *$\mathcal{A}$ can make signature queries on messages m_i to which the challenger responds with* Sign(sk, m_i).
- *$\mathcal{A}$ produces a forgery candidate* (m, σ).

$\mathcal{A}$ is said to win the game if m $\neq m_i$ *for any i and* Ver(pk, m, σ) = acc. *The signature* (Gen, Sign, Ver) *is said to be (post-quantum[2]) existentially unforgeable, a.k.a. (post-quantum) EUF-CMA secure, if for all (resp., quantum) ppt adversaries $\mathcal{A}$, the winning probability in the above game is negligible in κ.*

Definition 8 (Trapdoor Permutations). *A trapdoor permutation (TDP) is a tuple of ppt algorithms* (Gen, f, f^{-1}) *where:*

Gen: *Takes as input 1^κ and generates a public/secret key pair* (pk, sk).
f: *Takes as input the public key* pk *and an element $x \in \{0,1\}^\kappa$ and returns $y \in \{0,1\}^\kappa$ such that* f(pk, $\cdot$) *is a bijection over $\{0,1\}^\kappa$.*
f^{-1}: *Takes as input the secret key* sk *and an element $y \in \{0,1\}^\kappa$ and returns $x \in \{0,1\}^\kappa$ such that* f(pk, x) = y.

A TDP (Gen, f, f^{-1}) *is said to be (quantum) one-way if for any (resp., quantum) ppt adversary $\mathcal{A}$,*

$$\Pr[\mathcal{A}(\mathsf{pk}, \mathsf{f}(\mathsf{pk}, x)) = x] \leq \mathsf{negl},$$

where (pk, sk) $\leftarrow$ Gen(1^κ), *and $x \leftarrow \{0,1\}^\kappa$ is chosen uniformly at random.*

---

[2] Note the distinction between "*post-quantum*" secure signatures and "*quantum*" secure signatures; in the former security notion, the adversary can only make *classical* signature queries, whereas in the latter, the adversary can ask for signatures of *quantum* superpositions of messages. This distinction also applies to encryption schemes w.r.t. classical/quantum decryption queries. See [9] for the precise quantum security definitions for signatures and encryption schemes.

3   The Non-Observable Quantum Random Oracle Model

We follow the outlines of the NO ROM of Ananth and Bhaskar [3] and make some adaptations to allow for queries in superpositions. For the sake of simplicity, we ignore that a random oracle could also be adaptively programmed during a reduction.[3] Further, we simply use a random function or random one-way permutation [24] to describe the model rather than using a stateful Turing machine as [3]. We remark that the quantum indistinguishability of random functions and random one-way permutations has been implicitly shown in [40]. During a security game, the reduction might replace this random function or random one-way permutation with a different function that is indistinguishable for an adversary with query access. Such a function might be for example a polynomial, where the degree of the polynomial depends on the maximum amount of adversarial queries. We allow this by adding a setup phase in which the oracle can be programmed. In Fig. 1, we describe the setup and query phase. During the query phase, an oracle algorithm can send its queries and receives a response. In case of a one-way permutation, the oracle is not answering queries for the inverse permutation which separates this model from an ideal cipher model.

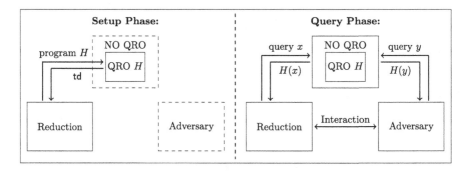

Fig. 1. The figure shows two phases, during the setup phase a reduction can program the quantum random oracle and might receive a polynomial size trapdoor information td. During the query phase, the reduction and adversary can query the quantum random oracle. The reduction cannot observe queries made by the adversary or measure them. We omit the case of adaptive programming, in which the reduction can program H during the query phase.

Following [8], a query can be a superposition over the domain of the oracle. Upon receiving a query for quantum state $|\phi\rangle := \sum \alpha_{x,y}|x, y\rangle$ the oracle responds with $\sum \alpha_{x,y}|x, y + H(x)\rangle$. We remark that an adversary does not actually need

---

[3] To the best of our knowledge it is unclear how useful an adaptive progammability of a ROM is if queries cannot be observed. We are not aware of any protocol or primitive in which adaptive programming is necessary during the reduction but observing the adversarial random oracle queries is not.

to send his quantum state. He can locally evaluate oracle H as long as he does not violate the only black box access requirement of the model.

In the following, we will consider non-uniform adversaries. To provide security against such adversaries we assume that H is rerandomized using a key or a salt. Further, when working with the NO QROM, we can leverage the above Lemmas 1, 2, 3, 4 and 5 since they do not require observing any query. This is crucial to establish our results.

4 Extractable Non-Malleable Commitments in the NO QROM

We revisit the definition of the standard hash-based commitment scheme.

Definition 9 (Standard Hash-based Commitment). *Let $\ell \in \mathbb{N}$, R be the randomness space and M the message space. For hash functions $H : R \times M \to \{0,1\}^\ell$, the standard hash-based commitment scheme is defined as follows.*

$\mathsf{Com}(1^\kappa, \mathsf{m})$**:** *Sample $r \leftarrow R$. Compute and output $\mathsf{c} := H(r, \mathsf{m})$, $\mathsf{o} := (r, \mathsf{m})$.*
$\mathsf{Open}(\mathsf{c}, \mathsf{o})$**:** *Parse $\mathsf{o} = (r, \mathsf{m})$ and output m if $\mathsf{c} = H(r, \mathsf{m})$ and otherwise output $\perp$.*

We now prove the computational and statistical binding properties, w.r.t. different parameters of the commitment schemes defined above.

Lemma 6 (Binding). *The standard hash-based commitment (Definition 9) is computationally (resp. statistically) binding, for $\ell \geq \omega(\log \kappa)$ (resp. $\ell \geq 2\log|\mathsf{M}| + 2\log|\mathsf{R}| + \omega(\log \kappa)$).*

Proof. We start with computationally binding. An unbounded algorithm $\mathcal{A}$ making at most q of quantum queries to the random oracle H breaking the binding property would output a commitment c such that there exist two openings o_0 and o_1 with $\mathsf{o}_0 \neq \mathsf{o}_1$. This implies that $H(\mathsf{o}_0) = \mathsf{c} = H(\mathsf{o}_1)$ and thus breaking the collision-resistance of H. However from Lemma 1, the latter probability is bounded by $O(q^3/2^\ell)$ which is negligible for $\ell \geq \omega(\log \kappa)$.

We now consider the statistical binding property. The commitments are determined by the randomness r and message m. Thus there are at most $|\mathsf{M}| \cdot |\mathsf{R}|$ many commitments. Further, the commitments are uniformly random over 2^ℓ due to the random oracles H. Therefore, the probability that there exists an r_0, r_1, m_0 and m_1 such that it results in the same commitment is bounded by $\frac{|\mathsf{R}|^2 \cdot |\mathsf{M}|^2}{2^\ell}$ which is negligible for $\ell \geq 2\log|\mathsf{M}| + 2\log|\mathsf{R}| + \omega(\log \kappa)$. $\square$

When we use random one-way permutations instead of random functions, we get better bounds on ℓ for the statistical binding case. Further, since random one-way permutations are computationally indistinguishable from random functions all other results such as extractability, hiding and non-malleability still hold. When replacing the one-way permutation with a degree $2q - 1$ polynomial, we might lose statistically binding since there might be up to $2q - 1$

preimages per image. Our extractor does this replacement and therefore unique extractability requires $\ell \geq \omega(\log \kappa)$ to prevent collisions of the $2q - 1$ preimages with overwhelming probability.

Lemma 7 (Statistical Binding for Permutations). *Let H be the hash function in Definition 9 and let H be defined as $H(r, m) = P(r, m) \| H'(r, m)$ where P is a one-way permutation and $H' : R \times M \rightarrow \{0, 1\}^{\ell'}$. Then, the standard hashed-based commitment is statistically binding (for any $\ell' \in \mathbb{N}$).*

Proof. The proof is almost identical to the proof of Lemma 6. The difference is that we get a much better bound on preventing a collision than the birthday bound due to the definition of a permutation which does not have such collisions. Therefore, such a collision can only happen with respect to oracle H'. However, the image of P uniquely defines r, m and therefore we can ignore collisions in the image of H'.   □

We now consider extractability of the commitent scheme. We first adapt the notion of extractability for a commitment scheme to the NO QROM described in Sect. 3. We allow an extractor similar to a reduction to program H during the setup phase. In this process, the extractor obtains a trapdoor information td which allows him to extract the message from a commitment.

Definition 10 (Extractability in the NO QROM). *We call a commitment scheme online-extractable in the NO QROM if there exists a ppt algorithm E which programs QRO H during the setup phase and might receive a polynomial length trapdoor information td within the process. During the query phase, E receives commitment c and outputs m, i.e. $m \leftarrow E(td, c)$, such that there exists an opening o with $Open(c, o) = m$. Otherwise, E outputs $\bot$.*

We now present two extraction techniques for the standard hash-based commitment scheme in the NO QROM. Both techniques follow a similar approach. Namely on a high-level, the corresponding extractor first simulates the QROs using finite-field polynomials with a sufficiently large degree, thanks to Lemma 2, and then uses an efficient *root-finding* algorithm over related polynomials to compute valid openings for a given commitment – *without* observing the queries made to the QROs. Nevertheless, the two techniques allow different parameter, security and extraction probability trade-offs.

We start with showing *perfect online-extractability* in the NO QROM based on finding roots of polynomials.

Theorem 1 (Extraction via Roots Finding). *As per Definition 9, let H be modeled as a QRO with the structure $H(r, m) = H'(r, m) \| H''(r, m)$, where H', H'' are QROs and $H' : R \times M \rightarrow R \times M$ whereas $H'' : R \times M \rightarrow \{0, 1\}^{\ell'}$ with $\ell' = \ell - \log |M| - \log |R|$. Then the standard hash-based commitment from Definition 9 is perfectly online-extractable in the NO QROM.*

Proof. We describe a ppt extractor E w.r.t. an adversary $\mathcal{A}$ which makes at most q queries to the QROs. In the setup phase, E replaces the true random oracle H' with an oracle f evaluating a uniformly random polynomial of degree $2q - 1$ over the finite field $\mathbb{F}_{2^\nu}$, where $\{0,1\}^\nu = \mathsf{R} \times \mathsf{M}$. From Lemma 2, the oracle f is *perfectly* indistinguishable from the QRO H' in $\mathcal{A}$'s view. E retains the (polynomial sized) description of f as the trapdoor information td.

Upon receiving a commitment $\mathsf{c} = (\mathsf{c}_1, \mathsf{c}_2) = (H'(r, \mathsf{m}), H''(r, \mathsf{m}))$ from $\mathcal{A}$ in the query phase, E first computes a set of roots S of the polynomial $f(x) - \mathsf{c}_1$. This can be done efficiently using for example the algorithm in [6]. Since the polynomial is of degree $2q - 1$, there are at most $2q - 1$ roots. For each of the roots (r, m), E makes a classical query to H'' and checks whether $H''(r, \mathsf{m}) = \mathsf{c}_2$. If there exists such a root (r, m), E picks one of them and outputs m as the result of its extraction, i.e. $\mathsf{m} \leftarrow \mathsf{E}(\mathsf{td}, \mathsf{c})$. Otherwise, E returns $\perp$. It's not hard to see that on one hand, when E outputs $\mathsf{m} \neq \perp$, then there exists an opening o such that $\mathsf{Open}(\mathsf{c}, \mathsf{o}) = \mathsf{m}$, namely $\mathsf{o} = (r, \mathsf{m}) \in S$. On the other hand, when E outputs $\perp$, there exists no valid opening for c. $\square$

The first approach has the disadvantage, that extraction is only possible if the commitment size at least matches the message plus randomness size. Our second approach requires much less overhead for the commitment size. However, it has the shortcoming that extraction needs superpolynomial space for a negligible distinguishability advantage between the normal and the extraction mode.

In the second approach, the extractor simulates the QROs using *small-range distributions*, as described in Lemma 3, and then (efficiently) iterates over the small output space of the QROs in order to compute valid openings for a given commitment – again while not observing any queries made to the QROs. For this approach, we first define a "small range mode" which allows extraction. In the small range mode, we replace oracle access to H with oracle access to $\hat{H}_{\mathsf{E}.\eta}$. $\hat{H}_{\mathsf{E}.\eta}$ is a very special oracle since it outputs the message m and masks it with an element from the small range set SR_η. More precisely, we denote the oracle in extraction mode with parameter η with $\hat{H}_{\mathsf{E}.\eta} : \mathsf{R} \times \mathsf{M} \to \{0,1\}^\ell$ with $\ell \geq \log|\mathsf{M}| + \log\eta$ and for any $r \in \mathsf{R}$, $\mathsf{m} \in \mathsf{M}$, $\hat{H}_{\mathsf{E},\eta}(r, \mathsf{m}) := \mathsf{SR}_\eta(r, \mathsf{m}) + (\mathsf{m}||0^{\ell'})$, where $\ell' := \ell - \log|\mathsf{M}|$.

Lemma 8. *Let $\hat{H}_{\mathsf{E},\eta}$ be the oracle in extraction mode with parameter η and H the oracle in the standard NO QROM mode. Then, for any unbounded distinguisher D making at most q queries,*

$$|\Pr[D^H = 1] - \Pr[D^{\hat{H}_{\mathsf{E},\eta}} = 1]| \leq \frac{14q^3}{\eta}.$$

Proof. Let $\tilde{H} : \mathsf{R} \times \mathsf{M} \to \{0,1\}^\ell$ defined as $\tilde{H}(r, \mathsf{m}) := H(r, \mathsf{m}) + (\mathsf{m}, 0^{\ell'})$ for all $r \in \mathsf{R}$, $\mathsf{m} \in \mathsf{M}$, where H is the QRO. Due to the uniformity of $H(r, \mathsf{m})$, the oracles H and $\tilde{H}$ are identically distributed and therefore indistinguishable.

By Lemma 3, we can replace $\tilde{H}$ with SR_η and this can be distinguished at most with probability $\frac{14q^3}{\eta}$. $\square$

Theorem 2 (Extraction via Small Range Distributions). *Let $H : \mathsf{R} \times \mathsf{M} \to \{0,1\}^\ell$ be modeled as a QRO and $\ell \geq \log|\mathsf{M}| + \log\eta$. Then the standard* *hash-based commitment from Definition 9 is perfectly online-extractable in the NO QROM extraction mode and* E *runs in time polynomial in* η.

Proof. Our extractor E is defined as follows. During the setup phase, E sets up the oracle such that it is in extraction mode, i.e. $\hat{H}_{E,\eta}$. E receives set $\mathbb{I}_\eta$ of SR_η as trapdoor information which has size at most η.

During the query phase, E receives a commitment $c = (c_1, c_2) \in M \times \{0,1\}^{\ell'}$. For any element $(\tilde{m}, x) \in \mathbb{I}_\eta$, E checks whether $x = c_2$. If this is the case, E outputs $m = c_1 - \tilde{m}$. If no such x exists, E outputs $\perp$.

Since $|\{0,1\}^{\ell'}| \geq \eta = |SR_\eta|$, E extracts the correct message and only outputs $\perp$ if c is not a valid commitment and therefore E is a correct extractor.   □

After establishing the (computational and statistical) binding and (perfect online) extractability properties of the standard hash-based commitment scheme in the NO QROM, we turn our attention towards proving their respective computational hiding properties. As discussed in Sect. 2 above, it suffices to show their *non-malleability* in the NO QROM instead because non-malleable commitments are also computationally hiding. We prove that they are computationally hiding in the settings when the schemes are statistically – respectively, computationally – binding by showing that they satisfy concurrent – respectively, *weak concurrent* – non-malleability in the NO QROM.

Theorem 3 (Non-Malleability when Statistically Binding). *Let the standard hash-based commitment from Definition 9 be set up such that it is statistically binding. Then, it is ε-concurrent non-malleable with respect to commitments in the NO QROM for $\varepsilon \leq$ negl as long as $\log |R| \geq \omega(\log \kappa)$.*

Proof. We can use the approach to puncture the random oracle and make the commitment to m independent of H and therefore uniform. Though there is one subtlety in the definition of non-malleable commitments. After the adversary sends his commitments, there is an exponential time routine that brute forces the commitments to extract the unique message. After the puncturing, it could happen that a commitment becomes invalid that was previously valid and instead of outputting the actual message, the brute force routine forwards $\perp$ to the distinguisher. Clearly, a distinguisher could then easily distinguish the punctured setting from the normal setting. Fortunately, in the standard hash-based commitment, the puncturing only affects a single commitment since we puncture H on point r, m which uniquely defines c. Further, if the adversary copies this commitment, the brute force routine forwards $\perp$ by default to the distinguisher such that it does not help to distinguish the punctured setting from the normal setting during the brute force routine.

We use a domain separation to define $H_{\hat{m}}$ for message $\hat{m} \in M$ such that for all $r \in R$, $H_{\hat{m}}(r) := H(r, \hat{m})$. We sample $\hat{r} \leftarrow R$, $\hat{y} \leftarrow \{0,1\}^\ell$ and define $\hat{G}_{\hat{m}}$ as follows. $\hat{G}_{\hat{m}}(\hat{r}) := \hat{y}$. For all other $r \in R \setminus \{\hat{r}\}$, we set $\hat{G}_{\hat{m}}(r) := H_{\hat{m}}(r)$.

To prove non-malleability, we define the following simple simulator. The simulator samples a random string $\hat{y} \leftarrow \{0,1\}^\ell$ and sends $\hat{y}$ to $\mathcal{A}$ as commitment. $\mathcal{A}$ then outputs commitments $c_1, \ldots, c_m$. For any $i \in [m]$ for which $c_i = \hat{y}$, sim sets

$m_i := \bot$. The random variable $\text{sim}^S_{\text{com}}(z)$ is generated from the view of $\mathcal{A}$ and the messages $m_1, \ldots, m_m$, where m_i is either $\bot$ or the unique message committed in c_i.

Afterwards, we use the puncturing technique to argue that the distinguisher cannot distinguish between $\text{sim}^S_{\text{com}}(z)$ and $\text{mim}^{\mathcal{A}}_{\text{com}}(z, \hat{m})$. The reduction uses D to distinguish between $\tilde{H}_{\hat{m}} = H_{\hat{m}}$ and $\tilde{H}_{\hat{m}} = \hat{G}_{\hat{m}}$. During the setup, the reduction programs H such that for a query $r, \hat{m}$ it outputs $\tilde{H}_{\hat{m}}(r)$. For all other messages $m \in M \setminus \{\hat{m}\}$, the reduction does not change H. Further, the reduction receives trapdoor information $\hat{y}$. During the query phase, the reduction sends $\hat{y}$ to $\mathcal{A}$ and uses $\mathcal{A}$'s view and commitments to define random variable X. If a commitment $c_i = \hat{y}$, it defines $m_i := \bot$.

When $\tilde{H}_{\hat{m}} = \hat{G}_{\hat{m}}$, $\hat{y}$ is a valid (and the only) commitment for $\hat{m}$ with randomness $\hat{r}$. In this case, $X = \text{mim}^{\mathcal{A}}_{\text{com}}(z, \hat{m})$. When $\tilde{H}_{\hat{m}} = H_{\hat{m}}$, $\hat{y}$ is statistically uniform and independent of $\hat{m}$. Further, due to the fact that input $\hat{r}, \hat{m}$ to $\tilde{H}$ defines a unique commitment, the puncturing of point $\hat{r}$ for $H_{\hat{m}}$ does not affect any commitment with $m \neq \hat{m}$ or $r \neq \hat{r}$. Therefore, during the exponential time brute force routine, there is no message m_i that is invalidated, i.e. set to $\bot$, due to the puncturing except messages derived from $\hat{y}$ which are in any case set to $\bot$. Thus, in this case $X = \text{sim}^S_{\text{com}}(z)$. When D distinguishes $\text{mim}^{\mathcal{A}}_{\text{com}}(z, \hat{m})$ from $\text{sim}^S_{\text{com}}(z)$ it implicitly distinguishes $H_{\hat{m}}$ from $\hat{G}_{\hat{m}}$ which is bounded by $4q\sqrt{2^{-\kappa}}$ by Lemma 5, where q is the amount of NO QRO queries of D and $\mathcal{A}$.   □

Theorem 4 (Weak Non-Malleability when Computationally Binding). *Let the standard hash-based commitment from Definition 9 be set up such that it is computationally binding. Then it is ε-weak-concurrent non-malleable with respect to commitments in the NO QROM for $\varepsilon \leq \text{negl}$ as long as $\log |R| \geq \omega(\log \kappa)$ and $|c| \geq \omega(\log \kappa)$.*

Proof. The proof follows essentially from the proof of Theorem 3 and we can use exactly the same simulator. We outline the differences. $\hat{c}$ received by $\mathcal{A}$ when generating wmim might be a commitment that has valid openings for multiple messages $\hat{m}_1, \ldots, \hat{m}_j$. Though due to the definition of the experiment, $\hat{m}_1, \ldots, \hat{m}_j$ are not contained in wmim and replaced with $\bot$. The puncturing of $\hat{c}$ again only affects $H(\hat{m}, \hat{r})$ as previously. Though there is another subtlety when considering the unbounded procedure that extracts the messages for the distinguisher. Using a uniformly random $\hat{y}$ instead of $\hat{c}$ could lead to replacing a different set of messages with $\bot$ such that wmim and wsim are distinguishable. However, this is only possible when collisions occur. Due to $|c| \geq \omega(\log \kappa)$ and Lemma 1, this happens at most with probability $q^3 2^{-\omega(\log \kappa)}$ which is negligible.   □

5   Signature Schemes in the NO QROM

In this section, we establish the post-quantum security of certain generic classes of signatures in the NO QROM. First we consider signature schemes whose proofs of security in the classical ROM involve so-called *history-free reductions* as defined in [8]; examples of such schemes include the lattice-based GPV signatures in [22] and *Fiat-Shamir* signatures analyzed in [26]. Then we shift our attention to the well-known generic *full domain hash (FDH)* signatures of Bellare and Rogaway [5] in the NO QROM.

5.1 Signatures with History-Free Reductions

Boneh *et. al.* [8] show that if the security proof of any signature scheme in the classical ROM follows a specific structure known as a *history-free reduction*, then the scheme is also provably secure in the QROM. On a high-level, in a history-free reduction, the responses to an adversary's random oracle queries are determined *independently* of the responses to previous queries. A more formal definition of a history-free reduction follows (taken from [8]):

Definition 11 (History-Free Reductions). *A random oracle signature scheme* $S^H = (\mathsf{Gen}, \mathsf{Sign}^H, \mathsf{Ver}^H)$ *has a history-free reduction from a hard problem* P *if the proof of security uses a classical ppt adversary* $\mathcal{A}$ *against* S^H *to construct a classical ppt algorithm* $\mathcal{B}$ *to solve problem* P *such that:*

- $\mathcal{B}$ *contains four classical algorithms:* START, RAND^{H_c}, SIGN^{H_c} *and* FINISH^{H_c}*; the latter three algorithms have access to a shared classical random oracle* H_c*. These algorithms are used as follows:*
  - *Given an instance* x *for problem* P, $\mathcal{B}$ *first runs* $\mathrm{START}(x)$ *to get* $(\mathsf{pk}, \mathsf{st})$ *where* pk *is a public key of* S^H *and* st *is some private state to be used by* $\mathcal{B}$*. Then* $\mathcal{B}$ *simulates the standard CMA security game (Definition 7) w.r.t.* S^H *by first forwarding* pk *to* $\mathcal{A}$*.*
  - *When* $\mathcal{A}$ *makes a classical RO query* $H(r)$, $\mathcal{B}$ *responds with* $\mathrm{RAND}^{H_c}(r, \mathsf{st})$*. Note here that* RAND^{H_c} *is only given the current query* r *as input, and in particular, is unaware of previous queries and responses.*
  - *When* $\mathcal{A}$ *makes a signature query* $\mathsf{Sign}^H(\mathsf{sk}, \mathsf{m})$*, where* sk *is the secret key corresponding to* pk, $\mathcal{B}$ *responds with* $\mathrm{SIGN}^{H_c}(\mathsf{m}, \mathsf{st})$*.*
  - *When* $\mathcal{A}$ *outputs a forgery candidate* (m, σ), $\mathcal{B}$ *outputs* $\mathrm{FINISH}^{H_c}(\mathsf{m}, \sigma, \mathsf{st})$*.*
- *There is an efficiently computable function* $\mathrm{INSTANCE}(\mathsf{pk})$ *which generates an instance* x *for problem* P *such that* $\mathrm{START}(x) = (\mathsf{pk}, \mathsf{st})$ *for some* st*. We also need the following distribution of* x *to be negligible close to the original distribution of* x *considered in problem* P*: first generate* $(\mathsf{pk}, \mathsf{sk}) \leftarrow \mathsf{Gen}(1^\kappa)$ *and compute* $x = \mathrm{INSTANCE}(\mathsf{pk})$*.*
- *Consider the classical oracle* $O(r) = \mathrm{RAND}^{H_c}(r, \mathsf{st})$*, for a fixed* st*. Define the corresponding quantum oracle* O_q *which maps* $|r\rangle |s\rangle \mapsto |r\rangle |s \oplus O(r)\rangle$*. We require* O_q *to be quantum computationally indistinguishable from a truly random oracle.*
- SIGN^{H_c} *either generates a valid signature relative to the oracle* $O(r) = \mathrm{RAND}^{H_c}(r, \mathsf{st})$ *with a distribution negligibly close to the correct signing algorithm, or it aborts (hence making* $\mathcal{B}$ *abort as well). The probability that none of* $\mathcal{A}$*'s signature queries result in an abort is non-negligible.*

– If the output (m, σ) of $\mathcal{A}$ is a valid signature forgery w.r.t. the received public key pk and oracle $O(r) = \mathrm{RAND}^{H_c}(r, \mathsf{st})$, then the output $\mathrm{FINISH}^{H_c}(\mathsf{m}, \sigma, \mathsf{st})$ of B solves the problem P w.r.t. instance x with non-negligible probability.

After defining history-free reductions for signature schemes, Boneh *et. al.* prove a general lifting theorem from ROM security to QROM security for such reductions [8, Theorem 1]. In the following, we extend their lifting theorem to show that signature schemes with history-free reductions are in fact secure in the *weaker* NO QROM heuristic.

Theorem 5. *Let* $\mathsf{S}^H = (\mathsf{Gen}, \mathsf{Sign}^H, \mathsf{Ver}^H)$ *be a random oracle signature scheme with a history-free reduction from a problem P assumed to be hard for polynomial-time quantum algorithms. Further assume that post-quantum one-way functions exist. Then* S^H *is post-quantum EUF-CMA secure when H is modelled in the NO QROM.*

The following proof essentially follows a similar strategy as the one by Boneh *et. al.* for "history-free signatures" in the plain QROM [8, Theorem 1] (however we provide a detailed sketch below for the sake of completeness). In addition, we adapt their proof in our NO QROM framework when it comes to simulating the responses to an adversary's quantum random oracle queries in the reduction.

Proof (Sketch). As per Definition 11, recall that the history-free reduction for signature $\mathsf{S}^H = (\mathsf{Gen}, \mathsf{Sign}^H, \mathsf{Ver}^H)$ above involves the classical algorithms START, RAND, SIGN, FINISH and INSTANCE. Now towards a contradiction, assume there is a quantum ppt adversary $\mathcal{A}$ that breaks the EUF-CMA security of S^H with non-negligible probability ε. The proof proceeds by a sequence of game-hybrids. Namely, let G_0 be the standard CMA game w.r.t. S^H (cf. Definition 7).

Now let the game G_1 be the following modification of G_0: after the challenger generates $(\mathsf{pk}, \mathsf{sk}) \leftarrow \mathsf{Gen}(1^\kappa)$, it computes $x = \mathrm{INSTANCE}(\mathsf{pk})$ and $(\mathsf{pk}, \mathsf{st}) \leftarrow \mathrm{START}(x)$. Then instead of using a truly random oracle to answer $\mathcal{A}$'s quantum queries to H, the challenger uses the quantum oracle O_q which maps $|r\rangle |s\rangle \mapsto |r\rangle |s \oplus \mathrm{RAND}^{H_c}(r, \mathsf{st})\rangle$; here H_c is a truly random quantum oracle which is not directly accessible to $\mathcal{A}$. From Definition 11, we have O_q to be quantum computationally indistinguishable from a truly random oracle. Hence, we have the winning probability of $\mathcal{A}$ in G_1 to be negligibly close to that in G_0; in other words, the probability is non-negligible like ε.

Let G_2 be the following modification of G_1: instead of generating $(\mathsf{pk}, \mathsf{sk}) \leftarrow \mathsf{Gen}(1^\kappa)$ and computing $x = \mathrm{INSTANCE}(\mathsf{pk})$, the challenger samples x from the *original* instance distribution w.r.t. problem P; it then uses the latter x to obtain $(\mathsf{pk}, \mathsf{st}) \leftarrow \mathrm{START}(x)$ before forwarding pk to $\mathcal{A}$. Furthermore, when $\mathcal{A}$ makes a signature query on m, the challenger responds with $\mathrm{SIGN}^{H_c}(\mathsf{m}, \mathsf{st})$. From the property of INSTANCE in Definition 11, we have the distributions of x in games G_1 and G_2 to be negligibly close. Also from the property of SIGN^{H_c}, we have with a non-negligible probability that all of $\mathcal{A}$'s signing queries are answered successfully (i.e., without aborting) with the corresponding signatures having a distribution negligibly close to the actual signatures in G_1. Hence as argued in the proof of [8, Theorem 1], it's not hard to see that $\mathcal{A}$'s winning probability in G_2 (i.e., probability of outputting a valid forgery) is non-negligible.

Finally let G_3 be the following modification of G_2: instead of using a truly random quantum oracle for evaluating H_c internally, the challenger uses a quantum-secure pseudorandom function PRF (cf. Definition 6). Specifically, the challenger first samples a random PRF key k. Then it replaces H_c with the quantum oracle $|\mathsf{PRF}(k,\cdot)\rangle$ which maps $|r\rangle\,|s\rangle \mapsto |r\rangle\,|s \oplus \mathsf{PRF}(k,r)\rangle$. Because of the quantum-security of PRF, it's not hard to see that the winning probabilities of $\mathcal{A}$ in games G_2 and G_3 are negligibly close. Hence we have the latter probability to be non-negligible as well. Also note that quantum-secure pseudorandom functions can be constructed (in a black-box manner) from post-quantum one-way functions, as shown by Zhandry [38].

After defining games $G_0 - G_3$ w.r.t. adversary $\mathcal{A}$, we now construct a polynomial-time quantum algorithm $\mathcal{B}$ that solves the underlying hard problem P in the NO QROM with non-negligible probability. Upon receiving an instance x w.r.t. problem P, $\mathcal{B}$ computes $(\mathsf{pk}, \mathsf{st}) \leftarrow \mathrm{START}(x)$. Then in the "setup phase" of the NO QROM (cf. Sect. 3), $\mathcal{B}$ samples a random PRF key k and programs the quantum random oracle H as:

$$H(r) := \mathrm{RAND}^{|\mathsf{PRF}(k,\cdot)\rangle}(r, \mathsf{st}),$$

as in game G_3. $\mathcal{B}$ also forwards pk to $\mathcal{A}$, and acts as the CMA-challenger in game G_3. Specifically in the "query phase" of the NO QROM:

- When $\mathcal{A}$ makes a signature query on message m, $\mathcal{B}$ responds with the value $\mathrm{SIGN}^{|\mathsf{PRF}(k,\cdot)\rangle}(\mathsf{m}, \mathsf{st})$.
- When $\mathcal{A}$ returns a forgery candidate (m, σ), $\mathcal{B}$ outputs $\mathrm{FINISH}^{|\mathsf{PRF}(k,\cdot)\rangle}(m, \sigma, \mathsf{st})$.

It's not hard to see that $\mathcal{B}$ perfectly simulates game G_3 towards $\mathcal{A}$, while importantly, also executing a valid reduction in the NO QROM. Because note that $\mathcal{B}$ never has to observe the quantum queries made by $\mathcal{A}$ to the random oracle H after the setup phase (also the above two steps in query phase can be seen as the "Interaction" in Fig. 1). Now since we have the winning probability of $\mathcal{A}$ in G_3 to be non-negligible, we also have the probability of $\mathcal{A}$ returning a valid forgery candidate (m, σ) to $\mathcal{B}$ in the above query phase to be non-negligible. So from the property of the FINISH algorithm in Definition 11, we note that the output $\mathrm{FINISH}^{|\mathsf{PRF}(k,\cdot)\rangle}(m, \sigma, \mathsf{st})$ of $\mathcal{B}$ solves the problem P w.r.t. given instance x with a non-negligible probability. This contradicts our starting assumption that P is hard for polynomial-time quantum algorithms. Hence, we have that the above signatures S^H with history-free reductions are indeed EUF-CMA secure in the NO QROM.   □

Following the results on history-free reductions in [8], quite a few works in the literature started devising "history-free versions" of classical ROM security proofs of important signature schemes in order to establish their post-quantum security in the QROM. Examples of such schemes include the lattice-based GPV signatures of [22], as analyzed in [8], and Fiat-Shamir signatures as analyzed in [26]. So a consequence of our lifting theorem (i.e., Theorem 5) above is that these classes of signature schemes are also provably secure in the weaker NO QROM. In other words, we explicitly establish that *weaker* heuristics – i.e., which do not require observing an adversary's quantum random oracle queries – are sufficient to prove post-quantum security of the above signature schemes.

5.2 FDH Based Signature Schemes

We first recall the definition of FDH signatures:

Definition 12 (FDH Signatures). *Let* $\mathsf{F} = (\mathsf{Gen}, \mathsf{f}, \mathsf{f}^{-1})$ *be a trapdoor permutation, and a hash function H that maps messages to the co-domain of f. Let $\mathsf{S}^H = (\mathsf{Gen}, \mathsf{Sign}^H, \mathsf{Ver}^H)$ be a signature scheme where:*

- $\mathsf{Sign}^H(\mathsf{sk}, \mathsf{m}) = \mathsf{f}^{-1}(\mathsf{sk}, H(\mathsf{m}))$
- $\mathsf{Ver}^H(\mathsf{pk}, \mathsf{m}, \sigma) = \begin{cases} \mathsf{acc} & \text{if } \mathsf{f}(\mathsf{pk}, \sigma) = H(m) \\ \mathsf{rej} & \text{otherwise} \end{cases}$

In the classical setting, Bellare and Rogaway [5] proved the EUF-CMA security of FDH signatures in the *classical* ROM while relying on one-wayness of the underlying TDP. At a high level, in their proof (via a reduction), the "TDP adversary" $\mathcal{B}$ – who is supposed to find a pre-image for a given challenge y – randomly guesses which of the random oracle queries the "signature adversary" $\mathcal{A}$ will use to produce a forgery w.r.t. the FDH scheme. $\mathcal{B}$ then *embeds* y into the response for this oracle query, and if both the guess is correct and $\mathcal{A}$ produces a valid forgery, then $\mathcal{B}$ will be able to find a pre-image for y.

However, as observed by Zhandry [39], the above approach will not work in the QROM setting because each of $\mathcal{A}$'s random oracle queries might be a superposition of exponentially many inputs; this makes it hard for $\mathcal{B}$ to meaningfully embed its challenge y into the oracle responses. Nevertheless, Zhandry [39] was able to overcome this barrier by introducing a class of oracle distributions called *Semi-Constant Distributions* (Definition 2) which allows for a specific random value to be embedded into a small but significant fraction of oracle inputs, while at the same time, ensuring that it is – in some sense – hard for a quantum algorithm to distinguish between this semi-constant oracle and a uniformly random oracle (cf. Lemma 4). This allowed Zhandry to translate the above embedding-based argument of Bellare and Rogaway to the quantum setting in order to show the EUF-CMA security of FDH signatures in the plain QROM based on one-wayness of the underlying TDP against *quantum* adversaries.[4]

However, upon a closer inspection of Zhandry's proof, we note that nowhere in the reduction is the "TDP adversary" $\mathcal{B}$ required to observe the "signature

---

[4] Though this should be seen as a theoretical result until there is an instantiation of such a quantum one-way trapdoor permutation.

adversary" $\mathcal{A}$'s quantum queries to the random oracle. In other words, by adapting Zhandry's proof in [39], the FDH signature scheme can be shown to be EUF-CMA secure in the *weaker* heuristic model of NO QROM – while still relying on the quantum one-wayness of the underlying TDP – wherein $\mathcal{B}$ would still have to (non-adaptively) program the random oracle by replacing it with a semi-constant oracle in the *setup phase* (see Sect. 3).

Theorem 6. *Let* $\mathsf{F} = (\mathsf{Gen}, \mathsf{f}, \mathsf{f}^{-1})$ *be a quantum one-way trapdoor permutation. Then the corresponding FDH signature scheme* $\mathsf{S}^H = (\mathsf{Gen}, \mathsf{Sign}^H, \mathsf{Ver}^H)$ *is post-quantum* EUF-CMA *secure when* H *is modelled in the NO QROM.*

The proof below mirrors the one given by Zhandry [39] for FDH signatures in the plain QROM. Here we adapt his proof to fit within our NO QROM framework, as described in Sect. 3.

Proof (Sketch). Towards a contradiction, assume there is a quantum ppt adversary $\mathcal{A}$ that breaks the FDH signature scheme $\mathsf{S}^H = (\mathsf{Gen}, \mathsf{Sign}^H, \mathsf{Ver}^H)$ with non-negligible probability ε. The proof proceeds by a sequence of game-hybrids. Let G_0 be the standard CMA game w.r.t. S^H (see Definition 7). Namely, the challenger generates the pair $(\mathsf{pk}, \mathsf{sk}) \leftarrow \mathsf{Gen}$ and sends pk to $\mathcal{A}$. The adversary $\mathcal{A}$ can make *classical* signature queries on messages m_i to which the challenger responds with $\mathsf{Sign}^H(\mathsf{sk}, \mathsf{m}_i)$, and *quantum* hash queries to the random oracle H. $\mathcal{A}$ wins if it produces a pair (m, σ) such that $\mathsf{m} \neq \mathsf{m}_i$ for any i and $\mathsf{Ver}^H(\mathsf{pk}, \mathsf{m}, \sigma) = \mathsf{acc}$. Also suppose $\mathcal{A}$ makes q_H hash queries and q_S signature queries.

Let $0 \leq \lambda \leq 1$ be a parameter to be chosen later, and let M be the message space of S^H. We now construct a subset $\mathcal{X} \subseteq \mathsf{M}$ as follows: for each $\mathsf{m} \in \mathsf{M}$, put $\mathsf{m} \in \mathcal{X}$ with probability λ. Now let the game G_1 be the same as G_0 except that we modify the winning conditions as follows: if $\mathcal{A}$ asks for a signature on message $\mathsf{m}_i \in \mathcal{X}$ or if $\mathcal{A}$ attempts to forge the signature for a message $\mathsf{m} \notin \mathcal{X}$, we abort G_1 and $\mathcal{A}$ loses; other than this, the winning condition in G_0 applies to G_1 as well. It is not hard to see that G_1 does not abort with probability at-least $\lambda(1 - \lambda q_S)$. Therefore, $\mathcal{A}$ wins G_1 with probability at-least $\lambda(1 - \lambda q_S)\varepsilon \geq \lambda\varepsilon - q_S\lambda^2$.

Let G_2 be the same as G_1 except that we reprogram the random oracle H (only) on inputs in $\mathcal{X}$ as follows: fix a uniformly random value y in the co-domain of f and set $H(x) := y$ for all $x \in \mathcal{X}$. We can see that the modified H is now an oracle with a λ-constant distribution (cf. Definition 2). As argued by Zhandry in [39, Claim 1]–using Lemma 4, among other things–we have that the probability $\mathcal{B}$ wins in G_2 is at-least $(\lambda\varepsilon - p(q_H, q_S)\lambda^2)$ for some polynomial $p(\cdot, \cdot)$.

After defining the games $\mathsf{G}_0 - \mathsf{G}_2$ w.r.t. adversary $\mathcal{A}$, we now construct a quantum ppt adversary $\mathcal{B}$ that breaks the underlying TDP $\mathsf{F} = (\mathsf{Gen}, \mathsf{f}, \mathsf{f}^{-1})$ in the NO QROM as follows. $\mathcal{B}$ first samples a $2(q_H + q_S + 1)$-wise independent function $O_1(\cdot)$ that maps M to the domain of f. Note that in the games $\mathsf{G}_0 - \mathsf{G}_2$, at-most $(q_H + q_S + 1)$ queries are made to the quantum oracle H (q_H quantum hash queries, q_S classical queries via the signature queries $\mathsf{Sign}^H(\mathsf{sk}, \mathsf{m}_i)$ and one classical query for checking $\mathcal{A}$'s forgery $\mathsf{Ver}^H(\mathsf{pk}, \mathsf{m}, \sigma)$). From Lemma 2, we have that $O_1(\cdot)$ is perfectly indistinguishable from a uniformly random oracle mapping M to the domain of f in the view of $\mathcal{A}$. Similarly, $\mathcal{B}$ simulates an oracle $O_2 : M \to \{0,1\}$ such that for each $m \in M$ $O_2(m) = 1$ with probability λ as follows (taken from [39, Section 6]): $\mathcal{B}$ approximates λ by a rational number a/b, with b being a prime power, and constructs a $2(q_H + q_S + 1)$-wise independent function $\hat{O}_2$ with range $\{1,\ldots,b\}$; it then constructs $O_2(\cdot)$ as

$$O_2(m) = \begin{cases} 1 & \text{if } \hat{O}_2(m) \leq a \\ 0 & \text{otherwise.} \end{cases}$$

Finally, $\mathcal{B}$ on input (pk, y) – for which it is supposed to find a pre-image w.r.t. F – proceeds in the "setup phase" of the NO QROM (cf. Section 3) by programming the quantum random oracle H as:

$$H(m) = \begin{cases} y & \text{if } O_2(m) = 1 \\ \mathsf{f}(\mathsf{pk}, O_1(m)) & \text{otherwise.} \end{cases}$$

$\mathcal{B}$ also sends pk to $\mathcal{A}$, playing the role of challenger in the game G_2.

In the "query phase":

- When $\mathcal{A}$ makes a signature query on message m_i, $\mathcal{B}$ computes $O_2(m_i)$ and aborts if the result is 1. Otherwise, $\mathcal{B}$ returns the response $O_1(m_i)$.
- When $\mathcal{A}$ returns a forgery candidate (m, σ), $\mathcal{B}$ checks if $O_2(m) = 1$ and $\mathsf{f}(\mathsf{pk}, \sigma) = y$. If satisfied, $\mathcal{B}$ returns the pre-image σ. Otherwise, it aborts.

We have $\mathcal{B}$ perfectly simulating the game G_2 towards $\mathcal{A}$, while at the same time, implementing a valid reduction in the NO QROM; note that $\mathcal{B}$ never has to observe the quantum hash queries made by $\mathcal{A}$ to oracle H, and the above two steps in the query phase can be seen as part of the "Interaction" in Fig. 1. Hence, by applying a similar analysis as that in [39, Theorem 5.1], we have $\mathcal{B}$'s advantage in breaking the underlying TDP F to be at-least the non-negligible quantity $\frac{\varepsilon^2}{4p(q_H, q_S)}$, when we set $\lambda = \frac{\varepsilon}{2p(q_H, q_S)}$. This shows that S^H is indeed quantum EUF-CMA secure in the NO QROM, given that F is a quantum one-way TDP. $\square$

6   Hinting PRGs in the NO QROM

In this section, we describe a simple and efficient construction of a special cryptographic primitive in the NO QROM called *hinting pseudorandom generator (PRG)*. This primitive is useful towards constructing CCA-secure encryption systems as will be detailed below. A hinting PRG is essentially a PRG with a stronger security property. It takes an n bit input $s \in \{0,1\}^n$ and outputs $(n+1) \cdot \ell$ bits $y_0, y_1, \ldots, y_n$ (where each y_i is an ℓ-bit string) such that the following two distributions $(r_0, (r_{i,0}, r_{i,1})_{i \in [n]})$ are computationally indistinguishable w.r.t. a uniformly random "seed" s: In the first distribution, $r_0 = y_0$, $r_{i,s_i} = y_i$ and $r_{i,1-s_i}$ is chosen uniformly from $\{0,1\}^\ell$ (where s_i is the i-th bit of s) for $i \in [n]$. In the second distribution, r_0, $r_{i,0}$ and $r_{i,1}$ are all chosen uniformly at random from $\{0,1\}^\ell$ for $i \in [n]$. Note that in the first distribution, the relative "placement" of pseudorandom values y_i (for $i \in [n]$) in the tuple $(r_{i,0}, r_{i,1})$ depends on the i-th bit of seed s; hence in some sense, the values $(r_{i,0}, r_{i,1})_{i \in [n]}$ give away a "hint" about the seed.

More formally, hinting PRGs are defined as follows:

Definition 13 (Hinting PRGs). *A hinting PRG is a deterministic polynomial-time algorithm* G *with parameters* n, ℓ, *such that* G *takes as input* 1^κ, *an n bit string s, and outputs an $(n+1) \cdot \ell$ bit string y. Moreover, it satisfies the following property for any ppt adversary* $\mathcal{A}$:

$$| \Pr[\mathcal{A}((y_0^0, (y_{i,0}^0, y_{i,1}^0)_{i \in [n]})) = 1] - \Pr[\mathcal{A}((y_0^1, (y_{i,0}^1, y_{i,1}^1)_{i \in [n]})) = 1]| \leq \mathsf{negl}.$$

where $s = (s_1, \ldots, s_n)$, y_0^1, $(y_{i,0}^1, y_{i,1}^1)_{i \in [n]}$ *and* $(y_{i,1-s_i}^0)_{i \in [n]}$ *are uniformly distributed whereas* $(y_0^0, (y_{1,s_1}^0, y_{n,s_n}^0)_{i \in [n]})$ *is the output of* $G(1^\kappa, s)$. *In more detail,* $s = (s_1, \ldots, s_n) \leftarrow \{0,1\}^n$, $G(1^\kappa, s) = (y_0^0, y_{1,s_1}^0, \ldots, y_{n,s_n}^0)$ *– with each* $y_{i,s_i}^0 \in \{0,1\}^\ell$ *– and* $y_{i,1-s_i}^0 \leftarrow \{0,1\}^\ell$ $\forall i \in [n]$, $y_0^1 \leftarrow \{0,1\}^\ell$ *and* $y_{i,b}^1 \leftarrow \{0,1\}^\ell$ $\forall i \in [n], b \in \{0,1\}$.

Let $G : \{0,1\}^n \to \{0,1\}^{(n+1) \cdot \ell}$ be a hash function, or alternatively, an *extendable output function*. Our main observation is that by modeling G as a random oracle in the NO QROM, we get the above hinting property from G *"for free"*. It's worth noting that very recently, Alamati and Patranabis [1] also realize hinting PRGs using a random oracle albeit in a *classical* setting.

Theorem 7. *The extendable output function* $G : \{0,1\}^n \to \{0,1\}^{(n+1) \cdot \ell}$ *when modelled in the NO QROM behaves as a hinting PRG.*

Proof. Consider any ppt adversary $\mathcal{A}$ that has quantum access to the random oracle G in the setup phase (cf. Sect. 3) and gets as input $y^0 = (y_0^0, (y_{i,0}^0, y_{i,1}^0)_{i \in [n]})$ where for a uniformly random seed $s = (s_1, \ldots, s_n) \leftarrow \{0,1\}^n$, we have $G(s) = (y_0^0, y_{1,s_1}^0, \ldots, y_{n,s_n}^0)$ – with each $y_{i,s_i}^0 \in \{0,1\}^\ell$ – and $y_{i,1-s_i}^0 \leftarrow \{0,1\}^\ell$ $\forall i \in [n]$. Now we replace G with another random oracle $H : \{0,1\}^n \to \{0,1\}^{(n+1) \cdot \ell}$ in the setup phase such that $\forall x \in \{0,1\}^n \setminus \{s\}$, $H(x) = G(x)$ and $H(s) = \hat{y}$ for a uniformly random and independent $\hat{y} \leftarrow \{0,1\}^{(n+1) \cdot \ell}$.

In the context of applying Lemma 5, it's not hard to see that we have $\Pr[\mathcal{A}^H(y^0) = 1] = \Pr[\mathcal{A}^G(y^1) = 1]$, where $y^1 = (y_0^1, (y_{i,0}^1, y_{i,1}^1)_{i \in [n]})$ with the uniformly random values $y_0^1 \leftarrow \{0,1\}^\ell$ and $y_{i,b}^1 \leftarrow \{0,1\}^\ell$ $\forall i \in [n], b \in \{0,1\}$; because in both cases, $\mathcal{A}$'s inputs y^0, y^1 have the same (uniformly random) distribution and are independent w.r.t. the oracle outputs $H(s), G(s)$ respectively. Hence if the ppt adversary $\mathcal{A}$ makes at-most q quantum oracle queries, then from Lemma 5 we have

$$| \Pr[\mathcal{A}^H(y^0) = 1] - \Pr[\mathcal{A}^G(y^0) = 1]|$$

$$= | \Pr[\mathcal{A}^G(y^1) = 1] - \Pr[\mathcal{A}^G(y^0) = 1]| \leq 4\sqrt{\frac{q(q+1)}{2^n}} = \mathsf{negl}.$$

This satisfies the hinting property specified in Definition 13 in the NO QROM. $\square$

CCA-Secure Encryption in the NO QROM. One of the main applications of hinting PRGs is to construct CCA-secure PKE schemes, and more advanced primitives such as CCA-secure *attribute-based encryption* (ABE) or CCA-secure *one-sided predicate encryption* schemes, from their CPA-secure counterparts in a black-box manner [27].

Hence, by replacing the hinting PRG in the black-box constructions of [27] with a standard hash function/extendable output function – later modeled as a random oracle – we obtain the above advanced CCA-secure encryption systems in the NO QROM; we can follow the proof strategies used in [27] w.r.t. their black-box constructions, in conjunction with Lemma 7 above, to prove CCA security of our corresponding constructions in the NO QROM in a relatively straightforward fashion. At the same time, we leave it as an open question to obtain more efficient constructions of the above CCA-secure primitives in the NO QROM.

References

1. Alamati, N., Patranabis, S.: Cryptographic primitives with hinting property. In: Agrawal, S., Lin, D. (eds.) ASIACRYPT 2022, Part I. LNCS, vol. 13791, pp. 33–62. Springer, Cham (2022). https://doi.org/10.1007/978-3-031-22963-3_2
2. Ambainis, A., Hamburg, M., Unruh, D.: Quantum security proofs using semi-classical oracles. In: Boldyreva, A., Micciancio, D. (eds.) CRYPTO 2019, Part II. LNCS, vol. 11693, pp. 269–295. Springer, Cham (2019). https://doi.org/10.1007/978-3-030-26951-7_10
3. Ananth, P., Bhaskar, R.: Non observability in the random oracle model. In: Susilo, W., Reyhanitabar, R. (eds.) ProvSec 2013. LNCS, vol. 8209, pp. 86–103. Springer, Heidelberg (2013). https://doi.org/10.1007/978-3-642-41227-1_5
4. Bellare, M., Boldyreva, A., O'Neill, A.: Deterministic and efficiently searchable encryption. In: Menezes, A. (ed.) CRYPTO 2007. LNCS, vol. 4622, pp. 535–552. Springer, Heidelberg (2007). https://doi.org/10.1007/978-3-540-74143-5_30
5. Bellare, M., Rogaway, P.: Random oracles are practical: a paradigm for designing efficient protocols. In: Dorothy, E.D., Pyle, R., Ganesan, R., Sandhu, R.S., Ashby, V.. (eds.) ACM CCS 93, pp. 62–73. ACM Press (1993)
6. Rabin, M.O.: Probabilistic algorithms in finite fields. In: 22nd FOCS, pp. 394–398. IEEE Computer Society Press (1981)
7. Bitansky, N., Lin, H., Shmueli, O.: Non-malleable commitments against quantum attacks. In: Dunkelman, O., Dziembowski, S. (eds.) EUROCRYPT 2022, Part III. LNCS, vol. 13277, pp. 519–550. Springer, Cham (2022). https://doi.org/10.1007/978-3-031-07082-2_19
8. Boneh, D., Dagdelen, Ö., Fischlin, M., Lehmann, A., Schaffner, C., Zhandry, M.: Random oracles in a quantum world. In: Lee, D.H., Wang, X. (eds.) ASIACRYPT 2011. LNCS, vol. 7073, pp. 41–69. Springer, Heidelberg (2011). https://doi.org/10.1007/978-3-642-25385-0_3
9. Boneh, D., Zhandry, M.: Secure signatures and chosen ciphertext security in a quantum computing world. In: Canetti, R., Garay, J.A. (eds.) CRYPTO 2013, Part II. LNCS, vol. 8043, pp. 361–379. Springer, Heidelberg (2013). https://doi.org/10.1007/978-3-642-40084-1_21

10. Brenner, H., Goyal, V., Richelson, S., Rosen, A., Vald, M.: Fast non-malleable commitments. In: Ray, I., Li, N., Kruegel, C., (eds.) ACM CCS 2015, pp. 1048–1057. ACM Press (2015)

11. Canetti, R., et al.: Fiat-Shamir: from practice to theory. In: Charikar, M., Cohen, E., (eds.) 51st ACM STOC, pp. 1082–1090. ACM Press (2019)

12. Canetti, R., Goldreich, O., Halevi, S.: The random oracle methodology, revisited (preliminary version). In: 30th ACM STOC, pp. 209–218. ACM Press (1998)

13. Di Crescenzo, G., Ishai, Y., Ostrovsky, R.: Non-interactive and non-malleable commitment. In: 30th ACM STOC, pp. 141–150. ACM Press (1998)

14. Dolev, D., Dwork, C., Naor, M.: Non-malleable cryptography (extended abstract). In: 23rd ACM STOC, pp. 542–552. ACM Press (1991)

15. Don, J., Fehr, S., Majenz, C., Schaffner, C.: Security of the Fiat-Shamir transformation in the quantum random-oracle model. In: Boldyreva, A., Micciancio, D. (eds.) CRYPTO 2019, Part II. LNCS, vol. 11693, pp. 356–383. Springer, Cham (2019). https://doi.org/10.1007/978-3-030-26951-7_13

16. Don, J., Fehr, S., Majenz, C., Schaffner, C.: Efficient NIZKs and signatures from commit-and-open protocols in the QROM. In: Dodis, Y., Shrimpton, T. (eds.) CRYPTO 2022, Part II. LNCS, vol. 13508, pp. 729–757. Springer, Cham (2022). https://doi.org/10.1007/978-3-031-15979-4_25

17. Don, J., Fehr, S., Majenz, C., Schaffner, C.: Online-extractability in the quantum random-oracle model. In: Dunkelman, O., Dziembowski, S. (eds.) EUROCRYPT 2022, Part III. LNCS, vol. 13277, pp. 677–706. Springer, Cham (2022). https://doi.org/10.1007/978-3-031-07082-2_24

18. Fiat, A., Shamir, A.: How to prove yourself: practical solutions to identification and signature problems. In: Odlyzko, A.M. (ed.) CRYPTO 1986. LNCS, vol. 263, pp. 186–194. Springer, Heidelberg (1987). https://doi.org/10.1007/3-540-47721-7_12

19. Fischlin, M., Fischlin, R.: Efficient non-malleable commitment schemes. In: Bellare, M. (ed.) CRYPTO 2000. LNCS, vol. 1880, pp. 413–431. Springer, Heidelberg (2000). https://doi.org/10.1007/3-540-44598-6_26

20. Fischlin, M., Lehmann, A., Ristenpart, T., Shrimpton, T., Stam, M., Tessaro, S.: Random oracles with(out) programmability. In: Abe, M. (ed.) ASIACRYPT 2010. LNCS, vol. 6477, pp. 303–320. Springer, Heidelberg (2010). https://doi.org/10.1007/978-3-642-17373-8_18

21. Fujisaki, E., Okamoto, T.: Secure integration of asymmetric and symmetric encryption schemes. In: Wiener, M. (ed.) CRYPTO 1999. LNCS, vol. 1666, pp. 537–554. Springer, Heidelberg (1999). https://doi.org/10.1007/3-540-48405-1_34

22. Gentry, C., Peikert, C., Vaikuntanathan, V.: Trapdoors for hard lattices and new cryptographic constructions. In: Ladner, R.E., Dwork, C., (eds.) 40th ACM STOC, pp. 197–206. ACM Press (2008)

23. Hövelmanns, K., Hülsing, A., Majenz, C.: Failing gracefully: decryption failures and the Fujisaki-Okamoto transform. In: Agrawal, S., Lin, D. (eds.) ASIACRYPT 2022, Part IV. LNCS, vol. 13794, pp. 414–443. Springer, Cham (2022). https://doi.org/10.1007/978-3-031-22972-5_15

24. Impagliazzo, R., Rudich, S.: Limits on the provable consequences of one-way permutations. In: Goldwasser, S. (ed.) CRYPTO 1988. LNCS, vol. 403, pp. 8–26. Springer, New York (1990). https://doi.org/10.1007/0-387-34799-2_2

25. Jiang, H., Zhang, Z., Chen, L., Wang, H., Ma, Z.: IND-CCA-secure key encapsulation mechanism in the quantum random oracle model, revisited. In: Shacham, H., Boldyreva, A. (eds.) CRYPTO 2018, Part III. LNCS, vol. 10993, pp. 96–125. Springer, Cham (2018). https://doi.org/10.1007/978-3-319-96878-0_4

26. Kiltz, E., Lyubashevsky, V., Schaffner, C.: A concrete treatment of Fiat-Shamir signatures in the quantum random-oracle model. In: Nielsen, J.B., Rijmen, V. (eds.) EUROCRYPT 2018, Part III. LNCS, vol. 10822, pp. 552–586. Springer, Cham (2018). https://doi.org/10.1007/978-3-319-78372-7_18

27. Koppula, V., Waters, B.: Realizing chosen ciphertext security generically in attribute-based encryption and predicate encryption. In: Boldyreva, A., Micciancio, D. (eds.) CRYPTO 2019, Part II. LNCS, vol. 11693, pp. 671–700. Springer, Cham (2019). https://doi.org/10.1007/978-3-030-26951-7_23

28. Lin, H., Pass, R., Venkitasubramaniam, M.: Concurrent non-malleable commitments from any one-way function. In: Canetti, R. (ed.) TCC 2008. LNCS, vol. 4948, pp. 571–588. Springer, Heidelberg (2008). https://doi.org/10.1007/978-3-540-78524-8_31

29. Liu, Q., Zhandry, M.: Revisiting post-quantum Fiat-Shamir. In: Boldyreva, A., Micciancio, D. (eds.) CRYPTO 2019, Part II. LNCS, vol. 11693, pp. 326–355. Springer, Cham (2019). https://doi.org/10.1007/978-3-030-26951-7_12

30. Lombardi, A., Ma, F., Spooner, N.: Post-quantum zero knowledge, revisited or: how to do quantum rewinding undetectably. In: 63rd IEEE Annual Symposium on Foundations of Computer Science, FOCS 2022, Denver, CO, USA, 31 October–3 November 2022, pp. 851–859. IEEE (2022)

31. Nielsen, M.A., Chuang, I.L.: Quantum Computation and Quantum Information. Cambridge University Press, Cambridge (2000)

32. Pass, R., Rosen, A.: Concurrent non-malleable commitments. In: 46th FOCS, pp. 563–572. IEEE Computer Society Press (2005)

33. Peikert, C., Shiehian, S.: Noninteractive zero knowledge for np from (plain) learning with errors. In: Boldyreva, A., Micciancio, D. (eds.) CRYPTO 2019, Part I. LNCS, vol. 11692, pp. 89–114. Springer, Cham (2019). https://doi.org/10.1007/978-3-030-26948-7_4

34. Pointcheval, D., Stern, J.: Security arguments for digital signatures and blind signatures. J. Cryptol. **13**(3), 361–396 (2000)

35. Targhi, E.E., Unruh, D.: Post-quantum security of the Fujisaki-Okamoto and OAEP transforms. In: Hirt, M., Smith, A. (eds.) TCC 2016, Part II. LNCS, vol. 9986, pp. 192–216. Springer, Heidelberg (2016). https://doi.org/10.1007/978-3-662-53644-5_8

36. Unruh, D.: Computationally binding quantum commitments. In: Fischlin, M., Coron, J.-S. (eds.) EUROCRYPT 2016, Part II. LNCS, vol. 9666, pp. 497–527. Springer, Heidelberg (2016). https://doi.org/10.1007/978-3-662-49896-5_18

37. Yamakawa, T., Zhandry, M.: Classical vs quantum random oracles. In: Canteaut, A., Standaert, F.-X. (eds.) EUROCRYPT 2021. LNCS, vol. 12697, pp. 568–597. Springer, Cham (2021). https://doi.org/10.1007/978-3-030-77886-6_20

38. Zhandry, M.: How to construct quantum random functions. In: 53rd FOCS, pp. 679–687. IEEE Computer Society Press (2012)

39. Zhandry, M.: Secure identity-based encryption in the quantum random oracle model. In: Safavi-Naini, R., Canetti, R. (eds.) CRYPTO 2012. LNCS, vol. 7417, pp. 758–775. Springer, Heidelberg (2012). https://doi.org/10.1007/978-3-642-32009-5_44

40. Zhandry, M.: A note on the quantum collision and set equality problems. Quantum Inf. Comput. **15**(7–8), 557–567 (2015)

41. Zhandry, M.: How to record quantum queries, and applications to quantum indifferentiability. In: Boldyreva, A., Micciancio, D. (eds.) CRYPTO 2019, Part II. LNCS, vol. 11693, pp. 239–268. Springer, Cham (2019). https://doi.org/10.1007/978-3-030-26951-7_9
42. Zhandry, M.: Augmented Random Oracles. In: Dodis, Y., Shrimpton, T. (eds.) CRYPTO 2022, Part III. LNCS, vol. 13509, pp. 35–65. Springer, Cham (2022). https://doi.org/10.1007/978-3-031-15982-4_2

Characterizing the qIND-qCPA (In)security of the CBC, CFB, OFB and CTR Modes of Operation

Tristan Nemoz[1,2,3(✉)], Zoé Amblard[1], and Aurélien Dupin[1]

[1] Thales SIX GTS, Gennevilliers, France
[2] Télécom Paris, Palaiseau, France
[3] EURECOM, Biot, France
nemoz@eurecom.fr

Abstract. We fully characterize the post-quantum security of the CBC, CFB, OFB and CTR modes of operation by considering all the possible notions of qIND-qCPA security defined by Carstens, Ebrahimi, Tabia and Unruh (TCC 2021), thus extending the work performed by Anand, Targhi, Tabia and Unruh (PQCrypto 2016).

We show that the results obtained by Anand et al. for the qIND-qCPA-P6 security of these modes carry on to the other IND-qCPA notions, namely the qIND-qCPA-P10 and qIND-qCPA-P11 ones. We also show that all of these modes are insecure according to all of the other notions, regardless of the block cipher they are used with.

We also provide two general results concerning the insecurity of commonly used properties of block ciphers, namely those preserving the length of their input and those using the XOR operation as a way to randomize the encryption. Finally, we use these results to highlight the need for new quantum semantic security notions.

Keywords: Post-quantum cryptography · Block ciphers · Modes of operation · qIND-qCPA security

1 Introduction

1.1 Context and Results

While it is now common knowledge that traditional asymmetric cryptography is threatened by quantum computers, notably due to Shor's algorithm [14], the security of the currently used symmetric primitives is still under consideration. Some work in this field includes for instance finding polynomial attacks against symmetric systems using Simon's algorithm [10], evaluating the security of AES in a quantum world [3,9] or defining quantum-aware security notions for cryptosystems [2,5–8].

The security of the CBC, CFB, OFB and CTR modes of operations has been traditionally assessed via the IND-CPA security notion. In this notion, the adversary can issue learning requests and challenge requests. Learning requests are

T. Johansson and D. Smith-Tone (Eds.): PQCrypto 2023, LNCS 14154, pp. 445–475, 2023.
https://doi.org/10.1007/978-3-031-40003-2_17

answered by an oracle implementing the encryption function which security is to be assessed. Challenge requests on the other hand are answered by an oracle which nature depends on the "world" the game is taking place in. In the "real" world, the challenge oracle behaves identically to the learning oracle. In the "random" world however, the oracle first applies a permutation chosen at random at the beginning of the game on the adversary's queries. The goal of the adversary is then to find out whether the game takes place in the real world or the random one. A system is said to be IND-CPA secure if the optimal strategy for such an adversary that runs in polynomial time provides low to no advantage when compared to simply guessing at random.

This notion however, requires that both learning and challenge requests are classical. Reasons for considering the security of cryptographic schemes when using superposition queries have previously been given in the literature [1,2,7]. The most sensible one is the fact that quantum communication protocols may arise from the upcoming advent of quantum computers. In such a situation where end-users communicate using quantum states, the question of encryption applied on superposed states and its associated security are to be considered. Another reason is that the security proof of a scheme that is meant to be used classically may use the security against quantum superposition of its internal schemes.

Boneh and Zhandry [2] showed that the immediate, natural translation of the IND-CPA notion in a quantum world was not achievable. Thus, they instead proposed the IND-qCPA notion, where learning queries are quantum, but challenge ones are still classical. In the light of this new notion, Anand et al. [1] proved the IND-qCPA (in)security of the aforementioned modes depending on whether they were used with a standard-secure block cipher or a quantum-secure one.

In the years following Boneh and Zhandry's IND-qCPA definition, some work has been performed to try to define other security notions for a quantum world where both learning and challenge requests are quantum [2,6,7,11]. These notions essentially make use of different quantum oracles and different challenge queries. Eventually, Carstens et al. [5] defined all possible remaining notions and studied the implications between them. This resulted in 14 distinct equivalence classes of qIND-qCPA notions. However, the relevance of these notions is still discussed because of their novelty.

1.2   Our Contributions

In this paper, we extend Anand et al.'s work [1] by studying the security of the CBC, CFB, OFB and CTR modes in all security notions defined by Carstens et al. [5]. These results are summarized in Table 1. Furthermore, we show two general results about the insecurity of two common practices. Firstly, we show that a scheme preserving the length of its input is not qIND-qCPA-P8 secure, thus generalizing a result from Gagliardoni et al. [7]. We also show that randomizing an encryption using a public function such as the XOR one while giving the associated randomness to the adversary makes the scheme qIND-qCPA-P5-insecure. The way all these are proved questions the relevance of some qIND-qCPA notions and highlights the need for equivalent quantum semantic security notions.

Table 1. Summary of our results. The ✓ symbol means that all denoted schemes are secure in this notion. The ✗ symbol means that no denoted scheme is secure in this notion. The ◆ symbol means that there is at least one scheme secure and one insecure in this notion. The superscripts indicate either the article in which this result was first proved, the theorem stating it or the security notion implying it.

	CTR/OFB with PRP/qPRP	CBC with PRP	CBC with qPRP	CFB with PRP	CFB with qPRP
P1	✗ [P13]	✗ [P13]	✗ [P13]	✗ [P13]	✗ [P13]
P2	✗ [6]	✗ [P12]	✗ [P12]	✗ [6]	✗ [6]
P3	✗ [P13]	✗ [P13]	✗ [P13]	✗ [P13]	✗ [P13]
P4	✗ [P13]	✗ [P13]	✗ [P13]	✗ [P13]	✗ [P13]
P5	✗ [P13]	✗ [P13]	✗ [P13]	✗ [P13]	✗ [P13]
P6	✓ [1]	◆ [1]	✓ [1]	◆ [1]	✓ [1]
P7	✗ [P13]	✗ [P13]	✗ [P13]	✗ [P13]	✗ [P13]
P8	✗ [P13]	✗ [P13]	✗ [P13]	✗ [P13]	✗ [P13]
P9	✗ [P13]	✗ [P13]	✗ [P13]	✗ [P13]	✗ [P13]
P10	✓ 6	◆ [P11]	✓ 9	◆ [P11]	✓ 9
P11	✓ [P6]	◆ 8	✓ [P6]	◆ 7	✓ [P6]
P12	✗ [5]	✗ [5]	✗ [5]	✗ [5]	✗ [5]
P13	✗ 1	✗ 3	✗ 3	✗ 2	✗ 2
P14	✓ [1]	✓ [1]	✓ [1]	✓ [1]	✓ [1]

IND-qCPA Security. We observe in Appendix A that the results found by Anand et al. for the IND-qCPA using a standard oracle (qIND-qCPA-P6) security notion carry on to the two other IND-qCPA notions, namely the one using an erasing oracle (qIND-qCPA-P10) and the one using an embedding oracle (qIND-qCPA-P11). In these notions, the adversary can perform their learning request on a quantum oracle but is limited to classical challenge queries. In fact, the proofs in these cases are adapted from the ones written in Anand et al.'s work [1]: simulating a quantum oracle that implements a CTR or OFB mode using classical queries remains possible; we use a variant of the One-way to Hiding Lemma to show the security of CBC and CFB when used with a qPRP and we use the same attack up to an extra step to show that these two modes may be insecure when used with a PRP.

qIND-qCPA-P13 Insecurity. Furthermore, we show in Subsects. 3.1 to 3.3 that these are the only security notions satisfied by these modes, since they are qIND-qCPA-P13 insecure, no matter what the underlying block cipher is. As shown on Fig. 1, the qIND-qCPA-P13 security notion is the weakest notion in which the challenge request is quantum. Thus, proving the insecurity of these modes with respect to this notion carry on to almost every other notion.

In the qIND-qCPA-P13 security notion, the adversary is allowed classical learning queries and a single real-or-random challenge query performed on an embedding oracle. It means that the adversary's challenge query undergoes the following transformation:

$$\sum_x \alpha_x \left| x \right\rangle \rightarrow \sum_x \alpha_x \left| x \right\rangle \left| \mathsf{Enc_k} \left(\pi^b(x) \right) \right) \rangle$$

with π being a random permutation. For the CFB, CTR and OFB modes of operation, we prove this by showing that it is possible for the adversary to disentangle the ciphertext register and the plaintext register in the real world, while it is not possible to do so in the random world. Concerning CBC, we show that for $\ell \geqslant 3$, with ℓ being the number of blocks, the adversary is able to separate the registers into two identical states in the real world, which is not possible in the random world with overwhelming probability. They are thus able to distinguish both cases using a SWAP test.

General Results and Relevance of the qIND-qCPA Notions. We show in Subsect. 3.4 two general insecurity results.

Firstly, we show that the way the encryption is randomized must be secretly kept in order for it to be qIND-qCPA-P5-secure. In particular, randomizing the encryption by XORing the input with a random string r which is provided to the adversary does not yield a qIND-qCPA-P5-secure scheme.

We then show that in order for a scheme to be qIND-qCPA-P8-secure, the length of the ciphertexts must be higher than that of the plaintexts. In particular, if the randomness is not part of the ciphertext and if the encryption function is bijective, the resulting scheme can not be qIND-qCPA-P8-secure.

We show as an example how the construction provided by Carstens et al. which is secured in all qIND-qCPA notions satisfies both these conditions. We then use these results to exhibit the need for new quantum semantic security notions.

1.3 Previous Work

Anand et al. [1] studied the security of the modes of operation under the standard IND-qCPA (qIND-qCPA-P6) security notion. Chevalier, Ebrahimi and Vu [6] showed that the CFB, OFB and CTR modes of operation cannot achieve qIND-qCPA-P2 security. This result was later improved by Carstens et al. [5] who showed that CBC, CFB, OFB and CTR are not qIND-qCPA-P12 secure as long as they use at least two blocks.

2   Prerequisites

2.1   Notations and Definitions

Notations. $[\![a\,;\,b]\!]$ represents the set $[a\,;\,b] \cap \mathbb{N}$. An adversary $\mathcal{A}$ having access to an oracle $\mathcal{O}$ is denoted $\mathcal{A}^{\mathcal{O}}$. For a given permutation π, we denote $\pi_{a \to b}$ the function which returns the bits of π from a to b inclusive, starting the indexing at 0. The security parameter of a system is denoted λ. For an arbitrary string a and a bit b, $a \cdot b$ is set to the all-zero string if b is equal to 0 and to a if $b = 1$.

The advantage of an adversary $\mathcal{A}$ in the experiment Exp using the symmetric scheme $\mathcal{S}$ is defined as, accordingly to the definition given in [11]:

$$\mathsf{Adv}_{\mathcal{A},\mathcal{S}}^{\exp}(\lambda) = \left| \Pr\left[\mathsf{Exp}_{\mathcal{S}}^0(\lambda, \mathcal{A}) = 1 \right] - \Pr\left[\mathsf{Exp}_{\mathcal{S}}^1(\lambda, \mathcal{A}) = 1 \right] \right|$$

where $\Pr\left[\mathsf{Exp}_{\mathcal{S}}^b(\lambda, \mathcal{A}) = 1 \right]$ is the probability that $\mathcal{A}$ returns 1 if the bit they have to guess is set to b. We define the real world to be the one where $b = 0$ and the random world to be the one where $b = 1$. Note that while the real-or-random notion we use has originally been introduced in [11], it was then named "real or permutation", and the convention for the real and random worlds was the opposite of ours.

We denote $\mathbf{H}$ the Hadamard gate and $\mathbf{X}$ the NOT gate. If we want to name a quantum register $|\psi\rangle$, we indicate its name as a subscript, like $|\psi\rangle_{\mathrm{Name}}$.

Modes of Operations. It is to be denoted that a key generation function is supposed to be defined in order to properly define an encryption scheme. For simplicity's sake, we did not include it within the following definitions, since it only consists in randomly choosing a key in $\{0,1\}^\lambda$.

Definition 1 (CBC mode, adapted from [1, Definition 6]). *For a given permutation $E_k : \{0,1\}^n \to \{0,1\}^n$, we define the CBC scheme with the following encryption and decryption functions:*

$\mathsf{Enc}_{E_k,\ell}^{\mathbf{CBC}}$: *For a message $m = m_1 \cdots m_\ell$, choose randomly c_0 and return c_0 along with $c = c_1 \cdots c_\ell$ where, for $i \in [\![1 \, ; \, \ell]\!]$, $c_i = E_k(m_i \oplus c_{i-1})$.*
$\mathsf{Dec}_{E_k,\ell}^{\mathbf{CBC}}$: *For a ciphertext $c = c_1 \cdots c_\ell$ and being given c_0, return $m = m_1 \cdots m_\ell$ where, for $i \in [\![1 \, ; \, \ell]\!]$, $m_i = E_k^{-1}(c_i) \oplus c_{i-1}$.*

Definition 2 (CFB mode, adapted from [1, Definition 7]). *For a given function $E_k : \{0,1\}^n \to \{0,1\}^n$, we define the CFB scheme with the following encryption and decryption functions:*

$\mathsf{Enc}_{E_k,\ell}^{\mathbf{CFB}}$: *For a message $m = m_1 \cdots m_\ell$, choose randomly c_0 and return c_0 along with $c = c_1 \cdots c_\ell$ where, for $i \in [\![1 \, ; \, \ell]\!]$, $c_i = m_i \oplus E_k(c_{i-1})$.*
$\mathsf{Dec}_{E_k,\ell}^{\mathbf{CFB}}$: *For a ciphertext $c = c_1 \cdots c_\ell$ and being given c_0, return $m = m_1 \cdots m_\ell$ where, for $i \in [\![1 \, ; \, \ell]\!]$, $m_i = E_k(c_{i-1}) \oplus c_i$.*

Definition 3 (OFB mode, adapted from [1, Definition 8]). *For a given function $E_k : \{0,1\}^n \to \{0,1\}^n$, we define the OFB scheme with the following encryption and decryption functions:*

$\mathsf{Enc}_{E_k,\ell}^{\mathbf{OFB}}$: *For a message $m = m_1 \cdots m_\ell$, choose randomly c_0 and return c_0 along with $c = c_1 \cdots c_\ell$ where $t_0 = E_k(c_0)$ and, for $i \in [\![1 \, ; \, \ell]\!]$, $c_i = t_i \oplus m_i$ and $t_i = E_k(t_{i-1})$.*

$\mathsf{Dec}^{\mathsf{OFB}}_{E_k, \ell}$: *For a ciphertext* $c = c_1 \cdots c_\ell$ *and being given* c_0, *computes* $t_0 = E_k(c_0)$ *and return* $m = m_1 \cdots m_\ell$ *where, for* $i \in [\![1; \ell]\!]$, $m_i = t_i \oplus c_i$ *and* $t_i = E_k(t_{i-1})$.

Definition 4 (CTR mode, adapted from [1, Definition 9]). *For a given function* $E_k : \{0,1\}^n \to \{0,1\}^n$, *we define the* CTR *scheme with the following encryption and decryption functions:*

$\mathsf{Enc}^{\mathsf{CTR}}_{E_k, \ell}$: *For a message* $m = m_1 \cdots m_\ell$, *choose randomly* c_0 *and return* c_0 *along with* $c = c_1 \cdots c_\ell$ *where, for* $i \in [\![1; \ell]\!]$, $c_i = m_i \oplus E_k(c_0 \oplus i - 1)$.

$\mathsf{Dec}^{\mathsf{CTR}}_{E_k, \ell}$: *For a ciphertext* $c = c_1 \cdots c_\ell$ *and being given* c_0, *return* $m = m_1 \cdots m_\ell$ *where, for* $i \in [\![1; \ell]\!]$, $m_i = c_i \oplus E_k(c_0 \oplus i - 1)$.

In these definitions, $c_0 \oplus i - 1$ *represents the bitwise* XOR *between* c_0 *and a fixed* n*-bit representation of* $i - 1$.

Some things are to be denoted with these definitions. First of all, in the literature, the initialization vector c_0 is often returned as part of the ciphertext. Since we want to apply these encryption schemes to quantum states, it is completely equivalent to consider that the adversary classically knows c_0 and receives the remaining of the ciphertext as a quantum state.

Furthermore, it is important to note that the maximal ℓ that such a mode of operation accepts is assumed to be polynomial in λ. In all of our proofs, ℓ is assumed to be constant, that is we assume that the oracle only accepts queries of size ℓ, which covers the case where the oracle accepts queries of variable length. Similarly, the block size, denoted n in the definitions, is also assumed to be polynomial in λ. This assumption is justified by the fact that often, $n = \lambda$ holds. The same assumption is made in [1], since the authors claim that CBC and CFB are qIND-qCPA-P6 secure when used with a qPRP by showing that the adversary's advantage is negligible with respect to n.

Security Notions

Definition 5 (Standard and quantum-secure pseudorandom permutation, adapted from [19, Definition 3.1]). *A permutation* π_k *depending on a key* k *is a standard-secure (respectively quantum-secure) pseudorandom permutation, which we denote* PRP *(respectively* qPRP*), if no polynomial quantum adversary* $\mathcal{A}$ *making classical (respectively quantum) queries to both the permutation and its inverse can distinguish between a truly random permutation and* π_k *for a randomly chosen* k.

Since we will consider different types of oracles in the following, we ought to be more precise about what a quantum query is in the previous definition. In particular, since an erasing oracle and a standard oracle can't simulate each other, the precision seems to have to be made. However, Carstens et al. [5, Lemma 6] showed that a permutation that is quantum-secure with standard queries is also secure with erasing queries, and reciprocally.

qIND-qCPA Notions. Carstens et al. [5] defined 14 different equivalence classes for qIND-qCPA notions. A notion is fully characterized by the oracle type on which the adversary performs its learning queries, the one on which they perform their challenge queries, the challenge type, like left-or-right or real-or-random, and the number of challenge queries they are allowed to perform.

Oracle Types. Let f be the function implemented by the oracle the adversary has access to. Note that it is sufficient to describe the behavior of an oracle on the basis states to fully describe it. Four types of oracle are considered in Carstens et al.'s work [5]:

Standard Oracle: On a basis state $|x, y\rangle$, the oracle returns $|x, y \oplus f(x)\rangle$.

Embedding Oracle: On a basis state $|x\rangle$, the oracle prepares a state $|0\rangle$ as the output register and acts as a standard oracle, returning $|x, f(x)\rangle$.

Erasing Oracle: This oracle requires f to be injective. On a basis state $|x\rangle$, it returns $|f(x)\rangle$.

Classical Oracle: This oracle only accepts classical queries.

It is important to note that the embedding oracle is the weakest of the three quantum oracles, since it is possible to simulate such an oracle using either one of the two others.

Challenge Type. Three challenge types are used in [5].

Real-Or-Random: On a challenge query, the oracle chooses a random permutation π and applies π^b to the plaintext register before encrypting it. This means that for a standard or an embedding challenge query, the oracle performs this mapping:

$$|x, y\rangle \rightarrow |x, y \oplus \mathsf{Enc}_k\left(\pi^b(x)\right)\rangle$$

while it performs this mapping for an erasing oracle:

$$|x\rangle \rightarrow |\mathsf{Enc}_k\left(\pi^b(x)\right)\rangle.$$

Note that such a permutation is chosen at random for each of the challenge queries the adversary performs.

Two-Ciphertexts. A challenge query is made of two states. On a challenge query on a standard or an embedding oracle, the oracle performs the following mapping:

$$|x_0, y_0\rangle |x_1, y_1\rangle \rightarrow |x_0, y_0 \oplus \mathsf{Enc}_k\left(x_b\right)\rangle |x_1, y_1 \oplus \mathsf{Enc}_k\left(x_{\bar{b}}\right)\rangle$$

while it performs the following mapping on an erasing oracle:

$$|x_0\rangle |x_1\rangle \rightarrow |\mathsf{Enc}_k\left(x_b\right)\rangle |\mathsf{Enc}_k\left(x_{\bar{b}}\right)\rangle.$$

One-Ciphertext. A challenge query is made of two states $|\psi_0\rangle$ and $|\psi_1\rangle$. The oracle first measures $|\psi_{\bar{b}}\rangle$ and throws away the result. It then performs the following mapping on a standard or an erasing oracle:

$$|x_0, y_0\rangle |x_1, y_1\rangle \rightarrow |x_b, y_b \oplus \mathsf{Enc}_k\left(x_b\right)\rangle$$

while it performs the following mapping on an erasing oracle:

$$|x_0\rangle |x_1\rangle \rightarrow |\mathsf{Enc}_k\left(x_b\right)\rangle.$$

It is immediate to see that the notions using the two-ciphertexts return type implies those with the one-ciphertext one when using the same number of challenge queries and the same learning scheme, since more information is given to the adversary. However, Carstens et al. [5] also showed that it just happens that the same property is true concerning the one-ciphertext return type and the real-or-random one. As such, the real-or-random return type is the weakest among all three.

A high-level overview of the differences between the notions used in this work is presented in Table 2.

Table 2. High-level overview of the different security notions considered in this work. Note that these notions belong to equivalence classes, as per Carstens et al.'s work [5]. For instance, one might replace the classical learning oracle of the qIND-qCPA-P5 notion by an Embedding one and still end up with a equivalent notion.

Notion	Oracle		Challenge	
	Learning	Challenge	Type	Number of queries
qIND-qCPA-P5	Classical	Embedding	Real-or-random	$\text{poly}(\lambda)$
qIND-qCPA-P8	Classical	Erasing	One-ciphertext	1
qIND-qCPA-P10	Erasing	Classical	One-ciphertext	$\text{poly}(\lambda)$
qIND-qCPA-P11	Embedding	Classical	One-ciphertext	$\text{poly}(\lambda)$
qIND-qCPA-P13	Classical	Embedding	Real-or-random	1

At the exception of the qIND-qCPA-P13 and IND-qCPA notions, every security notion is used at most once in our work. Thus, for clarity's sake, we define these notions just before their associated proof of (in)security. The IND-qCPA notions are put with the associated proofs in Appendix A and we define the qIND-qCPA-P13 security notion here since it is widely used throughout this work.

Definition 6 (qIND-qCPA-P13 game, adapted from [5]). *Let E be a cryptographic scheme: $E = (\mathsf{KGen}, \mathsf{Enc}, \mathsf{Dec})$. We denote by M the set of messages E operates on, by CL-Enc the classical oracle implementing* Enc *and by EM-Enc the embedding oracle implementing* Enc. *We say that E is qIND-qCPA-P13-secure if no polynomial time quantum adversary $\mathcal{A}$ has an advantage larger than $\frac{1}{2} + \varepsilon$ in the following experiment, with ε being negligible with respect to λ.*

$$
\begin{array}{l}
\hline
\textit{Experiment } \textit{qIND-qCPA-P13}_E^b(\lambda, \mathcal{A}) \\
\hline
\mathsf{k} \leftarrow_{\$} \mathsf{KGen}\left(1^\lambda\right) \\[4pt]
\pi \leftarrow_{\$} \mathfrak{S}_{|M|} \\[4pt]
(\mathsf{state}, |\varphi\rangle) \leftarrow_{\$} \mathcal{A}^{\mathsf{CL-Enc}(\mathsf{k}, \cdot)}() \\[4pt]
|\psi\rangle \leftarrow_{\$} \mathsf{EM\text{-}Enc}\left(\mathsf{k}, \left|\pi^b(\varphi)\right\rangle\right) \\[4pt]
b' \leftarrow_{\$} \mathcal{A}^{\mathsf{CL-Enc}(\mathsf{k}, \cdot)}(|\varphi, \psi\rangle, \mathsf{state}) \\[4pt]
\mathbf{return }\ b' \\
\hline
\end{array}
$$

Intuitively, this notion is the weakest one can come up with using a quantum challenge request. Indeed, the classical learning queries greatly limits the power of the adversary, and they are allowed a single challenge query on the weakest quantum oracle, using the weakest return type. This intuition has been shown by Carstens et al. [5] and is shown on Fig. 1.

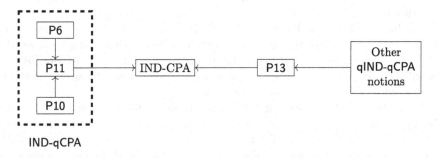

Fig. 1. Relationships between qIND-qCPA notions, adapted from [5]. The IND-CPA and qIND-qCPA-P6 (in)security of the CBC, CFB, OFB and CTR modes are known from [1,17]. Thus, proving their qIND-qCPA-P13 insecurity and their qIND-qCPA-P11 insecurity or their qIND-qCPA-P10 security fully characterizes them.

Note that the qIND-qCPA-P6 (in)security of the CBC, CFB, OFB and CTR modes of operation is known from [1], and that the IND-CPA security of these modes is also known (see for example [17]). As such, these implications show that in order to completely characterize the security of these modes, proving their qIND-qCPA-P13 insecurity and their qIND-qCPA-P10 security or their qIND-qCPA-P11 insecurity is sufficient.

2.2   Lemmas

Lemma 1. *We consider the quantum state $\frac{1}{\sqrt{2^m}} \sum_x |x\rangle |f(x)\rangle$ with f being a function from $\{0,1\}^m$ to $\{0,1\}^n$. Applying an $\mathbf{H}$ gate to the first register and then measuring it returns $|0\rangle$ with probability $\frac{1}{2^{2m}} \sum_y |f^{-1}(y)|^2$.*

Proof. We first apply the $\mathbf{H}$ gate on the system, which puts it in the state:

$$\frac{1}{2^m} \sum_x \sum_k (-1)^{x \cdot k} |k\rangle |f(x)\rangle = \frac{1}{2^m} |0\rangle \sum_x |f(x)\rangle + \frac{1}{2^m} \sum_x \sum_{k \neq 0} (-1)^{x \cdot k} |k\rangle |f(x)\rangle . \tag{1}$$

The probability of measuring $|0\rangle$ is thus given by:

$$\Pr\left[|0\rangle\right] = \left\| \frac{1}{2^m} |0\rangle \sum_x |f(x)\rangle \right\|^2 = \frac{1}{2^{2m}} \sum_y |f^{-1}(y)|^2 . \tag{2}$$

$\square$

2.3   IND-qCPA Security of CBC, CFB, CTR and OFB

In 2016, Anand et al. [1] characterized the security of the CBC, CFB, CTR and OFB modes of operation. The notion they used is the IND-qCPA notion defined in [2]. As its name suggests, in this notion the adversary is allowed to perform quantum learning queries but is restricted to classical challenge queries. Arguably, the term "IND-qCPA" is now ambiguous, for instance because of the different quantum oracles that can be used to answer the quantum queries.

In this work, IND-qCPA refers to all the notions defined by Carstens et al. [5] that can be identified using the previous description. This includes the qIND-qCPA-P6 notion, which is the one defined in [2], and the qIND-qCPA-P10 and qIND-qCPA-P11 ones. The former uses an erasing oracle to answer learning queries, while the latter uses an embedding one.

While these notions are not equivalent, their similarities allow us to reuse almost identically the proofs proposed by Anand et al. to show the (in)security of the CBC, CFB, CTR and OFB modes of operation with respect to the qIND-qCPA-P6 security in the qIND-qCPA-P10 and qIND-qCPA-P11 cases. As such, we put these proofs and the relevant definitions in Appendix A.

3   Our Results

3.1   qIND-qCPA-P13 Insecurity of CTR and OFB

In this section, we show that, according to Fig. 1, the only security notions that CTR and OFB satisfy are the IND-qCPA ones by exhibiting an attack against their qIND-qCPA-P13 security.

This proof only relies on the fact that in order to produce the ciphertext, CTR and OFB perform a XOR between the message and a pseudorandom string s. As such, our proof can also be applied to stream ciphers, and we will denote $m \oplus s$ an encryption of the message m using such a scheme. Note however that this proof assumes that the ciphertext can be written as $x \oplus s$ entirely. As such, it doesn't carry on to the GCM mode of operation which, though it uses the CTR mode of operation, adds a tag at the end of the ciphertext.

Theorem 1 (Originally written in [12]). *CTR and OFB are qIND-qCPA-P13 insecure, no matter what the underlying block cipher is.*

Proof. $\mathcal{A}$ prepares the state $|+\rangle$ and performs their challenge query using it. They thus receive:

$$\begin{cases} \sum_x |x\rangle\, |x \oplus s\rangle & \text{if } b = 0 \\ \sum_x |x\rangle\, |\pi(x) \oplus s\rangle & \text{if } b = 1 \end{cases} \tag{3}$$

for a random permutation π. By performing an **X** gate on the second register controlled by the first one, the state becomes:

$$\begin{cases} \sum_x |x\rangle\, |s\rangle & \text{if } b = 0 \\ \sum_x |x\rangle\, |x \oplus \pi(x) \oplus s\rangle & \text{if } b = 1 \end{cases} . \tag{4}$$

Thus, if $b = 0$, the two registers are not entangled: applying an $\mathbf{H}$ gate on the first register and measuring it yields $|0\rangle$ with certainty. If $b = 1$ however, such a procedure yields $|0\rangle$ with negligible probability. We can apply Lemma 1 with $f = x \mapsto x \oplus \pi(x) \oplus s$ to show this formally. The probability to measure $|0\rangle$ if $b = 1$ is thus given by:

$$\Pr\left[|0\rangle \mid b = 1\right] = \frac{1}{2^{2\ell n}} \sum_y \left|f^{-1}(y)\right|^2 . \tag{5}$$

Since the sum is going through all possible y, it is completely equivalent to redefine f to be $x \mapsto x \oplus \pi(x)$.

We have, for a given y^1:

$$\left|f^{-1}(y)\right| = \sum_x \mathbb{1}_{\pi(x)=x\oplus y} \tag{6}$$

thus:

$$\left|f^{-1}(y)\right|^2 = \sum_{x_1} \sum_{x_2} \mathbb{1}_{[\pi(x_1)=x_1\oplus y]\cap[\pi(x_2)=x_2\oplus y]} \tag{7}$$

thus:

$$\mathbb{E}\left[\left|f^{-1}(y)\right|^2\right] = \sum_{x_1} \sum_{x_2} \Pr\left[[\pi(x_1) = x_1 \oplus y] \cap [\pi(x_2) = x_2 \oplus y]\right] \tag{8a}$$

$$= \sum_{x_1} \Pr\left[\pi(x_1) = x_1 \oplus y\right] + \tag{8b}$$
$$\sum_{x_1} \sum_{x_2 \neq x_1} \Pr\left[[\pi(x_1) = x_1 \oplus y] \cap [\pi(x_2) = x_2 \oplus y]\right].$$

Since π is a random permutation, all the events in $(\pi(x_1) = x_1 \oplus y)_{x_1}$ have the same probability. As such:

$$\mathbb{E}\left[\left|f^{-1}(y)\right|^2\right] = 1 + \frac{1}{2^{\ell n}} \sum_{x_1} \sum_{x_2 \neq x_1} \Pr\left[\pi(x_2) = x_2 \oplus y \mid \pi(x_1) = x_1 \oplus y\right]. \tag{8c}$$

Similarly, since π is a random permutation, the events in $(\pi(x_2) = x_2 \oplus y)_{x_2 \neq x_1}$ have all the same probability being given that $\pi(x_1) = x_1 \oplus y$. Thus, we have:

$$\mathbb{E}\left[\left|f^{-1}(y)\right|^2\right] = 2. \tag{8d}$$

Finally, the probability of measuring $|0\rangle$ if $b = 1$ is given by:

$$\Pr\left[|0\rangle \mid b = 1\right] = \frac{1}{2^{\ell n-1}}. \tag{9}$$

All in all, the adversary's advantage is given by:

$$\mathsf{Adv}_{\mathcal{A},\mathrm{CTR/OFB}}^{\mathsf{qind\text{-}qcpa\text{-}p13}}(\lambda) = 1 - \frac{1}{2^{\ell n-1}}. \tag{10}$$

In particular, it is not negligible with respect to λ. $\square$

---

[1] The reasoning from Eq. 6 to Eq. 8d is a rewriting of a proof proposed by Iosif Pinelis.

3.2   qIND-qCPA-P13 Insecurity of CFB

Similarly to the CTR and OFB modes, we show that an adversary can win with non-negligible advantage in the qIND-qCPA-P13 security game of the CFB mode, no matter what the underlying block cipher is. Along with its IND-qCPA (in)security proven in Appendix A, this fully characterizes it, according to Fig. 1.

The qIND-qCPA-P13 insecurity of CFB, just like CTR and OFB, comes from the fact that the adversary can disentangle the ciphertext register from the plaintext register, which is not possible in the random world. The same strategy as for these two modes can thus be used to distinguish both worlds.

Theorem 2 (Originally written in [12]). *CFB is qIND-qCPA-P13 insecure, no matter what the underlying block cipher is.*

Proof. $\mathcal{A}$ prepares the following state, where each register is made of n qubits:

$$\frac{1}{\sqrt{2^n}} \left(\bigotimes_{k=1}^{\ell-1} |0\rangle \right) \sum_x |x\rangle \tag{11}$$

and performs their challenge query using it. They thus receive, ignoring the first $\ell - 1$ registers which are not entangled with the others:

$$\begin{cases} \frac{1}{\sqrt{2^n}} \sum_x |x\rangle \left(\bigotimes_{i=1}^{\ell-1} \left| E_k^i(c_0) \right\rangle \right) \left| x \oplus E_k^\ell(c_0) \right\rangle & \text{if } b = 0 \\ \frac{1}{\sqrt{2^n}} \sum_x |x\rangle \bigotimes_{i=1}^{\ell} \left| \pi_{(i-1)n \to in-1}(0 \| \cdots \| 0 \| x) \oplus E_k(c_{i-1}(x)) \right\rangle & \text{if } b = 1 \end{cases} \tag{12}$$

for a random permutation π, where c_0 is a random constant function and where we have defined:

$$c_i(x) \overset{\text{def}}{=} \pi_{(i-1)n \to in-1}(0 \| \cdots \| 0 \| x) \oplus E_k(c_{i-1}(x)). \tag{13}$$

By performing an **X** gate on the second register controlled by the first one, the state becomes:

$$\begin{cases} \frac{1}{\sqrt{2^n}} \sum_x |x\rangle \left(\bigotimes_{i=1}^{\ell-1} \left| E_k^i(c_0) \right\rangle \right) \left| E_k^\ell(c_0) \right\rangle & \text{if } b = 0 \\ \frac{1}{\sqrt{2^n}} \sum_x |x\rangle \left| f_{c_0,\pi}(x) \right\rangle & \text{if } b = 1 \end{cases} \tag{14}$$

with $f_{c_0,\pi}$ being defined as:

$$f_{c_0,\pi}(x) \overset{\text{def}}{=} x \mapsto c_1(x) \| \cdots \| c_{\ell-1}(x) \| (x \oplus c_\ell(x)). \tag{15}$$

Thus, if $b = 0$, the two registers are not entangled: applying an **H** gate on the first register and measuring it yields $|0\rangle$ with certainty. If $b = 1$ however, such a procedure yields $|0\rangle$ with negligible probability. We can use Lemma 1 to prove it. The probability to measure $|0\rangle$ if $b = 1$ is given by:

$$\Pr\left[|0\rangle \mid b = 1\right] = \frac{1}{2^{2n}} \sum_y \left| f_{c_0,\pi}^{-1}(y) \right|^2. \tag{16}$$

We have, for a given y^2:

$$\left| f_{c_0,\pi}^{-1}(y) \right| = \sum_x \mathbb{1}_{f_{c_0,\pi}(x)=y} \tag{17}$$

thus:

$$\left| f_{c_0,\pi}^{-1}(y) \right|^2 = \sum_{x_1} \sum_{x_2} \mathbb{1}_{[f_{c_0,\pi}(x_1)=y] \cap [f_{c_0,\pi}(x_2)=y]} \tag{18}$$

thus:

$$\mathbb{E}\left[\left| f_{c_0,\pi}^{-1}(y) \right|^2 \right] = \sum_{x_1} \sum_{x_2} \Pr\left[[f_{c_0,\pi}(x_1)=y] \cap [f_{c_0,\pi}(x_2)=y] \right] \tag{19a}$$

$$= \sum_{x_1} \Pr\left[f_{c_0,\pi}(x_1)=y \right] + \tag{19b}$$
$$\sum_{x_1} \sum_{x_2 \neq x_1} \Pr\left[[f_{c_0,\pi}(x_1)=y] \cap [f_{c_0,\pi}(x_2)=y] \right].$$

Since π is a random permutation, $\pi(x)$ is uniformly random. As such, any bitslice $\pi_{(i-1)n \to (in-1)}(x)$ is also uniformly random. Note also that it is independent from $E_k(c_{i-1}(x))$, thus every $c_i(x)$ is uniformly random. This property does not depend on its input, hence this remains true for $x \oplus c_\ell(x)$. As a consequence, $f_{c_0,\pi}$ is uniformly random and we have:

$$\mathbb{E}\left[\left| f_{c_0,\pi}^{-1}(y) \right|^2 \right] = \frac{2^n}{2^{\ell n}} + \frac{1}{2^{\ell n}} \sum_{x_1} \sum_{x_2 \neq x_1} \Pr\left[f_{c_0,\pi}(x_2)=y \mid f_{c_0,\pi}(x_1)=y \right]. \tag{19c}$$

Since the value of $f_{c_0,\pi}(x_1)$ is known, it means that $\pi(x_1)$ has been specified. As such, $\pi(x_2)$ can be equal to any value except $\pi(x_1)$.

Note that the probability that we want to compute is the probability that $c_i(x_1) = c_i(x_2)$ for $i \in [\![1\,;\,\ell-1]\!]$ and that $c_\ell(x_1) \oplus x_1 = c_i(x_2) \oplus x_2$. Using the definition of c_i, this is equivalent to computing the probability that $\pi(x_1)$ and $\pi(x_2)$ have the same $(\ell-1)n$ first bits and that their last n bits XOR up to $x_1 \oplus x_2$. The probability of the first event is $\frac{2^n-1}{2^{\ell n}}$, since we can freely choose the last n bits of $\pi(x_2)$ as long as they are not equal to those of $\pi(x_1)$, and the probability for the second event being given the first one is $\frac{1}{2^n-1}$ using the same reasoning. All in all, we have:

$$\mathbb{E}\left[\left| f_{c_0,\pi}^{-1}(y) \right|^2 \right] = \frac{2^n}{2^{\ell n}} + \frac{1}{2^{\ell n}} \sum_{x_1} \sum_{x_2 \neq x_1} \frac{1}{2^{\ell n}-1} = \frac{2^n}{2^{\ell n}} + \frac{2^n(2^n-1)}{2^{\ell n}(2^{\ell n}-1)}. \tag{19d}$$

Thus, the probability of measuring $|0\rangle$ being given that $b=1$ is given by:

$$\Pr\left[|0\rangle \mid b=1 \right] = \frac{1}{2^{2n}} \sum_y \left(\frac{2^n}{2^{\ell n}} + \frac{2^n(2^n-1)}{2^{\ell n}(2^{\ell n}-1)} \right) = \frac{1}{2^n}\left(1 + \frac{2^n-1}{2^{\ell n}-1} \right). \tag{20}$$

---

[2] The reasoning from Eq. 17 to Eq. 19d is an adaptation of the aforementioned proof proposed by Iosif Pinelis.

Thus, $\mathcal{A}$'s advantage is given by:

$$\mathsf{Adv}_{\mathcal{A},\mathsf{CFB}}^{\mathsf{qind\text{-}qcpa\text{-}p13}}(\lambda) = 1 - \frac{1}{2^n}\left(1 + \frac{2^n - 1}{2^{\ell n} - 1}\right). \tag{21}$$

In particular, this advantage is not negligible with respect to λ. □

3.3 qIND-qCPA-P13 Insecurity of CBC

Finally, we show that CBC is qIND-qCPA-P13 insecure, no matter what the underlying block cipher is. Contrarily to the three other modes, it is not possible to disentangle the ciphertext register from the plaintext one in this case. However, we show that an adversary is able to separate the answer to its challenge query into two identical registers in the real world, while it isn't possible in the random one. Thus, performing a SWAP test allows to distinguish both cases.

Theorem 3. *CBC is qIND-qCPA-P13 insecure if it uses more than 3 blocks, no matter what the underlying block cipher is.*

Proof. Let us assume for now that ℓ can be written as $\ell = 2L + 1$ with $L \geqslant 1$. $\mathcal{A}$ sends $|+\rangle$ as their unique challenge query. They thus receive, if $b = 0$:

$$\frac{1}{\sqrt{2^{\ell n}}} \sum_{x_1,\cdots,x_\ell} |x_1\rangle_{M_1} \cdots |x_\ell\rangle_{M_\ell} |E_k(x_1 \oplus c_0)\rangle_{C_1} |E_k(x_2 \oplus E_k(x_1 \oplus c_0))\rangle_{C_2} \cdots \tag{22}$$

Since they know c_0, they can apply $\mathbf{X}$ gates accordingly on M_1 to XOR it with c_0, thus creating the following state:

$$\frac{1}{\sqrt{2^{\ell n}}} \sum_{x_1,\cdots,x_\ell} |x_1\rangle_{M_1} \cdots |x_\ell\rangle_{M_\ell} |E_k(x_1)\rangle_{C_1} |E_k(x_2 \oplus E_k(x_1))\rangle_{C_2} \cdots \tag{23}$$

Note that this state doesn't depend on c_0 anymore. This is the state the adversary would have had if c_0 was nil. They now measure C_{L+1}, thus getting the associated value c_{L+1} and disturbing the superposition. Indeed, the following equation must hold:

$$c_{L+1} = E_k(x_{L+1} \oplus E_k(x_L \oplus E_k(\cdots \oplus E_k(x_1)\cdots))) \tag{24a}$$

$$\Longleftrightarrow x_{L+1} = E_k^{-1}(c_{L+1}) \oplus E_k(x_L \oplus E_k(\cdots \oplus E_k(x_1)\cdots)). \tag{24b}$$

This equation shows that the value of the M_{L+1} register is now $E_k^{-1}(c_{L+1}) \oplus C_L$. Thus, performing an $\mathbf{X}$ gate on M_{L+1} controlled by C_L sets the value of M_{L+1} to $E_k^{-1}(c_{L+1})$. As such, it is no longer entangled with the other registers. Furthermore, the ciphertext registers $C_{L+2},\cdots,C_{2L}$ are only function of c_{L+1} and the plaintext registers $M_{L+2},\cdots,M_{2L}$. Hence, the state is now separable and can be written as:

$$\left(\frac{1}{\sqrt{2^{Ln}}} \sum_{x_1,\cdots,x_L} |x_1,\cdots,x_L\rangle \left|\mathsf{Enc}^{\mathsf{CBC}}_{E_k,L,0}(x_1 \| \cdots \| x_L)\right\rangle\right) \otimes$$

$$\left(\frac{1}{\sqrt{2^{Ln}}} \sum_{x_{L+2},\cdots,x_{2L}} |x_{L+2},\cdots,x_{2L}\rangle \left|\mathsf{Enc}^{\mathsf{CBC}}_{E_k,L,c_{L+1}}(x_{L+2} \| \cdots \| x_{2L})\right\rangle\right) \tag{25}$$

where $\mathsf{Enc}^{\mathsf{CBC}}_{E_k,L,r}$ is the encryption function using the CBC mode of operation with E_k as its block cipher, operating on L blocks and using r as its initialization vector. Note that for any set of messages $(x_i)_{i\in[\![L+2\,;\,2L]\!]}$, the following holds:

$$\mathsf{Enc}^{\mathsf{CBC}}_{E_k,L,c_{L+1}}(x_{L+2} \| \cdots \| x_{2L}) = \mathsf{Enc}^{\mathsf{CBC}}_{E_k,L,0}((x_{L+2} \oplus c_{L+1}) \| \cdots \| x_{2L}). \tag{26}$$

Since $\mathcal{A}$ knows c_{L+1} from the measurement of C_{L+1}, they can apply $\mathbf{X}$ gates on M_{L+2} to XOR it with c_{L+1}, thus creating the state:

$$\left(\frac{1}{\sqrt{2^{Ln}}} \sum_{x_1,\cdots,x_L} |x_1,\cdots,x_L\rangle \left|\mathsf{Enc}^{\mathsf{CBC}}_{E_k,L,0}(x_1 \| \cdots \| x_L)\right\rangle\right) \otimes$$

$$\left(\frac{1}{\sqrt{2^{Ln}}} \sum_{x_{L+2},\cdots,x_{2L}} |x_{L+2},\cdots,x_{2L}\rangle \left|\mathsf{Enc}^{\mathsf{CBC}}_{E_k,L,0}(x_{L+2} \| \cdots \| x_{2L})\right\rangle\right) \tag{27}$$

$$= \left(\frac{1}{\sqrt{2^{Ln}}} \sum_x |x\rangle \left|\mathsf{Enc}^{\mathsf{CBC}}_{E_k,L,0}(x)\right\rangle\right) \otimes \left(\frac{1}{\sqrt{2^{Ln}}} \sum_x |x\rangle \left|\mathsf{Enc}^{\mathsf{CBC}}_{E_k,L,0}(x)\right\rangle\right). \tag{28}$$

$\mathcal{A}$ now performs a SWAP test [4] on these two states, which is an algorithm that runs in constant time, taking two quantum states $|\varphi\rangle$ and $|\psi\rangle$ and returning $|0\rangle$ with probability $\frac{1}{2} + \frac{1}{2}|\langle\varphi|\psi\rangle|^2$. Here, since these two states are identical, performing a SWAP test on them will return $|0\rangle$ with probability 1.

Let us consider the case $b = 1$ now. The oracle $\mathcal{A}$ interacts with is depicted on Fig. 2.

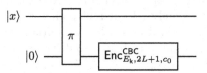

Fig. 2. The oracle the adversary interacts with in the random world in the qIND-qCPA-P13 security game of CBC. Note that $\mathsf{Enc}^{\mathsf{CBC}}_{E_k,2L+1,c_0}$ can be implemented as an erasing oracle since it is bijective. π is a random permutation freshly chosen and implemented as an embedding oracle.

Since π is freshly chosen and is implemented as an embedding oracle, we can use [5, Corollary 11] to measure the input register before applying the embedding oracle implementing π. This corollary ensures that $\mathcal{A}$ can distinguish the previous oracle from this new one with probability at most $\frac{1+C}{2^{\ell n}}$, with C being an universal constant defined in [18, Theorem 3.1].

Upon measurement, the input register collapses to a random message x and is then passed to the encryption oracle. The resulting state is:

$$|x_1, \cdots, x_{2L}\rangle |c_1, \cdots, c_{2L}\rangle \tag{29a}$$

with c_i being defined as:

$$\forall i \in [\![1\,;2L]\!], c_i = E_k \left(\pi_{in \to (i+1)n-1} \left(x_1 \parallel x_{2L} \right) \oplus c_{i-1} \right) \tag{29b}$$

and with c_0 being chosen uniformly at random. $\mathcal{A}$ firstly measures c_{L+1} and performs a XOR operation between c_0 and x_1 and between c_{L+1} and x_{L+1}. $\mathcal{A}$ will thus perform the SWAP test between $|x_1 \oplus c_0, x_2, \cdots, x_L\rangle |c_1, \cdots, c_L\rangle$ and $|x_{L+2} \oplus c_{L+1}, x_{L+3}, \cdots, x_{2L}\rangle |c_{L+2}, \cdots, c_{2L}\rangle$. Since these two states are basis states, they are either equal or orthogonal. If they are equal, the SWAP test returns $|0\rangle$ with probability 1. If they are orthogonal, it returns $|0\rangle$ with probability $\frac{1}{2}$. Note that the following holds:

$$[\forall i, x_i = x_{L+i+1}] \implies [\forall i, c_i = c_{L+i+1}]. \tag{30}$$

Thus, the probability that these two states are equal is the probability that each x_i is equal to x_{L+i+1}, which happens with probability $\frac{1}{2^{Ln}}$. All in all, the probability of measuring $|0\rangle$ on average is equal to:

$$\Pr[|0\rangle] = \frac{1}{2^{Ln}} + \frac{1}{2}\left(1 - \frac{1}{2^{LN}}\right) = \frac{1}{2} + \frac{1}{2^{Ln+1}}. \tag{31}$$

Thus, the following holds about $\mathcal{A}$'s advantage:

$$\mathsf{Adv}_{\mathcal{A},\mathsf{CBC}}^{\mathsf{qind\text{-}qcpa\text{-}p13}}(\lambda) \geqslant \frac{1}{2} - \frac{1}{2^{\lfloor \frac{\ell-1}{2}\rfloor n+1}} - \frac{1+C}{2^{\ell n}}. \tag{32}$$

In particular, this advantage is not negligible with respect to λ. Note that if ℓ is even, the adversary can simply set the first plaintext register to $|0\rangle$. That way, the first ciphertext register will be used as an initialization vector. $\mathcal{A}$ can thus measure it and apply the same strategy as outlined above.   □

3.4   General Results and Discussion

The original idea of the IND-CPA security was intuitively to show that an adversary does not even learn a bit of information by looking at the ciphertext. In a quantum world, such a bit can represent quite abstract information, such as the fact that the plaintext register can be disentangled with the corresponding ciphertext register, as shown by Theorems 1 and 2. The fact that such strategies can be applied to security notions gives rise to questioning their relevance. This can be taken to the extreme, where commonly used practices kill the potential security of a scheme with respect to some qIND-qCPA notions.

In this section, we prove two general insecurity results about schemes that uses a public function to randomize their encryption (such as the XOR one for instance) and those preserving the length of the messages they encrypt. The former concerns the qIND-qCPA-P5 security notion, which we define below.

Definition 7 (qIND-qCPA-P5 game, adapted from [5]). *Let E be a cryptographic scheme: $E = (\mathsf{KGen}, \mathsf{Enc}, \mathsf{Dec})$. We denote by M the set of messages E operates on, by $\mathsf{CL\text{-}Enc}$ the classical oracle implementing Enc and by $\mathsf{EM\text{-}Enc}$ the embedding oracle implementing Enc. We say that E is qIND-qCPA-P5-secure if no polynomial time quantum adversary $\mathcal{A}$ has an advantage larger than $\frac{1}{2} + \varepsilon$ in the following experiment, with ε being negligible with respect to λ.*

$$
\begin{array}{l}
\hline
Experiment~qIND\text{-}qCPA\text{-}P5^b_E(\lambda, \mathcal{A}) \\
\hline
\mathsf{k} \leftarrow_\$ \mathsf{KGen}\left(1^\lambda\right) \\[4pt]
\pi \leftarrow_\$ \mathfrak{S}_{|M|} \\[4pt]
b' \leftarrow_\$ \mathcal{A}^{\mathsf{CL\text{-}Enc}(\mathsf{k},\cdot),\mathsf{EM\text{-}Enc}(\mathsf{k},\cdot)\circ\pi^b}() \\[4pt]
\textbf{return}~b' \\
\hline
\end{array}
$$

Intuitively, the qIND-qCPA-P5 security experiment is very similar to the qIND-qCPA-P13 one. In fact, the only difference between these two experiments is that the adversary is allowed to perform multiple challenge queries instead of a single one.

We show that when using a public function to randomize the encryption and providing the adversary with the randomness used, an adversary can manage to get states independent of the said function and randomness in the real world. As such, they can create two identical states and perform a SWAP test on them to measure $|0\rangle$ with probability 1. In the random world however, a fresh permutation is applied on the input register beforehand, making the overlap $\langle \varphi | \psi \rangle$ exponentially small with high probability. The adversary can thus get an advantage close to $\frac{1}{2}$ by exploiting this method, which is what's described in Theorem 4 and its associated proof.

Theorem 4. *Let Enc be a randomized encryption function from $\{0,1\}^m \times \{0,1\}^p$ to $\{0,1\}^n$, with m being the message length and p being the randomness length. If the randomness r is given to the adversary and if Enc can be written as:*

$$\mathsf{Enc}(x; r) = f(g(x; r))$$

with g being a public, efficient bijective function with respect to r, then there is an adversary which has an advantage of $\frac{1}{2} - \frac{1}{2^m}$ in the qIND-qCPA-P5 security game of Enc.

Proof. First of all, let us consider the case $b = 0$. On a challenge request, if $\mathcal{A}$ sends $|+\rangle$, they will receive the following state:

$$\frac{1}{\sqrt{2^m}} \sum_x |x\rangle \, |f(g(x;r))\rangle . \tag{33}$$

Since they know r, they can apply an erasing oracle implementing $g(\cdot;r)$ on the first register to create the following state:

$$|\psi\rangle = \frac{1}{\sqrt{2^m}} \sum_x |g(x;r)\rangle \, |f(g(x;r))\rangle = \frac{1}{\sqrt{2^m}} \sum_x |x\rangle \, |f(x)\rangle . \tag{34}$$

Thus, they are able to create a state which is independent of the randomness that is used. As such, they can perform two challenge requests using this method to get $|\psi\rangle \otimes |\psi\rangle$. They can then perform a SWAP test using these two registers, which will return $|0\rangle$ with probability 1.

Let us now consider the case $b = 1$. Using the same method, $\mathcal{A}$ will get the state:

$$\frac{1}{2^m} \left(\sum_{x_0} |g(x_0; r_0)\rangle \, |f(g(\pi_0(x_0);r_0))\rangle \right) \otimes \left(\sum_{x_1} |g(x_1; r_1)\rangle \, |f(g(\pi_1(x_1);r_1))\rangle \right)$$
$$\tag{35}$$

and we show that the probability of measuring $|0\rangle$ using the same strategy is close to $\frac{1}{2}$. In order to compute this probability, we need to compute the scalar product of these two states. This scalar product is equal to:

$$\frac{1}{2^m} \sum_{x_0, x_1} \langle g(x_0; r_0), f(g(\pi_0(x_0);r_0)) | g(x_1;r_1), f(g(\pi_1(x_1);r_1))\rangle \tag{36a}$$

$$= \frac{1}{2^m} \sum_{x_0} \langle f(g(\pi_0(x_0);r_0)) | f(g(\pi_1(g^{-1}(g(x_0;r_0);r_1));r_1))\rangle . \tag{36b}$$

This scalar product is thus equal to $\frac{k}{2^m}$, where k is the number of messages x_0 such that the following equation is true:

$$f(g(\pi_0(x_0);r_0)) = f(g(\pi_1(g^{-1}(g(x_0;r_0);r_1));r_1)) . \tag{37}$$

Since f has to be injective, the previous equation can be rewritten as:

$$g^{-1}(g(\pi_0(x_0);r_0);r_1) = \pi_1(g^{-1}(g(x_0;r_0);r_1)) . \tag{38}$$

We now consider k and π_0 to be fixed and we ought to compute the number of permutations π_1 such that exactly k of these equations are satisfied.

Note that the number of permutations such that at least k of these equations are satisfied is $\binom{2^m}{k} (2^m - k)! \sum_{i=0}^{2^m-k} \frac{(-1)^i}{i!}$. Thus, the probability that exactly k

of these equations are satisfied is $\frac{1}{k!} \sum_{i=0}^{2^m-k} \frac{(-1)^i}{i!}$. It is thus possible to compute the expected probability of measuring $|0\rangle$:

$$\mathbb{E}\left[\mathbb{P}[|0\rangle]\right] = \frac{1}{2} + \frac{1}{2^{m+1}} \sum_{k=0}^{2^m-1} \frac{k^2}{k!} \underbrace{\sum_{i=0}^{2^m-k} \frac{(-1)^i}{i!}}_{2 \text{ for } m \geqslant 1} = \frac{1}{2} + \frac{1}{2^m}. \tag{39}$$

Thus, $\mathcal{A}$'s advantage is equal to $\frac{1}{2} - \frac{1}{2^m}$.   □

We now show an insecurity result with respect to the qIND-qCPA-P8 security notion, which we define below.

Definition 8 (qIND-qCPA-P8 game, adapted from [5]). *Let E be a cryptographic scheme: $E = (\mathsf{KGen}, \mathsf{Enc}, \mathsf{Dec})$. We denote by $\mathsf{CL\text{-}Enc}$ the classical oracle implementing Enc, by $\mathsf{ER\text{-}Enc}$ the erasing oracle implementing Enc and by $\mathcal{M}|\psi\rangle$ the measurement in the computational basis of a given register $|\psi\rangle$. We say that E is qIND-qCPA-P8-secure if no polynomial time quantum adversary $\mathcal{A}$ has an advantage larger than $\frac{1}{2} + \varepsilon$ in the following experiment, with ε being negligible with respect to λ.*

Experiment $qIND\text{-}qCPA\text{-}P8_E^b(\lambda, \mathcal{A})$
$k \leftarrow_{\$} \mathsf{KGen}\left(1^{\lambda}\right)$
$(\text{state}, |\varphi_0\rangle, |\varphi_1\rangle) \leftarrow_{\$} \mathcal{A}^{\mathsf{CL\text{-}Enc}(k, \cdot)}()$
$\mathcal{M}|\varphi_{\overline{b}}\rangle$
$|\psi\rangle \leftarrow_{\$} \mathsf{ER\text{-}Enc}(k, |\varphi_b\rangle)$
$b' \leftarrow_{\$} \mathcal{A}^{\mathsf{CL\text{-}Enc}(k, \cdot)}(|\psi\rangle, \text{state})$
return b'

We show that an adversary can get an advantage of 2^{-d} in the qIND-qCPA-P8 security game of a cryptographic scheme, where d is the difference in bitlengths between the ciphertexts and the plaintexts. In particular, an encryption scheme preserving the length of its input can't be qIND-qCPA-P8-secure. This generalizes a result from Gagliardoni et al. [7], who showed this result for the qIND-qCPA-P1 security notion, which implies the qIND-qCPA-P8 one.

Theorem 5. *Let Enc be a randomized encryption function from $\{0,1\}^m \times \{0,1\}^p$ to $\{0,1\}^n$, with m being the message length and p being the randomness length. There is an adversary which has an advantage of $\frac{2^m}{2^n}$ in the qIND-qCPA-P8 security game of Enc.*

Proof. $\mathcal{A}$ prepares the following states:

$$|+\rangle^m = \frac{1}{\sqrt{2^m}} \sum_x |x\rangle \tag{40a}$$

and

$$|+\rangle^{m-1} |-\rangle = \frac{1}{\sqrt{2^m}} \sum_x (-1)^x |x\rangle \tag{40b}$$

and performs their challenge query using them. They thus receive:

$$\frac{1}{\sqrt{2^m}} \sum_x (-1)^{b \cdot x} |\mathsf{Enc}\,(x, r_0)\rangle \tag{41}$$

They now apply an **H** gate on this state, which results in the following state:

$$\frac{1}{\sqrt{2^{m+n}}} \sum_x (-1)^{b \cdot x} \sum_y (-1)^{y \cdot \mathsf{Enc}(x, r_0)} |y\rangle \tag{42a}$$

$$= \frac{1}{\sqrt{2^{m+n}}} \sum_x (-1)^{b \cdot x} |0\rangle + \frac{1}{\sqrt{2^{m+n}}} \sum_x (-1)^{b \cdot x} \sum_{y \neq 0} (-1)^{y \cdot \mathsf{Enc}(x, r_0)} |y\rangle \tag{42b}$$

$\mathcal{A}$ now measures this state. Note that the probability of measuring $|0\rangle$ is:

$$\left(\frac{1}{\sqrt{2^{m+n}}} \sum_x (-1)^{b \cdot x} \right)^2 = \begin{cases} \frac{2^m}{2^n} & \text{if } b = 0 \\ 0 & \text{otherwise} \end{cases} . \tag{43}$$

The adversary can thus return $b = 0$ if they measure $|0\rangle$ and $b = 1$ otherwise. $\square$

Thus, these two theorems give two necessary conditions for a scheme to be qIND-qCPA-P1 and qIND-qCPA-P2-secure, since both these notions imply the qIND-qCPA-P5 one. Additionally, they give another necessary condition to be qIND-qCPA-P1-secure, since this notion implies the qIND-qCPA-P8 one. The security with respect to these two notions is important, since Carstens et al. proved that being secure with respect to these two notions implied the security with respect to any qIND-qCPA notion [5].

For instance, Carstens et al. showed that the following construction is both qIND-qCPA-P1 and qIND-qCPA-P2-secure:

$$\mathsf{Enc}_k\,(m; r; r') = \mathsf{qPRP}_r\,(r' \parallel m) \parallel \mathsf{PRP}_k(r).$$

Note that we can consider the second part of the ciphertext to be classically given to the adversary. As such, the ciphertext is p bits longer than the plaintext, with p being the bitlength of the randomness r', which lower-bounds the advantage of an adversary in the qIND-qCPA-P8 security game by $\frac{1}{2^p}$, using Theorem 5. Furthermore, it is to be noted that the randomization of the encryption is not done using a public function, which prevents Theorem 4 from breaking its qIND-qCPA-P5, and as such its qIND-qCPA-P1 and qIND-qCPA-P2 security.

It is however important to consider what these results actually mean regarding the security of the studied encryption scheme. For instance, one could argue that in Theorems 1, 2 and 5, the adversary is able to win in the associated security game without learning anything whatsoever about the encryption scheme, which questions the relevance of the associated notions. While this adversary did manage to win in these security games, it is not yet clear what does that imply concerning the confidentiality of the plaintexts for instance.

In the classical setting, this problem is solved by the semantic security notion, which is equivalent to the IND-CPA one. The intuition behind this notion is that there is low to no difference for an algorithm to be provided with a ciphertext or to be provided with no ciphertext at all. In the quantum setting however, a single quantum semantic security notion has been defined, which is equivalent to the qIND-qCPA-P1 security notion [7]. In order to fully understand what the insecurity with respect to the qIND-qCPA-P5, qIND-qCPA-P8 or qIND-qCPA-P13 security notions means, it is necessary to define the equivalent quantum semantic security notions. Such a task will not only provide a better understanding of these notions and of their relations, but will also help in defining what standard should be adopted to evaluate the quantum security of an encryption scheme.

4 Conclusion

In this paper, we have shown that the standard IND-qCPA security results proven by Anand et al. [1] carry on to the erasing and embedding IND-qCPA notions defined by Carstens et al. [5].

We have also shown however that CBC, CTR, OFB, CFB are qIND-qCPA-P13 insecure, no matter what the underlying block cipher is. Since all the security notions but the IND-qCPA ones and the IND-CPA one imply the qIND-qCPA-P13 one, this fully characterizes the security of these modes.

Finally, we gave two general insecurity results on the schemes using a public function to randomize their encryption and on those preserving the length of their input. These two results give necessary conditions for a scheme to be secure with respect to all qIND-qCPA notions and we used these to highlight the need for new quantum semantic security notions.

A   Adapting Anand et al.'s Work to the More General IND-qCPA Notions

A.1   Definitions

Similarly to [1], we define last and droplast as the functions which return respectively the last bit of their input and their input without their last bit.

We denote BC_k the block cipher introduced by Anand et al. [1], which maps x to:

$$\begin{cases} E_{h_1(k)}\left[\text{droplast}\,(x)\right] \,\|\, t_{h_2(k)}(x) & \text{if } \text{last}(x) = 0 \\ E_{h_1(k)}\left[\text{droplast}\,[x \oplus (k \,\|\, 1)]\right] \,\|\, \left[t_{h_2(k)}\,[x \oplus (k \,\|\, 1)] \oplus 1\right] & \text{if } \text{last}(x) = 1 \end{cases} \quad (44)$$

with E being a PRP taking as inputs a key of length $\lambda - 1$ and a message of length $\lambda - 1$ and returns a ciphertext of length $\lambda - 1$, t being a PRF taking as input a key of size λ and a message of size λ and returns a single bit and with h_1

and h_2 being two random oracles used to generate appropriate keys for E and t from the master key k. Anand et al. showed that this block cipher is a PRP [1].

We also define the relevant security notions.

Definition 9 (qIND-qCPA-P10{11} game, adapted from [5]). *Let E be a cryptographic scheme:* $E = (\mathsf{KGen}, \mathsf{Enc}, \mathsf{Dec})$. *We denote by M the set of messages E operates on, by* CL-1ct-b-Enc *the classical oracle implementing* Enc *in its 1-ciphertext version: it takes two inputs m_0 and m_1 and returns the encryption of m_b. We also denote* ER{EM}-Enc *the erasing {embedding} oracle implementing* Enc. *We say that E is* qIND-qCPA-P10{11}-*secure if no polynomial time quantum adversary $\mathcal{A}$ has an advantage larger than $\frac{1}{2} + \varepsilon$ in the following experiment, with ε being negligible with respect to λ.*

$$
\begin{array}{|l|}
\hline
\textit{Experiment } \textsf{qIND-qCPA-P10\{11\}}_E^b(\lambda, \mathcal{A}) \\
\hline
\mathsf{k} \leftarrow_\$ \mathsf{KGen}\left(1^\lambda\right) \\[4pt]
b' \leftarrow_\$ \mathcal{A}^{\mathsf{ER\{EM\}\text{-}Enc}(\mathsf{k},\cdot),\mathsf{CL\text{-}1}ct\text{-}b\text{-}\mathsf{Enc}(\mathsf{k},\cdot)}() \\[4pt]
\textbf{return } b' \\
\hline
\end{array}
$$

These notions simply mean that in the qIND-qCPA-P10 game, the adversary is allowed to perform erasing queries on the encryption function, while it is only permitted embedded queries in the qIND-qCPA-P11 one.

According to Fig. 1, we ought to show the insecurity of the CBC, CFB, OFB and CTR modes in the qIND-qCPA-P11 notion or their security in the qIND-qCPA-P10 one to fully characterize them.

A.2   Lemmas

Lemma 2 (Simon's algorithm, adapted from [15]). *Let s be a fixed n-bit string. Being given $n-1$ states that can be written as $|x\rangle + |x \oplus s\rangle$, it is possible to recover s in polynomial time with probability at least $\frac{1}{4}$.*

Lemma 3 (One-way to Hiding Lemma, originally written in [12]). *Let $H : \{0,1\}^n \to \{0,1\}^n$ be a random bijective function and $\mathcal{A}$ be an algorithm making at most q requests to H using either a standard oracle or an erasing one, taking as input two n-bit strings x and y and returning a single bit b. We define an algorithm $\mathcal{B}$ taking inputs similar to those of $\mathcal{A}$ and behaving as follows. $\mathcal{B}$ chooses $i \in [\![1 ; q]\!]$ uniformly at random and runs $\mathcal{A}^H(x,y)$ until just before the i-th query to H, at which point it measures the input register in the computational basis and returns the result. If $\mathcal{A}$ makes less than i requests to H, $\mathcal{B}$ returns $\perp \notin \{0,1\}^n$.*

For x being chosen uniformly at random, we define $P_\mathcal{A}^1$ to be the expected probability that $\mathcal{A}$ returns 1 if its inputs are x and $H(x)$. For y also being chosen uniformly at random, we define $P_\mathcal{A}^2$ to be the expected probability that $\mathcal{A}$ returns 1 if its entries are x and y. Finally, we define $P_\mathcal{B}$ to be the expected probability that $\mathcal{B}$ returns x or $H^{-1}(y)$ if its inputs are x and y. Then:

$$\left| P_\mathcal{A}^1 - P_\mathcal{A}^2 \right| \leqslant 2q\sqrt{P_\mathcal{B}}. \tag{45}$$

This lemma is a variant of the original One-way to Hiding Lemma introduced by Unruh [16], the only differences being the function being bijective, the possibility to use an erasing oracle and the natural redefinition of $P_{\mathcal{B}}$. As such, Unruh's original proof can almost be reused unmodified. Interested readers can find the proof in the full version of this article [13].

A.3   IND-qCPA Security of CTR and OFB

In this section, we show that Anand et al.'s argument [1] to prove the qIND-qCPA-P6 security of CTR and OFB can also be applied to prove its qIND-qCPA-P10 security.

Theorem 6 (Originally written in [12]). *A system using a PRP in CTR or OFB mode is qIND-qCPA-P10 secure.*

Proof. We adapt the argument used by Anand et al.: a reduction $\mathcal{R}$ having a classical access to the encryption function can perfectly simulate an erasing oracle.

Indeed, without loss of generality, let us assume that the adversary has an ancilla register and a query register, so that the sent state could be written as:

$$\sum_{x,y} \alpha_{x,y} \, |x,y\rangle . \tag{46}$$

The reduction queries for the encryption of 0 and receives $s \oplus 0 = s$, since CTR and OFB operate as stream ciphers. $\mathcal{R}$ can then apply $\mathbf{X}$ gates accordingly on the register it received, effectively creating the state

$$\sum_{x,y} \alpha_{x,y} \, |x,y \oplus s\rangle \tag{47}$$

which is exactly the state the adversary would have received, had they interacted with an erasing oracle.

Thus, the qIND-qCPA-P10 security of CTR and OFB can be reduced to their IND-CPA security, which they satisfy as long as they are used with a PRP.   □

A.4   Potential IND-qCPA Insecurity of CFB Used with a PRP

We now show that, similarly to Anand et al.'s results [1], there is a PRP which, when used in CFB mode, yields an IND-qCPA insecure scheme. We use the same block cipher as Anand et al. and performs the same attack up to one detail: Anand et al. used the fact that the adversary is allowed to query a uniform superposition on the last qubit so that it is not entangled with the other register. Using an embedding oracle, we cannot use such a trick and are forced to explicitly disentangle this last qubit with the remaining of the state.

Theorem 7 (Originally written in [12]). *There is a PRP such that the system using it as a block cipher in CFB mode is qIND-qCPA-P11 insecure.*

Proof. We use the same block cipher $\mathsf{BC_k}$ as Anand et al. [1], as described in Eq. 44. The adversary can prepare the state:

$$\left(\bigotimes_{i=1}^{\ell-2} |0\rangle\right) \sum_x |x\rangle |0\rangle \tag{48}$$

and performs a learning request using it, thus receiving the state, omitting the registers that are not entangled with the others:

$$\sum_x |x\rangle_M \left|\mathsf{BC_k^{\ell-1}}(c_0) \oplus x\right\rangle_{C_1} \left|\mathsf{BC_k}\left(\mathsf{BC_k^{\ell-1}}(c_0) \oplus x\right)\right\rangle_{C_2}. \tag{49}$$

The adversary then performs an **X** gate on M controlled by C_1, thus putting it in the basis state $\left|\mathsf{BC_k^{\ell-1}}(c_0)\right\rangle$, which disentangles it from the other registers. Hence, the state can now be written as:

$$\sum_x \left|\mathsf{BC_k^{\ell-1}}(c_0) \oplus x\right\rangle_{C_1} \left|\mathsf{BC_k}\left(\mathsf{BC_k^{\ell-1}}(c_0) \oplus x\right)\right\rangle_{C_2} \tag{50a}$$

$$= \sum_x |x\rangle_{C_1} |\mathsf{BC_k}(x)\rangle_{C_2} \tag{50b}$$

$$= \sum_x |x\rangle_{C_1} |\mathsf{droplast}(\mathsf{BC_k}(x))\rangle_{C_{2,2}} |\mathsf{last}(\mathsf{BC_k}(x))\rangle_{C_{2,2}}. \tag{50c}$$

$\mathcal{A}$ then measures the $C_{2,1}$ register and gets a value z, disturbing the superposition. Indeed, a message x still present in the superposition must satisfy:

$$z = E_{h_1(k)}(\mathsf{droplast}(x \oplus [(\mathsf{k} \| 1) \cdot \mathsf{last}(x)])) \tag{51a}$$

$$\Longleftrightarrow x \oplus [(\mathsf{k} \| 1) \cdot \mathsf{last}(x)] = \begin{cases} E_{h_1(k)}^{-1}(z) \| 0 \\ E_{h_1(k)}^{-1}(z) \| 1 \end{cases}. \tag{51b}$$

However, we know that for all Y, $\mathsf{last}(Y \oplus [(\mathsf{k} \| 1) \cdot \mathsf{last}(Y)]) = 0$ holds. As such, a valid message x must satisfy, denoting $Z = E_{h_1(k)}^{-1}(z) \| 0$ for conciseness' sake:

$$x \oplus [(\mathsf{k} \| 1) \cdot \mathsf{last}(x)] = Z \tag{51c}$$

$$\Longleftrightarrow x = \begin{cases} Z \\ Z \oplus (\mathsf{k} \| 1) \end{cases}. \tag{51d}$$

Thus, the resulting state is, omitting the now measured $C_{2,1}$ register:

$$|Z\rangle_{C_1} \left|t_{h_2(k)}(Z)\right\rangle_{C_{2,2}} + |Z \oplus (\mathsf{k} \| 1)\rangle_{C_1} \left|t_{h_2(k)}(Z) \oplus 1\right\rangle_{C_{2,2}}. \tag{52}$$

Finally, $\mathcal{A}$ can perform an **X** gate on $C_{2,2}$ controlled by the last qubit of C_1. This results in the $C_{2,2}$ register now being disentangled from C_1, since it is now in the basis state $\left|t_{h_2(k)}(Z)\right\rangle$. Hence, the state the adversary is left with is:

$$|Z\rangle + |Z \oplus (\mathsf{k} \| 1)\rangle. \tag{53}$$

The adversary is able to create such a state for each of their learning queries. In particular, they can now make use of Lemma 2 to recover (k ‖ 1) and as such k. They are now able to easily win in the qIND-qCPA-P11 game by performing a classical challenge query.   □

A.5 Potential IND-qCPA Insecurity of CBC Used with a PRP

We now show a similar attack on the qIND-qCPA-P11 security of CBC used with a PRP to the one used for CFB.

Theorem 8. *There is a PRP such that the system using it as a block cipher in CBC mode is qIND-qCPA-P11 insecure.*

Proof. We use the same block cipher BC_k as Anand et al. [1], as described in Eq. 44. The adversary can prepare the state:

$$\left(\bigotimes_{i=1}^{\ell-1} |0\rangle\right) \sum_x |x\rangle \tag{54}$$

and performs a learning request using it, thus receiving the state, omitting the registers that are not entangled with the others:

$$\sum_x |x\rangle_M \left| BC_k\left(BC_k^{\ell-1}(c_0) \oplus x\right)\right\rangle_C. \tag{55}$$

Note that $\mathcal{A}$ gets to know the value of $BC_k^{\ell-1}(c_0)$ using the previous ciphertext register, which is not entangled with the others. Thus, $\mathcal{A}$ can apply **X** gates on M to XOR it with this value, thus creating the state written in Eq. 50b. From there, they can apply the same method to recover k and win in the qIND-qCPA-P11 security game.   □

A.6 IND-qCPA Security of CBC and CFB Used with a qPRP

We show that Anand et al.'s proof [1] for showing that CBC and CFB are qIND-qCPA-P6 secure when used with a qPRP can be adapted to show that they are also qIND-qCPA-P10 secure. Similarly to their work, we perform the proof for the qIND-qCPA-P10 security of CFB and point out the differences with the one for CBC in brackets.

Theorem 9 (Originally written in [12]). *A system using a qPRP in CFB {CBC} mode is qIND-qCPA-P10 secure.*

Proof. We adapt Anand et al.'s proof [1] to the qIND-qCPA-P10 security notion. In particular, $\mathcal{A}$ is allowed to perform their learning queries on an erasing oracle. We first show a very similar lemma to Anand et al.'s Lemma 6.   □

Lemma 4 (Originally written in [12]**).** *For a random permutation* H, *we define* Enc^i *as the function that returns* $i + 1$ *blocks of randomness, including the IV* c_0, *and then behaves like a standard CFB {CBC} mode to compute the other blocks using* H *as its underlying block cipher. We stress that for* $i = 0$, Enc^i *is bijective, and as such can be implemented as an erasing oracle. Let* b *be a random bit. For every adversary* $\mathcal{A}$ *performing at most* q *quantum encryption queries, the following holds:*

$$
\begin{aligned}
\Big| \Pr & \Big[\mathcal{A}^{\mathsf{Enc}^0} \left(\mathsf{Enc}^i \left(M_b \right) \right) = b \mid M_0, M_1 \leftarrow \mathcal{A}^{\mathsf{Enc}^0} \Big] - \\
& \Pr \Big[\mathcal{A}^{\mathsf{Enc}^0} \left(\mathsf{Enc}^{i+1} \left(M_b \right) \right) = b \mid M_0, M_1 \leftarrow \mathcal{A}^{\mathsf{Enc}^0} \Big] \Big| \leqslant \mathcal{O} \left(\sqrt{\frac{\ell^3 q^3}{2^n}} \right).
\end{aligned}
\tag{56}
$$

Proof. For simplicity, we denote $\mathsf{Enc} = \mathsf{Enc}^0$. We define:

$$
\begin{aligned}
\varepsilon(\lambda, n) \overset{\text{def}}{=} \Big| \Pr & \Big[\mathcal{A}^{\mathsf{Enc}} \left(\mathsf{Enc}^i \left(M_b \right) \right) = b \mid M_0, M_1 \leftarrow \mathcal{A}^{\mathsf{Enc}} \Big] - \\
& \Pr \Big[\mathcal{A}^{\mathsf{Enc}} \left(\mathsf{Enc}^{i+1} \left(M_b \right) \right) = b \mid M_0, M_1 \leftarrow \mathcal{A}^{\mathsf{Enc}} \Big] \Big|.
\end{aligned}
\tag{57}
$$

Similarly to Anand et al.'s proof [1], we also define:

$$
\widetilde{\mathsf{Enc}}^i \left(M, c_0, \cdots, c_i \right) = \hat{c}_0 \ldots \hat{c}_\ell
\tag{58}
$$

where $\hat{c}_j = c_j$ if $j \leqslant i$ and $\hat{c}_j = m_j \oplus H \left(\hat{c}_{j-1} \right) \{ H \left(m_j \oplus \hat{c}_{j-1} \right) \}$ otherwise. We thus have, for $c_0, \ldots, c_{i+1}$ being uniformly random:

$$
\begin{aligned}
\varepsilon(\lambda, n) = \Big| \Pr & \Big[\mathcal{A}^{\mathsf{Enc}} \left(\widetilde{\mathsf{Enc}}^i \left(M_b, c_0, \ldots, c_i \right) \right) = b \mid M_0, M_1 \leftarrow \mathcal{A}^{\mathsf{Enc}} \Big] - \\
& \Pr \Big[\mathcal{A}^{\mathsf{Enc}} \left(\widetilde{\mathsf{Enc}}^{i+1} \left(M_b, c_0, \ldots, c_{i+1} \right) \right) = b \mid M_0, M_1 \leftarrow \mathcal{A}^{\mathsf{Enc}} \Big] \Big|.
\end{aligned}
\tag{59}
$$

We can then replace c_i and c_{i+1} by respectively $x \{ x \oplus m_b^{i+1} \}$ and $y \oplus m_b^{i+1} \{ y \}$, where x and y are chosen uniformly at random, giving us the following value for $\varepsilon(\lambda, n)$:

$$
\begin{aligned}
\Big| \Pr & \Big[\mathcal{A}^{\mathsf{Enc}} \left(\widetilde{\mathsf{Enc}}^i \left(M_b, c_0, \ldots, c_{i-1}, x \right) \right) = b \mid M_0, M_1 \leftarrow \mathcal{A}^{\mathsf{Enc}} \Big] - \\
& \Pr \Big[\mathcal{A}^{\mathsf{Enc}} \left(\widetilde{\mathsf{Enc}}^{i+1} \left(M_b, c_0, \ldots, c_{i-1}, x, y \oplus m_b^{i+1} \right) \right) = b \mid M_0, M_1 \leftarrow \mathcal{A}^{\mathsf{Enc}} \Big] \Big|.
\end{aligned}
\tag{60}
$$

$$
\begin{aligned}
\Big\{ \Big| \Pr & \Big[\mathcal{A}^{\mathsf{Enc}} \left(\widetilde{\mathsf{Enc}}^i \left(M_b, c_0, \ldots, c_{i-1}, x \oplus m_b^{i+1} \right) \right) = b \mid M_0, M_1 \leftarrow \mathcal{A}^{\mathsf{Enc}} \Big] - \\
& \Pr \Big[\mathcal{A}^{\mathsf{Enc}} \left(\widetilde{\mathsf{Enc}}^{i+1} \left(M_b, c_0, \ldots, c_{i-1}, x \oplus m_b^{i+1}, y \right) \right) = b \mid M_0, M_1 \leftarrow \mathcal{A}^{\mathsf{Enc}} \Big] \Big| \Big\}.
\end{aligned}
\tag{60}
$$

By definition of $\widetilde{\mathsf{Enc}}^{i+1}$, this is also equal to:

$$\left| \Pr\left[\mathcal{A}^{\mathsf{Enc}} \left(\widetilde{\mathsf{Enc}}^{i+1} \left(M_b, c_0, \ldots, c_{i-1}, x, H(x) \oplus m_b^{i+1} \right) \right) = b \mid M_0, M_1 \leftarrow \mathcal{A}^{\mathsf{Enc}} \right] - \right.$$
$$\left. \Pr\left[\mathcal{A}^{\mathsf{Enc}} \left(\widetilde{\mathsf{Enc}}^{i+1} \left(M_b, c_0, \ldots, c_{i-1}, x, y \oplus m_b^{i+1} \right) \right) = b \mid M_0, M_1 \leftarrow \mathcal{A}^{\mathsf{Enc}} \right] \right|.$$

$$(61)$$

$$\left\{ \left| \Pr\left[\mathcal{A}^{\mathsf{Enc}} \left(\widetilde{\mathsf{Enc}}^{i+1} \left(M_b, c_0, \ldots, c_{i-1}, x, H(x) \right) \right) = b \mid M_0, M_1 \leftarrow \mathcal{A}^{\mathsf{Enc}} \right] - \right. \right.$$
$$\left. \left. \Pr\left[\mathcal{A}^{\mathsf{Enc}} \left(\widetilde{\mathsf{Enc}}^{i+1} \left(M_b, c_0, \ldots, c_{i-1}, x, y \oplus m_b^{i+1} \right) \right) = b \mid M_0, M_1 \leftarrow \mathcal{A}^{\mathsf{Enc}} \right] \right| \right\}.$$

$$(61)$$

Thus, similarly to Anand et al.'s proof, we can define the following adversary, which can interact with a standard {erasing} oracle implementing H.

Adversary $\mathcal{A}_{O2H}^{H}(x, y)$

$M_0, M_1 \leftarrow \mathcal{A}^{\mathsf{Enc}}$

$b \leftarrow \{0, 1\}$

$c_0, \ldots, c_{i-1} \leftarrow \{0, 1\}^n$

$c_i = x \left\{ x \oplus m_b^{i+1} \right\}$

$c_{i+1} = y \oplus m_b^{i+1} \{y\}$

for j **in** $[\![j+2; \ell]\!]$

$\qquad c_j = m_b^j \oplus H(c_{j-1}) \left\{ H\left(m_b^j \oplus c_{j-1} \right) \right\}$

$b' \leftarrow \mathcal{A}^{\mathsf{Enc}}(c_0 \cdots c_\ell)$

return $b = b'$

We now show that $\mathcal{A}_{O2H}$ is able to answer $\mathcal{A}$'s queries, since they are able to implement an erasing oracle implementing H.

$\mathcal{A}_{O2H}$ uses a standard oracle to create c_k from c_{k-1} by simply feeding c_{k-1} and m_k to the standard oracle, which results in leaving the first register unchanged and the second one in the state $|m_k \oplus H(c_{k-1})\rangle$, which is c_k by definition.

{$\mathcal{A}_{O2H}$ uses an erasing oracle to create c_k from c_{k-1} by applying an **X** gate on m_k controlled by c_{k-1}, and then feeds this register to the erasing oracle, resulting in the state $|H(m_k \oplus c_{k-1})\rangle$, which is c_k by definition.}

We denote q_{O2H} the number of queries to H that this adversary performs. For each query that $\mathcal{A}$ performs to compute M_0 and M_1, $\mathcal{A}_{O2H}$ performs ℓ queries to H. They will then perform $\ell - i - 1$ requests to H in order to compute the ciphertext, and finally will answer $\mathcal{A}$'s queries one more time. All in all, $\mathcal{A}_{O2H}$ performs at most $(q+1)\ell - i - 1$ queries to H. Similarly to Anand et al.'s proof [1], we respectively denote q_1, q_2 and q_3 the number of queries performed by $\mathcal{A}_{O2H}$ before, during and after the challenge query. $\varepsilon(\lambda, n)$ is then easily seen to be:

$$\varepsilon(\lambda, n) = \left| \Pr\left[\mathcal{A}_{O2H}^{H}(x, H(x)) = 1 \right] - \Pr\left[\mathcal{A}_{O2H}^{H}(x, y) = 1 \right] \right| \qquad (62)$$

with x and y being chosen uniformly at random. This allows us to use the O2H lemma. We thus consider the adversary $\mathcal{B}$ associated to $\mathcal{A}_{O2H}$ as defined in the lemma and denote the number of the query during which $\mathcal{B}$ measures $\mathcal{A}_{O2H}$'s input register by j and the associated probability by $P_{\mathcal{B}}^{j}$.

If $j \leqslant q_1$: In this case, the challenge query hasn't yet been performed by $\mathcal{A}$. As such, $\mathcal{A}$ does not know the arguments x and y using which $\mathcal{A}_{O2H}$ has been instantiated. Thus, its queries are independent from those parameters and we have, by denoting $(\mathcal{M} = z)$ the event where $\mathcal{B}$'s measure of $\mathcal{A}_{O2H}$'s register results in the string z:

$$P_{\mathcal{B}}^{j} = \Pr\left[\left[\mathcal{B}(x,y) = x\right] \cup \left[\mathcal{B}(x,y) = H^{-1}(y)\right] \mid j \leqslant q_1\right] \tag{63a}$$

$$\leqslant \sum_{x'=0}^{2^n-1} \Pr\left[\mathcal{M} = x' \mid j \leqslant q_1, x' = x\right] \frac{1}{2^n} + \tag{63b}$$

$$\sum_{y'=0}^{2^n-1} \Pr\left[\mathcal{M} = y' \mid j \leqslant q_1, y' = H^{-1}(y)\right] \frac{1}{2^n}$$

$$\leqslant \frac{1}{2^{n-1}}. \tag{63c}$$

If $q_1 < j \leqslant q_1 + q_2$: In this case, the previous reasoning still applies to x, we thus have:

$$P_{\mathcal{B}}^{j} \leqslant \frac{1}{2^n} + \frac{1}{2^n} \sum_{y'=0}^{2^n-1} \Pr\left[\mathcal{M} = y' \mid q_1 < j \leqslant q_2, y' = H^{-1}(y)\right]. \tag{64}$$

In this case however, $\mathcal{A}_{O2H}$ performs their queries with inputs depending on y. Note that the first query done to H is $y \oplus m_b^{i+1}$. Since $\mathcal{A}$ does not know y when performing their challenge query, y and m_b^{i+1} are independent, which means that $y \oplus m_b^{i+1}$ is uniformly random, since y is uniformly random. Using a similar reasoning, each other query on H can be written as $m_b^k \oplus H(c_{k-1})$ $\left\{m_b^k \oplus c_{k-1}\right\}$, with c_{k-1} being uniformly random and independent from m_b^k. Every string has thus the same probability to be measured, even being given that $y' = H^{-1}(y)$. This is thus similar to the previous case and we have:

$$P_{\mathcal{B}}^{j} \leqslant \frac{1}{2^{n-1}}. \tag{65}$$

If $q_1 + q_2 < j$: In this case, the query is performed after $\mathcal{A}$ has received the challenge query. Note that we can use a similar reasoning to Anand et al.'s one to argue that we can consider the queries as being classical. Indeed, as described above, $\mathcal{A}_{O2H}$ only applies permutation matrices on the state they receive from $\mathcal{A}$. We can thus move the measurement performed by $\mathcal{B}$ before the first call to H to answer $\mathcal{A}$'s query, which allows us to consider this query classical.

Like the previous case, the queries performed on H can be written as $m_b^k \oplus H(c_{k-1}) \left\{m_b^k \oplus c_{k-1}\right\}$. For $k = 1$, it is obvious that this quantity is uniformly random, since c_0 is chosen independently of m_b^1. We thus now only have to show that for c_{k-1} being uniformly random, $m_b^k \oplus H(c_{k-1})\{m_b^k \oplus c_{k-1}\}$ is also uniformly random. It is for this enough to show that $\mathcal{A}$ did not get to know $H(c_{k-1})\{H(m_b^{k-1} \oplus c_{j-2})\}$. Since H is a random permutation queried at most q_{O2H} times, $\mathcal{A}$ got to know this value with probability at most $\frac{q_{O2H}}{2^n}$. We can actually do better by arguing that this probability upper-bounds the one that at least one of the queries to H isn't uniformly random. In order to upper-bound $P_\mathcal{B}^j$, we consider the trivial upper-bound in the case where $\mathcal{A}$ learned at least one such value, which happens with probability at most $\frac{q_{O2H}}{2^n}$, with 1. The other case is similar to the previous ones, which means that $\mathcal{B}$ will return x or $H^{-1}(y)$ with probability $\frac{1}{2^n}$. We upper-bound the probability of being in this case by the trivial upper-bound, that is 1. All in all, the following holds:

$$P_\mathcal{B}^j \leqslant \frac{1}{2^n} + \frac{q_{O2H}}{2^n}. \tag{66}$$

Now, we can use the previous upper-bound for every j, which ensures that:

$$P_\mathcal{B}^j = \sum_{j=1}^{q_{O2H}} P_\mathcal{B}^j \frac{1}{q_{O2H}} \leqslant \frac{1 + q_{O2H}}{2^n}. \tag{67}$$

Finally, we have, according to the O2H lemma:

$$\varepsilon(\lambda, n) \leqslant 2q_{O2H} \sqrt{\frac{1 + q_{O2H}}{2^n}} = \mathcal{O}\left(\sqrt{\frac{\ell^3 q^3}{2^n}}\right). \tag{68}$$

$\square$

We can now use this lemma to show the qIND-qCPA-P10 security of CFB {CBC}. Since the underlying block cipher is a qPRP, we can replace it with a truly random permutation H while only increasing $\mathcal{A}$'s advantage by a negligible amount. Using triangle inequality and the previous lemma, the following then holds:

$$\left| \Pr\left[\mathcal{A}^{\mathsf{Enc}}\left(\mathsf{Enc}\left(M_b\right)\right) = b \mid M_0, M_1 \leftarrow \mathcal{A}^{\mathsf{Enc}}\right] - \right.$$
$$\left. \Pr\left[\mathcal{A}^{\mathsf{Enc}}\left(\mathsf{Enc}^\ell\left(M_b\right)\right) = b \mid M_0, M_1 \leftarrow \mathcal{A}^{\mathsf{Enc}}\right]\right| \tag{69a}$$

$$\leqslant \sum_{i=0}^{\ell-1} \left[\left|\Pr\left[\mathcal{A}^{\mathsf{Enc}}\left(\mathsf{Enc}\left(M_b\right)\right) = b \mid M_0, M_1 \leftarrow \mathcal{A}^{\mathsf{Enc}}\right] - \right.\right.$$
$$\left.\left. \Pr\left[\mathcal{A}^{\mathsf{Enc}}\left(\mathsf{Enc}^\ell\left(M_b\right)\right) = b \mid M_0, M_1 \leftarrow \mathcal{A}^{\mathsf{Enc}}\right]\right|\right] \tag{69b}$$

$$\leqslant \mathcal{O}\left(\sqrt{\frac{\ell^5 q^3}{2^n}}\right). \tag{69c}$$

$\Pr\left[\mathcal{A}^{\mathsf{Enc}}\left(\mathsf{Enc}^\ell\left(M_b\right)\right) = b \mid M_0, M_1 \leftarrow \mathcal{A}^{\mathsf{Enc}}\right]$ is easily seen to be equal to $\frac{1}{2}$, since in this setup we returned to the adversary a uniformly random string that is independent of their challenge query. This allows us to upper-bound $\mathcal{A}$'s advantage:

$$\mathsf{Adv}_{\mathcal{A},\mathsf{CFB}}^{\mathsf{qind\text{-}qcpa\text{-}p13}}(\lambda) \leqslant \mathcal{O}\left(\sqrt{\frac{\ell^5 q^3}{2^n}}\right) + \mathsf{negl}(\lambda) \tag{70}$$

where $\mathsf{negl}(\lambda)$ is $\mathcal{A}$'s advantage in distinguishing the underlying block cipher from a truly random permutation. ℓ and n being polynomial in λ, this ensures that $\mathcal{A}$'s advantage is negligible with respect to λ. $\qquad\qquad\square$

References

1. Anand, M.V., Targhi, E.E., Tabia, G.N., Unruh, D.: Post-quantum security of the CBC, CFB, OFB, CTR, and XTS modes of operation. In: Takagi, T. (ed.) PQCrypto 2016. LNCS, vol. 9606, pp. 44–63. Springer, Cham (2016). https://doi. org/10.1007/978-3-319-29360-8_4
2. Boneh, D., Zhandry, M.: Secure signatures and chosen ciphertext security in a quantum computing world. In: Canetti, R., Garay, J.A. (eds.) CRYPTO 2013. LNCS, vol. 8043, pp. 361–379. Springer, Heidelberg (2013). https://doi.org/10. 1007/978-3-642-40084-1_21
3. Bonnetain, X., Naya-Plasencia, M., Schrottenloher, A.: Quantum security analysis of AES. IACR Trans. Symmetric Cryptol. **2019**(2), 55–93 (2019). https://doi.org/ 10.13154/tosc.v2019.i2.55-93
4. Buhrman, H., Cleve, R., Watrous, J., de Wolf, R.: Quantum fingerprinting. Phys. Rev. Lett. **87**(16) (2001). https://doi.org/10.1103/physrevlett.87.167902
5. Carstens, T.V., Ebrahimi, E., Tabia, G.N., Unruh, D.: Relationships between quantum IND-CPA notions. In: Nissim, K., Waters, B. (eds.) TCC 2021. LNCS, vol. 13042, pp. 240–272. Springer, Cham (2021). https://doi.org/10.1007/978-3-030-90459-3_9
6. Chevalier, C., Ebrahimi, E., Vu, Q.H.: On security notions for encryption in a quantum world. Cryptology ePrint Archive, Report 2020/237 (2020). https://eprint. iacr.org/2020/237
7. Gagliardoni, T., Hülsing, A., Schaffner, C.: Semantic security and indistinguishability in the quantum world. In: Robshaw, M., Katz, J. (eds.) CRYPTO 2016. LNCS, vol. 9816, pp. 60–89. Springer, Heidelberg (2016). https://doi.org/10.1007/ 978-3-662-53015-3_3
8. Gagliardoni, T., Krämer, J., Struck, P.: Quantum indistinguishability for public key encryption. In: Cheon, J.H., Tillich, J.-P. (eds.) PQCrypto 2021 2021. LNCS, vol. 12841, pp. 463–482. Springer, Cham (2021). https://doi.org/10.1007/978-3-030-81293-5_24
9. Grassl, M., Langenberg, B., Roetteler, M., Steinwandt, R.: Applying Grover's algorithm to AES: quantum resource estimates. In: Takagi, T. (ed.) PQCrypto 2016. LNCS, vol. 9606, pp. 29–43. Springer, Cham (2016). https://doi.org/10.1007/978-3-319-29360-8_3
10. Kaplan, M., Leurent, G., Leverrier, A., Naya-Plasencia, M.: Breaking symmetric cryptosystems using quantum period finding. In: Robshaw, M., Katz, J. (eds.) CRYPTO 2016. LNCS, vol. 9815, pp. 207–237. Springer, Heidelberg (2016). https://doi.org/10.1007/978-3-662-53008-5_8
11. Mossayebi, S., Schack, R.: Concrete security against adversaries with quantum superposition access to encryption and decryption oracles (2016)
12. Nemoz, T.: Cryptanalyse quantique d'algorithmes symétriques. Master's thesis, EURECOM (2021)

13. Nemoz, T., Amblard, Z., Dupin, A.: Characterizing the qIND-qCPA (in)security of the CBC, CFB, OFB and CTR modes of operation. Cryptology ePrint Archive, Report 2022/236 (2022). https://eprint.iacr.org/2022/236
14. Shor, P.W.: Polynomial-time algorithms for prime factorization and discrete logarithms on a quantum computer. SIAM J. Comput. **26**(5), 1484–1509 (1997). https://doi.org/10.1137/s0097539795293172
15. Simon, D.R.: On the power of quantum computation. In: 35th Annual Symposium on Foundations of Computer Science, Santa Fe, NM, USA, pp. 116–123. IEEE Computer Society Press (1994). https://doi.org/10.1109/SFCS.1994.365701
16. Unruh, D.: Revocable quantum timed-release encryption. In: Nguyen, P.Q., Oswald, E. (eds.) EUROCRYPT 2014. LNCS, vol. 8441, pp. 129–146. Springer, Heidelberg (2014). https://doi.org/10.1007/978-3-642-55220-5_8
17. Wooding, M.: New proofs for old modes. Cryptology ePrint Archive, Report 2008/121 (2008). https://eprint.iacr.org/2008/121
18. Zhandry, M.: A note on the quantum collision and set equality problems. Quantum Inf. Comput. **15**(7&8), 557–567 (2015). https://doi.org/10.26421/QIC15.7-8-2
19. Zhandry, M.: A note on quantum-secure PRPs. Cryptology ePrint Archive, Report 2016/1076 (2016). https://eprint.iacr.org/2016/1076

Breaking the Quadratic Barrier: Quantum Cryptanalysis of Milenage, Telecommunications' Cryptographic Backbone

Vincent Quentin Ulitzsch[1(✉)] and Jean-Pierre Seifert[1,2]

[1] Technische Universität Berlin – SECT, Berlin, Germany
vincent@sect.tu-berlin.de, jean-pierre.seifert@tu-berlin.de
[2] Fraunhofer Institute for Secure Information Technology, Darmstadt, Germany

Abstract. The potential advent of large-scale quantum computers in the near future poses a threat to contemporary cryptography. One ubiquitous usage of cryptography is currently present in the vibrant field of cellular networks. The cryptography of cellular networks is centered around seven secret-key algorithms $f_1, \ldots, f_5, f_1^*, f_5^*$, aggregated into an authentication and key agreement algorithm set. Still, to the best of our knowledge, these secret key algorithms have not yet been subject to quantum cryptanalysis. Instead, many quantum security considerations for telecommunication networks argue that the threat posed by quantum computers is restricted to public-key cryptography. However, various recent works have presented quantum attacks on secret key cryptography that exploit quantum period finding to achieve more than a quadratic speedup compared to the best known classical attacks. Motivated by this quantum threat to symmetric cryptography, this paper presents a quantum cryptanalysis for the Milenage algorithm set, the prevalent instantiation of the seven secret-key $f_1, \ldots, f_5, f_1^*, f_5^*$ algorithms that underpin cellular security. Building upon recent quantum cryptanalytic results, we show attacks that go beyond a quadratic speedup. Concretely, we provide quantum attack scenarios for all Milenage algorithms, including exponential speedups distinguishable by different quantum attack models. Our results do not constitute a quantum break of the Milenage algorithms, but they do show that Milenage suffers from structural weaknesses making it susceptible to quantum attacks.

Keywords: Quantum cryptanalysis · Simon's Algorithm · Quantum Security · Milenage · Cellular network · AKA protocol · Post-quantum cryptography

1 Introduction

Telecommunication operators are evidently expecting the advent of general purpose quantum computers, as indicated by their funding of various research projects investigating the new technologies' potential [31]. As part of these

© The Author(s), under exclusive license to Springer Nature Switzerland AG 2023
T. Johansson and D. Smith-Tone (Eds.): PQCrypto 2023, LNCS 14154, pp. 476–504, 2023.
https://doi.org/10.1007/978-3-031-40003-2_18

efforts, telecommunication standardization bodies also pay increasing attention to post-quantum security in telecommunication networks. As a result, the sixth generation of telecommunication networks (6G) is intended to be post-quantum secure, and proposals for extensions of the fifth generation (5G) already integrate quantum security considerations, cf. [13, 27, 38]. These security considerations are often focused on the threat quantum computers pose to asymmetric cryptography. To mitigate this threat, telecommunication protocols can replace the vulnerable cryptographic primitives with post-quantum secure cryptography, which does not rely on the hardness of factoring or the discrete logarithm problem. The National Institute of Standards and Technology (NIST), a standardization body, leads an ongoing process to evaluate and standardize asymmetric post-quantum primitives [28]. This process is now in its final stages, with four candidate algorithms already selected for standardization and an ongoing fourth round to analyze additional alternative constructions [29]. Multiple works have already demonstrated how the now standardized post-quantum secure public key cryptographic schemes can replace the (quantum) vulnerable public-key cryptography in present telecommunication protocols [11, 36].

In contrast to public key cryptography, quantum security considerations for cellular networks often do not consider the aspect of quantum attacks against symmetric cryptography. Instead, they assume symmetric cryptography to be unaffected by quantum cryptananalysis, except for a quadratic speed-up of exhaustive search due to Grover's algorithm. Hence, so the argument goes, increasing the key size of symmetric cryptography used in 6G to 256-bit would provide sufficient protection against quantum adversaries [27, 38].

In light of recent quantum cryptanalytic results however, this common belief can no longer be assumed to be trivially true. Starting with the seminal works of Kuwakado and Morii [23, 24], various works have shown that *quantum period finding* – through Simon's algorithm [35] – can speed up attacks on symmetric-key cryptography schemes beyond best known classical bounds [9, 10, 12, 21, 33]. The attacks demonstrate that, depending on the assumed attacker capabilities, quantum computers can be used to either efficiently break certain symmetric-key cryptography schemes or reduce the time needed to attack them. The distinguishing feature in the attacker capabilities for quantum cryptanalysis is the kind of oracle access that is provided to the attacker, commonly referred to as Q_2 and Q_1. In the Q_2 setting, also called the quantum known plaintext attack, the attacker can make superposition queries to an encryption oracle. This model enables quantum attackers to significantly reduce the security of classically secure symmetric ciphers. For example, in the Q_2 setting, Simon's algorithm enables attackers to execute forgery attacks against an otherwise *classically* secure CBC-MACs in polynomial time [21]. However, due to its powerful attacker model, the Q_2 model remains of mainly theoretical interest. In the Q_1 model the attacker has access to a general purpose quantum computer, but can only make classical queries to an encryption oracle. Attacks in this model can be executed as soon as general-purpose quantum computers come into existence. In the Q_1 model, symmetric cryptography can be attacked as well. Bonnetain et al. [10] demonstrated Q_1 attacks on symmetric cryptography that improve upon the best-known classical bounds. Their attacks extend quantum-cryptanalysis of symmetric ciphers that was rooted in the Q_2 model, i.e., relied on superposition queries to an encryption oracle. The cornerstone of these attacks is the offline Simon's algorithm [9], which combines quantum search and quantum period finding to transfer the Q_2 attacks to the Q_1 model.

These results call for a careful re-evaluation of the truism that has guided quantum security considerations for 6G so far. Doubling the key-size might not be sufficient to ensure long-term security of telecommunication protocols. Instead, symmetric-key cryptographic schemes used in telecommunications protocols must be evaluated towards their resilience against quantum enabled adversaries as well.

1.1   Contributions

We conduct such a quantum cryptanalysis for the Milenage algorithm set, a set of symmetric-key cryptographic algorithms ubiquitously used in the cellular world. The Milenage algorithm set's main usage is the Authentication and Key Agreement (AKA) protocol, used for authentication and session establishment in cellular networks. All Milenage algorithms make use of the network authentication key K, a secret key shared between the subscriber (stored in his network provider's SIM card) and the network. The algorithm set consists of the functions $f1, \ldots, f5, f1^*, f5^*$, and makes use of the AES block cipher.

In summary, when a user wants to authenticate to the network, the operator generates a random challenge and calculates the output of one of the Milenage algorithms, keyed with the network authentication key K. If the user, upon receiving the challenge, replies with the correct response, thus demonstrating knowledge of K, the authentication request is accepted. Other functions of the Milenage algorithm set are used to calculate a Message Authentication Code (MAC) or derive keys for later usage. Breaking the Milenage algorithm set would therefore allow attackers to perform account takeover attacks. Thus, the security of Milenage algorithms is crucial for the security of pervasive cellular networks in general. As such, the algorithms underpin the security of the worldwide cellular networks and provide a great starting point for the required quantum cryptanalysis of symmetric ciphers.

In conducting the quantum cryptanalysis, we take a gentle approach that can be followed by researchers who are not familiar with the internals of quantum computing. First, in Sect. 3, we distill a *quantum toolbox* from the various works on quantum cryptanalysis and quantum algorithms, i.e., a minimum set of quantum algorithms and results about their complexity that have proven to be useful in quantum cryptanalysis. For each algorithm in the toolbox, we explain the requirements that an attacker needs to meet in order to use the respective algorithm. For example, whether a quantum algorithm requires superposition access or can also be executed with only classical oracle access to the encryption under attack. Once equipped with this quantum toolbox, no more detailed understanding of quantum computing is required. The attacker then only needs to construct a function that meets the respective requirements, after which the algorithms can be applied as a black-box.

Leveraging this minimum quantum toolbox, we develop multiple attacks on the Milenage algorithm set inspired by various prior works. The quantum cryptanalysis of Milenage is the main contribution of this paper and can be found in Sect. 4. We analyze the Milenage set from several dimensions. In the two different query models Q_1 and Q_2, considering different attacker goals such as full key recovery or existential forgery and considering more powerful attacker models such as the related key model. Our results show that the quantum toolbox can be utilized to provide speedups over classical attacks in all dimensions, and even leads to polynomial time attacks in the Q_2 model. As a helpful overview, Table 1 summarizes the breadth of our results. The complexity analysis is additionally parameterized by three circuit complexities. First, T_{QAES} refers to the depth of a quantum circuit computing an AES encryption, as presented for example in Ref. [19]. Second, T_{AES} refers to runtime-complexity of a classical circuit computing an AES encryption. Finally, T_O refers to the time required for an oracle query. We find that a Q_2 attacker can execute existential forgery attacks against Milenage in polynomial time. It is an explicit design goal of Milenage to resist existential forgery attacks of classical adversaries (the design document does not consider a quantum adversary model) [4]. Less powerful adversaries are still able to significantly speed up their attacks, albeit not to an extent that fully breaks the algorithm set.

In summary, the attacks show that the Milenage algorithms exhibit a structure that can be exploited by quantum computers to obtain attacks that are more efficient than Grover's search. In the Q_2 model, Milenage must be considered broken, as it is vulnerable to a polynomial-time existential forgery attack. We emphasize that the Q_2 attacks remain of mainly theoretical interest for now, and *do not* imply that Milenage is broken once general purpose quantum computers come into existence. Notably however, the Q_2 attacker model encompasses all potential Q_1 attacks. An absence of Q_2 attacks would have implied an absence of Q_1 attacks as well. Given its vulnerability in the Q_2 model, further Q_1 attacks against Milenage cannot be ruled out. We encourage further quantum cryptanalysis and security proofs for Milenage, and its alternative TUAK, based on the Keccack-f-permutation [2], to lay the ground for post-quantum secure cellular networks.

2 Background

2.1 Notation

Throughout this paper, we will make use of a block cipher encryption function E, which takes as input an m-bit message, an n-bit key and returns an m-bit output. We denote by $E_K[m]$ the encryption of bit-string m under block cipher E with secret K. Similarly, if a function f takes as input a secret key k and a message m, we denote by $f_k(m)$ the invocation of that function with k and

Table 1. Summary of the results. $|K|$ is the length of the message authentication key, $|OP_C|$ is the length of the OP_c bitstring and $|M|$ is the block length of the underlying block cipher. In the case of Milenage, $|K| = |OP_C| = |M| = 128$. For all complexity estimates, the big-O notation hides only a very small multiplicative constant.

Attack	Model	Classical Queries	Superposition Queries	Circuit Depth Complexity	Best Known Classical Attack	Sec
Grover's attack for key recovery, OP known	Q_1	$O(1)$	0	$O\left(2^{|K|/2} \cdot T_{\mathrm{QAES}}\right)$	$O\left(2^{|K|} \cdot T_{\mathrm{AES}}\right)$	Sect. 4.1
Grover's attack for key recovery, OP unknown	Q_1	$O(1)$	0	$O\left(2^{(|K|+|OP_c|)/2} \cdot T_{\mathrm{QAES}}\right)$	$O\left(2^{|K|+|OP_c|} \cdot T_{\mathrm{AES}}\right)$	Sect. 4.1
Key Recovery $f2$, OP unknown	Q_2	0	$O(|M|)$	$\tilde{O}\left((|M| \cdot T_{\mathrm{QAES}}) \cdot 2^{|K|/2}\right)$	$O\left(2^{\frac{M}{2}} \cdot T_O + 2^{|K|+\frac{|M|}{2}} \cdot T_{\mathrm{AES}}\right)$	Sect. 4.2
Offline Key Recovery $f2$, OP unknown	Q_1	$O(2^{|M|})$	0	$\tilde{O}\left(2^{|M|} \cdot T_O + (|M| \cdot T_{\mathrm{QAES}}) \cdot 2^{\frac{|K|}{2}}\right)$	$O\left(2^{\frac{M}{2}} \cdot T_O + 2^{|K|+\frac{|M|}{2}} \cdot T_{\mathrm{AES}}\right)$	Sect. 4.2
Existential Forgery $f1$	Q_2	$O(1)$	$O(|M|)$	$O(|M| \cdot T_O)$	$O(2^{|M|/2} \cdot T_O)$	Sect. 4.3
Related Key Attack $f1, \ldots, f5$	Q_2	0	$O(|K| + |OP_c|)$	$\tilde{O}((|K| + |OP_c|) \cdot T_O)$	$O(S \cdot T_O + S \cdot T_{\mathrm{AES}})$ where $S = 2^{\frac{|K|+|OP_c|}{2}}$	Sect. 4.4
Offline Related Key Attack $f1, \ldots, f5$	Q_1	$O\left(2^{\frac{|K|+|OP_c|}{3}}\right)$	0	$\tilde{O}(S \cdot T_O + S \cdot T_{\mathrm{QAES}})$ where $S = 2^{\frac{|K|+|OP_c|}{3}}$	$O(S \cdot T_O + S \cdot T_{\mathrm{AES}})$ where $S = 2^{\frac{|K|+|OP_c|}{2}}$	Sect. 4.4

message m. For a bit-string $x \in \{0,1\}^*$, we denote by $|x|$ the length of the bit-string. We write 0^n to denote the bit-string of n zeros.

Additionally, we define the function $rot_r(x)$ and $rot_r^{-1}(x)$ which are the results of cyclically rotating the 128-bit value x by r bit positions towards the most significant or least significant bit, respectively. If $x = x[0]||x[1]||\ldots x[127]$, and $y = rot_r(x)$, then $y = x[r]||x[r+1]||\ldots x[127]||x[0]||x[1]||x[r-1]$. Of course, it holds that $rot_r(rot_r^{-1}(x)) = x$ and $rot_r^{-1}(rot_r(x)) = x$.

To state complexities, we use the big-O notation, where we use $O(f(n))$ to hide constant factors and $\tilde{O}(f(n))$ to hide polynomial factors.

2.2   The AKA Protocol and Milenage Algorithms

Cellular protocols base their security on seven secret-key cryptographic functions, referred to as a authentication and key generation algorithm set. Upon session establishment between the home network and the subscriber, these algorithms are used to authenticate the subscriber to the network and derive keys that are in turn used protect subsequent communication. To this end, telecommunication operators assign each subscriber a secret key, the network authentication key, denoted as K. The operator provisions each subscriber's SIM card with their individual network authentication key. To authenticate itself to the network, the subscriber then takes part in a challenge-response protocol, the so-called AKA protocol. The use of the AKA protocol is mandated through standardization bodies—all cellular networks follow this protocol.

The AKA protocol is built around a set of cryptographic functions $f1, \ldots, f5$ and $f1^*, f5^*$, keyed with the network authentication key K. In summary, the protocol follows a challenge-response structure. The subscriber sends the telecommunication operator an authentication request, containing the subscriber's identity. The operator then generates a random challenge $RAND$ and uses one of the provided cryptographic functions to calculate a corresponding response [5]. The operator then sends the challenge $RAND$ to the subscriber's device, which derives the response using the same cryptographic function and sends the derived response to the network. If the derived response and the expected response match, the subscriber has successfully authenticated themselves to the operator. In addition, the cryptographic functions $f1, \ldots, f5^*$ serve to a derive a MAC and additional key material used for encryption and integrity protection of subsequent messages as well as transferred user data. Figure 1 describes the authentication towards the network as implemented in the 4th generation of cellular networks (LTE), using the AKA protocol and the functions $f1, \ldots, f5$.

The exact details of the AKA protocol are not required to understand the present analysis—however, it is important to note that the results of the functions $f1$ and $f2$ are sent in cleartext over the network upon authentication. The AKA protocol itself has been subject to formal security analysis [5,15], proving AKA's security under the assumption that the function $f1, \ldots, f5$ and $f1^*, f5^*$ are pseudorandom. The analysis resulted in improvement suggestions to harden the protocol's privacy guarantees. A more detailed protocol description is given in Appendix B.

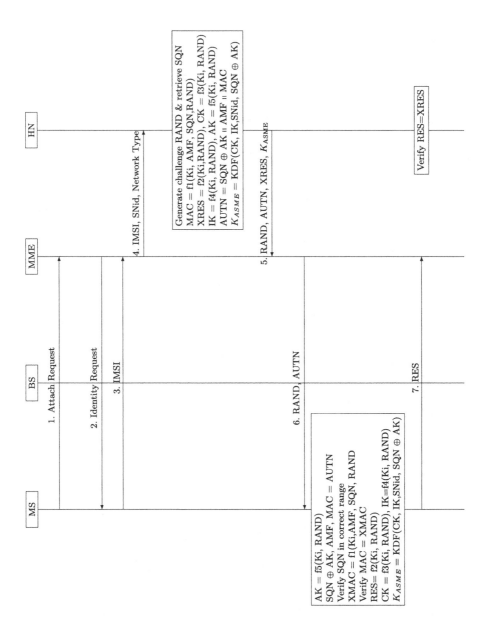

Fig. 1. The Authentication and Key Agreement (AKA) protocol as used in Long-Term Evolution (LTE). The user's device, referred to as Mobile Station (MS), communicates with the Base Station (BS) to authenticate towards the network. The BS forwards the request to the Mobility Management Entity (MME), which in turn forwards it to the Home Network (HN). The home network uses the function $f1, \ldots, f5$ to calculate session information and secret key material and forwards the necessary information back to the Mobility Management Entity (MME).

Note that if an attacker obtains a subscriber's secret key K, the attacker can impersonate the respective subscriber towards the home network. This amounts to a complete account takeover. In addition, an attacker can derive all keys used for encryption and integrity protection and thus eavesdrop on all communication between the subscriber and the home network. Therefore, the security of cellular networks is completely contingent on the security of the cryptographic functions used in the AKA protocol.

The most commonly used set of functions for the AKA protocol is the Milenage authentication and key generation algorithm set. The Milenage algorithm set consists of five basis functions, $h1, \ldots, h5,^1$ whose outputs are mapped to the seven required outputs for the functions $f1, \ldots, f5^*$. Figure 2 describes the Milenage algorithm set, standardized through the 3rd Generation Partnership Project (3GPP) [3]. All five functions take as input the random 128-bit challenge $RAND$, generated by the operator upon registration of the subscriber's device towards the network. The second to fifth basis function, $h2, \ldots, h5$, take this random challenge as an input and output:

$$hi_{K,OP_c}(RAND) = E_K[c_i \oplus rot_{r_i}(OP_c \oplus E_K[RAND \oplus OP_c])] \oplus OP_c,$$

where the function E_K, also referred to as the kernel, is a block cipher with block length of 128-bit.

The first basis function $h1$ takes as an additional input a 128 bit-string $IN1$, that is composed of the concatenation of a sequence number SQN and a fixed authentication management field AMF. The Sequence Number (SQN) acts as sequential counter to prevent replay attacks. The Authentication Management Field (AMF) specifies the type of authentication to be used and is usually fixed [1]. The function $h1$ is then defined as:

$$h1_{K,OP_c}(RAND, IN1) = E_K[TEMP \oplus rot_{r_1}(IN1 \oplus OP_c) \oplus c_1] \oplus OP_c,$$

where $TEMP = E_K[RAND \oplus OP_C]$.

The output of the basis functions is mapped to the seven required outputs $f1, \ldots, f5^*$ as follows. The first 64 bits of the $h1$ output are mapped to represent the output of $f1$, the last 64 bits of $h1$'s output are used as the output of $f1^*$. The output of $h2$ is split in the same vein, to obtain the outputs for $f5$ and $f2$. The basis function $h3, h4, h5$ are used as-is for the output of $f3, f4, f5^*$. To highlight this almost one-to-one relation between the basis functions and their respective AKA counterparts and to support an intuitive understanding of the implications of our attacks, we will simply refer to the basis function $h1, \ldots, h5$ as the functions $f1, \ldots, f5$ for the remainder of this paper. This is also done to emphasize that vulnerabilities in the basis functions translate into immediate insecurities of their respective AKA counterparts.

All functions in the Milenage algorithm use AES as the underlying block cipher E_K. The cipher is keyed with the network authentication key K, a 128-bit-string shared between the operator and the subscriber. The bit-strings $c_1, \ldots, c_5$

---

^{1} The standard denotes the basis functions as $OUT1, \ldots, OUT5$.

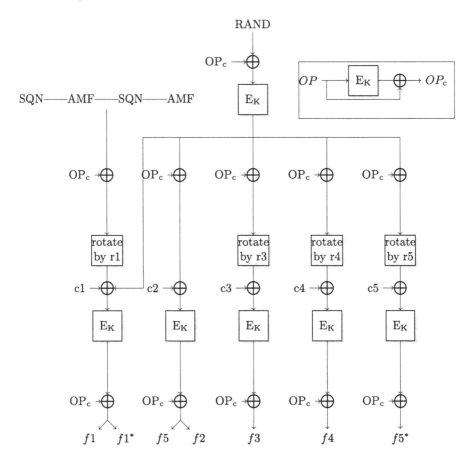

Fig. 2. The Milenage algorithm set as standardized by 3GPP [3]. The outputs of the five Milenage basis functions are mapped almost one-to-one to the seven required outputs.

and $r_1, \ldots, r_5$ are public constants which are defined in the standard. Notably, $r_2 = 0$ and $c_1 = 0$. As additional key material, the OP_c bit-string is derived from a (potentially secret) constant OP, defined by the operator. The operator provides the additional 128-bit string OP, which was intended to provide separation between different operators [3]. The per-subscriber secret OP_c is then derived as $OP_c = E_K[OP] \oplus OP$. Note that the OP-bit string is never used directly in the Milenage algorithm set, only the derived value OP_c. As such, it suffices to store the OP_c bit-string on a subscriber's SIM card, without ever revealing the operator constant OP.

There are no requirements on how the operators generate and manage the OP-bit string. It is conceivable that each operator uses the same OP bit-string for all handed-out SIM cards, but the operator could also rotate the OP for every batch of produced SIM cards. Although the Milenage algorithm set is designed to be secure even if the OP is public, in practice, operators do not reveal the value of OP. Instead of the OP, they store the OP_c bit-string on the SIM card. In the present analysis, we will show attacks for both the case when the OP bit-string is known and when it is secret.

2.3 Classical Cryptanalysis of Milenage algorithms

The Milenage algorithm set was designed to fulfill the following security requirements, as specified in [4]:

1. *Without knowledge of secret keys, the functions f1, f1*, f2, f3, f4, f5 and f5* should be practically indistinguishable from independent random functions of their inputs (RAND——SQN——AMF) and RAND. Examples: Knowledge of the values of one function on a fairly large number of given inputs should not enable its values to be predicted on other inputs [...]*
2. *It should be infeasible to determine any part of the secret key K, or the operator variant configuration field, OP, by manipulation of the inputs and examination of the outputs to the algorithm.*
3. *Events tending to violate criteria 1 and 2 should be regarded as insignificant if they occur with probability approximately 2^{-128} or less (or require approximately 2^{128} operations).*
4. *Events tending to violate criteria 1 and 2 should be examined if they occur with probability approximately 2^{-64} (or require approximately 2^{64} operations) to ensure that they do not have serious consequences. Serious consequences would include recovery of a secret key, or ability to emulate the algorithm on a large number of future inputs.*

So far, no attack violating this criteria has been identified. Simplified versions (not using the constant OP_c) of the Milenage algorithm set have been proven to be pseudorandom under the assumption that the kernel function E_K is a random permutation [4,16]. The proof gives rise to a lower bound of 2^{64} queries for attacks on the Milenage algorithms. This lower bound is tight, i.e., 2^{64} queries suffice to identify collisions between the functions $f1$ and $f2$ or in the function $f1$ itself. Once identified, a collision allows an attacker to perform existential forgery [4]. For a full key recovery however, no attacks that perform better than exhaustive search are known. The brute-force attacks amount to a complexity of $O\left(2^{|K|}\right)$ if the OP bit-string is known, and $O\left(2^{|K|+|OP_c|}\right)$ if OP is unknown.

2.4 Quantum Computation

For a thorough introduction to quantum computing, we refer to the accessible exposition of [32]. Briefly, quantum computation can be described as follows. Quantum computation is usually modelled in the quantum circuit model. A quantum circuit consists of a sequence of quantum gates, acting on logical qubits. A *qubit* is encoded in the state of a system, which is described by a vector in a 2-dimensional Hilbert space. This vector describes a complex linear superposition of two computational basis state vectors $|0\rangle$ and $|1\rangle$, i.e.,

$\alpha_0 |0\rangle + \alpha_1 |1\rangle$, where α_0, α_1 are called the complex amplitudes of the basis states and adhere to the normalization constraint $|\alpha_0|^2 + |\alpha_1|^2 = 1$. An n-qubit state $|\psi\rangle$ is described by the complex linear superposition over all 2^n computational basis states $|\psi\rangle = \sum_{x \in \{0,1\}^n} \alpha_x |x_1, \ldots, x_n\rangle$, where again it must hold that $\sum_x |\alpha_x|^2 = 1$. *Measuring* a state $|\psi\rangle$ will output the label x with probability $|\alpha_x|^2$ and leave the system in state $|x\rangle$. *Quantum gates* that act on n qubits are unitary operators U that transform a quantum state $|\psi\rangle$ into a quantum state $U|\psi\rangle$.

Quantum Oracles and Quantum Complexity. When acting on a function $f : \{0,1\}^n \rightarrow \{0,1\}^n$, quantum computation requires some kind of oracle access to this function. The oracle access is usually given through a unitary operator $\mathcal{O}_f$, that performs the following calculation $\mathcal{O}_f : |x\rangle \otimes |y\rangle \rightarrow |x\rangle |y \oplus f(x)\rangle$, where $x, y \in \{0,1\}^n$ and $|x\rangle, |y\rangle$ are the corresponding quantum states.

There are multiple ways to measure the complexity of quantum algorithms. We will focus here on two fundamental dimensions. The *query* complexity and the *time* complexity. Query complexity measures the number of accesses to the oracle $\mathcal{O}_f$, while *time* complexity is measured by the depth of the respective quantum circuit consisting of elementary gate operators from a universal quantum gate set, cf. [32]. We will use the terms *time* complexity and *depth* of a quantum circuit interchangeably.

We note here that this model abstracts away constraints that arise when actually implementing physical systems for quantum computation. For example, instead of measuring just the depth of the circuit, it has been proposed to include also the number of qubits (the width of the circuit) [20], to account for the fact that ensuring coherence of idle qubits might be costly. Unless otherwise mentioned, our work will focus on the time and query complexity of the described attacks. Accounting for other metrics would require to model the designed circuits in more detail, which we leave as future work.

2.5   Attacker Model

Almost all attacks described in this paper assume access to an encryption oracle which can be queried with arbitrary plaintexts. This follows the security model of a chosen plaintext attack. In quantum cryptanalysis, the attacker's capabilities are additionally determined by the kind of queries that are allowed to this oracle, namely whether only classical or also superposition queries are allowed.

In more detail, let $F = \{f_k : \{0,1\}^n \rightarrow \{0,1\}^n\}_{k \in \{0,1\}^n}$ be a family of functions indexed by k and assume that for any given $k, x \in \{0,1\}^n$, there exists a polynomial-time algorithm to compute $f_k(x)$. Intuitively, each function f_k defines encryption under key k. For a given function f_k sampled from F, the attacker is given oracle access to f_k, denoted by $\mathcal{O}_{f_k}$. Following other quantum cryptanalytic works [22,39], we will consider two quantum adversary models, distinguished by the capabilities of their oracle access.

In the *standard security* model, or Q_1 model, the attacker can only make classical queries to the function f_k. In this case, the oracle $\mathcal{O}_{f_k}$ is a classical function $\mathcal{O}_{f_k} : \{0,1\}^n \mapsto \{0,1\}^n$.

In the *quantum security model*, or Q_2 model, the attacker is allowed to query the oracle in superposition. That is, the attacker can provide as input to the oracle $\mathcal{O}_{f_k}$ a superposition $\sum_{x,y} \lambda_{x,y} |x\rangle |y\rangle$ and the oracle will return the output $\sum_{x,y} \lambda_{x,y} |x\rangle |y \oplus f_k(x)\rangle$. Note that quantum security implies standard security.

We stress that even in the Q_1 model, the attacker can still guess the key k and then construct (and access) a quantum circuit that, given any $k, x \in \{0,1\}^n$, efficiently evaluates $f_k(x)$. This quantum circuit can receive as input any superposition of k and x. We will make use of this *offline* computation later on.

Note that all Milenage functions $f1, \ldots, f5$ can be viewed as a function family F, where generating a random secret key k amounts to sampling a function from the family F. The attacker is given access to an oracle $\mathcal{O}_{f_k}$, which evaluates a function f_k with a fixed key k, where k is not known by the attacker.

3   The Quantum Cryptanalysis Toolbox

In recent years, symmetric cryptography has received increasing scrutiny with respect to resilience against quantum attacks. This quantum cryptanalysis of symmetric cryptography has mostly uncovered new attacks in the Q_2 model, but also yielded more than quadratic speedups (over classical attacks) in the Q_1 model [9,10,24]. Most of the cryptanalytic works present quantum algorithms that equip quantum attackers with powerful attack primitives that can be used as a black box. We follow this approach and present in this section a *quantum toolbox*. I.e., a set of algorithms that facilitate cryptanalytic attacks on symmetric key cryptography. To keep our work accessible to researchers outside of the quantum community, we will hereafter use these algorithms only as a black box.

The quantum cryptanalysis presented in this paper is based on three algorithms. Grover's algorithm to speed up exhaustive search, Simon's algorithm to identify a hidden period, and the offline version of Simon's algorithm, which combines the two former algorithms to speed up attacks in the Q_1 model. In this section, we will briefly describe the intuition of the relevant algorithms, the problems they solve, the requirements for their usage and their respective complexity. For the remainder of this work, we will then use these algorithms as a black box and focus our analysis on classical constructions that will then allow us to employ quantum algorithms in a simple fashion.

3.1   Grover's Algorithm: Fast Unstructured Search

In his seminal work, Grover [17] described an algorithm that achieves a quadratic speedup when performing an unstructured, brute-force search. We state the main result as relevant for this paper as follows, where we ignore small constants in Grover's time and query complexity and also the extremely high success probability for better readability.

Theorem 1 (Grover's Algorithm). *Consider a function $f : \{0,1\}^n \rightarrow \{0,1\}$, such that 2^t inputs map to 1 and the rest maps to 0. Given quantum oracle access to the function f, Grover's algorithm finds a preimage of 1, i.e., a $k \in \{0,1\}^n$ satisfying $f(k) = 1$, in $O\left(\sqrt{2^n/2^t}\right)$ time and oracle queries. If there is exactly one preimage of 1, i.e. only one k such that $f(k) = 1$, then Grover's algorithm finds this k in $O\left(\sqrt{2^n}\right)$ time.*

Intuitively, Grover's algorithm "cooks" a solution k_0, such that $f(k_0) = 1$, by constructing an equal superposition over all inputs in the domain of f and repeating a sub-procedure that increases the amplitude of k_0 while decreasing all other amplitudes. For a detailed explanation, we refer the reader to the standard literature [17,32]. Note that Grover's algorithm requires quantum oracle access to f.

In quantum cryptanalysis, Grover's algorithm is typically used to speed up the exhaustive search (bruteforce) of a key. To this end, an attacker can construct a quantum circuit for a given cipher, e.g., AES. This circuit will take as input a message and a key guess k^* and will return the encryption of the message under the key k^*. To then bruteforce the key for a fixed but unknown key k, the attacker first captures enough plaintext-ciphertext pairs so that the secret key is uniquely determined by those pairs. An attacker can then easily construct a quantum circuit for a function f that, on input of a key guess k^* returns 1 if k^* is equal to the correct k and zero otherwise. The construction works as follows. The quantum circuit encrypts the collected plaintexts under the key guess k^* and compares the resulting ciphertexts with the captured ciphertexts. If they match, f returns 1, otherwise f returns 0. Thus, an attacker can construct a quantum cirucit for f and then leverage Grover's algorithm to find the key k with $2^{|k|/2}$ queries to the quantum circuit implementing f.

The effectiveness of Grover attacks are limited by two factors. First, the search cannot be parallelized [6,14]. Second, by the complexity of the circuit actually implementing the oracle f. For example, Jang et al. [19] present a circuit for AES-128 encryption which results in a circuit depth of roughly 2^{80} gates in an end-to-end key recovery attack using Grover's search. To the best of our knowledge, this is the most efficient quantum circuit for AES presented so far.

3.2   Simon's Algorithm: Quantum Period Finding

Simon's algorithm can identify hidden period in a function f in polynomial time, given quantum oracle access to this function. This powerful primitive has been successfully used in various quantum attacks on symmetric cryptography [9,21,25] and to show *quantum separation*, i.e., the existence of functions that are learnable in the quantum setting, but not in the classical setting (under standard cryptographic assumptions) [34]. Formally, Simon's algorithm solves the following problem:

Definition 1 (Simon's problem). *Let $f : \{0,1\}^n \to \{0,1\}^n$ be a function that is either injective, or there exists a single period $s \neq 0^n$ such that*

$$\forall x \neq x': f(x) = f(x') \iff x' = x \oplus s;$$

determine s.

Given quantum oracle access to f through an oracle $\mathcal{O}_f$, this problem can be solved with $O(n)$ quantum queries to f and $O(n^3)$ time using Simon's algorithm [35]. In summary, Simon's algorithm relies on a quantum subroutine which queries the function f with a superposition query and returns a random value y, s.t. $y \oplus s = 0$ or a random y if f is injective. After $c \cdot n$ invocations of Simon's quantum subroutine (for a small constant $c \geq 1$), we obtain n linear independent vectors $y_1, \ldots, y_n$, such that $y_i \oplus s = 0$. This gives rise to an equation system and allows us to recover s via Gaussian elimination.

Note that for cryptanalytic purposes, where f represents some sort of cryptographic construction, f does not necessarily fulfill the requirement of Simon's problem perfectly. Instead, there might be unwanted collisions in f. Kaplan et al. [21] showed that Simon's algorithm can still recover the period s efficiently, provided that the probability of an unwanted collision is bounded away from 1. They prove the following theorem.

Theorem 2 (Simon's algorithm with approximate promise). *Let $f : \{0,1\}^n \to X$ be a function with period s. Define the probability of an unwanted collision as*

$$\varepsilon(f, s) = \max_{t \in \{0,1\}^n \setminus \{0,s\}} Pr_x[f(x) = f(x \oplus t)].$$

If $\varepsilon(f, s) \leq p_0 < 1$, then with $c \cdot n$ calls of the quantum subroutine, Simon's algorithm returns s with probability at least

$$1 - \left(2 \cdot \left(\frac{1 + p_0}{2} \right)^c \right)^n.$$

Note that the theorem also holds for cases where the codomain of the function is smaller than the domain, i.e., $|X| < 2^n$. It follows from Theorem 2 that as long as $c \geq 3/(1 - p_0)$ the error probability decreases exponentially in n. Thus, given a constant bound on p_0 on the probability of unwanted collision for a function f, we can recover that function's period s with $O(n)$ quantum queries and polynomial time. Throughout this paper, we will make implicit use of a related theorem. For almost all functions with large enough outputs (in terms of bit length), the impact of unwanted collisions on the query cost is negligible, c.f. [8]. This allows us to ignore the issue of unwanted collisions for the remainder of this paper at all, since we will only deal with functions that have large enough outputs.

3.3 Offline Simon's Algorithm: Attacks Without Superposition Queries

In the Q_1 model, superposition queries to an oracle $\mathcal{O}_f$ are not possible. Instead, the attacker can only query $\mathcal{O}_f$ classically. Many quantum cryptanalytic attacks on symmetric ciphers thus are not applicable in the Q_1 setting, since the attacks require superposition queries to the attacked cipher. However, even in the Q_1 setting, quantum computers can speed up attacks. Indeed, Bonnetain et al. [9] introduced a new algorithm, called the "Offline Simon's Algorithm", which leverages structural properties of cryptographic schemes to execute quantum attacks which are ways faster than their known classical counterparts [9,10]. The "Offline Simon's Algorithm" can be divided into two phases. An online phase, in which the attacker makes classical queries to the oracle. The results of the classical queries are then used to assemble a database of function inputs/outputs in superposition. Once this database is established, an offline phase follows. In the offline phase the attacker uses the database to run a quantum search and period finding algorithms. The key idea of the offline Simon's algorithm is that the database can be reused throughout the whole offline phase, without any further additional oracle queries. Reusing the database leads can be exploited to reduce query complexity, speedup existing algorithms, or reduce memory requirements. [9].

In more detail, the offline Simon's algorithm is applicable in the following situation. Consider a function $g : \{0,1\}^n \to \{0,1\}^l$ to which an attacker has only classical oracle access and a family of functions $F = \{f_i : \{0,1\}^n \to \{0,1\}^l, i \in \{0,1\}^m\}$. Assume that given any $(i,x) \in \{0,1\}^m \times \{0,1\}^n$, there exists a polynomial-time quantum circuit to compute $F(i,x) = f_i(x)$. For example, g might be an encryption oracle for an encryption under a fixed (and unknown) key k with a cipher E, while the function $F(i,x)$ is an encryption through the cipher E under a key i that is provided as input to the circuit. Further assume that there exists an $i_0 \in \{0,1\}^m$ such that $f_{i_0} \oplus g$ has a hidden period, i.e., $f_{i_0}(x) \oplus g(x) = f_{i_0}(x \oplus s) \oplus g(x \oplus s)$ for some $s \in \{0,1\}^n$.

The following result due to Bonnetain et al. [9] shows that in this setting, the strategy described above can be used to achieve a substantial speed up over classical algorithms when searching for the value i_0 and the period s.

Theorem 3 (Asymmetric Search of a Period). *Let $F = \{f_i : \{0,1\}^n \to \{0,1\}^l, i \in \{0,1\}^m\}$ be a family of functions, define $F(i,\cdot) = f_i(\cdot)$ and let g be a function $g : \{0,1\}^n \to \{0,1\}^l$. Assume that we are given quantum oracle access to F. Further, assume that there exists exactly one $i_0 \in \{0,1\}^m$ such that $f_{i_0} \oplus g$ has a hidden period, i.e., for all $x \in \{0,1\}^n$ it holds that $f_{i_0}(x) \oplus g(x) = f_{i_0}(x \oplus s) \oplus g(x \oplus s)$ for some s. Moreover, let the probability of unwanted collisions for all $f_i \oplus g$ be bounded from above by $1/2$, i.e.,*

$$\max_{\substack{i \in \{0,1\}^m \setminus \{i_0\} \\ t \in \{0,1\}^n \setminus \{0^n\}}} Pr_x[f_i(x) \oplus g(x) = f_i(x \oplus t) \oplus g(x)] \leq \frac{1}{2}.$$

Then, offline Simon's algorithm can identify i_0 with the following complexities:

1. *If we are given classical oracle access to g, then we can identify i_0 with extremely high success probability using $O(2^n)$ classical queries to g and additional computations with a time complexity of $O((n^3 + nT_F) \cdot 2^{m/2})$, where T_F is the time required to evaluate F once.*
2. *If we are given quantum oracle access to g, then we can identify i_0 with extremely high success probability, using $O(n)$ quantum queries to g and additional computations with time complexity $O((n^3 + nT_F) \cdot 2^{m/2})$.*

The offline version of Simon's algorithm leverages Grover's algorithm to search for the i_0 such that $f_{i_0} \oplus g$ has a period, and uses Simon's algorithm as a sub-procedure in that search to verify that a given guess i^* indeed results in a period for the function $f_{i^*} \oplus g$.

In the case where only classical access to g is provided, Bonnetain et al. [9] first build up a database of all $O(2^n)$ input-outputs pairs of g to obtain a superposition

$$|\phi_g\rangle = \bigotimes^{c \cdot n} \left(\sum_{x \in \{0,1\}^n} |x\rangle |g(x)\rangle \right),$$

where $\bigotimes$ is the usual tensor product, cf. [32]. This database can then be used to run the above-mentioned combination of Grover and Simon without any additional classical or quantum queries to g. In the case where quantum access to g is provided, this database can be built faster by querying g in superposition directly. Note that once that i_0 such that $f_{i_0} \oplus g$ has a period s is identified, we can recover the actual period s in polynomial time using Simon's algorithm—again reusing the g-database $|\phi_g\rangle$.

Throughout this paper, we will make use of the fact that the offline Simon's algorithm is also applicable in a more generalized setting, where the attacker combines the function g with a quantum circuit through means other than xoring the results [8,9].

Theorem 4 (Generalized Offline Simon's Algorithm). *Consider a family of functions $F_i : \{0,1\}^n \times \{0,1\}^l \rightarrow \{0,1\}^l$, indexed by $i \in \{0,1\}^m$. Let g be a function $g : \{0,1\}^n \rightarrow \{0,1\}^l$ to which the attacker has classical or quantum oracle access and $p_i : \{0,1\}^n \rightarrow \{0,1\}^n$ be a permutation. Assume that for the index value i_0, the function $F_{i_0}(x, g(p_{i_0}(x)))$ has some period s. The Offline Simon's algorithm can identify i_0 with extremely high success probability, with the following complexities:*

1. *If we are given classical oracle access to g, then we can identify i_0 using $O(2^n)$ classical queries to g and additional computations with time complexity $O((n^3 + nT_F) \cdot 2^{m/2})$, where T_F is the time required to evaluate F once.*
2. *If we are given quantum oracle access to g, then we can identify i_0 using $O(n)$ quantum queries to g and additional computations with time complexity $O((n^3 + nT_F) \cdot 2^{m/2})$.*

In the same vein as Simon's algorithm, the offline Simon's algorithm can deal with unwanted collisions; again, for functions with large enough output the impact of unwanted collisions can be neglected [8].

4 Quantum Cryptanalysis of the Milenage Algorithms

The main idea of this paper is to leverage the above described quantum toolbox to perform a quantum cryptanalysis of the Milenage algorithm set. To this end, we extend existing attacks on symmetric ciphers to perform forgery attacks or recover the secret key K and the bit-string OP_c.

To describe the complexities of the presented attacks, we will consider three parameters:

- the length of the secret key K,
- the length of the OP_c bit-string, and
- the block length of the underlying block-cipher E_K, which we denote by $|M|$.

Note that for the current Milenage configuration it holds that $|K| = 128, |OP_c| = 128$ and $|M| = 128$. Quantum security considerations for 5G have proposed to increase the key-size $|K|$ to 256 bits [27,38]. With this we can summarize our four different attacks as follows.

1. For reasons of (exposition) completeness, we include the trivial Grover attack that results in a quadratic reduction of the query complexity of exhaustive key search.
2. A quantum slide attack against the $f2$ function, which reduces the complexity of recovering the secret key material in case the OP bit-string is not known. If quantum superposition access to $f2$ is granted, the attacker can acquire the OP_c and the key K with only $O(|M|)$ superposition queries and $\tilde{O}\left(2^{|K|/2} \cdot \mathrm{T_{QAES}}\right)$ time. If the attacker is given only classical access to $f2$, then we require $O(2^{|M|})$ online classical queries, and the attack has a time complexity of $\tilde{O}\left(2^{|M|} \cdot \mathrm{T}_O + \mathrm{T_{QAES}} \cdot 2^{\frac{|K|}{2}}\right)$. To the best of our knowledge, recovering the network authentication key K as well as the OP_c bit-string via a classical slide attack requires $O\left(2^{\frac{M}{2}}\right)$ oracle quries and $O\left(2^{|K|+\frac{|M|}{2}}\right)$ operations.
3. A quantum polynomial time existential forgery attack on the MAC function $f1$, assuming quantum superposition access to $f1$. Classical attacks that achieve existential forgery on the $f1$ cipher require $O(2^{|M|/2})$ operations and queries.
4. A quantum related key attack against Milenage, which can recover the secret key in polynomial time in the Q_2 model, and in $\tilde{O}\left(2^{(|K|+|OP_c|)/3}\right)$ time and queries in the Q_1 model.

4.1 The Grover Key Recovery for $f1, \ldots, f5$

We first describe the most obvious attack on the Milenage algorithms, that gives an upper bound on the complexity of quantum attacks. Note that the Milenage algorithms only rely on AES encryption and the xor operation—both of these operations can be fully simulated by a quantum computer [40]. We can thus use Grover to execute the following attack:

1. Using classical oracle access to one of the functions $f1, \ldots, f5$, obtain enough function input/outputs pairs $(c_1, m_1), \ldots, (c_r, m_r)$ to uniquely determine the network authentication key K and—if required—the bitstring OP_c.
2. Given these plaintext/ciphertext pairs, we can construct a quantum circuit for the following function f: on input of a key guess K^*, OP_C^*, return 1 if $K^* = K$ and $OP_c^* = OP_c$ and zero otherwise. This circuit can be constructed as described in Sect. 3.1.
3. By this quantum circuit, we now have quantum oracle access to the function f. This allows us to apply Grover's algorithm to search for the key K and the bit-string OP_c.

With Theorem 1, the attack can recover the key with a circuit of depth $O\left(2^{|K|/2} \cdot \mathrm{T_{QAES}}\right)$ or $O\left(2^{\frac{|K|+|OP_c|}{2}} \cdot \mathrm{T_{QAES}}\right)$ if the bit-string OP_c is not known.

4.2   Quantum Slide Attacks Against f_2

Bonnetain et al. [9] describe that the offline Simon algorithm can be used to execute a quantum slide attack against a 2-round self-similar cipher. A self-similar cipher builds upon a block cipher E to encrypt a message m, using two keys k_1, k_2 in the following way:

$$iFX(m) = E_{k_2}[E_{k_2}[m \oplus k_1] \oplus k_1] \oplus k_1.$$

The attack described by Bonnetain et al. [9] yields a speedup compared to classical attacks. This *quantum slide attack* can be adapted to work on the $f2$ function as well.

To this end, we first show how the $f2$ function can be transformed into a 2-round self-similar cipher and then describe how the attack described by Bonnetain et al. [9] can be applied to our construction. This leads to an attack that reduces the additional security provided by the OP_c bit-string, a value which is unknown in practice.

In more detail, recall that function f_2 is defined as

$$f2(m) = E_K[rot_{r_2}(E_K[m \oplus OP_C] \oplus OP_C) \oplus c_2] \oplus OP_c.$$

Now, the standard defines r_2 as $r_2 = 0$, which simplifies $f2$ to

$$f2(m) = E_K[E_K[m \oplus OP_C] \oplus OP_C \oplus c_2] \oplus OP_c.$$

To transform $f2$ into a self-similar cipher, we define the function f_2', which for each input m instead queries f_2 for $m \oplus c_2$ and then xors the result with c_2. I.e.,

$$f2'(m) \stackrel{\text{def}}{=} f2(m \oplus c_2) \oplus c_2$$
$$= E_K[E_K[m \oplus c_2 \oplus OP_C] \oplus OP_C \oplus c_2] \oplus OP_c \oplus c_2.$$

Note that c_2 is public. As a result, if the attacker has (quantum) oracle access to $f2$, the attacker can easily construct a quantum circuit to also have (quantum) oracle access $f2'$. Clearly, $f2'$ follows the description of a self-similar cipher, as visualized in Fig. 3.

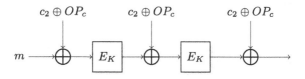

Fig. 3. The $f2'$ function, which now resembles an iterated FX cipher.

This enables us to execute the attack presented in [9], which we now describe in the following. Define the functions p_i, F_i, g as follows:

$$F_i((b,x),y) \overset{\text{def}}{=} \begin{cases} y \oplus x & \text{if } b = 0 \\ E_i(y) \oplus x & \text{if } b = 1 \end{cases} \qquad p_i((b,x)) \overset{\text{def}}{=} \begin{cases} E_i(x) & \text{if } b = 0 \\ x & \text{if } b = 1 \end{cases}$$

$$g(x) \overset{\text{def}}{=} f2'(x).$$

We combine now the above functions into a function F_i^*, indexed by i, which will have the desired hidden period,

$$F_i^*(b,x) \overset{\text{def}}{=} F_i((b,x), g(p_i(b,x))).$$

Note that for a given i, an attacker can easily construct an efficient quantum circuit for $F_i((b,x),y)$ and $F_i^*(b,x)$.

The function $F_k^*(b,x) = F_k((b,x), g(p_k(b,x)))$ has a hidden period $(1, OP_c \oplus c_2)$, as shown in Appendix C. This is sufficient to apply the offline Simon's algorithm. Armed with Theorem 4 and the above definitions, we arrive at the following complexities.

- In the Q_2 setting, the attack requires $O(|M|)$ superposition queries to $f2$ and $\tilde{O}\left((|M| \cdot \mathsf{T}_{\text{QAES}}) \cdot 2^{|K|/2}\right)$ time.
- In the Q_1 setting, the attack requires more time and queries to prepare the database of g's input-output pairs. To this end, the attacker needs to query $f2'(x)$ for all possible $2^{|M|}$ inputs. Once the database is prepared, the attacker can recover the key K as well as the OP_c bit-string via the offline Simon's algorithm. As such, the attack requires $O(2^{|M|})$ online classical queries, and has an *additional* time complexity of $\tilde{O}\left(|M| \cdot \mathsf{T}_{\text{QAES}}) \cdot 2^{\frac{|K|}{2}}\right)$. For the current Milenage configuration, this results in $c \cdot 2^{128}$ superposition queries and altogether $c \cdot (2^{128} \cdot \mathsf{T}_O + \mathsf{T}_{\text{QAES}} \cdot 2^{64})$ operations for a small constant c. Note that

while this is no improvement over the trivial Grover attack if $|K| = 128$, the advantage of the quantum slide attack shows when increasing the AES key length to 256 bit. Then, the quantum slide attack requires $c \cdot (2^{128} + 2^{128} \cdot T_{QAES})$ operations, while the Grover attack requires $c \cdot (2^{384/2}) \cdot T_{QAES} = c \cdot 2^{192} \cdot T_{QAES}$ operations, for a small constant c.

To the best of our knowledge, the best classical attack against the $f2$ construction—when both the OP bit-string as well the network authentication key K are unknown—is a slide attack as well. The attacker guesses a key $i \in \mathcal{K}$ and tries to find a collision in the function $F_i^*(b, x)$ to recover the period $(1, OP_c \oplus c_2)$. The attack requires $O\left(2^{\frac{M}{2}}\right)$ classical queries to the encryption oracle and approximately $O\left(2^{|K| + \frac{|M|}{2}}\right)$ time.

Therefore, the presented quantum slide attack reduces the additional security provided by the OP_c bit-string significantly.

4.3   Existential Forgery of $f1$

Our third attack is based on the seminal work of Kaplan et al. [21], who describe a polynomial time existential forgery attack against a CBC-MAC construction in the Q_2 model. As a result, if superposition queries against the CBC-MAC oracle are allowed, CBC-MACs must be considered insecure. The attack can be extended to an attack that allows for polynomial time existential forgery against the $f1$ function from the Milenage algorithm set. In the following, we provide the details of our novel quantum attack.

In summary, the attack assumes superposition access to an oracle $\mathcal{O}_{f1_{K,OP_C}}(x, y) = f1_{K,OP_c}(x, y)$, invoking the function $f1$ on input (x, y) with a fixed network authentication key K and fixed value OP_c. Given this access, the attacker can efficiently construct $q + 1$ outputs of the function $f1_{K,OP_c}$ after issuing a total of q quantum and classical queries to the function $f1_{K,OP_c}$.

Before we provide the details of the attack, recall that the function $f1$ is defined as

$$f1_{K,OP_c}(RAND, IN1)$$
$$\stackrel{\text{def}}{=} E_K[E_K[RAND \oplus OP_C] \oplus rot_{r_1}(IN1 \oplus OP_c) \oplus c_1] \oplus OP_c.$$

Also, for the sake of brevity, we will set $x = RAND$, and $y = IN1$, where $x, y \in \{0, 1\}^{|M|}$. Then, the function $f1$ can be a bit "shortened" to

$$f1_{K,OP_c}(x, y) = E_K[E_K[x \oplus OP_C] \oplus rot_{r_1}(y \oplus OP_c) \oplus c_1] \oplus OP_c.$$

To now perform an existential forgery attack, pick two arbitrary bit-strings $\alpha_0, \alpha_1 \in \{0, 1\}^{|M|}$ with $\alpha_0 \neq \alpha_1$. We then define the following function $f' : \{0, 1\} \times \{0, 1\}^{|M|} \to \{0, 1\}^{|M|}$ by

$$f'(b, y)$$
$$\stackrel{\text{def}}{=} f1_{K,OP_c}(\alpha_b, y)$$
$$= E_K[E_K[\alpha_b \oplus OP_C] \oplus rot_{r_1}(y) \oplus rot_{r1}(OP_c) \oplus c_1] \oplus OP_c.$$

Clearly, if an attacker has access to a quantum oracle for $f1_{K,OP_C}$, the attacker can construct an efficient quantum circuit for f' as well. As shown in Appendix D, the function f' has the hidden period $(1, rot_{r1}^{-1}(\alpha_0^* \oplus \alpha_1^*))$, where $\alpha_b^* = E_k[\alpha_b \oplus OP_c]$. This hidden period can be recovered in polynomial time using Simon's algorithm. Once an attacker obtained the period $(1, rot_{r_1}^{-1}(\alpha_0^* \oplus \alpha_1^*))$, the attacker can easily perform an existential forgery. Assume the attacker knows the value $t = f1_{K,OP_c}(\alpha_0, x)$, where $x \in \{0,1\}^{|M|}$. Then he also knows the output of the function call $f1_{K,OP_c}(\alpha_1, x \oplus rot_r^{-1}(\alpha_0^* \oplus \alpha_1^*)) = f1_{K,OP_c}(\alpha_0, x) = t$. Since the $f1$ function is intended to be used as a MAC, this amounts to an existential forgery attack.

The attacks proceeds then as follows.

1. Recover the hidden period $(1, rot_{r1}^{-1}(\alpha_0^* \oplus \alpha_1^*))$ using Simon's algorithm. Let q' denote the number of quantum queries made through running Simon's algorithm.
2. Repeat the following steps $q' + 1$ times:
   (a) Pick an arbitrary bit-string $y \in \{0,1\}^{|M|}$.
   (b) Query the function $f1_{K,OP_c}$ on input (α_0, y) to obtain $t = f1_{K,OP_c}(\alpha_0, y)$.
   (c) The same value t is also a value output/MAC tag for the input $(\alpha_1, y \oplus rot_r^{-1}(\alpha_0^* \oplus \alpha_1^*))$

This will produce a total of $2q' + 2$ tags after issuing only $2q' + 1$ queries. Overall the attack has a query complexity of $O(|M|)$ quantum queries to $f1_{K,OP_c}$ and $O(|M|^3)$ classical computation time. For the Milenage key lengths, this translates to $c \cdot 128$ quantum queries for a small constant c and a negligible amount of computation.

Resistance against classical existential forgery attacks is a design goal of the $f1$ function [4] – our *quantum existential forgery* attack demonstrates that this resistance does not transfer to the quantum security setting.

4.4   Quantum Related Key Attacks Against $f1, \ldots, f5$

Related key attacks, as introduced by Biham [7], consider attackers that can request encryption under multiple related keys. The exact values of the keys are unknown, but the way in which the keys are related is known to the attacker. The attacks can be modelled through a related key oracle, which provides the attacker access to encryption of a chosen-plaintext under related keys. Related key attacks are of interest because they have practical implications, for example when conducting fault-injection attacks. Recent works have shown that related key attacks on block ciphers can be sped up through quantum computers, both in the Q_2 as well as the Q_1 model. In the Q_2 model, with quantum superposition queries to the related key oracle, related key attacks can break any block cipher in polynomial time [33]. Using the offline Simon algorithm, the attack from [33] can be adapted to yield a super-quadratic speedup in the Q_1 model as well. Both attacks assume the following attacker model. For a given block-cipher E with a fixed secret K, the attacker has access to a related key oracle $\mathcal{O}_{E,K}$ defined as follows. The oracle $\mathcal{O}_{E_K}$ takes as input a bitmask L and a bit string x and outputs $E_{K \oplus L}(x)$.

Considering this attacker model, classical related key attacks on an ideal block cipher require at least $2^{n/2}$ operations, where n is the key length and the bound is tight, cf. [37].

In this section, we will describe the attacks in detail and show how to apply these attacks to the Milenage algorithm set, yielding a polynomial time attack in the Q_2 model, and a super-quadratic speedup over classical attacks in the Q_1 model. The described attacks can be mounted on all Milenage functions $f1, \ldots, f5$, regardless of whether the OP bit string is known or unknown. To focus on an intuitive understanding, we will assume that the OP bitstring is public and thus the functions $f1, \ldots, f5$ take only the network authentication K as key material. The analysis for the case when OP is unknown follows in an analogue fashion.

In the following, we denote by f the Milenage function under attack. Then, for a given function f_K, we assume that the attacker has access to an $\mathcal{O}_{f_K}$ that takes as input a bitmask $L \in \{0,1\}^n$ and a bit string $x \in \{0,1\}^n$ and outputs $f_{K \oplus L}(x)$, i.e., $\mathcal{O}_{f_k}(L, x) = f_{K \oplus L}(x)$. In the Q_2 model, the attacker has superposition access to this oracle, while in the Q_1 model, the attacker only has classical access.

Quantum Related Key Attacks with Superposition Access. The quantum related key attacks described by Roetteler and Steinwandt [33] can be transferred in a one-to-one fashion to attack the Milenage algorithm set in the attacker model described above. Their attack works as follows.

Let $c = (c_1, \ldots, c_l)$ and $m = (m_1, \ldots, m_l)$ be a set of output-inputs pairs $c = (f_K(m_1), \ldots, f_K(m_l))$ such that (c, m) uniquely determines K. Assume an attacker has superposition access to a related key oracle for

$$\mathcal{O}_{f_K}(s, m) = f_{K \oplus s}(m) = (f_{K \oplus s}(m_1), \ldots, f_{K \oplus s}(m_l)).$$

Then, define the following mapping

$$f'(s) \stackrel{\text{def}}{=} \{f_{K \oplus s}(m), f_s(m)\}.$$

Given quantum access to a related key oracle oracle $\mathcal{O}_{f_K}(s, m)$ for f_K, one can construct an efficient quantum circuit for f'. To be efficiently encodable, f' outputs can be encoded as integers [33].

The mapping f' is two-to-one with period K, as shown below. Using Simon's algorithm, we can recover this period efficiently with only a linear number of queries to the related key oracle.

To see why f' is 2-to-1 with period K, let s, s' be two different bit-strings such that $f'(s) = f'(s')$ and assume $K \neq 0^n$. We consider two cases.

1. Assume $f_s(m) = f_{s'}(m)$. As we choose the plaintexts $m = (m_1, \ldots, m_l)$ so that they uniquely determine the key, this would imply $s = s'$, which contradicts our assumption.
2. Now let $f_s(m) \neq f_{s'}(m)$. Thus, if $f'(s) = f'(s')$, then $f_{K \oplus s}(m) = f_{s'}(m)$. The choice of plaintexts implies $K \oplus s = s'$.

Quantum Related Key Attacks Without Superposition Access. In the Q_1 setting, the attacker only has classical access to the related key oracle $\mathcal{O}_{f_K}(s, m)$. However, leveraging the offline Simon's algorithm, the attacker can still achieve a super-quadratic speedup over classical attacks [9]. We now show how to apply the offline Simon related key attack as stated by Bonnetain et al. [9] to the Milenage algorithm set.

Intuitively, the attack works by dividing the key k and the bitmask l into two parts, i.e., $k = k_1||k_2$, $l = l_1||l_2$ where $l_1, k_1 \in \{0,1\}^{|M|/3}$. We then query the oracle $\mathcal{O}_{f_K}$ for each possible l_1 and construct a quantum circuit F so that $F_{k_2}(l) \oplus g(l)$ has period k_1, where g is a function derived from the related key oracle. This allows us to employ the offline Simon algorithm.

Let $l = l_1||l_2$, where $l_1 \in \{0,1\}^{|M|/3}$, $l_2 \in \{0,1\}^{|M| \cdot 2/3}$ and define the following function $g : \{0,1\}^{|M|/3} \to \{0,1\}^{l \cdot |M|}$ by

$$g(l_1) \stackrel{\text{def}}{=} \mathcal{O}(l_1||0^{n\frac{2}{3}}) = f_{(k_1||k_2) \oplus (l_1||0^{2/3 \cdot |M|})}(m).$$

Moreover let F be a family of functions indexed by h so that

$$F_h(j) = f_{j||h}(m).$$

Clearly F can be efficiently represented as a quantum circuit, while querying g requires oracle access. The function $F_{k_2}(l) \oplus g(l)$ has period k_1. Thus, we have a family of functions F such that there exists a k_2 so that $f_{k_2} \oplus g$ has a hidden period. This suffices to apply the offline Simon's algorithm to recover the key part k_2. Once we obtain the k_2, we can efficiently recover k_1 as well.

Applying now Theorem 3, the attack requires $O(2^{|K|/3})$ classical queries to the related key oracle and a has a time complexity of $\tilde{O}\left(2^{\frac{|K|}{3}} \cdot T_{\text{QAES}}\right)$. If the OP bit-string is known, this translates to approximately 2^{43} oracle queries and encryption operations. If the OP bit-string is not known, then the attack requires approximately $2^{85.3}$ oracle queries and encryption operations.

To see why the function $F_{k_2}(l) \oplus g(l)$ has period k_1 note that

$$
\begin{aligned}
F_{k_2}(l \oplus k_1) \oplus g(l \oplus k_1) &= f_{l \oplus k_1||k_2}(m) \oplus f_{(k_1 \oplus l \oplus k_1)||k_2}(m) \\
&= f_{l \oplus k_1||k_2}(m) \oplus f_{l||k_2}(m) \\
&= g(l) \oplus F_{k_2}(l).
\end{aligned}
$$

5   Discussion

The presented attacks expose a structural weakness in the Milenage algorithm set, namely that it exhibits a structure that makes it susceptible to quantum period finding attacks. The attacks *do not* imply the Milenage is broken once general quantum computer come into existence, since the required superposition oracle is not given to the attacker in Milenage's typical use-cases.

However, they do show that Milenage cannot be considered secure in the quantum security (Q_2) setting. This result has merit in and of itself, as an absence of Q_2 attacks would have implied an absence of Q_1 attacks as well. Further research is thus required to assess whether the vulnerability in the Q_2 model transfers to further attacks in the Q_1 model or security proofs for Milenage can be established. For other ciphers, Q_2 attacks have already been elevated to the Q_1 model [10]. In addition, the Q_1 attacks we presented already improve on best-known classical attacks, as well as the trivial Grover, "quantum bruteforce" attack (depending on Milenage's configuration). On the other hand, other works have managed to established security proofs for FX-constructions in the Q_1 model [18].

The 3GPP has also standardized an alternative instantiation of the secret key functions $f1, \ldots, f5$, the TUAK algorithm set [2]. The TUAK algorithm set is based on the Keccak-f-permutation, which so far withstood quantum cryptanalysis and seemingly does not exhibit the structural properties that enabled the presented attacks. We thus conjecture it be secure against the "quantum period finding" attacks presented in this paper. In addition, the TUAK algorithm set was found to provide sufficient performance to be executed on a SIM card [26], and thus poses a (great) alternative to the Milenage algorithm set.

6   Conclusion

Given that experts increasingly view large-scale quantum computers as likely [30] and faced with the slow nature of standardization bodies, quantum security considerations for cellular networks and infrastructure need to start now.

Bringing together research results from recent quantum cryptanalytic works and synthesizing their results into a quantum toolbox, we took a step in this direction. We present various novel attacks against the Milenage algorithm set. Against the strongest (but purely theoretical) quantum adversary, Milenage must be considered insecure. We see the following research directions as necessary to ensure the security of telecommunication networks against quantum adversaries.

1. Symmetric cryptography that is used in telecommunication networks needs to be subject to scrutiny, investigating the resilience against quantum-enabled attacks. With the synthesized quantum toolbox, we hope to make this work accessible to non-quantum experts in the research community as well. This scrutiny should also encompass the investigation whether the results of our attacks can be improved or proofs of security can be established.
2. It is necessary to clarify what security guarantees suffice and what kind of quantum adversary models can be ignored in quantum security considerations for cellular networks. The answer to this question can then guide the choice for appropriate cryptographic algorithms.

Standardizing an algorithm which later turns out to be vulnerable to quantum adversaries would be a disaster in a post-quantum world and should be prevented under any circumstances. To this end, this work should serve as a starting point to spark further investigations into the above-mentioned questions now, to ensure a smooth transition into quantum-resistant telecommunication networks in the future.

Acknowledgements. The work described in this paper has been supported by the Einstein Research Unit "Perspectives of a quantum digital transformation: Near-term quantum computational devices and quantum processors" of the Berlin University Alliance. The authors acknowledge the financial support by the Federal Ministry of Education and Research of Germany in the programme of "Souverän. Digital. Vernetzt." Joint project 6G-RIC, project identification number: 16KISK030. We would like to thank Ryan Sweke and Xavier Bonnetain for their valuable input which greatly improved the paper. We would like to thank Shinjo Park for his valuable input on cellular network protocols.

A   List of Abbreviations

3GPP   Third Generation Partnership Project
AK   Anomity Key
AKA   Authentication and Key Agreement
AMF   Authentication Management Field
SQN   Sequence Number
MAC   Message Authentication Code
HN   Home Network
MME   Mobility Management Entity
BS   Base Station
MS   Mobile Station
LTE   Long-Term Evolution
EAP   Extensible Authentication Protocol
3GPP   3rd Generation Partnership Project

B   The AKA Protocol

The Milenage algorithm set's main usage is the AKA protocol, used for authentication and session establishment in cellular networks as well as other cellular related applications, e.g., as a variant of the Extensible Authentication Protocol (EAP), the EAP-AKA.

In summary, the LTE-AKA protocol is a challenge-response protocol that allows the subscriber to authenticate themselves to the network. The AKA protocol also derives a session key K_{ASME} that is used for encryption and integrity protection of communication at later points. The functions $f1, \ldots, f4$ from the Milenage algorithm set serve to derive a MAC, an expected response to a challenge, and the confidentiality and integrity keys (commonly denoted as CK and IK), which are in turn used to derive session keys. The function $f5$ is used to derive an Anomity Key (AK). The AK serves to mask the SQN, where the purpose of the SQN itself is to prevent replay attacks.

The authentication procedure in the fifth generation (5G) of cellular networks add various security and privacy enhancements to the LTE-AKA protocol, but uses the functions $f1, \ldots, f5$ in the same way. Given that the functions provide authentication and serve as a basis for later encryption and integrity protection, the security of cellular networks is completely contigent on the security of the functions $f1, \ldots, f5$.

C   Proof of the Hidden Period Required for the Quantum Slide Attack

To see why $F_k^*(b, x) = F_k((b, x), g(p_k(b, x)))$ indeed has the hidden period $(1, OP_c \oplus c_2)$, first observe that

$$f2'(E_K(x \oplus OP_c^*)) \oplus (x \oplus OP_c^*) = E_K(f2'(x)) \oplus x, \tag{1}$$

where we write $OP_c^* = OP_c \oplus c_2$ for the sake of brevity. To see why Eq. 1 holds, note that:

$$
\begin{aligned}
&f2'(E_K[x \oplus OP_c^*]) \oplus (x \oplus OP_c^*) \\
&= E_K[E_K[E_K[x \oplus OP_c^*] \oplus OP_c^*] \oplus OP_c^*] \oplus OP_c^* \oplus (x \oplus OP_c^*) \\
&= E_K[E_K[E_K[x \oplus OP_c^*] \oplus OP_c^*] \oplus OP_c^*] \oplus x
\end{aligned}
$$

and

$$
\begin{aligned}
&E_K(f2'(x)) \oplus x \\
&= E_K[E_K[E_K[x \oplus OP_c^*] \oplus OP_c^*] \oplus OP_c^*] \oplus x \\
&= f2'(E_K[x \oplus OP_c^*]) \oplus (x \oplus OP_c^*).
\end{aligned}
$$

Thus, it follows that $F_k^*(1, x) = F_k^*(0, x \oplus OP_c \oplus c_2)$ because

$$
\begin{aligned}
F_k^*(1, x) &= F_k((1, x), g(p_k(1, x))) \\
&= F_k((1, x), g(x)) \\
&= F_k((1, x), f_2'((x))) \\
&= E_k(f_2'(x)) \oplus x
\end{aligned}
$$

and

$$
\begin{aligned}
&F_k^*(0, x \oplus OP_c \oplus c_2) \\
&= F_k((0, x \oplus OP_c^*), g(p_k(0, x \oplus OP_c^*))) \\
&= F_k((0, x \oplus OP_c^*), g(E_k(x \oplus OP_c^*))) \\
&= f2'(E_k(x \oplus OP_c^*)) \oplus x \oplus OP_c^* \\
&= E_k(f2'(x)) \oplus x,
\end{aligned}
$$

where the last step follows from Eq. 1.

D   Proof of the Hidden Period Required for the Existential Forgery Attack

It remains to be shown that f' as defined in Sect. 4.3 indeed has the hidden period $(1, rot_{r1}^{-1}(\alpha_0^* \oplus \alpha_1^*))$. To this end, we need to show that

$$f'(0, y) = f'(1, y \oplus rot_{r1}^{-1}(E_k[\alpha_0 \oplus OP_c] \oplus E_k[\alpha_1 \oplus OP_c])).$$

First, observe that by linearity of rotation it holds that

$$f1_{K,OP_c}(x,y)$$
$$= E_K[E_K[x \oplus OP_C] \oplus rot_{r_1}(y \oplus OP_c) \oplus c_1] \oplus OP_c$$
$$= E_K[E_K[x \oplus OP_C] \oplus rot_{r_1}(y) \oplus rot_{r_1}(OP_c) \oplus c_1] \oplus OP_c.$$

Thus, we have

$$f'(0,y) = E_K[\alpha_0^* \oplus rot_{r1}(y) \oplus rot_{r1}(OP_c) \oplus c_1] \oplus OP_c,$$

and

$$f'(1, y \oplus rot_r^{-1}(\alpha_0^* \oplus \alpha_1^*))$$
$$= E_K[\alpha_1^* \oplus rot_{r_1}(y \oplus rot_{r_1}^{-1}(\alpha_0^* \oplus \alpha_1^*)) \oplus rot_{r_1}(OP_c) \oplus c_1] \oplus$$
$$OP_c$$
$$= E_K[\alpha_1^* \oplus rot_{r_1}(y) \oplus rot_{r_1}(rot_{r_1}^{-1}(\alpha_0^* \oplus \alpha_1^*)) \oplus$$
$$rot_{r_1}(OP_c) \oplus c_1] \oplus OP_c.$$

Now, using $rot_{r_1}(rot_{r_1}^{-1}(x)) = x$ we can continue as

$$= E_K[\alpha_1^* \oplus rot_{r_1}(y) \oplus \alpha_0^* \oplus \alpha_1^* \oplus rot_{r_1}(OP_c) \oplus c_1] \oplus OP_c$$
$$= E_K[rot_{r_1}(y) \oplus \alpha_0^* \oplus rot_{r_1}(OP_c) \oplus c_1] \oplus OP_c$$
$$= f'(0,y),$$

which indeed yields $f'(0,y) = f'(1, y \oplus rot_r^{-1}(\alpha_0^* \oplus \alpha_1^*))$.

References

1. 3GPP: ETSI TR 135 102. Technical Report (TR) 35.102, 3rd Generation Partnership Project (3GPP) (2013). https://www.etsi.org/deliver/etsi_ts/133100_133199/133102/11.05.01_60/ts_133102v110501p.pdf, version11.5.1
2. 3GPP: ETSI TR 135 231. Technical Report (TR) 35.231, 3rd Generation Partnership Project (3GPP) (2014). https://www.etsi.org/deliver/etsi_ts/135200_135299/135231/12.01.00_60/ts_135231v120100p.pdf, version12.1.0
3. 3GPP: ETSI TR 135 206. Technical Report (TR) 35.206, 3rd Generation Partnership Project (3GPP) (2016). https://www.etsi.org/deliver/etsi_ts/135200_135299/135206/14.00.00_60/ts_135206v140000p.pdf, version14.0.0
4. 3GPP: ETSI TR 135 909. Technical Report (TR) 35.909, 3rd Generation Partnership Project (3GPP) (2019). https://www.etsi.org/deliver/etsi_tr/135900_135999/135909/07.00.00_60/tr_135909v070000p.pdf, version15.0.0
5. Alt, S., Fouque, P.-A., Macario-rat, G., Onete, C., Richard, B.: A cryptographic analysis of UMTS/LTE AKA. In: Manulis, M., Sadeghi, A.-R., Schneider, S. (eds.) ACNS 2016. LNCS, vol. 9696, pp. 18–35. Springer, Cham (2016). https://doi.org/10.1007/978-3-319-39555-5_2
6. Aumasson, J.P.: Too much crypto. Cryptology ePrint Archive (2019)
7. Biham, E.: New types of cryptanalytic attacks using related keys. J. Cryptol. **7**(4), 229–246 (1994). https://doi.org/10.1007/BF00203965

8. Bonnetain, X.: Tight bounds for Simon's algorithm. In: Longa, P., Ràfols, C. (eds.) LATINCRYPT 2021. LNCS, vol. 12912, pp. 3–23. Springer, Cham (2021). https://doi.org/10.1007/978-3-030-88238-9_1

9. Bonnetain, X., Hosoyamada, A., Naya-Plasencia, M., Sasaki, Yu., Schrottenloher, A.: Quantum attacks without superposition queries: the offline Simon's algorithm. In: Galbraith, S.D., Moriai, S. (eds.) ASIACRYPT 2019. LNCS, vol. 11921, pp. 552–583. Springer, Cham (2019). https://doi.org/10.1007/978-3-030-34578-5_20

10. Bonnetain, X., Schrottenloher, A., Sibleyras, F.: Beyond quadratic speedups in quantum attacks on symmetric schemes. In: Dunkelman, O., Dziembowski, S. (eds.) EUROCRYPT 2022. Lecture Notes in Computer Science, vol. 13277, pp. 315–344. Springer International Publishing, Cham (2022). https://doi.org/10.1007/978-3-031-07082-2_12

11. Damir, M.T., Meskanen, T., Ramezanian, S., Niemi, V.: A beyond-5G authentication and key agreement protocol. In: Yuan, X., Bai, G., Alcaraz, C., Majumdar, S. (eds.) Network and System Security, NSS 2022. Lecture Notes in Computer Science, vol. 13787, pp. 249–264. Springer, Cham (2022). https://doi.org/10.1007/978-3-031-23020-2_14

12. Dong, X., Dong, B., Wang, X.: Quantum attacks on some Feistel block ciphers. Des. Codes Crypt. 88(6), 1179–1203 (2020)

13. Fettweis, G.P., Boche, H.: On 6G and trustworthiness. Commun. ACM 65(4), 48–49 (2022)

14. Fluhrer, S.: Reassessing Grover's algorithm. Cryptology ePrint Archive (2017)

15. Fouque, P.A., Onete, C., Richard, B.: Achieving better privacy for the 3GPP AKA protocol. Proc. Priv. Enhancing Technol. 2016(4), 255–275 (2016). https://doi.org/10.1515/popets-2016-0039

16. Gilbert, H.: The security of "one-block-to-many" modes of operation. In: Johansson, T. (ed.) FSE 2003. LNCS, vol. 2887, pp. 376–395. Springer, Heidelberg (2003). https://doi.org/10.1007/978-3-540-39887-5_27

17. Grover, L.K.: A fast quantum mechanical algorithm for database search. In: Proceedings of the twenty-eighth annual ACM symposium on Theory of computing, pp. 212–219 (1996)

18. Jaeger, J., Song, F., Tessaro, S.: Quantum key-length extension. In: Nissim, K., Waters, B. (eds.) TCC 2021. LNCS, vol. 13042, pp. 209–239. Springer, Cham (2021). https://doi.org/10.1007/978-3-030-90459-3_8

19. Jang, K., Baksi, A., Kim, H., Song, G., Seo, H., Chattopadhyay, A.: Quantum analysis of AES - lowering limit of quantum attack complexity (2022)

20. Jaques, S., Schrottenloher, A.: Low-gate quantum golden collision finding. In: Dunkelman, O., Jacobson, Jr., M.J., O'Flynn, C. (eds.) SAC 2020. LNCS, vol. 12804, pp. 329–359. Springer, Cham (2021). https://doi.org/10.1007/978-3-030-81652-0_13

21. Kaplan, M., Leurent, G., Leverrier, A., Naya-Plasencia, M.: Breaking symmetric cryptosystems using quantum period finding. In: Robshaw, M., Katz, J. (eds.) CRYPTO 2016. LNCS, vol. 9815, pp. 207–237. Springer, Heidelberg (2016). https://doi.org/10.1007/978-3-662-53008-5_8

22. Kaplan, M., Leurent, G., Leverrier, A., Naya-Plasencia, M.: Quantum differential and linear cryptanalysis. IACR Trans. Symmetric Cryptology 2016(1), 71–94 (2016). https://doi.org/10.13154/tosc.v2016.i1.71-94, https://tosc.iacr.org/index.php/ToSC/article/view/536. ISSN 2519-173X

23. Kuwakado, H., Morii, M.: Quantum distinguisher between the 3-round Feistel cipher and the random permutation. In: 2010 IEEE International Symposium on Information Theory, pp. 2682–2685. IEEE (2010)

24. Kuwakado, H., Morii, M.: Security on the quantum-type Even-Mansour cipher. In: 2012 International Symposium on Information Theory and its Applications, pp. 312–316. IEEE (2012)
25. Leander, G., May, A.: Grover meets Simon – quantumly attacking the FX-construction. In: Takagi, T., Peyrin, T. (eds.) ASIACRYPT 2017. LNCS, vol. 10625, pp. 161–178. Springer, Cham (2017). https://doi.org/10.1007/978-3-319-70697-9_6
26. Mayes, K., Babbage, S., Maximov, A.: Performance evaluation of the new Tuak mobile authentication algorithm. Proc. ICONS/EMBEDDED, 38–44 (2016)
27. Mitchell, C.J.: The impact of quantum computing on real-world security: a 5g case study. Comput. Secur. **93**, 101825 (2020)
28. NIST: Submission requirements and evaluation criteria for the post-quantum cryptography standardization process. Technical report, National Institute of Standards and Technology (NIST), Washington, D.C. (2017). https://csrc.nist.gov/Projects/post-quantum-cryptography/post-quantum-cryptography-standardization
29. NIST: Announcing four candidates to be standardized, plus fourth round candidates (2022). https://csrc.nist.gov/News/2022/pqc-candidates-to-be-standardized-and-round-4#fourth-round
30. Piani, M., Mosca, M.: Quantum threat timeline report 2021 (2021)
31. PlankQK: Plankqk: Konsortium (2022). https://planqk.stoneone.de/partner/
32. Rieffel, E.G., Polak, W.H.: Quantum Computing: A Gentle Introduction. MIT Press, Cambridge (2011)
33. Roetteler, M., Steinwandt, R.: A note on quantum related-key attacks. Inf. Process. Lett. **115**(1), 40–44 (2015)
34. Servedio, R.A., Gortler, S.J.: Equivalences and separations between quantum and classical learnability. SIAM J. Comput. **33**(5), 1067–1092 (2004)
35. Simon, D.R.: On the power of quantum computation. SIAM J. Comput. **26**(5), 1474–1483 (1997)
36. Ulitzsch, V.Q., Park, S., Marzougui, S., Seifert, J.P.: A post-quantum secure subscription concealed identifier for 6G. In: Proceedings of the 15th ACM Conference on Security and Privacy in Wireless and Mobile Networks, pp. 157–168 (2022)
37. Winternitz, R., Hellman, M.: Chosen-key attacks on a block cipher. Cryptologia **11**(1), 16–20 (1987)
38. Yang, J., Johansson, T.: An overview of cryptographic primitives for possible use in 5g and beyond. Sci. China Inf. Sci. **63**(12), 1–22 (2020)
39. Zhandry, M.: How to construct quantum random functions. In: 2012 IEEE 53rd Annual Symposium on Foundations of Computer Science, pp. 679–687. IEEE (2012)
40. Zou, J., Wei, Z., Sun, S., Liu, X., Wu, W.: Quantum circuit implementations of AES with fewer qubits. In: Moriai, S., Wang, H. (eds.) ASIACRYPT 2020. LNCS, vol. 12492, pp. 697–726. Springer, Cham (2020). https://doi.org/10.1007/978-3-030-64834-3_24

Time and Query Complexity Tradeoffs for the Dihedral Coset Problem

Maxime Remaud[1], André Schrottenloher[2(✉)], and Jean-Pierre Tillich[3]

[1] Inria and Eviden Quantum Lab, Paris, France
[2] Univ Rennes, Inria, CNRS, IRISA, Rennes, France
andre.schrottenloher@inria.fr
[3] Inria, Paris, France

Abstract. The Dihedral Coset Problem (DCP) in $\mathbb{Z}_N$ has been extensively studied in quantum computing and post-quantum cryptography, as for instance, the Learning with Errors problem reduces to it. While the Ettinger-Høyer algorithm is known to solve the DCP in $O(\log N)$ queries, it runs inefficiently in time $O(N)$. The first time-efficient algorithm was introduced (and later improved) by Kuperberg (SIAM J. Comput. 2005). These algorithms run in a *subexponential* amount of time and queries $\tilde{O}\left(2^{\sqrt{c_{DCP} \log N}}\right)$, for some constant c_{DCP}.

The sieving algorithms á la Kuperberg admit many trade-offs between quantum and classical time, memory and queries. Some of these trade-offs allow the attacker to reduce the number of queries if they are particularly costly, which is notably the case in the post-quantum key-exchange CSIDH. Such optimizations have already been studied, but they typically fall into two categories: the resulting algorithm is either based on Regev's approach of reducing the DCP with quadratic queries to a subset-sum instance, or on a re-optimization of Kuperberg's sieve where the time and queries are both subexponential.

In this paper, we introduce the first algorithm to improve in the linear queries regime over the Ettinger-Høyer algorithm. We then show that we can in fact interpolate between this algorithm and Kuperberg's sieve, by using the latter in a pre-processing step to create several quantum states, and solving a *quantum* subset-sum instance to recover the full secret in one pass from the obtained states. This allows to interpolate smoothly between the linear queries-exponential time complexity case and the subexponential query and time complexity case, thus allowing a fine tuning of the complexity taking into account the query cost. We also give on our way a precise study of quantum subset-sum algorithms in the non-asymptotic regime.

Keywords: Dihedral Hidden Subgroup Problem · Subset-sum · Dihedral Coset Problem · Quantum Algorithms

1 Introduction

Hidden Subgroup Problem. Let G be a known group and H be an unknown subgroup of G. Finding H is a problem known as the Hidden Subgroup Problem

© The Author(s), under exclusive license to Springer Nature Switzerland AG 2023
T. Johansson and D. Smith-Tone (Eds.): PQCrypto 2023, LNCS 14154, pp. 505–532, 2023.
https://doi.org/10.1007/978-3-031-40003-2_19

(HSP). To solve it, we can query a function f which satisfies a certain property with respect to H:

Definition 1 (HSP). *The hidden subgroup problem is defined as:*

- *Given: a function $f : G \to S$ that is constant and distinct on the left cosets of an unknown subgroup H of a group G, S being a finite set,*
- *Find: (a generating set of) H.*

Many problems used to construct primitives can be reduced to an HSP instance, for example the Discrete Logarithm and Shortest Vector problems. Shor's algorithm [32], which solves the DLP and breaks the RSA cryptosystem [31] in polynomial time, can actually be extended to solve the HSP for an abelian group G. In the general case, it is well known that the problem requires only a *polynomial* (in $\log_2 |G|$) number of queries to the function f [19]. However, time-efficient quantum algorithms are only known for very specific instances, including abelian groups, and it is widely admitted that the generic problem remains difficult for quantum algorithms.

*Dihedral Hidden Subgroup Problem (*DHSP*).* While the HSP in an abelian group is quantumly easy to solve, many post-quantum primitives are related to the HSP in the *dihedral group*. In this case, even if the group is very close to be abelian (it has namely an abelian subgroup of index 2) no polynomial-time algorithm is known. This is the case of cryptosystems based on the Unique Shortest Vector Problem (uSVP) in lattice-based cryptography (such as [1,29]) or on any problem that can be reduced to the uSVP (because of a chain of reductions between several problems [25,28,33]). More concretely, the security of several primitives reduces to the DHSP. The most prominent example is the isogeny-based post-quantum key-exchange CSIDH [11], which is similar to the Diffie-Hellman protocol [16] except that it does not rely on the period-finding problem in an abelian group (which is solvable in quantum polynomial time), but on the difficulty to invert the group action. Several related constructions [3] such as the signature schemes SeaSign [14,15] and CSI-FiSh [6] also rely on the same problem. It should be noted that these isogeny-based cryptosystems are the only major contenders for which the quantum attacker enjoys more than a quadratic speedup, as opposed to the lattice- and hash-based finalists of the NIST post-quantum standardization process [2,26].

As it has been shown in [9,12,27], a better understanding of the security of CSIDH comes from a careful analysis of quantum DHSP algorithms. This is the motivation of our work.

From the DHSP *to the* DCP. Solving the HSP for the dihedral group of order $2N$ is known to reduce to the specific case where the hidden subgroup is $\{(0,0),(s,1)\}$, where $s \in \mathbb{Z}_N$, which can in turn be reduced to a problem known as the Dihedral Coset Problem (see [18]).

Definition 2 (DCP). *The dihedral coset problem is defined as:*

- *Given: an oracle outputting coset states of the form* $\frac{1}{\sqrt{2}} \left(|0\rangle \, |x\rangle + |1\rangle \, |x+s\rangle \right)$ *for random* $x \in [\![0, N]\!]$,
- *Find:* $s \in [\![0, N]\!]$

While the Ettinger-Høyer algorithm [18] solves the DCP with a linear number of queries ($O(\log N)$), it runs in exponential time $O(N)$. This algorithm basically consists in measuring $O(\log N)$ coset states and then classically looking among all possible values for the secret s the one that matches the best a statistical test. It is possible to improve over this running time by reducing the resolution of the DCP to a subset-sum problem, as described by [7,9], at the cost of squaring the query complexity. Though it remains exponential, the time complexity becomes $\tilde{O}(N^{c_{ss}})$, where c_{ss} is a constant smaller than 1 that depends on the invoked subset-sum subroutine.

In a seminal work [23], Kuperberg initiated a family of *sieving* algorithms which reach subexponential time complexities (at the cost of a subexponential query complexity). The idea here is to iterate a process of combining states to build new ones with a stronger and stronger structure, until building a very specific state that allows us to guess a bit of the secret when measured. The first algorithm [23] requires subexponential quantum time *and* space, but it was quickly followed by an algorithm of Regev [30] which requires only polynomial space. Later, Kuperberg proposed his second algorithm [24], which generalized Regev's while improving its exponents, giving in the end a complexity in time (classical and quantum) and classical space of $\tilde{O}\left(2^{\sqrt{2\log N}}\right)$ with a quantum space of $O(\text{polylog } N)$ and $\tilde{O}\left(2^{\sqrt{2\log N}}\right)$ queries, which is the state of the art so far.

Our Contributions. Let $n \overset{\text{def}}{=} \lceil \log_2 N \rceil$. We first propose a new algorithm using a linear number of queries. It is somewhat analogous to Regev's algorithm where instead of reducing the DCP to a classical subset-sum problem, it reduces the DCP to a *quantum* subset-sum problem. In the first case, the algorithm makes $O(n)$ queries to find one bit of the secret, meaning it has to be iterated $O(n)$ times. With this new algorithm, which is inspired by [28,33], we only need $O(1)$ quantum subset-sum instances, *i.e.*, $O(n)$ queries, to find the whole secret.

Second, we present a simple and natural method of interpolation between Kuperberg's second algorithm (which is the state of the art) and the new algorithm we mentioned above. It consists in using Kuperberg's algorithm to more or less preprocess the states given as input to our algorithm. The difficulty of solving the inherent quantum subset-sum problem instance will depend on the preprocessing step.

Finally, as a building block of our algorithms, we study quantum subset-sum algorithms when the problem to solve is partially in superposition. We show here that we can still improve over Grover's search even under the constraint of a polynomial quantum memory, using an exponential classical memory, with or without quantum access. Specifically, we show that the QRACM-based algorithm of [8] adapts to this case and reaches a complexity $\tilde{O}\left(2^{0.2356n}\right)$. Without

QRACM, we reach a quantum time $\tilde{O}\left(2^{0.4165n}\right)$ using $O\left(2^{0.2334n}\right)$ bits of classical memory, improving over a previous algorithm by Helm and May [21]. In both cases, we also give non-asymptotic estimates of their complexity.

All together, we can summarize the complexity exponents of the different algorithms for solving the DCP in Table 1, including the new one we propose.

Table 1. Costs of algorithms for finding the whole secret s.

Algorithm	Queries	Classical Time	Quantum Time	Classical Space
Kuperberg II	$\sqrt{2n} + \frac{1}{2}\log n + 3$	$\sqrt{2n} + \frac{1}{2}\log n + 3$	$\sqrt{2n} + \frac{1}{2}\log n + 3$	$\sqrt{2n}$
Regev	$\frac{3}{2}\log n + 3$	$0.283n + \frac{1}{2}\log n + 3$	$\frac{3}{2}\log n + 3$	$0.283n$
Ettinger-Hoyer	$\log n + 6.5$	n	$\log n + 6.5$	$\log n$
Algorithm 4 w/ QRACM	$\log n + 3$	$0.238n + 12$	$0.238n + \frac{3}{2}\log n + 12$	$0.238n$
Algorithm 4 w/o QRACM	$\log n + 3$	$< 0.2324n$	$0.418n + \frac{3}{2}\log n + 15.5$	$< 0.2324n$

We propose two versions of our algorithm, one with QRACM and one without, both using polynomial quantum space. Note that our algorithm with QRACM outperforms other algorithms using a linear number of queries when we look at the complexity in classical time + quantum time.

Impact on CSIDH. Although Kuperberg's second algorithm is the one with the best time complexity for solving the DCP, it is still interesting to look at algorithms that only use a linear number of queries, since for example, CSIDH cryptanalysis via the resolution of the DCP involves the use of a very expensive oracle.

We give in Table 2 a few examples of complexity exponents for parameters of CSIDH.

Table 2. Complexity exponents for some parameters of CSIDH. The quantum space is polynomial in n.

	Algorithm	Queries	Classical Time	Quantum Time	Classical Space
CSIDH-512	Regev	15	80	15	73
$(n = 256)$	Algorithm 4 w/ QRACM	11	73	85	61
CSIDH-1024	Regev	17	153	17	145
$(n = 512)$	Algorithm 4 w/ QRACM	12	134	148	122
CSIDH-1792	Regev	18	262	18	254
$(n = 896)$	Algorithm 4 w/ QRACM	13	226	240	214
CSIDH-3072	Regev	19	443	19	435
$(n = 1536)$	Algorithm 4 w/ QRACM	14	378	394	366
CSIDH-4096	Regev	20	589	20	580
$(n = 2048)$	Algorithm 4 w/ QRACM	14	500	516	488

Organization of the Paper. In Sect. 2, we give some preliminaries on sieving algorithms for the DCP, and subset-sum algorithms that we will use as black boxes afterwards. In Sect. 3, we recall the reduction from the DCP to the subset-sum problem, and introduce our new idea of using a *quantum* subset-sum solver. Our interpolation between the sieving and subset-sum approaches is detailed in Sect. 4. Finally, our contributions on quantum subset-sum algorithms, and the details of the black boxes that we used throughout the paper, are provided in Sect. 5.

2   Preliminaries

In this section, we cover the main principles of sieving algorithms for the DCP, including Kuperberg's and Regev's algorithms [13,23,24,30]. We assume knowledge of the quantum circuit model, *i.e.*, the $|\cdot\rangle$ notation of quantum states, and basic quantum operations such as CNOT, Toffoli, the Quantum Fourier Transform (QFT), *etc.*

We estimate the *time* complexity of a quantum algorithm in the quantum circuit model, as a number of *n-bit arithmetic operations*. That is, instead of counting precisely the quantum gates, we count the n-bit XORs, additions, subtractions, comparisons, QFTs, depending on the complexity parameter n.

We work with different types of memory:

- quantum memory (*i.e.*, qubits): some DCP algorithms (*e.g.*, Kuperberg's first algorithm [23]) need to store many coset states, which creates a subexponential quantum memory requirement;
- classical memory with quantum random-access (QRACM): the QRACM (or qRAM, QROM in some papers) is a specialized hardware which stores classical data and accesses this data in quantum superposition. That is, we assume that given a classical memory of M bits $y_0, \ldots, y_{M-1}$, the following unitary operation:

$$|x\rangle |i\rangle \xmapsto{\text{Access}} |x \oplus y_i\rangle |i\rangle$$

can be implemented in time $O(1)$. QRACM is a very common assumption in quantum computing, and it appears in several works on the DCP [24,27] but also on collision-finding [10] and subset-sum algorithms [8].
- classical memory without quantum random-access: the Access operation can be implemented in M arithmetic operations using a sequential circuit. This removes the QRACM assumption, and we fall back on the basic quantum circuit model. Some algorithms using QRACM can be re-optimized in a non-trivial way when memory access is costly, and this is the case of subset-sum [21].

2.1 Phase Vectors and Kuperberg's First Algorithm

We will consider in what follows that we have access to an oracle outputting *phase vectors* denoted by $|\psi_k\rangle$ and defined as:

$$|\psi_k\rangle \overset{\text{def}}{=} \frac{1}{\sqrt{2}}\left(|0\rangle + \omega_N^{sk}|1\rangle\right)$$

where $\omega_N = \exp(2\iota\pi/N)$, $\iota = \sqrt{-1}$, and k is a *known* uniformly distributed random element of $\mathbb{Z}_N$. They are obtained from coset states (the input states of the DCP) by applying a QFT on $\mathbb{Z}_N$ on the first register and then measuring this register, since we have

$$(QFT_N \otimes \mathbf{I})\left(\frac{1}{\sqrt{2}}\left(|x\rangle|0\rangle + |x+s\rangle|1\rangle\right)\right) = \frac{1}{\sqrt{N}}\sum_{k\in\mathbb{Z}_N}\omega_N^{kx}|k\rangle|\psi_k\rangle.$$

Finding $s \in [\![0, N-1]\!]$ from a collection of phase vectors $|\psi_k\rangle$ for known uniformly distributed random $k \in [\![0, N-1]\!]$ solves both the DCP and the DHSP.

Subexponential Algorithms. We will now give more details on the algorithms solving the DCP in subexponential time. Until the end of this section, it can be assumed that $N = 2^n$ for the sake of simplicity, but the algorithms discussed here work for any value of N.

Kuperberg's initial observation is that one can combine two phase vectors $|\psi_p\rangle$ and $|\psi_q\rangle$ to construct a new phase vector. Indeed, we have:

$$|\psi_p, \psi_q\rangle \xmapsto{\text{CNOT}} \frac{1}{\sqrt{2}}\left(|\psi_{p+q}, 0\rangle + \omega_N^{yq}|\psi_{p-q}, 1\rangle\right).$$

A measurement of the second qubit will leave the first one either in the state $|\psi_{p-q}\rangle$, or $|\psi_{p+q}\rangle$, depending on the bit measured. With probability $1/2$, we get $|\psi_{p-q}\rangle$. By noticing on the other hand that $|\psi_{N/2}\rangle = \mathbf{H}|\text{lsb}(s)\rangle$ ($\text{lsb}(s)$ being the least significant bit of s), Kuperberg designed a quite simple algorithm which groups the phase vectors according to their last non-zero bits. They are then combined two by two using CNOT gates. Half of the time, the difference is obtained, and it contains as many zeroes as there were bits in common. The resulting phase vectors are regrouped and the process is reiterated. As proven in [23], the target state $|\psi_{N/2}\rangle$ is then obtained in subexponential time.

2.2 Regev's Algorithm

Kuperberg's first algorithm requires to store, at each time, a subexponential number of phase vectors; thus, it has subexponential quantum memory complexity. Regev [30] modified the combination routine to reduce the number of qubits to polynomial, while keeping the time complexity subexponential.

The new routine combines m phase vectors for a well-chosen m (to minimize the overall complexity).

Let B be some chosen, arbitrary value. We start with m phase vectors $|\psi_{k_1}\rangle, \ldots, |\psi_{k_m}\rangle$. We tensor the vectors, $i.e.$, we obtain a sum:

$$\bigotimes_i |\psi_{k_i}\rangle = \sum_{\mathbf{b} \in \{0,1\}^m} \omega_N^{s\langle \mathbf{b}, \mathbf{k} \rangle} |\mathbf{b}\rangle$$

We compute $\lfloor \langle \mathbf{b}, \mathbf{k} \rangle / B \rfloor$ into a new qubit register, and measure a value V. This projects the state on the vectors $\mathbf{b}$ such that $\lfloor \langle \mathbf{b}, \mathbf{k} \rangle / B \rfloor = V$. We choose m and the size of B such that on average two solutions $\mathbf{b}$ and $\mathbf{b}'$ occur. The state becomes proportional to:

$$|\mathbf{b}\rangle + \omega_N^{s(\langle \mathbf{b}, \mathbf{k} \rangle - \langle \mathbf{b}', \mathbf{k} \rangle)} |\mathbf{b}'\rangle .$$

Finally, we remap $\mathbf{b}, \mathbf{b}'$ to $0, 1$ respectively. We have obtained a phase vector $|\psi_k\rangle$ with a label $k = \langle \mathbf{b}, \mathbf{k} \rangle - \langle \mathbf{b}', \mathbf{k} \rangle \leq B$. Then, step by step, we can make the labels decrease until we obtain the label 1. As remarked in [9], we can also obtain any label whose value is invertible modulo N, by multiplying all initial labels by their inverse, and applying normally the algorithm afterwards. In particular, when N is odd, we can obtain all powers of two.

Regev [30] and later Childs, Jao and Soukharev [13] used this combination routine to get an algorithm with $\tilde{O}\left(2^{\sqrt{2n \log_2 n}}\right)$ queries and $O(n)$ quantum memory.

2.3   Kuperberg's Second Algorithm

Like the two previous ones, Kuperberg's *collimation sieve* [24] is a hybrid quantum/classical procedure starting from the initial phase vectors, where we need to perform both quantum computations which create new vectors, and classical computations which give their description. The difference is that phase vectors are now multi-labeled:

$$|\psi_{k_1, \ldots, k_\ell}\rangle = \frac{1}{\sqrt{\ell}} \sum_i \omega_N^{sk_i} |i\rangle .$$

In order to control these new phase vectors, we need to know the list of all their labels. These lists will become of subexponential size, although the vector itself requires only a polynomial amount of qubits. This is why the algorithm combines a polynomial quantum memory with a subexponential *classical* memory.

The combination subroutine is similar to Regev's, except that it does not necessarily reduce the list of labels down to 2. Instead, the two phase vectors are combined into a new one holding a similar number of labels, as shown in Algorithm 1.

Originally, Kuperberg uses classical memory with quantum random-access (QRACM), an approach later followed by Peikert [27]. However it only improves the trade-offs with respect to the total quantum time, and it is not necessary to reach the optimal complexity. Also, the collimation procedure presented here

---

Algorithm 1. Combination routine in the collimation sieve.

Input: $|\psi_{k_1,\dots,k_\ell}\rangle, \dots, \left|\psi_{k'_1,\dots,k'_{\ell'}}\right\rangle$ such that $\forall i \leq \ell, \forall j \leq \ell', k_i < 2^a, k'_j < 2^a$, the lists of the labels

Output: $\left|\psi_{v_1,\dots,v_{\ell''}}\right\rangle$ such that $\forall i, v_i < 2^{a-r}$

1: *Quantum:* Tensor the vectors: $\sum_{i \leq \ell, j \leq \ell'} \omega_N^{s(k_i + k'_j)} |i\rangle |j\rangle$
2: *Quantum:* Compute the function $i, j \mapsto \lfloor (k_i + k'_j)/2^{a-r} \rfloor$ into an ancilla register
3: *Quantum:* Measure the register, obtain a value V. The state collapses to:

$$\sum_{i,j \,|\, \lfloor (k_i + k'_j)/2^{a-r} \rfloor = V} \omega_N^{s(k_i + k'_j)} |i\rangle |j\rangle$$

4: *Classical:* Compute $\{(i,j) \,|\, \lfloor (k_i + k'_j)/2^{a-r} \rfloor = V\}$, of size ℓ''
5: *Quantum:* Apply to the state a transformation that maps the pairs (i,j) to $[\![0, \ell'' - 1]\!]$.
6: Return the state and the vector of corresponding labels $k_i + k'_j$.

---

is from later works such as [27], as it allows to easily deal with arbitrary group orders.

Without QRACM, Steps 2 and 5 in Algorithm 1 require a time complexity $O(\max(\ell, \ell', \ell''))$. This is also the classical time complexity required by Step 4, assuming that the lists of labels are sorted.

The Algorithm as a Merging Tree. Starting from a certain set of multi-labeled phase vectors, we can identify them with the classical lists of their labels. The combination step operates on these lists like a purely classical list-merging algorithm, in which new lists of labels are formed from the pairs of labels satisfying a certain condition. This algorithm can be represented as a *merging tree* in which all nodes are lists of labels (resp. phase vectors).

On the classical side, Kuperberg's algorithm is thus similar to Wagner's generalized birthday algorithm [34], which is a binary merging tree of depth $\sqrt{n}$. In Wagner's algorithm, the goal is to impose stronger conditions at each level which culminate in a full-zero sum. Here, the same conditions are imposed on the labels in the phase vectors. A success in the list-merging routine is equivalent to a success in the collimation routine (we obtain a phase vector with the wanted label).

The query, time and memory complexities depend on the shape of the tree. Even though the conditions are actually chosen at random at the measurement step in Algorithm 1, we can consider them chosen at random *before* the combination to analyze the algorithm.

Example: Optimal Time. The optimal time complexity is obtained with a tree with $\sqrt{2n}$ levels. It starts with lists of size 2, *i.e.*, two-labeled phase vectors. At level i starting from the leaves, the lists have (expected) size 2^i, and they are merged pairwise into a list of size 2^{i+1}. This means that we can eliminate $2i - (i+1) = i - 1$ bits. So we should use h levels, where:

$$1 + \ldots + h - 1 = n \implies h \simeq \sqrt{2n} \ .$$

Since each level of merging doubles the number of lists, there are in total $2^{\sqrt{2n}}$ leaves (hence queries). The (classical) cost of merging, over the whole tree, is equal to the sum of all list sizes. It is also the (quantum) cost of the relabeling operations: $\sum_i 2^{\sqrt{2n}-i} \times 2^i = O\left(\sqrt{2n}2^{\sqrt{2n}}\right)$.

To compute the memory complexity, one must note that it is not required to store whole levels of the merging tree. Instead, we compute the lists (resp. the phase vectors) depth-first, and store only one node of each level at most, i.e. $\sqrt{2n}$ phase vectors. For the same reason, the classical memory complexity is $O\left(2^{\sqrt{2n}}\right)$.

Precise Analysis. The analysis above is only performed on average, and in practice, there is a significant variance in the list sizes. More precise analyses were performed in [12, 27]. It follows from them that the list size after merging should be considered smaller than the expected one by an "adjusting factor" $\sqrt{3/(2\pi)}$. Furthermore, the combination may create lists that are too large, which must be discarded. The empirical analysis of Peikert [27] gives a factor $(1 - \delta)$ of loss at each level, with $\delta = 0.02$.

The smaller factor in list sizes simply means that at level i, we will not exactly eliminate $i-1$ bits, but $i-c$ where $c = \log_2\left(1 + \sqrt{\frac{3}{2\pi}}\right) \simeq 0.76$. (We can control the interval size in Algorithm 1 very precisely.) Thus h is solution to:

$$\sum_{i=1}^{h}(i - c) = n \implies \frac{h^2}{2} - ch = n \implies h \simeq c + \sqrt{2n + 4c^2} \ .$$

Finally, the loss at each level induces a global multiplicative factor $(1-\delta)^{-h} = 2^{-\log_2(1-\delta)h} \simeq 2^{0.029h}$ on the complexity. Therefore, accounting for the adjusting factor and discards, the query complexity of the sieve is:

$$2^{1.029\left(0.76+\sqrt{2n+2.30}\right)} \tag{1}$$

and the quantum time complexity multiplies this by a factor $0.76 + \sqrt{2n + 2.30}$. The difference with the exact $2^{\sqrt{2n}}$ is not negligible, but not large either. At $n = 4608$, the two exponents are respectively 99.6 and 96.

Obtaining All the Bits of the Solution. The analysis above applies if we want to obtain a specific label, e.g., the label 1. Afterwards, the algorithm can be repeated n times. For a generic N (not a power of 2), one typically produces all labels which are powers of 2 and uses a QFT to directly recover the secret. This is done for example in [9]. Peikert [27] proposed a more advanced method to recover multiple bits of the secret with each phase vector.

Lemma 1. *Let $\alpha > 0$ and n be a positive integer. We have*

$$\sum_{i=1}^{n} 2^{\alpha\sqrt{i}} = O\left(\sqrt{n}2^{\alpha\sqrt{n}}\right).$$

Proof. When i is a perfect square, let say $i = j^2$, we have that $2^{\alpha\sqrt{i}} = 2^{\alpha j}$. Now for any i between the two perfect squares $(j-1)^2$ and j^2, we have the upper bound $2^{\alpha\sqrt{i}} < 2^{\alpha j}$. In order to use this, we rewrite the sum:

$$\sum_{i=1}^{n} 2^{\alpha\sqrt{i}} \leq \sum_{j=0}^{\lceil\sqrt{n}\rceil-1} \sum_{k=j^2+1}^{(j+1)^2} 2^{\alpha\sqrt{k}}$$

$$\leq \sum_{j=0}^{\lceil\sqrt{n}\rceil-1} \sum_{k=j^2+1}^{(j+1)^2} 2^{\alpha(j+1)}$$

$$= \sum_{j=0}^{\lceil\sqrt{n}\rceil-1} (2j+1)2^{\alpha(j+1)}$$

Using the formula for geometric series, we obtain:

$$\sum_{i=1}^{n} 2^{\alpha\sqrt{i}} \leq 2^{\alpha+1}\frac{(2^\alpha-1)\lceil\sqrt{n}\rceil 2^{\alpha\lceil\sqrt{n}\rceil} - 2^\alpha(2^{\alpha\lceil\sqrt{n}\rceil}-1)}{(2^\alpha-1)^2} + 2^\alpha\frac{2^{\alpha\lceil\sqrt{n}\rceil}-1}{2^\alpha-1}$$

$$= \frac{2^\alpha}{2^\alpha-1}\left((2\lceil\sqrt{n}\rceil+1)2^{\alpha\lceil\sqrt{n}\rceil} - \frac{2^{\alpha+1}}{2^\alpha-1}(2^{\alpha\lceil\sqrt{n}\rceil}-1) - 1\right)$$

$$\leq \frac{2^\alpha}{2^\alpha-1}(2\lceil\sqrt{n}\rceil+1)2^{\alpha\lceil\sqrt{n}\rceil} .$$

which allows us to conclude the proof, α being fixed.   □

Obtaining Partially Collimated Labels. In this paper, we will consider the task of obtaining labels which, instead of reaching a prescribed k, match k on a certain number of bits only (we can say that the phase vectors are *partially collimated*), let say i: this complexity is of order $2^{\sqrt{2i}}$. By Lemma 1, we can obtain a sequence of i phase vectors collimated on $1, \ldots, i$ bits with a query complexity: $\sum_{j=1}^{i} 2^{\sqrt{2j}} = O\left(\sqrt{i}2^{\sqrt{2i}}\right)$.

2.4   The Subset-Sum Problem

As we will see in Sect. 3, the DCP can be reduced to the Subset-sum problem; this leads to the most query-efficient algorithms, and depending on the cost of queries, to the best optimization for some instances.

Definition 3 (Subset-sum). *A subset-sum instance is given by $(v, \mathbf{k})$, $v \in \mathbb{Z}_N$, $\mathbf{k} \in \mathbb{Z}_N^m$ for some modulus N and integer m. The problem is to find a vector (or all vectors) $\mathbf{b} \in \{0, 1\}^m$ such that $\langle \mathbf{b}, \mathbf{k}\rangle = v \mod N$.*

When $m \simeq n = \lceil \log_2 N \rceil$, there is one solution on average. The instance is said to be of *density one*. Heuristic classical and quantum algorithms based on the *representation technique* [4,22] allow to solve it in exponential time in n. In the following, we will use these algorithms as black boxes. We first need a classical subset-sum solver.

Fact 1. *We have a classical algorithm $\mathscr{S}^C$ which, on input a subset-sum instance $(v, \mathbf{k})$ of density one, finds all solutions. It has a time complexity in $\tilde{O}(2^{c_{cSS}n})$ where $c_{cSS} < 1$.*

Here, the parameter c_{cSS} is the best asymptotic exponent that we can obtain for classical subset-sum algorithms. If there are no constraints on the memory, we can take $c_{cSS} = 0.283$ which is the best value known at the moment [8].

In this paper, we will also need (quantum) algorithms solving a more difficult problem, in which $\mathbf{k}$ is fixed, but the target v is *in superposition*. We will call this type of algorithm a *quantum subset-sum solver*.

Fact 2. *We have a quantum algorithm $\mathscr{S}^Q$ which has a complexity cost in $\tilde{O}(2^{c_{qSS}n})$ (where $c_{qSS} < 1$), which, given an error bound ε, given a known (classical) $\mathbf{k} \in \mathbb{Z}_N^m$ and on input a quantum v, maps:*

$$|v\rangle |\mathbf{b}\rangle \mapsto |v\rangle |\mathbf{b} \oplus \mathscr{S}^Q(v)\rangle$$

where, for a proportion at least $1 - \varepsilon$ of all v admitting a solution, $\mathscr{S}^Q(v)$ is selected u.a.r. from the solutions to the subset-sum problem, i.e., from the set $\{\mathbf{b}| \langle \mathbf{b}, \mathbf{k} \rangle = v\}$.

Notice that in the way we implement the solver, we can only guarantee that it succeeds on a large proportion of inputs (there remains some probability of error). However, it depends on some precomputations that we can redo, to obtain a heuristically independent solver which allows to reduce ε and/or to ensure that we get more solutions.

Though we could implement the function $\mathscr{S}^Q$ by running an available classical (or quantum) subset-sum algorithm, it would then require exponential amounts of qubits. Using only $\mathsf{poly}(n)$ qubits, we know for sure that $c_{qSS} \leq 0.5$, because we can use Grover's algorithm to exhaustively search for a solution $\mathbf{b}$. This search uses $\mathsf{poly}(n)$ qubits only. In Sect. 5, we will show that we can reach smaller values for c_{qSS}, which differ depending on whether we allow QRACM or not.

3   Reducing DCP To a Subset-Sum Problem

Recall that we note $n = \lceil \log_2 N \rceil$, where N is not necessarily a power of 2. We will focus in this section on two algorithms to solve the DCP: the first one (from Regev [30]) uses a classical subset-sum solver and the other (ours) uses a quantum one.

Algorithm 2. Finding lsb(s) using a classical subset-sum solver $\mathscr{S}^{\mathrm{C}}$

Require: $|\psi_{k_1}\rangle, \ldots, |\psi_{k_n}\rangle$ with $\mathbf{k} \overset{\text{def}}{=} (k_1 \ldots k_n) \in \mathbb{Z}_N^n$.
Ensure: lsb(s).
1: Tensor the phase vectors and append a register on $\mathbb{F}_2^{n-1}$

$$\bigotimes_{i=1}^{n} |\psi_{k_i}\rangle = \frac{1}{\sqrt{2^n}} \sum_{\mathbf{b} \in \mathbb{F}_2^n} \omega_N^{s\langle \mathbf{b}, \mathbf{k}\rangle} |\mathbf{b}\rangle$$

2: Compute the inner product of $\mathbf{b}$ and $\mathbf{k}$ in the ancillary register

$$\frac{1}{\sqrt{2^n}} \sum_{\mathbf{b} \in \mathbb{F}_2^n} \omega_N^{s\langle \mathbf{b}, \mathbf{k}\rangle} |\mathbf{b}\rangle \left| \langle \mathbf{b}, \mathbf{k}\rangle \mod 2^{n-1}\right\rangle$$

3: Measure the ancillary register   ▷ Z is a normalizing constant

$$\frac{1}{\sqrt{Z}} \sum_{\substack{\mathbf{b} \in \mathbb{F}_2^n: \\ \langle \mathbf{b}, \mathbf{k}\rangle = z \mod 2^{n-1}}} \omega_N^{s\langle \mathbf{b}, \mathbf{k}\rangle} |\mathbf{b}\rangle |z\rangle$$

4: Search for vectors $\mathbf{b_i}$ such that $\langle \mathbf{b_i}, \mathbf{k}\rangle = z \mod 2^{n-1}$ using $\mathscr{S}^{\mathrm{C}}$
5: Project the superposition onto a pair of solutions, *e.g.*, $(\mathbf{b}_1, \mathbf{b}_2)$

$$\frac{1}{\sqrt{2}} \left(\omega_N^{s\langle \mathbf{b_1}, \mathbf{k}\rangle} |\mathbf{b}_1\rangle + \omega_N^{s\langle \mathbf{b_2}, \mathbf{k}\rangle} |\mathbf{b}_2\rangle \right)$$

6: Relabel the basis states to $(|0\rangle, |1\rangle)$, resulting in

$$\frac{\omega_N^{s\langle \mathbf{b_1}, \mathbf{k}\rangle}}{\sqrt{2}} \left(|0\rangle + \omega_N^{s\langle \mathbf{b_2} - \mathbf{b_1}, \mathbf{k}\rangle} |1\rangle \right)$$

7: Apply a Hadamard gate on the qubit, measure it and output the result.

3.1   Using a Classical Subset-Sum Solver

By reducing Regev's algorithm to a single level, as described in [9], we can directly produce lsb(s) from n phase vectors. This is detailed in Algorithm 2.

It can be proven that in Step 4, the number of solutions is quite small but generally enough for our purpose. In Step 5, the solution vectors we want to project our superposition on are marked in an ancillary register which is then measured. Either we will get what we want, or we will end up with a superposition of the solution vectors that were not marked, in which case we start the process again with two other solution vectors. For more details, we refer to the extensive study of Regev's algorithm by Childs, Jao and Soukharev [13].

The following lemma gives us the complexity of Algorithm 2, derived from Regev's algorithm.

Lemma 2 (Subsect. 3.3 [9]). *There exists an algorithm which finds* lsb(s) *with* $O(n)$ *queries and quantum time and space. It has the same usage in classical time and space as the subset-sum solver* $\mathscr{S}^{\mathrm{C}}$.

Algorithm 2 finds one bit of the secret. In order to retrieve the whole secret, we will have to repeat this procedure n times. Thus, we get an algorithm using a quadratic number of calls to the oracle, exponential classical time and space because of the subset-sum solver, linear quantum space and quadratic quantum time.

It turns out that we could solve the classical subset-sum problem on the side with a quantum computer, leading to some tradeoffs described in [7]. But we show hereafter that we can also build an algorithm which directly uses a quantum subset-sum solver instead of having to measure the ancillary register to get a classical instance of a subset-sum problem.

3.2   Using a Quantum Subset-Sum Solver

The main observation that led to the design of the algorithm we introduce hereafter is that on one hand, we would like to build the superposition

$$\frac{1}{\sqrt{N}} \sum_{j \in \mathbb{Z}_N} \omega_N^{sj} |j\rangle \tag{2}$$

since applying the inverse QFT on $\mathbb{Z}_N$ on it would directly give the secret s, and on the other hand, we know that it would be possible, thanks to a quantum subset-sum solver, to prepare the state

$$\frac{1}{\sqrt{Z(\mathbf{k})}} \sum_{\mathbf{b} \in \mathbb{F}_2^m} \omega_N^{s\langle \mathbf{b}, \mathbf{k}\rangle} |\langle \mathbf{b}, \mathbf{k}\rangle \mod N\rangle \tag{3}$$

where $Z(\mathbf{k})$ is a normalizing constant depending on $\mathbf{k}$. Indeed, preparing this state is done by using Regev's trick (see [28,33]), i.e.,

(i) by tensoring m phase vectors

$$\frac{1}{\sqrt{M}} \sum_{\mathbf{b} \in \mathbb{F}_2^m} \omega_N^{s\langle \mathbf{b}, \mathbf{k}\rangle} |\mathbf{b}\rangle |0_n\rangle,$$

(ii) then computing the subset-sum in the second register to get the entangled state

$$\frac{1}{\sqrt{M}} \sum_{\mathbf{b} \in \mathbb{F}_2^m} \omega_N^{s\langle \mathbf{b}, \mathbf{k}\rangle} |\mathbf{b}\rangle |\langle \mathbf{b}, \mathbf{k}\rangle \mod N\rangle,$$

(iii) and finally disentangle it thanks to a quantum subset-sum algorithm which from $\langle \mathbf{b}, \mathbf{k}\rangle \mod N$ and $\mathbf{k}$ (which is classical) recovers $\mathbf{b}$ and subtracts it from the first register to get the state we want.

As one can see, if we could take $m = n$ and have an isomorphism between the vectors $\mathbf{b}$ and the knapsack sums $\langle \mathbf{b}, \mathbf{k}\rangle \mod N$, the prepared state (3) would be exactly the superposition (2).

Algorithm 3. Ideal algorithm

Require: A parameter $m < n$ and phase vectors $|\psi_{k_i}\rangle$ for $i \in [\![1, m]\!]$.
Ensure: An element $j \in \mathbb{Z}_N$.
1: Tensor the m phase vectors and append a register on $\mathbb{Z}_N$

$$\bigotimes_{i=1}^{m} |\psi_{k_i}\rangle |0_n\rangle = \frac{1}{\sqrt{M}} \sum_{\mathbf{b} \in \mathbb{F}_2^m} \omega_N^{s\langle \mathbf{b}, \mathbf{k} \rangle} |\mathbf{b}\rangle |0_n\rangle$$

2: Compute the inner product of $\mathbf{b}$ and $\mathbf{k}$ in the ancillary register

$$\frac{1}{\sqrt{M}} \sum_{\mathbf{b} \in \mathbb{F}_2^m} \omega_N^{s\langle \mathbf{b}, \mathbf{k} \rangle} |\mathbf{b}\rangle |\langle \mathbf{b}, \mathbf{k} \rangle \mod N\rangle$$

3: Uncompute $\mathbf{b}$ thanks to $\mathbf{k}$ and $|\langle \mathbf{b}, \mathbf{k} \rangle \mod N\rangle$

$$\frac{1}{\sqrt{Z(\mathbf{k})}} \sum_{\mathbf{b} \in \mathbb{F}_2^m} \omega_N^{s\langle \mathbf{b}, \mathbf{k} \rangle} |0_m\rangle |\langle \mathbf{b}, \mathbf{k} \rangle \mod N\rangle$$

4: Apply the inverse QFT on $\mathbb{Z}_N$ on the second register

$$\frac{1}{\sqrt{N}} \sum_{j \in \mathbb{Z}_N} \left(\frac{1}{\sqrt{Z(\mathbf{k})}} \sum_{\mathbf{b} \in \mathbb{F}_2^m} \omega_N^{(s-j)\langle \mathbf{b}, \mathbf{k} \rangle} \right) |0_m\rangle |j\rangle$$

5: Measure the state and output the resulting j.

However, there would be many cases in which multiple solutions to the subset-sum problem exist. Thus we take $m < n$ and define $M \stackrel{\text{def}}{=} 2^m < N$. This is different from Algorithm 2, where such collisions are needed. We obtain Algorithm 3, which uses Regev's trick with a quantum subset-sum solver in Step 3.

Despite M being smaller than N, some cases still yield multiple solutions, and furthermore the subset-sum solver (as given by Fact 2) fails on some instances. This is why we distinguish between Algorithm 3 in which we consider the quantum subset-sum solver to be ideal (*i.e.*, it finds back $\mathbf{b}$ from $\langle \mathbf{b}, \mathbf{k} \rangle$ and $\mathbf{k}$ with certainty), and the algorithm that we actually build in practice: Algorithm 4.

The analysis of Algorithm 4 is related to the set of $\mathbf{b}$ on which the quantum subset-sum solver succeeds: $\mathscr{S}^{\mathbb{Q}}(\langle \mathbf{b}, \mathbf{k} \rangle) = \mathbf{b}$ for a fixed $\mathbf{k}$.

Notation 3. *Let us denote by $\mathscr{G}(\mathbf{k})$ the set of $\mathbf{b}$'s that are correctly found back by $\mathscr{S}^{\mathbb{Q}}$ for a given $\mathbf{k}$:*

$$\mathscr{G}(\mathbf{k}) \stackrel{\text{def}}{=} \{\mathbf{b} \in \mathbb{F}_2^m : \mathscr{S}^{\mathbb{Q}}(\langle \mathbf{b}, \mathbf{k} \rangle) = \mathbf{b}\}$$

and let $G(\mathbf{k})$ be the size of the set $\mathscr{G}(\mathbf{k})$.

We apply in Step 4 a measurement in order to disentangle the superposition we have, so we can apply an inverse QFT in the same natural way as in the ideal algorithm. We show that the probability of success of the measurement (*i.e.*, of

---

Algorithm 4. Finding s using a quantum subset-sum solver $\mathscr{S}^Q$

Require: A parameter $m < n$ and phase vectors $|\psi_{k_i}\rangle$ for $i \in [\![1, m]\!]$.
Ensure: An element $j \in \mathbb{Z}_N$.
1: Tensor the phase vectors and append a register on $\mathbb{Z}_N$

$$\bigotimes_{i=1}^{m} |\psi_{k_i}\rangle |0_n\rangle = \frac{1}{\sqrt{M}} \sum_{\mathbf{b} \in \mathbb{F}_2^m} \omega_N^{s\langle \mathbf{b}, \mathbf{k}\rangle} |\mathbf{b}\rangle |0_n\rangle$$

2: Compute the inner product of $\mathbf{b}$ and $\mathbf{k}$ in the ancillary register

$$\frac{1}{\sqrt{M}} \sum_{\mathbf{b} \in \mathbb{F}_2^m} \omega_N^{s\langle \mathbf{b}, \mathbf{k}\rangle} |\mathbf{b}\rangle |\langle \mathbf{b}, \mathbf{k}\rangle \mod N\rangle$$

3: Apply $\mathscr{S}^Q$ to uncompute $\mathbf{b}$

$$\frac{1}{\sqrt{M}} \sum_{\mathbf{b} \in \mathbb{F}_2^m} \omega_N^{s\langle \mathbf{b}, \mathbf{k}\rangle} \left| \mathbf{b} \oplus \mathscr{S}^Q(\langle \mathbf{b}, \mathbf{k}\rangle) \right\rangle |\langle \mathbf{b}, \mathbf{k}\rangle \mod N\rangle$$

4: Measure the first register. If the result is not $\mathbf{0}_m$, abort and restart with new coset states. Otherwise, we obtain

$$\frac{1}{\sqrt{G(\mathbf{k})}} \sum_{\mathbf{b} \in \mathscr{G}} \omega_N^{s\langle \mathbf{b}, \mathbf{k}\rangle} |\mathbf{0}_m\rangle |\langle \mathbf{b}, \mathbf{k}\rangle \mod N\rangle$$

5: Apply the inverse QFT on $\mathbb{Z}_N$ on the second register

$$\frac{1}{\sqrt{N}} \sum_{j \in \mathbb{Z}_N} \left(\frac{1}{\sqrt{G(\mathbf{k})}} \sum_{\mathbf{b} \in \mathscr{G}} \omega_N^{(s-j)\langle \mathbf{b}, \mathbf{k}\rangle} \right) |\mathbf{0}_m\rangle |j\rangle$$

6: Measure the state and output the resulting j.

---

measuring 0) is good enough for our purpose when taking m close to n. We also prove under the same assumption that the algorithm outputs the secret with good probability. All in all, these two properties lead to our main result.

Theorem 4. *There exists an algorithm which finds s using $O(n)$ queries and the same usage in time and space as the subset-sum solver $\mathscr{S}^Q$.*

In order to analyze Algorithm 4 and prove Theorem 4, we will proceed in two steps.

Step 1. The first step is to give a lower bound on $\mathbb{E}_{\mathbf{k}}[G(\mathbf{k})]$. This lower bound is given by estimating the number of vectors which admit more than one possible solution.

To arrive here, we first take a look at the normalization constant $Z(\mathbf{k})$ and we compute $\mathbb{E}_{\mathbf{k}_\mathbf{k}}[Z(\mathbf{k})]$ (the average over all choices of $\mathbf{k}$). This can be done by simply looking at the measurement step in Algorithm 3.

Lemma 3. *We have*

$$\mathbb{E}\,\mathbf{k}_{\mathbf{k}}[Z(\mathbf{k})] = M\left(1 + \frac{M-1}{N}\right).$$

Proof. Fix $\mathbf{k} = (k_1, \cdots, k_m)$. For all $j \in \mathbb{Z}_N$, the measurement in Algorithm 3 returns j with probability:

$$\mathbb{P}_{ideal}\,[j|\mathbf{k}] = \frac{1}{NZ(\mathbf{k})}\left|\sum_{\mathbf{b}\in\mathbb{F}_2^m} \omega_N^{(s-j)\langle\mathbf{b},\mathbf{k}\rangle}\right|^2$$

$$= \frac{1}{NZ(\mathbf{k})}\left|\prod_{i=1}^{m}\left(1 + \omega_N^{(s-j)k_i}\right)\right|^2 \qquad = \frac{1}{NZ(\mathbf{k})}\prod_{i=1}^{m}\left|1 + \omega_N^{(s-j)k_i}\right|^2$$

$$= \frac{1}{NZ(\mathbf{k})}\prod_{i=1}^{m}4\cos^2\left(\pi k_i\frac{s-j}{N}\right) \qquad = \frac{M^2}{NZ(\mathbf{k})}\prod_{i=1}^{m}\cos^2\left(\pi k_i\frac{s-j}{N}\right).$$

Furthermore, we have $\sum_{j\in\mathbb{Z}_N}\mathbb{P}_{ideal}\,[j|\mathbf{k}] = 1$, so we can write:

$$Z(\mathbf{k}) = \frac{M^2}{N}\sum_{j\in\mathbb{Z}_N}\prod_{i=1}^{m}\cos^2\left(\pi k_i\frac{s-j}{N}\right) \tag{4}$$

It follows that

$$\mathbb{E}\,\mathbf{k}_{\mathbf{k}}[Z(\mathbf{k})] = \frac{M^2}{N}\sum_{j\in\mathbb{Z}_N}\mathbb{E}\left[\prod_{i=1}^{m}\cos^2\left(\pi k_i\frac{s-j}{N}\right)\right]$$

and since the k_i are i.i.d., we have

$$\mathbb{E}\,\mathbf{k}_{\mathbf{k}}[Z(\mathbf{k})] = \frac{M^2}{N}\left(1 + \sum_{j\in\mathbb{Z}_N\setminus\{s\}}\prod_{i=1}^{m}\mathbb{E}\left[\cos^2\left(\pi k_i\frac{s-j}{N}\right)\right]\right)$$

$$= \frac{M^2}{N}\left(1 + (N-1)\prod_{i=1}^{m}\frac{1}{2}\right) = \frac{M}{N}(N+M-1). \qquad \square$$

Next, we give a relation between $G(\mathbf{k})$ and $Z(\mathbf{k})$.

Lemma 4. *For any* $\mathbf{k}$*:*

$$G(\mathbf{k}) \geq (1-\varepsilon)\,(2M - Z(\mathbf{k})).$$

Proof. Fix $\mathbf{k}$. Let $\mathscr{B}(j)$ be the set of vectors whose knapsack sum is j:

$$\mathscr{B}(j) \overset{\text{def}}{=} \{\mathbf{b}\in\mathbb{F}_2^m|\,\langle\mathbf{b},\mathbf{k}\rangle = j \mod N\}$$

and let $\mathscr{C}_i$ be the set of vectors $\mathbf{b}$ that have i collisions:

$$\mathscr{C}_i \overset{\text{def}}{=} \{\mathbf{b}\in\mathbb{F}_2^m|\,\#\mathscr{B}(\langle\mathbf{b},\mathbf{k}\rangle) = i\}.$$

We denote by C_i the size of the set $\mathscr{C}_i$.

If we take a closer look at $Z(\mathbf{k})$, we have that

$$
\begin{aligned}
Z(\mathbf{k}) &= \sum_{j\in\mathbb{Z}_N}\left|\sum_{\mathbf{b}\in B(j)}\omega_N^{s\langle\mathbf{b},\mathbf{k}\rangle}\right|^2 & &= \sum_{j\in\mathbb{Z}_N}\left|\omega_N^{sj}\right|^2\left|\sum_{\mathbf{b}\in B(j)}1\right|^2 \\
&= \sum_{j\in\mathbb{Z}_N}\sum_{\mathbf{b}\in B(j)}\sum_{\mathbf{b}'\in B(j)}1 & &= \sum_{j\in\mathbb{Z}_N}\sum_{\mathbf{b}\in B(j)}\sum_{\mathbf{b}'\in B(\langle\mathbf{b},\mathbf{k}\rangle)}1 \\
&= \sum_{j\in\mathbb{Z}_N}\sum_{\mathbf{b}\in B(j)}\#\mathscr{B}(\langle\mathbf{b},\mathbf{k}\rangle) & &= \sum_{\mathbf{b}\in\mathbb{F}_2^m}\#\mathscr{B}(\langle\mathbf{b},\mathbf{k}\rangle) \\
&= \sum_{i\geq 1}\sum_{\mathbf{b}\in\mathbb{F}_2^m\,:\,\#\mathscr{B}(\langle\mathbf{b},\mathbf{k}\rangle)=i}i & &= \sum_{i\geq 1}iC_i
\end{aligned}
$$

Letting $C_{>1}$ be the number of vectors $\mathbf{b}$ with at least one collision (i.e., for which there exists $\mathbf{b}'\neq\mathbf{b}$ such that they have the same knapsack sum), we have $C_{>1}=\sum_{i>1}C_i$. From

$$
Z(\mathbf{k}) = \sum_{i\geq 1}iC_i = C_1 + 2\sum_{i\geq 2}C_i + \sum_{i\geq 3}(i-2)C_i ,
$$

it follows that we have the lower bound:

$$
Z(\mathbf{k}) \geq C_1 + 2C_{>1} .
$$

Injecting twice the equation $C_1 = M - C_{>1}$ in this inequality and using the trivial bound $G(\mathbf{k}) \geq (1-\varepsilon)C_1$, we conclude the proof.   □

From Lemma 3 and 4, we immediately deduce:

Lemma 5.
$$
\mathbb{E}_{\mathbf{k}}[G(\mathbf{k})] \geq (1-\varepsilon)M\left(1 - \frac{M-1}{N}\right).
$$

Step 2. The second step in our proof computes the probability of success of the "real" algorithm by relating it to $\mathbb{E}_{\mathbf{k}}[G(\mathbf{k})]$.

Lemma 6. *Algorithm 4 outputs the secret s with probability* $\geq (1-\varepsilon)\frac{M(N-M+1)}{N^2}$.

Proof. We compute the probability of measuring $j \in \mathbb{Z}_N$ at the end of Algorithm 4. In particular, we have for s

$$
\mathbb{P}_{real}[s|\mathbf{k}] = \frac{1}{NG(\mathbf{k})}\left|\sum_{\mathbf{b}\in\mathscr{G}}\omega_N^0\right|^2 = \frac{G(\mathbf{k})}{N}
$$

We have by Lemma 5 that $\mathbb{E}[G(\mathbf{k})] \geq (1-\varepsilon)M\left(1-\frac{M-1}{N}\right)$. We finish the proof by observing that $\mathbb{P}_{real}[s] = \mathbb{E}[\mathbb{P}_{real}[s|\mathbf{k}]] \geq (1-\varepsilon)\frac{M(N-M+1)}{N^2}$.   □

Finally, we can prove Theorem 4.

Proof. Step 4 of Algorithm 4 succeeds with average probability $\frac{\mathbb{E}\,[G(\mathbf{k})]}{M}$ which is greater than $(1-\varepsilon)\frac{N-M+1}{N}$ (by Lemma 5). The final measurement of the algorithm outputs the secret with probability $\geq (1-\varepsilon)\frac{M(N-M+1)}{N^2}$ (by Lemma 6). We will thus have to repeat the algorithm an expected number smaller than $\frac{N^3}{(1-\varepsilon)^2 M(N-M+1)^2}$ times. By letting m be equal to $n-1$, we obtain that the algorithm will have to be repeated less than $8/(1-\varepsilon)^2$ times. Thus, we can conclude that our algorithm needs $O(n)$ queries and has complexity costs identical to the ones of the subset-sum solver, since the subset-sum resolution is the only exponential step of the algorithm. □

4   Interpolation Algorithm

If we take a look at the ideal algorithm and consider that there is no collision, we can see that we would like 2^m to be as close to N as possible in order for the sum

$$\frac{1}{\sqrt{M}} \sum_{\mathbf{b}\in\mathbb{F}_2^m} \omega_N^{(s-j)\langle\mathbf{b},\mathbf{k}\rangle}$$

to contain as many as possible elements of the sum

$$\frac{1}{\sqrt{N}} \sum_{\mathbf{b}\in\mathbb{F}_2^n} \omega_N^{(s-j)\langle\mathbf{b},\mathbf{k}\rangle}.$$

In the mean time, it is clear that the closest M gets to N, the more likely collisions $\langle\mathbf{b_1},\mathbf{k}\rangle = \langle\mathbf{b_2},\mathbf{k}\rangle$ for $\mathbf{b_1}\neq\mathbf{b_2}$ become. We thus have to find a compromise on the value m or more interestingly play with the values k_i used in the algorithm, to avoid collisions and to simplify the resolution of the subset-sum problem.

In fact, we can reduce the size of the subset-sum problem we have to solve by pre-processing the states to get values of k_i that will allow us to solve the subset-sum problem on some bits by Gaussian elimination. Constructing these k_i's can be achieved by Kuperberg's second algorithm (or any improvement). Given a threshold parameter $t \in [\![1,m]\!]$, we can consider the following configuration for the k_i to use as inputs in Algorithm 4 (dots represent unknown bits and the i-th bit of the j-th row is the j-th bit of the binary expansion of k_i):

$$
\begin{array}{c}
\\ k_1 \\ k_2 \\ \vdots \\ k_{m-t} \\ k_{m-t+1} \\ \vdots \\ k_m
\end{array}
\begin{array}{c}
\begin{array}{ccccccc}
1 & 2 & \cdots & m-t & m-t+1 & \cdots & n
\end{array} \\
\left(\begin{array}{ccccccc}
1 & \bullet & \cdots & \bullet & \bullet & \cdots & \bullet \\
0 & 1 & \ddots & \bullet & \bullet & \cdots & \bullet \\
\vdots & \vdots & \ddots & \ddots & \vdots & \cdots & \bullet \\
0 & 0 & \cdots & 1 & \bullet & \cdots & \bullet \\
0 & 0 & \cdots & 0 & \bullet & \cdots & \bullet \\
\vdots & \vdots & & \vdots & \vdots & \cdots & \bullet \\
0 & 0 & \cdots & 0 & \bullet & \cdots & \bullet
\end{array}\right)
\end{array}
\qquad (5)
$$

In Algorithm 4, it turns out that we can keep a good probability of finding the secret s by letting m be equal to $n-1$ so that is what we will assume afterwards.

To build phase vectors that satisfy the configuration in (5), we will approximately have to query the oracle

$$\sum_{i=1}^{n-t} 2^{\sqrt{c_{\mathsf{DCP}} i}} + t 2^{\sqrt{c_{\mathsf{DCP}}(n-t)}}$$

leading to a query and time complexities of $O\left((\sqrt{n-t}+t)2^{\sqrt{c_{\mathsf{DCP}}(n-t)}}\right)$ (by Lemma 1), where c_{DCP} is the constant of the algorithm used to construct the states ($c_{\mathsf{DCP}} = 2$ for Kuperberg's second algorithm). For the subset-sum problem, solving it on the first $n-t$ bits is easy (thanks to a Gaussian elimination), the difficulty comes from the last t bits, leading to a complexity in $O\left(2^{c_{q\mathsf{ss}}t}\right)$ time, where $c_{q\mathsf{SS}}$ is the complexity exponent of the quantum subset-sum solver. This parameter t can be used in a natural way to obtain an interpolation algorithm, since it allows to obtain a tradeoff between the preparation of the states and the resolution of the problem (which amounts to solving a quantum subset-sum problem).

We can now give an interpolation algorithm derived from Algorithm 4. We note that letting q be the query complexity exponent, it is possible to determine t from n and the value q we can afford. Using Kuperberg's second algorithm (or any improvement) to compute suitable phase vectors as described before and then giving them as inputs to Algorithm 4, we can retrieve the secret s as described by Algorithm 5 with the complexities given by Sect. 5.

Algorithm 5. Interpolation algorithm (using a quantum SS solver)

Require: q such that 2^q is the number of queries we are allowed to do.
Ensure: The secret s.
  1: Use Kuperberg's second algorithm (or any improvement) to create states $|\psi_{k_i}\rangle$ for $i \in [\![1, m]\!]$ satisfying the configuration represented by Matrix (5), where $t \approx \frac{q}{c_{\mathsf{SS}}}$.
  2: Apply Algorithm 4 on these m states to obtain a value $j \in \mathbb{Z}_N$.
  3: Check if j is the secret. If not, return to Step 1. Otherwise, output j.

Theorem 5. *Let* $t \in [\![1, m]\!]$. *Algorithm 5 finds* s *with* $O\left((\sqrt{n-t}+t)\right.$ $\left.2^{\sqrt{c_{\mathsf{DCP}}(n-t)}}\right)$ *queries in* $O\left((\sqrt{n-t}+t)2^{\sqrt{c_{\mathsf{DCP}}(n-t)}} + 2^{c_{q\mathsf{ss}}t}\right)$ *quantum time,* *classical space* $O\left(2^{\sqrt{c_{\mathsf{DCP}}(n-t)}} + 2^{c_{q\mathsf{ss}}t}\right)$ *and* $O\left(\mathrm{poly}(n)\right)$ *quantum space.*

We notice that when $t = m$, the k_i are kept random and we have to solve the "full rank" subset-sum, matching with Algorithm 4. On the other side, when $t = 1$, we fall back on Kuperberg's second algorithm since we have in this case to construct a collection of states divisible by all the successive powers of 2, see Sect. 2.3. Finally, when $1 < t < m$, we have new algorithms working for any number of queries between $O(n)$ and $\tilde{O}\left(2^{\sqrt{c_{DCP}n}}\right)$.

5   Quantum Subset-Sum Algorithms

In this section, we consider quantum algorithms solving the *quantum* subset-sum problem introduced in Sect. 2.4. We give both asymptotic complexities and numerical estimates.

Recall that we consider a subset-sum instance $(v, \mathbf{k}), \mathbf{k} \in \mathbb{Z}_N^m$, where v is *in superposition*, and $\mathbf{k}$ will remain fixed. The problem is to find $\mathbf{b}$ such that $\langle \mathbf{b}, \mathbf{k} \rangle = v \mod N$ for a given (fixed) modulus N. For a given v, if there are many solutions, we want to find one selected uniformly at random (under heuristics). If we want all solutions, then we can run multiple instances of the solver (we will have to redo the pre-computations that we define below). A given solver, defined for a specific $\mathbf{k}$, is expected to work only for some (large) proportion $1 - \varepsilon$ of v. We can check whether the output is a solution or not and measure the obtained bit to collapse on the cases of success.

5.1   Algorithms Based on Representations

The best algorithms to solve the subset-sum problem with density one are list-merging algorithms using the *representation technique* [4,22]. The best asymptotic complexities (both classical and quantum) are given in [8]. We detail the representation framework following the depiction given in [8]. To ease the description, we start with the case $v = 0$, *i.e.*, the *homogeneous* case, and we will show below how to extend it easily to $v \neq 0$.

Guessed Weight. We assume that the solution $\mathbf{b}$ is of weight $\lceil m/2 \rceil$. This is true only with probability: $p_m := 2^{-m}\binom{m}{\lceil m/2 \rceil} = 1/\mathsf{poly}(m)$. If not, we re-randomize the subset-sum instance by multiplying $\mathbf{b}$ by a random invertible matrix. Thus if we manage to solve an instance of weight $\lceil m/2 \rceil$, the total complexity to solve any instance will introduce a multiplicative factor $\frac{1}{p_m}$ that we will have to estimate.

Distributions. We consider *distributions* of vectors having certain relative weights: $D^m[\alpha] \subseteq \{0,1\}^m$ is the set of vectors having weight αm. The basic idea of representations is to write the solution $\mathbf{b}$ as a sum of vectors of smaller relative weights, *e.g.*, $\mathbf{b} = \mathbf{b}_1 + \mathbf{b}_2$ where $\mathbf{b}_1 \in D^m[\alpha_1], \mathbf{b}_2 \in D^m[\alpha_2]$ and $\alpha_1 + \alpha_2 = \frac{1}{2}$. In this paper, we consider only representations with coefficients 0 or 1. Extended representations can be considered, using more coefficients (which have to cancel out each other). However, the advantage of using extended representations becomes quickly insignificant in practice. It is also harder to compute the number of representations, or the filtering probabilities that we define below.

Merging Tree. A subset-sum algorithm is defined by a *merging tree*. A node in this tree is a *list* $L[\ell, \alpha, c]$, which represents a set of vectors drawn from $\{0, 1\}^m$ under several conditions: 1. the size of the list is $2^{m\ell}$; 2. the vectors are sampled u.a.r. from a prescribed distribution $D^m[\alpha]$; 3. the vectors satisfy a *modular condition* of cm bits. With $v = 0$, the following condition can be used: $\langle \mathbf{e}, \mathbf{k} \rangle$ mod $N \in [-N/2^{cm}; N/2^{cm}]$ for some number c. More generally, the modular conditions can be chosen arbitrarily, as long as they remain compatible with the target v.

Once the tree structure is chosen, its parameters are optimized under several constraints. First, the lists have a certain maximal size. A distribution $D^m[\alpha]$ has size $\binom{m}{\alpha m}$, which is asymptotically estimated as $\simeq 2^{h(\alpha)m}$ where $h(x) := -x \log_2 x - (1-x) \log_2(1-x)$ is the Hamming entropy. This creates the constraint $\ell \leq h(\alpha) - c$. Second, we expect the root list to contain the solution of the problem, *i.e.*, $\ell = 0$ (one element), $\alpha = \frac{1}{2}$ and $c = 1$. Finally, each non-leaf list L has its parameters determined by its two children L_1, L_2. Indeed, it is obtained via the *merging-filtering* operation which selects, among all pairs of vectors $(\mathbf{e}_1, \mathbf{e}_2) \in L_1 \times L_2$, the pairs such that: $\mathbf{e}_1 + \mathbf{e}_2$ satisfies the modular condition (merging) and satisfies the weight condition (filtering). The parameters are:

$$\begin{cases} \alpha = \alpha_1 + \alpha_2 \text{ (increasing weights)} \\ \ell = \ell_1 + \ell_2 - (c - \min(c_1, c_2)) - \mathsf{pf}(\alpha_1, \alpha_2) \end{cases} \tag{6}$$

Here, pf is the probability that two vectors chosen u.a.r. in their respective distributions will not have colliding 1s.

Lemma 7 (Lemma 1 in [8]). *Let $\mathbf{e}_1, \mathbf{e}_2$ be drawn u.a.r. from $D^m[\alpha_1], D^m[\alpha_2]$ with $\alpha_1 + \alpha_2 \leq 1$. The probability that $\mathbf{e}_1 + \mathbf{e}_2 \in D^m[\alpha_1 + \alpha_2]$ is equal to:*

$$\mathsf{PF}(\alpha_1, \alpha_2, m) := \binom{m - \alpha_1 m}{\alpha_2 m} \Big/ \binom{m}{\alpha_2 m} \simeq 2^{m\mathsf{pf}(\alpha_1, \alpha_2)}$$

where $\mathsf{pf}(\alpha_1, \alpha_2) := h\left(\frac{1-\alpha_2}{\alpha_1}\right)\alpha_1 - h(\alpha_1)$.

Classical Computation of the Tree. To any correctly parameterized merging tree corresponds a classical subset-sum algorithm that runs as follows: it creates the leaf lists by sampling their distributions at random. It then builds the parent lists by *merging-filtering* steps. The *merging* operation is efficient, since elements can be ordered according to the modular condition to be satisfied.

Lemma 8 (Lemma 2 in [8]). *Let L_1, L_2 be two sorted lists stored in classical memory with random access. In $\log_2$, relatively to m, the parent list L can be built in time:* $\max(\min(\ell_1, \ell_2), \ell_1 + \ell_2 - (c - \min(c_1, c_2)))$ *and in memory* $\max(\ell_1, \ell_2, \ell)$.

Quantum Computation of the Tree. While the more advanced quantum subset-sum algorithms use quantum walks [5, 8, 20], we want to focus here on algorithms using few qubits, which at the moment, rely only on quantum merging with Grover search. They replace the classical merging operation by the following.

Lemma 9 (Lemma 4 in [8]). *Let L_2 be a sorted list stored in QRACM. Assume given a unitary U that produces, in time t_{L_1}, a uniform superposition of elements of L_1. Then there exists a unitary U' that produces a uniform superposition of elements of L, in time $O\left(\frac{t_{L_1}}{\sqrt{\mathsf{pf}(\alpha_1,\alpha_2)}} \max(\sqrt{2^{cm}/|L_2|}, 1)\right)$.*

Since the goal is only to sample u.a.r. from the root list, only half of the lists in the tree need actually to be stored in QRACM. The others are sampled using the unitary operators given by Lemma 9. In short, the obtained subset-sum algorithm is a sequence of Grover searches which use existing lists stored in memory to sample elements in new lists with more constraints.

Heuristics. The standard subset-sum heuristic assumes that the elements of all lists in the tree (not only the leaf lists) behave as if they were uniformly sampled from the set of vectors of right weight, satisfying the modular condition. This heuristic ensures that the list sizes are very close to their average: for each L obtained by merging and filtering $L_1[\ell_1, \alpha_1, c_1]$ and $L_2[\ell_2, \alpha_2, c_2]$, we have:

$$|L| \simeq \frac{|L_1||L_2|}{2^{m(c-\min(c_1,c_2))}\mathsf{PF}(\alpha_1,\alpha_2,m)} \quad,$$

where the approximation is exact down to a factor 2. This is true with over-whelming probability for all lists of large expected size via Chernoff-Hoeffding bounds, and even if the root list is of expected size 1, the probability that it actually ends up empty is smaller than $e^{-0.5} \simeq 0.61$.

5.2   From Asymptotic to Exact Optimizations

As the time and memory complexities of a subset-sum algorithm are determined by its merging tree, we seek to select a tree which minimizes these parameters. Given a certain subset-sum problem, we first select a tree shape. As an example, the best subset-sum algorithm with low qubits (using QRACM) is the "quantum HGJ" algorithm of [8], whose structure is reproduced in Fig. 1. At level 3, it splits the vectors into two halves, and merges without filtering. While all lists are obtained via quantum merging/filtering, the main computation is performed after obtaining L_1^3, L_1^2, L_1^1, where the main branch is explored using Grover's algorithm: we search through the lists $L_0^3, L_0^2 L_0^1$ without representing them in memory. The quadratic speedup of Grover search makes the tree unbalanced, which is reflected on the naming of its parameters in Fig. 1.

The *asymptotic* time complexity of the algorithms has the form $\tilde{O}\left(2^{\beta m}\right)$, and is the result of summing together the costs of all merging steps. Through the approximation of binomial coefficients, the list sizes are approximated in $\log_2$ and relatively to m. The parameters (relative weights, modular conditions and sizes) are numerically optimized. The optimization of Fig. 1 in [8] yields the complexity $\tilde{O}\left(2^{0.2356m}\right)$.

In this paper, we also perform non-asymptotic optimizations for a given m. Since we use only $\{0, 1\}$-representations, the filtering probability is well known

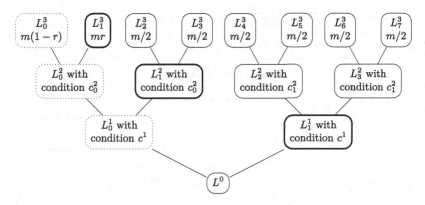

Fig. 1. Quantum HGJ algorithm. Dotted lists are search spaces (they are not stored). Bold lists are stored in QRACM. The first level uses a left-right split of vectors, without filtering.

and has a simple expression (Lemma 7). Since the binomial coefficients can be extended as functions of $\mathbb{R}^2$, we can perform an exact numerical optimization of list sizes for a given m. Afterwards, the numbers obtained are rounded, in particular the weights of representations, and we take the point which gives us the best results: smallest complexity and biggest average size for L^0.

Example. Let us take $n = \log_2 N = 256$, $m = n - 1 = 255$, and the structure of Fig. 1. We adapt the optimization code of [8] by taking the exact exponents (not relative to n) and optimize numerically under the constraint $|L^0| = 2^2$ (to ensure that there are solutions). The asymptotic formula would give $2^{0.2356n} \sim 2^{60.31}$. Numerical optimization gives us a time $2^{63.81}$, but this admits non-integer parameters and it is only the *maximum* between all steps. By rounding the parameters well, we obtain Fig. 2.

To compute the quantum time complexity, we consider the list sizes to be exact and use the formula of Lemma 9 without the O. The subtrees on the right can be computed in $2^{65.71}$ operations; the slight increase is due to the fact that we take a sum of their respective terms and not a maximum. In the left branch, we sample from L^0 in $2^{63.48}$ operations.

The actual time complexity is slightly bigger, due to the variation in list sizes, and the constant complexity overhead ($\pi/2$) of Grover search. More importantly, these operations require: • to recompute a sum, using m (controlled) additions modulo N; • to test membership in some distribution; • to sample from input distributions D^n. The latter can be done using a circuit given in [17], which for a weight k and n bits, has a gate count $\tilde{O}(nk)$ and uses $n + 2\lceil \log(k+1) \rceil$ qubits. All of this boils down to m arithmetic operations or $O(m^2)$ quantum gates.

Finally, this sampler works only for a proportion $\frac{1}{p_m} = 2^{-5.33}$ of subset-sum instances, so we need to re-randomize accordingly. After running the optimization for $128 \leq m \leq 1024$ and $n = m + 1$, we found that the subset-sum solver would use approximately $2^{0.238m+9.203}$ arithmetic operations, for a final list L^0

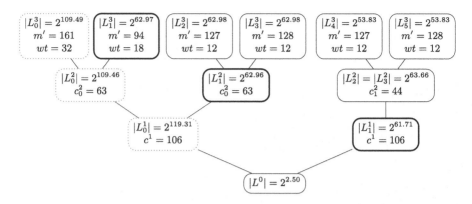

Fig. 2. Optimization of Fig. 1 for $m = 255$. The size of the support is indicated by m' and the weight by wt.

of size 2 on average. Under the subset-sum heuristic, we assume an independence between all tuples of elements in the initial lists. Using Chernoff-Hoeffding bounds the probability that the final list is empty is smaller than $e^{-1} \simeq 0.37$. To reduce it to a smaller constant ε, we may simply run multiple independent instances of the solver. This increases the asymptotic complexity by a factor $O(-\log \varepsilon)$.

5.3   Solving Subset-Sum in Superposition

We now show that we can reuse the structure of the QRACM-based subset-sum algorithm of Fig. 1 to solve the problem in *superposition* over the target v, while still keeping the number of qubits polynomial.

The basic idea is to reduce the problem with a given $v \neq 0$ to $v = 0$: $\langle \mathbf{k'}, \mathbf{b} \rangle = 0 \mod N$, where $\mathbf{k'}$ is a length $m + 1$ vector where we append $-v$ to $\mathbf{k}$. We can then modify *any* existing tree-based subset-sum algorithm solving this instance to force all vectors in the leftmost leaf list to have a 1 in the last coordinate, and all vectors in the other leaves to have 0 in this coordinate. Then only the lists in the left branch of the tree depend on v. The complexity is unchanged.

Following the tree structure of Fig. 1, we create the lists L_1^3, L_1^2, L_1^1 in a pre-computation step. Then we define a quantum algorithm that outputs an element in L^0 (or a superposition of such elements), and we run this algorithm in superposition over v.

Subset-Sum without QRACM. Helm and May [21] showed that quantum subset-sum algorithms using a small classical memory (without quantum access) can have better time-memory tradeoffs than classical ones. They obtained a time $\tilde{O}(2^{0.428m})$ for a memory $O(2^{0.285m})$, however their algorithm does not have an unbalanced structure like ours.

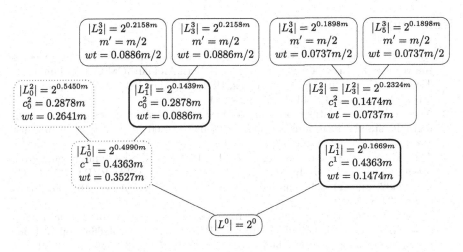

Fig. 3. Asymptotic optimization of our quantum subset-sum algorithm without QRACM. The lists on the right of the tree are constructed with classical computations, using classical RAM. The lists L_1^2 and L_1^1 are stored in classical memory without random access.

We improve on this time-memory tradeoff by adapting the tree of Fig. 1 as follows: we remove L_0^3 and L_1^3 and their parameters, and directly sample in L_0^2. Assuming that the lists L_1^2 and L_1^1 are precomputed classically, we sample from L^0 with the same algorithm, except that it replaces each QRACM access (in time 1) by a sequential memory access (in time $|L_1^2|$ and $|L_1^1|$ for L_1^2 and L_1^1 respectively), *i.e.*, a quantum circuit which encodes the elements of the lists as a sequence of standard gates. The asymptotic optimization gives a time $\tilde{O}\left(2^{0.4165m}\right)$ with a memory $O\left(2^{0.2324m}\right)$. The parameters are displayed in Fig. 3.

The difference between asymptotic and non-asymptotic optimization is bigger here. For $m = n - 1 = 127$, with the constraint $|L^0| = 2^2$, we obtain a time $2^{60.01} > 2^{128\times0.4165} = 2^{53.31}$ and a memory $2^{26.82} < 2^{128\times0.2324} = 2^{29.75}$. On top of this, we must also take p_m into account.

After running optimizations for $n = 128$ to 1024, we obtained a count of about $2^{0.418m+12.851}$ blocks of m arithmetic operations (m^2 quantum gates). The point at which the algorithm starts improving over Grover search lies around $n = 157$.

Acknowledgments. This work has been partially supported by the French Agence Nationale de la Recherche through the France 2030 program under grant agreement No. ANR-22-PETQ-0008 PQ-TLS.

References

1. Ajtai, M., Dwork, C.: A public-key cryptosystem with worst-case/average-case equivalence. In: Proceedings of the Twenty-Ninth Annual ACM Symposium on the Theory of Computing, El Paso, Texas, USA, 4–6 May 1997, pp. 284–293 (1997). http://doi.acm.org/10.1145/258533.258604

2. Alagic, G., et al.: Status report on the third round of the nist post-quantum cryptography standardization process (2022–07-05 04:07:00 2022). https://tsapps.nist.gov/publication/get_pdf.cfm?pub_id=934458

3. Alamati, N., De Feo, L., Montgomery, H., Patranabis, S.: Cryptographic group actions and applications. In: Moriai, S., Wang, H. (eds.) ASIACRYPT 2020. LNCS, vol. 12492, pp. 411–439. Springer, Cham (2020). https://doi.org/10.1007/978-3-030-64834-3_14

4. Becker, A., Coron, J.-S., Joux, A.: Improved generic algorithms for hard knapsacks. In: Paterson, K.G. (ed.) EUROCRYPT 2011. LNCS, vol. 6632, pp. 364–385. Springer, Heidelberg (2011). https://doi.org/10.1007/978-3-642-20465-4_21

5. Bernstein, D.J., Jeffery, S., Lange, T., Meurer, A.: Quantum algorithms for the subset-sum problem. In: Gaborit, P. (ed.) PQCrypto 2013. LNCS, vol. 7932, pp. 16–33. Springer, Heidelberg (2013). https://doi.org/10.1007/978-3-642-38616-9_2

6. Beullens, W., Kleinjung, T., Vercauteren, F.: CSI-FiSh: efficient isogeny based signatures through class group computations. In: Galbraith, S.D., Moriai, S. (eds.) ASIACRYPT 2019. LNCS, vol. 11921, pp. 227–247. Springer, Cham (2019). https://doi.org/10.1007/978-3-030-34578-5_9

7. Bonnetain, X.: Improved low-qubit hidden shift algorithms (2019). arXiv:1901.11428

8. Bonnetain, X., Bricout, R., Schrottenloher, A., Shen, Y.: Improved classical and quantum algorithms for subset-sum. In: Moriai, S., Wang, H. (eds.) ASIACRYPT 2020. LNCS, vol. 12492, pp. 633–666. Springer, Cham (2020). https://doi.org/10.1007/978-3-030-64834-3_22

9. Bonnetain, X., Schrottenloher, A.: Quantum security analysis of CSIDH. In: Canteaut, A., Ishai, Y. (eds.) EUROCRYPT 2020. LNCS, vol. 12106, pp. 493–522. Springer, Cham (2020). https://doi.org/10.1007/978-3-030-45724-2_17

10. Brassard, G., HØyer, P., Tapp, A.: Quantum cryptanalysis of hash and claw-free functions. In: Lucchesi, C.L., Moura, A.V. (eds.) LATIN 1998. LNCS, vol. 1380, pp. 163–169. Springer, Heidelberg (1998). https://doi.org/10.1007/BFb0054319

11. Castryck, W., Lange, T., Martindale, C., Panny, L., Renes, J.: CSIDH: an efficient post-quantum commutative group action. In: Peyrin, T., Galbraith, S. (eds.) ASIACRYPT 2018. LNCS, vol. 11274, pp. 395–427. Springer, Cham (2018). https://doi.org/10.1007/978-3-030-03332-3_15

12. Chávez-Saab, J., Chi-Domínguez, J., Jaques, S., Rodríguez-Henríquez, F.: The SQALE of CSIDH: sublinear vélu quantum-resistant isogeny action with low exponents. J. Cryptogr. Eng. **12**(3), 349–368 (2022)

13. Childs, A., Jao, D., Soukharev, V.: Constructing elliptic curve isogenies in quantum subexponential time. J. Math. Cryptol. **8**(1), 1–29 (2014)

14. De Feo, L., Galbraith, S.D.: SeaSign: compact isogeny signatures from class group actions. In: Ishai, Y., Rijmen, V. (eds.) EUROCRYPT 2019. LNCS, vol. 11478, pp. 759–789. Springer, Cham (2019). https://doi.org/10.1007/978-3-030-17659-4_26

15. Decru, T., Panny, L., Vercauteren, F.: Faster SeaSign signatures through improved rejection sampling. In: Ding, J., Steinwandt, R. (eds.) PQCrypto 2019. LNCS, vol.

11505, pp. 271–285. Springer, Cham (2019). https://doi.org/10.1007/978-3-030-25510-7_15

16. Diffie, W., Hellman, M.: New directions in cryptography. IEEE Trans. Inf. Theory **22**(6), 644–654 (1976)

17. Esser, A., Ramos-Calderer, S., Bellini, E., Latorre, J.I., Manzano, M.: An optimized quantum implementation of ISD on scalable quantum resources. IACR Cryptology ePrint Archive, p. 1608 (2021)

18. Ettinger, M., Høyer, P.: On quantum algorithms for noncommutative hidden subgroups. In: Meinel, C., Tison, S. (eds.) STACS 1999. LNCS, vol. 1563, pp. 478–487. Springer, Heidelberg (1999). https://doi.org/10.1007/3-540-49116-3_45

19. Ettinger, M., Høyer, P., Knill, E.: The quantum query complexity of the hidden subgroup problem is polynomial (2004). arXiv:quant-ph/0401083

20. Helm, A., May, A.: Subset sum quantumly in 1.17^n. In: Jeffery, S. (ed.) TQC 2018. Leibniz International Proceedings in Informatics (LIPIcs), vol. 111, pp. 5:1–5:15. Schloss Dagstuhl-Leibniz-Zentrum fuer Informatik, Dagstuhl, Germany (2018)

21. Helm, A., May, A.: The power of few qubits and collisions – subset sum below Grover's bound. In: Ding, J., Tillich, J.-P. (eds.) PQCrypto 2020. LNCS, vol. 12100, pp. 445–460. Springer, Cham (2020). https://doi.org/10.1007/978-3-030-44223-1_24

22. Howgrave-Graham, N., Joux, A.: New generic algorithms for hard knapsacks. In: Gilbert, H. (ed.) EUROCRYPT 2010. LNCS, vol. 6110, pp. 235–256. Springer, Heidelberg (2010). https://doi.org/10.1007/978-3-642-13190-5_12

23. Kuperberg, G.: A subexponential-time quantum algorithm for the dihedral hidden subgroup problem. SIAM J. Comput. **35**(1), 170–188 (2005). https://doi.org/10.1137/S0097539703436345

24. Kuperberg, G.: Another subexponential-time quantum algorithm for the dihedral hidden subgroup problem. In: TQC. LIPIcs, vol. 22, pp. 20–34. Schloss Dagstuhl - Leibniz-Zentrum für Informatik (2013)

25. Lyubashevsky, V., Micciancio, D.: On bounded distance decoding, unique shortest vectors, and the minimum distance problem. In: Halevi, S. (ed.) CRYPTO 2009. LNCS, vol. 5677, pp. 577–594. Springer, Heidelberg (2009). https://doi.org/10.1007/978-3-642-03356-8_34

26. NIST: Submission requirements and evaluation criteria for the post-quantum cryptography standardization process (2016). https://csrc.nist.gov/CSRC/media/Projects/Post-Quantum-Cryptography/documents/call-for-proposals-final-dec-2016.pdf

27. Peikert, C.: He gives C-sieves on the CSIDH. In: Canteaut, A., Ishai, Y. (eds.) EUROCRYPT 2020. LNCS, vol. 12106, pp. 463–492. Springer, Cham (2020). https://doi.org/10.1007/978-3-030-45724-2_16

28. Regev, O.: Quantum computation and lattice problems. In: FOCS, pp. 520–529. IEEE Computer Society (2002)

29. Regev, O.: New lattice-based cryptographic constructions. J. ACM **51**(6), 899–942 (2004)

30. Regev, O.: A subexponential time algorithm for the dihedral hidden subgroup problem with polynomial space (2004). arXiv:quant-ph/0406151

31. Rivest, R.L., Shamir, A., Adleman, L.M.: A method for obtaining digital signatures and public-key cryptosystems. Commun. ACM **21**(2), 120–126 (1978)

32. Shor, P.W.: Algorithms for quantum computation: discrete logarithms and factoring. In: Proceedings 35th Annual Symposium on Foundations of Computer Science, pp. 124–134 (1994)

33. Stehlé, D., Steinfeld, R., Tanaka, K., Xagawa, K.: Efficient public key encryption based on ideal lattices. In: Matsui, M. (ed.) ASIACRYPT 2009. LNCS, vol. 5912, pp. 617–635. Springer, Heidelberg (2009). https://doi.org/10.1007/978-3-642-10366-7_36
34. Wagner, D.: A generalized birthday problem. In: Yung, M. (ed.) CRYPTO 2002. LNCS, vol. 2442, pp. 288–304. Springer, Heidelberg (2002). https://doi.org/10.1007/3-540-45708-9_19

Post-Quantum Protocols

Post-Quantum Signatures in DNSSEC via Request-Based Fragmentation

Jason Goertzen and Douglas Stebila[✉][iD]

University of Waterloo, Waterloo, ON, Canada
{jgoertze,dstebila}@uwaterloo.ca

Abstract. The Domain Name System Security Extensions (DNSSEC) provide authentication of DNS responses using digital signatures. DNS operates primarily over UDP, which leads to several constraints: notably, DNS packets should be at most 1232 bytes long to avoid problems during transmission. Larger DNS responses would either need to be fragmented into several UDP responses or the request would need to be repeated over TCP, neither of which is sufficiently reliable in today's DNS ecosystem. While RSA or elliptic curve digital signatures are sufficiently small to avoid this problem, even for DNSSEC packets containing both a public key and a signature, this problem is unavoidable when considering the larger sizes of post-quantum schemes.

We propose ARRF, a method of fragmenting DNS resource records at the application layer (rather than the transport layer) that is *request-based*, meaning the initial response contains a truncated fragment and then the requester sends follow-up requests for the remaining fragments. Using request-based fragmentation avoids problems identified for several previously proposed—and rejected—application-level DNS fragmentation techniques. We implement our approach and evaluate its performance in a simulated network when used for the three post-quantum digital signature schemes selected by NIST for standardization (Falcon, Dilithium, and SPHINCS+) at the 128-bit security level. Our experiments show that our request-based fragmentation approach provides substantially lower resolution times compared to standard DNS over UDP with TCP fallback, for all the tested post-quantum algorithms, and with less data transmitted in the case of both Falcon and Dilithium. Furthermore, our request-based fragmentation design can be implemented relatively easily: our implementation is in fact a small daemon that can sit in front of a DNS name server or resolver to fragment/reassemble transparently. As well, our request-based application-level fragmentation over UDP may avoid problems that arise on poorly configured network devices with other approaches for handling large DNS responses.

Keywords: Domain Name System · DNSSEC · Post-quantum cryptography

1 Introduction

The Domain Name System (DNS) is a mission critical service for the Internet. DNS is responsible for translating human-readable domain names into

© The Author(s), under exclusive license to Springer Nature Switzerland AG 2023
T. Johansson and D. Smith-Tone (Eds.): PQCrypto 2023, LNCS 14154, pp. 535–564, 2023.
https://doi.org/10.1007/978-3-031-40003-2_20

machine-understandable IP addresses and is used by billions of devices daily. Ensuring that these translations are correct and not forged is critical to prevent users from being directed to malicious servers instead of their intended destination. The Domain Name System Security Extensions (DNSSEC) [23] provide data integrity by using digital signatures. DNSSEC ensures that the received DNS message is indeed from a server authorized to respond to the query, and that the message has not been modified in transit.

Today's DNSSEC uses digital signatures that rely on traditional security assumptions such as factoring and discrete logarithms, which would not resist attacks by a cryptographically relevant quantum computer. To continue to provide its intended security guarantees in the face of such threats, DNSSEC must be updated to accommodate quantum-resistant algorithms. The post-quantum cryptography standardization project of the United States National Institute of Standards and Technology (NIST) announced in July 2022 [2] three post-quantum digital signatures algorithms to be standardized: CRYSTALS-Dilithium [16], Falcon [21], and SPHINCS+ [14]. All of these selected algorithms have one thing in common: the amount of data transmission required in order to perform a verification is substantially larger than their non-post-quantum counterparts: both public keys and signatures. This increase in size can cause substantial issues for pre-existing network protocols; DNS and DNSSEC are particularly sensitive to this issue.

Constraints on DNS and DNSSEC. There is an extremely large quantity of DNS traffic, so DNSSEC must be sufficiently efficient to support this high volume, which leads to the need for highly performant signature verification and, to a somewhat lesser extent, signature generation (signatures are often done offline and then transferred to the servers). DNS relies primarily on UDP for communicating between servers. UDP has the benefit of being very lightweight and data efficient, however it has limitations that impact DNS: namely any UDP packet that exceeds 1500 bytes must be fragmented. UDP fragmentation is fragile and is generally not considered a reliable method for delivering large messages. With this in mind, accounting for the size of IPv6 headers, it is recommended that the DNS message sizes should not exceed 1232 bytes [7,19]. As we will note below, for all three of the post-quantum signature algorithms selected by NIST, 1232 bytes is not enough to send both a public key and a signature, as is needed in some parts of DNS.

Admittedly, this 1232 byte limit does not mean that large DNS message cannot in principle be sent. When a DNS response exceeds 1232 bytes, a truncated response is sent instead indicating to the requester that they should then switch to using TCP instead of UDP. Unfortunately, a non-trivial number of name servers are estimated to not support TCP communication, preventing them from sending and receiving large DNS messages. A 2016 study [19,22] observes that 11% of DNS servers do not support DNS over TCP. A 2022 study by Mao, Rabinovich, and Schomp [17] finds that 4.8% of domains using ADNS fail sometimes or always using DNS-over-TCP; the sample set in [17] is a set of "10.6 million domains queried in a week through a resolution service operated by [a] major

CDN". They also have data indicating that this 4.8% of domains accounts for a roughly proportionate (4.4%) of the overall query volume. (Interestingly, [17, §4.5] also notes that the TCP-fallback-incapable resolvers happen to have above average EDNS0 support, which bodes well for our solution which utilizes the increased DNS message sizes that ENDS0 provides.)

There have been two proposed mechanisms to solve the large DNS message issue [26,27], both of which ultimately failed at getting standardized for use. Both mechanisms moved message fragmentation from the transport layer into the application layer, thus removing concerns of UDP fragmentation fragility and the lack of support of TCP. If a large DNS message needed to be sent, both of these mechanisms would split the DNS message into chunks and send each chunk one after the other. Fundamentally, both these mechanisms sent many, potentially large, packets, in response to a single request. There were significant concerns about the impacts these mechanisms would have. First, sending many, potentially large, packets in response to a single request increases the risk and impact of denial of server amplification attacks. Second, sending many UDP packets in response to a single UDP request is an unusual behaviour, and some networks are configured to only accept a single UDP response packet to a single UDP request; the rest would trigger ICMP 'destination unreachable' packets, leading to concerns about ICMP flooding (which could reduce the utility of ICMP packets in debugging network issues).

Application level fragmentation is not the only solution presented for delivering large messages. Beernink presented in his thesis the idea of delivering large DNSKEYs out-of-band from DNS. The idea is that when a large DNSKEY is required, such as when using the now defunct round 3 candidate Rainbow [6], for verification the requesting server would initiate a HTTP or FTP request to fetch the large key.

Implications for Post-quantum DNSSEC. When considering which post-quantum algorithms to standardize for DNSSEC, we must consider both the algorithms' operation performance as well as the sizes of its signatures and public keys. Müller et al. [19] began this discussion by evaluating the NIST Round 3 candidates in the context of DNSSEC. They established several requirements for a scheme to fulfil if it were to be used for DNSSEC signatures. As noted above, fragmentation is a major concern for DNSSEC and the recommended maximum DNS response size, including any signatures and public keys, should not exceed 1232 bytes. However, due to public keys not needing to be transmitted as often as signatures, larger public keys may be acceptable. Müller et al. also noted the requirement that a resolver should be able to validate at least 1000 signatures per second. The final requirement noted by Müller et al. is that zones should be able to sign 100 records per second.

Müller et al. identified three of the NIST Round 3 candidate algorithms that had the potential to fulfill these requirements: Falcon-512 [21], Rainbow-I_a [6] and RedGeMSS128 [5]. On first inspection it would appear that Falcon-512 is the clear winner as it is the only scheme that completely meets the requirements set above, however, both Rainbow-I_a and RedGeMSS128 have significantly smaller

Table 1. Resolution times and data transfer sizes for standard DNS (over UDP using TCP fallback) and parallel ARRF in one network scenario.

Algorithm	Standard DNS	Parallel ARRF
Resolution time (ms) with 10ms latency		
and 50 megabytes per second bandwidth		
Falcon-512	82.11	61.96
Dilithium2	82.24	62.52
SPHINCS+-SHA256-128S	82.59	63.45
RSA 2048 with SHA256	41.50	—
ECDSA P256	47.78	—
Data transfer (bytes)		
Falcon-512	3,112	2,557
Dilithium2	8,623	8,367
SPHINCS+-SHA256-128S	26,073	26,140
RSA 2048 with SHA256	1,081	—
ECDSA P256	504	—

signatures sizes which made them appealing: Falcon-512 has a signature size of 0.7kB whereas the other two schemes have signature sizes of 66 bytes and 35 bytes respectively. The requirement that both Rainbow-I_a and RedGeMSS128 failed was that their public keys are 158kB and 375kB respectively, versus Falcon-512's much smaller size of 0.9kB. (Since the 2020 study of Müller et al., both Rainbow and GeMSS have succumbed to cryptanalysis that substantially undermines their claimed security [3,4], and they were not selected by NIST to advance beyond Round 3.) A conclusion of Müller et al. was that they expect that DNSSEC specification changes will be required before quantum safe cryptography can be deployed in order to support larger key sizes.

1.1 Our Contributions

Given the inherent conflict between the larger public key and signature sizes of post-quantum algorithms and the practical 1232-byte limit on DNS packet size, we revisit fragmentation in hopes of finding a practical way forward. In this work we propose A Resource Record Fragmentation mechanism, or ARRF for short. ARRF is a *request-based* lightweight DNS fragmentation solution which removes the fragility of large DNS messages over UDP while being designed with backwards compatibility in mind. Similarly to previously proposed mechanisms, fragmentation is moved from the transport layer to the application layer, thus avoiding the fragility of UDP fragmentation. Whereas previously proposed mechanisms sent several response fragments for a single request, ARRF requires that fragments of specific resource records be explicitly requested. In particular, for large responses, the first response packet is truncated but includes sufficient information to allow the requester to make separate requests for each additional fragment, either in sequential or in parallel (the latter of which we called "batched ARRF"). Our fragmentation approach based on explicit requests for fragments improves both backwards compatibility and addresses the concern over ICMP flooding. ARRF is also designed in such a way that it can be implemented with low impact on existing servers; in fact we were able to implement it as a transparent daemon sitting in front of an ARRF-unaware requester and resolver at both ends of a DNS lookup request, reducing the burden of deployment.

To evaluate our approach, we implemented the three post-quantum digital signature algorithms selected by NIST – specifically, parameter sets Falcon-512, Dilithium2, and SPHINCS+-SHA256-128S – in BIND using liboqs [28], as well as a daemon implementing ARRF sitting in front of the requester and resolver, transparently carrying out the ARRF fragmentation/reassembly. We were then able to carry out a variety of experiments on a simulated network with different latencies and bandwidth and different fragmentation sizes to evaluate the performance of ARRF compared to DNS over UDP with TCP fallback, measuring the total resolution time and the amount of data transmitted.

Detailed results across all the various scenarios can be found in Sect. 4. Table 1 shows the results for a low-latency (10ms) network scenario, when restricting DNS messages to be at most 1232 bytes. In this scenario, ARRF in batched mode (meaning with additional fragments requested in parallel) yields resolution times of approximately 62–63ms for our three post-quantum algorithms, compared to approximately 82ms when using standard DNS over UDP with TCP fallback. ARRF is also more data efficient for Falcon-512 and Dilithium2, with the small additional overhead on each ARRF fragment packet being outweighed by the cost of falling back to TCP and retransmitting the first fragment.

In all our tested scenarios, we found that Falcon-512 performs better than Dilithium2 due to Falcon-512's smaller signatures, suggesting that Falcon-512 may be the most suitable option currently available to be standardized for DNSSEC. We did however find that even with the improved performance of post-quantum algorithms in ARRF compared to standard DNS over UDP with TCP fallback, post-quantum algorithms incurred a performance penalty compared to non-post-quantum algorithms currently in use with DNSSEC (RSA and ECDSA) due to the unavoidable cost of transmitting more data. Overall, we conclude that ARRF is a promising option for transitioning to post-quantum DNSSEC: it has less performance degradation compared to standard DNS over UDP with TCP fallback.

It remains to evaluate the backwards compatibility of ARRF in real-world deployments, where there may be misconfigured network devices or poorly written software that incorrectly handles unrecognized fields. We did design ARRF to avoid some known problems by using EDNS(0) pseudo resource records and using request-based fragmentation rather than responder fragmentation. Assessing the success of this approach in real-world network scenarios is an important next step.

2   The Domain Name System

The Domain Name System is a distributed database primarily responsible for translating human readable domain names to machine understandable IP addresses. The DNS is broken up into *zones*, each responsible for a specific level of granularity of the translation process. Each zone is contains various types of *resource records* which correspond to *labels*. Resource records can be used to look up IP addresses associated to domain names, name servers of a zone, as well as many other types of data.

To assist with explaining how DNS translations are performed, we will suppose there is a client which wants the IP address for `example.com`. The client will generally send a query to a caching resolver to handle the rest of the translation on behalf of the client. Assuming a resolver without cached data, it will then query the root name servers for the name servers responsible for `.com` domain names. Once the resolver receives a reply from the root name servers, it will then query the name servers responsible for `.com` for the name servers responsible for `example.com`. Finally, once the resolver learns of the name servers responsible for `example.com`, it will query those servers for the IP address associated with `example.com`, and finally receive and forward the response to the client. The responses to each of the intermediate queries can be cached to reduce the resolution time and reduce load on name servers.

The original design of DNS did not incorporate security measures. However, over the years, security-focused DNS extensions have been designed and standardized. DNS-over-TLS [11], DNS-over-HTTPS [10], and DNS-over-QUIC [13] focus on providing clients privacy when querying resolvers and are not used as part of the recursive lookup that resolvers perform. DNSSEC, on the other hand, provides data integrity to the resolver's recursive lookup process and in practice is rarely used between the client and resolver; DNSSEC will be the primary focus of this work.

DNSSEC adds digital signatures to DNS to maintain data integrity. Resource record labels are not required to be unique, so all resource records of a specified type and a specified label are grouped together as a RRSet. These RRSets are then signed by a specified digital signature algorithm, and the signature is stored inside of an RRSIG resource record. The public key is published to the zone inside of a DNSKEY resource record. There are generally two types of key pairs generated: Zone Signing Keys (ZSK), and Key Signing Keys (KSK). The ZSKs are responsible for signing and verifying the resources records in the zone, and the KSKs are responsible for signing the ZSKs and are what allows the chain of trust to be constructed.

As queries are made from the root servers to its children, and its children's children, eventually reaching the appropriate name server to answer the query, a chain of trust is constructed. Each zone that is queried must have a digest of the public KSK being used stored in a delegate signer (DS) record in its parent's zone, otherwise the public ZSK which is transmitted by the name server cannot be trusted. The one zone which does not publish a DS record is the root zone, due to its lack of parent. The public KSK of the root zone must be retrieved out-of-band from DNS; most modern operating systems have the root zone's public KSK pre-installed, removing the need for the user to fetch and configure the key themselves.

DNS as original specified only allows for DNS messages of at most 512 bytes over UDP, which quickly became too small to transport DNS messages, especially with DNSSEC being deployed. Extension Mechanisms for DNS (EDNS(0)) [25] introduced a way for resolvers to advertise the maximum sized UDP message they can receive, with a theoretical maximum of 2^{16} bytes. In reality, however, UDP/IP fragmentation can pose a significant issue for reliable delivery and thus the maximum recommended DNS message size over UDP is 1232 bytes [7].

3   Request-Based Fragmentation

As DNS is most reliable with limited size, single packets running over UDP, and given that post-quantum digital signature schemes have public key and signature sizes larger than can be accommodated in that limited size, something must change in order to reliably support post-quantum cryptography in DNSSEC. In a perfect world, we could simply send the larger DNS messages with little to no concern of them arriving. However, UDP fragmentation can cause significant problems for delivering large DNS message via UDP. The current solution to solving this problem is falling back to TCP; however, a non-trivial number of DNS name servers do not support TCP, and fallback to TCP can also incur a performance penalty. We look to solve this problem by moving DNS message fragmentation from UDP (transport layer) to DNS itself (application layer), while addressing concerns raised to previously proposed mechanisms. In this section we present our solution, A Resource Record Fragmentation mechanism, or ARRF for short.

3.1   Resource Record Fragments

When a DNS message is too large to fit into the maximum advertised UDP size, some of the message must be omitted while still containing meaningful information to the requester. We introduce a new type of pseudo-resource record: Resource Record Fragments (RRFRAGs). Like OPT [25], another pseudo-resource record, RRFRAGs are not explicitly in DNS zones. Rather they are created only when they are needed. RRFRAGs are designed similarly to the OPT pseudo-resource record; they use the standard resource record wire format but repurpose some of the fields. An RRFRAG contains the following fields:

- **NAME**: Must always be root (.) to reduce the amount of overhead required to send a RRFRAG while respecting the generic resource record format.
- **TYPE**: Used to identify that this pseudo-resource record is an RRFRAG.
- **RRID**: Used to indicate the particular resource record that is being fragmented. Since labels do not necessarily have distinct resource records attached to them, this allows a requester to be explicit in its request while not requiring

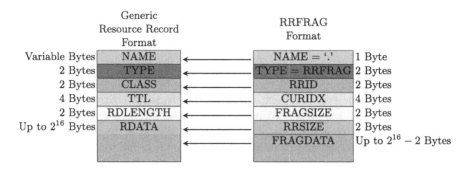

Fig. 1. The mapping of the RRFRAG format onto the generic resource record format.

the responder to remember which particular resource record it fragmented. The RRID of a particular resource record can be arbitrarily assigned, but must not change.

- **CURIDX**: The current index in the byte array of the original resource record which is being fragmented.
- **FRAGSIZE**: The total number of bytes contained in FRAGDATA plus two bytes to account for the extra space needed for the RRSIZE field. FRAGSIZE has two different meanings depending on the context. If the RRFRAG is part of a query, then this indicates how large the responding server should make this particular fragment. If the RRFRAG is part of a response, this field indicates how much data was sent in this particular fragment.
- **RRSIZE**: The size of the original non-fragmented resource record. This is used by the requester to determine how much data it still needs to request from the responder in order to reassemble that particular resource record.
- **FRAGDATA**: The raw bytes of the fragment of the original resource record. In queries this is always empty. In responses this will contain FRAGSIZE bytes starting at CURIDX. It is possible for FRAGDATA to contain zero bytes in responses, which we will elaborate on later.

Figure 1 depicts how an RRFRAG maps onto the generic resource record format. Similar to a DNSKEY resource record where the extra fields required are inside RDATA, an RRFRAG stores the RRSIZE alongside FRAGDATA inside RDATA. This was done to handle the case where an implementation which does not support ARRF blindly copies RDLENGTH, or in our case FRAGSIZE, bytes into a buffer prior to branching based on resource record type.

3.2   Using RRFRAGs

When a DNS response is too large to fit in the maximum advertised UDP size, RRFRAGs are used to split the data across multiple queries with each response's size below the advertised threshold. Resource records are replaced with RRFRAGs in place. That is to say, that if a resource record being fragmented is in a particular section of the DNS message, the RRFRAG replacing the resource record will be inserted into the same section. This is essential so that the original message format, once all resource records are assembled, will remain intact. It is important to note that the OPT pseudo-resource record must not be fragmented as it contains important meta data about the response, such as the DNS cookie. DNS messages that contain RRFRAGs should send as much data as they are able without surpassing the advertised threshold.

The initial response containing at least one RRFRAG can be considered a "map" of the non-fragmented message. This map is used by the requester to determine what the non-fragmented DNS message will look like upon reassembly. The requester can now determine what fragments it is missing in order to complete the original large DNS message, and can now send a new query for the missing RRFRAGs. It is the responsibility of the requester to specify which resource records it desires, how large the fragments should be, and where the fragments start. This is done by adding a RRFRAG for each distinct RRID the requester is requesting a fragment for in the query's additional section. If the response contains any non-RRFRAG resource records, it should store them until it is possible to reassemble the entire DNS message.

When the responder sees a query containing a RRFRAG, it just has to construct a standard DNS response by inserting the corresponding RRFRAGs into the answers section. The Fragdata being sent is a simple copy of the bytes of the desired resource record starting at CURIDX and ending at CURIDX + FRAGSIZE. This request/response cycle continues until the requester is able to reassemble the original large non-fragmented message. Note that, after receiving the initial response containing the map, nothing prevents the requester from making the subsequent RRFRAG requests in parallel.

For backwards compatibility reasons, whenever a response is sent which contains an RRFRAG, the truncated flag (TC) must be set in the DNS message header.

If a requester asks for a fragment which cannot be constructed, such as an RRID which does not map to a specific resource record, the responder should respond with a return code of FORMERR to indicate that the query was malformed.

3.3   Example Execution of ARRF

To better solidify how ARRF works, we will now work through an example DNS query whose response is larger than the MTU. This example has had some details abstracted away and should not be used in place of the above specification when implementing ARRF. Figure 2 illustrates our example execution. This example begins at the last stage of name resolution for the query "example.com". We have two parties: the resolver making the DNSSEC-enabled query for example.com., and the example.com. name server.

First the resolver makes a standard request for the A record and its associated RRSIG. Upon receiving the request, the name server observes that the DNS response is too large to fit within the confines of the MTU, and thus replaces the large RRSIG with an RRFRAG. This RRFRAG will contain as much of

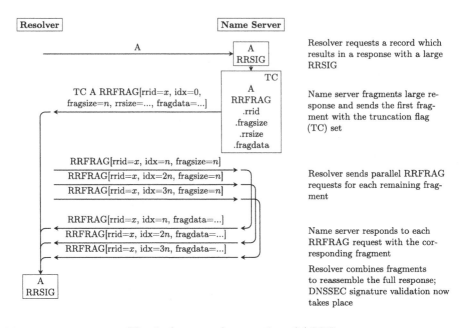

Fig. 2. An example execution of ARRF

the original RRSIG as possible, and will inform the resolver how much of the original RRSIG is missing. Once the resolver receives the DNS response, it will copy both the entire A record as well as the RRFRAG and allocating enough space for the rest of the missing record. The resolver will then send another DNS query, but this time asking for an RRFRAG and sending its own RRFRAG indicating the next range of data it needs. Once the name server receives the RRFRAG query, it will use the RRFRAG in the additional section to determine the starting position and size of the fragment of the original RRSIG is being requested. The name server will construct a new DNS response containing the rest of our missing RRSIG inside of an RRFRAG and send the new response to the resolver. Finally the resolver will copy the newly received RRFRAG into its state, reassemble the original RRSIG, and finally reconstruct the original large DNS response. DNSSEC validation now takes place, and if verification is successful the records are cached by the resolver.

3.4   Caching and DNSSEC Considerations

RRFRAGs themselves should never be cached. Once a DNS message is reassembled, and its DNSSEC authenticaiton validated if appropriate, then non-fragmented resource records may be cached. If RRFRAGs could be cached, this would allow for malicious data to be accepted prior to validation. Caching complete resource records as opposed to RRFRAGs also allows for intermediate resolvers to send different fragment sizes than they originally received which allows for more flexibility to handle varying advertised UDP sizes.

4 Evaluation

In this section we evaluate the performance of post-quantum signature algorithms in DNSSEC without and with our request-based fragmentation technique ARRF.

4.1 Experiment Setup

Algorithms. The algorithms we selected for the experiment are level-1 (128-bit-security) parameter sets of the three algorithms selected for standardization by NIST at the end of round 3: Falcon-512, Dilithium2-AES, and SPHINCS+-SHA256-128S (sometimes we abbreviate this to SPHINCS+ to save space).We also include results for RSA 2048 with SHA256 and ECDSA P256 for the sake of comparison.

Other post-quantum signature options include stateful hash-based signature schemes XMSS and XMSS^{MT} [12] and LMS [18], but we omit these from our study as their sizes do not yield smaller communication sizes than the options we do consider. The smallest XMSS or XMSS^{MT} signatures start at 2,500 bytes. For LMS, there are parameter sets with signatures between 1,616–1,936 for 2^{15} to 2^{25} signatures, but these are still not smaller than Falcon-512, even if one considers DNS responses containing both a public key and signature ($32 + 1616 = 1648$ for the smallest LMS, $897 + 690 = 1587$ for Falcon-512). These types of signatures would also require DNS zones to manage state which is difficult for online signing DNS zones [8].

Adding Post-quantum Algorithms to BIND. We evaluate these algorithms both using DNSSEC as defined today, as well as with ARRF. To perform this evaluation we used Internet Systems Consortium's BIND9 9.17.9 [15] as our DNS server software. We then added support for the three selected algorithms to BIND9 using Open Quantum Safe's liboqs 0.7.1 and OpenSSL 1.1.1l fork [1,28]. To construct a test network environment, we used Docker and Docker's built in networking as well as Linux's 'tc' (traffic control) to simulate network bandwidth and latency.

Daemon Implementing ARRF. Rather than implementing ARRF directly into BIND9, we constructed a daemon which intercepts all incoming and outgoing network traffic and implements ARRF transparently for both the resolver and all name servers. We used libnetfilter-queue 1.0.3-1 to intercept packets.

We will now describe how the daemon behaves. When the machine acting as the name server receives a DNS query, the daemon on the name server's side will modify the maximum advertised UDP message size to the maximum value of 65355 bytes.[1] The daemon then sends the message to the DNS software, which responds with a UDP message up to 65355 bytes. The daemon on the name

---

[1] Modifications to BIND9 were required as the maximum DNS message size BIND9 supports is 4096.

server side receives this response and copies the entire message into its state. It outputs a response that is either the original message, if it fits within the requester's maximum UDP message size, or the first fragment if fragmentation is required. Whenever a fragment is requested in the future the daemon will use its state if possible rather than sending the request to the DNS software.

On the side of the DNS resolver, there is another copy of the daemon which intercepts incoming DNS responses and processes them before passing them on to the DNS resolver. When the resolver-side daemon receives a DNS response containing an RRFRAG, the daemon will intercept the message. The daemon will create a state for that individual transaction containing the metadata provided by the initial response's map and copy any data included into the state. The daemon will then execute ARRF and request the remaining fragments until the entire message can be reconstructed, at which point in time the daemon transparently sends the reconstructed message to the DNS resolver software.

DNS Network Design. We construct a simple DNS network consisting of a client, a resolver, and a name server each running in their own Docker container on the same machine. The name server zone contains 1000 'A' records, each with a unique label and signature. We query for each of these A records and measure the total resolution time for each one. The zone also contains 1 'primer' name record. We first query for this primer resource record so that our resolver has the DNSKEYs and NS records of our test domain, which means that we can evaluate ARRF's effect on an individual query. To model the worst case response size, we disabled 'minimal responses', and as such each response will contain 1 question, 1 A record, 1 NS record, 1 SOA record, and 3 RRSIGs. We use 'dig' to issue each query and measure the total resolution time of said query.

We evaluated using the following four network conditions:

- low bandwidth, low delay: 10ms of delay and 128 kilobytes per second bandwidth;
- high bandwidth, low delay: 10ms of delay and 50 megabytes per second bandwidth;
- moderate bandwidth, high delay: 100 ms of delay and 50 megabytes per second bandwidth; and
- ideal network: no delay, unlimited bandwidth (the only cost being processing the messages).

All experiments were run on a c5.2xlarge Amazon Web Services instance which provides 8 cores of a 3 GHz Intel Xeon Platinum 8124M and 16 gigabytes of RAM.

4.2 Algorithm Performance

To put the network results in context, it is important to understand the performance of the verification function of each of the algorithms. We use the Open Quantum Safe OpenSSL fork's speed command to measure each algorithm's

Table 2. Algorithm runtime measured using OQS-OpenSSL Speed

Algorithm	Sign (ms)	Verify (ms)
Falcon-512	0.2810	0.0438
Dilithium2	0.0753	0.0268
SPHINCS+-SHA256-128S	373.1	1.36
RSA 2048 with SHA256	0.6019	0.0177
ECDSA P256	0.0219	0.0677

signing and verification performance and report the results in Table 2. These results provide a baseline of the raw cryptography performance against which later protocol-level results can be compared.

4.3 Post-quantum with Standard DNSSEC

In this section we measured how the post-quantum algorithms perform if they are deployed in DNSSEC as it is currently specified, under two scenarios and five different network conditions. We first measured how the algorithms would perform with a maximum UDP size of 1232. For messages larger than 1232 bytes, the DNS servers will fall back to TCP. The second scenario is the exclusive use of UDP for DNS communication, which provides an idealized view of the best case performance we can achieve using a particular algorithm; in this scenario, responses larger than the maximum advertised UDP message size will be fragmented *by the responder*, resulting in multiple UDP packets being sent in response to a single UDP packet request. Table 3 shows the average resolution times with standard deviation for the various network conditions. RSA 2048 with SHA256 and ECDSA P256 only have results recorded for standard DNS as the signatures of these algorithms are small enough to ensure they can fit in a single DNS message without fragmentation.

One main take away from Table 3 is the near doubling of latency for post-quantum algorithms using standard DNS (on connections with non-zero latency), due to the extra round trips. The first section of the table also shows the impact of restricted bandwidth on latency due to the larger signatures of post-quantum algorithms.

4.4 Post-quantum with ARRF

In this section we evaluate how each of the algorithms perform when using two different flavours of ARRF. First, we consider a "sequential" version. This version sends a request, receives a response, then looks what it needs to request and sends another request. This process is repeated until the entire message is received. Next, we consider a "parallel" version where once the first response is received

Table 3. Mean resolution times (and standard deviation) in milliseconds for DNS without ARRF

Algorithm	Standard DNS	DNS using only UDP
10 ms of latency and 128 kilobytes per second bandwidth		
Falcon-512	107.3 ± 1.786	61.52 ± 2241
Dilithium2	147.9 ± 1.478	102.0 ± 1.898
SPHINCS+	275.4 ± 2.114	229.4 ± 2.040
RSA 2048	52.20 ± 1.242	—
ECDSA P256	47.78 ± 1.949	—
10 ms of latency and 50 megabytes per second bandwidth		
Falcon-512	82.11 ± 2.331	40.56 ± 2.115
Dilithium2	82.24 ± 2.216	40.77 ± 2.251
SPHINCS+	82.59 ± 2.096	41.16 ± 2.192
RSA 2048	41.50 ± 2.157	—
ECDSA P256	47.49 ± 1.919	—
100 ms of latency and 50 megabytes per second bandwidth		
Falcon-512	802.1 ± 2.115	401.6 ± 1.991
Dilithium2	802.4 ± 2.032	401.5 ± 1.962
SPHINCS+	802.5 ± 1.940	401.9 ± 2.021
RSA 2048	401.3 ± 2.022	—
ECDSA P256	401.2 ± 2.176	—
0 ms of latency and unlimited bandwidth		
Falcon-512	2.480 ± 3.884	1.1222 ± 2.034
Dilithium2	2.282 ± 3.318	1.240 ± 2.156
SPHINCS+	2.38 ± 3.500	1.176 ± 1.935
RSA 2048	1.672 ± 3.046	—
ECDSA P256	1.567 ± 2.711	—

the name server sends all of the requests for the remaining fragments at once, essentially parallelizing the ARRF mechanism. We consider several scenarios where the maximum DNS message size varies across all of the various network conditions described above.

Our daemon implementation is a prototype; with that in mind, it is important to understand the raw overhead that the daemon incurs. By setting the maximum DNS message size to be larger than any response (say, 65355 bytes), we can see how much of a cost we are paying just by having the proof of concept daemon involved. We then also evaluate what we would expect most operators would use as their maximum DNS message size of 1232 bytes. In order to see how ARRF scales, we also provide some smaller maximum DNS message sizes of 512

Table 4. Mean resolution times (with standard deviation) with ARRF using daemon in sequential mode

Algorithm	ARRF in sequential mode			
	Resolution times (ms) for each max. message size			
	65355 bytes	1232 bytes	512 bytes	256 bytes
10ms of latency and 128 kilobytes per second bandwidth				
Falcon-512	62.61 ± 2.052	84.414 ± 1.451	148.5 ± 1.587	275.8 ± 1.738
Dilithium2	103.2 ± 1.753	231.7 ± 1.841	422.7 ± 2.409	803.9 ± 1.344
SPHINCS+	230.7 ± 1.879	635.1 ± 2.088	1271 ± 1.963	2480 ± 1.916
10ms of latency and 50 megabytes per second bandwidth				
Falcon-512	41.77 ± 2.135	62.07 ± 2.278	122.5 ± 2.197	243.0 ± 2.269
Dilithium2	41.91 ± 2.108	162.9 ± 2.240	343.8 ± 1.899	705.6 ± 2.379
SPHINCS+	42.45 ± 2.160	424.7 ± 1.811	1028 ± 2.465	2173 ± 2.123
100 ms of latency and 50 megabytes per second bandwidth				
Falcon-512	401.97 ± 2.060	601.1 ± 2.865	1203 ± 1.912	2404 ± 1.123
Dilithium2	402.1 ± 2.005	1604 ± 1.754	3405 ± 2.113	7008 ± 1.708
SPHINCS+	402.7 ± 1.957	4207 ± 2.166	10210 ± 1.843	21620 ± 1.440
0 ms of latency and unlimited bandwidth				
Falcon-512	1.644 ± 2.334	1.992 ± 2.594	2.172 ± 2.361	2.668 ± 2.606
Dilithium2	1.804 ± 2.641	2.344 ± 2.495	2.932 ± 2.184	4.176 ± 1.291
SPHINCS+	1.992 ± 2.408	3.564 ± 1.460	5.692 ± 2.243	5.673 ± 2.389

(the minimum DNS message size that must be supported) and 256 bytes. Table 4 shows the measured mean resolution time in milliseconds for the daemon running in sequential mode for the various network conditions measured, and Table 5 contains the results for the parallel daemon. Figures 3, 4, 5, and 6 illustrate all measured resolution times for standard DNS and DNS using ARRF for all network conditions.

4.5 Data Transmission

In order to understand the full implications of deploying ARRF, we must also consider the amount of data transmitted compared to that of the DNS as it is currently standardized. Table 6 shows the total number of bytes required to transmit a complete DNS message signed with Falcon-512, Dilithium2, and SPHINCS-SHA256-128S both with and without ARRF deployed.

4.6 Results

Resolution Times for Standard DNS without ARRF. When considering standard DNS, RSA and ECDSA have the shortest resolution times with the best performing post-quantum algorithm being twice as slow across all network conditions.

Table 5. Mean resolution times (with standard deviation) with ARRF using daemon in parallel mode

Algorithm	ARRF in parallel mode			
	Resolution times (ms) for each max. message size			
	65355 bytes	1232 bytes	512 bytes	256 bytes
10 ms of latency and 128 kilobytes per second bandwidth				
Falcon-512	62.80 ± 2.161	84.68 ± 1.765	86.15 ± 2.296	89.50 ± 2.120
Dilithium2	103.1 ± 1.855	127.9 ± 1.551	132.9 ± 2.038	142.7 ± 2.024
SPHINCS+	230.7 ± 1.908	262.9 ± 2.050	279.7 ± 1.720	311.6 ± 2.070
10 ms of latency and 50 megabytes per second bandwidth				
Falcon-512	41.62 ± 2.060	61.96 ± 2.140	62.14 ± 2.343	62.16 ± 2.156
Dilithium2	41.02 ± 2.170	62.52 ± 2.240	62.96 ± 2.590	62.45 ± 2.590
SPHINCS+	42.35 ± 2.164	63.45 ± 2.241	64.44 ± 1.865	66.808 ± 2.247
100 ms of latency and 50 megabytes per second bandwidth				
Falcon-512	400.6 ± 1.965	601.1 ± 2.212	601.2 ± 2.208	601.7 ± 2.168
Dilithium2	400.9 ± 2.044	601.7 ± 2.271	601.7 ± 2.209	602.4 ± 1.947
SPHINCS+	401.5 ± 2.145	602.4 ± 1.870	603.4 ± 1.638	605.5 ± 2.3638
0 ms of latency and unlimited bandwidth				
Falcon-512	1.224 ± 2.428	1.471 ± 2.250	1.650 ± 2.310	1.769 ± 2.520
Dilithium2	1.185 ± 2.052	1.698 ± 2.365	1.875 ± 2.010	2.496 ± 1.871
SPHINCS+	1.436 ± 2.143	2.406 ± 1.876	3.461 ± 1.618	5.673 ± 2.389

This is due to the response sizes being too large for a single UDP packet, causing it to be truncated and thus effectively making the initial query a wasted trip. The resolver must then fall back to the less performant TCP protocol to complete the lookup. When standard DNS using only UDP (with name-server-based fragmentation) is used, ECDSA and RSA only beat Falcon-512 and Dilithium2 when bandwidth was restricted to 128 kilobytes per second; this is likely due to the verification functions of Falcon-512 and Dilithium2 being more efficient than ECDSA and RSA.

Basic Overhead of ARRF Daemon. When considering the cases where the ARRF daemon is running, but not actively fragmenting resource records, we see comparable performance to standard DNS using only UDP. When comparing the post-quantum algorithms on standard DNS using only UDP versus the ARRF daemon using a maximum message size of 65355 bytes, we see a minimal overhead never exceeding 1.25 ms. Given that this is the overhead for our prototype daemon running as a separate process, we conclude that ARRF itself has very low overhead when fragmentation is not required.

Parallel Versus Sequential ARRF. When the ARRF daemon is fragmenting resource records, we see that the parallel daemon has a performance improvement

Table 6. Total data transmitted when performing a DNS lookup

Algorithm	Bytes transmitted during DNS lookup			
	Standard	ARRF		
		maximum message size		
	DNS	1232	512	256
		bytes	bytes	bytes
Falcon-512	3,112	2,557	2,947	3,637
Dilithium2	8,623	8,367	9,402	11,322
SPHINCS+	26,073	26,140	29,620	36,175

of approximately 20% over TCP for all algorithms and all maximum messages sizes. This is due to the parallel nature of the parallel daemon effectively only paying the latency cost once after receiving the initial response, whereas TCP has a limited sized window restricting its parallelization, which causes the latency cost to be paid more times compared to the unlimited parallelization of parallel ARRF. The sequential daemon even outperforms TCP for Falcon-512 with a maximum messages size of 1232 bytes across all tested network conditions. This is due to the Falcon-512 signed response only requiring one additional round trip to reassemble the message, whereas the TCP fallback needs to receive the entire message from scratch (it cannot make use of the truncated response returned in the UDP response).

The sequential daemon performs worse in all other cases and is greatly affected by increased latency. This is due to the sequential daemon needing to wait for each request to be fulfilled before requesting the next piece, and TCP being able to achieve some parallelism due to its sliding window.

In the scenarios with latency and bandwidth restrictions, we see that, as the maximum message size is reduced, parallel ARRF scales very nicely due to parallelizing the requests, whereas sequential ARRF scales roughly by the factor that the maximum message size is reduced by.

Post-quantum Versus Non-post-quantum. When comparing post-quantum to non-post-quantum algorithms, Falcon-512 comes the closest to RSA and ECDSA in all constrained network scenarios, but is still slower despite the efficient verification function. Falcon-512 is affected primarily by bandwidth and is 60% slower than RSA and 76% slower than ECDSA in the 128 kilobytes per second scenario even when using parallel ARRF. If bandwidth is not a concern, then Falcon-512 performs better, but is still 49% slower than both RSA and ECDSA in both scenarios with 50 megabytes per second bandwidth. Unsurprisingly, Dilithium2 and SPHINCS+-SHA256-128S perform far worse than Falcon-512 and the non-post-quantum algorithms; roughly 1.5 and 3 times slower than Falcon-512 when using parallel ARRF, and even worse when using sequential ARRF.

Data Overhead. When DNS messages sizes are at the recommended size of 1232 bytes, we can see that ARRF actually uses less data to transmit a DNSSEC response signed with Falcon-512 and Dilithium2. This is due to how DNS handles switching to TCP, essentially causing the three-way TCP handshake to turn into a five-way handshake, which we now explain. First the resolver sends a UDP request to the name server. The name server then sends a response identical to the request and marks the response as truncated. The resolver switches over to TCP and performs the standard TCP three-way handshake. TCP also sends an acknowledgement packet for each packet the requester receives, essentially offsetting the fragment requests in ARRF. With these factors, combined with UDP packet headers being 12 bytes smaller than those of TCP, ARRF allows efficient communication for both Falcon-512 and Dilithium2.

However, TCP becomes more data efficient compared to ARRF once many fragments are requested and sent, such as for SPHINCS+-SHA256-128S. Due to maintaining backwards compatibility, ARRF must surround all requests and responses inside of a DNS message and all fragments inside of an RRFRAG. TCP, on the other hand, is a stream which only sends a single DNS message header and sends the raw resource records themselves rather than sending the extra bytes that RRFRRAGs require. As mentioned earlier TCP sends acknowledgement packets for each TCP segment received (or cumulative acknowledgements after some batch). These acknowledgements are smaller than a UDP packet containing an ARRF request. The size difference depends on how many RRFRAGs are being requested, but the most common ARRF request in our experiments was 60 bytes including UDP, IP, and DNS message headers, and the largest request being 75 bytes, whereas TCP's acknowledgement packets are 52 bytes in size. If a DNS message is quite large, as is the case with SPHINCS+-SHA256-128S signed messages, these small savings end up making up for wasting the initial UDP request.

5   Discussion

Having seen the results of the experiments, we now discuss ARRF and consider whether if it is a viable solution for sending large DNS message.

5.1   Performance

Parallel ARRF is by far the most performant solution for larger responses, beating out TCP fallback in all cases despite how many requests and responses are required to transmit the original large DNS message. Sequential ARRF also outperforms TCP in cases where messages are only slightly larger than what can fit in a single UDP packet. However, parallel ARRF's performance does not come for free. On a busy resolver these parallel requests could eat up available bandwidth quite quickly and could potentially overwhelm middle boxes. We hypothesize that a production-ready version of ARRF would have a maximum window size similar to TCP in an effort to reduce request flooding, and therefore performance would lie somewhere between the ideal version of parallel ARRF and TCP. Despite there not being considerable differences between DNS with only UDP and the ARRF daemon running but not fragmenting, there are likely optimizations, such as multithreading, that can be made to the daemon. If ARRF was integrated directly into DNS software, it would also increase efficiency. We leave experimenting and evaluating these potential optimizations as well as evaluating window sizes as future work.

5.2 Backwards Compatibility

As DNS is a distributed system managed by many different entities, in any deployment there will be requesters and name servers which do not understand ARRF. We now consider what happens in two such scenarios: when the requester implements ARRF but the responder does not, and when the requester does not implement ARRF but the responder does. We also discuss the impact ARRF has on middle boxes.

Requester Implements ARRF but Responder Does Not. When a requester which supports ARRF receives a response from a name server which does not support ARRF, it will, as per the current DNS specifications, receive a truncated DNS message with the TC flag set. It can then gracefully fallback to TCP and retry the query, therefore maintaining backwards compatibility.

Requester does Not Implement ARRF but Responder Does. Since the requester does not actually indicate its support of ARRF, it may appear at first glance that ARRF may cause issues when the requester receives a response containing an RRFRAG, as it will not be able to understand what an RRFRAG is, nor what it should do with it. Fortunately, older resolvers ignore unknown resource record types, so they will gracefully fallback to repeating the request over TCP as they will see that the TC flag is set. This results in no additional round trips compared to if ARRF was not being used.

Middle Box Support. By fragmenting at the DNS level, we should ensure that the majority of middle boxes will not cause issues for ARRF. From a middle box's perspective (even one unaware of ARRF), all messages sent using ARRF look like standard DNS messages which should not require any state to be properly routed. However, if there exist middle boxes which look inside DNS messages and view the types of the message's resource records, the new RRFRAG type could potentially cause those middle boxes to reject the message. Additional work would be required to determine if there are middle boxes with that behaviour, and how widespread they are.

5.3 Security Considerations

Denial of Service Attacks. ARRF is designed to not increase the scope of DoS attacks. Since fragments must be explicitly requested, a querier can reject any fragments it is not expecting (unlike responder-based fragmenting). When combined with DNS cookies, off-path attacks become infeasible. An adversary who is on-path could modify the values in responses which contain RRFRAGs, which could cause a querier to ask for fragments which do not exist. Middle boxes could also inject malicious data into individual RRFRAG's FRAGDATA fields. If DNSSEC is used, then this will cause the validation to eventually fail. This is acceptable as this validation failure, although denying service, is no worse than DNS without ARRF deployed (where a middle box adversary simply modifies the body or signature of a DNSSEC response). ARRF also limits the impact of amplification DoS attacks as it restricts the response sizes and each response needs a corresponding request. If a response arrives with the wrong id or DNS cookie, it should be discarded.

DNS Cache Poisoning. Since RRFRAGs themselves should not be cached, DNS cache poisoning is no more of a concern than it is in traditional DNS. If DNSSEC is used, then DNS cache poisoning is not a concern assuming a secure algorithm is used.

Memory Exhaustion Attacks. ARRF as specified is susceptible to memory exhaustion attacks. Although DNS cookies make this less of a concern for off-path adversaries, there is nothing stopping an on-path adversary from changing the RRSIZE fields in the initial response. Since the requester uses this initial response as a map without any validation thereof, an adversary could insert many RRFRAGs advertising they are fragments of extremely large resource records. The requester would likely then allocate enough memory to store the intermediate state until reassembly is possible, and could only detect the attack once trying to verify the signature. One potential solution to this would be to use some heuristics to determine if a RRFRAG map makes sense. Based on what the requester could expect to receive for a query of some form, the requester can check to see if the response it actually received fits within those expectations. For example, if the requester indicated that it only supported Falcon-512 signatures, it can check that the advertised sizes of the fragments are no larger than 690 bytes. We leave this issue for future exploration.

Unreliable Networks. In this work we did not evaluate how ARRF performs when UDP packets do not reach their destination. BIND9 uses a default timeout of 800ms to determine whether it should try the request again or not, but it is unclear if that timeout duration would make sense for ARRF or not. This question must be answered before ARRF can be deployed and we leave this for future work.

Downgrade Attacks. Heftrig, Shulman, and Waidner [9] observed that under certain conditions some resolvers do not validate DNSSEC signatures when DNS responses contain new algorithms, which could include the case when post-quantum algorithms are deployed in DNSSEC. They recommend clearer description of the preferred behaviour in the DNSSEC standards and that buggy implementations be fixed.

5.4   Comparing ARRF against Previous DNS Fragmentation Proposals

ARRF is not the first attempt at a DNS-level fragmentation mechanism. Since Sivaraman's draft "DNS message fragments" [26] was not as developed as Additional Truncated Response (ATR) [27], we will be primarily focusing on ATR in this section. ATR, Sivaraman's draft, and ARRF, all rely on DNS-level fragmentation. The DNS servers are required to fragment messages and re-assemble them rather than relying on the transport layer to handle message fragmentation for them. All three mechanisms are transport layer agnostic and could therefore be used on both UDP and TCP. It may seem unclear why someone would want to run any of these mechanisms over TCP, however by doing so there is the potential for sending DNS messages larger than the 64 kilobyte maximum. ATR and Sivaraman's draft could in theory allow resource records of 64 kilobytes to be transmitted; whereas ARRF could allow for resource records of arbitrary length. This is due to the difference in granularity of fragmentation that the three mechanisms use. ATR and Sivaraman's draft fragment the DNS message as a whole, where as ARRF fragments individual resource records. Although there are no resource records that require an increase to the maximum DNS message size, and therefore maximum resource record size, it is not entirely unrealistic to see this issue potentially arising.

Before being broken [4], the Rainbow [6] post-quantum signature scheme was quite appealing due to its relatively small signature sizes; however it had large public keys of 161600 bytes. Since DNSKEYS are sent much less frequently than signatures, this might have been a reasonable trade off had Rainbow not been broken. It is entirely possible that a new, secure post-quantum signature scheme is created which has similar signature and public key sizes. (In fact, this is specifically mentioned as a desirable design characteristic in NIST's September 2022 call for additional post-quantum digital signature schemes [20].) In order to fully support arbitrary-sized resource records, the resource record format would need to be modified to support larger RDATA regions, and RRSIZE would need to be updated to the proper integer width.

One of the major criticisms of ATR [27] was that, since the mechanism would blindly send its additional message as part of its response, it would cause a flood of ICMP 'destination unreachable' packets to be created by resolvers which did not support ATR. Many implementations close their sockets immediately after receiving a response, so by the time the additional message is received the socket would no longer be accessible. This would make debugging considerably more challenging and reduce the usefulness of ICMP messages as a whole. Another issue arises with firewalls that have the policy of only receiving a single DNS message per query, and thus compounding the ICMP flood issue. ARRF does not suffer from these issues. Firstly, responses are only sent when they are explicitly queried for. A DNS server implementing ARRF will never send an additional response blindly and will never send additional messages to resolvers that don't support ARRF as they will never ask for them. Similarly, all DNS messages containing RRFrags will have an associated query and will therefore not get dropped by firewalls implementing the above policy. As ARRF does not suffer from either of those issues, there will not be a flood of ICMP packets that caused so much concern.

ATR also requires a slight delay between the first message being sent and the trailing messages being sent in order to maintain message ordering. Receiving messages out of order is not an issue for ARRF as the requesting server will know what to expect after receiving the first message containing the RRFRAG map of the whole DNS message. All responses after the first one will have been explicitly asked for and are not dependent on any other responses.

Where as ATR is quite lightweight, ARRF does have some additional transportation costs. ATR costs a single round trip plus the delay required to maintain message ordering, whereas ARRF has $\left\lceil \frac{\text{Original response size}}{\text{Maximum message size}} \right\rceil$ round trips. With the exception of the initial round trip, these round trips can be performed in parallel, thus reducing the overall resolution time. ARRF also requires more data to be sent, specifically as part of requesting the additional fragments. RRFRAGs in requests are 15 bytes in size, and the number sent depends on the number of resource records, how large they are, and how much data can fit in the maximum message size.

Sivaraman's draft [26] was built off of EDNS(0)'s OPT resource record requiring three fragmentation related options support to be assigned by ICANN. ARRF does not use the OPT pseudo-resource record and therefore does not require any options to be defined by ICANN.

Finally both ARRF and ATR can be implemented as a daemon on the resolver side without any changes required to the DNS software being used. This would make deployment much simpler as it would not require a DNS operator to update their resolver software and potentially have version incompatibilities. The reassembly could be performed entirely transparently to the resolver.

6   Future Work

Although ARRF appears to be a viable solution to solving DNS message fragmentation and therefore opening the door for post-quantum DNSSEC, additional work needs to be done. The backwards compatibility of ARRF needs to be further explored and evaluated in real-world deployments, exploring if there are middle boxes which cause ARRF to fail. ARRF as specified in this work is susceptible to memory exhaustion attacks and additional work needs to be done to prevent these attacks. It is also likely that operators will want to limit the number of concurrent requests when using parallel ARRF and therefore research into selecting a reasonable limit must be done.

In this work we provide a proof of concept daemon which transparently implements ARRF. Directly integrating ARRF into DNS implementations may uncover unexpected surprises.

Our experiments only considered the case of lossless packet delivery. In reality, UDP packet delivery is not guaranteed, so research is needed on how ARRF behaves in unreliable networks. Work also needs to be done to measure any additional processing/memory overhead introduced by ARRF and whether that overhead is reasonable.

Any future standardization of ARRF would depend both on ARRF itself being evaluated by the Internet Engineering Task Force as well as appropriate post-quantum algorithms being specified for use in DNSSEC.

Key material sizes are not the only challenges that we need to overcome if we are to have a seamless transition to post-quantum DNSSEC. In particular, one major open question is "how would a zone serve older resolvers which do not support post-quantum cryptography?" In principle it is possible to have a zone signed by multiple algorithms, however DNSSEC does not currently have the notion of algorithm negotiation [24], so there is no way for a resolver to indicate whether it wants a post-quantum algorithm or not. We leave these issues as open questions, and encourage the DNSSEC community to begin discussions on these topics sooner rather than later.

7   Conclusion

Post-quantum cryptography will inevitably need to be integrated into the DNSSEC ecosystem, however it looks like it will not be as smooth of a transition as we would like. Of our current options, Falcon-512 is by far the most performant but even with parallel ARRF is still significantly slower than currently used classical signing algorithms. There has been recent work on shrinking Falcon-512 signatures significantly which would improve its performance. Dilithium2 is perhaps viable as an alternative option, but considering the DNSSEC community's previous stance of "we can avoid sending large message by shaping their contents better (smaller signatures, less additional data)" [29], Dilithium2 may receive significant resistance if proposed for use in DNSSEC. SPHINCS+-SHA256-128S is by far the worst performing of the three NIST post-quantum selections due to its slow verification and extremely large signatures which causes very large resolution times.

Message sizes are not the only thing to consider when discussing which post-quantum signing algorithm to standardize for DNSSEC, as the security of the algorithms must also be considered. So far major attacks have been found against several candidates fairly late in the NIST selection process. To make matters worse, those algorithms were broken with traditional computers, therefore making the attacks much more practical. Although the three selected algorithms are believed to be secure now, will they hold up to additional scrutiny? Only time will tell. It is likely that using a hybrid of a classical signing scheme and post-quantum scheme will be desirable for some time to ensure that the signatures are at least as strong as what are currently standardized. This will come at a further performance cost and also increase communication sizes, and we plan to evaluate this additional cost in the future.

A final option is to wait for new post-quantum signature schemes to be invented and hope that signature sizes become more reasonable. NIST has requested additional post-quantum signature schemes be submitted for consideration standardization [20]. However, waiting several years for a better scheme to emerge is eating into the valuable time needed to prepare for securing DNS against a quantum adversary. It is best that we plan for the worst case of signatures sizes not improving, and be pleasantly surprised if such a scheme arises. With that in mind, we recommend Falcon-512 as a suitable signature algorithm for use in DNSSEC with ARRF as its delivery mechanism to achieve reasonable resolution times.

Acknowledgments. We gratefully acknowledge helpful discussion with Roland van Rijswijk-Deij, Andrew Fregly and Burt Kaliski, Sofía Celi, and Michael Baentsch. D.S. was supported by Natural Sciences and Engineering Research Council of Canada (NSERC) Discovery grants RGPIN-2016-05146 and RGPIN-2022-0318, and a donation from VeriSign, Inc.

Data Availibility Statement. The software implementing the daemon and experiment is available at https://github.com/Martyrshot/ARRF-experiments/.

A   Appendix – Performance Graphs

Figures 3, 4, 5, and 6 visualize the performance of ARRF in batched and sequential mode in various network scenarios and at different maximum UDP packet sizes compared with standard DNS with TCP fallback or UDP only mode.

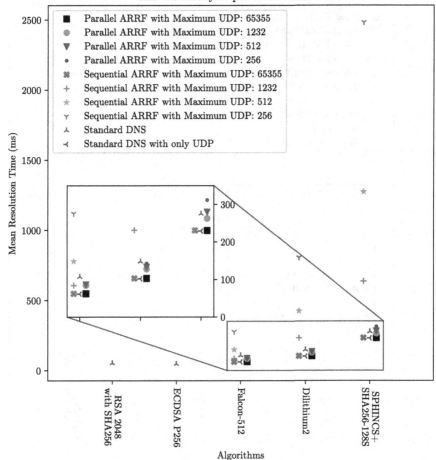

Fig. 3. Mean resolution times in milliseconds with 10 ms latency and 128 kilobytes per second bandwidth

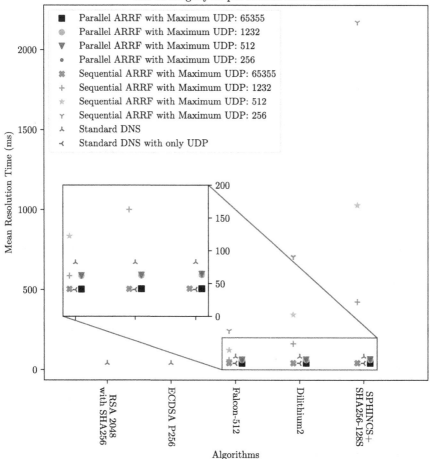

Fig. 4. Mean resolution times in milliseconds with 10 ms latency and 50 megabytes per second bandwidth

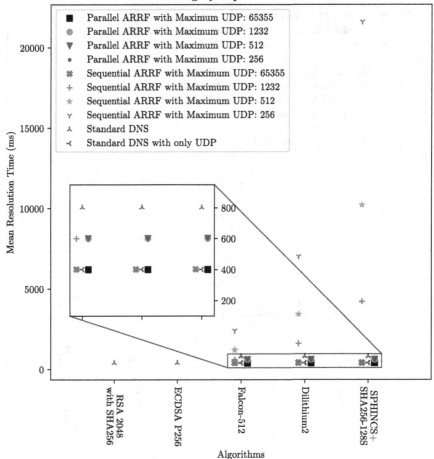

Fig. 5. Mean resolution times in milliseconds with 10 ms latency and 50 megabytes per second bandwidth

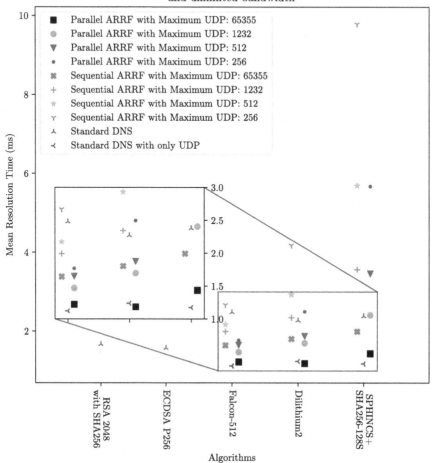

Fig. 6. Mean resolution times in milliseconds with 0 ms latency and unlimited bandwidth

References

1. The Open Quantum Safe project (2022). https://openquantumsafe.org
2. Alagic, G., et al.: Status report on the third round of the NIST post-quantum cryptography standardization process (2022). https://doi.org/10.6028/NIST.IR.8413
3. Beullens, W.: Improved cryptanalysis of UOV and rainbow. In: Canteaut, A., Standaert, F.-X. (eds.) EUROCRYPT 2021. LNCS, vol. 12696, pp. 348–373. Springer, Cham (2021). https://doi.org/10.1007/978-3-030-77870-5_13
4. Beullens, W.: Breaking Rainbow takes a weekend on a laptop. Cryptology ePrint Archive, Report 2022/214 (2022). https://eprint.iacr.org/2022/214

5. Casanova, A., Faugère, J.C., Macario-Rat, G., Patarin, J., Perret, L., Ryckeghem, J.: GeMSS. Technical report, National Institute of Standards and Technology (2020). https://csrc.nist.gov/projects/post-quantum-cryptography/round-3-submissions
6. Ding, J., et al.: Rainbow. Technical report, National Institute of Standards and Technology (2020). https://csrc.nist.gov/projects/post-quantum-cryptography/round-3-submissions
7. DNS-Violations: DNS flag day 2020 (2020). https://dnsflagday.net/2020/
8. Fregly, A., van Rijswijk-Deij, R.: Stateful hash-based signatures for DNSSEC. Internet-Draft draft-afrvrd-dnsop-stateful-hbs-for-dnssec-00, Internet Engineering Task Force, March 2022. https://datatracker.ietf.org/doc/draft-afrvrd-dnsop-stateful-hbs-for-dnssec/00/
9. Heftrig, E., Shulman, H., Waidner, M.: Poster: the unintended consequences of algorithm agility in DNSSEC, pp. 3363–3365. ACM (2022). https://doi.org/10.1145/3548606.3563517
10. Hoffman, P.E., McManus, P.: DNS Queries over HTTPS (DoH). RFC 8484, RFC Editor, October 2018. https://doi.org/10.17487/RFC8484, https://www.rfc-editor.org/info/rfc8484
11. Hu, Z., Zhu, L., Heidemann, J., Mankin, A., Wessels, D., Hoffman, P.E.: Specification for DNS over Transport Layer Security (TLS). RFC 7858, RFC Editor, May 2016. https://doi.org/10.17487/RFC7858,https://www.rfc-editor.org/info/rfc7858
12. Huelsing, A., Butin, D., Gazdag, S.L., Rijneveld, J., Mohaisen, A.: XMSS: eXtended Merkle Signature Scheme. RFC 8391, RFC Editor, May 2018. https://doi.org/10.17487/RFC8391, https://www.rfc-editor.org/info/rfc8391
13. Huitema, C., Dickinson, S., Mankin, A.: DNS over Dedicated QUIC Connections. RFC 9250, RFC Editor, May 2022. https://doi.org/10.17487/RFC9250, https://www.rfc-editor.org/info/rfc9250
14. Hulsing, A., et al.: SPHINCS+. Technical report, National Institute of Standards and Technology (2020). https://csrc.nist.gov/projects/post-quantum-cryptography/round-3-submissions
15. Internet Systems Consortium: BIND 9 (2021). https://www.isc.org/bind
16. Lyubashevsky, V., et al.: CRYSTALS-DILITHIUM. Technical report, National Institute of Standards and Technology (2020). https://csrc.nist.gov/projects/post-quantum-cryptography/round-3-submissions
17. Mao, J., Rabinovich, M., Schomp, K.: Assessing support for DNS-over-TCP in the wild. In: Hohlfeld, O., Moura, G., Pelsser, C. (eds.) PAM 2022. LNCS, vol. 13210, pp. 487–517. Springer, Cham (2022). https://doi.org/10.1007/978-3-030-98785-5_22
18. McGrew, D., Curcio, M., Fluhrer, S.: Leighton-Micali Hash-Based Signatures. RFC 8554, RFC Editor, April 2019. https://doi.org/10.17487/RFC8554,https://www.rfc-editor.org/info/rfc8554
19. Müller, M., de Jong, J., van Heesch, M., Overeinder, B., van Rijswijk-Deij, R.: Retrofitting post-quantum cryptography in internet protocols: a case study of DNSSEC. ACM SIGCOMM Comput. Commun. Rev. 50(4), 49–57 (2020)
20. National Institute of Standards and Technology: Call for additional digital signature schemes for the post-quantum cryptography standardization process, September 2022. https://csrc.nist.gov/csrc/media/Projects/pqc-dig-sig/documents/call-for-proposals-dig-sig-sept-2022.pdf
21. Prest, T., et al.: FALCON. Technical report, National Institute of Standards and Technology (2020). https://csrc.nist.gov/projects/post-quantum-cryptography/round-3-submissions

22. van Rijswijk, R.M., Jonker, M., Sperotto, A., Pras, A.: A high-performance, scalable infrastructure for large-scale active DNS measurements. IEEE J. Sel. Areas Commun. **34**(6), 1877–1888 (2016)

23. Rose, S., Larson, M., Massey, D., Austein, R., Arends, R.: Dns. RFC 4033, RFC Editor. https://rfc-editor.org/rfc/rfc4033.txt

24. Shrishak, K., Shulman, H.: Negotiating PQC for DNSSEC. In: 2021 51st Annual IEEE/IFIP International Conference on Dependable Systems and Networks - Supplemental Volume (DSN-S), pp. 9–10 (2021). https://doi.org/10.1109/DSN-S52858.2021.00015

25. da Silva Damas, J., Graff, M., Vixie, P.A.: Extension Mechanisms for DNS (EDNS(0)). RFC 6891, April 2013. https://doi.org/10.17487/RFC6891, https://www.rfc-editor.org/info/rfc6891

26. Sivaraman, M., Kerr, S., Song, L.: DNS message fragments, July 2015. https://datatracker.ietf.org/doc/draft-muks-dns-message-fragments/00/

27. Song, L., Wang, S.: ATR: Additional Truncation Response for Large DNS Response, March 2019. https://datatracker.ietf.org/doc/draft-song-atr-large-resp/03/

28. Stebila, D., Mosca, M.: Post-quantum key exchange for the internet and the open quantum safe project. In: Avanzi, R., Heys, H. (eds.) SAC 2016. LNCS, vol. 10532, pp. 14–37. Springer, Cham (2017). https://doi.org/10.1007/978-3-319-69453-5_2

29. Vixie, P.: Re: [dnsop] call for adoption: draft-song-atr-large-resp (2019). https://mailarchive.ietf.org/arch/msg/dnsop/JdhkwdWT2hGzIwfVx6CrX15KCfk/

Hash-Based Direct Anonymous Attestation

Liqun Chen[1]([✉])[ID], Changyu Dong[2][ID], Nada El Kassem[1][ID],
Christopher J. P. Newton[1][ID], and Yalan Wang[1][ID]

[1] University of Surrey, Guildford, UK
liqun.chen@surrey.ac.uk
[2] Guangzhou University, Guangzhou, China

Abstract. Direct Anonymous Attestation (DAA) was designed for the
Trusted Platform Module (TPM) and versions using RSA and elliptic curve cryptography have been included in the TPM specifications
and in ISO/IEC standards. These standardised DAA schemes have their
security based on the factoring or discrete logarithm problems and are
therefore insecure against quantum attackers. Research into quantum-
resistant DAA has resulted in several lattice-based schemes. Now in this
paper, we propose the first post-quantum DAA scheme from symmetric primitives. We make use of a hash-based signature scheme, which
is a slight modification of SPHINCS+, as a DAA credential. A DAA
signature, proving the possession of such a credential, is a multiparty
computation-based non-interactive zero-knowledge proof. The security
of our scheme is proved under the Universal Composability (UC) model.
While maintaining all the security properties required for a DAA scheme,
we try to make the TPM's workload as low as possible. Our DAA scheme
can handle a large group size (up to 2^{60} group members), which meets
the requirements of rapidly developing TPM applications.

Keywords: Hash-based signatures · Direct anonymous attestation

1 Introduction

Direct Anonymous Attestation (DAA) [7] is a group type of anonymous signature
scheme, which allows users in a group to sign messages such that the signatures
can be verified using a group public key, and the actual signers' identities are
not revealed (beyond the fact that they belong to the group). Unlike group
signatures [21], DAA signatures are not traceable, there is no group tracer who
can find out which signer created a given signature. However, DAA has two
properties that aim to stop a malicious signer from abusing anonymity: rogue
key-based revocation and user-controlled linkability. These two properties were
designed for using DAA in a remote attestation service that allows a Trusted
Platform Module (TPM) to serve as a root of trust for attesting to the host
platform that it is embedded in. The first property guarantees that a TPM whose

T. Johansson and D. Smith-Tone (Eds.): PQCrypto 2023, LNCS 14154, pp. 565–600, 2023.
https://doi.org/10.1007/978-3-031-40003-2_21

key has been revealed will not be allowed to make any attestation reports. The second property allows a user to include a *basename* in the signature. If the same basename is used for two signatures then they can be linked, even though the anonymity of the signer is maintained. This property allows a verifier to build a revocation list based on a link token which is a deterministic function of the TPM's key and a basename.

When using a TPM in a platform's attestation service, the group signer's role is split into two with a principal signer (the TPM) and an assistant signer (the host). They jointly create attestation reports on the state of the platform. These reports include information on the boot sequence and the software running in the host. These attestation reports convince a remote verifier that the computer platform it is communicating with is running on top of the trusted computing technology and using the correct software and hardware. Using DAA allows such attestations to be made in a privacy-preserving manner. That is, the verifier can check that an attestation report originates from a legitimate TPM, but it does not learn the identity of the particular TPM that generated the DAA signature.

The first RSA-based DAA scheme was standardised as part of the Trusted Computing Group's TPM 1.2 specification [53] published in 2004. The TPM specification was updated in 2014 and this newer TPM 2.0 specification [54] supports elliptic curve based DAA (EC-DAA) and an Intel variant called Enhanced Privacy ID (EPID) [11]. All of these versions of DAA (RSA-DAA, EC-DAA and EPID) have also been standardised by ISO/IEC as standard ISO/IEC 20008-2 [42]. Since the first proposal of DAA, many extensions and works to improve security and efficiency have been proposed [8–10,13,15,17,18,23,26–30,38,59]. Researchers have also paid attention to studying the security model and proofs of DAA, e.g. [16,27,56,58].

As reported by the Trusted Computing Group (TCG), which is the industry standards body that develops the TPM specifications, more than a billion devices include TPM technology; in particular almost all enterprise PCs, many servers and embedded systems make use of the TPM as trusted hardware anchors.

Authentication and attestation are important mechanisms used to protect computer systems and with increasing attention and awareness being given to privacy concerns, practical interest in DAA is growing. An anonymous attestation service is particularly important in automotive applications such as vehicle-to-vehicle communication, where the tracking of drivers should be prevented but the authenticity of the communication must also be guaranteed [39,57]. A DAA protocol has also been integrated into the Fast IDentity Online (FIDO) authentication framework [14]. Another DAA-based application is a privacy-enhancing cloud service architecture to protect user's data, using DAA to let users control the extent of data sharing among their service accounts [55].

DAA schemes that are currently supported by the TPM are based on either the factorization problem (for RSA-DAA) or the discrete logarithm problem (for EC-DAA and EPID). Since the factorization and discrete logarithm problems are known to be vulnerable to quantum computer attacks, all standardised DAA schemes are not post-quantum secure, i.e. an adversary with a powerful quantum computer could break the TPM's security and privacy. There is therefore a need to update the standard DAA schemes to be quantum resistant. Many proposed post-quantum cryptographic primitives are built on the top of code-, hash-, lattice-, isogeny- and multivariate-based problems, and could possibly be used as the basis for the development of post-quantum DAA schemes. Recently, El Bansarkhani et al. [1], El Kassem et al. [34,35,44], Chen et al. [24], and Chen et al. [22] proposed several post-quantum DAA schemes from lattice assumptions. Due to their expensive storage and computational cost, research in lattice-based DAA is still ongoing.

Among all post-quantum approaches, the symmetric key approach is considered as the most conservative approach. The security of symmetric primitives is the most well-understood and easier to evaluate, hence it serves as a safety net if the security of other approaches were endangered by newly discovered threats. Symmetric primitives have been used to build several variants of anonymous signature schemes, such as group signatures [12,33,45,52,60,61], ring signatures [36,45] and EPID [5]. However, due to the use of a single Merkle tree for membership credentials in a group, these group signature and EPID schemes can only handle a small group size, which is not suitable for TPM use.

Our Contribution. In this paper, we propose the first DAA scheme from symmetric primitives, which meets all the requirements on DAA, particularly:

- *Signer splitting:* To allow the DAA signer role to be split between a TPM and its host, we introduce a novel approach to splitting an MPC-in-the-Head scheme into two portions. The TPM keeps the key material secure and performs a small part of the work. Most of the work necessary is done by the host. The TPM and the host's contributions work together seamlessly to form a DAA signature.
- *Support a large group size:* our DAA scheme can support a large group size (up to 2^{60}). To achieve this, we make use of a slightly modified SPHINCS+ signature rather than a Merkle signature as a group membership credential.
- *Security proof:* the security of the proposed DAA scheme is proved under the Universal Composability (UC) model [16].

The remaining part of this paper is arranged as follows: Sect. 2 describes relevant preliminaries, Sect. 3 presents the proposed DAA construction, Sects. 4 to 7 provide security notions and proofs, and finally Sect. 8 concludes this paper.

2 Preliminaries

2.1 Hash-Based Signatures

Digital signature schemes can be built exclusively using cryptographic hash functions. In a hash-based signature scheme, a private key is composed of a series of randomly generated strings, while the corresponding public key is obtained by applying hash functions to the private key. Early hash-based signature schemes, such as the Lamport scheme [47] and the Winternitz scheme [48], were one-time signatures (OTS), meaning that each key pair can only be used to sign a single message. The Merkle signature scheme [48] is the first hash-based few-time signatures (FTS). It generates several OTS key pairs and aggregates their public keys using a Merkle tree. The root of the tree serves as the overall public key. Every signature uses one OTS private key, and it is comprised of the corresponding OTS and the Merkle tree authentication path for the OTS public key. As a result, the verifier can authenticate the signature using only the Merkle tree root. More recent FTS schemes, such as FORS [3], can be more efficient, as they utilize a large set of secret random strings that can be obtained from a pseudorandom function applied to the private key. Signatures are then generated by selecting elements from the set based on the message to be signed. While each signature discloses some secret strings in the set, the set size is large, and the number of signatures can be controlled to make it infeasible to forge a signature by mixing and matching secret strings from previously generated signatures.

All previously discussed multi-time signature schemes are characterized as stateful, as the signer is required to maintain a state containing information such as the number of signed messages and the keys utilized. In comparison, SPHINCS+ [3] is a stateless hash-based signature scheme. It employs a hypertree, i.e., a tree of trees, to organize OTS and FTS key pairs. Each SPHINCS+ signature constitutes a chain of signatures, with the initial signature Σ_0 being generated from the message, and each subsequent signature Σ_i being a signature of the public key that verifies the preceding signature Σ_{i-1}. By using the root public key, the authenticity of the signature chain can be verified. Although SPHINCS+ also has an upper limit on the number of signatures that can be generated per key pair, it can be set to an extremely large value (e.g. 2^{60}), making it highly unlikely to reach this limit in practical scenarios. SPHINCS+ has been chosen as one of the three digital signature schemes by the National Institute of Standards and Technology (NIST) to become a part of its postquantum cryptographic standard [49].

2.2   MPC-in-the-Head and Picnic-Style Signatures

This is a paradigm for zero-knowledge proofs introduced by Ishai et al. [40]. Roughly speaking, given a public value x, the prover needs to prove knowing a witness w such that $f(w) = x$. To do so, the prover simulates, by itself, an MPC (multi-party computation) protocol between m parties that realizes f, in which w is secretly shared as an input to the parties. After simulation, the prover commits to the views and internal state of each individual party. Next, the verifier challenges the prover to open a subset of these commitments, checks them and decides whether to accept or not. If the MPC realizes f properly, then obviously this protocol is complete, meaning a valid statement will always be accepted. The protocol is also zero-knowledge because only the views and internal states of a subset of the parties are available to the verifier, and by the privacy guarantee of the underlying MPC protocol, no information about w can be leaked. For soundness, if the prover tries to prove a false statement, then the joint views of some of the parties must be inconsistent, and with some probability, the verifier can detect that. The soundness error of a single MPC run can be high, but by repeating this process independently enough times, the soundness error can be made negligible. The interactive ZK proofs can be made non-interactive through techniques such as Fiat-Shamir transformation.

There are multiple frameworks for constructing MPC-in-the-head ZK proofs, e.g., IKOS [40], ZKBoo [37], ZKB++ [20], KKW [45], Ligero++ [4], Limbo [51], BBQ [50], Banquet [2], BN++ [43], Rainer [31] and AIMer [46]. They follow the same paradigm, but are different in the underlying MPC protocols and have different concrete/asymptotic efficiency. In this paper, to describe our scheme, we do not need to touch the low level details, hence we will use MPC-in-the-head (for Boolean circuits) in an abstract way. We will use the following syntax to describe a ZK proof:

$$\pi = \mathcal{P}\{(\texttt{public params}); (\texttt{witness})|\texttt{relation to be proved}\}$$

For example, to prove the same key sk is used in two different instantiations of a pseudorandom function F with different data inputs, we write:

$$\pi = \mathcal{P}\{(C_1, P_1), (C_2, P_2)); (sk)|C_1 = F(sk, P_1) \wedge C_2 = F(sk, P_2)\}$$

MPC-in-the-head has been used to generate signature schemes from a symmetric key setting. As the first scheme is named Picnic [19,20,62], this type of signature is called a Picnic-style signature, in which the secret signing key is k and the public verification key is a pair (c, p), and the key pair satisfy the equation $c = E(k, p)$ where E is a block cipher, k is a secret key, and p and c are respectively a plaintext and ciphertext block. Signing a message m essentially is to generate a non-interactive MPC-in-the-head proof of knowing the private key:

$$\pi = \mathcal{P}\{(c, p)); (k)|c = E(k, p)\}(m)$$

Note that this signature is based on the Fiat-Shamir transformation. The message m is included as a part of the input for the challenge hash in the transformation. Again, to describe our scheme, we do not need to explain the details of the E algorithm, and any secure Picnic-style signature scheme can be used.

2.3 DAA Concept

A DAA scheme involves the following players:

- **An issuer** manages the group membership, decides who can be a group member, and issues group membership credentials.
- **Group members** create DAA signatures. Each member is formed by two entities: the TPM serves as a principal signer and the host an assistant signer.
- **Verifiers** verify DAA signatures. A verifier also has two other roles: as a **linker** to check whether two given signatures using the same basename were created by the same signer or not; as a **revocation authority** to decide whether a group member should be removed from the group based on the verifier local revocation.

A DAA scheme consists of the following algorithms/protocols:

- Init(n): In the initialization algorithm, the issuer takes a security parameter n as the input, and outputs a master (group) key pair (mpk, msk). The master public key mpk is made public and the master secret key msk is stored privately by the issuer. In all other algorithms and protocols, we will assume mpk along with the security parameter n as an implicit input for all parties. The issuer also initializes its internal states.
- Join(msk): the joining protocol is an interactive protocol between the issuer and the user (a TPM and its host) who wants to join the group. The issuer has a private input msk and the user does not have input. At the end of the protocol, the issuer outputs a decision: accept or reject. If reject, then stop. If accept, the user obtains its signing key $gsk_u = (sk_u$, $cred_u)$ where sk_u is a secret key, and $cred_u$ is a group membership credential. sk_u is chosen and held by the TPM, and $cred_u$ is generated by the issuer and is given to the host. The issuer also updates its internal states.
- Sign(gsk_u, msg, bsn): the signing algorithm allows a TPM and its host to produce a signature Σ on a message $msg \in \{0, 1\}^*$ using its signing key gsk_u. If a basename $bsn \neq \perp$, Σ will include a link token.
- Verify($msg, bsn, \Sigma, \textbf{keyRL}, \textbf{linkRL}$): the verification algorithm allows a verifier to verify whether a signature Σ is a valid signature of msg/bsn and whether the signing key has been listed on a rogue key list **keyRL** or whether a link token in the signature has been listed on a link revocation list **linkRL**.
- Link($msg_1, \Sigma_1, msg_1, \Sigma_2, bsn$): the linking algorithm allows a verifier to check whether given two DAA signatures Σ_1 and Σ_2 with the same bsn value are signed using the same gsk_u or not.
- Revocation the revocation algorithm allows a verifier to add a revealed signing key in **keyRL** and to add a link token from a signature generated by a revoked signer in **linkRL**.

A DAA scheme needs to satisfy multiple security requirements, including:

- **Correctness** covers three aspects: (1) an honest user can successfully join the group, despite the existence of malicious users; (2) a signature generated by an honest and not revoked group member should always be valid when being verified; (3) user-controlled linkability, i.e., two valid signatures with the same bsn values and signed under the same gsk_u should be linked to each other.
- **Anonymity** means that a DAA signature does not reveal the identity of its signer, i.e., an adversary cannot distinguish which one of the two honest signers has signed a targeted message while both signers and the message are at the adversary's choice. Furthermore, given two signatures, w.r.t. two different basenames, the adversary cannot distinguish whether both signatures were created by one honest signer or two different signers.
- **Non-frameability** means that even if the rest of the group, as well as the issuer and the host of an honest TPM, are corrupted, they cannot falsely attribute a signature to the TPM who did not produce it. This property

covers three special cases: (1) no adversary can create a signature w.r.t. a basename that links to another signature created by an honest TPM for the same basename; (2) when the issuer and all TPMs are honest, no adversary can provide a signature on a message msg w.r.t. a basename bsn when no TPM signed this (msg, bsn) pair; (3) When the issuer is honest, an adversary can only sign in the name of corrupt TPMs. More precisely, if n TPMs are corrupt, the adversary can create at most n unlinkable signatures for the same basename.

These requirements will be described in detail under the DAA UC model in Sect. 6. Note that the host in a secure DAA scheme is trusted to correctly execute the protocol and to maintain anonymity. This trust requirement is necessary, as the host is a contributor to a DAA signature, so a malicious host is able to not provide correct input or to break anonymity by demonstrating the connection between a DAA signature and the corresponding TPM's public key and credential. We assume that the host represents the user so it is interested in creating valid DAA signatures and maintaining user privacy. However, for non-frameability, there is no requirement for the host to be trusted. Without the TPM, the host can neither receive a DAA credential nor generate a DAA signature. Several types of TPM have been considered in applications: (1) concrete hardware TPM, (2) integrated TPM, (3) firmware TPM, (4) virtual TPM, and (5) software TPM. Although the TPM tamper-resistant property level decreases from the highest case (1) to the lowest one (5), the trust requirements on the host are the same.

3 Construction

3.1 F-SPHINCS+ and M-FORS

To construct a DAA scheme from symmetric primitives, the first design choice is to select group membership credentials. A credential essentially is a signature on the user's keys generated by the issuer. Because we use only symmetric primitives, the credential can be in the form of the following: (1) a Merkle signature; (2) a SPHINCS+ style signature; (3) a Picnic-style signature. The first option is ruled out because it cannot handle a large group size. The last option is also ruled out because of practical considerations: we have to create a ZKP on that another ZKP (i.e. the Picnic-style signature) is valid. Unfortunately, the circuit for verifying a Picnic-style signature is too big, which results in prohibitively high computation costs and large proof size. Therefore, we focused on utilizing a SPHINCS+ style signature as the group credential.

   In the above descriptions, we said "SPHINCS+ style" rather than "SPHINCS+". This is because SPHINCS+ is still too heavy when being verified in zero knowledge. The main problem comes from the WOTS+ signature scheme. In WOTS+, verification involves verifying k blocks of d-bit strings. When verified in the clear, each block requires at most $2^d - 1$ hash operations to verify and the exact number of hash operations required depends on the content of the block. However, in a zero-knowledge proof, we will have to hash each block exactly $2^d - 1$ times then choose the right hash value in the chain blindly, to ensure the verifier is oblivious about the content of the block. Hence in total, $(2^d - 1) \cdot k$ hashes are required to verify a WOTS+ signature. Plug in concrete parameters, that means 510 hashes at 128-bit security, and 990 hashes at 256-bit security. The circuit implementing the hash function typically has 10^3 AND gates. So verifying one WOTS+ signature requires a circuit with over a million AND gates and in total we need to verify h WOTS+ signatures, where h is at least 7 in SPHINCS+.

To fix the problem, we propose a new variant of SPHINCS+ called F-SPHINCS+. As depicted in Fig. 1, in F-SPHINCS+ we use a hyper-tree that is a tree of M-FORS trees. The M-FORS signature scheme is depicted in Fig. 2. Recall that FORS is a few-time signature scheme such that each key pair can be used to sign up to q signatures. M-FORS, short for Merkle FORS, differs from FORS in that, the public key is generated as the root of a Merkle tree. The leaf nodes in this Merkle tree are the root nodes of Merkle trees that authenticate

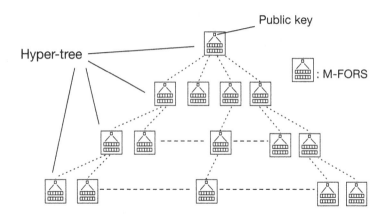

Fig. 1. F-SPHINCS+ signatures.

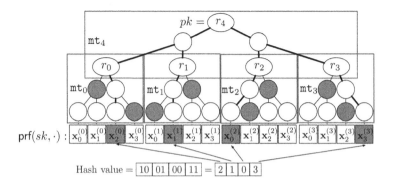

Fig. 2. M-FORS signatures.

each block of the hash value being signed. So with M-FORS, the hyper-tree in F-SPHINCS+ is a q-ary tree such that the public key in a child node is signed by the signing key in the parent node, and the signing key in the leaf node signs the actual message hash. An F-SPHINCS+ signature then contains a list of $h+1$ signatures, where h is the height of the hyper-tree. The benefit of M-FORS over XMSS that is used in the original SPHINCS+ scheme is the lower verification cost. To verify a message hash that is k blocks of d-bit string, the cost is $d \cdot k + k - 1$ hash operations. This is much less than the $(2^d - 1) \cdot k$ hashes for verifying a WOTS+ signature. On the other hand, the signing time is more than that of WOTS+. However, this is a lesser concern because in our case signing will be done in the clear (while verification needs to be done with zero knowledge).

We now describe M-FORS and F-SPHINCS+. M-FORS consists of the algorithms below. For readability and the page limitation, we abstract away certain low-level details such as how the Merkle trees are built.

- keyGen(seed, n, d, k, aux): it takes as input a random seed seed, a security parameter n, two positive integers d and k, and aux that is either an empty string or some optional data. If seed is an empty string, an n-bit random string will be chosen and assigned to it. Then a pseudorandom function prf is used to expand seed into k lists $(\mathbf{x}^{(0)}, \cdots, \mathbf{x}^{(k-1)})$, where each $\mathbf{x}^{(i)}$ contains 2^d distinct n-bit pseudorandom strings. Then $k + 1$ Merkle trees $\mathbf{T} = (\mathtt{mt}_0, \cdots, \mathtt{mt}_k)$ are built. In particular, each of $\mathtt{mt}_0, \cdots, \mathtt{mt}_{k-1}$ has 2^d leaf nodes. The jth leaf node in $\mathtt{mt}_i$ is the hash of $\mathbf{x}_j^{(i)}$. The leaf nodes of $\mathtt{mt}_k$ are $r_0, \cdots, r_{k-1}$ that are the roots of $(\mathtt{mt}_0, \cdots, \mathtt{mt}_{k-1})$. keyGen outputs $(pk, sk, param)$, such that the public key $pk = r_k$ where r_k is the root of $\mathtt{mt}_k$, the private key $sk = $ seed, and the public parameters $mp = (n, d, k, \mathtt{aux})$.
- sign(sk, MD, mp): to sign a message hash $MD \in \{0,1\}^{k \cdot d}$, parse it into k blocks, each block is interpreted as a d-bit unsigned integers $(p_0, \cdots, p_{k-1})$. Then for the i-th block p_i, $\mathbf{x}^{(i)}$ and $\mathtt{mt}_i$ (obtained by expanding sk) are used to generate authpath$^{(i)}$, which is the authentication path of the p_i-th leaf node in the i-th Merkle tree. Then $(\mathbf{x}_{p_i}^{(i)}, \mathtt{authpath}^{(i)})$ is put into the signature. The signature is a list of k pairs $\boldsymbol{\sigma} = \{(\mathbf{x}_{p_0}^{(0)}, \mathtt{authpath}^{(0)}), \cdots, (\mathbf{x}_{p_{k-1}}^{(k-1)}, \mathtt{authpath}^{(k-1)})\}$.
- recoverPK(σ, MD, mp): This algorithm outputs the public key recovered from a signature σ and the message hash MD. First MD is parsed into k blocks $(p_0', \cdots, p_{k-1}')$. Then for $0 \le i \le k - 1$, $\sigma_i = (x_i, \mathtt{authpath}^{(i)})$ and p_i' are used to re-generate a Merkle tree root and get the value r_i' (p_i' is used to determine the order of the siblings at each layer). Finally, $r_0', \cdots, r_{k-1}'$ are used to compute $\mathtt{mt}_k'$ and its root r_k' is returned.
- verify(σ, pk, MD, mp): to verify a signature, call recoverPK(σ, MD, mp). If the recovered public key is the same as pk, accept the signature, otherwise reject.

The hyper-tree nodes in F-SPHINCS+ are addressed by a pair (a, b) where a is its layer and b is its index within the layer. The root node is at layer 0, and the layer number of all other nodes is the layer number of its parent plus 1. All nodes within a layer are viewed as an ordered list, and index each node in the list from left to right, starting from 0. F-SPHINCS+ consists of the following algorithms:

- keyGen(n, q, h): This algorithm outputs (sk, pk, fp). It takes as input a security parameter n, the degree of non-leaf nodes in the hyper-tree q, and the height of the hyper-tree h. Then it chooses d, k that are the parameters for the underlying M-FORS signature scheme. The public parameters are $fp = (n, q, h, d, k)$. It also chooses an n-bit random string as the private key sk. It generates the M-FORS key pair for the root node by calling genNode$((0, 0), sk, fp)$, and set the public key pk to be the M-FORS public key $pk_{0,0}$.

- genNode$(nodeAdr, sk, fp)$: This algorithm generates a node in the hyper-tree given the address $nodeAdr = (a, b)$. With the private key sk used as a *seed*, the algorithm first generates a subseed with a pseudorandom function $\text{seed}_{a,b} = \text{prf}(seed, a\|b)$, then it calls M-FORS key generation algorithm M-FORS.keyGen $(\text{seed}_{a,b}, n, d, k, a\|b)$. The output $(pk_{a,b}, sk_{a,b}, mp_{a,b})$ is the content of the node at (a, b).

- mHash(msg, gr):This algorithm produces message hash and the leaf node index used in generating the F-SPHINCS+ signature. The input msg is the message to be signed, gr is a random string. The algorithm produces $MD\|idx \leftarrow H_3(msg\|gr)$, where $H_3 : \{0,1\}^* \rightarrow \{0,1\}^{d \cdot k + (\log_2 q) \cdot h}$ is a public hash function, MD is $d \cdot k$ bit long and idx is interpreted as an $(\log_2 q) \cdot h$ bit long unsigned integer.

- sign(msg, sk, fp): This algorithm produces the F-SPHINCS+ signature as a chain of M-FORS signature along the path from a leaf node to the root node of the hyper-tree. It chooses an n-bit random string gr. Then obtain $MD\|idx \leftarrow \text{mHash}(msg, gr)$. A leaf node at (h, idx) is then generated by calling genNode$((h, idx), sk, fp)$. The M-FORS signing key $sk_{h,idx}$ is used to sign MD and generate σ_0. The parent node of (h, idx) is then generated by calling genNode$((h-1, b), sk, fp)$ where $(h-1, b)$ is the address of the parent node. Then the parent secret key $sk_{h-1,b}$ is used to sign the child public key $pk_{h,idx}$, and the signature is σ_1. Repeat the signing process until obtaining σ_h that is signed by $sk_{0,0}$ on $pk_{1,b'}$ for some b'. The F-SPHINCS+ signature is then $\Sigma = (gr, (\sigma_0, \cdots, \sigma_h))$.

- verify(msg, Σ, pk, fp): This algorithm verifies every M-FORS signature chained up in Σ. Given $\Sigma = (gr, (\sigma_0, \cdots, \sigma_h))$, first compute $MD\|idx \leftarrow H_3(msg\|gr)$. Then obtain $pk_0 \leftarrow \text{recoverPK}(\sigma_0, MD, mp_0)$, $pk_1 \leftarrow \text{recoverPK}(\sigma_1, pk_0, mp_1)$, repeat until $pk_h \leftarrow \text{recoverPK}(\sigma_h, pk_{h-1}, mp_h)$. If $pk = pk_h$, accept the signature, otherwise reject.

Remark 1. In M-FORS algorithms, we use two tweakable hash functions [3] $H_1 : \{0,1\}^* \rightarrow \{0,1\}^n$ and $H_2 : \{0,1\}^* \rightarrow \{0,1\}^{d \cdot k}$. Almost all hash operations are done using H_1. H_2 is only used to map the k-th Merkle tree to the $k \cdot d$-bit M-FORS public key, so that when used in F-SPHINCS+ the public key is of the right size to be signed by the parent node. If M-FORS is to be used as a stand-alone signature scheme, these two hash functions can be the same.

Remark 2. The tweakable hash functions follow Construction 7 for tweakable hash functions in [3]. Namely, the hash of an input M is produced by calling a hash function with additional input as $H(\mathsf{P}||\mathsf{ADD}||M)$, where P is a public hash key and ADD acts as the tweak. The tweak is the address where the hash operation takes place within the hyper-tree, and it is a five part string $a_1||b_1||v||a_2||b_2$:

- (a_1, b_1), where $0 \le a_1 \le h, 0 \le b_1 \le 2^{a_1} - 1$, is the address of an hyper-tree node. Within the node, an M-FORS key pair that is based on $k + 1$ Merkle trees are stored.
- $0 \le v \le k$ is the index of a Merkle tree in the M-FORS key pair stored in the hyper-tree node (a_1, b_1). When $0 \le v \le k - 1$, the Merkle tree (of height d) is used to sign the v-th block of the message; when $v = k$, the Merkle tree (of height $\lceil \log_2 k \rceil$) is used to accumulated the roots of all the previous Merkle trees into the public key.
- (a_2, b_2) is the address of an Merkle tree node. When $0 \le v \le k - 1, 0 \le a_2 \le d$ and $0 \le b_2 \le 2^{a_2} - 1$; When $v = k$, $0 \le a_2 \le \lceil \log_2 k \rceil - 1$ and $0 \le b_2 \le 2^{a_2} - 1$.

The security analysis of F-SPHINCS+ is given in Sect. 4.

3.2 The DAA Scheme

Overall, the DAA signature scheme is designed in this way: the issuer generates an F-SPHINCS+ key pair as the group master key pair. When a user (including a TPM and its host) joins the group, the TPM generates a secret signing key. The issuer decides whether the user should be admitted into the group, if so a group credential is generated as an F-SPHINCS+ signature on an entry token (a commitment of the user's signing key). The credential is accessible to the host. When signing a message, the TPM and its host work together to produce an MPC-in-the-head (MPCitH) non-interactive zero-knowledge (NIZK) proof to show it possesses a group credential and the signature is generated on the hash of the message and a random data string under the key authorized by the group credential. We have created a novel approach that allows the TPM and its host each to make a partial signature and a DAA signature is a combination of these two. In particular, the TPM proves its possession of the signing key and the host proves the credential. These two proofs are glued seamlessly in a zero-knowledge manner. Verifying the DAA signature involves checking the NIZK proof so the verifier is convinced of a group membership. Each DAA signature also includes a link token, essentially it is a pseudorandom function output of a basename bsn produced using the signing key as a secret. This link token will be used for user-controlled linkability, key-based revocation and link-based revocation.

We now present the concrete construction of algorithms and protocols.

- **Initialization** $\mathsf{Init}(n)$: Given a security parameter n, the issuer does the following: Choose the hyper-tree node degree q and the tree height h, the values (d, k) for the underlying M-FORS scheme, a pseudorandom function prf, three hash functions $H_1 : \{0,1\}^* \to \{0,1\}^n$, $H_2 : \{0,1\}^* \to \{0,1\}^{d \cdot k}$, $H_3 : \{0,1\}^* \to \{0,1\}^{d \cdot k + (\log_2 q) \cdot h}$, and a keyed pseudorandom function $F :$

$\{0,1\}^n \times \{0,1\}^n \to \{0,1\}^n$; Run $(sk, rpk, gp) \leftarrow$ F-SPHINCS+.keyGen(n, q, h), where (rpk, sk) is the F-SPHINCS+ key pair, $gp = (n, q, h, d, k)$ are the hyper-tree parameters; Publish $mpk = (gp,\ rpk,\ H_1,\ H_2,\ H_3,\ F,\ \mathsf{prf})$ and keep $msk = sk$ private. The issuer provides a non-interactive zero-knowledge (NIZK) proof $\pi_\mathcal{I}$ to demonstrate that the key pair is generated correctly, meaning that the secret and public keys are associated with each other. This NIZK proof can be achieved by signing its own public key rpk using F-SPHINCS+.sign, which is similar to the issuer creating a group membership credential in the joining protocol described below. In addition, the issuer initializes a group list **GL**, and each verifier initializes two revocation lists: a key revocation list **keyRL** and a link token revocation list **linkRL**. All these lists are empty when initialized.

- **DAA joining protocol** Join(msk, mpk): The joining protocol is run between a user (a TPM and its host) and the issuer. Note that this protocol involves the authentication of the TPM by the issuer. The issuer has an authentic copy of the TPM's endorsement key, which is used to establish a secure and authenticated channel between the TPM and the issuer. In the following protocol description, it is assumed the existence of such a channel, and the reader is recommended to find the detail regarding how to establish such a channel from [25]. The protocol includes the following steps:

  1. A unique session ID u is assigned to the user. For simplicity we can think the session ID as a monotonically increasing counter, and each invocation of the joining protocol will increase it by 1. Alternatively, the value u can be computed from the TPM's endorsement key, which is unique to the TPM.
  2. The TPM chooses a random secret key: $sk_u \xleftarrow{R} \{0,1\}^n$ as its signing key.
  3. The host computes the group identifier $gid = H_1(rpk)$ and sends it to its TPM.
  4. The TPM then generates and returns its entry token $et_u = F(sk_u, gid)$ together with the NIZK proof π_u:

  $$\pi_u : \mathcal{P}\{(gp,\ gid,\ et_u); (sk_u) | et_u = F(sk_u,\ gid)\}$$

  5. The host then chooses a random string $cr \xleftarrow{R} \{0,1\}^n$ and computes a commitment $ct = H_1(et_u \| cr)$. The host sends (u, ct) to the issuer to request joining the group.
  6. Upon receiving (u, ct), the issuer checks whether an entry with the same u is in **GL**. If yes, rejects the user. Otherwise, if the issuer would like to accept the user, the issuer chooses a random string $gr_u \xleftarrow{R} \{0,1\}^n$ and sends it to the host, who responds by sending (et_u, cr, π_u) back. The issuer verifies $ct = H_1(et_u \| cr)$ and the NIZK proof π_u. If both verifications pass, the issuer computes the group credential $(gr_u, \mathbf{S}) \leftarrow$ F-SPHINCS+.sign$(et_u \| gr_u, msk, gp)$; otherwise the issuer rejects the user. The credential is sent to the TPM through the secure and authenticated channel between the TPM and issuer and then forwarded it to the host. The issuer adds $(u,\ et_u,\ gr_u, \mathbf{S})$ to **GL**.

7. The user, if accepted by the issuer, sets its group membership secret key $gsk_u = (sk_u, gr_u, \mathbf{S})$. More specifically, the TPM will record sk_u and the host will record the remaining values.

- **DAA signature generation** $\mathsf{DSig}(gsk_u, msg, bsn)$: To produce a DAA signature on a message msg and a basename bsn, the TPM and its host jointly create a DAA signature using $gsk_u = (sk_u, gr_u, \mathbf{S})$ as follows:

1. The host computes the link identifier $lid = H_1(bsn)$, the signature identifier $sid = H_1(msg\|str)$, where $str \xleftarrow{R} \{0,1\}^n$, and the group identifier $gid = H_1(rpk)$, and sends these three identifier values to the TPM.
2. The TPM computes the group membership entry token $et_u = F(sk_u, gid)$, the signature link token $slt = F(sk_u, lid)$ and the signature signing token $sst = F(sk_u, sid)$ together with the NIZK proof π_{D_T}. The TPM then sends sst and π_{D_T} back to the host.

$$
\begin{aligned}
\pi_{D_T} : \mathcal{P}\{(gp,\ sid,\ gid,\ lid,\ slt,\ hk,\ cet_u);\ (sk_u,\ sst,\ et_u)| \\
slt = F(sk_u,\ lid) \wedge sst = F(sk_u,\ sid) \wedge et_u = F(sk_u,\ gid) \\
\wedge hk = H_1(sst) \wedge cet_u = F(sst,\ et_u)\}
\end{aligned}
$$

Note that π_{D_T} proves that these three tokens are computed under the same sk_u and also provides a hook (hk, cet_u), which allows the host to carry on proving the group credential for et_u.

3. The host then computes $mt_u\|idx = H_3(et_u\|gr_u)$ and $com = H_1(sst\|pk_h\|\cdots\|rpk)\}$, where $pk_h, \cdots, rpk$ are the public keys for verifying the signatures in $\mathbf{S}$, from the layer h to layer 0 (the public key at the layer 0 is rpk). Here $H_3(et_u\|gr_u)$ is used as F-SPHINCS+.mHash(et_u, gr_u). The host also computes an NIZK proof π_{D_H}:

$$
\begin{aligned}
\pi_{D_H} : \mathcal{P}\{(gp,\ rpk,\ slt,\ com,\ hk,\ cet_u);\ (et_u,\ sst,\ gr_u,\ \mathbf{S} = \{\sigma_h, \cdots, \sigma_0\})| \\
hk = H_1(sst) \wedge cet_u = F(sst,\ et_u) \wedge mt_u\|idx = H_3(et_u\|gr_u) \\
\wedge pk_h = \mathsf{recoverPK}(\sigma_h, mt_u, (n, d, k, (h, idx))) \\
\wedge pk_{h-1} = \mathsf{recoverPK}(\sigma_{h-1}, pk_h, (n, d, k, (h-1, \lfloor \tfrac{idx}{q} \rfloor))) \wedge \cdots \\
\wedge rpk = \mathsf{recoverPK}(\sigma_0, pk_1, (n, d, k, (0, 0))) \\
\wedge com = H_1(sst\|pk_h\|\cdots\|rpk)\}
\end{aligned}
$$

4. The signature $\Sigma = (str,\ slt,\ com,\ \pi_D)$, where π_D is the combination of π_{D_T} and π_{D_H}, i.e., $\pi_D = (\pi_{D_T}, \pi_{D_H})$. hk and cet_u appearing in both π_{D_T} and π_{D_H} play the role that glues these two MPCitH instances together. From a verifier's point of view, π_D produces the following NIZK proof:

$$\pi_D : \mathcal{P}\{(gp,\ rpk,\ gid,\ sid,\ lid,\ slt,\ com);$$
$$(sk_u, et_u,\ sst,\ gr_u,\ \mathbf{S} = \{\sigma_h, \cdots, \sigma_0\})|$$
$$slt = F(sk_u,\ lid) \wedge sst = F(sk_u,\ sid) \wedge et_u = F(sk_u,\ gid)$$
$$\wedge\ mt_u \| idx = H_3(et_u \| gr_u)$$
$$\wedge\ pk_h = \mathsf{recoverPK}(\sigma_h, mt_u, (n, d, k, (h, idx)))$$
$$\wedge\ pk_{h-1} = \mathsf{recoverPK}(\sigma_{h-1}, pk_h, (n, d, k, (h-1, \lfloor \frac{idx}{q} \rfloor))) \wedge \cdots$$
$$\wedge\ rpk = \mathsf{recoverPK}(\sigma_0, pk_1, (n, d, k, (0, 0)))$$
$$\wedge\ com = H_1(sst \| pk_h \| \cdots \| rpk)\}$$

More details of π_D will follow in Sect. 3.3.

- **DAA signature verification** $\mathsf{DVf}(msg, bsn, \Sigma, \mathbf{keyRL}, \mathbf{linkRL})$: Given $\Sigma = (str, slt, com, \pi_D), msg, bsn$, together with two revocation lists **keyRL** and **linkRL**, the verifier first rejects Σ if $(bsn, slt) \in \mathbf{linkRL}$. Otherwise, the verifier recomputes $lid = H_1(bsn)$, and $\forall sk_u^* \in \mathbf{keyRL}$ computes $slt^* = F(sk_u^*, lid)$. If any $slt^* = slt$, rejects Σ. Otherwise, the verifier verifies π_D. Accept if the verification succeeds; otherwise reject.
- **DAA link algorithm** $\mathsf{Link}(\Sigma, \Sigma')$: Given two valid DAA signatures $\Sigma = (str, slt, com, \pi_D)$ and $\Sigma' = (str', slt', com', \pi_D')$ associated with the same bsn, the verifier checks if $slt = slt'$ holds. If so output linked, otherwise not linked.
- **DAA revocation** There are two cases to revoke the group membership of the user u: (1) Given sk_u, a verifier adds it in **keyRL**[1]; (2) Given a pair (bsn, slt) associated with a DAA signature signed by the user u to be revoked, a verifier adds this pair in **linkRL**.

3.3   The Proof π_D

The most important part in the DAA signature $\Sigma = (str,\ slt,\ com,\ \pi_D = (\pi_{D_T}, \pi_{D_H}))$ is the proof π_D. In this section we dissect it to show the design rationale and explain two changes we made to MPC-in-the-Head, which greatly improves the efficiency and may be of independent interest.

As Σ is a signature of a message msg, the foremost thing π_D needs to prove is that the signer knows a group signing key $gsk_u = (\ sk_u,\ gr_u,\ \mathbf{S})$ and it was used to sign msg. Besides that, π_D also needs to prove that gsk_u is authorized by the issuer. To do that, in π_D the following is done:

1. It proves that the same signing key sk_u is used to generate three values et_u, slt and sst, where et_u is bound with the group root public key rpk (as it is computed from $gid = H_1(rpk)$), slt is bound with the base name bsn (as it is computed from $lid = H_1(bsn)$), and sst is bound with the message msg and random string str (as it is computed from $sid = H_1(msg \| str)$). slt is revealed in Σ, and et_u and sst are hidden.

---

[1] It is an open problem for creating a validation check on **keyRL** that doesn't take $O(N)$ time, where N is the size of the list.

2. It proves that two revealed values slt and com are produced using the same sk_u. It binds com to sst (by using sst in computing com). The commitment com also binds Σ to all public keys used to blindly verify the signatures in **S**.
3. It proves that mt_u, which is computed from et_u, is signed under a private key in a leaf node of the hyper-tree generated by the group issuer. This is done by verifying all the signatures in **S** such that mt_u and σ_h produce the leaf public key pk_h, which in turn with σ_{h-1} produces pk_{h-1}, and so on until reaching the root. The last public key produced is rpk which is published by the group issuer. All public keys recovered in this process match those committed in the commitment com.

The first challenge for implementing π_D with MPCitH comes from splitting the signer role into two parts, the principal signer TPM and the assistant signer host, where the TPM holds sk_u and the host holds **S**. A straightforward choice is to let the TPM and host be involved in the same MPCitH instance. This will result in a large communication cost between these two entities. Our solution is to split π_D into two MPCinH instances, π_{D_T} and π_{D_H}, each is performed by one entity. The difficulty now is how to glue these two instances together seamlessly in a zero-knowledge manner. We let (sst, et_u) serve as a hidden hook and $hk = H_1(sst)$ and $cet_u = F(sst, et_u)$ as a commitment of sst and et_u. Both π_{D_T} and π_{D_H} include the same MPCitH proofs of hk and cet_u. The collision-resistance property of the functions F and H_1 guarantees that the same pair of (sst, et_u) are in π_{D_T} and π_{D_H}. The preimage resistance property of these two functions guarantees that neither et_u nor sst is revealed. The MPC instance of π_{D_T} is shown in MPCitH 1.

MPCitH 1: π_{D_T} – MPC instance for the TPM's part of π_D

  Public: $gp = (n,\ q,\ h,\ d,\ k),\ sid,\ gid,\ lid,\ slt$
  Private: $[\![sk_u]\!]$
  Output: $slt',\ hk,\ cet_u$
  Check: $slt' = slt \land hk' = hk \land cet'_u = cet_u$
1 $slt' = \mathsf{MPC\_F}([\![sk_u]\!],\ lid)$;
2 $[\![sst]\!] = \mathsf{MPC\_F}([\![sk_u]\!],\ sid)$;
3 $[\![et_u]\!] = \mathsf{MPC\_F}([\![sk_u]\!],\ gid)$;
4 $hk' = \mathsf{MPC\_H1}([\![sst]\!])$;
5 $cet'_u = \mathsf{MPC\_F}([\![sst]\!],\ [\![et_u]\!])$;

Let us first introduce the notation used in such an MPCitH algorithm: $[\![x]\!]$ means that the value x is secret-shared when using an MPC algorithm, meaning that it is known by the prover but not the verifier. $\mathsf{MPC\_X}$ means the MPC subroutine implementing the function X (e.g. $\mathsf{MPC\_F}$, $\mathsf{MPC\_H1}$, $\mathsf{MPC\_H2}$ and $\mathsf{MPC\_H3}$ implement F, H_1, H_2 and H_3). This notation will be used throughout the paper. Based on [41], in an implementation $\mathsf{MPC\_F}$ can be used as a building block for the hash functions that we need.

In MPCitH 1, the TPM performs the $\mathsf{MPC\_F}$ algorithm four times and the $\mathsf{MPC\_H1}$ algorithm once when computing the signature link token $slt =$

MPC_F($[\![sk_u]\!]$, lid), the signature signing token $[\![sst]\!]$ = MPC_F($[\![sk_u]\!]$, sid), the entry token $[\![et_u]\!]$ = MPC_F($[\![sk_u]\!]$, gid), the hash value hk = MPC_H1($[\![sst]\!]$), and the connection entry token cet_u = MPC_F($[\![sst]\!]$, $[\![et_u]\!]$). These five operations are performed in the same MPCinH knowledge-proof routine, where sk_u, sst and et_u are kept secret. The TPM outputs the proof along with slt', hk, and cet_u. The proof demonstrates that the same sk_u value was used in steps 1) - 3), and steps 4) and 5) are used to pass sst and et_u to the host, which allows the latter to carry on the MPCinH knowledge-proof π_{D_H} for the DAA credential associated with et_u. In an implementation this reduces to 5 calls to MPC_F.

The second challenge for implementing π_D with MPCitH comes from the cost of $h + 1$ M-FORS signature verifications required by the proof in π_{D_H}. Recall that in an M-FORS signature (Sect. 3.1, also the example in Fig. 2), the message hash to be signed is broken into k blocks, and each block is authenticated with a Merkle-tree of height d. Then the k Merkle tree roots are organized into a new Merkle tree whose root is the public key. Verifying the full signature means to check whether the public key can be recovered from the message hash, the secret strings corresponding to the hash blocks ($\mathbf{x}_{p_i}^{(i)}$), and the hashes along the Merkle tree authentication paths. In total, to verify a single M-FORS signature, $k \cdot (d+1) + (k-1) = kd + 2k - 1$ hashes are needed, which is in the order of 10^2 for a practical setting (with an extra factor of 2 if implementing with MPC_F). The $h + 1$ factor means that if implemented naively, the MPC used in π_{D_H} would need to call thousands of times the sub-procedure that implements the hash function, and the size of the circuit for the whole MPC can go easily above a million-gates. Even worse, to reduce the soundness error, the same circuit needs to be executed tens to hundreds of times in an MPCitH proof. Thus, a naive implementation of π_{D_H} will result in a very large signature size and a high computational cost.

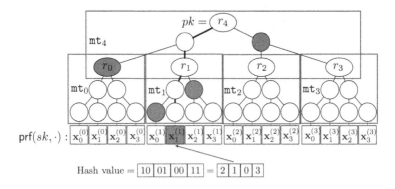

Fig. 3. M-FORS Patial Verification.

Our more efficient strategy for implementing π_{D_H} is: in MPCitH, rather than repeating t times a MPC procedure in which the M-FORS signatures are fully verified, we run $t' \geq k$ MPC procedures in which the M-FORS signatures are partially verified, one block in each run (see the example of partial verification in Fig. 3). More precisely, we extend the M-FORS with the following algorithms:

- partial-sig(σ, MD, i, mp): to extract a partial signature of the i-th block of MD from $\sigma = \{(x_0, \mathbf{authpath}^{(0)}), \cdots, (x_{k-1}, \mathbf{authpath}^{(k-1)})\}$. The Merkle tree $\mathtt{mt}_k$ can be recomputed from σ. The partial signature is $\partial_{\sigma,i} = (x_i, \mathbf{authpath}^{(i)}, \mathbf{authpath}^{(k,i)})$ where $(x_i, \mathbf{authpath}^{(i)})$ is a copy of the i-th pair in σ, and $\mathbf{authpath}^{(k,i)}$ is the authentication path of r_i (the root of the i-th Merkle tree) in $\mathtt{mt}_k$.
- partial-rec($\partial_{\sigma,i}, p_i, i, mp$): This algorithm recovers the public key from $\partial_{\sigma,i}$ and p_i. Given $\partial_{\sigma,i} = (x, \mathbf{authpath}, \mathbf{authpath}')$, first compute the Merkle tree root r_i from $(x, \mathbf{authpath}, p_i)$, then compute the Merkle tree root pk from $(r_i, \mathbf{authpath}', i)$. Output pk.

With partial-rec, only one path is used to recover the M-FORS public key instead of k paths.

The MPC procedure for proving the v-th block in π_{D_H} is shown in MPCitH 2. The first 2 steps of this algorithm are the same as steps 4) and 5) in MPCitH 1. This duplication can glue the TPM part π_{D_T} and the host part π_{D_H} together.

MPCitH 2: π_{D_H} – MPC instance for the v-th block in the host's part of π_D

> **Public:** $gp = (n, q, h, d, k)$, rpk, com, v, hk, cet_u
> **Private:** $[\![sst]\!]$, $[\![etu]\!]$, $[\![gr_u]\!]$, $[\![\partial_{\sigma_h,v}]\!]$, $\cdots$, $[\![\partial_{\sigma_0,v}]\!]$
> **Output:** pk_0, hk', cet'_u, com'
> **Check:** $pk_0 = rpk \wedge hk' = hk \wedge cet'_u = cet_u \wedge com' = com$
> 1 $hk' = \mathsf{MPC\_H1}([\![sst]\!])$;
> 2 $cet'_u = \mathsf{MPC\_F}([\![sst]\!], [\![et_u]\!])$;
> 3 $[\![mt_u]\!] \| [\![idx]\!] = \mathsf{MPC\_H3}([\![et_u]\!] \| [\![gr_u]\!])$;
> 4 $[\![M]\!] = [\![mt_u]\!]$;
> 5 $[\![COM]\!] = [\![sst]\!]$;
> 6   **for** $l = h;\ l \geq 0;\ l--$ **do**
> 7   parse $[\![M]\!]$ into k blocks $[\![p_0]\!], \cdots, [\![p_{k-1}]\!]$, each block is d-bit;
> 8 $[\![M]\!] = \mathsf{MPC\_pRec}([\![\partial_{\sigma_l,v}]\!], [\![p_v]\!], [\![idx]\!], gp, l, v)$;
> 9 $[\![COM]\!] = \mathsf{MPC\_H1}([\![COM]\!] \| [\![M]\!])$;
> 10 $[\![idx]\!] = [\![\lfloor idx/q \rfloor]\!]$;
> 11   **end**
> 12 $com' = [\![COM]\!]$;
> 13 $pk_0 = \mathsf{Reveal}([\![M]\!])$;

The host uses partial signatures in the MPC. Recall that in the group signing key gsk_u, a list $\mathbf{S} = \{\sigma_h, \cdots, \sigma_0\}$ of $h+1$ signatures are stored, one for each layer in the hyper-tree of F-SPHINCS+. The signer can extract a partial signature for the v-th block from each signature, i.e. $\{\partial_{\sigma_h,v}, \cdots, \partial_{\sigma_0,v}\}$. In Line 8, an MPC subroutine MPC_pRec that implements partial-rec is used. This subroutine uses the input to compute the corresponding public key at the l-th layer in the hyper-tree (stored in $[\![M]\!]$ and also appended to $[\![COM]\!]$). After the last iteration, $[\![COM]\!]$ is hashed and $[\![M]\!]$ is revealed. The results will be checked by the verifier to see whether they match com and rpk. If so, the signer is likely to possess valid partial signatures along the path from the idx-th leaf node to the root node in the hyper-tree.

Why does this strategy make sense? In an MPCitH proof, the same procedure is run multiple times. Each run has a soundness ϵ that a cheating prover can get away without being detected. Thus t runs are needed so that ϵ^t is negligibly small. In our case, the main cost of the MPC procedure comes from verifying all the M-FORS signatures. The full verification requires every block of the message digest or the child public key to be verified. Our observation is that if a prover has to cheat, then it has to cheat in more than 1 blocks with a high probability. If the prover has to cheat in n out of k blocks, then using partial verification with t', such that $t' \cdot n/k \geq t$, ensures that the prover has to cheat in more than t runs, and hence with a negligible success probability. As we analyzed, an implementation with full signature verification requires $t \cdot (h+1) \cdot (k \cdot d + 2k - 1)$ calls to the MPC hash procedure. The partial verification based implementation, on the other hand, requires only $t' \cdot (h + 1) \cdot (d + 1 + \lceil \log k \rceil)$ MPC hash calls. The improvement is roughly $\frac{tk}{t'}$ times.

The soundness analysis of π_D is given in Sect. 5.

4 Security Analysis of F-SPHINCS+

The standard security definition for digital signature schemes is existential unforgeability under adaptive chosen-message attacks (EU-CMA). It can be extended to few-time signature by limiting the adversary's call to the sign oracle to q_s times where q_s is the maximum number of signatures that the few-time signature scheme is allowed to generate for each signing key. Let $SIG = (kg, sign, vf)$ be a q_s-time signature scheme, Fig. 4 shows the q_s-EU-CMA game.

Experiment $\text{Exp}_{\text{SIG},A}^{q_s\text{-EU-CMA}}(n)$

- $(sk, pk) \leftarrow kg(n)$, where kg is the key generation algorithm.
- $(M^*, \sigma^*) \leftarrow A^{sign(sk,\cdot)}(pk)$, and A can query the $sign$ oracle at most q_s times
- Return 1 iff $vf(pk, M^*, \sigma^*) = 1 \wedge M^* \notin \{M_i\}_{i=1}^{q_s}$, where vf is the verification algorithm and $\{M_i\}_{i=1}^{q_s}$ is the set of messages queried by the adversary in the previous step.

Fig. 4. q_s-EU-CMA game.

Definition 1 (q_s-EU-CMA). *Let SIG be a digital signature scheme. It is said to be q_s-EU-CMA secure, if for any adversary A, the following holds:*

$$Succ_{SIG}^{q_s\text{-}EU\text{-}CMA}(A(n)) = Pr\left[Exp_{SIG,A}^{q_s\text{-}EU\text{-}CMA}(n) = 1\right] \leq negl(n)$$

Theorem 1. *Following the definitions of SM-TCR (single function, multi-target-collision resistance), SM-DSPR (single function, multi-target decisional second-preimage resistance), TSR (target subset resilience), and ITSR (interleaved target subset resilience) given in [3], for suitable parameters, n, d, k, h, q, the F-SPHINCS+ signature is q^h-EU-CMA secure if:*

- *H_1 is SM-TCR and SM-DSPR secure;*
- *H_2 is TSR secure with at most q queries;*
- *H_3 is ITSR secure with at most q^h queries;*
- *prf is a secure pseudorandom function.*

Proof. To successfully forge an issuer's signature on a message M chosen by the adversary, there are the following mutually exclusive cases:

1 Let $MD\|idx = H_3(M\|gr)$ for some gr. In the forged signature, all secret strings corresponding to $MD = p_0\|\cdots\|p_{k-1}$, i.e. $\{\mathbf{x}_{p_i}^{(i)}\}_{i=0}^{k-1}$, are the same as generated from leaf_{idx}'s secret key. This case consists of the following sub-cases:

  1.1 The adversary learns all secret strings from signatures obtained in the query phase.

  1.2 Some secret strings are not leaked from previous signatures, and for each of them, the adversary either:

    1.2.1 learns it by breaking the pseudorandom function that is used to expand the secret key into $\mathbf{x}_i$;

    1.2.2 or learns it by looking at their H_1 hash values and find the pre-images.

2 Let $MD\|idx = H_3(M\|gr)$ for some gr. In the forged signature, some secret strings corresponding to $MD = p_0\|\cdots\|p_{k-1}$, i.e. $\{\mathbf{x}_{p_i}^{(i)}\}_{i=0}^{k-1}$, are NOT the same as generated from leaf_{idx}'s secret key. Then let $\mathbf{S}$ be the list of $h+1$ M-FORS signatures in the forged signature, we can find i such that when verifying the i-th signature ($0 \leq i \leq h$), we obtain the same public key as would be generated by the signer, but for all $0 \leq j < i$, we obtain a different public key as would be generated by the signer. This means:

  2.1 The adversary has found at least one second-preimages of H_1 so that some Merkle trees in the ith signature are computed with the second-preimages. They end up having the same roots as the trees computed by the issuer.

  2.2 The adversary knows all secret strings corresponding to the public key produced from verifying the $(i-1)$th signature. This public key is different from the public key at the same location generated by the issuer. This can be done by either:

2.2.1 learning all from previous signature queries;

2.2.2 or breaking the pseudoranodm function;

2.2.3 or finding some pre-images of H_1.

Given the above, we analyze the F-SPHINCS+ signature scheme through a series of games:

Game 0: The original EU-CMA game in which the adversary needs to forge a valid issuer's signature after q_s queries.

Game 1: Exactly as Game 0 except all output of prf are replaced by truly random n-bit strings. We eliminate from the above list Case 1.2.1 and 2.2.2 by this modification. Since each call to prf uses a secret key and a distinct value as input, assuming prf is a pseudorandom function, we have:

$$|\text{Succ}^{Game0}(A(n)) - \text{Succ}^{Game1}(A(n))| \leq negl(n)$$

Game 2: Game 2 differs from Game 1 in that we consider the adversary lost if the adversary outputs a forgery by breaking the ITSR security of H_3. This modification eliminates from the above list Case 1.1. The winning condition in Fig. 4 is changed to:

– Return 1 iff $ITSR(H_3, M^*) = 0 \wedge vf(pk, M^*, \sigma^*) = 1 \wedge M^* \notin \{M_i\}_{i=1}^{q^h}$.

The predicate $ITSR$ is defined as the following:

– Let M^* be the message that the adversary chooses to generate the forgery on, and gr^* the random string used by the adversary to compute $MD^*||idx^* = H_3(M^*||gr^*)$.

– Parse $MD^* = p_0^*||\cdots||p_{k-1}^*$ where each $p_j^* \in [0, 2^d - 1]$. From the above we obtain a set $C^* = ((idx^*, 0, p_0^*), \cdots, (idx^*, k-1, p_{k-1}^*))$.

– For each message queried in the query phase M_i ($1 \leq i \leq q^h$), and gr_i the random string, compute $MD_i||idx_i = H_3(M_i||gr_i)$ and obtain $C_i = ((idx_i, 0, p_{i,0}), \cdots, (idx_i, k-1, p_{i,k-1}))$.

– Return 1 iff $C^* \subseteq \bigcup_{i=1}^{q^h} C_i$.

We can see that $ITSR(H_3, M^*) = 0$ iff the adversary can break the ITSR security of H_3. Hence, we have:

$$|\text{Succ}^{Game1}(A(n)) - \text{Succ}^{Game2}(A(n))| \leq \text{Succ}_{H_3, q^h}^{ITSR}(A) \leq negl(n)$$

Game 3: Game 3 differs from Game 2 in that we consider the adversary lost if the forgery contains a second preimage for an input to H_1 that was part of a signature returned as a signing-query response. Here the second preimage can be included explicitly in the signature, or implicitly observed when verifying the signature. This eliminates from the above list Case 2.1. Then we have:

$$|\text{Succ}^{Game2}(A(n)) - \text{Succ}^{Game3}(A(n))| \leq \text{Succ}_{H_1, q}^{SM-TCR}(A) \leq negl(n)$$

Game 4: Game 4 differs from Game 3 in that we consider the adversary lost if the adversary outputs a forgery by breaking the TSR security of H_2, which allows the adversary to forge an intermediate signature in **S**, and then any signature earlier in the chain. This eliminates from the above list Case 2.2.1. The winning condition in Fig. 4 is changed to:

- Return 1 iff $TSR(H_2, M^*) = 0 \land ITSR(H_3, M^*) = 0 \land vf(pk, M^*, \sigma^*) = 1 \land M^* \notin \{M_i\}_{i=1}^{q^h}$.

The predicate TSR is defined as the following:

- The adversary chooses an intermediate node in the hyper-tree at address (a, b), and two n-bit string L^*, R^*.
- For each signature obtained in the query phase, if $\mathbf{S}_i$ includes a signature generated using the secret key in node (a, b) over the public key in one of its child node, parse this public key into k blocks, each of d-bit $pk_i = p_{i,0}|| \cdots ||p_{i,k-1}$, and generate a set $C_i = \{(j, p_{i,j})\}_{j=0}^{k-1}$.
- Compute $pk^* = H_2(\mathbf{aux}||k||0||0||L^*||R^*)$, parse pk^* into $p_0^*|| \cdots ||p_{k-1}^*$, and generate a set $C^* = \{(j, p_j^*)\}_{j=0}^{k-1}$.
- Return 1 iff $C^* \subseteq \bigcup_{i=1}^{q} C_i$.

Note that each M-FORS public key is the root of a Merkle tree generated from pseudorandom strings. Also for each intermediate node in a hyper-tree, it has at most q children, hence no more than q signatures signed by the secret key in this intermediate node can be obtained by the adversary. So $TSR(H_2, M^*) = 0$ iff the adversary can break the TSR security of H_2. Hence, we have:

$$|\text{Succ}^{Game3}(A(n)) - \text{Succ}^{Game4}(A(n))| \leq \text{Succ}_{H_2,q}^{TSR}(A) \leq negl(n)$$

Now the cases in which the adversary can forge a signature are all eliminated except Case 1.2.2 and 2.2.3, which requires the adversary to find a pre-image of at least one hash value produced by H_1. The success probability of finding a pre-image is as analyzed in [3]:

$$\text{Succ}^{Game4}(A) \leq 3 \cdot \text{Succ}_{H_1,p}^{SM-TCR}(A) + \text{Adv}_{H_1,p}^{SM-DSPR}(A) \leq negl(n)$$

So overall, the advantage of the adversary is negligible.

TSR Security of H_2. In any case, q signatures can be generated under the secret key of a non-leaf node in the hyper-tree. Assuming the adversary knows all of them, then for each block of the chosen pk^*, the probability of the secret string has been leaked is $1 - (1 - \frac{1}{2^d})^q$, so all secret string have been leaked is $(1 - (1 - \frac{1}{2^d})^q)^k$. For $d = 16, q = 1024, k = 68$, this probability is $2^{-468.87}$, if $k = 35$, this probability is $2^{-210.39}$.

ITSR Security of H_3. For a leaf node of the hyper-tree, it may have been used to sign γ signatures out of the total q_s signature queries. So the probability that all secret string of a chosen message M being leaked through query is:

$$\sum_{\gamma} (1 - (1 - \frac{1}{2^d})^\gamma)^k \binom{q_s}{\gamma} (1 - \frac{1}{q^h})^{q_s - \gamma} \frac{1}{q^{h\gamma}}$$

For $d = 16, q = 1024, k = 68, h = 6, q_s = 2^{60}$, this probability is $2^{-407.32}$, if $k = 35$, this probability is $2^{-208.95}$.

5   Soundness Analysis of π_D

In π_D, k instances of MPC are run. In the ith instance, the partial verification procedure is used to verify every M-FORS signature in **S**, but only the i-th block of the hash value being signed. Out of the k blocks, the adversary may have learned the secret strings correspond to λ_1 blocks through queries, and has to cheat in all the remaining $k - \lambda_1$ blocks. For each MPC instance, the verifier opens the views of a subset of the MPC parties and a cheat prover can be detected with a probability $1 - \epsilon$. Therefore, if using an MPC protocol without pre-processing, then the soundness error is;

$$\sum_{i=0}^{k} \Pr[\lambda_1 = i] \cdot \epsilon^{k-i}$$

If using an MPC protocol with pre-processing, then the adversary can also cheat in the pre-processing phase. If the adversary cheats in λ_2 (out of M) copies of pre-processing data, and not being detected when checking the pre-processing data (the probability is denoted as $\mathrm{Succ}^{pre}(\lambda_2, k, M)$), then it needs to cheat in $k - \lambda_1 - \lambda_2$ MPC instances. The soundness error is:

$$\sum_{i=0}^{k} \Pr[\lambda_1 = i] \left(\sum_{\lambda_2=0}^{k-\lambda_1} \mathrm{Succ}^{pre}(\lambda_2, k, M) \cdot \epsilon^{k-\lambda_1-\lambda_2} \right)$$

As a concrete example, let us consider a case in which we implement π_D using KKW [45]. Then we have:

$$\Pr[\lambda_1 = i] = \binom{k}{i}(1 - (1 - 2^{-d})^q)^i((1 - 2^{-d})^q)^{k-i},$$

$$\mathrm{Succ}^{pre}(\lambda_2, k, M) = \frac{\binom{M-\lambda_2}{M-k}}{\binom{M}{M-k}}, \quad \epsilon = \frac{1}{N}$$

In the above, d, k, q are the parameters for the M-FORS signature, M is the number of pre-processing data generated, and N is the number of MPC parties. When $d = 16, k = 70, q = 1024, M = 1120$, and $N = 16$, then the soundness error is $2^{-257.769}$; when $d = 16, k = 35, q = 1024, M = 560$, and $N = 16$, then the soundness error is $2^{-128.987}$.

6   UC Security Model for DAA

Security in the Universal Composability (UC) framework follows the simulation-based paradigm, where a protocol is secure when it is as secure as an ideal functionality that performs the desired tasks in a way that is secure by design. In this framework, an environment $\mathcal{E}$ passes inputs and outputs to the protocol parties. The network is controlled by an adversary $\mathcal{A}$ that may communicate freely with $\mathcal{E}$. The framework includes an ideal world and a real world. In the ideal world, the parties forward their inputs to the ideal functionality $\mathcal{F}$, which then (internally) performs the defined task and creates outputs that are forwarded to $\mathcal{E}$ by the parties. A real-world protocol Π is said to securely realize a functionality $\mathcal{F}$, if the real world is indistinguishable from the ideal world, meaning that for every adversary performing an attack in the real world, there is an ideal world adversary (often called simulator) $\mathcal{S}$ that performs the same attack in the ideal world. More precisely, a protocol Π is secure if for every adversary $\mathcal{A}$, there exists a simulator $\mathcal{S}$ such that no environment $\mathcal{E}$ can distinguish executing the real world with Π and $\mathcal{A}$, and executing the ideal world with $\mathcal{F}$ and $\mathcal{S}$. Another key point of UC, towards reducing the computational complexity of the specified protocol, is the composition theorem: It guarantees composition with arbitrary sets of parties and executed computational tasks. This ensures that UC-security proofs, for any subroutine of $\mathcal{F}$, are also transferred to the security model of the entire protocol Π.

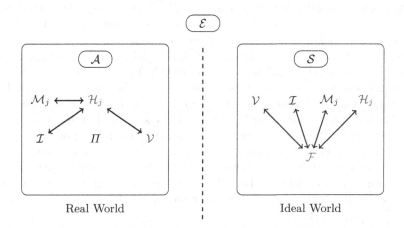

Fig. 5. UC security model for DAA

Now we employ the UC model for the security of our DAA protocol Π. Figure 5 depicts the network topology of the real and ideal worlds. The endmost goal is to prove the completeness and soundness of the DAA protocol by proving that an adversary cannot gain any significant advantage when monitoring the operations and interacting tasks that take place in the real world; i.e., be indistinguishable from the case where all the DAA internal phases are executed in the ideal world. Security of our DAA protocol Π is captured by the fact that every attack $\mathcal{A}$ mounted in the real world, $\mathcal{S}$ carries out in the ideal world. Protocol security is implied since such attacks cannot be mounted in the ideal world. We have then that the output $\mathcal{E}$ retrieved from the execution of Π in the ideal world with $\mathcal{S}$ and from the execution of Π with the real-world entities and $\mathcal{A}$ are indistinguishably distributed. This ensures that a real-world DAA protocol Π *securely realizes* all internal cryptographic tasks (e.g., JOIN, SIGN, VERIFY, and LINK) if for any real-world adversary $\mathcal{A}$ that interacts with the DAA players, running Π, there exists an ideal world simulator $\mathcal{S}$ that interacts with the ideal functionality $\mathcal{F}$, and the notional entities executing DAA protocol so that no probabilistic polynomial time environment $\mathcal{E}$ can distinguish whether it is interacting with the real world adversary $\mathcal{A}$ or the ideal world adversary $\mathcal{S}$.

We follow the UC security model for DAA given by Camenisch et al. in [16], where the ideal functionality $\mathcal{F}$ assumes static corruptions, i.e., the adversary decides upfront which parties are corrupt and makes this information known to the functionality. The UC framework allows us to focus the analysis on a single protocol instance with a globally unique session identifier sid. $\mathcal{F}$ uses session identifiers of the form $sid = (\mathcal{I}, sid')$ for some issuer $\mathcal{I}$ and a unique string sid'.

The ideal functionality $\mathcal{F}$ is further parametrized by a leakage function $l : \{0,1\}^* \rightarrow \{0,1\}^*$, that models the information leakage occurred in the communication between a host $\mathcal{H}_j$ and its TPM $\mathcal{M}_j$. We define $\mathcal{F}$ by using two "macros" to determine if a TPM's signing key sk_u is consistent with the internal functionality records or not. This is checked at several places in the functionality and also depends on whether the sk_u belongs to an honest or corrupt TPM. The first macro CheckTtdHonest is used when the functionality stores a new TPM key sk_u that belongs to an honest TPM, and checks that none of the existing valid signatures is identified as belonging to this TPM key. The second macro CheckTtdCorrupt is used when storing a new sk_u that belongs to a corrupt TPM, and checks that the new sk_u does not break the identifiability of signatures, i.e., it checks that there is no other known TPM key sk_u', unequal to sk_u, such that both keys are identified as the owner of a signature. Both functions output a bit b where $b = 1$ indicates that the new sk_u is consistent with the stored information, whereas $b = 0$ signals an invalid key. We also define the JOIN and SIGN sub-sessions by $jsid$ and $ssid$. In addition $\mathcal{F}$ maintains a group member list ML, a key record list DomainKeys, a signature record list Signed, and a verification result list VerResults.

We adopt two sub-functionalities introduced in [16] and they are available to all parties. The first one is a certificate authority functionality $\mathcal{F}_{ca}$ that allows the issuer to register their public key. The second is the common reference string functionality $\mathcal{F}_{crs}$, which is used to provide all entities with the system parameters comprising the random seed to generate the commitments and the issuer's public key. Note that for the communication between the TPM and issuer (via the host) in the join protocol we adopt the key binding protocol introduced in [25] that provides a secure and authenticated channel between the TPM and the issuer even in the presence of a corrupt host, therefore no need for the semi-authenticated channel $\mathcal{F}_{auth}^*$ in our model. We now define the algorithms that will be used inside the ideal functionality as follows:

- ukgen(n): A probabilistic algorithm that takes a security parameter n as input and generates a key sk_u for a honest TPM.
- sign(sk_u, msg, bsn): A probabilistic algorithm used by a honest TPM; input is a key sk_u, a message msg and a basename bsn, and output is a signature Σ.

- verify(Σ, msg, bsn): A deterministic algorithm that is used in the VERIFY interface. On input of a signature Σ, a message msg and a basename bsn, it outputs $f = 1$ if the signature is valid, and $f = 0$ otherwise.
- link($\Sigma_1, msg_1, \Sigma_2, msg_2, bsn$): A deterministic algorithm that is used in the LINK interface. Given two signatures with the same bsn, it outputs 1 if both Σ_1 and Σ_2 were generated by the same TPM, and outputs 0 otherwise.
- identify(sk_u, Σ, msg, bsn): A deterministic algorithm that is used to ensure consistency with the ideal functionality $\mathcal{F}$'s internal records. It outputs 1 if a key sk_u was used to produce a signature Σ, and outputs 0 otherwise.

We explain the interfaces of the ideal functionality $\mathcal{F}$ in the UC framework:

Setup

1. **Issuer Setup.** On input (SETUP, sid) from issuer $\mathcal{I}$,
   - Verify that $sid = (\mathcal{I}, sid')$ and output (SETUP, sid) to $\mathcal{S}$.
2. **Set Algorithms.** On input (ALG, sid, ukgen, sign, verify, link, identify) from $\mathcal{S}$,
   - Check that verify, link and identify are deterministic (i).
   - Store (sid, ukgen, sign, verify, link, identify) and output (SETUPDONE, sid) to $\mathcal{I}$.

Join

3. **Join Request.** On input (JOIN, $sid, jsid, \mathcal{M}_j$) from host $\mathcal{H}_j$,
   - Create a join session record $\langle jsid, \mathcal{M}_j, \mathcal{H}_j, status \rangle$ with $status \leftarrow request$.
   - Output (JOINSTART, $sid, jsid, \mathcal{M}_j, \mathcal{H}_j$) to $\mathcal{S}$.
4. **Join Request Delivery.** On input (JOINSTART, $sid, jsid$) from $\mathcal{S}$,
   - Update the session record $\langle jsid, \mathcal{M}_j, \mathcal{H}_j, status \rangle$ to $status \leftarrow delivered$.
   - Output (JOINPROCEED, $sid, jsid, \mathcal{M}_j$) to $\mathcal{I}$.
5. **Join Proceed.** On input (JOINPROCEED, $sid, jsid$) from $\mathcal{I}$,
   - Update the session record $\langle jsid, \mathcal{M}_j, \mathcal{H}_j, status \rangle$ to $status \leftarrow complete$.
   - Output (JOINCOMPLETE, $sid, jsid$) to $\mathcal{S}$.
6. **Platform Key Generation.** On input (JOINCOMPLETE, $sid, jsid, sk_j$) from $\mathcal{S}$,
   - Look up record $\langle jsid, \mathcal{M}_j, \mathcal{H}_j, status \rangle$ with $status = complete$.
   - Abort if $\mathcal{I}$ or $\mathcal{M}_j$ is honest and a record $\langle \mathcal{M}_j, *, * \rangle \in$ ML already exists (ii).
   - If $\mathcal{M}_j$ and $\mathcal{H}_j$ are honest, set $sk_j \leftarrow \bot$.
   - Else, verify that the provided sk_j is eligible by checking
     - CheckTtdHonest(sk_j) = 1 if $\mathcal{H}_j$ is corrupt (iii) and $\mathcal{M}_j$ is honest, or
     - CheckTtdCorrupt(sk_j) = 1 if $\mathcal{M}_j$ is corrupt (iv).
   - Insert $\langle \mathcal{M}_j, \mathcal{H}_j, sk_j \rangle$ into ML and output (JOINED, $sid, jsid$) to $\mathcal{H}_j$.

Sign

7. **Sign Request.** On input (SIGN, $sid, ssid, \mathcal{M}_j, msg, bsn$) from host $\mathcal{H}_j$,
   - If $\mathcal{I}$ is honest and no entry $\langle \mathcal{M}_j, \mathcal{H}_j, * \rangle$ exists in ML, abort.

- Create a sign session record $\langle ssid, \mathcal{M}_j, \mathcal{H}_j, msg, bsn, status \rangle$ with $status \leftarrow request$.
- Output (SIGNSTART, sid, $ssid$, $l(msg, bsn)$, $\mathcal{M}_j, \mathcal{H}_j$) to $\mathcal{S}$.

8. **Sign Request Delivery.** On input (SIGNSTART, sid, $ssid$) from $\mathcal{S}$,
   - Update the session record $\langle ssid, \mathcal{M}_j, \mathcal{H}_j, msg, bsn, status \rangle$ to $status \leftarrow delivered$.
   - Output (SIGNPROCEED, sid, $ssid$, msg, bsn) to $\mathcal{M}_j$.

9. **Sign Proceed.** On input (SIGNPROCEED, sid, $ssid$) from $\mathcal{M}_j$,
   - Look up record $\langle ssid, \mathcal{M}_j, \mathcal{H}_j, msg, bsn, status \rangle$ with $status = delivered$.
   - Output (SIGNCOMPLETE, sid, $ssid$) to $\mathcal{S}$.

10. **Signature Generation.** On input (SIGNCOMPLETE, sid, $ssid$, Σ) from $\mathcal{S}$,
    - If $\mathcal{M}_j$ and $\mathcal{H}_j$ are honest, ignore the adversary's signature and internally generate the signature for a fresh or established sk_j:
      - If $bsn \neq \bot$, retrieve sk_j from $\langle \mathcal{M}_j, bsn, sk_j \rangle \in$ DomainKeys for $(\mathcal{M}_j, bsn)$. If no such sk_j exists or $bsn = \bot$, set $sk_j \leftarrow$ ukgen(). Check CheckTtdHonest(sk_j) = 1 (v) and store $\langle \mathcal{M}_j, bsn, sk_j \rangle$ in DomainKeys.
      - Compute signature as $\Sigma \leftarrow$ sign(sk_j, msg, bsn) and check verify(Σ, msg, bsn) = 1 (vi).
      - Check identify(Σ, msg, bsn, sk_j) = 1 (vii) and check that there is no $\mathcal{M}'_j \neq \mathcal{M}_j$ with key sk'_j registered in ML or DomainKeys such that identify(Σ, msg, bsn, sk'_j) = 1 (viii).
    - If $\mathcal{M}_j$ is honest, store $\langle \Sigma, msg, bsn, \mathcal{M}_j \rangle$ in Signed.
    - Output (SIGNATURE, sid, $ssid$, Σ) to $\mathcal{H}_j$.

Verify

11. **Verify.** On input (VERIFY, sid, msg, bsn, Σ, **keyRL**, **linkRL**) from some party $\mathcal{V}$,
    - Retrieve all pairs $(sk_j, \mathcal{M}_j)$ from $\langle \mathcal{M}_j, *, sk_j \rangle \in$ ML and $\langle \mathcal{M}_j, *, sk_j \rangle \in$ DomainKeys where identify(Σ, msg, bsn, sk_j) = 1. Set $f \leftarrow 0$ if at least one of the following conditions holds:
      - More than one key sk_j was found (ix).
      - $\mathcal{I}$ is honest and no pair $(sk_j, \mathcal{M}_j)$ was found (x).
      - There is an honest $\mathcal{M}_j$ but no entry $\langle *, msg, bsn, \mathcal{M}_j \rangle \in$ Signed exists (xi).
      - There is a $sk'_u \in$ **keyRL** where identify(Σ, msg, bsn, sk'_u) = 1 and no pair $(sk_j, \mathcal{M}_j)$ for an honest $\mathcal{M}_j$ was found, or there exists $(slt', msg', bsn') \in$ **linkRL** such that identify(slt', msg', bsn', sk_j) = 1. (xii).
    - If $f \neq 0$, set $f \leftarrow$ verify(Σ, msg, bsn) (xiii).
    - Add $\langle \Sigma, msg, bsn, \textbf{keyRL}, \textbf{linkRL}, f \rangle$ to VerResults, output (VERIFIED, sid, f) to $\mathcal{V}$.

Link

12. **Link.** On input (LINK, sid, Σ, msg, Σ', msg', $bsn \neq \bot$) from some party $\mathcal{V}$,

- Output $\perp$ to $\mathcal{V}$ if at least one signature tuple (Σ, msg, bsn) or (Σ', msg', bsn) is not valid (verified via the verify interface with $\mathbf{keyRL} = \emptyset$ and $\mathbf{linkRL} = \emptyset$) (xiv).
- For each sk_i in ML and DomainKeys compute $b_i \leftarrow$ identify(Σ, msg, bsn, sk_i) and $b'_i \leftarrow$ identify$(\Sigma', msg', bsn, sk_i)$ and do the following:
  - Set $f \leftarrow 0$ if $b_i \neq b'_i$ for some i (xv).
  - Set $f \leftarrow 1$ if $b_i = b'_i = 1$ for some i (xvi).
- If f is not defined yet, set $f \leftarrow$ link$(\Sigma, msg, \Sigma', msg', bsn)$.
- Output (LINK, sid, f) to $\mathcal{V}$.

We highlight that our model catches all the security requirements discussed in Sect. 2.3 (correctness, anonymity and non-frameability):

- The *correctness* of our scheme is guaranteed in our model. When an honest signer (including both the TPM and Host) successfully creates a signature, honest Verifiers will always accept this signature. This is due to the checks v, vi, vii, and viii performed by $\mathcal{F}$ in the **Sign** interface.
- The *anonymity* in our scheme is also guaranteed by $\mathcal{F}$ due to the random choice of sk_j that will be later used for the construction of DAA signatures as part of the **Sign** interface. In the case of corrupt devices, the Simulator is allowed to provide a signature that will convey the signer's identity, as the signing key can be extracted from the respective device key pair. This reflects that the anonymity of the DAA signer is guaranteed if both the TPM and the Host are honest.
- The *non-frameability* property guarantees that a signature created by an adversary cannot be linked to a legitimate signature created by the target device, this is due to the check ix in our model. CheckTtdHonest prevents registering an honest sk_j in the Join interface that matches an existing signature so that conflicts can be avoided and signatures can always be traced back to the original signer. This ensures that honest signers are not revoked due to the identify algorithm being deterministic in our model. Consider an adversary aiming to create a signature on a message that has not been signed by an honest device, checks x and xi in the **Verify** interface ensure the scheme *unforgeability* property, which dictates that it is computationally infeasible to maliciously forge signatures.

7 UC Security Proof of the DAA Scheme

7.1 High-Level Description of Our Proof

We start with the real-world protocol execution in Game 1. In the next game, we construct one entity C that runs the real-world protocol for all honest parties. Then we split C into two pieces, an ideal functionality $\mathcal{F}$ and a simulator $\mathcal{S}$ that simulates the real-world parties. Initially, we start with an "empty" functionality $\mathcal{F}$. With each game, we gradually change $\mathcal{F}$ and update $\mathcal{S}$ accordingly, moving from the real world to the ideal world, and culminating in the full ideal functionality $\mathcal{F}$ being realized as part of the ideal world, thus, proving our proposed security model presented in Sect. 6. The endmost goal of our proof is to prove the indistinguishability between Game 1 and Game 16, i.e., between the complete real world and the fully functional ideal world. This is done by proving that each game is indistinguishable from the previous one. We use the "$\approx$" sign to express games indistinguishably between games.

The ideal functionality $\mathcal{F}$ is introduced in Game 3; at this stage $\mathcal{F}$ only forwards its inputs to the simulator $\mathcal{S}$ who simulates the real world. From Game 4 onward, $\mathcal{F}$ starts executing the setup interface on behalf of the Issuer. Moving on to Game 5, $\mathcal{F}$ handles simple verification and identification checks without performing any detailed checks at this stage; i.e., it only checks if the signer belongs to a revocation list separately. In Games 6–8, $\mathcal{F}$ executes the Join interface while performing checks to keep the consistency of registered keys. It also adds checks that allow only the signers that have successfully been enrolled to create signatures. Game 9 proves the anonymity of our protocol by letting $\mathcal{F}$ handle the sign queries on behalf of honest signers. To do this, $\mathcal{F}$ creates signatures using freshly generated random keys instead of running the signing algorithm using the signer's signing key. At the end of this game, we prove that by relying on the ZKP constructions, an external environment will notice no change from previous games where the real-world Sign algorithm was executed. Now moving to Games 10–16, we let $\mathcal{F}$ perform all other checks that are explained in Sect. 6.

7.2   The DAA Scheme Proof

Due to the limited space, we provide a sketch of the security proof of the proposed DAA protocol, including a sequence of games based on the model of Camenish et al. in [16]. A detailed proof will be given in the full paper. The proof in [16] is constructed under the Discrete Logarithm (DL) and Decisional Diffie-Hellman (DDH) assumptions and the unforgeability of the Camenisch-Lysyanskaya (CL) signatures. Other DAA signatures such as [24,35] are proved based on lattice hard problems, namely Ring-LWE and Ring-SIS, and the unforgeability is supported on the modified Boyen or Dilithium signature scheme [6,32]. In contrast to the previous DAA schemes, our game indistinguishability is based on the perfect simulation of the MPCitH-based NIZK proofs, the soundness, completeness and zero-knowledge properties of the proofs $\pi_{\mathcal{I}}$ and π_D, the unforgeability of the F-SPHINCS+ signature scheme, and the security properties of the tweakable hash functions, H_1, H_2 and H_3, and the pseudorandom function F. The sequence of games is as follows:

Proof (sketch)
   Game 1: (Real-World execution of the protocol): This is the start.
   Game 2: (Introducing C): An entity C is introduced; C receives all inputs from the parties and simulates the real-world protocol for them. This is equivalent to Game 1.

Game 3: (Reconstruction of C): We now split C into two parts, $\mathcal{F}$ and $\mathcal{S}$, where $\mathcal{F}$ behaves as an ideal functionality. $\mathcal{F}$ receives all the inputs and forwards them to $\mathcal{S}$, who simulates the real-world protocol for honest parties, and sends the outputs to $\mathcal{F}$. $\mathcal{F}$ then forwards the outputs to the environment $\mathcal{E}$. This game is simply Game 2 but with different structure, so Game 3 $\approx$ Game 2.

Game 4: ($\mathcal{F}$ handles the setup queries): $\mathcal{F}$ now behaves differently in the setup interface and stores the algorithms for the issuer $\mathcal{I}$. $\mathcal{F}$ also does checks to ensure that the structure of sid is correct for an honest $\mathcal{I}$, and aborts if not. In case $\mathcal{I}$ is corrupt, $\mathcal{S}$ extracts the secret key for $\mathcal{I}$ and proceeds in the setup interface on behalf of $\mathcal{I}$. Clearly $\mathcal{E}$ will notice no change, so Game 4 $\approx$ Game 3.

Game 5: ($\mathcal{F}$ handles the verification and linking queries): $\mathcal{F}$ now performs the verification and linking checks instead of forwarding them to $\mathcal{S}$. There are no protocol messages and the outputs are exactly as in the real-world protocol. However, the only difference is that the verification algorithm used by $\mathcal{F}$ does not contain a revocation check. $\mathcal{F}$ performs this check separately thus the outcomes are equal, so Game 5 $\approx$ Game 4.

Game 6: ($\mathcal{F}$ handles the join queries): The join interface of $\mathcal{F}$ is now changed, and $\mathcal{F}$ stores the joined member information in the Member List ML . If $\mathcal{I}$ is honest, $\mathcal{F}$ stores the secret key sk_u, extracted from $\mathcal{S}$, for corrupt TPM's. $\mathcal{S}$ always has enough information to simulate the real-world protocol except when the issuer is the only honest party. In this case, $\mathcal{S}$ does not know who initiated the join since the host does not authenticate towards the issuer in the real world, so $\mathcal{S}$ can't make a join query with $\mathcal{F}$ on a corrupt host's behalf. Thus, to deal with this case, $\mathcal{F}$ can safely choose any corrupt host and put it into ML, the identities of hosts are only used to create signatures for platforms with an honest TPM or honest host, so fully corrupted platforms do not matter. In the only case, where the TPM has already been registered in ML, $\mathcal{F}$ may abort the protocol, but $\mathcal{I}$ should have already tested this case before continuing with the query JOINPROCEED, hence $\mathcal{F}$ will not abort. Thus in all cases, $\mathcal{F}$ and $\mathcal{S}$ can interact to simulate the real-world protocol, so Game 6 $\approx$ Game 5.

Game 7: ($\mathcal{F}$ knows bsn and msg to be signed or $l(msg, bsn)$): $\mathcal{F}$ now no longer informs $\mathcal{S}$ about the message and the basename that are being signed. If the whole signer is honest, $\mathcal{S}$ can learn nothing about the message msg and the basename bsn. Instead, $\mathcal{S}$ knows only the leakage $l(msg, bsn)$. To simulate the real world, $\mathcal{S}$ chooses a pair (msg', bsn') such that $l(msg', bsn') = l(msg, bsn)$. Therefore Game 7 $\approx$ Game 6.

Game 8: ($\mathcal{F}$ performs pre-sign checks): If $\mathcal{I}$ is honest, $\mathcal{F}$ only allows the signer that has joined to sign. An honest host will always check whether it has joined with its TPM in the real-world protocol, so no difference for honest hosts. Also, an honest TPM only signs when it has joined with the host before. In the case that an honest $\mathcal{M}_i$ performs a join protocol with a corrupt host $\mathcal{H}_j$ and the honest issuer, the simulator $\mathcal{S}$ will make a join query with $\mathcal{F}$, to ensure that $\mathcal{M}_i$ and $\mathcal{H}_j$ are in ML. Therefore, Game 8 $\approx$ Game 7.

Game 9: ($\mathcal{F}$ handles the sign queries, i.e., simulating the TPM without knowing its secret): In this game, $\mathcal{F}$ creates anonymous signatures for honest signers by running the algorithms defined in the setup interface. Let us start by defining Game $9.k.k'$, in this game $\mathcal{F}$ handles the first k' signing inputs of $\mathcal{M}_k$, and subsequent inputs are then forwarded to $\mathcal{S}$. For $i < k$, $\mathcal{F}$ handles all the signing queries with $\mathcal{M}_i$ using algorithms. For $i > k$, $\mathcal{F}$ forwards all signing queries with $\mathcal{M}_i$ to $\mathcal{S}$ who creates signatures as before. Now from the definition of Game $9.k.k'$, we note that Game $9.0.0 =$ Game 8. For increasing k', Game $9.k.k'$ will be at some stage equal to Game $9.k + 1.0$, this is because there can only be a polynomial number of signing queries to be processed. Therefore, for large enough k and k', $\mathcal{F}$ handles all the signing queries of all TPMs, and Game 9 is indistinguishable from Game $9.k.k'$. We want to prove now that Game $9.k.k' + 1$ is indistinguishable from Game $9.k.k'$. Suppose that there exists an environment that can distinguish a signature of an honest party using sk_u from a signature using a different sk'_u, then the environment can break the pseudorandom property of the function F.

The first $j \leq k'$ signing queries on behalf of $\mathcal{M}_k$ are forwarded by $\mathcal{F}$ to $\mathcal{S}$, which calls the real-world protocol. Now suppose that $\mathcal{E}$ is given tuples $\Sigma = (str, slt, com, \pi_D)$ and it is challenged to decide if $\Sigma = (str, slt, com, \pi_D)$ is calculated from uniform random $r \leftarrow \{0,1\}^n$ or from a certified TPM secret key sk_u. In the reduction, we have to be able to simulate the TPM without knowing the secret sk_u. The issuer's zero-knowledge proof $\pi_\mathcal{I}$ for the correctness of the master secret and public key pair allows the simulator $\mathcal{S}$ extracts the master secret key. Furthermore, the zero-knowledge proof of the group membership credential π_D helps $\mathcal{S}$ extract the TPM's secret key sk_u for corrupt TPM and create signatures on behalf of the TPM as in the real world scenario. Let r be a randomly sampled key from $\{0,1\}^n$ that will be used to generate signatures on behalf of honest TPMs rather than using the real TPM secret key sk_u. Since the issuer's secret key msk can be extracted from $\pi_\mathcal{I}$ due to the soundness of the proof $\pi_\mathcal{I}$ and getting access to $\mathcal{F}_{crs}$, then a credential can be created on $et'_u = F(r, \; gid)$ by running the signing algorithm of F-SPHINCS+, $\mathsf{sign}(et'_u, msk, gp)$. After getting a credential on et'_u, slt and sst are calculated as functions of r, i.e. $slt = F(r, \; lid)$ and $sst = F(r, \; sid)$. Then all other parts of the signature follow exactly the same as the real-world protocol (i.e. when using the TPM's sk_u). The commitment com is calculated as our defined sign algorithm and the proof π_D can then be perfectly simulated using the random secret r. Due to the zero-knowledge property of the proof π_D and the pseudorandom outputs of the function F, we argue that an external environment cannot distinguish between 1) a signature generated using the TPM's (sk_u, et_u). 2) a signature generated by a random (r, et'_u). Therefore, Game 9 $\approx$ Game 8.

Game 10 ($\mathcal{F}$ performs key consistency checks): When storing a new sk_u, $\mathcal{F}$ checks $\mathsf{CheckTtdHonest}(sk_u) = 1$ or $\mathsf{CheckTtdCorrupt}(sk_u) = 1$. We want to show that these checks will always pass. In fact, valid signatures always satisfy $slt = F(sk_u, lid)$, $et_u = F(sk_u, gid)$, $(gr_u, \mathbf{S}) \leftarrow$ F-SPHINCS+.$\mathsf{sign}(et_u, msk, gp)$ and $sst = F(sk_u, sid)$. By the soundness property of π_D, there exists only one secret sk_u satisfying the slt construction, and there exists one sst that matches this signature by the soundness of the $hk = \mathsf{MPC\_H1}(\llbracket sst \rrbracket)$. Thus,

CheckTtdCorrupt(sk_u) = 1 will always give the correct output. On the other hand, the keys for honest TPMs are chosen uniformly at random from an exponentially large group $\{0,1\}^n$, due to the large min-entropy of the uniform distribution the probability that sampling a selected sk_u is negligible for large n with probability equal to $1/2^n$, thus with overwhelming probability, there does not exist a signature already using the same sk_u, which implies that CheckTtdHonest(sk_u) = 1 will always give the correct output. Hence, Game 10 $\approx$ Game 9.

Game 11: ($\mathcal{F}$ checks the correctness of the protocol): In this game $\mathcal{F}$ checks that any honestly generated signature $\Sigma = (str, slt, com, \pi_D)$ is always valid due to the completeness property of π_D and the correctness of the F-SPHINCS+ signature. A valid proof π_D on the credential ensures that the credential has the correct structure, follows the correct authentication path, and always leads to the issuer's public key rpk due to the soundness of π_D and the correctness of the F-SPHINCS+ signature. Second, $\mathcal{F}$ makes sure identify(Σ, msg, bsn, sk_u) = 1, this is also achieved in the real-world protocol due to the soundness of π_D. $\mathcal{F}$ checks, using its internal records ML and DomainKeys that honest users are not sharing the same secret key sk_u. If there exists a key $sk'_u \neq sk_u$ in DomainKeys such that $slt = F(sk'_u, lid) = F(sk_u, lid)$, then this breaks the collision resistance property of the function F. Therefore Game 11 $\approx$ Game 10.

Game 12 ($\mathcal{F}$ checks that valid signatures are deterministic): Add Check (ix) to ensure that there are no multiple sk_u values matching to one signature. A signature Σ includes $slt = F(sk_u, lid)$, $com = H_1(F(sk_u, sid)||pk_h|| \cdots ||rpk)$ and π_D. Due to the soundness of the function F and the proof π_D, and also due to the collision resistance and second-preimage properties of H_1, two different keys cannot create the same signature and two different signatures cannot share the same sk_u. Therefore a valid signature should be identified to one sk_u only. Hence, Game 12 $\approx$ Game 11.

Game 13 ($\mathcal{F}$ checks the unforgeability of the credential): To prevent accepting a signature that was not generated by using a group membership credential issued by an honest issuer, $\mathcal{F}$ adds Check (x). A credential is an F-SPHINCS+ signature on $mt_u||idx$, using the tweakable hash functions H_1, H_2 and H_3. Following the proof of Theorem 1 in Sect. 4, the F-SPHINCS+ signature scheme is unforgeable due to the security properties of H_1, H_2 and H_3, so this check is always passed and Game 13 $\approx$ Game 12.

Game 14 ($\mathcal{F}$ checks the unforgeability of signatures): Check (xi) is added to $\mathcal{F}$ to prevent an adversary from forging signatures using honest signer's credential key $gsk_u = (sk_u, gr_u, \mathbf{S})$. As discussed before, a DAA signature Σ is proof of the correct construction of slt, com and π_D, which form a NIZK proof of an F-SPHINCS+ signature associated with a single key sk_u. If the signature is verified, due to the unforgeability of F-SPHINCS+, the binding property of the commitment scheme used to generate $com = H_1(F(sk_u, sid)||pk_h|| \cdots ||rpk)$, and the soundness of the function F used to compute slt and com, sk_u belonging to an honest TPM must be involved. If the adversary uses a different key sk'_u to create this signature. Due to the soundness of π_D analyzed in Sect. 5, the proof π_D cannot be simulated with overwhelming probability unless $sk'_u = sk_u$, so Game 14 ≈ Game 13.

Game 15 ($\mathcal{F}$ checks the correct revocation): Check (xii) is added to $\mathcal{F}$ to ensure that an honest TPM with sk_u are not being revoked. If there exists a matching revoked key sk^*_u ($\neq sk_u$) ∈ **keyRL** such that $slt = F(sk^*_u, lid) = F(sk_u, lid)$, then this breaks the collision resistance property of the function F. For the same reason, there does not exist (slt', msg', bsn') ∈ **linkRL** such that $slt' = F(sk'_u, lid') = F(sk_u, lid')$ and $sk'_u \neq sk_u$. Therefore, our protocol ensures the correct revocation. So Game 15 ≈ Game 14.

Game 16 ($\mathcal{F}$ checks the linkability): Checks (xv and xvi) of the ideal functionality $\mathcal{F}$ that are related to link queries are now included. The output of $\mathcal{F}$ based on these checks is still consistent with the output which the link algorithm would give: If there is an sk_u that matches two signatures signed under the same bsn, by the soundness of π_D we have that the pseudonyms based on the same sk_u must be equal, resulting in link outputting 1. If there is an sk_u that matches one signature but not the other, by the soundness of π_D we have that the pseudonyms slt that are not generated using sk_u must also differ from those generated by a different key $sk'_u \neq sk_u$ which results in link outputting 0. Therefore, Game 16 ≈ Game 15. This concludes the proof.

8   Conclusion

This paper proposes the first DAA scheme from symmetric primitives and this scheme has some interesting features. We make use of a modified SPHINCS+ signature as a group membership credential and use of a Picnic-style signature to prove the possession of that credential. Our DAA scheme splits the signer role between a TPM and its host and allows the TPM to have a much smaller workload than the host. This scheme can handle a large group size (up to 2^{60}), which is suitable for rapidly increasing trusted computing applications. This research topic is still in its early stage. Improving the performance of this DAA scheme is challenging and it will be possible if either a more efficient stateless hash-based signature scheme than F-SPHINCS+ or an efficient Picnic-style signature scheme is developed.

Acknowledgments. We thank the European Union's Horizon research and innovation program for support under grant agreement numbers: 101069688 (CONNECT), 101070627 (REWIRE), 779391 (FutureTPM), 952697 (ASSURED), 101019645 (SECANT) and 101095634 (ENTRUST). These projects are funded by the UK government's Horizon Europe guarantee and administered by UKRI. We also thank the National Natural Science Foundation of China for support under grant agreement numbers: 62072132 and 62261160651. We would like to thank Qingju Wang and Scott Fluhrer for helpful discussions. We also thank the anonymous reviewers from PQCrypto for their valuable comments.

References

1. Bansarkhani, R.E., Kaafarani, A.E.: Direct anonymous attestation from lattices. IACR Cryptology ePrint Archive **2017**, 1022 (2017)
2. Baum, C., de Saint Guilhem, C.D., Kales, D., Orsini, E., Scholl, P., Zaverucha, G.: Banquet: short and fast signatures from AES. In: Garay, J.A. (ed.) PKC 2021. LNCS, vol. 12710, pp. 266–297. Springer, Cham (2021). https://doi.org/10.1007/978-3-030-75245-3_11
3. Bernstein, D.J., Hülsing, A., Kölbl, S., Niederhagen, R., Rijneveld, J., Schwabe, P.: The SPHINCS$^+$ signature framework. In: ACM CCS, pp. 2129–2146 (2019)
4. Bhadauria, R., Fang, Z., Hazay, C., Venkitasubramaniam, M., Xie, T., Zhang, Y.: Ligero++: a new optimized sublinear IOP. In: ACM CCS, pp. 2025–2038 (2020)
5. Boneh, D., Eskandarian, S., Fisch, B.: Post-quantum EPID signatures from symmetric primitives. In: Matsui, M. (ed.) CT-RSA 2019. LNCS, vol. 11405, pp. 251–271. Springer, Cham (2019). https://doi.org/10.1007/978-3-030-12612-4_13
6. Boyen, X.: Lattice mixing and vanishing trapdoors: a framework for fully secure short signatures and more. In: Nguyen, P.Q., Pointcheval, D. (eds.) PKC 2010. LNCS, vol. 6056, pp. 499–517. Springer, Heidelberg (2010). https://doi.org/10.1007/978-3-642-13013-7_29
7. Brickell, E.F., Camenisch, J., Chen, L.: Direct anonymous attestation. In: ACM CCS, pp. 132–145 (2004)
8. Brickell, E., Chen, L., Li, J.: A new direct anonymous attestation scheme from bilinear maps. In: Lipp, P., Sadeghi, A.-R., Koch, K.-M. (eds.) Trust 2008. LNCS, vol. 4968, pp. 166–178. Springer, Heidelberg (2008). https://doi.org/10.1007/978-3-540-68979-9_13
9. Brickell, E., Chen, L., Li, J.: Simplified security notions of direct anonymous attestation and a concrete scheme from pairings. Int. J. Inf. Secur. **8**, 315–300 (2009)
10. Brickell, E., Li, J.: A pairing-based DAA scheme further reducing TPM resources. Trust **6101**, 181–195 (2010)
11. Brickell, E., Li, J.: Enhanced privacy ID: a direct anonymous attestation scheme with enhanced revocation capabilities. IEEE Trans. Dependable Secur. Comput. **9**(3), 345–360 (2012)
12. Buser, M., Liu, J.K., Steinfeld, R., Sakzad, A., Sun, S.-F.: DGM: a dynamic and revocable group Merkle signature. In: Sako, K., Schneider, S., Ryan, P.Y.A. (eds.) ESORICS 2019. LNCS, vol. 11735, pp. 194–214. Springer, Cham (2019). https://doi.org/10.1007/978-3-030-29959-0_10
13. Camenisch, J., Chen, L., Drijvers, M., Lehmann, A., Novick, D., Urian, R.: One TPM to bind them all: fixing TPM 2.0 for provably secure anonymous attestation. In: IEEE S&P, pp. 901–920 (2017)
14. Camenisch, J., Drijvers, M., Edgington, A., Lehmann, T.A., Urian, R.: FIDO ECDAA algorithm (2018). http://fidoalliance.org/specs/fido-v2.0-id-20180227/fido-ecdaa-algorithm-v2.0-id-20180227.html
15. Camenisch, J., Drijvers, M., Lehmann, A.: Anonymous attestation using the strong Diffie Hellman assumption revisited. In: Franz, M., Papadimitratos, P. (eds.) Trust 2016. LNCS, vol. 9824, pp. 1–20. Springer, Cham (2016). https://doi.org/10.1007/978-3-319-45572-3_1
16. Camenisch, J., Drijvers, M., Lehmann, A.: Universally composable direct anonymous attestation. In: Cheng, C.-M., Chung, K.-M., Persiano, G., Yang, B.-Y. (eds.) PKC 2016. LNCS, vol. 9615, pp. 234–264. Springer, Heidelberg (2016). https://doi.org/10.1007/978-3-662-49387-8_10

17. Camenisch, J., Drijvers, M., Lehmann, A.: Anonymous attestation with subverted TPMs. In: Katz, J., Shacham, H. (eds.) CRYPTO 2017. LNCS, vol. 10403, pp. 427–461. Springer, Cham (2017). https://doi.org/10.1007/978-3-319-63697-9_15

18. Casey, M., Chen, L., Giannetsos, T., Newton, C., Sasse, R., Whitefield, J.: Direct anonymous attestation in the wild. Presentation at Real World Crypto (2019). https://rwc.iacr.org/2019/slides/DAA.pdf

19. Chase, M., et al.: The Picnic signature scheme design document (2020). https://microsoft.github.io/Picnic/

20. Chase, M., et al.: Post-quantum zero-knowledge and signatures from symmetric-key primitives. In: ACM CCS, pp. 1825–1842 (2017)

21. Chaum, D., van Heyst, E.: Group signatures. In: Davies, D.W. (ed.) EUROCRYPT 1991. LNCS, vol. 547, pp. 257–265. Springer, Heidelberg (1991). https://doi.org/10.1007/3-540-46416-6_22

22. Chen, L., Tu, T., Yu, K., Zhao, M., Wang, Y.: V-LDAA: a new lattice-based direct anonymous attestation scheme for VANETs system. Secur. Commun. Netw. **2021**, 1–13 (2021)

23. Chen, L.: A DAA scheme requiring less TPM resources. In: Bao, F., Yung, M., Lin, D., Jing, J. (eds.) Inscrypt 2009. LNCS, vol. 6151, pp. 350–365. Springer, Heidelberg (2010). https://doi.org/10.1007/978-3-642-16342-5_26

24. Chen, L., El Kassem, N., Lehmann, A., Lyubashevsky, V.: A framework for efficient lattice-based DAA. In: Proceedings of the 1st ACM Workshop on Cyber-Security Arms Race, pp. 23–34 (2019)

25. Chen, L., El Kassem, N., Newton, C.J.: How to bind a TPM's attestation keys with its endorsement key. Comput. J. bxad037 (2023)

26. Chen, L., Li, J.: Flexible and scalable digital signatures in TPM 2.0. In: ACM CCS, pp. 37–48 (2013)

27. Chen, L., Morrissey, P., Smart, N.P.: On proofs of security for DAA schemes. In: Baek, J., Bao, F., Chen, K., Lai, X. (eds.) ProvSec 2008. LNCS, vol. 5324, pp. 156–175. Springer, Heidelberg (2008). https://doi.org/10.1007/978-3-540-88733-1_11

28. Chen, L., Page, D., Smart, N.P.: On the design and implementation of an efficient DAA scheme. In: Gollmann, D., Lanet, J.-L., Iguchi-Cartigny, J. (eds.) CARDIS 2010. LNCS, vol. 6035, pp. 223–237. Springer, Heidelberg (2010). https://doi.org/10.1007/978-3-642-12510-2_16

29. Chen, L., Urian, R.: DAA-A: direct anonymous attestation with attributes. In: Conti, M., Schunter, M., Askoxylakis, I. (eds.) Trust 2015. LNCS, vol. 9229, pp. 228–245. Springer, Cham (2015). https://doi.org/10.1007/978-3-319-22846-4_14

30. Dai, Y., Zhang, F., Zhao, C.A.: Fast hashing to G_2 in direct anonymous attestation. Cryptology ePrint Archive (2022/996)

31. Dobraunig, C., Kales, D., Rechberger, C., Schofnegger, M., Zaverucha, G.: Shorter signatures based on tailor-made minimalist symmetric-key crypto. In: ACM CCS, pp. 843–857 (2022)

32. Ducas, L., et al.: Crystals-Dilithium: a lattice-based digital signature scheme. IACR Trans. Cryptographic Hardw. Embed. Syst. 238–268 (2018)

33. El Bansarkhani, R., Misoczki, R.: G-Merkle: a hash-based group signature scheme from standard assumptions. In: Lange, T., Steinwandt, R. (eds.) PQCrypto 2018. LNCS, vol. 10786, pp. 441–463. Springer, Cham (2018). https://doi.org/10.1007/978-3-319-79063-3_21

34. El Kassem, N.: Lattice-based direct anonymous attestation. Ph.D. thesis, University of Surrey (2020)

35. El Kassem, N., et al.: More efficient, provably-secure direct anonymous attestation from lattices. Futur. Gener. Comput. Syst. **99**, 425–458 (2019)
36. Fujisaki, E., Suzuki, K.: Traceable ring signature. In: Okamoto, T., Wang, X. (eds.) PKC 2007. LNCS, vol. 4450, pp. 181–200. Springer, Heidelberg (2007). https://doi.org/10.1007/978-3-540-71677-8_13
37. Giacomelli, I., Madsen, J., Orlandi, C.: ZKBoo: faster zero-knowledge for Boolean circuits. In: USENIX Security, pp. 1069–1083 (2016)
38. Greveler, U., Justus, B., Loehr, D.: Direct anonymous attestation: enhancing cloud service user privacy. In: Meersman, R., et al. (eds.) OTM 2011. LNCS, vol. 7045, pp. 577–587. Springer, Heidelberg (2011). https://doi.org/10.1007/978-3-642-25106-1_11
39. Hicks, C., Garcia, F.D.: A vehicular DAA scheme for unlinkable ECDSA pseudonyms in V2X. In: EuroS&P, pp. 460–473 (2020)
40. Ishai, Y., Kushilevitz, E., Ostrovsky, R., Sahai, A.: Zero-knowledge from secure multiparty computation. In: STOC, pp. 21–30 (2007)
41. ISO/IEC 10118-2:2010: Information technology - Security techniques - Hash-functions - Part 2: Hash-functions using an n-bit block cipher. Standard, International Organization for Standardization (2010)
42. ISO/IEC 20008-2: 2013: Information technology - Security techniques - Anonymous digital signatures - Part 2: Mechanisms using a group public key. Standard, International Organization for Standardization (2013)
43. Kales, D., Zaverucha, G.: Efficient lifting for shorter zero-knowledge proofs and post-quantum signatures. Cryptology ePrint Archive (2022/588)
44. Kassem, N.E., et al.: Lattice-based direct anonymous attestation (LDAA). Cryptology ePrint Archive (2018/401)
45. Katz, J., Kolesnikov, V., Wang, X.: Improved non-interactive zero knowledge with applications to post-quantum signatures. In: ACM CCS, pp. 525–537 (2018)
46. Kim, S., et al.: AIM: symmetric primitive for shorter signatures with stronger security. Cryptology ePrint Archive (2022/1387)
47. Lamport, L.: Constructing digital signatures from a one-way function. Technical report: SRI International Computer Science Laboratory (1979)
48. Merkle, R.C.: A certified digital signature. In: Brassard, G. (ed.) CRYPTO 1989. LNCS, vol. 435, pp. 218–238. Springer, New York (1990). https://doi.org/10.1007/0-387-34805-0_21
49. NIST: NIST announces first four quantum resistant cryptographic algorithms (2022). https://www.nist.gov/news-events/news/2022/07/nist-announces-first-four-quantum-resistant-cryptographic-algorithms
50. de Saint Guilhem, C.D., De Meyer, L., Orsini, E., Smart, N.P.: BBQ: using AES in picnic signatures. In: Paterson, K.G., Stebila, D. (eds.) SAC 2019. LNCS, vol. 11959, pp. 669–692. Springer, Cham (2020). https://doi.org/10.1007/978-3-030-38471-5_27
51. de Saint Guilhem, C.D., Orsini, E., Tanguy, T.: Limbo: efficient zero-knowledge MPCitH-based arguments. In: ACM CCS, pp. 3022–3036 (2021)
52. Shafieinejad, M., Esfahani, N.N.: A scalable post-quantum hash-based group signature. Des. Codes Crypt. **89**(5), 1061–1090 (2021). https://doi.org/10.1007/s10623-021-00857-9
53. TCG: TPM 1.2 Main Specification. Rev 116, Trusted Computing Group (2011). https://trustedcomputinggroup.org/resource/tpm-main-specification/
54. TCG: Trusted Platform Module 2.0 Library Specification. Rev 01.59, Trusted Computing Group (2019). https://trustedcomputinggroup.org/resource/tpm-library-specification/

55. Wang, H.Z., Huang, L.S.: An improved trusted cloud computing platform model based on DAA and privacy CA scheme. In: 2010 International Conference on Computer Application and System Modeling (ICCASM 2010), pp. 13–33 (2010)
56. Wesemeyer, S., Newton, C.J., Treharne, H., Chen, L., Sasse, R., Whitefield, J.: Formal analysis and implementation of a TPM 2.0-based direct anonymous attestation scheme. In: AsiaCCS, pp. 784–798 (2020)
57. Whitefield, J., Chen, L., Giannetsos, T., Schneider, S., Treharne, H.: Privacy-enhanced capabilities for VANETs using direct anonymous attestation. In: IEEE Vehicular Networking Conference (VNC), pp. 123–130 (2017)
58. Whitefield, J., Chen, L., Sasse, R., Schneider, S., Treharne, H., Wesemeyer, S.: A symbolic analysis of ECC-based direct anonymous attestation. In: EuroS&P, pp. 127–141 (2019)
59. Yang, K., Chen, L., Zhang, Z., Newton, C.J.P., Yang, B., Xi, L.: Direct anonymous attestation with optimal TPM signing efficiency. IEEE Trans. Inf. Forensics Secur. **16**, 2260–2275 (2021). https://doi.org/10.1109/TIFS.2021.3051801
60. Yehia, M., AlTawy, R., Gulliver, T.A.: GM^{MT}: a revocable group Merkle multi-tree signature scheme. In: Conti, M., Stevens, M., Krenn, S. (eds.) CANS 2021. LNCS, vol. 13099, pp. 136–157. Springer, Cham (2021). https://doi.org/10.1007/978-3-030-92548-2_8
61. Yehia, M., AlTawy, R., Gulliver, T.A.: Security analysis of DGM and GM group signature schemes instantiated with XMSS-T. In: Yu, Yu., Yung, M. (eds.) Inscrypt 2021. LNCS, vol. 13007, pp. 61–81. Springer, Cham (2021). https://doi.org/10.1007/978-3-030-88323-2_4
62. Zaverucha, G.: The Picnic signature algorithm specification. Supporting Documentation (2020). https://github.com/Microsoft/Picnic

Muckle+: End-to-End Hybrid Authenticated Key Exchanges

Sonja Bruckner[1], Sebastian Ramacher[2]([✉])(iD), and Christoph Striecks[2](iD)

[1] University of Applied Sciences Upper Austria, Hagenberg, Austria
sonja.bruckner@scch.at
[2] AIT Austrian Institute of Technology, Vienna, Austria
{sebastian.ramacher,christoph.striecks}@ait.ac.at

Abstract. End-to-end authenticity in public networks plays a significant role. Namely, without authenticity, the adversary might be able to retrieve even confidential information straight away by impersonating others. Proposed solutions to establish an authenticated channel cover pre-shared key-based, password-based, and certificate-based techniques. To add confidentiality to an authenticated channel, authenticated key exchange (AKE) protocols usually have one of the three solutions built in. As an amplification, hybrid AKE (HAKE) approaches are getting more popular nowadays and were presented in several flavors to incorporate classical, post-quantum, or quantum-key-distribution components. The main benefit is redundancy, i.e., if some of the components fail, the primitive still yields a confidential and authenticated channel. However, current HAKE instantiations either rely on pre-shared keys (which yields inefficient end-to-end authenticity) or only support one or two of the three above components (resulting in reduced redundancy and flexibility).

In this work, we present an extension of a modular HAKE framework due to Dowling, Brandt Hansen, and Paterson (PQCrypto'20) that does not suffer from the above constraints. While their instantiation, dubbed Muckle, requires pre-shared keys (and hence yields inefficient end-to-end authenticity), our extended instantiation called Muckle+ utilizes post-quantum digital signatures. While replacing pre-shared keys with digital signatures is rather straightforward in general, this turned out to be surprisingly non-trivial when applied to HAKE frameworks (resulting in adapted proof techniques).

Keywords: end-to-end security · hybrid authenticated key exchange · post-quantum cryptography

1 Introduction

Authenticated key exchanges (AKEs) are an essential building block of our connected world [7,32,58]. From user-to-user to server-to-server communication,

---

S. Bruckner—The work was conducted while the author was at AIT Austrian Institute of Technology.

data exchanged between any two parties is expected to be confidential even in the event of potentially active attacks on the communication channel. Ensuring confidentiality between two parties first requires that one can distinguish friend from foe. Specifically, if an adversary can impersonate a party in the system, all confidentiality guarantees are void since in that case the communication with the adversary is secured against outsiders, but the adversary itself may gain access to all data. Therefore, authenticity is a necessary requirement for achieving confidentiality on any level in any system and in the specific context of communication we thus require *end-to-end* authenticity. That is, both parties can directly verify the authenticity of the other party regardless of how many untrusted network links are located between them.

For network protocols on public or untrusted networks, well-established protocols such as Transport Layer Security (TLS) [67], IPsec [50], QUIC [47], Wire-Guard [34] employ various forms of an end-to-end AKE [7]; on the one hand to authenticate the other peer and on the other hand to establish an ephemeral session key to secure the communication channel. Depending on the concrete application, AKE protocols offer certificate-based authentication, password-based authentication, pre-shared key-based authentication whereas the secret keys are exchanged often using an ephemeral Diffie-Hellman key exchange or – on a more abstract level – with a key exchange using ephemeral key encapsulation mechanism (KEM) keys. Authentication in those protocols may be unilateral, e.g., only the initiator verifies the authenticity of the responder which is the default deployment mode of TLS on the web as the authentication of users is managed on the application layer, or mutual.

End-to-End Authentication Techniques. We will now discuss different techniques to achieve authenticity for key-exchange protocols: in a key exchange with pre-shared keys (PSK), both peers are required to agree on a secret key off-channel. This key is then part of the key-exchange protocol (e.g., is used as input in the key derivation function to derive the session keys) and only if the key is known, the protocol can be completed successfully. As a folklore consequence, networks with n peers necessitate the initial setup of $\mathcal{O}(n^2)$ PSKs to uniquely identify each peer. Otherwise, i.e., where 3 or more peers share the same PSK, peers would be unable to distinguish one communication partner from the other. Moreover, dynamically changing the network components becomes inefficient, e.g., if a new peer is added to the network, fresh PSKs have to be distributed to all other peers off-channel.

Password-based authenticated key exchanges [6,15] are of interest in a multi-client, single-sever scenario where each client is uniquely identified using a (low-entropy) password. Similar to the PSK approach, the password is an intrinsic part of the exchange which cannot be completed without knowledge of the specific password. As the scenario we are considering is not a multi-client single-server scenario and, more importantly, the password-based authentication is related to a PSK authentication scenario, we will omit further discussions of this type of key exchange.

Finally, with certificate-based protocols, peers have long-term public keys (typically of a digital signature scheme) whereas certificate authorities ensure the authenticity of these keys and establish a chain of trust. During a protocol run, peers are then required to sign certain messages to authenticate the exchange. A prominent example of such a protocol is SIGMA [51] which serves as a prototype for the key exchange deployed in IPsec [50], for example. Recently, due to the bandwidth requirements of post-quantum signature schemes, variants with long-term KEM keys such as KEMTLS [70] are also gaining interest as such variants are able to provide implicit server-to-client authentication. In this protocol, instead of signing the handshake transcript, after establishing an ephemeral secret, the client encapsulates another secret using the long-term KEM key embedded in the server's certificates. The server can only provide a valid key confirmation message if it is able to decapsulate the ciphertext with respect to the long-term key and thereby implicitly proves knowledge of the corresponding long-term secret key. This change in the protocol incurs the cost of an additional message but KEMTLS benefits from reduced runtime and bandwidth requirements.

While PSK key exchanges can be implemented solely from symmetric-key primitives, managing the required keys is a complex task. As no key material is available during system setup, those keys need to be securely exchanged via trusted couriers, installed on devices in the fab, or other methods are required to allow the keys be installed without relying on a yet unsecured communication channel. This task becomes more complex as the network grows and infeasible if parties have no trivial way to securely exchange the PSK.

Authenticated Key Exchanges Resilient Against Quantum Attacks.
End-to-end post-quantum AKE protocols have already been studied, e.g., most prominently in the area of Transport Layer Security (TLS) [13,53,54,62,70]. Moreover, standardization efforts towards post-quantum (hybrid) key exchanges are already in progress while NIST is expected to publish the first standards on post-quantum key-exchange mechanisms and digital signatures soon.[1] For most practical use-cases that require security against cryptographically relevant quantum computers, the post-quantum cryptography (PQC) paradigm seems to be a strong fit, although some techniques are rather recent and severe attacks are happening [11,19].

For highly secure use-cases, quantum-key distribution (QKD) [2,59] is gaining quite some attention recently with an expected market growth of 12 billion USD in 10 years.[2] Moreover, the European initiative for a quantum communication infrastructure named EuroQCI was recently established.[3] The benefit of a QKD system is that it guarantees information-theoretic security (ITS) compared to

---

[1] https://www.ietf.org/archive/id/draft-ietf-tls-hybrid-design-05.html, https://csrc.nist.gov/projects/post-quantum-cryptography.

[2] https://www.reuters.com/article/us-toshiba-cyber-idUSKBN2730KW.

[3] https://digital-strategy.ec.europa.eu/en/policies/european-quantum-communication-infrastructure-euroqci.

conjectured computational security of post-quantum primitives. However, QKD comes with significant limitations such as range and costly hardware.

To achieve ITS, QKD must use ITS authentication mechanisms [61] which can be enforced by relying on PSK-based authentication methods. Noteworthy, the PSKs for the individual QKD links are not enough to establish authenticity for the full path through the network as they only ensure authenticity for one link. Moreover, given the limited range of QKD link transmissions, all nodes in between are turned into so-called *trusted nodes* [59]. With trusted nodes, however, deployment in large-scale networks may become even more complex.[4] Hence, practical end-to-end authenticity guarantees for the to-be-anticipated QKD networks are still under investigation.

Since both, the PQC and QKD paradigms, have benefits and downsides, and following the approach "Don't put all your eggs in one basket," we are interested in how to achieve end-to-end authentication and confidentiality for key exchanges with the best possible security guarantees against future threats. One promising approach is using hybrid[5] techniques.

Hybrid Authenticated Key Exchanges (with Forward and Post-Compromise Security). Hybrid AKE (HAKE) approaches are getting more popular nowadays and were presented in several flavors to incorporate classical (or, non-quantum-safe), PQC, or QKD components [12,16,36,60]. The main benefit is redundancy, i.e., if some of the components fail, the primitive still yields a confidential and authenticated channel. Moreover, HAKE provides an approach towards the transition of non-quantum-secure networks to quantum-secure ones.

Particularly interesting is the recently proposed HAKE framework with its instantiation dubbed Muckle due to Dowling, Brandt Hansen, and Paterson [36]. Muckle combines secret keys obtained from a QKD network with session keys obtained from a classical and post-quantum secure key encapsulation mechanisms (KEMs). The combination of the keys is performed using a sequence of pseudo-random function evaluations.

Importantly, Muckle inherits desirable advanced security guarantees which are de-facto standard features nowadays for key exchanges, namely, *forward* and *post-compromise security*. Forward security is an important security feature and has a long body of literature in several domains such as interactive key-exchange protocols (prominently in TLS 1.3, QUIC, & Double Ratcheting) [26,33,41,68], public-key encryption [18,40], digital signatures [5,37], search on encrypted data [14], 0-RTT key exchange [22,28,29,42], updatable cryptography [71], mobile

---

[4] Interestingly, while some approaches even backed by patents (https://www.ipo. gov.uk/p-ipsum/Case/PublicationNumber/GB2590064) claim to provide long-range QKD networks without trusted nodes (i.e., establishing a secure channel between any two nodes), a recent work [46] demonstrates that such claim cannot be met.

[5] We are sticking to the term "hybrid" here as it was coined in prior work on AKEs [36] in the meaning of combining classical (or, non-quantum-safe), QKD, and post-quantum cryptographic primitives. Other works may use the term "quantum-safe" to combine QKD and PQC primitives, or different terms.

Cloud backups [27], proxy cryptography [30], new approaches to Tor [56], and content-delivery networks [31], among others.

The main property of forward security is that it hedges against "store-now-decrypt-later" attacks by evolving secret key material over epochs such that access to older ciphertexts or signing capabilities is revoked after the key material was updated. Nowadays, over 99% of Internet sites[6] support some form of forward security which is also due to the high recognition for such security feature by large companies such as Apple, Google, Cloudflare, Meta, and Microsoft.

In the concrete hybrid key-exchange setting, forward security guarantees that prior session keys cannot be retrieved even if the current session and long-term keys leak. Moreover, even if *all* classic KEM key material is leaked (e.g., in the event of a cryptographically relevant quantum computer), old session keys stay safe due to the PQC and QKD guarantees. Moreover, if additionally *all* post-quantum KEM keys should leak, an adversary cannot retrieve old sessions keys due to the QKD guarantees. Conversely, if *all* QKD keys leak, the security features of the post-quantum KEM component prevent an adversary from retrieving old session keys. Moreover, post-compromise security guarantees that future sessions are safe again (once an adversary does not compromise the system anymore). Thereby, we strictly require that at least one of the classic, PQC, or QKD components stays secure against a then-passive attacker.

The Muckle authentication, however, solely relies on the presence of pre-shared keys. Consequently, Muckle inherits the key management problem of PSKs in large-scale networks discussed above. In this work, we present an extension of the HAKE framework in [36] via an amplification of their Muckle scheme with end-to-end authenticity and better efficiency (given that we can rely on multi-path QKD) while no sacrifices on the security guarantees have to be made.

1.1 Contribution

Our contribution can be summarized as follows:

- We extend Muckle with a certificate-based authentication mechanism via digital signatures and dub it Muckle+. While replacing pre-shared keys with digital signatures is rather straightforward in general, this turned out to be surprisingly non-trivial when applied to HAKE frameworks (resulting in adapted proof techniques). The benefits are that we avoid the usage of PSKs (with its inherent quadratic blow-up to achieve end-to-end authenticity) which results in more efficient end-to-end HAKE instantiation than previously known. While gaining significant efficiency and flexibility with our approach compared to Muckle, to retrieve the same security guarantees, we need that the QKD keys are distributed via multi-path techniques.
- We implement the Muckle+ protocol and validated its functionality using a small QKD network in the field. To the best of our knowledge, such a proof-of-concept experiment for HAKEs is the first one with QKD hardware.

---

[6] Due to Qualys SSL Labs, https://www.ssllabs.com/ssl-pulse/, accessed in June 2023.

Thereby, we can demonstrate the added authenticity guarantees that ensure an end-to-end secure connection between the initiator and responder.

More on Muckle+ and the Differences to Muckle. The Muckle protocol uses a hybrid approach combining classical, PQC, and QKD keys through the use of a key derivation function. Muckle requires a classical and post-quantum KEM as well as data from a QKD channel to create the final shared secret. Additionally, the protocol relies on a secure pseudorandom function and a message authentication code (MAC). The latter is used in combination with a QKD pre-shared key to ensure the authenticity of the key exchange. To avoid such pre-shared keys for authentication, we carefully extend Muckle to allow certificate-based authentication. Technically, we use digital signatures as a building block instead of PSKs for authentication.

However, replacing PSKs with digital signatures in HAKE is not straightforward. Using PSKs yield an interesting cryptographic feature, namely, it guarantees that a sender and a receiver share a common secret key for end-to-end authentication (leaving the quadratic blow-up in that case on the side for a moment). Now, if digital signatures are used, we cannot build on such guarantee anymore (as we are in the public-key setting).

The key observation in the HAKE realm is that in the latter case, we either require a post-quantum KEM or we need multi-path approaches for the QKD part to guarantee end-to-end authenticity again. As we want to allow the post-quantum KEM components to fail (as in Muckle), we need that the QKD keys are distributed using a multi-path approach (essentially, by distributing key components via mutually disjoint paths from the initiator to the responder such that no individual trusted node knows all of the key material depending on some bound of colluding nodes). This is different to Muckle where Muckle only requires a "single path" to distribute the QKD key. However, as Muckle+ shows its full potential in larger-scale quantum-secure networks with many nodes, we assume that multiple paths between initiators and responders are available.

Through this alteration, we achieve the desired security properties, i.e., we are able to endure all security claims from original Muckle (in particular, forward and post-compromise security) while avoiding PSKs, which we show by formally proving our variant Muckle+ secure in the HAKE framework. Moreover, our instantiation allows for an efficient approach to achieve end-to-end security which we justify via an implementation.

Implementing Muckle+. The implementation of Muckle+ to demonstrate its efficacy follows the typical structure of both a QKD security application in the sense of the ETSI QKD GS standard documents (and in particular, ETSI QKD GS 014 [38]) and an authenticated key exchange using application well-understood from their use on the modern web. Thereby, the initiator of the connection obtains a key ID and the corresponding key material from a QKD device and transmits the key ID as part of the initial authenticated key exchange message to the receiver.

By providing an interface the applications that follow the structure of deployed authenticated key exchanges, we expect to reduce the required effort to integrate the use of QKD keys into applications that are already using TLS [67], QUIC [55], or similar protocols. Except for configuring the connection to the local QKD end-point, no further configuration will be necessary to establish secure channels with any service deployed on the QKD network.

On Further Directions to Achieve End-to-End HAKEs. We expect that end-to-end HAKEs can be built using further directions. Notably, Schwabe, Stebila and Wiggers proposed KEMTLS [70], a unilaterally authenticated key exchange protocol where authentication of the responders is performed using a long-term KEM key. The basic idea is, that after establishing an ephemeral key, the initiator encapsulates a secret with respect to the responder's long-term KEM key. The responder can only produce the authentication tags for session authentication if it can decapsulate using its long term KEM key. Thereby, the responder is implicitly authenticated via its knowledge of the corresponding private key. We chose to build Muckle+ with digital signatures for end-to-end authentication as a natural first step and leave extending Muckle+ with KEMTLS approaches for future work.

1.2 Related Work

Authenticated key exchanges have a long history and are still a very active area of research as they represent the core component of any protocol for secure communication. Notably, Krawczyk's Sign-and-MAC (SIGMA) protocols [51] serve as a template for many of the protocols used in practice. The basic idea of this template is to combine an ephemeral key exchange using key encapsulation methods (KEMs) to exchange a fresh shared secret, a signature scheme for authentication of the communication parties as well as a MAC to authenticate the shared secret. Keys are derived using a pseudorandom function (PRF). One execution then runs roughly as follows: the initiator produces a new ephemeral KEM key and sends the public key to the responder. The responder then performs the key encapsulation using the received public key, signs the produced ciphertext together with the first message to authenticate itself, and derives a shared secret to authenticate the session using the MAC. Ciphertext, authentication tag and signature are sent to the initiator. The initiator then decapsulates the shared secret key, verifies the received signature as well as the authentication tag. In a mutual authentication setting, the initiator also authenticates itself using the signature scheme, but the session is also always authenticated by the initiator using the MAC. This information is sent to the responder for verification. Afterwards, the two parties share an authenticated and fresh secret key.

While SIGMA was originally proposed using Diffie–Hellman for the ephemeral key exchange, presenting it in terms of KEMs allows us to consider it in a post-quantum setting as we then can instantiate all build blocks using post-quantum secure schemes. It can also be extended with responder or initiator privacy features [63,69,74], whereas the latter be observed in practice as part of the TLS handshake. With the migration towards post-quantum secure protocols, work on adapting and improving key exchange protocols based on the performance and bandwidth characteristics of post-quantum secure key encapsulation mechanisms and digital signature schemes has commenced [13,43,45,72], though.

In the area of QKD networks, proposals exist to address the trusted-node problem with secret-sharing-based multipath protocols, e.g. [64,65], to exchange the secret key. In a similar vein, multipath authentication protocols have been proposed too, whereas those are built on the assumption that an adversary is unable to compromise multiple nodes in the network. When considering network topologies with many routes available for connecting any two nodes, it is therefore possible to split sensitive information into parts (e.g., via secret sharing) and to send the shares via multiple paths instead of one.

For example, Rass and Schartner [66] introduced a MAC-based multipath authentication protocol specifically for the application in quantum networks. In the scenario they consider, two nodes wanting to communicate in a QKD network may not necessarily establish pre-shared keys. There are however shared QKD secrets between every node and each of its immediate neighbors. The protocol uses those secrets in combination with a multipath approach to share an authenticated message between the nodes and relies on the assumptions that (a) keys created by two adjacent nodes via the QKD channel are secure, and (b) every node shares a secret key with its neighboring nodes. While the protocol is secure against $k < n$ compromised paths when executed with n disjoint paths, it does not fit into the typical notion of an authenticated key exchange and it lacks end-to-end authenticity.

Finally, secure multipath key exchange (SMKEX) [24] utilizes two disjoint paths to facilitate authentication and key exchange. The protocol is based on a typical key exchange, but in addition the second channel is used to send a random nonce that is authenticated using the secret key exchanged via the first channel. SMKEX therefore ensures unilateral authenticity and computational security against an active adversary as long as only one path is compromised.

2   Preliminaries

In this section, we briefly recall notions related to (hybrid) authenticated key exchanges.

2.1   Cryptographic Primitives and Schemes

Definition 1 (PRF). *Let $\mathcal{F} : \mathcal{S} \times D \to \mathsf{R}$ be a family of functions and let Γ be the set of all functions $D \to \mathsf{R}$. For a PPT distinguisher $\mathcal{D}$ we define the advantage function as*

$$\mathsf{Adv}^{\mathsf{PRF}}_{\mathcal{D},\mathcal{F}}(\kappa) = \left| \Pr\left[s \xleftarrow{R} \mathcal{S} : \mathcal{D}^{\mathcal{F}(s,\cdot)}(1^{\kappa}) = 1 \right] - \Pr\left[f \xleftarrow{R} \Gamma : \mathcal{D}^{f(\cdot)}(1^{\kappa}) = 1 \right] \right|.$$

$\mathcal{F}$ *is a pseudorandom function (family) if it is efficiently computable and for all PPT distinguishers $\mathcal{D}$ there exists a negligible function $\varepsilon(\cdot)$ such that*

$$\mathsf{Adv}^{\mathsf{PRF}}_{\mathcal{D},\mathcal{F}}(\kappa) \le \varepsilon(\kappa).$$

A PRF $\mathcal{F}$ is a dual PRF [4], if $\mathcal{G} : D \times \mathcal{S} \to \mathsf{R}$ defined as $\mathcal{G}(d, s) = \mathcal{F}(s, d)$ is also a PRF.

We recall the notion of message authentication codes as well as digital signature schemes, and the standard unforgeability notions below.

Definition 2 (Message Authentication Codes). *A message authentication code* MAC *is a triple* (KGen, Sign, Ver) *of PPT algorithms, which are defined as:*

KGen(1^κ): *This algorithm takes a security parameter κ as input and outputs a secret key* sk.

Auth(sk, m): *This algorithm takes a secret key* sk $\in \mathcal{K}$ *and a* $m \in \mathcal{M}$ *and outputs an authentication tag τ.*

Ver(sk, m, τ): *This algorithm takes a secret key* sk, *a message* $m \in \mathcal{M}$ *and an authentication tag τ as input and outputs a bit $b \in \{0, 1\}$.*

A MAC is correct if for all $\kappa \in \mathbb{N}$, for all sk $\leftarrow$ KGen(1^κ) and for all $m \in \mathcal{M}$, it holds that $\Pr\left[\mathsf{Ver}(\mathsf{sk}, m, \mathsf{Auth}(\mathsf{sk}, m)) = 1\right] = 1$, where the probability is taken over the random coins of KGen.

Definition 3 (EUF-CMA). *For a PPT adversary $\mathcal{A}$, we define the advantage function in the sense of existential unforgeability under chosen message attacks (EUF-CMA) as*

$$\mathsf{Adv}^{\mathsf{euf\text{-}cma}}_{\mathcal{A},\mathsf{MAC}}(1^\kappa) = \Pr\left[\mathsf{Exp}^{\mathsf{euf\text{-}cma}}_{\mathcal{A},\mathsf{MAC}}(1^\kappa) = 1\right],$$

where the corresponding experiment is depicted in Experiment 1. If for all PPT adversaries $\mathcal{A}$ there is a negligible function $\varepsilon(\cdot)$ such that $\mathsf{Adv}^{\mathsf{euf\text{-}cma}}_{\mathcal{A},\mathsf{MAC}}(1^\kappa) \le \varepsilon(\kappa)$, *we say that* MAC *is* EUF-CMA *secure.*

Definition 4 (Signature Scheme). *A signature scheme Σ is a triple* (KGen, Sign, Ver) *of PPT algorithms, which are defined as follows:*

KGen(1^κ): *This algorithm takes a security parameter κ as input and outputs a secret (signing) key* sk *and a public (verification) key* pk *with associated message space $\mathcal{M}$ (we may omit to make the message space $\mathcal{M}$ explicit).*

Sign(sk, m): *This algorithm takes a secret key* sk *and a message $m \in \mathcal{M}$ as input and outputs a signature σ.*

Ver(pk, m, σ): *This algorithm takes a public key* pk, *a message $m \in \mathcal{M}$ and a signature σ as input and outputs a bit $b \in \{0, 1\}$.*

For correctness, we require that for all $\kappa \in \mathbb{N}$, for all (sk, pk) $\leftarrow$ KGen(1^κ) and for all $m \in \mathcal{M}$ it holds that $\Pr\left[\mathsf{Ver}(\mathsf{pk}, m, \mathsf{Sign}(\mathsf{sk}, m)) = 1\right] = 1$, where the probability is taken over the random coins of KGen and Sign.

$\mathsf{Exp}_{\mathcal{A},\mathsf{MAC}}^{\mathsf{euf\text{-}cma}}(1^\kappa)$:

    $\mathsf{sk} \leftarrow \mathsf{KGen}(1^\kappa), \mathcal{Q} \leftarrow \emptyset$

    $(m^*, \tau^*) \leftarrow \mathcal{A}^{\mathsf{Auth}', \mathsf{Ver}'}()$

       where oracle $\mathsf{Auth}'(m)$:

          $\mathcal{Q} \leftarrow \mathcal{Q} \cup \{m\}$

          return $\mathsf{Auth}(\mathsf{sk}, m)$

       where oracle $\mathsf{Ver}'(m, \tau)$:

          return $\mathsf{Ver}(\mathsf{sk}, m, \tau)$

    return 1, if $\mathsf{Ver}(\mathsf{sk}, m^*, \tau^*) = 1 \ \wedge \ m^* \notin \mathcal{Q}$, return 0, otherwise

Experiment 1: EUF-CMA security experiment for a MAC MAC.

Definition 5 (EUF-CMA). *For a PPT adversary $\mathcal{A}$, we define the advantage function in the sense of existential unforgeability under chosen message attacks (EUF-CMA) as*

$$\mathsf{Adv}_{\mathcal{A},\Sigma}^{\mathsf{euf\text{-}cma}}(1^\kappa) = \Pr\left[\mathsf{Exp}_{\mathcal{A},\Sigma}^{\mathsf{euf\text{-}cma}}(1^\kappa) = 1\right],$$

where the corresponding experiment is depicted in Experiment 2. If for all PPT adversaries $\mathcal{A}$ there is a negligible function $\varepsilon(\cdot)$ such that $\mathsf{Adv}_{\mathcal{A},\Sigma}^{\mathsf{euf\text{-}cma}}(1^\kappa) \leq \varepsilon(\kappa)$, we say that Σ is EUF-CMA secure.

$\mathsf{Exp}_{\mathcal{A},\Sigma}^{\mathsf{euf\text{-}cma}}(1^\kappa)$:

    $(\mathsf{sk}, \mathsf{pk}) \leftarrow \mathsf{KGen}(1^\kappa), \mathcal{Q} \leftarrow \emptyset$

    $(m^*, \sigma^*) \leftarrow \mathcal{A}^{\mathsf{Sign}}(\mathsf{pk})$

       where oracle $\mathsf{Sign}'(m)$:

          $\mathcal{Q} \leftarrow \mathcal{Q} \cup \{m\}$

          return $\mathsf{Sign}(\mathsf{sk}, m)$

    return 1, if $\mathsf{Ver}(\mathsf{pk}, m^*, \sigma^*) = 1 \ \wedge \ m^* \notin \mathcal{Q}$, return 0, otherwise

Experiment 2: EUF-CMA security experiment for a digital signature scheme Σ.

We recall the notion of key-encapsulations mechanisms, and the standard chosen-plaintext and chosen-ciphertext notions below.

Definition 6 *A key-encapsulation mechanism (KEM) scheme KEM with key space $\mathcal{K}$ consists of the three PPT algorithms* $(\mathsf{KGen}, \mathsf{Enc}, \mathsf{Dec})$:

$\mathsf{KGen}(1^\kappa)$: *This algorithm takes a security parameter κ as input and outputs public and secret keys* $(\mathsf{pk}, \mathsf{sk})$.

$\mathsf{Exp}^{\mathsf{ind}\text{-}T}_{\mathcal{A},\mathsf{KEM}}(\kappa)$:

    $(\mathsf{sk},\mathsf{pk}) \leftarrow \mathsf{KGen}(1^\kappa)$

    $(c^*, K_0) \leftarrow \mathsf{Enc}(\mathsf{pk}), K_1 \xleftarrow{R} \mathcal{K}$

    $\mathcal{Q} \leftarrow \emptyset, b \xleftarrow{R} \{0,1\}^\kappa$

    $b^* \leftarrow \mathcal{A}^{\mathcal{O}}(\mathsf{pk}, c^*, K_b)$

        where $\mathcal{O} = \{\mathsf{Dec}'\}$ if $T = \mathsf{cca}$ with oracle $\mathsf{Dec}'(c)$:

            $\mathcal{Q} \leftarrow \mathcal{Q} \cup \{c\}$

            return $\mathsf{Dec}(\mathsf{sk}, c)$

    return 1, if $b = b^* \wedge c^* \notin \mathcal{Q}$, return otherwise 0

Experiment 3: IND-T security experiments for KEM with $T \in \{\mathsf{cpa}, \mathsf{cca}\}$.

$\mathsf{Enc}(\mathsf{pk})$: *This algorithm takes a public key* pk *as input, and outputs a ciphertext c and key K.*

$\mathsf{Dec}(\mathsf{sk}, c)$: *This algorithm takes a secret key* sk *and a ciphertext c as input, and outputs K or $\{\bot\}$.*

We call a KEM correct if for all $\kappa \in \mathbb{N}$, for all $(\mathsf{pk}, \mathsf{sk}) \leftarrow \mathsf{KGen}(\kappa)$, for all $(c, K) \leftarrow \mathsf{Enc}(\mathsf{pk})$, we have that $\Pr[\mathsf{Dec}(\mathsf{sk}, c) = K] = 1$, where the probability is taken over the random coins of KGen and Enc.

Definition 7. *For a PPT adversary $\mathcal{A}$, we define the advantage function in the sense of indistinguishability under chosen-plaintext attacks (IND-CPA) and indistinguishability under chosen-ciphertexts attacks (IND-CCA) as*

$$\mathsf{Adv}^{\mathsf{ind}\text{-}\mathsf{cpa}}_{\mathcal{A},\mathsf{KEM}}(1^\kappa) = \left| \Pr\left[\mathsf{Exp}^{\mathsf{ind}\text{-}\mathsf{cpa}}_{\mathcal{A},\mathsf{KEM}}(1^\kappa) = 1\right] - \frac{1}{2} \right|, \text{ and}$$

$$\mathsf{Adv}^{\mathsf{ind}\text{-}\mathsf{cca}}_{\mathcal{A},\mathsf{KEM}}(1^\kappa) = \left| \Pr\left[\mathsf{Exp}^{\mathsf{ind}\text{-}\mathsf{cca}}_{\mathcal{A},\mathsf{KEM}}(1^\kappa) = 1\right] - \frac{1}{2} \right|$$

where the corresponding experiments are depicted in Experiment 3, respectively. If for all PPT adversaries $\mathcal{A}$ there is a negligible function $\varepsilon(\cdot)$ such that

$$\mathsf{Adv}^{\mathsf{ind}\text{-}\mathsf{cpa}}_{\mathcal{A},\mathsf{KEM}}(1^\kappa) \leq \varepsilon(\kappa) \text{ or } \mathsf{Adv}^{\mathsf{ind}\text{-}\mathsf{cca}}_{\mathcal{A},\mathsf{KEM}}(1^\kappa) \leq \varepsilon(\kappa),$$

then we say that KEM is IND-CPA or IND-CCA secure, respectively.

2.2 Hybrid Authenticated Key Exchange

We recall the hybrid authenticated key exchange (HAKE) security model due to Dowling et al. [36] which already foresees the use of long-term post-quantum digital signature keys. For a general treatment of authenticated key exchanges (AKE), we refer the reader to [33, 49].

Execution Environment. We consider a set of n_P parties $P_1, \ldots, P_{n_P}$ which are able to run up to n_S sessions of a key exchange protocol between them, where each session may consist of n_T different stages of the protocol. Each party P_i has access to its long-term key pair $(\mathsf{pk}_i, \mathsf{sk}_i)$ and to the public keys of all other parties. Each session is described by a set of session parameters:

- $\rho \in \{\mathsf{init}, \mathsf{resp}\}$: The role (initiator or responder) of the party during the current session.
- $pid \in n_P$: The communication partner of the current session.
- $stid \in n_T$: The current stage of the session.
- $\alpha \in \{\mathsf{active}, \mathsf{accept}, \mathsf{reject}, \bot\}$: The status of the session. Initialized with $\bot$.
- $m_i[stid], i \in \{s, r\}$: All messages sent $(i = s)$ or received $(i = r)$ by a session up to the stage $stid$. Initialized with $\bot$.
- $k[stid]$: All session keys created up to stage $stid$. Initialized with $\bot$.
- $exk[stid], x \in \{q, c, s\}$: All ephemeral post-quantum (q), classical (c) or symmetric (s) secret keys created up to stage $stid$. Initialized with $\bot$.
- $pss[stid]$: The per-session secret state (SecState) that is created during the stage $stid$ for the use in the next stage.
- $st[stid]$: Storage for other states used by the session in each stage.

We describe the protocol as a set of algorithms $(f, \mathsf{KGen}XY, \mathsf{KGen}ZS)$:

- $f(\kappa, \mathsf{pk}_i, \mathsf{sk}_i, pskid_i, psk_i, \pi, m) \to (m', \pi')$: a probabilistic algorithm that represents an honest execution of the protocol. It takes a security parameter κ, the long-term keys $\mathsf{pk}_i, \mathsf{sk}_i$, the session parameters π representing the current state of the session and a message m and outputs a response m' and the updated session state π'.
- $\mathsf{KGen}XY(\kappa) \to (\mathsf{pk}, \mathsf{sk})$: a probabilistic asymmetric key-generation algorithm that takes a security parameter κ and creates a public-key, secret-key pair $(\mathsf{pk}, \mathsf{sk})$. $X \in \{E, L\}$ determines whether the created key is an ephemeral (E) or long-term (L) secret. $Y \in \{Q, C\}$ determines whether the key is classical (C) or post-quantum (Q).
- $\mathsf{KGen}ZS(\kappa) \to (psk, pskid)$: a probabilistic symmetric key-generation algorithm that takes a security parameter κ and outputs symmetric keying material (psk). $Z \in \{E, L\}$ determines whether the created key is an ephemeral (E) or long-term (L) secret.

For each party $P_1, \ldots, P_{n_P}$, classical as well as post-quantum long-term keys are created using the corresponding $\mathsf{KGen}XY$ algorithms. The challenger then queries a uniformly random bit $b \leftarrow \{0, 1\}$ that will determine the key returned by the Test query. From this point on, the adversary may interact with the challenger using the queries defined in the next section. At some point during the execution of the protocol, the adversary $\mathcal{A}$ may issue the Test query and present a guess for the value of b. If $\mathcal{A}$ guesses correctly and the session satisfies the cleanness predicate, the adversary wins the key-indistinguishability experiment.

Adversarial Interaction. The HAKE framework defines a range of queries that allow the attacker to interact with the communication:

- Create$(i, j, role) \rightarrow \{(s), \bot\}$: Initializes a new session between party P_i with role *role* and the partner P_j. If the session already exists, then the query returns $\bot$, otherwise the session (s) is returned.
- Send$(i, s, m) \rightarrow \{m', \bot\}$: Enables $\mathcal{A}$ to send messages to sessions and receive the response m' by running f for the session π_i^s. Returns $\bot$ if the session is not active.
- Reveal(i, s, t): Provides $\mathcal{A}$ with the session keys corresponding to a session π_i^s if the session is in the accepted state. Otherwise, $\bot$ is returned.
- Test$(i, s, t) \rightarrow \{k_b, \bot\}$: Provides $\mathcal{A}$ with the real (if $b = 1$) or random ($b = 0$) session key for the key-indistinguishably experiment.
- Corrupt$XY(i) \rightarrow \{key, \bot\}$: Provides $\mathcal{A}$ with the long-term $XY \in \{SK, QK, CK\}$ keys for P_i. If the key has been corrupted previously, then $\bot$ is returned. Specifically:
  - CorruptSK: Reveals the long-term symmetric secret (if available).
  - CorruptQK: Reveals the post-quantum long-term key (if available).
  - CorruptCK: Reveals the classical long-term key (if available).
- Compromise$XY(i, s, t) \rightarrow \{key, \bot\}$: Provides $\mathcal{A}$ with the ephemeral $XY \in \{QK, CK, SK, SS\}$ keys created during the session π_i^s prior to stage t. If the ephemeral key has already been compromised, then $\bot$ is returned. Specifically:
  - CompromiseQK: Reveals the ephemeral post-quantum key.
  - CompromiseCK: Reveals the ephemeral classical key.
  - CompromiseSK: Reveals the ephemeral quantum key.
  - CompromiseSS: Reveals the ephemeral per session state (SecState).

Matching Sessions. Furthermore, we recall the definitions of matching sessions [57] and origin sessions [25] which covers that the two parties involved in a session have the same view of their conversation.

Definition 8 (Matching sessions). *We consider two sessions π_i^s and π_j^r in stage t to be matching if all messages sent by the former session $\pi_i^s.m_s[t]$ match those received by the later $\pi_j^r.m_r[t]$ and all messages sent by the later session $\pi_j^r.m_s[t]$ are received by the former $\pi_i^s.m_r[t]$.*

π_i^s is considered to be prefix-matching with π_j^r if $\pi_i^s.m_s[t] = \pi_j^r.m_r[t]'$ where $\pi_j^r.m_r[t]$ is truncated to the length of $\pi_i^s.m_s[t]$ resulting in $\pi_j^r.m_r[t]'$.

Definition 9 (Origin sessions). *We consider a session π_i^s to have an origin session with π_j^r if π_i^s matches π_j^r or if π_i^s prefix-matches π_j^r.*

Security. Dowling et al. [36] define key indistinguishability with respect to a predicate clean. However, their predicate is specific to Muckle and, hence, we therefore only give the security notion and postpone the discussion of the predicate to Sect. 3.3.

Definition 10. *Let Π be a key-exchange protocol and $n_P, n_S, n_T \in \mathbb{N}$. For a predicate* clean *and an adversary $\mathcal{A}$, we define the advantage of $\mathcal{A}$ in the HAKE key-indistinguishability game as*

$$\mathsf{Adv}^{\mathsf{HAKE,clean},\mathcal{A}}_{\Pi,n_P,n_S,n_T}(\kappa) = \left| \mathrm{Pr}\left[\mathsf{Exp}^{HAKE,\mathsf{clean},\mathcal{A}}_{\Pi,n_P,n_S,n_T}(\kappa) = 1 \right] \right|.$$

We say that Π is HAKE-secure if $\mathsf{Adv}^{\mathsf{HAKE,clean},\mathcal{A}}_{\Pi,n_P,n_S,n_T}(\kappa)$ is negligible in the security parameter κ for all $\mathcal{A}$.

3   Extending Muckle with Signature-Based Authentication

In this section, we recap Muckle [36] and present our novel variant Muckle+.

3.1   Muckle

The Muckle protocol combines classical, PQC, and QKD keys through the use of a key derivation function. More concretely, Muckle requires classical and post-quantum key encapsulation mechanisms (KEMs) as well as data from a QKD channel (i.e., a symmetric key k_q) to create the final shared secret between communication partners.

Muckle is a multi-stage protocol. While a Muckle instance is active between two parties, a single stage is run repeatedly, creating a pair of session keys during each execution. The communication that occurs during one stage of the protocol is detailed in Fig. 1.

The Muckle key exchange requires a symmetric pre-shared key PSK and unique party identifiers (implicit in ℓ_I and ℓ_R) to be distributed to the communication partners before the key exchange. The parties also have to set an initial value for the session secret state SecState. To begin a new session, the initiator uses the classical KEM KEM_c and post-quantum KEM KEM_{pq} to create a classical key pair $(\mathsf{pk}_c, \mathsf{sk}_c)$ and a post-quantum key pair $(\mathsf{pk}_{pq}, \mathsf{sk}_{pq})$, respectively. Both public keys are then combined with a header containing meta-data into the message m_0. The PRF $\mathcal{F}$ is applied over PSK and SecState to create a unique value for the current session, which is then used as an input in another round of the PRF with the value ℓ_I resulting in the message key $mkey_I$. The key $mkey_I$ is used as the MAC key to create a tag τ_0 for the message m_0. The message m_0 and the tag τ_0 are then sent to the responder.

Receiving the transmission, the responder will check the authenticity of the message m_0 by verifying the tag τ_0 with its $mkey_I$ (where $mkey_I$ is derived via PSK, shared SecState, and ℓ_I). If the verification succeeds, the responder can now use the encapsulation functions of the KEMs to create the keys $rkey_c$ and $rkey_{pq}$ as well as the ciphertexts c_c and c_{pq}, respectively. The responder proceeds to create a message m_1 and a tag τ_1 analogously to the initiator's MAC procedure, but using the ciphertexts instead of the public keys and the responder value $header_R$.

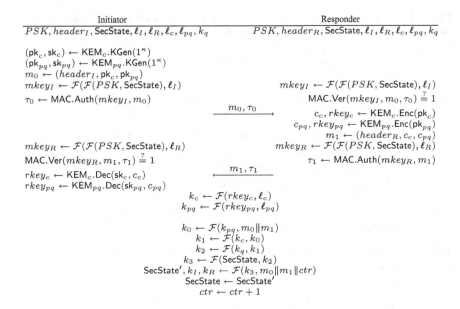

Fig. 1. One stage of the Muckle protocol [36] with a classical KEM KEM_c, a post-quantum KEM KEM_{pq}, a MAC MAC, and a PRF $\mathcal{F}$ whereas k_q represents the symmetric key from the QKD component (provided out-of-band).

m_1 and τ_1 are then transmitted to the initiator, who can use them in the KEM decapsulation function to get the keys $rkey_c$ and $rkey_{pq}$ (after successful verification of m_1). From this point on, the initiator and responder share the same information and proceed with the same steps.

First the both keys are entered into the PRF $\mathcal{F}$ together with labels ℓ_c and ℓ_{pq} to create the further keys. Then the key schedule starts combining all the keys into a final shared secret k_I, k_R and setting a new session state as well as incrementing the session counter.

Muckle offers mutual authentication, forward security, and post-compromise security. Post-compromise security is guaranteed under the condition that at least one previous stage has been completed without the attacker compromising all the ephemeral (classical, QKD, post-quantum and session secret) secrets, and that the attacker has been only acting passively since then.

3.2 Extending Muckle with Signature-Based Authentication

In Table 1, we compare the security properties of the protocols we have discussed in the introduction and Muckle. From this comparison, we can conclude that Muckle offers the most features and is therefore a suitable candidate for realizing end-to-end secure hybrid authenticated key exchanges. However, the protocol relies on PSKs for end-to-end authentication. As the other components including the QKD-layer do not provide end-to-end authentication (cf. Sect. 3.1),

Table 1. Comparison of the protocols in terms of provided security guarantees: KC (key confirmation), PFS (perfect forward secrecy), PCS (post-compromise security).

	protocol	authentication		KC	PFS	PCS
multipath	MAC-based [66]		initiator			
	SMKEX [24]		responder		*	*
post-quantum	SIGMA [51]	explicit	mutual	✓	✓	
	KEMTLS [70]	explicit[a]	responder/mutual	✓[b]	✓	?[c]
	Muckle [36]	explicit	mutual	✓	✓	✓[d]

* not applicable (no long-term secret)
[a] implicit for client during mutual authentication
[b] only for responder authentication
[c] PCS is not explicitly shown
[d] under the conditions discussed in Sect. 3.1

Table 2. Values for the contexts used in the Muckle+ key schedule. The context inputs follow the choices in the TLS 1.3 handshake [35].

Label	Context Input	Label	Context Input
H_ε	" "	H_0	$H(" ")$
H_1	$H(m_1 \| m_2)$	H_2	$H(m_1 \| \ldots \| m_3)$
H_3	$H(m_1 \| \ldots \| m_4)$		

we extend Muckle to also offer mutual signature-based authentication. Through this alteration, we preserve the desirable security whilst avoiding the issues associated with PSKs (given that we can rely on multi-path QKD). We will from now on refer to this new protocol as Muckle+.

Like Muckle, Muckle+ is a multi-stage protocol. One such stage is detailed in Fig. 2. The basic structure of Muckle+ is very similar to the original Muckle protocol. Up to the computation of the final chaining key, the PSK-based authentication is replaced with signature-based authentication and the addition of two random nonces n_I and n_R to avoid issues with the reuse of signatures. We note that the modifications essentially correspond to changing to a SIGMA-style key exchange with multiple KEMs and an additional ephemeral secret that is provided by the QKD link. We note that the correctness of the protocol follows directly from the correctness of the employed primitives.

3.3 Security of Muckle+

Similar to Muckle, Muckle+ achieves the same security properties including forward security, or, mostly called perfect forward secrecy (PFS) in the AKE regime, and post-compromise security (PCS). In this section, we formally proof this claim. The presented security analysis of the Muckle+ protocol is based on the HAKE framework as introduced by Dowling et al. [36]. We will use the

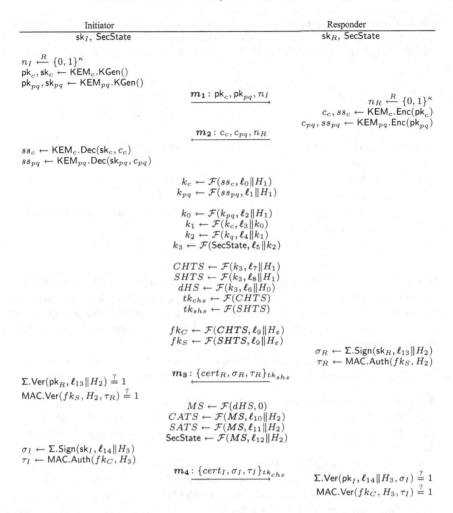

Fig. 2. One stage of the Muckle+ protocol. Messages $m : \{m_1, \ldots\}_k$ denote that $m_1, \ldots$ is encrypted with an authenticated encryption scheme using the secret key k. The various contexts and labels are given in Tables 2 and 3.

definitions and notations use in the HAKE framework in this analysis unless stated otherwise.

An adversary $\mathcal{A}$ has access all queries defined in the HAKE framework. As no pre-shared key exists in the Muckle+ protocol, the query CorruptSK will return $\bot$ if called. As multiple sessions keys are created in the new protocol, we specify that the key to be guessed during the Test query is the master secret MS.

We define a new cleanness predicate $\text{clean}_{\text{Muckle+}}$ for our protocol that captures the same goals – post-compromise security and perfect forward secrecy – but adapt it to match our setting. As our protocol does not require a long term PSK, we can omit handling compromise of the PSK in our predicate. We however

Table 3. Values for the labels used in the Muckle+ key schedule for domain separation. Some of these labels are directly based on the corresponding labels in the TLS 1.3 handshake [35]. The concrete value of these labels is unimportant as long as they are unique.

Label	Label Input	Label	Label Input
ℓ_0	"derive k c"	ℓ_1	"derive k pq"
ℓ_2	"first ck"	ℓ_3	"second ck"
ℓ_4	"third ck"	ℓ_5	"fourth ck"
ℓ_6	"derived"	ℓ_7	"c hs traffic"
ℓ_8	"s hs traffic"	ℓ_9	"finished"
ℓ_{10}	"c ap traffic"	ℓ_{11}	"s ap traffic"
ℓ_{12}	"secstate"	ℓ_{13}	"TLS 1.3, server CertificateVerify"
ℓ_{14}	"TLS 1.3, client CertificateVerify"		

have to take care of long-term signature keys instead. Hence, we consider their compromise in $\mathsf{clean}_{\mathrm{Muckle+}}$ as well. Overall, the goal of the cleanness predicate is to handle the compromise of as many combinations as possible as long as one set of keys – the post-quantum secure keys or the keys obtained from the QKD link – stay secure.

More formally, we define the cleanness of a session as follows: A session π_i^s in stage t is considered clean under the predicate $\mathsf{clean}_{\mathrm{Muckle+}}$ if:

- $\mathsf{Reveal}(i, s, t)$ has not been issued for session π_i^s.
- $\mathsf{Reveal}(j, r, t)$ has not been issued for all sessions π_j^r matching π_i^s at stage t.
- If π_i^s has a matching session π_j^r, at least one of the following conditions has been met:
  - No $\mathsf{CompromiseQK}(i, s, t)$ or $\mathsf{CompromiseQK}(j, r, t)$ have been issued.
  - No $\mathsf{CompromiseSK}(i, s, t)$ or $\mathsf{CompromiseSK}(j, r, t)$ have been issued.
  - No $\mathsf{CompromiseQK}(i, s, t')$ or $\mathsf{CompromiseQK}(j, r, t)$ have been issued with π_i^s matching π_j^r in stages u where $t' \leq u \leq t$. No $\mathsf{CompromiseSS}(i, s, u)$ or $\mathsf{CompromiseSS}(j, r, u)$ have been issued.
  - No $\mathsf{CompromiseSK}(i, s, t')$ or $\mathsf{CompromiseSK}(j, r, t')$ have been issued with π_i^s matching π_j^r in stages u where $t' \leq u \leq t$. No $\mathsf{CompromiseSS}(i, s, u)$ or $\mathsf{CompromiseSS}(j, r, u)$ have been issued.
- If there exists no $(j, r, t) \in [n_P] \times [n_S] \times [n_T]$ such that π_j^r is an origin session of π_i^s in stage t, then either $\mathsf{CompromiseSK}(i, j, t)$ and $\mathsf{CompromiseSK}(j, i, t)$ or $\mathsf{CorruptQK}(i)$ and $\mathsf{CorruptQK}(j)$ have not been issues before $\pi_i^s.\alpha[t] \leftarrow \mathsf{accept}$. If there exists $(j, r, t) \in [n_P] \times [n_S] \times [n_T]$ such that π_j^r is an origin session of π_i^s in stage t, then either $\mathsf{CompromiseSK}(i, j, t)$ and $\mathsf{CompromiseSK}(j, i, t)$ or $\mathsf{CorruptQK}(i)$ and $\mathsf{CorruptQK}(j)$ have not been issued before $\pi_i^r.\alpha[t] \leftarrow \mathsf{accept}$.

The first condition ensures, that the session key of the session used in the Test query has not been revealed to the adversary through the use of the Reveal query. Similarly, the second condition specifies that no session matching the test session may have been targeted by a Reveal query either, as any matching session will own the same session key as the test session. The third condition ensures that at least one ephemeral secret is not compromised by $\mathcal{A}$ or that the secret session state in the multi-stage setting. Finally, the forth case restricts access to one of the long-term secrets for the first round without origin session to exclude otherwise trivial impersonation attacks.

We note that similar to $\mathsf{clean}_{\text{Muckle}}$, we can define classical and quantum variants of the predicate to also reflect compromise of the classical keys. In that case, $\mathsf{clean}_{\text{cMuckle+}}$ is extended to include the following two conditions for matching sessions π_i^s and π_j^r:

- No $\mathsf{CompromiseCK}(i, s, t)$ or $\mathsf{CompromiseCK}(j, r, t)$ have been issued.
- No $\mathsf{CompromiseCK}(i, s, t')$ or $\mathsf{CompromiseCK}(j, r, t')$ have been issued with π_i^s matching π_j^r in stages u where $t' \leq u \leq t$. No $\mathsf{CompromiseSS}(i, s, u)$ or $\mathsf{CompromiseSS}(j, r, u)$ have been issued.

We will now proof that the proposed protocol is secure with the cleanness predicate $\mathsf{clean}_{\text{Muckle+}}$. In order to do so, we analyze the five cases corresponding to the conditions that are necessary to fulfil the $\mathsf{clean}_{\text{Muckle+}}$ predicate.

Theorem 1. *The Muckle+ key exchange protocol is HAKE-secure with the cleanness predicate* $\mathsf{clean}_{\text{Muckle+}}$ *assuming that the PRF $\mathcal{F}$ is a dual PRF, the MAC MAC is EUF-CMA secure, the KEMs KEM_c and KEM_{pq} are IND-CPA secure and the signature scheme Σ is EUF-CMA secure. If the security of $\mathcal{F}$, MAC, KEM_{pq} and Σ or of QKD hold against a quantum adversary, then so does the security of Muckle+.*

Proof. We divide the proof into different cases where the query $\mathsf{Test}(i, s, t)$ has been issued and prove them separately:

1. The session π_i^s (where $\pi_i^s.\rho = \mathsf{init}$) has no origin session in stage t.
2. The session π_i^s (where $\pi_i^s.\rho = \mathsf{resp}$) has no origin session in stage t.
3. The session π_i^s in stage t has a matching session.

Similar to the proof of Muckle, we show the first and third case. The second case follows analogously to the first case.

Case 1: Test init session without origin session. In case 1, we show that $\mathcal{A}$ has negligible chance of getting a session to reach the accept state if a $\mathsf{CorruptQK}$ or a $\mathsf{CompromiseSK}$ query has been issued. If the session does not reach the accept stage, the Test query will always return $\perp$, preventing $\mathcal{A}$ from winning the indistinguishability game. First we consider the case that no $\mathsf{CorruptQK}$ query has been issue.

Game 0: Standard HAKE-Game

$$\mathsf{Adv}_{\text{Muckle+},n_P,n_S,n_T}^{\text{HAKE},\mathsf{clean}_{\text{Muckle+}},\mathcal{A},C_1}(\kappa) = \Pr[S_0]$$

Game 1: In Game 1, the parameters (i, s, t) for a session and its matching session (j, r, t) are guessed. If a $\mathsf{Test}(i', s', t)$ query is issued for any session $\pi_{i'}^{s'}$ that is not the test session π_i^s the game aborts.

$$\Pr[S_0] \leq n_P^2 n_S n_T \cdot \Pr[S_1]$$

Game 2: Game 2 aborts, if the test session π_i^s ever reaches the status reject. As the Test query will always return $\perp$ is the session reaches this status, the advantage gained by $\mathcal{A}$ is 0.

$$\Pr[S_0] \leq n_P^2 n_S n_T \cdot \Pr[S_2]$$

Game 3: Game 3 aborts, if the session reaches the status accept.

$$\Pr[S_0] \leq n_P^2 n_S n_T \cdot \Pr[S_3]$$

We now bound the probability of $\mathcal{A}$ reaching the abort event. Assuming that the session reaches the status accept, we construct an EUF-CMA adversary against Σ. The challenge pk is used as the party's public key. For all other sessions, the signing oracle is used to produce the corresponding signatures. Now, if the test session reaches accept stage, we output the signature σ_I as forgery on the message $\ell_{14} \| H_3$. The signature verifies since accept stage was reached and has not been queried to the signing oracle (except for collisions of the hash function H). Hence, we obtain:

$$\Pr[S_0] \leq n_P^2 n_S n_T \cdot \left(\mathsf{Adv}_{\Sigma,\mathcal{A}}^{\mathsf{euf\text{-}cma}}(\kappa) \right)$$

The case that no CompromiseSK query has been issued before reaching the accept stage, follows analogously to [36, Theorem 1, Case 1] and is not repeated here.

Case 3: Test session with matching session. We will show that any adversary $\mathcal{A}$ has a negligible chance of winning the key-indistinguishability game using a sequence of games for each of the four cases. We denote with S_i the event of the adversary winning game i. Note that the proofs are the same regardless of whether $\mathsf{KEM} \in \{\mathsf{KEM}_c, \mathsf{KEM}_{pq}\}$, whereas security against a quantum adversary can only be achieved for $\mathsf{KEM} = \mathsf{KEM}_{pq}$. We split the proof into several subcases.

Subcase 1: No CompromiseQK(i, s, t) *or* CompromiseQK(j, r, t) *have been issued.* Subcase 1 shows, that if the attacker issues a Test query to a session that is clean due to the secrecy of the ephemeral post-quantum key, he has a negligible advantage in guessing the test bit. In this scenario all ephemeral secrets except the post-quantum key as well as the long-term classical and post-quantum secrets are known to the attacker.

Game 0: Standard HAKE-Game

$$\mathsf{Adv}_{\mathsf{Muckle+},n_P,n_S,n_T}^{\mathsf{HAKE,clean_{Muckle+}},\mathcal{A},C_2}(\kappa) = \Pr[S_0]$$

Games 1–7: Games 1 to 7 for Muckle are equivalent to the Games 1 to 7 of the proof of case 3.1 as described in [36], resulting in the following advantage:

$$\Pr[S_0] \leq n_P^2 n_S^2 n_T \cdot \left(\mathsf{Adv}_{\mathsf{KEM},\mathcal{A}}^{\mathsf{ind\text{-}cpa}}(\kappa) + 2 \cdot \mathsf{Adv}_{\mathcal{F},\mathcal{A}}^{\mathsf{prf}}(\lambda) + 3 \cdot \mathsf{Adv}_{\mathcal{F},\mathcal{A}}^{\mathsf{dual\text{-}prf}}(\lambda) \right)$$

Game 8: In Game 8, the computation of the derived handshake secret dHS is replaced by a uniformly random value. To achieve this, ℓ_6 is queried together with the context input H_0 and a PRF challenger is initialized for the computation. The output of the challenger is used to replace the dHS secret. As k_3 is uniformly random by Game 7, this is a valid replacement. To distinguish between the case where $dHS \leftarrow \mathcal{F}(k_3, \ell_6, H_0)$ or $dH \xleftarrow{R} \{0,1\}^\kappa$ the attacker would have to break the **prf** security of PRF and thus has the following advantage:

$$\Pr[S_0] \leq n_P^2 n_S^2 n_T \cdot \left(\mathsf{Adv}_{\mathsf{KEM},\mathcal{A}}^{\mathsf{ind\text{-}cpa}}(\kappa) + 3 \cdot \mathsf{Adv}_{\mathcal{F},\mathcal{A}}^{\mathsf{prf}}(\lambda) + 3 \cdot \mathsf{Adv}_{\mathcal{F},\mathcal{A}}^{\mathsf{dual\text{-}prf}}(\lambda) \right)$$

Game 9: In Game 9, the derivation of the master secret MS is replaced by a uniformly random value. A PRF challenger is initialised and its output used to replace MS. Since dHS is already random by Game 8, this is a valid substitution. To distinguish between the case, where $MS \leftarrow \mathcal{F}(dHS, 0)$ or $M \xleftarrow{R} \{0,1\}^\kappa$, $\mathcal{A}$ would have to break the **prf** security of PRF which leafs the attacker with the following advantage:

$$\Pr[S_0] \leq n_P^2 n_S^2 n_T \cdot \left(\mathsf{Adv}_{\mathsf{KEM},\mathcal{A}}^{\mathsf{ind\text{-}cpa}}(\kappa) + 4 \cdot \mathsf{Adv}_{\mathcal{F},\mathcal{A}}^{\mathsf{prf}}(\lambda) + 3 \cdot \mathsf{Adv}_{\mathcal{F},\mathcal{A}}^{\mathsf{dual\text{-}prf}}(\lambda) \right)$$

Game 10: In Game 10, the application traffic secrets (CATS,SATS) and the session state SecState are replaced by a uniformly random value. This is done by initializing a PRF challenger for each computation and querying the labels 10, 11 and 12 as well as the context input H_3 and replacing the corresponding value with the output from the challenger. Since the master secret MS is already random by Game 9, this is a valid substitution. For $\mathcal{A}$ to distinguish between the case where $CATS, SATS, \mathsf{SecState} \leftarrow \mathcal{F}(MS, \ell_{\{10,11,12\}}, H_3)$ or $CATS, SATS, \mathsf{SecState} \xleftarrow{R} \{0,1\}^{\mathcal{F}}$ he would have to break the **prf** security of PRF.

At this point the application traffic secrets and the session state are shown to be uniformly random under the condition of case 2 and $\mathcal{A}$ has an advantage of

$$\Pr[S_0] \leq n_P^2 n_S^2 n_T \cdot \left(\mathsf{Adv}_{\mathsf{KEM},\mathcal{A}}^{\mathsf{ind\text{-}cpa}}(\kappa) + 5 \cdot \mathsf{Adv}_{\mathcal{F},\mathcal{A}}^{\mathsf{prf}}(\lambda) + 3 \cdot \mathsf{Adv}_{\mathcal{F},\mathcal{A}}^{\mathsf{dual\text{-}prf}}(\lambda) \right)$$

Subcase 2: No CompromiseSK(i, s, t) *or* CompromiseSK(j, r, t) *have been issued.* This case shows, that if the attacker issues a Test query to a session that is clean due to the secrecy of the ephemeral quantum key, he has a negligible advantage in guessing the test bit. In this scenario all ephemeral secrets except the quantum key as well as the long-term classical and post-quantum secrets are known to the attacker.

Game 0: Standard HAKE-Game

$$\mathsf{Adv}_{\mathsf{Muckle+},n_P,n_S,n_T}^{\mathsf{HAKE,clean_{Muckle+}},\mathcal{A},\mathcal{C}_3}(\kappa) = \Pr[S_0]$$

Games 1–3: Games 1 to 3 for Muckle are equivalent to Games 1 to 3 of the proof of case 3.2 as described in [36], resulting in the following advantage:

$$\Pr[S_0] \leq n_P^2 n_S^2 n_T \cdot \left(\mathsf{Adv}^{\mathsf{prf}}_{\mathcal{F},\mathcal{A}}(\kappa) + \mathsf{Adv}^{\mathsf{dual\text{-}prf}}_{\mathcal{F},\mathcal{A}}(\lambda) \right)$$

Games 4–6: Games 4 to 6 are equivalent to Games 8 to 10 in subcase 1, resulting in the final advantage of

$$\Pr[S_0] \leq n_P^2 n_S^2 n_T \cdot \left(4 \cdot \mathsf{Adv}^{\mathsf{prf}}_{\mathcal{F},\mathcal{A}}(\kappa) + \mathsf{Adv}^{\mathsf{dual\text{-}prf}}_{\mathcal{F},\mathcal{A}}(\lambda) \right)$$

Subcase 3: No CompromiseQK(i, s, t') *or* CompromiseQK(j, r, t') *have been issued with* π_i^s *matching* π_j^r *in stages* u *where* $t' \leq u \leq t$. *No* CompromiseSS(i, s, u) *or* CompromiseSS(j, r, u) *have been issued.* This case shows, that if a previous session has been completed cleanly under the predicate clean$_{\mathrm{Muckle+}}$ and $\mathcal{A}$ has not compromised the session state SecState since then, the attacker has a negligible advantage in guessing the test bit of the current session.

Game 0: Standard HAKE-Game

$$\mathsf{Adv}^{\mathsf{HAKE},\mathsf{clean}_{\mathrm{Muckle+}},\mathcal{A},C_4}_{\mathrm{Muckle+},n_P,n_S,n_T}(\kappa) = \Pr[S_0]$$

Game 1: In Game 1 the parameters (i, s, t) for a session and its matching session (j, r, t), as well as the stage t' are guessed. If $\mathcal{A}$ issues a Test(i', s', t) query for any session $\pi_{i'}^{s'}$ that is not the test session π_i^s the game aborts.

$$\Pr[S_0] \leq n_P^2 n_S^2 n_T^2$$

Games 2–10: Games 2 to 10 are equivalent to Games 2 to 10 in subcase 1.

$$\Pr[S_0] \leq n_P^2 n_S^2 n_T^2 \cdot \left(\mathsf{Adv}^{\mathsf{ind\text{-}cpa}}_{\mathsf{KEM},\mathcal{A}}(\kappa) + 5 \cdot \mathsf{Adv}^{\mathsf{prf}}_{\mathcal{F},\mathcal{A}}(\lambda) + 3 \cdot \mathsf{Adv}^{\mathsf{dual\text{-}prf}}_{\mathcal{F},\mathcal{A}}(\lambda) \right)$$

After Game 10 the session π_i^s has been completed cleanly in stage t'. The following Games take place in each stage u and are therefore executed not once, but u-times. To represent the worst case scenario where $\mathcal{A}$ has compromised every stage after the first one, we replace the factor u by n_T.

Game 11: In Game 11 the computation of k_3 is replaced by a uniformly random value. This is done by initializing a post-quantum PRF challenger with the value k_2 and replacing k_3 with the output. As SecState is uniformly random by Game 10, this is a valid substitution. To distinguish between the case of $k_3 \leftarrow \mathcal{F}(\mathsf{SecState}, k_2)$ or $k_3 \xleftarrow{R} \{0, 1\}^{\mathcal{F}}$ the attacker would have to break the **prf** security of the PRF resulting in the advantage:

$$\Pr[S_0] \leq n_P^2 n_S^2 n_T^2 \cdot \left(\mathsf{Adv}^{\mathsf{ind\text{-}cpa}}_{\mathsf{KEM},\mathcal{A}}(\kappa) + (5 + n_T) \cdot \mathsf{Adv}^{\mathsf{prf}}_{\mathcal{F},\mathcal{A}}(\lambda) + 3 \cdot \mathsf{Adv}^{\mathsf{dual\text{-}prf}}_{\mathcal{F},\mathcal{A}}(\lambda) \right)$$

Games 12–14: Games 12 to 14 are equivalent to Games 8 to 10 in case 2

$$\Pr[S_0] \leq n_P^2 n_S^2 n_T^2 \cdot \left(\mathsf{Adv}^{\mathsf{ind\text{-}cpa}}_{\mathsf{KEM},\mathcal{A}}(\kappa) + (5 + 4n_T) \cdot \mathsf{Adv}^{\mathsf{prf}}_{\mathcal{F},\mathcal{A}}(\lambda) + 3 \cdot \mathsf{Adv}^{\mathsf{dual\text{-}prf}}_{\mathcal{F},\mathcal{A}}(\lambda) \right)$$

Subcase 4: No CompromiseSK(i, s, t') *or* CompromiseSK(j, r, t') *have been issued with* π_i^s *matching* π_j^r *in stages* u *where* $t' \leq u \leq t$. *No* CompromiseSS(i, s, u) *or* CompromiseSS(j, r, u) *have been issued.* This case shows, that if a previous session has been completed cleanly under the predicate clean$_{\text{Muckle+}}$ and $\mathcal{A}$ has not compromised the session state SecState since then, the attacker has a negligible advantage in guessing the test bit of the current session.

Game 0: Standard HAKE-Game

$$\text{Adv}^{\text{HAKE,clean}_{\text{Muckle+}},\mathcal{A},C_5}_{\text{Muckle+},n_p,n_s,n_t}(\kappa) = \Pr[S_0]$$

Game 1: In Game 1 the parameters (i, s, t) for a session and its matching session (j, r, t), as well as the stage t' are guessed. If $\mathcal{A}$ issues a Test query for any session that is not the test session π_i^s the game aborts.

$$\Pr[S_0] \leq n_P^2 n_S^2 n_T^2 \cdot \Pr[S_1]$$

Games 2–6: Games 2 to 6 are equivalent to Games 2 to 6 in subcase 2

$$\Pr[S_0] \leq n_P^2 n_S^2 n_T^2 \cdot \left(4 \cdot \text{Adv}^{\text{prf}}_{\mathcal{F},\mathcal{A}}(\kappa) + \text{Adv}^{\text{dual-prf}}_{\mathcal{F},\mathcal{A}}(\lambda) \right)$$

After Game 6 the session π_i^s has been completed cleanly in stage t'. The following Games take place in each stage u and are therefore executed not once, but u-times. To represent the worst case scenario where $\mathcal{A}$ has compromised every stage after the first one, we replace the factor u by n_T.

Games 7–10: Games 7 to 10 are equivalent to Games 11 to 14 in subcase 3.

$$\Pr[S_0] \leq n_P^2 n_S^2 n_T^2 \cdot \left((4 + 4n_T) \cdot \text{Adv}^{\text{prf}}_{\mathcal{F},\mathcal{A}}(\kappa) + \text{Adv}^{\text{dual-prf}}_{\mathcal{F},\mathcal{A}}(\lambda) \right)$$

Finally, we obtain the following advantage.

$$\text{Adv}^{\text{HAKE,clean}_{\text{Muckle+}},\mathcal{A}}_{\text{Muckle+},n_P,n_S,n_T}(\kappa) \leq$$
$$n_P^2 n_S n_T \cdot \text{Adv}^{\text{euf-cma}}_{\Sigma,\mathcal{A}}(\kappa) +$$
$$n_P^2 n_S^2 n_T \cdot \left(\text{Adv}^{\text{ind-cpa}}_{\text{KEM},\mathcal{A}}(\kappa) + 9 \cdot \text{Adv}^{\text{prf}}_{\mathcal{F},\mathcal{A}}(\lambda) + 4 \cdot \text{Adv}^{\text{dual-prf}}_{\mathcal{F},\mathcal{A}}(\lambda) \right) +$$
$$n_P^2 n_S^2 n_T^2 \cdot \left(\text{Adv}^{\text{ind-cpa}}_{\text{KEM},\mathcal{A}}(\kappa) + (9 + 8n_T) \cdot \text{Adv}^{\text{prf}}_{\mathcal{F},\mathcal{A}}(\kappa) + 4 \cdot \text{Adv}^{\text{dual-prf}}_{\mathcal{F},\mathcal{A}}(\lambda) \right)$$

3.4 Instantiating Muckle+

Finally, we discuss some possible choices when instantiating the primitives used in Muckle+. Especially in QKD networks providing high bandwidth communication, the sizes of ciphertexts and signatures might not be a limiting factor. For the choice of signature schemes, we can thus consider candidates that are built from hash functions such as XMSS [17,44] and SPHINCS+ [10] or block ciphers such as Picnic [20,48] and its variant built from AES [3]. Considering that in high bandwidth networks, the use of these symmetric primitives is perfectly valid to reduce the consumption of QKD keys, the use of these signature schemes does not require the addition of any new hardness assumptions to the overall system. We however want to note this chance comes with an increased runtime cost compared to KEM-based authentication as in KEMTLS.

We however want to note, that with the introduction of a signature-based authentication mechanism, the question arises on how to authenticate the other peer's public key. Note though, that even if all public keys are shared a priori, the complexity is reduced to n keys instead of $\mathcal{O}(n^2)$ pre-shared keys. With the introduction of a Public Key Infrastructure (PKI) such as PKIX [23], the amount of pre-installed public keys that then serve as certificate authority (CA) can be drastically reduced. In a setting with only one provider, this can be a single CA. With more providers, various different scenarios can be considered with one external CA or multiple CAs where, for example, each provider handles the certification of the public keys used by their network components.

For QKD networks with trusted nodes, we note that all trusted nodes have access to the QKD key. In the HAKE security model, we thus need to assume that CompromiseSK has been queried and therefore the security of Muckle+ solely relies on the security of the KEM and signature scheme. To achieve fault tolerance in such a setting, we can consider multipath QKD systems that apply a typical secret-sharing-based approaches, e.g., [39,52]. Thereby, the QKD key is shared on the initiator side and the shares are transported via mutually disjoint paths in the QKD network to the receiver. Such an approach has been considered to some extent in the literature specifically for QKD networks, e.g., to boost throughput [73] and with semi-trusted and fully-trusted paths [21] to increase the security of the network. The latter focuses specifically on the routing algorithms without going into details on the method to share the keys. By applying the techniques, e.g., from [52] to the QKD keys, and under the assumption that at least one path is non-compromised or more specifically – similar to the non-collusion in multiparty computation systems – that none of the nodes on disjunct paths collude, the risk stemming from trusted nodes can be mitigated.

4   Implementation and Evaluation

In order to evaluate the performance of Muckle+ in practical application, we implemented a prototype of the protocol. This prototype was implemented in Python using bindings[7] of liboqs [72] for the support of post-quantum primitives and the cryptography[8] module for all classically-secure schemes. As displayed Fig. 3, the Muckle+ protocol operates on the application layer. The quantum key material is fetched by all endpoints by their respective key managements services (KMS) that provide key material to applications via the interfaces from ETSI GS QKD 014 [38].

---

[7] https://github.com/open-quantum-safe/liboqs-python.
[8] https://pypi.org/project/cryptography/.

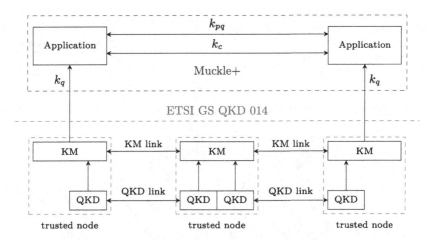

Fig. 3. Architecture of a Muckle+ Implementation with a single intermediate node.

While the Muckle+ protocol allows for server-only, as well as mutual authentication, we benchmarked the implementation with mutual authentication. Authentication of both parties is achieved through the use of hybrid certificates containing both post-quantum and classical long term public keys. Certificates were signed with classical (EdDSA [9]) and post-quantum signatures. We assumed a 2-tier certificate hierarchy to simulate a PKI hierarchy for Muckle+ reflecting current practice, e.g., similar to Let's Encrypt [1].

Our Muckle+ implementation was set up using a small network with three QKD links offering two mutually disjoint paths between endpoints. Initiator and responder of the protocol were executed on a notebook running Windows 10 with an Intel i5 2.60GHz CPU and 8 GB of RAM. Several instantiations of the protocol using different post-quantum KEMs and signature schemes were tested, resulting in the execution times displayed in Fig. 4 for directly linked nodes. For all executions of the protocol, the remaining primitives have been instantiated with X25519 [8] as KEM_c, HKDF-SHA2 as PRF and HMAC-SHA2 as MAC.

Figure 4 depicts the runtime of the initiator for various choices of signature schemes and KEMs for the initiator.[9] For the majority of the evaluated schemes, the runtime for a single Muckle+ stage ranged from 0.4 to 1.6 s. An average of ≈0.3 s of this runtime can be attributed to the retrieval of the QKD key. Hence, we could demonstrate that the determining factor in the performance of the Muckle+ protocol is the key rate of the QKD link as in the original Muckle protocol. While the use of signature-based incurs an overhead compared to Muckle, it is comparatively small in relation to the costs of accessing QKD keys.

---

[9] We observed no significant differences for the initiator and responder.

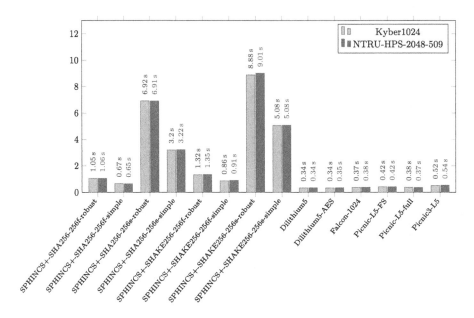

Fig. 4. Execution time of a single Muckle+ stage with mutual authentication. Times are in seconds.

An exception to the observation above is the small and robust SHA256 and SHAKE variants of SPHINCS+ where the slower runtime is attributed to the lack of support for the AVX2 instruction set in `liboqs` for SPHINCS+ on Windows.[10] Hence, we expect the performance of SPHINCS+ to be less of an issue with the availability of optimized implementation on Windows.

In Fig. 5, the results of the same experiment with a multi-path setup are depicted. The additional delay is caused by the intermediate nodes fetching additional key material in a serial manner. The overall execution time of the protocol is thus influenced by the slowest path which in our setup corresponds to the longest path. Overall, we can thus conclude that the overhead of our end-to-end secure protocol for hybrid networks is mainly influenced by the performance of the key rate provided by the QKD network.

---

[10] See https://github.com/open-quantum-safe/liboqs/issues/1476 for some background on this issue.

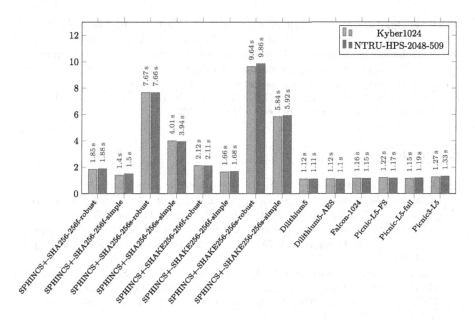

Fig. 5. Execution time of a single Muckle+ stage with mutual authentication in a multi-path setting. Times are in seconds.

5   Conclusion and Outlook

With Muckle+, we extend the hybrid authenticated key exchange protocol Muckle with signature-based authentication. Thereby, we are able to provide both certificate-based mutual or unilateral authentication depending on the intended use-case. Our implementation and evaluation of the protocol within a small QKD network demonstrates its practical feasibility. With our intended message flow of the protocol, Muckle+ may be integrated in typical scenarios where especially the authenticity of the responder is essential. We however note that there might be other trade-offs in the order and structure the messages if different privacy properties are required for an application, e.g., SIGMA with responder privacy or a protocol with forward privacy [63,69].

Note also that the Muckle+ protocol offers features that are interesting for a wide range of applications in a similar setting as found in many of today's applications. Indeed, if one considers classical client-server uses on the web, it is expected that one can connect to almost any server on the network without additional configuration. Hence, handling shared state such as the pre-shared keys is not desired due to scalability issues as well as the out-of-band communication. Considering more high-level use-cases that are envisioned in EuroQCI where network-wide key management systems will provide QKD keys to security applications, ensuring authenticity with certificate-based mechanisms will provide better scalability especially considering that nowadays process for certificate management can be fully automated [1].

Acknowledgements. The authors want to thank Christian Rechberger and Felix Wissel for insightful discussions, and Florian Kutschera for helping with the setup of the QKD devices. This work received funding from the Austrian Research Promotion Agency (FFG) under grant agreement number FO999886370 ("QKD4GOV"), from the European Defence Industrial Development Programme (EDIDP) under grant agreement number SI2858093 ("DISCRETION"), and from the Digital Europe Program under grant agreement number 101091642 ("QCI-CAT").

References

1. Aas, J., et al.: Let's encrypt: an automated certificate authority to encrypt the entire web. In: Cavallaro, L., Kinder, J., Wang, X., Katz, J. (eds.) ACM CCS 2019, pp. 2473–2487. ACM Press (2019). https://doi.org/10.1145/3319535.3363192

2. Alléaume, R., et al.: Using quantum key distribution for cryptographic purposes: a survey. Theor. Comput. Sci. **560**, 62–81 (2014). https://doi.org/10.1016/j.tcs.2014.09.018

3. Baum, C., de Saint Guilhem, C.D., Kales, D., Orsini, E., Scholl, P., Zaverucha, G.: Banquet: short and fast signatures from AES. In: Garay, J.A. (ed.) PKC 2021. LNCS, vol. 12710, pp. 266–297. Springer, Cham (2021). https://doi.org/10.1007/978-3-030-75245-3_11

4. Bellare, M., Lysyanskaya, A.: Symmetric and dual PRFs from standard assumptions: a generic validation of an HMAC assumption. Cryptology ePrint Archive, Report 2015/1198 (2015). https://eprint.iacr.org/2015/1198

5. Bellare, M., Miner, S.K.: A forward-secure digital signature scheme. In: Wiener, M. (ed.) CRYPTO 1999. LNCS, vol. 1666, pp. 431–448. Springer, Heidelberg (1999). https://doi.org/10.1007/3-540-48405-1_28

6. Bellare, M., Pointcheval, D., Rogaway, P.: Authenticated key exchange secure against dictionary attacks. In: Preneel, B. (ed.) EUROCRYPT 2000. LNCS, vol. 1807, pp. 139–155. Springer, Heidelberg (2000). https://doi.org/10.1007/3-540-45539-6_11

7. Bellare, M., Rogaway, P.: Provably secure session key distribution: the three party case. In: 27th ACM STOC, pp. 57–66. ACM Press (1995). https://doi.org/10.1145/225058.225084

8. Bernstein, D.J.: Curve25519: new Diffie-Hellman speed records. In: Yung, M., Dodis, Y., Kiayias, A., Malkin, T. (eds.) PKC 2006. LNCS, vol. 3958, pp. 207–228. Springer, Heidelberg (2006). https://doi.org/10.1007/11745853_14

9. Bernstein, D.J., Duif, N., Lange, T., Schwabe, P., Yang, B.-Y.: High-speed high-security signatures. In: Preneel, B., Takagi, T. (eds.) CHES 2011. LNCS, vol. 6917, pp. 124–142. Springer, Heidelberg (2011). https://doi.org/10.1007/978-3-642-23951-9_9

10. Bernstein, D.J., Hülsing, A., Kölbl, S., Niederhagen, R., Rijneveld, J., Schwabe, P.: The SPHINCS$^+$ signature framework. In: Cavallaro, L., Kinder, J., Wang, X., Katz, J. (eds.) ACM CCS 2019, pp. 2129–2146. ACM Press (2019). https://doi.org/10.1145/3319535.3363229

11. Beullens, W.: Breaking rainbow takes a weekend on a laptop. In: Dodis, Y., Shrimpton, T. (eds.) CRYPTO 2022. LNCS, vol. 13508, pp. 464–479. Springer, Heidelberg (2022). https://doi.org/10.1007/978-3-031-15979-4_16

12. Bindel, N., Brendel, J., Fischlin, M., Goncalves, B., Stebila, D.: Hybrid key encapsulation mechanisms and authenticated key exchange. In: Ding, J., Steinwandt,

R. (eds.) PQCrypto 2019. LNCS, vol. 11505, pp. 206–226. Springer, Cham (2019). https://doi.org/10.1007/978-3-030-25510-7_12

13. Bos, J.W., Costello, C., Naehrig, M., Stebila, D.: Post-quantum key exchange for the TLS protocol from the ring learning with errors problem. In: 2015 IEEE Symposium on Security and Privacy, pp. 553–570. IEEE Computer Society Press (2015). https://doi.org/10.1109/SP.2015.40

14. Bost, R., Minaud, B., Ohrimenko, O.: Forward and backward private searchable encryption from constrained cryptographic primitives. In: Thuraisingham, B.M., Evans, D., Malkin, T., Xu, D. (eds.) ACM CCS 2017, pp. 1465–1482. ACM Press (2017). https://doi.org/10.1145/3133956.3133980

15. Boyko, V., MacKenzie, P., Patel, S.: Provably secure password-authenticated key exchange using Diffie-Hellman. In: Preneel, B. (ed.) EUROCRYPT 2000. LNCS, vol. 1807, pp. 156–171. Springer, Heidelberg (2000). https://doi.org/10.1007/3-540-45539-6_12

16. Brendel, J., Fischlin, M., Günther, F.: Breakdown resilience of key exchange protocols: newhope, TLS 1.3, and hybrids. In: Sako, K., Schneider, S., Ryan, P.Y.A. (eds.) ESORICS 2019. LNCS, vol. 11736, pp. 521–541. Springer, Cham (2019). https://doi.org/10.1007/978-3-030-29962-0_25

17. Buchmann, J., Dahmen, E., Hülsing, A.: XMSS - a practical forward secure signature scheme based on minimal security assumptions. In: Yang, B.-Y. (ed.) PQCrypto 2011. LNCS, vol. 7071, pp. 117–129. Springer, Heidelberg (2011). https://doi.org/10.1007/978-3-642-25405-5_8

18. Canetti, R., Halevi, S., Katz, J.: A forward-secure public-key encryption scheme. In: Biham, E. (ed.) EUROCRYPT 2003. LNCS, vol. 2656, pp. 255–271. Springer, Heidelberg (2003). https://doi.org/10.1007/3-540-39200-9_16

19. Castryck, W., Decru, T.: An efficient key recovery attack on SIDH. In: Hazay, C., Stam, M. (eds.) EUROCRYPT 2023. LNCS, vol. 14008, pp. 423–447. Springer, Heidelberg (2023). https://doi.org/10.1007/978-3-031-30589-4_15

20. Chase, M., et al.: Post-quantum zero-knowledge and signatures from symmetric-key primitives. In: Thuraisingham, B.M., Evans, D., Malkin, T., Xu, D. (eds.) ACM CCS 2017, pp. 1825–1842. ACM Press (2017). https://doi.org/10.1145/3133956.3133997

21. Chen, L., Chen, J., Chen, Q., Zhao, Y.: A quantum key distribution routing scheme for hybrid-trusted QKD network system. Quantum Inf. Process. **22**(1), 75 (2023). https://doi.org/10.1007/s11128-022-03825-x

22. Cini, V., Ramacher, S., Slamanig, D., Striecks, C.: CCA-secure (puncturable) KEMs from encryption with non-negligible decryption errors. In: Moriai, S., Wang, H. (eds.) ASIACRYPT 2020. LNCS, vol. 12491, pp. 159–190. Springer, Cham (2020). https://doi.org/10.1007/978-3-030-64837-4_6

23. Cooper, D., Santesson, S., Farrell, S., Boeyen, S., Housley, R., Polk, W.T.: Internet X.509 public key infrastructure certificate and certificate revocation list (CRL) profile. RFC **5280**, 1–151 (2008). https://doi.org/10.17487/RFC5280

24. Costea, S., Choudary, M.O., Gucea, D., Tackmann, B., Raiciu, C.: Secure opportunistic multipath key exchange. In: Lie, D., Mannan, M., Backes, M., Wang, X. (eds.) ACM CCS 2018, pp. 2077–2094. ACM Press (2018). https://doi.org/10.1145/3243734.3243791

25. Cremers, C., Feltz, M.: Beyond eCK: perfect forward secrecy under actor compromise and ephemeral-key reveal. In: Foresti, S., Yung, M., Martinelli, F. (eds.) ESORICS 2012. LNCS, vol. 7459, pp. 734–751. Springer, Heidelberg (2012). https://doi.org/10.1007/978-3-642-33167-1_42

26. Dallmeier, F., et al.: Forward-secure 0-RTT goes live: implementation and performance analysis in QUIC. In: Krenn, S., Shulman, H., Vaudenay, S. (eds.) CANS 2020. LNCS, vol. 12579, pp. 211–231. Springer, Cham (2020). https://doi.org/10.1007/978-3-030-65411-5_11

27. Dauterman, E., Corrigan-Gibbs, H., Mazières, D.: SafetyPin: encrypted backups with human-memorable secrets. In: 14th USENIX Symposium on Operating Systems Design and Implementation, OSDI 2020, Virtual Event, 4–6 November 2020, pp. 1121–1138. USENIX Association (2020)

28. Derler, D., Gellert, K., Jager, T., Slamanig, D., Striecks, C.: Bloom filter encryption and applications to efficient forward-secret 0-RTT key exchange. J. Cryptol. **34**(2), 13 (2021)

29. Derler, D., Jager, T., Slamanig, D., Striecks, C.: Bloom filter encryption and applications to efficient forward-secret 0-RTT key exchange. In: Nielsen, J.B., Rijmen, V. (eds.) EUROCRYPT 2018. LNCS, vol. 10822, pp. 425–455. Springer, Cham (2018). https://doi.org/10.1007/978-3-319-78372-7_14

30. Derler, D., Krenn, S., Lorünser, T., Ramacher, S., Slamanig, D., Striecks, C.: Revisiting proxy re-encryption: forward secrecy, improved security, and applications. In: Abdalla, M., Dahab, R. (eds.) PKC 2018. LNCS, vol. 10769, pp. 219–250. Springer, Cham (2018). https://doi.org/10.1007/978-3-319-76578-5_8

31. Derler, D., Ramacher, S., Slamanig, D., Striecks, C.: Fine-grained forward secrecy: allow-list/deny-list encryption and applications. In: Borisov, N., Diaz, C. (eds.) FC 2021. LNCS, vol. 12675, pp. 499–519. Springer, Heidelberg (2021). https://doi.org/10.1007/978-3-662-64331-0_26

32. Diffie, W., Hellman, M.E.: New directions in cryptography. IEEE Trans. Inf. Theory **22**(6), 644–654 (1976). https://doi.org/10.1109/TIT.1976.1055638

33. Diffie, W., van Oorschot, P.C., Wiener, M.J.: Authentication and authenticated key exchanges. Des. Codes Cryptogr. **2**(2), 107–125 (1992)

34. Donenfeld, J.A.: WireGuard: next generation kernel network tunnel. In: NDSS 2017. The Internet Society (2017)

35. Dowling, B., Fischlin, M., Günther, F., Stebila, D.: A cryptographic analysis of the TLS 1.3 handshake protocol. J. Cryptol. **34**(4), 37 (2021). https://doi.org/10.1007/s00145-021-09384-1

36. Dowling, B., Hansen, T.B., Paterson, K.G.: Many a mickle makes a muckle: a framework for provably quantum-secure hybrid key exchange. In: Ding, J., Tillich, J.-P. (eds.) PQCrypto 2020. LNCS, vol. 12100, pp. 483–502. Springer, Cham (2020). https://doi.org/10.1007/978-3-030-44223-1_26

37. Drijvers, M., Gorbunov, S., Neven, G., Wee, H.: Pixel: multi-signatures for consensus. In: Capkun, S., Roesner, F. (eds.) USENIX Security 2020, pp. 2093–2110. USENIX Association (2020)

38. ETSI: Quantum key distribution (QKD): Protocol and data format of rest-based key delivery API (2019). https://www.etsi.org/deliver/etsi_gs/QKD/001_099/014/01.01.01_60/gs_qkd014v010101p.pdf

39. Fitzi, M., Franklin, M., Garay, J., Vardhan, S.H.: Towards optimal and efficient perfectly secure message transmission. In: Vadhan, S.P. (ed.) TCC 2007. LNCS, vol. 4392, pp. 311–322. Springer, Heidelberg (2007). https://doi.org/10.1007/978-3-540-70936-7_17

40. Groth, J.: Non-interactive distributed key generation and key resharing. Cryptology ePrint Archive, Report 2021/339 (2021). https://eprint.iacr.org/2021/339

41. Günther, C.G.: An identity-based key-exchange protocol. In: Quisquater, J.-J., Vandewalle, J. (eds.) EUROCRYPT 1989. LNCS, vol. 434, pp. 29–37. Springer, Heidelberg (1990). https://doi.org/10.1007/3-540-46885-4_5

42. Günther, F., Hale, B., Jager, T., Lauer, S.: 0-RTT key exchange with full forward secrecy. In: Coron, J.-S., Nielsen, J.B. (eds.) EUROCRYPT 2017. LNCS, vol. 10212, pp. 519–548. Springer, Cham (2017). https://doi.org/10.1007/978-3-319-56617-7_18

43. Hövelmanns, K., Kiltz, E., Schäge, S., Unruh, D.: Generic authenticated key exchange in the quantum random oracle model. In: Kiayias, A., Kohlweiss, M., Wallden, P., Zikas, V. (eds.) PKC 2020. LNCS, vol. 12111, pp. 389–422. Springer, Cham (2020). https://doi.org/10.1007/978-3-030-45388-6_14

44. Hülsing, A., Butin, D., Gazdag, S., Rijneveld, J., Mohaisen, A.: XMSS: extended Merkle signature scheme. RFC **8391**, 1–74 (2018). https://doi.org/10.17487/RFC8391

45. Hülsing, A., Ning, K.C., Schwabe, P., Weber, F., Zimmermann, P.R.: Post-quantum WireGuard. In: 2021 IEEE Symposium on Security and Privacy, pp. 304–321. IEEE Computer Society Press (2021). https://doi.org/10.1109/SP40001.2021.00030

46. Huttner, B., et al.: Long-range QKD without trusted nodes is not possible with current technology. npj Quantum Inf. **8**(1), 1–5 (2022)

47. Iyengar, J., Thomson, M.: QUIC: a UDP-based multiplexed and secure transport. RFC **9000**, 1–151 (2021). https://doi.org/10.17487/RFC9000

48. Katz, J., Kolesnikov, V., Wang, X.: Improved non-interactive zero knowledge with applications to post-quantum signatures. In: Lie, D., Mannan, M., Backes, M., Wang, X. (eds.) ACM CCS 2018, pp. 525–537. ACM Press (2018). https://doi.org/10.1145/3243734.3243805

49. Katz, J., Lindell, Y.: Introduction to Modern Cryptography, 2nd edn. CRC Press (2014). https://www.crcpress.com/Introduction-to-Modern-Cryptography-Second-Edition/Katz-Lindell/p/book/9781466570269

50. Kaufman, C.: Internet key exchange (IKEv2) protocol. RFC **4306**, 1–99 (2005). https://doi.org/10.17487/RFC4306

51. Krawczyk, H.: SIGMA: the "SIGn-and-MAc" approach to authenticated Diffie-Hellman and its use in the IKE protocols. In: Boneh, D. (ed.) CRYPTO 2003. LNCS, vol. 2729, pp. 400–425. Springer, Heidelberg (2003). https://doi.org/10.1007/978-3-540-45146-4_24

52. Kumar, M.V.N.A., Goundan, P.R., Srinathan, K., Rangan, C.P.: On perfectly secure communication over arbitrary networks. In: Ricciardi, A. (ed.) 21st ACM PODC, pp. 193–202. ACM (2002). https://doi.org/10.1145/571825.571858

53. Kwiatkowski, K., Sullivan, N., Langley, A., Levin, D., Mislove, A.: Measuring TLS key exchange with post-quantum KEM. In: Workshop Record of the Second PQC Standardization Conference (2019). https://csrc.nist.gov/CSRC/media/Events/Second-PQC-Standardization-Conference/documents/accepted-papers/kwiatkowski-measuring-tls.pdf

54. Langley, A.: Cecpq1 results. Blog post (2016). https://www.imperialviolet.org/2016/11/28/cecpq1.html

55. Langley, A., et al.: The QUIC transport protocol: design and internet-scale deployment. In: Proceedings of the Conference of the ACM Special Interest Group on Data Communication, SIGCOMM 2017, Los Angeles, CA, USA, 21–25 August 2017, pp. 183–196. ACM (2017). https://doi.org/10.1145/3098822.3098842

56. Lauer, S., Gellert, K., Merget, R., Handirk, T., Schwenk, J.: T0RTT: non-interactive immediate forward-secret single-pass circuit construction. PoPETs **2020**(2), 336–357 (2020). https://doi.org/10.2478/popets-2020-0030

57. Li, J., Kim, K., Zhang, F., Chen, X.: Aggregate proxy signature and verifiably encrypted proxy signature. In: Susilo, W., Liu, J.K., Mu, Y. (eds.) ProvSec 2007.

LNCS, vol. 4784, pp. 208–217. Springer, Heidelberg (2007). https://doi.org/10.1007/978-3-540-75670-5_15

58. Maurer, U.M.: Protocols for secret key agreement by public discussion based on common information. In: Brickell, E.F. (ed.) CRYPTO 1992. LNCS, vol. 740, pp. 461–470. Springer, Heidelberg (1993). https://doi.org/10.1007/3-540-48071-4_32

59. Mehic, M., et al.: Quantum key distribution: a networking perspective. ACM Comput. Surv. **53**(5), 96:1–96:41 (2020). https://doi.org/10.1145/3402192

60. Mosca, M., Stebila, D., Ustaoğlu, B.: Quantum key distribution in the classical authenticated key exchange framework. In: Gaborit, P. (ed.) PQCrypto 2013. LNCS, vol. 7932, pp. 136–154. Springer, Heidelberg (2013). https://doi.org/10.1007/978-3-642-38616-9_9

61. Pacher, C., et al.: Attacks on quantum key distribution protocols that employ non-its authentication. Quantum Inf. Process. **15**(1), 327–362 (2016). https://doi.org/10.1007/s11128-015-1160-4

62. Paquin, C., Stebila, D., Tamvada, G.: Benchmarking post-quantum cryptography in TLS. In: Ding, J., Tillich, J.-P. (eds.) PQCrypto 2020. LNCS, vol. 12100, pp. 72–91. Springer, Cham (2020). https://doi.org/10.1007/978-3-030-44223-1_5

63. Ramacher, S., Slamanig, D., Weninger, A.: Privacy-preserving authenticated key exchange: stronger privacy and generic constructions. In: Bertino, E., Shulman, H., Waidner, M. (eds.) ESORICS 2021. LNCS, vol. 12973, pp. 676–696. Springer, Cham (2021). https://doi.org/10.1007/978-3-030-88428-4_33

64. Rashidi, L., et al.: More than a fair share: network data remanence attacks against secret sharing-based schemes. In: NDSS 2021. The Internet Society (2021)

65. Rass, S., König, S.: Indirect eavesdropping in quantum networks. In: ICQNM 2011: The Fifth International Conference on Quantum, Nano and Micro Technologies (2011)

66. Rass, S., Schartner, P.: Multipath authentication without shared secrets and with applications in quantum networks. In: Arabnia, H.R., et al. (eds.) Proceedings of the 2010 International Conference on Security & Management, SAM 2010, Las Vegas Nevada, USA, 12–15 July 2010, vol. 2, pp. 111–115. CSREA Press (2010)

67. Rescorla, E.: The transport layer security (TLS) protocol version 1.3. RFC **8446**, 1–160 (2018). https://doi.org/10.17487/RFC8446

68. Rösler, P., Slamanig, D., Striecks, C.: Unique-path identity based encryption with applications to strongly secure messaging. In: Hazay, C., Stam, M. (eds.) EUROCRYPT 2023. LNCS, vol. 14008, pp. 3–34. Springer, Heidelberg (2023). https://doi.org/10.1007/978-3-031-30589-4_1

69. Schäge, S., Schwenk, J., Lauer, S.: Privacy-preserving authenticated key exchange and the case of IKEv2. In: Kiayias, A., Kohlweiss, M., Wallden, P., Zikas, V. (eds.) PKC 2020. LNCS, vol. 12111, pp. 567–596. Springer, Cham (2020). https://doi.org/10.1007/978-3-030-45388-6_20

70. Schwabe, P., Stebila, D., Wiggers, T.: Post-quantum TLS without handshake signatures. In: Ligatti, J., Ou, X., Katz, J., Vigna, G. (eds.) ACM CCS 2020, pp. 1461–1480. ACM Press (2020). https://doi.org/10.1145/3372297.3423350

71. Slamanig, D., Striecks, C.: Puncture 'em all: updatable encryption with no-directional key updates and expiring ciphertexts. Cryptology ePrint Archive, Report 2021/268 (2021). https://eprint.iacr.org/2021/268

72. Stebila, D., Mosca, M.: Post-quantum key exchange for the internet and the open quantum safe project. In: Avanzi, R., Heys, H. (eds.) SAC 2016. LNCS, vol. 10532, pp. 14–37. Springer, Cham (2017). https://doi.org/10.1007/978-3-319-69453-5_2

73. Yu, X., et al.: Multi-path-based quasi-real-time key provisioning in quantum-key-distribution enabled optical networks (QKD-on). Opt. Express **29**(14), 21225–21239 (2021). https://doi.org/10.1364/OE.425562

74. Zhao, Y.: Identity-concealed authenticated encryption and key exchange. In: Weippl, E.R., Katzenbeisser, S., Kruegel, C., Myers, A.C., Halevi, S. (eds.) ACM CCS 2016, pp. 1464–1479. ACM Press (2016). https://doi.org/10.1145/2976749.2978350

Side-Channel Cryptanalysis and Countermeasures

WrapQ: Side-Channel Secure Key Management for Post-quantum Cryptography

Markku-Juhani O. Saarinen[1,2(✉)]

[1] PQShield Ltd., Oxford, UK
mjos@pqshield.com
[2] Tampere University, Tampere, Finland
markku-juhani.saarinen@tuni.fi

Abstract. Transition to PQC brings complex challenges to builders of secure cryptographic hardware. PQC keys usually need to be stored off-module and protected via symmetric encryption and message authentication codes. Only a short, symmetric Key-Encrypting Key (KEK) can be managed on-chip with trusted non-volatile key storage. For secure use, PQC key material is handled in masked format; as randomized shares. Due to the masked encoding of the key material, algorithm-specific techniques are needed to protect the side-channel security of the PQC key import and export processes.

In this work, we study key handling techniques used in real-life secure Kyber and Dilithium hardware. We describe WrapQ, a masking-friendly key-wrapping mechanism designed for lattice cryptography. On a high level, WrapQ protects the integrity and confidentiality of key material and allows keys to be stored outside the main security boundary of the module. Significantly, its wrapping and unwrapping processes minimize side-channel leakage from the KEK integrity/authentication keys as well as the masked Kyber or Dilithium key material payload.

We demonstrate that masked Kyber or Dilithium private keys can be managed in a leakage-free fashion from a compact WrapQ format without updating its encoding in non-volatile (or read-only) memory. WrapQ has been implemented in a side-channel secure hardware module. Kyber and Dilithium wrapping and unwrapping functions were validated with 100K traces of ISO 17825/TVLA-type leakage assessment.

Keywords: Side-Channel Security · Masking Countermeasures · Key Wrapping · Kyber · Dilithium

1 Introduction

With the standardization of CRYSTALS suite algorithms Kyber [3] and Dilithium [5] as the preferred NIST Post-Quantum Cryptography (PQC) methods for key agreement and digital signatures [1], their secure and efficient implementation has become one of the most important engineering challenges in cryptography. NSA has also selected these two algorithms for the CNSA 2.0 suite for protecting classified information in National Security Systems [30].

© The Author(s), under exclusive license to Springer Nature Switzerland AG 2023
T. Johansson and D. Smith-Tone (Eds.): PQCrypto 2023, LNCS 14154, pp. 637–657, 2023.
https://doi.org/10.1007/978-3-031-40003-2_23

1.1   Side-Channel Countermeasures for Lattice Cryptography

Kyber and Dilithium are gradually replacing older RSA and Elliptic Curve Cryptography in systems where it is a requirement that a device (such as a mobile phone, authentication token, or a smart card) does not leak sensitive information even if an adversary has physical access to the device or its close proximity. A related (System-on-Chip) PQC use case is *platform security*, where cryptographic signatures and protocols are used to protect system firmware/bitstream integrity and updates against unauthorized modification and other attacks.

Side-Channel Attacks (SCA) use external physical measurements to derive information about the data being processed. Some of the most important considerations are Timing Attacks (TA) [22], Differential Power Analysis (DPA) [23], and Differential Electromagnetic Analysis (DEMA) [33]. Almost any implementation can be rapidly attacked with these methods if appropriate countermeasures are not in place. Mitigations against TA, DPA, DEMA non-invasive attacks are required for FIPS 140-3/ISO 19790 certification [20,21] at higher levels.

Masking [12] has emerged as the most prominent and effective way to secure lattice-based cryptography against side-channel attacks. Masking is based on randomly splitting all secret variables into two or more shares.

Definition 1. *Order-d masked encoding $[[x]]$ of a group element $x \in G$ consists of a tuple of $d + 1$ shares $(x_0, x_1, \cdots, x_d), x_i \in G$ with $x_0 + x_1 + \cdots + x_d \equiv x$.*

The addition operation can be defined in an arbitrary finite group G; Boolean masking uses the exclusive-or operation $\oplus$, while arithmetic masking uses modular addition. Vectors, matrices, and polynomials can be represented as shares.

A fundamental security requirement is that the shares are randomized so that all $d + 1$ shares are required to reconstruct x, and any subset of only d shares reveals no statistical information about x itself. There are $|G|^d$ possible representations $[[x]]$ for x; *Mask refreshing* refers to a re-randomization procedure that maps $[[x]]$ to another encoding $[[x]]'$ of x.

Computation of cryptographic functions $[[y]] = f([[x]])$ is organized in a way that avoids directly combining the shares, thereby limiting leakage. Arbitrary circuits can be transformed to use masking with quadratic $O(d^2)$ overhead [19]. It has been shown that the amount of side channel information required to learn x or y grows exponentially in relation to masking order d [12]. Hence masking is asymptotically efficient.

Several abstract models have been proposed for the purpose of providing theoretical proofs of security for masked implementations, including the Ishai-Sahai-Wagner probing model [19] and Prouff-Rivain noisy leakage model [32,35]. Designers often proceed by describing a set of generic "gadgets" that make up the secured portion of the algorithm and then providing analysis for the composition. The SNI (Strong Non-Interference) [6] property allows better composability.

In addition to theoretical soundness, an essential advantage of masking countermeasures for PQC is that they are generally less dependent on the physical details of the implementation when compared to logic-level techniques such as dual-rail countermeasures [2]. However, it is essential to verify the leakage properties experimentally. There are standard approaches to physical leakage assessment [14, 21, 38].

1.2 Sensitivity Analysis: Private Keys and Secret Variables

Side-channel leakage can be exploited in any component that handles secret key material. In a broader sensitivity analysis (such as the one performed on Dilithium in [18]), it is apparent that the key management processes must meet the same security requirements as the key generation or private key operations.

Often the "zeroth" step of an asymmetric private-key operation such as signing or decapsulation is "load private key." In SCA-protected implementation, the private key clearly cannot really be stored in non-masked plaintext format.

Masking generally requires that the shares are refreshed (re-randomized) every time they are used. A trivial solution is to write back the refreshed keys to non-volatile memory after each usage. However, this is not practical with ROM or Flash keys. Furthermore, masked representations significantly increase the secret key storage requirement. Secure, non-volatile key storage is an expensive resource. Standard-format Kyber1024 private keys are 25,344 bits, while Dilithium5 secret keys are 38,912 bits (Table 3). This is an order of magnitude more than typical RSA keys and two orders of magnitude more than the keys of Elliptic Curve Cryptography schemes.

Key Wrapping [15, 37] is a process where Authenticated Encryption (AE) is used to protect the confidentiality and integrity of other key material, such as asymmetric keys. Key wrapping reduces much of the problem of secure key management to that of protecting (or deriving) the shorter, symmetric AE wrapping key(s). However, the standard AES-based techniques can't easily protect the plaintext payload from side-channel leakage, just the AES/KEK key itself.

1.3 Outline of this Work and Our Contributions

There exists a body of work discussing the side-channel protection of lattice cryptography schemes, including GLP [7], Dilithium [4, 26] and Kyber [11, 18]. The key management issue has not been addressed previously; keys have been assumed to be immediately available in a dynamically refreshable masked form.

We define the *side-channel secure key wrapping* problem and outline the WrapQ approach. Here the key import function performs a simultaneous unwrapping (symmetric decryption) and refreshing of PQC private key masks. No writeback of refreshed keys is necessary. WrapQ enables compact storage of PQC secret keys on an untrusted medium and their side-channel secure use.

We describe a real-life implementation of WrapQ for Kyber and Dilithium. Side-channel security requires a sensitivity analysis and classification of these algorithms' Critical Security Parameters (CSPs) so that each variable in the secret key is appropriately handled. We then describe an FPGA implementation and perform a leakage assessment of masked Kyber and Dilithium key import and key export functions. No leakage was found in 100K traces.

2   Masked Key Wrapping

Most works on side-channel secure implementations of symmetric ciphers (such as AES) focus on protecting the symmetric key; in a standard model, the attacker can observe and even choose both plaintext and ciphertext. For Key Wrapping, we have an additional goal: its "plaintext" (i.e., the wrapped asymmetric key payload) must also remain invisible to side-channel measurements.

For lattice-based secret keys, an approach that first decrypts a standard serialization of a secret key and only then splits it into randomized shares (Definition 1) will leak information in repeat observations; even partial information about coefficients can be used to accelerate attacks. One can also consider encrypting the individual masked shares, which significantly increases the size of the key blob. However, when importing the same static key blob multiple times, the decrypted masked key is always the same: Not a unique, random representation as required for masking security.

A potential solution would be to write a refreshed, re-encrypted secret key back every time the key is used, but this approach has severe practical disadvantages in addition to a much larger key blob, such as reliability risks.

2.1   High Level Interface

WrapQ implements masked Key Wrapping (protection of the confidentiality and integrity of cryptographic keys [15]) for lattice cryptography with a special type of Authenticated Encryption with Associated Data (AEAD) [36] mechanism. An abstract high-level interface for a masked key wrapping and unwrapping is:

$$C \leftarrow \mathsf{WrapQ}([[K]], [[P]], AD) \tag{1}$$

$$\{[[P]], \mathsf{FAIL}\} \leftarrow \mathsf{WrapQ}^{-1}([[K]], C, AD). \tag{2}$$

Double square brackets $[[\cdot]]$ denote masked variables:

- $[[\mathbf{K}]]$ **Key Encrypting Key (KEK):** Symmetric secret for integrity and confidentiality (short, Boolean-masked key.)
- $[[\mathbf{P}]]$ **Payload:** Asymmetric key material to be encrypted (a set of masked arithmetic and Boolean variables.)
- $\mathbf{AD}$ **Authenticated Associated Data:** Additional elements that only require integrity protection (e.g. the public key.)
- $\mathbf{C}$ **Wrapped key:** Encrypted P, authentication information for AD and P, and internal auxiliary information such as nonces.

Each unwrapping call WrapQ^{-1} produces a fresh, randomized masking representation for $[[P]]$ variables, or FAIL in case of authentication (integrity) failure. In addition to standard AEAD security goals, the primitives guarantee that long-term secrets K or P do not leak while operating WrapQ and WrapQ^{-1} thousands of times.

3   WrapQ 1.0 Design Outline

Our solution makes several design choices motivated by its particular use case; a side-channel secure hardware module that implements lattice-based cryptography. It is hardware-oriented and is not intended as an "universal" format.

3.1   Design Choices

Key Import and Export. Importing may occur during device start-up or if there is a change of keys. Key export is required when new keys are generated or if KEK changes. Side-channel considerations are equally important in both use cases. The term "import" does not necessarily imply interaction with external devices. The import function simply prepares and loads a private key from static storage to be used by a cryptographic processor.

Key Encryption Key. We primarily want to secure the process of local, automatic, unsupervised loading of secret keys for immediate use. For example, some hardware devices may use a device-unique key or a Physically Unclonable Function (PUF) to derive the KEK, with the idea that keys exported to a less trusted storage can only be imported back into the same physical module [24]. Since the main goal is side-channel security, the storage format may be modified to accommodate implementation-specific requirements.

Non-determinism is Preferable. Rogaway and Shrimpton [37] argue that a key wrapping operation should be fully deterministic; the inputs K, P, A fully determine C without randomization. Their motivation is that removing the randomization nonce from C will save some bandwidth. We prioritize side-channel security and observe that randomization helps to eliminate leakage in the export function.

Secondary Encryption. WrapQ only encrypts critical portions of the key material. It is a "feature" that algorithm identifiers and the public key hash are unencrypted; this makes it possible to retrieve a matching public key before validating the secret key blob. WrapQ key blobs do not have complete confidentiality properties, such as indistinguishability from random. However, the resulting blob is much safer to handle as critical variables are encrypted; a secondary confidentiality step can use arbitrary mechanisms to re-encrypt it.

Not (Necessarily) a Key Interchange Format. Export can also occur between devices; sometimes, the term "Key Exchange Key" is used to export a key from one HSM to another or from an on-premises system to the cloud [25]. In such "one-off" manual use cases, side-channel protections may be less critical, and mechanisms such as PKCS #12 [27] can be used (after additional authorization).

3.2 Masked XOF and Domain Separation

WrapQ uses a masked XOF (extensible output function [28]) as a building block for all of its side-channel secure cryptographic functionality.

Definition 2. *An Order-d masked extensible output function* $[[h]]$ $\leftarrow$ $\mathsf{XOF}_n([[m]])$ *processes an arbitrary-length masked input* $[[m]]$ *into n-byte output shares* $[[h]]$ *while maintaining Order-d security (under some applicable definition).*

The XOF (Definition 2) is instantiated with a masked Keccak [1600] [28] permutation. Note that a masked SHA3/SHAKE (and hence a masked Keccak permutation) is required to process secret variables in Kyber (G, PRF, KDF) and in Dilithium (H, ExpandS, ExpandMask). Hence this primitive can be expected to be available in masked Kyber and Dilithium implementations.

Frame Header. We construct a non-secret frame header for all XOF inputs from four fixed-length components:

$$frame = (ID \parallel DS \parallel ctr \parallel IV) \tag{3}$$

ID 32-bit identifier for algorithm type, parameter set, authentication frame structure, key blob structure, WrapQ version; all serialization details.

DS 8-bit Domain Separation identifier. This specifies frame purpose: hash, keyed MAC, encryption, etc.

ctr A 24-bit block index $0, 1, 2, \ldots$ for encrypting multi-block material. Set to 0 for authentication (unless the authentication process is parallelized).

IV Nonce: a 256-bit Initialization Vector, chosen randomly for the key blob. Its frames share the *IV*.

The main security property of the frame header is that it creates non-repeating, domain-separated inputs for the XOF.

- For a fixed secret key protecting many key blobs, this is due to the randomization of *IV*. There is a birthday bound of 2^{128} wrapping operations for a given key.
- Within a key blob (fixed *IV*, key), frames are made unique thanks to (*DS*, *ctr*) being different.
- Across versions. Any functional change in WrapQ serialization requires a new *ID*. This identifier unambiguously defines the structure of the key blob, the interpretation of the contents, the frame header, etc.

There are predefined domain separation bytes; DS_{hash} and DS_{mac} for authentication (Algorithm 1) and DS_{enc} for encryption/decryption (Algorithms 2 and 3.) Frame headers with these domain separation fields are denoted $frame_{\mathrm{hash}}$, $frame_{\mathrm{mac}}$ and $frame_{\mathrm{enc}}$.

Algorithm 1: $T = \mathsf{AuthTag}(\ A, [[K]], ID, ctr, IV\ )$

Input: A, Authenticated data, including ciphertext.
Input: $[[K]]$, Message Integrity Key (Boolean masked.)
Input: ID, ctr, IV: Used to construct $frame_{DS}$ headers.
Output: T, Resulting authentication tag/code.

1: $h \leftarrow \mathsf{Hash}(\ frame_{\mathrm{hash}} \parallel A\ )$
2: $[[T]] \leftarrow \mathsf{XOF}_{|T|}(\ frame_{\mathrm{mac}} \parallel [[K]] \parallel h\ )$
3: $[[K]] \leftarrow \mathsf{Refresh}([[K]])$
4: **return** $T = \mathsf{Decode}([[T]])$

3.3 Integrity Protection: Masked MAC Computation

Algorithm 1 describes the authentication tag computation process. The authentication tag is always checked before any decryption is performed.

For performance reasons, we first use a non-masked hash function $\mathsf{Hash}()$ to process A (Step 1) and only use a masked XOF to bind the hash result h with the (masked) authentication key $[[K]]$ and other variables (Step 2). Furthermore, randomized hashing [17] with a frame header containing the IV is used to make the security of h more resilient to collision attacks. The random prefix IV is included in the *frame* construction (Eq. (3)) and used again in the masked key binding step. It is domain-separated via DS from encryption/decryption frames in case the same $[[K]]$ is used. After this single masked step, $[[K]]$ is refreshed, and the authentication tag $[[T]]$ can be unmasked (collapsed) into T.

Cryptographic Security Notes. In the terminology of [9], WrapQ is an Encrypt-then-MAC (EtM) scheme; ciphertext is authenticated rather than plaintext. Upon a mismatch between the calculated T' and the tag T, a FAIL is returned – no partial decrypted payload. Since WrapQ is an Authenticated Encryption with Associated Data (AEAD) [36] scheme, input tuple A includes data items that do not need to be decrypted in addition to ciphertext C. Unambiguous serialization is used to guarantee domain separation between data items. The ID identifier in *frame* defines the contents and ordering of fixed-length fields in A and all other variables.

3.4 Confidentiality Protection: Encrypting Masked Plaintext

We use the masked XOF in "counter mode" to encrypt/decrypt data. Data is processed in blocks. For Sponge-based primitives such as SHA3/SHAKE [28], the appropriate block size is related to the "rate" parameter, which depends on the security level. Generally, one wants to minimize the number of permutation invocations. SHAKE256 has a data rate of $(1600 - 2*256)/8 = 136$ bytes for each permutation, while SHAKE128 has a 168-byte rate.

Algorithm 2 outlines the process of encrypting a single block; using stream cipher terminology, it uses the masked XOF to produce a block of keystream shares (Step 1), which are exclusive-ored with the plaintext to produce ciphertext

(Step 2). Key blocks must be used only once before being refreshed (Step 3). Plaintext must also be refreshed unless it is discarded (Step 4). The ciphertext is no longer sensitive, so it can be decoded back into unmasked format (Step 5).

Algorithm 2: $C = \mathsf{EncBlock}([[P]], [[K]], ID, ctr, IV)$

Input: $[[P]]$, Payload block (Boolean masked.)
Input: $[[K]]$, Key Encryption Key (Boolean Masked).
Input: ID, ctr, IV: Used to construct header $frame_{enc}$.
Output: C, Resulting ciphertext block.

1: $[[x]] \leftarrow \mathsf{XOF}_{|P|}(\ frame_{enc}\ \|\ [[K]]\ )$
2: $[[C]] \leftarrow [[P]] \oplus [[x]]$ ▷ "Stream cipher."
3: $[[K]] \leftarrow \mathsf{Refresh}([[K]])$
4: $[[P]] \leftarrow \mathsf{Refresh}([[P]])$ ▷ (Unless discarded.)
5: **return** $C = \mathsf{Decode}([[C]])$

Algorithm 3 describes the decryption process, which is also illustrated in Fig. 1. A necessary feature of the block decryption (import) function (Algorithm 3) is that the ciphertext C is first converted into masked encoding (Step 1). The secret cover $[[x]]$ is also in randomized shares (Step 2). Hence decryption occurs in masked form (Step 3), avoiding collapsing $[[P]]$.

Algorithm 3: $[[P]] = \mathsf{DecBlock}(C, [[K]], ID, ctr, IV)$

Input: C, Ciphertext block.
Input: $[[K]]$, Key Encryption Key (Boolean Masked).
Input: ID, ctr, IV: Used to construct $frame_{enc}$.
Output: $[[P]]$, key material payload (Boolean masked.)

1: $[[C]] \leftarrow \mathsf{Encode}(C)$
2: $[[x]] \leftarrow \mathsf{XOF}_{|P|}(\ frame_{enc}\ \|\ [[K]]\ )$
3: $[[P]] \leftarrow [[C]] \oplus [[x]]$ ▷ "Stream cipher."
4: $[[K]] \leftarrow \mathsf{Refresh}([[K]])$
5: **return** $[[P]] = \mathsf{Refresh}([[P]])$

Cryptographic Security Notes. Algorithms 2 and 3 are analogous to counter-mode (CTR) encryption/decryption, except that the payload $[[P]]$ is masked. Confidentiality of ciphertext C follows from the one-wayness and random-indistinguishability of the XOF function (as it would without masking), assuming that the frame identifiers never repeat for the same secret key $[[K]]$.

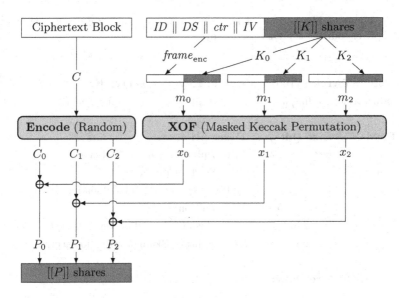

Fig. 1. The WrapQ^{-1} key import function uses a masked XOF in counter mode to decrypt ciphertext blocks C into randomized Boolean shares $[[P]]$. The Keccak Permutation (pictured here with three shares) exists in secure implementations of Dilithium and Kyber; WrapQ just reuses the component.

4 Kyber and Dilithium Private Keys

Cryptographic module security standards (FIPS 140-3 [29]/ISO 19790 [20]) expect that implementors classify all variables based on the impact of their potential compromise.

- **CSP** (Critical Security Parameter): Security-related information whose disclosure or modification can compromise the security of a cryptographic module. CSPs require both integrity and confidentiality protection.
- **PSP** (Public Security Parameter): Security-related public information whose modification can compromise the security of a cryptographic module. PSPs require only integrity protection (authentication).
- **SSP** (Sensitive Security Parameter): Either a CSP or PSP, or a mixture of both. Essentially all variables in a cryptographic module are SSPs.

The parts of secret key material whose disclosure can compromise cryptographic security are CSPs. Additionally, all internally derived or temporary variables whose leakage will compromise security are CSPs. In the FIPS 140-3/ISO 19790 context, the (non-invasive) side-channel leakage protection requirement only applies to CSPs [20, Sect 7.8], not PSPs.

Table 1. Kyber public and secret key components: Variable sensitivity classification and WrapQ encoding for Kyber secret keys.

CRYSTALS-Kyber Standard encoding [3]:		Public Key $pk = (\hat{\mathbf{t}}, \rho)$	Secret Key $sk = (\hat{\mathbf{s}}, pk, pkh), z)$
Field	**Size (bits)**	**Description**	
$\hat{\mathbf{t}}$	$k \times 12 \times 256$	PSP: Public vector, NTT domain.	
ρ	256	PSP: Seed for public $\mathbf{A}$.	
$\hat{\mathbf{s}}$	$k \times 12 \times 256$	CSP: Secret vector, NTT domain.	
pk	$|\hat{\mathbf{t}}| + 256$	PSP: Full public key.	
pkh	256	PSP: Hash of the public key $\mathsf{SHA3}(pk)$.	
z	256	CSP: Fujisaki-Okamoto rejection secret.	
WrapQ Secret Key:		$sk_{wq} = (ID, T, IV, pkh, z, \mathbf{s})$	
Field	**Size (bits)**	**Description**	
ID	32	Algorithm and serialization type identifier.	
T	256	Authentication tag (Algorithm 1).	
IV	256	Random nonce.	
pkh	256	Authenticated: Public key hash $\mathsf{SHA3}(pk)$.	
z	256	Encrypted: FO Transform secret.	
$\mathbf{s}$	$k \times 4 \times 256$	Encrypted: Secret key polynomials.	

4.1 CRYSTALS-Kyber

Table 1 contains a classification of Kyber key variables. WrapQ encrypts and authenticates masked CSPs $(\mathbf{s}, z)$ and only authenticates the rest of the parameters. For the underlying MLWE problem $\mathbf{t} = \mathbf{As} + \mathbf{e}$ the public key consists of $(\mathbf{A}, \mathbf{t})$ and the secret key is $\mathbf{s}$ (ephemeral error $\mathbf{e}$ is not stored.) In Kyber, the $\mathbf{A}$ matrix is represented by a SHAKE128 seed ρ that deterministically generates it.

Kyber standard secret key encoding stores $\mathbf{s}$ in the NTT-domain representation $\hat{\mathbf{s}}$. To conserve storage space and also Boolean-to-Arithmetic transformation effort, we instead store normal-domain $\hat{\mathbf{s}}$, where coefficients are in the range $[-\eta, \eta]$ and would fit into 3 bits (in Kyber, we have $\eta \in \{2, 3\}$, depending on the security level.) However, WrapQ uses four bits per coefficient for Boolean masking conversion convenience.

The z variable is a secret quantity used to generate a deterministic response to an invalid ciphertext in the Fujisaki-Okamoto transform. The security proofs assume it to be secret (we implement the entire FO transform as masked); hence, this 256-bit quantity is handled as a Boolean masked secret.

Table 2. Dilithium public and secret key components: Variable sensitivity classification and WrapQ encoding for Dilithium secret keys.

CRYSTALS-Dilithium	Public Key	Secret Key
Standard encoding [5]	$pk = (\rho, \mathbf{t}_1)$	$sk = (\rho, K, tr, \mathbf{s}_1, \mathbf{s}_2, \mathbf{t}_0)$

Field	Size (bits)	Description
ρ	256	PSP: Seed for public $\mathbf{A}$.
$\mathbf{t}_1$	$k \times 10 \times 256$	PSP: Upper half of public $\mathbf{t}$.
K	256	CSP: Seed for deterministic signing.
tr	$256^\star$	PSP: Hash of public key $tr = H(\rho \parallel \mathbf{t}_1)$.
$\mathbf{s}_1$	$\ell \times d_\eta \times 256$	CSP: Secret vector 1, coefficients $[-\eta, \eta]$.
$\mathbf{s}_2$	$k \times d_\eta \times 256$	CSP: Secret vector 2, coefficients $[-\eta, \eta]$.
$\mathbf{t}_0$	$k \times 13 \times 256$	PSP: Lower half of public $\mathbf{t}$.

WrapQ Secret Key:	$sk_{wq} = (ID, T, IV, \rho, K, tr, \mathbf{s}_1, \mathbf{s}_2)$	

Field	Size (bits)	Description
ID	32	Algorithm and serialization type identifier.
T	256	Authentication tag (Algorithm 1).
IV	256	Random nonce.
ρ	256	Authenticated: Public seed for $\mathbf{A}$.
K	256	Encrypted: Seed for deterministic signing.
tr	$256^\star$	Authenticated: Hash $tr = \mathsf{SHAKE256}(pk)$.
$\mathbf{t}_0$	$k \times 13 \times 256$	Authenticated: Lower half of public $\mathbf{t}$.
$\mathbf{s}_1$	$\ell \times 4 \times 256$	Encrypted: Secret vector 1.
$\mathbf{s}_2 f$	$k \times 4 \times 256$	Encrypted: Secret vector 2.

In standard encoding, the Kyber secret key contains a full copy of the public key. It also contains $H(pk)$, purely as a performance optimization. We also retain and authenticate the $H(pk)$ quantity, but for a different reason: it can be used to authenticate a separately supplied public key.

4.2   CRYSTALS-Dilithium

Table 2 contains a classification of Dilithium key variables. WrapQ encrypts and authenticates masked CSPs $(K, \mathbf{s}_1, \mathbf{s}_2)$ and only authenticates the rest of the parameters. In the underlying equation $\mathbf{t} = \mathbf{A}\mathbf{s}_1 + \mathbf{s}_2$, variables $(\mathbf{A}, \mathbf{t})$ are public and $(\mathbf{s}_1, \mathbf{s}_2)$ are secret. The $\mathbf{A}$ matrix is expanded from SHAKE128 seed ρ.

Note that Dilithium's public variable $\mathbf{t}$ is split into two halves to minimize the size of the public key, with $\mathbf{t}_1$ placed in the public key and the $\mathbf{t}_0$ in private key (as high bits are sufficient for verification.) However, from a cryptanalytic viewpoint, the entire $\mathbf{t}$ is a public variable. Hence $\mathbf{t}_0$ is placed within the secret key blob but as a PSP. There is no need to encrypt $\mathbf{t}_0$; we just authenticate it.

The tr quantity is a 256-bit* hash of the public key $tr = \mathsf{SHAKE256}(\rho \parallel \mathbf{t}_1)$. Only the hash is required for signature generation (as a collision-resilient message processing). Since tr is an authenticated part of the key blob, we also use this quantity to verify that a separately supplied public key is valid.

The distribution of both $\mathbf{s}_1$ and $\mathbf{s}_2$ is uniform in $[-\eta, +\eta]$. Depending on the security parameters, we have $\eta \in \{2, 4\}$. While the standard encoding uses $d_\eta = \lceil \log_2(2\eta + 1) \rceil$ bits (either 3 or 4), WrapQ uses 4 Boolean masked bits per coefficient with all security parametrizations.

The K variable is a secret "seed" value used in deterministic signing (making the signature a deterministic, non-randomized function of the private key and the message to be signed). We treat K as a 256-bit Boolean-masked quantity. However, from a side-channel security perspective, it is preferable to randomize the signing process, in which case K is not used.

5   Parameter Selection and Algorithm Analysis

Cryptography in WrapQ is entirely built from SHA3/SHAKE (FIPS 202 [28]) components, which in turn are based on the Keccak permutation. The $\mathsf{XOF}()$ function (Definition 2) uses a masked version while $\mathsf{Hash}()$ (Sect. 3.3) is non-masked. A straightforward first-order threshold implementation of masked Keccak is roughly three times larger [10] than the unmasked one, and the complexity grows quadratically with the masking order [6]. Other operations in the process are related to mask refreshing or trivial ones such as linear XORs, packing of bits, etc.

Algorithm 1 requires $\lceil (|frame| + |A| + |\text{padding}|)/r \rceil$ unmasked Keccak permutations to compute h with $\mathsf{Hash}()$, where r is the block rate. For SHAKE256, we have $r = 136$ bytes. Additionally, there is a single invocation of masked $\mathsf{XOF}()$ permutation to compute $[[T]]$.

Algorithms 2 and 3 require $\lceil |P|/r \rceil$ invocations of the masked permutation in $\mathsf{XOF}()$. This is also the minimum when computation is organized in a "counter mode" fashion where $[[P]]$ is split into block-sized chunks and ctr is used as an input index. It is not economical to encrypt blocks substantially smaller than r, as that will result in an increased number of permutations and slower speed. However, for some parameters, we sacrifice optimality for the logical separation of data items, simplifying implementation.

---

* The size of tr is 256 bits in Dilithium 3.1 [5]. It may change to 512 bits in a future revision of Dilithium [31].

5.1 Wrapping Process

In the implementation of the key wrapping operation WrapQ (Eq. (1)), all CSPs are converted to Boolean shares (Tables 1 and 2). For internal secret $[[\hat{s}]]$ shares, this involves Inverse-NTT operations to $[[s]]$ since 4-bit packing is used, followed by an Arithmetic-to-Boolean conversion.

After conversions required for the construction of $[[P]]$, we choose a random *IV* for the entire key blob. The $[[P]]$ input, comprising of CSP data, is divided into blocks and fed to Algorithm 2 to produce ciphertext C.

For Dilithium and Kyber, we can process one polynomial at a time since the resulting $(4 \times 256)/8 = 128$-byte block fits the 136-byte data rate of SHAKE256. This has the advantage of "random access" – each secret polynomial can be decrypted only when needed, reducing the RAM requirement. The 4-bit encoding is not optimal of all $[-\eta, +\eta]$ ranges present in these algorithms but is simpler to decode.

The Boolean CSPs (K or z) have $ctr = 0$, block and polynomial CSPs are $1 \leq ctr \leq k$ with Kyber and $1 \leq ctr \leq k + \ell$ with Dilithium. The ciphertext blocks and the PSP data items are then combined into blob A; their serialization is the same as given in Tables 1 and 2, although ID, T, IV are omitted.

Finally, A is passed to Algorithm 1 to produce T; then the final WrapQ key blob is combined from (ID, T, IV, A).

5.2 Unwrapping Process

The unwrapping operation WrapQ^{-1} (Eq. (2)) starts with consistency checks; we parse *ID* from the beginning of the blob and see if the size of the blob matches with it. We also check that the *pkh* (Kyber) or *tr* (Dilithium) fields match with a hash of the public key that is separately provided.

The rest of unwrapping proceeds in inverse order from wrapping; authentication first, then decryption. We extract *IV* and A (the remaining part after *IV* in the blob) and pass those to Algorithm 1 to obtain a check value T'. If we have a mismatch $T \neq T'$, we return FAIL and abort.

Upon success, we proceed to decrypt CSP fields into payload shares $[[P]]$ using Algorithm 3. The conversion of arithmetic CSPs also follows an inverse route; Boolean-to-Arithmetic conversion, followed by an NTT transform as the implementation keeps secret keys "ready" in the NTT domain.

5.3 Size Metrics

Table 3 summarizes the sizes of both standard encodings for Kyber and Dilithium keypairs. We observe that each randomized arithmetic CSP share would be larger than the WrapQ format (even if packed to $\lceil \log_2 q \rceil$ bits per coefficient). For several parameter sizes, the WrapQ size could be further reduced by encoding the $[-\eta, +\eta]$ coefficients in less than 4 bits, but this would complicate the implementation.

Note that the NIST standardization process will likely bring some changes to Kyber 3.02 [3] and Dilithium 3.1 [5].

Table 3. The size of a WrapQ secret key (Tables 1 and 2) does not depend on the masking order. Each individual internal (unpacked) masking share is larger, as are Kyber's "standard serialization" secret keys due to a lack of bit packing.

Algorithm			Masking Per Share	Std. Encoding		WrapQ
Parameters	k	ℓ		$|pk|$	$|sk|$	$|sk_{wq}|$
Kyber512	2		768	800	1,632	**388**
Kyber768	3		1,152	1,184	2,400	**516**
Kyber1024	4		1,536	1,568	3,168	**644**
Dilithium2	4	4	5,888	1,312	2,528	**2,852**
Dilithium3	6	5	8,096	1,952	4,000	**4,068**
Dilithium5	8	7	11,040	2,592	4,864	**5,412**

6   Implementation and Leakage Assessment

WrapQ grew out of a need to be able to manage Kyber and Dilithium private keys in a commercial side-channel secure hardware module. For leakage testing, the hardware platform was instantiated on an FPGA target. A secret key conversion program was written in Python for interoperability testing.

6.1   FPGA Platform Overview

A first-order implementation of WrapQ was tested with an FPGA module that also implements first-order masked Dilithium and Kyber. We outline its relevant components.

- A low-area 64-bit RISC-V control processor.
- Lattice accelerator that can support Kyber and Dilithium $\mathbb{Z}_q$ polynomials and NTT ring arithmetic. The unit can also perform vectorized bit manipulation operations for tasks such as masking conversions (A2B, B2A).
- Ascon-based random mask generator. This is used by the lattice unit for refreshing Boolean and Arithmetic (mod q) shares. The unit can be continuously seeded from an entropy source.
- A compact first-order, three-share Threshold Implementation [10,13] of the masked Keccak permutation. See discussion in Sect. 3.
- A faster, non-masked 1600-bit Keccak permutation used for public **A** matrix generation and also to compute PSP hashes (e.g., the h value in Algorithm 1).

For first-order security, we use trivial refresh gadgets $\mathsf{Refresh}([[x]]) = (x_0 \oplus r, x_1 \oplus r)$ with $r = \mathsf{Random}()$ and $\mathsf{Encode}(x) = (x \oplus r, r)$ with $r = \mathsf{Random}()$. The function $\mathsf{Decode}([[x]]) = x_0 \oplus x_1 \oplus \cdots x_d = x$ simply unmasks x.

6.2   Implementation Overview

The implementation supported all main versions of Kyber and Dilithium (Table 3). In the internal representation, the algorithms hold two copies of the secret CSP variables in Tables 1 and 2 either in compressed or uncompressed format. Kyber polynomials are manipulated at 16 bits per coefficient for arithmetic operations, while Dilithium polynomials use 32 bits. Hence a two-share unpacked Kyber1024 $[[s]]$ requires 4 kB of internal storage while Dilithium5 $([[s_1]], [[s_2]])$ needs 30 kB. These polynomials are handled using (mod q) arithmetic masking. The 256-bit quantities z (Kyber) and K (Dilithium) were Boolean masked in the internal representation.

The confidentiality algorithm used in the test target matches the details of Algorithms 2 and 3 in Sect. 2.1. Authentication was enabled in the import and export functions, but the tests were performed using a "platform security" parameterization; 128-bit IV and T fields, and a slightly different arrangement of hashes in Algorithm 1.

6.3   Leakage Assessment: Fixed-vs-Random Experiments

Our methodology broadly follows the ISO/IEC WD 17825:2021(E) "General Testing Procedure," [21, Figure 7] with statistical corrections. This, in turn, was based on Test Vector Leakage Assessment (TVLA) proposed by CRI/Rambus in 2011 [16] and refined in [14,38].

Traditionally a critical value C of ± 4.5 has been used for $L = 1$, which matches an $\alpha < 10^{-5}$ in that case [8,34]. Since we have long traces (large L), this choice would cause false positives. We adjust the critical value C based on L using the Mini-p procedure from Zhang et al. [14]. Let $\alpha_L = 1 - (1 - \alpha)^{(1/L)}$ be the adjusted significance level. Since the degrees of freedom are very large, we can approximate using the normal distribution: $C = \mathsf{CDF}^{-1}(1 - \frac{\alpha_L}{2})$.

KEK Leakage Testing. The test aims to find leakage from the key K itself, and its set-up is similar to "fixed-vs-random key" TVLA tests performed on block ciphers such as AES [21,34]. Set A has a fixed K, while set B has a random K. Note that the plaintext payload data (i.e., Kyber and Dilithium keys) is randomized in this test; only the symmetric keys are manipulated.

CSP Leakage Testing. For fixed-vs-random testing, confidentiality (encryption) is only provided in WrapQ for CSP (actually non-public) variables. Kyber has two CSPs: ring vector s (decryption key), and FO secret z (Table 1) while Dilithium's CSPs are the ring vectors s_1, s_2 (signing key) and the deterministic seed K (Table 2). All other variables are PSPs (public).

6.4   Trace Acquisition and Results

The experiments were performed with XC7A100T2FTG256 Artix 7 FPGA chip on a ChipWhisperer CW305-A100 board, clocked at 50 MHz. The processor

Table 4. Summary of Random-vs-Fixed tests on WrapQ key import and export functions. The tests were designed to test leakage from both the KEK (Key-Encrypting Key) and the payload CSPs (PQC Secret Keys.) See traces in Fig. 2.

Test	Function	Set A	Set B	Both A&B
#1	Kyber Import	Fix CSP	Rand CSP	Fix KEK
#2	Kyber Import	Fix KEK	Rand KEK	Rand CSP
#3	Dilithium Import	Fix CSP	Rand CSP	Fix KEK
#4	Dilithium Import	Fix KEK	Rand KEK	Rand CSP
#5	Kyber Export	Fix CSP	Rand CSP	Fix KEK
#6	Kyber Export	Fix KEK	Rand KEK	Rand CSP
#7	Dilithium Export	Fix CSP	Rand CSP	Fix KEK
#8	Dilithium Export	Fix KEK	Rand KEK	Rand CSP

and coprocessor bitstreams were synthesized with Xilinx Vivado 2021.2. The C language firmware was with complied GCC, under `-Os` size optimization and `-mabi=lp64 -march=rv64imac` architectural flags.

Signal acquisition was performed with Picoscope 6434E oscilloscopes with a 156.25 MHz sampling rate connected to the SMA connectors on the CW305 board. The DUT generated a cycle-precise trigger.

Table 4 summarizes the various Fixed-vs-Random tests performed on the implementation. The tests were carried out on all three proposed security levels of Kyber and Dilithium, but due to space constraints, we only include graphs for the (highest) Category 5 versions, Kyber1024 and Dilithium5.

The functions passed the tests with 100,000 traces. Even though the critical value C has been adjusted for long traces (as discussed above), from Fig. 2, we can see that the t values are generally bound at a much smaller range. The target unit also performs side-channel secure Kyber and Dilithium operations (key generation, signatures, encapsulation, decapsulation), but those tests are out of scope for the present work.

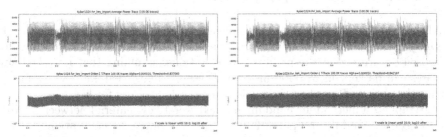

Kyber1024 WrapQ Key Import Random-vs-Fixed CSP (#1 left), KEK (#2 right).

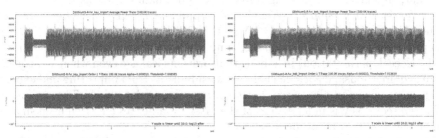

Dilithium5 WrapQ Key Import Random-vs-Fixed CSP (#3 left), KEK (#4 right).

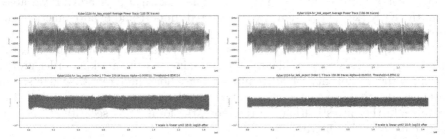

Kyber1024 WrapQ Key Export Random-vs-Fixed CSP (#5 left), KEK (#6 right).

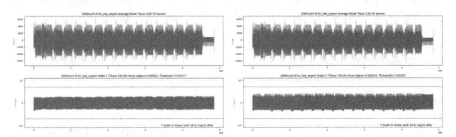

Dilithium5 WrapQ Key Export Random-vs-Fixed CSP (#7 left), KEK (#8 right).

Fig. 2. Kyber and Dilithium average power traces and TVLA t-traces for WrapQ key import and export functions (See Table 4). 100,000 traces were measured for each test. The TVLA results were well within leakage assessment boundaries (red lines). (Color figure online)

7   Conclusions and Future Work

When building side-channel secure implementations of asymmetric algorithms, it is easy to sidestep the key management problem. Academic works have generally focused on protecting the private key operations, assuming that refreshed key shares can be kept in working memory. However, many real-life devices do not have the option of having refreshable non-volatile memory for keys.

WrapQ is a method for handling masked secret key material between a hardware security module and potentially untrusted storage. Its encryption, decryption, and authentication modes can manage wrapped key material in masked format, significantly increasing resilience to side-channel attacks.

We detail a version of WrapQ that supports CRYSTALS-Kyber 3.02 Key Encapsulation Mechanism and CRYSTALS-Dilithium 3.1 signature scheme. The implementation leverages a masked implementation of FIPS 202/SHAKE256 (the Keccak permutation) in a mode that prevents leakage even when an attacker can acquire thousands of side-channel measurements from importing and exporting secret keys and also access the resulting WrapQ data itself. The size of the WrapQ secret key is independent of the masking order and is often even smaller than the standard encoding.

We have performed a TVLA leakage assessment and validation of a WrapQ implementation for Kyber and Dilithium. The leakage of payload CSP variables and the KEK (key encryption key) was tested. Import and export functions for both algorithms pass TVLA testing for up to 100K traces.

Our experimental work has focused on first-order protections. However, the file format works also with higher-order masking. As the masking order grows, so does the complexity of all nonlinear operations and refresh gadgets. We acknowledge that the construction of higher-order gadgets for WrapQ (Sect. 2.1) requires further investigation. Furthermore, the formal SNI security of the gadgets remains to be shown.

Acknowledgments. The author wishes to thank Ben Marshall for running the leakage assessment tests and Oussama Danba and Kevin Law for helping to make the FPGA test target operational. Further thanks to Thomas Prest, Rafael del Pino, and Melissa Rossi for the technical and theoretical discussions. The author is to blame for all errors and omissions.

References

1. Alagic, G., et al.: Status report on the third round of the NIST post-quantum cryptography standardization process. Interagency or internal report, National Institute of Standards and Technology (2022). https://doi.org/10.6028/NIST.IR.8413-upd1. https://csrc.nist.gov/publications/detail/nistir/8413/final
2. Alioto, M., Bongiovanni, S., Djukanovic, M., Scotti, G., Trifiletti, A.: Effectiveness of leakage power analysis attacks on DPA-resistant logic styles under process variations. IEEE Trans. Circ. Syst. I Regul. Pap. **61**(2), 429–442 (2014). https://doi.org/10.1109/TCSI.2013.2278350

3. Avanzi, R., et al.: CRYSTALS-Kyber: algorithm specifications and supporting documentation (version 3.02). NIST PQC Project, 3rd Round Submission Update (2021). https://pq-crystals.org/kyber/data/kyber-specification-round3-20210804.pdf

4. Azouaoui, M., et al.: Leveling Dilithium against leakage: revisited sensitivity analysis and improved implementations. Cryptology ePrint Archive, Paper 2022/1406 (2022). https://eprint.iacr.org/2022/1406. Fourth PQC Standardization Conference, NIST (Virtual) 29 November–1 December 2022

5. Bai, S., et al.: CRYSTALS-Dilithium: algorithm specifications and supporting documentation (version 3.1). NIST PQC Project, 3rd Round Submission Update (2021). https://pq-crystals.org/dilithium/data/dilithium-specification-round3-20210208.pdf

6. Barthe, G., et al.: Strong non-interference and type-directed higher-order masking. In: Weippl, E.R., Katzenbeisser, S., Kruegel, C., Myers, A.C., Halevi, S. (eds.) CCS 2016: Proceedings of the 2016 ACM SIGSAC Conference on Computer and Communications Security, Vienna, Austria, 24–28 October 2016, pp. 116–129. ACM (2016). https://doi.org/10.1145/2976749.2978427. http://dl.acm.org/citation.cfm?id=2976749

7. Barthe, G., et al.: Masking the GLP lattice-based signature scheme at any order. In: Nielsen, J.B., Rijmen, V. (eds.) EUROCRYPT 2018. LNCS, vol. 10821, pp. 354–384. Springer, Cham (2018). https://doi.org/10.1007/978-3-319-78375-8_12. https://eprint.iacr.org/2018/381

8. Becker, G., et al.: Test vector leakage assessment (TVLA) methodology in practice. Presented at International Cryptography Module Conference - ICMC 2013 (2013)

9. Bellare, M., Namprempre, C.: Authenticated encryption: relations among notions and analysis of the generic composition paradigm. J. Cryptol. 21(4), 469–491 (2008). https://doi.org/10.1007/s00145-008-9026-x

10. Bertoni, G., Daemen, J., Peeters, M., Assche, G.V.: Building power analysis resistant implementations of Keccak (2010). https://csrc.nist.gov/Events/2010/The-Second-SHA-3-Candidate-Conference

11. Bos, J.W., Gourjon, M., Renes, J., Schneider, T., van Vredendaal, C.: Masking kyber: first- and higher-order implementations. IACR Trans. Cryptogr. Hardw. Embed. Syst. 2021(4), 173–214 (2021). https://doi.org/10.46586/tches.v2021.i4.173-214

12. Chari, S., Jutla, C.S., Rao, J.R., Rohatgi, P.: Towards sound approaches to counteract power-analysis attacks. In: Wiener [39], pp. 398–412. https://doi.org/10.1007/3-540-48405-1_26

13. Daemen, J.: Changing of the guards: a simple and efficient method for achieving uniformity in threshold sharing. In: Fischer, W., Homma, N. (eds.) CHES 2017. LNCS, vol. 10529, pp. 137–153. Springer, Cham (2017). https://doi.org/10.1007/978-3-319-66787-4_7

14. Ding, A.A., Zhang, L., Durvaux, F., Standaert, F.-X., Fei, Y.: Towards sound and optimal leakage detection procedure. In: Eisenbarth, T., Teglia, Y. (eds.) CARDIS 2017. LNCS, vol. 10728, pp. 105–122. Springer, Cham (2018). https://doi.org/10.1007/978-3-319-75208-2_7

15. Dworkin, M.: Recommendation for block cipher modes of operation: methods for key wrapping. NIST Special Publication SP 800-38F (2012). https://doi.org/10.6028/NIST.SP.800-38F

16. Goodwill, G., Jun, B., Jaffe, J., Rohatgi, P.: A testing methodology for side-channel resistance validation. CMVP & AIST Non-Invasive Attack Testing Work-

shop (NIAT 2011) (2011). https://csrc.nist.gov/csrc/media/events/non-invasive-attack-testing-workshop/documents/08_goodwill.pdf

17. Halevi, S., Krawczyk, H.: Strengthening digital signatures via randomized hashing. In: Dwork, C. (ed.) CRYPTO 2006. LNCS, vol. 4117, pp. 41–59. Springer, Heidelberg (2006). https://doi.org/10.1007/11818175_3

18. Heinz, D., Kannwischer, M.J., Land, G., Pöppelmann, T., Schwabe, P., Sprenkels, D.: First-order masked Kyber on ARM Cortex-M4. IACR ePrint 2022/058 (2022). https://eprint.iacr.org/2022/058

19. Ishai, Y., Sahai, A., Wagner, D.: Private circuits: securing hardware against probing attacks. In: Boneh, D. (ed.) CRYPTO 2003. LNCS, vol. 2729, pp. 463–481. Springer, Heidelberg (2003). https://doi.org/10.1007/978-3-540-45146-4_27

20. ISO: Information technology - security techniques - security requirements for cryptographic modules. Standard ISO/IEC WD 19790:2022(E), International Organization for Standardization (2022)

21. ISO: Information technology - security techniques - testing methods for the mitigation of non-invasive attack classes against cryptographic modules. Draft International Standard ISO/IEC DIS 17825:2022(E), International Organization for Standardization (2023)

22. Kocher, P.C.: Timing attacks on implementations of Diffie-Hellman, RSA, DSS, and other systems. In: Koblitz, N. (ed.) CRYPTO 1996. LNCS, vol. 1109, pp. 104–113. Springer, Heidelberg (1996). https://doi.org/10.1007/3-540-68697-5_9

23. Kocher, P.C., Jaffe, J., Jun, B.: Differential power analysis. In: Wiener [39], pp. 388–397. https://doi.org/10.1007/3-540-48405-1_25

24. Menhorn, N.: External secure storage using the PUF. Application Note: Zynq UltraScale+ Devices, XAPP1333 (v1.2) (2022). https://docs.xilinx.com/r/en-US/xapp1333-external-storage-puf

25. Microsoft: Bring your own key specification. Online documentation: Azure Key Vault/Microsoft Learn (2022). https://learn.microsoft.com/en-us/azure/key-vault/keys/byok-specification. Accessed 12 Oct 2022

26. Migliore, V., Gérard, B., Tibouchi, M., Fouque, P.-A.: Masking Dilithium. In: Deng, R.H., Gauthier-Umaña, V., Ochoa, M., Yung, M. (eds.) ACNS 2019. LNCS, vol. 11464, pp. 344–362. Springer, Cham (2019). https://doi.org/10.1007/978-3-030-21568-2_17

27. Moriarty, K.M., Nystrom, M., Parkinson, S., Rusch, A., Scott, M.: PKCS #12: personal information exchange syntax v1.1. IETF RFC 7292 (2014). https://doi.org/10.17487/RFC7292

28. NIST: SHA-3 standard: permutation-based hash and extendable-output functions. Federal Information Processing Standards Publication FIPS 202 (2015). https://doi.org/10.6028/NIST.FIPS.202

29. NIST: Security requirements for cryptographic modules. Federal Information Processing Standards Publication FIPS 140-3 (2019). https://doi.org/10.6028/NIST.FIPS.140-3

30. NSA: Announcing the commercial national security algorithm suite 2.0. National Security Agency, Cybersecurity Advisory (2022). https://media.defense.gov/2022/Sep/07/2003071834/-1/-1/0/CSA_CNSA_2.0_ALGORITHMS_.PDF

31. Perlner, R.: Planned changes to the Dilithium spec. Posting on PQC Forum (2023). https://groups.google.com/a/list.nist.gov/g/pqc-forum/c/3pBJsYjfRw4/m/GjJ2icQkAQAJ

32. Prouff, E., Rivain, M.: Masking against side-channel attacks: a formal security proof. In: Johansson, T., Nguyen, P.Q. (eds.) EUROCRYPT 2013. LNCS, vol.

7881, pp. 142–159. Springer, Heidelberg (2013). https://doi.org/10.1007/978-3-642-38348-9_9

33. Quisquater, J.-J., Samyde, D.: ElectroMagnetic Analysis (EMA): measures and counter-measures for smart cards. In: Attali, I., Jensen, T. (eds.) E-smart 2001. LNCS, vol. 2140, pp. 200–210. Springer, Heidelberg (2001). https://doi.org/10.1007/3-540-45418-7_17

34. Rambus: Test vector leakage assessment (TVLA) derived test requirements (DTR) with AES. Rambus CRI Technical Note (2015). https://www.rambus.com/wp-content/uploads/2015/08/TVLA-DTR-with-AES.pdf

35. Rivain, M., Prouff, E.: Provably secure higher-order masking of AES. In: Mangard, S., Standaert, F.-X. (eds.) CHES 2010. LNCS, vol. 6225, pp. 413–427. Springer, Heidelberg (2010). https://doi.org/10.1007/978-3-642-15031-9_28

36. Rogaway, P.: Authenticated-encryption with associated-data. In: Atluri, V. (ed.) Proceedings of the 9th ACM Conference on Computer and Communications Security, CCS 2002, Washington, DC, USA, 18–22 November 2002, pp. 98–107. ACM (2002). https://doi.org/10.1145/586110.586125. http://dl.acm.org/citation.cfm?id=586110

37. Rogaway, P., Shrimpton, T.: A provable-security treatment of the key-wrap problem. In: Vaudenay, S. (ed.) EUROCRYPT 2006. LNCS, vol. 4004, pp. 373–390. Springer, Heidelberg (2006). https://doi.org/10.1007/11761679_23

38. Schneider, T., Moradi, A.: Leakage assessment methodology. In: Güneysu, T., Handschuh, H. (eds.) CHES 2015. LNCS, vol. 9293, pp. 495–513. Springer, Heidelberg (2015). https://doi.org/10.1007/978-3-662-48324-4_25

39. Wiener, M. (ed.): CRYPTO 1999. LNCS, vol. 1666. Springer, Heidelberg (1999). https://doi.org/10.1007/3-540-48405-1

Faulting Winternitz One-Time Signatures to Forge LMS, XMSS, or SPHINCS$^+$ Signatures

Alexander Wagner[1,2]($^{\boxtimes}$)(iD), Vera Wesselkamp[2](iD), Felix Oberhansl[1](iD), Marc Schink[1,2], and Emanuele Strieder[1,2](iD)

[1] Fraunhofer Institute for Applied and Integrated Security (AISEC), Garching near Munich, Germany
{alexander.wagner,felix.oberhansl,marc.schink, emanuele.strieder}@aisec.fraunhofer.de
[2] Technical University of Munich, Munich, Germany
{alexander.wagner,vera.wesselkamp,marc.schink,emanuele.strieder}@tum.de

Abstract. Hash-based signature (HBS) schemes are an efficient method of guaranteeing the authenticity of data in a post-quantum world. The stateful schemes LMS and XMSS and the stateless scheme SPHINCS$^+$ are already standardised or will be in the near future. The Winternitz one-time signature (WOTS) scheme is one of the fundamental building blocks used in all these HBS standardisation proposals. We present a new fault injection attack targeting WOTS that allows an adversary to forge signatures for arbitrary messages. The attack affects both the signing and verification processes of all current stateful and stateless schemes. Our attack renders the checksum calculation within WOTS useless. A successful fault injection allows at least an existential forgery attack and, in more advanced settings, a universal forgery attack. While checksum computation is clearly a critical point in WOTS, and thus in any of the relevant HBS schemes, its resilience against a fault attack has never been considered. To fill this gap, we theoretically explain the attack, estimate its practicability, and derive the brute-force complexity to achieve signature forgery for a variety of parameter sets. We analyse the reference implementations of LMS, XMSS and SPHINCS$^+$ and pinpoint the vulnerable points. To harden these implementations, we propose countermeasures and evaluate their effectiveness and efficiency. Our work shows that exposed devices running signature generation or verification with any of these three schemes must have countermeasures in place.

Keywords: fault injection · post-quantum cryptography · hash-based signatures · winternitz one-time signatures · LMS · XMSS · SPHINCS+

1 Introduction

Hash-based signature (HBS) schemes have been known for decades but they were not really considered for further research or practical applications in the past.

© The Author(s), under exclusive license to Springer Nature Switzerland AG 2023
T. Johansson and D. Smith-Tone (Eds.): PQCrypto 2023, LNCS 14154, pp. 658–687, 2023.
https://doi.org/10.1007/978-3-031-40003-2_24

This changed when the need for post-quantum cryptography (PQC) emerged that could withstand attacks by quantum computers.

The standardization of stateful HBS schemes started with the publications of the IETF RFCs for the eXtended Merkle Signature Scheme (XMSS) and Leighton-Micali hash-based signature (LMS) in 2018 and 2019, respectively [HBG+18,MMC19]. The National Institute of Standards and Technology (NIST) published a supplement to their digital signature standard recommending parameters for both of these algorithms in 2020 [CAD+]. The French national agency for the security of information systems (ANSSI) and the German federal office for information security (BSI) also specify both algorithms in their own publications [ANS22,BSI22]. The stateless scheme SPHINCS$^+$ was selected in 2022 at the end of the third round of the process to standardize quantum-resistant public key cryptographic algorithms [MAA+].

Since their standardization, stateful HBS algorithms have been deployed in several products ranging from embedded devices up to servers [Rai22,Cis19, gen20]. Due to their inherent nature of statefulness, the number of signatures that can be created with a key pair is limited, which also limits the range of applications. In practice, they are most applicable to verify the integrity and authenticity of data that rarely changes, such as the firmware of embedded devices. The verification procedure then takes place during a secure boot or firmware update process. In past works, the research community has investigated hardware and software optimizations for this use case [WOS22,WJW+,KPC+,KGC+20] and vendors brought forward products [Rai22]. The standard for SPHINCS$^+$ is yet to be published sometime between today and 2024, but the scheme is already considered for adoption [MAA+]. For example, the OpenTitan project considers to integrate SPHINCS$^+$ into their open source hardware root of trust for firmware verification [goo].

These efforts demonstrate the need for a post-quantum secure boot and firmware update process. An adversary who can circumvent such a process can execute malicious firmware, which compromises the security of embedded devices completely. Over time, researchers have established that fault attacks pose a considerable threat to exposed embedded devices, e.g. by allowing exactly such a circumvention of the secure boot process [BFP19,Rot19]. Developers of secure boot libraries such as MCUboot[1] and microcontroller manufacturers have recognized this by introducing countermeasures against such attacks in the basic control flow [AdGHB]. The cryptographic implementations, however, remained unprotected. We present a fault attack, which demonstrates that such an assumption could prove fatal for an exposed embedded device that uses any of the three HBS schemes: LMS, XMSS, and SPHINCS$^+$.

Attack Overview. Instead of trying to entirely skip a secure boot or firmware update process, our fault attack targets the internal structure of HBS schemes. Our attack grants the adversary signature forgery for arbitrary malicious payloads. We want to emphasize the impact of such an attack, if executed success-

---

[1] https://github.com/mcu-tools/mcuboot.

fully. It is common practice to rely on one entity for signing firmware updates with one key pair for a complete line of products. Therefore, forging a single signature for a malicious payload that seems valid with respect to the entity's public key allows the adversary to corrupt any device. We introduce the idea behind the attack itself in detail in Sect. 3 and the adversarial model in Sect. 3.5. The attack can target either the signing or the verifying entity, is applicable to LMS, XMSS, and SPHINCS$^+$, and consists of two phases. In one phase, a fault is introduced into the Winternitz one-time signature (WOTS) signing or verifying procedure. The other phase is responsible for brute-forcing a forgery candidate. The order of these phases depends on whether it is applied to the signer or the verifier. Further, the effort and success probability of the brute-force phase (analyzed in Sect. 4) depends on the algorithmic part targeted during fault injection. We demonstrate how our attack can be used on the reference implementations of LMS, XMSS, and SPHINCS$^+$ in Sect. 6.

Related Work. The only fault attack known in the context of HBS is the 'Grafting Trees' attack, proposed in [CMP18]. Effective and efficient countermeasures have not yet been sufficiently developed [Gen23]. Practicable evaluations of this fault injection attack were shown in [GKPM18, ALCZ20]. It targets the signature generation of multi-tree schemes, therefore it only affects SPHINCS$^+$ and the multi-tree variants of LMS and XMSS. The adversary tampers with the signing procedure, such that the signer unknowingly leaks secret information. A few tries suffice for the adversary to be able to reconstruct the signer's secret key. The attack has the advantage of very lax requirements with respect to the fault model and the temporal precision. Once the adversary extracts the secret key, she can sign arbitrary messages. The disadvantage is that the attack can only be carried out on the signer. Therefore, it is not applicable in the context of firmware updates or secure boot, as the adversary typically does not have physical access to the signing entity.

Contributions. We present the first attack that allows to tamper the signing as well as the verification operation of HBS schemes in general. Our attack is applicable to all variants of LMS, XMSS, and SPHINCS$^+$, by targeting the checksum mechanism in the fundamental WOTS scheme. The attack consists of two phases. The first phase is a brute-force search for a suitable message digest. This phase happens offline, i.e. there are no strict timing requirements on the adversary. We derive the brute-force complexity and success probability depending on the fault model and algorithmic parameters. Further, we estimate the cost of the brute-forcing capabilities needed in practice. The second phase covers the physical attack on the victim device, typically an embedded system to which the adversary has physical access. We analyze real world implementations for weak spots and show the applicability of our attack with respect to the capabilities of the adversary. In combination with the brute-force cost, our analysis shows that attacking reference implementations of all considered HBS schemes, namely LMS, XMSS, and SPHINCS$^+$ is feasible. To conclude, we outline different countermeasures to mitigate our attack, estimate their effectiveness and costs, and stress their importance for exposed devices.

2 Hash-Based Signatures

We briefly introduce the structure of WOTS and explain how it is used as a fundamental building block in the HBS algorithms LMS [MMC19], XMSS [HBG+18], and SPHINCS$^+$ [HBD+20].

2.1 Winternitz One-Time Signatures

Figure 1 depicts the principle behind WOTS+ as described in [Hü]. In the following we refer to WOTS+ as WOTS, unless clearly stated otherwise, as it is the foundation for all "WOTS-like" algorithms in LMS, XMSS, and SPHINCS$^+$, the most relevant HBS schemes to date.

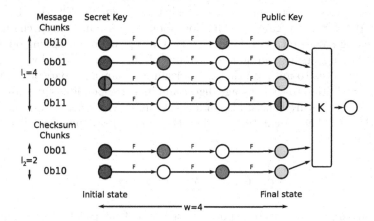

Fig. 1. Simplified Winternitz one-time signature – $w = 4$ and $n = 1$ – with the nodes of the secret key (●), the public key (○), and the signature (◑) highlighted. (Color figure online)

A WOTS signature consists of l hash chains and of these l_1 are required for the message digest and l_2 for the checksum, which are defined as

$$l = l_1 + l_2, \ l_1 = \left\lceil \frac{8n}{log_2(w)} \right\rceil, \ l_2 = \left\lfloor \frac{log_2(l_1(w-1))}{log_2(w)} \right\rfloor + 1. \tag{1}$$

To generate a WOTS signature, a message is hashed into an n-byte value m. The message digest m is split into l_1 chunks. Each chunk is interpreted as a value $m_i = \mathcal{N}(m, i)$, i.e. the function $\mathcal{N}$ maps the i-th chunk of m to m_i, where $m_i \in [0, w-1]$ and $i \in [0, l_1 - 1]$. The parameter w is the Winternitz parameter. Each of the values m_i is assigned an individual hash chain consisting of w nodes, each represented by an n-byte value. The start node is the one-time signature (OTS) secret key (●), and the end node the OTS public key (○). Advancing from one node to another is realized by applying a function $\mathcal{F}$ to the current node. The output of $\mathcal{F}$ serves as the next node. The end nodes are combined by applying the function $\mathcal{K}$ to obtain the compressed OTS public key. Although the exact implementations of $\mathcal{F}$ and $\mathcal{K}$ may differ, we assume both to be single calls to a cryptographic hash function. In reality, before being hashed, the node data might be - depending on the scheme - pre-processed with masks and keys, which are also the output of a hash function.

To **sign** (●→●) or **verify** (●→○) a m_i the corresponding hash chain is advanced by applying $\mathcal{F}$. For signing, $\mathcal{F}$ is applied m_i times to the respective secret key node (○) and the resulting node (●) is taken as part of the WOTS signature. For verifying, the signature node (●) is taken as basis and advanced $w - 1 - m_i$ times. If this does not yield the public key (○), the verifier rejects the signature.

If the WOTS scheme were used just with the l_1 hash chains representing the message digest m, an adversary could trivially sign any message, where the digest r consists only of chunks r_i, where $r_i \geq m_i, \forall i \in [0, l_1 - 1]$. This is because the adversary gains information about intermediate hash chain nodes from the original signature. Information that was prior to the signing operation, private. The adversary can simply advance all signature nodes by $r_i - m_i$ to forge a signature. To mitigate this, a checksum mechanism is part of the WOTS scheme. In addition to the message digest and its corresponding signature nodes, each WOTS signature consist also of a checksum c, which has its own signature nodes (Fig. 1). The calculation of the checksum c for a message digest m is denoted as

$$c = \mathcal{C}(m) = \sum_{i=0}^{l_1-1} (w - 1 - m_i). \tag{2}$$

Put in simple terms, c corresponds to the sum of "steps left" over all message hash chains. The value c is split into l_2 checksum chunks c_k, where $k \in [0, l_2 - 1]$ and l_2 is defined in Eq. (1). The mapping between c and checksum chunks c_k is defined by the function $\mathcal{N}(c, k)$, similar to the mapping between message digest m and message chunks m_i. For the final signature, message chunks and checksum chunks are appended, s.t. $m_0 | m_1 | \ldots | m_{l_1-1} | c_0 | c_1 | \ldots | c_{l_2-1}$. By doing an index transformation from $k \in [0, l_2 - 1]$ to $j \in [l_1, l - 1]$, we map $c_k = m_j$, s.t. we can simplify our signature to a continuous series of $m_0 | m_1 | \ldots | m_{l-1}$, where m_i are nodes corresponding to message chunks and m_j are nodes corresponding to checksum chunks. With the checksum nodes, it is now guaranteed that for a malicious message digest r for which $r_i \geq m_i, \forall i \in [0, l_1 - 1]$ the checksum $c' < c$. Therefore, the adversary would have to get to a lower node from a higher node for at least one checksum chain. This is impossible from an algorithmic perspective, as these lower nodes are neither public nor computable.

The WOTS scheme used today (WOTS+ [Hü]) is a result of optimizing the original scheme by Winternitz [Mer90] and the updated version from [BDE+11]. Its actual instantiations in LMS, XMSS and SPHINCS$^+$ differ, but the parts relevant for this paper are equivalent. This includes the Winternitz one-time signature with tweakable hash functions (WOTS-TW) scheme, the WOTS scheme used in SPHINCS$^+$, which was formally extracted and equipped with a new security proof in [HK22], after a flaw in the original proof was found. The Compressed Winternitz one-time signature (WOTS+C) scheme [KHRY22], however, differs in the fact that no checksum chains are required. Instead, a short random bit string (salt) is introduced in the signing procedure. The salt is sampled randomly until a message digest with a pre-defined value for c is found. This modification was proposed as part of the efforts to compress SPHINCS$^+$ signatures, as it makes the checksum signature nodes obsolete.

2.2   LMS, XMSS, and SPHINCS$^+$

For most of today's applications of digital signatures, a one-time signature scheme like WOTS alone can hardly ever be used. Therefore, many-time signatures (MTSs) like XMSS and LMS combine WOTS with one or multiple Merkle trees. The idea of Merkle signature schemes (MSSs) can be traced back to [Mer90]. Its structure is depicted in Fig. 2a. These schemes are stateful, i.e. the amount of signatures that can be created with one key pair is greater than one but still limited and the signer needs to keep track of the signatures that were already used (maintain a state). As in the previous subsection, WOTS is used to sign the initial message digest. The WOTS public key nodes (○) correspond to the leaf nodes of a Merkle tree. The root node of the tree (◉), in turn, corresponds to the LMS or XMSS public key. Therefore, a Merkle tree with a tree height of h can authenticate 2^h WOTS key pairs, each of which can be used once.

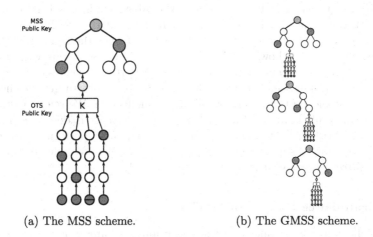

(a) The MSS scheme.   (b) The GMSS scheme.

Fig. 2. MTS variants with one (MSS) and multiple (GMSS) levels of Merkle trees.

To sign a message, the signing entity publishes the WOTS signature (●) and the so-called authentication path (●). These nodes are used by the verifying entity to compute the root node and check whether it matches the MSS public key (○).

For a large number of signatures, MSS schemes still proof impractical. For larger tree heights h, the runtime of key and signature generation is no longer feasible. The generalized Merkle signature scheme (GMSS) [BDK+] addresses this issue, by stacking up d Merkle trees of smaller height $h' = h/d$ instead of using one large tree of height h (see Fig. 2b). The WOTSs of the top and intermediate Merkle trees are used to authenticate the root nodes of the respective Merkle trees below (sub-trees). The WOTSs of the Merkle trees on the lowest layer are used to sign message digests. The multi-tree variants of XMSS, XMSS-MT, and LMS, hierarchical signature system (HSS), specify different parameter sets for d and h, which can be chosen depending on the number of required signatures.

For SPHINCS$^+$, a limited subset of parameters exist. The SPHINCS$^+$ scheme is an stateless signature scheme. Theoretically, a bound for the maximum number of allowed signatures can be derived, but due to a careful combination of parameters, this number is too high to pose a limitation for real-world applications. Additionally, the message digest in SPHINCS$^+$ is not signed with WOTS, but a few-time signature (FTS) scheme called forest of random subsets (FORS). Since the usage of FORS is not of importance for our attack, we omit an explanation here and refer the interested reader to [HBD+20] instead.

3   Attack Sketch

Our attack enables an adversary to choose an arbitrary message and create a valid signature, which we refer to as forged signature throughout this paper. The forged signature can be generated if the adversary has at least one signature which was signed with the secret key. In contrast to existing fault attacks in the context of HBSs, the adversary can either target the signing or the verifying entity. In the following, we abbreviate the two scenarios with $\mathcal{FS}$ and $\mathcal{FV}$ for *faulting the signer* or *faulting the verifier*, respectively. Both scenarios, described in detail in Sect. 3.4, share that the injected faults target the checksum mechanism of the WOTS scheme to render it ineffective. We refer to the phase in which this fault is injected as *fault injection phase*, it is described in detail in Sect. 3.2. Also, in both scenarios, the adversary must perform a brute-force search to generate a signature for its malicious message. We refer to this phase as *brute-force phase* and it is described in Sect. 3.1.

3.1   Brute-Force Forgery of WOTS

In the following we assume that the checksum mechanism is not part of the WOTS scheme, i.e. is ineffective due to the injected fault. Without the checksum, a WOTS of the message digest m created by an entity A can be used to sign other message digests, e.g. to forge a signature for a malicious payload. This is possible as the hash chains can be advanced by repeatedly hashing the signature chunks. To be able to exploit this, the adversary needs to be in possession of a message digest r, s.t. $r_i \geq m_i \; \forall i \; (r_i = \mathcal{N}(r, i)$ and $m_i = \mathcal{N}(m, i)$, see Sect. 2.1). The forged signature behaves as if A had signed r using its secret key. Finding a message which maps to such a message digest r is only possible through brute-force search, due to the preimage resistance of the underlying hash function. The number of trials that is necessary for an adversary to succeed in such a search is analyzed in Sect. 4.1. Section 6.1 reviews the means by which an adversary can efficiently perform the brute-force search.

3.2 Fault Attack on WOTS Checksum Chains

If the adversary is in possession of a malicious message digest r, s.t. $r_i \geq m_i \; \forall i$, the checksum of r will always be lower than that of m. The checksums cannot be equal as this would imply that all chunks of m and r are equal. We disregard the case where the adversary selects its malicious message to be equal to the original message, as this would be of no benefit. And, further, if the digests r and m are equal but not the messages, this would resemble an infeasible second preimage attack.

However, for some checksum chunks $r_j = \mathcal{N}(\mathcal{C}(r), j)$ and $m_j = \mathcal{N}(\mathcal{C}(m), j)$, $r_j \geq m_j$ may still hold. For these, the adversary can simply reuse or advance chains of the signature of m for her forgery. But, if $r_j < m_j$, the adversary must know prior nodes of the OTS checksum hash chain. Recovering prior nodes by inverting F is impossible as it is based on a cryptographic hash function. To overcome this issue, we instead propose a fault attack: The injected fault shall force a node to a lower level on the chain than required by the respective checksum chunk. Consider a value $v \in [0, w - 1]$ for checksum chunk $m_j = v$. Then, either the corresponding secret key node sk_j (during signing) or the signature node sig_j (during verification) is advanced v or $w - v - 1$ times, i.e. $\mathcal{F}^v(sk_j)$ or $\mathcal{F}^{w-v-1}(sig_j)$. Our fault attack forces the implementation to use values smaller than the actual v, or $w - v - 1$, respectively. If the signing entity is attacked, prior nodes than the actual signature nodes are revealed. If the verifying entity is attacked, a correct public WOTS key is derived from nodes too far progressed. With the fault, the adversary is able to forge a valid WOTS for r.

We describe both attack variants in Sect. 3.4. For our theoretic analysis in Sect. 4.1 we assume that the adversary is able to completely skip the checksum calculations. In this case we do not need to care about individual checksum chunks and whether we can forge them or not. We refine this by limiting our attacker capabilities to skip or tamper single or multiple calculations in the theoretic analysis in Sect. 4.2. We show the practicability of our fault attack in Sect. 6.

3.3 Faulting WOTS to Break LMS, XMSS, and SPHINCS$^+$

So far we have established how an adversary can forge a WOTS signature with fault injection. This section establishes that faulting WOTS is sufficient to break any of the HBS algorithms introduced in Sect. 2.2 and describes the attacks an adversary can mount on the respective schemes.

For the single tree variants of LMS and XMSS, the adversary is limited to attacking the only WOTS instance within these schemes, the one signing the actual message digest. A successfully forged WOTS signature is also valid for LMS and XMSS, as the Merkle tree in those schemes only authenticates the WOTS public key.

For the many-time signatures HSS and XMSS-MT, the adversary has more possibilities to mount an attack. If she chooses to attack the lowest WOTS, which signs the actual message, the attack is equivalent to the attack on a single tree scheme described above. However, choosing one of the intermediate WOTSs, which authenticates the root of the respective lower Merkle tree, allows an adversary to sign arbitrary malicious messages. This is because, if the attack on an intermediate WOTS succeeds, the adversary gains the capability to forge a signature for a root node of a lower Merkle tree. Once such a signature is forged, the adversary can arbitrarily construct an entire tree and is therefore in possession of a secret key, which can be used to sign (a limited amount of) arbitrary messages. For the brute-force phase we propose to use the topmost authentication node of the targeted intermediate tree as a counter to efficiently search for suitable root node candidates.

This also applies to the stateless signature scheme SPHINCS$^+$. The only difference between attacks on SPHINCS$^+$ and attacks on HSS and XMSS-MT is, that SPHINCS$^+$ uses FORS instead of WOTS to sign the actual message. However, this structural difference does not impact the adversary's capabilities to forge an entire Merkle tree.

3.4   Attack Variants

The two scenarios to which our attack applies, faulting the signer or verifier ($\mathcal{FS}$ or $\mathcal{FV}$), differ in the order in which the fault injection and brute-force phase take place.

Faulting the Signer ($\mathcal{FS}$). In case of the $\mathcal{FS}$ scenario, the message and therefore the digest m is only known to the adversary after the signature was generated. Nevertheless, the adversary manipulates the WOTS checksum mechanism during signing. The general goal is to force the signer to not advance any checksum hash chain up to the needed signature node, i.e. manipulating $\mathcal{F}^v(sk_j)$ to $\mathcal{F}^{v'}(sk_j)$, where $v' < v$. This reveals nodes which need to be kept secret. Depending on the adversary capabilities described in Sect. 3.5, we show in Sect. 4.2 that there are different strategies to achieve this outcome.

The fault was successful, if the result is a tampered signature revealing enough prior nodes in the checksum hash chains. To forge a valid signature for the malicious payload, the tampered signature is used as an input for the brute-force phase. Here, the selected fault strategy also has an impact on the probabilities for finding a message digest which is suitable to forge a signature.

The malicious payload is forwarded with the forged signature to the victim for verification, e.g. during a secure boot or firmware update. Since the adversary crafted a dedicated payload for the tampered signature, the victim's verification of the message with the public key stored on the device yields a valid signature.

Faulting the Verifier ($\mathcal{FV}$). In the $\mathcal{FV}$ scenario, the adversary is able to collect a set of signatures. These signatures are used as an input for the brute-force phase. Depending on the faulting capabilities of the adversary, the success probability of the brute-force phase, and therefore also the computational cost, vary.

During the fault injection, the adversary tries to force the verifier to not advance a checksum hash chain as determined by the respective checksum chunk, i.e. manipulate $\mathcal{F}^{w-v-1}(sig_j)$ to $\mathcal{F}^o(sig_j)$, where $o < w-v-1$. A straightforward approach for the adversary is to manipulate the victim, s.t. $o = 0$. In this case, the chain calculation of a checksum chunk is skipped entirely and the sig_j node of the forged signature is forwarded directly to the computation of the WOTS public key candidate. To achieve verification, the adversary sets sig_j to the top value of the respective chain, s.t. the correct public key is computed. In Sect. 4.2, we evaluate both relaxed assumptions on the adversary, where setting $o = 0, \forall j$ is possible and more constrained assumptions, where only individual checksum hash chains are (partly) skipped. As described above, these scenarios imply different degrees of freedom for the brute-force phase.

The malicious payload and the forged signature are forwarded to the target device for verification. To trick the verifier into accepting the invalid signature containing invalid OTSs for the checksum, an adversary applies the fault attack as described above. The fault injection was not successful, if the verifier advances this hash chain too far and calculates an invalid compressed OTS public key, which fails verification. If the fault injection was successful, the verifier derives the correct WOTS public key, the signature is verified as valid, and the malicious payload is accepted by the target device.

3.5   Adversarial Model

In this section, we introduce the faulting and brute-force capabilities of the adversary.

Faulting Capabilities. A fault attack has the purpose of manipulating the control or data flow of an application to achieve an outcome that is desired by the adversary. Typical fault attacks we deem applicable to this work are clock and voltage glitching, electromagnetic fault injection (EMFI), laser fault injection (LFI) or software-based hardware attacks like Rowhammer. To simplify analysis, we condense all these attacks into two basic fault models. Please note, that this is not sufficient to fully analyze an implementation. To do so, fault models specific to the underlying hardware need to be derived and used for analysis of the exact data and control flow.

The first fault model we deem reasonable allows an adversary to *skip a single instruction*. This fault model is frequently reported in literature and has been demonstrated on various embedded devices [OSS17, GTSC, O'F19].

The second fault model allows the adversary to tamper data. More precisely, we assume that the adversary is able to *inject single or multiple bit-flips* into registers or memory [SZK+18,FKK+22]. By applying both fault models and showing vulnerable spots within the HBS implementations (Sect. 6), we want to highlight the general applicability of our attack to several devices in different environments and scenarios.

Brute-Forcing Capabilities. As this attacks bears some computational complexity, we need to evaluate its feasibility depending on the adversary's capabilities. To do so, we base our categorisation on [Aum19], which classifies security strengths below 100 bits as *weakened*, and below 80 bits as *broken*. This is commonly used in similar scenarios like side-channel analysis [VCGS13,HMU+20]. In Sect. 6.1, we evaluate different hardware platforms (CPUs, GPUs, or ASICs) to give an estimate for the economic costs connected to this attack.

4   Probabilistic Analysis

In the previous section, we established that the complexity of the fault attack, and the complexity of the brute-force search for a suitable message digest to forge a signature are connected. In the following section, we first analyze the computational complexity for the brute-force phase when assuming that the checksum is rendered completely ineffective by the fault attack (Sect. 4.1). We refine these probabilities and the cost of the attack wrt. the faulting capabilities of the attacker in Sect. 4.2.

4.1   Probabilities

For the attack, the adversary needs to find a digest whose signature is forgeable by using a set M of signed random message digests. We assume the adversary has intercepted the set M of signed digests $m \in M$. As the attacker does not have an influence on the digests contained in M, its capabilities are those of a random message attack (RMA). She now performs the calculation of digests r of messages that are usable for the attack. The set of these trials is R. Even if the adversary has a specific target message, e.g. in the form of a binary, an infinite number of potential forgery targets can be generated by appending a counter to the payload. Among others, this principle was also used in [BHRVV] to efficiently generate a vast amount of different message digests. If it is not possible to append a counter to the selected message, an attacker can exploit the fact that for LMS and XMSS the message is digested using a method called randomised hashing. The hashing instance is initialised with a seed chosen by the signer. An attacker can therefore choose arbitrary values. For SPHINCS+ a different approach is used, with similar capabilities, which is described in more detail at the end of this section. We thus assume that, if needed, the adversary can generate any amount of candidate digests, only limited by its computational resources. In the following, we describe the attack scenario for the adversary goals of universal forgery (UF), selective forgery (SF), and existential forgery (EF). These goals were also used in [GBH18] to evaluate their attack.

To model the probability, we need to know the distribution of values the signed message can take. More precisely, we require the distribution of the message digest, as the message is always hashed prior to signing. We are not interested in weaknesses of the underlying hash functions, therefore we assume that $\mathcal{F}$ behaves like an oracle with uniformly randomly distributed output.

Universal Forgery (UF). An UF is a the strongest forgery attack as it enables an adversary to sign any given digest r. When applied to WOTS, it is necessary for the attacker to possess a valid signature of a message digest m that consists of all zeros – which is rarely the case. However, if the adversary has obtained such a signature, she has obtained all OTS secret keys. Hence, each hash chain can be advanced to an arbitrary node, signing any message. The probability for a single hash chain of length w to be equal to zero is $\frac{1}{w}$. The probability that this is the case for all hash chains is

$$p_{UF} = \left(\frac{1}{w}\right)^{l_1} = 2^{-8n}.$$

Given a set of M validly signed message hashes, the probability that one of them is a zero-hash can be modeled by the CDF of a geometric distribution with parameter p_{UF} as following

$$Pr_{break}[M, R] = 1 - (1 - p_{UF})^{|M|}.$$

The adversary has no possibility to increase the overall probability as its brute-force set R has no influence. As $n \in [16, 24, 32]$ – for the NIST security levels of one, three, and five, respectively – the success probability to achieve UF-RMA when our attack is applied only to WOTS is infeasible. By extending our attack to HBS schemes with multiple trees, we show how an attacker can still achieve UF-RMA within certain constraints. This extension is described in Sect. 3.3.

Selective Forgery (SF). In case of a SF, an adversary chooses a fixed digest r before gaining knowledge of the set M. Based on [GBH18], we model this scenario as follows: To maximize the likeliness that the chosen r is a forgery candidate for the unknown set M, the adversary chooses a threshold $b \in [0, w - 1]$. Now, an r where for each chunk r_i it holds that $r_i \geq b$ is pre-calculated. The attack succeeds with such a chosen r, if M contains a message hash m where for each chunk m_i holds $m_i \leq b$. In this case, the adversary has knowledge of an r for which holds that $r_i \geq m_i, \forall i$. Thus, m can be misused to forge a signature for r. Due to the equally distributed output of the hash function, the probabilities that $r_i \geq b$ and $m_i \leq b\ \forall i$ are given as

$$p_{SF_{\geq b}} = \left(\frac{w - b}{w}\right)^{l_1}, \; p_{SF_{\leq b}} = \left(\frac{b}{w}\right)^{l_1}.$$

Each of the two cases applied to the whole set, i.e. $\exists m \in M \mid m_i \leq b$ and $\exists r \in R \mid r_i \geq b \; \forall i$, can again be modeled as the CDF of a geometric distribution dependent on the size of the set. Thus, the joint probability of both occurring is

$$Pr_{break}[M, R] = \left(1 - (1 - p_{SF_{\leq b}})^{|M|}\right)$$
$$\cdot \left(1 - (1 - p_{SF_{\geq b}})^{|R|}\right).$$

The selection of the threshold b constitutes a trade-off, as a higher b leads to a higher $p_{SF_{\leq b}}$ allowing for a smaller set M, but at the same time raises the necessary pre-computation for the set R as $p_{SF_{\geq b}}$ drops. In the case that $\exists m \in M \mid m_i \leq b \; \forall i$ a signature m can still be leveraged for the forgery, if $\exists m \in M$ and $\exists r \in R \mid m_i \leq r_i \; \forall i$. Thus the actual probability is *at least* the above.

The SF scenario corresponds to cases where the computation of the forgery candidate needs to occur before the attacker gets access to m. We deem this as less relevant and therefore do not further investigate this scenario within this work.

Existential Forgery (EF). In case of EF, an adversary succeeds in signing one arbitrary digest. To achieve this when given set of signed digests M, the adversary performs a calculation of forgery candidates r for each $m \in M$, i.e. the size of both sets are equal: $|M| = |R|$. The probability that one chunk r_i of the candidate is greater or equal to the corresponding chunk m_i of the message m can be described using the law of total probability

$$Pr[r_i \geq m_i] =$$
$$= \sum_{x=0}^{w-1} Pr[r_i \geq m_i | m_i = x] \cdot Pr[m_i = x]$$
$$= \sum_{x=0}^{w-1} \left(\frac{w-x}{w}\right) \frac{1}{w} = \frac{w+1}{2w}.$$

This leads to the overall probability for l_1 chunks of r being larger than m with $|R|$ number of trials:

$$Pr_{break}[M, R] = 1 - \left(1 - \left(\frac{w+1}{2w}\right)^{l_1}\right)^{|R|}. \tag{3}$$

The results for different parameters are plotted in Fig. 3. As we assume for each forgery trial to draw an unseen m, we model the probability for each trial as independent event. While this case allows an exact calculation of the corresponding probabilities, it can only be used to roughly estimate the order of complexity for cases where $|M| = I$ and $|R| \gg I$. Hence, it remains unclear how many trials are required in the adversaries scenario and a more exact representation of the probability is needed.

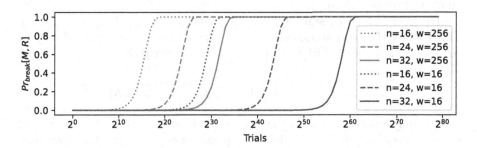

Fig. 3. The success probability of an EF-RMA with $|M| = |R|$.

A different approach is to calculate the probability of a forgery for each m individually. For a certain m we can calculate the probability that all l_1 chunks r_i of the candidate are greater or equal to the corresponding chunks m_i:

$$Pr\left[r_i \geq m_i, \forall i\right] = \prod_i^{l_1} \frac{w - m_i}{w}.$$

In contrast to the previous scenarios, this probability is dependent on m. It is thus not possible to derive a general p_{EU}. The probability of breaking a non-fixed message m using a set R is the sum of probabilities for all possible m, each of which occurs with the same probability:

$$Pr_{break}[m, R] = \sum_{m \in M} (1 - (1 - Pr[r_i \geq m_i, \forall i])^{|R|}) \cdot Pr[m]$$

$$= \sum_{m \in M} (1 - (1 - Pr[r_i \geq m_i, \forall i])^{|R|}) \cdot \frac{1}{w^{l_1}}.$$

For a set M, the overall probability thus becomes

$$Pr_{break}[M, R] = 1 - (1 - Pr_{break}[m, R])^{|M|}. \tag{4}$$

To calculate the probability $Pr_{break}[m, R]$, all valid digests $m \in M$ need to be evaluated. Due to the amount of possible outputs of a cryptographic hash function, this is infeasible to compute. Therefore, we propose to approximate the expected probabilities with the help of simulations. If the values from Fig. 3 are taken as a reference point to estimate the complexity for simulating the attack, it becomes obvious that a high resource usage is required. For example, the experiment with $n = 32, w = 16$ might require up to 2^{60} trials. Further, we would have to run the experiment a significant number of times to draw conclusions from it and the simulation only allows to draw conclusions for the number of trials performed.

To circumvent this issue, we instead simulate $Pr_{break}[M, R]$ for $|M| > 1$. This reduces the computational effort and, thus, allows to use general-purpose computing equipment. With these results we can approximate $Pr_{break}[m, R]$, i.e. $|M| = 1$ as

$$Pr_{break}\left[m, \frac{R}{|M|}\right] = 1 - \sqrt[|M|]{1 - Pr_{break}[M, R]}. \tag{5}$$

Figure 4 shows our results. Please note that the analysis of the $w = 16$, $n = 32$ parameter set exceeded our available computing resources and is therefore omitted. For the parameter set of $w = 16, n = 24$, we have run our simulations with $|M| = 131072$. Due to the high count of $|M|$ and limited computing resources, we selected 4096 messages from M, for which the brute-force search had the highest success probability based on Eq. (3) – effectively reducing the input to the brute-force search by 32. Hence, Pr_{break} for $w = 16, n = 24$ is *at least* as high as given by the results of our simulations. To reflect this in the plots, we marked the count of the message set with $|M^*|$.

Extending Existential Forgery to Universal Forgery. The results shown so far demonstrate that, if only a single WOTS signing a message is targeted, an adversary can only achieve EF with reasonable high probabilities. This changes if the attack is applied to any of the multi-tree algorithms, i.e. the HSS variant of LMS, XMSS-MT, and SPHINCS$^+$. By exploiting the dependency between trees, the adversary is able to extend its forging capabilities such that UF can be achieved. Section 3.3 established that an adversary may target WOTS instances that authenticate sub-trees. This affects the brute-force complexities slightly. The input to the signing or verifying operation is no longer a message, which can be chosen freely, but the root node of a sub-tree. During the brute-force phase, the adversary must generate a new sub-tree with a suitable root node. For this, the secret key (a seed which is used to generate all the leaf nodes) is chosen freely. Then, the adversary constructs the tree from the secret key and divides it into signature and authentication nodes (see Sect. 2.2). The top-most node of the authentication path can be replaced with a counter which is iterated until a suitable root node is found. The difference to attacking a WOTS instance signing a message is that the adversary is now capable of authenticating a key pair and is in possession of the secret key. Therefore, the adversary gains the possibility to sign messages without any additional effort. If a message-signing WOTS instance is attacked, every new message requires a new brute-force phase. Hence, the attack is extend from EF to UF.

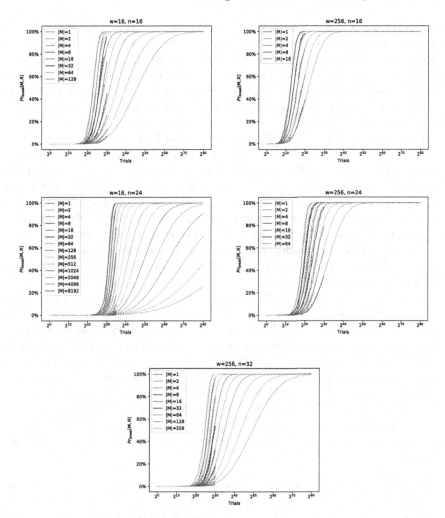

Fig. 4. Simulated (solid line), and approximated (dotted line) probability of finding suitable hash for different Winternitz parameters w, hash output lengths n, and signature set sizes $|M|$, with respect to the number of trials $|R|$. All results for a certain set size $|M|$ are plotted using the same color. The dashed lines represent the approximations obtained from the respective maximum $|M|$. The solid lines show actual simulation results to verify the estimated data.

4.2 Probabilities wrt. Adversary Capabilities

In this section, we empirically derive the theoretic probability that an adversary can produce a valid forgery with a digest r derived from the brute-force phase by means of fault injection. The general probability to find such a digest r can be obtained from Fig. 4. Recall, that in Sect. 4.1 and Fig. 4, the assumption was that the complete checksum computation can be skipped. Now the probabilities that

r is suitable for a forgery in more constrained fault models are analyzed. Recall that for a forged signature to be accepted, each chunk of the faulted checksum $\mathcal{C}(r)$ needs to be larger or equal to the corresponding chunk of $\mathcal{C}(m)$. Therefore, suitable in this context means that faults corresponding to certain models can be used to manipulate the checksum in this manner. We define this probability as Pr_{valid}. Obviously, this probability varies depending on the adversary's fault injection (FI) capabilities.

Two properties factor into Pr_{valid}: the type of fault attack and the number of independent faults injected during one operation, either during signing or verifying. We introduced the general FI capabilities of the attacker in Sect. 3.5. We simplified our evaluation by assuming two fault models, control flow and data corruption. For control flow corruption we only consider single instruction skips, for data corruption we analyze single and double bit-flips. We assume bit-flips for arbitrary positions with no positional constraints. Further, in the case of double bit-flips, both are independent from each other and behave as two single bit-flip faults. From these fault models, we derive three concrete fault scenarios, which are listed in the following.

In Sect. 3.4, two variants of our attack were introduced, $\mathcal{FS}$ for applying the fault attack to the signer, and $\mathcal{FV}$ for applying the fault attack to the verifier. For the $\mathcal{FS}$ scenario, the adversary needs a strategy to fault the signing operation without knowledge of the message and its signature, s.t. the probability to find a forged signature in the brute-force phase is as high as possible. For all listed scenarios we list the highest achievable probability with the respective strategy in Table 2. In the $\mathcal{FV}$ scenario, the attacker is already in possession of a forged signature obtained in the brute-force phase and therefore knows how the checksum computation needs to be manipulated. Therefore, for the listed probabilities in Table 1 it is not necessary to differentiate between different strategies.

Single hash chain skip. The attacker skips the calculation of one OTS checksum hash chain by means of a single instruction skip. In our practical analysis in Sect. 6, we show that this is a reasonable assumption. We assume that the adversary is able to skip one chosen checksum hash chain precisely. The exact point in time of individual checksum hash chains depends on m and therefore is not constant in time. However, in the $\mathcal{FV}$ scenario, the adversary knows the order of operations as r is known. In case of the $\mathcal{FS}$ scenario, the adversary could obtain such informations via a side-channel inspection. If the hash chain calculation is skipped, the chain will not be advanced by the signer or verifier at all, but execution stalls with the input node. Therefore, the input node is used as-is for the further execution of the algorithm.

Single bit-flip. The attacker corrupts the value of one of the checksum chunks with a single induced bit-flip. Ideally, this manipulates the checksum operation, s.t. instead of advancing by v steps, i.e. $\mathcal{F}^v$, the chain is only advanced by $v' < v$. In contrast to hash chain skips, timing might be less of an issue as the data can be targeted while stored in memory.

Double bit-flip. The attacker corrupts the value of at least one of the checksum chunks with two induced bit-flips. We do not differentiate between cases where both bit-flips target the same chunk and cases where the bit-flips apply to different chunks. In contrast to the single bit-flip scenario, a double bit-flip has more possible outcomes in terms of how the checksum chunks are manipulated. Therefore, $v' < v$ can hold for one or two checksum hash chains.

Table 1. The average probability Pr_{valid} in case of $\mathcal{FV}$ for a single suitable hash r depending on the attacker capabilities.

Fault type	Scenario	w = 16		w = 256		
		n = 16	n = 24	n = 16	n = 24	n = 32
Control flow corruption	Single hash chain skip	54.1%	44.1%	46.8%	39.6%	51.0%
Data corruption	Single bit-flip	54.1%	34.8%	46.8%	39.6%	51.0%
	Double bit-flip	89.1%	65.8%	81.2%	72.0%	83.8%

Table 2. The average probability Pr_{valid} for the most suitable fault locations in case of $\mathcal{FS}$ for a single suitable hash r depending on the attacker capabilities.

Fault type	Scenario	w = 16		w = 256		
		n = 16	n = 24	n = 16	n = 24	n = 32
Control flow corruption	Single hash chain skip	54.1% $r_j\|j = 0$	34.8% $r_j\|j = 0$	46.8% $r_j\|j = 0$	39.6% $r_j\|j = 0$	51.0% $r_j\|j = 0$
Data corruption	Single bit-flip	54.1% bit 8	28.0% bit 8	46.8% bit 11	17.3% bit 11	51.0% bit 12
	Double bit-flip	56.6% bit 8, 7	29.3% bit 8, 7	48.0% bit 11, 5	22.5% bit 11, 10	51.4% bit 12, 4

Table 1 shows the average Pr_{valid} for the scenarios of $\mathcal{FV}$. A value of $Pr_{valid} = 54.1\%$ for $\mathcal{FV}$, $w = 16$, $n = 16$, and *single hash chain skip*, reads as "slightly more than half of all digests found in the brute-force phase described in Sect. 4.1 can be realized in scenarios, where only one fault can be applied, s.t. a single hash chain calculation is skipped". Obviously, an adversary can determine directly from r, whether an attack will succeed within a certain fault scenario. Therefore, the fault injection phase is only performed for digests r for which $Pr_{valid}(r) = 1$. In the $\mathcal{FS}$ scenario, Table 2 additionally shows which strategy an adversary needs pursue to achieve the highest probability Pr_{valid}. A value of $Pr_{valid} = 54.1\%$ with $r_j|j = 0$ for $\mathcal{FS}$, $w = 16$, $n = 16$, and *single hash chain skip*, reads as "if during signing, a checksum chain with index $r_j|j = 0$ is skipped, slightly more than half of all digests found in the brute-force phase described in

Sect. 4.1 can be used to forge a signature". For the fault type of data corruption we list Pr_{valid} along the bits that needs to be targeted during signing to achieve this probability, e.g. for the parameter $w = 16$ and $n = 16$ the adversary has the highest probability of 54.1% or 56.6% if fault attacks with single-bit flips target bit 8 or with double bit-flips target bit 8 and 7, respectively. This is due to the fact that the brute-force phase described in Sect. 4.1 does not have any constraints on the checksum and its chunks, but only on the message chunks ($r_i \geq m_i \ \forall i$). These constraints are introduced by the fact that candidates found in the brute-force phase can only used for forgery with a probability of Pr_{valid}.

The analysis of the probabilities in general and the strategies for $\mathcal{FS}$ is based on the simulation results displayed in Fig. 4. For each pair of (r, m) we applied any possible fault for the three listed fault scenarios. We applied the fault to the checksum of m or r for $\mathcal{FS}$ or $\mathcal{FV}$, respectively. We calculated Pr_{valid} by dividing the number of suitable sets (r, m) for forgery by the total number of generated candidates r which fulfill the constraints of $r_i \geq m_i \ \forall i$.

5   Countermeasures

To protect HBS implementations against the presented attack, different measures are applicable depending on the two attack variants, $\mathcal{FS}$ and $\mathcal{FV}$. In the case of $\mathcal{FS}$, hardening the implementation is straightforward. As a consequence of the tampered signature generation, the signer generates an invalid signature. This weakness of the attack can be used to design a countermeasure (CM). If the signer verifies the signature after generation, the attack will be detected. Since the cost of verification is minimal compared to signature generation, this step can easily be added by the signing entity. In the case of $\mathcal{FV}$, the countermeasures are more diverse and costly. We describe their design in the following sections. However, due to the more complex approach, we evaluate their efficiency and effectiveness in detail in Sect. 6.

Hash Chain Length Calculations. Any error introduced into the calculation of the hash chain length can lead to a wrongly calculated, but potentially exploitable, hash chain length value. Repetition and comparison of the calculated hash lengths allows any tampering to be detected. The cost of this countermeasure is small, as this part of the algorithm is negligible in terms of overall performance.

Hash Chain Calculations. The countermeasures for the hash chain calculations can be divided into two independent levels: skipping partial and full hash chain calculations.

The attack vector of a *partial skip* of a hash calculation can be avoided by using a memory comparison of the input and output buffers. This will detect if the hash operation was skipped and thus render the attack vector ineffective. This countermeasure only needs to be performed during the first iteration, as an adversary must skip from the first iteration onwards. This is due to the fact that the iteration index is an input to each hash step calculation. To ensure successful verification, the verifier must be tricked to combine the malicious checksum node with the correct iteration index. Therefore, it is not possible to swap hash steps and the skip must be introduced from the first iteration onwards.

The *complete skip* of the hash chain calculation can be countered by assuring that at least one hash chain calculation is performed. Combined with the countermeasure to disable a partial skip of the hash calculation, this makes this attack vector impossible to execute. In practice, an implementation can simply return the iteration counter. The calling function compares the returned value with the maximum value for the iteration. If it does not match, a fault has been introduced and execution is aborted.

WOTS+C. WOTS+C is designed to compress WOTSs [KHRY22] as introduced in Sect. 2.1. The key idea behind this study is to skip the checksum chains in favor of a checksum with a fixed value. This makes control flow attacks to skip a checksum chain no longer feasible. The applicability of data errors needs to be investigated, as well as any impact on the brute-force phase. Operations such as checksum comparison may be suitable targets for FI and must therefore be hardened.

6   Attack in Practice

In this section we describe a real-world scenario to demonstrate the practicability and severity of our attack. The target is an embedded device based on the commonly used ARM Cortex-M4 processor. The attacker's goal is to run malicious firmware on the embedded device. To protect the firmware execution on the device against tampering from physical adversaries, secure boot is used directly after power-up to verify any firmware after loading it into the internal memory and before execution. For verification one of the hash-based signature schemes is used. The secure boot implementation is based on MCUboot [mcu]. We assume that the attacker has physical access and therefore is able to modify or exchange the off-chip stored firmware before it is loaded into the internal memory and to execute a fault attack.

Fault Model and Hardening. If MCUboot is used, the secure boot implementation is partially hardened against FI attacks [mcu]. The scope of the hardenings is to, for example, protect against an instruction skip. Therefore, instruction skip fault attacks that target the generic secure boot flow, e.g. ensuring that only valid images are booted, will not be successful. The cryptographic implementations are only partially hardened with similar countermeasures [Ban] and may therefore still be vulnerable to FI attacks.

PQ Secure Boot. To fulfill the requirements of a post-quantum secure boot, the targeted embedded device verifies each stage using a HBS scheme instead of classical asymmetric cryptography. Please note that MCUboot does not yet support PQC schemes, but plans to do so [Bro]. We select the algorithms and the respective parameters based on the results in Fig. 4, related research works [KPC+]

and public available information on embedded devices, which employ HBSs for secure boot or firmware updates or plan to do so [Phi22]. The probabilistic analysis in Sect. 4.1 has shown that – for the analyzed parameters – the parameter set of $w = 16$ and $n = 24$ has the highest brute-force complexity. Therefore, we deem it relevant to be investigated within this scenario. As we select these parameters, we assume either LMS or XMSS with a single tree, reflecting the worst case for the attacker based on our results. In [KPC+], HSS and SPHINCS$^+$ with 192-bit key length, $w = 256$, and three or five Merkle trees, respectively, is considered as relevant for UEFI secure boot. In [Phi22], SPHINCS$^+$ with 128-bit key length is reported as suitable for the secure boot of an embedded device. As the tree structure is not specified, but a reduced maximum signature count is requested, we assume a similar tree structure as in [KPC+], and set the Winternitz parameter as $w = 16$ based on the statement in [Phi22] that performance is a constraint.

In summary, this results in these distinct algorithms and parameter sets for our practical analysis: LMS or XMSS with $w = 16$ and $n = 24$; HSS with three Merkle trees, $w = 256$ and $n = 24$ [KPC+]; SPHINCS$^+$ with five Merkle trees, $w = 16$ and $n = 16$, and $w = 256$ and $n = 24$ [KPC+, Phi22].

6.1   Brute-Force Forgery of WOTS

As described in Sect. 3.1, the brute-force phase requires at least one WOTS message-signature pair as input, in this scenario we use the more suitable term of firmware-signature pair. Within this attack, the adversary has access to the external memory, which contains firmware and the corresponding signature. Because the device receives updates, the adversary is even capable to collect several pairs for the brute-force. To reflect different update intervals we analyze the scenario with the assumption that the adversary can collect firmware-signature pairs with a count out of $[1, 10, 100, 1000]$.

By applying our fault injection attack, a verifier is tricked to assume a malicious signature as valid. Before the actual fault attack, the attacker must forge this signature. This brute-force process can happen "offline" and "off-site", i.e. there are no strict timing requirements. Depending on the HBS scheme the adversary achieves existential or universal forgery as described in Sect. 3.3 and Sect. 4.1. In practice, the efficiency of signature forging boils down to the number of hash calculations per timespan, i.e. the hash rate, the attacker can

Table 3. Hash rates of SHA-256 for different platforms.

Hardware	Type	Hash rate
Intel i7-9700K [Son19]	CPU	299 MH/s
Nvidia RTX 3090 [Cro20]	GPU	9.71 GH/s
Nvidia RTX 4090 [Cro22]	GPU	22.0 GH/s
Antminer S19 XP [Bit22]	ASIC	140 TH/s

achieve. Table 3 shows different platforms with their respective hash rates. For central processing units (CPUs) and graphics processing units (GPUs), the benchmarks were performed with hashcat.

In comparison to CPUs and GPUs, application-specific integrated circuits (ASICs) achieve the best performance. However, we deem ASICs less relevant since their dedicated design would make them very expensive. GPUs are, however, attractive due their combination of high performance and flexibility. The attacker can easily gain access to many devices, e.g. from cloud computing providers. We selected a single Nvidia RTX 4090 GPU to estimate the time required for a brute-force search for the selected parameters. The results in Fig. 5 show that, for all three parameter sets based on a multi-tree structure, a forgery succeeds ($Pr_{break} \geq 90\%$) in less than an hour. We achieve these results even if an adversary has only access to a single firmware-signature pair. While the effort is significantly larger for single tree structures ($d = 1$), it is still feasible, e.g. if multiple GPUs are available.

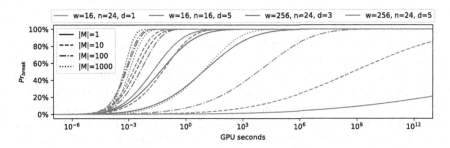

Fig. 5. Cost estimation for brute-force forgery of the selected parameter and structure with a single GPU. Estimations are displayed for the number of firmware-signature pairs for the values of 1, 10, 100, and 1000.

6.2 Fault Attack on Hash-Based Signatures

Having the possibility to forge a signature for a malicious firmware image brings the attacker one step closer to the goal of executing malicious code. The missing piece is to inject a fault to circumvent the signature verification. To assess the possibility of a successful fault attack we search for weak spots within the reference implementations of LMS, XMSS, and SPHINCS+. We base our analysis on an extensive emulation of all possible faults based on the instruction skip fault model using ARCHIE [HGA+21]. The emulation is performed for the ARM Cortex-M4 processor. We analyse two different scenarios reflecting the two different approaches to optimising for performance or size and their impact on fault injection resilience. Therefore, the firmware is compiled for the two scenarios with either of the two optimisation levels: -*O2* and -*Os*.

Table 4. Number of instructions that will lead to a successful verification of an invalid signature if only one is skipped.

	Optimization	CMs	Generic FI			WOTS FI		
			(1)	(2)	(3)	(1)	(2)	(3)
LMS	-O2	No	20	–	15	32	–	27
		Yes	1	–	0	1	–	0
	-Os	No	18	–	18	33	–	33
		Yes	2	–	0	2	–	0
XMSS	-O2	No	6	2	1	17	13	12
		Yes	5	1	0	5	1	0
	-Os	No	13	10	0	21	18	8
		Yes	13	10	0	13	10	0
SPHINCS$^+$	-O2	No	2	1	1	7	6	6
		Yes	1	0	0	1	0	0
	-Os	No	5	4	0	10	5	5
		Yes	5	4	0	5	4	0

We include both generic and WOTS-specific fault attacks in the analysis. Generic fault attacks are more straightforward for an attacker, as no brute-force phase is required. However, systems that require physical security can easily be protected against such attacks, without a detailed understanding of the underlying algorithms. In the following, we will demonstrate this by hardening a reference implementation with generic countermeasures. In contrast, we show that mitigating WOTS-specific attacks is not as straightforward. One needs to be aware of them and the vulnerable points they cause during execution. We demonstrate that generic countermeasures do not consider these points and that WOTS-specific attacks require a more thorough understanding in order to design integrated countermeasures. We apply the countermeasures proposed in Sect. 5 and evaluate their effectiveness and efficiency. The comparison of both types of attacks allows to understand their different leverage points. Furthermore, this analysis demonstrates the severity of an unprotected implementation and shows that countermeasures are feasible.

Table 5. Code size [B] of the signature verification routine for the different HBS schemes, optimisation levels, and CM tiers.

	Optimization	Code size	Code size increase by CMs		
			(1)	(2)	(3)
LMS	-O2	2650	+206	–	+258
SHA2_10_256	-Os	2380	+164	–	+216
XMSS	-O2	4380	+126	+138	+162
SHA2_10_192	-Os	3870	+98	+114	+134
SPHINCS$^+$-s	-O2	10400	+106	+118	+134
sha2-128s	-Os	9550	+84	+100	+112

Table 6. Cycle count [cc] of the signature verification for the different HBS schemes, optimisation levels, and CM tiers.

	Optimization	Cycle count	Cycle count increase by CMs		
			(1)	(2)	(3)
LMS	-O2	8.5M	+3.94k	–	+5.15k
SHA2_10_256	-Os	8.7M	+3.80k	–	+5.02k
XMSS	-O2	31.6M	+3.93k	+3.93k	+4.10k
SHA2_10_192	-Os	32.3M	+4.11k	+4.11k	+4.27k
SPHINCS$^+$-s	-O2	17.9M	+15.3k	+15.3k	+15.4k
sha2-128s	-Os	18.3M	+17.8k	+17.8k	+17.9k

The XMSS and SPHINCS$^+$ APIs provide a device with several ways to evaluate the result of the signature verification. As is common practice, the return value of the signature verification routine indicates whether an error has occurred or not. In addition, two other values, the message and its length, can be used to evaluate the result. In the event of an error, the message points to a array initialized with zeros and the corresponding length is set to zero. In the following, we will outline how these variants significantly increase the fault injection resilience. Hence, making fault attacks more difficult to execute. For this purpose, we group these variants into three enumerated categories with increased cost to the verifier: the verifier checks (1) the return code, (2) the return code and the message length, or (3) the return code, the message length, and the message. The original implementation of LMS does not support this functionality. To allow for a similar analysis, we add the ability to check the return code as well as the message. In the following this variant is labeled as (3).

Note that none of the reference implementations claim to be fault injection resilient. At the time of writing, there are no other HBS implementations available stating any countermeasures against fault attacks. Table 4 shows the overall fault injection resilience for the different scenarios. The count is the number of instructions where skipping one is sufficient to bypass the signature check. Therefore, a higher count corresponds to a lower resilience. Table 5 and Table 6 list the increased code size and execution time of the signature verification routine introduced by the variants for checking the returned values and the countermeasures.

Generic Fault Attack. Comparing the two stateful reference implementations, the XMSS implementation is more resilient to generic FI attacks. The main reason for this is the return of multiple values as described above and its internal structure. Most importantly, the comparison of the public key and the computed candidate directly triggers the writing of the return values. Furthermore, XMSS does not contain any bridging functions that may introduce exploitable weaknesses. However, despite the relatively high level of resilience, we still found vulnerable spots in XMSS that could be exploited with a generic FI attack. The existence of vulnerabilities depends on the level of compiler optimisation chosen. For the speed optimisation a countermeasure is needed to harden the comparison of the public key with its computed candidate. For all the experiments carried out, two measures were sufficient to protect this potentially fragile point. The first is to check that the length which is an input to the *memcmp* function is equal to zero. If this condition is met, an error is thrown and the execution is aborted. This is necessary because the *memcmp* function will always return zero for a length of zero despite the values contained in the two pointers. And the second part is to mark the returned value as volatile to allow for a repeated comparison of the returned value. The combination of these two measures effectively prevents tampering with this operation.

The LMS implementation differs fundamentally from the XMSS implementation. The major difference in terms of the fault injection resilience is that it only returns a single value to check the status of the signature verification. In general, the implementation contains more bridging functions, which has the effect that more measures to harden the implementation are required. As a result the required code size for the countermeasures listed in Table 5 is larger than for the other two implementations. The countermeasures required are similar to the hardening of the *memcmp* routine described above. As with the other two implementations, the comparison of the public key and the computed candidate must be hardened. In addition, for each returning bridging function, the check on the return value must be hardened by duplicated checks, and if it returns a Boolean value, it must be cast to an integer. The integer casting is required because we have experienced that for Boolean return values the compiler most often compares if the value is not equal to zero, resulting in false positives. Another necessary countermeasure is to initialise the error state with an initial error code. This way, any premature return will return the uncleared error statement and allow potential malicious tampering to be detected.

The SPHINCS$^+$ reference implementation is very similar to the XMSS implementation. The analysis showed a fairly resilient implementation. Nevertheless, SPHINCS$^+$ also requires a hardening of the public key comparison with its computed candidate. The hardening of this operation can be done with the same countermeasures as described above.

In conclusion, all three reference implementations of the HBS schemes can be hardened with simple measures so that there are no vulnerable instructions that could be skipped to lead to a successful verification of an invalid signature using a generic fault attack. This is reflected within the results in Table 4 showing that there are non weak spots left for a generic fault attack, if the proposed countermeasures are applied. Neither executing the generic attack nor designing countermeasures against it required any special knowledge of the running algorithms. The weak spots targeted by a generic fault attack are easy to spot for an attacker as well as the defender. Hence, an implementation is more likely to be resilient against a generic fault attack.

WOTS-Specific Fault Attack. The results in Table 4 demonstrate that while an implementation can be hardened, there may still be potential vulnerabilities to a specific attack. In the worst case, including a WOTS-specific attack triples the number of vulnerable locations. Even worse, some implementations, such as the size-optimised XMSS with three return values, appear to be resistant to fault injection, but are not when a WOTS-specific attack is executed. We can therefore conclude that the generic countermeasures are effective, but do not protect against WOTS-specific attacks. However, this is different for the WOTS-specific countermeasures proposed in Sect. 5. When the countermeasures are used together with the three return value variant, all implementations for all scenarios are resilient against each of the two types of attack. In spite of the different code bases of the three reference implementations, all of them allow for similar countermeasure approaches without any loss of effectiveness. This is, of course, mainly due to the high degree of similarity between the three algorithms, which is also reflected in their implementations.

Effectiveness and Efficiency of CMs. Due to the countermeasures applied, the implementations suffer in terms of performance and increased code size. The increase in execution time is listed in Table 6. Surprisingly, the performance is hardly changed by the countermeasures. Due to the adapted design of the countermeasures, a small impact was expected. But for all three implementations, the impact of the changed execution time is only about one permille or less. The impact on code size, listed in Table 5, is much more significant. The increase is in the range of one to ten percent. The additional size of the countermeasures is about 100 to 250 bytes, depending on the reference implementation, the level of optimisation and the number of return values. Due to the similarity of XMSS and SPHINCS$^+$, the implemented countermeasures are very similar and therefore the absolute impact on code size is comparable. The relative difference varies mostly due to a different implementation of the underlying hash function. In both relative and absolute terms, the LMS reference implementation has the largest code size increase due to the countermeasures. This is because this implementation has the smallest initial code size, but also required the most changes to be resilient. Overall, the proposed countermeasures, both generic and specific, make the reference implementations resilient to fault attacks with minimal impact on performance and size.

7   Conclusion

In this paper we present the first fault attack that directly targets the WOTS schema, which is an integral part of all currently standardised HBS schemes. Therefore, it affects LMS, XMSS and SPHINCS$^+$. Furthermore, our attack affects both signature generation and signature verification. Although the attack requires brute-force computation of an appropriate digest, we have demonstrated its feasibility. Our research shows that for a Winternitz parameter $w = 16$, signatures are forgeable for all algorithms with a NIST security level up to 3. For $w = 256$, signatures generated by all algorithms considered are forgeable, regardless of the chosen security level. The complexity of the attack is at most affected by the choice of the Winternitz parameter and the internal tree structure. Choosing a larger value for w combined with a multi-tree structure leads to parameter sets that can be broken within seconds with a single GPU. To defend against this attack, appropriate countermeasures must be in place. The analysis of the proposed countermeasures shows their effectiveness and efficiency against the WOTS-specific attack. Furthermore, our proposed generic countermeasures harden the implementations so that a fault attack is no longer feasible within this scenario. However, despite the advanced progress in standardisation, our research has shown that the analysis of the implementation security of HBS algorithms is still an ongoing task. With our work, we aim to stimulate further research in this area. The recent selection of SPHINCS$^+$ for standardisation makes this particularly important, as this will lead to more vendors looking to incorporate HBS schemes into their products. We also see a need for a more thorough analysis of implementation security in general. A combination of algorithmically formalised knowledge and automated analysis could ensure a higher probability of early detection of vulnerabilities in implementations. Efforts in this direction will allow the development of hardened PQC implementations in a secure and rapid manner.

Acknowledgements. This work was partly funded by the German Federal Ministry of Education and Research (BMBF) in the project APRIORI under grant number 16KIS1390.

References

[AdGHB] Atilano, E., de Grandmaison, A., Heydemann, K., Bouffard, G.: Assessing the effectiveness of MCUboot protections against fault injection attacks

[ALCZ20] Amiet, D., Leuenberger, L., Curiger, A., Zbinden, P.: FPGA-based SPHINCS$^+$ implementations: mind the glitch. In: 2020 23rd Euromicro Conference on Digital System Design (DSD), pp. 229–237 (2020)

[ANS22] ANSSI: ANSSI views on the Post-Quantum Cryptography transition (2022). https://www.ssi.gouv.fr/en/publication/anssi-views-on-the-post-quantum-cryptography-transition/

[Aum19] Aumasson, J.-P.: Too much crypto (2019). https://eprint.iacr.org/2019/1492.pdf

[Ban] Ban, T.: HW Fault Injection Mitigation - Trusted Firmware M. https://www.trustedfirmware.org/docs/TF-M_fault_injection_mitigation.pdf

[BDE+11] Buchmann, J., Dahmen, E., Ereth, S., Hülsing, A., Rückert, M.: On the security of the Winternitz one-time signature scheme. Cryptology ePrint Archive, Paper 2011/191 (2011). https://eprint.iacr.org/2011/191

[BDK+] Buchmann, J., Dahmen, E., Klintsevich, E., Okeya, K., Vuillaume, C.: Merkle signatures with virtually unlimited signature capacity. In: Katz, J., Yung, M. (eds.) ACNS 2007. LNCS, vol. 4521, pp. 31–45. Springer, Heidelberg (2007). https://doi.org/10.1007/978-3-540-72738-5_3

[BFP19] Bozzato, C., Focardi, R., Palmarini, F.: Shaping the glitch: optimizing voltage fault injection attacks. IACR Trans. Cryptogr. Hardw. Embed. Syst. **2019**(2), 199–224 (2019)

[BHRVV] Bos, J.W., Hülsing, A., Renes, J., Van Vredendaal, C.: Rapidly verifiable XMSS signatures, pp. 137–168 (2021)

[Bit22] Bitmain Antminer S19 XP (140Th) profitability (2022). https://www.asicminervalue.com/miners/bitmain/antminer-s19-xp-140th

[Bro] Brown, D.: Post-quantum cryptography. https://github.com/mcu-tools/mcuboot/discussions/1099?sort=top

[BSI22] BSI: BSI - Technische Richtlinie: Kryptographische Verfahren: Empfehlungen und Schluessellaengen (2022). https://www.bsi.bund.de/SharedDocs/Downloads/DE/BSI/Publikationen/TechnischeRichtlinien/TR02102/BSI-TR-02102.pdf?__blob=publicationFile

[CAD+] Cooper, D.A., Apon, D.C., Dang, Q.H., Davidson, M.S., Dworkin, M.J., Miller, C.A.: Recommendation for stateful hash-based signature schemes (2020)

[Cis19] Cisco: Post quantum trust anchors (2019). https://www.cisco.com/c/dam/en_us/about/doing_business/trust-center/docs/post-quantum-trust-anchors-wp.pdf

[CMP18] Castelnovi, L., Martinelli, A., Prest, T.: Grafting trees: a fault attack against the SPHINCS framework. In: Lange, T., Steinwandt, R. (eds.) PQCrypto 2018. LNCS, vol. 10786, pp. 165–184. Springer, Cham (2018). https://doi.org/10.1007/978-3-319-79063-3_8

[Cro20] Croley, S.: Hashcat v6.1.1 benchmark on the Nvidia RTX 3090 (2020). https://gist.github.com/Chick3nman/32e662a5bb63bc4f51b847bb42222 2fd

[Cro22] Croley, S.: Hashcat v6.2.6 benchmark on the Nvidia RTX 4090 (2022). https://gist.github.com/Chick3nman/32e662a5bb63bc4f51b847bb42222 2fd

[FKK+22] Fahr, M., et al.: When Frodo Flips: end-to-end key recovery on FrodoKEM via Rowhammer. In: Proceedings of the 2022 ACM SIGSAC Conference on Computer and Communications Security, Los Angeles, CA, USA, November 2022, pp. 979–993. ACM (2022)

[GBH18] Groot Bruinderink, L., Hülsing, A.: "Oops, i did it again" – security of one-time signatures under two-message attacks. In: Adams, C., Camenisch, J. (eds.) SAC 2017. LNCS, vol. 10719, pp. 299–322. Springer, Cham (2018). https://doi.org/10.1007/978-3-319-72565-9_15

[gen20] IT Security Solutions From Genua Withstand Attacks With Quantum Computers (2020). https://www.genua.eu/knowledge-base/it-security-solutions-from-genua-withstand-attacks-with-quantum-computers

[Gen23] Genêt, A.: On protecting SPHINCS+ against fault attacks. IACR Trans. Cryptogr. Hardw. Embed. Syst. 80–114 (2023)

[GKPM18] Genêt, A., Kannwischer, M.J., Pelletier, H., McLauchlan, A.: Practical fault injection attacks on SPHINCS (2018). https://eprint.iacr.org/2018/674

[goo] https://groups.google.com/a/list.nist.gov/g/pqc-forum/c/LUczQNCw7HA/m/f50WvA3RBAAJ

[GTSC] Gratchoff, J., Timmers, N., Spruyt, A., Chmielewski, L.: Proving the wild jungle jump. Technical report, University of Amsterdam (2015)

[HBD+20] Hülsing, A., et al.: SPHINCS+ - submission to the NIST post-quantum project, vol. 3 (2020). https://csrc.nist.gov/projects/post-quantum-cryptography/round-3-submissions

[HBG+18] Huelsing, A., Butin, D., Gazdag, S., Rijneveld, J., Mohaisen, A.: XMSS: eXtended Merkle signature scheme (2018). https://datatracker.ietf.org/doc/html/rfc8391

[HGA+21] Hauschild, F., Garb, K., Auer, L., Selmke, B., Obermaier, J.: ARCHIE: A QEMU-Based framework for architecture-independent evaluation of faults. In: 2021 Workshop on Fault Detection and Tolerance in Cryptography (FDTC), pp. 20–30 (2021)

[HK22] Hülsing, A., Kudinov, M.: Recovering the tight security proof of $SPHINCS^+$. Cryptology ePrint Archive, Paper 2022/346 (2022). https://eprint.iacr.org/2022/346

[HMU+20] Heyszl, J., et al.: Investigating profiled side-channel attacks against the DES key schedule. IACR Trans. Cryptogr. Hardw. Embed. Syst. **2020**(3), 22–72 (2020)

[Hü] Hülsing, A.: W-OTS+ – shorter signatures for hash-based signature schemes. In: Youssef, A., Nitaj, A., Hassanien, A.E. (eds.) AFRICACRYPT 2013. LNCS, vol. 7918, pp. 173–188. Springer, Heidelberg (2013). https://doi.org/10.1007/978-3-642-38553-7_10

[KGC+20] Kumar, V.B.Y., Gupta, N., Chattopadhyay, A., Kasper, M., Krauß, C., Niederhagen, R.: Post-quantum secure boot. In: 2020 Design, Automation Test in Europe Conference Exhibition (DATE), pp. 1582–1585 (2020)

[KHRY22] Kudinov, M., Hülsing, A., Ronen, E., Yogev, E.: SPHINCS+C: compressing SPHINCS+ with (almost) no cost. Cryptology ePrint Archive, Paper 2022/778 (2022). https://eprint.iacr.org/2022/778

[KPC+] Kampanakis, P., Panburana, P., Curcio, M., Shroff, C., Alam, M.: Post-quantum LMS and SPHINCS+ hash-based signatures for UEFI secure boot, p. 22 (2021)

[MAA+] Moody, D., et al.: Status report on the third round of the NIST post-quantum cryptography standardization process (2022)

[mcu] MCUboot documentation. https://docs.mcuboot.com/

[Mer90] Merkle, R.C.: A certified digital signature. In: Brassard, G. (ed.) CRYPTO 1989. LNCS, vol. 435, pp. 218–238. Springer, New York (1990). https://doi.org/10.1007/0-387-34805-0_21

[MMC19] McGrew, D., Fluhrer, S., Curcio, M.: Leighton-Micali hash-based signatures (2019). https://datatracker.ietf.org/doc/html/rfc8554

[O'F19] O'Flynn, C.: MIN()imum failure: EMFI attacks against USB stacks. In: 13th USENIX Workshop on Offensive Technologies (WOOT 2019), Santa Clara, CA, August 2019. USENIX Association (2019)

[OSS17] Obermaier, J., Specht, R., Sigl, G.: Fuzzy-glitch: a practical ring oscillator based clock glitch attack. In: 2017 International Conference on Applied Electronics (AE), pp. 1–6 (2017)

[Phi22] Philipoom, J.: Request for feedback on possible SPHINCS+ variant (2022). https://groups.google.com/a/list.nist.gov/g/pqc-forum/c/LUczQNCw7HA/m/f50WvA3RBAAJ

[Rai22] Raimbault, G.: Welcome to a new generation of future-proof TPMs: OPTIGA TPM SLB 9672 (2022). https://www.infineon.com/dgdl/Infineon-OPTIGA-TPM-SLB9672.pdf?fileId=8ac78c8b7e7122d1017f071c3f6b00d2

[Rot19] Roth, T.: TrustZone-M(eh): Breaking ARMv8-M's security (2019)

[Son19] Sondero: Hashcat v5.1.0 benchmark on the Intel(R) Core(TM) i7-9700K (2019). https://hashcat.net/forum/thread-9042-post-47927.html#pid47927

[SZK+18] Selmke, B., Zinnecker, K., Koppermann, P., Miller, K., Heyszl, J., Sigl, G.: Locked out by latch-up? An empirical study on laser fault injection into Arm Cortex-M processors. In: 2018 Workshop on Fault Diagnosis and Tolerance in Cryptography (FDTC), Amsterdam, Netherlands, September 2018, pp. 7–14. IEEE (2018)

[VCGS13] Veyrat-Charvillon, N., Gérard, B., Standaert, F.-X.: Security evaluations beyond computing power. In: Johansson, T., Nguyen, P.Q. (eds.) EURO-CRYPT 2013. LNCS, vol. 7881, pp. 126–141. Springer, Heidelberg (2013). https://doi.org/10.1007/978-3-642-38348-9_8

[WJW+] Wang, W., Jungk, B., Wälde, J., Deng, S., Gupta, N., Szefer, J., Nieder-hagen, R.: XMSS and embedded systems. In: Paterson, K.G., Stebila, D. (eds.) SAC 2019. LNCS, vol. 11959, pp. 523–550. Springer, Cham (2020). https://doi.org/10.1007/978-3-030-38471-5_21

[WOS22] Wagner, A., Oberhansl, F., Schink, M.: To be, or not to be stateful: post-quantum secure boot using hash-based signatures. In: Proceedings of the 2022 Workshop on Attacks and Solutions in Hardware Security, ASHES 2022, pp. 85–94. Association for Computing Machinery, New York (2022)

Breaking and Protecting the Crystal: Side-Channel Analysis of Dilithium in Hardware

Hauke Steffen[1] , Georg Land[2(✉)] , Lucie Kogelheide[3(✉)] ,
and Tim Güneysu[2,4]

[1] TÜV Informationstechnik GmbH, Essen, Germany
h.steffen@tuvit.de
[2] Horst Görtz Institute for IT Security, Ruhr University Bochum, Bochum, Germany
mail@georg.land, tim.gueneysu@rub.de
[3] BWI GmbH, Bonn, Germany
lucie.kogelheide@bwi.de
[4] DFKI GmbH, Cyber-Physical Systems, Bremen, Germany

Abstract. The lattice-based CRYSTALS-Dilithium signature scheme
has been selected for standardization by the NIST. As part of the selection process, a large number of implementations for platforms like x86,
ARM Cortex-M4, or – on the hardware side – Xilinx Artix-7 have been
presented and discussed by experts. While software implementations
have been subject to side-channel analysis with several attacks being
published, an analysis of Dilithium hardware implementations and their
peculiarities has not taken place. With this work, we aim to fill this gap,
presenting an analysis of vulnerable operations and practically showing a
successful profiled Simple Power Analysis (SPA) and a Correlation Power
Analysis (CPA) on a recent hardware implementation by Beckwith et al.
Our SPA attack requires 700 000 profiling traces and targets the first
Number-Theoretic Transform (NTT) stage. After finishing profiling, we
can identify pairs of coefficients with 1 101 traces. The full CPA attack
finds secret coefficients with as low as 66 000 traces. In response, we
present specific countermeasures and show that they effectively prevent
both attacks.

Keywords: Dilithium · Side-Channel Analysis · FPGA · SPA · CPA ·
PQC

1 Introduction

Quantum computers pose a real threat to communication security. Currently
deployed symmetric schemes can be adapted easily to withstand attacks even
from large-scale quantum computers. In contrast, asymmetric schemes like RSA
and ECC-based schemes can be broken without significant effort through Shor's

L. Kogelheide—The respective work has been conducted as an employee of TÜV Informationstechnik GmbH.

T. Johansson and D. Smith-Tone (Eds.): PQCrypto 2023, LNCS 14154, pp. 688–711, 2023.
https://doi.org/10.1007/978-3-031-40003-2_25

algorithms [25]. Although it is not yet clear whether this threat will become a reality in the near future, it is undisputed that action needs to be taken early to prevent prospective damage. Therefore, the United States National Institute for Standards and Technology (NIST) launched standardization efforts for post-quantum secure schemes for Key Encapsulation Mechanisms (KEMs) and digital signatures in 2017.

After three rounds, with several schemes being dropped due to cryptanalytic attacks, lacking efficiency, or missing confidence in their security assumptions, NIST announced the schemes to be standardized in July 2022. As KEM, Kyber has been selected, while four other schemes proceed to a fourth round and are considered for standardization in the future. For signature schemes, Dilithium, Falcon, and SPHINCS+ are being standardized, with Dilithium being the primary choice.

Dilithium has undergone a thorough cryptanalytic process and guarantees security against Strong Existential Unforgeability under Chosen Message Attacks (SUF-CMA). Besides, concrete implementations can be attacked by employing side-channel analysis, exploiting dependencies of physical characteristics on secret values during computation. Several side-channel analyses have been published on Dilithium software implementations in this context. In [22], Ravi et al. show a signature forgery attack enabled by finding a partial secret key using a power analysis. This work is extended to fault attacks on pqm4 implementations of Dilithium and qTesla [23], also presenting a mitigation approach. Migliore et al. carry out a side-channel evaluation targeting the ARM Cortex-M4 platform [21]. They are also the first to introduce concrete masking countermeasures. Following this, Chen et al. present an efficient CPA attack on the Dilithium pqm4 software implementation [9], succeeding with only 157 power measurements. Karabulut et al. show that sampling of fixed-weight polynomials in Dilithium, NTRU, and NTRU Prime is vulnerable to side-channel analysis [16]. Finally, Marzougui et al. present a novel side-channel attack that exploits a vulnerability in a sampling procedure [20]. However, their attack requires many measurements and complex post-processing. Finally, a recent work by Azouaoui et al. [1] presents a thorough analysis of side-channel requirements for Dilithium, including state-of-the-art countermeasures.

All these works have in common that they target *software* platforms. At the same time, there is *no* dedicated side-channel analysis targeting hardware implementations, which is a glaring lack in light of Dilithium already being chosen for standardization. Our work aims to close this gap by analyzing a recent Field-Programmable Gate Array (FPGA) implementation, presenting a profiled SPA and a CPA attack. Additionally, we investigate and implement countermeasures, evaluating their efficacy against the before-proposed attacks.

Contribution. Hence, our contribution can be summarized as follows:

- We present the first power side-channel results of a Dilithium implementation in reconfigurable hardware.
- We show several profiled SPA attacks on Dilithium-2 and -5, including:

- an evaluation of single-trace attacks on the decoding and the first NTT stage, with up to 94.2% success probability to recover the correct coefficient.
- multi-trace attacks on decoding with 50 000 profiling traces, capable of recovering the target coefficient with 130 traces during attack phase.
- multi-trace attacks on first NTT stage with 350 000 profiling traces that enable full key recovery with a pair of target coefficients using 1 101 traces.
– We also show a CPA on the polynomial multiplication, recovering secret coefficients with 66 000 traces, which are agnostic to the parameter set and enable full key recovery.
– We present an analysis of how to apply masking as a countermeasure by proposing arithmetic masking, effectively prohibiting the presented attacks.

2   Preliminaries

2.1   Notation

Throughout this work, we will use and assume the following notation. Let n and q be two integers, such that $n = 256$ and $q = 2^{23} - 2^{13} + 1$. Further, let $\mathcal{R}_q$ be a polynomial ring with $\mathcal{R}_q = \mathbb{Z}_q[X]/(X^n + 1)$. The infinity norm $||x||_\infty$ of a polynomial x is defined as the maximum absolute value among all its coefficients. For polynomial vectors, this norm is defined as the maximum infinity norm of all polynomials in the vector. Then, S_b denotes the set of polynomials in $\mathcal{R}_q$ with infinity norm b and $\tilde{S}_b$ denotes the same set but excluding coefficients with value $-b$. Furthermore, the set of polynomials in $\mathcal{R}_q$ with exactly τ non-zero coefficients and infinity norm 1 is denoted as B_τ. In addition, let us denote vectors in bold lower-case letters, e.g., $\mathbf{v}$, while matrices are denoted in bold upper-case letters, e.g., $\mathbf{A}$. Polynomials in NTT domain are indicated by a hat, e.g., $\hat{c}$. This is also used transitively; thus, $\hat{\mathbf{A}}$ denotes that each polynomial in $\mathbf{A}$ is transformed to NTT domain individually. Finally, we denote the pointwise multiplication with $\circ$.

2.2   CRYSTALS-Dilithium

As common for digital signature schemes, Dilithium provides the three core procedures for *key generation*, *signature generation*, and *signature verification*. In the following, we briefly explain the key generation and signing and leave a fully detailed description of the scheme to the official documentation [11].

Key Generation. Algorithm 1 shows the key generation of Dilithium. As can be seen there, finding the secret key from knowing the public key is basically the M-LWE problem. Moreover, once an attacker obtains either $\mathbf{s}_1$ or $\mathbf{s}_2$, she can directly obtain the other value since $\mathbf{A}$ and $\mathbf{t}$ are public values. However, Dilithium makes an interesting modification in moving the lower d bits of each coefficient in $\mathbf{t}$ to the secret key in order to reduce the public key size, which is what the function Power2Round does. Still, the polynomial vector $\mathbf{t}_0$, which contains these lower bits, is considered public information.

Algorithm 1. Dilithium key generation

1: $\zeta \leftarrow \{0,1\}^{256}$
2: $(\rho, \rho', K) \in \{0,1\}^{256} \times \{0,1\}^{512} \times \{0,1\}^{256} := \text{SHAKE-256}(\zeta)$
3: sample $\mathbf{A} \in \mathcal{R}_q^{k \times \ell}$ deterministically in NTT domain from the output stream of SHAKE-128(ρ)
4: sample $(\mathbf{s}_1, \mathbf{s}_2) \in S_\eta^\ell \times S_\eta^k$ from the output stream of SHAKE-256(ρ')
5: $\mathbf{t} := \mathbf{As}_1 + \mathbf{s}_2$
6: $(\mathbf{t}_1, \mathbf{t}_0) := \text{Power2Round}_q(\mathbf{t}, d)$
7: $tr \in \{0,1\}^{256} := \text{SHAKE-256}(\rho \| \mathbf{t}_1)$
8: **return** $(pk = (\rho, \mathbf{t}_1), sk = (\rho, K, tr, \mathbf{s}_1, \mathbf{s}_2, \mathbf{t}_0))$

Algorithm 2. Dilithium signature generation

Require: secret key sk, message M
1: $\kappa := 0$, sample $\mathbf{A}$ as in key generation
2: $\mu \in \{0,1\}^{512} := \text{SHAKE-256}(tr \| M)$
3: $\rho' \in \{0,1\}^{512} := \text{SHAKE-256}(K \| \mu)$ for deterministic signing
   $\rho' \leftarrow \{0,1\}^{512}$ for randomized signing
4: **while** true **do**
5:     sample $\mathbf{y} \in \tilde{S}_{\gamma_1}^\ell$ deterministically based on ρ', κ
6:     $\mathbf{w} := \mathbf{Ay}$
7:     $\mathbf{w}_1 := \text{HighBits}_q(\mathbf{w}, 2\gamma_2)$
8:     $\tilde{c} \in \{0,1\}^{256} := \text{SHAKE-256}(\mu \| \mathbf{w}_1)$
9:     $c \in B_\tau := \text{SampleInBall}(\tilde{c})$
10:    $\mathbf{z} := \mathbf{y} + c\mathbf{s}_1$
11:    $\mathbf{r}_0 := \text{LowBits}_q(\mathbf{w} - c\mathbf{s}_2, 2\gamma_2)$
12:    **if** $\|\mathbf{z}\|_\infty < \gamma_1 - \beta$ **and** $\|\mathbf{r}_0\|_\infty < \gamma_2 - \beta$ **then**
13:        $\mathbf{h} := \text{MakeHint}_q(-c\mathbf{t}_0, \mathbf{w} - c\mathbf{s}_2 + c\mathbf{t}_0, 2\gamma_2)$
14:        **if** $\|c\mathbf{t}_0\|_\infty < \gamma_2$ **and** the # of 1's in $\mathbf{h}$ is less than or equal to ω **then**
15:            **return** $(\mathbf{z}, \mathbf{h}, \tilde{c})$
16:    $\kappa := \kappa + \ell$

Signature Generation. Algorithm 2 describes the signature generation for a given message and secret key. Most notably, there is a big rejection loop that only terminates if the signature is approved not to leak any information on the secret key, which is ensured by the checks starting in Line 13. Inside the loop, the signing algorithm chooses a masking polynomial vector $\mathbf{y}$ with coefficients from $[-\gamma_1, \gamma_1)$, computes $\mathbf{w} = \mathbf{Ay}$, and rounds each coefficient of the resulting polynomial vector according to the HighBits_q function. From this and the message, the challenge polynomial c is sampled, which has precisely τ non-zero coefficients, which are either 1 or -1. Then, a signature candidate $\mathbf{z}$ is computed as $\mathbf{y} + c\mathbf{s}_1$. Following this, it is checked whether the broad "noise" generated by $\mathbf{y}$ actually hides $c\mathbf{s}_1$. Finally, using the MakeHint_q function, the signing algorithm generates "hints" for the verifier to compensate for the missing lower bits of $\mathbf{t}_0$. Note that all polynomial multiplications are performed using the NTT for efficiency.

Parameters. For Dilithium, three parameter sets are proposed, which aim at the NIST security categories 2, 3, and 5. The security is scaled primarily via increasing the matrix and vector dimensions (k, ℓ), which are $(4, 4)$ for level 2, $(6, 5)$ for level 3, and $(8, 7)$ for level 5. Another relevant parameter that changes over the parameter sets is the secret key range η, which is 2 for levels 2 and 5, and 4 for level 3.

2.3   Side-Channel Analysis

The field of side-channel analysis has been established with Kocher's seminal work [17] on timing side-channels. In the following, we briefly explain the two relevant approaches for our work.

Simple Power Analysis. This technique aims to analyze power traces directly to learn operations that have been executed and processed secrets. In the best case, a single measurement is sufficient to completely recover the key. The most important extension of SPA is *profiled* or template SPA. Here, the attack is performed in two phases. In the *profiling phase*, the attacker measures the target device performing several operations with known or chosen secret input, obtaining information about the device's behavior depending on the input. In the *attack phase*, she uses the knowledge from the first phase to recover the secret by measuring the target device performing the operation with secret input.

This requires an extension of the attacker model. When introducing profiling, the attacker must now have extended access to the target device, knowing or even being able to choose several usually secret inputs. She may use one or multiple traces in the attack phase, resulting in *single-trace* or *multi-trace* attacks.

Finding Points of Interest. To determine Points of Interest (POIs) that correspond to differences between the observed classes, we use the sum of squared pairwise t-differences (SOST) as the metric, which has been introduced in [13]. The idea is to measure many traces for each class, then compute the t-test traces between any possible pair of classes, square them point-wise, and accumulate the results. We then consider points if their SOST exceeds an adaptively chosen threshold based on the overall noise level.

Matching Power Traces to a Template. To match new traces to the prepared templates, we follow the approach first introduced in [8]. A template for a single class consists of a mean trace and the pooled noise covariance matrix (for a comprehensive definition, we refer to [10]). In the attack phase, when measuring a power trace, we compute the probability of matching each template using the probability density function of the multivariate normal distribution.

Updating the Ranking for Multi-trace Attacks. Starting with one trace, we obtain probabilities for matching each class, as explained before. Subsequently, we analogously compute the probabilities for the following trace and update the classification probabilities according to Bayes' theorem.

Correlation Power Analysis. CPA [5] has a very different concept, as the attacker obtains many power measurements here. The idea then is to test all possible hypotheses for a part of a key (e.g., a single coefficient) by correlating a power model of an intermediate value that depends on the targeted key part with the power traces. For this, the attacker either must be able to choose or at least know the public input, which is in contrast to the profiled SPA, where she also is required to know or choose *secret* inputs in the first phase. In our case, for a digital signature scheme, the model is either the known or chosen message attacker for the CPA.

Finally, the hypothesis with the highest absolute correlation coefficient is identified as the correct key part. For this, Pearson's correlation is used, i.e., the covariance of power model output and sample value normalized over the product of the standard deviations of each of the two. As significance bound, we use $\sqrt{28/N}$, where N is the number of processed traces [19].

Countermeasures. Many countermeasures have been proposed to mitigate side-channel attacks. The straightforward idea is to purposefully decrease the target devices' signal-to-noise ratio (SNR) (where the signal is the leaking information). For instance, this can be achieved by noise generators that run in parallel to sensitive operations [15]. However, this usually aims to increase the number of measurements required for an attack.

If the algorithm whose implementation is to be secured allows re-ordering of operations, *shuffling* [26] can be an option to counter single-trace SPA. By this, the attacker may be able to recover the secret value but not its position within the complete secret. For a CPA, shuffling only decreases the SNR because a certain fraction of the measurements will have the operation that leaks the secret aligned, with all other measurements being noise concerning the attack.

Thus, *masking* has been introduced [7,14] to counter this attack as well, which has its foundations in Shamir's secret sharing. Here, a secret value x is split into multiple uniform random shares. Regarding PQC, the two most common masking schemes are *Boolean* and *additive* masking, splitting secrets either in Boolean or additive shares. In order to process secret data, any linear function in the masking domain can be performed share-wise. Non-linear functions have a higher complexity growth and usually require refreshing the mask(s) during intermediate steps.

Consequently, the CPA attacker does not obtain any information about the secret, as only uniform random values are processed. This, of course, is only true if the attacker is restricted to only one probe. Once she can probe both shares, she can perform the same attack again. It follows that the masking degree is always chosen according to a given attacker model.

3   Conceptual Considerations

The first reported implementation of the current specification was presented by Land et al. [18]. This implementation heavily depends on Digital Signal Processors (DSPs) that speed up the NTT significantly. However, it is relatively slow and big compared to newer implementations. Instead, we target the state-of-the-art implementation by Beckwith et al. [4]. We are aware of the more recent work by Zhao et al. [27], which was unavailable at the start of our work. However, since the operations we exploit are rather algorithmic-specific, we expect broad applicability of our techniques. In the following, we explain and analyze several operations within the target implementation.

3.1 Bit-Packing and Decoding of Secret Polynomials s_1, s_2

In general, the specification describes encoding as follows: An integer $x \in [-\eta, \eta]$ is packed as $\eta - x$ such that the encoded value is non-negative. Particularly, $\eta = 2$ for Dilithium security levels 2 and 5, and $\eta = 4$ for security level 3. Five consecutive resulting three-bit values are packed to three bytes for all parameter sets. In our target implementation, chunks of 64 bits are processed rather than single coefficients, which is implemented with a FIFO, and then four coefficients are decoded in parallel.

Since the implementation uses an unsigned representation, the decoding operation (a subtraction) is modulo q. Thus, the decoded values are either close to zero or close to q. This results in vastly different HWs for the cases depicted in Table 1. As can be seen there, the particular value $q = 2^{23} - 2^{13} + 1$ additionally enables a clear distinction between the low-HW outputs, $q - 2$, and the high-HW outputs. We expect that the significant differences in the HW to lead to a distinguishable amount of power consumption, enabling SPA attacks.

3.2 Number-Theoretic Transform

After unpacking the secret polynomials in s_1 and s_2, they are transformed into NTT representation. The NTT, as used in Dilithium, can be seen as a discrete Fourier transform over polynomials in $\mathcal{R}_q$, where modular arithmetic of the

Table 1. Hamming weight (HW) differences of decoded coefficients in s_1 and s_2

(a) $\eta = 2$			(b) $\eta = 2$		
in	out $= \eta -$ in mod q	HW(out)	in	out $= \eta -$ in mod q	HW(out)
0	0x000002	1	0	0x000004	1
1	0x000001	1	1	0x000003	2
2	0x000000	0	2	0x000002	1
3	0x7fe000	10	3	0x000001	1
4	0x7fdfff	22	4	0x000000	0
			5	0x7fe000	10
			6	0x7fdfff	22
			7	0x7fdffe	21
			8	0x7fdffd	21

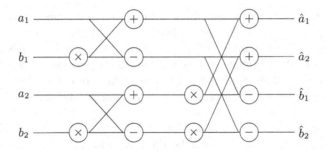

Fig. 1. 2 × 2 BFU construction

polynomial coefficients replaces the complex arithmetic. Since the ring structure enables negative wrapped convolution, we can use an n-point NTT for fast polynomial multiplication. For this, we transform both factor polynomials to the NTT domain, multiply coefficient-wise in the NTT domain, and then apply the inverse transform to the result to obtain the final product polynomial.

The core operation of the NTT is the so-called butterfly. Generally, the NTT is easily parallelizable and thus, it is possible to make a design choice of how many butterflies to instantiate. For the given $n = 256$, eight NTT layers must be processed. However, in the targeted implementation, a 2 × 2-Butterfly Unit (BFU) is deployed, which means that four butterflies are instantiated in a way that four input coefficients are processed first through two butterflies and then through the two others in order to perform two layers of NTT consecutively. This is depicted in Fig. 1. In the following, we refer to this as one stage of the NTT.

Note that for the butterfly, each output depends on all input values. Moreover, a_1 is spread without multiplication, b_1 is processed through one multiplication, a_2 through two multiplications, and b_2 through three. As the multiplications are with primitive roots of unity, which range over the whole $\mathbb{Z}_q$, intermediate values seem to be distributed uniformly in $\mathbb{Z}_q$ regardless of the input distribution. However, for s_1 and s_2 the input space to the first layer is bounded by η, which implicitly bounds the set of possible intermediate results and outputs of the BFU. We expect that this results in more distinguishable power signatures, facilitating more powerful SPA attacks.

3.3 Polynomial Multiplication

In Algorithm 2, we see that the secrets s_1 and s_2 are multiplied with the challenge polynomial c. If the signature candidate is accepted, the hash $\tilde{c}$ that is used to generate the challenge deterministically is part of the signature and thus publicly known. Besides, $\tilde{c}$ is the hash of μ, which directly depends on the message M, and w_1. Therefore, for the deterministic signing procedure, c deterministically depends on the message. On the other hand, if randomized signing is deployed

– introduced initially to counter fault attacks – c is also randomized even for a fixed message M through the randomization of $\mathbf{y}$, which is used to compute $\mathbf{w_1}$.

Moreover, the polynomial multiplications are performed in the NTT domain, which is essentially a coefficient-wise modular multiplication between $\hat{c}$ and the vectors $\hat{s}_1$ and $\hat{s}_2$. This renders the aforementioned polynomial multiplications a natural target for a CPA attack since we can target the polynomial vector $\hat{s}_1$ coefficient by coefficient.

The advantage of such an attack would be its weak attacker model. For the deterministic case, messages must be distinct, while for the randomized case there is no restriction on the messages. In both cases, though, the attacker must be able to trigger enough signings under the same secret key.

3.4 Measurement Setup

We perform all our attacks on a Xilinx Artix-7 100T FPGA – the hardware platform recommended by NIST for comparison of hardware implementations – running at 100 MHz. We measured the power consumption via peripheral components. Using an electromagnetic (EM) near-field probe, we measure the electromagnetic field of a capacitor on the board with a particularly low capacity of 47 nF. Since this capacitor is placed very close to the FPGA and in its power path, the capacitor's electromagnetic emanation directly depends on the power consumption of the FPGA. The advantage of this procedure is that no physical modifications are required on the target board. All measurements have been performed with 20 GS/s and a quantization of 12bit.

4 Simple Power Analysis

In the following, we focus on the case $\eta = 2$ (Dilithium-2 and -5), which is more promising. Still, we evaluate and discuss the case $\eta = 4$ (Dilithium-3) at the end of this section.

4.1 Targeting Single Coefficients

As a first step towards a practical attack, we target single coefficients. We start by applying an attacker model, in which three out of the four secret coefficients decoded simultaneously are known, and the other one is attempted to recover. In practice this means that during the profiling phase, the attacker builds the templates knowing the three other secret coefficients. This results in less noise compared to the more realistic scenario in which the attacker does not know the other coefficients and thus would choose them randomly.

Interestingly, our countermeasures work also against this attacker. This results in an extended efficacy guarantee by deducting that the countermeasures effectively hinder *any weaker* SPA attacker, i.e., also the attacker that does not know the other three coefficients.

Attacking the Decoding Step. For this, we measure 55 000 traces, using a secret key as input fixed for all coefficients but one chosen randomly. We divide this trace set into the profiling set of 50 000 traces and the attack set of 5 000 traces. Subsequently, we prepare templates for three different attacks:

1. Five classes, aiming for the classification of the exact coefficient value
2. Four classes, aiming to distinguish between input classes
    - 0, 1 (yielding output HW 1)
    - 2 (yielding output HW 0)
    - 3 (yielding output HW 10)
    - 4 (yielding output HW 22)
3. Three classes, aiming to distinguish between input classes
    - 0, 1, 2 (yielding output HW 1 or 0)
    - 3 (yielding output HW 10)
    - 4 (yielding output HW 22)

Finally, we perform the three attacks on each subset of the attack set with the same key, obtaining the single-trace success probabilities.

As can be seen in Table 2, the results match the expectations, and classification works best for the case where three classes each internally have a very similar HW, recovering with high probability whether the targeted output is 4 or 3 or a member of the set $\{0, 1, 2\}$. Nevertheless, the classification model with the worst results, which is finding the exact coefficient value, also classifies each class correctly with a significantly higher probability than guessing, which would be 20%.

When extending this attack to the multi-trace setting, the picture changes drastically. After at most 130 traces only, we can recover the correct coefficient for all classes.

Attacking the First NTT Layer. As explained before in Sect. 3.2, the four input coefficients to the BFU propagate differently as a_1 is only added or subtracted, while the others are also multiplied. We expect to classify coefficients for attacking this first NTT stage better than for targeting the decoding. That is because a small set of potential inputs is multiplied and reduced with the same constants, which results in a more diversified power signature and thus can be classified easier.

Table 2. Success rates of single-trace SPA on the decoder

Class					Avg.
0	1	2	3	4	
48.8%	34.7%	49.5%	80.4%	99.4%	64.1%
64.6%		57.7%	86.0%	99.3%	74.4%
92.9%			88.1%	99.4%	93.2%

Table 3. Success rates for attacking the first NTT stage in the single- and multi-trace setting for $\eta = 2$ and $\eta = 4$

Target	$\eta = 2$							$\eta = 4$	
	Class					Avg.	Multi-t.: # Traces	Avg.	Multi-t.: # Traces
	0	1	2	3	4				
a_1	60.1%	59.1%	92.2%	89.6%	97.8%	79.8%	34	57.3%	87
b_1	89.1%	88.4%	100.0%	89.3%	92.4%	91.8%	4	74.5%	10
a_2	83.5%	88.1%	93.8%	96.6%	100.0%	92.5%	4	84.0%	45
b_2	88.0%	90.2%	99.8%	94.6%	97.7%	94.2%	3	76.2%	23
Avg.	80.2%	81.5%	96.5%	92.5%	97.0%	89.6%		73.0%	

The results in the left part of Table 3 show that the expectations again are met. Overall, this attack yields better results for all classes, as now, we can recover single coefficients that are processed as b_1, a_2, b_2 with a probability of over 90%. In contrast, as expected, a_1 can be recovered with a lower probability.

Furthermore, Fig. 2 visualizes the results of the single-trace attacks. The confusion matrices depict the probabilities of assigning each class during the attack phase given each (known) correct class. There, the darkness of a square quantifies the probability that, given the correct class for a trace (y-axis), a specific class (x-axis) has been assigned by the attack. As shown in Fig. 2a, the attack on a_1 mainly confuses class 1 for class 0 with low probability while correctly classifying all other classes with high probability. Note that the diagonals in Fig. 2 represent the single rows in Table 3.

For the multi-trace setting, Table 3 also shows how many traces are required to recover the correct coefficient with 100% probability. This demonstrates the power of this attack, which requires at most 34 traces to recover any secret coefficient.

4.2 Extension to Multiple Coefficients

We extend our approach of targeting a single secret coefficient on the first NTT stage to attacking two coefficients simultaneously. A straightforward approach here would be to target all possible 5^4 combinations of (a_1, b_1, a_2, b_2). However, this would be a computationally very complex approach. Instead, we only target the first half of the BFU. The same operation is applied to the input tuples (a_1, b_1) and (a_2, b_2) independently. Thus, we can classify each possible input tuple by targeting $5 \times 5 = 25$ classes instead of 5^4. This comes at the cost of more profiling traces. Here, we require a profiling trace set with chosen secret coefficients, where (a_2, b_2) are kept steady for attacking (a_1, b_1) and vice versa. We increase the number of traces to 375 000 and divide them into 350 000 profiling traces and 25 000 attack traces to ensure the same number per class as for targeting single coefficients.

Figure 3b shows the confusion matrix of this attack. As can be seen there, this attack succeeds with a high probability of assigning the correct class (the

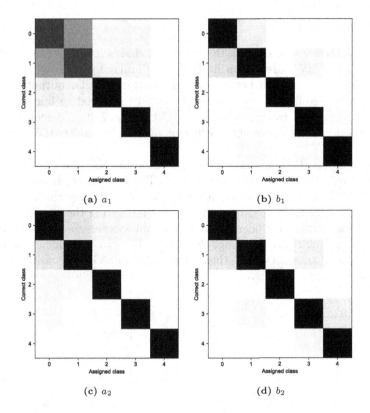

Fig. 2. Single-trace SPA confusion matrices for attacks on the first NTT stage with $\eta = 2$

diagonal) but also shows some symmetry for assigning wrong classes, primarily due to confusing (a_1, b_1) with (b_1, a_1). On average, the attack succeeds in classifying the correct tuple with a probability of 51.5%, vastly better than guessing, which would have a probability of 1/25. Moreover, in Fig. 3a, we see that the correct guess is within the top 5 with an overwhelming probability of 94.8%.

Ultimately, we have also performed this attack in the multi-trace setting. Here, we are able to recover the correct combination of both secret coefficients after 1 101 traces. Using this approach, an attacker in the profiled SPA setting is able to recover the full secret polynomials s_1 and s_2 with 700 000 profiling traces. In particular, the attacker would profile the device under test with 350 000 traces for all possible combinations of (a_1, b_1) and repeat the same for all possible combinations of (a_2, b_2). Then, according to our experiments, the device would be queried to perform 1 101 signing procedures (processing the secret key) and measure the first NTT stage of all secret polynomials either for s_1 or s_2 to recover it.

4.3   Attack on $\eta = 4$

For security level 3, where $\eta = 4$, the amount of classes increases from 5 to 9. The possible output HWs are shown in Table 1b. Similar to the results in Table 4, we can clearly distinguish between all groups with similar output HW when targeting the decoding. A multi-trace attack on the decoding finds the correct coefficient after 2 267 traces, compared to 130 for $\eta = 2$. This demonstrates that the increased number of possible coefficient values with similar HW downgrades the attack.

Targeting the BFU, we have performed experiments using 90 000 traces for profiling (i.e., 10 000 per class as for $\eta = 2$). The results are shown in the right part of Table 3. As expected and as it is the case for $\eta = 2$, the attack works better than those on the decoding, being capable of recovering the correct coefficient after one trace with a significantly higher probability than guessing, which would be $1/9$. In the multi-trace setting, classifying the correct coefficient is possible after at most 87 traces. Overall, the SPA on Dilithium-3 is less feasible compared to the other parameter sets.

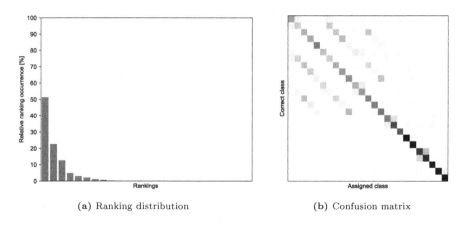

(a) Ranking distribution   (b) Confusion matrix

Fig. 3. Single-trace SPA results for NTT inputs a_1 and b_1.

Table 4. Success probabilities for single-trace SPA on the combined a_1, b_1.

		b_1				
		0	1	2	3	4
a_1	0	37.1%	25.8%	34.1%	35.6%	48.8%
	1	30.9%	27.2%	36.1%	40.2%	42.8%
	2	34.4%	39.4%	46.1%	46.9%	48.2%
	3	46.6%	60.2%	55.7%	73.3%	75.5%
	4	64.1%	66.9%	76.3%	78.5%	83.2%

5   Correlation Power Analysis on the Polynomial Multiplication

In addition to our SPA, we perform a CPA on the polynomial multiplication module, employing a weaker attacker model, as explained in Sect. 3.3.

For this attack, we observe many signature generations under the same secret key, and then, given the public challenge polynomial c, we target the pointwise multiplication $\hat{c} \circ \hat{s}_1$. In this attack, we cannot exploit that each coefficient of s_1 has a bounded norm since, during multiplication, the polynomial is processed in the NTT domain. Therefore, we have q hypotheses per coefficient in general.

5.1   Power Model

As a first approach, we chose to employ a HW model. As can be seen in Fig. 4, we show that the correct hypothesis reaches the first rank after 80 000 traces. However, there are also multiple wrong hypotheses exceeding the significance bound significantly.

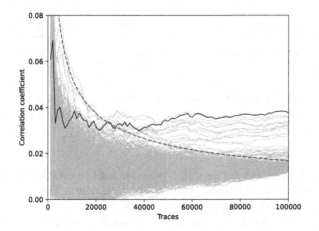

Fig. 4. CPA results – HW model, 1 000 most promising hypotheses shown, correct hypothesis in black, targeting $\hat{c} \circ \hat{t}_0$

Instead, we adapt an idea from [9, Sec. III.B], where a software implementation is attacked and the hypothesis space is reduced by using the correlation peak polarity as additional information. We identify that targeting the least significition bit (LSB) of the product between the challenge polynomial coefficient and the hypotheses yields better results (i.e., no wrong hypotheses exceeding the significance bound significantly). Moreover, this approach allows cutting the number of hypotheses in half, resulting in a computationally less complex attack. We observe that for each hypothesis $h \in \mathbb{Z}_q \backslash \{0\}$ and each challenge polynomial coefficient $\hat{c}_i \in \mathbb{Z}_q \backslash \{0\}$ of the challenge $\hat{c}$, the following equation holds:

$$\mathsf{lsb}(\hat{c}_i \cdot h \bmod q) = 1 \oplus \mathsf{lsb}(\hat{c}_i \cdot (-h) \bmod q) \tag{1}$$

It follows that for this power model, the hypotheses h and $-h \bmod q$ yield inverted correlations. This can be used to halve the number of possible hypotheses to the range $[0, \lfloor q/2 \rfloor]$ by the following procedure. Figure 5a shows the correlation of the LSB of the public coefficient $\hat{c}_i$ and the correlation with the LSB of the negative value. Note how there is first a positive peak and then a negative peak for the known $\hat{c}_i$. Correlations with other coefficients of the public polynomial c might also show an inverse peak polarity: first negative, then positive. In any case, the information of the correlation peak polarity is purely based on *public* information, and thus can be computed by the attacker in any case.

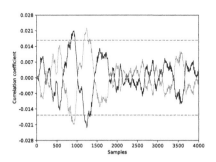
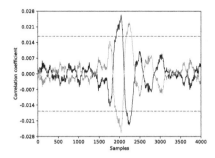

(a) Correlation of LSB of $\hat{c}_i$ (black) and $q - \hat{c}_i$ (gray)

(b) Correlation of LSB of $\hat{c}_i \cdot h \bmod q$ (black) and $\hat{c}_i \cdot (-h) \bmod q$ (gray)

Fig. 5. Correlation for 100 000 traces of the LSB of $\hat{c}_i$ and $\hat{c}_i \cdot h \bmod q$. For the highlighted (black) case, h is the correct hypothesis since both have a positive peak first, then a negative one.

Figure 5b then shows very similar behavior for the correlation of the LSB of $\hat{c}_i \cdot h \bmod q$ and $\hat{c}_i \cdot (-h) \bmod q$. Our observation now is that if the correlation peak polarity is the same for the power correlation of $\hat{c}_i$ and $\hat{c}_i \cdot h \bmod q$ (where h is the hypothesis that yields the highest absolute correlation), h is the correct hypothesis. Otherwise, if the peak polarity does not match, $q - h$ is the correct hypothesis.

Thus, the attacker only needs to compute the correlations for half the hypotheses and then, after finding a hypothesis h with maximum absolute correlation coefficient, decides between h and $q - h$ based on whether the respective $\hat{c}_i$ yields

1. a positive, then a negative correlation peak. Then, if h yields
   (a) a positive, then a negative correlation peak, h is the sought coefficient.
   (b) a negative, then a positive correlation peak, $q - h$ is the sought coefficient.
2. a negative, then a positive correlation peak. Then, if h yields
   (a) a positive, then a negative correlation peak, $q - h$ is the sought coefficient.
   (b) a negative, then a positive correlation peak, h is the sought coefficient.

5.2   Noise

In the targeted implementation, the Keccak core works during all multiplications that include s_1 or s_2. This core generates most of the design's power consumption. This causes the problem that a lower quantization precision is left for the targeted value since the Keccak power consumption is noise to it. Both issues lead to requiring an increased number of traces for an attack. Thus, we investigate the attack in two different scenarios:

1. Evaluate $\hat{c} \circ \hat{t}_0$, where no Keccak runs in parallel, and
2. Evaluate $\hat{c} \circ \hat{s}_1$.

Compared to the first scenario, the concurrently operating Keccak module reduces the SNR by a factor of 25.

   Therefore, the first scenario is a low-noise setting, and the second one is a high-noise setting, enabling a clear comparison between both. We expect that opening the FPGA packaging and probing the polynomial multiplication module locally using an EM near-field probe would result in a similar low-noise setting as for the first scenario.

5.3   Attacks

When targeting $\hat{c} \circ \hat{t}_0$, we are able to recover the correct coefficients of $\hat{t}_0$ after 66 000 traces, as can be seen in Fig. 6a. Moreover, after 22 000traces, the correct hypothesis is within the top 2048 candidates, and after 57 000traces, it is within the top 32 candidates.

   In Fig. 6b, it can be seen that the very same approach is becoming more difficult for attacking s_1 for the reasons mentioned above due to a decreased SNR. Still, after 1 million traces, we can recover the correct coefficient. For this attack, the correct hypothesis is in the top 2048 after 240 000 traces and the top 32 after 850 000 traces.

   In summary, it is possible to recover the secret in any case, even assuming a high-noise setting. Moreover, no invasive methods, such as opening the FPGA packaging, are required, which would be a much more specialized attack measuring the direct near-field EM emanation of the polynomial multiplication module. Finally, we want to stress that, contrary to the SPA, this attack works independently of η and thus is equally applicable to all security levels.

6   Countermeasures

6.1   Integration of Decoding into the First NTT Stage

Decoding the secrets s_1 and s_2 is an affine operation and thus can also be processed easily in a later phase of signature generation. Therefore, our first approach aims at removing the parts of the decoder unit that process the targeted secret coefficients and integrate the decoding step into the first level of the NTT.

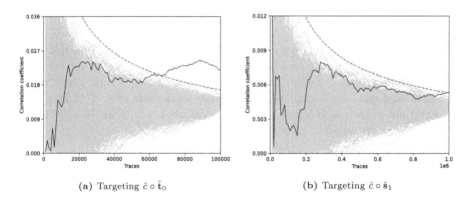

(a) Targeting $\hat{c} \circ \hat{t}_0$ (b) Targeting $\hat{c} \circ \hat{s}_1$

Fig. 6. CPA results – LSB model, 1 000 most promising hypotheses shown, correct hypothesis in black

As explained before, we assume that the leakage of the decoding mainly depends on the differences of the HWs of the decoded values. Therefore, keeping all processed coefficients at a similar level of HW would be advantageous. We integrate the decoding into the BFU by feeding $q + \eta - x$ into each BFU input, where x is an encoded coefficient.

6.2   Masking

Masking must be deployed to counter both attacks through a comprehensive countermeasure. A comprehensive masking approach, where secret data is never processed nor transferred unmasked, requires that the secret key is already masked in the first place. In particular, we have the option to either apply arithmetic or Boolean masking. Applying arithmetic masking on s_1 and s_2, however, is not possible *efficiently* as it would induce an unnecessary high overhead factor for storing the masked key, since the coefficients are uniformly bounded by η rather than uniform in $\mathbb{Z}_q$. Because memory is an expensive resource on embedded hardware devices and the masking shares pose an overhead already, a masking countermeasure that requires no additional overhead would be desirable.

Specifically, in a real-world device, the secret key usually would be stored in a permanent memory outside of the FPGA, which would then have to be dimensioned bigger by a factor of 23/3 to account for the larger shares, and the key transfer would take equivalently longer compared to Boolean masking. The problem intensifies when the system includes multiple keys. In this case, external memory is virtually inevitable. Moreover, a smaller arithmetic masking domain could also be used, but this would also require a similarly expensive masking conversion compared to our proposal. Thus, only Boolean masking is feasible, which raises the necessity of converting efficiently from the encoded, Boolean-masked representation of s_1 and s_2, to a decoded and arithmetically masked representation.

Algorithm 3. First-order secure combined masking conversion and decoding, adapted from [12, Alg. 12]

Require: b_0, b_1 such that $b = b_0 \oplus b_1$
Ensure: a_0, a_1 such that $a = a_0 + a_1 = \eta - b \bmod q$
1: $X, R \leftarrow \mathbb{Z}_q \times \mathbb{Z}_{2^{23}}$
2: $Y_0 := ((X - \eta) + (2^{23} - q)) \oplus R$
3: $Y_1 := R$
4: $Z_0, Z_1 \leftarrow \mathsf{SecAdd}_q((b_0, b_1), (Y_0, Y_1))$ $\triangleright$ instantiate with SecAdd_q from [12, Alg. 8]
5: **return** $a_0 = X, a_1 = q - (Z_0 \oplus Z_1)$

As already introduced in [3] and further developed in [12], an efficient conversion from Boolean to arithmetic masking modulo q can be performed using a secure adder over Boolean shares, which have been studied extensively in [2,24]. It is possible to adapt this procedure to integrate the decoding step into the masking conversion.

The original idea from [12] is to sample a uniform random $A \in \mathbb{Z}_q$, then generate a fresh Boolean sharing of $(q - A) + (2^{23} - q)$ and add this with a secure adder as described in [12, Alg. 8] to the masked input. Note that in order to enable an easy reduction modulo q, this secure adder has the special property to subtract an additional constant of $2^{23} - q$, which explains the uncommon form of the input. The unmasked result of this operation then is one arithmetic share, and A is the other.

Instead, to include the decoding into the masking conversion, we adapt this procedure as shown in Algorithm 3:

1. We need two statistically random integers for the conversion, as shown in Line 1.
2. We generate a fresh Boolean sharing of $(X - \eta) + (2^{23} - q)$ in Lines 2 and 3 using R and X. Note that this operation can also be done offline or – for hardware – in parallel.
3. In Line 4, the Boolean masked input coefficient is added to the constructed Boolean sharing using the aforementioned special adder [12, Alg. 8], yielding a Boolean sharing of $X - \eta + 2^{23} - q + b - (2^{23} - q) = X - \eta + b$. Since X is uniformly random, it serves as an arithmetic mask and we can unmask the Boolean sharing without revealing the secret b.
4. In order to obtain a valid arithmetic sharing of $\eta - x$, we need to subtract the unmasked result from q, resulting in $\eta - b - X \bmod q$. Setting X as the other arithmetic share, we have completed the conversion with implicit decoding.

Following this, we can perform all linear operations in the masking domain simply by applying the function to each share. This includes both the NTT and multiplication with non-secret values like c. An implementation of this approach requires two different secure adders over Boolean shares:

1. For Step 1 in [12, Alg. 8], a 3 plus 23 bit adder is required.

2. For Step 4 in [12, Alg. 8], a 23 plus 23 bit adder with 12 of the input bits being hardcoded to zero, which enables substantial improvements compared to a generic secure adder

Note that this approach is not restricted to hardware implementations alone, but could very well also be done efficiently in a software implementation. For this, a secure bit-sliced adder, as proposed by [6], could be utilized, enabling parallelized processing of 32 or more coefficients.

It is possible to adapt this approach to an arbitrary masking order. For this, [6, Alg. 11] can be modified analogously to our method above. This requires an additional arithmetic-to-Boolean conversion to generate the Boolean sharing from Lines 2 and 3 in Algorithm 3. The additional conversion can be also performed offline and does not induce a further delay, even for higher orders.

6.3 Evaluation

Decoding in the First NTT Stage. Integrating the decoding into the first NTT stage obviously eliminates the possibility of attacking the decoding as a standalone step. Nonetheless, we evaluate the effect of this countermeasure on the leakage of the BFU by performing the same single-coefficient attacks as explained before. Table 5 shows the attack's results compared to Table 3. Notably, even though the countermeasure is not intended to prevent this attack, it mitigates the SPA on the BFU. Additionally, the number of traces required to recover the coefficients is doubled. We suppose that Table 5 quantifies the impact of the diverse HWs of the first NTT stage while not altering the diversification of the power signature after the arithmetic operations.

Arithmetic Masking. We also evaluate the efficacy of arithmetic masking against the SPA and the CPA. First, we test whether the exact same CPA works as before. Figure 7 shows the results for the low-noise setting that targets $\hat{c} \circ \hat{t}_0$. As seen there, the correct hypothesis stays at about the same rank even after 1 million traces. Also, the absolute correlation does not come close to the higher-ranked hypotheses or even the significance threshold. Since the attack does not work in the low-noise setting, we deduct that it does also not work when the Keccak module produces noise in parallel.

Table 5. SPA results on BFU with integrated decoding given as percent points (resp. difference of traces required in the multi-trace setting) with the $\eta = 2$ part of Table 3 as reference

Target	Class					Average	$\Delta\#$Traces
	0	1	2	3	4		
a_1	−3.4%	−3.8%	+2.9%	−18.0%	−8.4%	−5.7%	+31
b_1	−23.0%	−5.6%	−17.7%	−14.7%	−14.1%	−15.1%	+3

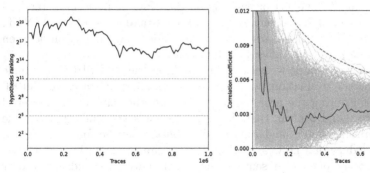

(a) Correct hypothesis ranking progression

(b) Absolute correlation progression for the 1 000 most promising hypotheses (gray) and the correct hypothesis (black)

Fig. 7. CPA results for multiplication of $\hat{c}$ with masked $\hat{t}_0$ for $1\,000\,000$ traces

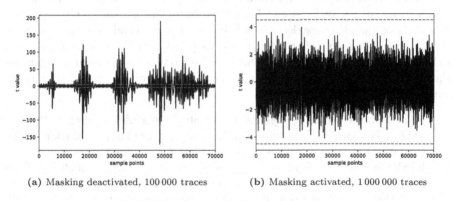

(a) Masking deactivated, 100 000 traces

(b) Masking activated, 1 000 000 traces

Fig. 8. Fixed-vs-random t-test for NTT

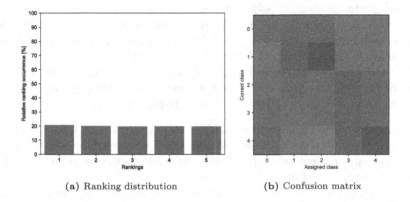

(a) Ranking distribution

(b) Confusion matrix

Fig. 9. SPA on NTT with masking, cf. Fig. 2

Then, to evaluate the effect of masking on the SPA, we perform a standard test-vector-based leakage assessment using a fixed-vs-random t-test on the NTT. As can be seen in Fig. 8, the masking effectively hinders any distinction between fixed and random input even after 1 000 000 traces.

Finally, we also attempt to perform the SPA on the whole BFU for single coefficients. For the evaluation, we increase the number of traces to 450 000 instead of 50 000 during the profiling phase, employ the same overly powerful attacker as before and confirm that the attack is not successful anymore. The respective confusion matrix and ranking distribution can be found in Fig. 9. From this, we deduce that no weaker SPA attacker can learn anything about the secret, e.g., also the one we present in Sect. 4.2. Finally, we could not recover any coefficient using a multi-trace attack with up to 10 000 traces per class.

7   Discussion and Future Work

Our work presents a first side-channel analysis of Dilithium in hardware. We demonstrate attack surfaces and feasibility for single- and multi-trace profiled SPA attacks, targeting the decoding of the secret polynomials and the first NTT stage. Beyond this strong attacker model of profiled SPA, we show a practical CPA attack on polynomial multiplication using power measurements. Regarding the applicability of these attacks on other implementations, we can summarize our findings as follow:

1. The SPA on the decoding exploits the specified range of the secret coefficients and their HW, which does not depend on our targeted implementation. Thus, we expect that the same attack surface exists for any implementation.
2. The SPA on the NTT similarly exploits the secret key range, benefitting from the more unique power signatures generated by the BFU. Following this, we expect that the attack works similarly for the implementations [18,27], which also contain BFUs (as necessary for computing an NTT). However, the co-processor [18] detaches a "pre-computation" step from the signing procedure, which performs the NTT of the secrets once and then stores the transformed polynomial vectors for all subsequent signings under the same secret key. This could mitigate the SPA attack by potentially preventing the collection of multiple traces of the NTT transformation on s_1 and s_2.
3. The CPA on the polynomial multiplication is rather generic, as all implementations will perform the polynomial multiplication using the NTT, even though the specification does not strictly require it.

Moreover, our work shows that random noise generated by a Keccak module running in parallel to the multiplication does not effectively hinder either attack. Finally, we also present countermeasures and evaluate that arithmetic masking effectively prohibits all presented attacks.

For future work, we leave both higher-order attacks and efficient higher-order masking conversions with integrated decoding open. On a higher level, a complete masked hardware implementation of Dilithium is desirable.

Acknowledgments. We thank the reviewers for their constructive comments. Furthermore, we thank Pascal Sasdrich for the fruitful discussions. This work was supported by the German Research Foundation under Germany's Excellence Strategy - EXC 2092 CASA - 390781972, through the H2020 project PROMETHEUS (grant agreement ID 780701), CONVOLVE (grant agreement ID 101070374), and by the Federal Ministry of Education and Research of Germany through the Quantum-RISC (16KIS1038), PQC4Med (16KIS1044), and 6GEM (16KISK038) projects.

References

1. Azouaoui, M., et al.: Protecting Dilithium against leakage: revisited sensitivity analysis and improved implementations. Cryptology ePrint Archive, Paper 2022/1406 (2022). https://eprint.iacr.org/2022/1406
2. Bache, F., Güneysu, T.: Boolean masking for arithmetic additions at arbitrary order in hardware. Appl. Sci. **12**(5), 2274 (2022)
3. Barthe, G., et al.: Masking the GLP lattice-based signature scheme at any order. In: Nielsen, J.B., Rijmen, V. (eds.) EUROCRYPT 2018. LNCS, vol. 10821, pp. 354–384. Springer, Cham (2018). https://doi.org/10.1007/978-3-319-78375-8_12
4. Beckwith, L., Nguyen, D.T., Gaj, K.: High-performance hardware implementation of CRYSTALS-Dilithium. In: International Conference on Field-Programmable Technology, (IC)FPT 2021, Auckland, New Zealand, 6–10 December 2021, pp. 1–10. IEEE (2021)
5. Brier, E., Clavier, C., Olivier, F.: Correlation power analysis with a leakage model. In: Joye, M., Quisquater, J.-J. (eds.) CHES 2004. LNCS, vol. 3156, pp. 16–29. Springer, Heidelberg (2004). https://doi.org/10.1007/978-3-540-28632-5_2
6. Bronchain, O., Cassiers, G.: Bitslicing arithmetic/Boolean masking conversions for fun and profit with application to lattice-based KEMs. IACR Trans. Cryptogr. Hardw. Embed. Syst. **2022**(4), 553–588 (2022)
7. Chari, S., Jutla, C.S., Rao, J.R., Rohatgi, P.: Towards sound approaches to counteract power-analysis attacks. In: Wiener, M. (ed.) CRYPTO 1999. LNCS, vol. 1666, pp. 398–412. Springer, Heidelberg (1999). https://doi.org/10.1007/3-540-48405-1_26
8. Chari, S., Rao, J.R., Rohatgi, P.: Template attacks. In: Kaliski, B.S., Koç, K., Paar, C. (eds.) CHES 2002. LNCS, vol. 2523, pp. 13–28. Springer, Heidelberg (2003). https://doi.org/10.1007/3-540-36400-5_3
9. Chen, Z., Karabulut, E., Aysu, A., Ma, Y., Jing, J.: An efficient non-profiled side-channel attack on the CRYSTALS-Dilithium post-quantum signature. In: 39th IEEE International Conference on Computer Design, ICCD 2021, Storrs, CT, USA, 24–27 October 2021, pp. 583–590. IEEE (2021)
10. Choudary, O., Kuhn, M.G.: Efficient template attacks. In: Francillon, A., Rohatgi, P. (eds.) CARDIS 2013. LNCS, vol. 8419, pp. 253–270. Springer, Cham (2014). https://doi.org/10.1007/978-3-319-08302-5_17
11. Ducas, L., et al.: CRYSTALS-Dilithium - algorithm specifications and supporting documentation (version 3.1). Technical report (2021). https://pq-crystals.org/dilithium/data/dilithium-specification-round3-20210208.pdf
12. Fritzmann, T., et al.: Masked accelerators and instruction set extensions for post-quantum cryptography. IACR Trans. Cryptogr. Hardw. Embed. Syst. **2022**(1), 414–460 (2022)

13. Gierlichs, B., Lemke-Rust, K., Paar, C.: Templates vs. stochastic methods. In: Goubin, L., Matsui, M. (eds.) CHES 2006. LNCS, vol. 4249, pp. 15–29. Springer, Heidelberg (2006). https://doi.org/10.1007/11894063_2

14. Goubin, L., Patarin, J.: DES and differential power analysis the "duplication" method. In: Koç, Ç.K., Paar, C. (eds.) CHES 1999. LNCS, vol. 1717, pp. 158–172. Springer, Heidelberg (1999). https://doi.org/10.1007/3-540-48059-5_15

15. Güneysu, T., Moradi, A.: Generic side-channel countermeasures for reconfigurable devices. In: Preneel, B., Takagi, T. (eds.) CHES 2011. LNCS, vol. 6917, pp. 33–48. Springer, Heidelberg (2011). https://doi.org/10.1007/978-3-642-23951-9_3

16. Karabulut, E., Alkim, E., Aysu, A.: Single-trace side-channel attacks on ω-small polynomial sampling: with applications to NTRU, NTRU Prime, and CRYSTALS-DILITHIUM. In: IEEE International Symposium on Hardware Oriented Security and Trust, HOST 2021, Tysons Corner, VA, USA, 12–15 December 2021, pp. 35–45. IEEE (2021)

17. Kocher, P.C.: Timing attacks on implementations of Diffie-Hellman, RSA, DSS, and other systems. In: Koblitz, N. (ed.) CRYPTO 1996. LNCS, vol. 1109, pp. 104–113. Springer, Heidelberg (1996). https://doi.org/10.1007/3-540-68697-5_9

18. Land, G., Sasdrich, P., Güneysu, T.: A hard crystal - implementing Dilithium on reconfigurable hardware. In: Grosso, V., Pöppelmann, T. (eds.) CARDIS 2021. LNCS, vol. 13173, pp. 210–230. Springer, Cham (2021). https://doi.org/10.1007/978-3-030-97348-3_12

19. Mangard, S., Oswald, E., Popp, T.: Power Analysis Attacks - Revealing the Secrets of Smart Cards. Springer, New York (2007). https://doi.org/10.1007/978-0-387-38162-6

20. Marzougui, S., Ulitzsch, V., Tibouchi, M., Seifert, J.-P.: Profiling side-channel attacks on Dilithium: a small bit-fiddling leak breaks it all. Cryptology ePrint Archive, Report 2022/106 (2022). https://eprint.iacr.org/2022/106

21. Migliore, V., Gérard, B., Tibouchi, M., Fouque, P.-A.: Masking Dilithium. In: Deng, R.H., Gauthier-Umaña, V., Ochoa, M., Yung, M. (eds.) ACNS 2019. LNCS, vol. 11464, pp. 344–362. Springer, Cham (2019). https://doi.org/10.1007/978-3-030-21568-2_17

22. Ravi, P., Jhanwar, M.P., Howe, J., Chattopadhyay, A., Bhasin, S.: Side-channel assisted existential forgery attack on Dilithium - a NIST PQC candidate. Cryptology ePrint Archive, Report 2018/821 (2018). https://eprint.iacr.org/2018/821

23. Ravi, P., Jhanwar, M.P., Howe, J., Chattopadhyay, A., Bhasin, S.: Exploiting determinism in lattice-based signatures: practical fault attacks on pqm4 implementations of NIST candidates. In: Galbraith, S.D., Russello, G., Susilo, W., Gollmann, D., Kirda, E., Liang, Z. (eds.) ASIACCS 2019: 14th ACM Symposium on Information, Computer and Communications Security, Auckland, New Zealand, 9–12 July 2019, pp. 427–440. ACM Press (2019)

24. Schneider, T., Moradi, A., Güneysu, T.: Arithmetic addition over Boolean masking. In: Malkin, T., Kolesnikov, V., Lewko, A.B., Polychronakis, M. (eds.) ACNS 2015. LNCS, vol. 9092, pp. 559–578. Springer, Cham (2015). https://doi.org/10.1007/978-3-319-28166-7_27

25. Shor, P.W.: Algorithms for quantum computation: discrete logarithms and factoring. In: 35th Annual Symposium on Foundations of Computer Science, Santa Fe, NM, USA, 20–22 November 1994, pp. 124–134. IEEE Computer Society Press (1994)

26. Veyrat-Charvillon, N., Medwed, M., Kerckhof, S., Standaert, F.-X.: Shuffling against side-channel attacks: a comprehensive study with cautionary note. In:

Wang, X., Sako, K. (eds.) ASIACRYPT 2012. LNCS, vol. 7658, pp. 740–757. Springer, Heidelberg (2012). https://doi.org/10.1007/978-3-642-34961-4_44

27. Zhao, C., et al.: A compact and high-performance hardware architecture for CRYSTALS-Dilithium. IACR Trans. Cryptogr. Hardw. Embed. Syst. **2022**(1), 270–295 (2022)

Author Index

T. Johansson and D. Smith-Tone (Eds.): PQCrypto 2023, LNCS 14154, pp. 713–714, 2023.
https://doi.org/10.1007/978-3-031-40003-2

Printed in the United States
by Baker & Taylor Publisher Services